FUNDAMENTALS OF
DATABASE SYSTEMS

FUNDAMENTALS OF
DATABASE SYSTEMS

Ramez Elmasri
Department of Computer Science Engineering
University of Texas at Arlington

Durvasula V.L.N. Somayajulu
Department of Computer Science and Engineering
National Institute of Technology at Warangal

Shamkant B. Navathe
College of Computing
Georgia Institute of Technology

Shyam K. Gupta
Department of Computer Science and Engineering
Indian Institute of Technology at New Delhi

Authorized adaptation from the United States edition, entitled *Fundamentals of Database Systems*, 4th Edition, ISBN: 0321122267 by Elmasri, Ramez; Navathe, Shamkant B., published by Pearson Education, Inc, Copyright © 2004

Indian Subcontinent Adaptation
Copyright © 2006 Dorling Kindersley (India) Pvt. Ltd.

ISBN 81-7758- 476-6

First Impression, 2006
Second Impression, 2006

This edition is manufactured in India and is authorized for sale only in India, Bangladesh, Bhutan, Pakistan, Nepal, Sri Lanka and the Maldives.

Published by Dorling Kindersley (India) Pvt. Ltd., licensees of Pearson Education in South Asia.

Head Office: 482 FIE, Patparganj, Delhi 110 092, India.
Registered Office: 14 Local Shopping Centre, Panchsheel Park, New Delhi 110 017, India.

Preface

This book introduces the fundamental concepts necessary for designing, using, and implementing database systems and applications. Our presentations stress the fundamentals of database modeling and design, the languages and facilities provided by database management systems, and system implementation techniques. The book is meant to be used as a textbook for a one- or two-semester course in database systems for B.E./ B.Tech., M.Sc. (CS), M.S. (CS), BCA, MCA, MBA and diploma courses, and as a reference book. We assume that the readers are familiar with elementary programming and data-structuring concepts and that they have had some exposure to basic computer organization.

We start, in Part 1, with an introduction to and a presentation of basic concepts, terminology, and database conceptual modeling principles. We conclude the book in Part 7 with an introduction to emerging technologies such as data mining, XML, data warehousing, security, and Web databases. Along the way we provide an in-depth treatment of the most important aspects of database fundamentals.

Key features of this book are:

- The entire book follows a self-contained, flexible organization that can be tailored to individual needs.

- Coverage of data modeling includes both the ER model and UML.

- A new advanced SQL chapter with material on SQL programming techniques, such as JDBC and SQL/CLI is included.

- Two examples running throughout the book—called COMPANY and UNIVERSITY—allow the reader to compare different approaches that use the same application.

- Coverage has been provided on security, mobile databases, GIS, and Genome data management.

- A new chapter on XML and Internet databases has been included.

- A new chapter on data mining has been added.

Organization

Part 1 describes the basic concepts necessary for a good understanding of database design and implementation, as well as the conceptual modeling techniques used in database systems. Chapters 1 and 2 introduce databases and their typical users; and DBMS concepts, terminology, and architecture. In Chapter 3, the concepts of the Entity-Relationship (ER) model and ER diagrams are presented and used to illustrate conceptual database design. The chapter also focuses on data abstraction and semantic data modeling concepts and extends the ER model to incorporate these ideas, leading to the enhanced-ER (EER) data model and EER diagrams. The concepts presented include subclasses, specialization, generalization, and union types (categories). The notation for the class diagrams of UML are also introduced in Chapter 3.

Part 2 describes the relational data model and relational DBMSs. Chapter 4 describes the basic relational model, its integrity constraints and update operations. Chapter 5 describes the operations of relational algebra and introduces relational calculus. Chapter 6 discusses relational database design using ER and EER-to-relational mapping. Chapter 7 gives a detailed overview of the SQL language, covering the SQL standard, implemented in most relational systems. Chapter 7 also covers SQL programming topics such as SQLJ, JDBC, and SQL/CLI.

Part 3 covers several topics related to database design. Chapter 8 covers the formalisms, theories, and algorithms developed for the relational database design by normalization. This material includes functional and other types of dependencies and normal forms of relations. Step-by-step intuitive normalization, and relational design algorithms are also covered.

Part 4 provides the description of the physical file structures and access methods used in database systems. Chapter 9 describes primary methods of organizing files of records on disk, including static and dynamic hashing, indexing techniques for files, including B-tree and B+-tree data structures and grid files. Chapter 10 introduces the basics of query processing and optimization.

Part 5 deals with transaction processing concepts. Chapter 11 discusses transaction processing, concurrency control, and recovery techniques, including discussions of how these concepts are realized in SQL.

Parts 6 and 7 cover a number of advanced topics and emerging technologies. Chapter 12 gives an overview of database security and authorization, including the SQL commands to GRANT and REVOKE privileges, and expanded coverage on security concepts such as encryption, roles, and flow control. For a single semester course based on this book, some chapters can be assigned as reading material. Chapter 13 introduces object-oriented concepts, detailed overview of the ODMG object model and its associated ODL and OQL languages, features of object-relational and extended-relational systems, overview of some of the features of the SQL3 standard, and the nested relational model. It also discusses several enhanced database models for advanced applications. These include active databases and triggers, temporal, spatial, multimedia, and deductive databases. Chapter 14 gives an introduction to distributed databases and the three-tier client-server architectures. Chapter 15 is a new chapter on XML (eXtended Markup Language). It first discusses the differences between structured, semi-structured, and unstructured models, then presents XML concepts, and finally compares the XML model to traditional database models. Chapter 16 on data mining has been expanded and updated. Chapter 17 introduces data warehousing concepts. Finally, Chapter 18 introduces the topics of mobile databases, multimedia databases, GIS (Geographic Information Systems), and Genome data management in bioinformatics.

Appendix A contains a number of alternative diagrammatic notations for displaying a conceptual ER or EER schema. These may be substituted for the notation we use, if the instructor so wishes. Appendix C gives more important physical parameters of disks. Appendixes B, E, and F are on the web site. Appendix B is a new case study that follows the design and implementation of a bookstore's database. Appendixes E and F cover legacy database systems, based on the network and hierarchical database models. These have been used for over thirty years as a basis for many existing commercial database applications and transaction-processing systems and will take decades to replace completely. We consider it important to expose students of database management to these long-standing approaches.

Guidelines for Using This Book

There are many different ways to teach a database course. The chapters in Parts 1 through 5 can be used in an introductory course on database systems in the order that they are given or in the order preferred by each individual instructor. Selected chapters and sections may be left out, and the instructor can add other chapters from the rest of the book, depending on the emphasis of the course. We suggest covering up to Chapter 12 in an introductory database course and including selected parts of other chapters, depending on the background of the students and the desired coverage.

Chapter 3 highlights conceptual modeling using the ER and EER models, and is important for a good conceptual understanding of databases. However, some of the sections/subsections may be partially covered, covered later in a course, or even left out if the emphasis is on DBMS implementation. Chapter 9 on file organizations and indexing may also be covered early on, later, or even left out if the emphasis is on database models and languages.

A total life-cycle database design and implementation project covers conceptual design (Chapter 3), data model mapping (Chapter 6), normalization (Chapter 8), and implementation in SQL (Chapter 7). Additional documentation in specific RDBMS would be required.

This book has been written so that it is possible to cover topics in a variety of orders. The chart included here shows the major dependencies between chapters. As the diagram illustrates, it is possible to start with several different topics following the first two introductory chapters. Although the chart may seem complex, it is important to note that if the chapters are covered in order, the dependencies are not lost. The chart can be consulted by instructors wishing to use an alternative order of presentation.

This book can also be used for a two-semester sequence. The first course, "Introduction to Database Management/Systems," at the B.E./B.Tech., M.Sc. (CS), M.S. (CS), BCA, MCA and MBA could cover most of Chapters 1 to 12. The second course, "Database Design and Implementation Techniques," (at the advanced level) can cover Chapters 13 to 18.

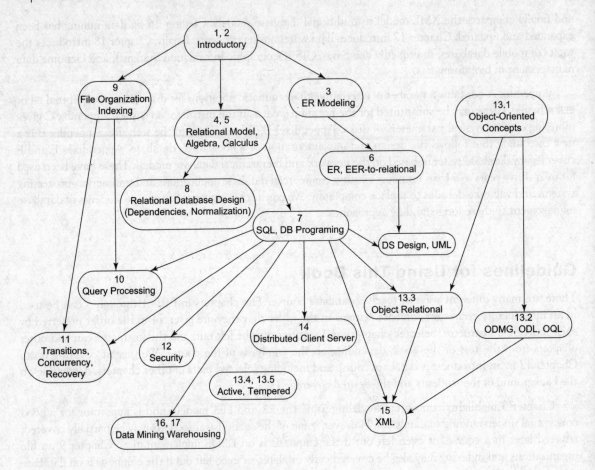

Acknowledgements

It is a great pleasure for us to acknowledge the assistance and contributions of a large number of individuals. First, we would like to thank our editors, Maite Suarez-Rivas, Katherine Harutunian, Daniel Rausch, and Juliet Silveri. We appreciated the contributions of the following reviewers: Phil Berhnard, *Florida Tech*; Zhengxin Chen, *University of Nebraska at Omaha*; Jan Chomicki, *University of Buffalo*; Hakan Ferhatosmagnoglu, *Ohio State University*; Len Fisk, *California State University, Chico*; William Hankley, *Kansas State University*; Ali R. Hurson, *Penn State University*; Vijay Kumar, *University of Missouri-Kansas City*; Peretz Shoval, *Ben-Guirion University, Israel*; Jason T. L. Wan, *New Jersey Institute of Technology*; and Ed Omiecinski of *Georgia Tech*, who contributed to Chapter 2.

Ramez Elmasri would like to thank his students Hyoil Han, Babak Hojabri, Jack Fu, Charley Li, Ande Swathi, and Steven Wu, who contributed to the material in Chapter 2. He would also like to acknowledge the support provided by the University of Texas at Arlington.

Sham Navathe would like to acknowledge Dan Forsythe and the following students at Georgia Tech: Weimin Feng, Angshuman Guin, Abrar Ul-Haque, Bin Liu, Ying Liu, Wanxia Xie and Waigen Yee.

We would like to repeat our thanks to Alan Apt, Don Batory, Scott Downing, Dennis Heimbinger, Julia Hodges, Yannis Ioannidis, Jim Larson, Dennis McLeod, Per-Ake Larson, Rahul Patel, Nicholas Roussopoulos, David Stemple, Michael Stonebraker, Frank Tompa, Kyu-Young Whang, Dan Joraanstad, Rafi Ahmed, Antonio Albano, David Beech, Jose Blakeley, Panos Chrysanthis, Suzanne Dietrich, Vic Ghorpadey, Goets Graefe, Eric Hanson, Junguk L. Kim, Roger King, Vram Kouramajian, Vijay Kumar, John Lowther, Sanjay Manchanda, Toshimi Minoura, Inderpal Mumick, Ed Omiecinski, Girish Pathak, Raghu Ramakrishnan, Ed Robertson, Eugene Sheng, David Stotts, Marianne Winslett, Stan Zdonick, Suzanne Dietrich, Ed Omiecinski, Rafi Ahmed, Francois Bancilhon, Jose Blakeley, Rick Cattell, Ann Chervenak, David W. Embley, Henry A. Etlinger, Leonidas Fegaras, Dan Forsyth, Farshad Fotouhi, Michael Franklin, Sreejith Gopinath, Goetz Craefe, Richard Hull, Sushil Jajodia, Ramesh K. Karne, Harish Kotbagi, Vijay Kumar, Tarcisio Lima, Ramon A. Mata-Toledo, Jack McCaw, Dennis McLeod, Rokia Missaoui, Magdi Morsi, M. Narayanaswamy, Carlos Ordonez, Joan Peckham, Betty Salzberg, Ming-Chien Shan, Junping Sun, Rajshekhar Sunderraman, Aravindan Veerasamy, and Emilia E. Villareal.

Last but not least, we gratefully acknowledge the support, encouragement, and patience of our families.

R.E.
S.B.N.
D.V.L.N.S.
S.K.G.

Contents

Preface   vii

PART 2 RELATIONAL MODEL: CONCEPTS, CONSTRAINTS, LANGUAGES, AND DESIGN   95

CHAPTER 4 The Relational Data Model and Relational Database Constraints
[Earlier Chapter Number 5]   **97**

CHAPTER 6 Relational Database Design by ER- and EER-to-Relational Mapping   156

CHAPTER 7 SQL-99: Schema Definition, Basic Constraints, and Queries [Earlier Chapter Number 8]   169

PART 3 DATABASE DESIGN THEORY AND METHODOLOGY   237

CHAPTER 8 Relational Database Design [Earlier Chapter Number 10]   239

PART 4 DATA STORAGE, INDEXING, AND QUERY PROCESSING 295

CHAPTER 9 File Organizations and Indexes   297

1

INTRODUCTION AND CONCEPTUAL MODELING

1

Databases and Database Users

Databases and database systems have become an essential component of everyday life in modern society. In the course of a day, most of us encounter several activities that involve some interaction with a database. For example, if we go to the bank to deposit or withdraw funds, if we make a hotel or airline reservation, if we access a computerized library catalog to search for a bibliographic item, or if we buy some item—such as a book, toy, or computer—from an Internet vendor through its Web page, chances are that our activities will involve someone or some computer program accessing a database. Even purchasing items from a supermarket nowadays in many cases involves an automatic update of various items of the Inventory Database.

These interactions are examples of what we may call **traditional database applications**, in which most of the information that is stored and accessed is either textual or numeric. In the past few years, advances in technology have been leading to exciting new applications of database systems. **Multimedia databases** can now store pictures, video clips, and sound messages. **Geographic information systems** (GIS) can store and analyze maps, weather data, and satellite images. **Data warehouses** and **online analytical processing** (OLAP) systems are used in many companies to extract and analyze useful information from very large databases for decision making. **Real-time** and **active database technology** is used in controlling industrial and manufacturing processes. And database search techniques are being applied to the World Wide Web to improve the search for information that is needed by users browsing the Internet.

To understand the fundamentals of database technology, however, we must start from the basics of traditional database applications. So, in Section 1.1 of this chapter we define what a database is, and then we give definitions of other basic terms. In Section 1.2, we provide a simple UNIVERSITY database example to illustrate our discussion. Section 1.3 describes some of the main characteristics of database systems, and

Sections 1.4 and 1.5 categorize the types of personnel whose jobs involve using and interacting with database systems. Sections 1.6, 1.7, and 1.8 offer a more thorough discussion of the various capabilities provided by database systems and discuss some typical database applications. Section 1.9 summarizes the chapter.

1.1 INTRODUCTION

Databases and database technology are having a major impact on the growing use of computers. It is fair to say that databases play a critical role in almost all areas where computers are used, including business, electronic commerce, engineering, medicine, law, education, and library science, to name a few. The word *database* is in such common use that we must begin by defining what a database is. Our initial definition is quite general.

A **database** is a collection of related data.[1] By **data**, we mean known facts that can be recorded and that have implicit meaning. For example, consider the names, telephone numbers, and addresses of the people you know. You may have recorded this data in an indexed address book, or you may have stored it on a hard drive, using a personal computer and software such as Microsoft Access, or Excel. This is a collection of related data with an implicit meaning and hence is a database.

The preceding definition of database is quite general. For example, we may consider the collection of words that make up this page of text to be related data and hence to constitute a database. However, the common use of the term *database* is usually more restricted. A database has the following implicit properties:

- A database represents some aspect of the real world, sometimes called the **miniworld** or the **universe of discourse (UoD)**. Changes to the miniworld are reflected in the database.

- A database is a logically coherent collection of data with some inherent meaning. A random assortment of data cannot correctly be referred to as a database.

- A database is designed, built, and populated with data for a specific purpose. It has an intended group of users and some preconceived applications in which these users are interested.

In other words, a database has some source from which data is derived, some degree of interaction with events in the real world, and an audience that is actively interested in the contents of the database.

A database can be of any size and of varying complexity. For example, the list of names and addresses referred to earlier may consist of only a few hundred records, each with a simple structure. On the other hand, the computerized catalog of a large library may contain half a million entries organized under different categories—by primary author's last name, by subject, by book title—with each category organized in alphabetic order. A database of even greater size and complexity is maintained by the Income Tax Department (ITD) to keep track of the tax forms filed by taxpayers. If we assume that there are 100 million taxpayers and if each taxpayer files an average of five forms with approximately 400 characters of information per form, we would get a database of $100 \times 10^6 \times 400 \times 5$ characters (bytes) of information. If the ITD keeps the past three returns for each taxpayer in addition to the current return, we would get a database of 8×10^{11} bytes (800 gigabytes). This huge amount of information must be organized and managed so that users can search for, retrieve, and update the data as needed.

A database may be generated and maintained manually or it may be computerized. For example, a library card catalog is a database that may be created and maintained manually. A computerized database may be created and maintained either by a group of application programs written specifically for that task or by a database management system. Of course, we are only concerned with computerized databases in this book.

---

1. We will use the word *data* as both singular and plural, as is common in database literature; context will determine whether it is singular or plural. In standard English, *data* is used only for plural; *datum* is used for singular.

A **database management system (DBMS)** is a collection of programs that enables users to create and maintain a database. The DBMS is hence a *general-purpose software system* that facilitates the processes of *defining, constructing, manipulating*, and *sharing* databases among various users and applications. **Defining** a database involves specifying the data types, structures, and constraints for the data to be stored in the database. **Constructing** the database is the process of storing the data itself on some storage medium that is controlled by the DBMS. **Manipulating** a database includes such functions as querying the database to retrieve specific data, updating the database to reflect changes in the miniworld, and generating reports from the data. **Sharing** a database allows multiple users and programs to access the database concurrently.

Other important functions provided by the DBMS include *protecting* the database and *maintaining* it over a long period of time. **Protection** includes both *system protection* against hardware or software malfunction (or crashes), and *security protection* against unauthorized or malicious access. A typical large database may have a life cycle of many years, so the DBMS must be able to **maintain** the database system by allowing the system to evolve as requirements change over time.

It is not necessary to use general-purpose DBMS software to implement a computerized database. We could write our own set of programs to create and maintain the database, in effect creating our own *special-purpose DBMS software*. In either case—whether we use a general-purpose DBMS or not—we usually have to deploy a considerable amount of complex software. In fact, most DBMSs are very complex software systems.

To complete our initial definitions, we will call the database and DBMS software together a **database system**. Figure 1.1 illustrates some of the concepts we discussed so far.

FIGURE 1.1 A simplified database system environment.

1.2 AN EXAMPLE

Let us consider a simple example that most readers may be familiar with: a UNIVERSITY database for maintaining information concerning students, courses, and grades in an university environment. Figure 1.2 shows the database structure and a few sample data for such a database. The database is organized as five files, each of which stores data records of the same type.[2] The STUDENT file stores data on each student, the COURSE file stores data on each course, the SECTION file stores data on each section of a course, the GRADE_REPORT file stores the grades that students receive in the various sections they have completed, and the PREREQUISITE file stores the prerequisites of each course.

STUDENT	Name	StudentNumber	Class	Major
	Uday	17	1	CS
	Nitin	8	2	CS

COURSE	CourseName	CourseNumber	CreditHours	Department
	Intro to Computer Science	CS1310	4	CS
	Data Structures	CS3320	4	CS
	Discrete Mathematics	MATH2410	3	MATH
	Database	CS3380	3	CS

SECTION	SectionIdentifier	CourseNumber	Semester	Year	Instructor
	85	MATH2410	First	98	Jain
	92	CS1310	First	98	Rao
	102	CS3320	Second	99	Ramesh
	112	MATH2410	First	99	Ravinder
	119	CS1310	First	99	Rao
	135	CS3380	First	99	Srinivas

GRADE_REPORT	StudentNumber	SectionIdentifier	Grade
	17	112	B
	17	119	C
	8	85	A
	8	92	A
	8	102	B
	8	135	A

PREREQUISITE	CourseNumber	PrerequisiteNumber
	CS3380	CS3320
	CS3380	MATH2410
	CS3320	CS1310

FIGURE 1.2 A database that stores student and course information.

---

2. We use the term file informally here. At a conceptual level, a file is a collection of records that may or may not be ordered.

To *define* this database, we must specify the structure of the records of each file by specifying the different types of **data elements** to be stored in each record. In Figure 1.2, each STUDENT record includes data to represent the student's Name, StudentNumber, Class (First year or 1, Second year or 2, ...), and Major (mathematics or math, computer science or CS, ...); each COURSE record includes data to represent the CourseName, CourseNumber, CreditHours, and Department (the department that offers the course); and so on. We must also specify a **data type** for each data element within a record. For example, we can specify that Name of STUDENT is a string of alphabetic characters, StudentNumber of STUDENT is an integer, and Grade of GRADE_REPORT is a single character from the set {A, B, C, D, F, I}. We may also use a coding scheme to represent the values of a data item. For example, in Figure 1.2 we represent the Class of a STUDENT as 1 for first year, 2 for second year, 3 for Third year, 4 for Final year, and 5 for Post graduate student.

To *construct* the UNIVERSITY database, we store data to represent each student, course, section, grade report, and prerequisite as a record in the appropriate file. Notice that records in the various files may be related. For example, the record for "Uday" in the STUDENT file is related to two records in the GRADE_REPORT file that specify Uday's grades in two sections. Similarly, each record in the PREREQUISITE file relates two course records: one representing the course and the other representing the prerequisite. Most medium-size and large databases include many types of records and have *many relationships* among the records.

Database *manipulation* involves querying and updating. Examples of queries are "retrieve the transcript—a list of all courses and grades—of Uday," "list the names of students who took the section of the Database course offered in first semester of 1999 and their grades in that section," and "what are the prerequisites of the Database course?" Examples of updates are "change the class of Uday to Second year," "create a new section for the Database course for this semester," and "enter a grade of A for Uday in the Database section of last semester." These informal queries and updates must be specified precisely in the query language of the DBMS before they can be processed.

1.3 CHARACTERISTICS OF THE DATABASE APPROACH

A number of characteristics distinguish the database approach from the traditional approach of programming with files. In traditional **file processing**, each user defines and implements the files needed for a specific software application as part of programming the application. For example, one user, the *grade reporting office*, may keep a file on students and their grades. Programs to print a student's transcript and to enter new grades into the file are implemented as part of the application. A second user, the *accounting office*, may keep track of students' fees and their payments. Although both users are interested in data about students, each user maintains separate files—and programs to manipulate these files—because each requires some data not available from the other user's files. This redundancy in defining and storing data results in wasted storage space and in redundant efforts to maintain common data up to date.

In the database approach, a single repository of data is maintained that is defined once and then is accessed by various users. The main characteristics of the database approach versus the file-processing approach are the following:

- Self-describing nature of a database system

- Insulation between programs and data, and data abstraction

- Support of multiple views of the data

- Sharing of data and multiuser transaction processing

We next describe each of these characteristics in a separate section. Additional characteristics of database systems are discussed in Sections 1.6 through 1.8.

1.3.1 Self-Describing Nature of a Database System

A fundamental characteristic of the database approach is that the database system contains not only the database itself but also a complete definition or description of the database structure and constraints. This definition is stored in the DBMS **catalog**, which contains information such as the structure of each file, the type and storage format of each data item, and various constraints on the data. The information stored in the catalog is called **meta-data**, and it describes the structure of the primary database (Figure 1.1).

The catalog is used by the DBMS software and also by database users who need information about the database structure. A general-purpose DBMS software package is not written for a specific database application, and hence it must refer to the catalog to know the structure of the files in a specific database, such as the type and format of data it will access. The DBMS software must work equally well with *any number of database applications*—for example, a university database, a banking database, or a company database—as long as the database definition is stored in the catalog.

In traditional file processing, data definition is typically part of the application programs themselves. Hence, these programs are constrained to work with only one *specific database*, whose structure is declared in the application programs. For example, an application program written in C++ may have struct or class declarations, and a COBOL program has Data Division statements to define its files. Whereas file-processing software can access only specific databases, DBMS software can access diverse databases by extracting the database definitions from the catalog and then using these definitions.

In the example shown in Figure 1.2, the DBMS catalog will store the definitions of all the files shown. These definitions are specified by the database designer prior to creating the actual database and are stored in the catalog. Whenever a request is made to access, say, the Name of a STUDENT record, the DBMS software refers to the catalog to determine the structure of the STUDENT file and the position and size of the Name data item within a STUDENT record. By contrast, in a typical file-processing application, the file structure and, in the extreme case, the exact location of Name within a STUDENT record are already coded within each program that accesses this data item.

1.3.2 Insulation between Programs and Data, and Data Abstraction

In traditional file processing, the structure of data files is embedded in the application programs, so any changes to the structure of a file may require *changing all programs* that access this file. By contrast, DBMS access programs do not require such changes in most cases. The structure of data files is stored in the DBMS catalog separately from the access programs. We call this property **program-data independence**. For example, a file access program may be written in such a way that it can access only STUDENT records of the structure shown in Figure 1.3. If we want to add another piece of data to each STUDENT record, say the Date of Birth, such a program will no longer work and must be changed. By contrast, in a DBMS environment, we just need to change the description of STUDENT records in the catalog to reflect the inclusion of the new data item Date of Birth; no programs are changed. The next time a DBMS program refers to the catalog, the new structure of STUDENT records will be accessed and used.

Program-operation independence is another term used in object-oriented and object-relational systems. In these systems, users can define operations on data as part of the database definitions. An **operation** (also called a *function* or *method*) is specified in two parts. The *interface* (or *signature*) of an operation includes the operation name and the data types of its arguments (or parameters). The *implementation* (or *method*) of the operation is specified separately and can be changed without affecting the interface. User application programs can operate on the data by invoking these operations through their names and arguments, regardless of how the operations are implemented.

Data Item Name	Starting Position in Record	Length in Characters (bytes)
Name	1	30
StudentNumber	31	4
Class	35	4
Major	39	4

FIGURE 1.3 Internal storage format for a STUDENT record.

The characteristic that allows program-data independence and program-operation independence is called **data abstraction**. A DBMS provides users with a **conceptual representation** of data that does not include many of the details of how the data is stored or how the operations are implemented. Informally, a **data model** is a type of data abstraction that is used to provide this conceptual representation. The data model uses logical concepts, such as objects, their properties, and their inter-relationships, that may be easier for most users to understand than computer storage concepts. Hence, the data model *hides* storage and implementation details that are not of interest to most database users.

For example, consider again Figure 1.2. The internal implementation of a file may be defined by its record length—the number of characters (bytes) in each record—and each data item may be specified by its starting byte within a record and its length in bytes. The STUDENT record would thus be represented as shown in Figure 1.3. But a typical database user is not concerned with the location of each data item within a record or its length; rather, the concern is that when a reference is made to Name of STUDENT, the correct value is returned. A conceptual representation of the STUDENT records is shown in Figure 1.2. Many other details of file storage organization—such as the access paths specified on a file—can be hidden from database users by the DBMS; we discuss storage details in Chapter 9.

In the database approach, the detailed structure and organization of each file are stored in the catalog. Database users and application programs refer to the conceptual representation of the files, and the DBMS extracts the details of file storage from the catalog when these are needed by the DBMS file access modules. Many data models can be used to provide this data abstraction to database users.

(a)

TRANSCRIPT	StudentName	Student Transcript				
		CourseNumber	Grade	Semester	Year	SectionId
	Uday	CS1310	C	First	99	119
		MATH2410	B	First	99	112
	Nitin	MATH2410	A	First	98	85
		CS1310	A	First	98	92
		CS3320	B	Second	99	102
		CS3380	A	First	99	135

(b)

PREREQUISITES	CourseName	CourseNumber	Prerequisites
	Database	CS3380	CS3320
			MATH2410
	Data Structures	CS3320	CS1310

FIGURE 1.4 Two views derived from the database in Figure 1.2. (a) The STUDENT TRANSCRIPT view (b) The COURSE PREREQUISITES view.

1.3.3 Support of Multiple Views of the Data

A database typically has many users, each of whom may require a different perspective or view of the database. A view may be a subset of the database or it may contain **virtual data** that is derived from the database files but is not explicitly stored. Some users may not need to be aware of whether the data they refer to is stored or derived. A multiuser DBMS whose users have a variety of distinct applications must provide facilities for defining multiple views. For example, one user of the database of Figure 1.2 may be interested only in accessing and printing the transcript of each student; the view for this user is shown in Figure 1.4a. A second user, who is interested only in checking that students have taken all the prerequisites of each course for which they register, may require the view shown in Figure 1.4b.

1.3.4 Sharing of Data and Multiuser Transaction Processing

A multiuser DBMS, as its name implies, must allow multiple users to access the database at the same time. This is essential if data for multiple applications is to be integrated and maintained in a single database. The DBMS must include **concurrency control** software to ensure that several users trying to update the same data do so in a controlled manner so that the result of the updates is correct. For example, when several reservation clerks try to assign a seat on an airline flight, the DBMS should ensure that each seat can be accessed by only one clerk at a time for assignment to a passenger. These types of applications are generally called **online transaction processing (OLTP)** applications. A fundamental role of multiuser DBMS software is to ensure that concurrent transactions operate correctly.

The concept of a **transaction** has become central to many database applications. A transaction is an *executing program* or *process* that includes one or more database accesses, such as reading or updating of database records. Each transaction is supposed to execute a logically correct database access if executed in its entirety without interference from other transactions. The DBMS must enforce several transaction properties. The **isolation** property ensures that each transaction appears to execute in isolation from other transactions, even though hundreds of transactions may be executing concurrently. The **atomicity** property ensures that either all the database operations in a transaction are executed or none are. We discuss transactions in detail in Chapter 11 of the textbook.

The preceding characteristics are most important in distinguishing a DBMS from traditional file-processing software. In Section 1.6 we discuss additional features that characterize a DBMS. First, however, we categorize the different types of users who work in a database system environment.

1.4 Actors on the Scene

For a small personal database, such as the list of addresses discussed in Section 1.1, one person typically defines, constructs, and manipulates the database, and there is no sharing. However, many persons are involved in the design, use, and maintenance of a large database with hundreds of users. In this section, we identify the people whose jobs involve the day-to-day use of a large database; we call them the "actors on the scene." In Section 1.5 we consider people who may be called "workers behind the scene"—those who work to maintain the database system environment but who are not actively interested in the database itself.

1.4.1 Database Administrators

In any organization where many persons use the same resources, there is a need for a chief administrator to oversee and manage these resources. In a database environment, the primary resource is the database itself, and the secondary resource is the DBMS and related software. Administering these resources is the responsibility of the **database administrator (DBA)**. The DBA is responsible for authorizing access to the database, for co-ordinating and monitoring its use, and for acquiring software and hardware resources as needed. The DBA is accountable for problems such as breach of security or poor system response time. In large organizations, the DBA is assisted by a staff that helps carry out these functions.

1.4.2 Database Designers

Database designers are responsible for identifying the data to be stored in the database and for choosing appropriate structures to represent and store this data. These tasks are mostly undertaken before the database is actually implemented and populated with data. It is the responsibility of database designers to communicate with all prospective database users in order to understand their requirements, and to come up with a design that meets these requirements. In many cases, the designers are on the staff of the DBA and may be assigned other staff responsibilities after the database design is completed. Database designers typically interact with each potential group of users and develop **views** of the database that meet the data and processing requirements of these groups. Each view is then analyzed and *integrated* with the views of other user groups. The final database design must be capable of supporting the requirements of all user groups.

1.4.3 End Users

End users are the people whose jobs require access to the database for querying, updating, and generating reports; the database primarily exists for their use. There are several categories of end users:

- **Casual end users** occasionally access the database, but they may need different information each time. They use a sophisticated database query language to specify their requests and are typically middle/ or high-level managers or other occasional browsers.

- **Naive** or **parametric end users** make up a sizable portion of database end users. Their main job function revolves around constantly querying and updating the database, using standard types of queries and updates—called **canned transactions**—that have been carefully programmed and tested. The tasks that such users perform are varied:

  Bank tellers check account balances and post withdrawals and deposits.

  Reservation clerks for airlines, hotels, and car rental companies check availability for a given request and make reservations.

  Clerks at receiving stations for courier mail enter package identifications via bar codes and descriptive information through buttons to update a central database of received and in-transit packages.

- **Sophisticated end users** include engineers, scientists, business analysts, and others who thoroughly familiarize themselves with the facilities of the DBMS so as to implement their applications to meet their complex requirements.

- **Stand-alone users** maintain personal databases by using ready-made program packages that provide easy-to-use menu-based or graphics-based interfaces. An example is the user of a tax package that stores a variety of personal financial data for tax purposes.

A typical DBMS provides multiple facilities to access a database. Naive end users need to learn very little about the facilities provided by the DBMS; they have to understand only the user interfaces of the standard transactions designed and implemented for their use. Casual users learn only a few facilities that they may use repeatedly. Sophisticated users try to learn most of the DBMS facilities in order to achieve their complex requirements. Stand-alone users typically become very proficient in using a specific software package.

1.4.4 System Analysts and Application Programmers (Software Engineers)

System analysts determine the requirements of end users, especially naive and parametric end users, and develop specifications for canned transactions that meet these requirements. **Application programmers** implement these specifications as programs; then they test, debug, document, and maintain these canned transactions. Such analysts and programmers—commonly referred to as **software engineers**—should be familiar with the full range of capabilities provided by the DBMS to accomplish their tasks.

1.5 WORKERS BEHIND THE SCENE

In addition to those who design, use, and administer a database, others are associated with the design, development, and operation of the DBMS *software and system environment*. These persons are typically not interested in the database itself. We call them the "workers behind the scene," and they include the following categories.

- DBMS **system designers and implementers** are persons who design and implement the DBMS modules and interfaces as a software package. A DBMS is a very complex software system that consists of many components, or **modules**, including modules for implementing the catalog, processing query language, processing the interface, accessing and buffering data, controlling concurrency, and handling data recovery and security. The DBMS must interface with other system software, such as the operating system and compilers for various programming languages.

- **Tool developers** include persons who design and implement **tools**—the software packages that facilitate database system design and use and that help improve performance. Tools are optional packages that are often purchased separately. They include packages for database design, performance monitoring, natural language or graphical interfaces, prototyping, simulation, and test data generation. In many cases, independent software vendors develop and market these tools.

- **Operators and maintenance personnel** are the system administration personnel who are responsible for the actual running and maintenance of the hardware and software environment for the database system.

Although these categories of workers behind the scene are instrumental in making the database system available to end users, they typically do not use the database for their own purposes.

1.6 ADVANTAGES OF USING THE DBMS APPROACH

In this section, we discuss some of the advantages of using a DBMS and the capabilities that a good DBMS should possess. These capabilities are in addition to the four main characteristics discussed in Section 1.3. The DBA must utilize these capabilities to accomplish a variety of objectives related to the design, administration, and use of a large multiuser database.

1.6.1   Controlling Redundancy

In traditional software development utilizing file processing, every user group maintains its own files for handling its data-processing applications. For example, consider the UNIVERSITY database example of Section 1.2; here, two groups of users might be the course registration personnel and the accounting office. In the traditional approach, each group independently keeps files on students. The accounting office also keeps data on registration and related billing information, whereas the registration office keeps track of student courses and grades. Much of the data is stored twice: once in the files of each user group. Additional user groups may further duplicate some or all of the same data in their own files.

This **redundancy** in storing the same data multiple times leads to several problems. First, there is the need to perform a single logical update—such as entering data on a new student—multiple times: once for each file where student data is recorded. This leads to *duplication of effort*. Second, *storage space is wasted* when the same data is stored repeatedly, and this problem may be serious for large databases. Third, files that represent the same data may become *inconsistent*. This may happen because an update is applied to some of the files but not to others. Even if an update—such as adding a new student—is applied to all the appropriate files, the data concerning the student may still be *inconsistent* because the updates are applied independently by each user group. For example, one user group may enter a student's date of birth erroneously as 19-JAN-1984, whereas the other user groups may enter the correct value of 29-JAN-1984.

In the database approach, the views of different user groups are integrated during database design. Ideally, we should have a database design that stores each logical data item—such as a student's name or birth date—in *only one place* in the database. This ensures consistency, and it saves storage space. However, in practice, it is sometimes necessary to use **controlled redundancy** for improving the performance of queries. For example, we may store StudentName and CourseNumber redundantly in a GRADE_REPORT file (Figure 1.5a) because whenever we retrieve a GRADE_REPORT record, we want to retrieve the student name and course number along with the grade, student number, and section identifier. By placing all the data together, we do not have to search multiple files to collect this data. In such cases, the DBMS should have the capability to *control* this redundancy so as to prohibit inconsistencies among the files. This may be done by automatically checking that the StudentName-StudentNumber values in any GRADE_REPORT record in Figure 1.5a match one of the Name-StudentNumber values of a STUDENT record (Figure 1.2). Similarly, the SectionIdentifier-CourseNumber values in GRADE_REPORT can be checked against SECTION records. Such checks can be specified to the DBMS during database design and automatically enforced by the DBMS whenever the GRADE_REPORT file is updated. Figure 1.5b shows a GRADE_REPORT record that is inconsistent with the STUDENT file of Figure 1.2, which may be entered erroneously if the redundancy is *not controlled*.

(a)

GRADE_REPORT	StudentNumber	StudentName	SectionIdentifier	CourseNumber	Grade
	17	Uday	112	MATH2410	B
	17	Uday	119	CS1310	C
	8	Nitin	85	MATH2410	A
	8	Nitin	92	CS1310	A
	8	Nitin	102	CS3320	B
	8	Nitin	135	CS3380	A

(b)

GRADE_REPORT	StudentNumber	StudentName	SectionIdentifier	CourseNumber	Grade
	17	Nitin	112	MATH2410	B

FIGURE 1.5 Redundant storage of StudentName and CourseNumber in GRADE_REPORT. (a) Consistent data. (b) Inconsistent record.

1.6.2 Restricting Unauthorized Access

When multiple users share a large database, it is likely that most users will not be authorized to access all information in the database. For example, financial data is often considered confidential, and hence only authorized persons are allowed to access such data. In addition, some users may be permitted only to retrieve data, whereas others are allowed both to retrieve and to update. Hence, the type of access operation—retrieval or update—must also be controlled. Typically, users or user groups are given account numbers protected by passwords, which they can use to gain access to the database. A DBMS should provide a **security and authorization subsystem**, which the DBA uses to create accounts and to specify account restrictions. The DBMS should then enforce these restrictions automatically. Notice that we can apply similar controls to the DBMS software. For example, only the DBA's staff may be allowed to use certain **privileged software**, such as the software for creating new accounts. Similarly, parametric users may be allowed to access the database only through the canned transactions developed for their use.

1.6.3 Providing Storage Structures for Efficient Query Processing

Database systems must provide capabilities for *efficiently executing queries and updates*. Because the database is typically stored on disk, the DBMS must provide specialized data structures to speed up disk search for the desired records. Auxiliary files called **indexes** are used for this purpose. Indexes are typically based on tree data structures or hash data structures, suitably modified for disk search. In order to process the database records needed by a particular query, those records must be copied from disk to memory. Hence, the DBMS often has a **buffering** module that maintains parts of the database in main memory buffers. In other cases, the DBMS may use the operating system to do the buffering of disk data.

The **query processing and optimization** module of the DBMS is responsible for choosing an efficient query execution plan for each query based on the existing storage structures. The choice of which indexes to create and maintain is part of *physical database design and tuning*, which is one of the responsibilities of the DBA staff.

1.6.4 Providing Backup and Recovery

A DBMS must provide facilities for recovering from hardware or software failures. The **backup and recovery subsystem** of the DBMS is responsible for recovery. For example, if the computer system fails in the middle of a complex update transaction, the recovery subsystem is responsible for making sure that the database is restored to the state it was in before the transaction started executing. Alternatively, the recovery subsystem could ensure that the transaction is resumed from the point at which it was interrupted so that its full effect is recorded in the database.

1.6.5 Providing Multiple User Interfaces

Because many types of users with varying levels of technical knowledge use a database, a DBMS should provide a variety of user interfaces. These include query languages for casual users, programming language interfaces for application programmers, forms and command codes for parametric users, and menu-driven interfaces and natural language interfaces for stand-alone users. Both forms-style interfaces and menu-driven interfaces are commonly known as **graphical user interfaces** (GUIs). Many specialized languages and environments exist for specifying GUIs. Capabilities for providing Web GUI interfaces to a database—or Web-enabling a database—are also quite common.

1.6.6 Representing Complex Relationships among Data

A database may include numerous varieties of data that are interrelated in many ways. Consider the example shown in Figure 1.2. The record for Nitin in the STUDENTfile is related to four records in the GRADE_REPORT file. Similarly, each section record is related to one course record as well as to a number of GRADE_REPORT records—one for each student who completed that section. A DBMS must have the capability to represent a variety of complex relationships among the data as well as to retrieve and update related data easily and efficiently.

1.6.7 Enforcing Integrity Constraints

Most database applications have certain **integrity constraints** that must hold for the data. A DBMS should provide capabilities for defining and enforcing these constraints. The simplest type of integrity constraint involves specifying a data type for each data item. For example, in Figure 1.2, we may specify that the value of the Class data item within each STUDENT record must be an integer between 1 and 5 and that the value of Name must be a string of no more than 30 alphabetic characters. A more complex type of constraint that frequently occurs involves specifying that a record in one file must be related to records in other files. For example, in Figure 1.2, we can specify that "every section record must be related to a course record." Another type of constraint specifies uniqueness on data item values, such as "every course record must have a unique value for CourseNumber." These constraints are derived from the meaning or **semantics** of the data and of the miniworld it represents. It is the database designers' responsibility to identify integrity constraints during database design. Some constraints can be specified to the DBMS and automatically enforced. Other constraints may have to be checked by update programs or at the time of data entry.

A data item may be entered erroneously and still satisfy the specified integrity constraints. For example, if a student receives a grade of A but a grade of C is entered in the database, the DBMS *cannot* discover this error automatically, because C is a valid value for the Grade data type. Such data entry errors can only be discovered manually (when the student receives the grade and complains) and corrected later by updating the database. However, a grade of Z can be rejected automatically by the DBMS, because Z is not a valid value for the Grade data type.

1.6.8 Permitting Inferencing and Actions Using Rules

Some database systems provide capabilities for defining *deduction rules* for *inferencing* new information from the stored database facts. Such systems are called **deductive database systems**. For example, there may be complex rules in the miniworld application for determining when a student is on probation. These can be specified *declaratively* as **rules**, which when compiled and maintained by the DBMS can determine all students on probation. In a traditional DBMS, an explicit *procedural program code* would have to be written to support such applications. But if the miniworld rules change, it is generally more convenient to change the declared deduction rules than to recode procedural programs. More powerful functionality is provided by **active database systems**, which provide active rules that can automatically initiate actions when certain events and conditions occur.

1.6.9 Additional Implications of Using the Database Approach

This section discusses some additional implications of using the database approach that can benefit most organizations.

Potential for Enforcing Standards. The database approach permits the DBA to define and enforce standards among database users in a large organization. This facilitates communication and co-operation among various departments, projects, and users within the organization. Standards can be defined for names and formats of data elements, display formats, report structures, terminology, and so on. The DBA can enforce standards in a centralized database environment more easily than in an environment where each user group has control of its own files and software.

Reduced Application Development Time. A prime selling feature of the database approach is that developing a new application—such as the retrieval of certain data from the database for printing a new report—takes very little time. Designing and implementing a new database from scratch may take more time than writing a single specialized file application. However, once a database is up and running, substantially less time is generally required to create new applications using DBMS facilities. Development time using a DBMS is estimated to be one-sixth to one-fourth of that for a traditional file system.

Flexibility. It may be necessary to change the structure of a database as requirements change. For example, a new user group may emerge that needs information not currently in the database. In response, it may be necessary to add a file to the database or to extend the data elements in an existing file. Modern DBMSs allow certain types of evolutionary changes to the structure of the database without affecting the stored data and the existing application programs.

Availability of Up-to-Date Information. A DBMS makes the database available to all users. As soon as one user's update is applied to the database, all other users can immediately see this update. This availability of up-to-date information is essential for many transaction-processing applications, such as reservation systems or banking databases, and it is made possible by the concurrency control and recovery subsystems of a DBMS.

Economies of Scale. The DBMS approach permits consolidation of data and applications, thus reducing the amount of wasteful overlap between activities of dataprocessing personnel in different projects or departments. This enables the whole organization to invest in more powerful processors, storage devices, or communication gear, rather than having each department purchase its own (weaker) equipment. This reduces overall costs of operation and management.

1.7 A Brief History of Database Applications

We now give a brief historical overview of the applications that use DBMSs, and how these applications provided the impetus for new types of database systems.

1.7.1 Early Database Applications Using Hierarchical and Network Systems

Many early database applications maintained records in large organzations, such as corporations, universities, hospitals, and banks. In many of these applications, there were large numbers of records of similar structure.

For example, in an university application, similar information would be kept for each student, each course, each grade record, and so on. There were also many types of records and many inter-relationships among them.

One of the main problems with early database systems was the intermixing of conceptual relationships with the physical storage and placement of records on disk. For example, the grade records of a particular student could be physically stored next to the student record. Although this provided very efficient access for the original queries and transactions that the database was designed to handle, it did not provide enough flexibility to access records efficiently when new queries and transactions were identified. In particular, new queries that required a different storage organization for efficient processing were quite difficult to implement efficiently. It was also quite difficult to reorganize the database when changes were made to the requirements of the application.

Another shortcoming of early systems was that they provided only programming language interfaces. This made it time-consuming and expensive to implement new queries and transactions, since new programs had to be written, tested, and debugged. Most of these database systems were implemented on large and expensive mainframe computers starting in the mid-1960s and through the 1970s and 1980s. The main types of early systems were based on three main paradigms: hierarchical systems, network model based systems, and inverted file systems.

1.7.2 Providing Application Flexibility with Relational Databases

Relational databases were originally proposed to separate the physical storage of data from its conceptual representation and to provide a mathematical foundation for databases. The relational data model also introduced high-level query languages that provided an alternative to programming language interfaces; hence, it was a lot quicker to write new queries. Relational representation of data somewhat resembles the example we presented in Figure 1.2. Relational systems were initially targeted to the same applications as earlier systems, but were meant to provide flexibility to quickly develop new queries and to reorganize the database as requirements changed.

Early experimental relational systems developed in the late 1970s and the commercial RDBMSs (relational database management systems) introduced in the early 1980s were quite slow, since they did not use physical storage pointers or record placement to access related data records. With the development of new storage and indexing techniques and better query processing and optimization, their performance improved. Eventually, relational databases became the dominant type of database systems for traditional database applications. Relational databases now exist on almost all types of computers, from small personal computers to large servers.

1.7.3 Object-Oriented Applications and the Need for More Complex Databases

The emergence of object-oriented programming languages in the 1980s and the need to store and share complex-structured objects led to the development of object-oriented databases. Initially, they were considered a competitor to relational databases, since they provided more general data structures. They also incorporated many of the useful object-oriented paradigms, such as abstract data types, encapsulation of operations, inheritance, and object identity. However, the complexity of the model and the lack of an early standard contributed to their limited use. They are now mainly used in specialized applications, such as engineering design, multimedia publishing, and manufacturing systems.

1.7.4 Interchanging Data on the Web for E-Commerce

The World Wide Web provided a large network of interconnected computers. Users can create documents using a Web publishing language, such as HTML (HyperText Markup Language), and store these documents on Web servers where other users (clients) can access them. Documents can be linked together through **hyperlinks**, which are pointers to other documents. In the 1990s, electronic commerce (e-commerce) emerged as a major application on the Web. It quickly became apparent that parts of the information on e-commerce Web pages were often dynamically extracted data from DBMSs. A variety of techniques were developed to allow the interchange of data on the Web. Currently, XML (eXtended Markup Language) is considered to be the primary standard for interchanging data among various types of databases and Web pages. XML combines concepts from the models used in document systems with database modeling concepts.

1.7.5 Extending Database Capabilities for New Applications

The success of database systems in traditional applications encouraged developers of other types of applications to attempt to use them. Such applications traditionally used their own specialized file and data structures. The following are examples of these applications:

- **Scientific** applications that store large amounts of data resulting from scientific experiments in areas such as high-energy physics or the mapping of the human genome.

- Storage and retrieval of **images**, from scanned news or personal photographs to satellite photograph images and images from medical procedures such as X-rays or MRI (magnetic resonance imaging).

- Storage and retrieval of **videos**, such as movies, or **video clips** from news or personal digital cameras.

- **Data mining** applications that analyze large amounts of data searching for the occurrences of specific patterns or relationships.

- **Spatial** applications that store spatial locations of data such as weather information or maps used in geographical information systems.

- **Time series** applications that store information such as economic data at regular points in time, for example, daily sales or monthly gross national product figures.

It was quickly apparent that basic relational systems were not very suitable for many of these applications, usually for one or more of the following reasons:

- More complex data structures were needed for modeling the application than the simple relational representation.

- New data types were needed in addition to the basic numeric and character string types.

- New operations and query language constructs were necessary to manipulate the new data types.

- New storage and indexing structures were needed.

This led DBMS developers to add functionality to their systems. Some functionality was general purpose, such as incorporating concepts from object-oriented databases into relational systems. Other functionality was special purpose, in the form of optional modules that could be used for specific applications. For example, users could buy a time series module to use with their relational DBMS for their time series application.

1.8 WHEN NOT TO USE A DBMS

In spite of the advantages of using a DBMS, there are a few situations in which such a system may involve unnecessary overhead costs that would not be incurred in traditional file processing. The overhead costs of using a DBMS are due to the following:

- High initial investment in hardware, software, and training
- The generality that a DBMS provides for defining and processing data
- Overhead for providing security, concurrency control, recovery, and integrity functions

Additional problems may arise if the database designers and DBA do not properly design the database or if the database systems applications are not implemented properly. Hence, it may be more desirable to use regular files under the following circumstances:

- The database and applications are simple, well defined, and not expected to change.
- There are stringent real-time requirements for some programs that may not be met because of DBMS overhead.
- Multiple-user access to data is not required.

1.9 SUMMARY

In this chapter, we defined a database as a collection of related data, where data means recorded facts. A typical database represents some aspect of the real world and is used for specific purposes by one or more groups of users. A DBMS is a generalized software package for implementing and maintaining a computerized database. The database and software together form a database system. We identified several characteristics that distinguish the database approach from traditional file-processing applications. We then discussed the main categories of database users, or the "actors on the scene." We noted that, in addition to database users, there are several categories of support personnel, or "workers behind the scene," in a database environment.

We then presented a list of capabilities that should be provided by the DBMS software to the DBA, database designers, and users to help them design, administer, and use a database. Following this, we gave a brief historical perspective on the evolution of database applications. Finally, we discussed the overhead costs of using a DBMS and discussed some situations in which it may not be advantageous to use a DBMS.

Review Questions

1.1. Define the following terms: *data, database, DBMS, database system, database catalog, program data independence, user view, DBA, end user, canned transaction, deductive database system, persistent object, meta-data, transaction-processing application.*

1.2. What three main types of actions involve databases? Briefly discuss each.

1.3. Discuss the main characteristics of the database approach and how it differs from traditional file systems.

1.4. What are the responsibilities of the DBA and the database designers?

1.5. What are the different types of database end users? Discuss the main activities of each.

1.6. Discuss the capabilities that should be provided by a DBMS.

Exercises

1.7. Identify some informal queries and update operations that you would expect to apply to the database shown in Figure 1.2.

1.8. What is the difference between controlled and uncontrolled redundancy? Illustrate with examples.

1.9. Name all the relationships among the records of the database shown in Figure 1.2.

1.10. Give some additional views that may be needed by other user groups for the database shown in Figure 1.2.

1.11. Cite some examples of integrity constraints that you think should hold on the database shown in Figure 1.2.

Selected Bibliography

The October 1991 issue of *Communications of the* ACM and *Kim* (1995) include several articles describing next-generation DBMSs; many of the database features discussed in the former are now commercially available. The March 1976 issue of ACM *Computing Surveys* offers an early introduction to database systems and may provide a historical perspective for the interested reader.

2

Database System— Concepts and Architecture

The architecture of DBMS packages has evolved from the early monolithic systems, where the whole DBMS software package was one tightly integrated system, to the modern DBMS packages that are modular in design, with a client/server system architecture. This evolution mirrors the trends in computing, where large centralized mainframe computers are being replaced by hundreds of distributed workstations and personal computers connected via communications networks to various types of server machines—Web servers, database servers, file servers, application servers, datawarehouse servers and so on.

In a basic client/server DBMS architecture, the system functionality is distributed between two types of modules.[1] A **client module** is typically designed so that it will run on a user workstation or personal computer. Typically, application programs and user interfaces that access the database run in the client module. Hence, the client module handles user interaction and provides the user-friendly interfaces such as forms- or menu-based GUIs (Graphical User Interfaces). The other kind of module, called a **server module**, typically handles data storage, access, search, and other functions. We discuss client/server architectures in more detail in Section 2.5. First, we must study more basic concepts that will give us a better understanding of modern database architectures.

In this chapter, we present the terminology and basic concepts that will be used throughout the book. We start, in Section 2.1, by discussing data models and defining the concepts of schemas and instances, which are fundamental to the study of database systems. We then discuss the three-schema DBMS architecture and

---

1. As we shall see in Section 2.5, there are variations on this simple *two-tier* client/server architecture.

data independence in Section 2.2; this provides a user's perspective on what a DBMS is supposed to do. In Section 2.3, we describe the types of interfaces and languages that are typically provided by a DBMS. Section 2.4 discusses the database system software environment. Section 2.5 gives an overview of various types of client/server architectures. Finally, Section 2.6 presents a classification of the types of DBMS packages. Section 2.7 summarizes the chapter.

2.1 DATA MODELS, SCHEMAS, AND INSTANCES

One fundamental characteristic of the database approach is that it provides some level of data abstraction by hiding details of data storage that are not needed by most database users. A **data model**—a collection of concepts that can be used to describe the structure of a database—provides the necessary means to achieve this abstraction.[2] By *structure of a database*, we mean the data types, relationships, and constraints that should hold for the data. Most data models also include a set of **basic operations** for specifying retrievals and updates on the database.

In addition to the basic operations provided by the data model, it is becoming more common to include concepts in the data model to specify the **dynamic aspect** or **behavior** of a database application. This allows the database designer to specify a set of valid **user-defined operations** that are allowed on the database objects.[3] An example of a user-defined operation could be COMPUTE_GPA, which can be applied to a STUDENT object. On the other hand, generic operations to insert, delete, modify, or retrieve any kind of object are often included in the *basic data model operations*. Concepts to specify behavior are fundamental to object-oriented data models but are also being incorporated in more traditional data models. For example, object-relational models extend the traditional relational model to include such concepts, among others.

2.1.1 Categories of Data Models

Many data models have been proposed, which we can categorize according to the types of concepts they use to describe the database structure. **High-level** or **conceptual data models** provide concepts that are close to the way many users perceive data, whereas **low-level** or **physical data models** provide concepts that describe the details of how data is stored in the computer. Concepts provided by low-level data models are generally meant for computer specialists, not for typical end users. Between these two extremes is a class of **representational** (or **implementation**) **data models**, which provide concepts that may be understood by end users but that are not too far removed from the way data is organized within the computer. Representational data models hide some details of data storage but can be implemented on a computer system in a direct way.

Conceptual data models use concepts such as entities, attributes, and relationships. An **entity** represents a real-world object or concept, such as an employee or a project, that is described in the database. An **attribute** represents some property of interest that further describes an entity, such as the employee's name or salary. A **relationship** among two or more entities represents an association among two or more entities. For example, a works-on relationship between an employee and a project. Chapter 3 presents the entity-relationship model—a popular high-level conceptual data model. Chapter 3 also describes additional conceptual data modeling concepts, such as generalization, specialization, and categories.

---

2. Sometimes the word *model* is used to denote a specific database description, or schema—for example, "the marketing data model." We will not use this interpretation.

3. The inclusion of concepts to describe behavior reflects a trend whereby database design and software design activities are increasingly being combined into a single activity. Traditionally, specifying behavior is associated with software design.

Representational or implementation data models are the models used most frequently in traditional commercial DBMSs. These include the widely used **relational data model**, as well as the so-called legacy data models—the **network** and **hierarchical models**—that have been widely used in the past. Chapters 4, 5 and 6 of this book are devoted to the relational data model, its operations and languages, and some of the techniques for programming relational database applications.[4] The SQL standard for relational databases is described in Chapter 7. Representational data models represent data by using record structures and hence are sometimes called **record-based data models**.

We can regard **object data models** as a new family of higher-level implementation data models that are closer to conceptual data models. Object data models are also frequently utilized as high-level conceptual models, particularly in the software engineering domain.

Physical data models describe how data is stored as files in the computer by representing information such as record formats, record orderings, and access paths. An **access path** is a structure that makes the search for particular database records efficient. We discuss physical storage techniques and access structures in Chapter 9.

2.1.2   Schemas, Instances, and Database State

In any data model, it is important to distinguish between the *description* of the database and the *database itself*. The description of a database is called the **database schema**, which is specified during database design and is not expected to change frequently.[5] Most data models have certain conventions for displaying schemas as diagrams.[6] A displayed schema is called a **schema diagram**. Figure 2.1 shows a schema diagram for the database shown in Figure 1.2; the diagram displays the structure of each record type but not the actual instances of records. We call each object in the schema—such as STUDENT or COURSE—a **schema construct**.

A schema diagram displays only *some aspects* of a schema, such as the names of record types and data items, and some types of constraints. Other aspects are not specified in the schema diagram. For example, Figure 2.1 shows neither the data type of each data item nor the relationships among the various files. Many types of constraints are not represented in schema diagrams. A constraint such as "students majoring in computer science must take CS1310 before the end of their second year" is quite difficult to represent.

The actual data in a database may change quite frequently. For example, the database shown in Figure 1.2 changes every time we add a student or enter a new grade for a student. The data in the database at a particular moment in time is called **a database state** or **snapshot**. It is also called the *current* set of **occurrences** or **instances** in the database. In a given database state, each schema construct has its own *current set* of instances. For example, the STUDENT construct will contain the set of individual student entities (records) as its instances. Many database states can be constructed to correspond to a particular database schema. Every time we insert or delete a record or change the value of a data item in a record, we change one state of the database into another state.

The distinction between database schema and database state is very important. When we **define** a new database, we specify its database schema only to the DBMS. At this point, the corresponding database state is the *empty state* with no data. We get the *initial state* of the database when the database is first **populated** or **loaded** with the initial data. From then on, every time an update operation is applied to the database, we get

---

4. A summary of the network and hierarchical data models is included in Appendices E and F. The full chapters from the second edition of this book are accessible from the Web site.

5. Schema changes are usually needed as the requirements of the database applications change. Newer database systems include operations for allowing schema changes, although the schema change process is more involved than simple database updates.

6. It is customary in database parlance to use *schemas* as the plural for *schema*, even though *schemata* is the proper plural form. The word *scheme* is sometimes used for a schema.

another database state. At any point in time, the database has a *current state*.[7] The DBMS is partly responsible for ensuring that *every* state of the database is a **valid state**—that is, a state that satisfies the structure and constraints specified in the schema. Hence, specifying a correct schema to the DBMS is extremely important, and the schema must be designed with the utmost care. The DBMS stores the descriptions of the schema constructs and constraints—also called the **meta-data**—in the DBMS catalog so that DBMS software can refer to the schema whenever it needs to. The schema is sometimes called the **intension**, and a database state an **extension** of the schema.

Although, as mentioned earlier, the schema is not supposed to change frequently, it is not uncommon that changes need to be occasionally applied to the schema as the application requirements change. For example, we may decide that another data item needs to be stored for each record in a file, such as adding the DateOfBirth to the STUDENT schema in Figure 2.1. This is known as **schema evolution**. Most modern DBMSs include some operations for schema evolution that can be applied while the database is operational.

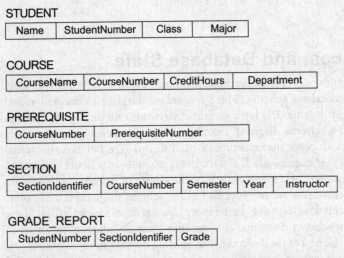

FIGURE 2.1 Schema diagram for the database in Figure 1.2.

2.2 THREE-SCHEMA ARCHITECTURE AND DATA INDEPENDENCE

Three of the four important characteristics of the database approach, listed in Section 1.3, are (1) insulation of programs and data (program-data and program-operation independence), (2) support of multiple user views, and (3) use of a catalog to store the database description (schema). In this section, we specify an architecture for database systems, called the **three-schema architecture**,[8] that was proposed to help achieve and visualize these characteristics. We then further discuss the concept of data independence.

---

7. The current state is also called the *current snapshot* of the database.

8. This is also known as the ANSI/SPARC architecture, after the committee that proposed it (Tsichritzis and Klug 1978).

2.2.1 The Three-Schema Architecture

The goal of the three-schema architecture, illustrated in Figure 2.2, is to separate the user applications and the physical database. In this architecture, schemas can be defined at the following three levels:

FIGURE 2.2 The three-schema architecture.

1. The **internal level** has an **internal schema**, which describes the physical storage structure of the database. The internal schema uses a physical data model and describes the complete details of data storage and access paths for the database.

2. The **conceptual level** has a **conceptual schema**, which describes the structure of the whole database for a community of users. The conceptual schema hides the details of physical storage structures and concentrates on describing entities, data types, relationships, user operations, and constraints. Usually, a representational data model is used to describe the conceptual schema when a database system is implemented. This *implementation conceptual schema* is often based on a *conceptual schema design* in a high-level data model.

3. The **external** or **view level** includes a number of **external schemas** or **user views**. Each external schema describes the part of the database that a particular user group is interested in and hides the rest of the database from that user group. As in the previous case, each external schema is typically implemented using a representational data model, possibly based on an external schema design in a high-level data model.

The three-schema architecture is a convenient tool with which the user can visualize the schema levels in a database system. Most DBMSs do not separate the three levels completely, but support the three-schema architecture to some extent. Some DBMSs may include physical-level details in the conceptual schema. In most DBMSs that support user views, external schemas are specified in the same data model that describes the conceptual-level information. Some DBMSs allow different data models to be used at the conceptual and external levels.

Notice that the three schemas are only *descriptions* of data; the only data that *actually* exists is at the physical level. In a DBMS based on the three-schema architecture, each user group refers only to its own external schema. Hence, the DBMS must transform a request specified on an external schema into a request against the conceptual schema, and then into a request on the internal schema for processing over the stored database. If the request is a database retrieval, the data extracted from the stored database must be reformatted to match the user's external view. The processes of transforming requests and results between levels are called **mappings**. These mappings may be time-consuming, so some DBMSs—especially those that are meant to support small databases—do not support external views. Even in such systems, however, a certain amount of mapping is necessary to transform requests between the conceptual and internal levels.

2.2.2 Data Independence

The three-schema architecture can be used to further explain the concept of **data independence**, which can be defined as the capacity to change the schema at one level of a database system without having to change the schema at the next higher level. We can define two types of data independence:

1. **Logical data independence** is the capacity to change the conceptual schema without having to change external schemas or application programs. We may change the conceptual schema to expand the database (by adding a record type or data item), to change constraints, or to reduce the database (by removing a record type or data item). In the last case, external schemas that refer only to the remaining data should not be affected. For example, the external schema of Figure 1.4a should not be affected by changing the GRADE_REPORT file shown in Figure 1.2 into the one shown in Figure 1.5a. Only the view definition and the mappings need to be changed in a DBMS that supports logical data independence. After the conceptual schema undergoes a logical reorganization, application programs that reference the external schema constructs must work as before. Changes to constraints can be applied to the conceptual schema without affecting the external schemas or application programs.

2. **Physical data independence** is the capacity to change the internal schema without having to change the conceptual schema. Hence, the external schemas need not be changed as well. Changes to the internal schema may be needed because some physical files had to be reorganized—for example, by creating additional access structures—to improve the performance of retrieval or update. If the same data as before remains in the database, we should not have to change the conceptual schema. For example, providing an access path to improve retrieval speed of SECTION records (Figure 1.2) by Semester and Year should not require a query such as "list all sections offered in First Semester of 1998" to be changed, although the query would be executed more efficiently by the DBMS by utilizing the new access path.

Whenever we have a multiple-level DBMS, its catalog must be expanded to include information on how to map requests and data among the various levels. The DBMS uses additional software to accomplish these mappings by referring to the mapping information in the catalog. Data independence occurs because when the schema is changed at some level, the schema at the next higher level remains unchanged; only the *mapping* between the two levels is changed. Hence, application programs referring to the higher-level schema need not be changed.

The three-schema architecture can make it easier to achieve true data independence, both physical and logical. However, the two levels of mappings create an overhead during compilation or execution of a query or program, leading to inefficiencies in the DBMS. Because of this, few DBMSs have implemented the full three-schema architecture.

2.3   DATABASE LANGUAGES AND INTERFACES

In Section 1.4 we discussed the variety of users supported by a DBMS. The DBMS must provide appropriate languages and interfaces for each category of users. In this section we discuss the types of languages and interfaces provided by a DBMS and the user categories targeted by each interface.

2.3.1   DBMS Languages

Once the design of a database is completed and a DBMS is chosen to implement the database, the first order of the day is to specify conceptual and internal schemas for the database and any mappings between the two. In many DBMSs where no strict separation of levels is maintained, one language, called the **data definition language (DDL)**, is used by the DBA and by database designers to define both schemas. The DBMS will have a DDL compiler whose function is to process DDL statements in order to identify descriptions of the schema constructs and to store the schema description in the DBMS catalog.

In DBMSs where a clear separation is maintained between the conceptual and internal levels, the DDL is used to specify the conceptual schema only. Another language, the **storage definition language (SDL)**, is used to specify the internal schema. The mappings between the two schemas may be specified in either one of these languages. For a true three-schema architecture, we would need a third language, the **view definition language (VDL)**, to specify user views and their mappings to the conceptual schema, but in most DBMSs the DDL is used to define both conceptual and external schemas.

Once the database schemas are compiled and the database is populated with data, users must have some means to manipulate the database. Typical manipulations include retrieval, insertion, deletion, and modification of the data. The DBMS provides a set of operations or a language called the **data manipulation language (DML)** for these purposes.

In current DBMSs, the preceding types of languages are usually *not considered distinct languages*; rather, a comprehensive integrated language is used that includes constructs for conceptual schema definition, view definition, and data manipulation. Storage definition is typically kept separate, since it is used for defining physical storage structures to fine-tune the performance of the database system, which is usually done by the DBA staff. A typical example of a comprehensive database language is the SQL relational database language (see Chapter 7), which represents a combination of DDL, VDL, and DML, as well as statements for constraint specification, schema evolution, and other features. The SDL was a component in early versions of SQL but has been removed from the language to keep it at the conceptual and external levels only.

There are two main types of DMLs. A **high-level** or **nonprocedural** DML can be used on its own to specify complex database operations in a concise manner. Many DBMSs allow high-level DML statements either to be entered interactively from a display monitor or terminal or to be embedded in a general-purpose programming language. In the latter case, DML statements must be identified within the program so that they can be extracted by a precompiler and processed by the DBMS. A **low-level** or **procedural** DML *must* be embedded in a general-purpose programming language. This type of DML typically retrieves individual records or objects from the database and processes each separately. Hence, it needs to use programming language constructs, such as looping, to retrieve and process each record from a set of records. Low-level DMLs are also called record-at-a-time DMLs because of this property. High-level DMLs, such as SQL, can specify and retrieve many records in a single DML statement and are hence called **set-at-a-time** or **set-oriented** DMLs. A query in a high-level DML often specifies *which* data to retrieve rather than *how* to retrieve it; hence, such languages are also called **declarative**.

Whenever DML commands, whether high-level or low-level, are embedded in a general-purpose programming language, that language is called the **host language** and the DML is called the **data sublanguage**.[9] On the other hand, a high-level DML used in a stand-alone interactive manner is called a **query language**. In general, both retrieval and update commands of a high-level DML may be used interactively and are hence considered part of the query language.[10]

Casual end users typically use a high-level query language to specify their requests, whereas programmers use the DML in its embedded form. For naive and parametric users, there usually are **user-friendly interfaces** for interacting with the database; these can also be used by casual users or others who do not want to learn the details of a high-level query language. We discuss these types of interfaces next.

2.3.2 DBMS Interfaces

User-friendly interfaces provided by a DBMS may include the following.

Menu-Based Interfaces for Web Clients or Browsing. These interfaces present the user with lists of options, called **menus**, that lead the user through the formulation of a request. Menus do away with the need to memorize the specific commands and syntax of a query language; rather, the query is composed step by step by picking options from a menu that is displayed by the system. Pull-down menus are a very popular technique in **Web-based user interfaces**. They are also often used in **browsing interfaces**, which allow a user to look through the contents of a database in an exploratory and unstructured manner.

Forms-Based Interfaces. A forms-based interface displays a **form** to each user. Users can fill out all of the form entries to insert new data, or they fill out only certain entries, in which case the DBMS will retrieve matching data for the remaining entries. Forms are usually designed and programmed for naive users as interfaces to canned transactions. Many DBMSs have **forms specification languages**, which are special languages that help programmers specify such forms. Some systems have utilities that define a form by letting the end user interactively construct a sample form on the screen.

Graphical User Interfaces. A graphical interface (GUI) typically displays a schema to the user in diagrammatic form. The user can then specify a query by manipulating the diagram. In many cases, GUIs utilize both menus and forms. Most GUIs use a **pointing device**, such as a mouse, to pick certain parts of the displayed schema diagram.

Natural Language Interfaces. These interfaces accept requests written in English or some other language and attempt to "understand" them. A natural language interface usually has its own "schema," which is similar to the database conceptual schema, as well as a dictionary of important words. The natural language interface refers to the words in its schema, as well as to the set of standard words in its dictionary, to interpret the request. If the interpretation is successful, the interface generates a high-level query corresponding to the natural language request and submits it to the DBMS for processing; otherwise, a dialogue is started with the user to clarify the request.

---

9. In object databases, the host and data sublanguages typically form one integrated language—for example, C++ with some extensions to support database functionality. Some relational systems also provide integrated languages—for example, Oracle's PL/SQL.

10. According to the meaning of the word *query* in English, it should really be used to describe only retrievals, not updates.

Interfaces for Parametric Users.   Parametric users, such as bank tellers, often have a small set of operations that they must perform repeatedly. Systems analysts and programmers design and implement a special interface for each known class of naive users. Usually, a small set of abbreviated commands is included, with the goal of minimizing the number of keystrokes required for each request. For example, function keys in a terminal can be programmed to initiate the various commands. This allows the parametric user to proceed with a minimal number of keystrokes.

Interfaces for the DBA.   Most database systems contain privileged commands that can be used only by the DBA's staff. These include commands for creating accounts, setting system parameters, granting account authorization, changing a schema, and reorganizing the storage structures of a database.

2.4   The Database System Environment

A DBMS is a complex software system. In this section, we discuss the types of software components that constitute a DBMS and the types of computer system software with which the DBMS interacts.

2.4.1   DBMS Component Modules

Figure 2.3 illustrates, in a simplified form, the typical DBMS components. The database and the DBMS catalog are usually stored on disk. Access to the disk is controlled primarily by the **operating system (OS)**, which schedules disk input/output. A higher-level **stored data manager** module of the DBMS controls access to DBMS information that is stored on disk, whether it is part of the database or the catalog. The dotted lines and circles marked A, B, C, D, and E in Figure 2.3 illustrate accesses that are under the control of this stored data manager. The stored data manager may use basic OS services for carrying out low-level data transfer between the disk and computer main storage, but it controls other aspects of data transfer, such as handling buffers in main memory. Once the data is in main memory buffers, it can be processed by other DBMS modules, as well as by application programs. Some DBMSs have their own **buffer manager module**, while others use the OS for handling the buffering of disk pages.

The **DDL** compiler processes schema definitions, specified in the DDL, and stores descriptions of the schemas (meta-data) in the DBMS catalog. The catalog includes information such as the names and sizes of files, names and data types of data items, storage details of each file, mapping information among schemas, and constraints, in addition to many other types of information that are needed by the DBMS modules. DBMS software modules then look up the catalog information as needed.

The **runtime database processor** handles database accesses at runtime; it receives retrieval or update operations and carries them out on the database. Access to disk goes through the stored data manager, and the buffer manager keeps track of the database pages in memory. The **query compiler** handles high-level queries that are entered interactively. It parses, analyzes, and compiles or interprets a query by creating database access code, and then generates calls to the runtime processor for executing the code.

The **precompiler** extracts DML commands from an application program written in a host programming language. These commands are sent to the DML compiler for compilation into object code for database access. The rest of the program is sent to the host language compiler. The object codes for the DML commands and the rest of the program are linked, forming a canned transaction whose executable code includes calls to the runtime database processor.

It is now common to have the **client program** that accesses the DBMS running on a separate computer from the computer on which the database resides. The former is called the **client computer**, and the latter is called the **database server**. In some cases, the client accesses a middle computer, called the **application server**, which in turn accesses the database server. We elaborate on this topic in Section 2.5.

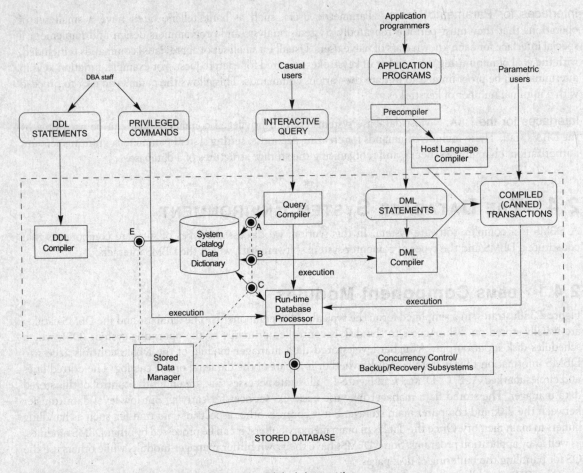

FIGURE 2.3 Component modules of a DBMS and their interactions.

Figure 2.3 is not meant to describe a specific DBMS; rather, it illustrates typical DBMS modules. The DBMS interacts with the operating system when disk accesses—to the database or to the catalog—are needed. If the computer system is shared by many users, the OS will schedule DBMS disk access requests and DBMS processing along with other processes. On the other hand, if the computer system is mainly dedicated to running the database server, the DBMS will control main memory buffering of disk pages. The DBMS also interfaces with compilers for general-purpose host programming languages, and with application servers and client programs running on separate machines through the system network interface.

2.4.2 Database System Utilities

In addition to possessing the software modules just described, most DBMSs have **database utilities** that help the DBA in managing the database system. Common utilities have the following types of functions:

- *Loading:* A loading utility is used to load existing data files—such as text files or sequential files—into the database. Usually, the current (source) format of the data file and the desired (target) database file structure are specified to the utility, which then automatically reformats the data and stores it in the database. With the proliferation of DBMSs, transferring data from one DBMS to another is becoming common in many organizations. Some vendors are offering products that generate the appropriate loading programs, given the existing source and target database storage descriptions (internal schemas). Such tools are also called **conversion tools**.

- *Backup:* A backup utility creates a backup copy of the database, usually by dumping the entire database onto tape. The backup copy can be used to restore the database in case of catastrophic failure. Incremental backups are also often used, where only changes since the previous backup are recorded. Incremental backup is more complex but saves space.

- *File reorganization:* This utility can be used to reorganize a database file into a different file organization to improve performance.

- *Performance monitoring:* Such a utility monitors database usage and provides statistics to the DBA. The DBA uses the statistics in making decisions such as whether or not to reorganize files to improve performance.

Other utilities may be available for sorting files, handling data compression, monitoring access by users, interfacing with the network, and performing other functions.

2.4.3 Tools, Application Environments, and Communications Facilities

Other tools are often available to database designers, users, and DBAs. **CASE** tools[11] are used in the design phase of database systems. Another tool that can be quite useful in large organizations is an expanded **data dictionary** (or **data repository**) **system**. In addition to storing catalog information about schemas and constraints, the data dictionary stores other information, such as design decisions, usage standards, application program descriptions, and user information. Such a system is also called an **information repository**. This information can be accessed *directly* by users or the DBA when needed. A data dictionary utility is similar to the DBMS catalog, but it includes a wider variety of information and is accessed mainly by users rather than by the DBMS software.

Application development environments, such as the PowerBuilder (Sybase) or JBuilder (Borland) system, are becoming quite popular. These systems provide an environment for developing database applications and include facilities that help in many facets of database systems, including database design, GUI development, querying and updating, and application program development.

The DBMS also needs to interface with **communications software**, whose function is to allow users at locations remote from the database system site to access the database through computer terminals, workstations, or their local personal computers. These are connected to the database site through data communications hardware such as phone lines, long-haul networks, local area networks, or satellite communication devices. Many commercial database systems have communication packages that work with the DBMS. The integrated DBMS and data communications system is called a DB/DC system. In addition, some distributed DBMSs are physically distributed over multiple machines. In this case, communications networks are needed to connect the machines. These are often **local area networks** (LANs), but they can also be other types of networks.

---

11. Although CASE stands for computer-aided software engineering, many CASE tools are used primarily for database design.

2.5 CENTRALIZED AND CLIENT/SERVER ARCHITECTURES FOR DBMSS

2.5.1 Centralized DBMSs Architecture

Architectures for DBMSs have followed trends similar to those for general computer system architectures. Earlier architectures used mainframe computers to provide the main processing for all functions of the system, including user application programs and user interface programs, as well as all the DBMS functionality. The reason was that most users accessed such systems via computer terminals that did not have processing power and only provided display capabilities. So, all processing was performed remotely on the computer system, and only display information and controls were sent from the computer to the display terminals, which were connected to the central computer via various types of communications networks.

As prices of hardware declined, most users replaced their terminals with personal computers (PCs) and workstations. At first, database systems used these computers in the same way as they had used display terminals, so that the DBMS itself was still a **centralized** DBMS in which all the DBMS functionality, application program execution, and user interface processing were carried out on one machine. Figure 2.4 illustrates the physical components in a centralized architecture. Gradually, DBMS systems started to exploit the available processing power at the user side, which led to client/server DBMS architectures.

FIGURE 2.4 A physical centralized architecture.

2.5.2   Basic Client/Server Architectures

We first discuss client/server architecture in general, then see how it is applied to DBMSs. The **client/server architecture** was developed to deal with computing environments in which a large number of PCs, workstations, file servers, printers, database servers, Web servers, and other equipment are connected via a network. The idea is to define **specialized servers** with specific functionalities. For example, it is possible to connect a number of PCs or small workstations as clients to a **file server** that maintains the files of the client machines. Another machine could be designated as a **printer server** by being connected to various printers; thereafter, all print requests by the clients are forwarded to this machine. **Web servers** or **e-mail servers** also fall into the specialized server category. In this way, the resources provided by specialized servers can be accessed by many client machines. The **client machines** provide the user with the appropriate interfaces to utilize these servers, as well as with local processing power to run local applications. This concept can be carried over to software, with specialized software—such as a DBMS or a CAD (computer-aided design) package—being stored on specific server machines and being made accessible to multiple clients. Figure 2.5 illustrates client/server architecture at the logical level, and Figure 2.6 is a simplified diagram that shows how the physical architecture would look. Some machines would be only client sites (for example, diskless workstations or workstations/PCs with disks that have only client software installed). Other machines would be dedicated servers. Still other machines would have both client and server functionality.

FIGURE 2.5 Logical two-tier client/server architecture.

The concept of client/server architecture assumes an underlying framework that consists of many PCs and workstations as well as a smaller number of mainframe machines, connected via local area networks and other types of computer networks. A **client** in this framework is typically a user machine that provides user interface capabilities and local processing. When a client requires access to additional functionality—such as database access—that does not exist at that machine, it connects to a server that provides the needed functionality. A **server** is a machine that can provide services to the client machines, such as file access, printing, archiving, or database access. In the general case, some machines install only client software, others only server software, and still others may include both client and server software, as illustrated in Figure 2.6. However, it is more common that client and server software usually run on separate machines. Two main types of basic DBMS architectures were created on this underlying client/server framework: two-tier and three-tier.[12] We discuss those next.

2.5.3   Two-Tier Client/Server Architectures for DBMSs

The client/server architecture is increasingly being incorporated into commercial DBMS packages. In relational DBMSs (RDBMSs), many of which started as centralized systems, the system components that were first moved

---

12. There are many other variations of client/server architectures. We only discuss the two most basic ones here. In Chapter 14, we discuss additional client/server and distributed architectures.

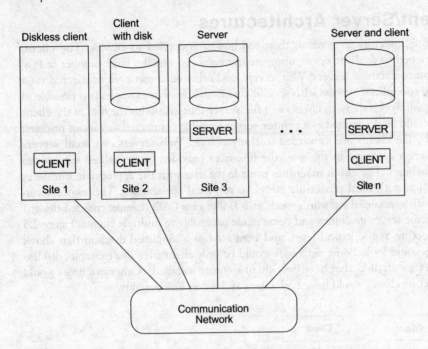

FIGURE 2.6 Physical two-tier client-server architecture.

to the client side were the user interface and application programs. Because SQL (see Chapter 7) provided a standard language for RDBMSs, this created a logical dividing point between client and server. Hence, the query and transaction functionality remained on the server side. In such an architecture, the server is often called a **query server** or **transaction server**, because it provides these two functionalities. In RDBMSs, the server is also often called an SQL **server**, since most RDBMS servers are based on the SQL language and standard.

In such a client/server architecture, the user interface programs and application programs can run on the client side. When DBMS access is required, the program establishes a connection to the DBMS (which is on the server side); once the connection is created, the client program can communicate with the DBMS. A standard called **Open Database Connectivity (ODBC)** provides an **application programming interface (API)**, which allows client-side programs to call the DBMS, as long as both client and server machines have the necessary software installed. Most DBMS vendors provide ODBC drivers for their systems. Hence, a client program can actually connect to several RDBMSs and send query and transaction requests using the ODBC API, which are then processed at the server sites. Any query results are sent back to the client program, which can process or display the results as needed. A related standard for the Java programming language, called JDBC, has also been defined. This allows Java client programs to access the DBMS through a standard interface.

The second approach to client/server architecture was taken by some object-oriented DBMSs. Because many of these systems were developed in the era of client/server architecture, the approach taken was to divide the software modules of the DBMS between client and server in a more integrated way. For example, the **server level** may include the part of the DBMS software responsible for handling data storage on disk pages, local concurrency control and recovery, buffering and caching of disk pages, and other such functions. Meanwhile, the **client level** may handle the user interface; data dictionary functions; DBMS interactions with programming language compilers; global query optimization, concurrency control, and recovery across multiple servers; structuring of complex objects from the data in the buffers; and other such functions. In this approach, the client/server interaction is more tightly coupled and is done internally by the DBMS modules— some of which reside on the client and some on the server—rather than by the users. The exact division of functionality varies from system to system. In such a client/server architecture, the server has been called a **data server**, because it provides data in disk pages to the client. This data can then be structured into objects for the client programs by the client-side DBMS software itself.

The architectures described here are called **two-tier architectures** because the software components are distributed over two systems: client and server. The advantages of this architecture are its simplicity and seamless compatibility with existing systems. The emergence of the World Wide Web changed the roles of clients and server, leading to the three-tier architecture.

2.5.4 Three-Tier Client/Server Architectures for Web Applications

Many Web applications use an architecture called the **three-tier architecture**, which adds an intermediate layer between the client and the database server, as illustrated in Figure 2.7. This intermediate layer or **middle tier** is sometimes called the **application server** and sometimes the **Web server**, depending on the application. This server plays an intermediary role by storing business rules (procedures or constraints) that are used to access data from the database server. It can also improve database security by checking a client's credentials before forwarding a request to the database server. Clients contain GUI interfaces and some additional application-specific business rules. The intermediate server accepts requests from the client, processes the request and sends database commands to the database server, and then acts as a conduit for passing (partially) processed data from the database server to the clients, where it may be processed further and filtered to be presented to users in GUI format. Thus, the *user interface*, *application rules*, and *data access* act as the three tiers.

Advances in encryption and decryption technology make it safer to transfer sensitive data from server to client in encrypted form, where it will be decrypted. The latter can be done by the hardware or by advanced software. This technology gives higher levels of data security, but the network security issues remain a major concern. Various technologies for data compression are also helping in transferring large amounts of data from servers to clients over wired and wireless networks.

FIGURE 2.7 Logical three-tier client/server architecture.

2.6 Classification of Database Management Systems

Several criteria are normally used to classify DBMSs. The first is the **data model** on which the DBMS is based. The main data model used in many current commercial DBMSs is the **relational data model**. The **object data model** was implemented in some commercial systems but has not had widespread use. Many legacy (older) applications still run on database systems based on the **hierarchical** and **network data models**. The relational DBMSs are evolving continuously, and, in particular, have been incorporating many of the concepts that were developed in object databases. This has led to a new class of DBMSs called **object-relational** DBMSs. We can hence categorize DBMSs based on the data model: relational, object, **object-relational**, hierarchical, network, and other.

The second criterion used to classify DBMSs is the **number of users** supported by the system. **Single-user systems** support only one user at a time and are mostly used with personal computers. **Multiuser systems,** which include the majority of DBMSs, support multiple users concurrently.

A third criterion is the **number of sites** over which the database is distributed. A DBMS is **centralized** if the data is stored at a single computer site. A centralized DBMS can support multiple users, but the DBMS and the database themselves reside totally at a single computer site. A **distributed** DBMS (DDBMS) can have the actual database and DBMS software distributed over many sites, connected by a computer network. **Homogeneous** DDBMSs use the same DBMS software at multiple sites. A recent trend is to develop software to access several autonomous preexisting databases stored under **heterogeneous** DBMSs. This leads to a **federated** DBMS (or **multidatabase system**), in which the participating DBMSs are loosely coupled and have a degree of local autonomy. Many DDBMSs use a client-server architecture.

A fourth criterion is the **cost** of the DBMS. The majority of DBMS packages cost between $10,000 and $100,000. Single-user low-end systems that work with microcomputers cost between $100 and $3000. At the other end of the scale, a few elaborate packages cost more than $100,000.

We can also classify a DBMS on the basis of the **types of access path** options for storing files. One well-known family of DBMSs is based on inverted file structures. Finally, a DBMS can be **general purpose** or **special purpose**. When performance is a primary consideration, a special-purpose DBMS can be designed and built for a specific application; such a system cannot be used for other applications without major changes. Many airline reservations and telephone directory systems developed in the past are special purpose DBMSs. These fall into the category of **online transaction processing (OLTP)** systems, which must support a large number of concurrent transactions without imposing excessive delays.

Let us briefly elaborate on the main criterion for classifying DBMSs: the data model. The basic relational data model represents a database as a collection of tables, where each table can be stored as a separate file. The database in Figure 1.2 is shown in a manner very similar to a relational representation. Most relational databases use the high-level query language called SQL and support a limited form of user views. We discuss the relational model, its languages and operations, and techniques for programming relational applications in Chapters 4 through 7.

The object data model defines a database in terms of objects, their properties, and their operations. Objects with the same structure and behavior belong to a **class**, and classes are organized into **hierarchies** (or **acyclic graphs**). The operations of each class are specified in terms of predefined procedures called **methods**. Relational DBMSs have been extending their models to incorporate object database concepts and other capabilities; these systems are referred to as **object-relational** or **extended relational systems**.

Two older, historically important data models, now known as legacy data models, are the network and hierarchical models. The **network model** represents data as record types and also represents a limited type of 1:N relationship, called a **set type**. Figure 2.8 shows a network schema diagram for the database of Figure 1.2, where record types are shown as rectangles and set types are shown as labeled directed arrows. The network model, also known as the CODASYL DBTG model,[13] has an associated record-at-a-time language that must be embedded in a host programming language. The **hierarchical model** represents data as hierarchical tree structures. Each hierarchy represents a number of related records. There is no standard language for the hierarchical model, although most hierarchical DBMSs have record-at-a-time languages. We give a brief overview of the network and hierarchical models in Appendices E and F.[14]

The **XML** (eXtended Markup Language) **model**, now considered the standard for data interchange over the Internet, also uses hierarchical tree structures. It combines database concepts with concepts from document representation models. Data is represented as elements, which can be nested to create complex hierarchical structures. This model conceptually resembles the object model, but uses different terminology.

FIGURE 2.8 The schema of Figure 2.1 in network model notation.

2.7 SUMMARY

In this chapter, we introduced the main concepts used in database systems. We defined a data model, and we distinguished three main categories of data models:

- High-level or conceptual data models (based on entities and relationships)

- Low-level or physical data models

- Representational or implementation data models (record-based, object-oriented)

We distinguished the schema, or description of a database, from the database itself. The schema does not change very often, whereas the database state changes every time data is inserted, deleted, or modified. We then described the three-schema DBMS architecture, which allows three schema levels:

- An internal schema describes the physical storage structure of the database.

- A conceptual schema is a high-level description of the whole database.

- External schemas describe the views of different user groups.

---

13. CODASYL DBTG stands for Conference on Data Systems Languages Data Base Task Group, which is the committee that specified the network model and its language.

14. The full chapters on the network and hierarchical models from the second edition of this book are available over the Internet from the Web site.

A DBMS that cleanly separates the three levels must have mappings between the schemas to transform requests and results from one level to the next. Most DBMSs do not separate the three levels completely. We used the three-schema architecture to define the concepts of logical and physical data independence.

We then discussed the main types of languages and interfaces that DBMSs support. A data definition language (DDL) is used to define the database conceptual schema. In most DBMSs, the DDL also defines user views and, sometimes, storage structures; in other DBMSs, separate languages (VDL, SDL) may exist for specifying views and storage structures. The DBMS compiles all schema definitions and stores their descriptions in the DBMS catalog. A data manipulation language (DML) is used for specifying database retrievals and updates. DMLs can be high-level (set-oriented, nonprocedural) or low-level (record-oriented, procedural). A high-level DML can be embedded in a host programming language, or it can be used as a stand-alone language; in the latter case it is often called a query language.

We discussed different types of interfaces provided by DBMSs, and the types of DBMS users with which each interface is associated. We then discussed the database system environment, typical DBMS software modules, and DBMS utilities for helping users and the DBA perform their tasks. We then gave an overview of the two-tier and three-tier architectures for database applications, which are now very common in most modern applications, particularly Web database applications.

In the final section, we classified DBMSs according to several criteria: data model, number of users, number of sites, cost, types of access paths, and generality. The main classification of DBMSs is based on the data model. We briefly discussed the main data models used in current commercial DBMSs.

Review Questions

2.1. Define the following terms: *data model, database schema, database state, internal schema, conceptual schema, external schema, data independence, DDL, DML, SDL, VDL, query language, host language, data sublanguage, database utility, catalog, client/server architecture.*

2.2. Discuss the main categories of data models.

2.3. What is the difference between a database schema and a database state?

2.4. Describe the three-schema architecture. Why do we need mappings between schema levels? How do different schema definition languages support this architecture?

2.5. What is the difference between logical data independence and physical data independence?

2.6. What is the difference between procedural and nonprocedural DMLs?

2.7. Discuss the different types of user-friendly interfaces and the types of users who typically use each.

2.8. With what other computer system software does a DBMS interact?

2.9. What is the difference between the two-tier and three-tier client/server architectures?

2.10. Discuss some types of database utilities and tools and their functions.

Exercises

2.11. Think of different users for the database of Figure 1.2. What types of applications would each user need? To which user category would each belong, and what type of interface would each need?

2.12. Choose a database application with which you are familiar. Design a schema and show a sample database for that application, using the notation of Figures 2.1 and 1.2. What types of additional information and constraints would you like to represent in the schema? Think of several users for your database, and design a view for each.

Selected Bibliography

Many database textbooks, including Date (2001), Silberschatz et al. (2001), Ramakrishnan and Gehrke (2002), Garcia-Molina et al (1999, 2001), and Abiteboul et al. (1995), provide a discussion of the various database concepts presented here. Tsichritzis and Lochovsky (1982) is an early textbook on data models. Tsichritzis and Klug (1978) and Jardine (1977) present the three-schema architecture, which was first suggested in the DBTG CODASYL report (1971) and later in an American National Standards Institute (ANSI) report (1975). An in-depth analysis of the relational data model and some of its possible extensions is given in Codd (1992). The proposed standard for object-oriented databases is described in Cattell (1997). Many documents describing XML are available on the Web, such as XML (2003).

Examples of database utilities are the ETI Extract Toolkit (www.eti.com) and the database administration tool DB Artisan from Embarcadero Technologies (www.embarcadero.com).

3

Data Modeling Using the Entity-Relationship Model

Conceptual modeling is a very important phase in designing a successful database application. Generally, the term **database application** refers to a particular database and the associated programs that implement the database queries and updates. For example, a BANK database application that keeps track of customer accounts would include programs that implement database updates corresponding to customers making deposits and withdrawals. These programs provide user-friendly graphical user interfaces (GUIs) utilizing forms and menus for the end users of the application—the bank tellers, in this example. Hence, part of the database application will require the design, implementation, and testing of these **application programs**. Traditionally, the design and testing of application programs has been considered to be more in the realm of the software engineering domain than in the database domain. As database design methodologies include more of the concepts for specifying operations on database objects, and as software engineering methodologies specify in more detail the structure of the databases that software programs will use and access, it is clear that these activities are strongly related.

In this chapter, we follow the traditional approach of concentrating on the database structures and constraints during database design. We present the modeling concepts of the **Entity-Relationship (ER) model**, which is a popular high-level conceptual data model. This model and its variations are frequently used for the conceptual design of database applications, and many database design tools employ its concepts. We describe the basic data-structuring concepts and constraints of the ER model and discuss their use in the design of conceptual schemas for database applications. We also present the diagrammatic notation associated with the ER model, known as **ER diagrams**.

Object modeling methodologies such as **UML** (**Universal Modeling Language**) are becoming increasingly popular in software design and engineering. These methodologies go beyond database design to specify detailed design of software modules and their interactions using various types of diagrams. An important part of these methodologies—namely, *class diagrams*[1]—are similar in many ways to the ER diagrams. In class diagrams, *operations* on objects are specified, in addition to specifying the database schema structure. Operations can be used to specify the *functional requirements* during database design, as discussed in Section 3.1. We present some of the UML notation and concepts for class diagrams that are particularly relevant to database design in Section 3.8, and briefly compare these to ER notation and concepts. In this chapter, we also describe features that have been proposed for semantic data models, and show how the ER model can be enhanced to include these concepts, leading to **enhanced ER**, or **EER model**.

This chapter is organized as follows. Section 3.1 discusses the role of high-level conceptual data models in database design. We introduce the requirements for an example database application in Section 3.2 to illustrate the use of concepts from the ER model. This example database is also used in subsequent chapters. In Section 3.3 we present the concepts of entities and attributes, and we gradually introduce the diagrammatic technique for displaying an ER schema. In Section 3.4 we introduce the concepts of binary relationships and their roles and structural constraints. Section 3.5 introduces weak entity types. Section 3.6 shows how a schema design is refined to include relationships. Section 3.7 reviews the notation for ER diagrams, summarizes the issues that arise in schema design, and discusses how to choose the names for database schema constructs. Section 3.8 introduces some UML class diagram concepts, compares them to ER model concepts, and applies them to the same database example. We then present the UML class diagram notation and concepts for representing specialization and generalization in Section 3.10, and briefly compare these with EER notation and concepts.

Section 3.11 discusses some of the more complex issues involved in the modeling of ternary and higher degree relationships. Section 3.12 summarizes the chapter.

3.1   USING HIGH-LEVEL CONCEPTUAL DATA MODELS FOR DATABASE DESIGN

Figure 3.1 shows a simplified description of the database design process. The first step shown is **requirements collection and analysis**. During this step, the database designers interview prospective database users to understand and document their **data requirements**. The result of this step is a concisely written set of users' requirements. These requirements should be specified in as detailed and complete a form as possible. In parallel with specifying the data requirements, it is useful to specify the known **functional requirements** of the application. These consist of the user-defined **operations** (or **transactions**) that will be applied to the database, including both retrievals and updates. In software design, it is common to use *data flow diagrams*, *sequence diagrams*, *scenarios*, and other techniques for specifying functional requirements.

Once all the requirements have been collected and analyzed, the next step is to create a **conceptual schema** for the database, using a high-level conceptual data model. This step is called **conceptual design** The conceptual schema is a concise description of the data requirements of the users and includes detailed descriptions of the entity types, relationships, and constraints; these are expressed using the concepts provided by the high-level data model. Because these concepts do not include implementation details, they are usually easier to understand and can be used to communicate with nontechnical users. The high-level conceptual schema can also be used as a reference to ensure that all users' data requirements are met and that the

---

1. A **class** is similar to an entity type in many ways.

requirements do not conflict. This approach enables the database designers to concentrate on specifying the properties of the data, without being concerned with storage details. Consequently, it is easier for them to come up with a good conceptual database design.

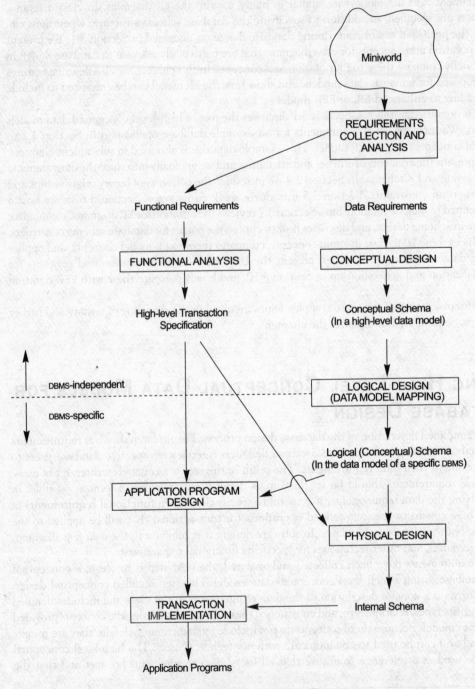

FIGURE 3.1 A simplified diagram to illustrate the main phases of database design.

During or after the conceptual schema design, the basic data model operations can be used to specify the high-level user operations identified during functional analysis. This also serves to confirm that the conceptual schema meets all the identified functional requirements. Modifications to the conceptual schema can be introduced if some functional requirements cannot be specified using the initial schema.

The next step in database design is the actual implementation of the database, using a commercial DBMS. Most current commercial DBMSs use an implementation data model—such as the relational or the object-relational database model—so the conceptual schema is transformed from the high-level data model into the implementation data model. This step is called **logical design** or **data model mapping**, and its result is a database schema in the implementation data model of the DBMS.

The last step is the **physical design** phase, during which the internal storage structures, indexes, access paths, and file organizations for the database files are specified. In parallel with these activities, application programs are designed and implemented as database transactions corresponding to the high-level transaction specifications.

3.2   AN EXAMPLE DATABASE APPLICATION

In this section, we describe an example database application, called COMPANY, that serves to illustrate the basic ER model concepts and their use in schema design. We list the data requirements for the database here, and then create its conceptual schema step by step as we introduce the modeling concepts of the ER model. The COMPANY database keeps track of a company's employees, departments, and projects. Suppose that after the requirements collection and analysis phase, the database designers provided the following description of the "miniworld"—the part of the company to be represented in the database:

1. The company is organized into departments. Each department has a unique name, a unique number, and a particular employee who manages the department. We keep track of the start date when that employee began managing the department. A department may have several locations.

2. A department controls a number of projects, each of which has a unique name, a unique number, and a single location.

3. We store each employee's name, employee's number, address, salary, sex, and date of birth. An employee is assigned to one department but may work on several projects, which are not necessarily controlled by the same department. We keep track of the number of hours per week that an employee works on each project. We also keep track of the direct supervisor of each employee.

4. We want to keep track of the dependents of each employee for insurance purposes. We keep each dependent's first name, sex, date of birth, and relationship to the employee.

Figure 3.2 shows how the schema for this database application can be displayed by means of the graphical notation known as **ER diagrams**. We describe the step-by-step process of deriving this schema from the stated requirements—and explain the ER diagrammatic notation—as we introduce the ER model concepts in the following section.

3.3   ENTITY TYPES, ENTITY SETS, ATTRIBUTES, AND KEYS

The ER model describes data as *entities*, *relationships*, and *attributes*. In Section 3.3.1 we introduce the concepts of entities and their attributes. We discuss entity types and key attributes in Section 3.3.2. Then, in Section 3.3.3, we specify the initial conceptual design of the entity types for the COMPANY database. Relationships are described in Section 3.4.

3.3.1 Entities and Attributes

Entities and Their Attributes. The basic object that the ER model represents is an **entity**, which is a "thing" in the real world with an independent existence. An entity may be an object with a physical existence (for example, a particular person, car, house, or employee) or it may be an object with a conceptual existence (for example, a company, a job, or a university course). Each entity has **attributes**—the particular properties that describe it. For example, an employee entity may be described by the employee's name, age, address, salary, and job. A particular entity will have a value for each of its attributes. The attribute values that describe each entity become a major part of the data stored in the database.

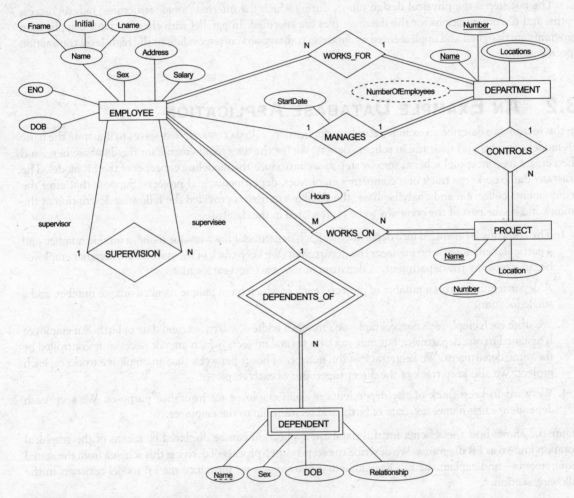

FIGURE 3.2 An ER schema diagram for the COMPANY database.

Figure 3.3 shows two entities and the values of their attributes. The employee entity e_1 has four attributes: Name, Address, Age, and HomePhone; their values are "Mahesh Kumar," "2311 Ameerpet, Hyderabad, AP 500001," "55," and "402459672," respectively. The company entity c_1 has three attributes: Name, Headquarters, and President; their values are "CDAC," "Hyderabad," and "Mahesh Kumar," respectively.

FIGURE 3.3 Two entities, employee e_1 and company c_1, and their attributes.

Several types of attributes occur in the ER model: *simple* versus *composite*, *single-valued* versus *multivalued*, and *stored* versus *derived*. We first define these attribute types and illustrate their use via examples. We then introduce the concept of a *null value* for an attribute.

Composite versus Simple (Atomic) Attributes. **Composite attributes** can be divided into smaller subparts, which represent more basic attributes with independent meanings. For example, the Address attribute of the employee entity shown in Figure 3.3 can be subdivided into StreetAddress, City, State, and Zip, with the values "2311 Ameerpet," "Hyderabad," "AP," and "500001." Attributes that are not divisible are called **simple** or **atomic attributes**. Composite attributes can form a hierarchy. For example, StreetAddress can be further subdivided into three simple attributes: Number, Street, and ApartmentNumber, as shown in Figure 3.4. The value of a composite attribute is the concatenation of the values of its constituent simple attributes.

FIGURE 3.4 A hierarchy of composite attributes.

Composite attributes are useful to model situations in which a user sometimes refers to the composite attribute as a unit but at other times refers specifically to its components. If the composite attribute is referenced only as a whole, there is no need to subdivide it into component attributes. For example, if there is no need to refer to the individual components of an address (zip code, street, and so on), then the whole address can be designated as a simple attribute.

Single-Valued versus Multivalued Attributes. Most attributes have a single value for a particular entity; such attributes are called **single-valued**. For example, Age is a single-valued attribute of a person. In some cases an attribute can have a set of values for the same entity—for example, a Colors attribute for a car, or a

CollegeDegrees attribute for a person. Cars with one color have a single value, whereas two-tone cars have two values for Colors. Similarly, one person may not have a college degree, another person may have one, and a third person may have two or more degrees; therefore, different persons can have different *numbers of values* for the CollegeDegrees attribute. Such attributes are called **multivalued**. A multivalued attribute may have lower and upper bounds to constrain the number of values allowed for each individual entity. For example, the Colors attribute of a car may have between one and three values, if we assume that a car can have at most three colors.

Stored versus Derived Attributes. In some cases, two (or more) attribute values are related—for example, the Age and DOB attributes of a person. For a particular person entity, the value of Age can be determined from the current (today's) date and the value of that person's date of birth (DOB). The Age attribute is hence called a **derived attribute** and is said to be **derivable from** the DOB attribute, which is called a **stored attribute**. Some attribute values can be derived from *related entities*. For example, an attribute NumberOfEmployees of a department entity can be derived by counting the number of employees related to (working for) that department.

Null Values. In some cases a particular entity may not have an applicable value for an attribute. For example, the ApartmentNumber attribute of an address applies only to addresses that are in apartment buildings and not to other types of residences, such as single-family homes. Similarly, a CollegeDegrees attribute applies only to persons with college degrees. For such situations, a special value called **null** is created. An address of a single-family home would have null for its ApartmentNumber attribute, and a person with no college degree would have null for CollegeDegrees. Null can also be used if we do not know the value of an attribute for a particular entity—for example, if we do not know the home phone of "Mahesh Kumar" in Figure 3.3. The meaning of the former type of null is *not applicable*, whereas the meaning of the latter is *unknown*. The "unknown" category of null can be further classified into two cases. The first case arises when it is known that the attribute value exists but is *missing*—for example, if the Height attribute of a person is listed as null. The second case arises when it is *not known* whether the attribute value exists—for example, if the HomePhone attribute of a person is null.

Complex Attributes. Notice that composite and multivalued attributes can be nested in an arbitrary way. We can represent arbitrary nesting by grouping components of a composite attribute between parentheses () and separating the components with commas, and by displaying multivalued attributes between braces { }. Such attributes are called **complex attributes**. For example, if a person can have more than one residence and each residence can have multiple phones, an attribute AddressPhone for a person can be specified as shown in Figure 3.5.

```
{AddressPhone( {Phone(AreaCode,PhoneNumber)},
Address(StreetAddress(Number,Street,ApartmentNumber),
                City,State,Zip) )}
```

FIGURE 3.5 A complex attribute: AddressPhone.

3.3.2 Entity Types, Entity Sets, Keys, and Value Sets

Entity Types and Entity Sets. A database usually contains groups of entities that are similar. For example, a company employing hundreds of employees may want to store similar information concerning each of the employees. These employee entities share the same attributes, but each entity has its *own value(s)* for each attribute. An **entity type** defines a *collection* (or *set*) of entities that have the same attributes. Each entity type in the database is described by its name and attributes. Figure 3.6 shows two entity types, named EMPLOYEE and COMPANY, and a list of attributes for each. A few individual entities of each type are also illustrated, along with the values of their attributes. The collection of all entities of a particular entity type in the database at any point in time is called an **entity set**; the entity set is usually referred to using the same name as the entity type. For example, EMPLOYEE refers to both a *type of entity* as well as the current *set of all employee entities* in the database.

An entity type is represented in ER diagrams[2] (see Figure 3.2) as a rectangular box enclosing the entity type name. Attribute names are enclosed in ovals and are attached to their entity type by straight lines. Composite attributes are attached to their component attributes by straight lines. Multivalued attributes are displayed in double ovals.

An entity type describes the **schema** or **intension** for a *set of entities* that share the same structure. The collection of entities of a particular entity type are grouped into an entity set, which is also called the **extension** of the entity type.

Key Attributes of an Entity Type.   An important constraint on the entities of an entity type is the **key** or **uniqueness constraint** on attributes. An entity type usually has an attribute whose values are distinct for each individual entity in the entity set. Such an attribute is called a **key attribute**, and its values can be used to identify each entity uniquely. For example, the Name attribute is a key of the COMPANY entity type in Figure 3.6, because no two companies are allowed to have the same name. Sometimes, several attributes together form a key, meaning that the *combination* of the attribute values must be distinct for each entity. If a set of attributes possesses this property, the proper way to represent this in the ER model that we describe here is to define a *composite attribute* and designate it as a key attribute of the entity type. Notice that such a composite key must be *minimal*; that is, all component attributes must be included in the composite attribute to have the uniqueness property.[3] In ER diagrammatic notation, each key attribute has its name **underlined** inside the oval, as illustrated in Figure 3.2.

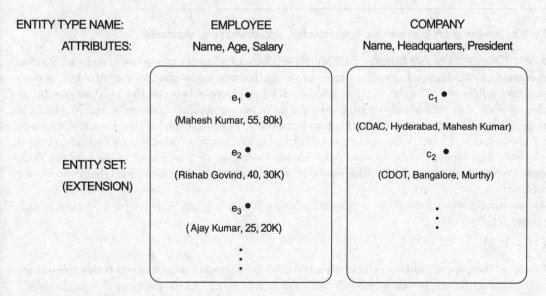

ENTITY TYPE NAME:	EMPLOYEE	COMPANY
ATTRIBUTES:	Name, Age, Salary	Name, Headquarters, President

e_1 •
(Mahesh Kumar, 55, 80k)

c_1 •
(CDAC, Hyderabad, Mahesh Kumar)

ENTITY SET:
(EXTENSION)

e_2 •
(Rishab Govind, 40, 30K)

c_2 •
(CDOT, Bangalore, Murthy)

e_3 •
(Ajay Kumar, 25, 20K)

FIGURE 3.6 Two entity types, EMPLOYEE and COMPANY, and some member entities of each.

---

2. We are using a notation for ER diagrams that is close to the original proposed notation (Chen 1976). Unfortunately, many other notations are in use. We illustrate some of the other notations in Appendix A and later in this chapter when we present UML class diagrams.

3. Superfluous attributes must not be included in a key; however, a **superkey** may include superfluous attributes, as explained in Chapter 4.

Specifying that an attribute is a key of an entity type means that the preceding uniqueness property must hold for *every entity set* of the entity type. Hence, it is a constraint that prohibits any two entities from having the same value for the key attribute at the same time. It is not the property of a particular extension; rather, it is a constraint on *all extensions* of the entity type. This key constraint (and other constraints we discuss later) is derived from the constraints of the miniworld that the database represents.

Some entity types have *more than one* key attribute. For example, each of the VehicleID and Registration attributes of the entity type CAR (Figure 3.7) is a key in its own right. The Registration attribute is an example of a composite key formed from two simple component attributes, RegistrationNumber and State, neither of which is a key on its own. An entity type may also have *no key*, in which case it is called a *weak entity type* (see Section 3.5).

CAR
Registration(RegistrationNumber, State), vehicleID, Make, Model, Year, {Color}

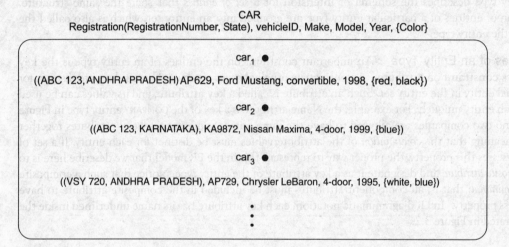

car_1 ●
((ABC 123, ANDHRA PRADESH) AP629, Ford Mustang, convertible, 1998, {red, black})

car_2 ●
((ABC 123, KARNATAKA), KA9872, Nissan Maxima, 4-door, 1999, {blue})

car_3 ●
((VSY 720, ANDHRA PRADESH), AP729, Chrysler LeBaron, 4-door, 1995, {white, blue})
⋮
⋮

FIGURE 3.7 The CAR entity type with two key attributes, Registration and VehicleID.

Value Sets (Domains) of Attributes. Each simple attribute of an entity type is associated with a **value set** (or **domain** of values), which specifies the set of values that may be assigned to that attribute for each individual entity. In Figure 3.6, if the range of ages allowed for employees is between 16 and 70, we can specify the value set of the Age attribute of EMPLOYEE to be the set of integer numbers between 16 and 70. Similarly, we can specify the value set for the Name attribute as being the set of strings of alphabetic characters separated by blank characters, and so on. Value sets are not displayed in ER diagrams. Value sets are typically specified using the basic **data types** available in most programming languages, such as integer, string, boolean, float, enumerated type, subrange, and so on. Additional data types to represent date, time, and other concepts are also employed.

Mathematically, an attribute A of entity type E whose value set is V can be defined as a function from E to the power set[4] $P(V)$ of V:

$$A : E \rightarrow P(V)$$

We refer to the value of attribute A for entity e as $A(e)$. The previous definition covers both single-valued and multivalued attributes, as well as nulls. A null value is represented by the *empty set*. For single-valued attributes, $A(e)$ is restricted to being a *singleton set* for each entity e in E, whereas there is no restriction on multivalued attributes.[5] For a composite attribute A, the value set V is the Cartesian product of $P(V_1)$,

---

4. The **power set** $P(V)$ of a set V is the set of all subsets of V.

5. A **singleton set** is a set with only one element (value).

$P(V_2), \ldots, P(V_n)$, where $V_1, V_2, \ldots, V_n$ are the value sets of the simple component attributes that form A:

$$V = P(V_1) \times P(V_2) \times \ldots \times P(V_n)$$

3.3.3   Initial Conceptual Design of the COMPANY Database

We can now define the entity types for the COMPANY database, based on the requirements described in Section 3.2. After defining several entity types and their attributes here, we refine our design in Section 3.4 after we introduce the concept of a relationship. According to the requirements listed in Section 3.2, we can identify four entity types—one corresponding to each of the four items in the specification (see Figure 3.8):

1. An entity type DEPARTMENT with attributes Name, Number, Locations, Manager, and ManagerStartDate. Locations is the only multivalued attribute. We can specify that both Name and Number are (separate) key attributes, because each was specified to be unique.

2. An entity type PROJECT with attributes Name, Number, Location, and ControllingDepartment. Both Name and Number are (separate) key attributes.

3. An entity type EMPLOYEE with attributes Name, ENO (for employee's number), Sex, Address, Salary, DOB, Department, and Supervisor. Both Name and Address may be composite attributes; however, this was not specified in the requirements. We must go back to the users to see if any of them will refer to the individual components of Name—FirstName, Initial, LastName—or of Address.

4. An entity type DEPENDENT with attributes Employee, DependentName, Sex, DOB, and Relationship (to the employee).

DEPARTMENT
Name, Number, {Locations}, Manager, ManagerStartDate

PROJECT
Name, Number, Location, ControllingDepartment

EMPLOYEE
Name (FName, Initial, LName), ENO, Sex, Address, Salary,
DOB, Department, Supervisor, {WorksOn (Project, Hours)}

DEPENDENT
Employee, DependentName, Sex, DOB, Relationship

FIGURE 3.8 Preliminary design of entity types for the COMPANY database.

So far, we have not represented the fact that an employee can work on several projects, nor have we represented the number of hours per week an employee works on each project. This characteristic is listed as part of requirement 3 in Section 3.2, and it can be represented by a multivalued composite attribute of EMPLOYEE called WorksOn with the simple components (Project, Hours). Alternatively, it can be represented as a multivalued composite attribute of PROJECT called Workers with the simple components (Employee, Hours) We choose the first alternative in Figure 3.8, which shows each of the entity types just described. The Name attribute of EMPLOYEE is shown as a composite attribute, presumably after consultation with the users.

3.4 RELATIONSHIP TYPES, RELATIONSHIP SETS, ROLES, AND STRUCTURAL CONSTRAINTS

In Figure 3.8 there are several *implicit relationships* among the various entity types. In fact, whenever an attribute of one entity type refers to another entity type, some relationship exists. For example, the attribute Manager of DEPARTMENT refers to an employee who manages the department; the attribute ControllingDepartment of PROJECT refers to the department that controls the project; the attribute Supervisor of EMPLOYEE refers to another employee (the one who supervises this employee); the attribute Department of EMPLOYEE refers to the department for which the employee works; and so on. In the ER model, these references should not be represented as attributes but as **relationships**, which are discussed in this section. The COMPANY database schema will be refined in Section 3.6 to represent relationships explicitly. In the initial design of entity types, relationships are typically captured in the form of attributes. As the design is refined, these attributes get converted into relationships between entity types.

This section is organized as follows. Section 3.4.1 introduces the concepts of relationship types, relationship sets, and relationship instances. We then define the concepts of relationship degree, role names, and recursive relationships in Section 3.4.2, and discuss structural constraints on relationships—such as cardinality ratios and existence dependencies—in Section 3.4.3. Section 3.4.4 shows how relationship types can also have attributes.

3.4.1 Relationship Types, Sets, and Instances

A **relationship type** R among n entity types $E_1, E_2, \ldots, E_n$ defines a set of associations—or a **relationship set**—among entities from these entity types. As for the case of entity types and entity sets, a relationship type and its corresponding relationship set are customarily referred to by the *same name*, R. Mathematically, the relationship set R is a set of **relationship instances** r_i, where each r_i associates n individual entities $(e_1, e_2, \ldots, e_n)$, and each entity e_j in r_i is a member of entity type E_j, $1 \leq j \leq n$. Hence, a relationship type is a mathematical relation on $E_1, E_2, \ldots, E_n$; alternatively, it can be defined as a subset of the Cartesian product $E_1 \times E_2 \times \ldots \times E_n$. Each of the entity types $E_1, E_2, \ldots, E_n$ is said to **participate** in the relationship type R_i; similarly, each of the individual entities $e_1, e_2, \ldots, e_n$ is said to participate in the relationship instance r_i $(e_1, e_2, \ldots, e_n)$.

Informally, each relationship instance r_i in R is an association of entities, where the association includes exactly one entity from each participating entity type. Each such relationship instance r_i represents the fact that the entities participating in r_i are related in some way in the corresponding miniworld situation. For example, consider a relationship type WORKS_FOR between the two entity types EMPLOYEE and DEPARTMENT, which associates each employee with the department for which the employee works. Each relationship instance in the relationship set WORKS_FOR associates one employee entity and one department entity. Figure 3.9 illustrates this example, where each relationship instance r_i is shown connected to the employee and department entities that participate in ri. In the miniworld represented by Figure 3.9, employees e_1, e_3, and e_6 work for department d_1; e_2 and e_4 work for d_2; and e_5 and e_7 work for d_3.

In ER diagrams, relationship types are displayed as diamond-shaped boxes, which are connected by straight lines to the rectangular boxes representing the participating entity types. The relationship name is displayed in the diamond-shaped box (see Figure 3.2).

EMPLOYEE   WORKS_FOR   DEPARTMENT

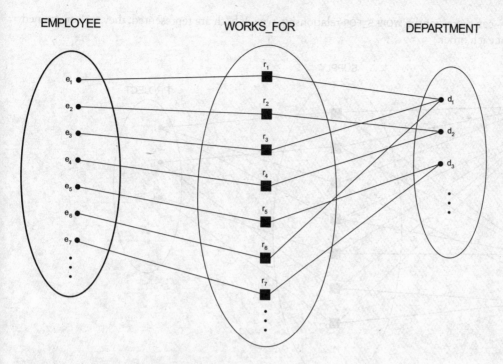

FIGURE 3.9 Some instances in the WORKS_FOR relationship set, which represents a relationship type WORKS_FOR between EMPLOYEE and DEPARTMENT.

3.4.2 Relationship Degree, Role Names, and Recursive Relationships

Degree of a Relationship Type. The **degree** of a relationship type is the number of participating entity types. Hence, the WORKS_FOR relationship is of degree two. A relationship type of degree two is called **binary**, and one of degree three is called **ternary**. An example of a ternary relationship is SUPPLY, shown in Figure 3.10, where each relationship instance r_i associates three entities—a supplier s, a part p, and a project j—whenever s supplies part p to project j. Relationships can generally be of any degree, but the ones most common are binary relationships. Higher-degree relationships are generally more complex than binary relationships; we characterize them further in Section 3.11.

Relationships as Attributes.   It is sometimes convenient to think of a relationship type in terms of attributes, as we discussed in Section 3.3.3. Consider the WORKS_FOR relationship type of Figure 3.9. One can think of an attribute called Department of the EMPLOYEE entity type whose value for each employee entity is (a reference to) the *department entity* that the employee works for. Hence, the value set for this Department attribute is the *set of all* DEPARTMENT *entities*, which is the DEPARTMENT entity set. This is what we did in Figure 3.8 when we specified the initial design of the entity type EMPLOYEE for the COMPANY database. However, when we think of a binary relationship as an attribute, we always have two options. In this example, the alternative is to think of a multivalued attribute Employees of the entity type DEPARTMENT whose values for each department entity is the *set of employee entities* who work for that department. The value set of this Employees attribute is the power set of the EMPLOYEE entity set. Either of these two attributes—Department of EMPLOYEE or Employees of DEPARTMENT—can represent the WORKS_FOR relationship type. If both are represented, they are constrained to be inverses of each other.[6]

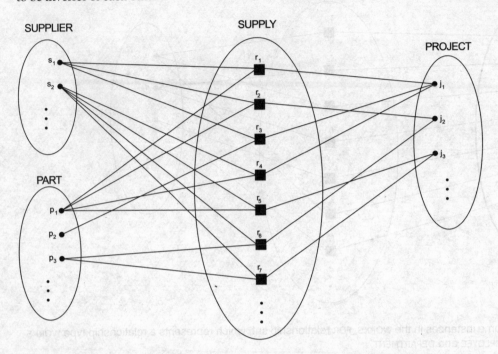

FIGURE 3.10 Some relationship instances in the SUPPLY ternary relationship set.

Role Names and Recursive Relationships.   Each entity type that participates in a relationship type plays a particular role in the relationship. The **role name** signifies the role that a participating entity from the entity type plays in each relationship instance, and helps to explain what the relationship means. For example, in the WORKS_FOR relationship type, EMPLOYEE plays the role of *employee* or *worker* and DEPARTMENT plays the role of *department* or *employer*.

Role names are not technically necessary in relationship types where all the participating entity types are distinct, since each participating entity type name can be used as the role name. However, in some cases the same *entity* type participates more than once in a relationship type in *different roles*. In such cases the role name becomes essential for distinguishing the meaning of each participation. Such relationship types are called **recursive relationships**. Figure 3.11 shows an example. The SUPERVISION relationship type relates an employee to a supervisor, where both employee and supervisor entities are members of the same EMPLOYEE entity type. Hence, the EMPLOYEE entity type *participates twice* in SUPERVISION: once in the role of *supervisor* (or *boss*), and once in the role of supervisee (or subordinate). Each relationship instance r_i in SUPERVISION associates two employee entities e_j and e_k, one of which plays the role of supervisor and the other the role of supervisee. In Figure 3.11, the lines marked "1" represent the supervisor role, and those marked "2" represent the supervisee role; hence, e_1 supervises e_2 and e_3, e_4 supervises e_6 and e_7, and e_5 supervises e_1 and e_4.

---

6. This concept of representing relationship types as attributes is used in a class of data models called **functional data models**. In relational databases (see Chapter 4), foreign keys are a type of reference attribute used to represent relationships.

3.4.3 Constraints on Relationship Types

Relationship types usually have certain constraints that limit the possible combinations of entities that may participate in the corresponding relationship set. These constraints are determined from the miniworld situation that the relationships represent. For example, in Figure 3.9, if the company has a rule that each employee must work for exactly one department, then we would like to describe this constraint in the schema. We can distinguish two main types of relationship constraints: *cardinality ratio* and *participation*.

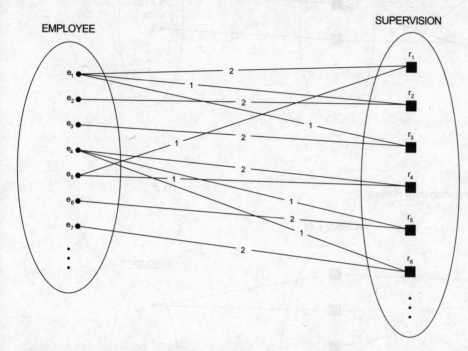

FIGURE 3.11 A recursive relationship SUPERVISION between EMPLOYEE in the supervisor role (1) and EMPLOYEE in the subordinate role (2).

Cardinality Ratios for Binary Relationships.   The **cardinality ratio** for a binary relationship specifies the *maximum* number of relationship instances that an entity can participate in. For example, in the WORKS_FOR binary relationship type, DEPARTMENT:EMPLOYEE is of cardinality ratio 1:N, meaning that each department can be related to (that is, employs) any number of employees,[7] but an employee can be related to (work for) only one department. The possible cardinality ratios for binary relationship types are 1:1, 1:N, N:1, and M:N.

An example of a 1:1 binary relationship is MANAGES (Figure 3.12), which relates a department entity to the employee who manages that department. This represents the miniworld constraints that—at any point in time—an employee can manage only one department and a department has only one manager. The relationship type WORKS_ON (Figure 3.13) is of cardinality ratio M:N, because the miniworld rule is that an employee can work on several projects and a project can have several employees.

Cardinality ratios for binary relationships are represented on ER diagrams by displaying 1, M, and N on the diamonds as shown in Figure 3.2.

---

7. N stands for any *number* of related entities (zero or more).

FIGURE 3.12 A 1:1 relationship, MANAGES.

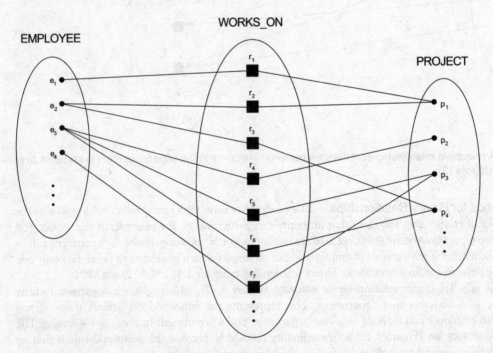

FIGURE 3.13 An M:N relationship, WORKS_ON.

Participation Constraints and Existence Dependencies. The **participation constraint** specifies whether the existence of an entity depends on its being related to another entity via the relationship type. This constraint specifies the *minimum* number of relationship instances that each entity can participate in, and is sometimes called the **minimum cardinality constraint**. There are two types of participation constraints—total and partial—which we illustrate by example. If a company policy states that every employee must work for a department, then an employee entity can exist only if it participates in at least one WORKS_FOR relationship instance (Figure 3.9). Thus, the participation of EMPLOYEE in WORKS_FOR is called **total participation**, meaning that every entity in "the total set" of employee entities must be related to a department entity via WORKS_FOR. Total participation is also called **existence dependency**. In Figure 3.12 we do not expect every employee to manage a department, so the participation of EMPLOYEE in the MANAGES relationship type is **partial**, meaning that some or "part of the set of " employee entities are related to some department entity via MANAGES, but not necessarily all. We will refer to the cardinality ratio and participation constraints, taken together, as the **structural constraints** of a relationship type.

In ER diagrams, total participation (or existence dependency) is displayed as a *double line* connecting the participating entity type to the relationship, whereas partial participation is represented by a *single line* (see Figure 3.2).

3.4.4   Attributes of Relationship Types

Relationship types can also have attributes, similar to those of entity types. For example, to record the number of hours per week that an employee works on a particular project, we can include an attribute Hours for the WORKS_ON relationship type of Figure 3.13. Another example is to include the date on which a manager started managing a department via an attribute StartDate for the MANAGES relationship type of Figure 3.12.

Notice that attributes of 1:1 or 1:N relationship types can be migrated to one of the participating entity types. For example, the StartDate attribute for the MANAGES relationship can be an attribute of either EMPLOYEE or DEPARTMENT, although conceptually it belongs to MANAGES. This is because MANAGES is a 1:1 relationship, so every department or employee entity participates in *at most one* relationship instance. Hence, the value of the StartDate attribute can be determined separately, either by the participating department entity or by the participating employee (manager) entity.

For a 1:N relationship type, a relationship attribute can be migrated *only* to the entity type on the N-side of the relationship. For example, in Figure 3.9, if the WORKS_FOR relationship also has an attribute StartDate that indicates when an employee started working for a department, this attribute can be included as an attribute of EMPLOYEE. This is because each employee works for only one department, and hence participates in at most one relationship instance in WORKS_FOR. In both 1:1 and 1:N relationship types, the decision as to where a relationship attribute should be placed—as a relationship type attribute or as an attribute of a participating entity type—is determined subjectively by the schema designer.

For M:N relationship types, some attributes may be determined by the *combination of participating entities* in a relationship instance, not by any single entity. Such attributes *must be specified as relationship attributes*. An example is the Hours attribute of the M:N relationship WORKS_ON (Figure 3.13); the number of hours an employee works on a project is determined by an employee-project combination and not separately by either entity.

3.5   WEAK ENTITY TYPES

Entity types that do not have key attributes of their own are called **weak entity types**. In contrast, **regular entity types** that do have a key attribute—which include all the examples we discussed so far—are called **strong entity types**. Entities belonging to a weak entity type are identified by being related to specific entities from another entity type in combination with one of their attribute values. We call this other entity type the **identifying** or **owner entity type**,[8] and we call the relationship type that relates a weak entity type to its owner the **identifying relationship** of the weak entity type.[9] A weak entity type always has a *total participation constraint* (existence dependency) with respect to its identifying relationship, because a weak entity cannot be identified without an owner entity. However, not every existence dependency results in a weak entity type. For example, a DRIVER_LICENSE entity cannot exist unless it is related to a PERSON entity, even though it has its own key (LicenseNumber) and hence is not a weak entity.

Consider the entity type DEPENDENT, related to EMPLOYEE, which is used to keep track of the dependents of each employee via a 1:N relationship (Figure 3.2). The attributes of DEPENDENT are Name (the first name of the dependent), DOB, Sex, and Relationship (to the employee). Two dependents of two distinct *employees* may, by chance, have the same values for Name, DOB, Sex, and Relationship, but they are still distinct entities. They are identified as distinct entities only after determining the *particular employee entity* to which each dependent is related. Each employee entity is said to **own** the dependent entities that are related to it.

A weak entity type normally has a **partial key**, which is the set of attributes that can uniquely identify weak entities that are *related to the same owner entity*.[10] In our example, if we assume that no two dependents of the same employee ever have the same first name, the attribute Name of DEPENDENT is the partial key. In the worst case, a composite attribute of *all the weak entity's attributes* will be the partial key.

In ER diagrams, both a weak entity type and its identifying relationship are distinguished by surrounding their boxes and diamonds with double lines (see Figure 3.2). The partial key attribute is underlined with a dashed or dotted line.

Weak entity types can sometimes be represented as complex (composite, multivalued) attributes. In the preceding example, we could specify a multivalued attribute Dependents for EMPLOYEE, which is a composite attribute with component attributes Name, DOB, Sex, and Relationship. The choice of which representation to use is made by the database designer. One criterion that may be used is to choose the weak entity type representation if there are many attributes. If the weak entity participates independently in relationship types other than its identifying relationship type, then it should *not* be modeled as a complex attribute.

In general, any number of levels of weak entity types can be defined; an owner entity type may itself be a weak entity type. In addition, a weak entity type may have more than one identifying entity type and an identifying relationship type of degree higher than two, as we illustrate in Section 3.11.

3.6 REFINING THE ER DESIGN FOR THE COMPANY DATABASE

We can now refine the database design of Figure 3.8 by changing the attributes that represent relationships into relationship types. The cardinality ratio and participation constraint of each relationship type are determined from the requirements listed in Section 3.2. If some cardinality ratio or dependency cannot be determined from the requirements, the users must be questioned further to determine these structural constraints.

In our example, we specify the following relationship types:

1. MANAGES, a 1:1 relationship type between EMPLOYEE and DEPARTMENT. EMPLOYEE participation is partial. DEPARTMENT participation is not clear from the requirements. We question the users, who say that a department must have a manager at all times, which implies total participation.[11] The attribute StartDate is assigned to this relationship type.

---

8. The identifying entity type is also sometimes called the **parent entity type** or the **dominant entity type**.

9. The weak entity type is also sometimes called the **child entity type** or the **subordinate entity type**.

10. The partial key is sometimes called the **discriminator**.

11. The rules in the miniworld that determine the constraints are sometimes called the *business rules*, since they are determined by the "business" or organization that will utilize the database.

2. WORKS_FOR, a 1:N relationship type between DEPARTMENT and EMPLOYEE. Both participations are total.

3. CONTROLS, a 1:N relationship type between DEPARTMENT and PROJECT. The participation of PROJECT is total, whereas that of DEPARTMENT is determined to be partial, after consultation with the users indicates that some departments may control no projects.

4. SUPERVISION, a 1:N relationship type between EMPLOYEE (in the supervisor role) and EMPLOYEE (in the supervisee role). Both participations are determined to be partial, after the users indicate that not every employee is a supervisor and not every employee has a supervisor.

5. WORKS_ON, determined to be an M:N relationship type with attribute Hours, after the users indicate that a project can have several employees working on it. Both participations are determined to be total.

6. DEPENDENTS_OF, a 1:N relationship type between EMPLOYEE and DEPENDENT, which is also the identifying relationship for the weak entity type DEPENDENT. The participation of EMPLOYEE is partial, whereas that of DEPENDENT is total.

After specifying the above six relationship types, we remove from the entity types in Figure 3.8 all attributes that have been refined into relationships. These include Manager and ManagerStartDate from DEPARTMENT; ControllingDepartment from PROJECT; Department, Supervisor, and WorksOn from EMPLOYEE; and Employee from DEPENDENT. It is important to have the least possible redundancy when we design the conceptual schema of a database. If some redundancy is desired at the storage level or at the user view level, it can be introduced later, as discussed in Section 1.6.1.

3.7   ER Diagrams, Naming Conventions, and Design Issues

3.7.1   Summary of Notation for ER Diagrams

Figures 3.9 through 3.13 illustrate examples of the participation of entity types in relationship types by displaying their extensions—the individual entity instances and relationship instances in the entity sets and relationship sets. In ER diagrams the emphasis is on representing the schemas rather than the instances. This is more useful in database design because a database schema changes rarely, whereas the contents of the entity sets change frequently. In addition, the schema is usually easier to display than the extension of a database, because it is much smaller.

Figure 3.2 displays the COMPANY ER database schema as an ER diagram. We now review the full ER diagram notation. Entity types such as EMPLOYEE, DEPARTMENT, and PROJECT are shown in rectangular boxes. Relationship types such as WORKS_FOR, MANAGES, CONTROLS, and WORKS_ON are shown in diamond-shaped boxes attached to the participating entity types with straight lines. Attributes are shown in ovals, and each attribute is attached by a straight line to its entity type or relationship type. Component attributes of a composite attribute are attached to the oval representing the composite attribute, as illustrated by the Name attribute of EMPLOYEE. Multivalued attributes are shown in double ovals, as illustrated by the Locations attribute of DEPARTMENT. Key attributes have their names underlined. Derived attributes are shown in dotted ovals, as illustrated by the NumberOfEmployees attribute of DEPARTMENT.

Weak entity types are distinguished by being placed in double rectangles and by having their identifying relationship placed in double diamonds, as illustrated by the DEPENDENT entity type and the DEPENDENTS_OF identifying relationship type. The partial key of the weak entity type is underlined with a dotted line.

In Figure 3.2 the cardinality ratio of each *binary* relationship type is specified by attaching a 1, M, or N on each participating edge. The cardinality ratio of DEPARTMENT:EMPLOYEE in MANAGES is 1:1, whereas it is 1:N for DEPARTMENT:EMPLOYEE in WORKS_FOR, and M:N for WORKS_ON. The participation constraint is specified by a single line for partial participation and by double lines for total participation (existence dependency).

In Figure 3.2 we show the role names for the SUPERVISION relationship type because the EMPLOYEE entity type plays both roles in that relationship. Notice that the cardinality is 1:N from supervisor to supervisee because each employee in the role of supervisee has at most one direct supervisor, whereas an employee in the role of supervisor can supervise zero or more employees.

Figure 3.14 summarizes the conventions for ER diagrams.

3.7.2 Proper Naming of Schema Constructs

When designing a database schema, the choice of names for entity types, attributes, relationship types, and (particularly) roles is not always straightforward. One should choose names that convey, as much as possible, the meanings attached to the different constructs in the schema. We choose to use *singular names* for entity types, rather than plural ones, because the entity type name applies to each individual entity belonging to that entity type. In our ER diagrams, we will use the convention that entity type and relationship type names are in uppercase letters, attribute names are capitalized, and role names are in lowercase letters. We have already used this convention in Figure 3.2.

As a general practice, given a narrative description of the database requirements, the *nouns* appearing in the narrative tend to give rise to entity type names, and the *verbs* tend to indicate names of relationship types. Attribute names generally arise from additional nouns that describe the nouns corresponding to entity types.

Another naming consideration involves choosing binary relationship names to make the ER diagram of the schema readable from left to right and from top to bottom. We have generally followed this guideline in Figure 3.2. To explain this naming convention further, we have one exception to the convention in Figure 3.2—the DEPENDENTS_OF relationship type, which reads from bottom to top. When we describe this relationship, we can say that the DEPENDENT entities (bottom entity type) are DEPENDENTS_OF (relationship name) an EMPLOYEE (top entity type). To change this to read from top to bottom, we could rename the relationship type to HAS_DEPENDENTS, which would then read as follows: An EMPLOYEE entity (top entity type) HAS_DEPENDENTS (relationship name) of type DEPENDENT (bottom entity type). Notice that this issue arises because each binary relationship can be described starting from either of the two participating entity types, as discussed in the beginning of Section 3.4.

3.7.3 Design Choices for ER Conceptual Design

It is occasionally difficult to decide whether a particular concept in the miniworld should be modeled as an entity type, an attribute, or a relationship type. In this section, we give some brief guidelines as to which construct should be chosen in particular situations.

Symbol	**Meaning**

FIGURE 3.14 Summary of the notation for ER diagrams.

In general, the schema design process should be considered an iterative refinement process, where an initial design is created and then iteratively refined until the most suitable design is reached. Some of the refinements that are often used include the following:

- A concept may be first modeled as an attribute and then refined into a relationship because it is determined that the attribute is a reference to another entity type. It is often the case that a pair of such attributes that are inverses of one another are refined into a binary relationship. We discussed this type of refinement in detail in Section 3.6.

- Similarly, an attribute that exists in several entity types may be elevated or promoted to an independent entity type. For example, suppose that several entity types in a UNIVERSITY database, such as STUDENT, INSTRUCTOR, and COURSE, each has an attribute Department in the initial design; the designer may then choose to create an entity type DEPARTMENT with a single attribute DeptName and relate it to the three entity types (STUDENT, INSTRUCTOR, and COURSE) via appropriate relationships. Other attributes/relationships of DEPARTMENT may be discovered later.

- An inverse refinement to the previous case may be applied—for example, if an entity type DEPARTMENT exists in the initial design with a single attribute DeptName and is related to only one other entity type, STUDENT. In this case, DEPARTMENT may be reduced or demoted to an attribute of STUDENT.

- In this chapter, we also discuss other refinements concerning specialization/generalization and relationships of higher degree.

3.7.4 Alternative Notations for ER Diagrams

There are many alternative diagrammatic notations for displaying ER diagrams. Appendix A gives some of the more popular notations. In Section 3.8, we introduce the Universal Modeling Language (UML) notation for class diagrams, which has been proposed as a standard for conceptual object modeling.

In this section, we describe one alternative ER notation for specifying structural constraints on relationships. This notation involves associating a pair of integer numbers (min, max) with each *participation* of an entity type E in a relationship type R, where $0 \leq$ min $\leq$ max and max ≥ 1. The numbers mean that for each entity e in E, e must participate in at least min and at most max relationship instances in R *at any point in time*. In this method, min $= 0$ implies partial participation, whereas min > 0 implies total participation.

Figure 3.15 displays the COMPANY database schema using the (min, max) notation.[12] Usually, one uses either the cardinality ratio/single-line/double-line notation *or* the (min,max) notation. The (min, max) notation is more precise, and we can use it easily to specify structural constraints for relationship types of *any degree*. However, it is not sufficient for specifying some key constraints on higher-degree relationships, as discussed in Section 3.11. Figure 3.15 displays all the role names for the COMPANY database schema.

---

12. In some notations, particularly those used in object modeling methodologies such as UML, the (min, max) is placed on the *opposite sides* to the ones we have shown. For example, for the WORKS_FOR relationship in Figure 3.15, the (1,1) would be on the DEPARTMENT side, and the (4,N) would be on the EMPLOYEE side. Here we used the original notation from Abrial (1974).

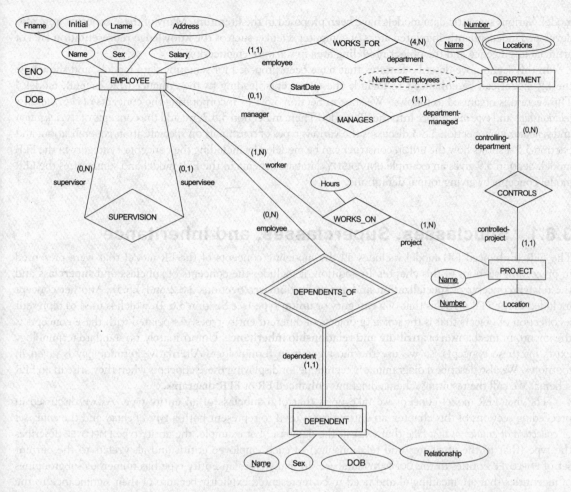

FIGURE 3.15 ER diagrams for the COMPANY schema, with structural constraints specified using (min, max) notation.

3.8 ENHANCED ENTITY-RELATIONSHIP (EER) MODELING

The ER modeling concepts discussed in the preceeding sections of this chapter are sufficient for representing many database schemas for "traditional" database applications, which mainly include dataprocessing applications in business and industry. Since the late 1970s, however, designers of database applications have tried to design more accurate database schemas that reflect the data properties and constraints more precisely. This was particularly important for newer applications of database technology, such as databases for engineering design and manufacturing (CAD/CAM[13]), telecommunications, complex software systems, and Geographic Information Systems (GIS), among many other applications. These types of databases have more complex requirements than do the more traditional applications. This led to the development of additional *semantic data modeling* concepts that were incorporated into conceptual data models such as the ER

---

13. CAD/CAM stands for computer-aided design/computer-aided manufacturing.

model. Various semantic data models have been proposed in the literature. Many of these concepts were also developed independently in related areas of computer science, such as the **knowledge representation** area of artificial intelligence and the **object modeling** area in software engineering.

In this section, we describe features that have been proposed for semantic data models, and show how the ER model can be enhanced to include these concepts, leading to the enhanced ER, or EER, model.[14] This section is organised as follows. We start in Section 3.8.1 by incorporating the concepts of *class/subclass relationships* and *type inheritance* into the ER model. Then, in Section 3.8.2, we add the concepts of *specialization* and *generalization*. Section 3.8.3 discusses the various types of *constraints* on specialization/generalization, and Section 3.8.4 shows how the UNION construct can be modeled by including the concept of category in the EER model. Section 3.9 gives an example UNIVERSITY database schema in the EER model and summarizes the EER model concepts by giving formal definitions.

3.8.1 Subclasses, Superclasses, and Inheritance

The EER (Enhanced ER) model includes all the modeling concepts of the ER model that were presented in preceeding sections of this chapter. In addition, it includes the concepts of **subclass** and **superclass** and the related concepts of **specialization** and **generalization** (see Sections 3.8.2 and 3.8.3). Another concept included in the EER model is that of a **category** or **union type** (see Section 3.8.4), which is used to represent a collection of objects that is the *union* of objects of different entity types. Associated with these concepts is the important mechanism of **attribute and relationship inheritance**. Unfortunately, no standard terminology exists for these concepts, so we use the most common terminology. Alternative terminology is given in footnotes. We also describe a diagrammatic technique for displaying these concepts when they arise in an EER schema. We call the resulting schema diagrams **enhanced ER** or **EER diagrams**.

The first EER model concept we take up is that of a **subclass** of an entity type. As we discussed in preceeding sections of this chapter, an entity type is used to represent both a *type of entity* and the *entity set* or *collection of entities of that type* that exist in the database. For example, the entity type EMPLOYEE describes the type (that is, the attributes and relationships) of each employee entity, and also refers to the current set of EMPLOYEE entities in the COMPANY database. In many cases an entity type has numerous subgroupings of its entities that are meaningful and need to be represented explicitly because of their significance to the database application. For example, the entities that are members of the EMPLOYEE entity type may be grouped further into SECRETARY, ENGINEER, MANAGER, TECHNICIAN, SALARIED_EMPLOYEE, HOURLY_EMPLOYEE, and so on. The set of entities in each of the latter groupings is a subset of the entities that belong to the EMPLOYEE entity set, meaning that every entity that is a member of one of these subgroupings is also an employee. We call each of these subgroupings a **subclass** of the EMPLOYEE entity type, and the EMPLOYEE entity type is called the **superclass** for each of these subclasses. Figure 3.16 shows how to diagramatically represent these concepts in EER diagrams.

We call the relationship between a superclass and any one of its subclasses a **superclass/subclass** or simply **class/subclass** relationship.[15] In our previous example, EMPLOYEE/SECRETARY and EMPLOYEE/TECHNICIAN are two class/subclass relationships. Notice that a member entity of the subclass represents the same real-world entity as some member of the superclass. For example, a SECRETARY entity 'Renuka' is also the EMPLOYEE 'Renuka'. Hence, the subclass member is the same as the entity in the superclass, but in a distinct *specific role*. When

---

14. EER has also been used to stand for *Extended* model.

15. A class/subclass relationship is often called an IS-A (or IS-AN) **relationship** because of the way we refer to the concept. We say "a SECRETARY is an EMPLOYEE," "a TECHNICIAN is an EMPLOYEE," and so on.

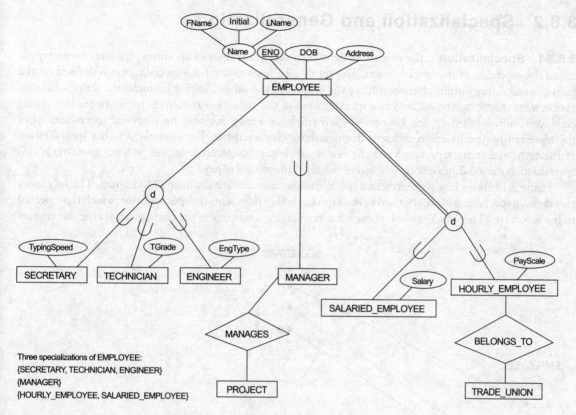

FIGURE 3.16 EER diagram notation to represent subclasses and specialization.

we implement a superclass/subclass relationship in the database system, however, we may represent a member of the subclass as a distinct database object—say, a distinct record that is related via the key attribute to its superclass entity. In Chapter 6, we discuss various options for representing superclass/subclass relationships in relational databases.

An entity cannot exist in the database merely by being a member of a subclass; it must also be a member of the superclass. Such an entity can be included optionally as a member of any number of subclasses. For example, a salaried employee who is also an engineer belongs to the two subclasses ENGINEER and SALARIED_ EMPLOYEE of the EMPLOYEE entity type. However, it is not necessary that every entity in a superclass be a member of some subclass.

An important concept associated with subclasses is that of **type inheritance**. Recall that the *type* of an entity is defined by the attributes it possesses and the relationship types in which it participates. Because an entity in the subclass represents the same real-world entity from the superclass, it should possess values for its specific attributes *as well as* values of its attributes as a member of the superclass. We say that an entity that is a member of a subclass **inherits** all the attributes of the entity as a member of the superclass. The entity also inherits all the relationships in which the superclass participates. Notice that a subclass, with its own specific (or local) attributes and relationships together with all the attributes and relationships it inherits from the superclass, can be considered an *entity type* in its own right.[16]

---

16. In some object-oriented programming languages, a common restriction is that an entity (or object) has *only one type*. This is generally too restrictive for conceptual database modeling.

3.8.2 Specialization and Generalization

3.8.2.1 Specialization is the process of defining a set of *subclasses* of an entity type; this entity type is called the *superclass* of the specialization. The set of subclasses that form a specialization is defined on the basis of some distinguishing characteristic of the entities in the superclass. For example, the set of subclasses {SECRETARY, ENGINEER, TECHNICIAN} is a specialization of the superclass EMPLOYEE that distinguishes among employee entities based on the *job type* of each employee entity. We may have several specializations of the same entity type based on different distinguishing characteristics. For example, another specialization of the EMPLOYEE entity type may yield the set of subclasses {SALARIED_EMPLOYEE, HOURLY_EMPLOYEE}; this specialization distinguishes among employees based on the *method of pay*.

Figure 3.17 shows how we represent a specialization diagrammatically in an EER diagram. The subclasses that define a specialization are attached by lines to a circle that represents the specialization, which is connected to the superclass. The subset symbol on each line connecting a subclass to the circle indicates the direction of

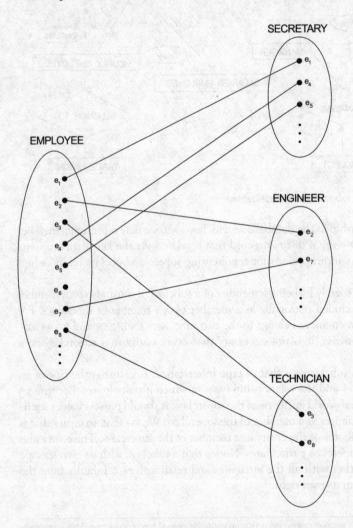

FIGURE 3.17 Instances of a specialization.

the superclass/subclass relationship.[17] Attributes that apply only to entities of a particular subclass—such as TypingSpeed of SECRETARY—are attached to the rectangle representing that subclass. These are called **specific attributes** (or **local attributes**) of the subclass. Similarly, a subclass can participate in **specific relationship types,** such as the HOURLY_EMPLOYEE subclass participating in the BELONGS_TO relationship in Figure 3.16. We will explain the **d** symbol in the circles of Figure 3.16 and additional EER diagram notation shortly.

Figure 3.17 shows a few entity instances that belong to subclasses of the {SECRETARY, ENGINEER, TECHNICIAN} specialization. Again, notice that an entity that belongs to a subclass represents the same *real-world entity* as the entity connected to it in the EMPLOYEE superclass, even though the same entity is shown twice. For example, e_1 is shown in both EMPLOYEE and SECRETARY in Figure 3.17. As this figure suggests, a superclass/ subclass relationship such as EMPLOYEE/SECRETARY somewhat resembles a 1:1 relationship at the *instance level* (see Figure 3.12). The main difference is that in a 1:1 relationship two *distinct entities* are related, whereas in a superclass/subclass relationship the entity in the subclass is the same real-world entity as the entity in the superclass but is playing a *specialized role*—for example, an EMPLOYEE specialized in the role of SECRETARY, or an EMPLOYEE specialized in the role of TECHNICIAN.

There are two main reasons for including class/subclass relationships and specializations in a data model. The first is that certain attributes may apply to some but not all entities of the superclass. A subclass is defined in order to group the entities to which these attributes apply. The members of the subclass may still share the majority of their attributes with the other members of the superclass. For example, in Figure 3.16 the SECRETARY subclass has the specific attribute TypingSpeed, whereas the ENGINEER subclass has the specific attribute EngType, but SECRETARY and ENGINEER share their other inherited attributes from the EMPLOYEE entity type.

The second reason for using subclasses is that some relationship types may be participated in only by entities that are members of the subclass. For example, if only HOURLY_EMPLOYEEs can belong to a trade union, we can represent that fact by creating the subclass HOURLY_EMPLOYEE of EMPLOYEE and relating the subclass to an entity type TRADE_UNION via the BELONGS_TO relationship type, as illustrated in Figure 3.16.

In summary, the specialization process allows us to do the following:

- Define a set of subclasses of an entity type
- Establish additional specific attributes with each subclass
- Establish additional specific relationship types between each subclass and other entity types or other subclasses

3.8.2.2   Generalization

We can think of a *reverse process* of abstraction in which we suppress the differences among several entity types, identify their common features, and **generalize** them into a single **superclass** of which the original entity types are special **subclasses**. For example, consider the entity types CAR and TRUCK shown in Figure 3.18a. Because they have several common attributes, they can be generalized into the entity type VEHICLE, as shown in Figure 3.18b. Both CAR and TRUCK are now subclasses of the **generalized superclass** VEHICLE. We use the term **generalization** to refer to the process of defining a generalized entity type from the given entity types.

Notice that the generalization process can be viewed as being functionally the inverse of the specialization process. Hence, in Figure 3.18 we can view {CAR, TRUCK} as a specialization of VEHICLE, rather than viewing VEHICLE as a generalization of CAR and TRUCK. Similarly, in Figure 3.16 we can view EMPLOYEE as a generalization of SECRETARY, TECHNICIAN, and ENGINEER. A diagrammatic notation to distinguish between generalization

---

17. There are many alternative notations for specialization; we present the UML notation in Section 3.10 and other proposed notations in Appendix A.

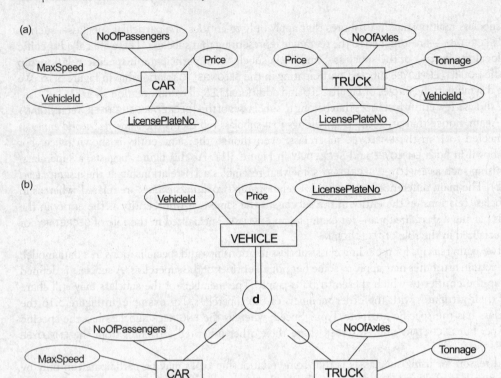

FIGURE 3.18 Generalization. (a) Two entity types, CAR and TRUCK. (b) Generalizing CAR and TRUCK into the superclass VEHICLE.

and specialization is used in some design methodologies. An arrow pointing to the generalized superclass represents a generalization, whereas arrows pointing to the specialized subclasses represent a specialization. We will *not* use this notation, because the decision as to which process is more appropriate in a particular situation is often subjective. Appendix A gives some of the suggested alternative diagrammatic notations for schema diagrams and class diagrams.

So far we have introduced the concepts of subclasses and superclass/subclass relationships, as well as the specialization and generalization processes. In general, a superclass or subclass represents a collection of entities of the same type and hence also describes an entity type; that is why superclasses and subclasses are shown in rectangles in EER diagrams, like entity types. We next discuss in more detail the properties of specializations and generalizations.

3.8.3 Constraints and Characteristics of Specialization and Generalization

We first discuss constraints that apply to a single specialization or a single generalization. For brevity, our discussion refers only to *specialization* even though it applies to *both* specialization and generalization. We then discuss differences between specialization/generalization *lattices* (*multiple inheritance*) and *hierarchies* (*single inheritance*), and elaborate on the differences between the specialization and generalization processes during conceptual database schema design.

3.8.3.1 Constraints on Specialization and Generalization In general, we may have several
specializations defined on the same entity type (or superclass), as shown in Figure 3.16. In such a case, entities may
belong to subclasses in each of the specializations. However, a specialization may also consist of a *single* subclass only,
such as the {MANAGER} specialization in Figure 3.16; in such a case, we do not use the circle notation.

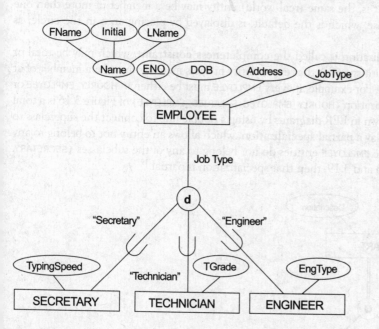

FIGURE 3.19 EER diagram notation for an attribute-defined specialization on JobType.

In some specializations we can determine exactly the entities that will become members of each subclass
by placing a condition on the value of some attribute of the superclass. Such subclasses are called **predicate-
defined** (or **condition-defined**) **subclasses**. For example, if the EMPLOYEE entity type has an attribute JobType,
as shown in Figure 3.19, we can specify the condition of membership in the SECRETARY subclass by the
condition (JobType = 'Secretary'), which we call the **defining predicate** of the subclass. This condition is a
constraint specifying that exactly those entities of the EMPLOYEE entity type whose attribute value for JobType is
'Secretary' belong to the subclass. We display a predicate-defined subclass by writing the predicate condition
next to the line that connects the subclass to the specialization circle.

If *all* subclasses in a specialization have their membership condition on the *same* attribute of the superclass,
the specialization itself is called an *attribute-defined specialization*, and the attribute is called the *defining attribute*
of the specialization.[18] We display an attribute-defined specialization by placing the defining attribute name
next to the arc from the circle to the superclass, as shown in Figure 3.19.

When we do not have a condition for determining membership in a subclass, the subclass is called **user-
defined**. Membership in such a subclass is determined by the database users when they apply the operation to
add an entity to the subclass; hence, membership is *specified individually for each entity by the user*, not by any
condition that may be evaluated automatically.

Two other constraints may apply to a specialization. The first is the **disjointness constraint**, which
specifies that the subclasses of the specialization must be disjoint. This means that an entity can be a member
of *at most one* of the subclasses of the specialization. A specialization that is attribute-defined implies the

---

18. Such an attribute is called a *discriminator in* UML terminology.

disjointness constraint if the attribute used to define the membership predicate is single-valued. Figure 3.19 illustrates this case, where the **d** in the circle stands for *disjoint*. We also use the **d** notation to specify the constraint that user-defined subclasses of a specialization must be disjoint, as illustrated by the specialization {HOURLY_EMPLOYEE, SALARIED_EMPLOYEE} in Figure 3.16. If the subclasses are not constrained to be disjoint, their sets of entities may **overlap**; that is, the same (real-world) entity may be a member of more than one subclass of the specialization. This case, which is the default, is displayed by placing an **o** in the circle, as shown in Figure 3.20.

The second constraint on specialization is called the **completeness constraint**, which may be total or partial. A **total specialization** constraint specifies that every entity in the superclass must be a member of at least one subclass in the specialization. For example, if every EMPLOYEE must be either an HOURLY_EMPLOYEE or a SALARIED_EMPLOYEE, then the specialization {HOURLY_EMPLOYEE, SALARIED_EMPLOYEE} of Figure 3.16 is a total specialization of EMPLOYEE. This is shown in EER diagrams by using a double line to connect the superclass to the circle. A single line is used to display a **partial specialization**, which allows an entity not to belong to any of the subclasses. For example, if some EMPLOYEE entities do not belong to any of the subclasses {SECRETARY, ENGINEER, TECHNICIAN} of Figures 3.16 and 3.19, then that specialization is partial.[19]

FIGURE 3.20 EER diagram notation for an overlapping (nondisjoint) specialization.

Notice that the disjointness and completeness constraints are independent. Hence, we have the following four possible constraints on specialization:

- Disjoint, total
- Disjoint, partial
- Overlapping, total
- Overlapping, partial

---

19. The notation of using single or double lines is similar to that for partial or total participation of an entity type in a relationship type.

Of course, the correct constraint is determined from the real-world meaning that applies to each specialization. In general, a superclass that was identified through the *generalization* process usually is **total**, because the superclass is *derived from* the subclasses and hence contains only the entities that are in the subclasses.

Certain insertion and deletion rules apply to specialization (and generalization) as a consequence of the constraints specified earlier. Some of these rules are as follows:

- Deleting an entity from a superclass implies that it is automatically deleted from all the subclasses to which it belongs.

- Inserting an entity in a superclass implies that the entity is mandatorily inserted in all *predicate-defined* (or *attribute-defined*) subclasses for which the entity satisfies the defining predicate.

- Inserting an entity in a superclass of a *total specialization* implies that the entity is mandatorily inserted in at least one of the subclasses of the specialization.

The reader is encouraged to make a complete list of rules for insertions and deletions for the various types of specializations.

3.8.3.2 Specialization and Generalization Hierarchies and Lattices

A subclass itself may have further subclasses specified on it, forming a hierarchy or a lattice of specializations. For example, in Figure 3.21 ENGINEER is a subclass of EMPLOYEE and is also a superclass of ENGINEERING_MANAGER; this represents the real-world constraint that every engineering manager is required to be an engineer. A **specialization hierarchy** has the constraint that every subclass participates *as a subclass in only one* class/subclass relationship; that is, each subclass has only one parent, which results in a tree structure. In contrast, for a **specialization lattice**, a subclass can be a subclass in *more than one* class/subclass relationship. Hence, Figure 3.21 is a lattice.

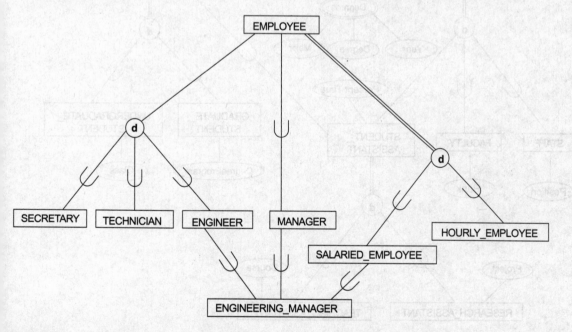

FIGURE 3.21 A specialization lattice with shared subclass ENGINEERING_MANAGER.

Figure 3.22 shows another specialization lattice of more than one level. This may be part of a conceptual schema for a UNIVERSITY database. Notice that this arrangement would have been a hierarchy except for the STUDENT_ASSISTANT subclass, which is a subclass in two distinct class/subclass relationships. In Figure 3.22, all person entities represented in the database are members of the PERSON entity type, which is specialized into

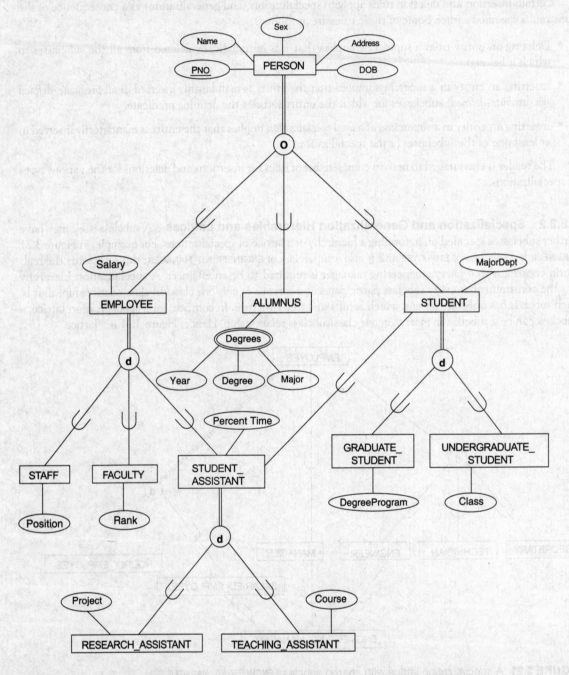

FIGURE 3.22 A specialization lattice with multiple inheritance for a UNIVERSITY database.

the subclasses {EMPLOYEE, ALUMNUS, STUDENT}. This specialization is overlapping. For example, an alumnus may also be an employee and may also be a student pursuing an advanced degree. The subclass STUDENT is the superclass for the specialization {GRADUATE_STUDENT, UNDERGRADUATE_STUDENT}, while EMPLOYEE is the superclass for the specialization {STUDENT_ASSISTANT, FACULTY, STAFF}. Notice that STUDENT_ASSISTANT is also a subclass of STUDENT. Finally, STUDENT_ASSISTANT is the superclass for the specialization into {RESEARCH_ASSISTANT, TEACHING_ASSISTANT}.

In such a specialization lattice or hierarchy, a subclass inherits the attributes not only of its direct superclass but also of all its predecessor superclasses *all the way to the root* of the hierarchy or lattice. For example, an entity in GRADUATE_STUDENT inherits all the attributes of that entity as a STUDENT *and* as a PERSON. Notice that an entity may exist in several leaf nodes of the hierarchy, where a **leaf node** is a class that has *no subclasses of its own*. For example, a member of GRADUATE_STUDENT may also be a member of RESEARCH_ASSISTANT.

A subclass with more than one superclass is called a **shared subclass**, such as ENGINEERING_ MANAGER in Figure 3.21. This leads to the concept known as **multiple inheritance**, where the shared subclass ENGINEERING_ MANAGER directly inherits attributes and relationships from multiple classes. Notice that the existence of at least one shared subclass leads to a lattice (and hence to *multiple inheritance*); if no shared subclasses existed, we would have a hierarchy rather than a lattice. An important rule related to multiple inheritance can be illustrated by the example of the shared subclass STUDENT_ASSISTANT in Figure 3.22, which inherits attributes from both EMPLOYEE and STUDENT. Here, both EMPLOYEE and STUDENT inherit *the same attributes* from PERSON. The rule states that if an attribute (or relationship) originating in the *same superclass* (PERSON) is inherited more than once via different paths (EMPLOYEE and STUDENT) in the lattice, then it should be included only once in the shared subclass (STUDENT_ASSISTANT). Hence, the attributes of PERSON are inherited only once in the STUDENT_ASSISTANT subclass of Figure 3.22.

It is important to note here that some models and languages *do not allow* multiple inheritance (shared subclasses). In such a model, it is necessary to create additional subclasses to cover all possible combinations of classes that may have some entity belong to all these classes simultaneously. Hence, any *overlapping* specialization would require multiple additional subclasses. For example, in the overlapping specialization of PERSON into {EMPLOYEE, ALUMNUS, STUDENT} (or {E, A, S} for short), it would be necessary to create seven subclasses of PERSON in order to cover all possible types of entities: E, A, S, E_A, E_S, A_S, and E_A_S. Obviously, this can lead to extra complexity.

It is also important to note that some inheritance mechanisms that allow multiple inheritance do not allow an entity to have multiple types, and hence an entity can be a member of only one class.[20] In such a model, it is also necessary to create additional shared subclasses as leaf nodes to cover all possible combinations of classes that may have some entity belong to all these classes simultaneously. Hence, we would require the same seven subclasses of PERSON.

Although we have used specialization to illustrate our discussion, similar concepts *apply equally* to generalization, as we mentioned at the beginning of this section. Hence, we can also speak of **generalization hierarchies** and **generalization lattices**.

3.8.3.3 Utilizing Specialization and Generalization in Refining Conceptual Schemas We now elaborate on the differences between the specialization and generalization processes, and how they are used to refine conceptual schemas during conceptual database design. In the specialization process, we typically start with an entity type and then define subclasses of the entity type by successive specialization; that is, we repeatedly define more specific groupings of the entity type. For example, when designing the specialization lattice in Figure 3.22, we may first specify an entity type PERSON for a university database. Then we discover that three types of persons will be represented in the database: university employees, alumni,

---

20. In some models, the class is further restricted to be a *leaf node* in the hierarchy or lattice.

and students. We create the specialization {EMPLOYEE, ALUMNUS, STUDENT} for this purpose and choose the overlapping constraint because a person may belong to more than one of the subclasses. We then specialize EMPLOYEE further into {STAFF, FACULTY, STUDENT_ASSISTANT}, and specialize STUDENT into {GRADUATE_STUDENT, UNDERGRADUATE_STUDENT}. Finally, we specialize STUDENT_ASSISTANT into {RESEARCH_ASSISTANT, TEACHING_ASSISTANT}. This successive specialization corresponds to a **top-down conceptual refinement process** during conceptual schema design. So far, we have a hierarchy; we then realize that STUDENT_ASSISTANT is a shared subclass, since it is also a subclass of STUDENT, leading to the lattice.

It is possible to arrive at the same hierarchy or lattice from the other direction. In such a case, the process involves generalization rather than specialization and corresponds to a **bottom-up conceptual synthesis**. In this case, designers may first discover entity types such as STAFF, FACULTY, ALUMNUS, GRADUATE_STUDENT, UNDERGRADUATE_STUDENT, RESEARCH_ASSISTANT, TEACHING_ASSISTANT, and so on; then they generalize {GRADUATE_STUDENT, UNDERGRADUATE_STUDENT} into STUDENT; then they generalize {RESEARCH_ASSISTANT, TEACHING_ASSISTANT} into STUDENT_ASSISTANT; then they generalize {STAFF, FACULTY, STUDENT_ASSISTANT} into EMPLOYEE; and finally they generalize {EMPLOYEE, ALUMNUS, STUDENT} into PERSON.

In structural terms, hierarchies or lattices resulting from either process may be identical; the only difference relates to the manner or order in which the schema superclasses and subclasses were specified. In practice, it is likely that neither the generalization process nor the specialization process is followed strictly, but that a combination of the two processes is employed. In this case, new classes are continually incorporated into a hierarchy or lattice as they become apparent to users and designers. Notice that the notion of representing data and knowledge by using superclass/subclass hierarchies and lattices is quite common in knowledge-based systems and expert systems, which combine database technology with artificial intelligence techniques. For example, frame-based knowledge representation schemes closely resemble class hierarchies. Specialization is also common in software engineering design methodologies that are based on the object-oriented paradigm.

3.8.4 Modeling of Union Types Using Categories

All of the superclass/subclass relationships we have seen thus far have a *single superclass*. A shared subclass such as ENGINEERING_MANAGER in the lattice of Figure 3.21 is the subclass in three *distinct* superclass/subclass relationships, where each of the three relationships has a *single* superclass. It is not uncommon, however, that the need arises for modeling a single superclass/subclass relationship with *more than one* superclass, where the superclasses represent different entity types. In this case, the subclass will represent a collection of objects that is a subset of the UNION of distinct entity types; we call such a *subclass* a **union type** or a **category**.[21]

For example, suppose that we have three entity types: PERSON, BANK, and COMPANY. In a database for vehicle registration, an owner of a vehicle can be a person, a bank (holding a lien on a vehicle), or a company. We need to create a class (collection of entities) that includes entities of all three types to play the role of *vehicle owner*. A category OWNER that is a *subclass of the* UNION of the three entity sets of COMPANY, BANK, and PERSON is created for this purpose. We display categories in an EER diagram as shown in Figure 3.23. The superclasses COMPANY, BANK, and PERSON are connected to the circle with the ∪ symbol, which stands for the *set union operation*. An arc with the subset symbol connects the circle to the (subclass) OWNER category. If a defining predicate is needed, it is displayed next to the line from the superclass to which the predicate applies. In Figure 3.23 we have two categories: OWNER, which is a subclass of the union of PERSON, BANK, and COMPANY; and REGISTERED_VEHICLE, which is a subclass of the union of CAR and TRUCK.

A category has two or more superclasses that may represent *distinct entity types*, whereas other superclass/subclass relationships always have a single superclass. We can compare a category, such as OWNER in Figure 3.23, with the ENGINEERING_MANAGER shared subclass of Figure 3.21. The latter is a subclass of *each of* the three

---

21. Our use of the term *category* is based on the ECR (Entity-Category-Relationship) model (Elmasri et al. 1985).

superclasses ENGINEER, MANAGER, and SALARIED_EMPLOYEE, so an entity that is a member of ENGINEERING_MANAGER must exist in *all three*. This represents the constraint that an engineering manager must be an

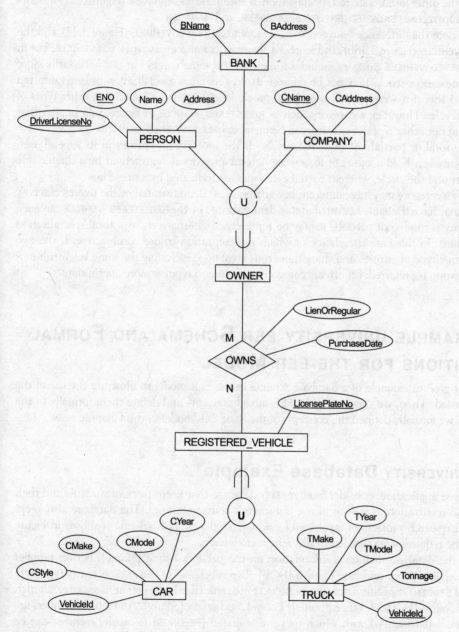

FIGURE 3.23 Two categories (union types): OWNER and REGISTERED_VEHICLE.

ENGINEER, a MANAGER, *and* a SALARIED_EMPLOYEE; that is, ENGINEERING_MANAGER is a subset of the *intersection* of the three subclasses (sets of entities). On the other hand, a category is a subset of the *union* of its superclasses. Hence, an entity that is a member of OWNER must exist in *only one* of the superclasses. This represents the constraint that an OWNER may be a COMPANY, a BANK, or a PERSON in Figure 3.23.

Attribute inheritance works more selectively in the case of categories. For example, in Figure 3.23 each OWNER entity inherits the attributes of a COMPANY, a PERSON, or a BANK, depending on the superclass to which the entity belongs. On the other hand, a shared subclass such as ENGINEERING_MANAGER (Figure 3.21) inherits *all* the attributes of its superclasses SALARIED_EMPLOYEE, ENGINEER, and MANAGER.

It is interesting to note the difference between the category REGISTERED_VEHICLE (Figure 3.23) and the generalized superclass VEHICLE (Figure 3.18b). In Figure 3.18b, every car and every truck is a VEHICLE; but in Figure 3.23, the REGISTERED_VEHICLE category includes some cars and some trucks but not necessarily all of them (for example, some cars or trucks may not be registered). In general, a specialization or generalization such as that in Figure 3.18b, if it were partial, would not preclude VEHICLE from containing other types of entities, such as motorcycles. However, a category such as REGISTERED_VEHICLE in Figure 3.23 implies that only cars and trucks, but not other types of entities, can be members of REGISTERED_VEHICLE.

A category can be **total** or **partial**. A total category holds the *union* of all entities in its superclasses, whereas a partial category can hold a *subset of the union*. A total category is represented by a double line connecting the category and the circle, whereas partial categories are indicated by a single line.

The superclasses of a category may have different key attributes, as demonstrated by the OWNER category of Figure 3.23, or they may have the same key attribute, as demonstrated by the REGISTERED_VEHICLE category. Notice that if a category is total (not partial), it may be represented alternatively as a total specialization (or a total generalization). In this case the choice of which representation to use is subjective. If the two classes represent the same type of entities and share numerous attributes, including the same key attributes, specialization/generalization is preferred; otherwise, categorization (union type) is more appropriate.

3.9 AN EXAMPLE UNIVERSITY EER SCHEMA AND FORMAL DEFINITIONS FOR THE EER MODEL

In this section, we first give an example of a database schema in the EER model to illustrate the use of the various concepts discussed. Then, we summarize the EER model concepts and define them formally in the same manner in which we formally defined the concepts of the basic EER model in this Chapter.

3.9.1 The UNIVERSITY Database Example

For our example database application, consider a UNIVERSITY database that keeps track of students and their majors, transcripts, and registration as well as of the university's course offerings. The database also keeps track of the sponsored research projects of faculty and graduate students. This schema is shown in Figure 3.24. A discussion of the requirements that led to this schema follows.

For each person, the database maintains information on the person's Name [Name], person number [eno], address [Address], sex [Sex], and date of birth [DOB]. Two subclasses of the PERSON entity type were identified: FACULTY and STUDENT. Specific attributes of FACULTY are rank [Rank] (assistant, associate, adjunct, research, visiting, etc.), office [FOffice], office phone [FPhone], and salary [Salary]. All faculty members are related to the academic department(s) with which they are affiliated [BELONGS] (a faculty member can be associated with several departments, so the relationship is M:N). A specific attribute of STUDENT is [Class] (first year = 1, second year = 2, . . . , graduate student = 4). Each student is also related to his or her major and minor departments, if known ([MAJOR] and [MINOR]), to the course sections he or she is currently attending [REGISTERED], and to the courses completed [TRANSCRIPT]. Each transcript instance includes the grade the student received [Grade] in the course section.

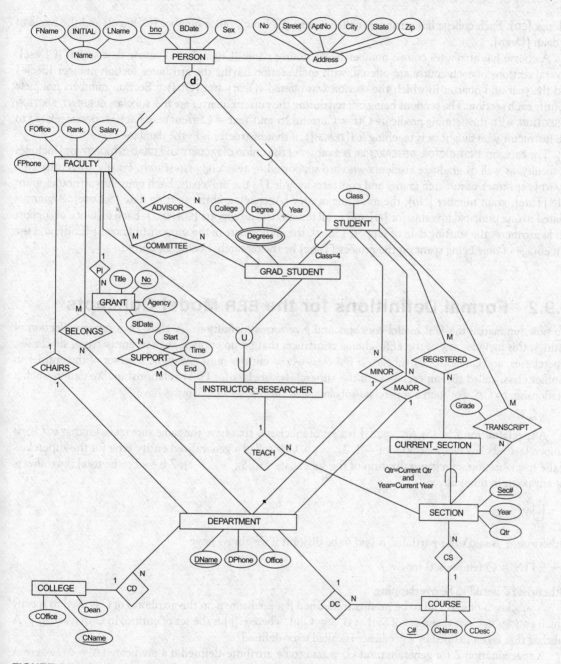

FIGURE 3.24 An EER conceptual schema for a UNIVERSITY database.

GRAD_STUDENT is a subclass of STUDENT, with the defining predicate Class = 4. For each graduate student, we keep a list of previous degrees in a composite, multivalued attribute [Degrees]. We also relate the graduate student to a faculty advisor [ADVISOR] and to a thesis committee [COMMITTEE], if one exists.

An academic department has the attributes name [DName], telephone [DPhone], and office number [Office] and is related to the faculty member who is its chairperson [CHAIRS] and to the college to which it belongs [CD]. Each college has attributes college name [CName], office number [COffice], and the name of its dean [Dean].

A course has attributes course number [C#], course name [Cname], and course description [CDesc]. Several sections of each course are offered, with each section having the attributes section number [Sec#] and the year and quarter in which the section was offered ([Year] and [Qtr]).[22] Section numbers uniquely identify each section. The sections being offered during the current quarter are in a subclass CURRENT_SECTION of SECTION, with the defining predicate Qtr = CurrentQtr and Year = CurrentYear. Each section is related to the instructor who taught or is teaching it ([TEACH]), if that instructor is in the database.

The category INSTRUCTOR_RESEARCHER is a subset of the union of FACULTY and GRAD_STUDENT and includes all faculty, as well as graduate students who are supported by teaching or research. Finally, the entity type GRANT keeps track of research grants and contracts awarded to the university. Each grant has attributes grant title [Title], grant number [No], the awarding agency [Agency], and the starting date [StDate]. A grant is related to one principal investigator [PI] and to all researchers it supports [SUPPORT]. Each instance of support has as attributes the starting date of support [Start], the ending date of the support (if known) [End], and the percentage of time being spent on the project [Time] by the researcher being supported.

3.9.2 Formal Definitions for the EER Model Concepts

We now summarize the EER model concepts and give formal definitions. A class[23] is a set or collection of entities; this includes any of the EER schema constructs that group entities, such as entity types, subclasses, superclasses, and categories. A subclass S is a class whose entities must always be a subset of the entities in another class, called the **superclass** C of the **superclass/subclass** (or IS-A) **relationship**. We denote such a relationship by C/S. For such a superclass/subclass relationship, we must always have

$S \subseteq C$

A **specialization** $Z = \{S_1, S_2, \ldots, S_n\}$ is a set of subclasses that have the same superclass G; that is, G/S_i is a superclass/subclass relationship for $i = 1, 2, \ldots, n$. G is called a **generalized entity type** (or the **superclass** of the specialization, or a **generalization** of the subclasses $\{S_1, S_2, \ldots, S_n\}$). Z is said to be **total** if we always (at any point in time) have

$$\bigcup_{i=1}^{n} S_i = G$$

Otherwise, z is said to be **partial**. Z is said to be **disjoint** if we always have

$S_i \cap S_j = \emptyset$ (empty set) for $i \neq j$

Otherwise, Z is said to be **overlapping**.

A subclass S of C is said to be **predicate-defined** if a predicate p on the attributes of C is used to specify which entities in C are members of S; that is, $S = C[p]$, where $C[p]$ is the set of entities in C that satisfy p. A subclass that is not defined by a predicate is called **user-defined**.

A specialization Z (or generalization G) is said to be **attribute-defined** if a predicate $(A = c_i)$, where A is an attribute of G and c_i is a constant value from the domain of A, is used to specify membership in each subclass S_i in Z. Notice that if $c_i \neq c_j$ for $i \neq j$, and A is a single-valued attribute, then the specialization will be disjoint.

---

22. We assume that the *quarter* system rather than the *semester* system is used in this university.

23. The use of the word *class* here differs from its more common use in object-oriented programming languages such as C++. In C++, a class is a structured type definition along with its applicable functions (operations).

A **category** T is a class that is a subset of the union of n defining superclasses $D_1, D_2, \ldots, D_n, n > 1$, and is formally specified as follows:

$$T \subseteq (D_1 \cup D_2 \ldots \cup D_n)$$

A predicate p_i on the attributes of D_i can be used to specify the members of each D_i that are members of T. If a predicate is specified on every D_i, we get

$$T = (D_1 [p_1] \cup D_2[p_2] \ldots \cup D_n[p_n])$$

We should now extend the definition of **relationship type** discussed earlier in this Chapter by allowing any class—not only any entity type—to participate in a relationship. Hence, we should replace the words *entity type* with class in that definition. The graphical notation of EER is consistent with ER because all classes are represented by rectangles.

FIGURE 3.25 The COMPANY conceptual schema in UML class diagram notation.

3.10 UML CLASS DIAGRAMS

The UML methodology is being extensively used in software design and has many types of diagrams for various software design purposes. We only briefly describe the basis of **UML class diagrams** here, and compare them with ER diagrams. In some ways, class diagrams can be considered as an alternative notation to ER diagrams. Additional UML notation and concepts are presented in Section 3.10.1. Figure 3.25 shows how the COMPANY ER database schema of Figure 3.15 can be displayed using UML class diagram notation. The entity types in Figure 3.15 are modeled as *classes* in Figure 3.25. An *entity* in ER corresponds to an *object* in UML.

In UML class diagrams, a **class** is displayed as a box (see Figure 3.25) that includes three sections: The top section gives the **class name**, the middle section includes the **attributes** for individual objects of the class; and the last section includes **operations** that can be applied to these objects. Operations are *not* specified in ER diagrams. Consider the EMPLOYEE class in Figure 3.25. Its attributes are Name, ENO, DOB, Sex, Address, and Salary. The designer can optionally specify the **domain** of an attribute if desired, by placing a colon (:) followed by the domain name or description, as illustrated by the Name, Sex, and DOB attributes of EMPLOYEE in Figure 3.25. A composite attribute is modeled as a **structured domain**, as illustrated by the Name attribute of EMPLOYEE. A multivalued attribute will generally be modeled as a separate class, as illustrated by the LOCATION class in Figure 3.25.

Relationship types are called **associations** in UML terminology, and relationship instances are called **links**. A **binary association** (binary relationship type) is represented as a line connecting the participating classes (entity types), and may optionally have a name. A relationship attribute, called a **link attribute**, is placed in a box that is connected to the association's line by a dashed line. The (min, max) notation described in Section 3.7.4 is used to specify relationship constraints, which are called **multiplicities** in UML terminology. Multiplicities are specified in the form *min..max*, and an asterisk (*) indicates no maximum limit on participation. However, the multiplicities are placed *on the opposite ends of the relationship* when compared with the notation discussed in Section 3.7.4 (compare Figures 3.25 and 3.15). In UML, a single asterisk indicates a multiplicity of 0..*, and a single 1 indicates a multiplicity of 1..1. A recursive relationship (see Section 3.4.2) is called a **reflexive association** in UML, and the role names—like the multiplicities—are placed at the opposite ends of an association when compared with the placing of role names in Figure 3.15.

In UML, there are two types of relationships: association and aggregation. **Aggregation** is meant to represent a relationship between a whole object and its component parts, and it has a distinct diagrammatic notation. In Figure 3.25, we modeled the locations of a department and the single location of a project as aggregations. However, aggregation and association do not have different structural properties, and the choice as to which type of relationship to use is somewhat subjective. In the ER model, both are represented as relationships.

UML also distinguishes between **unidirectional** and **bidirectional** associations (or aggregations). In the unidirectional case, the line connecting the classes is displayed with an arrow to indicate that only one direction for accessing related objects is needed. If no arrow is displayed, the bidirectional case is assumed, which is the default. For example, if we always expect to access the manager of a department starting from a DEPARTMENT object, we would draw the association line representing the MANAGES association with an arrow from DEPARTMENT to EMPLOYEE. In addition, relationship instances may be specified to be ordered. For example, we could specify that the employee objects related to each department through the WORKS_FOR association (relationship) should be ordered by their DOB attribute value. Association (relationship) names are optional in UML, and relationship attributes are displayed in a box attached with a dashed line to the line representing the association/aggregation (see StartDate and Hours in Figure 3.25).

The operations given in each class are derived from the functional requirements of the application, as we discussed in Section 3.1. It is generally sufficient to specify the operation names initially for the logical operations that are expected to be applied to individual objects of a class, as shown in Figure 3.25. As the design is refined, more details are added, such as the exact argument types (parameters) for each operation, plus a functional description of each operation. UML has *function descriptions* and *sequence diagrams* to specify some of the operation details, but these are beyond the scope of our discussion.

Weak entities can be modeled using the construct called **qualified association** (or **qualified aggregation**) in UML; this can represent both the identifying relationship and the partial key, which is placed in a box attached to the owner class. This is illustrated by the DEPENDENT class and its qualified aggregation to EMPLOYEE in Figure 3.25. The partial key DependentName is called the **discriminator** in UML terminology, since its value distinguishes the objects associated with (related to) the same EMPLOYEE. Qualified associations are not restricted to modeling weak entities, and they can be used to model other situations in UML.

3.10.1   Representing Specialization/Generalization and Inheritance in UML Class Diagrams

We discuss the UML notation for generalization/specialization and inheritance. Figure 3.26 illustrates a possible class diagram corresponding to the EER diagram in Figure 3.22. The basic notation for generalization is to connect the subclasses by vertical lines to a horizontal line, which has a triangle connecting the horizontal line through another vertical line to the superclass (see Figure 3.26). A blank triangle indicates a specialization/generalization with the disjoint constraint, and a filled triangle indicates an *overlapping* constraint. The root superclass is called the base class, and leaf nodes are called *leaf classes*. Both single and multiple inheritance are permitted.

FIGURE 3.26 A UML class diagram corresponding to the EER diagram in Figure 3.22, illustrating UML notation for specialization/generalization.

There are many details that we have not discussed because they are outside the scope of this book and are mainly relevant to software engineering. For example, classes can be of various types:

- Abstract classes define attributes and operations but do not have objects corresponding to those classes. These are mainly used to specify a set of attributes and operations that can be inherited.

- Concrete classes can have objects (entities) instantiated to belong to the class.
- Template classes specify a template that can be further used to define other classes.

In database design, we are mainly concerned with specifying concrete classes whose collections of objects are permanently (or persistently) stored in the database. The bibliographic notes at the end of this chapter give some references to books that describe complete details of UML.

3.11 RELATIONSHIP TYPES OF DEGREE HIGHER THAN TWO

In Section 3.4.2 we defined the **degree** of a relationship type as the number of participating entity types and called a relationship type of degree two binary and a relationship type of degree three ternary. In this section, we elaborate on the differences between *binary* and higher-degree relationships, when to choose higher-degree or binary relationships, and constraints on higher-degree relationships.

3.11.1 Choosing between Binary and Ternary (or Higher-Degree) Relationships

The ER diagram notation for a ternary relationship type is shown in Figure 3.27a, which displays the schema for the SUPPLY relationship type that was displayed at the instance level in Figure 3.10. Recall that the relationship set of SUPPLY is a set of relationship instances (s, j, p), where s is a SUPPLIER who is currently supplying a PART p to a PROJECT j. In general, a relationship type R of degree n will have n edges in an ER diagram, one connecting R to each participating entity type.

Figure 3.27b shows an ER diagram for the three binary relationship types CAN_SUPPLY, USES, and SUPPLIES. In general, a ternary relationship type represents different information than do three binary relationship types. Consider the three binary relationship types CAN_SUPPLY, USES, and SUPPLIES. Suppose that CAN_SUPPLY, between SUPPLIER and PART, includes an instance (s, p) whenever supplier s *can supply* part p (to any project); USES, between PROJECT and PART, includes an instance (j, p) whenever project j uses part p; and SUPPLIES, between SUPPLIER and PROJECT, includes an instance (s, j) whenever supplier s *supplies some part* to project j. The existence of three relationship instances (s, p), (j, p), and (s, j) in CAN_SUPPLY, USES, and SUPPLIES, respectively, does not necessarily imply that an instance (s, j, p) exists in the ternary relationship SUPPLY, because the *meaning is different*. It is often tricky to decide whether a particular relationship should be represented as a relationship type of degree n or should be broken down into several relationship types of smaller degrees. The designer must base this decision on the semantics or meaning of the particular situation being represented. The typical solution is to include the ternary relationship *plus* one or more of the binary relationships, if they represent different meanings and if all are needed by the application.

Some database design tools are based on variations of the ER model that permit only binary relationships. In this case, a ternary relationship such as SUPPLY must be represented as a weak entity type, with no partial key and with three identifying relationships. The three participating entity types SUPPLIER, PART, and PROJECT are together the owner entity types (see Figure 3.27c). Hence, an entity in the weak entity type SUPPLY of Figure 3.27c is identified by the combination of its three owner entities from SUPPLIER, PART, and PROJECT.

Another example is shown in Figure 3.28. The ternary relationship type OFFERS represents information on instructors offering courses during particular semesters; hence it includes a relationship instance (i, s, c) whenever INSTRUCTOR i offers COURSE c during SEMESTER s. The three binary relationship types shown in Figure 3.28 have the following meanings: CAN_TEACH relates a course to the instructors who can teach that course, TAUGHT_DURING relates a semester to the instructors who *taught some course* during that semester,

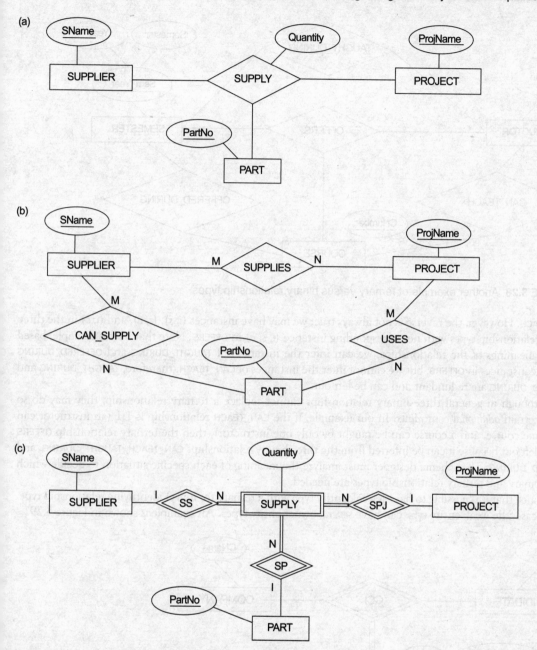

FIGURE 3.27 Ternary relationship types. (a) The SUPPLY relationship. (b) Three binary relationships not equivalent to SUPPLY. (c) SUPPLY represented as a weak entity type.

and OFFERED_DURING relates a semester to the courses offered during that semester by any instructor. These ternary and binary relationships represent different information, but certain constraints should hold among the relationships. For example, a relationship instance (i, s, c) should not exist in OFFERS unless an instance (i, s) exists in TAUGHT_DURING, an instance (s, c) exists in OFFERED_DURING, and an instance (i, c) exists in

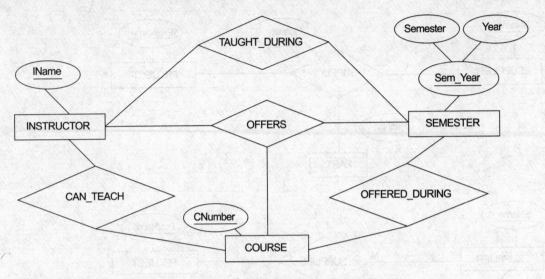

FIGURE 3.28 Another example of ternary versus binary relationship types.

CAN_TEACH. However, the reverse is not always true; we may have instances (i, s), (s, c), and (i, c) in the three binary relationship types with no corresponding instance (i, s, c) in OFFERS. Note that in this example, based on the meanings of the relationships, we can infer the instances of TAUGHT_DURING and OFFERED_DURING from the instances in OFFERS, but we cannot infer the instances of CAN_TEACH; therefore, TAUGHT_DURING and OFFERED_DURING are redundant and can be left out.

Although in general three binary relationships cannot replace a ternary relationship, they may do so under certain *additional constraints*. In our example, if the CAN_TEACH relationship is 1:1 (an instructor can teach one course, and a course can be taught by only one instructor), then the ternary relationship OFFERS can be left out because it can be inferred from the three binary relationships CAN_TEACH, TAUGHT_DURING, and OFFERED_DURING. The schema designer must analyze the meaning of each specific situation to decide which of the binary and ternary relationship types are needed.

Notice that it is possible to have a weak entity type with a ternary (or n-ary) identifying relationship type. In this case, the weak entity type can have *several* owner entity types. An example is shown in Figure 3.29.

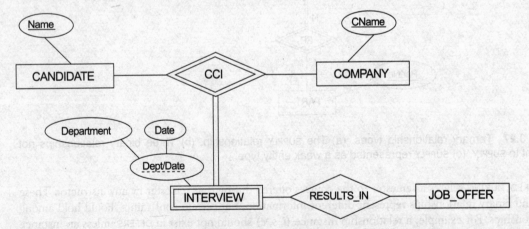

FIGURE 3.29 A weak entity type INTERVIEW with a ternary identifying relationship type.

3.11.2 Constraints on Ternary (or Higher-Degree) Relationships

There are two notations for specifying structural constraints on n-ary relationships, and they specify different constraints. They should thus *both be used* if it is important to fully specify the structural constraints on a ternary or higher-degree relationship. The first notation is based on the cardinality ratio notation of binary relationships displayed in Figure 3.2. Here, a 1, M, or N is specified on each participation arc (both M and N symbols stand for many or any number).[24] Let us illustrate this constraint using the SUPPLY relationship in Figure 3.27.

Recall that the relationship set of SUPPLY is a set of relationship instances (s, j, p), where s is a SUPPLIER, j is a PROJECT, and p is a PART. Suppose that the constraint exists that for a particular project-part combination, only one supplier will be used (only one supplier supplies a particular part to a particular project). In this case, we place 1 on the SUPPLIER participation, and M, N on the PROJECT, PART participations in Figure 3.27. This specifies the constraint that a particular (j, p) combination can appear *at most once* in the relationship set because each such (project, part) combination uniquely determines a single supplier. Hence, any relationship instance (s, j, p) is *uniquely identified* in the relationship set by its (j, p) combination, which makes (j, p) a key for the relationship set. In this notation, the participations that have a one specified on them are not required to be part of the identifying key for the relationship set.[25]

The second notation is based on the (min, max) notation displayed in Figure 3.15 for binary relationships. A (min, max) on a participation here specifies that each entity is related to at least *min* and at most *max* relationship instances in the relationship set. These constraints have no bearing on determining the key of an n-ary relationship, where $n > 2$,[26] but specify a different type of constraint that places restrictions on how many relationship instances each entity can participate in.

3.12 SUMMARY

In this chapter we presented the modeling concepts of a high-level conceptual data model, the Entity-Relationship (ER) model. We started by discussing the role that a high level data model plays in the database design process, and then we presented an example set of database requirements for the COMPANY database, which is one of the examples that is used throughout this book. We then defined the basic ER model concepts of entities and their attributes. We discussed null values and presented the various types of attributes, which can be nested arbitrarily to produce complex attributes:

- Simple or atomic
- Composite
- Multivalued

We also briefly discussed stored versus derived attributes. We then discussed the ER model concepts at the schema or "intension" level:

- Entity types and their corresponding entity sets
- Key attributes of entity types
- Value sets (domains) of attributes

---

24. This notation allows us to determine the key of the relationship relation, as we discuss in Chapter 6.

25. This is also true for cardinality ratios of binary relationships.

26. The (min, max) constraints can determine the keys for binary relationships, though.

- Relationship types and their corresponding relationship sets
- Participation roles of entity types in relationship types

We presented two methods for specifying the structural constraints on relationship types. The first method distinguished two types of structural constraints:

- Cardinality ratios (1:1, 1:N, M:N for binary relationships)
- Participation constraints (total, partial)

We noted that, alternatively, another method of specifying structural constraints is to specify minimum and maximum numbers (min, max) on the participation of each entity type in a relationship type. We discussed weak entity types and the related concepts of owner entity types, identifying relationship types, and partial key attributes.

Entity-Relationship schemas can be represented diagrammatically as ER diagrams. We showed how to design an ER schema for the COMPANY database by first defining the entity types and their attributes and then refining the design to include relationship types. We displayed the ER diagram for the COMPANY database schema. Finally, we discussed some of the basic concepts of UML class diagrams and how they relate to ER model concepts.

The ER modeling concepts we have presented thus far—entity types, relationship types, attributes, keys, and structural constraints—can model traditional business dataprocessing database applications. In this chapter, we also discussed extensions to the ER model that improve its representational capabilities. We called the resulting model the enhanced ER or EER model. The concept of subclass and its superclass and the related mechanism of attribute/relationship inheritance were presented. We saw how it is sometimes necessary to create additional classes of entities, either because of additional specific attributes or because of specific relationship types. We discussed two main processes for defining superclass/subclass hierarchies and lattices: specialization and generalization.

We then showed how to display these new constructs in an EER diagram. We also discussed the various types of constraints that may apply to specialization or generalization. The two main constraints are total/partial and disjoint/overlapping. In addition, a defining predicate for a subclass or a defining attribute for a specialization may be specified. We discussed the differences between user-defined and predicate-defined subclasses and between user-defined and attribute-defined specializations. Finally, we discussed the concept of a category or union type, which is a subset of the union of two or more classes, and we gave formal definitions of all the concepts presented.

We then introduced some of the notation and terminology of UML for representing specialization and generalization. We also discussed some of the issues concerning the difference between binary and higher-degree relationships, under which circumstances each should be used when designing a conceptual schema, and how different types of constraints on n-ary relationships may be specified.

Review Questions

3.1. Discuss the role of a high-level data model in the database design process.

3.2. List the various cases where use of a null value would be appropriate.

3.3. Define the following terms: *entity, attribute, attribute value, relationship instance, composite attribute, multivalued attribute, derived attribute, complex attribute, key attribute, value set (domain)*.

3.4. What is an entity type? What is an entity set? Explain the differences among an entity, an entity type, and an entity set.

3.5. Explain the difference between an attribute and a value set.

3.6. What is a relationship type? Explain the differences among a relationship instance, a relationship type, and a relationship set.

3.7. What is a participation role? When is it necessary to use role names in the description of relationship types?

3.8. Describe the two alternatives for specifying structural constraints on relationship types. What are the advantages and disadvantages of each?

3.9. Under what conditions can an attribute of a binary relationship type be migrated to become an attribute of one of the participating entity types?

3.10. When we think of relationships as attributes, what are the value sets of these attributes? What class of data models is based on this concept?

3.11. What is meant by a recursive relationship type? Give some examples of recursive relationship types.

3.12. When is the concept of a weak entity used in data modeling? Define the terms *owner entity type, weak entity type, identifying relationship type,* and *partial key.*

3.13. Can an identifying relationship of a weak entity type be of a degree greater than two? Give examples to illustrate your answer.

3.14. Discuss the conventions for displaying an ER schema as an ER diagram.

3.15. Discuss the naming conventions used for ER schema diagrams.

3.16. What is a subclass? When is a subclass needed in data modeling?

3.17. Define the following terms: *superclass of a subclass, superclass/subclass relationship, is-a relationship, specialization, generalization, category, specific (local) attributes, specific relationships.*

3.18. Discuss the mechanism of attribute/relationship inheritance. Why is it useful?

3.19. Discuss user-defined and predicate-defined subclasses, and identify the differences between the two.

3.20. Discuss user-defined and attribute-defined specializations, and identify the differences between the two.

3.21. Discuss the two main types of constraints on specializations and generalizations.

3.22. What is the difference between a specialization hierarchy and a specialization lattice?

3.23. What is the difference between specialization and generalization? Why do we not display this difference in schema diagrams?

3.24. How does a category differ from a regular shared subclass? What is a category used for? Illustrate your answer with examples.

3.25. For each of the following UML terms, discuss the corresponding term in the EER model, if any: *object, class, association, aggregation, generalization, multiplicity, attributes, discriminator, link, link attribute, reflexive association, qualified association.*

3.26. Discuss the main differences between the notation for EER schema diagrams and UML class diagrams by comparing how common concepts are represented in each.

3.27. Discuss the two notations for specifying constraints on *n*-ary relationships, and what each can be used for.

3.28. Consider the following set of requirements for a university database that is used to keep track of students' transcripts. This is similar but not identical to the database shown in Figure 1.2:

a. The university keeps track of each student's name, student number, current address and phone, permanent address and phone, DOB, sex, class (First year, Second year, . . . , graduate), major department, minor department (if any), and degree program (B.A., B.S., . . . , Ph.D.). Some user applications need to refer to the city, state, and zip code of the student's permanent address and to the student's last name. Both personal number and student number have unique values for each student.

b. Each department is described by a name, department code, office number, office phone, and college. Both name and code have unique values for each department.

c. Each course has a course name, description, course number, number of semester hours, level, and offering department. The value of the course number is unique for each course.

d. Each section has an instructor, semester, year, course, and section number. The section number distinguishes sections of the same course that are taught during the same semester/year; its values are 1, 2, 3, . . . , up to the number of sections taught during each semester.

e. A grade report has a student, section, letter grade, and numeric grade (0, 1, 2, 3, or 4).

Design an ER schema for this application, and draw an ER diagram for that schema. Specify key attributes of each entity type, and structural constraints on each relationship type. Note any unspecified requirements, and make appropriate assumptions to make the specification complete.

3.29. Composite and multivalued attributes can be nested to any number of levels. Suppose we want to design an attribute for a STUDENT entity type to keep track of previous college education. Such an attribute will have one entry for each college previously attended, and each such entry will be composed of college name, start and end dates, degree entries (degrees awarded at that college, if any), and transcript entries (courses completed at that college, if any). Each degree entry contains the degree name and the month and year the degree was awarded, and each transcript entry contains a course name, semester, year, and grade. Design an attribute to hold this information. Use the conventions of Figure 3.5.

3.30. Show an alternative design for the attribute described in Exercise 3.29 that uses only entity types (including weak entity types, if needed) and relationship types.

3.31. Consider the ER diagram of Figure 3.30, which shows a simplified schema for an airline reservations system. Extract from the ER diagram the requirements and constraints that produced this schema. Try to be as precise as possible in your requirements and constraints specification.

3.32. In Chapters 1 and 2, we discussed the database environment and database users. We can consider many entity types to describe such an environment, such as DBMS, stored database, DBA, and catalog/data dictionary. Try to specify all the entity types that can fully describe a database system and its environment; then specify the relationship types among them, and draw an ER diagram to describe such a general database environment.

3.33. Design an ER schema for keeping track of information about votes taken in the U.S. House of Representatives during the current two-year congressional session. The database needs to keep track of each U.S. STATE's Name (e.g., Texas, New York, California) and include the Region of the state (whose domain is {Northeast, Midwest, Southeast, Southwest, West}). Each CONGRESSPERSON in the House of Representatives is described by his or her Name, plus the District represented, the StartDate when the congressperson was first elected, and the political Party to which he or she belongs (whose domain is {Republican, Democrat, Independent, Other}). The database keeps track of each BILL (i.e., proposed law), including the BillName, the DateOfVote on the bill, whether the bill PassedOrFailed (whose domain is {Yes, No}), and the Sponsor (the congressperson(s) who sponsored— that is, proposed—the bill). The database keeps track of how each congressperson

FIGURE 3.30 An ER diagram for an AIRLINE database schema.

voted on each bill (domain of vote attribute is {Yes, No, Abstain, Absent}). Draw an ER schema diagram for this application. State clearly any assumptions you make.

3.34. A database is being constructed to keep track of the teams and games of a sports league. A team has a number of players, not all of whom participate in each game. It is desired to keep track of the players participating in each game for each team, the positions they played in that game, and the result of the game. Design an ER schema diagram for this application, stating any assumptions you make. Choose your favorite sport (e.g., soccer, baseball, football).

3.35. Consider the ER diagram shown in Figure 3.31 for part of a BANK database. Each bank can have multiple branches, and each branch can have multiple accounts and loans.

a. List the (nonweak) entity types in the ER diagram.

b. Is there a weak entity type? If so, give its name, partial key, and identifying relationship.

c. What constraints do the partial key and the identifying relationship of the weak entity type specify in this diagram?

FIGURE 3.31 An ER diagram for a BANK database schema.

d. List the names of all relationship types, and specify the (min, max) constraint on each participation of an entity type in a relationship type. Justify your choices.

e. List concisely the user requirements that led to this ER schema design.

f. Suppose that every customer must have at least one account but is restricted to at most two loans at a time, and that a bank branch cannot have more than 1000 loans. How does this show up on the (min, max) constraints?

3.36. Consider the ER diagram in Figure 3.32. Assume that an employee may work in up to two departments or may not be assigned to any department. Assume that each department must have one and may have up to three phone numbers. Supply (min, max) constraints on this diagram. *State clearly any additional assumptions you make.* Under what conditions would the relationship HAS_PHONE be redundant in this example?

3.37. Consider the ER diagram in Figure 3.33. Assume that a course may or may not use a textbook, but that a text by definition is a book that is used in some course. A course may not use more than five books. Instructors teach from two to four courses. Supply (min, max) constraints on this diagram. *State clearly any additional assumptions you make.* If we add the relationship ADOPTS between INSTRUCTOR and TEXT, what (min, max) constraints would you put on it? Why?

3.38. Consider an entity type SECTION in a UNIVERSITY database, which describes the section offerings of courses. The attributes of SECTION are SectionNumber, Semester, Year, CourseNumber, Instructor,

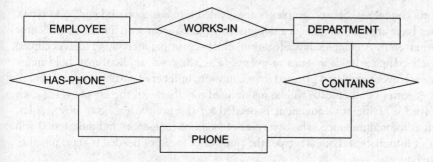

FIGURE 3.32 Part of an ER diagram for a COMPANY database.

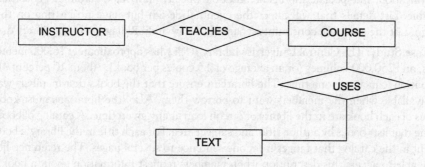

FIGURE 3.33 Part of an ER diagram for a COURSES database.

RoomNo (where section is taught), Building (where section is taught), Weekdays (domain is the possible combinations of weekdays in which a section can be offered {MWF, MW, TT, etc.}), and Hours (domain is all possible time periods during which sections are offered {9–9:50 A.M., 10–10:50 A.M., . . . , 3:30–4:50 P.M., 5:30–6:20 P.M., etc.}). Assume that SectionNumber is unique for each course within a particular semester/year combination (that is, if a course is offered multiple times during a particular semester, its section offerings are numbered 1, 2, 3, etc.). There are several composite keys for SECTION, and some attributes are components of more than one key. Identify three composite keys, and show how they can be represented in an ER schema diagram.

3.39. Design an EER schema for a database application that you are interested in. Specify all constraints that should hold on the database. Make sure that the schema has at least five entity types, four relationship types, a weak entity type, a superclass/ subclass relationship, a category, and an *n*-ary (*n* > 2) relationship type.

3.40. Consider the BANK ER schema of Figure 3.31, and suppose that it is necessary to keep track of different types of ACCOUNTS (SAVINGS_ACCTS, CHECKING_ACCTS, . . .) and LOANS (CAR_LOANS, HOME_LOANS, . . .). Suppose that it is also desirable to keep track of each account's TRANSACTIONs (deposits, withdrawals, checks, . . .) and each loan's PAYMENTs; both of these include the amount, date, and time. Modify the BANK schema, using ER and EER concepts of specialization and generalization. State any assumptions you make about the additional requirements.

3.41. The following narrative describes a simplified version of the organization of Olympic facilities planned for the summer Olympics. Draw an EER diagram that shows the entity types, attributes, relationships, and specializations for this application. State any assumptions you make. The Olympic facilities are divided into sports complexes. Sports complexes are divided into *one-sport* and *multisport* types. Multisport complexes have areas of the complex designated for each sport with a location indicator (e.g., center, NE corner, etc.). A complex has a location, chief organizing individual, total occupied area, and so on. Each complex holds a series of events (e.g., the track stadium may hold many different races). For each event there is a planned date, duration, number of participants, number of officials, and so on. A roster of all officials will be maintained together with the list of events each official will be involved in. Different equipment is needed for the events (e.g., goal posts, poles, parallel bars) as well as for maintenance. The two types of facilities (one-sport and multisport) will have different types of information. For each type, the number of facilities needed is kept, together with an approximate budget.

3.42. Identify all the important concepts represented in the library database case study described here. In particular, identify the abstractions of classification (entity types and relationship types), aggregation, identification, and specialization/generalization. Specify (min, max) cardinality constraints whenever possible. List details that will affect the eventual design but have no bearing on the conceptual design. List the semantic constraints separately. Draw an EER diagram of the library database.

Case Study: The Central University Library (CUL) has approximately 16,000 members, 100,000 titles, and 250,000 volumes (or an average of 2.5 copies per book). About 10 percent of the volumes are out on loan at any one time. The librarians ensure that the books that members want to borrow are available when the members want to borrow them. Also, the librarians must know how many copies of each book are in the library or out on loan at any given time. A catalog of books is available online that lists books by author, title, and subject area. For each title in the library, a book description is kept in the catalog that ranges from one sentence to several pages. The reference librarians want to be able to access this description when members request information about a book. Library staff is divided into chief librarian, departmental associate librarians, reference librarians, check-out staff, and library assistants.

Books can be checked out for 21 days. Members are allowed to have only five books out at a time. Members usually return books within three to four weeks. Most members know that they have one week of grace before a notice is sent to them, so they try to get the book returned before the grace period ends. About 5 percent of the members have to be sent reminders to return a book. Most overdue books are returned within a month of the due date. Approximately 5 percent of the overdue books are either kept or never returned. The most active members of the library are defined as those who borrow at least ten times during the year. The top 1 percent of membership does 15 percent of the borrowing, and the top 10 percent of the membership does 40 percent of the borrowing. About 20 percent of the members are totally inactive in that they are members but never borrow.

To become a member of the library, applicants fill out a form including their Identification number, campus and home mailing addresses, and phone numbers. The librarians then issue a numbered, machine-readable card with the member's photo on it. This card is good for four years. A month before a card expires, a notice is sent to a member for renewal. Professors at the institute are considered automatic members. When a new faculty member joins the institute, his or her information is pulled from the employee records and a library card is mailed to his or her campus address. Professors are allowed to check out books for three-month intervals and have a two-week grace period. Renewal notices to professors are sent to the campus address.

The library does not lend some books, such as reference books, rare books, and maps. The librarians must differentiate between books that can be lent and those that cannot be lent. In addition, the librarians have a list of some books they are interested in acquiring but cannot obtain, such as rare or out-of-print books and books that were lost or destroyed but have not been replaced. The librarians must have a system that keeps track of books that cannot be lent as well as books that they are interested in acquiring. Some books may have the same title; therefore, the title cannot be used as a means of identification. Every book is identified by its International Standard Book Number (ISBN), a unique international code assigned to all books. Two books with the same title can have different ISBNs if they are in different languages or have different bindings (hard cover or soft cover). Editions of the same book have different ISBNs.

The proposed database system must be designed to keep track of the members, the books, the catalog, and the borrowing activity.

3.43. Design a database to keep track of information for an art museum. Assume that the following requirements were collected:

- The museum has a collection of ART_OBJECTs. Each ART_OBJECT has a unique IdNo, an Artist (if known), a Year (when it was created, if known), a Title, and a Description. The art objects are categorized in several ways, as discussed below.

- ART_OBJECTs are categorized based on their type. There are three main types: PAINTING, SCULPTURE, and STATUE, plus another type called OTHER to accommodate objects that do not fall into one of the three main types.

- A PAINTING has a PaintType (oil, watercolor, etc.), material on which it is DrawnOn (paper, canvas, wood, etc.), and Style (modern, abstract, etc.).

- A SCULPTURE or a STATUE has a Material from which it was created (wood, stone, etc.), Height, Weight, and Style.

- An art object in the OTHER category has a Type (print, photo, etc.) and Style.

- ART_OBJECTs are also categorized as PERMANENT_COLLECTION, which are owned by the museum (these have information on the DateAcquired, whether it is OnDisplay or stored, and Cost) or BORROWED, which has information on the Collection (from which it was borrowed), DateBorrowed, and DateReturned.

- ART_OBJECTs also have information describing their country/culture using information on country/culture of Origin (Italian, Egyptian, American, Indian, etc.) and Epoch (Renaissance, Modern, Ancient, etc.).

- The museum keeps track of ARTIST's information, if known: Name, DateBorn (if known), DateDied (if not living), CountryOfOrigin, Epoch, MainStyle, and Description. The Name is assumed to be unique.

- Different EXHIBITIONs occur, each having a Name, StartDate, and EndDate. EXHIBITIONs are related to all the art objects that were on display during the exhibition.

- Information is kept on other COLLECTIONs with which the museum interacts, including Name (unique), Type (museum, personal, etc.), Description, Address, Phone, and current ContactPerson.

Draw an EER schema diagram for this application. Discuss any assumptions you made, and that justify your EER design choices.

3.44. Figure 3.34 shows an example of an EER diagram for a small private airport database that is used to keep track of airplanes, their owners, airport employees, and pilots. From the requirements for this database, the following information was collected: Each AIRPLANE has a registration number [Reg#], is of a particular plane type [OF_TYPE], and is stored in a particular hangar [STORED_IN]. Each PLANE_

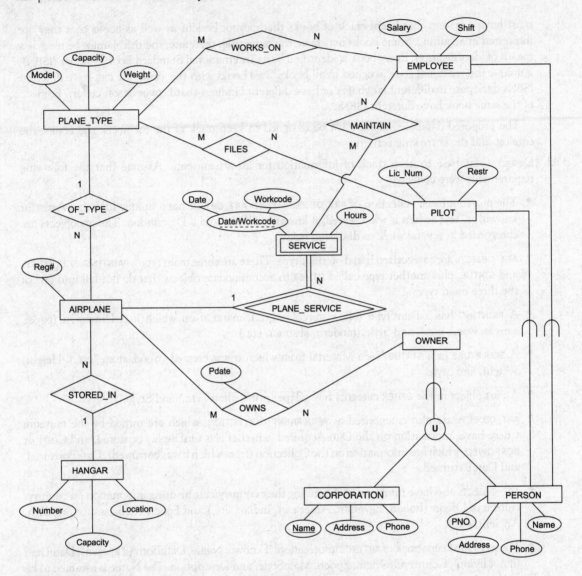

FIGURE 3.34 EER schema for a SMALL AIRPORT database.

TYPE has a model number [Model], a capacity [Capacity], and a weight [Weight]. Each HANGAR has a number [Number], a capacity [Capacity], and a location [Location]. The database also keeps track of the OWNERs of each plane [OWNS] and the EMPLOYEEs who have maintained the plane [MAINTAIN]. Each relationship instance in OWNS relates an airplane to an owner and includes the purchase date [Pdate]. Each relationship instance in MAINTAIN relates an employee to a service record [SERVICE]. Each plane undergoes service many times; hence, it is related by [PLANE_SERVICE] to a number of service records. A service record includes as attributes the date of maintenance [Date], the number of hours spent on the work [Hours], and the type of work done [Workcode]. We use a weak entity type [SERVICE] to represent airplane service, because the airplane registration number is used to identify a service record. An owner is either a person or a corporation. Hence, we use a union type (category) [OWNER] that is a subset of the union of corporation [CORPORATION] and person [PERSON] entity types. Both pilots [PILOT] and employees [EMPLOYEE] are subclasses of PERSON. Each pilot has specific attributes license number [Lic_Num] and restrictions [Restr]; each employee has specific attributes salary [Salary] and shift worked [Shift]. All PERSON entities in the database have data kept on their Personal Number [PNO], name [Name], address [Address], and telephone number [Phone]. For CORPORATION entities, the data kept includes name [Name], address [Address], and telephone number [Phone]. The database also keeps track of the types of planes each pilot is authorized to fly [FLIES] and the types of planes each employee can do maintenance work on [WORKS_ON]. Show how the SMALL AIRPORT EER schema of Figure 3.34 may be represented in UML notation. (*Note:* We have not discussed how to represent categories (union types) in UML, so you do not have to map the categories in this and the following question.)

3.45.   Show how the UNIVERSITY EER schema of Figure 3.24 may be represented in UML notation.

Selected Bibliography

The Entity-Relationship model was introduced by Chen (1976), and related work appears in Schmidt and Swenson (1975), Wiederhold and Elmasri (1979), and Senko (1975). Since then, numerous modifications to the ER model have been suggested and formalized in Ng (1981). We have incorporated some of these in our presentation. Structural constraints on relationships are discussed in Abrial (1974), Elmasri and Wiederhold (1980), and Lenzerini and Santucci (1983). Multivalued and composite attributes are incorporated in the ER model in Elmasri et al. (1985). Although we did not discuss languages for the entity-relationship model and its extensions, there have been several proposals for such languages. Elmasri and Wiederhold (1981) proposed the GORDAS query language for the ER model. Another ER query language was proposed by Markowitz and Raz (1983). Senko (1980) presented a query language for Senko's DIAM model. A formal set of operations called the ER algebra was presented by Parent and Spaccapietra (1985). Gogolla and Hohenstein (1991) presented another formal language for the ER model. Campbell et al. (1985) presented a set of ER operations and showed that they are relationally complete. A conference for the dissemination of research results related to the ER model has been held regularly since 1979. The conference, now known as the International Conference on Conceptual Modeling, has been held in Los Angeles (ER 1979, ER 1983, ER 1997), Washington, D.C. (ER 1981), Chicago (ER 1985), Dijon, France (ER 1986), New York City (ER 1987), Rome (ER 1988), Toronto (ER 1989), Lausanne, Switzerland (ER 1990), San Mateo, California (ER 1991), Karlsruhe, Germany (ER 1992), Arlington, Texas (ER 1993), Manchester, England (ER 1994), Brisbane, Australia (ER 1995), Cottbus, Germany (ER 1996), Singapore (ER 1998), Salt Lake City, Utah (ER 1999), Yokohama, Japan (ER 2001), and Tampere, Finland (ER 2002).

Many papers have proposed conceptual or semantic data models. We give a representative list here. One group of papers, including, Senko's DIAM model (1975), the NIAM method (Verheijen and VanBekkum 1982), and Bracchi et al. (1976), presents semantic models that are based on the concept of binary relationships. Another group of early papers discusses methods for extending the relational model to enhance its modeling capabilities. This includes the papers by Schmid and Swenson (1975), Navathe and Schkolnick (1978), Codd's RM/T model (1979), Furtado (1978), and the structural model of Wiederhold and Elmasri (1979).

Since then, numerous extensions of its modeling capabilities have been proposed, as in Scheuermann et al. (1979), Dos Santos et al. (1979), Teorey et al. (1986), Gogolla and Hohenstein (1991), and the entity-category-relationship (ECR) model of Elmasri et al. (1985). Smith and Smith (1977) present the concepts of generalization and aggregation. The semantic data model of Hammer and McLeod (1981) introduced the concepts of class/subclass lattices, as well as other advanced modeling concepts.

A survey of semantic data modeling appears in Hull and King (1987). Eick (1991) discusses design and transformations of conceptual schemas. Analysis of constraints for *n*-ary relationships is given in Soutou (1998). UML is described in detail in Booch, Rumbaugh, and Jacobson (1999). Fowler and Scott (2000) and Stevens and Pooley (2000) give concise introductions to UML concepts.

2

RELATIONAL MODEL: CONCEPTS, CONSTRAINTS, LANGUAGES, AND DESIGN

4

The Relational Data Model and Relational Database Constraints

[Earlier Chapter Number 5]

The relational model was first introduced by Ted Codd of IBM Research in 1970 in a classic paper (Codd 1970), and attracted immediate attention due to its simplicity and mathematical foundation. The model uses the concept of a *mathematical relation*—which looks somewhat like a table of values—as its basic building block, and has its theoretical basis in set theory and first-order predicate logic. In this chapter we discuss the basic characteristics of the model and its constraints.

The first commercial implementations of the relational model became available in the early 1980s, such as the Oracle DBMS and the SQL/DS system on the MVS operating system by IBM. Since then, the model has been implemented in a large number of commercial systems. Current popular relational DBMSs (RDBMSs) include DB2 and Informix Dynamic Server (from IBM), Oracle and Rdb (from Oracle), and SQL Server and Access (from Microsoft).

Chapter 5 covers the operations of the relational algebra and introduces the relational calculus notation for two types of calculi—tuple calculus and domain calculus. Chapter 6 relates the relational model data structures to the constructs of the ER and EER models, and presents algorithms for designing a relational database schema by mapping a conceptual schema in the ER or EER model (see Chapter 3) into a relational representation. These mappings are incorporated into many database design and CASE[1] tools. In Chapter 7, we describe the SQL query language, which is the standard for commercial relational DBMSs. Chapter 7 discusses the programming techniques used to access database systems, and presents additional topics concerning

---

1. CASE stands for computer-aided software engineering.

the SQL language—constraints, views, and the notion of connecting to relational databases via ODBC and JDBC standard protocols. Chapter 8 also present another aspect of the relational model, namely the formal constraints of functional and multivalued dependencies; these dependencies are used to develop a relational database design theory based on the concept known as *normalization*.

Data models that preceded the relational model include the hierarchical and network models. They were proposed in the 1960s and were implemented in early DBMSs during the 1970s and 1980s. Because of their historical importance and the large existing user base for these DBMSs, we have included a summary of the highlights of these models in appendices, which are available on the Web site for the book. These models and systems will be with us for many years and are now referred to as *legacy database systems*.

In this chapter, we concentrate on describing the basic principles of the relational model of data. We begin by defining the modeling concepts and notation of the relational model in Section 4.1. Section 4.2 is devoted to a discussion of relational constraints that are now considered an important part of the relational model and are automatically enforced in most relational DBMSs. Section 4.3 defines the update operations of the relational model and discusses how violations of integrity constraints are handled.

4.1 RELATIONAL MODEL CONCEPTS

The relational model represents the database as a collection of *relations*. Informally, each relation resembles a table of values or, to some extent, a "flat" file of records. For example, the database of files that was shown in Figure 1.2 is similar to the relational model representation. However, there are important differences between relations and files, as we shall soon see.

When a relation is thought of as a **table** of values, each row in the table represents a collection of related data values. We introduced entity types and relationship types as concepts for modeling real-world data in Chapter 3. In the relational model, each row in the table represents a fact that typically corresponds to a real-world entity or relationship. The table name and column names are used to help in interpreting the meaning of the values in each row. For example, the first table of Figure 1.2 is called STUDENT because each row represents facts about a particular student entity. The column names—Name, StudentNumber, Class, and Major—specify how to interpret the data values in each row, based on the column each value is in. All values in a column are of the same data type.

In the formal relational model terminology, a row is called a *tuple*, a column header is called an *attribute*, and the table is called a *relation*. The data type describing the types of values that can appear in each column is represented by a *domain* of possible values. We now define these terms—*domain, tuple*, attribute, and *relation*—more precisely.

4.1.1 Domains, Attributes, Tuples, and Relations

A **domain** D is a set of atomic values. By **atomic** we mean that each value in the domain is indivisible as far as the relational model is concerned. A common method of specifying a domain is to specify a data type from which the data values forming the domain are drawn. It is also useful to specify a name for the domain, to help in interpreting its values. Some examples of domains follow:

- Set_of_phone_numbers: The set of valid phone numbers in India.

- Local_phone_numbers: The set of valid phone numbers within a particular area code in India.

- Student_roll_numbers: The set of valid student roll numbers.

- Names: The set of character strings that represent names of persons.

- Grade_point_averages: Possible values of computed grade point averages; each must be a real (floating-point) number between 0 and 4.

- Employee_ages: Possible ages of employees of a company; each must be a value between 15 and 80 years old.

- Academic_department_names: The set of academic department names in a university, such as Computer Science, Economics, and Physics.

- Academic_department_codes: The set of academic department codes, such as CS, ECON, and PHYS.

The preceding are called *logical* definitions of domains. A **data type** or **format** is also specified for each domain. For example, the data type for the domain Set_phone_numbers can be declared as of character strings. The data type for Employee_ages is an integer number between 15 and 80. For Academic_department_names, the data type is the set of all character strings that represent valid department names. A domain is thus given a name, data type, and format. Additional information for interpreting the values of a domain can also be given. For example, a numeric domain such as Person_weights should have the units of measurement, such as pounds or kilograms.

A **relation schema**[2] R, denoted by $R(A_1, A_2, \ldots, A_n)$, is made up of a relation name R and a list of attributes $A_1, A_2, \ldots, A_n$. Each attribute A_i is the name of a role played by some domain D in the relation schema R. D is called the **domain** of A_i and is denoted by $\mathbf{dom}(A_i)$. A relation schema is used to *describe* a relation; R is called the **name** of this relation. The **degree** (or **arity**) of a relation is the number of attributes n of its relation schema.

An example of a relation schema for a relation of degree seven, which describes university students, is the following:

STUDENT(Name, RollNo, HomePhone, Address, OfficePhone, Age, GPA)

Using the data type of each attribute, the definition is sometimes written as:

STUDENT(Name: string, RollNo: string, HomePhone: string, Address: string, OfficePhone: string, Age: integer, GPA: real)

For this relation schema, STUDENT is the name of the relation, which has seven attributes. In the above definition, we showed assignment of generic types such as string or integer to the attributes. More precisely, we can specify the following previously defined domains for some of the attributes of the STUDENT relation: dom(Name) = Names; dom(RollNo) = Student_Roll_numbers; dom(HomePhone) = Local_phone_numbers, dom(OfficePhone) = Local_phone_numbers, and dom(GPA) = Grade_point_averages. It is also possible to refer to attributes of a relation schema by their position within the relation; thus, the second attribute of the STUDENT relation is RollNo, whereas the fourth attribute is Address.

A **relation** (or **relation state**)[3] r of the relation schema $R(A_1, A_2, \ldots, A_n)$, also denoted by $r(R)$, is a set of n-tuples $r = \{t_1, t_2, \ldots, t_m\}$. Each **$n$-tuple** t is an ordered list of n values $t = \langle v_1, v_2, \ldots, v_n \rangle$, where each value v_i, $1 \leq i \leq n$, is an element of dom(A_i) or is a special **null** value. The ith value in tuple t, which corresponds to the attribute A_i, is referred to as $t[A_i]$ (or $t[i]$ if we use the positional notation). The terms **relation intension** for the schema R and **relation extension** for a relation state $r(R)$ are also commonly used.

---

2. A relation schema is sometimes called a **relation scheme**.

3. This has also been called a **relation instance**. We will not use this term because *instance* is also used to refer to a single tuple or row.

Figure 4.1 shows an example of a STUDENT relation, which corresponds to the STUDENT schema just specified. Each tuple in the relation represents a particular student entity. We display the relation as a table, where each tuple is shown as a *row* and each attribute corresponds to a *column header* indicating a role or interpretation of the values in that column. *Null values* represent attributes whose values are unknown or do not exist for some individual STUDENT tuple.

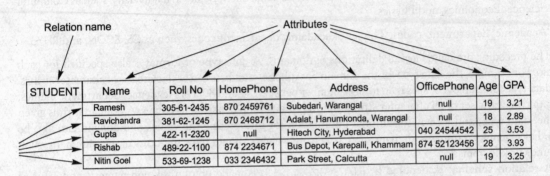

FIGURE 4.1 The attributes and tuples of a relation STUDENT.

The earlier definition of a relation can be *restated* more formally as follows. A relation (or relation state) $r(R)$ is a **mathematical relation** of degree n on the domains $\text{dom}(A_1)$, $\text{dom}(A_2)$, . . . , $\text{dom}(A_n)$, which is a **subset** of the **Cartesian product** of the domains that define R:

$$r(R) \subseteq (\text{dom}(A_1) \times \text{dom}(A_2) \times \ldots \times \text{dom}(A_n))$$

The Cartesian product specifies all possible combinations of values from the underlying domains. Hence, if we denote the total number of values, or **cardinality**, in a domain D by $|D|$ (assuming that all domains are finite), the total number of tuples in the Cartesian product is

$$|\text{dom}(A_1)| \times |\text{dom}(A_2)| \times \ldots \times |\text{dom}(A_n)|$$

Of all these possible combinations, a relation state at a given time—the **current relation state**—reflects only the valid tuples that represent a particular state of the real world. In general, as the state of the real world changes, so does the relation, by being transformed into another relation state. However, the schema R is relatively static and does *not* change except very infrequently—for example, as a result of adding an attribute to represent new information that was not originally stored in the relation.

It is possible for several attributes to *have the same domain*. The attributes indicate different **roles**, or interpretations, for the domain. For example, in the STUDENT relation, the same domain Local_phone_numbers plays the role of HomePhone, referring to the "home phone of a student," and the role of OfficePhone, referring to the "office phone of the student."

4.1.2 Characteristics of Relations

The earlier definition of relations implies certain characteristics that make a relation different from a file or a table. We now discuss some of these characteristics.

Ordering of Tuples in a Relation.   A relation is defined as a *set* of tuples. Mathematically, elements of a set have *no order* among them; hence, tuples in a relation do not have any particular order. However, in a file, records are physically stored on disk (or in memory), so there always is an order among the records. This ordering indicates first, second, *i*th, and last records in the file. Similarly, when we display a relation as a table, the rows are displayed in a certain order.

Tuple ordering is not part of a relation definition, because a relation attempts to represent facts at a logical or abstract level. Many logical orders can be specified on a relation. For example, tuples in the STUDENT relation in Figure 4.1 could be logically ordered by values of Name, or by RollNo, or by Age, or by some other attribute. The definition of a relation does not specify any order: There is *no preference* for one logical ordering over another. Hence, the relation displayed in Figure 4.2 is considered *identical* to the one shown in Figure 4.1. When a relation is implemented as a file or displayed as a table, a particular ordering may be specified on the records of the file or the rows of the table.

Ordering of Values within a Tuple, and an Alternative Definition of a Relation.

According to the preceding definition of a relation, an *n*-tuple is an *ordered list* of *n* values, so the ordering of values in a tuple—and hence of attributes in a relation schema—is important. However, at a logical level, the order of attributes and their values is *not* that important as long as the correspondence between attributes and values is maintained.

An **alternative definition** of a relation can be given, making the ordering of values in a tuple *unnecessary*. In this definition, a relation schema $R = \{A_1, A_2, \ldots, A_n\}$ is a *set* of attributes, and a relation state $r(R)$ is a finite set of mappings $r = \{t_1, t_2, \ldots, t_m\}$, where each tuple t_i is a **mapping** from R to D, and D is the union of the attribute domains; that is, $D = \text{dom}(A_1) \cup \text{dom}(A_2) \cup \ldots \cup \text{dom}(A_n)$. In this definition, $t[A_i]$ must be in $\text{dom}(A_i)$ for $1 \le i \le n$ for each mapping t in r. Each mapping t_i is called a tuple.

According to this definition of tuple as a mapping, a **tuple** can be considered as a **set** of (<attribute>, <value>) pairs, where each pair gives the value of the mapping from an attribute A_i to a value v_i from $\text{dom}(A_i)$. The ordering of attributes is *not* important, because the attribute name appears with its value. By this definition, the two tuples shown in Figure 4.3 are identical. This makes sense at an abstract or logical level, since there really is no reason to prefer having one attribute value appear before another in a tuple.

When a relation is implemented as a file, the attributes are physically ordered as fields within a record. We will generally use the **first definition** of relation, where the attributes and the values within tuples *are ordered*, because it simplifies much of the notation. However, the alternative definition given here is more general.[4]

Values and Nulls in the Tuples.

Each value in a tuple is an **atomic** value; that is, it is not divisible into components within the framework of the basic relational model. Hence, composite and multivalued attributes (see Chapter 3) are not allowed. This model is sometimes called the **flat relational model**. Much of the theory behind the relational model was developed with this assumption in mind, which is called the **first normal form** assumption.[5] Hence, multivalued attributes must be represented by separate relations, and composite attributes are represented only by their simple component attributes in the basic relational model.[6]

An important concept is that of **nulls**, which are used to represent the values of attributes that may be unknown or may not apply to a tuple. A special value, called **null**, is used for these cases. For example, in Figure 4.1, some student tuples have null for their office phones because they do not have an office (that is, office phone *does not apply* to these students). Another student has a null for home phone, presumably because either he does not have a home phone or he has one but we do not know it (value is *unknown*). In general, we can have *several meanings* for null values, such as "value unknown," "value exists but is not

---

4. As we shall see, the alternative definition of relation is useful when we discuss query processing in Chapter 10.

5. We discuss this assumption in more detail in Chapter 8.

6. Extensions of the relational model remove these restrictions. For example, object-relational systems allow complex-structured attributes, as do the **non-first normal form** or **nested** relational models.

available," or "attribute does not apply to this tuple." An example of the last type of null will occur if we add an attribute Visa_status to the STUDENT relation that applies only to tuples that represent foreign students. It is possible to devise different codes for different meanings of null values. Incorporating different types of null values into the relational model operations (see Chapter 5) has proven difficult and is outside the scope of our presentation.

STUDENT	Name	SSN	HomePhone	Address	OfficePhone	Age	GPA
	Gupta	422-11-2320	null	Hitech City, Hyderabad	040 2454542	25	3.53
	Nitin Goel	533-69-1238	033 2346432	Park Street, Calcutta	null	19	3.25
	Rishab	489-22-1100	874 2234671	Bus Depot, Karepalli, Khammam	874 52123456	28	3.93
	Ravichandra	381-62-1245	870 2468712	Adalat, Hanumkonda, Warangal	null	18	2.89
	Ramesh	305-61-2435	870 2459761	Subedari, Warangal	null	19	3.21

FIGURE 4.2 The relation STUDENT from Figure 4.1 with a different order of tuples.

t = < (Name, Gupta),(RollNo, 422-11-2320), (HomePhone, null), (Address, HiTech City, Hyderabad),
      (OfficePhone, 0402454542),(Age, 25),GPA, 3.53)>

t = < (Address, HiTech City, Hyderabad), (Name, Gupta), (RollNo 422-11-2320), (Age, 25),
      (OfficePhone, 0402454542),GPA, 3.53) (HomePhone,null)>

FIGURE 4.3 Two identical tuples when the order of attributes and values is not part of relation definition.

Interpretation (Meaning) of a Relation.   The relation schema can be interpreted as a declaration or a type of **assertion**. For example, the schema of the STUDENT relation of Figure 4.1 asserts that, in general, a student entity has a Name, RollNo, HomePhone, Address, OfficePhone, Age, and GPA. Each tuple in the relation can then be interpreted as a **fact** or a particular instance of the assertion. For example, the first tuple in Figure 4.1 asserts the fact that there is a student whose name is Ramesh, RollNo is 305-61-2435, Age is 19, and so on.

Notice that some relations may represent facts about *entities*, whereas other relations may represent facts about *relationships*. For example, a relation schema MAJORS (Student, RollNo, DepartmentCode) asserts that students major in academic departments. A tuple in this relation relates a student to his or her major department. Hence, the relational model represents facts about both entities and relationships *uniformly* as relations. This sometimes compromises understandability because one has to guess whether a relation represents an entity type or a relationship type. The mapping procedures in Chapter 6 show how different constructs of the ER and EER models get converted to relations.

An alternative interpretation of a relation schema is as a **predicate**; in this case, the values in each tuple are interpreted as values that *satisfy* the predicate. This interpretation is quite useful in the context of logic programming languages, such as Prolog, because it allows the relational model to be used within these languages.

4.1.3 Relational Model Notation

We will use the following notation in our presentation:

- A relation schema R of degree n is denoted by $R(A_1, A_2, \ldots, A_n)$.

- An n-tuple t in a relation r(R) is denoted by $t = <v_1, v_2, \ldots, v_n>$, where v_i is the value corresponding to attribute A_i. The following notation refers to **component values** of tuples:

- Both $t[A_i]$ and $t.A_i$ (and sometimes $t[i]$) refer to the value v_i in t for attribute A_i.

- Both $t[A_u, A_w, \ldots, A_z]$ and $t.(A_u, A_w, \ldots, A_z)$, where $A_u, A_w, \ldots, A_z$ is a list of attributes from R, refer to the subtuple of values $<vu, vw, \ldots, vz>$ from t corresponding to the attributes specified in the list.

- The letters Q, R, S denote relation names.

- The letters q, r, s denote relation states.

- The letters t, u, v denote tuples.

- In general, the name of a relation schema such as STUDENT also indicates the current set of tuples in that relation—the *current relation state*—whereas STUDENT(Name, RollNo, . . .) refers only to the relation schema.

- An attribute A can be qualified with the relation name R to which it belongs by using the *dot notation* $R.A$—for example, STUDENT.Name or STUDENT.Age. This is because the same name may be used for two attributes in different relations. However, all attribute names *in a particular relation* must be distinct.

As an example, consider the tuple t = <'Nitin goel', '533-69-1238', '0332346432', 'Parkstreet, Calcultta', null, 19, 3.25> from the STUDENT relation in Figure 4.1; we have $t[Name]$ = <'Nitin goel'>, and $t[RollNo, GPA, Age]$ = <'533-69-1238', 3.25, 19>.

4.2 RELATIONAL MODEL CONSTRAINTS AND RELATIONAL DATABASE SCHEMAS

So far, we have discussed the characteristics of single relations. In a relational database, there will typically be many relations, and the tuples in those relations are usually related in various ways. The state of the whole database will correspond to the states of all its relations at a particular point in time. There are generally many restrictions or **constraints** on the actual values in a database state. These constraints are derived from the rules in the miniworld that the database represents, as we discussed in Section 1.6.7.

In this section, we discuss the various restrictions on data that can be specified on a relational database in the form of constraints. Constraints on databases can generally be divided into three main categories:

1. Constraints that are inherent in the data model. We call these inherent **model-based constraints**.
2. Constraints that can be directly expressed in the schemas of the data model, typically by specifying them in the DDL (data definition language, see Section 2.3.1). We call these **schema-based constraints**.
3. Constraints that cannot be directly expressed in the schemas of the data model, and hence must be expressed and enforced by the application programs. We call these **application-based constraints**.

The characteristics of relations that we discussed in Section 4.1.2 are the inherent constraints of the relational model and belong to the first category. For example, the constraint that a relation cannot have duplicate tuples is an inherent constraint. The constraints we discuss in this section are of the second category, namely, constraints that can be expressed in the schema of the relational model via the DDL. Constraints in the third category are more general and are difficult to express and enforce within the data model, so they are usually checked within application programs.

Another important category of constraints is *data dependencies*, which include *functional dependencies* and *multivalued dependencies*. They are used mainly for testing the "goodness" of the design of a relational database and are utilized in a process called *normalization*, which is discussed in Chapter 8.

We now discuss the main types of constraints that can be expressed in the relational model—the schema-based constraints from the second category. These include domain constraints, key constraints, constraints on nulls, entity integrity constraints, and referential integrity constraints.

4.2.1   Domain Constraints

Domain constraints specify that within each tuple, the value of each attribute A must be an atomic value from the domain dom(A). We have already discussed the ways in which domains can be specified in Section 4.1.1. The data types associated with domains typically include standard numeric data types for integers (such as short integer, integer, and long integer) and real numbers (float and double-precision float). Characters, booleans, fixed-length strings, and variable-length strings are also available, as are date, time, time-stamp, and, in some cases, money data types. Other possible domains may be described by a subrange of values from a data type or as an enumerated data type in which all possible values are explicitly listed. Rather than describe these in detail here, we discuss the data types offered by the SQL-99 relational standard in Section 7.1.

4.2.2   Key Constraints and Constraints on Null Values

A *relation* is defined as a set of *tuples*. By definition, all elements of a set are distinct; hence, all tuples in a relation must also be distinct. This means that no two tuples can have the same combination of values for *all* their attributes. Usually, there are other **subsets of attributes** of a relation schema R with the property that no two tuples in any relation state r of R should have the same combination of values for these attributes. Suppose that we denote one such subset of attributes by SK; then for any two *distinct* tuples t_1 and t_2 in a relation state r of R, we have the constraint that

$$t_1[SK] \neq t_2[SK]$$

Any such set of attributes SK is called a **superkey** of the relation schema R. A superkey SK specifies a *uniqueness constraint* that no two distinct tuples in any state r of R can have the same value for SK. Every relation has at least one default superkey—the set of all its attributes. A superkey can have redundant attributes, however, so a more useful concept is that of a *key*, which has no redundancy. A **key** K of a relation schema R is a superkey of R with the additional property that removing any attribute A from K leaves a set of attributes K' that is not a superkey of R any more. Hence, a key satisfies two constraints:

1. Two distinct tuples in any state of the relation cannot have identical values for (all) the attributes in the key.

2. It is a *minimal superkey*—that is, a superkey from which we cannot remove any attributes and still have the uniqueness constraint in condition 1 hold.

The first condition applies to both keys and superkeys. The second condition is required only for keys. For example, consider the STUDENT relation of Figure 4.1. The attribute set {RollNo} is a key of STUDENT because no two student tuples can have the same value for RollNo.[7] Any set of attributes that includes RollNo—for example, {RollNo, Name, Age}—is a superkey. However, the superkey {RollNo, Name, Age} is not a key of STUDENT, because removing Name or Age or both from the set still leaves us with a superkey. In general, any superkey formed from a single attribute is also a key. A key with multiple attributes must require all its attributes to have the uniqueness property hold.

---

7. Note that ROLLNO is also a superkey.

The value of a key attribute can be used to identify uniquely each tuple in the relation. For example, the RollNo value 305-61-2435 identifies uniquely the tuple corresponding to Ramesh in the STUDENT relation. Notice that a set of attributes constituting a key is a property of the relation schema; it is a constraint that should hold on *every* valid relation state of the schema. A key is determined from the meaning of the attributes, and the property is *time-invariant*: It must continue to hold when we insert new tuples in the relation. For example, we cannot and should not designate the Name attribute of the STUDENT relation in Figure 4.1 as a key, because it is possible that two students with identical names will exist at some point in a valid state.[8]

CAR	LicenseNumber	EngineSerialNumber	Make	Model	Year
	Delhi ABC-739	A69352	Ford	Mustang	96
	Chennai TVP-347	B43696	Oldsmobile	Cutlass	99
	Calcutta MPO-22	X83554	Oldsmobile	Delta	95
	Mumbai 432-TFY	C43742	Mercedes	190-D	93
	Mumbai RSK-629	Y82935	Toyota	Camry	98
	Delhi RSK-629	U028365	Jaguar	XJS	98

FIGURE 4.4 The CAR relation, with two candidate keys: LicenseNumber and EngineSerialNumber.

In general, a relation schema may have more than one key. In this case, each of the keys is called a **candidate key**. For example, the CAR relation in Figure 4.4 has two candidate keys: LicenseNumber and EngineSerialNumber. It is common to designate one of the candidate keys as the **primary key** of the relation. This is the candidate key whose values are used to *identify* tuples in the relation. We use the convention that the attributes that form the primary key of a relation schema are underlined, as shown in Figure 4.4. Notice that when a relation schema has several candidate keys, the choice of one to become the primary key is arbitrary; however, it is usually better to choose a primary key with a single attribute or a small number of attributes.

Another constraint on attributes specifies whether null values are or are not permitted. For example, if every STUDENT tuple must have a valid, nonnull value for the Name attribute, then Name of STUDENT is constrained to be NOT NULL.

4.2.3 Relational Databases and Relational Database Schemas

The definitions and constraints we have discussed so far apply to single relations and their attributes. A relational database usually contains many relations, with tuples in relations that are related in various ways. In this section we define a relational database and a relational database schema. A **relational database schema** S is a set of relation schemas $S = \{R_1, R_2, \ldots, R_m\}$ and a set of **integrity constraints** IC. A **relational database state**[9] DB of S is a set of relation states DB $= \{r_1, r_2, \ldots, r_m\}$ such that each r_i is a state of R_i and such that the r_i relation states satisfy the integrity constraints specified in IC. Figure 4.5 shows a relational database schema that we call COMPANY $= \{$EMPLOYEE, DEPARTMENT, DEPT_LOCATIONS, PROJECT, WORKS_ON, DEPENDENT$\}$. The

---

8. Names are sometimes used as keys, but then some artifact—such as appending an ordinal number—must be used to distinguish between identical names.

9. A relational database *state* is sometimes called a relational database *instance*. However, as we mentioned earlier, we will not use the term *instance* since it also applies to single tuples.

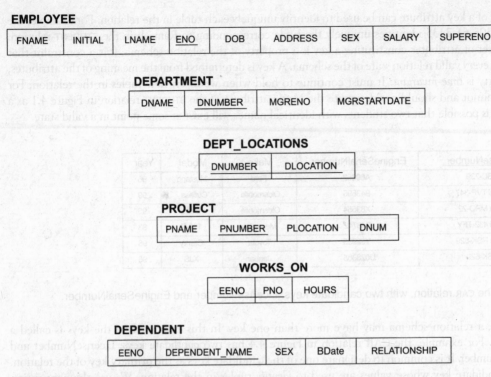

FIGURE 4.5 Schema diagram for the COMPANY relational database schema.

underlined attributes represent primary keys. Figure 4.6 shows a relational database state corresponding to the COMPANY schema. We will use this schema and database state in this chapter and in Chapter 5 through 7 for developing example queries in different relational languages. When we refer to a relational database, we implicitly include both its schema and its current state. A database state that does not obey all the integrity constraints is called an **invalid state**, and a state that satisfies all the constraints in IC is called a **valid state**.

In Figure 4.5, the DNUMBER attribute in both DEPARTMENT and DEPT_LOCATIONS stands for the same real-world concept—the number given to a department. That same concept is called DNO in EMPLOYEE and DNUM in PROJECT. Attributes that represent the same real-world concept may or may not have identical names in different relations. Alternatively, attributes that represent different concepts may have the same name in different relations. For example, we could have used the attribute name NAME for both PNAME of PROJECT and DNAME of DEPARTMENT; in this case, we would have two attributes that share the same name but represent different real-world concepts—project names and department names.

In some early versions of the relational model, an assumption was made that the same real-world concept, when represented by an attribute, would have *identical* attribute names in all relations. This creates problems when the same real-world concept is used in different roles (meanings) in the same relation. For example, the concept of employee number (ENO) appears twice in the EMPLOYEE relation of Figure 4.5: once in the role of the employee's number, and once in the role of the supervisor's number (who is also an employee). We gave them distinct attribute names—ENO and SUPERENO, respectively—in order to distinguish their meaning.

Each relational DBMS must have a data definition language (DDL) for defining a relational database schema. Current relational DBMSs are mostly using SQL for this purpose. We present the SQL DDL in Chapter 7.

Integrity constraints are specified on a database schema and are expected to hold on every valid database state of that schema. In addition to domain, key, and NOT NULL constraints, two other types of constraints are considered part of the relational model: entity integrity and referential integrity.

EMPLOYEE	FNAME	INITIAL	LNAME	ENO	BDATE	ADDRESS	SEX	SALARY	SUPERENO	DNO
	Mahesh	B	Kumar	123456789	09-01-1965	731, Ameerpet, Hyderapad, AP	M	30000	333445555	5
	Karthik	T	Chandra	333445555	08-12-1955	638, Begampet, Hyderabad, AP	M	40000	888665555	5
	Swetha	J	Narayan	999887777	19-01-1968	3321, Hauzkhar, New Delhi	F	25000	987654321	4
	Priya	S	Ganesh	987654321	20-06-1941	291, Majestic Street, Bangalore	F	43000	888665555	4
	Ramesh	K	Narayan	666884444	15-09-1962	975 Hauzkhas, New Delhi	M	38000	333445555	5
	Kiran	A	Goyal	453453453	31-07-1972	5631 Abids, Hyderabad, AP	F	25000	333445555	5
	Kikndra	V	Nath	987987987	29-03-1963	980, Koti, Hyderabad, AP	M	25000	987654321	4
	Gaurav	E	Kishan	888665555	10-11-1937	450 Abids, Hyderabad, AP	M	55000	null	1

DEPT_LOCATIONS	DNUMBER	DLOCATION
	1	Hyderabad
	4	Chennai
	5	Bangalore
	5	New Delhi
		Hyderabad

DEPARTMENT	DNAME	DNUMBER	MGRENO	MGRSTARTDATE
	Research	5	333445555	1988-05-22
	Administration	4	987654321	1995-01-01
	Headquarters	1	888665555	1981-06-19

WORKS_ON	EENO	PNO	HOURS
	123456789	1	32.5
	123456789	2	7.5
	666884444	3	40.0
	453453453	1	20.0
	453453453	2	20.0
	333445555	2	10.0
	333445555	3	10.0
	333445555	10	10.0
	333445555	20	10.0
	999887777	30	30.0
	999887777	10	10.0
	987987987	10	35.0
	987987987	30	5.0
	987654321	30	20.0
	987654321	20	15.0
	888665555	20	null

PROJECT	PNAME	PNUMBER	PLOCATION	DNUM
	ProductX	1	Bangalore	5
	ProductY	2	New Delhi	5
	ProductZ	3	Hyderabad	5
	Computerization	10	Chennai	4
	Reorganization	20	Hyderabad	1
	Newbenefits	30	Chennai	4

DEPENDENT	EENO	DEPENDENT_NAME	SEX	BDATE	RELATIONSHIP
	333445555	Archana	F	05-04-1986	DAUGHTER
	333445555	Tejpaul	M	25-10-1983	SON
	333445555	Jyothi	F	03-05-1958	SPOUSE
	987654321	Anand	M	28-02-1942	SPOUSE
	123456789	Manikam	M	04-01-1988	SON
	123456789	Arpitha	F	30-12-1988	DAUGHTER
	123456789	Pratyusa	F	05-05-1967	SPOUSE

FIGURE 4.6 One possible database state for the COMPANY relational database schema.

4.2.4   Entity Integrity, Referential Integrity, and Foreign Keys

The **entity integrity constraint** states that no primary key value can be null. This is because the primary key value is used to identify individual tuples in a relation. Having null values for the primary key implies that we cannot identify some tuples. For example, if two or more tuples had null for their primary keys, we might not be able to distinguish them if we tried to reference them from other relations.

Key constraints and entity integrity constraints are specified on individual relations. The **referential integrity** constraint is specified between two relations and is used to maintain the consistency among tuples in the two relations. Informally, the referential integrity constraint states that a tuple in one relation that refers to another relation must refer to an *existing tuple* in that relation. For example, in Figure 4.6, the attribute DNO of EMPLOYEE gives the department number for which each employee works; hence, its value in every EMPLOYEE tuple must match the DNUMBER value of some tuple in the DEPARTMENT relation.

To define referential integrity more formally, we first define the concept of a *foreign key*. The conditions for a foreign key, given below, specify a referential integrity constraint between the two relation schemas R_1 and R_2. A set of attributes FK in relation schema R_1 is a **foreign key** of R_1 that **references** relation R_2 if it satisfies the following two rules:

1. The attributes in FK have the same domain(s) as the primary key attributes PK of R_2; the attributes FK are said to **reference** or **refer** to the relation R_2.

2. A value of FK in a tuple t_1 of the current state $r_1(R_1)$ either occurs as a value of PK for some tuple t_2 in the current state $r_2(R_2)$ *or is null*. In the former case, we have $t_1[FK] = t_2[PK]$, and we say that the tuple t_1 **references** or **refers** to the tuple t_2.

In this definition, R_1 is called the **referencing relation** and R_2 is the **referenced relation**. If these two conditions hold, a **referential integrity constraint** from R_1 to R_2 is said to hold. In a database of many relations, there are usually many referential integrity constraints.

To specify these constraints, we must first have a clear understanding of the meaning or role that each set of attributes plays in the various relation schemas of the database. Referential integrity constraints typically arise from the *relationships among the entities* represented by the relation schemas. For example, consider the database shown in Figure 4.6. In the EMPLOYEE relation, the attribute DNO refers to the department for which an employee works; hence, we designate DNO to be a foreign key of EMPLOYEE referring to the DEPARTMENT relation. This means that a value of DNO in any tuple t_1 of the EMPLOYEE relation must match a value of the primary key of DEPARTMENT—the DNUMBER attribute—in some tuple t_2 of the DEPARTMENT relation, or the value of DNO *can be null* if the employee does not belong to a department. In Figure 4.6 the tuple for employee 'Mahesh Kumar' references the tuple for the 'Research' department, indicating that 'Mahesh Kumar' works for this department.

Notice that a foreign key can *refer to its own relation*. For example, the attribute SUPERENO in EMPLOYEE refers to the supervisor of an employee; this is another employee, represented by a tuple in the EMPLOYEE relation. Hence, SUPERENO is a foreign key that references the EMPLOYEE relation itself. In Figure 4.6 the tuple for employee 'Mahesh Kumar' references the tuple for employee 'Karthik Chandra,' indicating that 'Karthik Chandra' is the supervisor of 'Mahesh Kumar.'

We can *diagrammatically display referential integrity constraints* by drawing a directed arc from each foreign key to the relation it references. For clarity, the arrowhead may point to the primary key of the referenced relation. Figure 4.7 shows the schema in Figure 4.5 with the referential integrity constraints displayed in this manner.

All integrity constraints should be specified on the relational database schema if we want to enforce these constraints on the database states. Hence, the DDL includes provisions for specifying the various types of constraints so that the DBMS can automatically enforce them. Most relational DBMSs support key and entity integrity constraints, and make provisions to support referential integrity. These constraints are specified as a part of data definition.

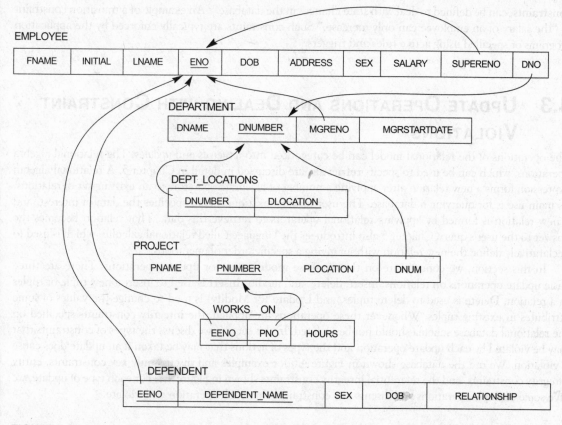

FIGURE 4.7 Referential integrity constraints displayed on the COMPANY relational database schema.

4.2.5 Other Types of Constraints

The preceding integrity constraints do not include a large class of general constraints, sometimes called *semantic integrity constraints*, that may have to be specified and enforced on a relational database. Examples of such constraints are "the salary of an employee should not exceed the salary of the employee's supervisor" and "the maximum number of hours an employee can work on all projects per week is 56." Such constraints can be specified and enforced within the application programs that update the database, or by using a general-purpose **constraint specification language**. Mechanisms called **triggers** and **assertions** can be used. In SQL-99, a CREATE ASSERTION statement is used for this purpose (see Chapter 7). It is more common to check for these types of constraints within the application programs than to use constraint specification languages, because the latter are difficult and complex to use correctly.

Another type of constraint is the *functional dependency* constraint, which establishes a functional relationship among two sets of attributes X and Y. This constraint specifies that the value of X determines the value of Y in all states of a relation; it is denoted as a functional dependency $X \rightarrow Y$. We use functional dependencies and other types of dependencies in Chapter 8 as tools to analyze the quality of relational designs and to "normalize" relations to improve their quality.

The types of constraints we discussed so far may be called **state constraints**, because they define the constraints that a *valid state* of the database must satisfy. Another type of constraint, called **transition**

constraints, can be defined to deal with state changes in the database.[10] An example of a transition constraint is: "the salary of an employee can only increase." Such constraints are typically enforced by the application programs or specified using active rules and triggers.

4.3 UPDATE OPERATIONS AND DEALING WITH CONSTRAINT VIOLATIONS

The operations of the relational model can be categorized into *retrievals* and *updates*. The relational algebra operations, which can be used to specify **retrievals**, are discussed in detail in Chapter 5. A relational algebra expression forms a new relation after applying a number of algebraic operators to an existing set of relations; its main use is for querying a database. The user formulates a query that specifies the data of interest, and a new relation is formed by applying relational operators to retrieve this data. That relation becomes the answer to the user's query. Chapter 5 also introduces the language called relational calculus, which is used to declaratively define the new relation without giving a specific order of operations.

In this section, we concentrate on the database **modification** or **update** operations. There are three basic update operations on relations: insert, delete, and modify. **Insert** is used to insert a new tuple or tuples in a relation, **Delete** is used to delete tuples, and **Update** (or **Modify**) is used to change the values of some attributes in existing tuples. Whenever these operations are applied, the integrity constraints specified on the relational database schema should not be violated. In this section we discuss the types of constraints that may be violated by each update operation and the types of actions that may be taken if an update does cause a violation. We use the database shown in Figure 4.6 for examples and discuss only key constraints, entity integrity constraints, and the referential integrity constraints shown in Figure 4.7. For each type of update, we give some example operations and discuss any constraints that each operation may violate.

4.3.1 The Insert Operation

The **Insert** operation provides a list of attribute values for a new tuple *t* that is to be inserted into a relation R. Insert can violate any of the four types of constraints discussed in the previous section. Domain constraints can be violated if an attribute value is given that does not appear in the corresponding domain. Key constraints can be violated if a key value in the new tuple *t* already exists in another tuple in the relation *r(R)*. Entity integrity can be violated if the primary key of the new tuple *t* is null. Referential integrity can be violated if the value of any foreign key in *t* refers to a tuple that does not exist in the referenced relation. Here are some examples to illustrate this discussion.

1. Insert <'Raju', 'V', 'Kanaka', null, '05-04-1960', '621, Dabagardens, Visakhapatnam, AP', M, 28000, null, 4> into EMPLOYEE.

   - This insertion violates the entity integrity constraint (null for the primary key ENO), so it is rejected.

2. Insert <'valli', 'V', 'Anjana', '999887777', '05-04-1960' '6357 Bhanu street, Hyderabad, AP,' F, 28000, '987654321', 4> into EMPLOYEE.

   - This insertion violates the key constraint because another tuple with the same ENO value already exists in the EMPLOYEE relation, and so it is rejected.

---

10. State constraints are sometimes called *static constraints*, and transition constraints are sometimes called *dynamic constraints*.

3. Insert <' Raju', 'V' 'Kanaka', '677678989', '05-04-1960', '6357, Bhanu street, Hyderabad', M, 28000, ' 987654321', 7 >.

- This insertion violates the referential integrity constraint specified on DNO because no DEPARTMENT tuple exists with DNUMBER = 7.

4. Insert <'Raju', 'V', 'Kanaka', '677678989', '04-05-1960', '6357, Bhanu street, Hyderabad, M, 28000, null, 4>.

- This insertion satisfies all constraints, so it is acceptable.

If an insertion violates one or more constraints, the default option is to *reject the insertion*. In this case, it would be useful if the DBMS could explain to the user why the insertion was rejected. Another option is to attempt to *correct the reason for rejecting the insertion*, but this is typically not used for violations caused by Insert; rather, it is used more often in correcting violations for Delete and Update. In operation 1 above, the DBMS could ask the user to provide a value for ENO and could accept the insertion if a valid ENO value were provided. In operation 3, the DBMS could either ask the user to change the value of DNO to some valid value (or set it to null), or it could ask the user to insert a DEPARTMENT tuple with DNUMBER = 7 and could accept the original insertion only after such an operation was accepted. Notice that in the latter case the insertion violation can **cascade** back to the EMPLOYEE relation if the user attempts to insert a tuple for department 7 with a value for MGRENO that does not exist in the EMPLOYEE relation.

4.3.2 The Delete Operation

The **Delete** operation can violate only referential integrity, if the tuple being deleted is referenced by the foreign keys from other tuples in the database. To specify deletion, a condition on the attributes of the relation selects the tuple (or tuples) to be deleted. Here are some examples.

1. Delete the WORKS_ON tuple with ENO = '999887777' and PNO = 10.

- This deletion is acceptable.

2. Delete the EMPLOYEE tuple with ENO = '999887777'.

- This deletion is not acceptable, because tuples in WORKS_ON refer to this tuple. Hence, if the tuple is deleted, referential integrity violations will result.

3. Delete the EMPLOYEE tuple with ENO = '333445555'.

- This deletion will result in even worse referential integrity violations, because the tuple involved is referenced by tuples from the EMPLOYEE, DEPARTMENT, WORKS_ON, and DEPENDENT relations.

Several options are available if a deletion operation causes a violation. The first option is to *reject the deletion*. The second option is to *attempt to cascade (or propagate) the deletion* by deleting tuples that reference the tuple that is being deleted. For example, in operation 2, the DBMS could automatically delete the offending tuples from WORKS_ON with ENO = '999887777'. A third option is to modify the referencing *attribute values* that cause the violation; each such value is either set to null or changed to reference another valid tuple. Notice that if a referencing attribute that causes a violation is *part of the primary key*, it cannot be set to null; otherwise, it would violate entity integrity.

Combinations of these three options are also possible. For example, to avoid having operation 3 cause a violation, the DBMS may automatically delete all tuples from WORKS_ON and DEPENDENT with ENO = '333445555'. Tuples in EMPLOYEE with SUPERENO = '333445555' and the tuple in DEPARTMENT with MGRENO = '333445555' can have their SUPERENO and MGRENO values changed to other valid values or to null.

Although it may make sense to delete automatically the WORKS_ON and DEPENDENT tuples that refer to an EMPLOYEE tuple, it may not make sense to delete other EMPLOYEE tuples or a DEPARTMENT tuple.

In general, when a referential integrity constraint is specified in the DDL, the DBMS will allow the user to *specify which of the options* applies in case of a violation of the constraint. We discuss how to specify these options in the SQL-99 DDL in Chapter 7.

4.3.3 The Update Operation

The **Update** (or **Modify**) operation is used to change the values of one or more attributes in a tuple (or tuples) of some relation R. It is necessary to specify a condition on the attributes of the relation to select the tuple (or tuples) to be modified. Here are some examples.

1. Update the SALARY of the EMPLOYEE tuple with ENO = '999887777' to 28000.

  - Acceptable.

2. Update the DNO of the EMPLOYEE tuple with ENO = '999887777' to 1.

  - Acceptable.

3. Update the DNO of the EMPLOYEE tuple with ENO = '999887777' to 7.

  - Unacceptable, because it violates referential integrity.

4. Update the ENO of the EMPLOYEE tuple with ENO = '999887777' to '987654321'.

  - Unacceptable, because it violates primary key and referential integrity constraints.

Updating an attribute that is neither a primary key nor a foreign key usually causes no problems; the DBMS need only check to confirm that the new value is of the correct data type and domain. Modifying a primary key value is similar to deleting one tuple and inserting another in its place, because we use the primary key to identify tuples. Hence, the issues discussed earlier in both Sections 4.3.1 (Insert) and 4.3.2 (Delete) come into play. If a foreign key attribute is modified, the DBMS must make sure that the new value refers to an existing tuple in the referenced relation (or is null). Similar options exist to deal with referential integrity violations caused by Update as those options discussed for the Delete operation. In fact, when a referential integrity constraint is specified in the DDL, the DBMS will allow the user to choose separate options to deal with a violation caused by Delete and a violation caused by Update (see Chapter 7).

4.4 SUMMARY

In this chapter we presented the modeling concepts, data structures, and constraints provided by the relational model of data. We started by introducing the concepts of domains, attributes, and tuples. We then defined a relation schema as a list of attributes that describe the structure of a relation. A relation, or relation state, is a set of tuples that conforms to the schema.

Several characteristics differentiate relations from ordinary tables or files. The first is that tuples in a relation are not ordered. The second involves the ordering of attributes in a relation schema and the corresponding ordering of values within a tuple. We gave an alternative definition of relation that does not require these two orderings, but we continued to use the first definition, which requires attributes and tuple values to be ordered, for convenience. We then discussed values in tuples and introduced null values to represent missing or unknown information.

We then classified database constraints into inherent model-based constraints, schema-based constraints and application-based constraints. We then discussed the schema constraints pertaining to the relational model, starting with domain constraints, then key constraints, including the concepts of superkey, candidate key, and primary key, and the NOT NULL constraint on attributes. We then defined relational databases and relational database schemas. Additional relational constraints include the entity integrity constraint, which prohibits primary key attributes from being null. The interrelation referential integrity constraint was then described, which is used to maintain consistency of references among tuples from different relations.

The modification operations on the relational model are Insert, Delete, and Update. Each operation may violate certain types of constraints. These operations were discussed in Section 4.3. Whenever an operation is applied, the database state after the operation is executed must be checked to ensure that no constraints have been violated.

Review Questions

4.1. Define the following terms: *domain, attribute, n-tuple, relation schema, relation state, degree of a relation, relational database schema, relational database state.*

4.2. Why are tuples in a relation not ordered?

4.3. Why are duplicate tuples not allowed in a relation?

4.4. What is the difference between a key and a superkey?

4.5. Why do we designate one of the candidate keys of a relation to be the primary key?

4.6. Discuss the characteristics of relations that make them different from ordinary tables and files.

4.7. Discuss the various reasons that lead to the occurrence of null values in relations.

4.8. Discuss the entity integrity and referential integrity constraints. Why is each considered important?

4.9. Define *foreign key*. What is this concept used for?

Exercises

4.10. Suppose that each of the following update operations is applied directly to the database state shown in Figure 4.6. Discuss *all* integrity constraints violated by each operation, if any, and the different ways of enforcing these constraints.

a. Insert <'Rohit', 'F', 'Kumar', '943775543', '21-06-1952', '2365 Infantry Rd, Bangalore, KA', M, 58000, '888665555', 1> into EMPLOYEE.

b. Insert <'ProductA', 4, 'Bangalore', 2> into PROJECT.

c. Insert <'Production', 4, '943775543', '01-10-1988'> into DEPARTMENT.

d. Insert <'677678989', null, '40.0'> into WORKS_ON.

e. Insert <'453453453', 'RAM', M, '12-12-1970', 'SPOUSE'> into DEPENDENT.

f. Delete the WORKS_ON tuples with EENO = '333445555'.

g. Delete the EMPLOYEE tuple with ENO = '987654321'.

h. Delete the PROJECT tuple with PNAME = 'ProductX'.

i. Modify the MGRENO and MGRSTARTDATE of the DEPARTMENT tuple with DNUMBER = 5 to '123456789' and '01-10-1999', respectively.

    j. Modify the SUPERENO attribute of the EMPLOYEE tuple with ENO = '999887777' to '943775543'.

    k. Modify the HOURS attribute of the WORKS_ON tuple with EENO = '999887777' and PNO = 10 to '5.0'.

4.11. Consider the AIRLINE relational database schema shown in Figure 4.8, which describes a database for airline flight information. Each FLIGHT is identified by a flight NUMBER, and consists of one or more FLIGHT_LEGS with LEG_NUMBERs 1, 2, 3, and so on. Each leg has scheduled arrival and departure times and airports and has many LEG_INSTANCES—one for each DATE on which the flight travels. FARES are kept for each flight. For each leg instance, SEAT_RESERVATIONS are kept, as are the AIR-PLANE used on the leg and the actual arrival and departure times and airports. An AIRPLANE is identified by an AIRPLANE_ID and is of a particular AIRPLANE_TYPE. CAN_LAND relates AIRPLANE_TYPEs to the AIRPORTs in which they can land. An AIRPORT is identified by an AIRPORT_CODE. Consider an update for the AIRLINE database to enter a reservation on a particular flight or flight leg on a given date.

    a. Give the operations for this update.

    b. What types of constraints would you expect to check?

    c. Which of these constraints are key, entity integrity, and referential integrity constraints, and which are not?

    d. Specify all the referential integrity constraints that hold on the schema shown in Figure 4.8.

4.12. Consider the relation CLASS(Course#, Univ_Section#, InstructorName, Semester, BuildingCode, Room#, TimePeriod, Weekdays, CreditHours). This represents classes taught in a university, with unique Univ_Section#. Identify what you think should be various candidate keys, and write in your own words the constraints under which each candidate key would be valid.

4.13. Consider the following six relations for an order-processing database application in a company:

    CUSTOMER(Cust#, Cname, City)

    ORDER(Order#, Odate, Cust#, Ord_Amt)

    ORDER_ITEM(Order#, Item#, Qty)

    ITEM(Item#, Unit_price)

    SHIPMENT(Order#, Warehouse#, Ship_date)

    WAREHOUSE(Warehouse#, City)

    Here, Ord_Amt refers to total dollar amount of an order; Odate is the date the order was placed; Ship_date is the date an order is shipped from the warehouse. Assume that an order can be shipped from several warehouses. Specify the foreign keys for this schema, stating any assumptions you make.

4.14. Consider the following relations for a database that keeps track of business trips of salespersons in a sales office:

    SALESPERSON(Sid, Name, Start_Year, Dept_No)

    TRIP(Sid, From_City, To_City, Departure_Date, Return_Date, Trip_ID)

    EXPENSE(Trip_ID, Account#, Amount)

    Specify the foreign keys for this schema, stating any assumptions you make.

4.15. Consider the following relations for a database that keeps track of student enrollment in courses and the books adopted for each course:

    STUDENT(StudNo, Name, Major, Bdate)

    COURSE(Course#, Cname, Dept)

AIRPORT

AIRPORT_CODE	NAME	CITY	STATE

FLIGHT

NUMBER	AIRLINE	WEEKDAYS

FLIGHT_LEG

FLIGHT_NUMBER	LEG_NUMBER	DEPARTURE_AIRPORT_CODE	SCHEDULED_DEPARTURE_TIME

ARRIVAL_AIRPORT_CODE	SCHEDULED_ARRIVAL_TIME

LEG_INSTANCE

FLIGHT_NUMBER	LEG_NUMBER	DATE	NUMBER_OF_AVAILABLE_SEATS	AIRPLANE_ID

DEPARTURE_AIRPORT_CODE	DEPARTURE_TIME	ARRIVAL_AIRPORT_CODE	ARRIVAL_TIME

FARES

FLIGHT_NUMBER	FARE_CODE	AMOUNT	RESTRICTIONS

AIRPLANE_TYPE

TYPE_NAME	MAX_SEATS	COMPANY

CAN_LAND

AIRPLANE_TYPE_NAME	AIRPORT_CODE

AIRPLANE

AIRPLANE_ID	TOTAL_NUMBER_OF_SEATS	AIRPLANE_TYPE

SEAT_RESERVATION

FLIGHT_NUMBER	LEG_NUMBER	DATE	SEAT_NUMBER	CUSTOMER_NAME	CUSTOMER_PHONE

FIGURE 4.8 The AIRLINE relational database schema.

ENROLL(StudNo, Course#, Quarter, Grade)

BOOK_ADOPTION(Course#, Quarter, Book_ISBN)

TEXT(Book_ISBN, Book_Title, Publisher, Author)

Specify the foreign keys for this schema, stating any assumptions you make.

4.16. Consider the following relations for a database that keeps track of auto sales in a car dealership (Option refers to some optional equipment installed on an auto):

CAR(Serial-No, Model, Manufacturer, Price)

OPTIONS(Serial-No, Option-Name, Price)

SALES(Salesperson-id, Serial-No, Date, Sale-price)

SALESPERSON(<u>Salesperson-id</u>, Name, Phone)

First, specify the foreign keys for this schema, stating any assumptions you make.

Next, populate the relations with a few example tuples, and then give an example of an insertion in the SALES and SALESPERSON relations that *violates* the referential integrity constraints and of another insertion that does not.

Selected Bibliography

The relational model was introduced by Codd (1970) in a classic paper. Codd also introduced relational algebra and laid the theoretical foundations for the relational model in a series of papers (Codd 1971, 1972, 1972a, 1974); he was later given the Turing award, the highest honor of the ACM, for his work on the relational model. In a later paper, Codd (1979) discussed extending the relational model to incorporate more meta-data and semantics about the relations; he also proposed a three-valued logic to deal with uncertainty in relations and incorporating NULLs in the relational algebra. The resulting model is known as RM/T. Childs (1968) had earlier used set theory to model databases. Later, Codd (1990) published a book examining over 300 features of the relational data model and database systems.

Since Codd's pioneering work, much research has been conducted on various aspects of the relational model. Todd (1976) describes an experimental DBMS called PRTV that directly implements the relational algebra operations. Schmidt and Swenson (1975) introduces additional semantics into the relational model by classifying different types of relations. Chen's (1976) entity-relationship model, which is discussed in Chapter 3, is a means to communicate the real-world semantics of a relational database at the conceptual level. Wiederhold and Elmasri (1979) introduces various types of connections between relations to enhance its constraints.

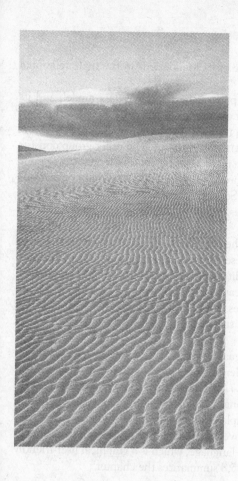

5

The Relational Algebra and Relational Calculus

In this chapter we discuss the two formal languages for the relational model: the relational algebra and the relational calculus. As we discussed in Chapter 2, a data model must include a set of operations to manipulate the database, in addition to the data model's concepts for defining database structure and constraints. The basic set of operations for the relational model is the **relational algebra**. These operations enable a user to specify basic retrieval requests. The result of a retrieval is a new relation, which may have been formed from one or more relations. The algebra operations thus produce new relations, which can be further manipulated using operations of the same algebra. A sequence of relational algebra operations forms a **relational algebra expression**, whose result will also be a relation that represents the result of a database query (or retrieval request).

The relational algebra is very important for several reasons. First, it provides a formal foundation for relational model operations. Second, and perhaps more important, it is used as a basis for implementing and optimizing queries in relational database management systems (RDBMSs). Third, some of its concepts are incorporated into the SQL standard query language for RDBMSs.

Whereas the algebra defines a set of operations for the relational model, the **relational calculus** provides a higher-level declarative notation for specifying relational queries. A relational calculus expression creates a new relation, which is specified in terms of variables that range over rows of the stored database relations (in tuple calculus) or over columns of the stored relations (in domain calculus). In a calculus expression, there is *no order of operations* to specify how to retrieve the query result—a calculus expression specifies only what information the result should contain. This is the main distinguishing feature between relational algebra and relational calculus. The relational calculus is important because it has a firm basis in mathematical logic and because the SQL (standard query language) for RDBMSs has some of its foundations in the tuple relational calculus.[1]

The relational algebra is often considered to be an integral part of the relational data model, and its operations can be divided into two groups. One group includes set operations from mathematical set theory; these are applicable because each relation is defined to be a set of tuples in the formal relational model. Set operations include UNION, INTERSECTION, SET DIFFERENCE, and CARTESIAN PRODUCT. The other group consists of operations developed specifically for relational databases—these include SELECT, PROJECT, and JOIN, among others. We first describe the SELECT and PROJECT operations in Section 5.1, because they are **unary operations** that operate on single relations. Then we discuss set operations in Section 5.2. In Section 5.3, we discuss JOIN and other complex **binary operations**, which operate on two tables. The COMPANY relational database shown in Figure 4.6 is used for our examples.

Some common database requests cannot be performed with the original relational algebra operations, so additional operations were created to express these requests. These include **aggregate functions**, which are operations that can *summarize* data from the tables, as well as additional types of JOIN and UNION operations. These operations were added to the original relational algebra because of their importance to many database applications, and are described in Section 5.4. We give examples of specifying queries that use relational operations in Section 5.5. Some of these queries are used in subsequent chapters to illustrate various languages.

In Sections 5.6 and 5.7 we describe the other main formal language for relational databases, the **relational calculus**. There are two variations of relational calculus. The tuple relational calculus is described in Section 5.6, and the domain relational calculus is described in Section 5.7. Some of the SQL constructs discussed in Chapter 8 are based on the tuple relational calculus. The relational calculus is a formal language, based on the branch of mathematical logic called predicate calculus.[2] In tuple relational calculus, variables range over tuples, whereas in domain relational calculus, variables range over the domains (values) of attributes. In Appendix D we give an overview of the QBE (*Query-By-Example*) language, which is a graphical user-friendly relational language based on domain relational calculus. Section 5.8 summarizes the chapter.

5.1 UNARY RELATIONAL OPERATIONS: SELECT AND PROJECT [Earlier Section Number 6.1]

5.1.1 The SELECT Operation

The SELECT operation is used to select a *subset* of the tuples from a relation that satisfy a **selection condition**. One can consider the SELECT operation to be a *filter* that keeps only those tuples that satisfy a qualifying condition. The SELECT operation can also be visualized as a *horizontal partition* of the relation into two sets of tuples—those tuples that satisfy the condition and are selected, and those tuples that do not satisfy the condition and are discarded. For example, to select the EMPLOYEE tuples whose department is 4, or those whose salary is greater than Rs 30,000, we can individually specify each of these two conditions with a SELECT operation as follows:

---

1. SQL is based on tuple relational calculus, but also incorporates some of the operations from the relational algebra and its extensions, as we shall see in Chapter 7.

2. In this chapter no familiarity with first-order predicate calculus—which deals with quantified variables and values—is assumed.

$$\sigma \rightarrow \sigma_{DNO = 4} \, (\text{EMPLOYEE})$$

$$\sigma \rightarrow \sigma_{SALARY>30000}(\text{EMPLOYEE})$$

In general, the SELECT operation is denoted by

$$\sigma_{<\text{selection condition}>}(R)$$

where the symbol σ (sigma) is used to denote the SELECT operator, and the selection condition is a Boolean expression specified on the attributes of relation R. Notice that R is generally a *relational algebra expression* whose result is a relation—the simplest such expression is just the name of a database relation. The relation resulting from the SELECT operation has the *same attributes* as R.

The Boolean expression specified in <selection condition> is made up of a number of **clauses** of the form

      <attribute name> <comparison op> <constant value>,

or

      <attribute name> <comparison op> <attribute name>

where <attribute name> is the name of an attribute of R, <comparison op> is normally one of the operators $\{=, <, \leq, >, \geq, \neq\}$, and <constant value> is a constant value from the attribute domain. Clauses can be arbitrarily connected by the Boolean operators AND, OR, and NOT to form a general selection condition. For example, to select the tuples for all employees who either work in department 4 and make over Rs 25,000 per year, or work in department 5 and make over Rs 30,000, we can specify the following SELECT operation:

$$\sigma_{(DNO=4 \text{ AND SALARY} >25000) \text{ OR } (DNO=5 \text{ AND SALARY}>30000)} \, (\text{EMPLOYEE})$$

The result is shown in Figure 5.1a.

Notice that the comparison operators in the set $\{=, <, \leq, >, \geq, \neq\}$ apply to attributes whose domains are *ordered values*, such as numeric or date domains. Domains of strings of characters are considered ordered based on the collating sequence of the characters. If the domain of an attribute is a set of *unordered values*, then only the comparison operators in the set $\{=, \neq\}$ can be used. An example of an unordered domain is the domain Color = {red, blue, green, white, yellow, ...} where no order is specified among the various colors. Some domains allow additional types of comparison operators. For example, a domain of character strings may allow the comparison operator SUBSTRING _ OF.

(a)

FNAME	INITIAL	LNAME	ENO	DOB	ADDRESS	SEX	SALARY	SUPERENO	DNO
Karthik	T	Chandra	333445555	08-12-1955	638, Begampet, Hyderabad, AP	M	40000	888665555	5
Priya	S	Ganesh	987654321	20-06-1941	291, Majestic Street, Bangalore	F	43000	888665555	4
Ramesh	K	Narayan	666884444	15-09-1962	975 Hauzkhas, New Delhi	M	38000	334445555	5

(b)

LNAME	FNAME	SALARY
Kumar	Mahesh	30000
Chandra	Karthik	40000
Narayan	Sweta	25000
Ganesh	Priya	43000
Narayan	Ramesh	38000
Goyal	Kiran	25000
Nath	Jitendra	25000
Kishan	Gaurav	55000

(c)

SEX	SALARY
M	30000
M	40000
F	25000
F	43000
M	38000
M	25000
M	55000

FIGURE 5.1 Results of SELECT and PROJECT operations. (a) $\sigma_{(DNO=4 \text{ AND SALARY}>25000) \text{ OR } (DNO=5 \text{ AND SALARY}>30000)}(\text{EMPLOYEE})$. (b) $\pi_{LNAME, FNAME, SALARY}(\text{EMPLOYEE})$. (c) $\pi_{SEX, SALARY}(\text{EMPLOYEE})$.

In general, the result of a SELECT operation can be determined as follows. The <selection condition> is applied independently to each tuple t in R. This is done by substituting each occurrence of an attribute Ai in the selection condition with its value in the tuple $t[A_i]$. If the condition evaluates to TRUE, then tuple t is **selected**. All the selected tuples appear in the result of the SELECT operation. The Boolean conditions AND, OR, and NOT have their normal interpretation, as follows:

- (cond1 AND cond2) is TRUE if both (cond1) and (cond2) are TRUE; otherwise, it is FALSE.
- (cond1 OR cond2) is TRUE if either (cond1) or (cond2) or both are TRUE; otherwise, it is FALSE.
- (NOT cond) is TRUE if cond is FALSE; otherwise, it is FALSE.

The SELECT operator is unary; that is, it is applied to a single relation. Moreover, the selection operation is applied to *each tuple individually*; hence, selection conditions cannot involve more than one tuple. The **degree** of the relation resulting from a SELECT operation—its number of attributes—is the same as the degree of R. The number of tuples in the resulting relation is always *less than or equal to* the number of tuples in R. That is, $|\sigma_c(R)| \leq |R|$ for any condition C. The fraction of tuples selected by a selection condition is referred to as the **selectivity** of the condition.

Notice that the SELECT operation is **commutative**; that is,

$$\sigma_{<cond1>}(\sigma_{<cond2>}(R)) = \sigma_{<cond2>}(\sigma_{<cond1>}(R))$$

Hence, a sequence of SELECTs can be applied in any order. In addition, we can always combine a cascade of SELECT operations into a single SELECT operation with a conjunctive (AND) condition; that is:

$$\sigma_{<cond1>}(\sigma_{<cond2>}(\ldots(\sigma_{<condn>}(R))\ldots)) = \sigma_{<cond1> \text{ AND } <cond2> \text{ AND} \ldots \text{ AND } <condn>}(R)$$

5.1.2 The PROJECT Operation

If we think of a relation as a table, the SELECT operation selects some of the *rows* from the table while discarding other rows. The PROJECT operation, on the other hand, selects certain *columns* from the table and discards the other columns. If we are interested in only certain attributes of a relation, we use the PROJECT operation to *project* the relation over these attributes only. The result of the PROJECT operation can hence be visualized as a *vertical partition* of the relation into two relations: one has the needed columns (attributes) and contains the result of the operation, and the other contains the discarded columns. For example, to list each employee's first and last name and salary, we can use the PROJECT operation as follows:

$\pi_{\text{LNAME, FNAME, SALARY}}(\text{EMPLOYEE})$

The resulting relation is shown in Figure 5.1(b). The general form of the PROJECT operation is

$\pi_{<\text{attribute list}>}(R)$

where π (pi) is the symbol used to represent the PROJECT operation, and <attribute list> is the desired list of attributes from the attributes of relation R. Again, notice that R is, in general, *a relational algebra expression* whose result is a relation, which in the simplest case is just the name of a database relation. The result of the PROJECT operation has only the attributes specified in <attribute list> *in the same order as they appear in the list*. Hence, its **degree** is equal to the number of attributes in <attribute list>.

If the attribute list includes only nonkey attributes of R, duplicate tuples are likely to occur. The PROJECT operation *removes* any *duplicate tuples*, so the result of the PROJECT operation is a set of tuples, and hence a valid relation.[3] This is known as **duplicate elimination**. For example, consider the following PROJECT operation:

$\pi_{\text{SEX, SALARY}}(\text{EMPLOYEE})$

---

3. If duplicates are not eliminated, the result would be a **multiset** or **bag** of tuples rather than a set. Although this is not allowed in the formal relation model, it is permitted in practice. We shall see in Chapter 7 that SQL allows the user to specify whether duplicates should be eliminated or not.

The result is shown in Figure 5.1c. Notice that the tuple <F, 25000> appears only once in Figure 5.1c, even though this combination of values appears twice in the EMPLOYEE relation.

The number of tuples in a relation resulting from a PROJECT operation is always less than or equal to the number of tuples in R. If the projection list is a superkey of R—that is, it includes some key of R—the resulting relation has the same number of tuples as R. Moreover,

$$\pi_{<list1>} (\pi_{<list2>}(R)) = \pi_{<list1>}(R)$$

as long as <list2> contains the attributes in <list1>; otherwise, the left-hand side is an incorrect expression. It is also noteworthy that commutativity *does not* hold on PROJECT.

5.1.3   Sequences of Operations and the RENAME Operation

The relations shown in Figure 5.1 do not have any names. In general, we may want to apply several relational algebra operations one after the other. Either we can write the operations as a single **relational algebra expression** by nesting the operations, or we can apply one operation at a time and create intermediate result relations. In the latter case, we must give names to the relations that hold the intermediate results. For example, to retrieve the first name, last name, and salary of all employees who work in department number 5, we must apply a SELECT and a PROJECT operation. We can write a single relational algebra expression as follows:

$$\pi_{FNAME, LNAME, SALARY}(\sigma_{DNO=5}(EMPLOYEE))$$

Figure 5.2a shows the result of this relational algebra expression. Alternatively, we can explicitly show the sequence of operations, giving a name to each intermediate relation:

$$DEP5\_EMPS \leftarrow \sigma_{DNO=5}(EMPLOYEE)$$

$$RESULT \leftarrow \pi_{FNAME, LNAME, SALARY}(DEP5\_EMPS)$$

(a)

FNAME	LNAME	SALARY
Mahesh	Kumar	30000
Karthik	Chandra	40000
Ramesh	Narayan	38000
Kiran	Goyal	25000

(b)

TEMP	FNAME	INITIAL	LNAME	ENO	DOB	ADDRESS	SEX	SALARY	SUPERENO	DNO
	Mahesh	B	Kumar	123456789	09-01-1965	731, Ameerpet, Hyderabad, AP	M	30000	333445555	5
	Karthik	T	Chandra	333445555	08-12-1955	638, Begampet, Hyderabad, AP	M	40000	888665555	5
	Ramesh	K	Narayan	666884444	15-09-1962	975 Hauzkhas, New Delhi	M	38000	333445555	5
	Kiran	A	Goyal	453453453	31-07-1972	5631 Abids, Hyderabad, AP	F	25000	333445555	5

R	FIRSTNAME	LASTNAME	SALARY
	Mahesh	Kumar	30000
	Karthik	Chandra	40000
	Ramesh	Narayan	38000
	Kiran	Goyal	25000

FIGURE 5.2 Results of a sequence of operations. (a) $\pi_{FNAME, LNAME, SALARY}(\sigma_{DNO=5}(EMPLOYEE))$. (b) Using intermediate relations and renaming of attributes.

It is often simpler to break down a complex sequence of operations by specifying intermediate result relations than to write a single relational algebra expression. We can also use this technique to **rename** the attributes in the intermediate and result relations. This can be useful in connection with more complex operations such as UNION and JOIN, as we shall see. To rename the attributes in a relation, we simply list the new attribute names in parentheses, as in the following example:

TEMP ← $\sigma_{DNO=5}$(EMPLOYEE)

R(FIRSTNAME, LASTNAME, SALARY) ←$\pi_{FNAME, LNAME, SALARY}$(TEMP)

These two operations are illustrated in Figure 5.2b.

If no renaming is applied, the names of the attributes in the resulting relation of a SELECT operation are the same as those in the original relation and in the same order. For a PROJECT operation with no renaming, the resulting relation has the same attribute names as those in the projection list and in the same order in which they appear in the list.

We can also define a formal **RENAME** operation—which can rename either the relation name or the attribute names, or both—in a manner similar to the way we defined SELECT and PROJECT. The general RENAME operation when applied to a relation R of degree n is denoted by any of the following three forms

$$\rho_{S(B_1, B_2, ..., B_n)}(R) \text{ or } \rho_S(R) \text{ or } \rho_{(B_1, B_2, ..., B_n)}(R)$$

where the symbol ρ (rho) is used to denote the RENAME operator, S is the new relation name, and $B_1, B_2, ..., B_n$ are the new attribute names. The first expression renames both the relation and its attributes, the second renames the relation only, and the third renames the attributes only. If the attributes of R are $(A_1, A_2, ..., A_n)$ in that order, then each A_i is renamed as B_i.

5.2 RELATIONAL ALGEBRA OPERATIONS FROM SET THEORY [Earlier Section Number 6.2]

5.2.1 The UNION, INTERSECTION, and MINUS Operations

The next group of relational algebra operations are the standard mathematical operations on sets. For example, to retrieve the employee numbers of all employees who either work in department 5 or directly supervise an employee who works in department 5, we can use the UNION operation as follows:

DEP5_EMPS ← $\sigma_{DNO=5}$(EMPLOYEE)

RESULT1 ← π_{ENO}(DEP5_EMPS)

RESULT2(ENO) ← $\pi_{SUPERENO(DEP5\_EMPS)}$

RESULT ← RESULT1 ∪ RESULT2

The relation RESULT1 has the employee's numbers of all employees who work in department 5, whereas RESULT2 has the numbers of all employees who directly supervise an employee who works in department 5. The UNION operation produces the tuples that are in either RESULT1 or RESULT2 or both (see Figure 5.3). Thus, the ENO value 333445555 appears only once in the result.

Several set theoretic operations are used to merge the elements of two sets in various ways, including **UNION, INTERSECTION,** and **SET DIFFERENCE** (also called MINUS). These are binary operations; that is, each is applied to two sets (of tuples). When these operations are adapted to relational databases, the two relations on which any of these three operations are applied must have the same **type of tuples**; this condition has been called *union compatibility*.

Two relations $R(A_1, A_2, \ldots, A_n)$ and $S(B_1, B_2, \ldots, B_n)$ are said to be **union compatible** if they have the same degree n and if $\mathrm{dom}(A_i) = \mathrm{dom}(B_i)$ for $1 \leq i \leq n$. This means that the two relations have the same number of attributes, and each corresponding pair of attributes has the same domain.

We can define the three operations UNION, INTERSECTION, and SET DIFFERENCE on two union-compatible relations R and S as follows:

- **union:** The result of this operation, denoted by $R \cup S$, is a relation that includes all tuples that are either in R or in S or in both R and S. Duplicate tuples are eliminated.

- **intersection:** The result of this operation, denoted by $R \cap S$, is a relation that includes all tuples that are in both R and S.

- **set difference** (or **MINUS**): The result of this operation, denoted by $R - S$, is a relation that includes all tuples that are in R but not in S.

We will adopt the convention that the resulting relation has the same attribute names as the *first* relation R. It is always possible to rename the attributes in the result using the rename operator.

Figure 5.4 illustrates the three operations. The relations STUDENT and INSTRUCTOR in Figure 5.4a are union compatible, and their tuples represent the names of students and instructors, respectively. The result of the UNION operation in Figure 5.4b shows the names of all students and instructors. Note that duplicate tuples appear only once in the result. The result of the INTERSECTION operation (Figure 5.4c) includes only those who are both students and instructors.

Notice that both UNION and INTERSECTION are *commutative operations*; that is,

$R \cup S = S \cup R$, and $R \cap S = S \cap R$

RESULT1	ENO
	123456789
	333445555
	666884444
	453453453

RESULT2	ENO
	333445555
	888665555

RESULT	ENO
	123456789
	333445555
	666884444
	453453453
	888665555

FIGURE 5.3 Result of the UNION operation RESULT ← RESULT1 ∪ RESULT2.

Both UNION and INTERSECTION can be treated as *n*-ary operations applicable to any number of relations because both are associative operations; that is,

$R \cup (S \cup T) = (R \cup S) \cup T$, and $(R \cap S) \cap T = R \cap (S \cap T)$

The MINUS operation is not *commutative*; that is, in general,

$R - S \neq S - R$

Figure 5.4d shows the names of students who are not instructors, and Figure 5.4e shows the names of instructors who are not students.

(a)

STUDENT	FN	LN
	Suresh	Rao
	Ramesh	Shah
	Jiven	Mishra
	Ravi	Reddy
	Amit	Bose
	Mohan	Varma
	Ashwin	Kumar

INSTRUCTOR	FNAME	LNAME
	Kishore	Das
	Rakesh	Agarwal
	Suresh	Rao
	Sushil	Sharma
	Ramesh	Shah

(b)

FN	LN
Suresh	Rao
Ramesh	Shah
Jiven	Mishra
Ravi	Reddy
Amit	Bose
Mohan	Varma
Ashwin	Kumar
Kishore	Das
Rakesh	Agarwal
Sushil	Sharma

(c)

FN	LN
Suresh	Rao
Ramesh	Shah

(d)

FN	LN
Jiven	Mishra
Ravi	Reddy
Amit	Bose
Mohan	Varma
Ashwin	Kumar

(e)

FNAME	LNAME
Kishore	Das
Rakesh	Agarwal
Sushil	Sharma

FIGURE 5.4 The set operations UNION, INTERSECTION, and MINUS. (a) Two union-compatible relations. (b) STUDENT ∪ INSTRUCTOR. (c) STUDENT ∩ INSTRUCTOR. (d) STUDENT − INSTRUCTOR. (e) INSTRUCTOR − STUDENT.

5.2.2 The CARTESIAN PRODUCT (or CROSS PRODUCT) Operation

Next we discuss the **CARTESIAN PRODUCT** operation—also known as **CROSS PRODUCT** or **CROSS JOIN**—which is denoted by x. This is also a binary set operation, but the relations on which it is applied do *not* have to be union compatible. This operation is used to combine tuples from two relations in a combinatorial fashion. In general, the result of $R(A_1, A_2, \ldots, A_n) \times S(B_1, B_2, \ldots, B_m)$ is a relation Q with degree $n + m$ attributes $Q(A_1, A_2, \ldots, A_n, B_1, B_2, \ldots, B_m)$, in that order. The resulting relation Q has one tuple for each combination of tuples—one from R and one from S. i.e. the first n-components and the last m-components of every tuple in Q belong to R and S respectively. Hence, if R has n_R tuples (denoted as $|R| = n_R$), and S has n_S tuples, then $R \times S$ will have $n_R * n_S$ tuples.

The operation applied by itself is generally meaningless. It is useful when followed by a selection that matches values of attributes coming from the component relations. For example, suppose that we want to retrieve a list of names of each female employee's dependents. We can do this as follows:

FEMALE_EMPS ← $\sigma_{SEX='F'}$(EMPLOYEE)

EMPNAMES ← $\pi_{FNAME, LNAME, ENO}$(FEMALE_EMPS)

EMP_DEPENDENTS ← EMPNAMES × DEPENDENT

ACTUAL_DEPENDENTS ← $\sigma_{ENO=EENO}$(EMP_DEPENDENTS)

RESULT ← $\pi_{FNAME, LNAME, DEPENDENT\_NAME}$(ACTUAL_DEPENDENTS)

The resulting relations from this sequence of operations are shown in Figure 5.5. The EMP_DEPENDENTS relation is the result of applying the CARTESIAN PRODUCT operation to EMPNAMES from Figure 5.5 with DEPENDENT from Figure 4.6. In EMP_DEPENDENTS, every tuple from EMPNAMES is combined with every tuple from DEPENDENT, giving a result that is not very meaningful. We want to combine a female employee tuple only with her particular dependents—namely, the DEPENDENT tuples whose EENO values match the ENO value of the EMPLOYEE tuple. The ACTUAL_DEPENDENTS relation accomplishes this. The EMP_DEPENDENTS relation is a good example of the case where relational algebra can be correctly applied to yield results that make no sense at all. It is therefore the responsibility of the user to make sure to apply only meaningful operations to relations.

The CARTESIAN PRODUCT creates tuples with the combined attributes of two relations. We can then SELECT only related tuples from the two relations by specifying an appropriate selection condition, as we did in the preceding example. Because this sequence of CARTESIAN PRODUCT followed by SELECT is used quite commonly to identify and select related tuples from two relations, a special operation, called JOIN, was created to specify this sequence as a single operation. We discuss the JOIN operation next.

5.3   Binary Relational Operations: Join and Division

[Earlier Section Number 6.3]

5.3.1   The Join Operation

The JOIN operation, denoted by ×, is used to combine *related tuples* from two relations into single tuples. This operation is very important for any relational database with more than a single relation, because it allows us to process relationships among relations. To illustrate JOIN, suppose that we want to retrieve the name of the manager of each department. To get the manager's name, we need to combine each department tuple with the employee tuple whose ENO value matches the MGRENO value in the department tuple. We do this by using the JOIN operation, and then projecting the result over the necessary attributes, as follows:

DEPT_MGR ← DEPARTMENT ⋈ $_{MGRENO=ENO}$ EMPLOYEE

RESULT ← $\pi_{DNAME, LNAME, FNAME}$(DEPT_MGR)

The first operation is illustrated in Figure 5.6. Note that MGRENO is a foreign key and that the referential integrity constraint plays a role in having matching tuples in the referenced relation EMPLOYEE.

The JOIN operation can be stated in terms of a CARTESIAN PRODUCT followed by a SELECT operation. However, JOIN is very important because it is used very frequently when specifying database queries. Consider

FEMALE_EMPS	FNAME	INITIAL	LNAME	ENO	DOB	ADDRESS	SEX	SALARY	SUPERENO	DNO
	Swetha	J	Narayan	999887777	19-07-1968	3321, Hauzkhas, New Delhi	F	25000	987654321	4
	Priya	S	Ganesh	987654321	20-06-1941	291, Majestic Street, Bangalore	F	43000	888665555	4
	Kiran	A	Goyal	453453453	31-07-1972	5631, Abids, Hyderabad, AP	F	25000	333445555	5

EMPNAMES	FNAME	LNAME	ENO
	Swetha	Narayan	999887777
	Priya	Ganesh	987654321
	Kiran	Goyal	453453453

EMP_DEPENDENTS	FNAME	LNAME	ENO	EENO	DEPENDENT_NAME	SEX	BDATE	• • •
	Swetha	Narayan	999887777	333445555	Archana	F	05-04-1986	• • •
	Swetha	Narayan	999887777	333445555	Tejpal	M	25-10-1983	• • •
	Swetha	Narayan	999887777	333445555	Jyothi	F	08-05-1958	• • •
	Swetha	Narayan	999887777	987654321	Anand	M	28-02-1942	• • •
	Swetha	Narayan	999887777	123456789	Manikanth	M	04-01-1988	• • •
	Swetha	Narayan	999887777	123456789	Arpitha	F	30-12-1988	• • •
	Swetha	Narayan	999887777	123456789	Pratyuga	F	05-05-1967	• • •
	Priya	Ganesh	987654321	333445555	Archana	F	05-04-1986	• • •
	Priya	Ganesh	987654321	333445555	Tejpal	M	25-10-1983	• • •
	Priya	Ganesh	987654321	333445555	Jyothi	F	03-05-1958	• • •
	Priya	Ganesh	987654321	987654321	Anand	M	28-02-1942	• • •
	Priya	Ganesh	987654321	123456789	Manikanth	M	04-01-1988	• • •
	Priya	Ganesh	987654321	123456789	Arpitha	F	30-12-1988	• • •
	Priya	Ganesh	987654321	123456789	Pratyuga	F	05-05-1967	• • •
	Kiran	Goyal	453453453	333445555	Archana	F	05-04-1986	• • •
	Kiran	Goyal	453453453	333445555	Tejpal	M	25-10-1983	• • •
	Kiran	Goyal	453453453	333445555	Jyothi	F	03-05-1958	• • •
	Kiran	Goyal	453453453	987654321	Anand	M	28-02-1942	• • •
	Kiran	Goyal	453453453	123456789	Manikanth	M	04-01-1988	• • •
	Kiran	Goyal	453453453	123456789	Arpitha	F	30-12-1988	• • •
	Kiran	Goyal	453453453	123456789	Pratyuga	F	05-05-1987	• • •

ACTUAL_DEPENDENTS	FNAME	LNAME	ENO	EENO	DEPENDENT_NAME	SEX	BDATE	• • •
	Priya	Ganesh	987654321	987654321	Anand	M	28-02-1942	• • •

RESULT	FNAME	LNAME	DEPENDENT_NAME
	Priya	Ganesh	Anand

FIGURE 5.5 The CARTESIAN PRODUCT (CROSS PRODUCT) operation.

the example we gave earlier to illustrate CARTESIAN PRODUCT, which included the following sequence of operations:

EMP_DEPENDENTS ← EMPNAMES × DEPENDENT

ACTUAL_DEPENDENTS ← $\sigma_{ENO=EENO}$(EMP_DEPENDENTS)

These two operations can be replaced with a single JOIN operation as follows:

ACTUAL_DEPENDENTS ← EMPNAMES ⋈ $_{ENO = EENO}$ (EMP_DEPENDENT)

The general form of a JOIN operation on two relations[4] $R(A_1, A_2, \ldots, A_n)$ and $S(B_1, B_2, \ldots, B_m)$ is

$$R \bowtie_{<\text{join condition}>} S$$

The result of the JOIN is a relation Q with $n + m$ attributes $Q(A_1, A_2, \ldots, A_n, B_1, B_2, \ldots, B_m)$ in that order; Q has one tuple for each combination of tuples—one from R and one from S—*whenever the combination satisfies the join condition*. This is the main difference between CARTESIAN PRODUCT and JOIN. In JOIN, only combinations of tuples *satisfying the join condition* appear in the result, whereas in the CARTESIAN PRODUCT all combinations of tuples are included in the result. The join condition is specified on attributes from the two relations R and S and is evaluated for each combination of tuples. Each tuple combination for which the join condition evaluates to TRUE is included in the resulting relation Q *as a single combined tuple*.

A general join condition is of the form

<condition> AND <condition> AND ... AND <condition>

where each condition is of the form $A_i \, \theta \, B_j$, A_i is an attribute of R, B_j is an attribute of S, A_i and B_j have the same domain, and θ (theta) is one of the comparison operators $\{=, <, \leq >, \geq, \neq\}$. A JOIN operation with such a general join condition is called a **THETA JOIN**. Tuples whose join attributes are null do *not* appear in the result. In that sense, the JOIN operation does *not* necessarily preserve all of the information in the participating relations.

DEPT_MGR	DNAME	DNUMBER	MGRENO	• • •	FNAME	INITIAL	LNAME	ENO	• • •
	Research	5	333445555	• • •	Karthik	T	Chandra	333445555	• • •
	Administration	4	987654321	• • •	Priya	S	Ganesh	987654321	• • •
	Headquarters	1	888665555	• • •	Gaurav	E	Kishan	888665555	• • •

FIGURE 5.6 Result of the JOIN operation DEPT_MGR ← DEPARTMENT $\times_{\text{MGRENO=ENO}}$ EMPLOYEE.

5.3.2 The EQUIJOIN and NATURAL JOIN Variations of JOIN

The most common use of JOIN involves join conditions with equality comparisons only. Such a JOIN, where the only comparison operator used is =, is called an EQUIJOIN. Both examples we have considered were EQUIJOINs. Notice that in the result of an EQUIJOIN we always have one or more pairs of attributes that have identical values in every tuple. For example, in Figure 5.6, the values of the attributes MGRENO and ENO are identical in every tuple of DEPT_MGR because of the equality join condition specified on these two attributes. Because one of each pair of attributes with identical values is superfluous, a new operation called NATURAL JOIN—denoted by *—was created to get rid of the second (superfluous) attribute in an EQUIJOIN condition.[5] The standard definition of NATURAL JOIN requires that the two join attributes (or each pair of join attributes) have the same name in both relations. If this is not the case, a renaming operation is applied first.

In the following example, we first rename the DNUMBER attribute of DEPARTMENT to DNUM—so that it has the same name as the DNUM attribute in PROJECT—and then apply NATURAL JOIN:

PROJ_DEPT ← PROJECT $*\rho_{\text{(DNAME,DNUM,MGRENO,MGRSTARTDATE)}}$(DEPARTMENT)

The same query can be done in two steps by creating an intermediate table DEPT as follows:

DEPT ← $\sigma_{\text{(DNAME,DNUM,MGRENO,MGRSTARTDATE)}}$(DEPARTMENT)

---

4. Again, notice that R and S can be any relations that result from general *relational algebra expressions*.

5. NATURAL JOIN is basically an EQUIJOIN followed by removal of the superfluous attributes.

PROJ_DEPT ← PROJECT * DEPT

The attribute DNUM is called the **join attribute**. The resulting relation is illustrated in Figure 5.7a. In the PROJ_DEPT relation, each tuple combines a PROJECT tuple with the DEPARTMENT tuple for the department that controls the project, but *only one join attribute* is kept.

If the attributes on which the natural join is specified already *have the same names in both relations*, renaming is unnecessary. For example, to apply a natural join on the DNUMBER attributes of DEPARTMENT and DEPT_LOCATIONS, it is sufficient to write

DEPT_LOCS ← DEPARTMENT * DEPT_LOCATIONS

The resulting relation is shown in Figure 5.7b, which combines each department with its locations and has one tuple for each location. In general, NATURAL JOIN is performed by equating *all* attribute pairs that have the same name in the two relations. There can be a list of join attributes from each relation, and each corresponding pair must have the same name.

(a)

PROJ_DEPT	PNAME	PNUMBER	PLOCATION	DNUM	DNAME	MGRENO	MGRSTARTDATE
	ProductX	1	Bangalore	5	Research	333445555	22-05-1988
	ProductY	2	New Delhi	5	Research	333445555	22-05-1988
	ProductZ	3	Hyderabad	5	Research	333445555	22-05-1988
	Computerization	10	Chennai	4	Administration	987654321	01-01-1995
	Reorganization	20	Hyderabad	1	Headquarters	888665555	19-06-1981
	Newbenefits	30	Chennai	4	Administration	987654321	01-01-1995

(b)

DEPT_LOCS	DNAME	DNUMBER	MGRENO	MGRSTARTDATE	LOCATION
	Headquarters	1	888665555	19-06-1981	Hyderabad
	Administration	4	987654321	01-01-1995	Chennai
	Research	5	333445555	22-05-1988	Bangalore
	Research	5	333445555	22-05-1988	New Delhi
	Research	5	333445555	22-05-1988	Hyderabad

FIGURE 5.7 Results of two NATURAL JOIN operations. (a) PROJ_DEPT ← PROJECT * DEPT. (b) DEPT_LOCS ← DEPARTMENT * DEPT_LOCATIONS.

A more general but nonstandard definition for NATURAL JOIN is

$$Q \leftarrow R *_{(<\text{list1}>),(<\text{list2}>)} S$$

In this case, <list1> specifies a list of i attributes from R, and <list2> specifies a list of i attributes from S. The lists are used to form equality comparison conditions between pairs of corresponding attributes, and the conditions are then ANDed together. Only the list corresponding to attributes of the first relation R—<list1>—is kept in the result Q.

Notice that if no combination of tuples satisfies the join condition, the result of a JOIN is an empty relation with zero tuples. In general, if R has n_R tuples and S has n_S tuples, the result of a JOIN operation $R_{<\text{join condition}>} S$ will have between zero and $n_R * n_S$ tuples. The expected size of the join result divided by the maximum size $n_R * n_S$ leads to a ratio called **join selectivity**, which is a property of each join condition. If there is no join condition, all combinations of tuples qualify and the JOIN degenerates into a CARTESIAN PRODUCT, also called CROSS PRODUCT or CROSS JOIN.

As we can see, the JOIN operation is used to combine data from multiple relations so that related information can be presented in a single table. These operations are also known as **inner joins**, to distinguish them from a different variation of join called *outer joins* (see Section 5.4.3). Note that sometimes a join may be specified between a relation and itself, as we shall illustrate in Section 5.4.2. The NATURAL JOIN or EQUIJOIN operation can also be specified among multiple tables, leading to an *n-way join*. For example, consider the following three-way join:

$$((\text{PROJECT} \times _{\text{DNUM=DNUMBER}} \text{DEPARTMENT}) \times _{\text{MGRENO=ENO}} \text{EMPLOYEE})$$

This links each project to its controlling department, and then relates the department to its manager employee. The net result is a consolidated relation in which each tuple contains this project-department-manager information.

5.3.3   A Complete Set of Relational Algebra Operations

It has been shown that the set of relational algebra operations $\{\sigma, \pi, \cup, -, \times\}$ is a complete set; that is, any of the other original relational algebra operations can be expressed as a *sequence of operations from this set*. For example, the INTERSECTION operation can be expressed by using UNION and MINUS as follows:

$$R \cap S \equiv (R \cup S) - ((R - S) \cup (S - R))$$

Although, strictly speaking, INTERSECTION is not required, it is inconvenient to specify this complex expression every time we wish to specify an intersection. As another example, a JOIN operation can be specified as a CARTESIAN PRODUCT followed by a SELECT operation, as we discussed:

$$R \bowtie_{<\text{condition}>} S \equiv \sigma_{<\text{condition}>} (R \times S)$$

Similarly, a NATURAL JOIN can be specified as a CARTESIAN PRODUCT preceded by RENAME and followed by SELECT and PROJECT operations. Hence, the various JOIN operations are also *not strictly necessary* for the expressive power of the relational algebra. However, they are important to consider as separate operations because they are convenient to use and are very commonly applied in database applications. Other operations have been included in the relational algebra for convenience rather than necessity. We discuss one of these—the DIVISION operation—in the next section.

5.3.4   The DIVISION Operation

The DIVISION operation, denoted by ÷, is useful for a special kind of query that sometimes occurs in database applications. An example is "Retrieve the names of employees who work on *all* the projects that 'Mahesh Kumar' works on." To express this query using the DIVISION operation, proceed as follows. First, retrieve the list of project numbers that 'Mahesh Kumar' works on in the intermediate relation MAHESH_PNOS:

$$\text{MAHESH} \leftarrow \sigma_{\text{FNAME='MAHESH' AND LNAME='KUMAR'}} (\text{EMPLOYEE})$$

$$\text{MAHESH\_PNOS} \leftarrow \pi_{\text{PNO}} (\text{WORKS\_ON} \bowtie _{\text{EENO=ENO}} \text{MAHESH})$$

Next, create a relation that includes a tuple <PNO, EENO> whenever the employee's number is EENO works on the project whose number is PNO in the intermediate relation ENO_PNOS:

$$\text{ENO\_PNOS} \leftarrow \sigma_{\text{EENO,PNO}} (\text{WORKS\_ON})$$

Finally, apply the DIVISION operation to the two relations, which gives the desired employees' social security numbers:

$$\text{ENOS(ENO)} \leftarrow \text{ENO\_PNOS} \_ \text{MAHESH\_PNOS}$$

RESULT ← $\pi_{\text{FNAME,LNAME}}$(ENOS * EMPLOYEE)

The previous operations are shown in Figure 5.8a.

(a)

ENO_PNOS	EENO	PNO
	123456789	1
	123456789	2
	666884444	3
	453453453	1
	453453453	2
	333445555	2
	333445555	3
	333445555	10
	333445555	20
	999887777	30
	999887777	10
	987987987	10
	987987987	30
	987654321	30
	987654321	20
	888665555	20

MAHESH_PNOS	PNO
	1
	2

ENOS	ENO
	123456789
	453453453

(b)

R	A	B
	a1	b1
	a2	b1
	a3	b1
	a4	b1
	a1	b2
	a3	b2
	a2	b3
	a3	b3
	a4	b3
	a1	b4
	a2	b4
	a3	b4

S	A
	a1
	a2
	.a3

T	B
	b1
	b4

FIGURE 5.8 The DIVISION operation. (a) Dividing ENO_PNOS by MAHESH_PNOS. (b) $T \leftarrow R \div S$.

In general, the DIVISION operation is applied to two relations $R(Z) \div S(X)$, where $X \subseteq Z$. Let $Y = Z - X$ (and hence $Z = X \cup Y$); that is, let Y be the set of attributes of R that are not attributes of S. The result of DIVISION is a relation $T(Y)$ that includes a tuple t if tuples t_R appear in R with $t_R[Y] = t$, and with $t_R[X] = t_S$ for every tuple t_S in S. This means that, for a tuple t to appear in the result T of the DIVISION, the values in t must appear in R in combination with every tuple in S. Note that in the formulation of the DIVISION operation, the tuples in the denominator relation restrict the numerator relation by selecting those tuples in the result that match all values present in the denominator. It is not necessary to know what those values are.

Figure 5.8b illustrates a DIVISION operation where $X = \{A\}$, $Y = \{B\}$, and $Z = \{A, B\}$. Notice that the tuples (values) b_1 and b_4 appear in R in combination with all three tuples in S; that is why they appear in the resulting relation T. All other values of B in R do not appear with all the tuples in S and are not selected: b_2 does not appear with a_2, and b_3 does not appear with a_1.

The DIVISION operation can be expressed as a sequence of $\pi, \times$, and $-$ operations as follows:

$$T1 \leftarrow \pi Y(R)$$

$$T2 \leftarrow \pi Y((S \times T_1) - R)$$

$$T \leftarrow T_1 - T_2$$

The DIVISION operation is defined for convenience for dealing with queries that involve "universal quantification" (see Section 5.6.6) or the all condition. Most RDBMS implementations with SQL as the primary query language do not directly implement division. SQL has a roundabout way of dealing with the type of query illustrated above (see Section 7.5). Table 5.1 lists the various basic relational algebra operations we have discussed.

5.4 ADDITIONAL RELATIONAL OPERATIONS

[Earlier Section Number 6.4]

Some common database requests—which are needed in commercial query languages for RDBMSs—cannot be performed with the original relational algebra operations described in Sections 5.1 through 5.3. In this section we define additional operations to express these requests. These operations enhance the expressive power of the original relational algebra.

5.4.1 Aggregate Functions and Grouping

The first type of request that cannot be expressed in the basic relational algebra is to specify mathematical **aggregate functions** on collections of values from the database. Examples of such functions include retrieving the average or total salary of all employees or the total number of employee tuples. These functions are used in simple statistical queries that summarize information from the database tuples. Common functions applied to collections of numeric values include SUM, AVERAGE, MAXIMUM, and MINIMUM. The COUNT function is used for counting tuples or values.

Another common type of request involves grouping the tuples in a relation by the value of some of their attributes and then applying an aggregate function independently to each group. An example would be to group employee tuples by DNO, so that each group includes the tuples for employees working in the same department. We can then list each DNO value along with, say, the average salary of employees within the department, or the number of employees who work in the department.

We can define an AGGREGATE FUNCTION operation, using the symbol $\Im$ (pronounced "script F"),[6] to specify these types of requests as follows:

$$\text{<grouping attributes>} \Im \text{<function list>} (R)$$

TABLE 5.1 OPERATIONS OF RELATIONAL ALGEBRA

Operation	Purpose	Notation
SELECT	Selects all tuples that satisfy the selection condition from a relation R.	$\sigma_{<\text{SELECTION CONDITION}>}(R)$
PROJECT	Produces a new relation with only some of the attributes of R, and removes duplicate tuples.	$\pi_{<\text{ATTRIBUTE LIST}>}(R)$
THETA JOIN	Produces all combinations of tuples from R_1 and R_2 that satisfy the join condition.	$R_1 \bowtie_{<\text{JOIN CONDITION}>} R_2$
EQUIJOIN	Produces all the combinations of tuples from R_1 and R_2 that satisfy a join condition with only equality comparisons.	$R_1 \bowtie_{<\text{JOIN CONDITION}>} R_2$, OR $R_1 (_{<\text{JOIN ATTRIBUTES 1}>}), (_{<\text{JOIN ATTRIBUTES 2}>}) R_2$
NATURAL JOIN	Same as EQUIJOIN except that the join attributes of R_2 are not included in the resulting relation; if the join attributes have the same names, they do not have to be specified at all.	$R_1 *_{<\text{JOIN CONDITION}>} R_2$, OR $R_1 *(_{<\text{JOIN ATTRIBUTES 1}>}), (_{<\text{JOIN ATTRIBUTES 2}>}) R_2$ OR $R_1 * R_2$
UNION	Produces a relation that includes all the tuples in R_1 or R_2 or both R_1 and R_2; R_1 and R_2 must be union compatible.	$R_1 \cup R_2$
INTERSECTION	Produces a relation that includes all the tuples in both R_1 and R_2; R_1 and R_2 must be union compatible.	$R_1 \cap R_2$
DIFFERENCE	Produces a relation that includes all the tuples in R_1 that are not in R_2; R_1 and R_2 must be union compatible.	R1 – R2
CARTESIAN PRODUCT	Produces a relation that has the attributes of R_1 and R_2 and includes as tuples all possible combinations of tuples from R_1 and R_2.	$R_1 \times R_2$
DIVISION	Produces a relation $R(X)$ that includes all tuples $t[X]$ in $R_1(Z)$ that appear in R_1 in combination with every tuple from $R_2(Y)$, where $Z = X \cup Y$.	$R_1(Z) \div R_2(Y)$

where <grouping attributes> is a list of attributes of the relation specified in R, and <function list> is a list of (<function> <attribute>) pairs. In each such pair, <function> is one of the allowed functions—such as SUM, AVERAGE, MAXIMUM, MINIMUM, COUNT—and <attribute> is an attribute of the relation specified

---

6. There is no single agreed-upon notation for specifying aggregate functions. In some cases a "script A" is used.

by R. The resulting relation has the grouping attributes plus one attribute for each element in the function list. For example, to retrieve each department number, the number of employees in the department, and their average salary, while renaming the resulting attributes as indicated below, we write:

$$\rho R_{(DNO, \ NO\_OF\_EMPLOYEES, \ AVERAGE\_SAL)}(DNO \ \Im \ COUNT_{ENO}, \ AVERAGE_{SALARY} \ (EMPLOYEE))$$

The result of this operation is shown in Figure 5.9a.

In the above example, we specified a list of attribute names—between parentheses in the RENAME operation—for the resulting relation R. If no renaming is applied, then the attributes of the resulting relation that correspond to the function list will each be the concatenation of the function name with the attribute name in the form <function>_<attribute>.[7] For example, Figure 5.9b shows the result of the following operation:

$$DNO \ \Im \ COUNT_{ENO}, \ AVERAGE_{SALARY} \ (EMPLOYEE)$$

If no grouping attributes are specified, the functions are applied to *all the tuples* in the relation, so the resulting relation has a *single tuple only*. For example, Figure 5.9c shows the result of the following operation:

$$\Im \ COUNT_{ENO}, \ AVERAGE_{SALARY} \ (EMPLOYEE)$$

(a)

R	DNO	NO_OF_EMPLOYEES	AVERAGE_SAL
	5	4	33250
	4	3	31000
	1	1	55000

(b)

DNO	COUNT_ENO	AVERAGE_SALARY
5	4	33250
4	3	31000
1	1	55000

(c)

COUNT_ENO	AVERAGE_SALARY
8	35125

FIGURE 5.9 The AGGREGATE FUNCTION operation. (a) $\rho R_{(DNO, \ NO\_OF\_EMPLOYEES, \ AVERAGE\_SAL)}$ $(DNO \ \Im \ COUNT_{ENO}$, $AVERAGE_{SALARY} \ (EMPLOYEE))$. (b) $DNO \ \Im \ COUNT_{ENO}$, $AVERAGE_{SALARY} \ (EMPLOYEE)$. (c) $\Im \ COUNT_{ENO}$, $AVERAGE_{SALARY} \ (EMPLOYEE)$.

It is important to note that, in general, duplicates are not eliminated when an aggregate function is applied; this way, the normal interpretation of functions such as SUM and AVERAGE is computed.[8] It is worth emphasizing that the result of applying an aggregate function is a relation, not a scalar number—even if it has a single value. This makes the relational algebra a closed system.

---

7. Note that this is an arbitrary notation we are suggesting. There is no standard notation.

8. In SQL, the option of eliminating duplicates before applying the aggregate function is available by including the keyword DISTINCT (see Chapter 7).

5.4.2 Recursive Closure Operations

Another type of operation that, in general, cannot be specified in the basic original relational algebra is **recursive closure**. This operation is applied to a **recursive relationship** between tuples of the same type, such as the relationship between an employee and a supervisor. This relationship is described by the foreign key SUPERENO of the EMPLOYEE relation in Figures 4.5 and 4.6, and it relates each employee tuple (in the role of supervisee) to another employee tuple (in the role of supervisor). An example of a recursive operation is to retrieve all supervisees of an employee e at all levels—that is, all employees e' directly supervised by e, all employees e'' directly supervised by each employee e'; all employees e''' directly supervised by each employee e''; and so on.

Although it is straightforward in the relational algebra to specify all employees supervised by e *at a specific level*, it is difficult to specify all supervisees at *all* levels. For example, to specify the ENOs of all employees e' directly supervised—*at level one*—by the employee e whose name is 'GAURAV KISHAN' (see Figure 4.6), we can apply the following operation:

KISHAN_ ENO ← $\sigma_{ENO}(\sigma_{FNAME='GAURAV' AND LNAME='KISHAN'}(EMPLOYEE))$

SUPERVISION(ENO1, ENO2) ← $\pi_{ENO, SUPERENO}$ (EMPLOYEE)

RESULT1(ENO) ← π_{ENO1}(SUPERVISION $\bowtie_{ENO2=ENO}$ KISHAN_ENO)

To retrieve all employees supervised by Kishan at level 2—that is, all employees e'' supervised by some employee e' who is directly supervised by Kishan—we can apply another

JOIN to the result of the first query, as follows:

RESULT2(ENO) ← π_{ENO1}(SUPERVISION $\bowtie_{ENO2= ENO}$ RESULT1)

To get both sets of employees supervised at levels 1 and 2 by 'Gaurav Kishan,' we can apply the UNION operation to the two results, as follows:

RESULT ← RESULT2 ∪ RESULT1

The results of these queries are illustrated in Figure 5.10. Although it is possible to retrieve employees at each level and then take their UNION, we cannot, in general, specify a query such as "retrieve the supervisees of 'Gaurav kishan' at all levels" without utilizing a looping mechanism.[9] An operation called the transitive closure of relations has been proposed to compute the recursive relationship as far as the recursion proceeds.

5.4.3 OUTER JOIN Operations

We now discuss some extensions to the JOIN operation that are necessary to specify certain types of queries. The JOIN operations described earlier match tuples that satisfy the join condition. For example, for a NATURAL JOIN operation $R * S$, only tuples from R that have matching tuples in S—and vice versa—appear in the result. Hence, tuples without a *matching* (or *related*) tuple are eliminated from the JOIN result. Tuples with null values in the join attributes are also eliminated. This amounts to loss of information, if the result of JOIN is supposed to be used to generate a report based on all the information in the component relations.

A set of operations, called **outer joins**, can be used when we want to keep all the tuples in R, or all those in S, or all those in both relations in the result of the JOIN, regardless of whether or not they have

---

9. The SQL3 standard includes syntax for recursive closure.

(Kishan's ENO is 888665555)

	(ENO)	(SUPERENO)
SUPERVISION	ENO1	ENO2
	123456789	333445555
	333445555	888665555
	999887777	987654321
	987654321	888665555
	666884444	333445555
	453453453	333445555
	987987987	987654321
	888665555	null

RESULT 1	ENO
	333445555
	987654321

(Supervised by Kishan)

RESULT 2	ENO
	123456789
	999887777
	666884444
	453453453
	987987987

(Supervised by Kishan's subordinates)

RESULT	ENO
	123456789
	999887777
	666884444
	453453453
	987987987
	333445555
	987654321

(RESULT1 ∪ RESULT2)

FIGURE 5.10 A two-level recursive query.

matching tuples in the other relation. This satisfies the need of queries in which tuples from two tables are to be combined by matching corresponding rows, but without losing any tuples for lack of matching values. The join operations we described earlier in Section 5.3, where only matching tuples are kept in the result, are called **inner joins**.

For example, suppose that we want a list of all employee names and also the name of the departments they manage *if they happen to manage a department*; if they do not manage any, we can so indicate with a null value. We can apply an operation LEFT OUTER JOIN, denoted by , to retrieve the result as follows:

TEMP ← (EMPLOYEE ⋈ $_{ENO=MGRENO}$ DEPARTMENT)

RESULT ← π $_{FNAME, INITIAL, LNAME, DNAME}$(TEMP)

The LEFT OUTER JOIN operation keeps every tuple in the *first*, or *left*, relation R in $R ⋈ S$; if no matching tuple is found in S, then the attributes of S in the join result are filled or "padded" with null values. The result of these operations is shown in Figure 5.11.

A similar operation, **RIGHT OUTER JOIN**, denoted by ⋈, keeps every tuple in the *second*, or *right*, relation S in the result of $R ⋈ S$. A third operation, FULL OUTER JOIN, denoted by ⋈ keeps all tuples in both the left and the right relations when no matching tuples are found, padding them with null values as needed. The three outer join operations are part of the SQL2 standard (see Chapter 7).

5.4.4 The OUTER UNION Operation

The OUTER UNION operation was developed to take the union of tuples from two relations if the relations are *not union compatible*. This operation will take the UNION of tuples in two relations $R(X, Y)$ and $S(X, Z)$ that are **partially compatible**, meaning that only some of their attributes, say X, are union compatible. The attributes that are union compatible are represented only once in the result, and those attributes that are not union compatible from either relation are also kept in the result relation $T(X, Y, Z)$.

Two tuples t_1 in R and t_2 in S are said to **match** if $t_1[X] = t_2[X]$, and are considered to represent the same entity or relationship instance. These will be combined (unioned) into a single tuple in T. Tuples in either relation that have no matching tuple in the other relation are padded with null values. For example, an OUTER UNION can be applied to two relations whose schemas are STUDENT(Name, ENO, Department, Advisor) and INSTRUCTOR(Name, ENO, Department, Rank). Tuples from the two relations are matched based on having the same combination of values of the shared attributes—Name, ENO, Department. The result relation, STUDENT_OR_INSTRUCTOR, will have the following attributes:

STUDENT_OR_INSTRUCTOR(Name, ENO, Department, Advisor, Rank)

RESULT	FNAME	INITIAL	LNAME	DNAME
	Mahesh	B	Kumar	null
	Karthik	T	Chandra	Research
	Swetha	J	Narayan	null
	Priya	S	Ganesh	Administration
	Ramesh	K	Narayan	null
	Kiran	A	Goyal	null
	Jitendra	V	Nath	null
	Gaurav	E	Kishan	Headquarters

FIGURE 5.11 The result of a LEFT OUTER JOIN operation.

All the tuples from both relations are included in the result, but tuples with the same (Name, ENO, Department) combination will appear only once in the result. Tuples appearing only in STUDENT will have a null for the Rank attribute, whereas tuples appearing only in INSTRUCTOR will have a null for the Advisor attribute. A tuple that exists in both relations, such as a student who is also an instructor, will have values for all its attributes.[10]

Notice that the same person may still appear twice in the result. For example, we could have a graduate student in the Mathematics department who is an instructor in the Computer Science department. Although the two tuples representing that person in STUDENT and INSTRUCTOR will have the same (Name, ENO) values, they will not agree on the Department value, and so will not be matched. This is because Department has two separate meanings in STUDENT (the department where the person studies) and INSTRUCTOR (the department where the person is employed as an instructor). If we wanted to union persons based on the same (Name, ENO) combination only, we should rename the Department attribute in each table to reflect that they have different meanings, and designate them as not being part of the union-compatible attributes.

Another capability that exists in most commercial languages (but not in the basic relational algebra) is that of specifying operations on values after they are extracted from the database. For example, arithmetic operations such as +, −, and * can be applied to numeric values that appear in the result of a query.

---

10. Notice that OUTER UNION is equivalent to a FULL OUTER JOIN if the join attributes are *all* the common attributes of the two relations.

5.5   EXAMPLES OF QUERIES IN RELATIONAL ALGEBRA

[Earlier Section Number 6.5]

We now give additional examples to illustrate the use of the relational algebra operations. All examples refer to the database of Figure 4.6. In general, the same query can be stated in numerous ways using the various operations. We will state each query in one way and leave it to the reader to come up with equivalent formulations.

QUERY 1

Retrieve the name and address of all employees who work for the 'Research' department.

RESEARCH_DEPT ← $\sigma_{DNAME='RESEARCH'}$ (DEPARTMENT)

RESEARCH_EMPS ← (RESEARCH_DEPT ⋈ $_{DNUMBER=DNOEMPLOYEE}$)

RESULT ← $\pi_{FNAME, LNAME, ADDRESS}$ (RESEARCH_EMPS)

This query could be specified in other ways; for example, the order of the JOIN and SELECT operations could be reversed, or the JOIN could be replaced by a NATURAL JOIN after renaming one of the join attributes.

QUERY 2

For every project located in 'Chennai', list the project number, the controlling department number, and the department manager's last name, address, and date of birth.

CHENNAI_PROJS ← $\sigma_{PLOCATION='CHENNAI'}$ (PROJECT)

CONTR_DEPT ← (CHENNAI_PROJS ⋈ $_{DNUM=DNUMBER}$ DEPARTMENT)

PROJ_DEPT_MGR ← (CONTR_DEPT ⋈ $_{MGRENO=ENO}$ EMPLOYEE)

RESULT ← $\pi_{NUMBER, DNUM, LNAME, ADDRESS, DOB}$ (PROJ_DEPT_MGR)

QUERY 3

Find the names of employees who work on all the projects controlled by department number 5.

DEPT5_PROJS(PNO) ← $\pi_{PNUMBER}$ ($\sigma_{DNUM=5}$ (PROJECT))

EMP_PROJ(SSN, PNO) ← $\pi_{EENO, PNO}$ (WORKS_ON)

RESULT_EMP_ ENOS ← EMP_PROJ _ DEPT5_PROJS

RESULT ← $\pi_{LNAME, FNAME}$ (RESULT_EMP_ ENOS * EMPLOYEE)

QUERY 4

Make a list of project numbers for projects that involve an employee whose last name is 'Kumar', either as a worker or as a manager of the department that controls the project.

KUMARS(EENO) ← π_{ENO} ($\sigma_{LNAME='KUMAR'}$ (EMPLOYEE))

KUMAR_WORKER_PROJ ← π_{PNO} (WORKS_ON * KUMARS)

MGRS ← $\pi_{LNAME, DNUMBER}$ (EMPLOYEE ⋈ $_{ENO=MGRENO}$ DEPARTMENT)

KUMAR_MANAGED_DEPTS(DNUM) ← $\pi_{\text{DNUMBER}}(\sigma_{\text{LNAME = 'KUMAR'}}(\text{MGRS}))$

KUMAR_MGR_PROJS(PNO) ← $\pi_{\text{PNUMBER}}(\text{KUMAR\_MANAGED\_DEPTS} * \text{PROJECT})$

RESULT ← (KUMAR_WORKER_PROJS ∪ KUMAR_MGR_PROJS)

QUERY 5

List the names of all employees with two or more dependents.

Strictly speaking, this query cannot be done in the *basic (original) relational algebra*. We have to use the AGGREGATE FUNCTION operation with the COUNT aggregate function. We assume that dependents of the same employee have distinct DEPENDENT_NAME values.

T1(ENO, NO_OF_DEPTS) ← EENO $\Im$ COUNT DEPENDENT_NAME

(DEPENDENT)

T2 ← $\sigma_{\text{NO\_OF\_DEPS} \geq 2}$ (T1)

RESULT ← $\pi_{\text{LNAME, FNAME}}(T2 * \text{EMPLOYEE})$

QUERY 6

Retrieve the names of employees who have no dependents.

This is an example of the type of query that uses the MINUS (SET DIFFERENCE) operation.

ALL_EMPS ← $\pi_{\text{ENO}}(\text{EMPLOYEE})$

EMPS_WITH_DEPS(ENO) ← π_{EENO} (DEPENDENT)

EMPS_WITHOUT_DEPS ← (ALL_EMPS − EMPS_WITH_DEPS)

RESULT ← $\pi_{\text{LNAME, FNAME}}(\text{EMPS\_WITHOUT\_DEPS} * \text{EMPLOYEE})$

QUERY 7

List the names of managers who have at least one dependent.

MGRS(ENO) ← $\pi_{\text{MGRENO}}(\text{DEPARTMENT})$

EMPS_WITH_DEPS(ENO) ← π_{EENO} (DEPENDENT)

MGRS_WITH_DEPS ← (MGRS ∩ EMPS_WITH_DEPS)

RESULT ← $\pi_{\text{LNAME, FNAME}}(\text{MGRS\_WITH\_DEPS} * \text{EMPLOYEE})$

As we mentioned earlier, the same query can in general be specified in many different ways. For example, the operations can often be applied in various orders. In addition, some operations can be used to replace others; for example, the INTERSECTION operation in Query 7 can be replaced by a NATURAL JOIN. As an exercise, try to do each of the above example queries using different operations.[11] In Chapter 7 and in Sections 5.6 and 5.7, we show how these queries are written in other relational languages.

---

11. When queries are optimized (see Chapter 10), the system will choose a particular sequence of operations that corresponds to an execution strategy that can be executed efficiently.

5.6   THE TUPLE RELATIONAL CALCULUS

In this and the next section, we introduce another formal query language for the relational model called **relational calculus**. In relational calculus, we write one **declarative** expression to specify a retrieval request, and hence there is no description of how to evaluate a query. A calculus expression specifies *what* is to be retrieved rather than *how* to retrieve it. Therefore, the relational calculus is considered to be a **nonprocedural** language. This differs from relational algebra, where we must write a *sequence of operations* to specify a retrieval request; hence, it can be considered as a **procedural** way of stating a query. It is possible to nest algebra operations to form a single expression; however, a certain order among the operations is always explicitly specified in a relational algebra expression. This order also influences the strategy for evaluating the query. A calculus expression may be written in different ways, but the way it is written has no bearing on how a query should be evaluated.

It has been shown that any retrieval that can be specified in the basic relational algebra can also be specified in relational calculus, and vice versa; in other words, the **expressive power** of the two languages is *identical*. This led to the definition of the concept of a relationally complete language. A relational query language L is considered **relationally complete** if we can express in L any query that can be expressed in relational calculus. Relational completeness has become an important basis for comparing the expressive power of high-level query languages. However, as we saw in Section 5.4, certain frequently required queries in database applications cannot be expressed in basic relational algebra or calculus. Most relational query languages are relationally complete but have *more expressive power* than relational algebra or relational calculus because of additional operations such as aggregate functions, grouping, and ordering. In this section and the next, all our examples again refer to the database shown in Figures 4.6 and 4.7. We will use the same queries that were used in Section 5.5.

5.6.1   Tuple Variables and Range Relations

The tuple relational calculus is based on specifying a number of **tuple variables**. Each tuple variable usually *ranges over* a particular database relation, meaning that the variable may take as its value any individual tuple from that relation. A simple tuple relational calculus query is of the form

$$\{t \mid COND(t)\}$$

where t is a tuple variable and $COND(t)$ is a conditional expression involving t. The result of such a query is the set of all tuples t that satisfy $COND(t)$. For example, to find all employees whose salary is above Rs 50,000, we can write the following tuple calculus expression:

$$\{t \mid EMPLOYEE(t) \textbf{ and } t.SALARY > 50000\}$$

The condition EMPLOYEE(t) specifies that the **range relation** of tuple variable t is EMPLOYEE. Each EMPLOYEE tuple t that satisfies the condition $t.SALARY > 50000$ will be retrieved. Notice that $t.SALARY$ references attribute SALARY of tuple variable t; this notation resembles how attribute names are qualified with relation names or aliases in SQL, as we shall see in Chapter 7. In the notation of Chapter 4, $t.SALARY$ is the same as writing $t[SALARY]$.

The above query retrieves all attribute values for each selected EMPLOYEE tuple t. To retrieve only *some* of the attributes—say, the first and last names—we write

$$\{t.FNAME, t.LNAME \mid EMPLOYEE(t) \text{ AND } t.SALARY > 50000\}$$

Informally, we need to specify the following information in a tuple calculus expression:

- For each tuple variable t, the **range relation** R of t. This value is specified by a condition of the form $R(t)$.
- A condition to select particular combinations of tuples. As tuple variables range over their respective range relations, the condition is evaluated for every possible combination of tuples to identify the **selected combinations** for which the condition evaluates to TRUE.
- A set of attributes to be retrieved, the **requested attributes**. The values of these attributes are retrieved for each selected combination of tuples.

Before we discuss the formal syntax of tuple relational calculus, consider another query.

QUERY 0

Retrieve the date of birth and address of the employee (or employees) whose name is 'Mahesh B. Kumar'.

Q0: $\{t.\text{DOB}, t.\text{ADDRESS} \mid \text{EMPLOYEE}(t) \text{ AND } t.\text{FNAME}=\text{'Mahesh' AND } t.\text{MINIT}=\text{'B' AND } t.\text{LNAME}=\text{'Kumar'}\}$

In tuple relational calculus, we first specify the requested attributes $t.\text{BDATE}$ and $t.\text{ADDRESS}$ for each selected tuple t. Then we specify the condition for selecting a tuple following the bar ($\mid$)—namely, that t be a tuple of the EMPLOYEE relation whose FNAME, NITIAL, and LNAME attribute values are 'Mahesh', 'B', and 'Kumar', respectively.

5.6.2 Expressions and Formulas in Tuple Relational Calculus

A general expression of the tuple relational calculus is of the form

$$\{t_1.A_j, t_2.A_k, \ldots, t_n.A_m \mid \text{COND}(t_1, t_2, \ldots, t_n, t_{n+1}, t_{n+2}, \ldots, t_{n+m})\}$$

where $t_1, t_2, \ldots, t_n, t_{n+1}, \ldots, t_{n+m}$ are tuple variables, each Ai is an attribute of the relation on which t_i ranges, and COND is a **condition** or **formula**[12] of the tuple relational calculus. A formula is made up of predicate calculus **atoms**, which can be one of the following:

1. An atom of the form $R(t_i)$, where R is a relation name and t_i is a tuple variable. This atom identifies the range of the tuple variable t_i as the relation whose name is R.

2. An atom of the form $t_i.A \text{ op } t_j.B$, where op is one of the comparison operators in the set $\{=, <, \leq, >, \geq, \neq\}$, t_i and t_j are tuple variables, A is an attribute of the relation on which t_i ranges, and B is an attribute of the relation on which t_j ranges.

3. An atom of the form $t_i.A \text{ op } c$ or $c \text{ op } t_j.B$, where op is one of the comparison operators in the set $\{=, <, \leq, >, \geq, \neq\}$, t_i and t_j are tuple variables, A is an attribute of the relation on which t_i ranges, B is an attribute of the relation on which t_j ranges, and c is a constant value.

Each of the preceding atoms evaluates to either TRUE or FALSE for a specific combination of tuples; this is called the **truth value** of an atom. In general, a tuple variable t ranges over all possible tuples "in the universe." For atoms of the form $R(t)$, if t is assigned to a tuple that is a *member of the specified relation R*, the

---

12. Also called a **well-formed formula**, or **wff**, in mathematical logic.

atom is TRUE; otherwise, it is FALSE. In atoms of types 2 and 3, if the tuple variables are assigned to tuples such that the values of the specified attributes of the tuples satisfy the condition, then the atom is TRUE.

A **formula** (condition) is made up of one or more atoms connected via the logical operators **AND, OR,** and **NOT** and is defined recursively as follows:

1. Every atom is a formula.

2. If F_1 and F_2 are formulas, then so are $(F_1 \text{ AND } F_2)$, $(F_1 \text{ OR } F_2)$, **NOT** (F_1), and **NOT** (F_2). The truth values of these formulas are derived from their component formulas F_1 and F_2 as follows:

    a. $(F_1 \text{ AND } F_2)$ is TRUE if both F_1 and F_2 are TRUE; otherwise, it is FALSE.

    b. $(F_1 \text{ OR } F_2)$ is FALSE if both F_1 and F_2 are FALSE; otherwise, it is TRUE.

    c. NOT(F_1) is TRUE if F_1 is FALSE; it is FALSE if F_1 is TRUE.

    d. NOT(F_2) is TRUE if F_2 is FALSE; it is FALSE if F_2 is TRUE.

5.6.3   The Existential and Universal Quantifiers

In addition, two special symbols called **quantifiers** can appear in formulas; these are the **universal quantifier** ($\forall$) and the **existential quantifier** ($\exists$). Truth values for formulas with quantifiers are described in rules 3 and 4 below; first, however, we need to define the concepts of free and bound tuple variables in a formula. Informally, a tuple variable t is bound if it is quantified, meaning that it appears in an ($\exists t$) or ($\forall t$) clause; otherwise, it is free. Formally, we define a tuple variable in a formula as **free** or **bound** according to the following rules:

* An occurrence of a tuple variable in a formula F that is an *atom* is free in F.

* An occurrence of a tuple variable t is free or bound in a formula made up of logical connectives—$(F_1$ AND $F_2)$, $(F_1$ OR $F_2)$, NOT(F_1), and NOT(F_2)—depending on whether it is free or bound in F_1 or F_2 (if it occurs in either). Notice that in a formula of the form $F = (F_1 \text{ AND } F_2)$ or $F = (F_1 \text{ OR } F_2)$, a tuple variable may be free in F_1 and bound in F_2, or vice versa; in this case, one occurrence of the tuple variable is bound and the other is free in F.

* All *free* occurrences of a tuple variable t in F are bound in a formula F' of the form $F' = (\exists t)(F)$ or $F' = (\forall t)(F)$. The tuple variable is bound to the quantifier specified in F'. For example, consider the following formulas:

    F_1 : D.DNAME='RESEARCH'

    F_2 : ($\exists$T)(D.DNUMBER=T.DNO)

    F_3 : ($\forall$D)(D.MGRENO='333445555')

The tuple variable d is free in both F_1 and F_2, whereas it is bound to the ($\forall$) quantifier in F_3. Variable t is bound to the ($\exists$) quantifier in F_2.

We can now give rules 3 and 4 for the definition of a formula we started earlier:

3. If F is a formula, then so is ($\exists t$)(F), where t is a tuple variable. The formula ($\exists t$)(F) is TRUE if the formula F evaluates to TRUE *for some* (at least one) tuple assigned to free occurrences of t in F; otherwise, ($\exists t$)(F) is FALSE.

4. If F is a formula, then so is ($\forall t$)(F), where t is a tuple variable. The formula ($\forall t$)(F) is TRUE if the formula F evaluates to TRUE for *every tuple* (in the universe) assigned to free occurrences of t in F; otherwise, ($\forall t$)(F) is FALSE.

The (∃) quantifier is called an existential quantifier because a formula (∃ t)(F) is TRUE if "there exists" some tuple that makes F TRUE. For the universal quantifier, (∀ t)(F) is TRUE if every possible tuple that can be assigned to free occurrences of t in F is substituted for t, and F is TRUE *for every such substitution*. It is called the universal or "for all" quantifier because every tuple in "the universe of" tuples must make F TRUE to make the quantified formula TRUE.

5.6.4   Example Queries Using the Existential Quantifier

We will use some of the same queries from Section 5.5 to give a flavor of how the same queries are specified in relational algebra and in relational calculus. Notice that some queries are easier to specify in the relational algebra than in the relational calculus, and vice versa.

QUERY 1

Retrieve the name and address of all employees who work for the 'Research' department.

Q1: {t.FNAME, t.LNAME, t.ADDRESS | EMPLOYEE(t) AND (∃d)

(DEPARTMENT(d) AND d.DNAME='Research' AND d.DNUMBER=t.DNO) }

The *only free tuple variables* in a relational calculus expression should be those that appear to the left of the bar (|). In Q_1, t is the only free variable; it is then *bound successively* to each tuple. If a tuple *satisfies the conditions* specified in Q1, the attributes FNAME, LNAME, and ADDRESS are retrieved for each such tuple. The conditions EMPLOYEE(t) and DEPARTMENT(d) specify the range relations for t and d. The condition d.DNAME = 'Research' is a **selection condition** and corresponds to a SELECT operation in the relational algebra, whereas the condition d.DNUMBER = t.DNO is a **join condition** and serves a similar purpose to the JOIN operation (see Section 5.3).

QUERY 2

For every project located in 'Chennai', list the project number, the controlling department number, and the department manager's last name, date of birth, and address.

Q2: {p.PNUMBER, p.DNUM, m.LNAME, m.DOB, m.ADDRESS | PROJECT(p) AND EMPLOYEE(m) AND p.PLOCATION='Chennai' AND ((∃d)(DEPARTMENT(d) AND p.DNUM=d.DNUMBER AND d.MGRENO=m.ENO))}

In Q_2 there are two free tuple variables, p and m. Tuple variable d is bound to the existential quantifier. The query condition is evaluated for every combination of tuples assigned to p and m; and out of all possible combinations of tuples to which p and m are bound, only the combinations that satisfy the condition are selected.

Several tuple variables in a query can range over the same relation. For example, to specify the query Q8—for each employee, retrieve the employee's first and last name and the first and last name of his or her immediate supervisor—we specify two tuple variables e and s that both range over the EMPLOYEE relation:

Q8: {e.FNAME, e.LNAME, s.FNAME, s.LNAME | EMPLOYEE(e) AND EMPLOYEE(s) AND e.SUPERENO=s.ENO}

QUERY 3

Find the name of each employee who works on *some* project controlled by department number 5. This is a variation of query 3 in which "all" is changed to "some." In this case we need two join conditions and two existential quantifiers.

Q3: {e.LNAME, e.FNAME | EMPLOYEE(e) AND (($\exists$ x)($\exists$ w) (PROJECT(x) AND WORKS_ON(w) AND x.DNUM=5 AND w.EENO=e.ENO AND x.PNUMBER=w.PNO))}

QUERY 4

Make a list of project numbers for projects that involve an employee whose last name is 'Kumar', either as a worker or as manager of the controlling department for the project.

Q4: {p.PNUMBER | PROJECT(p) AND (($\exists$ e)($\exists$ w)(EMPLOYEE(e) AND WORKS_ON(w) AND w.PNO=p. PNUMBER AND e.LNAME='Kumar' AND e.ENO=w.EENO))

or

(($\exists$ m)($\exists$ d)(EMPLOYEE(m) AND DEPARTMENT(d) AND p.DNUM=d.DNUMBER AND d.MGRENO=m.ENO AND m.LNAME='Kumar'))) }

Compare this with the relational algebra version of this query in Section 5.5. The UNION operation in relational algebra can usually be substituted with an OR connective in relational calculus. In the next section we discuss the relationship between the universal and existential quantifiers and show how one can be transformed into the other.

5.6.5 Transforming the Universal and Existential Quantifiers

We now introduce some well-known transformations from mathematical logic that relate the universal and existential quantifiers. It is possible to transform a universal quantifier into an existential quantifier, and vice versa, to get an equivalent expression. One general transformation can be described informally as follows: Transform one type of quantifier into the other with negation (preceded by **NOT**); **AND** and **OR** replace one another; a negated formula becomes unnegated; and an unnegated formula becomes negated. Some special cases of this transformation can be stated as follows, where the $\equiv$ symbol stands for **equivalent to**:

($\forall$ x) (P(x)) $\int$ NOT ($\exists$ x) (NOT (P(x)))

($\exists$ x) (P(x)) $\int$ NOT ($\forall$ x) (NOT (P(x)))

($\forall$ x) (P(x) AND Q(x)) $\int$ NOT ($\exists$ x) (NOT (P(x)) OR NOT (Q(x)))

($\forall$ x) (P(x) OR Q(x)) $\int$ NOT ($\exists$ x) (NOT (P(x)) AND NOT (Q(x)))

($\exists$ x) (P(x)) OR Q(x)) $\int$ NOT ($\forall$ x) (NOT (P(x)) AND NOT (Q(x)))

($\exists$ x) (P(x) AND Q(x)) $\int$ NOT ($\forall$ x) (NOT (P(x)) OR NOT (Q(x)))

Notice also that the following is TRUE, where the $\Rightarrow$ symbol stands for **implies**:

($\forall$ x) (P(x)) $\Rightarrow$ ($\exists$ x) (P(x))

NOT ($\exists$ x) (P(x)) $\Rightarrow$ NOT ($\forall$ x) (P(x))

5.6.6 Using the Universal Quantifier

Whenever we use a universal quantifier, it is quite judicious to follow a few rules to ensure that our expression makes sense. We discuss these rules with respect to Query 3.

QUERY 3

Find the names of employees who work on all the projects controlled by department number 5. One way of specifying this query is by using the universal quantifier as shown.

Q3: {e.LNAME, e.FNAME | EMPLOYEE(e) AND ((∀ x)(NOT(PROJECT(x)) OR

NOT (x.DNUM=5)

OR ((∃ w)(WORKS_ON(w) AND w.EENO=e.ENO AND x.PNUMBER=w.PNO)))) }

We can break up Q3 into its basic components as follows:

Q3: {e.LNAME, e.FNAME | EMPLOYEE(e) AND F' }

$F' = ((∀ x)(NOT(PROJECT(x)) OR F_1))$

$F_1 = NOT(x.DNUM=5) OR F_2$

$F_2 = ((∃ w)(WORKS\_ON(w) AND w.EENO = e.ENO AND x.PNUMBER=w.PNO))$

We want to make sure that a selected employee e works on *all the projects* controlled by department 5, but the definition of universal quantifier says that to make the quantified formula TRUE, the inner formula must be TRUE *for all tuples in the universe*. The trick is to exclude from the universal quantification all tuples that we are not interested in by making the condition TRUE *for all such tuples*. This is necessary because a universally quantified tuple variable, such as x in Q3, must evaluate to TRUE *for every possible tuple* assigned to it to make the quantified formula TRUE. The first tuples to exclude (by making them evaluate automatically to TRUE) are those that are not in the relation R of interest. In Q3, using the expression NOT(PROJECT(x)) inside the universally quantified formula evaluates to TRUE all tuples x that are not in the PROJECT relation. Then we exclude the tuples we are not interested in from R itself. In Q3, using the expression NOT(x.DNUM=5) evaluates to TRUE all tuples x that are in the PROJECT relation but are not controlled by department 5. Finally, we specify a condition F_2 that must hold on all the remaining tuples in R. Hence, we can explain Q_3 as follows:

1. For the formula F' = (∀ x)(F) to be TRUE, we must have the formula F be TRUE *for all tuples in the universe that can be assigned to x*. However, in Q3 we are only interested in F being TRUE for all tuples of the PROJECT relation that are controlled by department 5. Hence, the formula F is of the form (NOT(PROJECT(x)) OR F_1). The 'NOT(PROJECT(x)) OR . . .' condition is TRUE for all tuples *not in the* PROJECT *relation* and has the effect of eliminating these tuples from consideration in the truth value of F_1. For every tuple in the PROJECT relation, F_1 must be TRUE if F' is to be TRUE.

2. Using the same line of reasoning, we do not want to consider tuples in the PROJECT relation that are not controlled by department number 5, since we are only interested in PROJECT tuples whose DNUM = 5. We can therefore write:

   IF (x.DNUM=5) THEN F_2

   which is equivalent to

   (NOT (x.DNUM=5) OR F_2)

3. Formula F_1, hence, is of the form NOT(x.DNUM=5) OR F_2. In the context of Q3, this means that, for a tuple x in the PROJECT relation, either its DNUM≠5 or it must satisfy F_2.

4. Finally, F_2 gives the condition that we want to hold for a selected EMPLOYEE tuple: that the employee works on *every* PROJECT *tuple that has not been excluded yet*. Such employee tuples are selected by the query.

In English, Q3 gives the following condition for selecting an EMPLOYEE tuple e: For every tuple x in the PROJECT relation with x.DNUM = 5, there must exist a tuple w in WORKS_ON such that w.EENO = e.ENO and w.PNO = x.PNUMBER. This is equivalent to saying that EMPLOYEE e works on every PROJECT x in DEPARTMENT number 5. (Whew!)

Using the general transformation from universal to existential quantifiers given in Section 5.6.5, we can rephrase the query in Q3 as shown in Q3A:

Q3A: $\{e$.LNAME, e.FNAME | EMPLOYEE(e) AND (NOT ($\exists x$) (PROJECT(x) AND $(x$.DNUM=5) AND (NOT ($\exists w$)(WORKS_ON(w) AND w.EENO=e.ENO AND x.PNUMBER=w.PNO)))) $\}$

We now give some additional examples of queries that use quantifiers.

QUERY 6

Find the names of employees who have no dependents.

Q6: $\{e$.FNAME, e.LNAME | EMPLOYEE(e) AND (NOT ($\exists d$)(DEPENDENT(d) AND e.ENO=d.EENO))$\}$

Using the general transformation rule, we can rephrase Q6 as follows:

Q6A: $\{e$.FNAME, e.LNAME | EMPLOYEE(e) AND (($\forall d$) (NOT(DEPENDENT(d)) OR NOT $(e$.ENO=d.EENO)))$\}$

QUERY 7

List the names of managers who have at least one dependent.

Q7: $\{e$.FNAME, e.LNAME | EMPLOYEE(e) AND (($\exists d$) ($\exists p$) (DEPARTMENT(d) AND DEPENDENT(p) AND e.ENO=d.MGRENO AND p.EENO=e.ENO))$\}$

This query is handled by interpreting "managers who have at least one dependent" as "managers for whom there exists some dependent."

5.6.7   Safe Expressions

Whenever we use universal quantifiers, existential quantifiers, or negation of predicates in a calculus expression, we must make sure that the resulting expression makes sense. A **safe expression** in relational calculus is one that is guaranteed to yield a *finite number of tuples* as its result; otherwise, the expression is called **unsafe**. For example, the expression

$\{t$ | NOT (EMPLOYEE(t))$\}$

is *unsafe* because it yields all tuples in the universe that are not EMPLOYEE tuples, which are infinitely numerous. If we follow the rules for Q_3 discussed earlier, we will get a safe expression when using universal quantifiers. We can define safe expressions more precisely by introducing the concept of the *domain of a tuple relational calculus expression*: This is the set of all values that either appear as constant values in the expression or exist in any tuple in the relations referenced in the expression. The domain of $\{t$ | NOT(EMPLOYEE(t))$\}$ is the set of all attribute values appearing in some tuple of the EMPLOYEE relation (for any attribute). The domain of the expression Q3A would include all values appearing in EMPLOYEE, PROJECT, and WORKS_ON (unioned with the value 5 appearing in the query itself).

An expression is said to be **safe** if all values in its result are from the domain of the expression. Notice that the result of $\{t \mid \text{NOT}(\text{EMPLOYEE}(t))\}$ is unsafe, since it will, in general, include tuples (and hence values) from outside the EMPLOYEE relation; such values are not in the domain of the expression. All of our other examples are safe expressions.

5.7 THE DOMAIN RELATIONAL CALCULUS

There is another type of relational calculus called the domain relational calculus, or simply, **domain calculus.** While SQL (see Chapter 7), a language based on tuple relational calculus, was being developed by IBM Research at San Jose, California, another language called QBE (Query-By-Example) that is related to domain calculus was being developed almost concurrently at IBM Research at Yorktown Heights, New York. The formal specification of the domain calculus was proposed after the development of the QBE system.

Domain calculus differs from tuple calculus in the *type of variables* used in formulas: Rather than having variables range over tuples, the variables range over single values from domains of attributes. To form a relation of degree n for a query result, we must have n of these **domain variables**—one for each attribute. An expression of the domain calculus is of the form

$$\{x_1, x_2, \ldots, x_n \mid \text{COND } (x_1, x_2, \ldots, x_n, x_{n+1}, x_{n+2}, \ldots, x_{n+m})\}$$

where $x_1, x_2, \ldots, x_n, x_n + 1, x_{n+2}, \ldots, x_{n+m}$ are domain variables that range over domains (of attributes), and COND is a **condition** or **formula** of the domain relational calculus.

A formula is made up of **atoms**. The atoms of a formula are slightly different from those for the tuple calculus and can be one of the following:

1. An atom of the form $R(x_1, x_2, \ldots, x_j)$, where R is the name of a relation of degree j and each x_i, $1 \le i \le j$, is a domain variable. This atom states that a list of values of $<x_1, x_2, \ldots, x_j>$ must be a tuple in the relation whose name is R, where x_i is the value of the ith attribute value of the tuple. To make a domain calculus expression more concise, we can *drop the commas* in a list of variables; thus, we can write

   $$\{x_1, x_2, \ldots, x_n \mid R(x_1 \ x_2 \ x_3) \text{ AND} \ldots\}$$

   instead of

   $$\{x_1, x_2, \ldots, x_n \mid R(x_1, x_2, x_3) \text{ AND} \ldots\}$$

2. An atom of the form $x_i \text{ op } x_j$, where **op** is one of the comparison operators in the set $\{=, <, \le, >, \ge, \ne\}$, and x_i and x_j are domain variables.

3. An atom of the form $x_i \text{ op } c$ or $c \text{ op } x_j$, where op is one of the comparison operators in the set $\{=, <, \le, >, \ge, \ne\}$, x_i and x_j are domain variables, and c is a constant value.

As in tuple calculus, atoms evaluate to either TRUE or FALSE for a specific set of values, called the **truth values** of the atoms. In case 1, if the domain variables are assigned values corresponding to a tuple of the specified relation R, then the atom is TRUE. In cases 2 and 3, if the domain variables are assigned values that satisfy the condition, then the atom is TRUE.

In a similar way to the tuple relational calculus, formulas are made up of atoms, variables, and quantifiers, so we will not repeat the specifications for formulas here. Some examples of queries specified in the domain calculus follow. We will use lowercase letters $l, m, n, \ldots, x, y, z$ for domain variables.

QUERY 0

Retrieve the date of birth (DOB) and address of the employee whose name is 'Mahesh B. Kumar'.

Q0: $\{uv \mid (\exists q)\ (\exists r)\ (\exists s)\ (\exists t)\ (\exists w)\ (\exists x)\ (\exists y)\ (\exists z)$

(EMPLOYEE($qrstuvwxyz$) **AND** $q=$'MAHESH' **AND** $r=$'B' **AND** $s=$'KUMAR')$\}$

We need ten variables for the EMPLOYEE relation, one to range over the domain of each attribute in order. Of the ten variables $q, r, s, \ldots, z$, only u and v are free. We first specify the requested attributes, DOB and ADDRESS, by the free domain variables u for DOB and v for ADDRESS. Then we specify the condition for selecting a tuple following the bar (|)—namely, that the sequence of values assigned to the variables qrstuvwxyz be a tuple of the EMPLOYEE relation and that the values for q (FNAME), r (NITIAL), and s (LNAME) be 'Mahesh', 'B', and 'Kumar', respectively. For convenience, we will quantify only those variables actually appearing in a condition (these would be q, r, and s in Q0) in the rest of our examples.[13]

An alternative shorthand notation, used in QBE, for writing this query is to assign the constants 'Mahesh', 'B', and 'Kumar' directly as shown in Q0A. Here, all variables not appearing to the left of the bar are implicitly existentially quantified:[14]

Q0A: $\{uv \mid$ EMPLOYEE('Mahesh','B','Kumar',t,u,v,w,x,y,z) $\}$

QUERY 1

Retrieve the name and address of all employees who work for the 'Research' department.

Q1: $\{qsv \mid (\exists . z)\ (\exists l)\ (\exists m)$ (EMPLOYEE($qrstuvwxyz$) **AND** DEPARTMENT($lmno$) **AND** $l=$'RESEARCH' **AND** $m=z)\}$

A condition relating two domain variables that range over attributes from two relations, such as $m = z$ in Q1, is a **join condition**; whereas a condition that relates a domain variable to a constant, such as $l =$ 'Research', is a **selection condition**.

QUERY 2

For every project located in 'Chennai', list the project number, the controlling department number, and the department manager's last name, date of birth (DOB), and address.

Q2: $\{iksuv \mid (\exists j)\ (\exists m)(\exists n)\ (\exists t)$ (PROJECT($hijk$) **AND** EMPLOYEE($qrstuvwxyz$) **AND** DEPARTMENT($lmno$) **AND** $k=m$ **AND** $n=t$ **AND** $j=$'CHENNAI')$\}$

QUERY 6

Find the names of employees who have no dependents.

Q6: $\{qs \mid (\exists t)$ (EMPLOYEE($qrstuvwxyz$) **AND** (**NOT**($\exists l$) (DEPENDENT($lmnop$) **AND** $t=l)))\}$

Query 6 can be restated using universal quantifiers instead of the existential quantifiers, as shown in Q6A:

Q6A: $\{qs \mid (\exists t)$ (EMPLOYEE($qrstuvwxyz$) **AND** ((∃ l) (**NOT**(DEPENDENT($lmnop$)) **OR NOT**($t=l$))))$\}$

---

13. Note that the notation of quantifying only the domain variables actually used in conditions and of showing a predicate such as EMPLOYEE($qrstuvwxyz$) without separating domain variables with commas is an abbreviated notation used for convenience; it is not the correct formal notation.

14. Again, this is not formally accurate notation.

QUERY 7

List the names of managers who have at least one dependent.

Q7: $\{sq \mid (\exists t) (\exists j) (\exists l) (\text{EMPLOYEE}(qrstuvwxyz)$ **AND** DEPARTMENT$(hijk)$

AND DEPENDENT$(lmnop)$ **AND** $t=j$ **AND** $l=t)\}$

As we mentioned earlier, it can be shown that any query that can be expressed in the relational algebra can also be expressed in the domain or tuple relational calculus. Also, any *safe expression* in the domain or tuple relational calculus can be expressed in the relational algebra.

The Query-By-Example (QBE) language was based on the domain relational calculus, although this was realized later, after the domain calculus was formalized. QBE was one of the first graphical query languages with minimum syntax developed for database systems. It was developed at IBM Research and is available as an IBM commercial product as part of the QMF (Query Management Facility) interface option to DB2. It has been mimicked by several other commercial products. Because of its important place in the field of relational languages, we have included an overview of QBE in Appendix D.

5.8 SUMMARY

In this chapter, we presented two formal languages for the relational model of data. They are used to manipulate relations and produce new relations as answers to queries. We discussed the relational algebra and its operations, which are used to specify a sequence of operations to specify a query. Then we introduced two types of relational calculi called tuple calculus and domain calculus; they are declarative in that they specify the result of a query without specifying how to produce the query result.

In Sections 5.1 through 5.3, we introduced the basic relational algebra operations and illustrated the types of queries for which each is used. The unary relational operators SELECT and PROJECT, as well as the RENAME operation, were discussed first. Then we discussed binary set theoretic operations requiring that relations on which they are applied be union compatible; these include UNION, INTERSECTION, and SET DIFFERENCE. The CARTESIAN PRODUCT operation is a set operation that can be used to combine tuples from two relations, producing all possible combinations. It is rarely used in practice; however, we showed how CARTESIAN PRODUCT followed by SELECT can be used to define matching tuples from two relations and leads to the JOIN operation. Different JOIN operations called THETA JOIN, EQUIJOIN, and NATURAL JOIN were introduced.

We then discussed some important types of queries that cannot be stated with the basic relational algebra operations but are important for practical situations. We introduced the AGGREGATE FUNCTION operation to deal with aggregate types of requests. We discussed recursive queries, for which there is no direct support in the algebra but which can be approached in a step-by-step approach, as we demonstrated. We then presented the OUTER JOIN and OUTER UNION operations, which extend JOIN and UNION and allow all information in source relations to be preserved in the result.

The last two sections described the basic concepts behind relational calculus, which is based on the branch of mathematical logic called predicate calculus. There are two types of relational calculi: (1) the tuple relational calculus, which uses tuple variables that range over tuples (rows) of relations, and (2) the domain relational calculus, which uses domain variables that range over domains (columns of relations). In relational calculus, a query is specified in a single declarative statement, without specifying any order or method for retrieving the query result. Hence, relational calculus is often considered to be a higher-level language than the relational algebra because a relational calculus expression states *what* we want to retrieve regardless of *how* the query may be executed.

We discussed the syntax of relational calculus queries using both tuple and domain variables. We also discussed the existential quantifier (∃) and the universal quantifier (∀). We saw that relational calculus variables are bound by these quantifiers. We described in detail how queries with universal quantification are written, and we discussed the problem of specifying safe queries whose results are finite. We also discussed rules for transforming universal into existential quantifiers, and vice versa. It is the quantifiers that give expressive power to the relational calculus, making it equivalent to relational algebra. There is no analog to grouping and aggregation functions in basic relational calculus, although some extensions have been suggested.

Review Questions

5.1. List the operations of relational algebra and the purpose of each.

5.2. What is union compatibility? Why do the UNION, INTERSECTION, and SET DIFFERENCE operations require that the relations on which they are applied be union compatible?

5.3. Discuss some types of queries for which renaming of attributes is necessary in order to specify the query unambiguously.

5.4. Discuss the various types of *inner join* operations. Why is theta join required?

5.5. What role does the concept of *foreign key* play when specifying the most common types of meaningful join operations?

5.6. What is the FUNCTION operation? What is it used for?

5.7. How are the OUTER JOIN operations different from the INNER JOIN operations? How is the OUTER UNION operation different from UNION?

5.8. In what sense does relational calculus differ from relational algebra, and in what sense are they similar?

5.9. How does tuple relational calculus differ from domain relational calculus?

5.10. Discuss the meanings of the existential quantifier (∃) and the universal quantifier (∀).

5.11. Define the following terms with respect to the tuple calculus: *tuple variable, range relation, atom, formula*, and *expression*.

5.12. Define the following terms with respect to the domain calculus: *domain variable, range relation, atom, formula*, and *expression*.

5.13. What is meant by a *safe expression* in relational calculus?

5.14. When is a query language called relationally complete?

Exercises

5.15. Show the result of each of the example queries in Section 5.5 as it would apply to the database state of Figure 4.6.

5.16. Specify the following queries on the database schema shown in Figure 4.5, using the relational operators discussed in this chapter. Also show the result of each query as it would apply to the database state of Figure 4.6.

   a. Retrieve the names of all employees in department 5 who work more than 10 hours per week on the 'ProductX' project.

b. List the names of all employees who have a dependent with the same first name as themselves.

c. Find the names of all employees who are directly supervised by 'Karthik Chandra'.

d. For each project, list the project name and the total hours per week (by all employees) spent on that project.

e. Retrieve the names of all employees who work on every project.

f. Retrieve the names of all employees who do not work on any project.

g. For each department, retrieve the department name and the average salary of all employees working in that department.

h. Retrieve the average salary of all female employees.

i. Find the names and addresses of all employees who work on at least one project located in Hyderabad but whose department has no location in Hyderabad.

j. List the last names of all department managers who have no dependents.

5.17. Consider the AIRLINE relational database schema shown in Figure 4.8, which was described in Exercise 4.11. Specify the following queries in relational algebra:

a. For each flight, list the flight number, the departure airport for the first leg of the flight, and the arrival airport for the last leg of the flight.

b. List the flight numbers and weekdays of all flights or flight legs that depart from Houston Intercontinental Airport (airport code 'IAH') and arrive in Los Angeles International Airport (airport code 'LAX').

c. List the flight number, departure airport code, scheduled departure time, arrival airport code, scheduled arrival time, and weekdays of all flights or flight legs that depart from some airport in the city of Houston and arrive at some airport in the city of Los Angeles.

d. List all fare information for flight number 'CO197'.

e. Retrieve the number of available seats for flight number 'CO197' on '1999-10-09'.

5.18. Consider the LIBRARY relational database schema shown in Figure 5.12, which is used to keep track of books, borrowers, and book loans. Referential integrity constraints are shown as directed arcs in Figure 5.12, as in the notation of Figure 4.7. Write down relational expressions for the following queries:

a. How many copies of the book titled *The Lost Tribe* are owned by the library branch whose name is 'Sharpstown'?

b. How many copies of the book titled *The Lost Tribe* are owned by each library branch?

c. Retrieve the names of all borrowers who do not have any books checked out.

d. For each book that is loaned out from the 'Sharpstown' branch and whose DueDate is today, retrieve the book title, the borrower's name, and the borrower's address.

e. For each library branch, retrieve the branch name and the total number of books loaned out from that branch.

f. Retrieve the names, addresses, and number of books checked out for all borrowers who have more than five books checked out.

g. For each book authored (or coauthored) by 'Stephen King,' retrieve the title and the number of copies owned by the library branch whose name is 'Central.'

5.19. Specify the following queries in relational algebra on the database schema given in Exercise 4.13:

 a. List the Order# and Ship_date for all orders shipped from Warehouse number 'W2'.

 b. List the Warehouse information from which the Customer named 'Jose Lopez' was supplied his orders. Produce a listing: Order#, Warehouse#.

 c. Produce a listing CUSTNAME, #OFORDERS, AVG_ORDER_AMT, where the middle column is the total number of orders by the customer and the last column is the average order amount for that customer.

 d. List the orders that were not shipped within 30 days of ordering.

 e. List the Order# for orders that were shipped from *all* warehouses that the company has in New York.

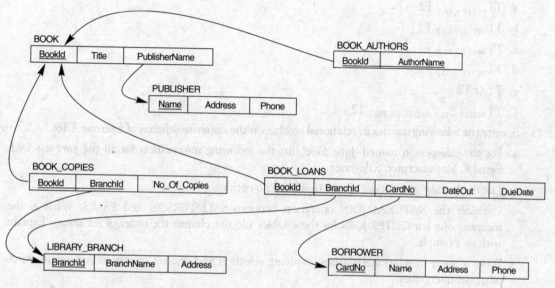

FIGURE 5.12 A relational database schema for a LIBRARY database.

5.20. Specify the following queries in relational algebra on the database schema given in Exercise 4.14:

 a. Give the details (all attributes of TRIP relation) for trips that exceeded Rs. 2000 in expenses.

 b. Print the ENO of salesman who took trips to 'Honolulu'.

 c. Print the total trip expenses incurred by the salesman with ENO = '234-56-7890'.

5.21. Specify the following queries in relational algebra on the database schema given in Exercise 4.15:

 a. List the number of courses taken by all students named 'Kishore Das' in Winter 1999 (i.e., Quarter = 'W99').

 b. Produce a list of textbooks (include Course#, Book_ISBN, Book_Title) for courses offered by the 'CS' department that have used more than two books.

 c. List any department that has all its adopted books published by 'AWL Publishing'.

5.22. Consider the two tables T1 and T2 shown in Figure 5.13. Show the results of the following operations:

Table T1

P	Q	R
10	a	5
15	b	8
25	a	6

Table T2

A	B	C
10	b	6
25	c	3
10	b	5

FIGURE 5.13 A database state for the relations T1 and T2.

a. $T1 \bowtie_{T1.P = T2.A} T2$

b. $T1 \bowtie_{T1.Q = T2.B} T2$

c. $T1 \bowtie_{T1.P = T2.A} T2$

d. $T1 \bowtie_{T1.Q = T2.B} T2$

e. $T1 \cup T2$

f. $T1 \bowtie_{(T1.P = T2.A \text{ AND } T1.R = T2.C)} T2$

5.23. Specify the following queries in relational algebra on the database schema of Exercise 4.16:

a. For the salesperson named 'Jane Doe', list the following information for all the cars she sold: Serial#, Manufacturer, Sale-price.

b. List the Serial# and Model of cars that have no options.

c. Consider the NATURAL JOIN operation between SALESPERSON and SALES. What is the meaning of a left OUTER JOIN for these tables (do not change the order of relations). Explain with an example.

d. Write a query in relational algebra involving selection and one set operation and say in words what the query does.

5.24. Specify queries a, b, c, e, f, i, and j of Exercise 5.16 in both tuple and domain relational calculus.

5.25. Specify queries a, b, c, and d of Exercise 5.17 in both tuple and domain relational calculus.

5.26. Specify queries c, d, f, and g of Exercise 5.18 in both tuple and domain relational calculus.

5.27. In a tuple relational calculus query with n tuple variables, what would be the typical minimum number of join conditions? Why? What is the effect of having a smaller number of join conditions?

5.28. Rewrite the domain relational calculus queries that followed Q0 in Section 5.7 in the style of the abbreviated notation of Q0A, where the objective is to minimize the number of domain variables by writing constants in place of variables wherever possible.

5.29. Consider this query: Retrieve the ENOs of employees who work on at least those projects on which the employee with ENO = 123456789 works. This may be stated as (FORALL x) (IF P THEN Q), where

- x is a tuple variable that ranges over the PROJECT relation.

- $P \equiv$ employee with ENO = 123456789 works on project x.

- $Q \equiv$ employee e works on project x.

Express the query in tuple relational calculus, using the rules

- $(\forall x)(P(x)) \equiv NOT(\exists x)(NOT(P(x)))$.
- (IF P THEN Q) $\equiv$ (NOT(P) OR Q).

5.30. Show how you may specify the following relational algebra operations in both tuple and domain relational calculus.

a. $\sigma_{A=C}(R(A, B, C))$

b. $\pi_{<A, B>}(R(A, B, C))$

c. $R(A, B, C) * S(C, D, E)$

d. $R(A, B, C) \cup S(A, B, C)$

e. $R(A, B, C) \cap S(A, B, C)$

f. $R(A, B, C) - S(A, B, C)$

g. $R(A, B, C) \times S(D, E, F)$

h. $R(A, B) \div S(A)$

5.31. Suggest extensions to the relational calculus so that it may express the following types of operations that were discussed in Section 5.4: (a) aggregate functions and grouping; (b) OUTER JOIN operations; (c) recursive closure queries.

5.32. With regard to expressive power of the formal query languages, which of the following statements is true/

a. Relational algebra is less powerful than tuple relational calculus

b. Relational algebra has the same power as tuple relational calculus

c. Relational algebra has the same power as safe tuple relational calculus

d. None of the above

5.33. How many distinct instances are there of a relation scheme with k attributes, each with a Boolean domain?

5.34. Which of the following is true?

a. Selection, projection, union, set difference, and Cartesian product are independent

b. Selection, projection, intersection, set difference, and Cartesian product are independent

c. Selection, projection, union, division, and Cartesian product are independent

d. All of the above

5.35. Given two relations R1 and R2 where R1 contains N1 tuples, R2 contains N2 tuples and N2 >N1>0. For what relational operations, the minimum and maximum sizes are 0 and N1 respectively

a. $R1 \cap R2$

b. $\sigma_{A=5}(R1)$

c. Both (A) and (B)

d. $\pi_A(R1)$

5.36. Given the two tables Name(drinker) and Likes(Drinker, Beer), the following relational query is intended to print. Here $\bowtie$ stands for natural join operation

Name - $\pi_{Name}((Name \bowtie \pi_{Beer}(Likes) - Likes)$

    a. List all the names of the drinkers who do not like beer

    b. List all the names of drinkers who take at least one kind of beer

    c. List all the names of the drinkers who likes all beers which are not in the beer table.

    d. List all the names the drinkers who likes all beers.

5.37. Consider the following relational schema pertaining to students database:

Student(*roll number, Student_Name, Address*)

Enroll(*roll number, Course, no. Course_Name*)

where the primary keys are shown underlined. The number of tuples in the *Student and Enroll* tables are 120 and 8 respectively. What are the maximum and minimum number of tuples that can be present the NA TURAL JOIN of the relation *Student with Course?*

5.38. Let R1 ($\underline{A}$,B,C) and R2($\underline{D}$,E) be two relation schemes, where the primary keys are shown underlined, and let C be a foreign key in R1 referencing to R2. Suppose there is no violation of the above referential integrity constraint in the corresponding relation instances r1 and r2. Which one of the following relational algebra expressions would necessarily produce an empty relation?

    a. $\pi_D(r_2) - \pi_C(r_1)$

    b. $\pi_C(r_1) - \pi_D(r_2)$

    c. $\pi_D(r_1 \Join_{C=D} r_2)$

    d. $\pi_C(r_1 \Join_{C=D} r_2)$

5.39. Consider the relation student (*name*, sex, marks) where the primary key is shown underlined, pertaining to students in a class that has at least one boy and one girl. What does the following relational algebra expression produce?

$$\pi_{name} (\sigma_{sex='female'} (student)) - \pi_{name} \left((student) \underset{\substack{sex='female' \\ \wedge X='male' \\ \wedge marks \leq m}}{\Join} \rho_{n,x,m} (student) \right)$$

Selected Bibliography

Codd (1970) defined the basic relational algebra. Date (1983a) discusses outer joins. Work on extending relational operations is discussed by Carlis (1986) and Ozsoyoglu et al. (1985). Cammarata et al. (1989) extends the relational model integrity constraints and joins.

    Codd (1971) introduced the language Alpha, which is based on concepts of tuple relational calculus. Alpha also includes the notion of aggregate functions, which goes beyond relational calculus. The original formal definition of relational calculus was given by Codd (1972), which also provided an algorithm that transforms any tuple relational calculus expression to relational algebra. The QUEL (Stonebraker et al. 1976) is based on tuple relational calculus, with implicit existential quantifiers but no universal quantifiers, and was implemented in the Ingres system as a commercially available language. Codd defined relational completeness of a query language to mean at least as powerful as relational calculus. Ullman (1988) describes a formal proof of the equivalence of relational algebra with the safe expressions of tuple and domain relational calculus. Abiteboul et al. (1995) and Atzeni and deAntonellis (1993) give a detailed treatment of formal relational languages.

Although ideas of domain relational calculus were initially proposed in the QBE language (Zloof 1975), the concept was formally defined by Lacroix and Pirotte (1977). The experimental version of the Query-By-Example system is described in Zloof (1977). The ILL (Lacroix and Pirotte 1977a) is based on domain relational calculus. Whang et al. (1990) extends QBE with universal quantifiers. Visual query languages, of which QBE is an example, are being proposed as a means of querying databases; conferences such as the Visual Database Systems Workshop (e.g., Arisawa and Catarci (2000) or Zhou and Pu (2002)) have a number of proposals for such languages.

6

Relational Database Design by ER- and EER-to-Relational Mapping

We now focus on how to design a **relational database schema** based on a conceptual schema design. This corresponds to the logical database design or data model mapping step discussed in Section 3.1 (see Figure 3.1). We present the procedures to create a relational schema from an entity-relationship (ER) or an enhanced ER (EER) schema. Our discussion relates the constructs of the ER and EER models, presented in Chapters 3, to the constructs of the relational model, presented in Chapters 4 and 5. Many CASE (computer-aided software engineering) tools are based on the ER or EER models, or other similar models, as we have discussed in Chapter 3. These computerized tools are used interactively by database designers to develop an ER or EER schema for a database application. Many tools use ER or EER diagrams or variations to develop the schema graphically, and then automatically convert it into a relational database schema in the DDL of a specific relational DBMS by employing algorithms similar to the ones presented in this chapter.

We outline a seven-step algorithm in Section 6.1 to convert the basic ER model constructs—entity types (strong and weak), binary relationships (with various structural constraints), n-ary relationships, and attributes (simple, composite, and multivalued) into relations. Then, in Section 6.2, we continue the mapping algorithm by describing how to map EER model constructs—specialization/generalization and union types (categories)— into relations.

6.1   RELATIONAL DATABASE DESIGN USING ER-TO-RELATIONAL MAPPING [Earlier Section Number 7.1]

6.1.1   ER-to-Relational Mapping Algorithm

We now describe the steps of an algorithm for ER-to-relational mapping. We will use the COMPANY database example to illustrate the mapping procedure. The COMPANY ER schema is shown again in Figure 6.1, and the corresponding COMPANY relational database schema is shown in Figure 6.2 to illustrate the mapping steps.

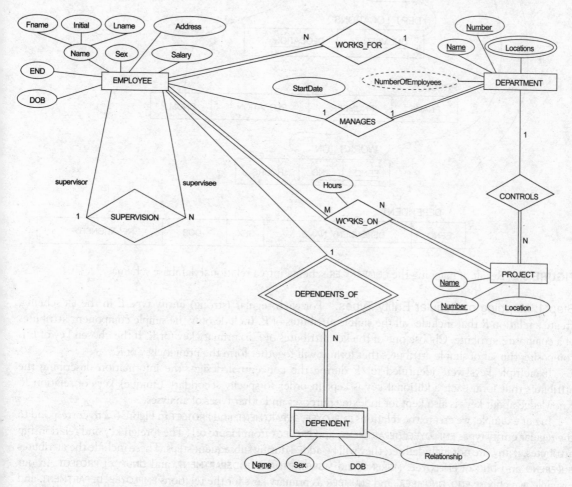

FIGURE 6.1 The ER conceptual schema diagram for the COMPANY database.

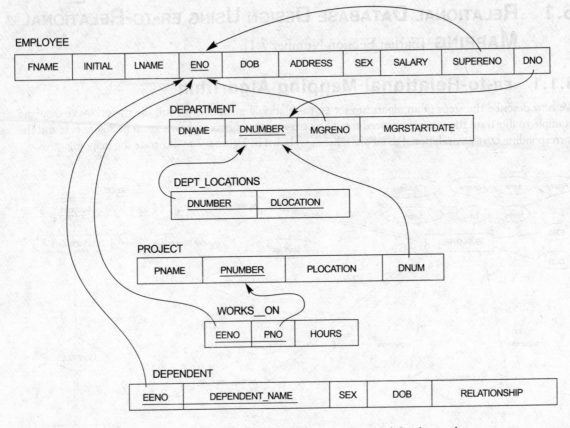

FIGURE 6.2 Result of mapping the COMPANY ER schema into a relational database schema.

Step 1: Mapping of Regular Entity Types. For each regular (strong) entity type E in the ER schema, create a relation R that includes all the simple attributes of E. Include only the simple component attributes of a composite attribute. Choose one of the key attributes of E as primary key for R. If the chosen key of E is composite, the set of simple attributes that form it will together form the primary key of R.

If multiple keys were identified for E during the conceptual design, the information describing the attributes that form each additional key is kept in order to specify secondary (unique) keys of relation R. Knowledge about keys is also kept for indexing purposes and other types of analyses.

In our example, we create the relations EMPLOYEE, DEPARTMENT, and PROJECT in Figure 6.2 to correspond to the regular entity types EMPLOYEE, DEPARTMENT, and PROJECT from Figure 6.1. The foreign key and relationship attributes, if any, are not included yet; they will be added during subsequent steps. These include the attributes SUPERENO and DNO of EMPLOYEE, MGRENO and MGRSTARTDATE of DEPARTMENT, and DNUM of PROJECT. In our example, we choose ENO, DNUMBER, and PNUMBER as primary keys for the relations EMPLOYEE, DEPARTMENT, and PROJECT, respectively. Knowledge that DNAME of DEPARTMENT and PNAME of PROJECT are secondary keys is kept for possible use later in the design.

The relations that are created from the mapping of entity types are sometimes called **entity relations** because each tuple (row) represents an entity instance.

Step 2: Mapping of Weak Entity Types. For each weak entity type W in the ER schema with owner entity type E, create a relation R and include all simple attributes (or simple components of composite attributes) of W as attributes of R. In addition, include as foreign key attributes of R the primary key attribute(s) of the relation(s) that correspond to the owner entity type(s); this takes care of the identifying relationship type of W. The primary key of R is the combination of the primary key(s) of the owner(s) and the partial key of the weak entity type W, if any.

If there is a weak entity type E_2 whose owner is also a weak entity type E_1, then E_1 should be mapped before E_2 to determine its primary key first.

In our example, we create the relation DEPENDENT in this step to correspond to the weak entity type DEPENDENT. We include the primary key ENO of the EMPLOYEE relation—which corresponds to the owner entity type—as a foreign key attribute of DEPENDENT; we renamed it EENO, although this is not necessary. The primary key of the DEPENDENT relation is the combination {EENO, DEPENDENT_NAME} because DEPENDENT_NAME is the partial key of DEPENDENT.

It is common to choose the propagate (CASCADE) option for the referential triggered action (see Section 7) on the foreign key in the relation corresponding to the weak entity type, since a weak entity has an existence dependency on its owner entity. This can be used for both ON UPDATE and ON DELETE.

Step 3: Mapping of Binary 1:1 Relationship Types.   For each binary 1:1 relationship type R in the ER schema, identify the relations S and T that correspond to the entity types participating in R. There are three possible approaches: (1) the foreign key approach, (2) the merged relationship approach, and (3) the cross-reference or relationship relation approach. Approach 1 is the most useful and should be followed unless special conditions exist, as we discuss below.

1. *Foreign key approach:* Choose one of the relations—S, say—and include as a foreign key in S the primary key of T. It is better to choose an entity type with *total participation* in R in the role of S. Include all the simple attributes (or simple components of composite attributes) of the 1:1 relationship type R as attributes of S.

   In our example, we map the 1:1 relationship type MANAGES from Figure 6.1 by choosing the participating entity type DEPARTMENT to serve in the role of S, because its participation in the MANAGES relationship type is total (every department has a manager). We include the primary key of the EMPLOYEE relation as foreign key in the DEPARTMENT relation and rename it MGRENO. We also include the simple attribute STARTDATE of the MANAGES relationship type in the DEPARTMENT relation and rename it MGRSTARTDATE.

   Note that it is possible to include the primary key of S as a foreign key in T instead. In our example, this amounts to having a foreign key attribute, say DEPARTMENT_MANAGED in the EMPLOYEE relation, but it will have a null value for employee tuples who do not manage a department. If only 10 percent of employees manage a department, then 90 percent of the foreign keys would be null in this case. Another possibility is to have foreign keys in both relations S and T redundantly, but this incurs a penalty for consistency maintenance.

2. *Merged relation option:* An alternative mapping of a 1:1 relationship type is possible by merging the two entity types and the relationship into a single relation. This may be appropriate when *both participations are total.*

3. *Cross-reference or relationship relation option:* The third alternative is to set up a third relation R for the purpose of cross-referencing the primary keys of the two relations S and T representing the entity types. As we shall see, this approach is required for binary M:N relationships. The relation R is called a **relationship relation,** (or sometimes a **lookup table**), because each tuple in R represents a relationship instance that relates one tuple from S with one tuple of T.

Step 4: Mapping of Binary 1:N Relationship Types.   For each regular binary 1:N relationship type R, identify the relation S that represents the participating entity type at the *N-side* of the relationship type. Include as foreign key in S the primary key of the relation T that represents the other entity type participating in R; this is done because each entity instance on the N-side is related to at most one entity instance on the 1-side of the relationship type. Include any simple attributes (or simple components of composite attributes) of the 1:N relationship type as attributes of S.

In our example, we now map the 1:N relationship types WORKS_FOR, CONTROLS, and SUPERVISION from Figure 6.1. For WORKS_FOR we include the primary key DNUMBER of the DEPARTMENT relation as foreign key in the EMPLOYEE relation and call it DNO. For SUPERVISION we include the primary key of the EMPLOYEE relation as foreign key in the EMPLOYEE relation itself—because the relationship is recursive—and call it SUPERENO. The CONTROLS relationship is mapped to the foreign key attribute DNUM of PROJECT, which references the primary key DNUMBER of the DEPARTMENT relation.

An alternative approach we can use here is again the relationship relation (cross-reference) option as in the case of binary 1:1 relationships. We create a separate relation R whose attributes are the keys of S and T, and whose primary key is the same as the key of S. This option can be used if few tuples in S participate in the relationship to avoid excessive null values in the foreign key.

Step 5: Mapping of Binary M:N Relationship Types.

For each binary M:N relationship type R, create a new relation S to represent R. Include as foreign key attributes in S the primary keys of the relations that represent the participating entity types; their combination will form the primary key of S. Also include any simple attributes of the M:N relationship type (or simple components of composite attributes) as attributes of S. Notice that we cannot represent an M:N relationship type by a single foreign key attribute in one of the participating relations (as we did for 1:1 or 1:N relationship types) because of the M:N cardinality ratio; we must create a separate *relationship relation* S.

In our example, we map the M:N relationship type WORKS_ON from Figure 6.1 by creating the relation WORKS_ON in Figure 6.2. We include the primary keys of the PROJECT and EMPLOYEE relations as foreign keys in WORKS_ON and rename them PNO and EENO, respectively. We also include an attribute HOURS in WORKS_ON to represent the HOURS attribute of the relationship type. The primary key of the WORKS_ON relation is the combination of the foreign key attributes {EENO, PNO}.

The propagate (CASCADE) option for the referential triggered action (see Chapter 7) should be specified on the foreign keys in the relation corresponding to the relationship R, since each relationship instance has an existence dependency on each of the entities it relates. This can be used for both ON UPDATE and ON DELETE.

Notice that we can always map 1:1 or 1:N relationships in a manner similar to M:N relationships by using the cross-reference (relationship relation) approach, as we discussed earlier. This alternative is particularly useful when few relationship instances exist, in order to avoid null values in foreign keys. In this case, the primary key of the relationship relation will be *only one* of the foreign keys that reference the participating entity relations. For a 1:N relationship, the primary key of the relationship relation will be the foreign key that references the entity relation on the N-side. For a 1:1 relationship, either foreign key can be used as the primary key of the relationship relation as long as no null entries are present in that relation.

Step 6: Mapping of Multivalued Attributes.

For each multivalued attribute A, create a new relation R. This relation R will include an attribute corresponding to A, plus the primary key attribute K—as a foreign key in R—of the relation that represents the entity type or relationship type that has A as an attribute. The primary key of R is the combination of A and K. If the multivalued attribute is composite, we include its simple components.

In our example, we create a relation DEPT_LOCATIONS. The attribute DLOCATION represents the multivalued attribute LOCATIONS of DEPARTMENT, while DNUMBER—as foreign key—represents the primary key of the DEPARTMENT relation. The primary key of DEPT_LOCATIONS is the combination of {DNUMBER, DLOCATION}. A separate tuple will exist in DEPT_LOCATIONS for each location that a department has.

The propagate (CASCADE) option for the referential triggered action (see Chapter 7) should be specified on the foreign key in the relation R corresponding to the multivalued attribute for both ON UPDATE and ON DELETE. We should also note that the key of R when mapping a composite, multivalued attribute requires some analysis of the meaning of the component attributes. In some cases when a multivalued attribute is composite, only some of the component attributes are required to be part of the key of R; these attributes are similar to a partial key of a weak entity type that corresponds to the multivalued attribute (see Section 3.5).

Figure 6.2 shows the COMPANY relational database schema obtained through steps 1 to 6, and Figure 4.6 shows a sample database state. Notice that we did not yet discuss the mapping of n-ary relationship types ($n > 2$), because none exist in Figure 6.1; these are mapped in a similar way to M:N relationship types by including the following additional step in the mapping algorithm.

Step 7: Mapping of N-ary Relationship Types. For each n-ary relationship type R, where $n > 2$, create a new relation S to represent R. Include as foreign key attributes in S the primary keys of the relations that represent the participating entity types. Also include any simple attributes of the n-ary relationship type (or simple components of composite attributes) as attributes of S. The primary key of S is usually a combination of all the foreign keys that reference the relations representing the participating entity types. However, if the cardinality constraints on any of the entity types E participating in R is 1, then the primary key of S should not include the foreign key attribute that references the relation E' corresponding to E (see Section 3.11).

For example, consider the relationship type SUPPLY of Figure 3.27a. This can be mapped to the relation SUPPLY shown in Figure 6.3, whose primary key is the combination of the three foreign keys {SNAME, PARTNO, PROJNAME}.

6.1.2 Discussion and Summary of Mapping for Model Constructs

Table 6.1 summarizes the correspondences between ER and relational model constructs and constraints.

SUPPLIER

SNAME	...

PROJECT

PROJNAME	...

PART

PARTNO	...

SUPPLY

SNAME	PROJNAME	PARTNO	QUANTITY

FIGURE 6.3 Mapping the n-ary relationship type SUPPLY from Figure 3.27a.

One of the main points to note in a relational schema, in contrast to an ER schema, is that relationship types are not represented explicitly; instead, they are represented by having two attributes A and B, one a primary key and the other a foreign key (over the same domain) included in two relations S and T. Two tuples in S and T are related when they have the same value for A and B. By using the EQUIJOIN operation (or NATURAL JOIN if the two join attributes have the same name) over S.A and T.B, we can combine all pairs of related tuples from S and T and materialize the relationship. When a binary 1:1 or 1:N relationship type is involved, a single join operation is usually needed. For a binary M:N relationship type, two join operations are needed, whereas for n-ary relationship types, n joins are needed to fully materialize the relationship instances.

TABLE 6.1 CORRESPONDENCE BETWEEN ER AND RELATIONAL MODELS

ER MODEL	RELATIONAL MODEL
Entity type	"Entity" relation
1:1 or 1:N relationship type	Foreign key (or "relationship" relation)
M:N relationship type	"Relationship" relation and two foreign keys
n-ary relationship type	"Relationship" relation and n foreign keys
Simple attribute	Attribute
Composite attribute	Set of simple component attributes
Multivalued attribute	Relation and foreign key
Value set	Domain
Key attribute	Primary (or secondary) key

For example, to form a relation that includes the employee name, project name, and hours that the employee works on each project, we need to connect each EMPLOYEE tuple to the related PROJECT tuples via the WORKS_ON relation of Figure 6.2. Hence, we must apply the EQUIJOIN operation to the EMPLOYEE and WORKS_ON relations with the join condition ENO = EENO, and then apply another EQUIJOIN operation to the resulting relation and the PROJECT relation with join condition PNO = PNUMBER. In general, when multiple relationships need to be traversed, numerous join operations must be specified. A relational database user must always be aware of the foreign key attributes in order to use them correctly in combining related tuples from two or more relations. This is sometimes considered to be a drawback of the relational data model because the foreign key/primary key correspondences are not always obvious upon inspection of relational schemas. If an equijoin is performed among attributes of two relations that do not represent a foreign key/primary key relationship, the result can often be meaningless and may lead to spurious (invalid) data. For example, the reader can try joining the PROJECT and DEPT_LOCATIONS relations on the condition DLOCATION = PLOCATION and examine the result (see also Chapter 8).

Another point to note in the relational schema is that we create a separate relation for *each* multivalued attribute. For a particular entity with a set of values for the multivalued attribute, the key attribute value of the entity is repeated once for each value of the multivalued attribute in a separate tuple. This is because the basic relational model does *not* allow multiple values (a list, or a set of values) for an attribute in a single tuple. For example, because department 5 has three locations, three tuples exist in the DEPT_LOCATIONS relation of Figure 4.6; each tuple specifies one of the locations. In our example, we apply EQUIJOIN to DEPT_LOCATIONS and DEPARTMENT on the DNUMBER attribute to get the values of all locations along with other DEPARTMENT attributes. In the resulting relation, the values of the other department attributes are repeated in separate tuples for every location that a department has.

The basic relational algebra does not have a NEST or COMPRESS operation that would produce from the DEPT_LOCATIONS relation of Figure 4.6 a set of tuples of the form {<1, Hyderabad>, <4, Chennai>,

<5,{Bangalore,NewDelhi,Hyderabad}>}. This is a serious drawback of the basic normalized or "flat" version of the relational model. On this score, the object-oriented model and the legacy hierarchical and network models have better facilities than does the relational model. The nested relational model and object-relational systems attempt to remedy this.

6.2 Mapping EER Model Constructs to Relations

We now discuss the mapping of EER model constructs to relations by extending the ER-to-relational mapping algorithm that was presented in Section 6.1.1.

6.2.1 Mapping of Specialization or Generalization

There are several options for mapping a number of subclasses that together form a specialization (or alternatively, that are generalized into a superclass), such as the {SECRETARY, TECHNICIAN, ENGINEER} subclasses of EMPLOYEE in Figure 3.19. We can add a further step to our ER-to-relational mapping algorithm from Section 6.1.1, which has seven steps, to handle the mapping of specialization. Step 8, which follows, gives the most common options; other mappings are also possible. We then discuss the conditions under which each option should be used. We use Attrs(R) to denote the *attributes of relation* R, and PK(R) to denote the *primary key of* R.

Step 8: Options for Mapping Specialization or Generalization. Convert each specialization with m subclasses $\{S_1, S_2, \ldots, S_m\}$ and (generalized) superclass C, where the attributes of C are $\{k, a_1, \ldots a_n\}$ and k is the (primary) key, into relation schemas using one of the four following options:

- **Option 8A: Multiple relations—Superclass and subclasses.** Create a relation L for C with attributes Attrs(L) = $\{k, a_1, \ldots, a_n\}$ and PK(L) = k. Create a relation L_i for each subclass S_i, $1 \le i \le m$, with the attributes Attrs(L_i) = $\{k\} \cup$ {attributes of S_i} and PK(L_i) = k. This option works for any specialization (total or partial, disjoint or over-lapping).

- **Option 8B: Multiple relations—Subclass relations only.** Create a relation L_i for each subclass S_i, $1 \le i \le m$, with the attributes Attrs(L_i) = {attributes of S_i} $\cup$ $\{k, a_1, \ldots, a_n\}$ and PK(L_i) = k. This option only works for a specialization whose subclasses are *total* (every entity in the superclass must belong to (at least) one of the subclasses).

- **Option 8C: Single relation with one type attribute.** Create a single relation L with attributes Attrs(L) = $\{k, a_1, \ldots, a_n\}$ $\cup$ {attributes of S_1} $\cup \ldots \cup$ {attributes of S_m} $\cup$ $\{t\}$ and PK(L) = k. The attribute t is called a *type* (or **discriminating**) attribute that indicates the subclass to which each tuple belongs, if any. This option works only for a specialization whose subclasses are *disjoint*, and has the potential for generating many null values if many specific attributes exist in the subclasses.

- **Option 8D: Single relation with multiple type attributes.** Create a single relation schema L with attributes Attrs(L) = $\{k, a_1, \ldots, a_n\}$ $\cup$ {attributes of S_1} $\cup \ldots \cup$ {attributes of S_m} $\cup$ $\{t_1, t_2, \ldots, t_m\}$ and PK(L) = k. Each t_i, $1 \le i \le m$, is a *Boolean type attribute* indicating whether a tuple belongs to subclass S_i. This option works for a specialization whose subclasses are *overlapping* (but will also work for a disjoint specialization).

Options 8A and 8B can be called the **multiple-relation options**, whereas options 8C and 8D can be called the **single-relation options**. Option 8A creates a relation L for the superclass C and its attributes, plus a relation L_i for each subclass S_i; each L_i includes the specific (or local) attributes of S_i, plus the primary key of the superclass C, which is propagated to L_i and becomes its primary key. An EQUIJOIN operation on the primary key between any L_i and L produces all the specific and inherited attributes of the entities in S_i. This option is illustrated in Figure 6.4a for the EER schema in Figure 3.19. Option 8A works for any constraints on the specialization: disjoint or overlapping, total or partial. Notice that the constraint

$$\pi_{<K>}(L_i) \subseteq \pi_{<K>}(L)$$

must hold for each L_i. This specifies a foreign key from each L_i to L, as well as an *inclusion dependency* $L_i.k < L.k$.

(a) EMPLOYEE

ENO	FName	Initial	LName	DOB	Address	JobType

SECRETARY		TECHNICIAN		ENGINEER	
ENO	TypingSpeed	ENO	TGrade	ENO	EngType

(b) CAR

VehicleId	LicensePlateNo	Price	MaxSpeed	NoOfPassengers

TRUCK

VehicleId	LicensePlateNo	Price	NoOfAxles	Tonnage

(c) EMPLOYEE

ENO	FName	Initial	LName	DOB	Address	JobType	TypingSpeed	TGrade	EngType

(d) PART

PartNo	Description	MFlag	DrawingNo	ManufactureDate	BatchNo	PFlag	SupplierName	ListPrice

FIGURE 6.4 Options for mapping specialization or generalization. (a) Mapping the EER schema in Figure 3.19 using option 8A. (b) Mapping the EER schema in Figure 3.18b using option 8B. (c) Mapping the EER schema in Figure 3.19 using option 8C. (d) Mapping Figure 3.20 using option 8D with Boolean type fields MFlag and PFlag.

In option 8B, the EQUIJOIN operation is *built* into the schema, and the relation L is done away with, as illustrated in Figure 6.4b for the EER specialization in Figure 3.18b. This option works well only when *both* the disjoint and total constraints hold. If the specialization is not total, an entity that does not belong to any of the subclasses S_i is lost. If the specialization is not disjoint, an entity belonging to more than one subclass will have its inherited attributes from the superclass C stored redundantly in more than one L_i. With option 8B, no relation holds all the entities in the superclass C; consequently, we must apply an OUTER UNION (or FULL OUTER JOIN) operation to the L_i relations to retrieve all the entities in C. The result of the outer union will be similar to the relations under options 8C and 8D except that the type fields will be missing. Whenever we search for an arbitrary entity in C, we must search all the m relations L_i.

Options 8C and 8D create a single relation to represent the superclass C and all its subclasses. An entity that does not belong to some of the subclasses will have null values for the specific attributes of these subclasses. These options are hence not recommended if many specific attributes are defined for the subclasses. If few specific subclass attributes exist, however, these mappings are preferable to options 8A and 8B because they do away with the need to specify EQUIJOIN and OUTER UNION operations and hence can yield a more efficient implementation.

Option 8C is used to handle disjoint subclasses by including a **single type** (or **image** or **discriminating**) **attribute** t to indicate the subclass to which each tuple belongs; hence, the domain of t could be $\{1, 2, \ldots, m\}$. If the specialization is partial, t can have null values in tuples that do not belong to any subclass. If the specialization is attribute defined, that attribute serves the purpose of t and t is not needed; this option is illustrated in Figure 6.4c for the EER specialization in Figure 3.19.

Option 8D is designed to handle overlapping subclasses by including m *Boolean* type fields, one for *each* subclass. It can also be used for disjoint subclasses. Each type field t_i can have a domain {yes, no}, where a value of yes indicates that the tuple is a member of subclass S_i. If we use this option for the EER specialization in Figure 3.19, we would include three types attributes—IsASecretary, IsAEngineer, and IsATechnician—instead of the JobType attribute in Figure 6.4c. Notice that it is also possible to create a single type attribute of m *bits* instead of the m type fields.

When we have a multilevel specialization (or generalization) hierarchy or lattice, we do not have to follow the same mapping option for all the specializations. Instead, we can use one mapping option for part of the hierarchy or lattice and other options for other parts. Figure 6.5 shows one possible mapping into relations for the EER lattice of Figure 3.21. Here we used option 8A for PERSON/{EMPLOYEE, ALUMNUS, STUDENT}, option 8C for EMPLOYEE/{STAFF, FACULTY, STUDENT_ASSISTANT}, and option 8D for STUDENT_ASSISTANT/{RESEARCH_ASSISTANT, TEACHING_ASSISTANT}, STUDENT/STUDENT_ASSISTANT (in STUDENT), and STUDENT/{GRADUATE_STUDENT, UNDERGRADUATE_STUDENT}. In Figure 6.5, all attributes whose names end with 'Type' or 'Flag' are type fields.

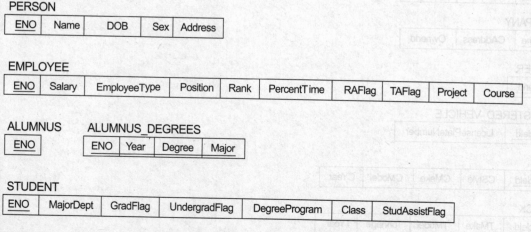

FIGURE 6.5 Mapping the EER specialization lattice in Figure 3.21 using multiple options.

6.2.2   Mapping of Shared Subclasses (Multiple Inheritance)

A shared subclass, such as ENGINEERING_MANAGER of Figure 3.21, is a subclass of several superclasses, indicating multiple inheritance. These classes must all have the same key attribute; otherwise, the shared subclass would be modeled as a category. We can apply any of the options discussed in step 8 to a shared subclass, subject to the restrictions discussed in step 8 of the mapping algorithm. In Figure 6.5, both options 8C and 8D are used for the shared subclass STUDENT_ASSISTANT. Option 8C is used in the EMPLOYEE relation (EmployeeType attribute) and option 8D is used in the STUDENT relation (StudAssistFlag attribute).

6.2.3 Mapping of Categories (Union Types)

We now add another step to the mapping procedure—step 9—to handle categories. A category (or union type) is a subclass of the *union* of two or more superclasses that can have different keys because they can be of different entity types. An example is the OWNER category shown in Figure 3.22, which is a subset of the union of three entity types PERSON, BANK, and COMPANY. The other category in that figure, REGISTERED_VEHICLE, has two superclasses that have the same key attribute.

Step 9: Mapping of Union Types (Categories).   For mapping a category whose defining superclasses have different keys, it is customary to specify a new key attribute, called a **surrogate key**, when creating a relation to correspond to the category. This is because the keys of the defining classes are different, so we cannot use any one of them exclusively to identify all entities in the category. In our example of Figure 3.22, we can create a relation OWNER to correspond to the OWNER category, as illustrated in Figure 6.6, and include any attributes of the category in this relation. The primary key of the OWNER relation is the surrogate key, which we called OwnerId. We also include the surrogate key attribute OwnerId as foreign key in each relation corresponding to a superclass of the category, to specify the correspondence in values between the surrogate key and the key of each superclass. Notice that if a particular PERSON (or BANK or COMPANY) entity is not a member of OWNER, it would have a null value for its OwnerId attribute in its corresponding tuple in the PERSON (or BANK or COMPANY) relation, and it would not have a tuple in the OWNER relation.

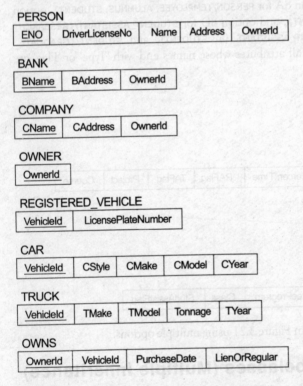

FIGURE 6.6 Mapping the EER categories (union types) in Figure 3.22 to relations.

For a category whose superclasses have the same key, such as VEHICLE in Figure 3.22, there is no need for a surrogate key. The mapping of the REGISTERED_VEHICLE category, which illustrates this case, is also shown in Figure 6.6.

6.3   SUMMARY

In Section 6.1, we showed how a conceptual schema design in the ER model can be mapped to a relational database schema. An algorithm for ER-to-relational mapping was given and illustrated by examples from the COMPANY database. Table 6.1 summarized the correspondences between the ER and relational model constructs and constraints. We then added additional steps to the algorithm in Section 6.2 for mapping the constructs from the EER model into the relational model. Similar algorithms are incorporated into graphical database design tools to automatically create a relational schema from a conceptual schema design.

Review Questions

6.1. Discuss the correspondences between the ER model constructs and the relational model constructs. Show how each ER model construct can be mapped to the relational model, and discuss any alternative mappings.

6.2. Discuss the options for mapping EER model constructs to relations.

Exercises

6.3. Try to map the relational schema of Figure 5.12 into an ER schema. This is part of a process known as *reverse engineering*, where a conceptual schema is created for an existing implemented database. State any assumptions you make.

FIGURE 6.6 An ER schema for a SHIP_TRACKING database.

6.4. Figure 6.7 shows an ER schema for a database that may be used to keep track of transport ships and their locations for maritime authorities. Map this schema into a relational schema, and specify all primary keys and foreign keys.

6.5. Map the BANK ER schema of Exercise 3.35 (shown in Figure 3.30) into a relational schema. Specify all primary keys and foreign keys. Repeat for the AIRLINE schema (Figure 3.34) of Exercise 3.32 and for the other schemas for Exercises 3.28 through 3.36.

6.6. Map the EER diagrams in Figures 3.26 into relational schemas. Justify your choice of mapping options.

Selected Bibliography

The original ER-to-relational mapping algorithm was described in Chen's classic paper (Chen 1976) that presented the original ER model.

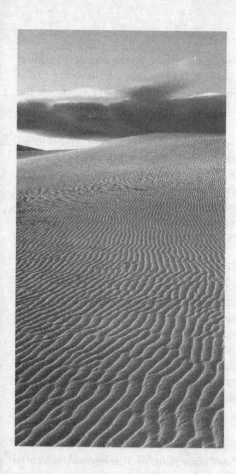

7

SQL-99: Schema Definition, Basic Constraints, and Queries

[Earlier Chapter Number 8]

The SQL language may be considered one of the major reasons for the success of relational databases in the commercial world. Because it became a standard for relational databases, users were less concerned about migrating their database applications from other types of database systems—for example, network or hierarchical systems—to relational systems. The reason is that even if users became dissatisfied with the particular relational DBMS product they chose to use, converting to another relational DBMS product would not be expected to be too expensive and time-consuming, since both systems would follow the same language standards. In practice, of course, there are many differences between various commercial relational DBMS packages. However, if the user is diligent in using only those features that are part of the standard, and if both relational systems faithfully support the standard, then conversion between the two systems should be much simplified. Another advantage of having such a standard is that users may write statements in a database application program that can access data stored in two or more relational DBMSs without having to change the database sublanguage (SQL) if both relational DBMSs support standard SQL.

This chapter presents the main features of the SQL standard for *commercial* relational DBMSs, whereas Chapter 4 presented the most important concepts underlying the *formal* relational data model. In Chapter 5 (Sections 5.1 through 5.5) we discussed the *relational algebra* operations, which are very important for understanding the types of requests that may be specified on a relational database. They are also important for query processing and optimization in a relational DBMS, as we shall see in Chapter 10. However, the relational algebra operations are considered to be too technical for most commercial DBMS users because a query in relational algebra is written as a sequence of operations that, when executed, produces the required result. Hence, the user must specify how—that is, *in what order*—to execute the query operations. On the other hand, the SQL language provides a higher-level *declarative* language interface, so the user only specifies *what* the result is to be, leaving the actual optimization and decisions on how to execute the query to the DBMS. Although SQL includes some features from relational algebra, it is based to a greater extent on the *tuple relational calculus*, which we described in Section 5.6. However, the SQL syntax is more user-friendly than either of the two formal languages.

The name **SQL** is derived from Structured Query Language. Originally, SQL was called SEQUEL (for Structured English QUEry Language) and was designed and implemented at IBM Research as the interface for an experimental relational database system called SYSTEM R. SQL is now the standard language for commercial relational DBMSs. A joint effort by ANSI (the American National Standards Institute) and ISO (the International Standards Organization) has led to a standard version of SQL (ANSI 1986), called SQL-86 or SQL1. A revised and much expanded standard called SQL2 (also referred to as SQL-92) was subsequently developed. The next version of the standard was originally called SQL3, but is now called SQL-99. We will try to cover the latest version of SQL as much as possible.

SQL is a comprehensive database language: It has statements for data definition, query, and update. Hence, it is both a DDL *and* a DML. In addition, it has facilities for defining views on the database, for specifying security and authorization, for defining integrity constraints, and for specifying transaction controls. It also has rules for embedding SQL statements into a general-purpose programming language such as Java or COBOL or C/C++.[1] We will discuss most of these topics in the following subsections.

Because the specification of the SQL standard is expanding, with more features in each version of the standard, the latest **SQL–99** standard is divided into a **core** specification plus optional specialized **packages**. The core is supposed to be implemented by all RDBMS vendors that are SQL-99 compliant. The packages can be implemented as optional modules to be purchased independently for specific database applications such as data mining, spatial data, temporal data, data warehousing, on-line analytical processing (OLAP), multimedia data, and so on.

In this chapter, Section 7.1 describes the SQL DDL commands for creating schemas and tables, and gives an overview of the basic data types in SQL. Section 7.2 presents how basic constraints such as key and referential integrity are specified. Section 7.3 discusses statements for modifying schemas, tables, and constraints. Section 7.4 describes the basic SQL constructs for specifying retrieval queries, and Section 7.5 goes over more complex features of SQL queries, such as aggregate functions and grouping. Section 7.6 describes the SQL commands for insertion, deletion, and updating of data. Section 7.7 lists some SQL features that are presented in other chapters of the book; these include transaction control in Chapter 11, security/authorization in Chapter 12, active databases (triggers), object-oriented features, and OLAP (OnLine Analytical Processing) features in Chapter 17.

We also present several additional aspects of SQL. We start in Section 7.8 by describing the CREATE ASSERTION statement, which allows the specification of more general constraints on the database. Then, in Section 7.9, we describe the SQL facilities for defining views on the database. Views are also called *virtual* or *derived tables* because they present the user with what appear to be tables; however, the information in those tables is derived from previously defined tables.

The next several sections of this chapter discuss various techniques for accessing databases from programs. Most database access in practical situations is through software programs that implement **database applications.** This software is usually developed in a general-purpose programming language such as JAVA, COBOL, or C/C++. Recall from Section 2.3.1 that when database statements are included in a program, the

---

1. Originally, SQL had statements for creating and dropping indexes on the files that represent relations, but these have been dropped from the SQL standard for some time.

general-purpose programming language is called the *host language*, whereas the database language—SQL, in our case—is called the *data sublanguage*. In some cases, special *database programming languages* are developed specifically for writing database applications. Although many of these were developed as research prototypes, some notable database programming languages have widespread use, such as ORACLE's PL/SQL (*Programming Language/SQL*).

We start our presentation of database programming in Section 7.10 with an overview of the different techniques developed for accessing a database from programs. Then, in Section 7.11, we discuss the rules for embedding SQL statements into a general-purpose programming language, generally known as *embedded* SQL. This section also briefly discusses *dynamic* SQL, in which queries can be dynamically constructed at runtime, and presents the basics of the SQLJ variation of embedded SQL that was developed specifically for the programming language JAVA. In Section 7.12, we discuss the technique known as SQL/CLI (Call Level Interface), in which a library of procedures and functions is provided for accessing the database. Various sets of library functions have been proposed. The SQL/CLI set of functions is the one given in the SQL standard. Another library of functions is ODBC (Open Data Base Connectivity). We do not describe ODBC because it is considered to be the predecessor to SQL/CLI. A third library of functions—which we do describe—is JDBC; this was developed specifically for accessing databases from JAVA. Finally, in Section 7.13, we discuss SQL/PSM (Persistent Stored Modules), which is a part of the SQL standard that allows program modules—procedures and functions—to be stored by the DBMS and accessed through SQL. Section 7.14 summarizes the chapter.

7.1 SQL DATA DEFINITION

SQL uses the terms **table, row,** and **column** for the formal relational model terms *relation, tuple,* and *attribute*, respectively. We will use the corresponding terms interchangeably. The main SQL command for data definition is the CREATE statement, which can be used to create schemas, tables (relations), and domains (as well as other constructs such as views, assertions, and triggers). Before we describe the relevant CREATE statements, we discuss schema and catalog concepts in Section 7.1.1 to place our discussion in perspective. Section 7.1.2 describes how tables are created, and Section 7.1.3 describes the most important data types available for attribute specification. Because the SQL specification is very large, we give a description of the most important features. Further details can be found in the various SQL standards documents (see bibliographic notes).

7.1.1 Schema and Catalog Concepts in SQL

Early versions of SQL did not include the concept of a relational database schema; all tables (relations) were considered part of the same schema. The concept of an SQL **schema** was incorporated starting with SQL2 in order to group together tables and other constructs that belong to the same database application. An SQL **schema** is identified by a **schema name**, and includes an **authorization identifier** to indicate the user or account who owns the schema, as well as **descriptors** for *each element* in the schema. Schema **elements** include tables, constraints, views, domains, and other constructs (such as authorization grants) that describe the schema. A schema is created via the CREATE SCHEMA statement, which can include all the schema elements' definitions. Alternatively, the schema can be assigned a name and authorization identifier, and the elements can be defined later. For example, the following statement creates a schema called COMPANY, owned by the user with authorization identifier MKUMAR:

CREATE SCHEMA COMPANY **AUTHORIZATION** MKUMAR;

In general, not all users are authorized to create schemas and schema elements. The privilege to create schemas, tables, and other constructs must be explicitly granted to the relevant user accounts by the system administrator or DBA.

In addition to the concept of a schema, SQL2 uses the concept of a **catalog**—a named collection of schemas in an SQL environment. An SQL **environment** is basically an installation of an SQL-compliant RDBMS on a computer system.[2] A catalog always contains a special schema called INFORMATION_SCHEMA, which provides information on all the schemas in the catalog and all the element descriptors in these schemas. Integrity constraints such as referential integrity can be defined between relations only if they exist in schemas within the same catalog. Schemas within the same catalog can also share certain elements, such as domain definitions.

7.1.2 The CREATE TABLE Command in SQL

The **CREATE TABLE** command is used to specify a new relation by giving it a name and specifying its attributes and initial constraints. The attributes are specified first, and each attribute is given a name, a data type to specify its domain of values, and any attribute constraints, such as NOT NULL. The key, entity integrity, and referential integrity constraints can be specified within the CREATE TABLE statement after the attributes are declared, or they can be added later using the ALTER TABLE command (see Section 7.3). Figure 7.1 shows sample data definition statements in SQL for the relational database schema shown in Figure 4.7.

Typically, the SQL schema in which the relations are declared is implicitly specified in the environment in which the CREATE TABLE statements are executed. Alternatively, we can explicitly attach the schema name to the relation name, separated by a period. For example, by writing

CREATE TABLE COMPANY.EMPLOYEE . . .

rather than

CREATE TABLE EMPLOYEE . . .

as in Figure 7.1, we can explicitly (rather than implicitly) make the EMPLOYEE table part of the COMPANY schema.

The relations declared through CREATE TABLE statements are called **base tables** (or base relations); this means that the relation and its tuples are actually created and stored as a file by the DBMS. Base relations are distinguished from **virtual relations**, created through the CREATE VIEW statement (see Section 7.9), which may or may not correspond to an actual physical file. In SQL the attributes in a base table are considered to be *ordered in the sequence in which they are specified* in the CREATE TABLE statement. However, rows (tuples) are not considered to be ordered within a relation.

7.1.3 Attribute Data Types and Domains in SQL

The basic **data types** available for attributes include numeric, character string, bit string, boolean, date, and time.

- **Numeric:** Numeric data types include integer numbers of various sizes (INTEGER or INT, and SMALLINT) and floating-point (real) numbers of various precision (FLOAT or REAL, and DOUBLE

---

2. SQL also includes the concept of a cluster of catalogs within an environment, but it is not very clear if so many levels of nesting are required in most applications.

(a)

```
CREATE TABLE EMPLOYEE
    (    FNAME              VARCHAR(15)        NOT NULL ,
         INITIAL            CHAR ,
         LNAME              VARCHAR(15)        NOT NULL ,
         ENO                CHAR(9)            NOT NULL ,
         DOB                DATE,
         ADDRESS            VARCHAR(30) ,
         SEX                CHAR ,
         SALARY             DECIMAL(10,2) ,
         SUPERENO           CHAR(9) ,
         DNO                INT                NOT NULL ,
    PRIMARY KEY (ENO),
    FOREIGN KEY (SUPERENO) REFERENCES EMPLOYEE(ENO),
    FOREIGN KEY (DNO) REFERENCES DEPARTMENT(DNUMBER) ) ;

CREATE TABLE DEPARTMENT
    (    DNAME              VARCHAR(15)        NOT NULL ,
         DNUMBER            INT                NOT NULL ,
         MGRENO             CHAR(9)            NOT NULL ,
         MGRSTARTDATE       DATE ,
    PRIMARY KEY (DNUMBER) ,
    UNIQUE (DNAME) ,
    FOREIGN KEY (MGRENO) REFERENCES EMPLOYEE(ENO) ) ;

CREATE TABLE DEPT_LOCATIONS
    (    DNUMBER            INT                NOT NULL ,
         DLOCATION          VARCHAR(15)        NOT NULL ,
    PRIMARY KEY (DNUMBER, DLOCATION) ,
    FOREIGN KEY (DNUMBER) REFERENCES DEPARTMENT(DNUMBER) ) ;

CREATE TABLE PROJECT
    (    PNAME              VARCHAR(15)        NOT NULL ,
         PNUMBER            INT                NOT NULL ,
         PLOCATION          VARCHAR(15) ,
         DNUM               INT                NOT NULL ,
    PRIMARY KEY (PNUMBER) ,
    UNIQUE (PNAME) ,
    FOREIGN KEY (DNUM) REFERENCES DEPARTMENT(DNUMBER) ) ;

CREATE TABLE WORKS_ON
    (    EENO               CHAR(9)            NOT NULL ,
         PNO                INT                NOT NULL ,
         HOURS              DECIMAL(3,1)       NOT NULL ,
    PRIMARY KEY (EENO, PNO),
    FOREIGN KEY (EENO) REFERENCES EMPLOYEE(ENO),
    FOREIGN KEY (PNO) REFERENCES PROJECT(PNUMBER) ) ;

CREATE TABLE DEPENDENT
    (    EENO               CHAR(9)            NOT NULL ,
         DEPENDENT_NAME     VARCHAR(15)        NOT NULL ,
         SEX                CHAR ,
         DOB                DATE ,
         RELATIONSHIP       VARCHAR(8) ,
    PRIMARY KEY (EENO, DEPENDENT_NAME),
    FOREIGN KEY (EENO) REFERENCES EMPLOYEE(ENO) ) ;
```

FIGURE 7.1 SQL CREATE TABLE data definition statements for defining the COMPANY schema from Figure 4.7.

PRECISION). Formatted numbers can be declared by using DECIMAL(i,j)—or DEC(i,j) or NUMERIC(i,j)—where i, the *precision*, is the total number of decimal digits and j, the *scale*, is the number of digits after the decimal point. The default for scale is zero, and the default for precision is implementation-defined.

- **Character**: Character data consists of a sequence of characters from an implementation defined character set. ASCII and EBCDIC are two sets commonly used Character-string. Data types are either fixed length—CHAR(n) or CHARACTER(n), where n is the number of characters—or varying length—VARCHAR(n) or CHAR VARYING(n) or CHARACTER VARYING(n), where n is the maximum number of characters. The default length of character string is 1. When specifying a literal string value, it is placed between single quotation marks (apostrophes), and it is *case sensitive* (a distinction is made between uppercase and lowercase).[3] For fixed-length strings, a shorter string is padded with blank characters to the right. For example, if the value 'Mahesh' is for an attribute of type CHAR(10), it is padded with six blank characters to become 'Mahesh' if needed. Padded blanks are generally ignored when strings are compared. For comparison purposes, strings are considered ordered in alphabetic (or lexicographic) order; if a string *str*1 appears before another string *str*2 in alphabetic order, then *str*1 is considered to be less than *str*2.[4] There is also a concatenation operator denoted by || (double vertical bar) that can concatenate two strings in SQL. For example, 'abc' || 'XYZ' results in a single string 'abcXYZ'.

- **Bit-string** data types are either of fixed length n—BIT(n)—or varying length—BIT VARYING(n), where n is the maximum number of bits. The default for n, the length of a character string or bit string, is 1. Literal bit strings are placed between single quotes but preceded by a B to distinguish them from character strings; for example, B'10101'.[5]

- A **boolean** data type has the traditional values of TRUE or FALSE. In SQL, because of the presence of NULL values, a three-valued logic is used, so a third possible value for a boolean data type is UNKNOWN. We discuss the need for UNKNOWN and the three valued logic in Section 7.5.1.

- New data types for **date** and **time** were added in SQL2. The DATE data type has ten positions, and its components are YEAR, DAY and MONTH, in the form YYYY-MM-DD[5a]. The TIME data type has at least eight positions, with the components HOUR, MINUTE, and SECOND in the form HH:MM:SS. Only valid dates and times should be allowed by the SQL implementation. The < (less than) comparison can be used with dates or times—*an earlier* date is considered to be smaller than a later date, and similarly with time. Literal values are represented by single-quoted strings preceded by the keyword DATE or TIME; for example, DATE '27-09-2002' or TIME '09:12:47'. In addition, a data type TIME(i), where i is called *time fractional seconds precision*, specifies $i + 1$ additional positions for TIME—one position for an additional separator character, and i positions for specifying decimal fractions of a second. A TIME WITH TIME ZONE data type includes an additional six positions for specifying the displacement from the standard universal time zone, which is in the range +13:00 to –12:59 in units of HOURS:MINUTES. If WITH TIME ZONE is not included, the default is the local time zone for the SQL session.

---

3. This is not the case with SQL keywords, such as CREATE or CHAR. With keywords, SQL is *case insensitive*, meaning that SQL treats uppercase and lowercase letters as equivalent in keywords.

4. For nonalphabetic characters, there is a defined order.

5. Bit strings whose length is a multiple of 4 can also be specified in *hexadecimal* notation, where the literal string is preceded by X and each hexadecimal character represents 4 bits.

5a. All dates are by default relative to "UST", format YYYY-MM-DD, with appropriate ranges (YYYY range 1 to 9999). But for explanation purpose in Indian context, this book will use DD-MM-YYYY format everywhere.

- A **timestamp** data type (TIMESTAMP) includes both the DATE and TIME fields, plus a minimum of six positions for decimal fractions of seconds and an optional WITH TIME ZONE qualifier. Literal values are represented by single-quoted strings preceded by the keyword TIMESTAMP, with a blank space between data and time; for example, TIMESTAMP '27-09-2002 09:12:47 648302'.

- Another data type related to DATE, TIME, and TIMESTAMP is the INTERVAL data type. This specifies an **interval**—a *relative value* that can be used to increment or decrement an absolute value of a date, time, or timestamp. Intervals are qualified to be either YEAR/MONTH intervals or DAY/TIME intervals.

- The format of DATE, TIME, and TIMESTAMP can be considered as a special type of string. Hence, they can generally be used in string comparisons by being cast (or coerced or converted) into the equivalent strings.

It is possible to specify the data type of each attribute directly, as in Figure 7.1; alternatively, a domain can be declared, and the domain name used with the attribute specification. This makes it easier to change the data type for a domain that is used by numerous attributes in a schema, and improves schema readability. For example, we can create a domain ENO_TYPE by the following statement:

CREATE DOMAIN ENO_TYPE AS CHAR(9);

We can use ENO_TYPE in place of CHAR(9) in Figure 7.1 for the attributes ENO and SUPERENO of EMPLOYEE, MGRENO of DEPARTMENT, EENO of WORKS_ON, and EENO of DEPENDENT. A domain can also have an optional default specification via a DEFAULT clause, as we discuss later for attributes.

7.2   Specifying Basic Constraints in SQL

We now describe the basic constraints that can be specified in SQL as part of table creation. These include key and referential integrity constraints, as well as restrictions on attribute domains and NULLs, and constraints on individual tuples within a relation. We discuss the specification of more general constraints, called assertions, in Secion 7.8.

7.2.1   Specifying Attribute Constraints and Attribute Defaults

Because SQL allows NULLs as attribute values, a *constraint* NOT NULL may be specified if NULL is not permitted for a particular attribute. This is always implicitly specified for the attributes that are part of the *primary key* of each relation, but it can be specified for any other attributes whose values are required not to be NULL, as shown in Figure 7.1.

It is also possible to define a *default value* for an attribute by appending the clause **DEFAULT** <value> to an attribute definition. The default value is included in any new tuple if an explicit value is not provided for that attribute. Figure 7.2 illustrates an example of specifying a default manager for a new department and a default department for a new employee. If no default clause is specified, the default *default value* is NULL for attributes *that do not have* the NOT NULL constraint.

Another type of constraint can restrict attribute or domain values using the **CHECK** clause following an attribute or domain definition.[6] For example, suppose that department numbers are restricted to integer numbers between 1 and 20; then, we can change the attribute declaration of DNUMBER in the DEPARTMENT table (see Figure 7.1) to the following:

DNUMBER INT **NOT NULL CHECK** (DNUMBER > 0 **AND** DNUMBER < 21);

The CHECK clause can also be used in conjunction with the CREATE DOMAIN statement. For example, we can write the following statement:

CREATE DOMAIN D_NUM AS INTEGER **CHECK**
(D_NUM > 0 **AND** D_NUM < 21);

We can then use the created domain D_NUM as the attribute type for all attributes that refer to department numbers in Figure 7.1, such as DNUMBER of DEPARTMENT, DNUM of PROJECT, DNO of EMPLOYEE, and so on.

7.2.2 Specifying Key and Referential Integrity Constraints

Because keys and referential integrity constraints are very important, there are special clauses within the CREATE TABLE statement to specify them. Some examples to illustrate the specification of keys and referential integrity are shown in Figure 7.1.[7] The **PRIMARY KEY** clause specifies one or more attributes that make up the primary key of a relation. If a primary key has a *single* attribute, the clause can follow the attribute directly. For example, the primary key of DEPARTMENT can be specified as follows (instead of the way it is specified in Figure 7.1):

DNUMBER INT **PRIMARY KEY**;

The UNIQUE clause specifies alternate (secondary) keys, as illustrated in the DEPARTMENT and PROJECT table declarations in Figure 7.1.

Referential integrity is specified via the **FOREIGN KEY** clause, as shown in Figure 7.1. As we discussed in Section 4.2.4, a referential integrity constraint can be violated when tuples are inserted or deleted, or when a foreign key or primary key attribute value is modified. The default action that SQL takes for an integrity violation is to **reject** the update operation that will cause a violation. However, the schema designer can specify an alternative action to be taken if a referential integrity constraint is violated, by attaching a **referential triggered action** clause to any foreign key constraint. The options include SET NULL, CASCADE, and SET DEFAULT. An option must be qualified with either ON DELETE or ON UPDATE. We illustrate this with the examples shown in Figure 7.2. Here, the database designer chooses SET NULL ON DELETE and CASCADE ON UPDATE for the foreign key SUPERENO of EMPLOYEE. This means that if the tuple for a supervising employee is *deleted*, the value of SUPERENO is automatically set to NULL for all employee tuples that were referencing the deleted employee tuple. On the other hand, if the ENO value for a supervising employee is *updated* (say, because it was entered incorrectly), the new value is *cascaded* to SUPERENO for all employee tuples referencing the updated employee tuple.

---

6. The CHECK clause can also be used for other purposes, as we shall see.

7. Key and referential integrity constraints were not included in early versions of SQL. In some earlier implementations, keys were specified implicitly at the internal level via the CREATE INDEX command.

```
CREATE TABLE EMPLOYEE
    (...,
     DNO                INT    NOT NULL    DEFAULT 1,
     CONSTRAINT EMPPK
       PRIMARY KEY (ENO),
     CONSTRAINT EMPSUPERFK
       FOREIGN KEY (SUPERENO) REFERENCES EMPLOYEE(ENO)
                    ON DELETE SET NULL    ON UPDATE CASCADE ,
     CONSTRAINT EMPDEPTFK
       FOREIGN KEY (DNO) REFERENCES DEPARTMENT(DNUMBER)
                    ON DELETE SET DEFAULT    ON UPDATE CASCADE );

CREATE TABLE DEPARTMENT
    (...,
     MGRENO   CHAR(9) NOT NULL DEFAULT '888665555' ,
     ...,
     CONSTRAINT DEPTPK
       PRIMARY KEY (DNUMBER) ,
     CONSTRAINT DEPTSK
       UNIQUE (DNAME),
     CONSTRAINT DEPTMGRFK
       FOREIGN KEY (MGRENO) REFERENCES EMPLOYEE(ENO)
            ON DELETE SET DEFAULT    ON UPDATE CASCADE );

CREATE TABLE DEPT_LOCATIONS
    (...,
     PRIMARY KEY (DNUMBER, DLOCATION),
     FOREIGN KEY (DNUMBER) REFERENCES DEPARTMENT(DNUMBER)
            ON DELETE CASCADE    ON UPDATE CASCADE ) ;
```

FIGURE 7.2 Example illustrating how default attribute values and referential triggered actions are specified in SQL.

In general, the action taken by the DBMS for SET NULL or SET DEFAULT is the same for both ON DELETE or ON UPDATE: The value of the affected referencing attributes is changed to NULL for SET NULL, and to the specified default value for SET DEFAULT. The action for CASCADE ON DELETE is to delete all the referencing tuples, whereas the action for CASCADE ON UPDATE is to change the value of the foreign key to the updated (new) primary key value for all referencing tuples. It is the responsibility of the database designer to choose the appropriate action and to specify it in the database schema. As a general rule, the CASCADE option is suitable for "relationship" relations (see Section 6.1), such as WORKS_ON; for relations that represent multivalued attributes, such as DEPT_LOCATIONS; and for relations that represent weak entity types, such as DEPENDENT.

7.2.3   Giving Names to Constraints

Figure 7.2 also illustrates how a constraint may be given a **constraint name**, following the keyword **CONSTRAINT.** The names of all constraints within a particular schema must be unique. A constraint name is used to identify a particular constraint in case the constraint must be dropped later and replaced with another constraint, as we discuss in Section 7.3. Giving names to constraints is optional.

7.2.4 Specifying Constraints on Tuples Using CHECK

In addition to key and referential integrity constraints, which are specified by special keywords, other *table constraints* can be specified through additional CHECK clauses at the end of a CREATE TABLE statement. These can be called **tuple-based** constraints because they apply to each tuple *individually* and are checked whenever a tuple is inserted or modified. For example, suppose that the DEPARTMENT table in Figure 7.1 had an additional attribute DEPT_CREATE_DATE, which stores the date when the department was created. Then we could add the following CHECK clause at the end of the CREATE TABLE statement for the DEPARTMENT table to make sure that a manager's start date is later than the department creation date:

> **CHECK** (DEPT_CREATE_DATE < MGRSTARTDATE);

The CHECK clause can also be used to specify more general constraints using the CREATE ASSERTION statement of SQL. We discuss this in Section 7.8 because it requires the full power of queries, which are discussed in Sections 7.3 and 7.4.

7.3 SCHEMA CHANGE STATEMENTS IN SQL

In this section, we give an overview of the **schema evolution commands** available in SQL, which can be used to alter a schema by adding or dropping tables, attributes, constraints, and other schema elements.

7.3.1 The DROP Command

The DROP command can be used to drop *named* schema elements, such as tables, domains, or constraints. One can also drop a schema. For example, if a whole schema is not needed any more, the DROP SCHEMA command can be used. There are two *drop behavior* options: CASCADE and RESTRICT. For example, to remove the COMPANY database schema and all its tables, domains, and other elements, the CASCADE option is used as follows:

> **DROP SCHEMA** COMPANY **CASCADE;**

If the RESTRICT option is chosen in place of CASCADE, the schema is dropped only if it has *no elements* in it; otherwise, the DROP command will not be executed.

If a base relation within a schema is not needed any longer, the relation and its definition can be deleted by using the DROP TABLE command. For example, if we no longer wish to keep track of dependents of employees in the COMPANY database of Figure 7.1, we can get rid of the DEPENDENT relation by issuing the following command:

> **DROP TABLE** DEPENDENT **CASCADE;**

If the RESTRICT option is chosen instead of CASCADE, a table is dropped only if it is *not referenced* in any constraints (for example, by foreign key definitions in another relation) or views (see Section 7.9). With the CASCADE option, all such constraints and views that reference the table are dropped automatically from the schema, along with the table itself.

The DROP command can also be used to drop other types of named schema elements, such as constraints or domains.

7.3.2 The ALTER Command

The definition of a base table or of other named schema elements can be changed by using the ALTER command. For base tables, the possible *alter table actions* include adding or dropping a column (attribute), changing a column definition, and adding or dropping table constraints. For example, to add an attribute for keeping track of jobs of employees to the EMPLOYEE base relations in the COMPANY schema, we can use the command

ALTER TABLE COMPANY.EMPLOYEE **ADD** JOB VARCHAR(12);

We must still enter a value for the new attribute JOB for each individual EMPLOYEE tuple. This can be done either by specifying a default clause or by using the UPDATE command (see Section 7.6). If no default clause is specified, the new attribute will have NULLs in all the tuples of the relation immediately after the command is executed; hence, the NOT NULL constraint is *not allowed* in this case.

To drop a column, we must choose either CASCADE or RESTRICT for drop behavior. If CASCADE is chosen, all constraints and views that reference the column are dropped automatically from the schema, along with the column. If RESTRICT is chosen, the command is successful only if no views or constraints (or other elements) reference the column. For example, the following command removes the attribute ADDRESS from the EMPLOYEE base table:

ALTER TABLE COMPANY.EMPLOYEE **DROP** ADDRESS **CASCADE;**

It is also possible to alter a column definition by dropping an existing default clause or by defining a new default clause. The following examples illustrate this clause:

ALTER TABLE COMPANY.DEPARTMENT **ALTER** MGRENO **DROP DEFAULT;**

ALTER TABLE COMPANY.DEPARTMENT **ALTER** MGRENO **SET DEFAULT** "333445555";

One can also change the constraints specified on a table by adding or dropping a constraint. To be dropped, a constraint must have been given a name when it was specified. For example, to drop the constraint named EMPSUPERFK in Figure 7.2 from the EMPLOYEE relation, we write:

ALTER TABLE COMPANY.EMPLOYEE
DROP CONSTRAINT EMPSUPERFK **CASCADE;**

Once this is done, we can redefine a replacement constraint by adding a new constraint to the relation, if needed. This is specified by using the **ADD** keyword in the ALTER TABLE statement followed by the new constraint, which can be named or unnamed and can be of any of the table constraint types discussed.

The preceding subsections gave an overview of the schema evolution commands of SQL. There are many other details and options, and we refer the interested reader to the SQL documents listed in the bibliographical notes. The next two sections discuss the querying capabilities of SQL.

7.4 BASIC QUERIES IN SQL

SQL has one basic statement for retrieving information from a database: the **SELECT** statement. The SELECT statement *has no relationship* to the SELECT operation of relational algebra, which was discussed in Chapter 5. There are many options and flavors to the SELECT statement in SQL, so we will introduce its features gradually. We will use example queries specified on the schema of Figure 4.5 and will refer to the sample database state shown in Figure 4.6 to show the results of some of the example queries.

Before proceeding, we must point out an important distinction between SQL and the formal relational model discussed in Chapter 4. SQL allows a table (relation) to have two or more tuples that are identical in all their attribute values. Hence, in general, an SQL table is not a set of *tuples*, because a set does not allow two identical members; rather, it is a **multiset** (sometimes called a *bag*) of tuples. Some SQL relations are *constrained to be sets* because a key constraint has been declared or because the DISTINCT option has been used with the SELECT statement (described later in this section). We should be aware of this distinction as we discuss the examples.

7.4.1 The SELECT-FROM-WHERE Structure of Basic SQL Queries

Queries in SQL can be very complex. We will start with simple queries, and then progress to more complex ones in a step-by-step manner. The basic form of the SELECT statement, sometimes called a **mapping** or a **select-from-where block**, is formed of the three clauses SELECT, FROM, and WHERE and has the following form:

SELECT   <attribute list>
FROM   <table list>
WHERE   <condition>;

where

- <attribute list> is a list of attribute names whose values are to be retrieved by the query.

- <table list> is a list of the relation names required to process the query.

- <condition> is a conditional (Boolean) expression that identifies the tuples to be retrieved by the query.

In SQL, the basic logical comparison operators for comparing attribute values with one another and with literal constants are =, <, <=, >, >=, and <>. These correspond to the relational algebra operators =, <, ≤, >, ≥, and ≠, respectively, and to the C/C++ programming language operators =, <, <=, >, >=, and !=. The main difference is the not equal operator. SQL has many additional comparison operators that we shall present gradually as needed.

We now illustrate the basic SELECT statement in SQL with some example queries. The queries are labeled here with the same query numbers that appear in Chapter 5 for easy cross reference.

QUERY 0

Retrieve the date of birth and address of the employee(s) whose name is 'Mahesh B. Kumar'.

Q0:   SELECT DOB, ADDRESS
        FROM   EMPLOYEE
        WHERE   FNAME='Mahesh' **AND** INITIAL='B' **AND** LNAME='Kumar';

This query involves only the EMPLOYEE relation listed in the FROM clause. The query selects the EMPLOYEE tuples that satisfy the condition of the WHERE clause, then *projects* the result on the DOB and ADDRESS attributes listed in the SELECT clause. Q0 is similar to the following relational algebra expression, except that duplicates, if any, would not be eliminated:

$$\pi_{\text{DOB,ADDRESS}}(\sigma_{\text{FNAME}}=\text{'Mahesh' AND INITIAL='B' AND LNAME='Kumar'}(\text{EMPLOYEE}))$$

Hence, a simple SQL query with a single relation name in the FROM clause is similar to a SELECT-PROJECT pair of relational algebra operations. The SELECT clause of SQL specifies the *projection attributes*, and the WHERE clause specifies the *selection condition*. The only difference is that in the SQL query we may get duplicate tuples in the result, because the constraint that a relation is a set is not enforced. Figure 7.3a shows the result of query Q0 on the database of Figure 4.6.

The query Q0 is also similar to the following tuple relational calculus expression, except that duplicates, if any, would again not be eliminated in the SQL query:

Q0: {t.DOB, t.ADDRESS | EMPLOYEE(t) **AND** t.FNAME='Mahesh' **AND** t.INITIAL='B' **AND** t.LNAME='Kumar'}

Hence, we can think of an implicit tuple variable in the SQL query ranging over each tuple in the EMPLOYEE table and evaluating the condition in the WHERE clause. Only those tuples that satisfy the condition—that is, those tuples for which the condition evaluates to TRUE after substituting their corresponding attribute values—are selected.

QUERY 1

Retrieve the name and address of all employees who work for the 'Research' department.

Q1:   **SELECT** FNAME, LNAME, ADDRESS
      FROM   EMPLOYEE, DEPARTMENT
      WHERE   DNAME='Research' **AND** DNUMBER=DNO;

Query Q1 is similar to a SELECT-PROJECT-JOIN sequence of relational algebra operations. Such queries are often called **select-project-join queries**. In the WHERE clause of Q1, the condition DNAME = 'Research' is a **selection condition** and corresponds to a SELECT operation in the relational algebra. The condition DNUMBER = DNO is a **join condition**, which corresponds to a JOIN condition in the relational algebra. The result of query Q1 is shown in Figure 7.3b. In general, any number of select and join conditions may be specified in a single SQL query. The next example is a select-project-join query with *two* join conditions.

QUERY 2

For every project located in 'Chennai', list the project number, the controlling department number, and the department manager's last name, and address.

Q2:   **SELECT** PNUMBER, DNUM, LNAME, ADDRESS,
      FROM   PROJECT, DEPARTMENT, EMPLOYEE
      WHERE   DNUM=DNUMBER **AND** MGRENO=ENO AND
              PLOCATION='Chennai';

The join condition DNUM = DNUMBER relates a project to its controlling department, whereas the join condition MGRENO = ENO relates the controlling department to the employee who manages that department. The result of query Q2 is shown in Figure 7.3c.

7.4.2   Ambiguous Attribute Names, Aliasing, and Tuple Variables

In SQL the same name can be used for two (or more) attributes as long as the attributes are in *different relations*. If this is the case, and a query refers to two or more attributes with the same name, we must **qualify** the attribute name with the relation name to prevent ambiguity. This is done by *prefixing* the relation name to the attribute name and separating the two by a period. To illustrate this, suppose that in Figures 4.5 and 4.6 the DNO and LNAME attributes of the EMPLOYEE relation were called DNUMBER and NAME, and the DNAME attribute of DEPARTMENT was also called NAME; then, to prevent ambiguity, query Q1 would be rephrased as

(a)

DOB	ADDRESS
09-01-1965	731 Ameerpet, Hyderabad, AP

(b)

FNAME	LNAME	ADDRESS
Mahesh	Kumar	731 Ameerpet, Hyderabad, AP
Karthik	Chandra	638 Begampet, Hyderabad, AP
Ramesh	Narayan	975 Hauzkhas, New Delhi
Kiran	Goyal	5631 Abids, Hyderabad

(c)

PNUMBER	DNUM	LNAME	ADDRESS
10	4	Priya	291 Majestic Street, Bangalore
30	4	Priya	291 Majestic Street, Bangalore

(d)

E.FNAME	E.LNAME	S.FNAME	S.LNAME
Mahesh	Kumar	Karthik	Chandra
Karthik	Chandra	Gaurav	Kishan
Swetha	Narayan	Priya	Ganesh
Priya	Ganesh	Gaurav	Kishan
Ramesh	Narayan	Karthik	Chandra
Kiran	Goyal	Karthik	Chandra
Jitendra	Nath	Priya	Ganesh

(e)

ENO
123456789
333445555
999887777
987654321
666884444
453453453
987987987
888665555

(f)

ENO	DNAME
123456789	Research
333445555	Research
999887777	Research
987654321	Research
666884444	Research
453453453	Research
987987987	Research
888665555	Research
123456789	Administration
333445555	Administration
999887777	Administration
987654321	Administration
666884444	Administration
453453453	Administration
987987987	Administration
888665555	Administration
123456789	Headquarters
333445555	Headquarters
999887777	Headquarters
987654321	Headquarters
666884444	Headquarters
453453453	Headquarters
987987987	Headquarters
888665555	Headquarters

(g)

FNAME	INITIAL	LNAME	ENO	DOB	ADDRESS	SEX	SALARY	SUPERENO	DNO
Mahesh	B	Kumar	123456789	01-09-1965	731 Ameerpet, Hyderabad, AP	M	30000	333445555	5
Karthik	T	Chandra	333445555	08-12-1955	638 Begampet, Hyderabad, AP	M	40000	888665555	5
Ramesh	K	Narayan	666884444	15-09-1962	975 Hauzkhas, New Delhi	M	38000	333445555	5
Kiran	A	Goyal	453453453	31-07-1972	5631 Abids, Hyderabad	F	25000	333445555	5

FIGURE 7.3 Results of SQL queries when applied to the COMPANY database state shown in Figure 4.6. (a) Q0. (b) Q1. (c) Q2. (d) Q8. (e) Q9. (f) Q10. (g) Q1C.

shown in Q1A. We must prefix the attributes NAME and DNUMBER in Q1A to specify which ones we are referring to, because the attribute names are used in both relations:

Q1A: **SELECT** FNAME, EMPLOYEE.NAME, ADDRESS
      FROM EMPLOYEE, DEPARTMENT
      WHERE DEPARTMENT.NAME='Research' **AND**
                DEPARTMENT.DNUMBER=EMPLOYEE.DNUMBER;

Ambiguity also arises in the case of queries that refer to the same relation twice, as in the following example.

QUERY 8

For each employee, retrieve the employee's first and last name and the first and last name of his or her immediate supervisor.

Q8:   **SELECT**   E.FNAME, E.LNAME, S.FNAME, S.LNAME
      FROM   EMPLOYEE **AS** E, EMPLOYEE **AS** S
      WHERE   E.SUPERENO=S.ENO;

In this case, we are allowed to declare alternative relation names E and S, called aliases or tuple variables, for the EMPLOYEE relation. An alias can follow the keyword AS, as shown in Q8, or it can directly follow the relation name—for example, by writing EMPLOYEE E, EMPLOYEE S in the FROM clause of Q8. It is also possible to rename the relation attributes within the query in SQL by giving them aliases. For example, if we write

EMPLOYEE **AS** E(FN, MI, LN, ENO, DOB, ADDR, SEX, SAL, EENO, DNO)

in the FROM clause, FN becomes an alias for DOB, MI for INITIAL, LN for LNAME, and so on.

In Q8, we can think of E and S as two *different copies* of the EMPLOYEE relation; the first, E, represents employees in the role of supervisees; the second, S, represents employees in the role of supervisors. We can now join the two copies. Of course, in reality there is *only one* EMPLOYEE relation, and the join condition is meant to join the relation with itself by matching the tuples that satisfy the join condition E.SUPERENO = S.ENO. Notice that this is an example of a one-level recursive query, as we discussed in Section 5.4.2. In earlier versions of SQL, as in relational algebra, it was not possible to specify a general recursive query, with an unknown number of levels, in a single SQL statement. A construct for specifying recursive queries has been incorporated into SQL-99.

The result of query Q8 is shown in Figure 7.3d. Whenever one or more aliases are given to a relation, we can use these names to represent different references to that relation. This permits multiple references to the same relation within a query. Notice that, if we want to, we can use this alias-naming mechanism in any SQL query to specify tuple variables for every table in the WHERE clause, whether or not the same relation needs to be referenced more than once. In fact, this practice is recommended since it results in queries that are easier to comprehend. For example, we could specify query Q1A as in Q1B:

Q1B: **SELECT**   E.FNAME, E.NAME, E.ADDRESS
       FROM   EMPLOYEE E, DEPARTMENT D
       WHERE   D.NAME='Research' **AND** D.DNUMBER=E.DNUMBER;

If we specify tuple variables for every table in the WHERE clause, a select-project-join query in SQL closely resembles the corresponding tuple relational calculus expression (except for duplicate elimination). For example, compare Q1B with the following tuple relational calculus expression:

Q1:   {**e**.FNAME, **e**.LNAME, **e**.ADDRESS | EMPLOYEE(**e**) **AND** (∃d)
       (DEPARTMENT(d) **AND** d.DNAME='Research' **AND** d.DNUMBER=**e**.DNO) }

Notice that the main difference—other than syntax—is that in the SQL query, the existential quantifier is not specified explicitly.

7.4.3   Unspecified WHERE Clause and Use of the Asterisk

We discuss two more features of SQL here. A *missing* WHERE clause indicates no condition on tuple selection; hence, *all tuples* of the relation specified in the FROM clause qualify and are selected for the query result. If more than one relation is specified in the FROM clause and there is no WHERE clause, then the CROSS

PRODUCT—all *possible tuple combinations*—of these relations is selected. For example, Query 9 selects all EMPLOYEE ENOs (Figure 7.3e), and Query 10 selects all combinations of an EMPLOYEE ENO and a DEPARTMENT DNAME (Figure 7.3f).

QUERIES 9 AND 10

Select all EMPLOYEE numbers (ENOs) (Q9), and all combinations of EMPLOYEE number (ENO) and DEPARTMENT DNAME (Q10) in the database.

Q9: **SELECT** ENO
     FROM   EMPLOYEE;

Q10: **SELECT** ENO, DNAME
     FROM   EMPLOYEE, DEPARTMENT;

It is extremely important to specify every selection and join condition in the WHERE clause; if any such condition is overlooked, incorrect and very large relations may result. Notice that Q10 is similar to a CROSS PRODUCT operation followed by a PROJECT operation in relational algebra. If we specify all the attributes of EMPLOYEE and DEPARTMENT in Q10, we get the CROSS PRODUCT (except for duplicate elimination, if any).

To retrieve all the attribute values of the selected tuples, we do not have to list the attribute names explicitly in SQL; we just specify an asterisk (*), which stands for *all the attributes.* For example, query Q1C retrieves all the attribute values of any EMPLOYEE who works in DEPARTMENT number 5 (Figure 7.3g), query Q1D retrieves all the attributes of an EMPLOYEE and the attributes of the DEPARTMENT in which he or she works for every employee of the 'Research' department, and Q10A specifies the CROSS PRODUCT of the EMPLOYEE and DEPARTMENT relations.

Q1C: **SELECT**   *
      FROM   EMPLOYEE
      WHERE   DNO=5;

Q1D: **SELECT**   *
      FROM   EMPLOYEE, DEPARTMENT
      WHERE   DNAME='Research' **AND** DNO=DNUMBER;

Q10A: **SELECT**   *
      FROM   EMPLOYEE, DEPARTMENT;

7.4.4   Tables as Sets in SQL

As we mentioned earlier, SQL usually treats a table not as a set but rather as a **multiset;** *duplicate tuples can appear more than once* in a table, and in the result of a query. SQL does not automatically eliminate duplicate tuples in the results of queries, for the following reasons:

- Duplicate elimination is an expensive operation. One way to implement it is to sort the tuples first and then eliminate duplicates.

- The user may want to see duplicate tuples in the result of a query.

- When an aggregate function (see Section 7.5.7) is applied to tuples, in most cases we do not want to eliminate duplicates.

An SQL table with a key is restricted to being a set, since the key value must be distinct in each tuple.[8] If we *do want* to eliminate duplicate tuples from the result of an SQL query, we use the keyword **DISTINCT** in the SELECT clause, meaning that only distinct tuples should remain in the result. In general, a query with SELECT DISTINCT eliminates duplicates, whereas a query with SELECT ALL does not. Specifying SELECT with neither ALL nor DISTINCT—as in our previous examples—is equivalent to SELECT ALL. For example, Query 11 retrieves the salary of every employee; if several employees have the same salary, that salary value will appear as many times in the result of the query, as shown in Figure 7.4a. If we are interested only in distinct salary values, we want each value to appear only once, regardless of how many employees earn that salary. By using the keyword DISTINCT as in Q11A, we accomplish this, as shown in Figure 7.4b.

QUERY 11

Retrieve the salary of every employee (Q11) and all distinct salary values (Q11A).

Q11:   **SELECT   ALL** SALARY
　　　　FROM 　　EMPLOYEE;

Q11A: **SELECT   DISTINCT** SALARY
　　　　FROM 　　EMPLOYEE;

SQL has directly incorporated some of the set operations of relational algebra. There are set union (**UNION**), set difference (**EXCEPT**), and set intersection (**INTERSECT**) operations. The relations resulting from these set operations are sets of tuples; that is, *duplicate tuples are eliminated from the result*. Because these set operations apply only to *union-compatible relations*, we must make sure that the two relations on which we apply the operation have the same attributes and that the attributes appear in the same order in both relations. The next example illustrates the use of UNION.

QUERY 4

Make a list of all project numbers for projects that involve an employee whose last name is 'Kumar', either as a worker or as a manager of the department that controls the project.

(a) SALARY	(b) SALARY
30000	30000
40000	40000
25000	25000
43000	43000
38000	38000
25000	55000
25000	
55000	

(c) FNAME	LNAME	(d) FNAME	LNAME
		Gaurav	Kishan

FIGURE 7.4 Results of additional SQL queries when applied to the COMPANY database state shown in Figure 4.6. (a) Q11. (b) Q11A. (c) Q16. (d) Q18.

---

8. In general, an SQL table is not required to have a key, although in most cases there will be one.

Q4:   (**SELECT DISTINCT** PNUMBER
        FROM   PROJECT, DEPARTMENT, EMPLOYEE
        WHERE   DNUM=DNUMBER **AND** MGRENO=ENO **AND** LNAME='Kumar')
        UNION
        (**SELECT DISTINCT** PNUMBER
        FROM   PROJECT, WORKS_ON, EMPLOYEE
        WHERE   PNUMBER=PNO **AND** EENO=ENO **AND** LNAME='Kumar');

The first SELECT query retrieves the projects that involve a 'Kumar' as manager of the department that controls the project, and the second retrieves the projects that involve a 'Kumar' as a worker on the project. Notice that if several employees have the last name 'Kumar', the project names involving any of them will be retrieved. Applying the UNION operation to the two SELECT queries gives the desired result.

SQL also has corresponding multiset operations, which are followed by the keyword ALL (UNION ALL, EXCEPT ALL, INTERSECT ALL). Their results are multisets (duplicates are not eliminated). The behavior of these operations is illustrated by the examples in Figure 7.5. Basically, each tuple—whether it is a duplicate or not—is considered as a different tuple when applying these operations.

FIGURE 7.5 The results of SQL multiset operations. (a) Two tables, R(A) and S(A). (b) R(A) UNION ALL S(A). (c) R(A) EXCEPT ALL S(A). (d) R(A) INTERSECT ALL S(A).

7.4.5 Substring Pattern Matching and Arithmetic Operators

In this section we discuss several more features of SQL. The first feature allows comparison conditions on only parts of a character string, using the **LIKE** comparison operator. This can be used for string **pattern matching**. Partial strings are specified using two reserved characters: % replaces an arbitrary number of zero or more characters, and the underscore (_) replaces a single character. For example, consider the following query.

QUERY 12

Retrieve all employees whose address is in Hyderabad, AP.

Q12:   **SELECT**   FNAME, LNAME
         FROM   EMPLOYEE
         WHERE   ADDRESS LIKE '%Hyderabad,AP%';

To retrieve all employees who were born during the 1950s, we can use Query 12A. Here, '5' must be the third character of the string (according to our format for date), so we use the value '‑‑‑‑‑‑‑‑5‑', with each underscore serving as a placeholder for an arbitrary character.

QUERY 12A

Find all employees who were born during the 1950s.

Q12A: **SELECT**   FNAME, LNAME
         FROM   EMPLOYEE
         WHERE   DOB LIKE '‑‑‑‑‑‑‑‑5‑';

If an underscore or % is needed as a literal character in the string, the character should be preceded by an *escape character*, which is specified after the string using the keyword ESCAPE. For example, 'AB_CD\%EF' ESCAPE '\' represents the literal string 'AB_CD%EF', because \ is specified as the escape character. Any character not used in the string can be chosen as the escape character. Also, we need a rule to specify apostrophes or single quotation marks (") if they are to be included in a string, because they are used to begin and end strings. If an apostrophe (') is needed, it is represented as two consecutive apostrophes ('') so that it will not be interpreted as ending the string.

Another feature allows the use of arithmetic in queries. The standard arithmetic operators for addition (+), subtraction (–), multiplication (*), and division (/) can be applied to numeric values or attributes with numeric domains. For example, suppose that we want to see the effect of giving all employees who work on the 'ProductX' project a 10 percent raise; we can issue Query 13 to see what their salaries would become. This example also shows how we can rename an attribute in the query result using AS in the SELECT clause.

QUERY 13

Show the resulting salaries if every employee working on the 'ProductX' project is given a 10 percent raise.

Q13:   **SELECT**   FNAME, LNAME, 1.1*SALARY **AS** INCREASED_SAL
         FROM   EMPLOYEE, WORKS_ON, PROJECT
         WHERE   ENO=EENO **AND** PNO=PNUMBER **AND**
                        PNAME='ProductX';

For string data types, the concatenate operator | | can be used in a query to append two string values. For date, time, timestamp, and interval data types, operators include incrementing (+) or decrementing (–) a date, time, or timestamp by an interval. In addition, an interval value is the result of the difference between two date, time, or timestamp values. Another comparison operator that can be used for convenience is BETWEEN, which is illustrated in Query 14.

QUERY 14

Retrieve all employees in department 5 whose salary is between Rs 30,000 and Rs 40,000.

Q14:   SELECT   *
             FROM   EMPLOYEE
             WHERE   (SALARY BETWEEN 30000 **AND** 40000) AND DNO = 5;

The condition (SALARY BETWEEN 30000 **AND** 40000) in Q14 is equivalent to the condition ((SALARY >= 30000) **AND** (SALARY <= 40000)).

7.4.6 Ordering of Query Results

SQL allows the user to order the tuples in the result of a query by the values of one or more attributes, using the **ORDER BY** clause. This is illustrated by Query 15.

QUERY 15

Retrieve a list of employees and the projects they are working on, ordered by department and, within each department, ordered alphabetically by last name, first name.

Q15:   SELECT   DNAME, LNAME, FNAME, PNAME
            FROM   DEPARTMENT, EMPLOYEE, WORKS_ON, PROJECT
            WHERE   DNUMBER=DNO AND ENO=EENO AND PNO=PNUMBER
            ORDER BY DNAME, LNAME, FNAME;

The default order is in ascending order of values. We can specify the keyword DESC if we want to see the result in a descending order of values. The keyword ASC can be used to specify ascending order explicitly. For example, if we want descending order on DNAME and ascending order on LNAME, FNAME, the ORDER BY clause of Q15 can be written as

ORDER BY DNAME **DESC**, LNAME **ASC**, FNAME **ASC**

7.5 MORE COMPLEX SQL QUERIES

In the previous section, we described some basic types of queries in SQL. Because of the generality and expressive power of the language, there are many additional features that allow users to specify more complex queries. We discuss several of these features in this section.

7.5.1 Comparisons Involving NULL and Three-Valued Logic

SQL has various rules for dealing with NULL values. Recall from Section 4.1.2 that NULL is used to represent a missing value, but that it usually has one of three different interpretations—value unknown (exists but is not known), value not available (exists but is purposely withheld), or attribute not applicable (undefined for this tuple). Consider the following examples to illustrate each of the three meanings of NULL.

1. *Unknown value:* A particular person has a date of birth but it is not known, so it is represented by NULL in the database.

2. *Unavailable or withheld value:* A person has a home phone but does not want it to be listed, so it is withheld and represented as NULL in the database.

3. *Not applicable attribute:* An attribute LastCollegeDegree would be NULL for a person who has no college degrees, because it does not apply to that person.

It is often not possible to determine which of the three meanings is intended; for example, a NULL for the home phone of a person can have any of the three meanings. Hence, SQL does not distinguish between the different meanings of NULL.

In general, each NULL is considered to be different from every other NULL in the database. When a NULL is involved in a comparison operation, the result is considered to be UNKNOWN (it may be TRUE or it may be FALSE). Hence, SQL uses a three-valued logic with values TRUE, FALSE, and UNKNOWN instead of the standard two-valued logic with values TRUE or FALSE. It is therefore necessary to define the results of three-valued logical expressions when the logical connectives AND, OR, and NOT are used. Table 7.1 shows the resulting values.

TABLE 7.1 LOGICAL CONNECTIVES IN THREE-VALUED LOGIC

AND	TRUE	FALSE	UNKNOWN
TRUE	TRUE	FALSE	UNKNOWN
FALSE	FALSE	FALSE	FALSE
UNKNOWN	UNKNOWN	FALSE	UNKNOWN

OR	TRUE	FALSE	UNKNOWN
TRUE	TRUE	TRUE	TRUE
FALSE	TRUE	FALSE	UNKNOWN
UNKNOWN	TRUE	UNKNOWN	UNKNOWN

NOT	
TRUE	FALSE
FALSE	TRUE
UNKNOWN	UNKNOWN

In select-project-join queries, the general rule is that only those combinations of tuples that evaluate the logical expression of the query to TRUE are selected. Tuple combinations that evaluate to FALSE or UNKNOWN are not selected. However, there are exceptions to that rule for certain operations, such as outer joins, as we shall see.

SQL allows queries that check whether an attribute value is **NULL**. Rather than using = or < > to compare an attribute value to NULL, SQL uses **IS** or **IS NOT**. This is because SQL considers each NULL value as being distinct from every other NULL value, so equality comparison is not appropriate. It follows that when a join condition is specified, tuples with NULL values for the join attributes are not included in the result (unless it is an OUTER JOIN; see Section 7.5.6). Query 18 illustrates this; its result is shown in Figure 7.4d.

QUERY 18

Retrieve the names of all employees who do not have supervisors.

Q18: SELECT   FNAME, LNAME
      FROM   EMPLOYEE
      WHERE   SUPERENO IS NULL;

7.5.2 Nested Queries, Tuples, and Set/Multiset Comparisons

Some queries require that existing values in the database be fetched and then used in a comparison condition. Such queries can be conveniently formulated by using **nested queries**, which are complete select-from-where blocks within the WHERE clause of another query. That other query is called the **outer query**. Query 4 is formulated in Q4 without a nested query, but it can be rephrased to use nested queries as shown in Q4A. Q4A introduces the comparison operator **IN**, which compares a value v with a set (or multiset) of values V and evaluates to **TRUE** if v is one of the elements in V.

```
Q4A:   SELECT    DISTINCT PNUMBER
       FROM      PROJECT
       WHERE     PNUMBER IN  (SELECT  PNUMBER
                              FROM     PROJECT, DEPARTMENT,
                                       EMPLOYEE
                              WHERE    DNUM=DNUMBER AND
                                       MGRENO=ENO AND
                                       LNAME='Kumar')

       OR
       PNUMBER IN  (SELECT   PNO
                    FROM      WORKS_ON, EMPLOYEE
                    WHERE     EENO=ENO AND
                              LNAME='Kumar');
```

The first nested query selects the project numbers of projects that have a 'Kumar' involved as manager, while the second selects the project numbers of projects that have a 'Kumar' involved as worker. In the outer query, we use the **OR** logical connective to retrieve a PROJECT tuple if the PNUMBER value of that tuple is in the result of either nested query.

If a nested query returns a single attribute *and* a single tuple, the query result will be a single (scalar) value. In such cases, it is permissible to use = instead of IN for the comparison operator. In general, the nested query will return a **table** (relation), which is a set or multiset of tuples.

SQL allows the use of **tuples** of values in comparisons by placing them within parentheses. To illustrate this, consider the following query:

```
SELECT   DISTINCT EENO
FROM     WORKS_ON
WHERE    (PNO, HOURS) IN (SELECT PNO, HOURS FROM WORKS_ON
                          WHERE ENO='123456789');
```

This query will select the employee numbers of all employees who work the same (project, hours) combination on some project that employee 'Mahesh Kumar' (whose ENO = '123456789') works on. In this example, the IN operator compares the subtuple of values in parentheses (PNO, HOURS) for each tuple in WORKS_ON with the set of union-compatible tuples produced by the nested query.

In addition to the IN operator, a number of other comparison operators can be used to compare a single value v (typically an attribute name) to a set or multiset V (typically a nested query). The = ANY (or = SOME) operator returns TRUE if the value v is equal to *some value* in the set V and is hence equivalent to IN. The keywords ANY and SOME have the same meaning. Other operators that can be combined with ANY (or SOME) include >, >=, <, <=, and <>. The keyword ALL can also be combined with each of these operators. For example, the comparison condition (v > ALL V) returns TRUE if the value v is greater than *all* the values in the set (or multiset) *V*. An example is the following query, which returns the names of employees whose salary is greater than the salary of all the employees in department 5:

> **SELECT**   LNAME, FNAME
> **FROM**   EMPLOYEE
> **WHERE**   SALARY > **ALL** (**SELECT** SALARY **FROM EMPLOYEE**
>   **WHERE** DNO=5);

In general, we can have several levels of nested queries. We can once again be faced with possible ambiguity among attribute names if attributes of the same name exist—one in a relation in the FROM clause of the *outer query*, and another in a relation in the FROM clause of the *nested query*. The rule is that a reference to an *unqualified attribute* refers to the relation declared in the **innermost nested query.** For example, in the SELECT clause and WHERE clause of the first nested query of Q4A, a reference to any unqualified attribute of the PROJECT relation refers to the PROJECT relation specified in the FROM clause of the nested query. To refer to an attribute of the PROJECT relation specified in the outer query, we can specify and refer to an *alias* (tuple variable) for that relation. These rules are similar to scope rules for program variables in most programming languages that allow nested procedures and functions. To illustrate the potential ambiguity of attribute names in nested queries, consider Query 16, whose result is shown in Figure 7.4c.

QUERY 16

Retrieve the name of each employee who has a dependent with the same first name and same sex as the employee.

> Q16:   **SELECT**   E.FNAME, E.LNAME
>   **FROM**   EMPLOYEE AS E
>   **WHERE**   E. ENO **IN**   (**SELECT**   EENO
>   **FROM**   DEPENDENT
>   **WHERE**   E.FNAME=DEPENDENT_NAME
>   **AND** E.SEX=SEX);

In the nested query of Q16, we must qualify E.SEX because it refers to the SEX attribute of EMPLOYEE from the outer query, and DEPENDENT also has an attribute called SEX. All unqualified references to SEX in the nested query refer to SEX of DEPENDENT. However, we do not have to qualify FNAME and ENO because the DEPENDENT relation does not have attributes called FNAME and ENO, so there is no ambiguity.

It is generally advisable to create tuple variables (aliases) for *all the tables referenced in an SQL query* to avoid potential errors and ambiguities.

7.5.3   Correlated Nested Queries

Whenever a condition in the WHERE clause of a nested query references some attribute of a relation declared in the outer query, the two queries are said to be **correlated.** We can understand a correlated query better by considering that the *nested query is evaluated once for each tuple* (or *combination of tuples*) in the *outer query*. For example, we can think of Q16 as follows: For each EMPLOYEE tuple, evaluate the nested query, which retrieves the EENO values for all DEPENDENT tuples with the same sex and name as that EMPLOYEE tuple; if the ENO value of the EMPLOYEE tuple is *in* the result of the nested query, then select that EMPLOYEE tuple.

In general, a query written with nested select-from-where blocks and using the = or IN comparison operators can *always* be expressed as a single block query. For example, Q16 may be written as in Q16A:

Q16A:	SELECT	E.FNAME, E.LNAME
	FROM	EMPLOYEE AS E, DEPENDENT AS D
	WHERE	E.ENO=D.EENO AND E.SEX=D.SEX AND
		E.FNAME=D.DEPENDENT_NAME;

The original SQL implementation on SYSTEM R also had a CONTAINS comparison operator, which was used to compare two sets or multisets. This operator was subsequently dropped from the language, possibly because of the difficulty of implementing it efficiently. Most commercial implementations of SQL do *not* have this operator. The CONTAINS operator compares two sets of values and returns TRUE if one set contains all values in the other set. Query 3 illustrates the use of the CONTAINS operator.

QUERY 3

Retrieve the name of each employee who works on *all* the projects controlled by department number 5.

Q3:	SELECT	FNAME, LNAME	
	FROM	EMPLOYEE	
	WHERE	(	(SELECT	PNO
			FROM	WORKS_ON
			WHERE	ENO=EENO)
			CONTAINS	
			(SELECT	PNUMBER
			FROM	PROJECT
			WHERE	DNUM=5));

In Q3, the second nested query (which is not correlated with the outer query) retrieves the project numbers of all projects controlled by department 5. For *each* employee tuple, the first nested query (which is correlated) retrieves the project numbers on which the employee works; if these contain all projects controlled by department 5, the employee tuple is selected and the name of that employee is retrieved. Notice that the CONTAINS comparison operator has a similar function to the DIVISION operation of the relational algebra (see Section 5.3.4) and to universal quantification in relational calculus (see Section 5.6.6). Because the CONTAINS operation is not part of SQL, we have to use other techniques, such as the EXISTS function, to specify these types of queries, as described in Section 7.5.4.

7.5.4 The EXISTS and UNIQUE Functions in SQL

The EXISTS function in SQL is used to check whether the result of a correlated nested query is empty (contains no tuples) or not. We illustrate the use of EXISTS—and NOT EXISTS—with some examples. First, we formulate Query 16 in an alternative form that uses EXISTS. This is shown as Q16B:

Q16B:	SELECT	E.FNAME, E.LNAME	
	FROM	EMPLOYEE AS E	
	WHERE	EXISTS	(SELECT	*
			FROM	DEPENDENT
			WHERE	E.ENO=EENO AND E.SEX=SEX
				AND E.FNAME=DEPENDENT_NAME);

EXISTS and NOT EXISTS are usually used in conjunction with a correlated nested query. In Q16B, the nested query references the ENO, FNAME, and SEX attributes of the EMPLOYEE relation from the outer query. We can think of Q16B as follows: For each EMPLOYEE tuple, evaluate the nested query, which retrieves all

DEPENDENT tuples with the same employee number, sex, and name as the EMPLOYEE tuple; if at least one tuple EXISTS in the result of the nested query, then select that EMPLOYEE tuple. In general, EXISTS(Q) returns **TRUE** if there is at least one tuple in the result of the nested query Q, and it returns **FALSE** otherwise. On the other hand, NOT EXISTS(Q) returns TRUE if there are *no tuples* in the result of nested query Q, and it returns **FALSE** otherwise. Next, we illustrate the use of NOT EXISTS.

QUERY 6

Retrieve the names of employees who have no dependents.

Q6:   SELECT   FNAME, LNAME
         FROM   EMPLOYEE
         WHERE   NOT EXISTS   (SELECT   *
                                     FROM   DEPENDENT
                                     WHERE   ENO=EENO);

In Q6, the correlated nested query retrieves all DEPENDENT tuples related to a particular EMPLOYEE tuple. If none exist, the EMPLOYEE tuple is selected. We can explain Q6 as follows: For each EMPLOYEE tuple, the correlated nested query selects all DEPENDENT tuples whose EENO value matches the EMPLOYEE ENO; if the result is empty, no dependents are related to the employee, so we select that EMPLOYEE tuple and retrieve its FNAME and LNAME.

QUERY 7

List the names of managers who have at least one dependent.

Q7:   SELECT   FNAME, LNAME
         FROM   EMPLOYEE
         WHERE   EXISTS   (SELECT   *
                                 FROM   DEPENDENT
                                 WHERE   ENO=EENO)
                      AND
                      EXISTS   (SELECT   *
                                 FROM   DEPARTMENT
                                 WHERE   ENO=MGRENO);

One way to write this query is shown in Q7, where we specify two nested correlated queries; the first selects all DEPENDENT tuples related to an EMPLOYEE, and the second selects all DEPARTMENT tuples managed by the EMPLOYEE. If at least one of the first and at least one of the second exists, we select the EMPLOYEE tuple. Can you rewrite this query using only a single nested query or no nested queries?

Query 3 ("Retrieve the name of each employee who works on *all* the projects controlled by department number 5," see Section 7.5.3) can be stated using EXISTS and NOT EXISTS in SQL systems. There are two options. The first is to use the well-known set theory transformation that (S1 CONTAINS S2) is logically equivalent to (S2 EXCEPT S1) is empty.[9] This option is shown as Q3A.

Q3A: SELECT   FNAME, LNAME
         FROM   EMPLOYEE
         WHERE   NOT EXISTS

---

9. Recall that EXCEPT is the set difference operator.

```
                    (SELECT    PNUMBER
                     FROM      PROJECT
                     WHERE     DNUM=5)
        EXCEPT
                    (SELECT    PNO
                     FROM      WORKS_ON
                     WHERE     ENO=EENO) );
```

In Q3A, the first subquery (which is not correlated) selects all projects controlled by department 5, and the second subquery (which is correlated) selects all projects that the particular employee being considered works on. If the set difference of the first subquery MINUS (EXCEPT) the second subquery is empty, it means that the employee works on all the projects and is hence selected.

The second option is shown as Q3B. Notice that we need two-level nesting in Q3B and that this formulation is quite a bit more complex than Q3, which used the CONTAINS comparison operator, and Q3A, which uses NOT EXISTS and EXCEPT. However, CONTAINS is not part of SQL, and not all relational systems have the EXCEPT operator even though it is part of SQL-99.

```
Q3B:    SELECT    LNAME, FNAME
        FROM      EMPLOYEE
        WHERE     NOT EXISTS
        (SELECT   *
        FROM      WORKS_ON B
        WHERE     (B.PNO IN   (SELECT    PNUMBER
                               FROM      PROJECT
                               WHERE     DNUM=5) )
                  AND
        NOT EXISTS (SELECT    *
                    FROM      WORKS_ON C
                    WHERE     C.EENO=ENO
                    AND       C.PNO=B.PNO) );
```

In Q3B, the outer nested query selects any WORKS_ON (B) tuples whose PNO is of a project controlled by department 5, *if* there is not a WORKS_ON (C) tuple with the same PNO and the same ENO as that of the EMPLOYEE tuple under consideration in the outer query. If no such tuple exists, we select the EMPLOYEE tuple. The form of Q3B matches the following rephrasing of Query 3: Select each employee such that there does not exist a project controlled by department 5 that the employee does not work on. It corresponds to the way we wrote this query in tuple relation calculus in Section 5.6.6.

There is another SQL function, UNIQUE(Q), which returns TRUE if there are no duplicate tuples in the result of query Q; otherwise, it returns FALSE. This can be used to test whether the result of a nested query is a set or a multiset.

7.5.5 Explicit Sets and Renaming of Attributes in SQL

We have seen several queries with a nested query in the WHERE clause. It is also possible to use an **explicit set of values** in the WHERE clause, rather than a nested query. Such a set is enclosed in parentheses in SQL.

QUERY 17

Retrieve the employee numbers (ENOs) of all employees who work on project numbers 1, 2, or 3.

Q17:   **SELECT**   DISTINCT EENO
       FROM   WORKS_ON
       WHERE   PNO **IN** (1, 2, 3);

In SQL, it is possible to rename any attribute that appears in the result of a query by adding the qualifier AS followed by the desired new name. Hence, the AS construct can be used to alias both attribute and relation names, and it can be used in both the SELECT and FROM clauses. For example, Q8A shows how query Q8 can be slightly changed to retrieve the last name of each employee and his or her supervisor, while renaming the resulting attribute names as EMPLOYEE_NAME and SUPERVISOR_NAME. The new names will appear as column headers in the query result.

Q8A: **SELECT**   E.LNAME **AS** EMPLOYEE_NAME, S.LNAME **AS**
                    SUPERVISOR_NAME
       FROM   EMPLOYEE AS E, EMPLOYEE **AS** S
       WHERE   E.SUPERENO=S.ENO;

7.5.6   **Joined Tables in** SQL

The concept of a **joined table** (or **joined relation**) was incorporated into SQL to permit users to specify a table resulting from a join operation *in the FROM clause* of a query. This construct may be easier to comprehend than mixing together all the select and join conditions in the WHERE clause. For example, consider query Q1, which retrieves the name and address of every employee who works for the 'Research' department. It may be easier first to specify the join of the EMPLOYEE and DEPARTMENT relations, and then to select the desired tuples and attributes. This can be written in SQL as in Q1A:

Q1A: **SELECT**   FNAME, LNAME, ADDRESS
       FROM   (EMPLOYEE **JOIN** DEPARTMENT **ON** DNO=DNUMBER)
       WHERE   DNAME='Research';

The FROM clause in Q1A contains a single *joined table*. The attributes of such a table are all the attributes of the first table, EMPLOYEE, followed by all the attributes of the second table, DEPARTMENT. The concept of a joined table also allows the user to specify different types of join, such as NATURAL JOIN and various types of OUTER JOIN. In a NATURAL JOIN on two relations R and S, no join condition is specified; an implicit equijoin condition for *each pair of attributes with the same name* from R and S is created. Each such pair of attributes is included only once in the resulting relation (see Section 5.4.3).

If the names of the join attributes are not the same in the base relations, it is possible to rename the attributes so that they match, and then to apply NATURAL JOIN. In this case, the AS construct can be used to rename a relation and all its attributes in the FROM clause. This is illustrated in Q1B, where the DEPARTMENT relation is renamed as DEPT and its attributes are renamed as DNAME, DNO (to match the name of the desired join attribute DNO in EMPLOYEE), MENO, and MSDATE. The implied join condition for this NATURAL JOIN is EMPLOYEE.DNO = DEPT.DNO, because this is the only pair of attributes with the same name after renaming.

Q1B:	SELECT	FNAME, LNAME, ADDRESS
	FROM	(EMPLOYEE **NATURAL JOIN**
		(DEPARTMENT **AS** DEPT (DNAME, DNO, MENO, MSDATE)))
	WHERE	DNAME='Research;

The default type of join in a joined table is an **inner join,** where a tuple is included in the result only if a matching tuple exists in the other relation. For example, in query Q8A, only employees that *have a supervisor* are included in the result; an EMPLOYEE tuple whose value for SUPERENO is NULL is excluded. If the user requires that all employees be included, an OUTER JOIN must be used explicitly (see Section 5.4.3 for the definition of OUTER JOIN). In SQL, this is handled by explicitly specifying the OUTER JOIN in a joined table, as illustrated in Q8B:

Q8B:	SELECT	E.LNAME **AS** EMPLOYEE_NAME,
		S.LNAME **AS** SUPERVISOR_NAME
	FROM	(EMPLOYEE **AS** E **LEFT OUTER JOIN** EMPLOYEE **AS** S
		ON E.SUPERENO=S.ENO);

The options available for specifying joined tables in SQL include INNER JOIN (same as JOIN), LEFT OUTER JOIN, RIGHT OUTER JOIN, and FULL OUTER JOIN. In the latter three options, the keyword OUTER may be omitted. If the join attributes have the same name, one may also specify the natural join variation of outer joins by using the keyword NATURAL before the operation (for example, NATURAL LEFT OUTER JOIN). The keyword CROSS JOIN is used to specify the Cartesian product operation (see Section 5.2.2), although this should be used only with the utmost care because it generates all possible tuple combinations.

It is also possible to *nest* join specifications; that is, one of the tables in a join may itself be a joined table. This is illustrated by Q2A, which is a different way of specifying query Q2, using the concept of a joined table:

Q2A:	SELECT	PNUMBER, DNUM, LNAME, ADDRESS
	FROM	((PROJECT JOIN DEPARTMENT **ON** DNUM=DNUMBER)
		JOIN EMPLOYEE ON MGRENO=ENO)
	WHERE	PLOCATION='Chennai';

7.5.7 Aggregate Functions in SQL

In Section 5.4.1, we introduced the concept of an aggregate function as a relational operation. Because grouping and aggregation are required in many database applications, SQL has features that incorporate these concepts. A number of built-in functions exist: **COUNT, SUM, MAX, MIN,** and **AVG.**[10] The COUNT function returns the number of tuples or values as specified in a query. The functions SUM, MAX, MIN, and AVG are applied to a set or multiset of numeric values and return, respectively, the sum, maximum value, minimum value, and average (mean) of those values. These functions can be used in the SELECT clause or in a HAVING clause (which we introduce later). The functions MAX and MIN can also be used with attributes that have nonnumeric domains if the domain values have a *total ordering* among one another.[11] We illustrate the use of these functions with example queries.

---

10. Additional aggregate functions for more advanced statistical calculation have been added in SQL-99.

11. Total order means that for any two values in the domain, it can be determined that one appears before the other in the defined order; for example, DATE, TIME, and TIMESTAMP domains have total orderings on their values, as do alphabetic strings.

QUERY 19

Find the sum of the salaries of all employees, the maximum salary, the minimum salary, and the average salary.

Q19:   SELECT   SUM (SALARY), MAX (SALARY), MIN (SALARY),
                  AVG (SALARY)
        FROM   EMPLOYEE;

If we want to get the preceding function values for employees of a specific department—say, the 'Research' department—we can write Query 20, where the EMPLOYEE tuples are restricted by the WHERE clause to those employees who work for the 'Research' department.

QUERY 20

Find the sum of the salaries of all employees of the 'Research' department, as well as the maximum salary, the minimum salary, and the average salary in this department.

Q20:   SELECT   SUM (SALARY), MAX (SALARY), MIN (SALARY),
                  AVG (SALARY)
        FROM   (EMPLOYEE JOIN DEPARTMENT ON DNO=DNUMBER)
        WHERE   DNAME='Research';

QUERIES 21 AND 22

Retrieve the total number of employees in the company (Q21) and the number of employees in the 'Research' department (Q22).

Q21:   SELECT   COUNT (*)
        FROM   EMPLOYEE;
Q22:   SELECT   COUNT (*)
        FROM   EMPLOYEE, DEPARTMENT
        WHERE   DNO=DNUMBER AND DNAME='Research';

Here the asterisk (*) refers to the *rows* (tuples), so COUNT (*) returns the number of rows in the result of the query. We may also use the COUNT function to count values in a column rather than tuples, as in the next example.

QUERY 23

Count the number of distinct salary values in the database.

Q23:   SELECT   COUNT (DISTINCT SALARY)
        FROM   EMPLOYEE;

If we write COUNT(SALARY) instead of COUNT(DISTINCT SALARY) in Q23, then duplicate values will not be eliminated. However, any tuples with NULL for SALARY will not be counted. In general, NULL values are **discarded** when aggregate functions are applied to a particular column (attribute).

The preceding examples summarize *a whole relation* (Q19, Q21, Q23) or a selected subset of tuples (Q20, Q22), and hence all produce single tuples or single values. They illustrate how functions are applied to retrieve a summary value or summary tuple from the database. These functions can also be used in selection conditions involving nested queries. We can specify a correlated nested query with an aggregate function, and then use the nested query in the WHERE clause of an outer query. For example, to retrieve the names of all employees who have two or more dependents (Query 5), we can write the following:

```
Q5:      SELECT   LNAME, FNAME
         FROM     EMPLOYEE
         WHERE    (SELECT  COUNT (*)
                  FROM     DEPENDENT
                  WHERE    ENO=EENO) >= 2;
```

The correlated nested query counts the number of dependents that each employee has; if this is greater than or equal to two, the employee tuple is selected.

7.5.8 Grouping: The GROUP BY and HAVING Clauses

In many cases we want to apply the aggregate functions to *subgroups of tuples in a relation*, where the subgroups are based on some attribute values. For example, we may want to find the average salary of employees *in each department* or the number of employees who work *on each project*. In these cases we need to **partition** the relation into nonoverlapping subsets (or **groups**) of tuples. Each group (partition) will consist of the tuples that have the same value of some attribute(s), called the **grouping attribute**(s). We can then apply the function to each such group independently. SQL has a **GROUP BY** clause for this purpose. The GROUP BY clause specifies the grouping attributes, which should also appear in the SELECT clause, so that the value resulting from applying each aggregate function to a group of tuples appears along with the value of the grouping attribute(s).

QUERY 24

For each department, retrieve the department number, the number of employees in the department, and their average salary.

```
Q24:     SELECT   DNO, COUNT (*), AVG (SALARY)
         FROM     EMPLOYEE
         GROUP BY DNO;
```

In Q24, the EMPLOYEE tuples are partitioned into groups—each group having the same value for the grouping attribute DNO. The COUNT and AVG functions are applied to each such group of tuples. Notice that the SELECT clause includes only the grouping attribute and the functions to be applied on each group of tuples. Figure 7.6a illustrates how grouping works on Q24; it also shows the result of Q24.

If NULLs exist in the grouping attribute, then a **separate group** is created for all tuples with a NULL *value in the grouping attribute*. For example, if the EMPLOYEE table had some tuples that had NULL for the grouping attribute DNO, there would be a separate group for those tuples in the result of Q24.

QUERY 25

For each project, retrieve the project number, the project name, and the number of employees who work on that project.

```
Q25:     SELECT   PNUMBER, PNAME, COUNT (*)
         FROM     PROJECT, WORKS_ON
         WHERE    PNUMBER=PNO
         GROUP BY PNUMBER, PNAME;
```

Q25 shows how we can use a join condition in conjunction with GROUP BY. In this case, the grouping and functions are applied *after* the joining of the two relations. Sometimes we want to retrieve the values of these functions only for *groups that satisfy certain conditions*. For example, suppose that we want to modify Query 25 so that only projects with more than two employees appear in the result. SQL provides a **HAVING** clause, which can appear in conjunction with a GROUP BY clause, for this purpose. **HAVING** provides a condition on the group of tuples associated with each value of the grouping attributes. Only the groups that satisfy the condition are retrieved in the result of the query. This is illustrated by Query 26.

QUERY 26

For each project *on which more than two employees work*, retrieve the project number, the project name, and the number of employees who work on the project.

(a)

FNAME	INITIAL	LNAME	ENO	• • •	SALARY	SUPERENO	DNO
Mahesh	B	Kumar	123456789		30000	333445555	5
Karthik	T	Chandra	333445555		40000	888665555	5
Swetha	K	Narayan	666884444		38000	333445555	5
Priya	A	Ganesh	453453453	• • •	25000	333445555	5
Ramesh	J	Narayan	999887777		25000	987654321	4
Kiran	S	Goyal	987654321		43000	888665555	4
Jitendra	V	Nath	987987987		25000	987654321	4
Gaurav	E	Kishan	888665555		55000	null	1

DNO	COUNT (*)	AVG (SALARY)
5	4	33250
4	3	31000
1	1	55000

Result of Q24.

Grouping EMPLOYEE tuples by the value of DNO.

(b)

PNAME	PNUMBER		EENO	PNO	HOURS
ProductX	1		123456789	1	32.5
ProductX	1		453453453	1	20.0
ProductY	2		123456789	2	7.5
ProductY	2		453453453	2	20.0
ProductY	2		333445555	2	10.0
ProductZ	3		666884444	3	40.0
ProductZ	3		333445555	3	10.0
Computerization	10	• • •	333445555	10	10.0
Computerization	10		999887777	10	10.0
Computerization	10		987987987	10	35.0
Reorganization	20		333445555	20	10.0
Reorganization	20		987654321	20	15.0
Reorganization	20		888665555	20	null
Newbenefits	30		987987987	30	5.0
Newbenefits	30		987654321	30	20.0
Newbenefits	30		999887777	30	30.0

These groups are not selected by the HAVING condition of Q26.

After applying the WHERE clause but before applying HAVING.

PNAME	PNUMBER		EENO	PNO	HOURS
ProductY	2		123456789	2	7.5
ProductY	2		453453453	2	20.0
ProductY	2		333445555	2	10.0
Computerization	10	• • •	333445555	10	10.0
Computerization	10		999887777	10	10.0
Computerization	10		987987987	10	35.0
Reorganization	20		333445555	20	10.0
Reorganization	20		987654321	20	15.0
Reorganization	20		888665555	20	null
Newbenefits	30		987987987	30	5.0
Newbenefits	30		987654321	30	20.0
Newbenefits	30		999887777	30	30.0

PNAME	COUNT (*)
ProductY	3
Computerization	3
Reorganization	3
Newbenefits	3

Result of Q26 (PNUMBER not shown).

After applying the HAVING clause condition.

FIGURE 7.6 Results of GROUP BY and HAVING. (a) Q24. (b) Q26.

```
Q26:    SELECT      PNUMBER, PNAME, COUNT (*)
        FROM        PROJECT, WORKS_ON
        WHERE       PNUMBER=PNO
        GROUP BY    PNUMBER, PNAME
        HAVING      COUNT (*) > 2;
```

Notice that, while selection conditions in the WHERE clause limit the tuples to which functions are applied, the HAVING clause serves to choose *whole groups*. Figure 7.6b illustrates the use of HAVING and displays the result of Q26.

QUERY 27

For each project, retrieve the project number, the project name, and the number of employees from department 5 who work on the project.

```
Q27:    SELECT      PNUMBER, PNAME, COUNT (*)
        FROM        PROJECT, WORKS_ON, EMPLOYEE
        WHERE       PNUMBER=PNO AND ENO=EENO AND DNO=5
        GROUP BY    PNUMBER, PNAME;
```

Here we restrict the tuples in the relation (and hence the tuples in each group) to those that satisfy the condition specified in the WHERE clause—namely, that they work in department number 5. Notice that we must be extra careful when two different conditions apply (one to the function in the SELECT clause and another to the function in the HAVING clause). For example, suppose that we want to count the *total* number of employees whose salaries exceed Rs. 40,000 in each department, but only for departments where more than five employees work. Here, the condition (SALARY > 40000) applies only to the COUNT function in the SELECT clause. Suppose that we write the following *incorrect* query:

```
SELECT          DNAME, COUNT (*)
FROM            DEPARTMENT, EMPLOYEE
WHERE           DNUMBER=DNO AND SALARY>40000
GROUP BY        DNAME
HAVING          COUNT (*)T > 5;
```

This is incorrect because it will select only departments that have more than five employees who *each earn more than* Rs. 40,000. The rule is that the WHERE clause is executed first, to select individual tuples; the HAVING clause is applied later, to select individual groups of tuples. Hence, the tuples are already restricted to employees who earn more than Rs. 40,000, *before* the function in the HAVING clause is applied. One way to write this query correctly is to use a nested query, as shown in Query 28.

QUERY 28

For each department that has more than five employees, retrieve the department number and the number of its employees who are making more than Rs. 40,000.

```
Q28:    SELECT      DNUMBER, COUNT (*)
        FROM        DEPARTMENT, EMPLOYEE
        WHERE       DNUMBER=DNO AND SALARY>40000 AND
                    DNO IN   (SELECT     DNO
                              FROM       EMPLOYEE
                              GROUP BY   DNO
                              HAVING     COUNT (*) > 5)
        GROUP BY    DNUMBER;
```

7.5.9   Discussion and Summary of SQL Queries

A query in SQL can consist of up to six clauses, but only the first two—SELECT and FROM—are mandatory. The clauses are specified in the following order, with the clauses between square brackets [. . .] being optional:

> **SELECT** <ATTRIBUTE AND FUNCTION LIST>
> **FROM** <TABLE LIST>
> **[WHERE** <CONDITION>**]**
> **[GROUP BY** <GROUPING ATTRIBUTE(S)>**]**
> **[HAVING** <GROUP CONDITION>**]**
> **[ORDER BY** <ATTRIBUTE LIST>**]**;

The SELECT clause lists the attributes or functions to be retrieved. The FROM clause specifies all relations (tables) needed in the query, including joined relations, but not those in nested queries. The WHERE clause specifies the conditions for selection of tuples from these relations, including join conditions if needed. GROUP BY specifies grouping attributes, whereas HAVING specifies a condition on the groups being selected rather than on the individual tuples. The built-in aggregate functions COUNT, SUM, MIN, MAX, and AVG are used in conjunction with grouping, but they can also be applied to all the selected tuples in a query without a GROUP BY clause. Finally, ORDER BY specifies an order for displaying the result of a query.

A query is evaluated *conceptually*[12] by first applying the FROM clause (to identify all tables involved in the query or to materialize any joined tables), followed by the WHERE clause, and then by GROUP BY and HAVING. Conceptually, ORDER BY is applied at the end to sort the query result. If none of the last three clauses (GROUP BY, HAVING, and ORDER BY) are specified, we can *think conceptually* of a query as being executed as follows: For *each combination of tuples*—one from each of the relations specified in the FROM clause—evaluate the WHERE clause; if it evaluates to TRUE, place the values of the attributes specified in the SELECT clause from this tuple combination in the result of the query. Of course, this is not an efficient way to implement the query in a real system, and each DBMS has special query optimization routines to decide on an execution plan that is efficient. We discuss query processing and optimization in Chapter 10.

In general, there are numerous ways to specify the same query in SQL. This flexibility in specifying queries has advantages and disadvantages. The main advantage is that users can choose the technique with which they are most comfortable when specifying a query. For example, many queries may be specified with join conditions in the WHERE clause, or by using joined relations in the FROM clause, or with some form of nested queries and the IN comparison operator. Some users may be more comfortable with one approach, whereas others may be more comfortable with another. From the programmer's and the system's point of view regarding query optimization, it is generally preferable to write a query with as little nesting and implied ordering as possible.

The disadvantage of having numerous ways of specifying the same query is that this may confuse the user, who may not know which technique to use to specify particular types of queries. Another problem is that it may be more efficient to execute a query specified in one way than the same query specified in an alternative way. Ideally, this should not be the case: The DBMS should process the same query in the same way regardless of how the query is specified. But this is quite difficult in practice, since each DBMS has different methods for processing queries specified in different ways. Thus, an additional burden on the user is to determine which of the alternative specifications is the most efficient. Ideally, the user should worry only about specifying the

---

12. The actual order of query evaluation is implementation dependent; this is just a way to conceptually view a query in order to correctly formulate it.

query correctly. It is the responsibility of the DBMS to execute the query efficiently. In practice, however, it helps if the user is aware of which types of constructs in a query are more expensive to process than others (see Chapter 10).

7.6 INSERT, DELETE, AND UPDATE STATEMENTS IN SQL

In SQL, three commands can be used to modify the database: INSERT, DELETE, and UPDATE. We discuss each of these in turn.

7.6.1 The INSERT Command

In its simplest form, INSERT is used to add a single tuple to a relation. We must specify the relation name and a list of values for the tuple. The values should be listed *in the same order* in which the corresponding attributes were specified in the CREATE TABLE command. For example, to add a new tuple to the EMPLOYEE relation shown in Figure 4.5 and specified in the CREATE TABLE EMPLOYEE . . . command in Figure 7.1, we can use U1:

U1:	INSERT INTO	EMPLOYEE
	VALUES	('Govardhan,' 'K', 'Gaurav', '653298653', '30-12-1962', '98 Kacheguda, Hyderabad, AP', 'M' 37000, '987654321,' 4);

A second form of the INSERT statement allows the user to specify explicit attribute names that correspond to the values provided in the INSERT command. This is useful if a relation has many attributes but only a few of those attributes are assigned values in the new tuple. However, the values must include all attributes with NOT NULL specification *and* no default value. Attributes with NULL allowed or DEFAULT values are the ones that can be *left out*. For example, to enter a tuple for a new EMPLOYEE for whom we know only the FNAME, LNAME, DNO, and ENO attributes, we can use U1A:

U1A:	INSERT INTO	EMPLOYEE (FNAME, LNAME, DNO, ENO)
	VALUES	('Govardhan', 'Gaurav', 4, '653298653');

Attributes not specified in U1A are set to their DEFAULT or to NULL, and the values are listed in the same order as the *attributes are listed in* the INSERT command itself. It is also possible to insert into a relation *multiple tuples* separated by commas in a single INSERT command. The attribute values forming *each tuple* are enclosed in parentheses.

A DBMS that fully implements SQL-99 should support and enforce all the integrity constraints that can be specified in the DDL. However, some DBMSs do not incorporate all the constraints, in order to maintain the efficiency of the DBMS and because of the complexity of enforcing all constraints. If a system does not support some constraint say, referential integrity—the users or programmers must enforce the constraint. For example, if we issue the command in U2 on the database shown in Figure 4.6, a DBMS not supporting referential integrity will do the insertion even though no DEPARTMENT tuple exists in the database with DNUMBER = 2. It is the responsibility of the user to check that any such constraints *whose checks are not implemented by the* DBMS are not violated. However, the DBMS must implement checks to enforce all the SQL integrity constraints *it supports*. A DBMS enforcing NOT NULL will reject an INSERT command in which an attribute declared to be NOT NULL does not have a value; for example, U2A would be *rejected* because no ENO value is provided.

U2:	INSERT INTO	EMPLOYEE (FNAME, LNAME, ENO, DNO)
	VALUES	('Sai', 'Prasad', '980760540', 2);

(* U2 is rejected if referential integrity checking is provided by dbms *)

U2A:	INSERT INTO	EMPLOYEE (FNAME, LNAME, DNO)
	VALUES	('Sai', 'Prasad', 5);

(* U2A is rejected if not null checking is provided by dbms *)

A variation of the INSERT command inserts multiple tuples into a relation in conjunction with creating the relation and loading it with the *result of a query*. For example, to create a temporary table that has the name, number of employees, and total salaries for each department, we can write the statements in U3A and U3B:

U3A:	CREATE TABLE	DEPTS_INFO
	(DEPT_NAME	VARCHAR(15),
	NO_OF_EMPS	INTEGER,
	TOTAL_SAL	INTEGER);
U3B:	INSERT INTO	DEPTS_INFO (DEPT_NAME, NO_OF_EMPS, TOTAL_SAL)
	SELECT	DNAME, COUNT (*), SUM (SALARY)
	FROM	(DEPARTMENT JOIN EMPLOYEE ON DNUMBER=DNO)
	GROUP BY	DNAME;

A table DEPTS_INFO is created by U3A and is loaded with the summary information retrieved from the database by the query in U3B. We can now query DEPTS_INFO as we would any other relation; when we do not need it any more, we can remove it by using the DROP TABLE command. Notice that the DEPTS_INFO table may not be up to date; that is, if we update either the DEPARTMENT or the EMPLOYEE relations after issuing U3B, the information in DEPTS_INFO *becomes outdated*. We have to create a view to keep such a table up to date.

7.6.2   The DELETE Command

The DELETE command removes tuples from a relation. It includes a WHERE clause, similar to that used in an SQL query, to select the tuples to be deleted. Tuples are explicitly deleted from only one table at a time. However, the deletion may propagate to tuples in other relations if *referential triggered actions* are specified in the referential integrity constraints of the DDL (see Section 7.2.2).[13] Depending on the number of tuples selected by the condition in the WHERE clause, zero, one, or several tuples can be deleted by a single DELETE command. A missing WHERE clause specifies that all tuples in the relation are to be deleted; however, the table remains in the database as an empty table.[14] The DELETE commands in U4A to U4D, if applied independently to the database of Figure 4.6, will delete zero, one, four, and all tuples, respectively, from the EMPLOYEE relation:

U4A:	DELETE FROM	EMPLOYEE
	WHERE	LNAME='Varma';
U4B:	DELETE FROM	EMPLOYEE

---

13. Other actions can be automatically applied through triggers (see Chapter 13) and other mechanisms.

14. We must use the DROP TABLE command to remove the table definition (see Section 7.3.1).

	WHERE	ENO='123456789';	
U4C:	DELETE FROM	EMPLOYEE	
	WHERE	DNO IN (SELECT	DNUMBER
		FROM	DEPARTMENT
		WHERE	DNAME='Research');
U4D:	DELETE FROM	EMPLOYEE;	

7.6.3 The UPDATE Command

The UPDATE command is used to modify attribute values of one or more selected tuples. As in the DELETE command, a WHERE clause in the UPDATE command selects the tuples to be modified from a single relation. However, updating a primary key value may propagate to the foreign key values of tuples in other relations if such a *referential triggered action* is specified in the referential integrity constraints of the DDL (see Section 7.2.2). An additional SET clause in the UPDATE command specifies the attributes to be modified and their new values. For example, to change the location and controlling department number of project number 10 to 'Bangalore' and 5, respectively, we use U5:

U5:	UPDATE	PROJECT
	SET	PLOCATION = 'Bangalore', DNUM = 5
	WHERE	PNUMBER=10;

Several tuples can be modified with a single UPDATE command. An example is to give all employees in the 'Research' department a 10 percent raise in salary, as shown in U6. In this request, the modified SALARY value depends on the original SALARY value in each tuple, so two references to the SALARY attribute are needed. In the SET clause, the reference to the SALARY attribute on the right refers to the old SALARY value *before modification*, and the one on the left refers to the new SALARY value *after modification*:

U6:	UPDATE	EMPLOYEE	
	SET	SALARY = SALARY *1.1	
	WHERE	DNO IN (SELECT	DNUMBER
		FROM	DEPARTMENT
		WHERE	DNAME='Research');

It is also possible to specify NULL or DEFAULT as the new attribute value. Notice that each UPDATE command explicitly refers to a single relation only. To modify multiple relations, we must issue several UPDATE commands.

7.7 ADDITIONAL FEATURES OF SQL

SQL has a number of additional features that we have not described in this chapter but discuss elsewhere in the book. These are as follows:

- SQL has the capability to specify more general constraints, called assertions, using the CREATE ASSERTION statement. This is described in Section 7.8.

- SQL has language constructs for specifying views, also known as virtual tables, using the CREATE VIEW statement. Views are derived from the base tables declared through the CREATE TABLE statement, and are discussed in Section 7.9.

- SQL has several different techniques for writing programs in various programming languages that can include SQL statements to access one or more databases. These include embedded (and dynamic) SQL, SQL/CLI (Call Language Interface) and its predecessor ODBC (Open Data Base Connectivity), and SQL/PSM (Program Stored Modules). We discuss the differences among these techniques in Section 7.10, then discuss each technique in Sections 7.11 through 7.13. We also discuss how to access SQL databases through the Java programming language using JDBC and SQLJ.

- Each commercial RDBMS will have, in addition to the SQL commands, a set of commands for specifying physical database design parameters, file structures for relations, and access paths such as indexes. We called these commands a *storage definition language* (SDL) in Chapter 2. Earlier versions of SQL had commands for **creating indexes**, but these were removed from the language because they were not at the conceptual schema level (see Chapter 2).

- SQL has transaction control commands. These are used to specify units of database processing for concurrency control and recovery purposes. We discuss these commands in Chapter 12 after we discuss the concept of transactions in more detail.

- SQL has language constructs for specifying the *granting and revoking of privileges* to users. Privileges typically correspond to the right to use certain SQL commands to access certain relations. Each relation is assigned an owner, and either the owner or the DBA staff can grant to selected users the privilege to use an SQL statement—such as SELECT, INSERT, DELETE, or UPDATE—to access the relation. In addition, the DBA staff can grant the privileges to create schemas, tables, or views to certain users. These SQL commands—called **GRANT** and **REVOKE**—are discussed in Chapter 12 where we discuss database security and authorization.

- SQL has language constructs for creating triggers. These are generally referred to as **active database** techniques, since they specify actions that are automatically triggered by events such as database updates. We discuss these features in Chapter 13, where we discuss active database concepts.

- SQL has incorporated many features from object-oriented models to have more powerful capabilities, leading to enhanced relational systems known as **object-relational.**

- SQL and relational databases can interact with new technologies such as XML (eXtended Markup Language; see Chapter 15s) and OLAP (On Line Analytical Processing for Data Warehouses; see Chapter 17).

7.8   Specifying General Constraints as Assertions

[Earlier Section Number 9.1]

In SQL, users can specify general constraints—those that do not fall into any of the categories described in Section 7.2—via **declarative assertions**, using the **CREATE ASSERTION** statement of the DDL. Each assertion is given a constraint name and is specified via a condition similar to the WHERE clause of an SQL query. For example, to specify the constraint that "the salary of an employee must not be greater than the salary of the manager of the department that the employee works for" in SQL, we can write the following assertion:

```
CREATE ASSERTION SALARY_CONSTRAINT
CHECK ( NOT EXISTS
        (SELECT *
        FROM    EMPLOYEE E, EMPLOYEE M, DEPARTMENT D
        WHERE   E.SALARY>M.SALARY AND
                E.DNO=D.DNUMBER AND
                D.MGRENO=M.ENO) );
```

The constraint name SALARY_CONSTRAINT is followed by the keyword CHECK, which is followed by a **condition** in parentheses that must hold true on every database state for the assertion to be satisfied. The constraint name can be used later to refer to the constraint or to modify or drop it. The DBMS is responsible for ensuring that the condition is not violated. Any WHERE clause condition can be used, but many constraints can be specified using the EXISTS and NOT EXISTS style of SQL conditions. Whenever some tuples in the database cause the condition of an ASSERTION statement to evaluate to FALSE, the constraint is **violated.** The constraint is **satisfied** by a database state if *no combination of tuples* in that database state violates the constraint.

The basic technique for writing such assertions is to specify a query that selects any tuples *that violate the desired condition.* By including this query inside a NOT EXISTS clause, the assertion will specify that the result of this query must be empty. Thus, the assertion is violated if the result of the query is not empty. In our example, the query selects all employees whose salaries are greater than the salary of the manager of their department. If the result of the query is not empty, the assertion is violated.

Note that the CHECK clause and constraint condition can also be used to specify constraints on attributes and domains (see Section 7.2.1) and on tuples (see Section 7.2.4). A major difference between CREATE ASSERTION and the other two is that the CHECK clauses on attributes, domains, and tuples are checked in SQL *only when tuples are inserted* or *updated.* Hence, constraint checking can be implemented more efficiently by the DBMS in these cases. The schema designer should use CHECK on attributes, domains, and tuples only when he or she is sure that the constraint *can only be violated by insertion* or *updating of tuples.* On the other hand, the schema designer should use CREATE ASSERTION only in cases where it is not possible to use CHECK on attributes, domains, or tuples, so that checks are implemented more efficiently by the DBMS.

Another statement related to CREATE ASSERTION in SQL is CREATE TRIGGER, but triggers are used in a different way. In many cases it is convenient to specify the type of action to be taken when certain events occur and when certain conditions are satisfied. Rather than offering users only the option of aborting an operation that causes a violation—as with CREATE ASSERTION—the DBMS should make other options available. For example, it may be useful to specify a condition that, if violated, causes some user to be informed of the violation. A manager may want to be informed if an employee's travel expenses exceed a certain limit by receiving a message whenever this occurs. The action that the DBMS must take in this case is to send an appropriate message to that user. The condition is thus used to **monitor** the database. Other actions may be specified, such as executing a specific *stored procedure* or triggering other updates. The CREATE TRIGGER statement is used to implement such actions in SQL. A **trigger** specifies an **event** (such as a particular database update operation), a **condition**, and an **action**. The action is to be executed automatically if the condition is satisfied when the event occurs. Triggers in detail in Chapter 13 when we describe *active databases.*

7.9 VIEWS (VIRTUAL TABLES) IN SQL [Earlier Section Number 9.2]

In this section, we introduce the concept of a view in SQL. We then show how views are specified, and we discuss the problem of updating a view, and how a view can be implemented by the DBMS.

7.9.1   Concept of a View in SQL [Earlier Section Number 9.2.1]

A **view** in SQL terminology is a single table that is derived from other tables.[15] These other tables could be base tables or previously defined views. A view does not necessarily exist in physical form; it is considered a **virtual table**, in contrast to base tables, whose tuples are actually stored in the database. This limits the possible update operations that can be applied to views, but it does not provide any limitations on querying a view.

We can think of a view as a way of specifying a table that we need to reference frequently, even though it may not exist physically. For example, in Figure 4.5 we may frequently issue queries that retrieve the employee name and the project names that the employee works on. Rather than having to specify the join of the EMPLOYEE, WORKS_ON, and PROJECT tables every time we issue that query, we can define a view that is a result of these joins. We can then issue queries on the view, which are specified as single-table retrievals rather than as retrievals involving two joins on three tables. We call the EMPLOYEE, WORKS_ON, and PROJECT tables the **defining tables** of the view.

7.9.2   Specification of Views in SQL [Earlier Section Number 9.2.2]

In SQL, the command to specify a view is **CREATE VIEW.** The view is given a (virtual) table name (or view name), a list of attribute names, and a query to specify the contents of the view. If none of the view attributes results from applying functions or arithmetic operations, we do not have to specify attribute names for the view, since they would be the same as the names of the attributes of the defining tables in the default case. The views in V1 and V2 create virtual tables whose schemas are illustrated in Figure 7.7 when applied to the database schema of Figure 4.5.

V1:	**CREATE VIEW**	WORKS_ON1
	AS SELECT	FNAME, LNAME, PNAME, HOURS
	FROM	EMPLOYEE, PROJECT, WORKS_ON
	WHERE	ENO=EENO AND PNO=PNUMBER;
V2:	**CREATE VIEW**	DEPT_INFO(DEPT_NAME,NO_OF_EMPS,TOTAL_SAL)
	AS SELECT	DNAME, **COUNT** (*), **SUM** (SALARY)
	FROM	DEPARTMENT, EMPLOYEE
	WHERE	DNUMBER=DNO
	GROUP BY	DNAME;

WORKS_ON

FNAME	LNAME	PNAME	HOURS

DEPT_ON1

DEPT_NAME	NO_OF_EMPS	TOTAL_SAL

FIGURE 7.7 Two views specified on the database schema of Figure 4.5.

---

15. As used in SQL, the term *view* is more limited than the term *user view* discussed in Chapters 1 and 2, since a user view would possibly include many relations.

In V1, we did not specify any new attribute names for the view WORKS_ON1 (although we could have); in this case, WORKS_ON1 inherits the names of the view attributes from the defining tables EMPLOYEE, PROJECT, and WORKS_ON. View V2 explicitly specifies new attribute names for the view DEPT_INFO, using a one-to-one correspondence between the attributes specified in the CREATE VIEW clause and those specified in the SELECT clause of the query that defines the view.

We can now specify SQL queries on a view—or virtual table—in the same way we specify queries involving base tables. For example, to retrieve the last name and first name of all employees who work on 'ProjectX', we can utilize the WORKS_ON1 view and specify the query as in QV1:

QV1:   SELECT   FNAME, LNAME
              FROM   WORKS_ON1
              WHERE   PNAME='ProjectX';

The same query would require the specification of two joins if specified on the base relations; one of the main advantages of a view is to simplify the specification of certain queries. Views are also used as a security and authorization mechanism (see Chapter 12).

A view is supposed to be *always up to date*; if we modify the tuples in the base tables on which the view is defined, the view must automatically reflect these changes. Hence, the view is not realized at the time of *view definition* but rather at the time we *specify a query* on the view. It is the responsibility of the DBMS and not the user to make sure that the view is up to date.

If we do not need a view any more, we can use the **DROP VIEW** command to dispose of it. For example, to get rid of the view V1, we can use the **SQL** statement in V1A:

V1A: **DROP VIEW** WORKS_ON1;

7.9.3   View Implementation and View Update

[Earlier Section Number 9.2.3]

The problem of efficiently implementing a view for querying is complex. Two main approaches have been suggested. One strategy, called **query modification**, involves modifying the view query into a query on the underlying base tables. For example, the query QV1 would be automatically modified to the following query by the DBMS:

SELECT   FNAME, LNAME
FROM   EMPLOYEE, PROJECT, WORKS_ON
WHERE   ENO=EENO **AND** PNO=PNUMBER
           AND PNAME='ProjectX';

The disadvantage of this approach is that it is inefficient for views defined via complex queries that are time-consuming to execute, especially if multiple queries are applied to the view within a short period of time. The other strategy, called **view materialization**, involves physically creating a temporary view table when the view is first queried and keeping that table on the assumption that other queries on the view will follow. In this case, an efficient strategy for automatically updating the view table when the base tables are updated must be developed in order to keep the view up to date. Techniques using the concept of **incremental update** have been developed for this purpose, where it is determined what new tuples must be inserted, deleted, or modified in a materialized view table when a change is applied to one of the defining base tables. The view is generally kept as long as it is being queried. If the view is not queried for a certain period of time, the system may then automatically remove the physical view table and recompute it from scratch when future queries reference the view.

Updating of views is complicated and can be ambiguous. In general, an update on a view defined on a *single table* without any *aggregate functions* can be mapped to an update on the underlying base table under certain conditions. For a view involving joins, an update operation may be mapped to update operations on the underlying base relations in *multiple ways*. To illustrate potential problems with updating a view defined on multiple tables, consider the WORKS_ON1 view, and suppose that we issue the command to update the PNAME attribute of 'Mahesh Kumar' from 'ProductX' to 'ProductY'. This view update is shown in UV1:

UV1:	UPDATE	WORKS_ON1
	SET	PNAME = 'ProductY'
	WHERE	LNAME='Kumar' AND FNAME='Mahesh' AND
		PNAME='ProductX';

This query can be mapped into several updates on the base relations to give the desired update effect on the view. Two possible updates, (a) and (b), on the base relations corresponding to UV1 are shown here:

(a):	UPDATE	WORKS_ON		
	SET	PNO =	(SELECT	PNUMBER
			FROM	PROJECT
			WHERE	PNAME='ProductY')
	WHERE	EENO IN	(SELECT	ENO
			FROM	EMPLOYEE
			WHERE	LNAME='Kumar' AND FNAME='Mahesh')
		AND		
		PNO =	(SELECT	PNUMBER
			FROM	PROJECT
			WHERE	PNAME='ProductX');
(b):	UPDATE	PROJECT	SET PNAME = 'ProductY'	
	WHERE	PNAME = 'ProductX';		

Update (a) relates 'Mahesh Kumar' to the 'ProductY' PROJECT tuple in place of the 'ProductX' PROJECT tuple and is the most likely desired update. However, (b) would also give the desired update effect on the view, but it accomplishes this by changing the name of the 'ProductX' tuple in the PROJECT relation to 'ProductY'. It is quite unlikely that the user who specified the view update UV1 wants the update to be interpreted as in (b), since it also has the side effect of changing all the view tuples with PNAME = 'ProductX'.

Some view updates may not make much sense. For example, modifying the TOTAL_SAL attribute of the DEPT_INFO view does not make sense because TOTAL_SAL is defined to be the sum of the individual employee salaries. This request is shown as UV2:

UV2:	UPDATE	DEPT_INFO
	SET	TOTAL_SAL=100000
	WHERE	DNAME='Research';

A large number of updates on the underlying base relations can satisfy this view update. A view update is feasible when only one *possible update* on the base relations can accomplish the desired update effect on the view. Whenever an update on the view can be mapped to *more than one update* on the underlying base relations, we must have a certain procedure for choosing the desired update. Some researchers have developed methods for choosing the most likely update, while other researchers prefer to have the user choose the desired update mapping during view definition.

In summary, we can make the following observations:

- A view with a single defining table is updatable if the view attributes contain the primary key of the base relation, as well as all attributes with the NOT NULL constraint that *do not have default* values specified.

- Views defined on multiple tables using joins are generally not updatable.

- Views defined using grouping and aggregate functions are not updatable.

In SQL, the clause **WITH CHECK OPTION** must be added at the end of the view definition if a view *is to be updated*. This allows the system to check for view updatability and to plan an execution strategy for view updates.

7.10 DATABASE PROGRAMMING: ISSUES AND TECHNIQUES

[Earlier Section Number 9.3]

We now turn our attention to the techniques that have been developed for accessing databases from programs and, in particular, to the issue of how to access SQL databases from application programs. Our presentation of SQL so far has focused on the language constructs for various database operations—from schema definition and constraint specification to querying, to updating, and the specification of views. Most database systems have an **interactive interface** where these SQL commands can be typed directly into a monitor and input to the database system. For example, in a computer system where the ORACLE RDBMS is installed, the command SQLPLUS will start the interactive interface. The user can type SQL commands or queries directly over several lines, ended by a semicolon and the Enter key (that is, "; <cr>"). Alternatively, a **file of commands** can be created and executed through the interactive interface by typing @<filename>. The system will execute the commands written in the file and display the results, if any.

The interactive interface is quite convenient for schema and constraint creation or for occasional ad hoc queries. However, the majority of database interactions in practice are executed through programs that have been carefully designed and tested. These programs are generally known as **application programs** or **database applications**, and are used as *canned transactions* by the end users, as discussed in Section 1.4.3. Another very common use of database programming is to access a database through an application program that implements a **Web interface**, for example, for making airline reservations or department store purchases. In fact, the vast majority of Web electronic commerce applications include some database access commands.

In this section, we first give an overview of the main approaches to database programming. Then we discuss some of the problems that occur when trying to access a database from a general-purpose programming language, and discuss the typical sequence of commands for interacting with a database from a software program.

7.10.1 Approaches to Database Programming

[Earlier Section Number 9.3.1]

Several techniques exist for including database interactions in application programs. The main approaches for database programming are the following:

1. *Embedding database commands in a general-purpose programming language:* In this approach, database statements are **embedded** into the host programming language, but they are identified by a special prefix. For example, the prefix for embedded SQL is the string EXEC SQL, which precedes all SQL commands

in a host language program.[16] A **precompiler** or **preproccessor** first scans the source program code to identify database statements and extract them for processing by the DBMS. They are replaced in the program by function calls to the DBMS-generated code.

2. *Using a library of database functions:* A **library of functions** is made available to the host programming language for database calls. For example, there could be functions to connect to a database, execute a query, execute an update, and so on. The actual database query and update commands, and any other necessary information, are included as parameters in the function calls. This approach provides what is known as an **Application Programming Interface (API)** for accessing a database from application programs.

3. *Designing a brand-new language:* A **database programming language** is designed from scratch to be compatible with the database model and query language. Additional programming structures such as loops and conditional statements are added to the database language to convert it into a full-fledged programming language.

In practice, the first two approaches are more common, since many applications are already written in general-purpose programming languages but require some database access. The third approach is more appropriate for applications that have intensive database interaction. One of the main problems with the first two approaches is *impedance mismatch*, which does not occur in the third approach. We discuss this next.

7.10.2   Impedance Mismatch [Earlier Section Number 9.3.2]

Impedance mismatch is the term used to refer to the problems that occur because of differences between the database model and the programming language model. For example, the practical relational model has three main constructs: attributes and their data types, tuples (records), and tables (sets or multisets of records). The first problem that may occur is that the data types of the programming language differ from the attribute data types in the data model. Hence, it is necessary to have a **binding** for each host programming language that specifies for each attribute type the compatible programming language types. It is necessary to have a binding for each programming language because different languages have different data types. For example, the data types available in C and JAVA are different, and both differ from the SQL data types.

Another problem occurs because the results of most queries are sets or multisets of tuples, and each tuple is formed of a sequence of attribute values. In the program, it is often necssary to access the individual data values within individual tuples for printing or processing. Hence, a binding is needed to map the *query result data structure*, which is a table, to an appropriate data structure in the programming language. A mechanism is needed to loop over the tuples in a query result in order to access a single tuple at a time and to extract individual values from the tuple. A **cursor** or **iterator variable** is used to loop over the tuples in a query result. Individual values within each tuple are typically extracted into distinct program variables of the appropriate type.

Impedance mismatch is less of a problem when a special database programming language is designed that uses the same data model and data types as the database model. One example of such a language is ORACLE's PL/SQL. For object databases, the object data model is quite similar to the data model of the JAVA programming language, so the impedance mismatch is greatly reduced when JAVA is used as the host language for accessing a JAVA-compatible object database. Several database programming languages have been implemented as research prototypes (see bibliographic notes).

---

16. Other prefixes are sometimes used, but this is the most common one.

7.10.3 Typical Sequence of Interaction in Database Programming [Earlier Section Number 9.3.3]

When a programmer or software engineer writes a program that requires access to a database, it is quite common for the program to be running on one computer system while the database is installed on another. Recall from Section 2.5 that a common architecture for database access is the client/server model, where a **client program** handles the logic of a software application, but includes some calls to one or more **database servers** to access or update the data.[17] When writing such a program, a common sequence of interaction is the following:

1. When the client program requires access to a particular database, the program must first *establish* or *open a* **connection** to the database server. Typically, this involves specifying the Internet address (URL) of the machine where the database server is located, plus providing a login account name and password for database access.

2. Once the connection is established, the program can interact with the database by submitting queries, updates, and other database commands. In general, most types of SQL statements can be included in an application program.

3. When the program no longer needs access to a particular database, it should *terminate* or *close* the connection to the database.

A program can access multiple databases if needed. In some database programming approaches, only one connection can be active at a time, whereas in other approaches multiple connections can be established at the same time.

In the next three sections, we discuss examples of each of the three approaches to database programming. Section 7.11 describes how SQL is *embedded* into a programming language. Section 7.12 discusses how *function calls* are used to access the database, and Section 7.13 discusses an extension to SQL called SQL/PSM that allows *general-purpose programming* constructs for defining modules (procedures and functions) that are stored within the database system.[18]

7.11 EMBEDDED SQL, DYNAMIC SQL, AND SQLJ

[Earlier Section Number 9.4]

7.11.1 Retrieving Single Tuples with Embedded SQL

[Earlier Section Number 9.4.1]

In this section, we give an overview of how SQL statements can be embedded in a generalpurpose programming language such as C, ADA, COBOL, or PASCAL. The programming language is called the **host language.** Most SQL statements—including data or constraint definitions, queries, updates, or view definitions—can be embedded in a host language program. An embedded SQL statement is distinguished from programming language statements by prefixing it with the keywords EXEC SQL so that a **preprocessor** (or **precompiler**) can separate embedded SQL statements from the host language code. The SQL statements can be terminated by a semicolon (;) or a matching END-EXEC.

---

17. As we discussed in Section 2.5, there are two-tier and three-tier architectures; to keep our discussion simple, we will assume a two-tier client/server architecture here. We discuss additional variations of these architectures in Chapter 14.

18. Although SQL/PSM is not considered to be a full-fledged programming language, it illustrates how typical general-purpose programming constructs—such as loops and conditional structures—can be incorporated into SQL.

To illustrate the concepts of embedded SQL, we will use C as the host programming language. Within an embedded SQL command, we may refer to specially declared C program variables. These are called **shared variables** because they are used in both the C program and the embedded SQL statements. Shared variables are prefixed by a colon (:) *when they appear in an* SQL *statement*. This distinguishes program variable names from the names of database schema constructs such as attributes and relations. It also allows program variables to have the same names as attribute names, since they are distinguishable by the ":" prefix in the SQL statement.

Names of database schema constructs—such as attributes and relations—can only be used within the SQL commands, but shared program variables can be used elsewhere in the C program without the ":" prefix.

Suppose that we want to write C programs to process the COMPANY database of Figure 4.5. We need to declare program variables to match the types of the database attributes that the program will process. The programmer can choose the names of the program variables; they may or may not have names that are identical to their corresponding attributes. We will use the C program variables declared in Figure 7.8 for all our examples, and we will show C program segments without variable declarations. Shared variables are declared within a **declare section** in the program, as shown in Figure 7.8 (lines 1 through 7).[19] A few of the common bindings of C types to SQL types are as follows. The SQL types INTEGER, SMALLINT, REAL, and DOUBLE are mapped to the C types long, short, float, and double, respectively. Fixed-length and varying-length strings (CHAR[i], VARCHAR[i]) in SQL can be mapped to arrays of characters (**char [i+1], varchar [i+1]**) in C that are one character longer than the SQL type, because strings in C are terminated by a "\0" (null) character, which is not part of the character string itself.[20]

Notice that the only embedded SQL commands in Figure 7.5 are lines 1 and 7, which tell the precompiler to take note of the C variable names between BEGIN DECLARE and END DECLARE because they can be included in embedded SQL statements—as long as they are preceded by a colon (:). Lines 2 through 5 are regular C program declarations. The C program variables declared in lines 2 through 5 correspond to the attributes of the EMPLOYEE and DEPARTMENT tables from the COMPANY database of Figure 4.5 that was declared by the SQL DDL in Figure 7.1. The variables declared in line 6—SQLCODE and SQLSTATE—are used to communicate errors and exception conditions between the database system and the program. Line 0 shows a program variable loop that will not be used in any embedded SQL statements, so it is declared outside the SQL declare section.

```
0)   int loop ;
1)   EXEC SQL BEGIN DECLARE SECTION ;
2)   varchar dname [16], fname [16], lname [16], address [31] ;
3)   char eno [10], dob [11], sex [2], initial [2] ;
4)   float salary, raise ;
5)   int dno, dnumber ;
6)   int SQLCODE ; char SQLSTATE [6] ;
7)   EXEC SQL END DECLARE SECTION ;
```

FIGURE 7.8 C program variables used in the embedded SQL examples E1 and E2.

---

19. We use line numbers in our code segments for easy reference; these numbers are not part of the actual code.

20. SQL strings can also be mapped to char* types in C.

Connecting to the Database. The SQL command for establishing a connection to a database has the following form:

> CONNECT TO <server name> AS <connection name>
> AUTHORIZATION <user account name and password> ;

In general, since a user or program can access several database servers, several connections can be established, but only one connection can be active at any point in time. The programmer or user can use the <connection name> to change from the currently active connection to a different one by using the following command:

> SET CONNECTION <connection name> ;

Once a connction is no longer needed, it can be terminated by the following command:

> DISCONNECT <connection name> ;

In the examples in this chapter, we assume that the appropriate connection has already been established to the COMPANY database, and that it is the currently active connection.

Communicating between the Program and the DBMS Using SQLCODE and SQLSTATE. The two special **communication variables** that are used by the DBMS to communicate exception or error conditions to the program are SQLCODE and SQLSTATE. The SQLCODE variable shown in Figure 7.8 is an integer variable. After each database command is executed, the DBMS returns a value in SQLCODE. A value of 0 indicates that the statement was executed successfully by the DBMS. If SQLCODE > 0 (or, more specifically, if SQLCODE = 100), this indicates that no more data (records) are available in a query result. If SQLCODE < 0, this indicates some error has occurred. In some systems—for example, in the ORACLE RDBMS—SQLCODE is a field in a record structure called SQLCA (SQL communication area), so it is referenced as SQLCA.SQLCODE. In this case, the definition of SQLCA must be included in the C program by including the following line:

> EXEC SQL include SQLCA ;

In later versions of the SQL standard, a communication variable called SQLSTATE was added, which is a string of five characters. A value of "00000" in SQLSTATE indicates no error or exception; other values indicate various errors or exceptions. For example, "02000" indicates "no more data" when using SQLSTATE. Currently, both SQLSTATE and SQLCODE are available in the SQL standard. Many of the error and exception codes returned in SQLSTATE are supposed to be standardized for all SQL vendors and platforms,[21] whereas the codes returned in SQLCODE are not standardized but are defined by the DBMS vendor. Hence, it is generally better to use SQLSTATE, because this makes error handling in the application programs independent of a particular DBMS. As an exercise, the reader should rewrite the examples given later in this chapter using SQLSTATE instead of SQLCODE.

Example of Embedded SQL Programming. Our first example to illustrate embedded SQL programming is a repeating program segment (loop) that reads an employee number of an employee and prints out some information from the corresponding EMPLOYEE record in the database. The C program code is shown as program segment E1 in Figure 7.9. The program reads (inputs) an employee number value and then retrieves the EMPLOYEE tuple with that social security number from the database via the embedded SQL command. The INTO **clause** (line 5) specifies the program variables into which attribute values from the database are retrieved. C program variables in the INTO clause are prefixed with a colon (:), as we discussed earlier.

---

21. In particular, SQLSTATE codes starting with the characters 0 through 4 or A through H are supposed to be standardized, whereas other values can be implementation-defined.

Line 7 in E1 illustrates the communication between the database and the program through the special variable SQLCODE. If the value returned by the DBMS in SQLCODE is 0, the previous statement was executed without errors or exception conditions. Line 7 checks this and assumes that if an error occurred, it was because no EMPLOYEE tuple existed with the given employee number; it therefore outputs a message to that effect (line 8).

In E1 a *single tuple* is selected by the embedded SQL query; that is why we are able to assign its attribute values directly to C program variables in the INTO clause in line 5. In general, an SQL query can retrieve many tuples. In that case, the C program will typically go through the retrieved tuples and process them one at a time. A *cursor* is used to allow tuple-at-a-time processing by the host language program. We describe cursors next.

7.11.2 Retrieving Multiple Tuples with Embedded SQL Using Cursors [Earlier Section Number 9.4.2]

We can think of a **cursor** as a pointer that points to a *single tuple* (*row*) from the result of a query that retrieves multiple tuples. The cursor is declared when the SQL query command is declared in the program. Later in the program, an **OPEN CURSOR** command fetches the query result from the database and sets the cursor to a position *before the first row* in the result of the query. This becomes the **current row** for the cursor. Subsequently, **FETCH** commands are issued in the program; each FETCH moves the cursor to the *next row* in the result of the query, making it the current row and copying its attribute values into the C (host language) program variables specified in the FETCH command by an INTO clause. The cursor variable is basically an **iterator** that iterates (loops) over the tuples in the query result—one tuple at a time. This is similar to traditional record-at-a-time file processing.

```
//Program Segment E1:
0)    loop = 1 ;
1)    while (loop) {
2)        prompt("Enter an Employee Number: ", eno) ;
3)        EXEC SQL
4)            select FNAME, INITIAL, LNAME, ADDRESS, SALARY
5)            into :fname, :initial, :lname, :address, :salary
6)            from EMPLOYEE where eno = :eno ;
7)        if (SQLCODE == 0) printf(fname, initial, lname, address, salary)
8)            else printf("Employee Number does not exist: ", eno) ;
9)        prompt("More Employee Numbers (enter 1 for Yes, 0 for No): ", loop) ;
10)  }
```

FIGURE 7.9 Program segment E1, a C program segment with embedded SQL.

To determine when all the tuples in the result of the query have been processed, the communication variable SQLCODE (or, alternatively, SQLSTATE) is checked. If a FETCH command is issued that results in moving the cursor past the last tuple in the result of the query, a positive value (SQLCODE > 0) is returned in SQLCODE, indicating that no data (tuple) was found (or the string "02000" is returned in SQLSTATE). The programmer uses this to terminate a loop over the tuples in the query result. In general, numerous cursors can be opened at the same time. A **CLOSE CURSOR** command is issued to indicate that we are done with processing the result of the query associated with that cursor.

An example of using cursors is shown in Figure 7.10, where a cursor called EMP is declared in line 4. We assume that appropriate C program variables have been declared as in Figure 7.8. The program segment in E2 reads (inputs) a department name (line 0), retrieves its department number (lines 1 to 3), and then retrieves the employees who work in that department via a cursor. A loop (lines 10 to 18) then iterates over each employee record, one at a time, and prints the employee name. The program then reads a raise amount for that employee (line 12) and updates the employee's salary in the database by the raise amount (lines 14 to 16).

```
//Program Segment E2:
0)      prompt("Enter the Department Name: ", dname) ;
1)      EXEC SQL
2)          select DNUMBER into :dnumber
3)          from DEPARTMENT where DNAME = :dname ;
4)      EXEC SQL DECLARE EMP CURSOR FOR
5)          select ENO, FNAME, INITIAL, LNAME, SALARY
6)          from EMPLOYEE where DNO = :dnumber
7)          FOR UPDATE OF SALARY ;
8)      EXEC SQL OPEN EMP ;
9)      EXEC SQL FETCH from EMP into :eno, :fname, :initial, :lname, :salary ;
10)     while (SQLCODE == 0) {
11)         printf("Employee name is:", fname, initial, lname)
12)         prompt("Enter the raise amount: ", raise) ;
13)         EXEC SQL
14)             update EMPLOYEE
15)             set SALARY = SALARY + :raise
16)             where CURRENT OF EMP ;
17)         EXEC SQL FETCH from EMP into :eno, :fname, :initial, :lname, :salary ;
18)     }
19)     EXEC SQL CLOSE EMP ;
```

FIGURE 7.10 Program segment E2, a C program segment that uses cursors with embedded SQL for update purposes.

When a cursor is defined for rows that are to be modified (updated), we must add the clause **FOR UPDATE OF** in the cursor declaration and list the names of any attributes that will be updated by the program. This is illustrated in line 7 of code segment E2. If rows are to be deleted, the keywords **FOR UPDATE** must be added without specifying any attributes. In the embedded UPDATE (or DELETE) command, the condition **WHERE CURRENT OF** <cursor name> specifies that the current tuple referenced by the cursor is the one to be updated (or deleted), as in line 16 of E2.

Notice that declaring a cursor and associating it with a query (lines 4 through 7 in E2) does not execute the query; the query is executed only when the OPEN <cursor name> command (line 8) is executed. Also notice that there is no need to include the **FOR UPDATE OF** clause in line 7 of E2 if the results of the query are to be used for *retrieval purposes only* (no update or delete).

Several options can be specified when declaring a cursor. The general form of a cursor declaration is as follows:

DECLARE <cursor name> [**INSENSITIVE**] [**SCROLL**] **CURSOR**
[**WITH HOLD**] **FOR** <query specification>
[**ORDER BY** <ordering specification>]
[**FOR READ ONLY** | **FOR UPDATE** [**OF** <attribute list>]] ;

We already briefly discussed the options listed in the last line. The default is that the query is for retrieval purposes (FOR READ ONLY). If some of the tuples in the query result are to be updated, we need to specify FOR UPDATE OF <attribute list> and list the attributes that may be updated. If some tuples are to be deleted, we need to specify FOR UPDATE without any attributes listed.

When the optional keyword SCROLL is specified in a cursor declaration, it is possible to position the cursor in other ways than for purely sequential access. A **fetch orientation** can be added to the FETCH command, whose value can be one of NEXT, PRIOR, FIRST, LAST, ABSOLUTE i, and RELATIVE i. In the latter two commands, i must evaluate to an integer value that specifies an absolute tuple position or a tuple position relative to the current cursor position, respectively. The default fetch orientation, which we used in our examples, is NEXT. The fetch orientation allows the programmer to move the cursor around the tuples in the query result with greater flexibility, providing random access by position or access in reverse order. When SCROLL is specified on the cursor, the general form of a FETCH command is as follows, with the parts in square brackets being optional:

FETCH [[<fetch orientation>] **FROM**] <cursor name> **INTO** <fetch target list> ;

The ORDER BY clause orders the tuples so that the FETCH command will fetch them in the specified order. It is specified in a similar manner to the corresponding clause for SQL queries (see Section 7.4.6). The last two options when declaring a cursor (INSENSITIVE and WITH HOLD) refer to transaction characteristics of database programs, which we discuss in Chapter 11.

7.11.3   Specifying Queries at Runtime Using Dynamic SQL
[Earlier Section Number 9.4.3]

In the previous examples, the embedded SQL queries were written as part of the host program source code. Hence, any time we want to write a different query, we must write a new program, and go through all the steps involved (compiling, debugging, testing, and so on). In some cases, it is convenient to write a program that can execute different SQL queries or updates (or other operations) *dynamically at runtime*. For example, we may want to write a program that accepts an SQL query typed from the monitor, executes it, and displays its result, such as the interactive interfaces available for most relational DBMSs. Another example is when a user-friendly interface generates SQL queries dynamically for the user based on point-and-click operations on a graphical schema (for example, a QBE-like interface; see Appendix D). In this section, we give a brief overview of **dynamic SQL**, which is one technique for writing this type of database program, by giving a simple example to illustrate how dynamic SQL can work.

Program segment E3 in Figure 7.11 reads a string that is input by the user (that string should be an SQL update command) into the string variable sqlupdatestring in line 3. It then prepares this as an SQL command in line 4 by associating it with the SQL variable **sql command.** Line 5 then executes the command. Notice that in this case no syntax check or other types of checks on the command are possible *at compile time*, since the command is not available until runtime. This contrasts with our previous examples of embedded SQL, where the query could be checked at compile time because its text was in the program source code.

Although including a dynamic update command is relatively straightforward in dynamic SQL, a dynamic query is much more complicated. This is because in the general case we do not know the type or the number of attributes to be retrieved by the SQL query when we are writing the program. A complex data structure is sometimes needed to allow for different numbers and types of attributes in the query result if no prior information is known about the dynamic query. Techniques similar to those that we discuss in Section 7.12 can be used to assign query results (and query parameters) to host program variables.

In E3, the reason for separating PREPARE and EXECUTE is that if the command is to be executed multiple times in a program, it can be prepared only once. Preparing the command generally involves syntax and other types of checks by the system, as well as generating the code for executing it. It is possible to combine the PREPARE and EXECUTE commands (lines 4 and 5 in E3) into a single statement by writing

EXEC SQL EXECUTE IMMEDIATE :sqlupdatestring ;

```
//Program Segment E3:
0)    EXEC SQL BEGIN DECLARE SECTION ;
1)    varchar sqlupdatestring [256] ;
2)    EXEC SQL END DECLARE SECTION ;
      ...
3)    prompt("Enter the Update Command: ", sqlupdatestring) ;
4)    EXEC SQL PREPARE sqlcommand FROM :sqlupdatestring ;
5)    EXEC SQL EXECUTE sqlcommand ;
      ...
```

FIGURE 7.11 Program segment E3, a C program segment that uses dynamic SQL for updating a table.

This is useful if the command is to be executed only once. Alternatively, one can separate the two to catch any errors after the PREPARE statement, if any.

7.11.4 SQLJ: Embedding SQL Commands in JAVA

In the previous sections, we gave an overview of how SQL commands can be embedded in a traditional programming language, using the C language in our examples. We now turn our attention to how SQL can be embedded in an object-oriented programming language,[22] in particular, the JAVA language. SQLJ is a standard that has been adopted by several vendors for embedding SQL in JAVA. Historically, SQLJ was developed after JDBC, which is used for accessing SQL databases from JAVA using function calls. We discuss JDBC in Section 7.12.2. In our discussion, we focus on SQLJ as it is used in the ORACLE RDBMS. An SQLJ translator will generally convert SQL statements into JAVA, which can then be executed through the JDBC interface. Hence, it is necessary to install a JDBC *driver* when using SQLJ.[23] In this section, we focus on how to use SQLJ concepts to write embedded SQL in a JAVA program.

Before being able to process SQLJ with JAVA in ORACLE, it is necessary to import several class libraries, shown in Figure 7.12. These include the JDBC and IO classes (lines 1 and 2), plus the additional classes listed in lines 3, 4, and 5. In addition, the program must first connect to the desired database using the function call getConnection, which is one of the methods of the oracle class in line 5 of Figure 7.14. The format of this function call, which returns an object of type *default context*,[24] is as follows:

```
public static DefaultContext
getConnection(String url, String user, String password, Boolean
autoCommit)
throws SQLException ;
```

For example, we can write the statements in lines 6 through 8 in Figure 7.12 to connect to an ORACLE database located at the URL <url name> using the login of <user name> and <password> with automatic commitment of each command,[25] and then set this connection as the **default context** for subsequent commands.

---

22. This section assumes familiarity with object-oriented concepts and basic JAVA concepts.

23. We discuss JDBC drivers in Section 7.12.2.

24. A *default context*, when set, applies to subsequent commands in the program until it is changed.

25. *Automatic commitment* roughly means that each command is applied to the database after it is executed. The alternative is that the programmer wants to execute several related database commands and then commit them together. We discuss commit concepts in Chapter 11 when we describe database transactions.

```
1)   import java.sql.* ;
2)   import java.io.* ;
3)   import sqlj.runtime.* ;
4)   import sqlj.runtime.ref.* ;
5)   import oracle.sqlj.runtime.* ;
     ...
6)   DefaultContext cntxt =
7)       oracle.getConnection("<url name>", "<user name>", "<password>", t
8)   DefaultContext.setDefaultContext(cntxt) ;
     ...
```

FIGURE 7.12 Importing classes needed for including SQLJ in JAVA programs in ORACLE, and establishing a connection and default context.

In the following examples, we will not show complete JAVA classes or programs since it is not our intention to teach JAVA. Rather, we will show program segments that illustrate the use of SQLJ. Figure 7.13 shows the JAVA program variables used in our examples. Program segment J1 in Figure 7.14 reads an employee's employee number and prints some of the employee's information from the database.

Notice that because JAVA already uses the concept of **exceptions** for error handling, a special exception called SQLException is used to return errors or exception conditions after executing an SQL database command. This plays a similar role to SQLCODE and SQLSTATE in embedded SQL. JAVA has many types of predefined exceptions. Each JAVA operation (function) must specify the exceptions that can be **thrown**—that is, the exception conditions that may occur while executing the JAVA code of that operation. If a defined exception occurs, the system transfers control to the JAVA code specified for exception handling. In J1, exception handling for an SQLException is specified in lines 7 and 8. Exceptions that can be thrown by the code in a particular operation should be specified as part of the operation declaration or *interface*—for example, in the following format:

```
<operation return type> <operation name>(<parameters>) throws
SQLException, IOException ;
```

In SQLJ, the embedded SQL commands within a JAVA program are preceded by #sql, as illustrated in J1 line 3, so that they can be identified by the preprocessor. SQLJ uses an INTO *clause*—similar to that used in embedded SQL—to return the attribute values retrieved from the database by an SQL query into JAVA program variables. The program variables are preceded by colons (:) in the SQL statement, as in embedded SQL.

```
1)   string dname, eno, fname, fn, lname, ln, dob, address ;
2)   char sex, initial, mi ;
3)   double salary, sal ;
4)   integer dno, dnumber ;
```

FIGURE 7.13 JAVA program variables used in SQLJ examples J1 and J2.

In J1 a single tuple is selected by the embedded SQLJ query; that is why we are able to assign its attribute values directly to JAVA program variables in the INTO clause in line 4. For queries that retrieve many tuples, SQLJ uses the concept of an *iterator*, which is somewhat similar to a cursor in embedded SQL.

7.11.5 Retrieving Multiple Tuples in SQLJ Using Iterators

In SQLJ, an **iterator** is a type of object associated with a collection (set or multiset) of tuples in a query result. The iterator is associated with the tuples and attributes that appear in a query result. There are two types of iterators:

1. A **named iterator** is associated with a query result by listing the attribute *names* and *types* that appear in the query result.

2. A **positional iterator** lists only the *attribute types* that appear in the query result.

In both cases, the list should be *in the same order* as the attributes that are listed in the SELECT clause of the query. However, looping over a query result is different for the two types of iterators, as we shall see. First, we show an example of using a *named* iterator in Figure 7.15, program segment J2A. Line 9 in Figure 7.15 shows how a named iterator type Emp is declared. Notice that the names of the attributes in a named iterator type must match the names of the attributes in the SQL query result. Line 10 shows how an iterator object e of type Emp is created in the program and then associated with a query (lines 11 and 12).

When the iterator object is associated with a query (lines 11 and 12 in Figure 7.15), the program fetches the query result from the database and sets the iterator to a position *before the first row* in the result of the query. This becomes the **current row** for the iterator. Subsequently, **next** operations are issued on the iterator; each moves the iterator to the *next row* in the result of the query, making it the current row. If the row exists, the operation retrieves the attribute values for that row into the corresponding program variables. If no more rows exist, the next operation returns null, and can thus be used to control the looping.

```
//Program Segment J1:
1)      ENO = readEntry("Enter a Employee Number: ") ;
2)      try {
3)          #sql{select FNAME, INITIAL, LNAME, ADDRESS, SALARY
4)              into :fname, :initial, :lname, :address, :salary
5)              from EMPLOYEE where ENO = :eno} ;
6)      }   catch (SQLException se) {
7)          System.out.println("employee number does not exist: " + eno) ;
8)          Return ;
9)      }
10)     System.out.println(fname + " " + initial + " " + lname + " " + address + " " + salary)
```

FIGURE 7.14 Program segment J1, a JAVA program segment with SQLJ.

In Figure 7.15, the command (e.next()) in line 13 performs two functions: It gets the next tuple in the query result and controls the while loop. Once we are done with the query result, the command e.close() (line 16) closes the iterator.

Next, consider the same example using *positional* iterators as shown in Figure 7.16 (program segment J2B). Line 9 in Figure 7.16 shows how a positional iterator type Emppos is declared. The main difference between this and the named iterator is that there are no attribute names in the positional iterator—only attribute types. They still must be compatible with the attribute types in the SQL query result and in the same order. Line 10 shows how a positional iterator variable e of type Emppos is created in the program and then associated with a query (lines 11 and 12).

The positional iterator behaves in a manner that is more similar to embedded SQL (see Section 7.11.2). A **fetch <iterator variable> into <program variables>** command is needed to get the next tuple in a query result. The first time fetch is executed, it gets the first tuple (line 13 in Figure 7.16). Line 16 gets the next tuple until no more tuples exist in the query result. To control the loop, a positional iterator function e.endFetch() is used. This function is set to a value of TRUE when the iterator is initially associated with an SQL query (line 11), and is set to FALSE each time a fetch command returns a valid tuple from the query result. It is set to TRUE again when a fetch command does not find any more tuples. Line 14 shows how the looping is controlled by negation.

```
//Program Segment J2A:
0)    dname = readEntry("Enter the Department Name: ") ;
1)    try {
2)        #sql{select DNUMBER into :dnumber
3)            from DEPARTMENT where DNAME = :dname} ;
4)    }  catch (SQLException se) {
5)        System.out.println("Department does not exist: " + dname) ;
6)        Return ;
7)    }
8)    System.out.printline("Employee information for Department: " + dname) ;
9)    #sql iterator Emp(String eno, String fname, String initial, String lname, double salary) ;
10)   Emp e = null ;
11)   #sql e ={select ENO, fname, initial, lname, salary
12)            from EMPLOYEE where DNO = :dnumber} ;
13)   while (e.next()) {
14)       System.out.printline(e.eno + " " + e.fname + " " + e.initial + " " + e.lname + " " + e.salar
15)   } ;
16)   e.close() ;
```

FIGURE 7.15 Program segment J2A, a JAVA program segment that uses a named iterator to print employee information in a particular department.

7.12 DATABASE PROGRAMMING WITH FUNCTION CALLS: SQL/CLI AND JDBC

Embedded SQL (see Section 7.11) is sometimes referred to as a **static** database programming approach because the query text is written within the program and cannot be changed without recompiling or reprocessing the source code. The use of function calls is a more **dynamic** approach for database programming than embedded SQL. We already saw one dynamic database programming technique—dynamic SQL—in Section 7.11.3. The techniques discussed here provide another approach to dynamic database programming. A **library of functions**, also known as an **application programming interface (API)**, is used to access the database. Although this provides more flexibility because no preprocessor is needed, one drawback is that syntax and other checks on SQL commands have to be done at runtime. Another drawback is that it sometimes requires more complex programming to access query results because the types and numbers of attributes in a query result may not be known in advance.

In this section, we give an overview of two function call interfaces. We first discuss **SQL/CLI** (Call Level Interface), which is part of the SQL standard. This was developed as a follow-up to the earlier technique know as ODBC (Open Data Base Connectivity). We use C as the host language in our SQL/CLI examples. Then we give an overview of **JDBC**, which is the call function interface for accessing databases from JAVA. Although it is commonly assumed that JDBC stands for Java Data Base Connectivity, JDBC is just a registered trademark of Sun Microsystems, not an acronym.

```
//Program Segment J2B:
0)      dname = readEntry("Enter the Department Name: ") ;
1)      try {
2)          #sql{select DNUMBER into :dnumber
3)              from DEPARTMENT where DNAME = :dname} ;
4)      }   catch (SQLException se) {
5)          System.out.println("Department does not exist: " + dname) ;
6)          Return ;
7)          }
8)      System.out.println("Employee information for Department: " + dname) ;
9)      #sql iterator Emppos(String, String, String, String, double) ;
10)     Emppos e = null ;
11)     #sql e ={select eno, fname, initial, lname, salary
12)         from EMPLOYEE where DNO = :dnumber} ;
13)     #sql {fetch :e into :eno, :fn, :mi, :ln, :sal} ;
14)     while (!e.endFetch()) {
15)         System.out.println(eno + " " + fn + " " + mi + " " + ln + " " + sal) ;
16)         #sql {fetch :e into :eno, :fn, :mi, :ln, :sal} ;
17)         } ;
18)     e.close() ;
```

FIGURE 7.16 Program segment J2B, a JAVA program segment that uses a positional iterator to print employee information in a particular department.

The main advantage of using a function call interface is that it makes it easier to access multiple databases within the same application program, even if they are stored under different DBMS packages. We discuss this further in Section 7.12.2 when we discuss JAVA database programming with JDBC, although this advantage also applies to database programming with SQL/CLI and ODBC (see Section 7.12.1).

7.12.1 Database Programming with SQL/CLI Using C as the Host Language

Before using the function calls in SQL/CLI, it is necessary to install the appropriate library packages on the database server. These packages are obtained from the vendor of the DBMS being used. We now give an overview of how SQL/CLI can be used in a C program. We shall illustrate our presentation with the example program segment CLI1 shown in Figure 7.17.

When using SQL/CLI, the SQL statements are dynamically created and passed as string parameters in the function calls. Hence, it is necessary to keep track of the information about host program interactions with the database in runtime data structures, because the database commands are processed at runtime. The information is kept in four types of records, represented as *structs* in C data types. **An environment record** is used as a container to keep track of one or more database connections and to set environment information. A **connection record** keeps track of the information needed for a particular database connection. A **statement record** keeps track of the information needed for one SQL statement. A description record keeps track of the information about tuples or parameters—for example, the number of attributes and their types in a tuple, or the number and types of parameters in a function call.

```
//Program CLI1:
0)      #include sqlcli.h ;
1)      void printSal() {
2)      SQLHSTMT stmt1 ;
3)      SQLHDBC con1 ;
4)      SQLHENV env1 ;
5)      SQLRETURN ret1, ret2, ret3, ret4 ;
6)      ret1 = SQLAllocHandle(SQL_HANDLE_ENV, SQL_NULL_HANDLE, &env1) ;
7)      if (!ret1) ret2 = SQLAllocHandle(SQL_HANDLE_DBC, env1, &con1) else exit ;
8)      if (!ret2) ret3 = SQLConnect(con1, "dbs", SQL_NTS, "js", SQL_NTS, "xyz", SQL_NTS) else exit ;
9)      if (!ret3) ret4 = SQLAllocHandle(SQL_HANDLE_STMT, con1, &stmt1) else exit ;
10)     SQLPrepare(stmt1, "select LNAME, SALARY from EMPLOYEE where ENO = ?", SQL_NTS) ;
11)     prompt("Enter a Employee : ", eno) ;
12)     SQLBindParameter(stmt1, 1, SQL_CHAR, &eno, 9, &fetchlen1) ;
13)     ret1 = SQLExecute(stmt1) ;
14)     if (!ret1) {
15)         SQLBindCol(stmt1, 1, SQL_CHAR, &lname, 15, &fetchlen1) ;
16)         SQLBindCol(stmt1, 2, SQL_FLOAT, &salary, 4, &fetchlen2) ;
17)         ret2 = SQLFetch(stmt1) ;
18)         if (!ret2) printf(eno, lname, salary)
19)             else printf("Employee Number does not exist: ", eno) ;
20)         }
21)   }
```

FIGURE 7.17 Program segment CLI1, a C program segment with SQL/CLI.

Each record is accessible to the program through a C pointer variable—called a **handle** to the record. The handle is returned when a record is first created. To create a record and return its handle, the following SQL/CLI function is used:

SQLAllocHandle(<handle_type>, <handle_1>, <handle_2>)

In this function, the parameters are as follows:

- **<handle_type>** indicates the type of record being created. The possible values for this parameter are the keywords SQL_HANDLE_ENV, SQL_HANDLE_DBC, SQL_HANDLE_STMT, or SQL_HANDLE_DESC, for an environment, connection, statement, or description record, respectively.

- **<handle_1>** indicates the container within which the new handle is being created. For example, for a connection record this would be the environment within which the connection is being created, and for a statement record this would be the connection for that statement.

- **<handle_2>** is the pointer (handle) to the newly created record of type **<handle_type>**.

When writing a C program that will include database calls through SQL/CLI, the following are the typical steps that are taken. We illustrate the steps by referring to the example CLI1 in Figure 7.17, which reads a employee number of an employee and prints the employee's last name and salary.

1. The *library of functions* comprising SQL/CLI must be included in the C program. This is called **sqlcli.h**, and is included using line 0 in Figure 7.17.

2. Declare *handle variables* of types SQLHSTMT, SQLHDBC, SQLHENV, and SQLHDESC for the statements, connections, environments, and descriptions needed in the program, respectively (lines 2 to 4).[26] Also declare variables of type SQLRETURN (line 5) to hold the return codes from the SQL/CLI function calls. A return code of 0 (zero) indicates *successful execution* of the function call.

---

26. We will not show description records here, to keep our presentation simple.

3. An *environment record* must be set up in the program using SQLAllocHandle. The function to do this is shown in line 6. Because an environment record is not contained in any other record, the parameter **<handle_1>** is the null handle SQL_ NULL_HANDLE (null pointer) when creating an environment. The handle (pointer) to the newly created environment record is returned in variable env1 in line 6.

4. A *connection record* is set up in the program using SQLAllocHandle. In line 7, the connection record created has the handle con1 and is contained in the environment env1. A **connection** is then established in con1 to a particular server database using the SQLConnect function of SQL/CLI (line 8). In our example, the database server name we are connecting to is "dbs", and the account name and password for login are "js" and "xyz", respectively.

5. A *statement record* is set up in the program using SQLAllocHandle. In line 9, the statement record created has the handle stmt1 and uses the connection con1.

6. The statement is *prepared* using the SQL/CLI function SQLPrepare. In line 10, this assigns the SQL statement string (the query in our example) to the statement handle stmt1. The question mark (?) symbol in line 10 represents a **statement parameter**, which is a value to be determined at runtime—typically by binding it to a C program variable. In general, there could be several parameters. They are distinguished by the order of appearance of the question marks in the statement (the first ? represents parameter 1, the second ? represents parameter 2, and so on). The last parameter in SQLPrepare should give the length of the SQL statement string in bytes, but if we enter the keyword SQL_NTS, this indicates that the string holding the query is a *null-terminated string* so that SQL can calculate the string length automatically. This also applies to other string parameters in the function calls.

7. Before executing the query, any parameters should be bound to program variables using the SQL/CLI function **SQLBindParameter**. In Figure 7.17, the parameter (indicated by ?) to the prepared query referenced by stmt1 is bound to the C program variable eno in line 12. If there are *n* parameters in the SQL statement, we should have *n* SQLBindParameter function calls, each with a different parameter position $(1, 2, ..., n)$.

8. Following these preparations, we can now execute the SQL statement referenced by the handle **stmt1** using the function **SQLExecute** (line 13). Notice that although the query will be executed in line 13, the query results have not yet been assigned to any C program variables.

9. In order to determine where the result of the query is returned, one common technique is the **bound columns** approach. Here, each column in a query result is bound to a C program variable using the **SQLBindCol** function. The columns are distinguished by their order of appearance in the SQL query. In Figure 7.17 lines 15 and 16, the two columns in the query (LNAME and SALARY) are bound to the C program variables **lname** and **salary**, respectively.[27]

10. Finally, in order to retrieve the column values into the C program variables, the function **SQLFetch** is used (line 17). This function is similar to the FETCH command of embedded SQL. If a query result has a collection of tuples, each SQLFetch call gets the next tuple and returns its column values into the bound program variables. SQLFetch returns an exception (nonzero) code if there are no more tuples.[28]

As we can see, using dynamic function calls requires a lot of preparation to set up the SQL statements and to bind parameters and query results to the appropriate program variables.

---

27. An alternative technique known as **unbound columns** uses different SQL/CLI functions, namely SQLGetCol or SQLGetData, to retrieve columns from the query result without previously binding them; these are applied after the SQLFetch command in step 17.

28. If unbound program variables are used, SQLFetch returns the tuple into a temporary program area. Each subsequent SQLGetCol (or SQLGetData) returns one attribute value in order.

In CLI1 a *single tuple* is selected by the SQL query. Figure 7.18 shows an example of retrieving multiple tuples. We assume that appropriate C program variables have been declared as in Figure 7.18. The program segment in CLI2 reads (inputs) a department number and then retrieves the employees who work in that department. A loop then iterates over each employee record, one at a time, and prints the employee's last name and salary.

7.12.2   JDBC: SQL Function Calls for JAVA Programming

We now turn our attention to how SQL can be called from the JAVA object-oriented programming language.[29] The function libraries for this access are known as **JDBC**.[30] The JAVA programming language was designed to be platform independent—that is, a program should be able to run on any type of computer system that has a JAVA interpreter installed. Because of this portability, many RDBMS vendors provide JDBC drivers so that it is possible to access their systems via JAVA programs. A **JDBC driver** is basically an implementation of the function calls specified in the JDBC API (Application Programming Interface) for a particular vendor's RDBMS. Hence, a JAVA program with JDBC function calls can access any RDBMS that has a JDBC driver available.

Because JAVA is object-oriented, its function libraries are implemented as **classes**. Before being able to process JDBC function calls with JAVA, it is necessary to import the **JDBC class libraries**, which are called **java.sql.***. These can be downloaded and installed via the Web.[31]

JDBC is designed to allow a single JAVA program to connect to several different databases. These are sometimes called the **data sources** accessed by the JAVA program. These data sources could be stored using RDBMSs from different vendors and could reside on different machines. Hence, different data source accesses within the same JAVA program may require JDBC drivers from different vendors. To achieve this flexibility, a special JDBC class called the **driver manager** class is employed, which keeps track of the installed drivers. A driver should be *registered* with the driver manager before it is used. The operations (methods) of the driver manager class include **getDriver, registerDriver,** and **deregisterDriver.** These can be used to add and remove drivers dynamically. Other functions set up and close connections to data sources, as we shall see.

To load a JDBC driver explicitly, the generic JAVA function for loading a class can be used. For example, to load the JDBC driver for the ORACLE RDBMS, the following command can be used:

```
Class.forName("oracle.jdbc.driver.OracleDriver")
```

This will register the driver with the driver manager and make it available to the program. It is also possible to load and register the driver(s) needed in the command line that runs the program, for example, by including the following in the command line:

```
-Djdbc.drivers = oracle.jdbc.driver
```

The following are typical steps that are taken when writing a JAVA application program with database access through JDBC function calls. We illustrate the steps by referring to the example JDBC1 in Figure 7.18, which reads a employee number of an employee and prints the employee's last name and salary.

---

29. This section assumes familiarity with object-oriented concepts and basic JAVA concepts.

30. As we mentioned earlier, JDBC is a registered trademark of Sun Microsystems, although it is commonly thought to be an acronym for Java Data Base Connectivity.

31. These are available from several Web sites—for example, through the Web site at the URL http://industry.java.sun.com/products/jdbc/drivers.

```
//Program Segment CLI2:
0)      #include sqlcli.h ;
1)      void printDepartmentEmps() {
2)      SQLHSTMT stmt1 ;
3)      SQLHDBC con1 ;
4)      SQLHENV env1 ;
5)      SQLRETURN ret1, ret2, ret3, ret4 ;
6)      ret1 = SQLAllocHandle(SQL_HANDLE_ENV, SQL_NULL_HANDLE, &env1) ;
7)      if (!ret1) ret2 = SQLAllocHandle(SQL_HANDLE_DBC, env1, &con1) else exit ;
8)      if (!ret2) ret3 = SQLConnect(con1, "dbs", SQL_NTS, "js", SQL_NTS, "xyz", SQL_NTS) else exit ;
9)      if (!ret3) ret4 = SQLAllocHandle(SQL_HANDLE_STMT, con1, &stmt1) else exit ;
10)     SQLPrepare(stmt1, "select LNAME, SALARY from EMPLOYEE where DNO = ?", SQL_NTS) ;
11)     prompt("Enter the Department Number: ", dno) ;
12)     SQLBindParameter(stmt1, 1, SQL_INTEGER, &dno, 4, &fetchlen1) ;
13)     ret1 = SQLExecute(stmt1) ;
14)     if (!ret1) {
15)         SQLBindCol(stmt1, 1, SQL_CHAR, &lname, 15, &fetchlen1) ;
16)         SQLBindCol(stmt1, 2, SQL_FLOAT, &salary, 4, &fetchlen2) ;
17)         ret2 = SQLFetch(stmt1) ;
18)         while (!ret2) {
19)             printf(lname, salary) ;
20)             ret2 = SQLFetch(stmt1) ;
21)         }
22)     }
23) }
```

FIGURE 7.18 Program segment CLI2, a C program segment that uses SQL/CLI for a query with a collection of tuples in its result.

1. The JDBC *library of classes* must be imported into the JAVA program. These classes are called java.sql.*, and can be imported using line 1 in Figure 7.19. Any additional JAVA class libraries needed by the program must also be imported.

2. Load the JDBC driver as discussed previously (lines 4 to 7). The JAVA exception in line 5 occurs if the driver is not loaded successfully.

3. Create appropriate variables as needed in the JAVA program (lines 8 and 9).

4. A **connection object** is created using the **getConnection** function of the **DriverManager** class of JDBC. In lines 12 and 13, the connection object is created by using the function call **getConnection(urlstring)**, where urlstring has the form

   jdbc:oracle:<driverType>:<dbaccount>/<password>

   An alternative form is
   getConnection(url, dbaccount, password)

   Various properties can be set for a connection object, but they are mainly related to transactional properties, which we discuss in Chapter 11.

5. A **statement object** is created in the program. In JDBC, there is a basic statement class, **Statement,** with two specialized subclasses: **PreparedStatement** and **CallableStatement.** This example illustrates how **PreparedStatement** objects are created and used. The next example (Figure 7.20) illustrates the other type of Statement objects. In line 14, a query string with a single parameter—indicated by the "?" symbol—is created in the variable stmt1. In line 15, an object **p** of type **PreparedStatement** is created based on the query string in stmt1 and using the connection object conn. In general, the programmer

should use **PreparedStatement** objects if a query is to be executed multiple times, since it would be prepared, checked, and compiled only once, thus saving this cost for the additional executions of the query.

6. The question mark (?) symbol in line 14 represents a **statement parameter,** which is a value to be determined at runtime, typically by binding it to a JAVA program variable. In general, there could be several parameters, distinguished by the order of appearance of the question marks (first ? represents parameter 1, second ? represents parameter 2, and so on) in the statement, as discussed previously.

7. Before executing a **PreparedStatement** query, any parameters should be bound to program variables. Depending on the type of the parameter, functions such as **setString, setInteger, setDouble,** and so on are applied to the **PreparedStatement** object to set its parameters. In Figure 7.19, the parameter (indicated by ?) in object **p** is bound to the JAVA program variable eno in line 18. If there are n parameters in the SQL statement, we should have n Set... functions, each with a different parameter position $(1, 2, ..., n)$. Generally, it is advisable to clear all parameters before setting any new values (line 17).

8. Following these preparations, we can now execute the SQL statement referenced by the object p using the function **executeQuery** (line 19). There is a generic function execute in JDBC, plus two specialized functions: **executeUpdate** and **executeQuery. executeUpdate** is used for SQL insert, delete, or update statements, and returns an integer value indicating the number of tuples that were affected. executeQuery is used for SQL retrieval statements, and returns an object of type ResultSet, which we discuss next.

```
//Program JDBC1:
0)      import java.io.* ;
1)      import java.sql.*
        ...
2)      class getEmpInfo {
3)          public static void main (String args []) throws SQLException, IOException {
4)          try { Class.forName("oracle.jdbc.driver.OracleDriver")
5)          }   catch (ClassNotFoundException x) {
6)                  System.out.println ("Driver could not be loaded") ;
7)                  }
8)          String dbacct, passwrd, eno, lname ;
9)          Double salary ;
10)         dbacct = readentry("Enter database account:") ;
11)         passwrd = readentry("Enter pasword:") ;
12)         Connection conn = DriverManager.getConnection
13)                 ("jdbc:oracle:oci8:" + dbacct + "/" + passwrd) ;
14)         String stmt1 = "select LNAME, SALARY from EMPLOYEE where ENO = ?" ;
15)         PreparedStatement p = conn.prepareStatement(stmt1) ;
16)         eno = readentry("Enter a Employee Number: ") ;
17)         p.clearParameters() ;
18)         p.setString(1, eno) ;
19)         ResultSet r = p.executeQuery() ;
20)         while (r.next()) {
21)                 lname = r.getString(1) ;
22)                 salary = r.getDouble(2) ;
23)                 system.out.printline(lname + salary) ;
24)         }       }
25)     }
```

FIGURE 7.19 Program segment JDBC1, a JAVA program segment with JDBC.

9. In line 19, the result of the query is returned in an object **r** of type ResultSet. This resembles a two-dimensional array or a table, where the tuples are the rows and the attributes returned are the columns. A **ResultSet** object is similar to a cursor in embedded SQL and an iterator in SQLJ. In our example, when the query is executed, r refers to a tuple before the first tuple in the query result. The **r.next()** function (line 20) moves to the next tuple (row) in the **ResultSet** object and returns null if there are no more objects. This is used to control the looping. The programmer can refer to the attributes in the current tuple using various **get...** functions that depend on the type of each attribute (for example, **getString, getInteger, getDouble**, and so on). The programmer can either use the attribute positions (1, 2) or the actual attribute names ("LNAME", "SALARY") with the get... functions. In our examples, we used the positional notation in lines 21 and 22.

In general, the programmer can check for SQL exceptions after each JDBC function call. Notice that JDBC does not distinguish between queries that return single tuples and those that return multiple tuples, unlike some of the other techniques. This is justifiable because a single tuple result set is just a special case.

In example JDBC1, a *single tuple* is selected by the SQL query, so the loop in lines 20 to 24 is executed at most once. The next example, shown in Figure 7.20, illustrates the retrieval of multiple tuples. The program segment in JDBC2 reads (inputs) a department number and then retrieves the employees who work in that department. A loop then iterates over each employee record, one at a time, and prints the employee's last name and salary. This example also illustrates how we can execute a query directly, without having to prepare it as in the previous example. This technique is preferred for queries that will be executed only once, since it is simpler to program. In line 17 of Figure 7.20, the programmer creates a **Statement** object (instead of **PreparedStatement**, as in the previous example) without associating it with a particular query string. The query string q is passed to the statement object **s** when it is executed in line 18.

```
//Program Segment JDBC2:
0)      import java.io.* ;
1)      import java.sql.*
        ...
2)      class printDepartmentEmps {
3)          public static void main (String args []) throws SQLException, IOException {
4)              try { Class.forName("oracle.jdbc.driver.OracleDriver")
5)              } catch (ClassNotFoundException x) {
6)                  System.out.println ("Driver could not be loaded") ;
7)              }
8)          String dbacct, passwrd, lname ;
9)          Double salary ;
10)         Integer dno ;
11)         dbacct = readentry("Enter database account:") ;
12)         passwrd = readentry("Enter pasword:") ;
13)         Connection conn = DriverManager.getConnection
14)             ("jdbc:oracle:oci8:" + dbacct + "/" + passwrd) ;
15)         dno = readentry("Enter a Department Number: ") ;
16)         String q = "select LNAME, SALARY from EMPLOYEE where DNO = " + dno.tostring()
17)         Statement s = conn.createStatement() ;
18)         ResultSet r = s.executeQuery(q) ;
19)         while (r.next()) {
20)             lname = r.getString(1) ;
21)             salary = r.getDouble(2) ;
22)             system.out.println(lname + salary) ;
23)         }   }
24) }
```

FIGURE 7.20 Program segment JDBC2, a JAVA program segment that uses JDBC for a query with a collection of tuples in its result.

This concludes our brief introduction to JDBC. The interested reader is referred to the Web site http://java.sun.com/docs/books/tutorial/jdbc/, which contains many further details on JDBC.

7.13   DATABASE STORED PROCEDURES AND SQL/PSM

We conclude this chapter with two additional topics **related** to database programming. In Section 7.13.1, we discuss the concept of stored procedures, which are program modules that are stored by the DBMS at the database server. Then in Section 7.13.2, we discuss the extensions to SQL that are specified in the standard to include general-purpose programming constructs in SQL. These extensions are known as SQL/PSM (SQL/Persistent Stored Modules) and can be used to write stored procedures. SQL/PSM also serves as an example of a database programming language that extends a database model and language—namely, SQL—with some programming constructs, such as conditional statements and loops.

7.13.1   Database Stored Procedures and Functions

In our presentation of database programming techniques so far, there was an implicit assumption that the database application program was running on a client machine that is different from the machine on which the database server—and the main part of the DBMS software package—is located. Although this is suitable for many applications, it is sometimes useful to create database program modules—procedures or functions—that are stored and executed by the DBMS at the database server. These are historically known as database **stored procedures**, although they can be functions or procedures. The term used in the SQL standard for stored procedures is **persistent stored modules**, because these programs are stored persistently by the DBMS, similarly to the persistent data stored by the DBMS.

Stored procedures are useful in the following circumstances:

- If a database program is needed by several applications, it can be stored at the server and invoked by any of the application programs. This reduces duplication of effort and improves software modularity.

- Executing a program at the server can reduce data transfer and hence communication cost between the client and server in certain situations.

- These procedures can enhance the modeling power provided by views by allowing more complex types of derived data to be made available to the database users. In addition, they can be used to check for complex constraints that are beyond the specification power of assertions and triggers.

In general, many commercial DBMSs allow stored procedures and functions to be written in a general-purpose programming language. Alternatively, a stored procedure can be made of simple SQL commands such as retrievals and updates. The general form of declaring a stored procedures is as follows:

CREATE PROCEDURE <procedure name> (<parameters>)
<local declarations>
<procedure body> ;

The parameters and local declarations are optional, and are specified only if needed. For declaring a function, a return type is necessary, so the declaration form is

CREATE FUNCTION <function name> (<parameters>)
RETURNS <return type>
<local declarations>
<function body> ;

If the procedure (or function) is written in a general-purpose programming language, it is typical to specify the language, as well as a file name where the program code is stored. For example, the following format can be used:

CREATE PROCEDURE <procedure name> (<parameters>)
LANGUAGE <programming language name>
EXTERNAL NAME <file path name> ;

In general, each parameter should have a **parameter type** that is one of the SQL data types. Each parameter should also have a **parameter mode**, which is one of IN, OUT, or INOUT. These correspond to parameters whose values are input only, output (returned) only, or both input and output, respectively.

Because the procedures and functions are stored persistently by the DBMS, it should be possible to call them from the various SQL interfaces and programming techniques. The **CALL statement** in the SQL standard can be used to invoke a stored procedure—either from an interactive interface or from embedded SQL or SQLJ. The format of the statement is as follows:

CALL <procedure or function name> (<argument list>) ;

If this statement is called from JDBC, it should be assigned to a statement object of type CallableStatement (see Section 7.12.2).

7.13.2 SQL/PSM: Extending SQL for Specifying Persistent Stored Modules

SQL/PSM is the part of the SQL standard that specifies how to write persistent stored modules. It includes the statements to create functions and procedures that we described in the previous section. It also includes additional programming constructs to enhance the power of SQL for the purpose of writing the code (or body) of stored procedures and functions.

In this section, we discuss the SQL/PSM constructs for conditional (branching) statements and for looping statements. These will give a flavor of the type of constructs that SQL/PSM has incorporated.[32] Then we give an example to illustrate how these constructs can be used.

The conditional branching statement in SQL/PSM has the following form:

IF <condition> **THEN** <statement list>
      ELSEIF <condition> **THEN** <statement list>
      ...
      ELSEIF <condition> **THEN** <statement list>
      ELSE <statement list>
      END IF ;

---

32. We only give a brief introduction to SQL/PSM here. There are many other features in the SQL/PSM standard.

Consider the example in Figure 7.21, which illustrates how the conditional branch structure can be used in an SQL/PSM function. The function returns a string value (line 1) describing the size of a department based on the number of employees. There is one IN integer parameter, deptno, which gives a department number. A local variable **NoOfEmps** is declared in line 2. The query in lines 3 and 4 returns the number of employees in the department, and the conditional branch in lines 5 to 8 then returns one of the values {"HUGE", "LARGE", "MEDIUM", "SMALL"} based on the number of employees.

SQL/PSM has several constructs for looping. There are standard while and repeat looping structures, which have the following forms:

WHILE <condition> DO
        <statement list>
END WHILE ;

```
//Function PSM1:
0)    CREATE FUNCTION DeptSize(IN deptno INTEGER)
1)    RETURNS VARCHAR [7]
2)    DECLARE NoOfEmps INTEGER ;
3)    SELECT COUNT(*) INTO NoOfEmps
4)    FROM EMPLOYEE WHERE DNO = deptno ;
5)    IF NoOfEmps > 100 THEN RETURN "HUGE"
6)       ELSEIF NoOfEmps > 25 THEN RETURN "LARGE"
7)       ELSEIF NoOfEmps > 10 THEN RETURN "MEDIUM"
8)       ELSE RETURN "SMALL"
9)    END IF ;
```

FIGURE 7.21 Declaring a function in SQL/PSM.

REPEAT
        <statement list>
UNTIL <condition>
END REPEAT ;

There is also a cursor-based looping structure. The statement list in such a loop is executed once for each tuple in the query result. This has the following form:

FOR <loop name> AS <cursor name> CURSOR FOR <query> DO
        <statement list>
END FOR ;

Loops can have names, and there is a **LEAVE <loop name>** statement to break a loop when a condition is satisfied. SQL/PSM has many other features, but they are outside the scope of our presentation.

7.14   SUMMARY

In this chapter we presented the SQL database language. This language or variations of it have been implemented as interfaces to many commercial relational DBMSs, including Oracle, IBM's DB2 and SQL/DS, Microsoft's SQL Server and ACCESS, INGRES, INFORMIX, and SYBASE. The original version of SQL was implemented in the experimental DBMS called SYSTEM R, which was developed at IBM Research. SQL is designed to be a comprehensive language that includes statements for data definition, queries, updates, view definition, and constraint specification. We discussed many of these in separate sections of this chapter. In the final section we discussed additional features that are described elsewhere in the book. Our emphasis was on the SQL-99 standard.

Table 7.2 summarizes the syntax (or structure) of various SQL statements. This summary is not meant to be comprehensive nor to describe every possible SQL construct; rather, it is meant to serve as a quick reference to the major types of constructs available in SQL. We use BNF notation, where nonterminal symbols are shown in angled brackets < . . . >, optional parts are shown in square brackets [. . .], repetitions are shown in braces { . . . }, and alternatives are shown in parentheses (. . . | . . . | . . .).[33]

We also presented additional features of the SQL database language. In particular, we presented an overview of the most important techniques for database programming. We started in Section 7.8 by presenting the features for specifying general constraints as assertions. Then we discussed the concept of a view in SQL. We then discussed the various approaches to database application programming in Sections 7.10 to 7.13.

TABLE 7.2 SUMMARY OF SQL SYNTAX

CREATE TABLE <table name>   (<column name> <column type> [<attribute constraint>]
                               {, <column name> <column type> [<attribute constraint>]}
                               [<table constraint> {,<table constraint>}])

DROP TABLE <table name>

ALTER TABLE <table name> ADD <column name> <column type>

SELECT [DISTINCT] <attribute list>
FROM (<table name>{<alias>} | <joined table>){,(<table name>{<alias>} | <joined>)}
[WHERE <condition>]
[GROUP BY <grouping attriputes>[HAVING <group selection condition>]]
[ORDER BY <column name>[<order>]{,<column name>[<order>]}]

<attribute list>::=(* | (<column name> | <function>(([DISTINCT]<column name> | *)))
                  {,(<column name> | <function>(([DISTINCT]<column name> | *))}))
<grouping attributes>::=<column name>{, <column name>}
<order>::=(ASC | DESC)

INSERT INTO <table name>[(<column name>{, <column name>})]
(VALUES(<constant value>, {<constant value>}){,(<constant value>{,<constant value>})}
| <select statement>)

DELETE FROM <table name>
[WHERE <selection condition>]

UPDATE <table name>
SET <column name>=<value expression>{,<column name>=<value expression>}
[WHERE <selection condition>]

CREATE [UNIQUE] INDEX <index name>
ON <table name> (<column name>[<order>]{, <column name>[<order>]})
[CLUSTER]

DROP INDEX <index name>

CREATE VIEW <view name>[(<column name>{, <column name>})]
AS <select statement>

DROP VIEW <view name>

---

*The last two commands are not part of standard SQL2.

---

33. The full syntax of SQL-99 is described in many voluminous documents of hundreds of pages.

Review Questions

7.1. How do the relations (tables) in SQL differ from the relations defined formally in Chapter 4? Discuss the other differences in terminology. Why does SQL allow duplicate tuples in a table or in a query result?

7.2. List the data types that are allowed for SQL attributes.

7.3. How does SQL allow implementation of the entity integrity and referential integrity constraints described in Chapter 4? What about referential triggered actions?

7.4. Describe the six clauses in the syntax of an SQL query, and show what type of constructs can be specified in each of the six clauses. Which of the six clauses are required and which are optional?

7.5. Describe conceptually how an SQL query will be executed by specifying the conceptual order of executing each of the six clauses.

7.6. Discuss how NULLs are treated in comparison operators in SQL. How are NULLs treated when aggregate functions are applied in an SQL query? How are NULLs treated if they exist in grouping attributes?

7.7. How does SQL allow implementation of general integrity constraints?

7.8. What is a view in SQL, and how is it defined? Discuss the problems that may arise when one attempts to update a view. How are views typically implemented?

7.9. List the three main approaches to database programming. What are the advantages and disadvantages of each approach?

7.10. What is the impedance mismatch problem? Which of the three programming approaches minimizes this problem?

7.11. Describe the concept of a cursor and how it is used in embedded SQL.

7.12. What is SQLJ used for? Describe the two types of iterators available in SQLJ.

Exercises

7.13. Consider the database shown in Figure 1.2, whose schema is shown in Figure 2.1. What are the referential integrity constraints that should hold on the schema? Write appropriate SQL DDL statements to define the database.

7.14. Repeat Exercise 7.13, but use the AIRLINE database schema of Figure 4.8.

7.15. Consider the LIBRARY relational database schema of Figure 5.12. Choose the appropriate action (reject, cascade, set to null, set to default) for each referential integrity constraint, both for *deletion* of a referenced tuple, and for *update* of a primary key attribute value in a referenced tuple. Justify your choices.

7.16. Write appropriate SQL DDL statements for declaring the LIBRARY relational database schema of Figure 5.12. Specify appropriate keys and referential triggered actions.

7.17. Write SQL queries for the LIBRARY database queries given in Exercise 5.18.

7.18. How can the key and foreign key constraints be enforced by the DBMS? Is the enforcement technique you suggest difficult to implement? Can the constraint checks be executed efficiently when updates are applied to the database?

7.19. Specify the queries of Exercise 5.16 in SQL. Show the result of each query if it is applied to the COMPANY database of Figure 4.6.

7.20. Specify the following additional queries on the database of Figure 4.5 in SQL. Show the query results if each query is applied to the database of Figure 4.6.

   a. For each department whose average employee salary is more than Rs. 30,000, retrieve the department name and the number of employees working for that department.

   b. Suppose that we want the number of *male* employees in each department rather than all employees (as in Exercise 7.20a). Can we specify this query in SQL? Why or why not?

7.21. Specify the updates of Exercise 4.10, using the SQL update commands.

7.22. Specify the following queries in SQL on the database schema of Figure 1.2.

   a. Retrieve the names of all senior students majoring in 'CS' (computer science).
   b. Retrieve the names of all courses taught by Professor Jain in 1998 and 1999.
   c. For each section taught by Professor Jain, retrieve the course number, semester, year, and number of students who took the section.
   d. Retrieve the name and transcript of each senior student (Class = 5) majoring in CS. A transcript includes course name, course number, credit hours, semester, year, and grade for each course completed by the student.
   e. Retrieve the names and major departments of all straight-A students (students who have a grade of A in all their courses).
   f. Retrieve the names and major departments of all students who do not have a grade of A in any of their courses.

7.23. Write SQL update statements to do the following on the database schema shown in Figure 1.2.

   a. Insert a new student, <'Johnson', 25, 1, 'MATH'>, in the database.
   b. Change the class of student 'Uday' to 2.
   c. Insert a new course, <'Knowledge Engineering', 'CS4390', 3, 'CS'>.
   d. Delete the record for the student whose name is 'Uday' and whose student number is 17.

7.24. Specify the queries and updates of Exercises 5.17 and 4.11, which refer to the AIRLINE database (see Figure 4.8), in SQL.

7.25. a. Design a relational database schema for your database application.
   b. Declare your relations, using the SQL DDL.
   c. Specify a number of queries in SQL that are needed by your database application.
   d. Based on your expected use of the database, choose some attributes that should have indexes specified on them.
   e. Implement your database, if you have a DBMS that supports SQL.

7.26. Specify the answers to Exercises 5.19 through 5.21 and Exercise 5.23 in SQL.

7.27. Consider the database shown in Figure 1.2, whose schema is shown in Figure 2.1. Write a program segment to read a student's name and print his or her grade point average, assuming that $A=4$, $B=3$, $C=2$, and $D=1$ points. Use embedded SQL with C as the host language.

7.28. Repeat Exercise 7.27, but use SQLJ with JAVA as the host language.

7.29. Consider the LIBRARY relational database schema of Figure 5.12. Write a program segment that retrieves the list of books that became overdue yesterday and that prints the book title and borrower name for each. Use embedded SQL with C as the host language.

7.30. Repeat Exercise 7.29, but use SQLJ with JAVA as the host language.

7.31. Repeat Exercises 7.27 and 7.29, but use SQL/CLI with C as the host language.

7.32. Repeat Exercises 7.27 and 7.29, but use JDBC with JAVA as the host language.

7.33. Repeat Exercise 7.27, but write a function in SQL/PSM.

7.34. Specify the following views in SQL on the COMPANY database schema shown in Figure 4.5.
   a. A view that has the department name, manager name, and manager salary for every department.
   b. A view that has the employee name, supervisor name, and employee salary for each employee who works in the 'Research' department.
   c. A view that has the project name, controlling department name, number of employees, and total hours worked per week on the project for each project.
   d. A view that has the project name, controlling department name, number of employees, and total hours worked per week on the project for each project *with more than one employee working on it.*

7.35. Consider the following view, DEPT_SUMMARY, defined on the COMPANY database of Figure 4.6:

CREATE VIEW	DEPT_SUMMARY (D, C, TOTAL_S, AVERAGE_S)
AS SELECT	DNO, **COUNT (*)**, **SUM** (SALARY), **AVG** (SALARY)
	FROM EMPLOYEE
	GROUP BY DNO;

State which of the following queries and updates would be allowed on the view. If a query or update would be allowed, show what the corresponding query or update on the base relations would look like, and give its result when applied to the database of Figure 4.6.

a.	**SELECT**	*
	FROM	DEPT_SUMMARY;
b.	**SELECT**	D, C
	FROM	DEPT_SUMMARY
	WHERE	TOTAL_S > 100000;
c.	**SELECT**	D, AVERAGE_S
	FROM	DEPT_SUMMARY
	WHERE	C > (**SELECT** C **FROM** DEPT_SUMMARY **WHERE** D=4);
d.	**UPDATE**	DEPT_SUMMARY
	SET	D=3
	WHERE	D=4;
e.	**DELETE**	**FROM** DEPT_SUMMARY
	WHERE	C > 4;

Selected Bibliography

The SQL language, originally named SEQUEL, was based on the language SQUARE (Specifying Queries as Relational Expressions), described by Boyce et al. (1975). The syntax of SQUARE was modified into SEQUEL (Chamberlin and Boyce 1974) and then into SEQUEL2 (Chamberlin et al. 1976), on which SQL is based. The original implementation of SEQUEL was done at IBM Research, San Jose, California.

Reisner (1977) describes a human factors evaluation of SEQUEL in which she found that users have some difficulty with specifying join conditions and grouping correctly. Date (1984b) contains a critique of the SQL language that points out its strengths and shortcomings. Date and Darwen (1993) describes SQL2. ANSI (1986) outlines the original SQL standard, and ANSI (1992) describes the SQL2 standard. Various vendor manuals describe the characteristics of SQL as implemented on DB2, SQL/DS, Oracle, INGRES, INFORMIX, and other commercial DBMS products. Melton and Simon (1993) is a comprehensive treatment of SQL2. Horowitz (1992) discusses some of the problems related to referential integrity and propagation of updates in SQL2.

The question of view updates is addressed by Dayal and Bernstein (1978), Keller (1982), and Langerak (1990), among others. View implementation is discussed in Blakeley et al. (1989). Negri et al. (1991) describes formal semantics of SQL queries.

3

DATABASE DESIGN THEORY
AND METHODOLOGY

3

DATABASE DESIGN THEORY AND METHODOLOGY

8

Relational Database Design

[Earlier Chapter Number 10]

In Chapters 4 through 7, we presented various aspects of the relational model and the languages associated with it. Each *relation schema* consists of a number of attributes, and the *relational database schema* consists of a number of relation schemas. So far, we have assumed that attributes are grouped to form a relation schema by using the common sense of the database designer or by mapping a database schema design from a conceptual data model such as the ER or enhanced ER (EER) or some other conceptual data model. These models make the designer identify entity types and relationship types and their respective attributes, which leads to a natural and logical grouping of the attributes into relations when the mapping procedures in Chapter 6 are followed. However, we still need some formal measure of why one grouping of attributes into a relation schema may be better than another. So far in our discussion of conceptual design in Chapter 3 and its mapping into the relational model in Chapter 6, we have not developed any measure of appropriateness or "goodness" to measure the quality of the design, other than the intuition of the designer. In this chapter we discuss some of the theory that has been developed with the goal of evaluating relational schemas for design quality—that is, to measure formally why one set of groupings of attributes into relation schemas is better than another.

There are two levels at which we can discuss the "goodness" of relation schemas. The first is the **logical** (or **conceptual**) **level**—how users interpret the relation schemas and the meaning of their attributes. Having good relation schemas at this level enables users to understand clearly the meaning of the data in the relations, and hence to formulate their queries correctly. The second is the **implementation** (or **storage**) **level**—how the tuples in a base relation are stored and updated. This level applies only to schemas of base relations—which will be physically stored as files—whereas at the logical level we are interested in schemas of both *base relations* and views (virtual relations). The relational database design theory developed in this chapter applies mainly to *base relations*, although some criteria of appropriateness also apply to views, as shown in Section 8.1.

As with many design problems, database design may be performed using two approaches: bottom-up or top-down. A **bottom-up design methodology** (also called *design by synthesis*) considers the basic relationships *among individual attributes* as the starting point and uses those to construct relation schemas. This approach is not very popular in practice[1] because it suffers from the problem of having to collect a large number of binary relationships among attributes as the starting point. In contrast, a **top-down design methodology** (also called *design by analysis*) starts with a number of groupings of attributes into relations that exist together naturally, for example, on an invoice, a form, or a report. The relations are then analyzed individually and collectively, leading to further decomposition until all desirable properties are met. The theory described in this chapter is applicable to both the top-down and bottom-up design approaches, but is more practical when used with the top-down approach.

In this chapter, we also describe some of these normalization algorithms as well as the other types of dependencies. We also describe the two desirable properties of nonadditive (lossless) joins and dependency preservation in more detail. The normalization algorithms typically start by synthesizing one giant relation schema, called the **universal relation**, which is a theoretical relation that includes all the database attributes. We then perform **decomposition**—breaking up into smaller relation schemas—until it is no longer feasible or no longer desirable, based on the functional and other dependencies specified by the database designer.

We start this chapter by informally discussing some criteria for good and bad relation schemas in Section 8.1. Then in Section 8.2 we define the concept of *functional dependency*, a formal constraint among attributes that is the main tool for formally measuring the appropriateness of attribute groupings into relation schemas. Properties of functional dependencies are also studied and analyzed. In Section 8.3 we show how functional dependencies can be used to group attributes into relation schemas that are in a *normal form*. A relation schema is in a normal form when it satisfies certain desirable properties. The process of *normalization* consists of analyzing relations to meet increasingly more stringent normal forms leading to progressively better groupings of attributes. Normal forms are specified in terms of functional dependencies—which are identified by the database designer—and key attributes of relation schemas. In Section 8.4 we discuss more general definitions of normal forms that can be directly applied to any given design and do not require step-by-step analysis and normalization. Then, we discuss the concept of Boyce-Codd normal form in Section 8.5.

We describe in Section 8.6 the two desirable **properties of decompositions**, namely, the dependency preservation property and the lossless (or nonadditive) join property, which are both used by the design algorithms to achieve desirable decompositions. It is important to note that it is *insufficient* to test the relation schemas *independently of one another* for compliance with higher normal forms like 2NF, 3NF, and BCNF. The resulting relations must collectively satisfy these two additional properties to qualify as a good design. Section 8.7 presents several normalization algorithms based on functional dependencies alone that can be used to design 3NF and BCNF schemas.

We then introduce other types of data dependencies, including multivalued dependencies and join dependencies, that specify constraints that *cannot* be expressed by functional dependencies. Presence of these dependencies leads to the definition of fourth normal form (4NF) and fifth normal form (5NF), respectively.

---

1. An exception in which this approach is used in practice is based on a model called the binary relational model. An example is the NIAM methodology (Verheijen and VanBekkum 1982).

8.1   INFORMAL DESIGN GUIDELINES FOR RELATION SCHEMAS

We discuss four *informal measures* of quality for relation schema design in this section:

- Semantics of the relation attributes
- Reducing the redundant values in tuples
- Reducing the null values in tuples
- Disallowing the possibility of generating spurious tuples

These measures are not always independent of one another, as we shall see.

8.1.1   Semantics of the Relation Attributes

Whenever we group attributes to form a relation schema, we assume that attributes belonging to one relation have certain real-world meaning and a proper interpretation associated with them. In Chapter 4 we discussed how each relation can be interpreted as a set of facts or statements. This meaning, or **semantics**, specifies how to interpret the attribute values stored in a tuple of the relation—in other words, how the attribute values in a tuple relate to one another. If the conceptual design is done carefully, followed by a systematic mapping into relations, most of the semantics will have been accounted for and the resulting design should have a clear meaning.

In general, the easier it is to explain the semantics of the relation, the better the relation schema design will be. To illustrate this, consider Figure 8.1, a simplified version of the COMPANY relational database schema of Figure 4.5, and Figure 8.2, which presents an example of populated relation states of this schema. The meaning of the EMPLOYEE relation schema is quite simple: Each tuple represents an employee, with values for the employee's name (ENAME), employee number (ENO), birth date (DOB), and address (ADDRESS), and the number of the department that the employee works for (DNUMBER). The DNUMBER attribute is a foreign key that represents an *implicit relationship* between EMPLOYEE and DEPARTMENT. The semantics of the DEPARTMENT and PROJECT schemas are also straightforward: Each DEPARTMENT tuple represents a department entity, and each PROJECT tuple represents a project entity. The attribute DMGRENO of DEPARTMENT relates a department to the employee who is its manager, while DNUM of PROJECT relates a project to its controlling department; both are foreign key attributes. The ease with which the meaning of a relation's attributes can be explained is an *informal measure* of how well the relation is designed.

The semantics of the other two relation schemas in Figure 8.1 are slightly more complex. Each tuple in DEPT_LOCATIONS gives a department number (DNUMBER) and *one of* the locations of the department (DLOCATION). Each tuple in WORKS_ON gives an employee number (ENO), the project number of *one of* the projects that the employee works on (PNUMBER), and the number of hours per week that the employee works on that project (HOURS). However, both schemas have a well-defined and unambiguous interpretation. The schema DEPT_LOCATIONS represents a multivalued attribute of DEPARTMENT, whereas WORKS_ON represents an M:N relationship between EMPLOYEE and PROJECT. Hence, all the relation schemas in Figure 8.1 may be considered as easy to explain and hence good from the standpoint of having clear semantics. We can thus formulate the following informal design guideline.

GUIDELINE 1.   Design a relation schema so that it is easy to explain its meaning. Do not combine attributes from multiple entity types and relationship types into a single relation. Intuitively, if a relation schema corresponds to one entity type or one relationship type, it is straightforward to explain its meaning.

Otherwise, if the relation corresponds to a mixture of multiple entities and relationships, semantic ambiguities will result and the relation cannot be easily explained.

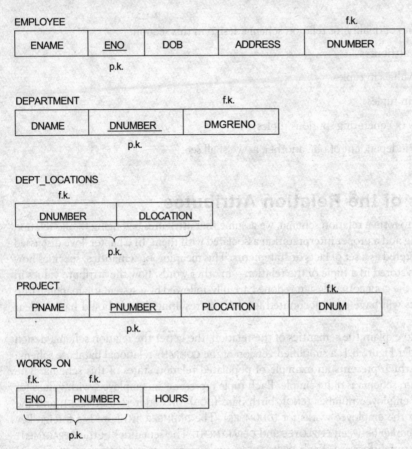

FIGURE 8.1 A simplified COMPANY relational database schema.

The relation schemas in Figures 8.3a and 8.3b also have clear semantics. (The reader should ignore the lines under the relations for now; they are used to illustrate functional dependency notation, discussed in Section 8.2.) A tuple in the EMP_DEPT relation schema of Figure 8.3a represents a single employee but includes additional information—namely, the name (DNAME) of the department for which the employee works and the number (DMGRENO) of the department manager. For the EMP_PROJ relation of Figure 8.3b, each tuple relates an employee to a project but also includes the employee name (ENAME), project name (PNAME), and project location (PLOCATION). Although there is nothing wrong logically with these two relations, they are considered poor designs because they violate Guideline 1 by mixing attributes from distinct real-world entities; EMP_DEPT mixes attributes of employees and departments, and EMP_PROJ mixes attributes of employees and projects. They may be used as views, but they cause problems when used as base relations, as we discuss in the following section.

EMPLOYEE

ENAME	ENO	DOB	ADDRESS	DNUMBER
Mahesh, B. Kumar	123456789	09-01-1965	731, Ameerpet, Hyderabad, AP	5
Karthik, T. Chandra	333445555	08-12-1955	638, Begumpet, Hyderabad, AP	5
Sweta, J. Narayanan	999887777	19-01-1968	332, Hauzkhas, New Delhi	4
Priya, S. Ganesh	987654321	20-06-1941	291, Majestic street, Bangalore	4
Ramesh, K. Narayan	666884444	15-09-1962	975, Hauzkhas, New Delhi	5
Kiran, A. Goyal	453453453	31-07-1972	5631, Abids, Hyderabad, AP	5
Jitendra, V. Nath	987987987	29-03-1969	980, Koti, Hyderabad, AP	4
Gaurav, E. Kishan	888665555	10-11-1937	450, Abids, Hyderabad, AP	1

DEPARTMENT

DNAME	DNUMBER	DMGRENO
Research	5	333445555
Administration	4	987654321
Headquarters	1	888665555

DEPT_LOCATIONS

DNUMBER	DLOCATION
1	Hyderabad
4	Chennai
5	Bangalore
5	New Delhi
5	Hyderabad

WORKS_ON

ENO	PNUMBER	HOURS
123456789	1	32.5
123456789	2	7.5
666884444	3	40.0
453453453	1	20.0
453453453	2	20.0
333445555	2	10.0
333445555	3	10.0
333445555	10	10.0
333445555	20	10.0
999887777	30	30.0
999887777	10	10.0
987987987	10	35.0
987987987	30	5.0
987654321	30	20.0
987654321	20	15.0
888665555	20	null

PROJECT

PNAME	PNUMBER	PLOCATION	DNUM
ProductX	1	Bangalore	5
ProductY	2	New Delhi	5
ProductZ	3	Hyderabad	5
Computerization	10	Chennai	4
Reorganization	20	Hyderabad	1
Newbenefits	30	Chennai	4

FIGURE 8.2 Example database state for the relational database schema of Figure 8.1.

8.1.2   Redundant Information in Tuples and Update Anomalies

One goal of schema design is to minimize the storage space used by the base relations (and hence the corresponding files). Grouping attributes into relation schemas has a significant effect on storage space. For example, compare the space used by the two base relations EMPLOYEE and DEPARTMENT in Figure 8.2 with that for an EMP_DEPT base relation in Figure 8.4, which is the result of applying the NATURAL JOIN operation to EMPLOYEE and DEPARTMENT. In EMP_DEPT, the attribute values pertaining to a particular department

(DNUMBER, DNAME, DMGRENO) are repeated for *every employee who works for that department*. In contrast, each department's information appears only once in the DEPARTMENT relation in Figure 8.2. Only the department number (DNUMBER) is repeated in the EMPLOYEE relation for each employee who works in that department. Similar comments apply to the EMP_PROJ relation (Figure 8.4), which augments the WORKS_ON relation with additional attributes from EMPLOYEE and PROJECT.

FIGURE 8.3 Two relation schemas suffering from update anomalies.

Another serious problem with using the relations in Figure 8.4 as base relations is the problem of **update anomalies**. These can be classified into insertion anomalies, deletion anomalies, and modification anomalies.[2]

Insertion Anomalies.   Insertion anomalies can be differentiated into two types, illustrated by the following examples based on the EMP_DEPT relation:

- To insert a new employee tuple into EMP_DEPT, we must include either the attribute values for the department that the employee works for, or nulls (if the employee does not work for a department as yet). For example, to insert a new tuple for an employee who works in department number 5, we must enter the attribute values of department 5 correctly so that they are consistent with values for department 5 in other tuples in EMP_DEPT. In the design of Figure 8.2, we do not have to worry about this consistency problem because we enter only the department number in the employee tuple; all other attribute values of department 5 are recorded only once in the database, as a single tuple in the DEPARTMENT relation.

- It is difficult to insert a new department that has no employees as yet in the EMP_DEPT relation. The only way to do this is to place null values in the attributes for employee. This causes a problem because ENO is the primary key of EMP_DEPT, and each tuple is supposed to represent an employee entity—not a department entity. Moreover, when the first employee is assigned to that department, we do not need this tuple with null values any more. This problem does not occur in the design of Figure 8.2, because a department is entered in the DEPARTMENT relation whether or not any employees work for it, and whenever an employee is assigned to that department, a corresponding tuple is inserted in EMPLOYEE.

Deletion Anomalies.   The problem of deletion anomalies is related to the second insertion anomaly situation discussed earlier. If we delete from EMP_DEPT an employee tuple that happens to represent the last

---

2. These anomalies were identified by Codd (1972a) to justify the need for normalization of relations, as we shall discuss in Section 8.3.

employee working for a particular department, the information concerning that department is lost from the database. This problem does not occur in the database of Figure 8.2 because DEPARTMENT tuples are stored

EMP_DEPT

redundancy

ENAME	ENO	DOB	ADDRESS	DNUMBER	DNAME	DMGRENO
Mahesh, B. Kumar	123456789	09-01-1965	731, Ameerpet, Hyderabad, AP	5	Research	333445555
Karthik, T. Chandra	333445555	08-12-1955	638, Begumpet, Hyderabad, AP	5	Research	333445555
Swetha, J. Narayan	999887777	19-07-1968	3321, Hauzkhas, New Delhi	4	Administration	987654321
Priya, S. Ganesh	987654321	20-06-1941	291, Majestic street, Bangalore	4	Administration	987654321
Ramesh, K. Narayan	666884444	15-09-1962	975, Hauzkhas, New Delhi	5	Research	333445555
Kiran, A. Goyal	453453453	31-07-1972	5631, Abids, Hyderabad, AP	5	Research	333445555
Jitendra, V. Nath	987987987	29-03-1969	980, Koti, Hyderabad, AP	4	Administration	987654321
Gaurav, E. kishan	888665555	10-11-1937	450, Abids, Hyderabad, AP	1	Headquarters	888665555

EMP_PROJ

redundancy   redundancy

ENO	PNUMBER	HOURS	ENAME	PNAME	PLOCATION
123456789	1	32.5	Mahesh, B. Kumar	ProductX	Bangalore
123456789	2	7.5	Mahesh, B. Kumar	ProductY	New Delhi
666884444	3	40.0	Ramesh, K. Narayan	ProductZ	Hyderabad
453453453	1	20.0	Kiran, A. Goyal	ProductX	Bangalore
453453453	2	20.0	Kiran, A. Goyal	ProductY	New Delhi
333445555	2	10.0	Karthik, T. Chandra	ProductY	New Delhi
333445555	3	10.0	Karthik, T. Chandra	ProductZ	Hyderabad
333445555	10	10.0	Karthik, T. Chandra	Computerization	Chennai
333445555	20	10.0	Karthik, T. Chandra	Reorganization	Hyderabad
999887777	30	30.0	Sweta, J. Narayan	Newbenefits	Chennai
999887777	10	10.0	Sweta, J. Narayan	Computerization	Chennai
987987987	10	35.0	Jitendra, V. Nath	Computerization	Chennai
987987987	30	5.0	Jitendra, V. Nath	Newbenefits	Chennai
987654321	30	20.0	Priya, S. Ganesh	Newbenefits	Chennai
987654321	20	15.0	Priya, S. Ganesh	Reorganization	Hyderabad
888665555	20	null	Gaurav, E. Kishan	Reorganization	Hyderabad

FIGURE 8.4 Example states for EMP_DEPT and EMP_PROJ resulting from applying NATURAL JOIN to the relations in Figure 8.2. These may be stored as base relations for performance reasons.

separately.

Modification Anomalies. In EMP_DEPT, if we change the value of one of the attributes of a particular department—say, the manager of department 5—we must update the tuples of all employees who work in that department; otherwise, the database will become inconsistent. If we fail to update some tuples, the same department will be shown to have two different values for manager in different employee tuples, which would be wrong.[3]

Based on the preceding three anomalies, we can state the guideline that follows.

GUIDELINE 2. Design the base relation schemas so that no insertion, deletion, or modification anomalies are present in the relations. If any anomalies are present, note them clearly and make sure that the programs that update the database will operate correctly.

---

3. This is not as serious as the other problems, because all tuples can be updated by a single SQL query.

The second guideline is consistent with and, in a way, a restatement of the first guideline. We can also see the need for a more formal approach to evaluating whether a design meets these guidelines. Sections 8.2 through 8.4 provide these needed formal concepts. It is important to note that these guidelines may sometimes *have to be violated* in order to *improve the performance* of certain queries. For example, if an important query retrieves information concerning the department of an employee along with employee attributes, the EMP_DEPT schema may be used as a base relation. However, the anomalies in EMP_DEPT must be noted and accounted for (for example, by using triggers or stored procedures that would make automatic updates) so that, whenever the base relation is updated, we do not end up with inconsistencies. In general, it is advisable to use anomaly-free base relations and to specify views that include the joins for placing together the attributes frequently referenced in important queries. This reduces the number of JOIN terms specified in the query, making it simpler to write the query correctly, and in many cases it improves the performance.[4]

8.1.3 Null Values in Tuples

In some schema designs we may group many attributes together into a "fat" relation. If many of the attributes do not apply to all tuples in the relation, we end up with many nulls in those tuples. This can waste space at the storage level and may also lead to problems with understanding the meaning of the attributes and with specifying JOIN operations at the logical level.[5] Another problem with nulls is how to account for them when aggregate operations such as COUNT or SUM are applied. Moreover, nulls can have multiple interpretations, such as the following:

- The attribute does *not apply* to this tuple.

- The attribute value for this tuple is *unknown*.

- The value is *known but absent*; that is, it has not been recorded yet.

Having the same representation for all nulls compromises the different meanings they may have. Therefore, we may state another guideline.

GUIDELINE 3.   As far as possible, avoid placing attributes in a base relation whose values may frequently be null. If nulls are unavoidable, make sure that they apply in exceptional cases only and do not apply to a majority of tuples in the relation.

Using space efficiently and avoiding joins are the two overriding criteria that determine whether to include the columns that may have nulls in a relation or to have a separate relation for those columns (with the appropriate key columns). For example, if only 10 percent of employees have individual offices, there is little justification for including an attribute OFFICE_NUMBER in the EMPLOYEE relation; rather, a relation EMP_OFFICES(EENO, OFFICE_NUMBER) can be created to include tuples for only the employees with individual offices.

---

4. The performance of a query specified on a view that is the join of several base relations depends on how the DBMS implements the view. Many RDBMSS materialize a frequently used view so that they do not have to perform the joins often. The DBMS remains responsible for updating the materialized view (either immediately or periodically) whenever the base relations are updated.

5. This is because inner and outer joins produce different results when nulls are involved in joins. The users must thus be aware of the different meanings of the various types of joins. Although this is reasonable for sophisticated users, it may be difficult for others.

8.1.4   Generation of Spurious Tuples

Consider the two relation schemas EMP_LOCS and EMP_PROJ1 in Figure 8.5a, which can be used instead of the single EMP_PROJ relation of Figure 8.3b. A tuple in EMP_LOCS means that the employee whose name is ENAME

(a)

EMP_LOCS

ENAME	PLOCATION

p.k.

EMP_PROJ1

ENO	PNUMBER	HOURS	PNAME	PLOCATION

p.k.

(b)

EMP_LOCS

ENAME	PLOCATION
Mahesh, B. Kumar	Bangalore
Mahesh, B. Kumar	New Delhi
Ramesh, K. Narayan	Hyderabad
Kiran, A. Goyal	Bangalore
Kiran, A. Goyal	New Delhi
Karthik, T. Chandra	New Delhi
Karthik, T. Chandra	Hyderabad
Karthik, T. Chandra	Chennai
Sweta, J. Narayan	Chennai
Jitendra, V. Nath	Chennai
Priya, S. Ganesh	Chennai
Priya, S. Ganesh	Hyderabad
Gaurav, E. Kishan	Hyderabad

EMP_PROJ1

ENO	PNUMBER	HOURS	PNAME	PLOCATION
123456789	1	32.5	Product X	Bangalore
123456789	2	7.5	Product Y	New Delhi
666884444	3	40.0	Product Z	Hyderabad
453453453	1	20.0	Product X	Bangalore
453453453	2	20.0	Product Y	New Delhi
333445555	2	10.0	Product Y	New Delhi
333445555	3	10.0	Product Z	Hyderabad
333445555	10	10.0	Computerization	Chennai
333445555	20	10.0	Reorganization	Hyderabad
999887777	30	30.0	Newbenefits	Chennai
999887777	10	10.0	Computerization	Chennai
987987987	10	35.0	Computerization	Chennai
987987987	30	5.0	Newbenefits	Chennai
987654321	30	20.0	Newbenefits	Chennai
987654321	20	15.0	Reorganization	Hyderabad
888665555	20	null	Reorganization	Hyderabad

FIGURE 8.5 Particularly poor design for the EMP_PROJ relation of Figure 8.3b. (a) The two relation schemas EMP_LOCS and EMP_PROJ1. (b) The result of projecting the extension of EMP_PROJ from Figure 8.4 onto the relations EMP_LOCS and EMP_PROJ1.

works on *some project* whose location is PLOCATION. A tuple in EMP_PROJ1 means that the employee whose employee number is ENO works HOURS per week on the project whose name, number, and location are PNAME, PNUMBER, and PLOCATION. Figure 8.5b shows relation states of EMP_LOCS and EMP_PROJ1 corresponding to the EMP_PROJ relation of Figure 8.4, which are obtained by applying the appropriate PROJECT (π) operations to EMP_PROJ (ignore the dotted lines in Figure 8.5b for now).

Suppose that we used EMP_PROJ1 and EMP_LOCS as the base relations instead of EMP_PROJ. This produces a particularly bad schema design, because we cannot recover the information that was originally in EMP_PROJ from EMP_PROJ1 and EMP_LOCS. If we attempt a NATURAL JOIN operation on EMP_PROJ1 and EMP_LOCS, the result produces many more tuples than the original set of tuples in EMP_PROJ. In Figure 8.6, the result of applying the join to only the tuples *above* the dotted lines in Figure 8.5b is shown (to reduce the size of the resulting relation). Additional tuples that were not in EMP_PROJ are called **spurious tuples** because they represent spurious or *wrong* information that is not valid. The spurious tuples are marked by asterisks (*) in Figure 8.6.

Decomposing EMP_PROJ into EMP_LOCS and EMP_PROJ1 is undesirable because, when we JOIN them back using NATURAL JOIN, we do not get the correct original information. This is because in this case PLOCATION is the attribute that relates EMP_LOCS and EMP_PROJ1, and PLOCATION is neither a primary key nor a foreign key in either EMP_LOCS or EMP_PROJ1. We can now informally state another design guideline.

ENO	PNUMBER	HOURS	PNAME	PLOCATION	ENAME
123456789	1	32.5	Product	Bangalore	Mahesh, B. Kumar
123456789	1	32.5	XProductX	Bangalore	Kiran, A. Goyal
123456789	2	7.5	ProductY	New Delhi	Mahesh, B. Kumar
123456789	2	7.5	ProductY	New Delhi	Kiran, A. Goyal
123456789	2	7.5	ProductY	New Delhi	Karthik, T. Chandra
666884444	3	40.0	ProductZ	Hyderabad	Ramesh, K. Narayan
666884444	3	40.0	ProductZ	Hyderabad	Karthik, T. Chandra
453453453	1	20.0	ProductX	Bangalore	Mahesh, B. Kumar
453453453	1	20.0	ProductX	Bangalore	Kiran, A. Goyal
453453453	2	20.0	ProductY	New Delhi	Mahesh, B. Kumar
453453453	2	20.0	ProductY	New Delhi	Kiran, A. Goyal
453453453	2	20.0	ProductY	New Delhi	Karthik, T. Chandra
333445555	2	10.0	ProductY	New Delhi	Mahesh, B. Kumar
333445555	2	10.0	ProductY	New Delhi	Kiran, A. Goyal
333445555	2	10.0	ProductY	New Delhi	Karthik, T. Chandra
333445555	3	10.0	ProductZ	Hydrabad	Ramesh, K. Narayan
333445555	3	10.0	ProductZ	Hyderabad	Karthik, T. Chandra
333445555	10	10.0	Computerization	Chennai	Karthik, T. Chandra
333445555	20	10.0	Reorganization	Hyderabad	Ramesh, K. Narayan
333445555	20	10.0	Reorganization	Hyderabad	Karthik, T. Chandra

FIGURE 8.6 Result of applying NATURAL JOIN to the tuples above the dotted lines in EMP_PROJ1 and EMP_LOCS of Figure 8.5. Generated spurious tuples are marked by asterisks.

GUIDELINE 4. Design relation schemas so that they can be joined with equality conditions on attributes that are either primary keys or foreign keys in a way that guarantees that no spurious tuples are generated. Avoid relations that contain matching attributes that are not (foreign key, primary key) combinations, because joining on such attributes may produce spurious tuples.

This informal guideline obviously needs to be stated more formally. In Section 8.7 of this chapter we discuss a formal condition, called the nonadditive (or lossless) join property, that guarantees that certain joins do not produce spurious tuples.

8.1.5 Summary and Discussion of Design Guidelines

In Sections 8.1.1 through 8.1.4, we informally discussed situations that lead to problematic relation schemas, and we proposed informal guidelines for a good relational design. The problems we pointed out, which can be detected without additional tools of analysis, are as follows:

- Anomalies that cause redundant work to be done during insertion into and modification of a relation, and that may cause accidental loss of information during a deletion from a relation

- Waste of storage space due to nulls and the difficulty of performing aggregation operations and joins due to null values

- Generation of invalid and spurious data during joins on improperly related base relations

In the rest of this chapter we present formal concepts and theory that may be used to define the "goodness" and "badness" of *individual* relation schemas more precisely. We first discuss functional dependency as a tool for analysis. Then we specify the three normal forms and Boyce-Codd normal form (BCNF) for relation schemas. In Sections 8.7, 8.8 and 8.9, we define additional normal forms that which are based on additional types of data dependencies called multivalued dependencies and join dependencies.

8.2 FUNCTIONAL DEPENDENCIES

The single most important concept in relational schema design theory is that of a functional dependency. In this section we formally define the concept, and in Section 8.3 we see how it can be used to define normal forms for relation schemas.

8.2.1 Definition of Functional Dependency

A **functional dependency** is a constraint between two sets of attributes from the database. Suppose that our relational database schema has n attributes $A_1, A_2, \ldots, A_n$; let us think of the whole database as being described by a single **universal** relation schema $R = \{A_1, A_2, \ldots, A_n\}$.[6] We do not imply that we will actually store the database as a single universal table; we use this concept only in developing the formal theory of data dependencies.[7]

Definition. A **functional dependency**, denoted by $X \rightarrow Y$, between two sets of attributes X and Y that are subsets of R specifies a *constraint* on the possible tuples that can form a relation state r of R. The constraint is that, for any two tuples t_1 and t_2 in r that have $t_1[X] = t_2[X]$, they must also have $t_1[Y] = t_2[Y]$.

This means that the values of the Y component of a tuple in r depend on, or are *determined by*, the values of the X component; alternatively, the values of the X component of a tuple uniquely (or **functionally**) *determine* the values of the Y component. We also say that there is a functional dependency from X to Y, or that Y is **functionally dependent** on X. The abbreviation for functional dependency is FD or **f.d.** The set of attributes X is called the **left-hand side** of the FD, and Y is called the **right-hand side.**

---

6. This concept of a universal relation is important when we discuss the algorithms for relational database design in Sections 8.6 and 8.7.

7. This assumption implies that every attribute in the database should have a *distinct name*. In Chapter 4 we prefixed attribute names by relation names to achieve uniqueness whenever attributes in distinct relations had the same name.

Thus, X functionally determines Y in a relation schema R if, and only if, whenever two tuples of $r(R)$ agree on their X-value, they must necessarily agree on their Y-value. Note the following:

- If a constraint on R states that there cannot be more than one tuple with a given X value in any relation instance $r(R)$—that is, X is a **candidate key** of R—this implies that $X \to Y$ for any subset of attributes Y of R (because the key constraint implies that no two tuples in any legal state $r(R)$ will have the same value of X).
- If $X \to Y$ in R, this does not say whether or not $Y \to X$ in R.

A functional dependency is a property of the **semantics** or **meaning of the attributes**. The database designers will use their understanding of the semantics of the attributes of R—that is, how they relate to one another—to specify the functional dependencies that should hold on *all* relation states (extensions) r of R. Whenever the semantics of two sets of attributes in R indicate that a functional dependency should hold, we specify the dependency as a constraint. Relation extensions $r(R)$ that satisfy the functional dependency constraints are called **legal relation states** (or **legal extensions**) of R. Hence, the main use of functional dependencies is to describe further a relation schema R by specifying constraints on its attributes that must hold at *all times*. Certain FDs can be specified without referring to a specific relation, but as a property of those attributes. For example, {STATE, DRIVER_LICENSE_NUMBER} $\to$ ENO should hold for any adult. It is also possible that certain functional dependencies may cease to exist in the real world if the relationship changes. For example, the FD ZIP_CODE $\to$ AREA_CODE used to exist as a relationship between postal codes and telephone number codes in the United States, but with the proliferation of telephone area codes it is no longer true.

Consider the relation schema EMP_PROJ in Figure 8.3b; from the semantics of the attributes, we know that the following functional dependencies should hold:

a. ENO $\to$ ENAME
b. PNUMBER $\to$ {PNAME, PLOCATION}
c. {ENO, PNUMBER} $\to$ HOURS

These functional dependencies specify that (a) the value of an employee's employee number (ENO) uniquely determines the employee name (ENAME), (b) the value of a project's number (PNUMBER) uniquely determines the project name (PNAME) and location (PLOCATION), and (c) a combination of ENO and PNUMBER values uniquely determines the number of hours the employee currently works on the project per week (HOURS). Alternatively, we say that ENAME is functionally determined by (or functionally dependent on) ENO, or "given a value of ENO, we know the value of ENAME," and so on.

A functional dependency is a *property of the relation schema R*, not of a particular legal relation state r of R. Hence, an FD *cannot* be inferred automatically from a given relation extension r but must be defined explicitly by someone who knows the semantics of the attributes of R. For example, Figure 8.7 shows a particular state of the TEACH relation schema. Although at first glance we may think that TEXT $\to$ COURSE, we cannot confirm this unless we know that it is true *for all possible legal states* of TEACH. It is, however, sufficient to demonstrate a *single counterexample* to disprove a functional dependency. For example, because 'Gupta' teaches both 'Data Structures' and 'Data Management', we can conclude that TEACHER *does not* functionally determine COURSE.

Figure 8.3 introduces a **diagrammatic notation** for displaying FDs: Each FD is displayed as a horizontal line. The left-hand-side attributes of the FD are connected by vertical lines to the line representing the FD, while the right-hand-side attributes are connected by arrows pointing toward the attributes, as shown in Figures 8.3a and 8.3b.

8.2.2   Inference Rules for Functional Dependencies

We denote by F the set of functional dependencies that are specified on relation schema R. Typically, the schema designer specifies the functional dependencies that are *semantically obvious*; usually, however, numerous other functional dependencies hold in *all* legal relation instances that satisfy the dependencies in F. Those other dependencies can be *inferred* or *deduced* from the FDs in F.

TEACH

TEACHER	COURSE	TEXT
Gupta	Data Structures	Wiess
Gupta	Data Management	Navathe
Srinivas	Compilers	Hoffman
Raju	Data Structures	Sahni

FIGURE 8.7 A relation state of TEACH with a *possible* functional dependency TEXT → COURSE. However, TEACHER → COURSE is ruled out.

In real life, it is impossible to specify all possible functional dependencies for a given situation. For example, if each department has one manager, so that DEPT_NO uniquely determines MANAGER_ENO (DEPT_NO → MGR_ENO), and a Manager has a unique phone number called MGR_PHONE (MGR_ENO → MGR_PHONE), then these two dependencies together imply that DEPT_NO → MGR_PHONE. This is an inferred FD and need *not* be explicitly stated in addition to the two given FDs. Therefore, formally it is useful to define a concept called *closure* that includes all possible dependencies that can be inferred from the given set F.

Definition.   Formally, the set of all dependencies that include F as well as all dependencies that can be inferred from F is called the **closure** of F; it is denoted by F^+.

For example, suppose that we specify the following set F of obvious functional dependencies on the relation schema of Figure 8.3a:

F = {ENO → {ENAME, DOB, ADDRESS, DNUMBER},

DNUMBER → {DNAME, DMGRENO}

Some of the additional functional dependencies that we can *infer* from F are the following:

ENO → {DNAME, DMGRENO}

ENO → ENO

DNUMBER → DNAME

An FD $X → Y$ is **inferred from** a set of dependencies F specified on R if $X → Y$ holds in *every* legal relation state r of R; that is, whenever r satisfies all the dependencies in F, $X → Y$ also holds in r. The closure F^+ of F is the set of all functional dependencies that can be inferred from F. To determine a systematic way to infer dependencies, we must discover a set of **inference rules** that can be used to infer new dependencies from a given set of dependencies. We consider some of these inference rules next. We use the notation $F \models X → Y$ to denote that the functional dependency $X → Y$ is inferred from the set of functional dependencies F.

In the following discussion, we use an abbreviated notation when discussing functional dependencies. We concatenate attribute variables and drop the commas for convenience. Hence, the FD {X,Y} → Z is abbreviated to $XY → Z$, and the FD {X, Y, Z} → {U, V} is abbreviated to $XYZ → UV$. The following six rules IR1 through IR6 are well-known inference rules for functional dependencies:

IR1 (reflexive rule[8]): If $X \supseteq Y$, then $X \rightarrow Y$.

IR2 (augmentation rule[9]): $\{X \rightarrow Y\} \models XZ \rightarrow YZ$.

IR3 (transitive rule): $\{X \rightarrow Y, Y \rightarrow Z\} \models X \rightarrow Z$.

IR4 (decomposition, or projective, rule): $\{X \rightarrow YZ\} \models X \rightarrow Y$.

IR5 (union, or additive, rule): $\{X \rightarrow Y, X \rightarrow Z\} \models X \rightarrow YZ$.

IR6 (pseudotransitive rule): $\{X \rightarrow Y, WY \rightarrow Z\} \models WX \rightarrow Z$.

The reflexive rule (IR1) states that a set of attributes always determines itself or any of its subsets, which is obvious. Because IR1 generates dependencies that are always true, such dependencies are called *trivial*. Formally, a functional dependency $X \rightarrow Y$ is **trivial** if $X \supseteq Y$; otherwise, it is **nontrivial**. The augmentation rule (IR2) says that adding the same set of attributes to both the left and right-hand sides of a dependency results in another valid dependency. According to IR3, functional dependencies are transitive. The decomposition rule (IR4) says that we can remove attributes from the right-hand side of a dependency; applying this rule repeatedly can decompose the FD $X \rightarrow \{A_1, A_2, \ldots, A_n\}$ into the set of dependencies $\{X \rightarrow A_1, X \rightarrow A_2, \ldots, X \rightarrow A_n\}$. The union rule (IR5) allows us to do the opposite; we can combine a set of dependencies $\{X \rightarrow A_1, X \rightarrow A_2, \ldots, X \rightarrow A_n\}$ into the single FD $X \rightarrow \{A_1, A_2, \ldots, A_n\}$.

One cautionary note regarding the use of these rules. Although $X \rightarrow A$ and $X \rightarrow B$ implies $X \rightarrow AB$ by the union rule stated above, $X \rightarrow A$, and $Y \rightarrow B$ does *not* imply that $XY \rightarrow AB$. Also, $XY \rightarrow A$ does not necessarily imply either $X \rightarrow A$ or $Y \rightarrow A$.

Each of the preceding inference rules can be proved from the definition of functional dependency, either by direct proof or **by contradiction**. A proof by contradiction assumes that the rule does not hold and shows that this is not possible. We now prove that the first three rules IR1 through IR3 are valid. The second proof is by contradiction.

PROOF OF IR1

Suppose that $X \supseteq Y$ and that two tuples t_1 and t_2 exist in some relation instance r of R such that $t_1[X] = t_2[X]$. Then $t_1[Y] = t_2[Y]$ because $X \supseteq Y$; hence, $X \rightarrow Y$ must hold in r.

PROOF OF IR2 (BY CONTRADICTION)

Assume that $X \rightarrow Y$ holds in a relation instance r of R but that $XZ \rightarrow YZ$ does not hold. Then there must exist two tuples t_1 and t_2 in r such that (1) $t_1[X] = t_2[X]$, (2) $t_1[Y] = t_2[Y]$, (3) $t_1[XZ] = t_2[XZ]$, and (4) $t_1[YZ] \neq t_2[YZ]$. This is not possible because from (1) and (3) we deduce (5) $t_1[Z] = t_2[Z]$, and from (2) and (5) we deduce (6) $t_1[YZ] = t_2[YZ]$, contradicting (4).

PROOF OF IR3

Assume that (1) $X \rightarrow Y$ and (2) $Y \rightarrow Z$ both hold in a relation r. Then for any two tuples t_1 and t_2 in r such that $t_1[X] = t_2[X]$, we must have (3) $t_1[Y] = t_2[Y]$, from assumption (1); hence we must also have (4) $t_1[Z] = t_2[Z]$, from (3) and assumption (2); hence $X \rightarrow Z$ must hold in r.

Using similar proof arguments, we can prove the inference rules IR4 to IR6 and any additional valid inference rules. However, a simpler way to prove that an inference rule for functional dependencies is valid is to prove it by using inference rules that have already been shown to be valid. For example, we can prove IR4 through IR6 by using IR1 through IR3 as follows.

---

8. The reflexive rule can also be stated as $X \rightarrow X$; that is, any set of attributes functionally determines itself.

9. The augmentation rule can also be stated as $\{X \rightarrow Y\} \models XZ \rightarrow Y$; that is, augmenting the left-hand side attributes of an FD produces another valid FD.

PROOF OF IR4 (USING IR1 THROUGH IR3)

1. $X \rightarrow YZ$ (given).
2. $YZ \rightarrow Y$ (using IR1 and knowing that $YZ \supseteq Y$).
3. $X \rightarrow Y$ (using IR3 on 1 and 2).

PROOF OF IR5 (USING IR1 THROUGH IR3)

1. $X \rightarrow Y$ (given).
2. $X \rightarrow Z$ (given).
3. $X \rightarrow XY$ (using IR2 on 1 by augmenting with X; notice that $XX = X$).
4. $XY \rightarrow YZ$ (using IR2 on 2 by augmenting with Y).
5. $X \rightarrow YZ$ (using IR3 on 3 and 4).

PROOF OF IR6 (USING IR1 THROUGH IR3)

1. $X \rightarrow Y$ (given).
2. $WY \rightarrow Z$ (given).
3. $WX \rightarrow WY$ (using IR2 on 1 by augmenting with W).
4. $WX \rightarrow Z$ (using IR3 on 3 and 2).

It has been shown by Armstrong (1974) that inference rules IR1 through IR3 are sound and complete. By **sound**, we mean that given a set of functional dependencies F specified on a relation schema R, any dependency that we can infer from F by using IR1 through IR3 holds in every relation state r of R that *satisfies the dependencies* in F. By **complete**, we mean that using IR1 through IR3 repeatedly to infer dependencies until no more dependencies can be inferred results in the complete set of *all possible dependencies* that can be inferred from F. In other words, the set of dependencies F^+, which we called the **closure** of F, can be determined from F by using only inference rules IR1 through IR3. Inference rules IR1 through IR3 are known as **Armstrong's inference rules**.[10]

Typically, database designers first specify the set of functional dependencies F that can easily be determined from the semantics of the attributes of R; then IR1, IR2, and IR3 are used to infer additional functional dependencies that will also hold on R. A systematic way to determine these additional functional dependencies is first to determine each set of attributes X that appears as a left-hand side of some functional dependency in F and then to determine the set of *all attributes* that are dependent on X. Thus, for each such set of attributes X, we determine the set X^+ of attributes that are functionally determined by X based on F; X^+ is called the **closure** of X under F. Algorithm 8.1 can be used to calculate X^+.

Algorithm 8.1: Determining X^+, the Closure of X under F

$X^+ := X$;
repeat
    old $X^+ := X^+$;
    for each functional dependency $Y \rightarrow Z$ in F do
    if $X^+ \supseteq Y$ then $X^+ := X^+ \cup Z$;
until ($X^+ =$ old X^+);

---

10. They are actually known as **Armstrong's axioms**. In the strict mathematical sense, the *axioms* (given facts) are the functional dependencies in F, since we assume that they are correct, whereas IR1 through IR3 are the *inference rules* for inferring new functional dependencies (new facts).

Algorithm 8.1 starts by setting X^+ to all the attributes in X. By IR1, we know that all these attributes are functionally dependent on X. Using inference rules IR3 and IR4, we add attributes to X^+, using each functional dependency in F. We keep going through all the dependencies in F (the *repeat* loop) until no more attributes are added to X^+ *during a complete cycle* (of the *for* loop) through the dependencies in F. For example, consider the relation schema EMP_PROJ in Figure 8.3b; from the semantics of the attributes, we specify the following set F of functional dependencies that should hold on EMP_PROJ:

$F = \{$ENO $\rightarrow$ ENAME,

     PNUMBER $\rightarrow$ {PNAME, PLOCATION},

     {ENO, PNUMBER} $\rightarrow$ HOURS$\}$

Using Algorithm 8.1, we calculate the following closure sets with respect to F:

     {ENO}+ = {ENO, ENAME}

     {PNUMBER}+ = {PNUMBER, PNAME, PLOCATION}

     {ENO, PNUMBER}+ = {ENO, PNUMBER, ENAME, PNAME, PLOCATION, HOURS}

Intuitively, the set of attributes in the right-hand side of each line represents all those attributes that are functionally dependent on the set of attributes in the left-hand side based on the given set F.

8.2.3 Equivalence of Sets of Functional Dependencies

In this section we discuss the equivalence of two sets of functional dependencies. First, we give some preliminary definitions.

Definition. A set of functional dependencies F is said to cover another set of functional dependencies E if every FD in E is also in F^+; that is, if every dependency in E can be inferred from F; alternatively, we can say that E is **covered by** F.

Definition. Two sets of functional dependencies E and F are **equivalent** if $E^+ = F^+$. Hence, equivalence means that every FD in E can be inferred from F, and every FD in F can be inferred from E; that is, E is equivalent to F if both the conditions E covers F *and* F covers E hold.

We can determine whether F covers E by calculating X^+ *with respect* to F for each FD $X \rightarrow Y$ in E, and then checking whether this X^+ includes the attributes in Y. If this is the case for every FD in E, then F covers E. We determine whether E and F are equivalent by checking that E covers F and F covers E.

8.2.4 Minimal Sets of Functional Dependencies

Informally, a **minimal cover** of a set of functional dependencies E is a set of functional dependencies F that satisfies the property that every dependency in E is in the closure F^+ of F. In addition, this property is lost if any dependency from the set F is removed; F must have no redundancies in it, and the dependencies in E are in a standard form. To satisfy these properties, we can formally define a set of functional dependencies F to be **minimal** if it satisfies the following conditions:

1. Every dependency in F has a single attribute for its right-hand side.

2. We cannot replace any dependency $X \rightarrow A$ in F with a dependency $Y \rightarrow A$, where Y is a proper subset of X, and still have a set of dependencies that is equivalent to F.

3. We cannot remove any dependency from F and still have a set of dependencies that is equivalent to F.

We can think of a minimal set of dependencies as being a set of dependencies in a *standard* or *canonical form* and with *no redundancies*. Condition 1 just represents every dependency in a canonical form with a single attribute on the right-hand side.[11] Conditions 2 and 3 ensure that there are no redundancies in the dependencies either by having redundant attributes on the left-hand side of a dependency (Condition 2) or by having a dependency that can be inferred from the remaining FDs in F (Condition 3). A **minimal cover** of a set of functional dependencies E is a minimal set of dependencies F that is equivalent to E. There can be several minimal covers for a set of functional dependencies. We can always find *at least one* minimal cover F for any set of dependencies E using Algorithm 8.2.

If several sets of FDs qualify as minimal covers of E by the definition above, it is customary to use additional criteria for "minimality." For example, we can choose the minimal set with the *smallest number of dependencies* or with the *smallest total length* (the total length of a set of dependencies is calculated by concatenating the dependencies and treating them as one long character string).

Algorithm 8.2: Finding a Minimal Cover F for a Set of Functional Dependencies E

1. Set $F := E$.

2. Replace each functional dependency $X \rightarrow \{A_1, A_2, \ldots, A_n\}$ in F by the n functional dependencies $X \rightarrow A_1, X \rightarrow A_2, \ldots, X \rightarrow A_n$.

3. For each functional dependency $X \rightarrow A$ in F

   for each attribute B that is an element of X

   if $\{ \{ F - \{X \rightarrow A\} \} \cup \{(X - \{B\}) \rightarrow A\} \}$ is equivalent to F,

   then replace $X \rightarrow A$ with $(X - \{B\}) \rightarrow A$ in F.

4. For each remaining functional dependency $X \rightarrow A$ in F

   if $\{ F - \{X \rightarrow A\} \}$ is equivalent to F,

   then remove $X \rightarrow A$ from F.

In the subsequent sections of this chapter, we will see how relations can be synthesized from a given set of dependencies E by first finding the minimal cover F for E.

8.3 NORMAL FORMS BASED ON PRIMARY KEYS

Having studied functional dependencies and some of their properties, we are now ready to use them to specify some aspects of the semantics of relation schemas. We assume that a set of functional dependencies is given for each relation, and that each relation has a designated primary key; this information combined with the tests (conditions) for normal forms drives the *normalization process* for relational schema design. Most practical relational design projects take one of the following two approaches:

- First perform a conceptual schema design using a conceptual model such as ER or EER and then map the conceptual design into a set of relations.

- Design the relations based on external knowledge derived from an existing implementation of files or forms or reports.

---

11. This is a standard form to simplify the conditions and algorithms that ensure no redundancy exists in F. By using the inference rule IR4, we can convert a single dependency with multiple attributes on the right-hand side into a set of dependencies with single attributes on the right-hand side.

Following either of these approaches, it is then useful to evaluate the relations for goodness and decompose them further as needed to achieve higher normal forms, using the normalization theory presented in this chapter and the next. We focus in this section on the first three normal forms for relation schemas and the intuition behind them, and discuss how they were developed historically. More general definitions of these normal forms, which take into account all candidate keys of a relation rather than just the primary key, are deferred to Section 8.4.

We start by informally discussing normal forms and the motivation behind their development, as well as reviewing some definitions from Chapter 4 that are needed here. We then discuss first normal form (1NF) in Section 8.3.4, and present the definitions of second normal form (2NF) and third normal form (3NF), which are based on primary keys, in Sections 8.3.5 and 8.3.6, respectively.

8.3.1 Normalization of Relations

The normalization process, as first proposed by Codd (1972a), takes a relation schema through a series of tests to "certify" whether it satisfies a certain **normal form**. The process, which proceeds in a top-down fashion by evaluating each relation against the criteria for normal forms and decomposing relations as necessary, can thus be considered as relational design by analysis. Initially, Codd proposed three normal forms, which he called first, second, and third normal form. A stronger definition of 3NF—called Boyce-Codd normal form (BCNF)—was proposed later by Boyce and Codd. All these normal forms are based on the functional dependencies among the attributes of a relation. Later, a fourth normal form (4NF) and a fifth normal form (5NF) were proposed, based on the concepts of multivalued dependencies and join dependencies, respectively; these are discussed in Sections 8.6, 8.7, 8.8, and 8.9. We also discuss how 3NF relations may be synthesized from a given set of FDs in Section 8.7. This approach is called *relational design by synthesis*.

Normalization of data can be looked upon as a process of analyzing the given relation schemas based on their FDs and primary keys to achieve the desirable properties of (1) minimizing redundancy and (2) minimizing the insertion, deletion, and update anomalies discussed in Section 8.1.2. Unsatisfactory relation schemas that do not meet certain conditions—the **normal form tests**—are decomposed into smaller relation schemas that meet the tests and hence possess the desirable properties. Thus, the normalization procedure provides database designers with the following:

- A formal framework for analyzing relation schemas based on their keys and on the functional dependencies among their attributes

- A series of normal form tests that can be carried out on individual relation schemas so that the relational database can be **normalized** to any desired degree

The **normal form** of a relation refers to the highest normal form condition that it meets, and hence indicates the degree to which it has been normalized. Normal forms, when considered in *isolation* from other factors, do not guarantee a good database design. It is generally not sufficient to check separately that each relation schema in the database is, say, in BCNF or 3NF. Rather, the process of normalization through decomposition must also confirm the existence of additional properties that the relational schemas, taken together, should possess. These would include two properties:

- The **lossless join** or **nonadditive join property**, which guarantees that the spurious tuple generation problem discussed in Section 8.1.4 does not occur with respect to the relation schemas created after decomposition

- The **dependency preservation property,** which ensures that each functional dependency is represented in some individual relation resulting after decomposition

The nonadditive join property is extremely critical and must be achieved at any cost, whereas the dependency preservation property, although desirable, is sometimes sacrificed, as we discuss in Section 8.6.2. We defer the presentation of the formal concepts and techniques that guarantee the above two properties to Section 8.6.

8.3.2 Practical Use of Normal Forms

Most practical design projects acquire existing designs of databases from previous designs, designs in legacy models, or from existing files. Normalization is carried out in practice so that the resulting designs are of high quality and meet the desirable properties stated previously. Although several higher normal forms have been defined, such as the 4NF and 5NF that we discuss in Sections 8.8 and 8.9, the practical utility of these normal forms becomes questionable when the constraints on which they are based are hard to understand or to detect by the database designers and users who must discover these constraints. Thus, database design as practiced in industry today pays particular attention to normalization only up to 3NF, BCNF, or 4NF.

Another point worth noting is that the database designers *need not* normalize to the highest possible normal form. Relations may be left in a lower normalization status, such as 2NF, for performance reasons, such as those discussed at the end of Section 8.1.2. The process of storing the join of higher normal form relations as a base relation—which is in a lower normal form—is known as **denormalization**.

8.3.3 Definitions of Keys and Attributes Participating in Keys

Before proceeding further, let us look again at the definitions of keys of a relation schema from Chapter 5.

Definition.   A **superkey** of a relation schema $R = \{A_1, A_2, \ldots, A_n\}$ is a set of attributes $S \subseteq R$ with the property that no two tuples t_1 and t_2 in any legal relation state r of R will have $t_1[S] = t_2[S]$. A **Key** K is a superkey with the additional property that removal of any attribute from K will cause K not to be a superkey any more.

The difference between a key and a superkey is that a key has to be *minimal*; that is, if we have a key $K = \{A_1, A_2, \ldots, A_k\}$ of R, then $K - \{A_i\}$ is not a key of R for any A_i, $1 \le i \le k$. In Figure 8.1, {ENO} is a key for EMPLOYEE, whereas {ENO}, {ENO, ENAME}, {ENO, ENAME, DOB}, and any set of attributes that includes ENO are all superkeys.

If a relation schema has more than one key, each is called a **candidate key**. One of the candidate keys is *arbitrarily* designated to be the **primary key**, and the others are called secondary keys. Each relation schema must have a primary key. In Figure 8.1, {ENO} is the only candidate key for EMPLOYEE, so it is also the primary key.

Definition.   An attribute of relation schema R is called a **prime attribute** of R if it is a member of *some* candidate key of R. An attribute is called **nonprime** if it is not a prime attribute—that is, if it is not a member of any candidate key.

In Figure 8.1 both ENO and PNUMBER are prime attributes of WORKS_ON, whereas other attributes of WORKS_ON are nonprime.

We now present the first three normal forms: 1NF, 2NF, and 3NF. These were proposed by Codd (1972a) as a sequence to achieve the desirable state of 3NF relations by progressing through the intermediate states of 1NF and 2NF if needed. As we shall see, 2NF and 3NF attack different problems. However, for historical reasons, it is customary to follow them in that sequence; hence we will assume that a 3NF relation *already satisfies* 2NF.

8.3.4 First Normal Form

First normal form (1NF) is now considered to be part of the formal definition of a relation in the basic (flat) relational model;[12] historically, it was defined to disallow multivalued attributes, composite attributes, and their combinations. It states that the domain of an attribute must include only *atomic* (simple, indivisible) *values* and that the value of any attribute in a tuple must be a *single value* from the domain of that attribute. Hence, 1NF disallows having a set of values, a tuple of values, or a combination of both as an attribute value for a single tuple. In other words, 1NF disallows "relations within relations" or "relations as attribute values within tuples." The only attribute values permitted by 1NF are single **atomic** (or **indivisible**) **values**.

Consider the DEPARTMENT relation schema shown in Figure 8.1, whose primary key is DNUMBER, and suppose that we extend it by including the DLOCATIONS attribute as shown in Figure 8.8a. We assume that each department can have *a number of* locations. The DEPARTMENT schema and an example relation state are shown in Figure 8.8. As we can see, this is not in 1NF because DLOCATIONS is not an atomic attribute, as illustrated by the first tuple in Figure 8.8b. There are two ways we can look at the DLOCATIONS attribute:

(a)

(b)

DNAME	DNUMBER	DMGRENO	DLOCATIONS
Research	5	333445555	{Bangalore, New Delhi, Hyderabad}
Administration	4	987654321	{Chennai}
Headquarters	1	888665555	{Hyderabad}

DEPARTMENT

(c)

DEPARTMENT

DNAME	DNUMBER	DMGRENO	DLOCATION
Research	5	333445555	Bangalore
Research	5	333445555	New Delhi
Research	5	333445555	Hyderabad
Administration	4	987654321	Chennai
Headquarters	1	888665555	Hyderabad

FIGURE 8.8 Normalization into 1NF. (a) A relation schema that is not in 1NF. (b) Example state of relation DEPARTMENT. (c) 1NF version of same relation with redundancy.

- The domain of DLOCATIONS contains atomic values, but some tuples can have a set of these values. In this case, DLOCATIONS *is not* functionally dependent on the primary key DNUMBER.

- The domain of DLOCATIONS contains sets of values and hence is nonatomic. In this case, DNUMBER → DLOCATIONS, because each set is considered a single member of the attribute domain.[13]

---

12. This condition is removed in the *nested relational model* and in *object-relational systems* (ORDBMSs), both of which allow *unnormalized relations*.

13. In this case we can consider the domain of DLOCATIONS to be the **power set** of the set of single locations; that is, the domain is made up of all possible subsets of the set of single locations.

In either case, the DEPARTMENT relation of Figure 8.8 is not in 1NF; in fact, it does not even qualify as a relation according to our definition of relation in Section 4.1. There are three main techniques to achieve first normal form for such a relation:

1. Remove the attribute DLOCATIONS that violates 1NF and place it in a separate relation DEPT_LOCATIONS along with the primary key DNUMBER of DEPARTMENT. The primary key of this relation is the combination {DNUMBER, DLOCATION}, as shown in Figure 8.2. A distinct tuple in DEPT_LOCATIONS exists for *each location* of a department. This decomposes the non-1NF relation into two 1NF relations.

2. Expand the key so that there will be a separate tuple in the original DEPARTMENT relation for each location of a DEPARTMENT, as shown in Figure 8.8c. In this case, the primary key becomes the combination {DNUMBER, DLOCATION}. This solution has the disadvantage of introducing *redundancy* in the relation.

3. If a *maximum number of values* is known for the attribute—for example, if it is known that *at most three locations* can exist for a department—replace the DLOCATIONS attribute by three atomic attributes: DLOCATION1, DLOCATION2, and DLOCATION3. This solution has the disadvantage of introducing *null values* if most departments have fewer than three locations. It further introduces a spurious semantics about the ordering among the location values that is not originally intended. Querying on this attribute becomes more difficult; for example, consider how you would write the query: "List the departments that have "Bangalore" as one of their locations" in this design.

Of the three solutions above, the first is generally considered best because it does not suffer from redundancy and it is completely general, having no limit placed on a maximum number of values. In fact, if we choose the second solution, it will be decomposed further during subsequent normalization steps into the first solution.

First normal form also disallows multivalued attributes that are themselves composite. These are called **nested relations** because each tuple can have a relation *within it*. Figure 8.9 shows how the EMP_PROJ relation could appear if nesting is allowed. Each tuple represents an employee entity, and a relation PROJS(PNUMBER, HOURS) *within each tuple* represents the employee's projects and the hours per week that employee works on each project. The schema of this EMP_PROJ relation can be represented as follows:

EMP_PROJ(ENO, ENAME, {PROJS(PNUMBER, HOURS)})

The set braces { } identify the attribute PROJS as multivalued, and we list the component attributes that form PROJS between parentheses ( ). Interestingly, recent trends for supporting complex objects and XML data using the relational model attempt to allow and formalize nested relations within relational database systems, which were disallowed early on by 1NF.

Notice that ENO is the primary key of the EMP_PROJ relation in Figures 8.9a and b, while PNUMBER is the **partial key** of the nested relation; that is, within each tuple, the nested relation must have unique values of PNUMBER. To normalize this into 1NF, we remove the nested relation attributes into a new relation and *propagate the primary key* into it; the primary key of the new relation will combine the partial key with the primary key of the original relation. Decomposition and primary key propagation yield the schemas EMP_PROJ1 and EMP_PROJ2 shown in Figure 8.9c.

This procedure can be applied recursively to a relation with multiple-level nesting to **unnest** the relation into a set of 1NF relations. This is useful in converting an unnormalized relation schema with many levels of nesting into 1NF relations. The existence of more than one multivalued attribute in one relation must be handled carefully. As an example, consider the following non-1NF relation:

PERSON (ENO, {CAR_LIC#}, {PHONE#})

This relation represents the fact that a person has multiple cars and multiple phones. If a strategy like the second option above is followed, it results in an all-key relation:

PERSON_IN_1NF (ENO, CAR_LIC#, PHONE#)

(a)

EMP_PROJ

ENO	ENAME	PROJS	
		PNUMBER	HOURS

(b)

EMP_PROJ

ENO	ENAME	PNUMBER	HOURS
123456789	Mahesh, B. Kumar	1	32.5
		2	7.5
666884444	Ramesh, K. Narayan	3	40.0
453453453	Kiran, A. Goyal	1	20.0
		2	20.0
333445555	Karthik, T. Chandra	2	10.0
		3	10.0
		10	10.0
		20	10.0
999887777	Sweta, J. Narayanan	30	30.0
		10	10.0
987987987	Jitendra, V. Nath	10	35.0
		30	5.0
987654321	Priya, S. Ganesh	30	20.0
		20	15.0
888665555	Gaurav, E. Kishan	20	null

(c)

EMP_PROJ1

ENO	ENAME

EMP_PROJ2

ENO	PNUMBER	HOURS

FIGURE 8.9 Normalizing nested relations into 1NF. (a) Schema of the EMP_PROJ relation with a "nested relation" attribute PROJS. (b) Example extension of the EMP_PROJ relation showing nested relations within each tuple. (c) Decomposition of EMP_PROJ into relations EMP_PROJ1 and EMP_PROJ2 by propagating the primary key.

To avoid introducing any extraneous relationship between CAR_LIC# and PHONE#, all possible combinations of values are represented for every ENO, giving rise to redundancy. This leads to the problems handled by multivalued dependencies and 4NF, which we discuss in Section 8.8. The right way to deal with the two multivalued attributes in PERSON above is to decompose it into two separate relations, using strategy 1 discussed above:

P1(SS#, CAR_LIC#) and P2(ENO, PHONE#).

8.3.5 Second Normal Form

Second normal form (2NF) is based on the concept of *full functional dependency*. A functional dependency $X \rightarrow Y$ is a **full functional dependency** if removal of any attribute A from X means that the dependency does not hold any more; that is, for any attribute $A \in X$, $(X - \{A\})$ does not functionally determine Y. A functional dependency $X \rightarrow Y$ is a **partial dependency** if some attribute $A \in X$ can be removed from X and the dependency still holds; that is, for some $A \in X$, $(X - \{A\}) \rightarrow Y$. In Figure 8.3b, {ENO, PNUMBER} $\rightarrow$ HOURS is a full dependency (neither ENO $\rightarrow$ HOURS nor PNUMBER $\rightarrow$ HOURS holds). However, the dependency {ENO, PNUMBER} $\rightarrow$ ENAME is partial because ENO $\rightarrow$ ENAME holds.

Definition.   A relation schema R is in **2NF** if every nonprime attribute A in R is *fully functionally dependent* on the primary key of R.

The test for 2NF involves testing for functional dependencies whose left-hand side attributes are part of the primary key. If the primary key contains a single attribute, the test need not be applied at all. The EMP_PROJ relation in Figure 8.3b is in 1NF but is not in 2NF. The nonprime attribute ENAME violates 2NF because of FD2, as do the nonprime attributes PNAME and PLOCATION because of FD3. The functional dependencies FD2 and FD3 make ENAME, PNAME, and PLOCATION partially dependent on the primary key {ENO, PNUMBER} of EMP_PROJ, thus violating the 2NF test.

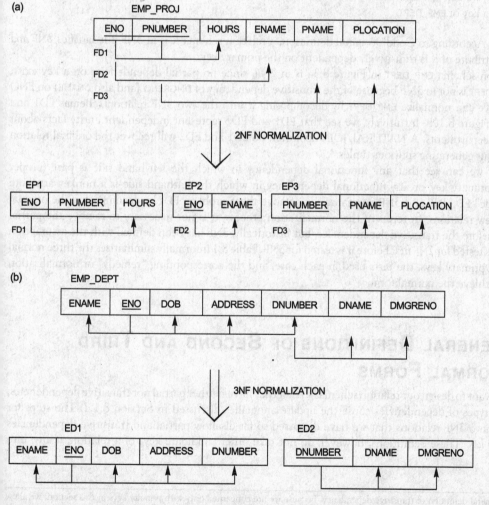

FIGURE 8.10. Normalizing into 2NF and 3NF. (a) Normalizing EMP_PROJ into 2NF relations. (b) Normalizing EMP_DEPT into 3NF relations.

If a relation schema is not in 2NF, it can be "second normalized" or "2NF normalized" into a number of 2NF relations in which nonprime attributes are associated only with the part of the primary key on which they are fully functionally dependent. The functional dependencies FD1, FD2, and FD3 in Figure 8.3b hence lead to the decomposition of EMP_PROJ into the three relation schemas EP1, EP2, and EP3 shown in Figure 8.10a, each of which is in 2NF.

8.3.6 Third Normal Form

Third normal form (3NF) is based on the concept of *transitive dependency*. A functional dependency $X \rightarrow Y$ in a relation schema R is a **transitive dependency** if there is a set of attributes Z that is neither a candidate key nor a subset of any key of R,[14] and both $X \rightarrow Z$ and $Z \rightarrow Y$ hold. The dependency ENO $\rightarrow$ DMGRENO is transitive through DNUMBER in EMP_DEPT of Figure 8.3a because both the dependencies ENO $\rightarrow$ DNUMBER and DNUMBER $\rightarrow$ DMGRENO hold and DNUMBER is neither a key itself nor a subset of the key of EMP_DEPT. Intuitively, we can see that the dependency of DMGRENO on DNUMBER is undesirable in EMP_DEPT since DNUMBER is not a key of EMP_DEPT.

Definition. According to Codd's original definition, a relation schema R is in 3NF if it satisfies 2NF *and* no nonprime attribute of R is transitively dependent on the primary key.

The relation schema EMP_DEPT in Figure 8.3a is in 2NF, since no partial dependencies on a key exist. However, EMP_DEPT is not in 3NF because of the transitive dependency of DMGRENO (and also DNAME) on ENO via DNUMBER. We can normalize EMP_DEPT by decomposing it into the two 3NF relation schemas ED1 and ED2 shown in Figure 8.10b. Intuitively, we see that ED1 and ED2 represent independent entity facts about employees and departments. A NATURAL JOIN operation on ED1 and ED2 will recover the original relation EMP_DEPT without generating spurious tuples.

Intuitively, we can see that any functional dependency in which the left-hand side is part (proper subset) of the primary key, or any functional dependency in which the lefthand side is a nonkey attribute is a "problematic" FD. 2NF and 3NF normalization remove these problem FDs by decomposing the original relation into new relations. In terms of the normalization process, it is not necessary to remove the partial dependencies before the transitive dependencies, but historically, 3NF has been defined with the assumption that a relation is tested for 2NF first before it is tested for 3NF. Table 8.1 informally summarizes the three normal forms based on primary keys, the tests used in each case, and the corresponding "remedy" or normalization performed to achieve the normal form.

8.4 GENERAL DEFINITIONS OF SECOND AND THIRD NORMAL FORMS

In general, we want to design our relation schemas so that they have neither partial nor transitive dependencies, because these types of dependencies cause the update anomalies discussed in Section 8.1.2. The steps for normalization into 3NF relations that we have discussed so far disallow partial and transitive dependencies on the *primary key*. These definitions, however, do not take other candidate keys of a relation, if any, into

---

14. This is the general definition of transitive dependency. Because we are concerned only with primary keys in this section, we allow transitive dependencies where X is the primary key but Z may be (a subset of) a candidate key.

account. In this section, we give the more general definitions of 2NF and 3NF that take all candidate keys of a relation into account. Notice that this does not affect the definition of 1NF, since it is independent of keys and functional dependencies. As a general definition of **prime attribute**, an attribute that is part of *any candidate key* will be considered as prime.

TABLE 8.1 Summary of Normal Forms Based on Primary Keys and Corresponding Normalization

NORMAL FORM	TEST	REMEDY (NORMALIZATION)
First (1NF)	Relation should have no nonatomic attributes or nested relations.	Form new relations for each nonatomic attribute or nested relation.
Second (2NF)	For relations where primary key contains multiple attributes, no nonkey attribute should be functionally dependent on a part of the primary key.	Decompose and set up a new relation for each partial key with its dependent attribute(s). Make sure to keep a relation with the original primary key and any attributes that are fully functionally dependent on it.
Third (3NF)	Relation should not have a nonkey attribute functionally determined by another nonkey attribute (or by a set of nonkey attributes.) That is, there should be no transitive dependency of a nonkey attribute on the primary key.	Decompose and set up a relation that includes the nonkey attribute(s) that functionally determine(s) other nonkey attribute(s).

Partial and full functional dependencies and transitive dependencies will now be considered *with respect to all candidate keys* of a relation.

8.4.1 General Definition of Second Normal Form

Definition. A relation schema R is in **second normal form (2NF)** if every nonprime attribute A in R is not partially dependent on *any* key of R.[15]

The test for 2NF involves testing for functional dependencies whose left-hand side attributes are *part of* the primary key. If the primary key contains a single attribute, the test need not be applied at all. Consider the relation schema LOTS shown in Figure 8.11a, which describes parcels of land for sale in various counties of a state. Suppose that there are two candidate keys: PROPERTY_ID# and {COUNTY_NAME, LOT#}; that is, lot numbers are unique only within each county, but PROPERTY_ID numbers are unique across counties for the entire state.

Based on the two candidate keys PROPERTY_ID# and {COUNTY_NAME, LOT#}, we know that the functional dependencies FD1 and FD2 of Figure 8.11a hold. We choose PROPERTY_ID# as the primary key, so it is underlined in Figure 8.11a, but no special consideration will be given to this key over the other candidate key. Suppose that the following two additional functional dependencies hold in LOTS:

FD3: COUNTY_NAME → TAX_RATE

FD4: AREA → PRICE

---

15. This definition can be restated as follows: A relation schema R is in 2NF if every nonprime attribute A in R is fully functionally dependent on *every* key of R.

(a)

(b)

(c)

(d)

FIGURE 8.11 Normalization into 2NF and 3NF. (a) The LOTS relation with its functional dependencies FD1 through FD4. (b) Decomposing into the 2NF relations LOTS1 and LOTS2. (c) Decomposing LOTS1 into the 3NF relations LOTS1A and LOTS1B. (d) Summary of the progressive normalization of LOTS.

In words, the dependency FD3 says that the tax rate is fixed for a given county (does not vary lot by lot within the same county), while FD4 says that the price of a lot is determined by its area regardless of which county it is in. (Assume that this is the price of the lot for tax purposes.)

The LOTS relation schema violates the general definition of 2NF because TAX_RATE is partially dependent on the candidate key {COUNTY_NAME, LOT#}, due to FD3. To normalize LOTS into 2NF, we decompose it into the two relations LOTS1 and LOTS2, shown in Figure 8.11b. We construct LOTS1 by removing the attribute TAX_RATE that violates 2NF from LOTS and placing it with COUNTY_NAME (the left-hand side of FD3 that causes the partial dependency) into another relation LOTS2. Both LOTS1 and LOTS2 are in 2NF. Notice that FD4 does not violate 2NF and is carried over to LOTS1.

8.4.2 General Definition of Third Normal Form

Definition. A relation schema R is in **third normal form (3NF)** if, whenever a nontrivial functional depen-dency $X \rightarrow A$ holds in R, either (a) X is a superkey of R, or (b) A is a prime attribute of R.

According to this definition, LOTS2 (Figure 8.11b) is in 3NF. However, FD4 in LOTS1 violates 3NF because AREA is not a superkey and PRICE is not a prime attribute in LOTS1. To normalize LOTS1 into 3NF, we decompose it into the relation schemas LOTS1A and LOTS1B shown in Figure 8.11c. We construct LOTS1A by removing the attribute PRICE that violates 3NF from LOTS1 and placing it with AREA (the left-hand side of FD4 that causes the transitive dependency) into another relation LOTS1B. Both LOTS1A and LOTS1B are in 3NF.

Two points are worth noting about this example and the general definition of 3NF:

- LOTS1 violates 3NF because PRICE is transitively dependent on each of the candidate keys of LOTS1 via the nonprime attribute AREA.

- This general definition can be applied *directly* to test whether a relation schema is in 3NF; it does not have to go through 2NF first. If we apply the above 3NF definition to LOTS with the dependencies FD1 through FD4, we find that both FD3 and FD4 violate 3NF. We could hence decompose LOTS into LOTS1A, LOTS1B, and LOTS2 directly. Hence the transitive and partial dependencies that violate 3NF can be removed in any order.

8.4.3 Interpreting the General Definition of Third Normal Form

A relation schema R violates the general definition of 3NF if a functional dependency $X \rightarrow A$ holds in R that violates *both* conditions (a) and (b) of 3NF. Violating (b) means that A is a nonprime attribute. Violating (a) means that X is not a superset of any key of R; hence, X could be nonprime or it could be a proper subset of a key of R. If X is nonprime, we typically have a transitive dependency that violates 3NF, whereas if X is a proper subset of a key of R, we have a partial dependency that violates 3NF (and also 2NF). Hence, we can state a **general alternative definition of 3NF** as follows: A relation schema R is in 3NF if every nonprime attribute of R meets both of the following conditions:

- It is fully functionally dependent on every key of R.

- It is nontransitively dependent on every key of R.

8.5 Boyce-Codd Normal Form

Boyce-Codd normal form (BCNF) was proposed as a simpler form of 3NF, but it was found to be stricter than 3NF. That is, every relation in BCNF is also in 3NF; however, a relation in 3NF is *not necessarily* in BCNF.

Intuitively, we can see the need for a stronger normal form than 3NF by going back to the LOTS relation schema of Figure 8.11a with its four functional dependencies FD1 through FD4. Suppose that we have thousands of lots in the relation but the lots are from only two counties: Dekalb and Fulton. Suppose also that lot sizes in Dekalb County are only 0.5, 0.6, 0.7, 0.8, 0.9, and 1.0 acres, whereas lot sizes in Fulton County are restricted to 1.1, 1.2, . . . , 1.9, and 2.0 acres. In such a situation we would have the additional functional dependency FD5: AREA → COUNTY_NAME. If we add this to the other dependencies, the relation schema LOTS1A still is in 3NF because COUNTY_NAME is a prime attribute.

The area of a lot that determines the county, as specified by FD5, can be represented by 16 tuples in a separate relation R(AREA, COUNTY_NAME), since there are only 16 possible AREA values. This representation reduces the redundancy of repeating the same information in the thousands of LOTS1A tuples. BCNF is a *stronger normal form* that would disallow LOTS1A and suggest the need for decomposing it.

Definition. A relation schema R is in **BCNF** if whenever a *nontrivial* functional dependency $X \to A$ holds in R, then X is a superkey of R.

The formal definition of BCNF differs slightly from the definition of 3NF. The only difference between the definitions of BCNF and 3NF is that condition (b) of 3NF, which allows A to be prime, is absent from BCNF. In our example, FD5 violates BCNF in LOTS1A because AREA is not a superkey of LOTS1A. Note that FD5 satisfies 3NF in LOTS1A because COUNTY_NAME is a prime attribute (condition b), but this condition does not exist in the definition of BCNF. We can decompose LOTS1A into two BCNF relations LOTS1AX and LOTS1AY, shown in Figure 8.12a. This decomposition loses the functional dependency FD2 because its attributes no longer coexist in the same relation after decomposition.

In practice, most relation schemas that are in 3NF are also in BCNF. Only if $X \to A$ holds in a relation schema R with X not being a superkey *and* A being a prime attribute will R be in 3NF but not in BCNF. The

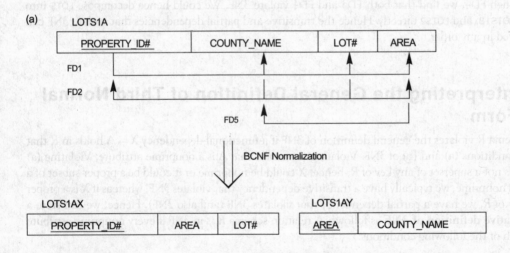

(a)
LOTS1A

| PROPERTY_ID# | COUNTY_NAME | LOT# | AREA |

FD1
FD2
FD5

BCNF Normalization

LOTS1AX

| PROPERTY_ID# | AREA | LOT# |

LOTS1AY

| AREA | COUNTY_NAME |

(b)

R

| A | B | C |

FD1
FD2

FIGURE 8.12 Boyce-Codd normal form. (a) BCNF normalization of LOTS1A with the functional dependency FD2 being lost in the decomposition. (b) A schematic relation with FDs; it is in 3NF, but not in BCNF.

relation schema R shown in Figure 8.12b illustrates the general case of such a relation. Ideally, relational database design should strive to achieve BCNF or 3NF for every relation schema. Achieving the normalization status of just 1NF or 2NF is not considered adequate, since they were developed historically as stepping stones to 3NF and BCNF.

As another example, consider Figure 8.13, which shows a relation TEACH with the following dependencies:

FD1: { STUDENT, COURSE } → INSTRUCTOR

FD2:[16] INSTRUCTOR → COURSE

Note that {STUDENT, COURSE} is a candidate key for this relation and that the dependencies shown follow the pattern in Figure 8.12b, with STUDENT as A, COURSE as B, and INSTRUCTOR as C. Hence this relation is in 3NF but not BCNF. Decomposition of this relation schema into two schemas is not straightforward because it may be decomposed into one of the three following possible pairs:

1. {STUDENT, INSTRUCTOR} and {STUDENT, COURSE}.
2. {COURSE, INSTRUCTOR } and {COURSE, STUDENT}.
3. {INSTRUCTOR, COURSE } and {INSTRUCTOR, STUDENT}.

TEACH

STUDENT	COURSE	INSTRUCTOR
Ramesh	Database	Mark
Mahesh	Database	Navathe
Mahesh	Operating Systems	Ammar
Mahesh	Theory	Schulman
Priya	Database	Mark
Priya	Operating Systems	Ahamad
Karthik	Database	Omiecinski
Swetha	Database	Navathe

FIGURE 8.13 A relation TEACH that is in 3NF but not BCNF.

All *three decompositions* "lose" the functional dependency FD1. The *desirable decomposition* of those just shown is 3, because it will not generate spurious tuples after a join.

A test to determine whether a decomposition is nonadditive (lossless) is discussed in Section 8.6.4 under Property LJ1. In general, a relation not in BCNF should be decomposed so as to meet this property, while possibly forgoing the preservation of all functional dependencies in the decomposed relations, as is the case in this example. Algorithm 8.5 does that and could be used above to give decomposition 3 for TEACH.

---

16. This dependency means that "each instructor teaches one course" is a constraint for this application.

8.6 PROPERTIES OF RELATIONAL DECOMPOSITIONS

[Sections: 8.6–8.9—Earlier Chapter Number 11]

In Section 8.6.1 we give examples to show that looking at an *individual* relation to test whether it is in a higher normal form does not, on its own, guarantee a good design; rather, a *set of relations* that together form the relational database schema must possess certain additional properties to ensure a good design. In Sections 8.6.2 and 8.6.3 we discuss two of these properties: the dependency preservation property and the lossless or nonadditive join property. Section 8.6.4 discusses binary decompositions, and Section 8.6.5 discusses successive nonadditive join decompositions.

8.6.1 Relation Decomposition and Insufficiency of Normal Forms

The relational database design algorithms that we present in Section 8.7 start from a single **universal relation schema** $R = \{A_1, A_2, \ldots, A_n\}$ that includes all the attributes of the database. We implicitly make the **universal relation assumption**, which states that every attribute name is unique. The set F of functional dependencies that should hold on the attributes of R is specified by the database designers and is made available to the design algorithms. Using the functional dependencies, the algorithms decompose the universal relation schema R into a set of relation schemas $D = \{R_1, R_2, \ldots, R_m\}$ that will become the relational database schema; D is called a **decomposition** of R.

We must make sure that each attribute in R will appear in at least one relation schema R_i in the decomposition so that no attributes are "lost"; formally, we have

$$\bigcup_{i=1}^{m} R_i = R$$

This is called the **attribute preservation** condition of a decomposition.

Another goal is to have each individual relation R_i in the decomposition D be in BCNF or 3NF. However, this condition is not sufficient to guarantee a good database design on its own. We must consider the decomposition of the universal relation as a whole, in addition to looking at the individual relations. To illustrate this point, consider the EMP_LOCS (ENAME, PLOCATION) relation of Figure 8.5, which is in 3NF and also in BCNF. In fact, any relation schema with only two attributes is automatically in BCNF.[17] Although EMP_LOCS is in BCNF, it still gives rise to spurious tuples when joined with EMP_PROJ (ENO, PNUMBER, HOURS, PNAME, PLOCATION), which is not in BCNF (see the result of the natural join in Figure 8.6). Hence, EMP_LOCS represents a particularly bad relation schema because of its convoluted semantics by which PLOCATION gives the location of *one of the projects* on which an employee works. Joining EMP_LOCS with PROJECT (PNAME, PNUMBER, PLOCATION, DNUM) of Figure 8.2—which is in BCNF—also gives rise to spurious tuples. This underscores the need for other criteria that, together with the conditions of 3NF or BCNF, prevent such bad designs. In the next three subsections we discuss such additional conditions that should hold on a decomposition D as a whole.

---

17. As an exercise, the reader should prove that this statement is true.

8.6.2 Dependency Preservation Property of a Decomposition

It would be useful if each functional dependency $X \rightarrow Y$ specified in F either appeared directly in one of the relation schemas R_i in the decomposition D or could be inferred from the dependencies that appear in some R_i. Informally, this is the *dependency preservation condition*. We want to preserve the dependencies because each dependency in F represents a constraint on the database. If one of the dependencies is not represented in some individual relation R_i of the decomposition, we cannot enforce this constraint by dealing with an individual relation; instead, we have to join two or more of the relations in the decomposition and then check that the functional dependency holds in the result of the JOIN operation. This is clearly an inefficient and impractical procedure.

It is not necessary that the exact dependencies specified in F appear themselves in individual relations of the decomposition D. It is sufficient that the union of the dependencies that hold on the individual relations in D be equivalent to F. We now define these concepts more formally.

Definition. Given a set of dependencies F on R, the **projection** of F on R_i, denoted by $\pi R_i(F)$ where R_i is a subset of R, is the set of dependencies $X \rightarrow Y$ in F^+ such that the attributes in $X \rightarrow Y$ are all contained in R_i. Hence, the projection of F on each relation schema R_i in the decomposition D is the set of functional dependencies in F^+, the closure of F, such that all their left- and right-hand-side attributes are in R_i. We say that a decomposition $D = \{R_1, R_2, \ldots, R_m\}$ of R is **dependency-preserving** with respect to F if the union of the projections of F on each R_i in D is equivalent to F; that is,

$$((\pi R_1 (F)) \cup \ldots \cup (\pi_{Rm} (F)))^+ = F^+$$

If a decomposition is not dependency-preserving, some dependency is lost in the decomposition. As we mentioned earlier, to check that a lost dependency holds, we must take the JOIN of two or more relations in the decomposition to get a relation that includes all left- and right-hand-side attributes of the lost dependency, and then check that the dependency holds on the result of the JOIN—an option that is not practical.

An example of a decomposition that does not preserve dependencies is shown in Figure 8.12a, in which the functional dependency FD2 is lost when LOTS1A is decomposed into {LOTS1AX, LOTS1AY}. The decompositions in Figure 8.11, however, are dependency-preserving. Similarly, for the example in Figure 8.13, no matter what decomposition is chosen for the relation TEACH(STUDENT, COURSE, INSTRUCTOR) from the three provided in the text, one or both of the dependencies originally present are lost. We state a claim below related to this property without providing any proof.

CLAIM 1

It is always possible to find a dependency-preserving decomposition D with respect to F such that each relation R_i in D is in 3NF.

In Section 8.7.1, we describe Algorithm 8.4, which creates a dependency-preserving decomposition $D = \{R_1, R_2, \ldots, R_m\}$ of a universal relation R based on a set of functional dependencies F, such that each R_i in D is in 3NF.

8.6.3 Lossless (Nonadditive) Join Property of a Decomposition

Another property that a decomposition D should possess is the lossless join or nonadditive join property, which ensures that no spurious tuples are generated when a NATURAL JOIN operation is applied to the relations in the decomposition. We already illustrated this problem in Section 8.1.4 with the example of Figures 8.5 and 8.6. Because this is a property of a decomposition of relation *schemas*, the condition of no spurious tuples should hold *on every legal relation state*—that is, every relation state that satisfies the functional dependencies in *F*. Hence, the lossless join property is always defined with respect to a specific set F of dependencies.

Definition. Formally, a decomposition $D = \{R_1, R_2, \ldots, R_m\}$ of R has the **lossless (nonadditive) join property** with respect to the set of dependencies *F* on R if, for *every* relation state r of R that satisfies F, the following holds, where * is the NATURAL JOIN of all the relations in D:

$$* (\pi_{R1} (r), \ldots, \pi_{Rm} (r)) = r$$

The word loss in *lossless* refers to *loss of information*, not to loss of tuples. If a decomposition does not have the lossless join property, we may get additional spurious tuples after the PROJECT (π) and NATURAL JOIN (*) operations are applied; these additional tuples represent erroneous information. We prefer the term nonadditive join because it describes the situation more accurately. If the property holds on a decomposition, we are guaranteed that no spurious tuples bearing wrong information are added to the result after the project and natural join operations are applied.

The decomposition of EMP_PROJ(ENO, PNUMBER, HOURS, ENAME, PNAME, PLOCATION) from Figure 8.3 into EMP_LOCS(ENAME, PLOCATION) and EMP_PROJ1(ENO, PNUMBER, HOURS, PNAME, PLOCATION) in Figure 8.5 obviously does not have the lossless join property, as illustrated by Figure 8.6. We will use a general procedure for testing whether any decomposition D of a relation into n relations is lossless (nonadditive) with respect to a set of given functional dependencies F in the relation; it is presented as Algorithm 8.3 below. It is possible to apply a simpler test to check if the decomposition is nonadditive for binary decompositions; that test is described in Section 8.6.4.

Algorithm 8.3: Testing for Lossless (nonadditive) Join Property

Input: A universal relation R, a decomposition $D = \{R_1, R_2, \ldots, R_m\}$ of R, and a set F of functional dependencies.

1. Create an initial matrix S with one row *i* for each relation R_i in D, and one column *j* for each attribute A_j in R.

2. Set $S(i, j) := b_{ij}$ for all matrix entries.
    (* each b_{ij} is a distinct symbol associated with indices (i, j) *)

3. For each row i representing relation schema R_i
    {for each column j representing attribute A_j
    {if (relation R_i includes attribute A_j) then set $S(i, j) := a_j$;};};
    (* each a_j is a distinct symbol associated with index (j) *)

4. Repeat the following loop until a *complete loop execution* results in no changes to S
    {for each functional dependency $X \rightarrow Y$ in F
    {for all rows in S *that have the same symbols* in the columns corresponding to attributes in X

    {make the symbols in each column that correspond to an attribute in Y be the same in all these rows as follows: If any of the rows has an "*a*" symbol for the column, set the other rows to that same "*a*" symbol in the column. If no "*a*" symbol exists for the attribute in any of the rows, choose one of the "*b*" symbols that appears in one of the rows for the attribute and set the other rows to that same "*b*" symbol in the column ;};};};

5. If a row is made up entirely of "*a*" symbols, then the decomposition has the lossless join property; otherwise, it does not.

Given a relation R that is decomposed into a number of relations $R_1, R_2, \ldots, R_m$, Algorithm 8.3 begins the matrix S that we consider to be some relation state r of R. Row i in S represents a tuple t_i (corresponding to relation R_i) that has "a" symbols in the columns that correspond to the attributes of R_i and "b" symbols in the remaining columns. The algorithm then transforms the rows of this matrix (during the loop of step 4) so that they represent tuples that satisfy all the functional dependencies in F. At the end of step 4, any two rows in S—which represent two tuples in r—that agree in their values for the left-hand-side attributes X of a functional dependency $X \rightarrow Y$ in F will also agree in their values for the right-hand-side attributes Y. It can be shown that after applying the loop of step 4, if any row in S ends up with all "a" symbols, then the decomposition D has the lossless join property with respect to F.

If, on the other hand, no row ends up being all "a" symbols, D does not satisfy the lossless join property. In this case, the relation state r represented by S at the end of the algorithm will be an example of a relation state r of R that satisfies the dependencies in F but does not satisfy the lossless join condition. Thus, this relation serves as a **counterexample** that proves that D does not have the lossless join property with respect to F. Note that the "a" and "b" symbols have no special meaning at the end of the algorithm

Figure 8.14a shows how we apply Algorithm 8.3 to the decomposition of the EMP_PROJ relation schema from Figure 8.3b into the two relation schemas EMP_PROJ1 and EMP_ LOCS of Figure 8.5a. The loop in step 4 of the algorithm cannot change any "b" symbols to "a" symbols; hence, the resulting matrix S does not have a row with all "a" symbols, and so the decomposition does not have the lossless join property.

Figure 8.14b shows another decomposition of EMP_PROJ (into EMP, PROJECT, and WORKS_ON) that does have the lossless join property, and Figure 8.14c shows how we apply the algorithm to that decomposition. Once a row consists only of "a" symbols, we know that the decomposition has the lossless join property, and we can stop applying the functional dependencies (step 4 of the algorithm) to the matrix S.

8.6.4 Testing Binary Decompositions for the Nonadditive Join Property

Algorithm 8.3 allows us to test whether a particular decomposition D into n relations obeys the lossless join property with respect to a set of functional dependencies F. There is a special case of a decomposition called a **binary decomposition**—decomposition of a relation R into two relations. We give an easier test to apply than Algorithm 8.3, but while it is very handy to use, it is *limited* to binary decompositions only.

PROPERTY LJ1 (LOSSLESS JOIN TEST FOR BINARY DECOMPOSITIONS)

A decomposition $D = \{R_1, R_2\}$ of R has the lossless (nonadditive) join property with respect to a set of functional dependencies F on R *if and only if* either

- The FD $((R_1 \cap R_2) \rightarrow (R_1 - R_2))$ is in F^+, or

- The FD $((R_1 \cap R_2) \rightarrow (R_2 - R_1))$ is in F^+

You should verify that this property holds with respect to our informal successive normalization examples in Sections 8.3 and 8.4.

(a)

$R = \{\text{ENO, ENAME, PNUMBER, PNAME, PLOCATION, HOURS}\}$ $D = \{R_1, R_2\}$
$R_1 = \text{EMP\_LOCS} = \{\text{ENAME, PLOCATION}\}$
$R_2 = \text{EMP\_PROJ1} = \{\text{ENO, PNUMBER, HOURS, PNAME, PLOCATION}\}$

$F = \{\text{ENO} \rightarrow \text{ENAME; PNUMBER} \rightarrow \{\text{PNAME, PLOCATION}\}; \{\text{ENO, PNUMBER}\} \rightarrow \text{HOURS}\}$

	ENO	ENAME	PNUMBER	PNAME	PLOCATION	HOURS
R_1	b_{11}	a_2	b_{13}	b_{14}	a_5	b_{16}
R_2	a_1	b_{22}	a_3	a_4	a_5	a_6

(no changes to matrix after applying functional dependencies)

(b)

EMP			PROJECT				WORKS_ON		
ENO	ENAME		PNUMBER	PNAME	PLOCATION		ENO	PNUMBER	HOURS

(c)

$R = \{\text{ENO, ENAME, PNUMBER, PNAME, PLOCATION, HOURS}\}$ $D = \{R_1, R_2, R_3\}$
$R_1 = \text{EMP} = \{\text{ENO, ENAME}\}$
$R_2 = \text{PROJ} = \{\text{PNUMBER, PNAME, PLOCATION}\}$
$R_3 = \text{WORKS\_ON} = \{\text{ENO, PNUMBER, HOURS}\}$

$F = \{\text{ENO} \rightarrow \text{ENAME; PNUMBER} \rightarrow \{\text{PNAME, PLOCATION}\}; \{\text{ENO, PNUMBER}\} \rightarrow \text{HOURS}\}$

	ENO	ENAME	PNUMBER	PNAME	PLOCATION	HOURS
R_1	a_1	a_2	b_{13}	b_{14}	b_{15}	b_{16}
R_2	b_{21}	b_{22}	a_3	a_4	a_5	b_{26}
R_3	a_1	b_{32}	a_3	b_{34}	b_{35}	a_6

(original matrix S at start of algorithm)

	ENO	ENAME	PNUMBER	PNAME	PLOCATION	HOURS
R_1	a_1	a_2	b_{13}	b_{14}	b_{15}	b_{16}
R_2	b_{21}	b_{22}	a_3	a_4	a_5	b_{26}
R_3	a_1	$b_{32}\,a_2$	a_3	$b_{34}\,a_4$	$b_{35}\,a_5$	a_6

(matrix S after applying the first two functional dependencies -
last row is all "a" symbols, so we stop)

FIGURE 8.14 Lossless (nonadditive) join test for *n*-ary decompositions. (a) Case 1: Decomposition of EMP_PROJ into EMP_PROJ1 and EMP_LOCS fails test. (b) A decomposition of EMP_PROJ that has the lossless join property. (c) Case 2: Decomposition of EMP_PROJ into EMP, PROJECT, and WORKS_ON satisfies test.

8.6.5   Successive Lossless (Nonadditive) Join Decompositions

We saw the successive decomposition of relations during the process of second and third normalization in Sections 8.3 and 8.4. To verify that these decompositions are nonadditive, we need to ensure another property, as set forth in Claim 2.

CLAIM 2 (Preservation of Nonadditivity in Successive Decompositions)

If a decomposition $D = \{R_1, R_2, \ldots, R_m\}$ of R has the nonadditive (lossless) join property with respect to a set of functional dependencies F on R, and if a decomposition $D_i = \{Q_1, Q_2, \ldots, Q_k\}$ of R_i has the nonadditive join property with respect to the projection of F on R_i, then the decomposition $D_2 = \{R_1, R_2, \ldots, R_{i-1}, Q_1, Q_2, \ldots, Q_k, R_{i+1}, \ldots, R_m\}$ of R has the nonadditive join property with respect to F.

8.7   ALGORITHMS FOR RELATIONAL DATABASE SCHEMA DESIGN

We now give three algorithms for creating a relational decomposition. Each algorithm has specific properties, as we discuss below.

8.7.1   Dependency-Preserving Decomposition into 3NF Schemas

Algorithm 8.4 creates a dependency-preserving decomposition $D = \{R_1, R_2, \ldots, R_m\}$ of a universal relation R based on a set of functional dependencies F, such that each R_i in D is in 3NF. It guarantees only the dependency-preserving property; it does *not* guarantee the lossless join property. The first step of Algorithm 8.4 is to find a minimal cover G for F; Algorithm 8.2 can be used for this step.

Algorithm 8.4: Relational Synthesis into 3NF with Dependency Preservation

Input: A universal relation R and a set of functional dependencies F on the attributes of R.

1. Find a minimal cover G for F (use Algorithm 8.2);

2. For each left-hand-side X of a functional dependency that appears in G, create a relation schema in D with attributes $\{X \cup \{A_1\} \cup \{A_2\} \ldots \cup \{A_k\}\}$, where $X \to A_1, X \to A_2, \ldots, X \to A_k$ are the only dependencies in G with X as the left-hand-side (X is the key of this relation);

3. Place any remaining attributes (that have not been placed in any relation) in a single relation schema to ensure the attribute preservation property.

CLAIM 3

Every relation schema created by Algorithm 8.4 is in 3NF. (We will not provide a formal proof here;[18] the proof depends on G being a minimal set of dependencies.)

---

18. See Maier (1983) or Ullman (1982) for a proof.

It is obvious that all the dependencies in G are preserved by the algorithm because each dependency appears in one of the relations R_i in the decomposition D. Since G is equivalent to F, all the dependencies in F are either preserved directly in the decomposition or are derivable using the inference rules from Section 8.2.2 from those in the resulting relations, thus ensuring the dependency preservation property. Algorithm 8.4 is called the relational synthesis algorithm, because each relation schema R_i in the decomposition is synthesized (constructed) from the set of functional dependencies in G with the same left-hand-side X.

8.7.2   Lossless (Nonadditive) Join Decomposition into BCNF Schemas

The next algorithm decomposes a universal relation schema $R = \{A_1, A_2, \ldots, A_n\}$ into a decomposition $D = \{R_1, R_2, \ldots, R_m\}$ such that each R_i is in BCNF and the decomposition D has the lossless join property with respect to F. Algorithm 8.5 utilizes Property LJ1 and Claim (preservation of nonadditivity in successive decompositions) to create a nonadditive join decomposition $D = \{R_1, R_2, \ldots, R_m\}$ of a universal relation R based on a set of functional dependencies F, such that each R_i in D is in BCNF.

Algorithm 8.5: Relational Decomposition into BCNF with Nonadditive Join Property

Input: A universal relation R and a set of functional dependencies F on the attributes of R.

1. Set $D := \{R\}$;

2. While there is a relation schema Q in D that is not in BCNF do

   {

   choose a relation schema Q in D that is not in BCNF;

   find a functional dependency $X \rightarrow Y$ in Q that violates BCNF;

   replace Q in D by two relation schemas $(Q - Y)$ and $(X \cup Y)$;

   };

Each time through the loop in Algorithm 8.5, we decompose one relation schema Q that is not in BCNF into two relation schemas. According to Property LJ1 for binary decompositions and Claim 2, the decomposition D has the nonadditive join property. At the end of the algorithm, all relation schemas in D will be in BCNF. The reader can check that the normalization example in Figures 8.11 and 8.12 basically follows this algorithm. The functional dependencies FD3, FD4, and later FD5 violate BCNF, so the LOTS relation is decomposed appropriately into BCNF relations, and the decomposition then satisfies the nonadditive join property. Similarly, if we apply the algorithm to the TEACH relation schema from Figure 8.13, it is decomposed into TEACH1(INSTRUCTOR, STUDENT) and TEACH2(INSTRUCTOR, COURSE) because the dependency FD2: INSTRUCTOR → COURSE violates BCNF.

In step 2 of Algorithm 8.5, it is necessary to determine whether a relation schema Q is in BCNF or not. One method for doing this is to test, for each functional dependency $X \rightarrow Y$ in Q, whether X^+ fails to include all the attributes in Q, thereby determining whether or not X is a (super)key in Q. Another technique is based on an observation that whenever a relation schema Q violates BCNF, there exists a pair of attributes A and B in Q such that $\{Q - \{A, B\}\} \rightarrow A$; by computing the closure $\{Q - \{A, B\}\}^+$ for each pair of attributes $\{A, B\}$ of Q, and checking whether the closure includes A (or B), we can determine whether Q is in BCNF.

8.7.3 Dependency-Preserving and Nonadditive (Lossless) Join Decomposition into 3NF Schemas

If we want a decomposition to have the nonadditive join property *and* to preserve dependencies, we have to be satisfied with relation schemas in 3NF rather than BCNF. A simple modification to Algorithm 8.4, shown as Algorithm 8.6, yields a decomposition D of R that does the following:

- Preserves dependencies

- Has the nonadditive join property

- Is such that each resulting relation schema in the decomposition is in 3NF

Algorithm 8.6: Relational Synthesis into 3NF with Dependency Preservation and Nonadditive (Lossless) Join Property

Input: A universal relation R and a set of functional dependencies F on the attributes of R.

1. Find a minimal cover G for F (use Algorithm 8.2).

2. For each left-hand-side X of a functional dependency that appears in G create a relation schema in D with attributes $\{X \cup \{A_1\} \cup \{A_2\} \dots \cup \{A_k\}\}$, where $X \to A_1, X \to A_2, \dots, X \to A_k$ are the only dependencies in G with X as left-hand-side (X is the key of this relation).

3. If none of the relation schemas in D contains a key of R, then create one more relation schema in D that contains attributes that form a key of R.

It can be shown that the decomposition formed from the set of relation schemas created by the preceding algorithm is dependency-preserving *and* has the nonadditive join property. In addition, each relation schema in the decomposition is in 3NF. This algorithm is an improvement over Algorithm 8.4 in that the former guaranteed only dependency preservation[19]

Step 3 of Algorithm 8.6 involves identifying a key K of R. Algorithm 8.7 can be used to identify a key K of R based on the set of given functional dependencies F. We start by setting K to all the attributes of R; we then remove one attribute at a time and check whether the remaining attributes still form a superkey. Notice that the set of functional dependencies used to determine a key in Algorithm 8.7 could be either F or G, since they are equivalent. Notice, too, that Algorithm 8.7 determines only *one* key out of the possible candidate keys for R; the key returned depends on the order in which attributes are removed from R in step 2.

Algorithm 8.7: Finding a Key K for R Given a set F of Functional Dependencies

Input: A universal relation R and a set of functional dependencies F on the attributes of R.

1. Set $K := R$.

2. For each attribute A in K

   {compute $(K - A)^+$ with respect to F;

   If $(K - A)^+$ contains all the attributes in R, then set $K := K - \{A\}$};

It is important to note that the theory of nonadditive join decompositions is based on the assumption that *no null values are allowed for the join attributes*. The next section discusses some of the problems that nulls may cause in relational decompositions.

---

19. Step 3 of Algorithm 8.4 is not needed in Algorithm 8.6 to preserve attributes because the key will include any unplaced attributes; these are the attributes that do not participate in any functional dependency.

8.7.4 Problems with Null Values and Dangling Tuples

We must carefully consider the problems associated with nulls when designing a relational database schema. There is no fully satisfactory relational design theory as yet that includes null values. One problem occurs when some tuples have null values for attributes that will be used to join individual relations in the decomposition. To illustrate this, consider the database shown in Figure 8.15a, where two relations EMPLOYEE and DEPARTMENT

(a)

EMPLOYEE

ENAME	ENO	DOB	ADDRESS	DNUM
Mahesh, B. Kumar	123456789	09-01-1965	731 Ameerpet, Hyderabad, AP	5
Karthik, T. Chandra	333445555	08-12-1955	638 Begampet ,Hyderabad ,AP	5
Swetha, J. Narayan	999887777	19-07-1968	3321 Hauzkhas, New Delhi	4
Priya, S. Ganesh	987654321	20-06-1941	291 Majestic Street, Bangalore	4
Ramesh, K. Narayan	666884444	15-09-1962	975 Hauzkhas, New Delhi	5
Kiran, A Goyal	453453453	31-07-1972	5631 Abids, Hyderabad, AP	5
Jitendra, V. Nath	987987987	29-03-1969	980 Koti, Hyderabad, AP	4
Gaurav, E. Kishan	888665555	10-11-1937	450 Abids, Hyderabad, AP	1
Srinivas, Naga C .	999775555	26-04-1965	6530 T.Nagar, Chennai, TN	null
Rakesh, Gupta M.	888664444	09-01-1963	7654 Beach Rd, Chennai, TN	null

DEPARTMENT

DNAME	DNUM	DMGRENO
Research	5	333445555
Administration	4	987654321
Headquarters	1	888665555

(b)

ENAME	ENO	DOB	ADDRESS	DNUM	DNAME	DMGRENO
Mahesh, B. Kumar	123456789	09-01-1965	731 Ameerpet, Hyderabad, AP	5	Research	333445555
Karthik, T. Chandra	333445555	08-12-1955	638 Begampet, Hyderabad, AP	5	Research	333445555
Swetha, J. Narayan	999887777	19-07-1968	3321 Hauzkhas, New Delhi	4	Administration	987654321
Priya, S. Ganesh	987654321	20-06-1941	291 Majestic Street, Bangalore	4	Administration	987654321
Ramesh, K. Narayan	666884444	15-09-1962	975 Hauzkhas, New Delhi	5	Research	333445555
Kiran, A Goyal	453453453	31-07-1972	5631 Abids, Hyderabad, AP	5	Research	333445555
Jitendra, V. Nath	987987987	29-03-1969	980 Koti, Hyderabad, AP	4	Administration	987654321
Gaurav, E. Kishan	888665555	10-11-1937	450 Abids, Hyderabad, AP	1	Headquarters	888665555

(c)

ENAME	ENO	DOB	ADDRESS	DNUM	DNAME	DMGRENO
Mahesh, B. Kumar	123456789	09-01-1965	731 Ameerpet, Hyderabad, AP	5	Research	333445555
Karthik, T. Chandra	333445555	08-12-1955	638 Begampet, Hyderabad, AP	5	Research	333445555
Swetha, J. Narayan	999887777	19-07-1968	3321 Hauzkhas, New Delhi	4	Administration	987654321
Priya, S. Ganesh	987654321	20-06-1941	291 Majestic Street, Bangalore	4	Administration	987654321
Ramesh, K. Narayan	666884444	15-09-1962	975 Hauzkhas, New Delhi	5	Research	333445555
Kiran, A Goyal	453453453	31-07-1972	5631 Abids, Hyderabad, AP	5	Research	333445555
Jitendra, V. Nath	987987987	29-03-1969	980 Koti, Hyderabad, AP	4	Administration	987654321
Gaurav, E. Kishan	888665555	10-11-1937	450 Koti, Hyderabad, AP	1	Headquarters	888665555
Srinivas, Naga C .	999775555	26-04-1965	6530 T.Nagar, Chennai, TN	null	null	null
Rakesh, Gupta M .	888664444	09-01-1963	7654 Beach Rd, Chennai, TN	null	null	null

FIGURE 8.15 Issues with null-value joins. (a) Some EMPLOYEE tuples have null for the join attribute DNUM. (b) Result of applying NATURAL JOIN to the EMPLOYEE and DEPARTMENT relations. (c) Result of applying LEFT OUTER JOIN to EMPLOYEE and DEPARTMENT.

are shown. The last two employee tuples—Srinivas and Rakesh—represent newly hired employees who have not yet been assigned to a department (assume that this does not violate any integrity constraints). Now suppose that we want to retrieve a list of (ENAME, DNAME) values for all the employees. If we apply the NATURAL JOIN operation on EMPLOYEE and DEPARTMENT (Figure 8.15b), the two aforementioned tuples will *not* appear in the result.

The OUTER JOIN operation, discussed in Chapter 5, can deal with this problem. Recall that if we take the LEFT OUTER JOIN of EMPLOYEE with DEPARTMENT, tuples in EMPLOYEE that have null for the join attribute will still appear in the result, joined with an "imaginary" tuple in DEPARTMENT that has nulls for all its attribute values. Figure 8.15c shows the result.

In general, whenever a relational database schema is designed in which two or more relations are interrelated via foreign keys, particular care must be devoted to watching for potential null values in foreign keys. This can cause unexpected loss of information in queries that involve joins on that foreign key. Moreover, if nulls occur in other attributes, such as SALARY, their effect on built-in functions such as SUM and AVERAGE must be carefully evaluated.

A related problem is that of *dangling tuples*, which may occur if we carry a decomposition too far. Suppose that we decompose the EMPLOYEE relation of Figure 8.15a further into EMPLOYEE_1 and EMPLOYEE_2, shown in Figure 8.16a and 8.16b.[20] If we apply the NATURAL JOIN operation to EMPLOYEE_1 AND EMPLOYEE_2, we get the original EMPLOYEE relation. However, we may use the alternative representation, shown in Figure 8.16c, where we do *not include a tuple* in EMPLOYEE_3 if the employee has not been assigned a department (instead of including a tuple with null for DNUM as in EMPLOYEE_2). If we use EMPLOYEE_3 instead of EMPLOYEE_2 and apply a NATURAL JOIN on EMPLOYEE_1 and EMPLOYEE_3, the tuples for Srinivas and Rakesh will not appear in the result; these are called **dangling tuples** because they are represented in only one of the two relations that represent employees and hence are lost if we apply an (INNER) JOIN operation.

8.7.5   Discussion of Normalization Algorithms

One of the problems with the normalization algorithms we described is that the database designer must first specify *all* the relevant functional dependencies among the database attributes. This is not a simple task for a large database with hundreds of attributes. Failure to specify one or two important dependencies may result in an undesirable design. Another problem is that these algorithms are not deterministic in general. For example, the *synthesis algorithms* (Algorithms 8.4 and 8.6) require the specification of a minimal cover G for the set of functional dependencies F. Because there may be in general many minimal covers corresponding to F, the algorithm can give different designs depending on the particular minimal cover used. Some of these designs may not be desirable. The *decomposition algorithm* (Algorithm 8.5) depends on the order in which the functional dependencies are supplied to the algorithm to check for BCNF violation. Again, it is possible that many different designs may arise corresponding to the same set of functional dependencies, depending on the order in which such dependencies are considered for violation of BCNF. Some of the designs may be quite superior, whereas others may be undesirable.

---

20. This sometimes happens when we apply vertical fragmentation to a relation in the context of a distributed database.

(a) EMPLOYEE_1

ENAME	ENO	DOB	ADDRESS
Mahesh, B. Kumar	123456789	09-01-1965	731 Ameerpet, Hyderabad, AP
Karthik, T. Chandra	333445555	08-12-1955	638 Begampet, Hyderabad, AP
Swetha, J. Narayan	999887777	19-07-1968	3321 Hauzkhos, New Delhi
Priya, S. Ganesh	987654321	20-06-1941	291 Majestic Street, bangalore
Ramesh, K. Narayan	666884444	15-09-1962	975 Hauzkhas, New Delhi
Kiran, A Goyal	453453453	31-07-1972	5631 Abids, Hyderabad, AP
Jitendra, V. Nath	987987987	29-03-1969	980 Koti, Hyderabad, AP
Gaurav, E. Kishan	888665555	10-11-1937	450 Abids, Hyderabad, AP
Srinivas, Naga C.	999775555	26-04-1965	6530 T.Nagar, Chennai, TN
Rakesh, Gupta M.	888664444	09-01-1963	7654 Beach Rd, Chennai, TN

(b) EMPLOYEE_2

ENO	DNUM
123456789	5
333445555	5
999887777	4
987654321	4
666884444	5
453453453	5
987987987	4
888665555	1
999775555	null
888664444	null

(c) EMPLOYEE_3

ENO	DNUM
123456789	5
333445555	5
999887777	4
987654321	4
666884444	5
453453453	5
987987987	4
888665555	1

FIGURE 8.16 The "dangling tuple" problem. (a) The relation EMPLOYEE_1 (includes all attributes of EMPLOYEE from Figure 11.2a except DNUM). (b) The relation EMPLOYEE_2 (includes DNUM attribute with null values). (c) The relation EMPLOYEE_3 (includes DNUM attribute but does not include tuples for which DNUM has null values).

It is not always possible to find a decomposition into relation schemas that preserves dependencies and allows each relation schema in the decomposition to be in BCNF (instead of 3NF as in Algorithm 8.6). We can check the 3NF relation schemas in the decomposition individually to see whether each satisfies BCNF. If some relation schema R_i is not in BCNF, we can choose to decompose it further or to leave it as it is in 3NF (with some possible update anomalies). The fact that we cannot always find a decomposition into relation schemas in BCNF that preserves dependencies can be illustrated by the examples in Figures 8.12 and 8.13. The relations LOTS1A (Figure 8.12a) and TEACH (Figure 8.13) are not in BCNF but are in 3NF. Any attempt to decompose either relation further into BCNF relations results in loss of the dependency FD2: {COUNTY_NAME, LOT#} → {PROPERTY_ID#, AREA} in LOTS1A or loss of FD1: {STUDENT, COURSE} → INSTRUCTOR in TEACH.

Table 8.2 SUMMARY OF THE ALGORITHMS DISCUSSED IN SECTIONS 8.6 AND 8.7

ALGORITHM	INPUT	OUTPUT	PROPERTIES/PURPOSE	REMARKS
8.3	A decomposition D of R and a set F of functional dependencies	Boolean result: yes or no for nonadditive join property	Testing for nonadditive join decomposition	See a simpler test in Section 8.6.4 for binary decompositions
8.4	Set of functional dependencies F	A set of relations in 3NF	Dependency preservation	No guarantee of satisfying lossless join property
8.5	Set of functional dependencies F	A set of relations in BCNF	Nonadditive join decomposition	No guarantee of dependency preservation
8.6	Set of functional dependencies F	A set of relations in 3NF	Nonadditive join AND dependency preserving decomposition	May not achieve BCNF
8.7	Relation schema R with a set of functional dependencies F	Key K of R	To find a key K (that is a subset of R)	The entire relation R is always a default superkey

8.8 MULTIVALUED DEPENDENCIES AND FOURTH NORMAL FORM

So far we have discussed only functional dependency, which is by far the most important type of dependency in relational database design theory. However, in many cases relations have constraints that cannot be specified as functional dependencies. In this section, we discuss the concept of *multivalued dependency* (MVD) and define *fourth normal form*, which is based on this dependency. Multivalued dependencies are a consequence of first normal form (1NF) (see Section 8.3.4), which disallows an attribute in a tuple to have a *set of values*. If we have two or more multivalued *independent* attributes in the same relation schema, we get into a problem of having to repeat every value of one of the attributes with every value of the other attribute to keep the relation state consistent and to maintain the independence among the attributes involved. This constraint is specified by a multivalued dependency.

For example, consider the relation EMP shown in Figure 8.17a. A tuple in this EMP relation represents the fact that an employee whose name is ENAME works on the project whose name is PNAME and has a dependent whose name is DNAME. An employee may work on several projects and may have several dependents, and the employee's projects and dependents are independent of one another.[21] To keep the relation state consistent, we must have a separate tuple to represent every combination of an employee's dependent and an employee's project. This constraint is specified as a multivalued dependency on the EMP relation. Informally, whenever two *independent* 1:N relationships A:B and A:C are mixed in the same relation, a MVD may arise.

---

21. In an ER diagram, each would be represented as a multivalued attribute or as a weak entity type (see Chapter 3).

(a) EMP

ENAME	PNAME	DNAME
Kumar	X	Rakesh
Kumar	Y	Rao
Kumar	X	Rao
Kumar	Y	Rakesh

(b) **EMP_PROJECTS**

ENAME	PNAME
Kumar	X
Kumar	Y

EMP_DEPENDENTS

ENAME	DNAME
Kumar	Rakesh
Kumar	Rao

(c) SUPPLY

SNAME	PARTNAME	PROJNAME
Kumar	Bolt	ProjX
Kumar	Nut	ProjY
Prakash	Bolt	ProjY
Ramesh	Nut	ProjZ
Prakash	Nail	ProjX
Prakash	Bolt	ProjX
Kumar	Bolt	ProjY

(d) R1

SNAME	PARTNAME
Kumar	Bolt
Kumar	Nut
Prakash	Bolt
Ramesh	Nut
Prakash	Nail

R2

SNAME	PROJNAME
Kumar	ProjX
Kumar	ProjY
Prakash	ProjY
Ramesh	ProjZ
Prakash	ProjX

R3

PARTNAME	PROJNAME
Bolt	ProjX
Nut	ProjY
Bolt	ProjY
Nut	ProjZ
Nail	ProjX

FIGURE 8.17 Fourth and fifth normal forms. (a) The EMP relation with two MVDs: ENAME →→ PNAME and ENAME →→ DNAME. (b) Decomposing the EMP relation into two 4NF relations EMP_PROJECTS and *EMP_DEPENDENTS*. (c) The relation SUPPLY with no MVDs is in 4NF but not in 5NF if it has the JD(R1, R2, R3). (d) Decomposing the relation SUPPLY into the 5NF relations R1, R2, R3.

8.8.1 Formal Definition of Multivalued Dependency

Definition. A multivalued dependency $X \twoheadrightarrow Y$ specified on relation schema R, where X and Y are both subsets of R, specifies the following constraint on any relation state r of R: If two tuples t_1 and t_2 exist in r such that $t_1[X] = t_2[X]$, then two tuples t_3 and t_4 should also exist in r with the following properties,[22] where we use Z to denote $(R - (X \cup Y))$:[23]

---

22. The tuples t_1, t_2, t_3, and t4 are not necessarily distinct.

23. Z is shorthand for the attributes remaining in R after the attributes in $(X \cup Y)$ are removed from R.

- $t_3[X] = t_4[X] = t_1[X] = t_2[X]$.

- $t_3[Y] = t_1[Y]$ and $t_4[Y] = t_2[Y]$.

- $t_3[Z] = t_2[Z]$ and $t_4[Z] = t_1[Z]$.

Whenever $X \twoheadrightarrow Y$ holds, we say that X **multidetermines** Y. Because of the symmetry in the definition, whenever $X \twoheadrightarrow Y$ holds in R, so does $X \twoheadrightarrow Z$. Hence, $X \twoheadrightarrow Y$ implies $X \twoheadrightarrow Z$, and therefore it is sometimes written as $X \twoheadrightarrow Y|Z$.

The formal definition specifies that given a particular value of X, the set of values of Y determined by this value of X is completely determined by X alone and *does not depend* on the values of the remaining attributes Z of R. Hence, whenever two tuples exist that have distinct values of Y but the same value of X, these values of Y must be repeated in separate tuples with *every distinct value of Z* that occurs with that same value of X. This informally corresponds to Y being a multivalued attribute of the entities represented by tuples in R.

In Figure 8.17a the MVDs ENAME $\twoheadrightarrow$ PNAME and ENAME $\twoheadrightarrow$ DNAME (or ENAME $\twoheadrightarrow$ PNAME|DNAME) hold in the EMP relation. The employee with ENAME 'KUMAR' works on projects with PNAME 'X' and 'Y' and has two dependents with DNAME 'Rakesh' and 'Rao'. If we stored only the first two tuples in EMP (<'Kumar', 'X', 'Rakesh'> and <'Kumar', 'Y', 'Rao'>), we would incorrectly show associations between project 'X' and 'Rakesh' and between project 'Y' and 'Rao'; these should not be conveyed, because no such meaning is intended in this relation. Hence, we must store the other two tuples (<'Kumar', 'X', 'Rao'> and <'Kumar', 'Y', 'Rakesh'>) to show that {'X','Y'} and {'Rakesh', 'Rao'} are associated only with 'Kumar'; that is, there is no association between PNAME and DNAME—which means that the two attributes are independent.

A MVD $X \twoheadrightarrow Y$ in R is called a **trivial** MVD if (a) Y is a subset of X, or (b) $X \cup Y = R$. For example, the relation EMP_PROJECTS in Figure 8.17b has the trivial MVD ENAME $\twoheadrightarrow$ PNAME. An MVD that satisfies neither (a) nor (b) is called a **nontrivial** MVD. A trivial MVD will hold in any relation state r of R; it is called trivial because it does not specify any significant or meaningful constraint on R.

If we have a nontrivial MVD in a relation, we may have to repeat values redundantly in the tuples. In the EMP relation of Figure 8.17a, the values 'X' and 'Y' of PNAME are repeated with each value of DNAME (or, by symmetry, the values 'Kumar' and 'Rao' of DNAME are repeated with each value of PNAME). This redundancy is clearly undesirable. However, the EMP schema is in BCNF because no functional dependencies hold in EMP. Therefore, we need to define a fourth normal form that is stronger than BCNF and disallows relation schemas such as EMP. We first discuss some of the properties of MVDs and consider how they are related to functional dependencies. Notice that relations containing nontrival MVDs tend to be **all -Key relations**—that is, their key is all their attributes taken together.

8.8.2   Inference Rules for Functional and Multivalued Dependencies

As with functional dependencies (FDs), inference rules for multivalued dependencies (MVDs) have been developed. It is better, though, to develop a unified framework that includes both FDs and MVDs so that both types of constraints can be considered together. The following inference rules IR1 through IR8 form a sound and complete set for inferring functional and multivalued dependencies from a given set of dependencies. Assume that all attributes are included in a "universal" relation schema $R = \{A_1, A_2, \ldots, A_n\}$ and that X, Y, Z, and W are subsets of R.

IR1 (reflexive rule for FDs): If $X \supseteq Y$, then $X \rightarrow Y$.

IR2 (augmentation rule for FDs): $\{X \rightarrow Y\} \models XZ \rightarrow YZ$.

IR3 (transitive rule for FDs): $\{X \to Y, Y \to Z\} \mid= X \to Z$.

IR4 (complementation rule for MVDs): $\{X \twoheadrightarrow Y\} \mid= \{X \twoheadrightarrow (R - (X \cup Y))\}$.

IR5 (augmentation rule for MVDs): If $X \twoheadrightarrow Y$ and $W \supseteq Z$, then $WX \twoheadrightarrow YZ$.

IR6 (transitive rule for MVDs): $\{X \twoheadrightarrow Y, Y \twoheadrightarrow Z\} \mid= X \twoheadrightarrow (Z - Y)$.

IR7 (replication rule for FD to MVD): $\{X \to Y\} \mid= X \twoheadrightarrow Y$.

IR8 (coalescence rule for FDs and MVDs): If $X \twoheadrightarrow Y$ and there exists W with the properties that (a) $W \cap Y$ is empty, (b) $W \to Z$, and (c) $Y \supseteq Z$, then $X \to Z$.

IR1 through IR3 are Armstrong's inference rules for FDs alone. IR4 through IR6 are inference rules pertaining to MVDs only. IR7 and IR8 relate FDs and MVDs. In particular, IR7 says that a functional dependency is a *special* case of a multivalued dependency; that is, every FD is also an MVD because it satisfies the formal definition of a MVD. However, this equivalence has a catch: A FD $X \to Y$ is a MVD $X \twoheadrightarrow Y$ with the *additional implicit restriction* that at most one value of Y is associated with each value of X.[24] Given a set F of functional and multivalued dependencies specified on $R = \{A_1, A_2, \ldots, A_n\}$, we can use IR1 through IR8 to infer the (complete) set of all dependencies (functional or multivalued) F^+ that will hold in every relation state r of R that satisfies F. We again call F^+ the **closure** of F.

8.8.3 Fourth Normal Form

We now present the definition of **fourth normal form (4NF),** which is violated when a relation has undesirable multivalued dependencies, and hence can be used to identify and decompose such relations.

Definition. A relation schema R is in 4NF with respect to a set of dependencies F (that includes functional dependencies and multivalued dependencies) if, for every nontrivial multivalued dependency $X \twoheadrightarrow Y$ in F^+, X is a superkey for R.

The EMP relation of Figure 8.17a is not in 4NF because in the nontrivial MVDs ENAME $\twoheadrightarrow$ PNAME and ENAME $\twoheadrightarrow$ DNAME, ENAME is not a superkey of EMP. We decompose EMP into EMP_PROJECTS and EMP_DEPENDENTS, shown in Figure 8.17b. Both EMP_PROJECTS and EMP_DEPENDENTS are in 4NF, because the MVDs ENAME $\twoheadrightarrow$ PNAME in EMP_PROJECTS and ENAME $\twoheadrightarrow$ DNAME in EMP_ DEPENDENTS are trivial MVDs. No other nontrivial MVDs hold in either EMP_PROJECTS or EMP_DEPENDENTS. No FDs hold in these relation schemas either.

To illustrate the importance of 4NF, Figure 8.18a shows the EMP relation with an additional employee, 'Gupta', who has three dependents ('Valli', 'Ravi', and 'Nath') and works on four different projects ('W', 'X', 'Y', and 'Z'). There are 16 tuples in EMP in Figure 8.18a. If we decompose EMP into EMP_PROJECTS and EMP_DEPENDENTS, as shown in Figure 8.18b, we need to store a total of only 11 tuples in both relations. Not only would the decomposition save on storage, but the update anomalies associated with multivalued dependencies would also be avoided. For example, if Brown starts working on a new project P, we must insert *three* tuples in EMP—one for each dependent. If we forget to insert any one of those, the relation violates the MVD and becomes inconsistent in that it incorrectly implies a relationship between project and dependent.

---

24. That is, the set of values of Y determined by a value of X is restricted to being a *singleton set* with only one value. Hence, in practice, we never view an FD as a MVD.

(a) **EMP**

ENAME	PNAME	DNAME
Kumar	X	Rakesh
Kumar	Y	Rao
Kumar	X	Rao
Kumar	Y	Rakesh
Gupta	W	Valli
Gupta	X	Valli
Gupta	Y	Valli
Gupta	Z	Valli
Gupta	W	Ravi
Gupta	X	Ravi
Gupta	Y	Ravi
Gupta	Z	Ravi
Gupta	W	Nath
Gupta	X	Nath
Gupta	Y	Nath
Gupta	Z	Nath

(b) **EMP_PROJECTS**

ENAME	PNAME
Kumar	X
Kumar	Y
Gupta	W
Gupta	X
Gupta	Y
Gupta	Z

EMP_DEPENDENTS

ENAME	DNAME
Kumar	Rao
Kumar	Rakesh
Gupta	Valli
Gupta	Ravi
Gupta	Nath

FIGURE 8.18 Decomposing a relation state of EMP that is not in 4NF. (a) EMP relation with additional tuples. (b) Two corresponding 4NF relations EMP_PROJECTS and EMP_DEPENDENTS.

If the relation has nontrivial MVDs, then insert, delete, and update operations on single tuples may cause additional tuples besides the one in question to be modified. If the update is handled incorrectly, the meaning of the relation may change. However, after normalization into 4NF, these update anomalies disappear. For example, to add the information that Brown will be assigned to project P, only a single tuple need be inserted in the 4NF relation EMP_PROJECTS.

The EMP relation in Figure 8.17a is not in 4NF because it represents two *independent* 1:N relationships—one between employees and the projects they work on and the other between employees and their dependents. We sometimes have a relationship among three entities that depends on all three participating entities, such as the SUPPLY relation shown in Figure 8.17c. (Consider only the tuples in Figure 8.17c *above* the dotted line for now.) In this case a tuple represents a supplier supplying a specific part to *a particular project*, so there are *no* nontrivial MVDs. The SUPPLY relation is already in 4NF and should not be decomposed.

8.8.4 Lossless (Nonadditive) Join Decomposition into 4NF Relations

Whenever we decompose a relation schema R into $R_1 = (X \cup Y)$ and $R_2 = (R - Y)$ based on an MVD $X \twoheadrightarrow Y$ that holds in R, the decomposition has the nonadditive join property. It can be shown that this is a necessary and sufficient condition for decomposing a schema into two schemas that have the nonadditive join property, as given by property LJ1' which is a further generalization of Property LJ1 given earlier. Property LJ1 dealt with FDs only, whereas LJ1' deals with both FDs and MVDs (recall that a FD is also a MVD).

PROPERTY LJ1'

The relation schemas R_1 and R_2 form a nonadditive join decomposition of R with respect to a set F of functional *and* multivalued dependencies if and only if

$(R_1 \cap R_2) \twoheadrightarrow (R_1 - R_2)$

or, by symmetry, if and only if

$(R_1 \cap R_2) \twoheadrightarrow (R_2 - R_1)$.

We can use a slight modification of Algorithm 8.5 to develop Algorithm 8.8, which creates a nonadditive join decomposition into relation schemas that are in 4NF (rather than in BCNF). As with Algorithm 8.5, Algorithm 8.8 does not necessarily produce a decomposition that preserves FDs.

Algorithm 8.8: Relational Decomposition into 4NF Relations with Nonadditive Join Property

Input: A universal relation R and a set of functional and multivalued dependencies F.

1. Set $D := \{ R \}$;
2. While there is a relation schema Q in D that is not in 4NF, do

   {choose a relation schema Q in D that is not in 4NF;

   find a nontrivial MVD $X \twoheadrightarrow Y$ in Q that violates 4NF;

   replace Q in D by two relation schemas $(Q - Y)$ and $(X \cup Y)$;

   };

8.9 JOIN DEPENDENCIES AND FIFTH NORMAL FORM

We saw that LJ1 and LJ1' give the condition for a relation schema R to be decomposed into two schemas R_1 and R_2, where the decomposition has the nonadditive join property. However, in some cases there may be no nonadditive join decomposition of R into two relation schemas, but there may be a nonadditive (lossless) join decomposition *into more than two* relation schemas. Moreover, there may be no functional dependency in R that violates any normal form up to BCNF, and there may be no nontrivial MVD present in R either that violates 4NF. We then resort to another dependency called the *join dependency* and, if it is present, carry out a *multiway decomposition* into fifth normal form (5NF). It is important to note that such a dependency is a very peculiar semantic constraint that is very difficult to detect in practice; therefore, normalization into 5NF is very rarely done in practice.

Definition. A **join dependency (JD)**, denoted by $JD(R_1, R_2, \ldots, R_n)$, specified on relation schema R, specifies a constraint on the states r of R. The constraint states that every legal state r of R should have a nonadditive join decomposition into $R_1, R_2, \ldots, R_n$; that is, for every such r we have

$$* \ (\pi_{R1} (r), \pi_{R2} (r), ..., \pi_{Rn} (r)) = r$$

Notice that an MVD is a special case of a JD where $n = 2$. That is, a JD denoted as JD(R1, R2) implies a MVD $(R_1 \cap R_2) \twoheadrightarrow (R_1 - R_2)$ (or, by symmetry, $(R_1 \cap R_2) \twoheadrightarrow (R_2 - R_1)$). A join dependency $JD(R_1, R_2, \ldots, R_n)$, specified on relation schema R, is a trivial JD if one of the relation schemas R_i in $JD(R_1, R_2, \ldots, R_n)$ is equal to R. Such a dependency is called trivial because it has the nonadditive join property for any relation state r of R and hence does not specify any constraint on R. We can now define fifth normal form, which is also called project-join normal form.

Definition. A relation schema R is in **fifth normal form (5NF)** (or **project-join normal form [PJNF]**) with respect to a set F of functional, multivalued, and join dependencies if, for every nontrivial join dependency $JD(R_1, R_2, \ldots, R_n)$ in F^+ (that is, implied by F), every R_i is a superkey of R.

For an example of a JD, consider once again the SUPPLY all-key relation of Figure 8.17c. Suppose that the following additional constraint always holds: Whenever a supplier s supplies part p, and a project j uses part p, and the supplier s supplies *at least one* part to project j, then supplier s will also be supplying part p to project j. This constraint can be restated in other ways and specifies a join dependency $JD(R1, R2, R3)$ among the three projections R1(SNAME, PARTNAME), R2(SNAME, PROJNAME), and R3(PARTNAME, PROJNAME) of SUPPLY. If this constraint holds, the tuples below the dotted line in Figure 8.17c must exist in any legal state of the SUPPLY relation that also contains the tuples above the dotted line. Figure 8.17d shows how the SUPPLY relation *with the join dependency* is decomposed into three relations R1, R2, and R3 that are each in 5NF. Notice that applying a natural join to any two of these relations *produces spurious tuples*, but applying a natural join to *all three together* does not. The reader should verify this on the example relation of Figure 8.17c and its projections in Figure 8.17d. This is because only the JD exists, but no MVDs are specified. Notice, too, that the $JD(R1, R2, R3)$ is specified on *all* legal relation states, not just on the one shown in Figure 8.17c.

Discovering JDs in practical databases with hundreds of attributes is next to impossible. It can be done only with a great degree of intuition about the data on the part of the designer. Hence, the current practice of database design pays scant attention to them.

8.10 SUMMARY

In this chapter we first discussed several pitfalls in relational database design using intuitive arguments. We identified informally some of the measures for indicating whether a relation schema is "good" or "bad," and provided informal guidelines for a good design. We then presented some formal concepts that allow us to do relational design in a top-down fashion by analyzing relations individually. We defined this process of design by analysis and decomposition by introducing the process of normalization.

We discussed the problems of update anomalies that occur when redundancies are present in relations. Informal measures of good relation schemas include simple and clear attribute semantics and few nulls in the extensions (states) of relations. A good decomposition should also avoid the problem of generation of spurious tuples as a result of the join operation.

We defined the concept of functional dependency and discussed some of its properties. Functional dependencies specify semantic constraints among the attributes of a relation schema. We showed how from a given set of functional dependencies, additional dependencies can be inferred using a set of inference rules. We defined the concepts of closure and cover related to functional dependencies. We then defined minimal cover of a set of dependencies, and provided an algorithm to compute a minimal cover. We also showed how to check whether two sets of functional dependencies are equivalent.

We then described the normalization process for achieving good designs by testing relations for undesirable types of "problematic" functional dependencies. We provided a treatment of successive normalization based on a predefined primary key in each relation, then relaxed this requirement and provided more general definitions of second normal form (2NF) and third normal form (3NF) that take all candidate keys of a relation into account. We presented examples to illustrate how by using the general definition of 3NF a given relation may be analyzed and decomposed to eventually yield a set of relations in 3NF.

Finally, we presented Boyce-Codd normal form (BCNF) and discussed how it is a stronger form of 3NF. We also illustrated how the decomposition of a non-BCNF relation must be done by considering the nonadditive decomposition requirement.

In this chapter we also presented several normalization algorithms. The *relational synthesis algorithms* create 3NF relations from a universal relation schema based on a given set of functional dependencies that has been specified by the database designer. The relational decomposition algorithms create BCNF (or 4NF) relations by successive nonadditive decomposition of unnormalized relations into two component relations at a time. We first discussed two important properties of decompositions: the lossless (nonadditive) join property, and the dependency-preserving property. An algorithm to test for lossless decomposition, and a simpler test for checking the losslessness of binary decompositions, were described. We saw that it is possible to synthesize 3NF relation schemas that meet both of the above properties; however, in the case of BCNF, it is possible to aim only for the nonadditiveness of joins—dependency preservation cannot be necessarily guaranteed. If one has to aim for one of these two, the nonadditive join condition is an absolute must.

We then defined additional types of dependencies and some additional normal forms. Multivalued dependencies, which arise from an improper combination of two or more independent multivalued attributes in the same relation, are used to define fourth normal form (4NF). Join dependencies, which indicate a lossless multiway decomposition of a relation, lead to the definition of fifth normal form (5NF), which is also known as project-join normal form (PJNF).

Review Questions

8.1. Discuss attribute semantics as an informal measure of goodness for a relation schema.

8.2. Discuss insertion, deletion, and modification anomalies. Why are they considered bad? Illustrate with examples.

8.3. Why should nulls in a relation be avoided as far as possible? Discuss the problem of spurious tuples and how we may prevent it.

8.4. State the informal guidelines for relation schema design that we discussed. Illustrate how violation of these guidelines may be harmful.

8.5. What is a functional dependency? What are the possible sources of the information that defines the functional dependencies that hold among the attributes of a relation schema?

8.6. Why can we not infer a functional dependency automatically from a particular relation state?

8.7. What role do Armstrong's inference rules—the three inference rules IR1 through IR3—play in the development of the theory of relational design?

8.8. What is meant by the completeness and soundness of Armstrong's inference rules?

8.9. What is meant by the closure of a set of functional dependencies? Illustrate with an example.

8.10. When are two sets of functional dependencies equivalent? How can we determine their equivalence?

8.11. What is a minimal set of functional dependencies? Does every set of dependencies have a minimal equivalent set? Is it always unique?

8.12. What does the term *unnormalized relation* refer to? How did the normal forms develop historically from first normal form up to Boyce-Codd normal form?

8.13. Define first, second, and third normal forms when only primary keys are considered. How do the general definitions of 2NF and 3NF, which consider all keys of a relation, differ from those that consider only primary keys?

8.14. What undesirable dependencies are avoided when a relation is in 2NF?

8.15. What undesirable dependencies are avoided when a relation is in 3NF?

8.16. Define Boyce-Codd normal form. How does it differ from 3NF? Why is it considered a stronger form of 3NF?

8.17. What is meant by the attribute preservation condition on a decomposition?

8.18. Why are normal forms alone insufficient as a condition for a good schema design?

8.19. What is the dependency preservation property for a decomposition? Why is it important?

8.20. Why can we not guarantee that BCNF relation schemas will be produced by dependency-preserving decompositions of non-BCNF relation schemas? Give a counter example to illustrate this point.

8.21. What is the lossless (or nonadditive) join property of a decomposition? Why is it important?

8.22. Between the properties of dependency preservation and losslessness, which one must definitely be satisfied? Why?

8.23. Discuss the null value and dangling tuple problems.

8.24. What is a multivalued dependency? What type of constraint does it specify? When does it arise?

8.25. Illustrate how the process of creating first normal form relations may lead to multivalued dependencies. How should the first normalization be done properly so that MVDs are avoided?

8.26. Define fourth normal form. When is it violated? Why is it useful?

8.27. Define join dependencies and fifth normal form. Why is 5NF also called project-join normal form (PJNF)?

8.28. Indicate which of the following statement is true:

A relational database which is in 3NF may still have undesirable data redundancy because there may exist:

a) transitive functional dependencies

b) non-trivial FOs involving prime attributes on the RHS

c) none trivial FDs involving prime attributes only on the LHS

d) non trivial FDs involving only prime attributes.

8.29. An instance of a relation schema R (ABC) has distinct values for attribute A. Can you conclude that A is a candidate key for R.

8.30. Consider the relation scheme $R(ABC)$ with FDs $AB \to C$ and $C \to A$ Show that the schema R is 3NF but not in BCNF. Also determine the minimal keys for R.

8.31. For a database relation $R(a, b, c, d)$ where its domain of a, b, c, d include only atomic values, only the following functional dependencies and those that can be inferred from them hold: $a \to e$ and $b \to d$. The relation is

a) in INF but not in 2NF

b) in 2NF but not in 3NF

c) in 3NF

d) none of the above

8.32. Consider the following database relation containing the attributes

Book-Id, Subject_Category_of-book, Name_of-author and Nationality-of-author.

With book_id as the primary key

a) What is the highest normal form satisfied by this relation?

b) Suppose the attributes Books_title and Author_address are added to the relation, and the primary key is changed to {name_of_Author, Book_title}, what will be the highest normal form satisfied by the relation?

8.33. Consider the schema R=(STUV) and the dependencies S→T, T→U, U→V and V→S. Let R = (R1 and R2) be a decomposition such that R1 ∩ R2 = φ. The Decomposition is

a) Not in 2NF

b) In 2NF but not in 3NF c) In 3NF but not in 2NF d) In both 2NF and 3NF.

8.34. Let R = (ABCDEF) be a relation scheme with the functional dependencies C→F, E→A, EC→D, A→B. Which of the following is a key for R?

a) CD   b) EC   c) AE   d) AC

8.35. Given the following relation instance,

$$\mathbf{X\,Y\,Z}$$
$$1\,4\,2$$
$$1\,5\,3$$
$$1\,6\,3$$
$$3\,2\,2$$

which of the following functional dependencies are satisfied by the instance?

a) XY → Z and Z →Y

b) YZ → X and Y → Z

c) YZ → X and X → Z

d) XZ → Y and Y → X

8.36. R(ABCD) is a relation. Which of the following does not have a lossless join, dependency preserving BCNF decomposition?

a) A → B, B → CD

b) A → B, B → C, C→ D

c) AB → C

d) A → BCD

8.37 Consider the schema R(ABCD) and functional dependencies A→B and C→D. Then the decomposition of R into Rl(AB) and R2(CD) is

a) Dependency preserving and lossless join

b) Lossless join but not dependency preserving

c) Dependency preserving but not lessless join

d) Not dependency preserving and not lossless join

8.38. Relation R with an associated set of functional dependencies F, is decomposed into BCNF. The redundancy (arising out of functional dependencies) in the resulting set of relations is

a) zero

b) proportional to the size of F^+

c) More than zero but less than that of an equivalent 3NF decomposition d) indeterminate

8.39 From the following instance of a relation schema R(A,B,C) we can conclude that:

A	B	C
1	1	1
1	1	0
2	3	2
2	3	2

a) A functionally determines B and B functionally determines C

b) A functionally determines B and B does not functionally determine C

c) B does not functionally determine C

d) A does not functionally determine B and B does not functionally determine C

8.40. Relation R is decomposed using a set of functional dependencies F, and relation S is decomposed using another set of functional dependencies G. One decomposition is definitely BCNF, the other is definitely 3NF, but it is not known which is which. To make a guaranteed identification, which one of the following tests should be used on the decompositions? (Assume that the closure of F and G are available).

a) dependency preservation

b) lossless join

c) BCNF definition

d) 3NF definition

8.41. Suppose that we have the following requirements for a university database that is used to keep track of students' transcripts:

a. The university keeps track of each student's name (SNAME), student number (SNUM), student roll number (SROLLNO), current address (SCADDR) and phone (SCPHONE), permanent address (SPADDR) and phone (SPPHONE), date of birth (DOB), sex (SEX), class (CLASS) (first year, second year, . . . , graduate), major department (MAJORCODE), minor department (MINORCODE) (if any), and degree program (PROG) (B.A., B.S., . . . , PH.D.). Both SROLLNO and student number have unique values for each student.

b. Each department is described by a name (DNAME), department code (DCODE), office number (DOFFICE), office phone (DPHONE), and college (DCOLLEGE). Both name and code have unique values for each department.

c. Each course has a course name (CNAME), description (CDESC), course number (CNUM), number of semester hours (CREDIT), level (LEVEL), and offering department (CDEPT). The course number is unique for each course.

d. Each section has an instructor (INAME), semester (SEMESTER), year (YEAR), course (SECCOURSE), and section number (SECNUM). The section number distinguishes different sections of the same course that are taught during the same semester/year; its values are 1, 2, 3, . . . , up to the total number of sections taught during each semester.

e. A grade record refers to a student (SRN), a particular section, and a grade (GRADE). Design a relational database schema for this database application. First show all the functional dependencies that should hold among the attributes. Then design relation schemas for the database that are each in 3NF or BCNF. Specify the key attributes of each relation. Note any unspecified requirements, and make appropriate assumptions to render the specification complete.

8.42. Prove or disprove the following inference rules for functional dependencies. A proof can be made either by a proof argument or by using inference rules IR1 through IR3. A disproof should be performed by demonstrating a relation instance that satisfies the conditions and functional dependencies in the left-hand side of the inference rule but does not satisfy the dependencies in the right-hand side.

 a. $\{W \rightarrow Y, X \rightarrow Z\} \models \{WX \rightarrow Y\}$

 b. $\{X \rightarrow Y\}$ and $Y \supseteq Z \models \{X \rightarrow Z\}$

 c. $\{X \rightarrow Y, X \rightarrow W, WY \rightarrow Z\} \models \{X \rightarrow Z\}$

 d. $\{XY \rightarrow Z, Y \rightarrow W\} \models \{XW \rightarrow Z\}$

 e. $\{X \rightarrow Z, Y \rightarrow Z\} \models \{X \rightarrow Y\}$

 f. $\{X \rightarrow Y, XY \rightarrow Z\} \models \{X \rightarrow Z\}$

 g. $\{X \rightarrow Y, Z \rightarrow W\} \models \{XZ \rightarrow YW\}$

 h. $\{XY \rightarrow Z, Z \rightarrow X\} \models \{Z \rightarrow Y\}$

 i. $\{X \rightarrow Y, Y \rightarrow Z\} \models \{X \rightarrow YZ\}$

 j. $\{XY \rightarrow Z, Z \rightarrow W\} \models \{X \rightarrow W\}$

8.43. Consider the following two sets of functional dependencies: $F = \{A \rightarrow C, AC \rightarrow D, E \rightarrow AD, E \rightarrow H\}$ and $G = \{A \rightarrow CD, E \rightarrow AH\}$. Check whether they are equivalent.

8.44. Consider the relation schema EMP_DEPT in Figure 8.3a and the following set G of functional dependencies on EMP_DEPT: $G = \{$ENO $\rightarrow \{$ENAME, DOB, ADDRESS, DNUMBER$\}$, DNUMBER $\rightarrow \{$DNAME, DMGRENO$\}\}$. Calculate the closures $\{$ENO$\}^+$ and $\{$DNUMBER$\}^+$ with respect to G.

8.45. Is the set of functional dependencies G in Exercise 8.44 minimal? If not, try to find a minimal set of functional dependencies that is equivalent to G. Prove that your set is equivalent to G.

8.46. What update anomalies occur in the EMP_PROJ and EMP_DEPT relations of Figures 8.3 and 8.4?

8.47. In what normal form is the LOTS relation schema in Figure 8.11a with respect to the restrictive interpretations of normal form that take *only the primary key* into account? Would it be in the same normal form if the general definitions of normal form were used?

8.48. Prove that any relation schema with two attributes is in BCNF.

8.49. Why do spurious tuples occur in the result of joining the EMP_PROJ1 and EMP_LOCS relations of Figure 10.5 (result shown in Figure 8.6)?

8.50. Consider the universal relation $R = \{A, B, C, D, E, F, G, H, I, J\}$ and the set of functional dependencies $F = \{\{A, B\} \rightarrow \{C\}, \{A\} \rightarrow \{D, E\}, \{B\} \rightarrow \{F\}, \{F\} \rightarrow \{G, H\}, \{D\} \rightarrow \{I, J\}\}$. What is the key for R? Decompose R into 2NF and then 3NF relations.

8.51. Repeat Exercise 8.50 for the following different set of functional dependencies $G = \{\{A, B\} \rightarrow \{C\}, \{B, D\} \rightarrow \{E, F\}, \{A, D\} \rightarrow \{G, H\}, \{A\} \rightarrow \{I\}, \{H\} \rightarrow \{J\}\}$.

8.52. Consider the following relation:

A	B	C	TUPLE#
10	b1	c1	#1
10	b2	c2	#2
11	b4	c1	#3
12	b3	c4	#4
13	b1	c1	#5
14	b3	c4	#6

a. Given the previous extension (state), which of the following dependencies may hold in the above relation? If the dependency cannot hold, explain why *by specifying the tuples that cause the violation.*

   i. A → B, ii. B → C, iii. C → B, iv. B → A, v. C → A

b. Does the above relation have a potential candidate key? If it does, what is it? If it does not, why not?

8.53. Consider a relation R(A, B, C, D, E) with the following dependencies:

$$AB \rightarrow C, CD \rightarrow E, DE \rightarrow B$$

Is AB a candidate key of this relation? If not, is ABD? Explain your answer.

8.54. Consider the relation R, which has attributes that hold schedules of courses and sections at an university; R = {CourseNo, SecNo, OfferingDept, Credit–Hours, CourseLevel, InstructorENO, Semester, Year, Days_Hours, RoomNo, NoOfStudents}. Suppose that the following functional dependencies hold on R:

{CourseNo} → {OfferingDept, CreditHours, CourseLevel}

{CourseNo, SecNo, Semester, Year} → {Days_Hours, RoomNo, NoOfStudents, InstructorENO}

{RoomNo, Days_Hours, Semester, Year} → {InstructorENO, CourseNo, SecNo}

Try to determine which sets of attributes form keys of R. How would you normalize this relation?

8.55. Consider the following relations for an order-processing application database at ABC, Inc.

ORDER (O#, Odate, Cust#, Total_amount)

ORDER-ITEM(O#, I#, Qty_ordered, Total_price, Discount%)

Assume that each item has a different discount. The TOTAL_PRICE refers to one item, ODATE is the date on which the order was placed, and the TOTAL_AMOUNT is the amount of the order. If we apply a natural join on the relations ORDER-ITEM and ORDER in this database, what does the resulting relation schema look like? What will be its key? Show the FDs in this resulting relation. Is it in 2NF? Is it in 3NF? Why or why not? (State assumptions, if you make any.)

8.56. Consider the following relation:

CAR_SALE(Car#, Date_sold, Salesman#, Commission%, Discount_amt)

Assume that a car may be sold by multiple salesmen, and hence {CAR#, SALESMAN#} is the primary key. Additional dependencies are Date_sold → Discount_amt and Salesman# → Commission%

Based on the given primary key, is this relation in 1NF, 2NF, or 3NF? Why or why not? How would you successively normalize it completely?

8.57. Consider the following relation for published books: BOOK (Book_title, Authorname, Book_type, Listprice, Author_affil, Publisher) Author_affil refers to the affiliation of author. Suppose the following dependencies exist:

Book_title → Publisher, Book_type

Book_type → Listprice

Authorname → Author-affil

a. What normal form is the relation in? Explain your answer.

b. Apply normalization until you cannot decompose the relations further. State the reasons behind each decomposition.

8.58. Show that the relation schemas produced by Algorithm 8.4 are in 3NF.

8.59. Show that, if the matrix S resulting from Algorithm 8.3 does not have a row that is all "a" symbols, projecting S on the decomposition and joining it back will always produce at least one spurious tuple.

8.60. Show that the relation schemas produced by Algorithm 8.5 are in BCNF.

8.61. Show that the relation schemas produced by Algorithm 8.6 are in 3NF.

8.62. Determine all 4NF violations for the relation schema $R(X,Y,Z,W)$ with multivalued dependencies $X \twoheadrightarrow Y$ and $X \twoheadrightarrow Z$.

8.63. Consider the following functional dependencies in a database.

Date_of_birth → Age, Age → eligibility, Name → roll_number, Course_number → Instructor, Roll_number → Name, Course_number → Course_name.

State the highest normal form of the relation (Roll_number, Name, Date_of_birth, Age)

8.64. Prove that a functional dependency satisfies the formal definition of multivalued dependency.

8.65. Consider the example of normalizing the LOTS relation in Section 8.4. Determine whether the decomposition of LOTS into {LOTS1AX, LOTS1AY, LOTS1B, LOTS2} has the lossless join property, by applying Algorithm 8.3 and also by using the test under Property LJ1.

8.66. Show how the MVDs ENAME → PNAME and ENAME → DNAME in Figure 8.17a may arise during normalization into 1NF of a relation, where the attributes PNAME and DNAME are multivalued.

8.67. Apply Algorithm 8.7 to the relation in Exercise 8.50 to determine a key for R. Create a minimal set of dependencies G that is equivalent to F, and apply the synthesis algorithm (Algorithm 8.6) to decompose R into 3NF relations.

8.68. Repeat Exercise 8.67 for the functional dependencies in Exercise 8.51.

8.69. Apply the decomposition algorithm (Algorithm 8.5) to the relation R and the set of dependencies F in Exercise 8.50. Repeat for the dependencies G in Exercise 8.51.

8.70. Apply Algorithm 8.7 to the relations in Exercises 8.53 and 8.54 to determine a key for R. Apply the synthesis algorithm (Algorithm 8.8) to decompose R into 3NF relations and the decomposition algorithm (Algorithm 8.5) to decompose R into BCNF relations.

8.71. Write programs that implement Algorithms 8.5 and 8.6.

8.72. Consider the following decompositions for the relation schema R of Exercise 8.50. Determine whether each decomposition has (i) the dependency preservation property, and (ii) the lossless join property, with respect to F. Also determine which normal form each relation in the decomposition is in.

a. $D_1 = \{R_1, R_2, R_3, R_4, R_5\}$; $R_1 = \{A, B, C\}$, $R_2 = \{A, D, E\}$, $R_3 = \{B, F\}$,

$R_4 = \{F,G,H\}$, $R_5 = \{D, I, J\}$

b. $D_2 = \{R_1, R_2, R_3\}$; $R_1 = \{A, B, C, D, E\}$, $R_2 = \{B, F, G, H\}$, $R_3 = \{D, I, J\}$

c. $D_3 = \{R_1, R_2, R_3, R_4, R_5\}$; $R_1 = \{A, B, C, D\}$, $R_2 = \{D, E\}$, $R_3 = \{B, F\}$,

$R_4 = \{F,G,H\}$, $R_5 = \{D, I, J\}$

8.73. Consider the relation REFRIG(MODEL#, YEAR, PRICE, MANUF_PLANT, COLOR), which is abbreviated as REFRIG(**M, Y, P, MP, C**), and the following set F of functional dependencies: $F = \{M \rightarrow MP, \{M, Y\} \rightarrow P, MP \rightarrow C\}$

a. Evaluate each of the following as a candidate key for REFRIG, giving reasons why it can or cannot be a key: {M}, {M, Y}, {M, C}.

b. Based on the above key determination, state whether the relation REFRIG is in 3NF and in BCNF, giving proper reasons.

c. Consider the decomposition of REFRIG into $D = \{R1(M, Y, P), R2(M, MP, C)\}$. Is this decomposition lossless? Show why. (You may consult the test under Property LJ1 in Section 8.6.4.)

Selected Bibliography

Functional dependencies were originally introduced by Codd (1970). The original definitions of first, second, and third normal form were also defined in Codd (1972a), where a discussion on update anomalies can be found. Boyce-Codd normal form was defined in Codd (1974). The alternative definition of third normal form is given in Ullman (1988), as is the definition of BCNF that we give here. Ullman (1988), Maier (1983), and Atzeni and De Antonellis (1993) contain many of the theorems and proofs concerning functional dependencies.

Armstrong (1974) shows the soundness and completeness of the inference rules IR1 through IR3. The books by Maier (1983) and Atzeni and De Antonellis (1992) include a comprehensive discussion of relational dependency theory. The decomposition algorithm (Algorithm 8.5) is due to Bernstein (1976). Algorithm 8.6 is based on the normalization algorithm presented in Biskup et al. (1979). Tsou and Fischer (1982) give a polynomialtime algorithm for BCNF decomposition.

The theory of dependency preservation and lossless joins is given in Ullman (1988), where proofs of some of the algorithms discussed here appear. The lossless join property is analyzed in Aho et al. (1979). Algorithms to determine the keys of a relation from functional dependencies are given in Osborn (1976); testing for BCNF is discussed in Osborn (1979). Testing for 3NF is discussed in Tsou and Fischer (1982). Algorithms for designing BCNF relations are given in Wang (1990) and Hernandez and Chan (1991).

Multivalued dependencies and fourth normal form are defined in Zaniolo (1976) and Nicolas (1978). Many of the advanced normal forms are due to Fagin: the fourth normal form in Fagin (1977), PJNF in Fagin (1979), and DKNF in Fagin (1981). The set of sound and complete rules for functional and multivalued dependencies was given by Beeri et al. (1977). Join dependencies are discussed by Rissanen (1977) and Aho et al. (1979). Inference rules for join dependencies are given by Sciore (1982). Inclusion dependencies are discussed by Casanova et al. (1981) and analyzed further in Cosmadakis et al. (1990). Their use in optimizing relational schemas is discussed in Casanova et al. (1989). Template dependencies are discussed by Sadri and Ullman (1982). Other dependencies are discussed in Nicolas (1978), Furtado (1978), and Mendelzon and Maier (1979). Abiteboul et al. (1995) provides a theoretical treatment of many of the ideas presented in this chapter.

4

DATA STORAGE, INDEXING, AND QUERY PROCESSING

9

File Organizations and Indexes

Databases are stored physically as files of records, which are typically stored on magnetic disks. This chapter deal with the organization of databases in storage and the techniques for accessing them efficiently using various algorithms, some of which require auxiliary data structures called indexes. We start in Section 9.1 by introducing the concepts of computer storage hierarchies and how they are used in database systems. Section 9.2 is devoted to a description of magnetic disk storage devices and their characteristics, and we also briefly describe magnetic tape storage devices. Having discussed different storage technologies, we then turn our attention to the methods for organizing data on disks. Section 9.3 covers the technique of double buffering, which is used to speed retrieval of multiple disk blocks. In Section 9.4 we discuss various ways of formatting and storing records of a file on disk. Section 9.5 discusses the various types of operations that are typically applied to records of a file. We then present three primary methods for organizing records of a file on disk: unordered records, discussed in Section 9.6; ordered records, in Section 9.7; and hashed records, in Section 9.8.

Section 9.9 very briefly discusses files of mixed records and other primary methods for organizing records, such as B-trees. These are particularly relevant for storage of object-oriented databases. Section 9.10 describes RAID (Redundant Arrays of Inexpensive (or Independent) Disks)—a data storage system architecture that is used commonly in large organizations for better reliability and performance. In Section 9.11 we describe storage area networks, a more recent approach for managing stored data on networks. Finally in Section 9.12, we discuss techniques for creating auxiliary data structures, called indexes, that speed up the search for and retrieval of records. These techniques involve storage of auxiliary data, called index files, in addition to the file records themselves. Section 9.13 summarizes the chapter.

9.1 INTRODUCTION

The collection of data that makes up a computerized database must be stored physically on some computer **storage medium**. The DBMS software can then retrieve, update, and process this data as needed. Computer storage media form a *storage hierarchy* that includes two main categories:

- **Primary storage.** This category includes storage media that can be operated on directly by the computer *central processing unit* (CPU), such as the computer main memory and smaller but faster cache memories. Primary storage usually provides fast access to data but is of limited storage capacity.

- **Secondary storage.** This category includes magnetic disks, optical disks, and tapes. These devices usually have a larger capacity, cost less, and provide slower access to data than do primary storage devices. Data in secondary storage cannot be processed directly by the CPU; it must first be copied into primary storage.

We will first give an overview of the various storage devices used for primary and secondary storage in Section 9.1.1 and will then discuss how databases are typically handled in the storage hierarchy in Section 9.1.2.

9.1.1 Memory Hierarchies and Storage Devices

In a modern computer system data resides and is transported throughout a hierarchy of storage media. The highest-speed memory is the most expensive and is therefore available with the least capacity. The lowest-speed memory is offline tape storage, which is essentially available in indefinite storage capacity.

At the *primary storage level*, the memory hierarchy includes at the most expensive end **cache memory**, which is a static RAM (Random Access Memory). Cache memory is typically used by the CPU to speed up execution of programs. The next level of primary storage is DRAM (Dynamic RAM), which provides the main work area for the CPU for keeping programs and data and is popularly called **main memory**. The advantage of DRAM is its low cost, which continues to decrease; the drawback is its volatility[1] and lower speed compared with static RAM. At the *secondary storage level*, the hierarchy includes magnetic disks, as well as **mass storage** in the form of CD-ROM (Compact Disk–Read-Only Memory) devices, and finally tapes at the least expensive end of the hierarchy. The **storage capacity** is measured in kilobytes (Kbyte or 1000 bytes), megabytes (Mbyte or 1 million bytes), gigabytes (Gbyte or 1 billion bytes), and even terabytes (1000 Gbytes).

Programs reside and execute in DRAM. Generally, large permanent databases reside on secondary storage, and portions of the database are read into and written from buffers in main memory as needed. Now that personal computers and workstations have hundreds of megabytes of data in DRAM, it is becoming possible to load a large fraction of the database into main memory. Eight to 16 gigabytes of RAM on a single server are becoming commonplace. In some cases, entire databases can be kept in main memory (with a backup copy on magnetic disk), leading to **main memory databases**; these are particularly useful in real-time applications that require extremely fast response times. An example is telephone switching applications, which store databases that contain routing and line information in main memory.

Between DRAM and magnetic disk storage, another form of memory, **flash memory**, is becoming common, particularly because it is nonvolatile. Flash memories are high-density, high-performance memories using EEPROM (Electrically Erasable Programmable Read-Only Memory) technology. The advantage of

---

1. Volatile memory typically loses its contents of a power outage, whereas nonvolatile memory does not.

flash memory is the fast access speed; the disadvantage is that an entire block must be erased and written over at a time.[2] Flash memory cards are appearing as the data storage medium in appliances with capacities ranging from a few megabytes to a few gigabytes. These are appearing in cameras, MP3 players, USB storage accessories, etc.

CD-ROM disks store data optically and are read by a laser. CD-ROMs contain prerecorded data that cannot be overwritten. WORM (Write-Once-Read-Many) disks are a form of optical storage used for archiving data; they allow data to be written once and read any number of times without the possibility of erasing. They hold about half a gigabyte of data per disk and last much longer than magnetic disks. **Optical juke box memories** use an array of CD-ROM platters, which are loaded onto drives on demand. Although optical juke boxes have capacities in the hundreds of gigabytes, their retrieval times are in the hundreds of milliseconds, quite a bit slower than magnetic disks.[3] This type of storage is continuing to decline because of the rapid decrease in cost and increase in capacities of magnetic disks. The DVD (Digital Video Disk) is a recent standard for optical disks allowing 4.5 to 15 gigabytes of storage per disk. Most personal computer disk drives now read CD-ROM and DVD disks.

Finally, **magnetic tapes** are used for archiving and backup storage of data. **Tape jukeboxes**—which contain a bank of tapes that are catalogued and can be automatically loaded onto tape drives—are becoming popular as **tertiary storage** to hold terabytes of data. For example, NASA's EOS (Earth Observation Satellite) system stores archived databases in this fashion.

Many large organizations are already finding it normal to have terabyte-sized databases. The term **very large database** cannot be defined precisely any more because disk storage capacities are on the rise and costs are declining. It may very soon be reserved for databases containing tens of terabytes.

9.1.2   **Storage of Databases**

Databases typically store large amounts of data that must *persist* over long periods of time. The data is accessed and processed repeatedly during this period. This contrasts with the notion of *transient* data structures that persist for only a limited time during program execution. Most databases are stored permanently (or *persistently*) on magnetic disk secondary storage, for the following reasons:

- Generally, database are too large to fit entirely in main memory.

- The circumstances that cause performance loss of stored data arise less frequently for disk secondary storage than for primary storage. Hence, we refer to disk—and other secondary storage devices—as **nonvolatile storage**, whereas main memory is often called **volatile storage**.

- The cost of storage per unit of data is an order of magnetic less for disk than for primary storage.

Some of the newer technologies—such as optical disks, DVDs, and tape jukeboxes—are likely to provide viable alternatives to the use of magnetic disks. Databases in the future may therefore reside at different levels of the memory hierarchy from those described in Section 9.1.1. However, it is anticipated that magnetic disks will continue to be the medium of primary choice for large databases for years to come. Hence, it is important to study and understand the properties and characteristics of magnetic disks and the way data files can be organized on disk in order to design effective databases with acceptable performance.

---

2. For example, the INTEL DD 28F032SA is a 32-megabit capacity flash memory with 70-nanosecond access speed, and 430 KB/second write transfer rate.

3. Their notational speeds are lower (around 400 rpm), giving higher latency delays and low transfer rates (around 100 to 200 KB/second).

Magnetic tapes are frequently used as a storage medium for backing up the database because storage on tape costs even less than storage on disk. However, access to data on tape is quite slow. Data stored on tapes is **offline**; that is, some intervention by an operator—or an automatic loading device—to load a tape is needed before this data becomes available. In contrast, disks are **online** devices that can be accessed directly at any time.

The techniques used to store large amounts of structured data on disk are important for database designers, the DBA, and implementers of a DBMS. Database designers and the DBA must know the advantages and disadvantages of each storage technique when they design, implement, and operate a database on a specific DBMS. Usually, the DBMS has several options available for organizing the data, and the process of **physical database design** involves choosing from among the options the particular data organization techniques that best suit the given application requirements. DBMS system implementers must study data organization techniques so that they can implement them efficiently and thus provide the DBA and users of the DBMS with sufficient options.

Typical database applications need only a small portion of the database at a time for processing. Whenever a certain portion of the data is needed, it must be located on disk, copied to main memory for processing, and then rewritten to the disk if the data is changed. The data stored on disk is organized as **files** of **records**. Each record is a collection of data values that can be interpreted as facts about entities, their attributes, and their relationships. Records should be stored on disk in a manner that makes it possible to locate them efficiently whenever they are needed.

There are several **primary file organizations**, which determine how the records of a file are *physically placed* on the disk, *and hence how the records can be accessed*. A *heap file* (or *unordered file*) places the records on disk in no particular order by appending new records at the end of the file, whereas a *sorted file* (or *sequential file*) keeps the records ordered by the value of a particular field (called the sort key). A *hashed file* uses a hash function applied to a particular field (called the hash key) to determine a record's placement on disk. Other primary file organizations, such as *B-trees*, use tree structures. We discuss primary file organizations in Sections 9.6 through 9.9. A **secondary organization** or **auxiliary access structure** allows efficient access to the records of a file based on *alternate fields* than those that have been used for the primary file organization. Most of these exist as indexes and will be discussed in Section 9.12.

9.2 SECONDARY STORAGE DEVICES

In this section, we describe some characteristics of magnetic disk and magnetic tape storage devices. Readers who have studied these devices already may just browse through this section.

9.2.1 Hardware Description of Disk Devices

Magnetic disks are used for storing large amounts of data. The most basic unit of data on the disk is a single bit of information. By magnetizing an area on disk in certain ways, one can make it represent a bit value of either 0 (zero) or 1 (one). To code information, bits are grouped into **bytes** (or **characters**). Byte sizes are typically 4 to 8 bits, depending on the computer and the device. We assume that one character is stored in a single byte, and we use the terms *byte* and *character* interchangeably. The **capacity** of a disk is the number of bytes it can store, which is usually very large. Small floppy disks used with microcomputers typically hold from 400 Kbytes to 1.5 Mbytes; hard disks for micros typically hold from several hundred Mbytes up to a few Gbytes; and large disk packs used with servers and mainframes have capacities that range up to a few tens or hundreds of Gbytes. Disk capacities continue to grow as technology improves.

Whatever their capacity, disks are all made of magnetic material shaped as a thin circular disk (Figure 9.1a) and protected by a plastic or acrylic cover. A disk is **single-sided** if it stores information on only one of its surfaces and **double-sided** if both surfaces are used. To increase storage capacity, disks are assembled into a **disk pack** (Figure 9.1b), which may include many disks and hence many surfaces. Information is stored on a disk surface in concentric circles of *small width*,[4] each having a distinct diameter. Each circle is called a **track**. For disk packs, the tracks with the same diameter on the various surfaces are called a **cylinder** because of the shape they would form if connected in space. The concept of a cylinder is important because data stored on one cylinder can be retrieved much faster than if it were distributed among different cylinders.

FIGURE 9.1   (a) A single-sided disk with read/write hardware. (b) A disk pack with read/write hardware.

The number of tracks on a disk ranges from a few hundred to a few thousand, and the capacity of each track typically ranges from tens of Kbytes to 150 Kbytes. Because a track usually contains a large amount of information, it is divided into smaller blocks or sectors. The division of a track into **sectors** is hard-coded on the disk surface and cannot be changed. One type of sector organization calls a portion of a track that subtends a fixed angle at the center as a sector (Figure 9.2a). Several other sector organizations are possible, one of which is to have the sectors subtend smaller angles at the center as one moves away, thus maintaining

---

4. In some disks, the circles are now connected into a kind of continuous spiral.

a uniform density of recording (Figure 9.2b). A technique called ZBR (Zone Bit Recording) allows a range of cylinders to have the same number of sectors per arc. For example, cylinders 0–99 may have one sector per track, 100–199 may have two per track, etc. Not all disks have their tracks divided into sectors.

FIGURE 9.2 Different sector organizations on disk. (a) Sectors subtending a fixed angle. (b) Sectors maintaining a uniform recording density.

The division of a track into equal-sized **disk blocks** (or **pages**) is set by the operating system during disk **formatting** (or **initialization**). Block size is fixed during initialization and cannot be changed dynamically. Typical disk block sizes range from 512 to 4096 bytes. A disk with hard-coded sectors often has the sectors subdivided into blocks during initialization. Blocks are separated by fixed-size **interblock gaps**, which include specially coded control information written during disk initialization. This information is used to determine which block on the track follows each interblock gap. Table 9.1 represents specifications of a typical disk.

There is continuous improvement in the storage capacity and transfer rates associated with disks; they are also progressively getting cheaper—currently costing only a fraction of a dollar per megabyte of disk storage. Costs are going down so rapidly that costs as low 0.1 cent/MB which translates to $1/GB and $1K/TB are not too far away.

A disk is a *random access* addressable device. Transfer of data between main memory and disk takes place in units of disk blocks. The **hardware address** of a block—a combination of a cylinder number, track number (surface number within the cylinder on which the track is located), and block number (within the track) is supplied to the disk I/O hardware. In many modern disk drives, a single number called LBA (Logical Block Address) which is a number between 0 and n (assuming the total capacity of the disk is $n+1$ blocks), is mapped automatically to the right block by the disk drive controller. The address of a **buffer**—a contiguous reserved area in main storage that holds one block—is also provided. For a **read** command, the block from disk is copied into the buffer; whereas for a **write** command, the contents of the buffer are copied into the disk block. Sometimes several contiguous blocks, called a **cluster**, may be transferred as a unit. In this case the buffer size is adjusted to match the number of bytes in the cluster.

TABLE 9.1 SPECIFICATIONS OF TYPICAL HIGH-END CHEETAH DISKS FROM SEAGATE

Description	Cheetah X15 36LP	Cheetah 10K.6
Model Number	ST336732LC	ST3146807LC
Form Factor (width)	3.5 inch	3.5 inch
Height	25.4 mm	25.4 mm
Width	101.6 mm	101.6 mm
Weight	0.68 Kg	0.73 Kg
Capacity/Interface		
Formatted Capacity	36.7 Gbytes	146.8 Gbytes
Interface Type	80-pin	80-pin
Configuration		
Number of disks (physical)	4	4
Number of heads (physical)	8	8
Number of Cylinders	18,479	49,854
Bytes per Sector	512	512
Areal Density	N/A	36,000 Mbits/sq.inch
Track Density	N/A	64,000 Tracks/inch
Recording Density	N/A	570,000 bits/inch
Performance		
Transfer Rates		
Internal Transfer Rate (min)	522 Mbits/sec	475 Mbits/sec
Internal Transfer Rate (max)	709 Mbits/sec	840 Mbits/sec
Formatted Int. Transfer Rate (min)	51 MBytes/sec	43 MBytes/sec
Formatted Int. Transfer Rate (max)	69 MBytes/sec	78 MBytes/sec
External I/O Transfer Rate (max)	320 MBytes/sec	320 MBytes/sec
Seek Times		
Avg. Seek Time (Read)	3.6 msec (typical)	4.7 msec (typical)
Avg. Seek Time (Write)	4.2 msec (typical)	5.2 msec (typical)
Track-to-track Seek, Read	0.5 msec (typical)	0.3 msec (typical)
Track-to-track Seek, Write	0.8 msec (typical)	0.5 msec (typical)
Average Latency	2 msec	2.99 msec
Other		
Default Buffer (cache) size	8,192 Kbytes	8,000 Kbytes
Spindle Speed	15K rpm	10K rpm
Reliability		
Mean Time Between Failure (MTBF)	1,200,000 Hours	1,200,000 Hours
Recoverable Read Errors	10 per 10^{12} bits	10 per 10^{12} bits
Nonrecoverable Read Errors	1 per 10^{15} bits	1 per 10^{15} bits
Seek Errors	10 per 10^8 bits	10 per 10^8 bits

(courtesy Seagate Technology)

The actual hardware mechanism that reads or writes a block is the disk **read/write head**, which is part of a system called a **disk drive**. A disk or disk pack is mounted in the disk drive, which includes a motor that rotates the disks. A read/write head includes an electronic component attached to a **mechanical arm**. Disk packs with multiple surfaces are controlled by several read/write heads—one for each surface (see Figure 9.1b). All arms are connected to an **actuator** attached to another electrical motor, which moves the read/write heads in unison and positions them precisely over the cylinder of tracks specified in a block address.

Disk drives for hard disks rotate the disk pack continuously at a constant speed (typically ranging between 5400 and 15,000 rpm). For a floppy disk, the disk drive begins to rotate the disk whenever a particular read or write request is initiated and ceases rotation soon after the data transfer is completed. Once the read/write head is positioned on the right track and the block specified in the block address moves under the read/write head, the electronic component of the read/write head is activated to transfer the data. Some disk units have fixed read/write heads, with as many heads as there are tracks. These are called **fixed-head** disks, whereas disk units with an actuator are called **movable-head disks**. For fixed-head disks, a track or cylinder is selected by electronically switching to the appropriate read/write head rather than by actual mechanical movement; consequently, it is much faster. However, the cost of the additional read/write heads is quite high, so fixed-head disks are not commonly used.

A **disk controller**, typically embedded in the disk drive, controls the disk drive and interfaces it to the computer system. One of the standard interfaces used today for disk drives on PC and workstations is called SCSI (Small Computer Storage Interface). The controller accepts high-level I/O commands and takes appropriate action to position the arm and causes the read/write action to take place. To transfer a disk block, given its address, the disk controller must first mechanically position the read/write head on the correct track. The time required to do this is called the **seek time**. Typical seek times are 7 to 10 msec on desktops and 3 to 8 msecs on servers. Following that, there is another delay—called the **rotational delay** or **latency**—while the beginning of the desired block rotates into position under the read/write head. It depends on the rpm of the disk. For example, at 15,000 rpm, the time per rotation is 4 msec and the average rotational delay is the time per half revolution, or 2 msec. Finally, some additional time is needed to transfer the data; this is called the **block transfer time**. Hence, the total time needed to locate and transfer an arbitrary block, given its address, is the sum of the seek time, rotational delay, and block transfer time. The seek time and rotational delay are usually much larger than the block transfer time. To make the transfer of multiple blocks more efficient, it is common to transfer several consecutive blocks on the same track or cylinder. This eliminates the seek time and rotational delay for all but the first block and can result in a substantial saving of time when numerous contiguous blocks are transferred. Usually, the disk manufacturer provides a **bulk transfer rate** for calculating the time required to transfer consecutive blocks. Appendix B contains a discussion of these and other disk parameters.

The time needed to locate and transfer a disk block is in the order of milliseconds, usually ranging from 12 to 60 msec. For contiguous blocks, locating the first block takes from 12 to 60 msec, but transferring subsequent blocks may take only 1 to 2 msec each. Many search techniques take advantage of consecutive retrieval of blocks when searching for data on disk. In any case, a transfer time in the order of milliseconds is considered quite high compared with the time required to process data in main memory by current CPUs. Hence, locating data on disk is *a major bottleneck* in database applications. The file structures we discuss here and in Chapter 9 attempt to *minimize the number of block transfers* needed to locate and transfer the required data from disk to main memory.

9.2.2 Magnetic Tape Storage Devices

Disks are **random access** secondary storage devices, because an arbitrary disk block may be accessed "at random" once we specify its address. Magnetic tapes are **sequential access** devices; to access the nth block on tape, we must first scan over the preceding $n - 1$ blocks. Data is stored on reels of high-capacity magnetic tape, somewhat similar to audio or videotapes. A **tape drive** is required to read the data from or to write the data to a **tape reel**. Usually, each group of bits that forms a byte is stored across the tape, and the bytes themselves are stored consecutively on the tape.

A read/write head is used to read or write data on tape. Data records on tape are also stored in blocks—although the blocks may be substantially larger than those for disks, and interblock gaps are also quite large. With typical tape densities of 1600 to 6250 bytes per inch, a typical interblock gap[5] of 0.6 inches corresponds to 960 to 3750 bytes of wasted storage space. For better space utilization it is customary to group many records together in one block.

The main characteristic of a tape is its requirement that we access the data blocks in **sequential order**. To get to a block in the middle of a reel of tape, the tape is mounted and then scanned until the required block gets under the read/write head. For this reason, tape access can be slow and tapes are not used to store online data, except for some specialized applications. However, tapes serve a very important function—that of **backing up** the database. One reason for backup is to keep copies of disk files in case the data is lost because of a disk crash, which can happen if the disk read/write head touches the disk surface because of mechanical malfunction. For this reason, disk files are copied periodically to tape. For many online critical applications such as airline reservation systems, to avoid any downtime, mirrored systems are used keeping three sets of identical disks—two in online operation and one as backup. Here, offline disks become a backup device. The three are rotated so that they can be switched in case there is a failure on one of the live disk drives. Tapes can also be used to store excessively large database files. Finally, database files that are seldom used or are outdated but are required for historical record keeping can be **archived** on tape. Recently, smaller 8-mm magnetic tapes (similar to those used in camcorders) that can store up to 50 Gbytes, as well as 4-mm helical scan data cartridges and writable CDs and DVDs have become popular media for backing up data files from workstations and personal computers. They are also used for storing images and system libraries. Backing up enterprise databases so that no transaction information is lost is a major undertaking. Currently tape libraries with slots for several hundred cartridges are used with Digital and Superdigital Linear Tapes (DLTs and SDLTs) having capacities in hundreds of gigabytes that record data on linear tracks. Robotic arms are used to write on multiple cartridges in parallel using multiple tape drives with automatic labeling software to identify the backup cartridges. An example of a giant library is the L5500 model of Storage Technology that can scale up to 13.2 Petabytes (Petabyte = 1000 TB) with a thruput rate of 55TB/hour. We defer the discussion of disk storage technology called RAID, and of storage area networks, to the end of the chapter.

9.3 BUFFERING OF BLOCKS

When several blocks need to be transferred from disk to main memory and all the block addresses are known, several buffers can be reserved in main memory to speed up the transfer. While one buffer is being read or written, the CPU can process data in the other buffer. This is possible because an independent disk I/O processor (controller) exists that, once started, can proceed to transfer a data block between memory and disk independent of and in parallel to CPU processing.

Figure 9.3 illustrates how two processes can proceed in parallel. Processes A and B are running **concurrently** in an **interleaved** fashion, whereas processes C and D are running **concurrently** in a **parallel** fashion. When a single CPU controls multiple processes, parallel execution is not possible. However, the processes can still run concurrently in an interleaved way. Buffering is most useful when processes can run

---

5. Called *interrecord gaps* in tape terminology.

concurrently in a parallel fashion, either because a separate disk I/O processor is available or because multiple CPU processors exist.

Figure 9.4 illustrates how reading and processing can proceed in parallel when the time required to process a disk block in memory is less than the time required to read the next block and fill a buffer. The CPU can start processing a block once its transfer to main memory is completed; at the same time the disk I/O processor can be reading and transferring the next block into a different buffer. This technique is called **double buffering** and can also be used to write a continuous stream of blocks from memory to the disk. Double buffering permits continuous reading or writing of data on consecutive disk blocks, which eliminates the seek time and rotational delay for all but the first block transfer. Moreover, data is kept ready for processing, thus reducing the waiting time in the programs.

FIGURE 9.3 Interleaved concurrency versus parallel execution.

FIGURE 9.4 Use of two buffers, A and B, for reading from disk.

9.4 PLACING FILE RECORDS ON DISK

In this section, we define the concepts of records, record types, and files. We then discuss techniques for placing file records on disk.

9.4.1 Records and Record Types

Data is usually stored in the form of **records**. Each record consists of a collection of related data **values** or **items**, where each value is formed of one or more bytes and corresponds to a particular **field** of the record. Records usually describe entities and their attributes. For example, an EMPLOYEE record represents an employee entity, and each field value in the record specifies some attribute of that employee, such as NAME, DOB, SALARY, or SUPERVISOR. A collection of field names and their corresponding data types constitutes a **record type** or **record format** definition. A **data type**, associated with each field, specifies the types of values a field can take.

The data type of a field is usually one of the standard data types used in programming. These include numeric (integer, long integer, or floating point), string of characters (fixed-length or varying), Boolean (having 0 and 1 or TRUE and FALSE values only), and sometimes specially coded **date** and **time** data types. The number of bytes required for each data type is fixed for a given computer system. An integer may require 4 bytes, a long integer 8 bytes, a real number 4 bytes, a Boolean 1 byte, a date 10 bytes (assuming a format of DD-MM-YYYY), and a fixed-length string of k characters k bytes. Variable-length strings may require as many bytes as there are characters in each field value. For example, an EMPLOYEE record type may be defined—using the C programming language notation—as the following structure:

```
struct employee{
    char name[30];
    char eno[9];
    int salary;
    int jobcode;
    char department[20];
};
```

In recent database applications, the need may arise for storing data items that consist of large unstructured objects, which represent images, digitized video or audio streams, or free text. These are referred to as **BLOBs** (Binary Large Objects). A BLOB data item is typically stored separately from its record in a pool of disk blocks, and a pointer to the BLOB is included in the record.

9.4.2 Files, Fixed-Length Records, and Variable-Length Records

A **file** is a *sequence* of records. In many cases, all records in a file are of the same record type. If every record in the file has exactly the same size (in bytes), the file is said to be made up of **fixed-length records**. If different records in the file have different sizes, the file is said to be made up of **variable-length records**. A file may have variable-length records for several reasons:

- The file records are of the same record type, but one or more of the fields are of varying size (**variable-length fields**). For example, the NAME field of EMPLOYEE can be a variable-length field.

- The file records are of the same record type, but one or more of the fields may have multiple values for individual records; such a field is called a **repeating field** and a group of values for the field is often called a **repeating group**.

- The file records are of the same record type, but one or more of the fields are **optional**; that is, they may have values for some but not all of the file records (**optional fields**).

- The file contains records of *different record types* and hence of varying size (**mixed file**). This would occur if related records of different types were *clustered* (placed together) on disk blocks; for example, the GRADE_REPORT records of a particular student may be placed following that STUDENT's record.

The fixed-length EMPLOYEE records in Figure 9.5a have a record size of 71 bytes. Every record has the same fields, and field lengths are fixed, so the system can identify the starting byte position of each field relative to the starting position of the record. This facilitates locating field values by programs that access such files. Notice that it is possible to represent a file that logically should have variable-length records as a fixed-length records file. For example, in the case of optional fields we could have *every field* included in *every file* record but store a special null value if no value exists for that field. For a repeating field, we could allocate as many spaces in each record as the *maximum number of values* that the field can take. In either case, space is wasted when certain records do not have values for all the physical spaces provided in each record. We now consider other options for formatting records of a file of variable length records.

FIGURE 9.5 Three record storage formats. (a) A fixed-length record with six fields and size of 71 bytes. (b) A record with two variable-length fields and three fixed-length fields. (c) A variable-field record with three types of separator characters.

For *variable-length fields*, each record has a value for each field, but we do not know the exact length of some field values. To determine the bytes within a particular record that represent each field, we can use special **separator** characters (such as ? or % or $)—which do not appear in any field value—to terminate variable length fields (Figure 9.5b), or we can store the length in bytes of the field in the record, preceding the field value.

A file of records with *optional fields* can be formatted in different ways. If the total number of fields for the record type is large but the number of fields that actually appear in a typical record is small, we can include in each record a sequence of <field-name, field-value> pairs rather than just the field values. Three types of separator characters are used in Figure 9.5c, although we could use the same separator character for the first two purposes—separating the field name from the field value and separating one field from the next field. A more practical option is to assign a short **field type** code—say, an integer number—to each field and include in each record a sequence of <field-type, field-value> pairs rather than <field-name, field-value> pairs.

A *repeating field* needs one separator character to separate the repeating values of the field and another separator character to indicate termination of the field. Finally, for a file that includes *records of different types*, each record is preceded by a **record type** indicator. Understandably, programs that process files of variable-length records—which are usually part of the file system and hence hidden from the typical programmers—need to be more complex than those for fixed-length records, where the starting position and size of each field are known and fixed.[6]

9.4.3 Record Blocking and Spanned Versus Unspanned Records

The records of a file must be allocated to disk blocks because a block is the *unit of data transfer* between disk and memory. When the block size is larger than the record size, each block will contain numerous records, although some files may have unusually large records that cannot fit in one block. Suppose that the block size is B bytes. For a file of fixed-length records of size R bytes, with $B \geq R$, we can fit $bfr = \lfloor B/R \rfloor$ records per block, where the $\lfloor (x) \rfloor$ (*floor function*) *rounds down* the number x to an integer. The value bfr is called the **blocking factor** for the file. In general, R may not divide B exactly, so we have some unused space in each block equal to

$$B - (bfr * R) \text{ bytes}$$

To utilize this unused space, we can store part of a record on one block and the rest on another. A **pointer** at the end of the first block points to the block containing the remainder of the record in case it is not the next consecutive block on disk. This organization is called **spanned**, because records can span more than one block. Whenever a record is larger than a block, we *must* use a spanned organization. If records are not allowed to cross block boundaries, the organization is called **unspanned**. This is used with fixed-length records having $B > R$ because it makes each record start at a known location in the block, simplifying record processing. For variable-length records, either a spanned or an unspanned organization can be used. If the average record is large, it is advantageous to use spanning to reduce the lost space in each block. Figure 9.6 illustrates spanned versus unspanned organization.

---

6. Other schemes are also possible for representing variable-length records.

For variable-length records using spanned organization, each block may store a different number of records. In this case, the blocking factor *bfr* represents the *average* number of records per block for the file. We can use *bfr* to calculate the number of blocks *b* needed for a file of *r* records:

$$b = \lceil (r/bfr) \rceil \text{ blocks}$$

where the $\lceil (x) \rceil$ (*ceiling function*) rounds the value x up to the next integer.

9.4.4 Allocating File Blocks on Disk

There are several standard techniques for allocating the blocks of a file on disk. In **contiguous allocation** the file blocks are allocated to consecutive disk blocks. This makes reading the whole file very fast using double buffering, but it makes expanding the file difficult. In **linked allocation** each file block contains a pointer to the next file block. This makes it easy to expand the file but makes it slow to read the whole file. A combination of the two allocates **clusters** of consecutive disk blocks, and the clusters are linked. Clusters are sometimes called **file segments** or **extents**. Another possibility is to use **indexed allocation**, where one or more index blocks contain pointers to the actual file blocks. It is also common to use combinations of these techniques.

FIGURE 9.6 Types of record organization. (a) Unspanned. (b) Spanned.

9.4.5 File Headers

A **file header** or **file descriptor** contains information about a file that is needed by the system programs that access the file records. The header includes information to determine the disk addresses of the file blocks as well as to record format descriptions, which may include field lengths and order of fields within a record for fixed-length unspanned records and field type codes, separator characters, and record type codes for variable-length records.

To search for a record on disk, one or more blocks are copied into main memory buffers. Programs then search for the desired record or records within the buffers, using the information in the file header. If the address of the block that contains the desired record is not known, the search programs must do a **linear search** through the file blocks. Each file block is copied into a buffer and searched either until the record is located or all the file blocks have been searched unsuccessfully. This can be very time consuming for a large file. The goal of a good file organization is to locate the block that contains a desired record with a minimal number of block transfers.

9.5 OPERATIONS ON FILES

Operations on files are usually grouped into **retrieval operations** and **update operations**. The former does not change any data in the file, but only locate certain records so that their field values can be examined and processed. The latter change the file by insertion or deletion of records or by modification of field values. In either case, we may have to **select** one or more records for retrieval, deletion, or modification based on a **selection condition** (or **filtering condition**), which specifies criteria that the desired record or records must satisfy.

Consider an EMPLOYEE file with fields NAME, ENO, SALARY, JOBCODE, and DEPARTMENT. A **simple selection condition** may involve an equality comparison on some field value—for example, (ENO = '123456789') or (DEPARTMENT = 'Research'). More complex conditions can involve other types of comparison operators, such as > or ≥; an example is (SALARY ≥ 30000). The general case is to have an arbitrary Boolean expression on the fields of the file as the selection condition.

Search operations on files are generally based on simple selection conditions. A complex condition must be decomposed by the DBMS (or the programmer) to extract a simple condition that can be used to locate the records on disk. Each located record is then checked to determine whether it satisfies the full selection condition. For example, we may extract the simple condition (DEPARTMENT = 'Research') from the complex condition ((SALARY ≥ 30000) AND (DEPARTMENT = 'Research')); each record satisfying (DEPARTMENT = 'Research') is located and then tested to see if it also satisfies (SALARY ≥ 30000).

When several file records satisfy a search condition, the *first* record—with respect to the physical sequence of file records—is initially located and designated the **current record**. Subsequent search operations commence from this record and locate the next record in the file that satisfies the condition.

Actual operations for locating and accessing file records vary from system to system. Below, we present a set of representative operations. Typically, high-level programs, such as DBMS software programs, access the records by using these commands, so we sometimes refer to **program variables** in the following descriptions:

- *Open:* Prepares the file for reading or writing. Allocates appropriate buffers (typically at least two) to hold file blocks from disk, and retrieves the file header. Sets the file pointer to the beginning of the file.

- *Reset:* Sets the file pointer of an open file to the beginning of the file.

- *Find* (or *Locate*): Searches for the first record that satisfies a search condition. Transfers the block containing that record into a main memory buffer (if it is not already there). The file pointer points to the record in the buffer and it becomes the *current record*. Sometimes, different verbs are used to indicate whether the located record is to be retrieved or updated.

- *Read* (or *Get*): Copies the current record from the buffer to a program variable in the user program. This command may also advance the current record pointer to the next record in the file, which may necessitate reading the next file block from disk.

- *FindNext:* Searches for the next record in the file that satisfies the search condition. Transfers the block containing that record into a main memory buffer (if it is not already there). The record is located in the buffer and becomes the current record.

- *Delete:* Deletes the current record and (eventually) updates the file on disk to reflect the deletion.

- *Modify:* Modifies some field values for the current record and (eventually) updates the file on disk to reflect the modification.

- *Insert:* Inserts a new record in the file by locating the block where the record is to be inserted, transferring that block into a main memory buffer (if it is not already there), writing the record into the buffer, and (eventually) writing the buffer to disk to reflect the insertion.

- *Close:* Completes the file access by releasing the buffers and performing any other needed cleanup operations.

The preceding (except for Open and Close) are called **record-at-a-time** operations, because each operation applies to a single record. It is possible to streamline the operations Find, FindNext, and Read into a single operation, Scan, whose description is as follows:

- *Scan:* If the file has just been opened or reset, Scan returns the first record; otherwise it returns the next record. If a condition is specified with the operation, the returned record is the first or next record satisfying the condition.

In database systems, additional **set-at-a-time** higher-level operations may be applied to a file. Examples of these are as follows:

- *Find All:* Locates all the records in the file that satisfy a search condition.

- *Find* (or *Locate*) *n:* Searches for the first record that satisfies a search condition and then continues to locate the next $n - 1$ records satisfying the same condition. Transfers the blocks containing the n records to the main memory buffer (if not already there).

- *FindOrdered:* Retrieves all the records in the file in some specified order.

- *Reorganize:* Starts the reorganization process. As we shall see, some file organizations require periodic reorganization. An example is to reorder the file records by sorting them on a specified field.

At this point, it is worthwhile to note the difference between the terms *file organization* and *access method*. A **file organization** refers to the organization of the data of a file into records, blocks, and access structures; this includes the way records and blocks are placed on the storage medium and interlinked. An **access method**, on the other hand, provides a group of operations—such as those listed earlier—that can be applied to a file. In general, it is possible to apply several access methods to a file organization. Some access methods, though, can be applied only to files organized in certain ways. For example, we cannot apply an indexed access method to a file without an index.

Usually, we expect to use some search conditions more than others. Some files may be **static**, meaning that update operations are rarely performed; other, more **dynamic** files may change frequently, so update operations are constantly applied to them. A successful file organization should perform as efficiently as possible the operations we expect to *apply frequently* to the file. For example, consider the EMPLOYEE file (Figure 9.5a), which stores the records for current employees in a company. We expect to insert records (when employees are hired), delete records (when employees leave the company), and modify records (say, when an employee's salary or job is changed). Deleting or modifying a record requires a selection condition to identify a particular record or set of records. Retrieving one or more records also requires a selection condition.

If users expect mainly to apply a search condition based on ENO, the designer must choose a file organization that facilitates locating a record given its ENO value. This may involve physically ordering the records by ENO value or defining an index on ENO. Suppose that a second application uses the file to generate employees' paychecks and requires that paychecks be grouped by department. For this application, it is best to store all employee records having the same department value contiguously, clustering them into blocks and perhaps ordering them by name within each department. However, this arrangement conflicts with ordering the records by ENO values. If both applications are important, the designer should choose an organization that allows both operations to be done efficiently. Unfortunately, in many cases there may not be an organization that allows all needed operations on a file to be implemented efficiently. In such cases a compromise must be chosen that takes into account the expected importance and mix of retrieval and update operations.

In the following sections, we discuss methods for organizing records of a file on disk. Several general techniques, such as ordering, hashing, and indexing, are used to create access methods. In addition, various general techniques for handling insertions and deletions work with many file organizations.

9.6 FILES OF UNORDERED RECORDS (HEAP FILES)

In this simplest and most basic type of organization, records are placed in the file in the order in which they are inserted, so new records are inserted at the end of the file. Such an organization is called a **heap** or **pile file**.[7] This organization is often used with additional access paths, such as the secondary indexes. It is also used to collect and store data records for future use.

Inserting a new record is *very efficient*: the last disk block of the file is copied into a buffer; the new record is added; and the block is then **rewritten** back to disk. The address of the last file block is kept in the file header. However, searching for a record using any search condition involves a **linear search** through the file block by block—an expensive procedure. If only one record satisfies the search condition, then, on the average, a program will read into memory and search half the file blocks before it finds the record. For a file of b blocks, this requires searching $(b/2)$ blocks, on average. If no records or several records satisfy the search condition, the program must read and search all b blocks in the file.

To delete a record, a program must first find its block, copy the block into a buffer, then delete the record from the buffer, and finally **rewrite the block** back to the disk. This leaves unused space in the disk block. Deleting a large number of records in this way results in wasted storage space. Another technique used for record deletion is to have an extra byte or bit, called a **deletion marker**, stored with each record. A record is deleted by setting the deletion marker to a certain value. A different value of the marker indicates a valid (not deleted) record. Search programs consider only valid records in a block when conducting their search. Both of these deletion techniques require periodic **reorganization** of the file to reclaim the unused space of deleted records. During reorganization, the file blocks are accessed consecutively, and records are packed by removing deleted records. After such a reorganization, the blocks are filled to capacity once more. Another possibility is to use the space of deleted records when inserting new records, although this requires extra bookkeeping to keep track of empty locations.

We can use either spanned or unspanned organization for an unordered file, and it may be used with either fixed-length or variable-length records. Modifying a variable length record may require deleting the old record and inserting a modified record, because the modified record may not fit in its old space on disk.

To read all records in order of the values of some field, we create a sorted copy of the file. Sorting is an expensive operation for a large disk file, and special techniques for **external sorting** are used (see Chapter 10).

For a file of unordered *fixed-length records using unspanned blocks* and *contiguous allocation*, it is straightforward to access any record by its **position** in the file. If the file records are numbered 0, 1, 2, ..., $r-1$ and the records in each block are numbered 0, 1, ..., $bfr-1$, where bfr is the blocking factor, then the ith record of the file is

---

7. Sometimes this organization is called a **sequential file**.

located in block $\lfloor (i/bfr) \rfloor$ and is the $(i \bmod bfr)^{\text{th}}$ record in that block. Such a file is often called a **relative** or **direct file** because records can easily be accessed directly by their relative positions. Accessing a record by its position does not help locate a record based on a search condition; however, it facilitates the construction of access paths on the file.

9.7 FILES OF ORDERED RECORDS (SORTED FILES)

We can physically order the records of a file on disk based on the values of one of their fields—called the **ordering field**. This leads to an **ordered** or **sequential** file.[8] If the ordering field is also a **key field** of the file—a field guaranteed to have a unique value in each record—then the field is called the **ordering key** for the file. Figure 9.7 shows an ordered file with NAME as the ordering key field (assuming that employees have distinct names).

Ordered records have some advantages over unordered files. First, reading the records in order of the ordering key values becomes extremely efficient, because no sorting is required. Second, finding the next record from the current one in order of the ordering key usually requires no additional block accesses, because the next record is in the same block as the current one (unless the current record is the last one in the block). Third, using a search condition based on the value of an ordering key field results in faster access when the binary search technique is used, which constitutes an improvement over linear searches, although it is not often used for disk files.

A **binary search** for disk files can be done on the blocks rather than on the records. Suppose that the file has b blocks numbered $1, 2, \ldots, b$; the records are ordered by ascending value of their ordering key field; and we are searching for a record whose ordering key field value is K. Assuming that disk addresses of the file blocks are available in the file header, the binary search can be described by Algorithm 9.1. A binary search usually accesses $\log_2(b)$ blocks, whether the record is found or not—an improvement over linear searches, where, on the average, $(b/2)$ blocks are accessed when the record is found and b blocks are accessed when the record is not found.

Algorithm 9.1: Binary search on an ordering key of a disk file.

```
l ← 1; u ← b; (* b is the number of file blocks*)
while (u ∃ 1) do
     begin i ← (1 + u) div 2;
     read block i of the file into the buffer;
     if K < (ordering key field value of the first record in block i)
     then u ← i ∃ 1
     else if K > (ordering key field value of the last record in block i)
             then 1 ← i + 1
             else if the record with ordering key field value = K is in the buffer
                     then goto found
                     else goto notfound;
     end;
  goto notfound;
```

---

8. The term sequential file has also been used to refer to unordered files.

	NAME	ENO	DOB	JOB	SALARY	SEX
block 1	Abbas					
	Achyuth					
	⋮					
	Adam					
block 2	Agarkar					
	Agarwal					
	⋮					
	Akram					
block 3	Akthar					
	Alexander					
	⋮					
	Anil					
block 4	Anitha					
	Anusha					
	⋮					
	Arvind					
block 5	Archana					
	Arjun					
	⋮					
	Arnold					
block 6	Arun					
	Asha					
	⋮					
	Azar					
⋮						
block n − 1	Wahab					
	Watson					
	⋮					
	Wazzid					
block n	Williams					
	Wright					
	⋮					
	Zamal					

FIGURE 9.7 Some blocks of an ordered (sequential) file of EMPLOYEE records with NAME as the ordering key field.

A search criterion involving the conditions >, <, ≥, and ≤ on the ordering field is quite efficient, since the physical ordering of records means that all records satisfying the condition are contiguous in the file. For example, referring to Figure 9.9, if the search criterion is (NAME < 'G')—where < means *alphabetically before*—the records satisfying the search criterion are those from the beginning of the file up to the first record that has a NAME value starting with the letter G.

Ordering does not provide any advantages for random or ordered access of the records based on values of the other *nonordering fields* of the file. In these cases we do a linear search for random access. To access the records in order based on a nonordering field, it is necessary to create another sorted copy—in a different order—of the file.

Inserting and deleting records are expensive operations for an ordered file because the records must remain physically ordered. To insert a record, we must find its correct position in the file, based on its ordering field value, and then make space in the file to insert the record in that position. For a large file this can be very time consuming because, on the average, half the records of the file must be moved to make space for the new record. This means that half the file blocks must be read and rewritten after records are moved among them. For record deletion, the problem is less severe if deletion markers and periodic reorganization are used.

One option for making insertion more efficient is to keep some unused space in each block for new records. However, once this space is used up, the original problem resurfaces. Another frequently used method is to create a temporary *unordered* file called an **overflow** or **transaction** file. With this technique, the actual ordered file is called the **main** or **master** file. New records are inserted at the end of the overflow file rather than in their correct position in the main file. Periodically, the overflow file is sorted and merged with the master file during file reorganization. Insertion becomes very efficient, but at the cost of increased complexity in the search algorithm. The overflow file must be searched using a linear search if, after the binary search, the record is not found in the main file. For applications that do not require the most up-to-date information, overflow records can be ignored during a search.

Modifying a field value of a record depends on two factors: (1) the search condition to locate the record and (2) the field to be modified. If the search condition involves the ordering key field, we can locate the record using a binary search; otherwise we must do a linear search. A nonordering field can be modified by changing the record and rewriting it in the same physical location on disk—assuming fixed-length records. Modifying the ordering field means that the record can change its position in the file, which requires deletion of the old record followed by insertion of the modified record.

Reading the file records in order of the ordering field is quite efficient if we ignore the records in overflow, since the blocks can be read consecutively using double buffering. To include the records in overflow, we must merge them in their correct positions; in this case, we can first reorganize the file, and then read its blocks sequentially. To reorganize the file, first sort the records in the overflow file, and then merge them with the master file. The records marked for deletion are removed during the reorganization.

TABLE 9.2 AVERAGE ACCESS TIMES FOR BASIC FILE ORGANIZATIONS

TYPE OF ORGANIZATION	ACCESS/SEARCH METHOD	AVERAGE TIME TO ACCESS A SPECIFIC RECORD
Heap (Unordered)	Sequential scan (Linear Search)	$b/2$
Ordered	Sequential scan	$b/2$
Ordered	Binary Search	$\log_2 b$

Table 9.2 summarizes the average access time in block accesses to find a specific record in a file with b blocks.

Ordered files are rarely used in database applications unless an additional access path, called a **primary index**, is used; this results in an **indexed-sequential file**. This further improves the random access time on the ordering key field. We discuss indexes in Section 9.12.

9.8 HASHING TECHNIQUES

Another type of primary file organization is based on hashing, which provides very fast access to records on certain search conditions. This organization is usually called a **hash file**.[9] The search condition must be an equality condition on a single field, called the **hash field** of the file. In most cases, the hash field is also a key field of the file, in which case it is called the **hash key**. The idea behind hashing is to provide a function h, called a **hash function** or **randomizing function**, that is applied to the hash field value of a record and yields the address of the disk block in which the record is stored. A search for the record within the block can be carried out in a main memory buffer. For most records, we need only a single-block access to retrieve that record.

FIGURE 9.8 Internal hashing data structures. (a) Array of M positions for use in internal hashing. (b) Collision resolution by chaining records.

---

9. A hash file has also been called a *direct file*.

Hashing is also used as an internal search structure within a program whenever a group of records is accessed exclusively by using the value of one field. We describe the use of hashing for internal files in Section 9.8.1; then we show how it is modified to store external files on disk in Section 9.8.2. In Section 9.8.3 we discuss techniques for extending hashing to dynamically growing files.

9.8.1 Internal Hashing

For internal files, hashing is typically implemented as a **hash table** through the use of an array of records. Suppose that the array index range is from 0 to $M - 1$ (Figure 9.8a); then we have M **slots** whose addresses correspond to the array indexes. We choose a hash function that transforms the hash field value into an integer between 0 and $M - 1$. One common hash function is the $h(K) = K \bmod M$ function, which returns the remainder of an integer hash field value K after division by M; this value is then used for the record address.

Noninteger hash field values can be transformed into integers before the mod function is applied. For character strings, the numeric (ASCII) codes associated with characters can be used in the transformation—for example, by multiplying those code values. For a hash field whose data type is a string of 20 characters, Algorithm 9.2a can be used to calculate the hash address. We assume that the code function returns the numeric code of a character and that we are given a hash field value K of type K: *array* [1..20] of *char* (in PASCAL) or *char* K[20] (in C).

Algorithm 9.2: Two simple hashing algorithms. (a) Applying the mod hash function to a character string K. (b) Collision resolution by open addressing.

```
(a) temp ← 1;
    for i ← 1 to 20 do temp ← temp * code(K[i]) mod M;
    hash_address ← temp mod M;
(b) i ← hash_address(K); a ← i;
    if location i is occupied
        then begin i ← (i + 1) mod M;
            while (i fi a) and location i is occupied
                do i ← (i + 1) mod M;
            if (i = a) then all positions are full
                else new_hash_address ← i;
        end;
```

Other hashing functions can be used. One technique, called **folding**, involves applying an arithmetic function such as *addition* or a logical function such as *exclusive or* to different portions of the hash field value to calculate the hash address. Another technique involves picking some digits of the hash field value—for example, the third, fifth, and eighth digits—to form the hash address.[10] The problem with most hashing functions is that they do not guarantee that distinct values will hash to distinct addresses, because the **hash field space**—the number of possible values a hash field can take—is usually much larger than the **address space**—the number of available addresses for records. The hashing function maps the hash field space to the address space.

---

10. A detailed discussion of hashing functions is outside the scope of our presentation.

A **collision** occurs when the hash field value of a record that is being inserted hashes to an address that already contains a different record. In this situation, we must insert the new record in some other position, since its hash address is occupied. The process of finding another position is called **collision resolution**. There are numerous methods for collision resolution, including the following:

- *Open addressing*: Proceeding from the occupied position specified by the hash address, the program checks the subsequent positions in order until an unused (empty) position is found. Algorithm 9.2b may be used for this purpose.

- *Chaining*: For this method, various overflow locations are kept, usually by extending the array with a number of overflow positions. In addition, a pointer field is added to each record location. A collision is resolved by placing the new record in an unused overflow location and setting the pointer of the occupied hash address location to the address of that overflow location. A linked list of overflow records for each hash address is thus maintained, as shown in Figure 9.8b.

- *Multiple hashing*: The program applies a second hash function if the first results in a collision. If another collision results, the program uses open addressing or applies a third hash function and then uses open addressing if necessary.

Each collision resolution method requires its own algorithms for insertion, retrieval, and deletion of records. The algorithms for chaining are the simplest. Deletion algorithms for open addressing are rather tricky. Data structures textbooks discuss internal hashing algorithms in more detail.

The goal of a good hashing function is to distribute the records uniformly over the address space so as to minimize collisions while not leaving many unused locations. Simulation and analysis studies have shown that it is usually best to keep a hash table between 70 and 90 percent full so that the number of collisions remains low and we do not waste too much space. Hence, if we expect to have r records to store in the table, we should choose M locations for the address space such that (r/M) is between 0.7 and 0.9. It may also be useful to choose a prime number for M, since it has been demonstrated that this distributes the hash addresses better over the address space when the mod hashing function is used. Other hash functions may require M to be a power of 2.

9.8.2   External Hashing for Disk Files

Hashing for disk files is called **external hashing**. To suit the characteristics of disk storage, the target address space is made of **buckets**, each of which holds multiple records. A bucket is either one disk block or a cluster of contiguous blocks. The hashing function maps a key into a relative bucket number, rather than assign an absolute block address to the bucket. A table maintained in the file header converts the bucket number into the corresponding disk block address, as illustrated in Figure 9.9.

The collision problem is less severe with buckets, because as many records as will fit in a bucket can hash to the same bucket without causing problems. However, we must make provisions for the case where a bucket is filled to capacity and a new record being inserted hashes to that bucket. We can use a variation of chaining in which a pointer is maintained in each bucket to a linked list of overflow records for the bucket, as shown in Figure 9.10. The pointers in the linked list should be **record pointers**, which include both a block address and a relative record position within the block.

Hashing provides the fastest possible access for retrieving an arbitrary record given the value of its hash field. Although most good hash functions do not maintain records in order of hash field values, some functions—called **order preserving**—do. A simple example of an order preserving hash function is to take the leftmost three digits of an invoice number field as the hash address and keep the records sorted by invoice number within each bucket. Another example is to use an integer hash key directly as an index to a relative file, if the hash key values fill up a particular interval; for example, if employee numbers in a company are assigned as 1, 2, 3, . . . up to the total number of employees, we can use the identity hash function that maintains order. Unfortunately, this only works if keys are generated in order by some application.

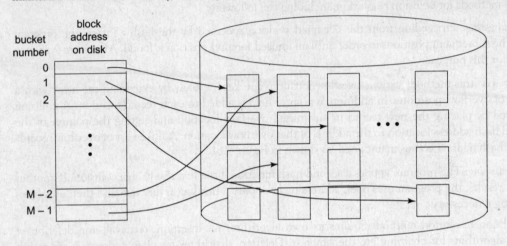

FIGURE 9.9 Matching bucket numbers to disk block addresses.

FIGURE 9.10 Handling overflow for buckets by chaining.

The hashing scheme described is called **static hashing** because a fixed number of buckets M is allocated. This can be a serious drawback for dynamic files. Suppose that we allocate M buckets for the address space and let m be the maximum number of records that can fit in one bucket; then at most $(m * M)$ records will fit in the allocated space. If the number of records turns out to be substantially fewer than $(m * M)$, we are left with a lot of unused space. On the other hand, if the number of records increases to substantially more than $(m * M)$, numerous collisions will result and retrieval will be slowed down because of the long lists of overflow records. In either case, we may have to change the number of blocks M allocated and then use a new hashing function (based on the new value of M) to redistribute the records. These reorganizations can be quite time consuming for large files. Newer dynamic file organizations based on hashing allow the number of buckets to vary dynamically with only localized reorganization (see Section 9.8.3).

When using external hashing, searching for a record given a value of some field other than the hash field is as expensive as in the case of an unordered file. Record deletion can be implemented by removing the record from its bucket. If the bucket has an overflow chain, we can move one of the overflow records into the bucket to replace the deleted record. If the record to be deleted is already in overflow, we simply remove it from the linked list. Notice that removing an overflow record implies that we should keep track of empty positions in overflow. This is done easily by maintaining a linked list of unused overflow locations.

Modifying a record's field value depends on two factors: (1) the search condition to locate the record and (2) the field to be modified. If the search condition is an equality comparison on the hash field, we can locate the record efficiently by using the hashing function; otherwise, we must do a linear search. A nonhash field can be modified by changing the record and rewriting it in the same bucket. Modifying the hash field means that the record can move to another bucket, which requires deletion of the old record followed by insertion of the modified record.

9.8.3   Hashing Techniques that Allow Dynamic File Expansion

A major drawback of the *static* hashing scheme just discussed is that the hash address space is fixed. Hence, it is difficult to expand or shrink the file dynamically. The schemes described in this section attempt to remedy this situation. The first scheme—extendible hashing—stores an access structure in addition to the file, and hence is somewhat similar to indexing. The main difference is that the access structure is based on the values that result after application of the hash function to the search field. In indexing, the access structure is based on the values of the search field itself. The second technique, called linear hashing, does not require additional access structures.

These hashing schemes take advantage of the fact that the result of applying a hashing function is a nonnegative integer and hence can be represented as a binary number. The access structure is built on the **binary representation** of the hashing function result, which is a string of **bits**. We call this the **hash value** of a record. Records are distributed among buckets based on the values of the *leading bits* in their hash values.

Extendible Hashing.   In extendible hashing, a type of **directory**—an array of 2^d bucket addresses—is maintained, where d is called the **global depth** of the directory. The integer value corresponding to the first (high-order) d bits of a hash value is used as an index to the array to determine a directory entry, and the address in that entry determines the bucket in which the corresponding records are stored. However, there does not have to be a distinct bucket for each of the 2^d directory locations. Several directory locations with the same first d' bits for their hash values may contain the same bucket address if all the records that hash to these locations fit in a single bucket. A **local depth** d'—stored with each bucket—specifies the number of bits on which the bucket contents are based. Figure 9.11 shows a directory with global depth $d = 3$.

FIGURE 9.11 Structure of the extendible hashing scheme.

The value of d can be increased or decreased by one at a time, thus doubling or halving the number of entries in the directory array. Doubling is needed if a bucket, whose local depth d' is equal to the global depth d, overflows. Halving occurs if $d > d'$ for all the buckets after some deletions occur. Most record retrievals require two block accesses—one to the directory and the other to the bucket.

To illustrate bucket splitting, suppose that a new inserted record causes overflow in the bucket whose hash values start with 01—the third bucket in Figure 9.11. The records will be distributed between two buckets: the first contains all records whose hash values start with 010, and the second all those whose hash values start with 011. Now the two directory locations for 010 and 011 point to the two new distinct buckets. Before the split, they pointed to the same bucket. The local depth d' of the two new buckets is 3, which is one more than the local depth of the old bucket.

If a bucket that overflows and is split used to have a local depth d' equal to the global depth d of the directory, then the size of the directory must now be doubled so that we can use an extra bit to distinguish the two new buckets. For example, if the bucket for records whose hash values start with 111 in Figure 9.11 overflows, the two new buckets need a directory with global depth $d = 4$, because the two buckets are now labeled 1110 and 1111, and hence their local depths are both 4. The directory size is hence doubled, and each of the other original locations in the directory is also split into two locations, both of which have the same pointer value as did the original location.

The main advantage of extendible hashing that makes it attractive is that the performance of the file does not degrade as the file grows, as opposed to static external hashing where collisions increase and the corresponding chaining causes additional accesses. In addition, no space is allocated in extendible hashing for future growth, but additional buckets can be allocated dynamically as needed. The space overhead for the directory table is negligible. The maximum directory size is 2^k, where k is the number of bits in the hash value. Another advantage is that splitting causes minor reorganization in most cases, since only the records in one bucket are redistributed to the two new buckets. The only time a reorganization is more expensive is when the directory has to be doubled (or halved). A disadvantage is that the directory must be searched before accessing the buckets themselves, resulting in two block accesses instead of one in static hashing. This performance penalty is considered minor and hence the scheme is considered quite desirable for dynamic files.

Linear Hashing.   The idea behind linear hashing is to allow a hash file to expand and shrink its number of buckets dynamically *without* needing a directory. Suppose that the file starts with M buckets numbered 0, 1, . . . , M – 1 and uses the mod hash function $h(K) = K \bmod M$; this hash function is called the initial hash function h_i. Overflow because of collisions is still needed and can be handled by maintaining individual overflow chains for each bucket. However, when a collision leads to an overflow record in any file bucket, the first bucket in the file—bucket 0—is split into two buckets: the original bucket 0 and a new bucket M at the end of the file. The records originally in bucket 0 are distributed between the two buckets based on a different hashing function $h_{i+1}(K) = K \bmod 2M$. A key property of the two hash functions h_i and h_{i+1} is that any records that hashed to bucket 0 based on h_i will hash to either bucket 0 or bucket M based on h_{i+1}; this is necessary for linear hashing to work.

As further collisions lead to overflow records, additional buckets are split in the *linear* order 1, 2, 3, ... If enough overflows occur, all the original file buckets 0, 1, . . . , M – 1 will have been split, so the file now has 2M instead of M buckets, and all buckets use the hash function h_{i+1}. Hence, the records in overflow are eventually redistributed into regular buckets, using the function h_{i+1} via a *delayed split* of their buckets. There is no directory; only a value n—which is initially set to 0 and is incremented by 1 whenever a split occurs—is needed to determine which buckets have been split. To retrieve a record with hash key value K, first apply the function h_i to K; if $h_i(K) < n$, then apply the function h_{i+1} on K because the bucket is already split. Initially, $n = 0$, indicating that the function h_i applies to all buckets; n grows linearly as buckets are split.

When $n = M$ after being incremented, this signifies that all the original buckets have been split and the hash function h_{i+1} applies to all records in the file. At this point, n is reset to 0 (zero), and any new collisions that cause overflow lead to the use of a new hashing function $h_{i+2}(K) = K \bmod 4M$. In general, a sequence of hashing functions $h_{i+j}(K) = K \bmod (2^j M)$ is used, where $j = 0, 1, 2, . . .$; a new hashing function h_{i+j+1} is needed whenever all the buckets 0, 1, . . . , $(2^j M) - 1$ have been split and n is reset to 0. The search for a record with hash key value K is given by Algorithm 9.3.

Splitting can be controlled by monitoring the file load factor instead of by splitting whenever an overflow occurs. In general, the **file load factor** l can be defined as $l = r/(bfr * N)$, where r is the current number of file records, *bfr* is the maximum number of records that can fit in a bucket, and N is the current number of file buckets. Buckets that have been split can also be recombined if the load of the file falls below a certain threshold. Blocks are combined linearly, and N is decremented appropriately. The file load can be used to trigger both splits and combinations; in this manner the file load can be kept within a desired range. Splits can be triggered when the load exceeds a certain threshold—say, 0.9—and combinations can be triggered when the load falls below another threshold—say, 0.7.

Algorithm 9.3: The search procedure for linear hashing.

```
if n = 0
    then m ← hj(K) (* m is the hash value of record with hash key K *)
    else begin
```

$m \leftarrow h_j(K)$;
if $m < n$ then $m \leftarrow h_{j+1}(K)$
end;
search the bucket whose hash value is m (and its overflow, if any);

9.9 OTHER PRIMARY FILE ORGANIZATIONS

9.9.1 Files of Mixed Records

The file organizations we have studied so far assume that all records of a particular file are of the same record type. The records could be of EMPLOYEEs, PROJECTs, STUDENTs, or DEPARTMENTs, but each file contains records of only one type. In most database applications, we encounter situations in which numerous types of entities are interrelated in various ways, as we saw in Chapter 3. Relationships among records in various files can be represented by **connecting fields**.[11] For example, a STUDENT record can have a connecting field MAJORDEPT whose value gives the name of the DEPARTMENT in which the student is majoring. This MAJORDEPT field refers to a DEPARTMENT entity, which should be represented by a record of its own in the DEPARTMENT file. If we want to retrieve field values from two related records, we must retrieve one of the records first. Then we can use its connecting field value to retrieve the related record in the other file. Hence, relationships are implemented by **logical field references** among the records in distinct files.

File organizations in object DBMSs, as well as legacy systems such as hierarchical and network DBMSs, often implement relationships among records as **physical relationships** realized by physical contiguity (or clustering) of related records or by physical pointers. These file organizations typically assign an **area** of the disk to hold records of more than one type so that records of different types can be **physically clustered** on disk. If a particular relationship is expected to be used very frequently, implementing the relationship physically can increase the system's efficiency at retrieving related records. For example, if the query to retrieve a DEPARTMENT record and all records for STUDENTs majoring in that department is very frequent, it would be desirable to place each DEPARTMENT record and its cluster of STUDENT records contiguously on disk in a mixed file. The concept of **physical clustering** of object types is used in object DBMSs to store related objects together in a mixed file.

To distinguish the records in a mixed file, each record has—in addition to its field values—a record type field, which specifies the type of record. This is typically the first field in each record and is used by the system software to determine the type of record it is about to process. Using the catalog information, the DBMS can determine the fields of that record type and their sizes, in order to interpret the data values in the record.

9.9.2 B-Trees and Other Data Structures as Primary Organization

Other data structures can be used for primary file organizations. For example, if both the record size and the number of records in a file are small, some DBMSs offer the option of a B-tree data structure as the primary file organization. We will describe B-trees in Section 9.12.3.1, when we discuss the use of the B-tree data structure for indexing. In general, any data structure that can be adapted to the characteristics of disk devices can be used as a primary file organization for record placement on disk.

---

11. The concept of foreign keys in the relational model (Chapter 4) and references among objects in object-oriented models are examples of connecting fields.

9.10   PARALLELIZING DISK ACCESS USING RAID TECHNOLOGY

With the exponential growth in the performance and capacity of semiconductor devices and memories, faster microprocessors with larger and larger primary memories are continually becoming available. To match this growth, it is natural to expect that secondary storage technology must also take steps to keep up in performance and reliability with processor technology.

A major advance in secondary storage technology is represented by the development of **RAID**, which originally stood for **Redundant Arrays of Inexpensive Disks**. Lately, the "I" in RAID is said to stand for Independent. The RAID idea received a very positive endorsement by industry and has been developed into an elaborate set of alternative RAID architectures (RAID levels 0 through 6). We highlight the main features of the technology below.

The main goal of RAID is to even out the widely different rates of performance improvement of disks against those in memory and microprocessors.[12] While RAM capacities have quadrupled every two to three years, disk *access times* are improving at less than 10 percent per year, and disk *transfer rates* are improving at roughly 20 percent per year. Disk *capacities* are indeed improving at more than 50 percent per year, but the speed and access time improvements are of a much smaller magnitude. Table 9.3 shows trends in disk technology in terms of 1993 parameter values and rates of improvement, as well as where these parameters are in 2003.

A second qualitative disparity exists between the ability of special microprocessors that cater to new applications involving processing of video, audio, image, and spatial data with corresponding lack of fast access to large, shared data sets.

The natural solution is a large array of small independent disks acting as a single higher-performance logical disk. A concept called **data striping** is used, which utilizes *parallelism* to improve disk performance. Data striping distributes data transparently over multiple disks to make them appear as a single large, fast disk. Figure 9.12 shows a file distributed or *striped* over four disks. Striping improves overall I/O performance by

TABLE 9.3 TRENDS IN DISK TECHNOLOGY

	1993 PARAMETER VALUES*	HISTORICAL RATE OF IMPROVEMENT PER YEAR (%)*	CURRENT (2003) VALUES**
Areal density	50–150 Mbits/sq. inch	27	36 Gbits/sq. inch
Linear density	40,000–60,000 bits/inch	13	570 Kbits/inch
Inter-track density	1500–3000 tracks/inch	10	64,000 tracks/inch
Capacity (3.5" form factor)	100–2000 MB	27	146 GB
Transfer rate	3–4 MB/s	22	43–78 MB/sec
Seek time	7–20 ms	8	3.5–6 msec

Source: From Chen, Lee, Gibson, Katz, and Patterson (1994), ACM *Computing Surveys*, Vol. 26, No. 2 (June 1994). Reprinted by permission.
**Source*: IBM Ultrastar 36XP and 18ZX hard disk drives.

---

12. This was predicted by Gordon Bell to be about 40 percent every year between 1974 and 1984 and is now supposed to exceed 50 percent per year.

allowing multiple I/Os to be serviced in parallel, thus providing high overall transfer rates. Data striping also accomplishes load balancing among disks. Moreover, by storing redundant information on disks using parity or some other error correction code, reliability can be improved. In Sections 9.10.1 and 9.10.2, we discuss how RAID achieves the two important objectives of improved reliability and higher performance. Section 9.10.3 discusses RAID organizations.

FIGURE 9.12 Data striping. File A is striped across four disks.

9.10.1 Improving Reliability with RAID

For an array of n disks, the likelihood of failure is n times as much as that for one disk. Hence, if the MTTF (Mean Time To Failure) of a disk drive is assumed to be 200,000 hours or about 22.8 years (typical times range up to 1 million hours), that of a bank of 100 disk drives becomes only 2000 hours or 83.3 days. Keeping a single copy of data in such an array of disks will cause a significant loss of reliability. An obvious solution is to employ redundancy of data so that disk failures can be tolerated. The disadvantages are many: additional I/O operations for write, extra computation to maintain redundancy and to do recovery from errors, and additional disk capacity to store redundant information.

One technique for introducing redundancy is called **mirroring** or **shadowing**. Data is written redundantly to two identical physical disks that are treated as one logical disk. When data is read, it can be retrieved from the disk with shorter queuing, seek, and rotational delays. If a disk fails, the other disk is used until the first is repaired. Suppose the mean time to repair is 24 hours, then the mean time to data loss of a mirrored disk system using 100 disks with MTTF of 200,000 hours each is $(200,000)^2/(2 * 24) = 8.33 * 10^8$ hours, which is 95,028 years.[13] Disk mirroring also doubles the rate at which read requests are handled, since a read can go to either disk. The transfer rate of each read, however, remains the same as that for a single disk.

Another solution to the problem of reliability is to store extra information that is not normally needed but that can be used to reconstruct the lost information in case of disk failure. The incorporation of redundancy must consider two problems: (1) selecting a technique for computing the redundant information, and (2) selecting a method of distributing the redundant information across the disk array. The first problem is addressed by using error correcting codes involving parity bits, or specialized codes such as Hamming codes. Under the parity scheme, a redundant disk may be considered as having the sum of all the data in the other disks. When a disk fails, the missing information can be constructed by a process similar to subtraction.

For the second problem, the two major approaches are either to store the redundant information on a small number of disks or to distribute it uniformly across all disks. The latter results in better load balancing. The different levels of RAID choose a combination of these options to implement redundancy, and hence to improve reliability.

---

13. The fomulas for MTTF calculations appear in Chen et al. (1994).

9.10.2   Improving Performance with RAID

The disk arrays employ the technique of data striping to achieve higher transfer rates. Note that data can be read or written only one block at a time, so a typical transfer contains 512 bytes. Disk striping may be applied at a finer granularity by breaking up a byte of data into bits and spreading the bits to different disks. Thus, **bit-level data striping** consists of splitting a byte of data and writing bit j to the jth disk. With 8-bit bytes, eight physical disks may be considered as one logical disk with an eightfold increase in the data transfer rate. Each disk participates in each I/O request and the total amount of data read per request is eight times as much. Bit-level striping can be generalized to a number of disks that is either a multiple or a factor of eight. Thus, in a four-disk array, bit n goes to the disk which is $(n \bmod 4)$.

The granularity of data interleaving can be higher than a bit; for example, blocks of a file can be striped across disks, giving rise to **block-level striping**. Figure 9.12 shows blocklevel data striping assuming the data file contained four blocks. With block-level striping, multiple independent requests that access single blocks (small requests) can be serviced in parallel by separate disks, thus decreasing the queuing time of I/O requests. Requests that access multiple blocks (large requests) can be parallelized, thus reducing their response time. In general, the more the number of disks in an array, the larger the potential performance benefit. However, assuming independent failures, the disk array of 100 disks collectively has a $1/100^{th}$ the reliability of a single disk. Thus, redundancy via error-correcting codes and disk mirroring is necessary to provide reliability along with high performance.

9.10.3   RAID Organizations and Levels

Different RAID organizations were defined based on different combinations of the two factors of granularity of data interleaving (striping) and pattern used to compute redundant information. In the initial proposal, levels 1 through 5 of RAID were proposed, and two additional levels—0 and 6—were added later.

RAID level 0 uses data striping, has no redundant data and hence has the best write performance since updates do not have to be duplicated. However, its read performance is not as good as RAID level 1, which uses mirrored disks. In the latter, performance improvement is possible by scheduling a read request to the disk with shortest expected seek and rotational delay. RAID level 2 uses memory-style redundancy by using Hamming codes, which contain parity bits for distinct overlapping subsets of components. Thus, in one particular version of this level, three redundant disks suffice for four original disks whereas, with mirroring—as in level 1—four would be required. Level 2 includes both error detection and correction, although detection is generally not required because broken disks identify themselves.

RAID level 3 uses a single parity disk relying on the disk controller to figure out which disk has failed. Levels 4 and 5 use block-level data striping, with level 5 distributing data and parity information across all disks. Finally, RAID level 6 applies the so-called $P + Q$ redundancy scheme using Reed-Soloman codes to protect against up to two disk failures by using just two redundant disks. The seven RAID levels (0 through 6) are illustrated in Figure 9.13 schematically.

Rebuilding in case of disk failure is easiest for RAID level 1. Other levels require the reconstruction of a failed disk by reading multiple disks. Level 1 is used for critical applications such as storing logs of transactions. Levels 3 and 5 are preferred for large volume storage, with level 3 providing higher transfer rates. Most popular use of RAID technology currently uses level 0 (with striping), level 1 (with mirroring) and level 5 with an extra drive for parity. Designers of a RAID setup for a given application mix have to confront many design decisions such as the level of RAID, the number of disks, the choice of parity schemes, and grouping of disks for block-level striping. Detailed performance studies on small reads and writes (referring to I/O requests for one striping unit) and large reads and writes (referring to I/O requests for one stripe unit from each disk in an error-correction group) have been performed.

9.11 STORAGE AREA NETWORKS

With the rapid growth of electronic commerce, Enterprise Resource Planning (ERP) systems that integrate application data across organizations, and data warehouses that keep historical aggregate information (see Chapter 17), the demand for storage has gone up substantially. For today's internet-driven organizations

Non-Redundant (RAID Level 0)

Mirrored (RAID Level 1)

Memory-styl ECC (RAID Level 2)

Bit-Interleaved parity (RAID Level 3)

Block-Interleaved parity (RAID Level 4)

Block-Interleaved Distribution-parity (RAID Level 5)

P+Q Redundancy (RAID Level 6)

FIGURE 9.13 Multiple levels of RAID. From Chen, Lee, Gibson, Katz, and Patterson (1994), ACM Computing Survey, Vol. 26, No. 2 (June 1994). Reprinted with permisson.

it has become necessary to move from a static fixed data center oriented operation to a more flexible and dynamic infrastructure for their information processing requirements. The total cost of managing all data is growing so rapidly that in many instances the cost of managing server attached storage exceeds the cost of the server itself. Furthermore, the procurement cost of storage is only a small fraction—typically, only 10 to 15 percent of the overall cost of storage management. Many users of RAID systems cannot use the capacity effectively because it has to be attached in a fixed manner to one or more servers. Therefore, large organizations are moving to a concept called **Storage Area Networks** (SANs). In a SAN, online storage peripherals are configured as nodes on a high-speed network and can be attached and detached from servers in a very flexible manner. Several companies have emerged as SAN providers and supply their own proprietary topologies. They allow storage systems to be placed at longer distances from the servers and provide different performance and connectivity options. Existing storage management applications can be ported into SAN configurations using Fiber Channel networks that encapsulate the legacy SCSI protocol. As a result, the SAN-attached devices appear as SCSI devices.

Current architectural alternatives for SAN include the following: point-to-point connections between servers and storage systems via fiber channel, use of a fiber-channel-switch to connect multiple RAID systems, tape libraries, etc. to servers, use of fiber channel hubs and switches to connect servers and storage systems in different configurations. Organizations can slowly move up from simpler topologies to more complex ones by adding servers and storage devices as needed. We do not provide further details here because they vary among vendors of SANs. The main advantages claimed are the following:

- Flexible many-to-many connectivity among servers and storage devices using fiber channel hubs and switches

- Up to 10 km separation between a server and a storage system using appropriate fiber optic cables.

- Better isolation capabilities allowing nondisruptive addition of new peripherals and servers.

SANs are growing very rapidly, but are still faced with many problems such as combining storage options from multiple vendors and dealing with evolving standards of storage management software and hardware. Most major companies are evaluating SAN as a viable option for database storage.

9.12 INDEXING STRUCTURES FOR FILES

In this Section, we assume that a file already exists with some primary organization such as the unordered, ordered, or hashed organizations that were described in preceding sections. We will describe additional auxiliary **access structures** called **indexes**, which are used to speed up the retrieval of records in response to certain search conditions. The index structures typically provide **secondary access paths**, which provide alternative ways of accessing the records without affecting the physical placement of records on disk. They enable efficient access to records based on the **indexing fields** that are used to construct the index. Basically, *any field* of the file can be used to create an index and *multiple indexes* on different fields can be constructed on the same file. A variety of indexes are possible; each of them uses a particular data structure to speed up the search. To find a record or records in the file based on a certain selection criterion on an indexing field, one has to initially access the index, which points to one or more blocks in the file where the required records are located. The most prevalent types of indexes are based on ordered files (single-level indexes) and tree data structures (multilevel indexes, B$^+$-trees). Indexes can also be constructed based on hashing or other search data structures.

This subsection is organized as follows. We describe different types of single-level ordered indexes—primary, secondary, and clustering—in Section 9.12.1. By viewing a single-level index as an ordered file, one can develop additional indexes for it, giving rise to the concept of multilevel indexes. A popular indexing scheme called ISAM (Indexed Sequential Access Method) is based on this idea. We discuss multilevel indexes in Section 9.12.2. In Section 9.12.3 we describe B-trees and B^+-trees, which are data structures that are commonly used in DBMSs to implement dynamically changing multilevel indexes. B^+-trees have become a commonly accepted default structure for generating indexes on demand in most relational DBMSs. Section 9.12.4 is devoted to the alternative ways of accessing data based on a combination of multiple keys. In Section 9.12.5, we discuss how other data structures—such as hashing—can be used to construct indexes. We also briefly introduce the concept of logical indexes, which give an additional level of indirection from physical indexes, allowing for the physical index to be flexible and extensible in its organization.

9.12.1 Types of Single-level Ordered Indexes

The idea behind an ordered index access structure is similar to that behind the index used in a textbook, which lists important terms at the end of the book in alphabetical order along with a list of page numbers where the term appears in the book. We can search an index to find a list of *addresses*—page numbers in this case—and use these addresses to locate a term in the textbook by *searching* the specified pages. The alternative, if no other guidance is given, would be to sift slowly through the whole textbook word by word to find the term we are interested in; this corresponds to doing a linear search on a file. Of course, most books do have additional information, such as chapter and section titles, that can help us find a term without having to search through the whole book. However, the index is the only exact indication of where each term occurs in the book.

For a file with a given record structure consisting of several fields (or attributes), an index access structure is usually defined on a single field of a file, called an **indexing field** (or **indexing attribute**).[14] The index typically stores each value of the index field along with a list of pointers to all disk blocks that contain records with that field value. The values in the index are *ordered* so that we can do a binary search on the index. The index file is much smaller than the data file, so searching the index using a binary search is reasonably efficient. Multilevel indexing (see Section 9.12.2) does away with the need for a binary search at the expense of creating indexes to the index itself.

There are several types of ordered indexes. A **primary index** is specified on the *ordering key field* of an ordered file of records. Recall from Section 9.7 that an ordering key field is used to *physically order* the file records on disk, and every record has a *unique value* for that field. If the ordering field is not a key field—that is, if numerous records in the file can have the same value for the ordering field—another type of index, called a **clustering index**, can be used. Notice that a file can have at most one physical ordering field, so it can have at most one primary index or one clustering index, *but not both*. A third type of index, called a **secondary index**, can be specified on any *nonordering* field of a file. A file can have several secondary indexes in addition to its primary access method. In the next three subsections we discuss these three types of single-level indexes.

9.12.1.1 Primary indexes
A **primary index** is an ordered file whose records are of fixed length with two fields. The first field is of the same data type as the ordering key field—called the **primary key**—of the data file, and the second field is a pointer to a disk block (a block address). There is one **index entry** (or **index record**) in the index file for each *block* in the data file. Each index entry has the value of the primary key field

---

14. We will use the terms *field* and *attribute* interchangeably in this chapter.

for the *first* record in a block and a pointer to that block as its two field values. We will refer to the two field values of index entry i as $<K(i), P(i)>$.

To create a primary index on the ordered file shown in Figure 9.7, we use the NAME field as primary key, because that is the ordering key field of the file (assuming that each value of NAME is unique). Each entry in the index has a NAME value and a pointer. The first three index entries are as follows:

$<K(1) = $ (Abbas), $P(1) = $ address of block 1>
$<K(2) = $ (Agarkar), $P(2) = $ address of block 2>
$<K(3) = $ (Akthar), $P(3) = $ address of block 3>

Figure 9.14 illustrates this primary index. The total number of entries in the index is the same as the *number of disk blocks* in the ordered data file. The first record in each block of the data file is called the **anchor record** of the block, or simply the **block anchor**.[15]

Indexes can also be characterized as dense or sparse. A **dense index** has an index entry for *every search key value* (and hence every record) in the data file. A **sparse** (or **nondense**) **index**, on the other hand, has index entries for only some of the search values. A primary index is hence a nondense (sparse) index, since it includes an entry for each disk block of the data file and the keys of its anchor record rather than for every search value (or every record).

The index file for a primary index needs substantially fewer blocks than does the data file, for two reasons. First, there are *fewer index entries* than there are records in the data file. Second, each index entry is typically *smaller in size* than a data record because it has only two fields; consequently, more index entries than data records can fit in one block. A binary search on the index file hence requires fewer block accesses than a binary search on the data file. Referring back to Table 9.2, note that the binary search for an ordered data file required $\log_2 b$ block accesses. But if the primary index file contains b_i blocks, then to locate a record with a search key value requires a binary search of that index and access to the block containing that record: a total of $\log_2 b_i + 1$ accesses.

A record whose primary key value is K lies in the block whose address is $P(i)$, where $K(i) \le K < K(i + 1)$. The ith block in the data file contains all such records because of the physical ordering of the file records on the primary key field. To retrieve a record, given the value K of its primary key field, we do a binary search on the index file to find the appropriate index entry i, and then retrieve the data file block whose address is $P(i)$.[16] Example 1 illustrates the saving in block accesses that is attainable when a primary index is used to search for a record.

EXAMPLE 1: Suppose that we have an ordered file with $r = 30,000$ records stored on a disk with block size $B = 1024$ bytes. File records are of fixed size and are unspanned, with record length $R = 100$ bytes. The blocking factor for the file would be $bfr = \lfloor B/R \rfloor = \lfloor (1024/100) \rfloor = 10$ records per block. The number of blocks needed for the file is $b = \lceil (r/bfr) \rceil = (30,000/10) = 3000$ blocks. A binary search on the data file would need approximately $\lceil \log_2 b = \log_2 3000 \rceil = 12$ block accesses.

Now suppose that the ordering key field of the file is $V = 9$ bytes long, a block pointer is $P = 6$ bytes long, and we have constructed a primary index for the file. The size of each index entry is $R_i = (9 + 6) = 15$ bytes, so the blocking factor for the index is $bfr_i = \lfloor (B/R_i) \rfloor = \lfloor (1024/15) \rfloor = 68$ entries per block. The total number of index entries r_i is equal to the number of blocks in the data file, which is 3000. The number of index blocks is hence $b_i = \lceil (r_i/bfr_i) \rceil = \lceil (3000/68) \rceil = 45$ blocks. To perform a binary search on the index file

---

15. We can use a scheme similar to the one described here, with the last record in each block (rather than the first) as the block anchor. This slightly improves the efficiency of the search algorithm.

16. Notice that the above formula would not be correct if the data file were ordered on a *nonkey field*; in that case the same index value in the block anchor could be repeated in the last records of the previous block.

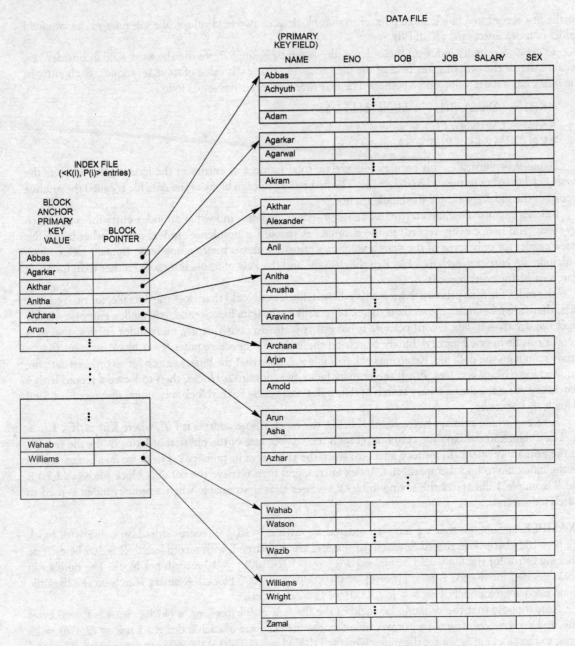

FIGURE 9.14 Primary index on the ordering key field of the file shown in Figure 9.7.

would need $\lceil (\log_2 b_i) \rceil = \lceil (\log_2 45) \rceil = 6$ block accesses. To search for a record using the index, we need one additional block access to the data file for a total of $6 + 1 = 7$ block accesses—an improvement over binary search on the data file, which required 12 block accesses.

A major problem with a primary index—as with any ordered file—is insertion and deletion of records. With a primary index, the problem is compounded because, if we attempt to insert a record in its correct position in the data file, we have to not only move records to make space for the new record but also change some index entries, since moving records will change the anchor records of some blocks. Using an unordered overflow file, as discussed in Section 9.7, can reduce this problem. Another possibility is to use a linked list of overflow records for each block in the data file. This is similar to the method of dealing with overflow records described with hashing in Section 9.8.2. Records within each block and its overflow linked list can be sorted to improve retrieval time. Record deletion is handled using deletion markers.

9.12.1.2   Clustering indexes

If records of a file are physically ordered on a nonkey field—which does not have a distinct value for each record—that field is called the **clustering field**. We can create a different type of index, called a **clustering index**, to speed up retrieval of records that have the same value for the

FIGURE 9.15 A clustering index on the DEPTNUMBER ordering nonkey field of an EMPLOYEE file.

FIGURE 9.16 Clustering index with a separate block cluster for each group of records that share the same value for the clustering field.

clustering field. This differs from a primary index, which requires that the ordering field of the data file have a *distinct value* for each record.

A clustering index is also an ordered file with two fields; the first field is of the same type as the clustering field of the data file, and the second field is a block pointer. There is one entry in the clustering index for each *distinct value* of the clustering field, containing the value and a pointer to the *first block* in the data file that has a record with that value for its clustering field. Figure 9.15 shows an example. Notice that record insertion and deletion still cause problems, because the data records are physically ordered. To alleviate the problem of insertion, it is common to reserve a whole block (or a cluster of contiguous blocks) for *each value* of the clustering field; all records with that value are placed in the block (or block cluster). This makes insertion and deletion relatively straightforward. Figure 9.16 shows this scheme.

A clustering index is another example of a *nondense* index, because it has an entry for every *distinct value* of the indexing field which is a nonkey by definition and hence has duplicate values rather than for every record in the file. There is some similarity between Figures 9.14 to 9.16, on the one hand, and Figure 9.11, on the other. An index is somewhat similar to the directory structures used for extendible hashing, described in Section 9.8.3. Both are searched to find a pointer to the data block containing the desired record. A main difference is that an index search uses the values of the search field itself, whereas a hash directory search uses the hash value that is calculated by applying the hash function to the search field.

9.12.1.3 Secondary indexes

A **secondary index** provides a secondary means of accessing a file for which some primary access already exists. The secondary index may be on a field which is a candidate key and has a unique value in every record, or a nonkey with duplicate values. The index is an ordered file with two fields. The first field is of the same data type as some *nonordering field* of the data file that is an **indexing field**. The second field is either a *block* pointer or a *record* pointer. There can be *many* secondary indexes (and hence, indexing fields) for the same file.

We first consider a secondary index access structure on a key field that has a *distinct value* for every record. Such a field is sometimes called a **secondary key**. In this case there is one index entry for *each record* in the data file, which contains the value of the secondary key for the record and a pointer either to the block in which the record is stored or to the record itself. Hence, such an index is **dense**.

We again refer to the two field values of index entry i as $<K(i), P(i)>$. The entries are **ordered** by value of $K(i)$, so we can perform a binary search. Because the records of the data file are *not* physically ordered by values of the secondary key field, we *cannot* use block anchors. That is why an index entry is created for each record in the data file, rather than for each block, as in the case of a primary index. Figure 9.17 illustrates a secondary index in which the pointers $P(i)$ in the index entries are *block pointers*, not record pointers. Once the appropriate block is transferred to main memory, a search for the desired record within the block can be carried out.

A secondary index usually needs more storage space and longer search time than does a primary index, because of its larger number of entries. However, the *improvement* in search time for an arbitrary record is much greater for a secondary index than for a primary index, since we would have to do a *linear search* on the data file if the secondary index did not exist. For a primary index, we could still use a binary search on the main file, even if the index did not exist. Example 2 illustrates the improvement in number of blocks accessed.

EXAMPLE 2: Consider the file of Example 1 with $r = 30,000$ fixed-length records of size $R = 100$ bytes stored on a disk with block size $B = 1024$ bytes. The file has $b = 3000$ blocks, as calculated in Example 1. To do a linear search on the file, we would require $b/2 = 3000/2 = 1500$ block accesses on the average. Suppose that we construct a secondary index on a nonordering key field of the file that is $V = 9$ bytes long. As in Example

1, a block pointer is $P = 6$ bytes long, so each index entry is $R_i = (9 + 6) = 15$ bytes, and the blocking factor for the index is $bfr_i = \lfloor (B/R_i) \rfloor = \lfloor (1024/15) \rfloor = 68$ entries per block. In a dense secondary index such as this, the total number of index entries r_i is equal to the *number of records* in the data file, which is 30,000. The number of blocks needed for the index is hence $b_i = \lceil (r_i/bfr_i) \rceil = \lceil (30,000/68) \rceil = 442$ blocks.

A binary search on this secondary index needs $\lceil (\log_2 b_i) \rceil = \lceil (\log_2 442) \rceil = 9$ block accesses. To search for a record using the index, we need an additional block access to the data file for a total of $9 + 1 = 10$ block accesses—a vast improvement over the 1500 block accesses needed on the average for a linear search, but slightly worse than the seven block accesses required for the primary index.

FIGURE 9.17 A dense secondary index (with block pointers) on a nonordering key field of a file.

We can also create a secondary index on a *nonkey field* of a file. In this case, numerous records in the data file can have the same value for the indexing field. There are several options for implementing such an index:

- Option 1 is to include several index entries with the same $K(i)$ value—one for each record. This would be a dense index.

- Option 2 is to have variable-length records for the index entries, with a repeating field for the pointer. We keep a list of pointers $<P(i,1), \ldots, P(i,k)>$ in the index entry for $K(i)$—one pointer to each block that contains a record whose indexing field value equals $K(i)$. In either option 1 or option 2, the binary search algorithm on the index must be modified appropriately.

- Option 3, which is more commonly used, is to keep the index entries themselves at a fixed length and have a single entry for each *index field value* but to create an extra level of indirection to handle the multiple pointers. In this nondense scheme, the pointer $P(i)$ in index entry $<K(i), P(i)>$ points to a *block of record pointers*; each record pointer in that block points to one of the data file records with value $K(i)$ for the indexing field. If some value $K(i)$ occurs in too many records, so that their record pointers cannot fit in a single disk block, a cluster or linked list of blocks is used. This technique is illustrated in Figure 9.18. Retrieval via the index requires one or more additional block accesses because of the extra level, but the algorithms for searching the index and (more importantly) for inserting of new records in the data file are straightforward. In addition, retrievals on complex selection conditions may be handled by referring to the record pointers, without having to retrieve many unnecessary file records (see Exercise 9.61).

Notice that a secondary index provides a **logical ordering** on the records by the indexing field. If we access the records in order of the entries in the secondary index, we get them in order of the indexing field.

9.12.1.4   Summary   To conclude this section, we summarize the discussion on index types in two tables. Table 9.4 shows the index field characteristics of each type of ordered single-level index discussed—primary, clustering, and secondary. Table 9.5 summarizes the properties of each type of index by comparing the number of index entries and specifying which indexes are dense and which use block anchors of the data file.

9.12.2   Multilevel Indexes

The indexing schemes we have described thus far involve an ordered index file. A binary search is applied to the index to locate pointers to a disk block or to a record (or records) in the file having a specific index field value. A binary search requires approximately $(\log_2 b_i)$ block accesses for an index with b_i blocks, because each step of the algorithm reduces the part of the index file that we continue to search by a factor of 2. This is why we take the log function to the base 2. The idea behind a **multilevel index** is to reduce the part of the index that we continue to search by bfr_i, the blocking factor for the index, which is larger than 2. Hence, the search space is reduced much faster. The value bfr_i is called the **fan-out** of the multilevel index, and we will refer to it by the symbol **fo**. Searching a multilevel index requires approximately $(\log_{fo} b_i)$ block accesses, which is a smaller number than for binary search if the fan-out is larger than 2.

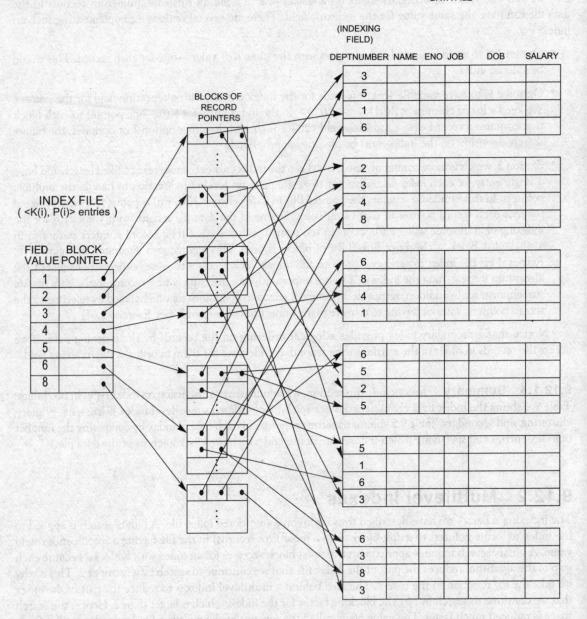

FIGURE 9.18 A secondary index (with record pointers) on a nonkey field implemented using one level of indirection so that index entries are of fixed length and have unique field values.

A multilevel index considers the index file, which we will now refer to as the **first** (or **base**) **level** of a multilevel index, as an *ordered file* with a *distinct value* for each K(i). Hence we can create a primary index for the first level; this index to the first level is called the **second level** of the multilevel index. Because the second level is a primary index, we can use block anchors so that the second level has one entry for *each block* of the first level. The blocking factor *bfr_i* for the second level—and for all subsequent levels—is the same as that for the first-level index, because all index entries are the same size; each has one field value and one block address. If the first level has r_1 entries, and the blocking factor—which is also the fan-out—for the index is $bfr_i = $ fo, then the first level needs $\lceil (r_1/\text{fo}) \rceil$ blocks, which is therefore the number of entries r_2 needed at the second level of the index.

TABLE 9.4 TYPES OF INDEXES BASED ON THE PROPERTIES OF THE INDEXING FIELD

	INDEX FIELD USED FOR ORDERING THE FILE	INDEX FIELD NOT USED FOR ORDERING THE FILE
Indexing field is key	Primary index	Secondary index (Key)
Indexing field is nonkey	Clustering index	Secondary index (NonKey)

We can repeat this process for the second level. The **third level**, which is a primary index for the second level, has an entry for each second-level block, so the number of third-level entries is $r_3 = \lceil (r_2/\text{fo}) \rceil$. Notice that we require a second level only if the first level needs more than one block of disk storage, and, similarly, we require a third level only if the second level needs more than one block. We can repeat the preceding process until all the entries of some index level t fit in a single block. This block at the tth level is called the top index level.[17] Each level reduces the number of entries at the previous level by a factor of fo—the index fan-out—so we can use the formula $1 \leq (r_1/((\text{fo})^t))$ to calculate t. Hence, a multilevel index with r_1 first-level entries will have approximately t levels, where $t = \lceil (\log_{\text{fo}}(r_1)) \rceil$.

The multilevel scheme described here can be used on any type of index, whether it is primary, clustering, or secondary—as long as the first-level index has *distinct values* for $K(i)$ and *fixed-length entries*. Figure 9.19 shows a multilevel index built over a primary index. Example 3 illustrates the improvement in number of blocks accessed when a multilevel index is used to search for a record.

TABLE 9.5 PROPERTIES OF INDEX TYPES

TYPE OF INDEX	NUMBER OF (FIRST-LEVEL) INDEX ENTRIES	DENSE OR NONDENSE	BLOCK ANCHORING ON THE DATA FILE
Primary	Number of blocks in data file	Nondense	Yes
Clustering	Number of distinct index field values	Nondense	Yes/no[a]
Secondary (key)	Number of records in data file	Dense	No
Secondary (nonkey)	Number of records[b] or Number of distinct index field values[c]	Dense or Nondense	No

[a]Yes if every distinct value of the ordering field starts a new block; no otherwise.
[b]For option 1.
[c]For options 2 and 3.

---

17. The numbering scheme for index levels used here is the reverse of the way levels are commonly defined for tree data structures. In tree data structures, t is referred to as level 0 (zero), $t - 1$ is level 1, etc.

FIGURE 9.19 A two-level primary index resembling ISAM (Indexed Sequential Access Method) organization.

EXAMPLE 3: Suppose that the dense secondary index of Example 2 is converted into a multilevel index. We calculated the index blocking factor $bfr_i = 68$ index entries per block, which is also the fan-out fo for the multilevel index; the number of first-level blocks $b_1 = 442$ blocks was also calculated. The number of second-level blocks will be $b_2 = \lceil (b_1/fo) \rceil = \lceil (442/68) \rceil = 7$ blocks, and the number of third-level blocks will be $b_3 = \lceil (b_2/fo) \rceil = \lceil (7/68) \rceil = 1$ block. Hence, the third level is the top level of the index, and $t = 3$. To access a record by searching the multilevel index, we must access one block at each level plus one block from the data file, so we need $t + 1 = 3 + 1 = 4$ block accesses. Compare this to Example 2, where 10 block accesses were needed when a single-level index and binary search were used.

Notice that we could also have a multilevel primary index, which would be nondense. Exercise 9.56(c) illustrates this case, where we *must* access the data block from the file before we can determine whether the record being searched for is in the file. For a dense index, this can be determined by accessing the first index level (without having to access a data block), since there is an index entry for *every* record in the file.

A common file organization used in business data processing is an ordered file with a multilevel primary index on its ordering key field. Such an organization is called an **indexed sequential file** and was used in a large number of early IBM systems. Insertion is handled by some form of overflow file that is merged periodically with the data file. The index is re-created during file reorganization. IBM's **ISAM** organization incorporates a twolevel index that is closely related to the organization of the disk. The first level is a cylinder index, which has the key value of an anchor record for each cylinder of a disk pack and a pointer to the track index for the cylinder. The track index has the key value of an anchor record for each track in the cylinder and a pointer to the track. The track can then be searched sequentially for the desired record or block.

Algorithm 9.4 outlines the search procedure for a record in a data file that uses a nondense multilevel primary index with t levels. We refer to entry i at level j of the index as $<K_j(i), P_j(i)>$, and we search for a record whose primary key value is K. We assume that any overflow records are ignored. If the record is in the file, there must be some entry at level 1 with $K_1(i) \leq K < K_1(i + 1)$ and the record will be in the block of the data file whose address is $P_1(i)$. Exercise 9.61 discusses modifying the search algorithm for other types of indexes.

Algorithm 9.4: Searching a nondense multilevel primary index with t levels.

```
p ← address of top level block of index;
for j ← t step − 1 to 1 do
    begin
    read the index block (at jth index level) whose address is p;
    search block p for entry i such that Kj(i) # K, Kj(i + 1) (if Kj(i)
    is the last entry in the block, it is sufficient to satisfy Kj(i)
    # K);
        p ← Pj(i) (* picks appropriate pointer at jth index level *)
    end;
    read the data file block whose address is p;
    search block p for record with key = K;
```

As we have seen, a multilevel index reduces the number of blocks accessed when searching for a record, given its indexing field value. We are still faced with the problems of dealing with index insertions and deletions, because all index levels are *physically ordered files*. To retain the benefits of using multilevel indexing while reducing index insertion and deletion problems, designers adopted a multilevel index that leaves some space in each of its blocks for inserting new entries. This is called a **dynamic multilevel index** and is often implemented by using data structures called B-trees and B$^+$-trees, which we describe in the next section.

9.12.3 Dynamic Multilevel Indexes using B-trees and B$^+$-trees

B-trees and B$^+$-trees are special cases of the well-known tree data structure. We introduce very briefly the terminology used in discussing tree data structures. A **tree** is formed of **nodes**. Each node in the tree, except for a special node called the **root**, has one **parent** node and several—zero or more—**child** nodes. The root node has no parent. A node that does not have any child nodes is called a **leaf** node; a nonleaf node is called an **internal** node. The **level** of a node is always one more than the level of its parent, with the level of the root node being zero.[18] A **subtree** of a node consists of that node and all its **descendant** nodes—its child nodes,

---

18. This standard definition of the level of a tree node, which we use throughout Section 9.12.3, is different from the one we gave for multilevel indexes in Section 9.12.2.

the child nodes of its child nodes, and so on. A precise recursive definition of a subtree is that it consists of a node n and the subtrees of all the child nodes of n. Figure 9.20 illustrates a tree data structure. In this figure the root node is A, and its child nodes are B, C, and D. Nodes E, J, C, G, H, and K are leaf nodes.

Usually, we display a tree with the root node at the top, as shown in Figure 9.20. One way to implement a tree is to have as many pointers in each node as there are child nodes of that node. In some cases, a parent pointer is also stored in each node. In addition to pointers, a node usually contains some kind of stored information. When a multilevel index is implemented as a tree structure, this information includes the values of the file's indexing field that are used to guide the search for a particular record.

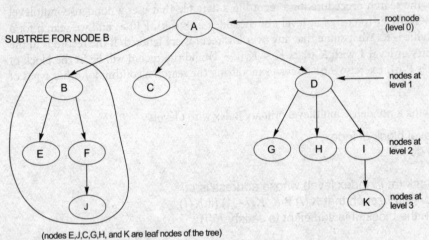

(nodes E,J,C,G,H, and K are leaf nodes of the tree)

FIGURE 9.20 A tree data structure that shows an unbalanced tree.

In Section 9.12.3.1, we introduce search trees and then discuss B-trees, which can be used as dynamic multilevel indexes to guide the search for records in a data file. B-tree nodes are kept between 50 and 100 percent full, and pointers to the data blocks are stored in both internal nodes and leaf nodes of the B-tree structure. In Section 9.12.3.2 we discuss B+-trees, a variation of B-trees in which pointers to the data blocks of a file are stored only in leaf nodes; this can lead to fewer levels and higher-capacity indexes.

9.12.3.1 Search trees and B-trees

A search tree is a special type of tree that is used to guide the search for a record, given the value of one of the record's fields. The multilevel indexes discussed in Section 9.12.2 can be thought of as a variation of a search tree; each node in the multilevel index can have as many as fo pointers and fo key values, where fo is the index fan-out. The index field values in each node guide us to the next node, until we reach the data file block that contains the required records. By following a pointer, we restrict our search at each level to a subtree of the search tree and ignore all nodes not in this subtree.

Search Trees. A search tree is slightly different from a multilevel index. A **search tree** of order p is a tree such that each node contains *at most* $p - 1$ search values and p pointers in the order $<P_1, K_1, P_2, K_2, \ldots, P_{q-1}, K_{q-1}, P_q>$, where $q \leq p$; each P_i is a pointer to a child node (or a null pointer); and each K_i is a search value from some ordered set of values. All search values are assumed to be unique.[19] Figure 9.21 illustrates a node in a search tree. Two constraints must hold at all times on the search tree:

---

19. This restriction can be relaxed. If the index is on a nonkey field, duplicate search values may exist and the node structure and the navigation rules for the tree may be modified.

1. Within each node, $K_1 < K_2 < ... < K_{q-1}$.
2. For all values X in the subtree pointed at by P_i, we have $K_{i-1} < X < K_i$ for $1 < i < q$; $X < K_i$ for $i = 1$; and $K_{i-1} < X$ for $i = q$ (see Figure 9.21).

FIGURE 9.21 A node in a search tree with pointers to subtrees below it.

Whenever we search for a value X, we follow the appropriate pointer P_i according to the formulas in condition 2 above. Figure 9.22 illustrates a search tree of order $p = 3$ and integer search values. Notice that some of the pointers P_i in a node may be null pointers.

We can use a search tree as a mechanism to search for records stored in a disk file. The values in the tree can be the values of one of the fields of the file, called the **search field** (which is the same as the index field if a multilevel index guides the search). Each key value in the tree is associated with a pointer to the record in the data file having that value. Alternatively, the pointer could be to the disk block containing that record. The search tree itself can be stored on disk by assigning each tree node to a disk block. When a new record is inserted, we must update the search tree by inserting an entry in the tree containing the search field value of the new record and a pointer to the new record.

Algorithms are necessary for inserting and deleting search values into and from the search tree while maintaining the preceding two constraints. In general, these algorithms do not guarantee that a search tree is **balanced**, meaning that all of its leaf nodes are at the same level.[20] The tree in Figure 9.20 is not balanced because it has leaf nodes at levels 1, 2, and 3. Keeping a search tree balanced is important because it guarantees that no nodes will be at very high levels and hence require many block accesses during a tree search. Keeping the tree balanced yields a uniform search speed regardless of the value of the search key. Another problem with search trees is that record deletion may leave some nodes in the tree nearly empty, thus wasting storage space and increasing the number of levels. The B-tree addresses both of these problems by specifying additional constraints on the search tree.

B-Trees.   The B-tree has additional constraints that ensure that the tree is always balanced and that the space wasted by deletion, if any, never becomes excessive. The algorithms for insertion and deletion, though, become more complex in order to maintain these constraints. Nonetheless, most insertions and deletions are simple processes; they become complicated only under special circumstances—namely, whenever we attempt an insertion into a node that is already full or a deletion from a node that makes it less than half full. More formally, a **B-tree** of **order** p, when used as an access structure on a *key field* to search for records in a data file, can be defined as follows:

---

20. The definition of *balanced* is different for binary trees. Balanced binary trees are known as AVL trees.

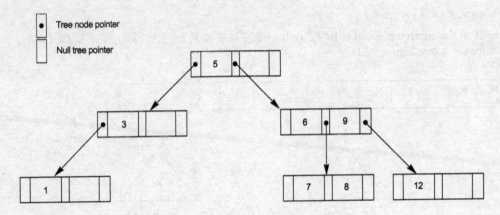

FIGURE 9.22 A search tree of order $p = 3$.

1. Each internal node in the B-tree (Figure 9.23a) is of the form

   $$<P_1, <K_1, Pr_1>, P_2, <K_2, Pr_2>, \ldots, <K_{q-1}, Pr_{q-1}>, P_q>$$

   where $q \leq p$. Each P_i is a **tree pointer**—a pointer to another node in the B-tree. Each Pr_i is a **data pointer** [21]—a pointer to the record whose search key field value is equal to K_i (or to the data file block containing that record).

2. Within each node, $K_1 < K_2 < \ldots < K_{q-1}$.

3. For all search key field values X in the subtree pointed at by P_i (the ith subtree, see Figure 9.23a), we have:

   $K_{i-1} < X < K_i$ for $1 < i < q$; $X < K_i$ for $i = 1$; and $K_{i-1} < X$ for $i = q$.

4. Each node has at most p tree pointers.

5. Each node, except the root and leaf nodes, has at least $\lceil (p/2) \rceil$ tree pointers. The root node has at least two tree pointers unless it is the only node in the tree.

6. A node with q tree pointers, $q \leq p$, has $q - 1$ search key field values (and hence has $q - 1$ data pointers).

7. All leaf nodes are at the same level. Leaf nodes have the same structure as internal nodes except that all of their *tree pointers* P_i are null.

Figure 9.23b illustrates a B-tree of order $p = 3$. Notice that all search values K in the B-tree are unique because we assumed that the tree is used as an access structure on a key field. If we use a B-tree *on a nonkey field*, we must change the definition of the file pointers Pr_i to point to a block—or cluster of blocks—that contain the pointers to the file records. This extra level of indirection is similar to Option 3, discussed in Section 9.12.1.3, for secondary indexes.

A B-tree starts with a single root node (which is also a leaf node) at level 0 (zero). Once the root node is full with $p - 1$ search key values and we attempt to insert another entry in the tree, the root node splits into two nodes at level 1. Only the middle value is kept in the root node, and the rest of the values are split evenly between the other two nodes. When a nonroot node is full and a new entry is inserted into it, that node is split into two nodes at the same level, and the middle entry is moved to the parent node along with two pointers

---

21. A data pointer is either a block address, or a record address; the latter is essentially a block address and a record offset within the block.

to the new split nodes. If the parent node is full, it is also split. Splitting can propagate all the way to the root node, creating a new level if the root is split. We do not discuss algorithms for B-trees in detail here; rather, we outline search and insertion procedures for B+-trees in the next section.

FIGURE 9.23 B-tree structures. (a) A node in a B-tree with $q - 1$ search values. (b) A B-tree of order $p = 3$. The values were inserted in the order 8, 5, 1, 7, 3, 12, 9, 6.

If deletion of a value causes a node to be less than half full, it is combined with its neighboring nodes, and this can also propagate all the way to the root. Hence, deletion can reduce the number of tree levels. It has been shown by analysis and simulation that, after numerous random insertions and deletions on a B-tree, the nodes are approximately 69 percent full when the number of values in the tree stabilizes. This is also true of B+- trees. If this happens, node splitting and combining will occur only rarely, so insertion and deletion become quite efficient. If the number of values grows, the tree will expand without a problem—although splitting of nodes may occur, so some insertions will take more time. Example 4 illustrates how we calculate the order p of a B-tree stored on disk.

EXAMPLE 4: Suppose the search field is $V = 9$ bytes long, the disk block size is $B = 512$ bytes, a record (data) pointer is $P_r = 7$ bytes, and a block pointer is $P = 6$ bytes. Each B-tree node can have *at most* p tree pointers, $p - 1$ data pointers, and $p - 1$ search key field values (see Figure 9.23a). These must fit into a single disk block if each B-tree node is to correspond to a disk block. Hence, we must have:

$$(p * P) + ((p - 1) * (P_r + V)) \leq B$$
$$(p * 6) + ((p - 1) * (7 + 9)) \leq 512$$
$$(22 * p) \leq 528$$

We can choose p to be a large value that satisfies the above inequality, which gives $p = 23$ ($p = 24$ is not chosen because of the reasons given next).

In general, a B-tree node may contain additional information needed by the algorithms that manipulate the tree, such as the number of entries q in the node and a pointer to the parent node. Hence, before we do the preceding calculation for p, we should reduce the block size by the amount of space needed for all such information. Next, we illustrate how to calculate the number of blocks and levels for a B-tree.

EXAMPLE 5: Suppose that the search field of Example 4 is a nonordering key field, and we construct a B-tree on this field. Assume that each node of the B-tree is 69 percent full. Each node, on the average, will have $p * 0.69 = 23 * 0.69$ or approximately 16 pointers and, hence, 15 search key field values. The **average fan-out** $fo = 16$. We can start at the root and see how many values and pointers can exist, on the average, at each subsequent level:

Root:	1 node	15 entries	16 pointers
Level 1:	16 nodes	240 entries	256 pointers
Level 2:	256 nodes	3840 entries	4096 pointers
Level 3:	4096 nodes	61,440 entries	

At each level, we calculated the number of entries by multiplying the total number of pointers at the previous level by 15, the average number of entries in each node. Hence, for the given block size, pointer size, and search key field size, a two-level B-tree holds $3840 + 240 + 15 = 4095$ entries on the average; a three-level B-tree holds 65,535 entries on the average.

B-trees are sometimes used as primary file organizations. In this case, whole records are stored within the B-tree nodes rather than just the <search key, record pointer> entries. This works well for files with a relatively *small number of records*, and a *small record size*. Otherwise, the fan-out and the number of levels become too great to permit efficient access.

In summary, B-trees provide a multilevel access structure that is a balanced tree structure in which each node is at least half full. Each node in a B-tree of order p can have at most $p - 1$ search values.

9.12.3.2 B⁺-Trees

Most implementations of a dynamic multilevel index use a variation of the B-tree data structure called a **B⁺-tree**. In a B-tree, every value of the search field appears once at some level in the tree, along with a data pointer. In a B⁺-tree, data pointers are stored *only at the leaf nodes* of the tree; hence, the structure of leaf nodes differs from the structure of internal nodes. The leaf nodes have an entry for *every* value of the search field, along with a data pointer to the record (or to the block that contains this record) if the search field is a key field. For a nonkey search field, the pointer points to a block containing pointers to the data file records, creating an extra level of indirection.

The leaf nodes of the B⁺-tree are usually linked together to provide ordered access on the search field to the records. These leaf nodes are similar to the first (base) level of an index. Internal nodes of the B⁺-tree correspond to the other levels of a multilevel index. Some search field values from the leaf nodes are *repeated* in the internal nodes of the B⁺-tree to guide the search. The structure of the *internal nodes* of a B⁺-tree of order p (Figure 9.24a) is as follows:

1. Each internal node is of the form

   $<P_1, K_1, P_2, K_2, \ldots, P_{q-1}, K_{q-1}, P_q>$

   where $q \leq p$ and each P_i is a **tree pointer**.

2. Within each internal node, $K_1 < K_2 < \ldots < K_{q-1}$.

3. For all search field values X in the subtree pointed at by P_i, we have $K_{i-1} < X \leq K_i$ for $1 < i < q$; $X \leq K_i$ for $i = 1$; and $K_{i-1} < X$ for $i = q$ (see Figure 9.24a).[22]

4. Each internal node has at most p tree pointers.

---

22. Our definition follows Knuth (1973). One can define a B⁺-tree differently by exchanging the $<$ and $\leq$ symbols ($K_{i-1} \leq X < K_i$; $X < K_1$; $K_{q-1} \leq X$), but the principles remain the same.

5. Each internal node, except the root, has at least $\lceil (p/2) \rceil$ tree pointers. The root node has at least two tree pointers if it is an internal node.

6. An internal node with q pointers, $q \le p$, has $q - 1$ search field values.

The structure of the leaf nodes of a B+-tree of order p (Figure 9.24b) is as follows:

1. Each leaf node is of the form

   $<<K_1, Pr_1>, <K_2, Pr_2>, ..., <K_{q-1}, Pr_{q-1}>, P_{next}>$

   where $q \le p$, each Pr_i is a data pointer, and P_{next} points to the next *leaf node* of the B$^+$-tree.

2. Within each leaf node, $K_1 < K_2 < ... < K_{q-1}, q \le p$.

3. Each Pr_i is a **data pointer** that points to the record whose search field value is K_i or to a file block containing the record (or to a block of record pointers that point to records whose search field value is K_i if the search field is not a key).

4. Each leaf node has at least $\lceil (p/2) \rceil$ values.

5. All leaf nodes are at the same level.

(a)

(b)

FIGURE 9.24 The nodes of a B$^+$-tree. (a) Internal node of a B$^+$-tree with $q-1$ search values. (b) Leaf node of a B$^+$-tree with $q-1$ search values and $q-1$ data pointers.

The pointers in internal nodes are *tree pointers* to blocks that are tree nodes, whereas the pointers in leaf nodes are *data pointers* to the data file records or blocks—except for the P_{next} pointer, which is a tree pointer to the next leaf node. By starting at the leftmost leaf node, it is possible to traverse leaf nodes as a linked list, using the P_{next} pointers. This provides ordered access to the data records on the indexing field. A $P_{previous}$ pointer can also be included. For a B$^+$-tree on a nonkey field, an extra level of indirection is needed similar to the one shown in Figure 9.18, so the Pr pointers are block pointers to blocks that contain a set of record pointers to the actual records in the data file, as discussed in Option 3 of Section 9.12.1.3.

Because entries in the *internal nodes* of a B$^+$-tree include search values and tree pointers without any data pointers, more entries can be packed into an internal node of a B$^+$-tree than for a similar B-tree. Thus, for the same block (node) size, the order p will be larger for the B$^+$-tree than for the B-tree, as we illustrate in

Example 6. This can lead to fewer B$^+$-tree levels, improving search time. Because the structures for internal and for leaf nodes of a B$^+$-tree are different, the order p can be different. We will use p to denote the order for *internal nodes* and p_{leaf} to denote the order for *leaf nodes*, which we define as being the maximum number of data pointers in a leaf node.

EXAMPLE 6: To calculate the order p of a B$^+$-tree, suppose that the search key field is $V = 9$ bytes long, the block size is $B = 512$ bytes, a record pointer is $P_r = 7$ bytes, and a block pointer is $P = 6$ bytes, as in Example 4. An internal node of the B$^+$-tree can have up to p tree pointers and $p - 1$ search field values; these must fit into a single block. Hence, we have:

$$(p * P) + ((p - 1) * V) \leq B$$
$$(p * 6) + ((p - 1) * 9) \leq 512$$
$$(15 * p) \leq 521$$

We can choose p to be the largest value satisfying the above inequality, which gives $p = 34$. This is larger than the value of 23 for the B-tree, resulting in a larger fan-out and more entries in each internal node of a B$^+$-tree than in the corresponding B-tree. The leaf nodes of the B$^+$-tree will have the same number of values and pointers, except that the pointers are data pointers and a next pointer. Hence, the order p_{leaf} for the leaf nodes can be calculated as follows:

$$(p_{leaf} * (P_r + V)) + P \leq B$$
$$(p_{leaf} * (7 + 9)) + 6 \leq 512$$
$$(16 * p_{leaf}) \leq 506$$

It follows that each leaf node can hold up to $p_{leaf} = 31$ key value/data pointer combinations, assuming that the data pointers are record pointers.

As with the B-tree, we may need additional information—to implement the insertion and deletion algorithms—in each node. This information can include the type of node (internal or leaf), the number of current entries q in the node, and pointers to the parent and sibling nodes. Hence, before we do the above calculations for p and p_{leaf}, we should reduce the block size by the amount of space needed for all such information. The next example illustrates how we can calculate the number of entries in a B$^+$-tree.

EXAMPLE 7: Suppose that we construct a B$^+$-tree on the field of Example 6. To calculate the approximate number of entries of the B$^+$-tree, we assume that each node is 69 percent full. On the average, each internal node will have 34 * 0.69 or approximately 23 pointers, and hence 22 values. Each leaf node, on the average, will hold 0.69 * p_{leaf} = 0.69 * 31 or approximately 21 data record pointers. A B$^+$-tree will have the following average number of entries at each level:

Root:	1 node	22 entries	23 pointers
Level 1:	23 nodes	506 entries	529 pointers
Level 2:	529 nodes	11,638 entries	12,167 pointers
Leaf level:	12,167 nodes	255,507 record pointers	

For the block size, pointer size, and search field size given above, a three-level B$^+$-tree holds up to 255,507 record pointers, on the average. Compare this to the 65,535 entries for the corresponding B-tree in Example 5.

Search, Insertion, and Deletion with B$^+$-Trees.
Algorithm 9.5 outlines the procedure using the B$^+$-tree as access structure to search for a record. Algorithm 9.6 illustrates the procedure for inserting a record in a file with a B$^+$-tree access structure. These algorithms assume the existence of a key search field, and they must be modified appropriately for the case of a B$^+$-tree on a nonkey field. We now illustrate insertion and deletion with an example.

Algorithm 9.5: Searching for a record with search key field value K, using a B⁺-tree.

```
n ← block containing root node of B⁺-tree;
read block n;
while (n is not a leaf node of the B+-tree) do
    begin
        q ← number of tree pointers in node n;
        if K # n.K₁ (*n.Kᵢ refers to the iᵗʰ search field value in node n*)
            then n ← n.P₁ (*n.Pᵢ refers to the iᵗʰ tree pointer in node n*)
            else if K > n.K_{q-1}
                then n ← n.P_q
                else begin
                search node n for an entry i such that n.K_{i-1} < K # n.Kᵢ;
                n ← n.Pᵢ
                end;
        read block n
        end;
search block n for entry (Kᵢ, Prᵢ) with K = Kᵢ; (* search leaf node *)
if found
    then read data file block with address Prᵢ and retrieve record
        else record with search field value K is not in the data file;
```

Algorithm 9.6: Inserting a record with search key field value K in a B⁺-tree of order p.

```
n ← block containing root node of B⁺-tree;
read block n; set stack S to empty;
while (n is not a leaf node of the B⁺-tree) do
    begin
        push address of n on stack S;
(*stack S holds parent nodes that are needed in case of split*)
        q ← number of tree pointers in node n;
        if K # n.K₁ (*n.Kᵢ refers to the iᵗʰ search field value in node n*)
        then n ← n.P₁ (*n.Pi refers to the iᵗʰ tree pointer in node n*)
        else if K > n.K_{q-1}
                then n ← n.P_q
                else begin
                search node n for an entry i such that n.K_{i-1} < K # n.Kᵢ;
                n ← n.Pᵢ
                end;
read block n
        end;
search block n for entry (Kᵢ,Prᵢ) with K = Kᵢ; (*search leaf node n*)
if found
    then record already in file—cannot insert
    else (*insert entry in B⁺-tree to point to record*)
    begin
    create entry (K,Pr) where Pr points to the new record;
    if leaf node n is not full
```

then insert entry (K, Pr) in correct position in leaf node n
else
begin (*leaf node n is full with p_{leaf} record pointers—is split*)
copy n to temp (*temp is an oversize leaf node to hold extra
entry*);
insert entry (K, Pr) in temp in correct position;
  (*temp now holds pleaf + 1 entries of the form (K_i, Pr_i)*)
new ← a new empty leaf node for the tree; new P_{next} ← n.P_{next};
j ← $\lceil (p_{leaf} 1)/2 \rceil$;
n ← first j entries in temp (up to entry (K_j, Pr_j)); n.P_{next} ← new;
new ← remaining entries in temp; K ← K_j;
(*now we must move (K,new) and insert in parent internal node
  —however, if parent is full, split may propagate*)
finished ← false;
repeat
if stack S is empty
    then (*no parent node—new root node is created for the tree*)
    begin
    root ← a new empty internal node for the tree;
    root ← <n, K, new>; finished ← true;
end
else
    begin
n ← pop stack S;
if internal node n is not full
    then
    begin (*parent node not full—no split*)
     insert (K, new) in correct position in internal node n;
    finished ← true
end
else
        begin (*internal node n is full with p tree pointers—is split*)
copy n to temp (*temp is an oversize internal node*);
insert (K,new) in temp in correct position;
    (*temp now has p+1 tree pointers*)
new ← a new empty internal node for the tree;
j ← $\lfloor ((p+1)/2) \rfloor$;
n ← entries up to tree pointer Pj in temp;
        (*n contains $<P_1, K_1, P_2, K_2, ..., P_{j-1}, K_{j-1}, Pj>$*)
new ← entries from tree pointer P_{j+1} in temp;
        (*new contains $< P_{j+1}, K_{j+1}, ..., K_{p-1}, P_p, K_p, P_{p+1} >$*)
K ← K_j
        (*now we must move (K,new) and insert in parent internal node*)
    end
  end
until finished
  end;
end;

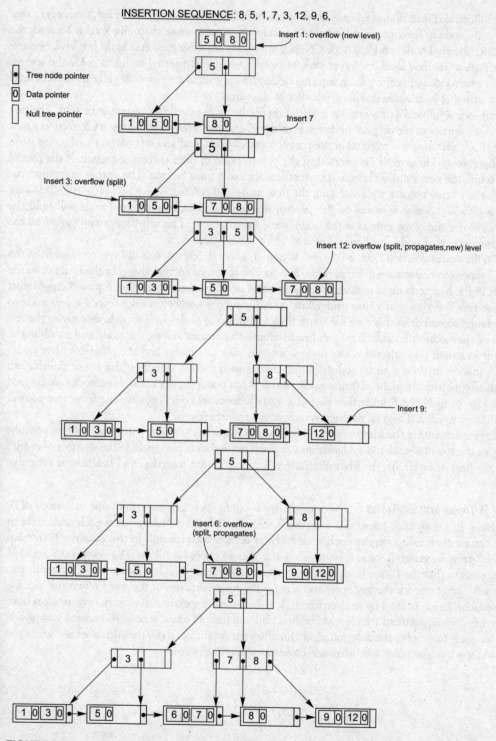

FIGURE 9.25 An example of insertion in a B+-tree with $p = 3$ and $p_{leaf} = 2$.

Figure 9.25 illustrates insertion of records in a B^+-tree of order $p = 3$ and $p_{leaf} = 2$. First, we observe that the root is the only node in the tree, so it is also a leaf node. As soon as more than one level is created, the tree is divided into internal nodes and leaf nodes. Notice that *every key value must exist at the leaf level*, because all data pointers are at the leaf level. However, only some values exist in internal nodes to guide the search. Notice also that every value appearing in an internal node also appears *as the rightmost value* in the leaf level of the subtree pointed at by the tree pointer to the left of the value.

When a *leaf node* is full and a new entry is inserted there, the node **overflows** and must be split. The first $j = \lceil ((p_{leaf} + 1)/2) \rceil$ entries in the original node are kept there, and the remaining entries are moved to a new leaf node. The jth search value is replicated in the parent internal node, and an extra pointer to the new node is created in the parent. These must be inserted in the parent node in their correct sequence. If the parent internal node is full, the new value will cause it to overflow also, so it must be split. The entries in the internal node up to P_j—the jth tree pointer after inserting the new value and pointer, where $j = \lfloor ((p + 1)/2) \rfloor$—are kept, while the jth search value is *moved* to the parent, not replicated. A new internal node will hold the entries from P_{j+1} to the end of the entries in the node (see Algorithm 9.6). This splitting can propagate all the way up to create a new root node and hence a new level for the B^+-tree.

Figure 9.26 illustrates deletion from a B^+-tree. When an entry is deleted, it is always removed from the leaf level. If it happens to occur in an internal node, it must also be removed from there. In the latter case, the value to its left in the leaf node must replace it in the internal node, because that value is now the rightmost entry in the subtree. Deletion may cause **underflow** by reducing the number of entries in the leaf node to below the minimum required. In this case we try to find a **sibling** leaf node—a leaf node directly to the left or to the right of the node with underflow—and **redistribute** the entries among the node and its sibling so that both are at least half full; otherwise, the node is merged with its siblings and the number of leaf nodes is reduced. A common method is to try redistributing entries with the left sibling; if this is not possible, an attempt to redistribute with the right sibling is made. If this is not possible either, the three nodes are merged into two leaf nodes. In such a case, underflow may propagate to **internal** nodes because one fewer tree pointer and search value are needed. This can propagate and reduce the tree levels.

Notice that implementing the insertion and deletion algorithms may require parent and sibling pointers for each node, or the use of a stack as in Algorithm 9.6. Each node should also include the number of entries in it and its type (leaf or internal). Another alternative is to implement insertion and deletion as recursive procedures.

Variations of B-Trees and B⁺-Trees.

To conclude this section, we briefly mention some variations of B-trees and B^+-trees. In some cases, constraint 5 on the B-tree (or B^+-tree), which requires each node to be at least half full, can be changed to require each node to be at least two-thirds full. In this case the B-tree has been called a **B*-tree**. In general, some systems allow the user to choose a **fill factor** between 0.5 and 1.0, where the latter means that the B-tree (index) nodes are to be completely full. It is also possible to specify two fill factors for a B^+- tree: one for the leaf level and one for the internal nodes of the tree. When the index is first constructed, each node is filled up to approximately the fill factors specified. Recently, investigators have suggested relaxing the requirement that a node be half full, and instead allow a node to become completely empty before merging, to simplify the deletion algorithm. Simulation studies show that this does not waste too much additional space under randomly distributed insertions and deletions.

DELETION SEQUENCE: 5, 12, 9

FIGURE 9.26 An example of deletion from a B+-tree.

9.12.4   Indexes on Multiple Keys

In our discussion so far, we assumed that the primary or secondary keys on which files were accessed were single attributes (fields). In many retrieval and update requests, multiple attributes are involved. If a certain combination of attributes is used very frequently, it is advantageous to set up an access structure to provide efficient access by a key value that is a combination of those attributes.

For example, consider an EMPLOYEE file containing attributes DNO (department number), AGE, STREET, CITY, ZIPCODE, SALARY and SKILL_CODE, with the key of ENO (employee number). Consider the query: "List the employees in department number 4 whose age is 59." Note that both DNO and AGE are nonkey attributes, which means that a search value for either of these will point to multiple records. The following alternative search strategies may be considered:

1. Assuming DNO has an index, but AGE does not, access the records having DNO = 4 using the index then select from among them those records that satisfy AGE = 59.

2. Alternately, if AGE is indexed but DNO is not, access the records having AGE = 59 using the index then select from among them those records that satisfy DNO = 4 .

3. If indexes have been created on both DNO and AGE, both indexes may be used; each gives a set of records or a set of pointers (to blocks or records). An intersection of these sets of records or pointers yields those records that satisfy both conditions, those records that satisfy both conditions, or the blocks in which records satisfying both conditions are located.

All of these alternatives eventually give the correct result. However, if the set of records that meet each condition (DNO = 4 or AGE = 59) individually are large, yet only a few records satisfy the combined condition, then none of the above is a very efficient technique for the given search request. A number of possibilities exist that would treat the combination <DNO, AGE>, or <AGE, DNO> as a search key made up of multiple attributes. We briefly outline these techniques below. We will refer to keys containing multiple attributes as **composite keys**.

9.12.4.1   Ordered index on multiple attributes   All the discussion in this chapter so far still applies if we create an index on a search key field that is a combination of <DNO, AGE>. The search key is a pair of values <4, 59> in the above example. In general, if an index is created on attributes <A_1, A_2, . . . , A_n>, the search key values are tuples with n values: <v_1, v_2,......., v_n>.

A lexicographic ordering of these tuple values establishes an order on this composite search key. For our example, all of department keys for department number 3 precede those for department 4. Thus <3, n> precedes <4, m> for any values of m and n. The ascending key order for keys with DNO = 4 would be <4, 18>, <4, 19>, <4, 20>, and so on. Lexicographic ordering works similarly to ordering of character strings. An index on a composite key of n attributes works similarly to any index discussed in this chapter so far.

9.12.4.2   Partitioned hashing   Partitioned hashing is an extension of static external hashing (Section 9.8.2) that allows access on multiple keys. It is suitable only for equality comparisons; range queries are not supported. In partitioned hashing, for a key consisting of n components, the hash function is designed to produce a result with n separate hash addresses. The bucket address is a concatenation of these n addresses. It is then possible to search for the required composite search key by looking up the appropriate buckets that match the parts of the address in which we are interested.

For example, consider the composite search key <DNO, AGE>. If DNO and AGE are hashed into a 3-bit and 5-bit address respectively, we get an 8-bit bucket address. Suppose that DNO = 4 has a hash address "100" and

AGE = 59 has hash address "10101". Then to search for the combined search value, DNO = 4 and AGE = 59, one goes to bucket address 100 10101; just to search for all employees with AGE = 59, all buckets (eight of them) will be searched whose addresses are "000 10101", "001 10101", . . . etc. An advantage of partitioned hashing is that it can be easily extended to any number of attributes. The bucket addresses can be designed so that high order bits in the addresses correspond to more frequently accessed attributes. Additionally, no separate access structure needs to be maintained for the individual attributes. The main drawback of partitioned hashing is that it cannot handle range queries on any of the component attributes.

9.12.4.3 Grid files

Another alternative is to organize the EMPLOYEE file as a grid file. If we want to access a file on two keys, say DNO and AGE as in our example, we can construct a grid array with one linear scale (or dimension) for each of the search attributes. Figure 9.27 shows a grid array for the EMPLOYEE file with one linear scale for DNO and another for the AGE attribute. The scales are made in a way as to achieve a uniform distribution of that attribute. Thus, in our example, we show that the linear scale for DNO has DNO = 1, 2 combined as one value 0 on the scale, while DNO = 5 corresponds to the value 2 on that scale. Similarly, AGE is divided into its scale of 0 to 5 by grouping ages so as to distribute the employees uniformly by age. The grid array shown for this file has a total of 36 cells. Each cell points to some bucket address where the records corresponding to that cell are stored. Figure 9.27 also shows assignment of cells to buckets (only partially).

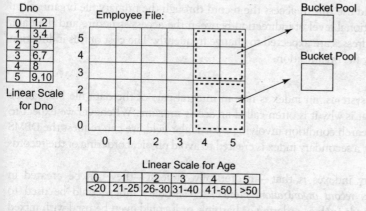

FIGURE 9.27 Example of a grid array on DNO and AGE attributes.

Thus our request for DNO = 4 and AGE = 59 maps into the cell (1, 5) corresponding to the grid array. The records for this combination will be found in the corresponding bucket. This method is particularly useful for range queries that would map into a set of cells corresponding to a group of values along the linear scales. Conceptually, the grid file concept may be applied to any number of search keys. For n search keys, the grid array would have n dimensions. The grid array thus allows a partitioning of the file along the dimensions of the search key attributes and provides an access by combinations of values along those dimensions. Grid files perform well in terms of reduction in time for multiple key access. However, they represent a space overhead in terms of the grid array structure. Moreover, with dynamic files, a frequent reorganization of the file adds to the maintenance cost.[23]

---

23. Insertion/deletion algorithms for grid files may be found in Nievergelt [1984].

9.12.5 Other Types of Indexes

9.12.5.1 Using hashing and other data structures as indexes
It is also possible to create access structures similar to indexes that are based on *hashing*. The index entries $<K, Pr>$ (or $<K, P>$) can be organized as a dynamically expandable hash file, using one of the techniques described in Section 9.8.3; searching for an entry uses the hash search algorithm on K. Once an entry is found, the pointer Pr (or P) is used to locate the corresponding record in the data file. Other search structures can also be used as indexes.

9.12.5.2 Logical versus Physical Indexes
So far, we have assumed that the index entries $<K,$ $Pr>$ (or $<K, P>$) always include a physical pointer Pr (or P) that specifies the physical record address on disk as a block number and offset. This is sometimes called a **physical index**, and it has the disadvantage that the pointer must be changed if the record is moved to another disk location. For example, suppose that a primary file organization is based on linear hashing or extendible hashing; then, each time a bucket is split, some records are allocated to new buckets and hence have new physical addresses. If there was a secondary index on the file, the pointers to those records would have to be found and updated—a difficult task.

To remedy this situation, we can use a structure called a **logical index**, whose index entries are of the form $<K, K_p>$. Each entry has one value K for the secondary indexing field matched with the value K_p of the field used for the primary file organization. By searching the secondary index on the value of K, a program can locate the corresponding value of K_p and use this to access the record through the primary file organization. Logical indexes thus introduce an additional level of indirection between the access structure and the data. They are used when physical record addresses are expected to change frequently. The cost of this indirection is the extra search based on the primary file organization.

9.12.5.3 Discussion
In many systems, an index is not an integral part of the data file but can be created and discarded dynamically. That is why it is often called an *access structure*. Whenever we expect to access a file frequently based on some search condition involving a particular field, we can request the DBMS to create an index on that field. Usually, a secondary index is created to avoid physical ordering of the records in the data file on disk.

The main advantage of secondary indexes is that—theoretically, at least—they can be created in conjunction with *virtually any primary record organization*. Hence, a secondary index could be used to complement other primary access methods such as ordering or hashing, or it could even be used with mixed files. To create a B^+-tree secondary index on some field of a file, we must go through all records in the file to create the entries at the leaf level of the tree. These entries are then sorted and filled according to the specified fill factor; simultaneously, the other index levels are created. It is more expensive and much harder to create primary indexes and clustering indexes dynamically, because the records of the data file must be physically sorted on disk in order of the indexing field. However, some systems allow users to create these indexes dynamically on their files by sorting the file during index creation.

It is common to use an index to enforce a *key constraint* on an attribute. While searching the index to insert a new record, it is straightforward to check at the same time whether another record in the file—and hence in the index tree—has the same key attribute value as the new record. If so, the insertion can be rejected.

A file that has a secondary index on every one of its fields is often called a **fully inverted file**. Because all indexes are secondary, new records are inserted at the end of the file; therefore, the data file itself is an unordered (heap) file. The indexes are usually implemented as B^+-trees, so they are updated dynamically to reflect insertion or deletion of records. Some commercial DBMSs, such as ADABAS of Software-AG, use this method extensively.

We referred to the popular IBM file organization called ISAM in Section 9.12.2. Another IBM method, the **virtual storage access method (VSAM)**, is somewhat similar to the B^+-tree access structure.

In this chapter we also presented file organizations that involve additional access structures, called indexes, to improve the efficiency of retrieval of records from a data file. These access structures may be used *in conjunction with* the primary file organizations which are used to organize the file records themselves on disk.

9.13 Summary

We began this chapter by discussing the characteristics of memory hierarchies and then concentrated on secondary storage devices. In particular, we focused on magnetic disks because they are used most often to store online database files.

Data on disk is stored in blocks; accessing a disk block is expensive because of the seek time, rotational delay, and block transfer time. Double buffering can be used when accessing consecutive disk blocks, to reduce the average block access time. Other disk parameters are discussed in Appendix B. We presented different ways of storing records of a file on disk. Records of a file are grouped into disk blocks and can be of fixed length or variable length, spanned or unspanned, and of the same record type or mixed types. We discussed the file header, which describes the record formats and keeps track of the disk addresses of the file blocks. Information in the file header is used by system software accessing the file records.

We then presented a set of typical commands for accessing individual file records and discussed the concept of the current record of a file. We discussed how complex record search conditions are transformed into simple search conditions that are used to locate records in the file.

Three primary file organizations were then discussed: unordered, ordered, and hashed. Unordered files require a linear search to locate records, but record insertion is very simple. We discussed the deletion problem and the use of deletion markers.

Ordered files shorten the time required to read records in order of the ordering field. The time required to search for an arbitrary record, given the value of its ordering key field, is also reduced if a binary search is used. However, maintaining the records in order makes insertion very expensive; thus the technique of using an unordered overflow file to reduce the cost of record insertion was discussed. Overflow records are merged with the master file periodically during file reorganization.

Hashing provides very fast access to an arbitrary record of a file, given the value of its hash key. The most suitable method for external hashing is the bucket technique, with one or more contiguous blocks corresponding to each bucket. Collisions causing bucket overflow are handled by chaining. Access on any nonhash field is slow, and so is ordered access of the records on any field. We then discussed two hashing techniques for files that grow and shrink in the number of records dynamically—namely, extendible and linear hashing.

We briefly discussed other possibilities for primary file organizations, such as B-trees, and files of mixed records, which implement relationships among records of different types physically as part of the storage structure. Finally, we reviewed the recent advances in disk technology represented by RAID (Redundant Arrays of Inexpensive [Independent] Disks).

We also presented file organizations, called indexes, to improve the efficiency of retrieval of records from a data file. These access structures may be used in conjunction with the primary file organizations, which are used to organize the file records on disk.

Three types of ordered single-level indexes were introduced: (1) primary, (2) clustering, and (3) secondary. Each index is specified on a field of the file. Primary and clustering indexes are constructed on the physical ordering field of a file, whereas secondary indexes are specified on nonordering fields. The field for a primary index must also be a key of the file, whereas it is a nonkey field for a clustering index. A single-level index is an ordered file and is searched using a binary search. We showed how multilevel indexes can be constructed to improve the efficiency of searching an index.

We then showed how multilevel indexes can be implemented as B-trees and B$^+$-trees, which are dynamic structures that allow an index to expand and shrink dynamically. The nodes (blocks) of these index structures are kept between half full and completely full by the insertion and deletion algorithms. Nodes eventually stabilize at an average occupancy of 69 percent full, allowing space for insertions without requiring reorganization of the index for the majority of insertions. B$^+$-trees can generally hold more entries in their internal nodes than can B-trees, so they may have fewer levels or hold more entries than does a corresponding B-tree.

We gave an overview of multiple key access methods, and showed how an index can be constructed based on hash data structures. We then introduced the concept of a logical index, and compared it with the physical indexes we described before. Finally, we discussed how combinations of the above organizations can be used. For example, secondary indexes are often used with mixed files, as well as with unordered and ordered files. Secondary indexes can also be created for hash files and dynamic hash files.

Review Questions

9.1. What is the difference between primary and secondary storage?

9.2. Why are disks, not tapes, used to store online database files?

9.3. Define the following terms: *disk, disk pack, track, block, cylinder, sector, interblock gap, read/write head.*

9.4. Discuss the process of disk initialization.

9.5. Discuss the mechanism used to read data from or write data to the disk.

9.6. What are the components of a disk block address?

9.7. Why is accessing a disk block expensive? Discuss the time components involved in accessing a disk block.

9.8. Describe the mismatch between processor and disk technologies.

9.9. What are the main goals of the RAID technology? How does it achieve them?

9.10. How does disk mirroring help improve reliability? Give a quantitative example.

9.11. What are the techniques used to improve performance of disks in RAID?

9.12. What characterizes the levels in RAID organization?

9.13. How does double buffering improve block access time?

9.14. What are the reasons for having variable-length records? What types of separator characters are needed for each?

9.15. Discuss the techniques for allocating file blocks on disk.

9.16. What is the difference between a file organization and an access method?

9.17. What is the difference between static and dynamic files?

9.18. What are the typical record-at-a-time operations for accessing a file? Which of these depend on the current record of a file?

9.19. Discuss the techniques for record deletion.

9.20. Discuss the advantages and disadvantages of using (a) an unordered file, (b) an ordered file, and (c) a static hash file with buckets and chaining. Which operations can be performed efficiently on each of these organizations, and which operations are expensive?

9.21. Discuss the techniques for allowing a hash file to expand and shrink dynamically. What are the advantages and disadvantages of each?

9.22. What are mixed files used for? What are other types of primary file organizations?

9.23. Define the following terms: *indexing field, primary key field, clustering field, secondary key field, block anchor, dense index,* and *nondense (sparse) index.*

9.24. What are the differences among primary, secondary, and clustering indexes? How do these differences affect the ways in which these indexes are implemented? Which of the indexes are dense, and which are not?

9.25. Why can we have at most one primary or clustering index on a file, but several secondary indexes?

9.26. How does multilevel indexing improve the efficiency of searching an index file?

9.27. What is the order p of a B-tree? Describe the structure of B-tree nodes.

9.28. What is the order p of a B$^+$-tree? Describe the structure of both internal and leaf nodes of a B$^+$-tree.

9.29. How does a B-tree differ from a B$^+$-tree? Why is a B$^+$-tree usually preferred as an access structure to a data file?

9.30. Explain what alternative choices exist for accessing a file based on multiple search keys.

9.31. What is partitioned hashing? How does it work? What are its limitations?

9.32. What is a grid file? What are its advantages and disadvantages?

9.33. Show an example of constructing a grid array on two attributes on some file.

9.34. What is a fully inverted file? What is an indexed sequential file?

9.35. How can hashing be used to construct an index? What is the difference between a logical index and a physical index?

Exercises

9.36. Consider a disk with the following characteristics (these are not parameters of any particular disk unit): block size $B = 512$ bytes; interblock gap size $G = 128$ bytes; number of blocks per track = 20; number of tracks per surface = 400. A disk pack consists of 15 double-sided disks.

a. What is the total capacity of a track, and what is its useful capacity (excluding interblock gaps)?

b. How many cylinders are there?

c. What are the total capacity and the useful capacity of a cylinder?

d. What are the total capacity and the useful capacity of a disk pack?

e. Suppose that the disk drive rotates the disk pack at a speed of 2400 rpm (revolutions per minute); what are the transfer rate (tr) in bytes/msec and the block transfer time (btt) in msec? What is the average rotational delay (rd) in msec? What is the bulk transfer rate? (See Appendix B.)

f. Suppose that the average seek time is 30 msec. How much time does it take (on the average) in msec to locate and transfer a single block, given its block address?

g. Calculate the average time it would take to transfer 20 random blocks, and compare this with the time it would take to transfer 20 consecutive blocks using double buffering to save seek time and rotational delay.

9.37. A file has r = 20,000 STUDENT records of *fixed length*. Each record has the following fields: NAME (30 bytes), ENO (9 bytes), ADDRESS (40 bytes), PHONE (9 bytes), DOB (8 bytes), SEX (1 byte), MAJORDEPTCODE (4 bytes), MINORDEPTCODE (4 bytes), CLASSCODE (4 bytes, integer), and DEGREEPROGRAM (3 bytes). An additional byte is used as a deletion marker. The file is stored on the disk whose parameters are given in Exercise 9.36.

a. Calculate the record size R in bytes.

b. Calculate the blocking factor *bfr* and the number of file blocks b, assuming an unspanned organization.

c. Calculate the average time it takes to find a record by doing a linear search on the file if (i) the file blocks are stored contiguously, and double buffering is used; (ii) the file blocks are not stored contiguously.

d. Assume that the file is ordered by ENO; calculate the time it takes to search for a record given its ENO value, by doing a binary search.

9.38. Suppose that only 80 percent of the STUDENT records from Exercise 9.37 have a value for PHONE, 85 percent for MAJORDEPTCODE, 15 percent for MINORDEPTCODE, and 90 percent for DEGREEPROGRAM; and suppose that we use a variable-length record file. Each record has a 1-byte *field type* for each field in the record, plus the 1-byte deletion marker and a 1-byte end-of-record marker. Suppose that we use a *spanned* record organization, where each block has a 5-byte pointer to the next block (this space is not used for record storage).

a. Calculate the average record length R in bytes.

b. Calculate the number of blocks needed for the file.

9.39. Suppose that a disk unit has the following parameters: seek time s = 20 msec; rotational delay rd = 10 msec; block transfer time btt = 1 msec; block size B = 2400 bytes; interblock gap size G = 600 bytes. An EMPLOYEE file has the following fields: ENO, 9 bytes; LASTNAME, 20 bytes; FIRSTNAME, 20 bytes; INITIAL, 1 byte; DOB, 10 bytes; ADDRESS, 35 bytes; PHONE, 12 bytes; SUPERVISORENO, 9 bytes; DEPARTMENT, 4 bytes; JOBCODE, 4 bytes; *deletion marker*, 1 byte. The EMPLOYEE file has r = 30,000 records, fixed-length format, and unspanned blocking. Write appropriate formulas and calculate the following values for the above EMPLOYEE file:

a. The record size R (including the deletion marker), the blocking factor *bfr*, and the number of disk blocks b.

b. Calculate the wasted space in each disk block because of the unspanned organization.

c. Calculate the transfer rate tr and the bulk transfer rate btr for this disk unit (see Appendix B for definitions of tr and btr).

d. Calculate the average *number of block accesses* needed to search for an arbitrary record in the file, using linear search.

e. Calculate in msec the average *time* needed to search for an arbitrary record in the file, using linear search, if the file blocks are stored on consecutive disk blocks and double buffering is used.

f. Calculate in msec the average time needed to search for an arbitrary record in the file, using linear search, if the file blocks are *not* stored on consecutive disk blocks.

g. Assume that the records are ordered via some key field. Calculate the average *number of block accesses* and the *average time* needed to search for an arbitrary record in the file, using binary search.

9.40. A PARTS file with Part# as hash key includes records with the following Part# values: 2369, 3760, 4692, 4871, 5659, 1821, 1074, 7115, 1620, 2428, 3943, 4750, 6975, 4981, 9208. The file uses eight buckets, numbered 0 to 7. Each bucket is one disk block and holds two records. Load these records into the file in the given order, using the hash function $h(K) = K \bmod 8$. Calculate the average number of block accesses for a random retrieval on Part#.

9.41. Load the records of Exercise 9.40 into expandable hash files based on extendible hashing. Show the structure of the directory at each step, and the global and local depths. Use the hash function $h(K) = K \bmod 128$.

9.42. Load the records of Exercise 9.40 into an expandable hash file, using linear hashing. Start with a single disk block, using the hash function $h_0 = K \bmod 2^0$, and show how the file grows and how the hash functions change as the records are inserted. Assume that blocks are split whenever an overflow occurs, and show the value of n at each stage.

9.43. Compare the file commands listed in Section 9.6 to those available on a file access method you are familiar with.

9.44. Suppose that we have an unordered file of fixed-length records that uses an unspanned record organization. Outline algorithms for insertion, deletion, and modification of a file record. State any assumptions you make.

9.45. Suppose that we have an ordered file of fixed-length records and an unordered overflow file to handle insertion. Both files use unspanned records. Outline algorithms for insertion, deletion, and modification of a file record and for reorganizing the file. State any assumptions you make.

9.46. Can you think of techniques other than an unordered overflow file that can be used to make insertions in an ordered file more efficient?

9.47. Suppose that we have a hash file of fixed-length records, and suppose that over-flow is handled by chaining. Outline algorithms for insertion, deletion, and modification of a file record. State any assumptions you make.

9.48. Can you think of techniques other than chaining to handle bucket overflow in external hashing?

9.49. Write pseudocode for the insertion algorithms for linear hashing and for extendible hashing.

9.50. Write program code to access individual fields of records under each of the following circumstances. For each case, state the assumptions you make concerning pointers, separator characters, and so forth. Determine the type of information needed in the file header in order for your code to be general in each case.

a. Fixed-length records with unspanned blocking.

b. Fixed-length records with spanned blocking.

c. Variable-length records with variable-length fields and spanned blocking.

d. Variable-length records with repeating groups and spanned blocking.

e. Variable-length records with optional fields and spanned blocking.

f. Variable-length records that allow all three cases in parts c, d, and e.

9.51. Suppose that a file initially contains $r = 120,000$ records of $R = 200$ bytes each in an unsorted (heap) file. The block size $B = 2400$ bytes, the average seek time $s = 16$ ms, the average rotational latency $rd = 8.3$ ms and the block transfer time $btt = 0.8$ ms. Assume that 1 record is deleted for every 2 records added until the total number of active records is 240,000.

a. How many block transfers are needed to reorganize the file?

b. How long does it take to find a record right before reorganization?

c. How long does it take to find a record right after reorganization?

9.52. Suppose we have a sequential (ordered) file of 100,000 records where each record is 240 bytes. Assume that $B = 2400$ bytes, $s = 16$ ms, $rd = 8.3$ ms, and $btt = 0.8$ ms. Suppose we want to make X independent random record reads from the file. We could make X random block reads or we could perform one exhaustive read of the entire file looking for those X records. The question is to decide when it would be more efficient to perform one exhaustive read of the entire file than to perform X individual random reads. That is, what is the value for X when an exhaustive read of the file is more efficient than random X reads? Develop this as a function of X.

9.53. Suppose that a static hash file initially has 600 buckets in the primary area and that records are inserted that create an overflow area of 600 buckets. If we reorganize the hash file, we can assume that the overflow is eliminated. If the cost of reorganizing the file is the cost of the bucket transfers (reading and writing all of the buckets) and the only periodic file operation is the fetch operation, then how many times would we have to perform a fetch (successfully) to make the reorganization cost-effective? That is, the reorganization cost and subsequent search cost are less than the search cost before reorganization. Support your answer. Assume $s = 16$ ms, $rd = 8.3$ ms, $btt = 1$ ms.

9.54. Suppose we want to create a linear hash file with a file load factor of 0.7 and a blocking factor of 20 records per bucket, which is to contain 112,000 records initially.

a. How many buckets should we allocate in the primary area?

b. What should be the number of bits used for bucket addresses?

9.55. Construct a B$^+$tree with fanout (the number of points per node) equal to 3 for the following set of key values 80, 50, 10, 70, 30, 100, 90. Assume that the tree is initially empty and the values are added in the order given.

a. Show the tree after insertion of 10, after insertion of 30, and after insertion of 90.

b. The key values 30 and 10 are now deleted from the tree in that order. Show the tree after each deletion.

9.56. Consider a disk with block size $B = 512$ bytes. A block pointer is $P = 6$ bytes long, and a record pointer is $P_R = 7$ bytes long. A file has $r = 30,000$ EMPLOYEE records of *fixed length*. Each record has the following fields: NAME (30 bytes), ENO (9 bytes), DEPARTMENTCODE (9 bytes), ADDRESS (40 bytes), PHONE (9 bytes), DOB (8 bytes), SEX (1 byte), JOBCODE (4 bytes), SALARY (4 bytes, real number). An additional byte is used as a deletion marker.

a. Calculate the record size R in bytes.

b. Calculate the blocking factor *bfr* and the number of file blocks b, assuming an nspanned organization.

c. Suppose that the file is *ordered* by the key field ENO and we want to construct a *primary index* on ENO. Calculate (i) the index blocking factor bfr_i (which is also the index fan-out fo); (ii) the number of first-level index entries and the number of first-level index blocks; (iii) the number of levels needed if we make it into a multilevel index; (iv) the total number of blocks required by the multilevel index; and (v) the number of block accesses needed to search for and retrieve a record from the file—given its ENO value—using the primary index.

d. Suppose that the file is *not ordered* by the key field ENO and we want to construct a *secondary index* on ENO. Repeat the previous exercise (part c) for the secondary index and compare with the primary index.

e. Suppose that the file is *not ordered* by the nonkey field DEPARTMENTCODE and we want to construct a *secondary index* on DEPARTMENTCODE, using option 3 of Section 9.12.1.3, with an extra level of indirection that stores record pointers. Assume there are 1000 distinct values of DEPARTMENTCODE and that the EMPLOYEE records are evenly distributed among these values. Calculate (i) the index blocking factor bfr_i (which is also the index fan-out fo); (ii) the number of blocks needed by the level of indirection that stores record pointers; (iii) the number of first-level index entries and the number of first-level index blocks; (iv) the number of levels needed if we make it into a multilevel index; (v) the total number of blocks required by the multilevel index and the blocks used in the extra level of indirection; and (vi) the approximate number of block accesses needed to search for and retrieve all records in the file that have a specific DEPARTMENTCODE value, using the index.

f. Suppose that the file is *ordered* by the nonkey field DEPARTMENTCODE and we want to construct a *clustering index* on DEPARTMENTCODE that uses block anchors (every new value of DEPARTMENTCODE starts at the beginning of a new block). Assume there are 1000 distinct values of DEPARTMENTCODE and that the EMPLOYEE records are evenly distributed among these values. Calculate (i) the index blocking factor bfr_i (which is also the index fan-out fo); (ii) the number of first-level index entries and the number of first-level index blocks; (iii) the number of levels needed if we make it into a multilevel index; (iv) the total number of blocks required by the multilevel index; and (v) the number of block accesses needed to search for and retrieve all records in the file that have a specific DEPARTMENTCODE value, using the clustering index (assume that multiple blocks in a cluster are contiguous).

g. Suppose that the file is not ordered by the key field ENO and we want to construct a B$^+$-tree access structure (index) on ENO. Calculate (i) the orders p and p_{leaf} of the B$^+$-tree; (ii) the number of leaf-level blocks needed if blocks are approximately 69 percent full (rounded up for convenience); (iii) the number of levels needed if internal nodes are also 69 percent full (rounded up for convenience); (iv) the total number of blocks required by the B$^+$-tree; and (v) the number of block accesses needed to search for and retrieve a record from the file—given its ENO value—using the B$^+$-tree.

h. Repeat part g, but for a B-tree rather than for a B$^+$-tree. Compare your results for the B-tree and for the B$^+$-tree.

9.57. A PARTS file with Part# as key field includes records with the following Part# values: 23, 65, 37, 60, 46, 92, 48, 71, 56, 59, 18, 21, 10, 74, 78, 15, 16, 20, 24, 28, 39, 43, 47, 50, 69, 75, 8, 49, 33, 38. Suppose that the search field values are inserted in the given order in a B$^+$-tree of order $p = 4$ and $p_{leaf} = 3$; show how the tree will expand and what the final tree will look like.

9.58. Repeat Exercise 9.57, but use a B-tree of order $p = 4$ instead of a B$^+$-tree.

9.59. Suppose that the following search field values are deleted, in the given order, from the B$^+$-tree of Exercise 9.57; show how the tree will shrink and show the final tree. The deleted values are 65, 75, 43, 18, 20, 92, 59, 37.

9.60. Repeat Exercise 9.59, but for the B-tree of Exercise 9.58.

9.61. Algorithm 9.4 outlines the procedure for searching a nondense multilevel primary index to retrieve a file record. Adapt the algorithm for each of the following cases:

a. A multilevel secondary index on a nonkey nonordering field of a file. Assume that option 3 of Section 9.12.1.3 is used, where an extra level of indirection stores pointers to the individual records with the corresponding index field value.

b. A multilevel secondary index on a nonordering key field of a file.

c. A multilevel clustering index on a nonkey ordering field of a file.

9.62. Suppose that several secondary indexes exist on nonkey fields of a file, implemented using option 3 of Section 9.12.1.3; for example, we could have secondary indexes on the fields DEPARTMENTCODE, JOBCODE, and SALARY of the EMPLOYEE file of Exercise 9.56. Describe an efficient way to search for and retrieve records satisfying a complex selection condition on these fields, such as (DEPARTMENTCODE = 5 AND JOBCODE = 12 AND SALARY = 50,000), using the record pointers in the indirection level.

9.63. Adapt Algorithms 9.5 and 9.6, which outline search and insertion procedures for a B+-tree, to a B-tree.

9.64. It is possible to modify the B+-tree insertion algorithm to delay the case where a new level is produced by checking for a possible *redistribution* of values among the leaf nodes. Figure 9.28 illustrates how this could be done for our example in Figure 9.25; rather than splitting the leftmost leaf node when 12 is inserted, we do a *left redistribution* by moving 7 to the leaf node to its left (if there is space in this node). Figure 9.28 shows how the tree would look when redistribution is considered. It is also possible to consider *right redistribution*. Try to modify the B+-tree insertion algorithm to take redistribution into account.

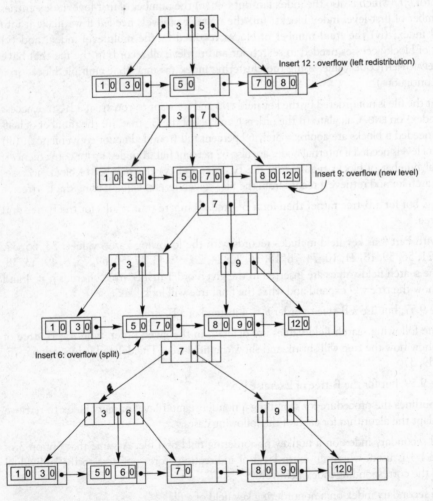

FIGURE 9.28 B+-tree insertion with left redistribution.

9.65.   Outline an algorithm for deletion from a B$^+$-tree.

9.66.   Repeat Exercise 9.65 for a B-tree.

Selected Bibliography

Wiederhold (1983) has a detailed discussion and analysis of secondary storage devices and file organizations. Optical disks are described in Berg and Roth (1989) and analyzed in Ford and Christodoulakis 1991. Flash memory is discussed by Dippert and Levy (1993). Ruemmler and Wilkes (1994) present a survey of the magnetic-disk technology. Most textbooks on databases include discussions of the material presented here. Most data structures textbooks, including Knuth (1973), discuss static hashing in more detail; Knuth has a complete discussion of hash functions and collision resolution techniques, as well as of their performance comparison. Knuth also offers a detailed discussion of techniques for sorting external files. Textbooks on file structures include Claybrook (1983), Smith and Barnes (1987), and Salzberg (1988); they discuss additional file organizations including tree structured files, and have detailed algorithms for operations on files. Additional textbooks on file organizations include Miller (1987), and Livadas (1989). Salzberg et al. (1990) describe a distributed external sorting algorithm. File organizations with a high degree of fault tolerance are described by Bitton and Gray (1988) and by Gray et al. (1990). Disk striping is proposed in Salem and Garcia Molina (1986). The first paper on redundant arrays of inexpensive disks (RAID) is by Patterson et al. (1988). Chen and Patterson (1990) and the excellent survey of RAID by Chen et al. (1994) are additional references. Grochowski and Hoyt (1996) discuss future trends in disk drives. Various formulas for the RAID architecture appear in Chen et al. (1994). Details of disk storage devices can be found at manufacturer sites; e.g., www.seagate.com, www.ibm.com, www.storagetek.com. IBM has a storage technology research center at IBM Almaden (www.almaden.ibm.com/sst/).

Morris (1968) is an early paper on hashing. Extendible hashing is described in Fagin et al. (1979). Linear hashing is described by Litwin (1980). Dynamic hashing, which we did not discuss in detail, was proposed by Larson (1978). There are many proposed variations for extendible and linear hashing; for examples, see Cesarini and Soda (1991), Du and Tong (1991), and Hachem and Berra (1992).

Bayer and McCreight (1972) introduced B-trees and associated algorithms. Comer (1979) provides an excellent survey of B-trees and their history, and variations of B-trees. Knuth (1973) provides detailed analysis of many search techniques, including B-trees and some of their variations. Nievergelt (1974) discusses the use of binary search trees for file organization. Textbooks on file structures including Wirth (1972), Claybrook (1983), Smith and Barnes (1987), Miller (1987), and Salzberg (1988) discuss indexing in detail and may be consulted for search, insertion, and deletion algorithms for B-trees and B$^+$-trees. Larson (1981) analyzes index-sequential files, and Held and Stonebraker (1978) compare static multilevel indexes with B-tree dynamic indexes. Lehman and Yao (1981) and Srinivasan and Carey (1991) did further analysis of concurrent access to B-trees. The books by Wiederhold (1983), Smith and Barnes (1987), and Salzberg (1988), among others, discuss many of the search techniques described in this chapter. Grid files are introduced in Nievergelt (1984). Partial-match retrieval, which uses partitioned hashing, is discussed in Burkhard (1976, 1979).

New techniques and applications of indexes and B$^+$-trees are discussed in Lanka and Mays (1991), Zobel et al. (1992), and Faloutsos and Jagadish (1992). Mohan and Narang (1992) discuss index creation. The performance of various B-tree and B$^+$-tree algorithms is assessed in Baeza-Yates and Larson (1989) and Johnson and Shasha (1993). Buffer management for indexes is discussed in Chan et al. (1992).

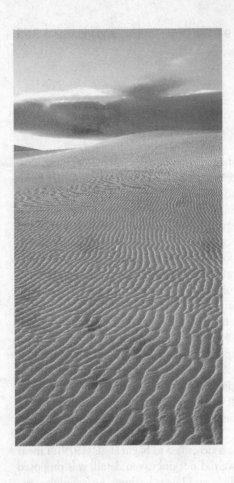

10

Algorithms for Query Processing and Optimization

In this chapter we discuss the techniques used by a DBMS to process, optimize, and execute high-level queries. A query expressed in a high-level query language such as SQL must first be scanned, parsed, and validated.[1] The **scanner** identifies the language tokens—such as SQL keywords, attribute names, and relation names—in the text of the query, whereas the **parser** checks the query syntax to determine whether it is formulated according to the syntax rules (rules of grammar) of the query language. The query must also be **validated**, by checking that all attribute and relation names are valid and semantically meaningful names in the schema of the particular database being queried. An internal representation of the query is then created, usually as a tree data structure called a **query tree**. It is also possible to represent the query using a graph data structure called a **query graph**. The DBMS must then devise an **execution strategy** for retrieving the result of the query from the database files. A query typically has many possible execution strategies, and the process of choosing a suitable one for processing a query is known as query optimization.

Different steps of processing a high-level query are shown in Figure 10.1. The query optimizer module has the task of producing an execution plan, and the **code generator** generates the code to execute that plan. The **runtime database processor** has the task of running the query code, whether in compiled or interpreted mode, to produce the query result. If a runtime error results, an error message is generated by the runtime database processor.

---

1. We will not discuss the parsing and syntax-checking phase of query processing here; this material is discussed in compiler textbooks.

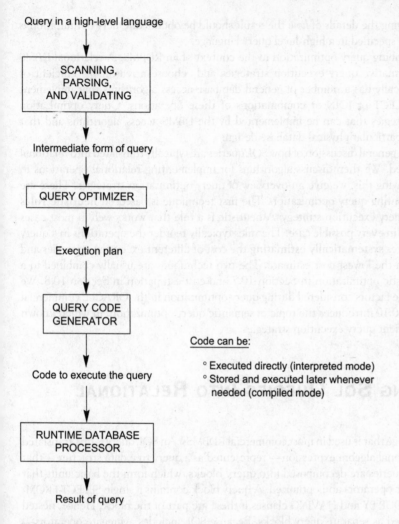

Query in a high-level language

SCANNING,
PARSING,
AND VALIDATING

Intermediate form of query

QUERY OPTIMIZER

Execution plan

QUERY CODE
GENERATOR

Code can be:

° Executed directly (interpreted mode)
° Stored and executed later whenever
  needed (compiled mode)

RUNTIME DATABASE
PROCESSOR

Result of query

FIGURE 10.1 Typical steps when processing a high-level query.

The term *optimization* is actually a misnomer because in some cases the chosen execution plan is not the optimal (best) strategy—it is just a *reasonably efficient strategy* for executing the query. Finding the optimal strategy is usually too time-consuming except for the simplest of queries and may require information on how the files are implemented and even on the contents of the files—information that may not be fully available in the DBMS catalog. Hence, *planning of an execution strategy* may be a more accurate description than *query optimization*.

For lower-level navigational database languages in legacy systems—such as the network DML or the hierarchical HDML (see Appendixes E and F)—the programmer must choose the query execution strategy while writing a database program. If a DBMS provides only a navigational language, there is *limited need or opportunity* for extensive query optimization by the DBMS; instead, the programmer is given the capability to choose the "optimal" execution strategy. On the other hand, a high-level query language—such as SQL for relational DBMSs (RDBMSs)—is more declarative in nature because it specifies what the intended results of the query are, rather than identifying the details of *how* the result should be obtained. Query optimization is thus necessary for queries that are specified in a high-level query language.

We will concentrate on describing query optimization in the context of an RDBMS. A relational DBMS must systematically evaluate alternative query execution strategies and choose a reasonably efficient or optimal strategy. Each DBMS typically has a number of general database access algorithms that implement relational operations such as SELECT or JOIN or combinations of these operations. Query optimization considers the only execution strategies that can be implemented by the DBMS access algorithms and that apply to the particular query and particular physical database design.

We start in Section 10.1 with a general discussion of how SQL queries are typically translated into relational algebra queries and then optimized. We then discuss algorithms for implementing relational operations in Sections 10.2 through 10.6. Following this, we give an overview of query optimization strategies. There are two main techniques for implementing query optimization. The first technique is based on **heuristic rules** for ordering the operations in a query execution strategy. A heuristic is a rule that works well in most cases but is not guaranteed to work well in every possible case. The rules typically reorder the operations in a query tree. The second technique involves **systematically estimating** the cost of different execution strategies and choosing the execution plan with the lowest cost estimate. The two techniques are usually combined in a query optimizer. We discuss heuristic optimization in Section 10.7 and cost estimation in Section 10.8. We then provide a brief overview of the factors considered during query optimization in the ORACLE commercial RDBMS in Section 10.9. Section 10.10 introduces the topic of semantic query optimization, in which known constraints are used to devise efficient query execution strategies.

10.1 TRANSLATING SQL QUERIES INTO RELATIONAL ALGEBRA

In practice, SQL is the query language that is used in most commercial RDBMSs. An SQL query is first translated into an equivalent extended relational algebra expression— represented as a query tree data structure—that is then optimized. Typically, SQL queries are decomposed into **query blocks**, which form the basic units that can be translated into the algebraic operators and optimized. A query block contains a single SELECT-FROM-WHERE expression, as well as GROUP BY and HAVING clauses if these are part of the block. Hence, nested queries within a query are identified as separate query blocks. Because SQL includes aggregate operators— such as MAX, MIN, SUM, and COUNT—these operators must also be included in the extended algebra, as we discussed in Section 5.4. Consider the following SQL query on the EMPLOYEE relation in Figure 4.5:

```
SELECT    LNAME, FNAME
FROM      EMPLOYEE
WHERE     SALARY >  (SELECT    MAX (SALARY)
                     FROM      EMPLOYEE
                     WHERE     DNO=5);
```

This query includes a nested subquery and hence would be decomposed into two blocks. The inner block is

```
(SELECT    MAX    (SALARY)
 FROM      EMPLOYEE
 WHERE     DNO=5)
```

and the outer block is

```
SELECT    LNAME, FNAME
FROM      EMPLOYEE
WHERE     SALARY  >  C
```

where c represents the result returned from the inner block. The inner block could be translated into the extended relational algebra expression

$$\Im_{MAX\ SALARY}(\sigma_{DNO=5}(EMPLOYEE))$$

and the outer block into the expression

$$\pi_{LNAME,FNAME}(\sigma_{SALARY>c}(EMPLOYEE))$$

The *query optimizer* would then choose an execution plan for each block. We should note that in the above example, the inner block needs to be evaluated only once to produce the maximum salary, which is then used—as the constant c—by the outer block. We called this an *uncorrelated nested query* in Chapter 7. It is much harder to optimize the more complex correlated nested queries (see Section 7.5), where a tuple variable from the outer block appears in the WHERE-clause of the inner block.

10.2   ALGORITHMS FOR EXTERNAL SORTING

Sorting is one of the primary algorithms used in query processing. For example, whenever an SQL query specifies an ORDER BY-clause, the query result must be sorted. Sorting is also a key component in sort-merge algorithms used for JOIN and other operations (such as UNION and INTERSECTION), and in duplicate elimination algorithms for the PROJECT operation (when an SQL query specifies the DISTINCT option in the SELECT clause). We will discuss one of these algorithms in this section. Note that sorting may be avoided if an appropriate index exists to allow ordered access to the records.

External sorting refers to sorting algorithms that are suitable for large files of records stored on disk that do not fit entirely in main memory, such as most database files.[2] The typical external sorting algorithm uses a **sort-merge strategy**, which starts by sorting small subfiles—called **runs**—of the main file and then merges the sorted runs, creating larger sorted subfiles that are merged in turn. The sort-merge algorithm, like other database algorithms, requires *buffer space* in main memory, where the actual sorting and merging of the runs is performed. The basic algorithm, outlined in Figure 10.2, consists of two phases: (1) the sorting phase and (2) the merging phase.

In the **sorting phase**, runs (portions or pieces) of the file that can fit in the available buffer space are read into main memory, sorted using an internal sorting algorithm, and written back to disk as temporary sorted subfiles (or runs). The size of a run and **number of initial runs (n_R)** is dictated by **the number of file blocks (b)** and the **available buffer space (n_B)**. For example, if $n_B = 5$ blocks and the size of the file $b = 1024$ blocks, then $n_R = \lceil (b/n_B) \rceil$, or 205 initial runs each of size 5 blocks (except the last run which will have 4 blocks). Hence, after the sort phase, 205 sorted runs are stored as temporary subfiles on disk.

In the **merging phase**, the sorted runs are merged during one or more **passes**. The **degree of merging (d_M)** is the number of runs that can be merged together in each pass. In each pass, one buffer block is needed to hold one block from each of the runs being merged, and one block is needed for containing one block of the merge result. Hence, d_M is the smaller of $(n_B - 1)$ and n_R, and the number of passes is $\lceil (\log_{d_M}(n_R)) \rceil$. In our example, $d_M = 4$ (four-way merging), so the 205 initial sorted runs would be merged into 52 at the end of the first pass, which are then merged into 13, then 4, then 1 run, which means that *four passes* are needed. The minimum d_M of 2 gives the worst-case performance of the algorithm, which is

$$(2 * b) + (2 * (b * (\log_2 b)))$$

---

2. *Internal sorting algorithms* are suitable for sorting data structures that can fit entirely in memory.

```
set    i ← 1;
       j ← b;.    {size of the file in blocks}
       k ← nB;    {size of buffer in blocks}
       m ← ⌈(j/k)⌉; .
{Sort Phase}
while (i <= m)
       do  {
              read next k blocks of the file into the buffer or if there are less than k blocks remaining,
                    then read in the remaining blocks;
              sort the records in the buffer and write as a temporary subfile;
              i ← i + 1;
              }
{Merge Phase: merge subfiles until only 1 remains}
set    i ← 1;
       P ← ⌈log_{k-1}m⌉;  ← {p is the number of passes for the merging phase}
       J ← m;
while (i <= p)
       do  {
              n ← 1;
              q ← ⌈(j/(k-1))⌉;    {number of subfiles to write in this pass}
              while (n <= q)
              do  {
                    read next k-1 subfiles or remaining subfiles (from previous pass) one block at a time;
                    merge and write as new subfile one block at a time;
                    n ← n + 1;
                    }
              j ← q;
              i ← i + 1;
              }
```

FIGURE 10.2 Outline of the sort-merge algorithm for external sorting.

The first term represents the number of block accesses for the sort phase, since each file block is accessed twice—once for reading into memory and once for writing the records back to disk after sorting. The second term represents the number of block accesses for the merge phase, assuming the worst-case d_M of 2. In general, the log is taken to the base d_M and the expression for number of block accesses becomes

$$(2 * b) + (2 * (b * (\log_{d_M} n_R)))$$

10.3 ALGORITHMS FOR SELECT AND JOIN OPERATIONS

10.3.1 Implementing the SELECT Operation

There are many options for executing a SELECT operation; some depend on the file having specific access paths and may apply only to certain types of selection conditions. We discuss some of the algorithms for implementing SELECT in this section. We will use the following operations, specified on the relational database of Figure 4.5, to illustrate our discussion:

(OP1): $\sigma_{ENO='123456789'}(EMPLOYEE)$

(OP2): $\sigma_{DNUMBER_5}(DEPARTMENT)$

(OP3): $\sigma_{DNO=5}(EMPLOYEE)$

(OP4): $\sigma_{DNO=5\ AND\ SALARY\_30000\ AND\ SEX='F'}(EMPLOYEE)$

(OP5): $\sigma_{EENO='123456789'\ AND\ PNO=10}(WORKS\_ON)$

Search Methods for Simple Selection.

A number of search algorithms are possible for selecting records from a file. These are also known as **file scans**, because they scan the records of a file to search for and retrieve records that satisfy a selection condition.[3]

If the search algorithm involves the use of an index, the index search is called an **index scan**. The following search methods (S1 through S6) are examples of some of the search algorithms that can be used to implement a select operation:

- S1. *Linear search (brute force)*: Retrieve *every record* in the file, and test whether its attribute values satisfy the selection condition.

- S2. *Binary search*: If the selection condition involves an equality comparison on a key attribute on which the file is ordered, binary search—which is more efficient than linear search—can be used. An example is OP1 if ENO is the ordering attribute for the EMPLOYEE file.[4]

- S3. *Using a primary index (or hash key)*: If the selection condition involves an equality comparison on a **key attribute** with a primary index (or hash key)—for example, ENO = '123456789' in OP1—use the primary index (or hash key) to retrieve the record. Note that this condition retrieves a single record (at most).

- S4. *Using a primary index to retrieve multiple records*: If the comparison condition is >, >=, <, or <= on a key field with a primary index—for example, DNUMBER > 5 in OP2—use the index to find the record satisfying the corresponding equality condition (DNUMBER = 5), then retrieve all subsequent records in the (ordered) file. For the condition DNUMBER < 5, retrieve all the preceding records.

- S5. *Using a clustering index to retrieve multiple records*: If the selection condition involves an equality comparison on a **non-key attribute** with a clustering index—for example, DNO = 5 in OP3—use the index to retrieve all the records satisfying the condition.

- S6. *Using a secondary (B^+-tree) index on an equality comparison*: This search method can be used to retrieve a single record if the indexing field is a **key** (has unique values) or to retrieve multiple records if the indexing field is **not a key**. This can also be used for comparisons involving >, >=, <, or <=.

In Section 10.8, we discuss how to develop formulas that estimate the access cost of these search methods in terms of number of block accesses and access time. Method S1 applies to any file, but all the other methods depend on having the appropriate access path on the attribute used in the selection condition. Methods S4 and S6 can be used to retrieve records in a certain *range*—for example, 30000 < =SALARY< =35000. Queries involving such conditions are called **range queries**.

---

3. A selection operation is sometimes called a **filter**, since it filters out the records in the file that do not satisfy the selection condition.

4. Generally, binary search is not used in database search because ordered files are not used unless they also have a corresponding primary index.

Search Methods for Complex Selection. If a condition of a SELECT operation is a **conjunctive condition**—that is, if it is made up of several simple conditions connected with the AND logical connective such as OP4 above—the DBMS can use the following additional methods to implement the operation:

- S7. *Conjunctive selection using an individual index*: If an attribute involved in any **single simple condition** in the conjunctive condition has an access path that permits the use of one of the Methods S2 to S6, use that condition to retrieve the records and then check whether each retrieved record satisfies the remaining simple conditions in the conjunctive condition.

- S8. *Conjunctive selection using a composite index*: If two or more attributes are involved in equality conditions in the conjunctive condition and a composite index (or hash structure) exists on the combined fields—for example, if an index has been created on the composite key (EENO, PNO) of the WORKS_ON file for OP5—we can use the index directly.

- S9. *Conjunctive selection by intersection of record pointers*:[5] If secondary indexes (or other access paths) are available on more than one of the fields involved in simple conditions in the conjunctive condition, and if the indexes include record pointers (rather than block pointers), then each index can be used to retrieve the **set of record pointers** that satisfy the individual condition. The **intersection** of these sets of record pointers gives the record pointers that satisfy the conjunctive condition, which are then used to retrieve those records directly. If only some of the conditions have secondary indexes, each retrieved record is further tested to determine whether it satisfies the remaining conditions.[6]

Whenever a single condition specifies the selection—such as OP1, OP2, or OP3—we can only check whether an access path exists on the attribute involved in that condition. If an access path exists, the method corresponding to that access path is used; otherwise, the brute force linear search approach of method S1 can be used. Query optimization for a SELECT operation is needed mostly for conjunctive select conditions whenever *more than one* of the attributes involved in the conditions have an access path. The optimizer should choose the access path that *retrieves the fewest records* in the most efficient way by estimating the different costs (see Section 10.8) and choosing the method with the least estimated cost.

When the optimizer is choosing between multiple simple conditions in a conjunctive select condition, it typically considers the selectivity of each condition. The **selectivity (s)** is defined as the ratio of the number of records (tuples) that satisfy the condition to the total number of records (tuples) in the file (relation), and thus is a number between zero and 1—zero selectivity means no records satisfy the condition and 1 means all the records satisfy the condition. Although exact selectivities of all conditions may not be available, **estimates of selectivities** are often kept in the DBMS catalog and are used by the optimizer. For example, for an equality condition on a key attribute of relation $r(R)$, $s = 1/|r(R)|$, where $|r(R)|$ is the number of tuples in relation $r(R)$. For an equality condition on an attribute with i *distinct values*, s can be estimated by $(|r(R)|/i)/|r(R)|$ or $1/i$, assuming that the records are evenly distributed among the distinct values.[7] Under this assumption, $|r(R)|/i$ records will satisfy an equality condition on this attribute. In general, the number of records satisfying a selection condition with selectivity s is estimated to be $|r(R)| * s$. The smaller this estimate is, the higher the desirability of using that condition first to retrieve records.

---

5. A record pointer uniquely identifies a record and provides the address of the record on disk; hence, it is also called the **record identifier** or **record id.**

6. The technique can have many variations—for example, if the indexes are *logical indexes* that store primary key values instead of record pointers.

7. In more sophisticated optimizers, histograms representing the distribution of the records among the different attribute values can be kept in the catalog.

Compared to a conjunctive selection condition, a **disjunctive condition** (where simple conditions are connected by the OR logical connective rather than by AND) is much harder to process and optimize. For example, consider OP49:

(OP49): $\sigma_{\text{DNO=5 OR SALARY>30000 OR SEX='F'}}$ (EMPLOYEE)

With such a condition, little optimization can be done, because the records satisfying the disjunctive condition are the union of the records satisfying the individual conditions. Hence, if any *one* of the conditions does not have an access path, we are compelled to use the brute force linear search approach. Only if an access path exists on *every* condition can we optimize the selection by retrieving the records satisfying each condition—or their record ids—and then applying the union operation to eliminate duplicates.

A DBMS will have available many of the methods discussed above, and typically many additional methods. The query optimizer must choose the appropriate one for executing each SELECT operation in a query. This optimization uses formulas that estimate the costs for each available access method, as we shall discuss in Section 10.8. The optimizer chooses the access method with the lowest estimated cost.

10.3.2   Implementing the JOIN Operation

The JOIN operation is one of the most time-consuming operations in query processing. Many of the join operations encountered in queries are of the EQUIJOIN and NATURAL JOIN varieties, so we consider only these two here. For the remainder of this chapter, the term **join** refers to an EQUIJOIN (or NATURAL JOIN). There are many possible ways to implement a **two-way join**, which is a join on two files. Joins involving more than two files are called **multiway joins**. The number of possible ways to execute multiway joins grows very rapidly. In this section we discuss techniques for implementing only two-way joins. To illustrate our discussion, we refer to the relational schema of Figure 4.5 once more—specifically, to the EMPLOYEE, DEPARTMENT, and PROJECT relations. The   algorithms we consider are for join operations of the form

$$R \bowtie_{A=B} S$$

where A and B are domain-compatible attributes of R and S, respectively. The methods we discuss can be extended to more general forms of join. We illustrate four of the most common techniques for performing such a join, using the following example operations:

(OP6): EMPLOYEE $\bowtie_{\text{DNO=DNUMBER}}$ DEPARTMENT
(OP7): DEPARTMENT $\bowtie_{\text{MGRENO=ENO}}$ EMPLOYEE

Methods for Implementing Joins

- J1. *Nested-loop join (brute force):* For each record t in R (outer loop), retrieve every record s from S (inner loop) and test whether the two records satisfy the join condition $t[A] = s[B]$.[8]

- J2. *Single-loop join (using an access structure to retrieve the matching records):* If an index (or hash key) exists for one of the two join attributes—say, B of S— retrieve each record t in R, one at a time (single loop), and then use the access structure to retrieve directly all matching records s from S that satisfy $s[B] = t[A]$.

---

8. For disk files, it is obvious that the loops will be over disk blocks so this technique has also been called *nested-block* join.

- J3. *Sort-merge join*: If the records of R and S are *physically sorted* (ordered) by value of the join attributes A and B, respectively, we can implement the join in the most efficient way possible. Both files are scanned concurrently in order of the join attributes, matching the records that have the same values for A and B. If the files are not sorted, they may be sorted first by using external sorting (see Section 10.2). In this method, pairs of file blocks are copied into memory buffers in order and the records of each file are scanned only once each for matching with the other file—unless both A and B are nonkey attributes, in which case the method needs to be modified slightly. A sketch of the sort-merge join algorithm is given in Figure 10.3a. We use $R(i)$ to refer to the ith record in R. A variation of the sort-merge join can be used when secondary indexes exist on both join attributes. The indexes provide the ability to access (scan) the records in order of the join attributes, but the records themselves are physically scattered all over the file blocks, so this method may be quite inefficient, as every record access may involve accessing a different disk block.

- J4. *Hash-join*: The records of files R and S are both hashed to the same hash file, using the same hashing function on the join attributes A of R and B of S as hash keys. First, a single pass through the file with fewer records (say, R) hashes its records to the hash file buckets; this is called the **partitioning phase**, since the records of R are partitioned into the hash buckets. In the second phase, called the **probing phase**, a single pass through the other file (S) then hashes each of its records to probe the appropriate bucket, and that record is combined with all matching records from R in that bucket. This simplified description of hash-join assumes that the smaller of the two files fits *entirely into memory buckets* after the first phase. We will discuss variations of hash-join that do not require this assumption below.

In practice, techniques J1 to J4 are implemented by accessing *whole disk blocks* of a file, rather than individual records. Depending on the available buffer space in memory, the number of blocks read in from the file can be adjusted.

Effects of Available Buffer Space and Join Selection Factor on Join Performance. The buffer space available has an important effect on the various join algorithms. First, let us consider the nested-loop approach (J1). Looking again at the operation OP6 above, assume that the number of buffers available in main memory for implementing the join is $n_B = 7$ blocks (buffers). For illustration, assume that the DEPARTMENT file consists of $r_D = 50$ records stored in $b_D = 10$ disk blocks and that the EMPLOYEE file consists of $r_E = 6000$ records stored in $b_E = 2000$ disk blocks. It is advantageous to read as many blocks as possible at a time into memory from the file whose records are used for the outer loop (that is, $n_B > 2$ blocks). The algorithm can then read one block at a time for the inner-loop file and use its records to **probe** (that is, search) the outer loop blocks in memory for matching records. This reduces the total number of block accesses. An extra buffer block is needed to contain the resulting records after they are joined, and the contents of this buffer block are appended to the **result file**—the disk file that contains the join result—whenever it is filled. This buffer block is then is reused to hold additional result records.

In the nested-loop join, it makes a difference which file is chosen for the outer loop and which for the inner loop. If EMPLOYEE is used for the outer loop, each block of EMPLOYEE is read once, and the entire DEPARTMENT file (each of its blocks) is read once for each time we read in $(n_B - 2)$ blocks of the EMPLOYEE file. We get the following:

Total number of blocks accessed for outer file $= b_E$
Number of times $(n_B - 2)$ blocks of outer file are loaded $= \lceil b_E/(n_B - 2) \rceil$
Total number of blocks accessed for inner file $= b_D * \lceil b_E/(n_B - 2) \rceil$

(a)
```
        sort the tuples in R on attribute A; (*assume R has n tuples (records) ")
        sort the tuples in S on attribute B; ("assume S has m tuples (records) ")
        set i ← 1; j ← 1;
        while (i ≤ n) and (j ≤ m)
        do{     if R(i)[A] > S(j)[B]
                    then            set j ← j+1
                elseif R(i)[A] < S(j)[B]
                    then            set i ← i+1
                    else    {       (* R(i) [A] = S(j)[B], so we output a matched tuple*)
                                    output the combined tuple < R(i), S(j) to T; .
                                    (*output other tuples that match R(i), it any.)
                                    set l ≤ j+1;
                                    while (l ≤ m) and (R(i)[A] = S(l)[B]) .
                                    do      {   output the combined tuple < R(i), S(l) to T;
                                                set l ← l+1;
                                            }
                                    (*output other tuples that match S(j), if any*)
                                    set k ← i + 1;
                                    while (k ≤ n) and (R(k)[A] = S(j)[B])
                                    do      {   output the combined tuple < R(k), S(j) to T;
                                                set k ← k+1
                                            }
                                    set i ← i + 1, j ← j+1
                            }
        }
```

(b)
```
        create a tuple t [<attribute list >] in T' for each tuple t in R;
                (*T 'contains the projection result before duplicate elimination*)
        if <attribute list> includes a key of R
            then T ← T'
            else {      sort the tuples in T';
                        set i ← 1, j ← 2;
                        while i ← n
                        do      {   output the tuple T'[i] to T;
                                    while T'[i] = T'[j] and j < n do j ← j+ 1; (*eliminate duplicates.)
                                    i ← j; j ← i+1
                                }
                 }
        (* T contains the projection result after duplicate elimination *) .
```

FIGURE 10.3 Implementing JOIN, PROJECT, UNION, INTERSECTION, and SET DIFFERENCE by using sort-merge, where R has n tuples and S has m tuples. (a) Implementing the operation $T \leftarrow R \bowtie_{A=B} S$. (b) Implementing the operation $T \leftarrow \pi_{<\text{attribute list}>}(R)$.

(c)   sort the tuples in R and S using the same unique sort attributes;
        set $i \leftarrow 1, j \leftarrow 1$;
        while $(i \leftarrow n)$ and $(j \leq m)$
        do   {   if $R(i) > S(j)$
                       then   {   output $S(j)$ to T;
                                        set $j \leftarrow j+1$
                                   }
                       elseif $R(i) < S(j)$
                       then   {   output $R(i)$ to T;
                                        set $i \leftarrow i+1$
                                   }
                       else set $j \leftarrow j+1$ (*$R(i) = S(j)$, so we skip one of the duplicate tuples*)
                  }
        if $(i \leq n)$ then add tuples $R(i)$ to $R(n)$ to T;
        if $(j \leq m)$ then add tuples $S(j)$ to $S(m)$ to T;

(d)   sort the tuples In R and S using the same unique sort attributes;
        set $i \leftarrow 1, j \leftarrow 1$;
        while $(i \leq n)$ and $(j \leq m)$
        do   {   if $R(I) > S(j)$
                       then   set $j \leftarrow j+1$
                       elseif $R(i) < S(j)$
                       then   set $j \leftarrow i+1$
                       else   {   output $R(i)$ to T; (* $R((i) = S(j)$, so we output the tuple *)
                                        set, $i \leftarrow i+1, i \leftarrow j+1$
                                   }
                  }

(e)   sort the tuples in R and S using the same unique sort attributes;
        set i $\leftarrow 1, j \leftarrow 1$;
        while $(i \leq n)$ and $(j \leq m)$
        do   {   if $R(i) > S(j)$
                       then   set} $j \leftarrow j+1$
                       elseif $R(i) < S(j)$
                       then   {   output $R(i)$ to T; (* $R(i)$ has no matching $S(j)$, so output $R(i)$*)
                                        set $i \leftarrow i+1$
                                   }
                       else   set $i \leftarrow i+1, j \leftarrow j+1$
                  }
        if $(i \leq n)$ then add tuples $R(i)$ to $R(n)$ to T;

FIGURE 10.3(CONTINUED)   Implementing JOIN, PROJECT, UNION, INTERSECTION, and SET DIFFERENCE by using sort-merge, where R has n tuples and S has m tuples. (c) Implementing the operation $T \leftarrow R \cup S$. (d) Implementing the operation $T \leftarrow R \cap S$. (e) Implementing the operation $T \leftarrow R - S$.

Hence, we get the following total number of block accesses:

$$b_E + (\lceil b_E/(n_B - 2)\rceil * b_D) = 2000 + (\lceil (2000/5)\rceil * 10) = 6000 \text{ block accesses}$$

On the other hand, if we use the DEPARTMENT records in the outer loop, by symmetry we get the following total number of block accesses:

$$b_D + (\lceil b_D/(n_B - 2) \rceil * b_E) = 10 + (\lceil (10/5) \rceil * 2000) = 4010 \text{ block accesses}$$

The join algorithm uses a buffer to hold the joined records of the result file. Once the buffer is filled, it is written to disk and reused.[9] If the result file of the join operation has b_{RES} disk blocks, each block is written once, so an additional b_{RES} block accesses should be added to the preceding formulas in order to estimate the total cost of the join operation. The same holds for the formulas developed later for other join algorithms. As this example shows, it is advantageous to use the file *with fewer blocks* as the outer-loop file in the nested-loop join.

Another factor that affects the performance of a join, particularly the single-loop method J2, is the percentage of records in a file that will be joined with records in the other file. We call this the **join selection factor**[10] of a file with respect to an equijoin condition with another file. This factor depends on the particular equijoin condition between the two files. To illustrate this, consider the operation OP7, which joins each DEPARTMENT record with the EMPLOYEE record for the manager of that department. Here, each DEPARTMENT record (there are 50 such records in our example) is expected to be joined with a single EMPLOYEE record, but many EMPLOYEE records (the 5950 of them that do not manage a department) will not be joined.

Suppose that secondary indexes exist on both the attributes ENO of EMPLOYEE and MGRENO of DEPARTMENT, with the number of index levels $x_{ENO} = 4$ and $x_{MGRENO} = 2$, respectively. We have two options for implementing method J2. The first retrieves each EMPLOYEE record and then uses the index on MGRENO of DEPARTMENT to find a matching DEPARTMENT record. In this case, no matching record will be found for employees who do not manage a department. The number of block accesses for this case is approximately

$$b_E + (r_E * (x_{MGRENO} + 1)) = 2000 + (6000 * 3) = 20,000 \text{ block accesses}$$

The second option retrieves each DEPARTMENT record and then uses the index on ENO of EMPLOYEE to find a matching manager EMPLOYEE record. In this case, every DEPARTMENT record will have one matching EMPLOYEE record. The number of block accesses for this case is approximately

$$b_D + (r_D * (x_{ENO} + 1)) = 10 + (50 * 5) = 260 \text{ block accesses}$$

The second option is more efficient because the join selection factor of DEPARTMENT with respect to the join condition ENO = MGRENO is 1, whereas the join selection factor of EMPLOYEE with respect to the same join condition is (50/6000), or 0.008. For method J2, either the smaller file or the file that has a match for every record (that is, the file with the high join selection factor) should be used in the (outer) join loop. It is also possible to create an index specifically for performing the join operation if one does not already exist.

The sort-merge join J3 is quite efficient if both files are already sorted by their join attribute. Only a single pass is made through each file. Hence, the number of blocks accessed is equal to the sum of the numbers of blocks in both files. For this method, both OP6 and OP7 would need $b_E + b_D = 2000 + 10 = 2010$ block accesses. However, both files are required to be ordered by the join attributes; if one or both are not, they may be sorted specifically for performing the join operation. If we estimate the cost of sorting an external file by (b $\log_2 b$) block accesses, and if both files need to be sorted, the total cost of a sort-merge join can be estimated by $(b_E + b_D + b_E \log_2 b_E + b_D \log_2 b_D)$.[11]

---

9. If we reserve two buffers for the result file, double buffering can be used to speed the algorithm (see Chapter 9.3).

10. This is different from the *join selectivity*, which we shall discuss in Section 10.8.

11. We can use the more accurate formulas from Section 10.2 if we know the number of available buffers for sorting.

Partition Hash Join and Hybrid Hash Join. The hash-join method J4 is also quite efficient. In this case only a single pass is made through each file, whether or not the files are ordered. If the hash table for the smaller of the two files can be kept entirely in main memory after hashing (partitioning) on its join attribute, the implementation is straightforward. If, however, parts of the hash file must be stored on disk, the method becomes more complex, and a number of variations to improve the efficiency have been proposed. We discuss two techniques: partition hash join and a variation called hybrid hash join, which has been shown to be quite efficient.

In the **partition hash join** algorithm, each file is first partitioned into M partitions using a **partitioning hash function** on the join attributes. Then, each pair of partitions is joined. For example, suppose we are joining relations R and S on the join attributes R.A and S.B:

$$R \bowtie_{A=B} S$$

In the **partitioning phase**, R is partitioned into the M partitions $R_1, R_2, \ldots, R_M$, and S into the M partitions $S_1, S_2, \ldots, S_M$. The property of each pair of corresponding partitions R_i, S_i is that records in R_i *only need to be joined* with records in S_i, and vice versa. This property is ensured by using the *same hash function* to partition both files on their join attributes—attribute A for R and attribute B for S. The minimum number of in-memory buffers needed for the partitioning phase is M + 1. Each of the files R and S are partitioned separately. For each of the partitions, a single in-memory buffer—whose size is one disk block—is allocated to store the records that hash to this partition. Whenever the in-memory buffer for a partition gets filled, its contents are appended to a **disk subfile** that stores this partition. The partitioning phase has *two iterations*. After the first iteration, the first file R is partitioned into the subfiles $R_1, R_2, \ldots, R_M$, where all the records that hashed to the same buffer are in the same partition. After the second iteration, the second file S is similarly partitioned.

In the second phase, called the **joining** or **probing phase**, M *iterations* are needed. During iteration *i*, the two partitions R_i and S_i are joined. The minimum number of buffers needed for iteration *i* is the number of blocks in the smaller of the two partitions, say R_i, plus two additional buffers. If we use a nested loop join during iteration *i*, the records from the smaller of the two partitions R_i are copied into memory buffers; then all blocks from the other partition S_i are read—one at a time—and each record is used to **probe** (that is, search) partition R_i for matching record(s). Any matching records are joined and written into the result file. To improve the efficiency of in-memory probing, it is common to use an *in-memory hash table* for storing the records in partition R_i by using a different hash function from the partitioning hash function.[12]

We can approximate the cost of this partition hash-join as $3 * (b_R + b_S) + b_{RES}$ for our example, since each record is read once and written back to disk once during the partitioning phase. During the joining (probing) phase, each record is read a second time to perform the join. The *main difficulty* of this algorithm is to ensure that the partitioning hash function is **uniform**—that is, the partition sizes are nearly equal in size. If the partitioning function is **skewed** (nonuniform), then some partitions may be too large to fit in the available memory space for the second joining phase.

Notice that if the available in-memory buffer space $n_B > (b_R + 2)$, where b_R is the number of blocks for the *smaller* of the two files being joined, say R, then there is no reason to do partitioning since in this case the join can be performed entirely in memory using some variation of the nested-loop join based on hashing and probing. For illustration, assume we are performing the join operation OP6, repeated below:

(OP6): EMPLOYEE $\bowtie_{DNO=DNUMBER}$ DEPARTMENT

---

12. If the hash function used for partitioning is used again, all records in a partition will hash to the same bucket again.

In this example, the smaller file is the DEPARTMENT file; hence, if the number of available memory buffers $n_B > (b_D + 2)$, the whole DEPARTMENT file can be read into main memory and organized into a hash table on the join attribute. Each EMPLOYEE block is then read into a buffer, and each EMPLOYEE record in the buffer is hashed on its join attribute and is used to probe the corresponding in-memory bucket in the DEPARTMENT hash table. If a matching record is found, the records are joined, and the result record(s) are written to the result buffer and eventually to the result file on disk. The cost in terms of block accesses is hence $(b_D + b_E)$, plus b_{RES}—the cost of writing the result file.

The **hybrid hash-join algorithm** is a variation of partition hash join, where the *joining* phase for *one of the partitions* is included in the *partitioning* phase. To illustrate this, let us assume that the size of a memory buffer is one disk block; that n_B such buffers are *available*; and that the hash function used is $h(K) = K$ mod M so that M partitions are being created, where $M < n_B$. For illustration, assume we are performing the join operation OP6. In the *first pass* of the partitioning phase, when the hybrid hash-join algorithm is partitioning the smaller of the two files (DEPARTMENT in OP6), the algorithm divides the buffer space among the M partitions such that all the blocks of the first *partition* of DEPARTMENT completely reside in main memory. For each of the other partitions, only a single in-memory buffer—whose size is one disk block—is allocated; the remainder of the partition is written to disk as in the regular partition hash join. Hence, at the end of the *first pass of the partitioning phase*, the first partition of DEPARTMENT resides wholly in main memory, whereas each of the other partitions of DEPARTMENT resides in a disk subfile.

For the second pass of the partitioning phase, the records of the second file being joined—the larger file, EMPLOYEE in OP6—are being partitioned. If a record hashes to the *first partition*, it is joined with the matching record in DEPARTMENT and the joined records are written to the result buffer (and eventually to disk). If an EMPLOYEE record hashes to a partition other than the first, it is partitioned normally. Hence, at the end of the second pass of the partitioning phase, all records that hash to the first partition have been joined. Now there are $M - 1$ pairs of partitions on disk. Therefore, during the second **joining** or **probing** phase, $M - 1$ *iterations* are needed instead of M. The goal is to join as many records during the partitioning phase so as to save the cost of storing those records back to disk and rereading them a second time during the joining phase.

10.4 ALGORITHMS FOR PROJECT AND SET OPERATIONS

A PROJECT operation $\pi_{<\text{attribute list}>}(R)$ is straightforward to implement if <attribute list> includes a key of relation R, because in this case the result of the operation will have the same number of tuples as R, but with only the values for the attributes in <attribute list> in each tuple. If <attribute list> does not include a key of R, *duplicate tuples must be eliminated*. This is usually done by sorting the result of the operation and then eliminating duplicate tuples, which appear consecutively after sorting. A sketch of the algorithm is given in Figure 10.3b. Hashing can also be used to eliminate duplicates: as each record is hashed and inserted into a bucket of the hash file in memory, it is checked against those already in the bucket; if it is a duplicate, it is not inserted. It is useful to recall here that in SQL queries, the default is not to eliminate duplicates from the query result; only if the keyword DISTINCT is included are duplicates eliminated from the query result.

Set operations—UNION, INTERSECTION, SET DIFFERENCE, and CARTESIAN PRODUCT—are sometimes expensive to implement. In particular, the CARTESIAN PRODUCT operation $R \times S$ is quite expensive, because its result includes a record for each combination of records from R and S. In addition, the attributes of the result include all attributes of R and S. If R has n records and j attributes and S has m records and k attributes, the result relation will have $n * m$ records and $j + k$ attributes. Hence, it is important to avoid the CARTESIAN PRODUCT operation and to substitute other equivalent operations during query optimization (see Section 10.7).

The other three set operations—UNION, INTERSECTION, and SET DIFFERENCE[13]—apply only to union-compatible relations, which have the same number of attributes and the same attribute domains. The customary way to implement these operations is to use variations of the **sort-merge technique**: the two relations are sorted on the same attributes, and, after sorting, a single scan through each relation is sufficient to produce the result. For example, we can implement the UNION operation, $R \cup S$, by scanning and merging both sorted files concurrently, and whenever the same tuple exists in both relations, only one is kept in the merged result. For the INTERSECTION operation, $R \cap S$, we keep in the merged result only those tuples that appear in *both relations*. Figure 10.3c to (e) sketches the implementation of these operations by sorting and merging. Some of the details are not included in these algorithms.

Hashing can also be used to implement UNION, INTERSECTION, and SET DIFFERENCE. One table is partitioned and the other is used to probe the appropriate partition. For example, to implement $R \cup S$, first hash (partition) the records of R; then, hash (probe) the records of S, but do not insert duplicate records in the buckets. To implement $R \cap S$, first partition the records of R to the hash file. Then, while hashing each record of S, probe to check if an identical record from R is found in the bucket, and if so add the record to the result file. To implement $R - S$, first hash the records of R to the hash file buckets. While hashing (probing) each record of S, if an identical record is found in the bucket, remove that record from the bucket.

10.5 Implementing Aggregate Operations and Outer Joins

10.5.1 Implementing Aggregate Operations

The aggregate operators (MIN, MAX, COUNT, AVERAGE, SUM), when applied to an entire table, can be computed by a table scan or by using an appropriate index, if available. For example, consider the following SQL query:

```
SELECT    MAX(SALARY)
FROM      EMPLOYEE;
```

If an (ascending) index on SALARY exists for the EMPLOYEE relation, then the optimizer can decide on using the index to search for the largest value by following the *rightmost* pointer in each index node from the root to the rightmost leaf. That node would include the largest SALARY value as its *last* entry. In most cases, this would be more efficient than a full table scan of EMPLOYEE, since no actual records need to be retrieved. The MIN aggregate can be handled in a similar manner, except that the *leftmost* pointer is followed from the root to leftmost leaf. That node would include the smallest SALARY value as its first entry.

The index could also be used for the COUNT, AVERAGE, and SUM aggregates, but only if it is a **dense index**—that is, if there is an index entry for every record in the main file. In this case, the associated computation would be applied to the values in the index. For a nondense index, the actual number of records associated with each index entry must be used for a correct computation (except for COUNT DISTINCT, where the number of distinct values can be counted from the index itself).

When a GROUP BY clause is used in a query, the aggregate operator must be applied separately to each group of tuples. Hence, the table must first be partitioned into subsets of tuples, where each partition (group)

---

13. SET DIFFERENCE is called EXCEPT in SQL.

has the same value for the grouping attributes. In this case, the computation is more complex. Consider the following query:

> **SELECT**   DNO, **AVG**(SALARY)
> **FROM**   EMPLOYEE
> **GROUP BY**   DNO;

The usual technique for such queries is to first use either **sorting** or **hashing** on the grouping attributes to partition the file into the appropriate groups. Then the algorithm computes the aggregate function for the tuples in each group, which have the same grouping attribute(s) value. In the example query, the set of tuples for each department number would be grouped together in a partition and the average salary computed for each group.

Notice that if a **clustering index** (see Chapter 9) exists on the grouping attribute(s), then the records are *already partitioned* (grouped) into the appropriate subsets. In this case, it is only necessary to apply the computation to each group.

10.5.2   Implementing Outer Join

In Section 6.4, the *outer join operation* was introduced, with its three variations: left outer join, right outer join, and full outer join. We also discussed in Chapter 7 how these operations can be specified in SQL. The following is an example of a left outer join operation in SQL:

> **SELECT** LNAME, FNAME, DNAME
> **FROM** (EMPLOYEE **LEFT OUTER JOIN** DEPARTMENT **ON** DNO=DNUMBER);

The result of this query is a table of employee names and their associated departments. It is similar to a regular (inner) join result, with the exception that if an EMPLOYEE tuple (a tuple in the *left* relation) *does not have an associated department*, the employee's name will still appear in the resulting table, but the department name would be *null* for such tuples in the query result.

Outer join can be computed by modifying one of the join algorithms, such as nested-loop join or single-loop join. For example, to compute a *left* outer join, we use the left relation as the outer loop or single-loop because every tuple in the left relation must appear in the result. If there are matching tuples in the other relation, the joined tuples are produced and saved in the result. However, if no matching tuple is found, the tuple is still included in the result but is padded with null value(s). The sort-merge and hash-join algorithms can also be extended to compute outer joins.

Alternatively, outer join can be computed by executing a combination of relational algebra operators. For example, the left outer join operation shown above is equivalent to the following sequence of relational operations:

1. Compute the (inner) JOIN of the EMPLOYEE and DEPARTMENT tables.

   TEMP 1 ← $\pi_{\text{LNAME, FNAME, DNAME}}$ (EMPLOYEE $\bowtie_{\text{DNO=DNUMBER}}$ DEPARTMENT)

2. Find the EMPLOYEE tuples that do not appear in the (inner) JOIN result.

   TEMP 2 ← $\pi_{\text{LNAME, FNAME}}$ (EMPLOYEE) − $\pi_{\text{LNAME, FNAME}}$ (TEMP 1)

3. Pad each tuple in TEMP 2 with a null DNAME field.

   TEMP 2 ← TEMP 2 × 'NULL'

4. Apply the UNION operation to TEMP 1, TEMP 2 to produce the LEFT OUTER JOIN result.

   RESULT ← TEMP 1 ∪ TEMP 2

The cost of the outer join as computed above would be the sum of the costs of the associated steps (inner join, projections, and union). However, note that step 3 can be done as the temporary relation is being constructed in step 2; that is, we can simply pad each resulting tuple with a null. In addition, in step 4, we know that the two operands of the union are disjoint (no common tuples), so there is no need for duplicate elimination.

10.6 COMBINING OPERATIONS USING PIPELINING

A query specified in SQL will typically be translated into a relational algebra expression that is a *sequence of relational operations*. If we execute a single operation at a time, we must generate temporary files on disk to hold the results of these temporary operations, creating excessive overhead. Generating and storing large temporary files on disk is time-consuming and can be unnecessary in many cases, since these files will immediately be used as input to the next operation. To reduce the number of temporary files, it is common to generate query execution code that correspond to algorithms for combinations of operations in a query.

For example, rather than being implemented separately, a JOIN can be combined with two SELECT operations on the input files and a final PROJECT operation on the resulting file; all this is implemented by one algorithm with two input files and a single output file. Rather than creating four temporary files, we apply the algorithm directly and get just one result file. In Section 10.7.2 we discuss how heuristic relational algebra optimization can group operations together for execution. This is called **pipelining** or **stream-based processing**.

It is common to create the query execution code dynamically to implement multiple operations. The generated code for producing the query combines several algorithms that correspond to individual operations. As the result tuples from one operation are produced, they are provided as input for subsequent operations. For example, if a join operation follows two select operations on base relations, the tuples resulting from each select are provided as input for the join algorithm in a **stream** or **pipeline** as they are produced.

10.7 USING HEURISTICS IN QUERY OPTIMIZATION

In this section we discuss optimization techniques that apply heuristic rules to modify the internal representation of a query—which is usually in the form of a query tree or a query graph data structure—to improve its expected performance. The parser of a high-level query first generates an *initial internal representation*, which is then optimized according to heuristic rules. Following that, a query execution plan is generated to execute groups of operations based on the access paths available on the files involved in the query.

One of the main **heuristic rules** is to apply SELECT and PROJECT operations *before* applying the JOIN or other binary operations. This is because the size of the file resulting from a binary operation—such as JOIN—is usually a multiplicative function of the sizes of the input files. The SELECT and PROJECT operations reduce the size of a file and hence should be applied *before* a join or other binary operation.

We start in Section 10.7.1 by introducing the query tree and query graph notations. These can be used as the basis for the data structures that are used for internal representation of queries. A query tree is used to represent a relational algebra or extended relational algebra expression, whereas a query graph is used to represent a relational calculus expression. We then show in Section 10.7.2 how heuristic optimization rules are applied to convert a query tree into an **equivalent query tree**, which represents a different relational algebra expression that is more efficient to execute but gives the same result as the original one. We also discuss the equivalence of various relational algebra expressions. Finally, Section 10.7.3 discusses the generation of query execution plans.

10.7.1   Notation for Query Trees and Query Graphs

A **query tree** is a tree data structure that corresponds to a relational algebra expression. It represents the input relations of the query as *leaf nodes* of the tree, and represents the relational algebra operations as internal nodes. An execution of the query tree consists of executing an internal node operation whenever its operands are available and then replacing that internal node by the relation that results from executing the operation. The execution terminates when the root node is executed and produces the result relation for the query.

Figure 10.4a shows a query tree for query Q2 of Chapters 4 to 7: For every project located in 'Chennai', retrieve the project number, the controlling department number, and the department manager's last name, address, and date of birth. This query is specified on the relational schema of Figure 4.5 and corresponds to the following relational algebra expression:

$$\pi_{\text{PNUMBER, DNUM, LNAME, ADDRESS, DOB}} \left(\left(\left(\sigma_{\text{PLOCATION='CHENNAI'}}(\text{PROJECT}) \right) \right) \right)$$

$$\Join_{\text{DNUM=DNUMBER}}(\text{DEPARTMENT}) \Join_{\text{MGRENO=ENO}}(\text{EMPLOYEE})$$

This corresponds to the following SQL query:

Q2:   **SELECT** P.PNUMBER, P.DNUM, E.LNAME, E.ADDRESS, E.DOB
       FROM   PROJECT **AS** P, DEPARTMENT **AS** D, EMPLOYEE **AS** E
       WHERE P.DNUM=D.DNUMBER **AND** D.MGRENO=E.ENO **AND**
              P.PLOCATION='CHENNAI';

In Figure 10.4a the three relations PROJECT, DEPARTMENT, and EMPLOYEE are represented by leaf nodes P, D, and E, while the relational algebra operations of the expression are represented by internal tree nodes. When this query tree is executed, the node marked (1) in Figure 10.4a must begin execution before node (2) because some resulting tuples of operation (1) must be available before we can begin executing operation (2). Similarly, node (2) must begin executing and producing results before node (3) can start execution, and so on.

As we can see, the query tree represents a specific order of operations for executing a query. A more neutral representation of a query is the **query graph** notation. Figure 10.4c shows the query graph for query Q2. Relations in the query are represented by **relation nodes**, which are displayed as single circles. Constant values, typically from the query selection conditions, are represented by **constant nodes**, which are displayed as double circles or ovals. Selection and join conditions are represented by the graph **edges**, as shown in Figure 10.4c. Finally, the attributes to be retrieved from each relation are displayed in square brackets above each relation.

The query graph representation does not indicate an order on which operations to perform first. There is only a single graph corresponding to each query.[14] Although some optimization techniques were based on query graphs, it is now generally accepted that query trees are preferable because, in practice, the query optimizer needs to show the order of operations for query execution, which is not possible in query graphs.

---

14. Hence, a query graph corresponds to a relational calculus expression (see Chapter 5).

(a)

(b)

(c)

FIGURE 10.4 Two query trees for the query Q2. (a) Query tree corresponding to the relational algebra expression for Q2. (b) Initial (canonical) query tree for SQL query Q2. (c) Query graph for Q2.

10.7.2 Heuristic Optimization of Query Trees

In general, many different relational algebra expressions—and hence many different query trees—can be equivalent; that is, they can correspond to the same query.[15] The query parser will typically generate a standard initial query tree to correspond to an SQL query, without doing any optimization. For example, for a select-project-join query, such as Q2, the initial tree is shown in Figure 10.4b. The CARTESIAN PRODUCT of the relations specified in the FROM clause is first applied; then the selection and join conditions of the WHERE clause are applied, followed by the projection on the SELECT clause attributes. Such a canonical query tree represents a relational algebra expression that is *very inefficient if executed directly*, because of the CARTESIAN PRODUCT (×) operations. For example, if the PROJECT, DEPARTMENT, and EMPLOYEE relations had record sizes of 100, 50, and 150 bytes and contained 100, 20, and 5000 tuples, respectively, the result of the CARTESIAN PRODUCT would contain 10 million tuples of record size 300 bytes each. However, the query tree in Figure 10.4b is in a simple standard form that can be easily created. It is now the job of the heuristic query optimizer to transform this initial query tree into a **final query tree** that is efficient to execute.

The optimizer must include rules for equivalence among relational algebra expressions that can be applied to the initial tree. The heuristic query optimization rules then utilize these equivalence expressions to transform the initial tree into the final, optimized query tree. We first discuss informally how a query tree is transformed by using heuristics. Then we discuss general transformation rules and show how they may be used in an algebraic heuristic optimizer.

Example of Transforming a Query. Consider the following query Q on the database of Figure 4.5: "Find the last names of employees born after 1957 who work on a project named 'Aquarius'." This query can be specified in SQL as follows:

```
Q:   SELECT    LNAME
     FROM      EMPLOYEE,   WORKS_ON,   PROJECT
     WHERE     PNAME='AQUARIUS' AND PNUMBER=PNO AND EENO=ENO
               AND DOB > '31-12-1957';
```

The initial query tree for Q is shown in Figure 10.5a. Executing this tree directly first creates a very large file containing the CARTESIAN PRODUCT of the entire EMPLOYEE, WORKS_ ON, and PROJECT files. However, this query needs only one record from the PROJECT relation— for the 'Aquarius' project—and only the EMPLOYEE records for those whose date of birth is after '31-12-1957'. Figure 10.5b shows an improved query tree that first applies the SELECT operations to reduce the number of tuples that appear in the CARTESIAN PRODUCT.

A further improvement is achieved by switching the positions of the EMPLOYEE and PROJECT relations in the tree, as shown in Figure 10.5c. This uses the information that PNUMBER is a key attribute of the project relation, and hence the SELECT operation on the PROJECT relation will retrieve a single record only. We can further improve the query tree by replacing any CARTESIAN PRODUCT operation that is followed by a join condition with a JOIN operation, as shown in Figure 15.5d. Another improvement is to keep only the attributes needed by subsequent operations in the intermediate relations, by including PROJECT (π) operations as early as possible in the query tree, as shown in Figure 10.5e. This reduces the attributes (columns) of the intermediate relations, whereas the SELECT operations reduce the number of tuples (records).

As the preceding example demonstrates, a query tree can be transformed step by step into another query tree that is more efficient to execute. However, we must make sure that the transformation steps always lead

---

15. A query may also be stated in various ways in a high-level query language such as SQL (see Chapter 7).

(a)

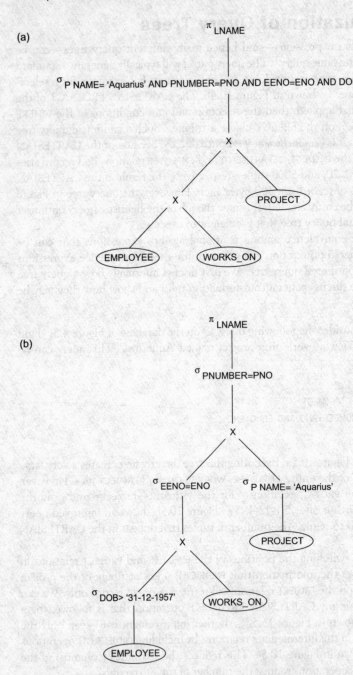

(b)

FIGURE 10.5 Steps in converting a query tree during heuristic optimization. (a) Initial (canonical) query tree for SQL query Q. (b) Moving SELECT operations down the query tree.

(c)

(d)

FIGURE 10.5(CONTINUED) Steps in converting a query tree during heuristic optimization. (c) Applying the more restrictive SELECT operation first. (d) Replacing CARTESIAN PRODUCT and SELECT with JOIN operations.

(e)

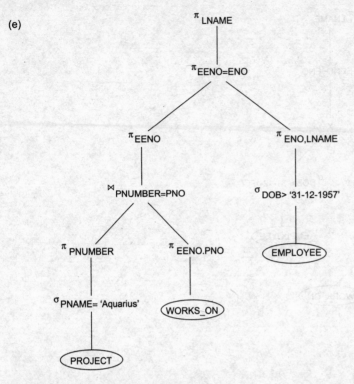

FIGURE 10.5(CONTINUED) Steps in converting a query tree during heuristic optimization. (e) Moving PROJECT operations down the query tree.

to an equivalent query tree. To do this, the query optimizer must know which transformation rules preserve this equivalence. We discuss some of these transformation rules next.

General Transformation Rules for Relational Algebra Operations. There are many rules for transforming relational algebra operations into equivalent ones. Here we are interested in the meaning of the operations and the resulting relations. Hence, if two relations have the same set of attributes in a *different order* but the two relations represent the same information, we consider the relations equivalent. In Section 4.1.2 we gave an alternative definition of relation that makes order of attributes unimportant; we will use this definition here. We now state some transformation rules that are useful in query optimization, without proving them:

1. Cascade of σ: A conjunctive selection condition can be broken up into a cascade (that is, a sequence) of individual σ operations:

   $$\sigma_{c1 \text{ AND } c2 \text{ AND} \ldots \text{ AND } cn}(R) \equiv \sigma_{c1}(\sigma_{c2}(\ldots(\sigma_{cn}(R))\ldots))$$

2. Commutativity of σ: The σ operation is commutative:

   $$\sigma_{c1}(\sigma_{c2}(R)) \equiv \sigma_{c2}(\sigma_{c1}(R))$$

3. Cascade of π: In a cascade (sequence) of π operations, all but the last one can be ignored:

   $$\pi_{List1}(\pi_{List2}(\ldots(\pi_{Listn}(R))\ldots)) \equiv \sigma_{List1}(R)$$

4. Commuting π with π: If the selection condition c involves only those attributes A1, ..., An in the projection list, the two operations can be commuted:

$$\pi_{A1, A2, \ldots, An} (\sigma_c (R)) \equiv \sigma_c (\pi_{A1, A2, \ldots, An} (R))$$

5. Commutativity of $\bowtie$ (and $\times$): The $\bowtie$ operation is commutative, as is the $\times$ operation:

$$R \bowtie_c S \equiv S \bowtie_c R$$

$$R \times S \equiv S \times R$$

Notice that, although the order of attributes may not be the same in the relations resulting from the two joins (or two cartesian products), the "meaning" is the same because order of attributes is not important in the alternative definition of relation.

6. Commuting σ with $\bowtie$ (or $\times$): If all the attributes in the selection condition c involve only the attributes of one of the relations being joined—say, R—the two operations can be commuted as follows:

$$\sigma_c (R \bowtie S) \equiv (\sigma_c (R)) \bowtie S$$

Alternatively, if the selection condition c can be written as ($c1$ AND $c2$), where condition $c1$ involves only the attributes of R and condition $c2$ involves only the attributes of S, the operations commute as follows:

$$\sigma_c (R \bowtie S) \equiv (\sigma_{c1} (R)) \bowtie (\sigma_{c2} (S))$$

The same rules apply if the $\bowtie$ is replaced by a $\times$ operation.

7. Commuting π with $\bowtie$ (or $\times$): Suppose that the projection list is $L = \{A_1, \ldots, A_n, B_1, \ldots, B_m\}$, where $A_1, \ldots, A_n$ are attributes of R and $B_1, \ldots, B_m$ are attributes of S. If the join condition c involves only attributes in L, the two operations can be commuted as follows:

$$\pi_L (R \bowtie_c S) \equiv (\pi_{A1, \ldots, An} (R)) \bowtie_c (\pi_{B1, \ldots, Bm} (S))$$

If the join condition c contains additional attributes not in L, these must be added to the projection list, and a final π operation is needed. For example, if attributes $A_{n+1}, \ldots, A_{n+k}$ of R and $B_{m+1}, \ldots, B_{m+p}$ of S are involved in the join condition c but are not in the projection list L, the operations commute as follows:

$$\pi_L (R \bowtie_c S) \equiv \pi_L ((\pi_{A1, \ldots, An, An+1, \ldots, An+k}(R)) \bowtie_c (\pi_{B1, \ldots, Bm, Bm+1, \ldots, Bm+p} (S)))$$

For $\times$, there is no condition c, so the first transformation rule always applies by replacing $\bowtie_c$ with $\times$.

8. Commutativity of set operations: The set operations $\cup$ and $\cap$ are commutative but $-$ is not.

9. Associativity of $\bowtie$, $\times$, $\cup$, and $\cap$: These four operations are individually associative; that is, if θ stands for any one of these four operations (throughout the expression), we have:

$$(R \theta S) \theta T \equiv R \theta (S \theta T)$$

10. Commuting σ with set operations: The σ operation commutes with $\cup$, $\cap$, and $-$. If θ stands for any one of these three operations (throughout the expression), we have:

$$\sigma_c (R \theta S) \equiv (\sigma_c (R)) \theta (\sigma_c (S))$$

11. The π operation commutes with _:

$$\pi_L (R \cup S) \equiv (\pi_L (R)) \cup (\pi_L (S))$$

12. Converting a (σ, $\times$) sequence into $\bowtie$: If the condition c of a σ that follows a $\times$ corresponds to a join condition, convert the (σ, $\times$) sequence into a $\bowtie$ as follows:

$$(\sigma_c (R \times S)) \equiv (R \bowtie_c S)$$

There are other possible transformations. For example, a selection or join condition c can be converted into an equivalent condition by using the following rules (DeMorgan's laws):

NOT (C1 **AND** C2) ≡ (**NOT** C1) **OR** (**NOT** C2)

NOT (C1 **OR** C2) ≡ (**NOT** C1) **AND** (**NOT** C2)

Additional transformations discussed in Chapters 4 and 5 are not repeated here. We discuss next how transformations can be used in heuristic optimization.

Outline of a Heuristic Algebraic Optimization Algorithm.   We can now outline the steps of an algorithm that utilizes some of the above rules to transform an initial query tree into an optimized tree that is more efficient to execute (in most cases). The algorithm will lead to transformations similar to those discussed in our example of Figure 10.5. The steps of the algorithm are as follows:

1. Using Rule 1, break up any SELECT operations with conjunctive conditions into a cascade of SELECT operations. This permits a greater degree of freedom in moving SELECT operations down different branches of the tree.

2. Using Rules 2, 4, 6, and 10 concerning the commutativity of SELECT with other operations, move each SELECT operation as far down the query tree as is permitted by the attributes involved in the select condition.

3. Using Rules 5 and 9 concerning commutativity and associativity of binary operations, rearrange the leaf nodes of the tree using the following criteria. First, position the leaf node relations with the most restrictive SELECT operations so they are executed first in the query tree representation. The definition of *most restrictive* SELECT can mean either the ones that produce a relation with the fewest tuples or with the smallest absolute size.[16] Another possibility is to define the most restrictive SELECT as the one with the smallest selectivity; this is more practical because estimates of selectivities are often available in the DBMS catalog. Second, make sure that the ordering of leaf nodes does not cause CARTESIAN PRODUCT operations; for example, if the two relations with the most restrictive SELECT do not have a direct join condition between them, it may be desirable to change the order of leaf nodes to avoid Cartesian products.[17]

4. Using Rule 12, combine a CARTESIAN PRODUCT operation with a subsequent SELECT operation in the tree into a JOIN operation, if the condition represents a join condition.

5. Using Rules 3, 4, 7, and 11 concerning the cascading of PROJECT and the commuting of PROJECT with other operations, break down and move lists of projection attributes down the tree as far as possible by creating new PROJECT operations as needed. Only those attributes needed in the query result and in subsequent operations in the query tree should be kept after each PROJECT operation.

6. Identify subtrees that represent groups of operations that can be executed by a single algorithm.

In our example, Figure 10.5(b) shows the tree of Figure 10.5(a) after applying steps 1 and 2 of the algorithm; Figure 10.5(c) shows the tree after step 3; Figure 10.5(d) after step 4; and Figure 10.5(e) after step 5. In step 6 we may group together the operations in the subtree whose root is the operation π_{EENO} into a single algorithm. We may also group the remaining operations into another subtree, where the tuples resulting from the first algorithm replace the subtree whose root is the operation π_{EENO}, because the first grouping means that this subtree is executed first.

---

16. Either definition can be used, since these rules are heuristic.

17. Note that a Cartesian product is acceptable in some cases—for example, if each relation has only a single tuple because each had a previous select condition on a key field.

Summary of Heuristics for Algebraic Optimization.   We now summarize the basic heuristics for algebraic optimization. The main heuristic is to apply first the operations that reduce the size of intermediate results. This includes performing as early as possible SELECT operations to reduce the number of tuples and PROJECT operations to reduce the number of attributes. This is done by moving SELECT and PROJECT operations as far down the tree as possible. In addition, the SELECT and JOIN operations that are most restrictive—that is, result in relations with the fewest tuples or with the smallest absolute size—should be executed before other similar operations. This is done by reordering the leaf nodes of the tree among themselves while avoiding Cartesian products, and adjusting the rest of the tree appropriately.

10.7.3   Converting Query Trees into Query Execution Plans

An execution plan for a relational algebra expression represented as a query tree includes information about the access methods available for each relation as well as the algorithms to be used in computing the relational operators represented in the tree. As a simple example, consider query Q1 from Chapter 4, whose corresponding relational algebra expression is

$$\pi_{\text{FNAME,LNAME,ADDRESS}} (\sigma_{\text{DNAME='RESEARCH'}} (\text{DEPARTMENT}) \bowtie_{\text{DNUMBER=DNO}} \text{EMPLOYEE})$$

The query tree is shown in Figure 10.6. To convert this into an execution plan, the optimizer might choose an index search for the SELECT operation (assuming one exists), a table scan as access method for EMPLOYEE, a nested-loop join algorithm for the join, and a scan of the JOIN result for the PROJECT operator. In addition, the approach taken for executing the query may specify a materialized or a pipelined evaluation.

With **materialized evaluation**, the result of an operation is stored as a temporary relation (that is, the result is *physically materialized*). For instance, the join operation can be computed and the entire result stored as a temporary relation, which is then read as input by the algorithm that computes the PROJECT operation, which would produce the query result table. On the other hand, with **pipelined evaluation**, as the resulting tuples of an operation are produced, they are forwarded directly to the next operation in the query sequence. For example, as the selected tuples from DEPARTMENT are produced by the SELECT operation, they are placed in a buffer; the JOIN operation algorithm would then consume the tuples from the buffer, and those tuples that result from the JOIN operation are pipelined to the projection operation algorithm. The advantage of pipelining is the cost savings in not having to write the intermediate results to disk and not having to read them back for the next operation.

FIGURE 10.6 A query tree for query Q1.

10.8 USING SELECTIVITY AND COST ESTIMATES IN QUERY OPTIMIZATION

A query optimizer should not depend solely on heuristic rules; it should also estimate and compare the costs of executing a query using different execution strategies and should choose the strategy with the *lowest cost estimate*. For this approach to work, accurate cost estimates are required so that different strategies are compared fairly and realistically. In addition, we must limit the number of execution strategies to be considered; otherwise, too much time will be spent making cost estimates for the many possible execution strategies. Hence, this approach is more suitable for **compiled queries** where the optimization is done at compile time and the resulting execution strategy code is stored and executed directly at runtime. For **interpreted queries**, where the entire process shown in Figure 10.1 occurs at runtime, a full-scale optimization may slow down the response time. A more elaborate optimization is indicated for compiled queries, whereas a partial, less time-consuming optimization works best for interpreted queries.

We call this approach **cost-based query optimization,**[18] and it uses traditional optimization techniques that search the *solution space* to a problem for a solution that minimizes an objective (cost) function. The cost functions used in query optimization are estimates and not exact cost functions, so the optimization may select a query execution strategy that is not the optimal one. In Section 10.8.1 we discuss the components of query execution cost. In Section 10.8.2 we discuss the type of information needed in cost functions. This information is kept in the DBMS catalog. In Section 10.8.3 we give examples of cost functions for the SELECT operation, and in Section 10.8.4 we discuss cost functions for *two-way* JOIN operations. Section 10.8.5 discusses multiway joins, and Section 10.8.6 gives an example.

10.8.1 Cost Components for Query Execution

The cost of executing a query includes the following components:

1. *Access cost to secondary storage:* This is the cost of searching for, reading, and writing data blocks that reside on secondary storage, mainly on disk. The cost of searching for records in a file depends on the type of access structures on that file, such as ordering, hashing, and primary or secondary indexes. In addition, factors such as whether the file blocks are allocated contiguously on the same disk cylinder or scattered on the disk affect the access cost.

2. *Storage cost:* This is the cost of storing any intermediate files that are generated by an execution strategy for the query.

3. *Computation cost:* This is the cost of performing in-memory operations on the data buffers during query execution. Such operations include searching for and sorting records, merging records for a join, and performing computations on field values.

4. *Memory usage cost:* This is the cost pertaining to the number of memory buffers needed during query execution.

5. *Communication cost:* This is the cost of shipping the query and its results from the database site to the site or terminal where the query originated.

For large databases, the main emphasis is on minimizing the access cost to secondary storage. Simple cost functions ignore other factors and compare different query execution strategies in terms of the number

---

18. This approach was first used in the optimizer for the SYSTEM R experimental DBMS developed at IBM.

of block transfers between disk and main memory. For smaller databases, where most of the data in the files involved in the query can be completely stored in memory, the emphasis is on minimizing computation cost. In distributed databases, where many sites are involved, communication cost must be minimized also. It is difficult to include all the cost components in a (weighted) cost function because of the difficulty of assigning suitable weights to the cost components. That is why some cost functions consider a single factor only—disk access. In the next section we discuss some of the information that is needed for formulating cost functions.

10.8.2 Catalog Information Used in Cost Functions

To estimate the costs of various execution strategies, we must keep track of any information that is needed for the cost functions. This information may be stored in the DBMS catalog, where it is accessed by the query optimizer. First, we must know the size of each file. For a file whose records are all of the same type, the **number of records (tuples) (r)**, the (average) **record size (R)**, and the **number of blocks (b)** (or close estimates of them) are needed. The **blocking factor (bfr)** for the file may also be needed. We must also keep track of the *primary access method* and the *primary access attributes* for each file. The file records may be unordered, ordered by an attribute with or without a primary or clustering index, or hashed on a key attribute. Information is kept on all secondary indexes and indexing attributes. The **number of levels (x)** of each multilevel index (primary, secondary, or clustering) is needed for cost functions that estimate the number of block accesses that occur during query execution. In some cost functions the **number of first-level index blocks (b_{I1})** is needed.

Another important parameter is the **number of distinct values (d)** of an attribute and its **selectivity (sl)**, which is the fraction of records satisfying an equality condition on the attribute. This allows estimation of the **selection cardinality (s = sl * r)** of an attribute, which is the *average* number of records that will satisfy an equality selection condition on that attribute. For a *key attribute*, $d = r$, $sl = 1/r$ and $s = 1$. For a *nonkey attribute*, by making an assumption that the d distinct values are uniformly distributed among the records, we estimate $sl = (1/d)$ and so $s = (r/d)$.[19]

Information such as the number of index levels is easy to maintain because it does not change very often. However, other information may change frequently; for example, the number of records r in a file changes every time a record is inserted or deleted. The query optimizer will need reasonably close but not necessarily completely up-to-the minute values of these parameters for use in estimating the cost of various execution strategies. In the next two sections we examine how some of these parameters are used in cost functions for a cost-based query optimizer.

10.8.3 Examples of Cost Functions for SELECT

We now give cost functions for the selection algorithms S1 to S8 discussed in Section 10.3.1 in terms of *number of block transfers* between memory and disk. These cost functions are estimates that ignore computation time, storage cost, and other factors. The cost for method Si is referred to as C_{Si} block accesses.

- S1. *Linear search (brute force) approach:* We search all the file blocks to retrieve all records satisfying the selection condition; hence, $C_{S1a} = b$. For an equality condition on a key, only half the file blocks are searched on the average before finding the record, so $C_{S1b} = (b/2)$ if the record is found; if no record satisfies the condition, $C_{S1b} = b$.

- S2. *Binary search:* This search accesses approximately $C_{S2} = \log_2 b + \lceil (s/bfr) \rceil - 1$ file blocks. This reduces to $\log_2 b$ if the equality condition is on a unique (key) attribute, because $s = 1$ in this case.

---

19. As we mentioned earlier, more accurate optimizers may store histograms of the distribution of records over the data values for an attribute.

- S3. *Using a primary index (S3a) or hash key (S3b) to retrieve a single record:* For a primary index, retrieve one more block than the number of index levels; hence, $C_{S3a} = x + 1$. For hashing, the cost function is approximately $C_{S3b} = 1$ for static hashing or linear hashing, and it is 2 for extendible hashing (see Chapter 9).

- S4. *Using an ordering index to retrieve multiple records:* If the comparison condition is $>$, $>=$, $<$, or $<=$ on a key field with an ordering index, roughly half the file records will satisfy the condition. This gives a cost function of $C_{S4} = x + (b/2)$. This is a very rough estimate, and although it may be correct on the average, it may be quite inaccurate in individual cases.

- S5. *Using a clustering index to retrieve multiple records:* Given an equality condition, s records will satisfy the condition, where s is the selection cardinality of the indexing attribute. This means that file blocks will be accessed, giving $C_{S5} = x + \lceil (s/bfr) \rceil$.

- S6. *Using a secondary (B^+-tree) index:* On an *equality* comparison, s records will satisfy the condition, where s is the selection cardinality of the indexing attribute. However, because the index is nonclustering, each of the records may reside on a different block, so the (worst case) cost estimate is $C_{S6a} = x + s$. This reduces to $x + 1$ for a key indexing attribute. If the comparison condition is $>$, $>=$, $<$, or $<=$ and half the file records are assumed to satisfy the condition, then (very roughly) half the first-level index blocks are accessed, plus half the file records via the index. The cost estimate for this case, approximately, is $C_{S6b} = x + (b_{I1}/2) + (r/2)$. The $r/2$ factor can be refined if better selectivity estimates are available.

- S7. *Conjunctive selection:* We can use either S1 or one of the methods S2 to S6 discussed above. In the latter case, we use one condition to retrieve the records and then check in the memory buffer whether each retrieved record satisfies the remaining conditions in the conjunction.

- S8. *Conjunctive selection using a composite index:* Same as S3a, S5, or S6a, depending on the type of index.

Example of Using the Cost Functions. In a query optimizer, it is common to enumerate the various possible strategies for executing a query and to estimate the costs for different strategies. An optimization technique, such as dynamic programming, may be used to find the optimal (least) cost estimate efficiently, without having to consider all possible execution strategies. We do not discuss optimization algorithms here; rather, we use a simple example to illustrate how cost estimates may be used. Suppose that the EMPLOYEE file of Figure 4.5 has $r_E = 10,000$ records stored in $b_E = 2000$ disk blocks with blocking factor $bfr_E = 5$ records/block and the following access paths:

1. A clustering index on SALARY, with levels $x_{SALARY} = 3$ and average selection cardinality $s_{SALARY} = 20$.

2. A secondary index on the key attribute ENO, with $x_{ENO} = 4$ ($s_{ENO} = 1$).

3. A secondary index on the nonkey attribute DNO, with $x_{DNO} = 2$ and first-level index blocks $b_{I1DNO} = 4$. There are $d_{DNO} = 125$ distinct values for DNO, so the selection cardinality of DNO is $s_{DNO} = (r_E/d_{DNO}) = 80$.

4. A secondary index on SEX, with $x_{SEX} = 1$. There are $d_{SEX} = 2$ values for the sex attribute, so the average selection cardinality is $s_{SEX} = (r_E/d_{SEX}) = 5000$.

We illustrate the use of cost functions with the following examples:

(OP1): $\sigma_{ENO='123456789'}$ (EMPLOYEE)

(OP2): $\sigma_{DNO>5}$ (EMPLOYEE)

(OP3): $\sigma_{DNO=5}$ (EMPLOYEE)

(OP4): $\sigma_{DNO=5\ AND\ SALARY>30000\ AND\ SEX='F'}$ (EMPLOYEE)

The cost of the brute force (linear search) option S1 will be estimated as $C_{S1a} = b_E = 2000$ (for a selection on a nonkey attribute) or $C_{S1b} = (b_E/2) = 1000$ (average cost for a selection on a key attribute). For OP1 we can use either method S1 or method S6a; the cost estimate for S6a is $C_{S6a} = x_{SSN} + 1 = 4 + 1 = 5$, and it is chosen over Method S1, whose average cost is $C_{S1b} = 1000$. For OP2 we can use either method S1 (with estimated cost $C_{S1a} = 2000$) or method S6b (with estimated cost $C_{S6b} = x_{DNO} + (b_{I1DNO}/2) + (r_E/2) = 2 + (4/2)$ $+ (10,000/2) = 5004$), so we choose the brute force approach for OP2. For OP3 we can use either method S1 (with estimated cost $C_{S1a} = 2000$) or method S6a (with estimated cost $C_{S6a} = x_{DNO} + s_{DNO} = 2 + 80 = 82$), so we choose method S6a.

Finally, consider OP4, which has a conjunctive selection condition. We need to estimate the cost of using any one of the three components of the selection condition to retrieve the records, plus the brute force approach. The latter gives cost estimate $C_{S1a} = 2000$. Using the condition (DNO = 5) first gives the cost estimate $C_{S6a} = 82$. Using the condition (SALARY > 30,000) first gives a cost estimate $C_{S4} = x_{SALARY} + (b_E/2)$ $= 3 + (2000/2) = 1003$. Using the condition (SEX = 'F') first gives a cost estimate $C_{S6a} = x_{SEX} + s_{SEX} = 1 +$ $5000 = 5001$. The optimizer would then choose method S6a on the secondary index on DNO because it has the lowest cost estimate. The condition (DNO = 5) is used to retrieve the records, and the remaining part of the conjunctive condition (SALARY > 30,000 AND SEX = 'F') is checked for each selected record after it is retrieved into memory.

10.8.4   Examples of Cost Functions for JOIN

To develop reasonably accurate cost functions for JOIN operations, we need to have an estimate for the size (number of tuples) of the file that results *after* the JOIN operation. This is usually kept as a ratio of the size (number of tuples) of the resulting join file to the size of the Cartesian product file, if both are applied to the same input files, and it is called the **join selectivity** (js). If we denote the number of tuples of a relation R by $|R|$, we have

$$js = |(R \bowtie_c S)| / |(R \times S)| = |(R \bowtie_c S)| / (|R| * |S|)$$

If there is no join condition c, then js = 1 and the join is the same as the CARTESIAN PRODUCT. If no tuples from the relations satisfy the join condition, then js = 0. In general, $0 \le js \le 1$. For a join where the condition c is an equality comparison R.A = S.B, we get the following two special cases:

1. If A is a key of R, then $|(R \bowtie_c S)| \le |S|$, so $js \le (1/|R|)$.
2. If B is a key of S, then $|(R \bowtie_c S)| \le |R|$, so $js \le (1/|S|)$.

Having an estimate of the join selectivity for commonly occurring join conditions enables the query optimizer to estimate the size of the resulting file after the join operation, given the sizes of the two input files, by using the formula $|(R \bowtie_c S)| = js * |R| * |S|$. We can now give some sample *approximate* cost functions for estimating the cost of some of the join algorithms given in Section 10.3.2. The join operations are of the form

$$R \bowtie_{A=B} S$$

where A and B are domain-compatible attributes of R and S, respectively. Assume that R has b_R blocks and that S has b_S blocks:

- J1. *Nested-loop join:* Suppose that we use R for the outer loop; then we get the following cost function to estimate the number of block accesses for this method, assuming *three memory buffers*. We assume that the blocking factor for the resulting file is b_{fRS} and that the join selectivity is known:

$$C_{J1} = b_R + (b_R * b_S) + ((js * |R| * |S|)/bfr_{RS})$$

The last part of the formula is the cost of writing the resulting file to disk. This cost formula can be modified to take into account different numbers of memory buffers, as discussed in Section 10.3.2.

- J2. *Single-loop join (using an access structure to retrieve the matching record(s)):* If an index exists for the join attribute B of S with index levels x_B, we can retrieve each record s in R and then use the index to retrieve all the matching records t from S that satisfy $t[B] = s[A]$. The cost depends on the type of index. For a secondary index where S_B is the selection cardinality for the join attribute B of S,[20] we get

$$C_{J2a} = b_R + (|R| * (x_B + s_B)) + ((js * |R| * |S|)/bfr_{RS})$$

For a clustering index where sB is the selection cardinality of B, we get

$$C_{J2b} = b_R + (|R| * (x_B + (s_B/bfr_B))) + ((js * |R| * |S|)/bfr_{RS})$$

For a primary index, we get

$$C_{J2c} = b_R + (|R| * (x_B + 1)) + ((js * |R| * |S|)/bfr_{RS})$$

If a hash key exists for one of the two join attributes—say, B of S—we get

$$C_{J2d} = b_R + (|R| * h) + ((js * |R| * |S|)/bfr_{RS})$$

where $h \geq 1$ is the average number of block accesses to retrieve a record, given its hash key value.

- J3. *Sort-merge join:* If the files are already sorted on the join attributes, the cost function for this method is

$$C_{J3a} = b_R + b_S + ((js * |R| * |S|)/bfr_{RS})$$

If we must sort the files, the cost of sorting must be added. We can use the formulas from Section 10.2 to estimate the sorting cost.

Example of Using the Cost Functions. Suppose that we have the EMPLOYEE file described in the example of the previous section, and assume that the DEPARTMENT file of Figure 4.5 consists of $r_D = 125$ records stored in $b_D = 13$ disk blocks. Consider the join operations

(OP6):   EMPLOYEE ⋈$_{DNO=DNUMBER}$ DEPARTMENT

(OP7):   DEPARTMENT ⋈$_{MGRENO=ENO}$ EMPLOYEE

Suppose that we have a primary index on DNUMBER of DEPARTMENT with $x_{DNUMBER} = 1$ level and a secondary index on MGRSSN of DEPARTMENT with selection cardinality $s_{MGRENO} = 1$ and levels $x_{MGRENO} = 2$. Assume that the join selectivity for OP6 is $js_{OP6} = (1/|DEPARTMENT|) = 1/125$ because DNUMBER is a key of DEPARTMENT. Also assume that the blocking factor for the resulting join file $b_{fr_{ED}} = 4$ records per block. We can estimate the worst case costs for the JOIN operation OP6 using the applicable methods J1 and J2 as follows:

1. Using Method J1 with EMPLOYEE as outer loop:

$$C_{J1} = b_E + (b_E * b_D) + ((js_{OP6} * r_E * r_D)/bfr_{ED})$$
$$= 2000 + (2000 * 13) + (((1/125) * 10,000 * 125)/4) = 30,500$$

---

20. *Selection cardinality* was defined as the average number of records that satisfy an equality condition on an attribute, which is the average number of records that have the same value for the attribute and hence will be joined to a single record in the other file.

2. Using Method J1 with DEPARTMENT as outer loop:

$$C_{J1} = b_D + (b_E * b_D) + ((js_{OP6} * r_E * r_D)/bfr_{ED})$$
$$= 13 + (13 * 2000) + (((1/125) * 10,000 * 125/4) = 28,513$$

3. Using Method J2 with EMPLOYEE as outer loop:

$$C_{J2c} = b_E + (r_E * (x_{DNUMBER} + 1)) + ((js_{OP6} * r_E * r_D)/bfr_{ED})$$
$$= 2000 + (10,000 * 2) + (((1/125) * 10,000 * 125/4) = 24,500$$

4. Using Method J2 with DEPARTMENT as outer loop:

$$C_{J2a} = b_D + (r_D * (x_{DNO} + s_{DNO})) + ((js_{OP6} * r_E * r_D)/bfr_{ED})$$
$$= 13 + (125 * (2 + 80)) + (((1/125) * 10,000 * 125/4) = 12,763$$

Case 4 has the lowest cost estimate and will be chosen. Notice that if 15 memory buffers (or more) were available for executing the join instead of just three, 13 of them could be used to hold the entire DEPARTMENT relation in memory, one could be used as buffer for the result, and the cost for Case 2 could be drastically reduced to just $b_E + b_D + ((js_{OP6} * r_E * r_D)/bfr_{ED})$ or 4513, as discussed in Section 10.3.2. As an exercise, the reader should perform a similar analysis for OP7.

10.8.5   Multiple Relation Queries and Join Ordering

The algebraic transformation rules in Section 10.7.2 include a commutative rule and an associative rule for the join operation. With these rules, many equivalent join expressions can be produced. As a result, the number of alternative query trees grows very rapidly as the number of joins in a query increases. In general, a query that joins n relations will have $n - 1$ join operations, and hence can have a large number of different join orders. Estimating the cost of every possible join tree for a query with a large number of joins will require a substantial amount of time by the query optimizer. Hence, some pruning of the possible query trees is needed. Query optimizers typically limit the structure of a (join) query tree to that of left-deep (or right-deep) trees. A **left-deep** tree is a binary tree where the right child of each nonleaf node is always a base relation. The optimizer would choose the particular left-deep tree with the lowest estimated cost. Two examples of left-deep trees are shown in Figure 10.7. (Note that the trees in Figure 10.5 are also left-deep trees.)

FIGURE 10.7 Two left-deep (join) query trees.

With left-deep trees, the right child is considered to be the inner relation when executing a nested-loop join. One advantage of left-deep (or right-deep) trees is that they are amenable to pipelining, as discussed in Section 10.6. For instance, consider the first left-deep tree in Figure 10.7 and assume that the join algorithm is the single-loop method; in this case, a disk page of tuples of the outer relation is used to probe the inner relation for matching tuples. As a resulting block of tuples is produced from the join of R1 and R2, it could be used to probe R3. Likewise, as a resulting page of tuples is produced from this join, it could be used to probe R4. Another advantage of left-deep (or right-deep) trees is that having a base relation as one of the inputs of each join allows the optimizer to utilize any access paths on that relation that may be useful in executing the join.

If materialization is used instead of pipelining (see Section 10.6), the join results could be materialized and stored as temporary relations. The key idea from the optimizer's standpoint with respect to join ordering is to find an ordering that will reduce the size of the temporary results, since the temporary results (pipelined or materialized) are used by subsequent operators and hence affect the execution cost of those operators.

10.8.6 Example to Illustrate Cost-Based Query Optimization

We will consider query Q2 and its query tree shown in Figure 10.4a to illustrate cost-based query optimization:

Q2:	SELECT	PNUMBER, DNUM, LNAME, ADDRESS, DOB
	FROM	PROJECT, DEPARTMENT, EMPLOYEE
	WHERE	DNUM=DNUMBER **AND** MGRENO=ENO **AND** PLOCATION='CHENNAI';

Suppose we have the statistical information about the relations shown in Figure 10.8. The LOW_VALUE and HIGH_VALUE statistics have been normalized for clarity. The tree in Figure 10.4a is assumed to represent the result of the algebraic heuristic optimization process and the start of cost-based optimization (in this example, we assume that the heuristic optimizer does not push the projection operations down the tree).

(a)

TABLE_NAME	COLUMN_NAME	NUM_DISTINCT	LOW_VALUE	HIGH_VALUE
PROJECT	PLOCATION	200	1	200
PROJECT	PNUMBER	2000	1	2000
PROJECT	DNUM	50	1	50
DEPARTMENT	DNUMBER	50	1	50
DEPARTMENT	MGRENO	50	1	50
EMPLOYEE	ENO	10000	1	10000
EMPLOYEE	DNO	50	1	50
EMPLOYEE	SALARY	500	1	500

(b)

TABLE_NAME	NUM_ROWS	BLOCKS
PROJECT	2000	100
DEPARTMENT	50	5
EMPLOYEE	10000	2000

(c)

INDEX_NAME	UNIQUENES	BLEVEL*	LEAF_BLOCKS	DISTINCT_KEYS
PROJ_PLOC	NONUNIQUE	1	4	200
EMP_ENO	UNIQUE	1	50	10000
EMP_SAL	NONUNIQUE	1	50	500

*BLEVEL is the number of levels without the leaf level.

FIGURE 10.8 Sample statistical information for relations in Q2. (a) Column information. (b) Table information. (c) Index information.

The first cost-based optimization to consider is join ordering. As previously mentioned, we assume the optimizer considers only left-deep trees, so the potential join orders—without Cartesian product—are

1. PROJECT ⋈ DEPARTMENT ⋈ EMPLOYEE

2. DEPARTMENT ⋈ PROJECT ⋈ EMPLOYEE

3. DEPARTMENT ⋈ EMPLOYEE ⋈ PROJECT

4. EMPLOYEE ⋈ DEPARTMENT ⋈ PROJECT

Assume that the selection operation has already been applied to the PROJECT relation. If we assume a materialized approach, then a new temporary relation is created after each join operation. To examine the cost of join order (1), the first join is between PROJECT and DEPARTMENT. Both the join method and the access methods for the input relations must be determined. Since DEPARTMENT has no index according to Figure 10.8, the only available access method is a table scan (that is, a linear search). The PROJECT relation will have the selection operation performed before the join, so two options exist: table scan (linear search) or utilizing its PROJ_PLOC index, so the optimizer must compare their estimated costs. The statistical information on the PROJ_PLOC index (see Figure 10.8) shows the number of index levels $x = 2$ (root plus leaf levels). The index is nonunique (because PLOCATION is not a key of PROJECT), so the optimizer assumes a uniform data distribution and estimates the number of record pointers for each PLOCATION value to be 10. This is computed from the tables in Figure 10.8 by multiplying SELECTIVITY * NUM_ROWS, where SELECTIVITY is estimated by 1/NUM_DISTINCT. So the cost of using the index and accessing the records is estimated to be 12 block accesses (2 for the index and 10 for the data blocks). The cost of a table scan is estimated to be 100 block accesses, so the index access is more efficient as expected.

In the materialized approach, a temporary file TEMP1 of size 1 block is created to hold the result of the selection operation. The file size is calculated by determining the Blocking factor using the formula NUM_ROWS/BLOCKS, which gives 2000/100 or 20 rows per block. Hence, the 10 records selected from the PROJECT relation will fit into a single block. Now we can compute the estimated cost of the first join. We will consider only the nested-loop join method, where the outer relation is the temporary file, TEMP1, and the inner relation is DEPARTMENT. Since the entire TEMP1 file fits in the available buffer space, we need to read each of the DEPARTMENT table's five blocks only once, so the join cost is six block accesses plus the cost of writing the temporary result file, TEMP2. The optimizer would have to determine the size of TEMP2. Since the join attribute DNUMBER is the key for DEPARTMENT, any DNUM value from TEMP1 will join with at most one record from DEPARTMENT, so the number of rows in TEMP2 will be equal to the number of rows in TEMP1, which is 10. The optimizer would determine the record size for TEMP2 and the number of blocks needed to store these 10 rows. For brevity, assume that the blocking factor for TEMP2 is five rows per block, so a total of two blocks are needed to store TEMP2.

Finally, the cost of the last join needs to be estimated. We can use a single-loop join on TEMP2 since in this case the index EMP_ENO (see Figure 10.8) can be used to probe and locate matching records from EMPLOYEE. Hence, the join method would involve reading in each block of TEMP2 and looking up each of the five MGRENO values using the EMP_ENO index. Each index lookup would require a root access, a leaf access, and a data block access ($x+1$, where the number of levels x is 2). So, 10 lookups require 30 block accesses. Adding the two block accesses for TEMP2 gives a total of 32 block accesses for this join.

For the final projection, assume pipelining is used to produce the final result, which does not require additional block accesses, so the total cost for join order (1) is estimated as the sum of the previous costs. The optimizer would then estimate costs in a similar manner for the other three join orders and choose the one with the lowest estimate. We leave this as an exercise for the reader.

10.9 OVERVIEW OF QUERY OPTIMIZATION IN ORACLE

The ORACLE DBMS provides two different approaches to query optimization: rule-based and cost-based. With the rule-based approach, the optimizer chooses execution plans based on heuristically ranked operations. ORACLE maintains a table of 15 ranked access paths, where a lower ranking implies a more efficient approach. The access paths range from table access by ROWID (most efficient)—where ROWID specifies the record's physical address that includes the data file, data block, and row offset within the block—to a full table scan (least efficient)—where all rows in the table are searched by doing multiblock reads. However, the rule-based approach is being phased out in favor of the cost-based approach, where the optimizer examines alternative access paths and operator algorithms and chooses the execution plan with lowest estimated cost. The estimated query cost is proportional to the expected elapsed time needed to execute the query with the given execution plan. The ORACLE optimizer calculates this cost based on the estimated usage of resources, such as I/O, CPU time, and memory needed. The goal of cost based optimization in ORACLE is to minimize the elapsed time to process the entire query.

An interesting addition to the ORACLE query optimizer is the capability for an application developer to specify **hints** to the optimizer.[21] The idea is that an application developer might know more information about the data than the optimizer. For example, consider the EMPLOYEE table shown in Figure 5.5. The SEX column of that table has only two distinct values. If there are 10,000 employees, then the optimizer would estimate that half are male and half are female, assuming a uniform data distribution. If a secondary index exists, it would more than likely not be used. However, if the application developer knows that there are only 100 male employees, a hint could be specified in an SQL query whose WHERE-clause condition is SEX = 'M' so that the associated index would be used in processing the query. Various hints can be specified, such as:

- The optimization approach for an SQL statement.

- The access path for a table accessed by the statement.

- The join order for a join statement.

- A particular join operation in a join statement.

The cost-based optimization of ORACLE is a good example of the sophisticated approach taken to optimize SQL queries in commercial RDBMSs.

10.10 SEMANTIC QUERY OPTIMIZATION

A different approach to query optimization, called **semantic query optimization**, has been suggested. This technique, which may be used in combination with the techniques discussed previously, uses constraints specified on the database schema—such as unique attributes and other more complex constraints—in order to modify one query into another query that is more efficient to execute. We will not discuss this approach in detail but only illustrate it with a simple example. Consider the SQL query:

```
SELECT    E.LNAME, M.LNAME
FROM      EMPLOYEE AS E, EMPLOYEE AS M
WHERE     E.SUPERENO=M.ENO AND E.SALARY > M.SALARY
```

This query retrieves the names of employees who earn more than their supervisors. Suppose that we had a constraint on the database schema that stated that no employee can earn more than his or her direct

---

21. Such hints have also been called query *annotations*.

supervisor. If the semantic query optimizer checks for the existence of this constraint, it need not execute the query at all because it knows that the result of the query will be empty. This may save considerable time if the constraint checking can be done efficiently. However, searching through many constraints to find those that are applicable to a given query and that may semantically optimize it can also be quite time-consuming. With the inclusion of active rules in database systems (see Chapter), semantic query optimization techniques may eventually be fully incorporated into the DBMSs of the future.

10.11 SUMMARY

In this chapter we gave an overview of the techniques used by DBMSs in processing and optimizing high-level queries. We first discussed how SQL queries are translated into relational algebra and then how various relational algebra operations may be executed by a DBMS. We saw that some operations, particularly SELECT and JOIN, may have many execution options. We also discussed how operations can be combined during query processing to create pipelined or stream-based execution instead of materialized execution.

Following that, we described heuristic approaches to query optimization, which use heuristic rules and algebraic techniques to improve the efficiency of query execution. We showed how a query tree that represents a relational algebra expression can be heuristically optimized by reorganizing the tree nodes and transforming it into another equivalent query tree that is more efficient to execute. We also gave equivalence-preserving transformation rules that may be applied to a query tree. Then we introduced query execution plans for SQL queries, which add method execution plans to the query tree operations.

We then discussed the cost-based approach to query optimization. We showed how cost functions are developed for some database access algorithms and how these cost functions are used to estimate the costs of different execution strategies. We presented an overview of the ORACLE query optimizer, and we mentioned the technique of semantic query optimization.

Review Questions

10.1. Discuss the reasons for converting SQL queries into relational algebra queries before optimization is done.

10.2. Discuss the different algorithms for implementing each of the following relational operators and the circumstances under which each algorithm can be used: SELECT, JOIN, PROJECT, UNION, INTERSECT, SET DIFFERENCE, CARTESIAN PRODUCT.

10.3. What is a query execution plan?

10.4. What is meant by the term *heuristic optimization*? Discuss the main heuristics that are applied during query optimization.

10.5. How does a query tree represent a relational algebra expression? What is meant by an execution of a query tree? Discuss the rules for transformation of query trees, and identify when each rule should be applied during optimization.

10.6. How many different join orders are there for a query that joins 10 relations?

10.7. What is meant by cost-based *query optimization*?

10.8. What is the difference between *pipelining* and *materialization*?

10.9. Discuss the cost components for a cost function that is used to estimate query execution cost. Which cost components are used most often as the basis for cost functions?

10.10. Discuss the different types of parameters that are used in cost functions. Where is this information kept?

10.11. List the cost functions for the SELECT and JOIN methods discussed in Section 10.8.

10.12. What is meant by semantic query optimization? How does it differ from other query optimization techniques?

Exercises

10.13. Consider SQL queries Q1, Q8, Q1B, Q4, and Q27 from Chapter 7.

    a. Draw at least two query trees that can represent each of these queries. Under what circumstances would you use each of your query trees?

    b. Draw the initial query tree for each of these queries, then show how the query tree is optimized by the algorithm outlined in Section 10.7.

    c. For each query, compare your own query trees of part (a) and the initial and final query trees of part (b).

10.14. A file of 4096 blocks is to be sorted with an available buffer space of 64 blocks. How many passes will be needed in the merge phase of the external sort-merge algorithm?

10.15. Develop cost functions for the PROJECT, UNION, INTERSECTION, SET DIFFERENCE, and CARTESIAN PRODUCT algorithms discussed in Section 10.4.

10.16. Develop cost functions for an algorithm that consists of two SELECTs, a JOIN, and a final PROJECT, in terms of the cost functions for the individual operations.

10.17. Can a nondense index be used in the implementation of an aggregate operator? Why or why not?

10.18. Calculate the cost functions for different options of executing the JOIN operation OP7 discussed in Section 10.3.2.

10.19. Develop formulas for the hybrid hash join algorithm for calculating the size of the buffer for the first bucket. Develop more accurate cost estimation formulas for the algorithm.

10.20. Estimate the cost of operations OP6 and OP7, using the formulas developed in Exercise 10.9.

10.21. Extend the sort-merge join algorithm to implement the left outer join operation.

10.22. Compare the cost of two different query plans for the following query:

$$\sigma_{SALARY > 40000} (\text{EMPLOYEE} \bowtie_{DNO=DNUMBER} \text{DEPARTMENT})$$

Use the database statistics in Figure 10.8.

Selected Bibliography

A survey by Graefe (1993) discusses query execution in database systems and includes an extensive bibliography. A survey paper by Jarke and Koch (1984) gives a taxonomy of query optimization and includes a bibliography of work in this area. A detailed algorithm for relational algebra optimization is given by Smith and Chang (1975). The Ph.D. thesis of Kooi (1980) provides a foundation for query processing techniques.

Whang (1985) discusses query optimization in OBE (Office-By-Example), which is a system based on QBE. Cost-based optimization was introduced in the SYSTEM R experimental DBMS and is discussed in Astrahan et al. (1976). Selinger et al. (1979) discuss the optimization of multiway joins in SYSTEM R. Join algorithms are discussed in Gotlieb (1975), Blasgen and Eswaran (1976), and Whang et al. (1982). Hashing algorithms for implementing joins are described and analyzed in DeWitt et al. (1984), Bratbergsengen (1984), Shapiro (1986), Kitsuregawa et al. (1989), and Blakeley and Martin (1990), among others. Approaches to finding a good join order are presented in Ioannidis and Kang (1990) and in Swami and Gupta (1989). A discussion of the implications of left-deep and bushy join trees is presented in Ioannidis and Kang (1991). Kim (1982) discusses transformations of nested SQL queries into canonical representations. Optimization of aggregate functions is discussed in Klug (1982) and Muralikrishna (1992). Salzberg et al. (1990) describe a fast external sorting algorithm. Estimating the size of temporary relations is crucial for query optimization. Sampling-based estimation schemes are presented in Haas et al. (1995) and in Haas and Swami (1995). Lipton et al. (1990) also discuss selectivity estimation. Having the database system store and use more detailed statistics in the form of histograms is the topic of Muralikrishna and DeWitt (1988) and Poosala et al. (1996).

Kim et al. (1985) discuss advanced topics in query optimization. Semantic query optimization is discussed in King (1981) and Malley and Zdonick (1986). More recent work on semantic query optimization is reported in Chakravarthy et al. (1990), Shenoy and Ozsoyoglu (1989), and Siegel et al. (1992).

5

TRANSACTION PROCESSING CONCEPTS

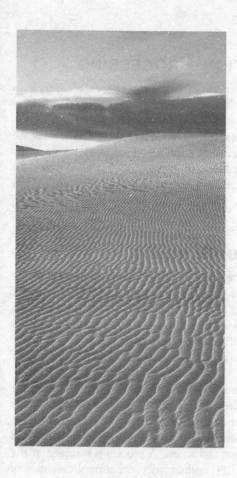

11

Introduction to Transaction Processing Concepts and Theory

The concept of transaction provides a mechanism for describing logical units of database processing. **Transaction processing systems** are systems with large databases and hundreds of concurrent users that are executing database transactions. Examples of such systems include systems for reservations, banking, credit card processing, stock markets, supermarket checkout, and other similar systems. They require high availability and fast response time for hundreds of concurrent users. In this chapter we present the concepts that are needed in transaction processing systems. We define the concept of a transaction, which is used to represent a logical unit of database processing that must be completed in its entirety to ensure correctness. We discuss the concurrency control problem, which occurs when multiple transactions submitted by various users interfere with one another in a way that produces incorrect results. We also discuss recovery from transaction failures.

Section 11.1 informally discusses why concurrency control and recovery are necessary in a database system. Section 11.2 introduces the concept of a transaction and ACID properties of transactions. In Section 11.3 we define first the concepts of schedules. Basic concurrency control techniques are described in Section 11.4. Section 11.5 describes an outline of typical recovery procedure, characterization of recovery algorithms and several recovery concepts. Section 11.6 presents an overview of recovery technique.

11.1 INTRODUCTION TO TRANSACTION PROCESSING

In this section we informally introduce the concepts of concurrent execution of transactions and recovery from transaction failures. Section 11.1.1 compares single-user and multiuser database systems and demonstrates how concurrent execution of transactions can take place in multiuser systems. Section 11.1.2 defines the concept of transaction and presents a simple model of transaction execution, based on read and write database operations, that is used to formalize concurrency control and recovery concepts. Section 11.1.3 shows by informal examples why concurrency control techniques are needed in multiuser systems. Finally, Section 11.1.4 discusses why techniques are needed to permit recovery from failure by discussing the different ways in which transactions can fail while executing.

11.1.1 Single-User Versus Multiuser Systems

One criterion for classifying a database system is according to the number of users who can use the system **concurrently**—that is, at the same time. A DBMS is **single-user** if at most one user at a time can use the system, and it is **multiuser** if many users can use the system—and hence access the database—concurrently. Single-user DBMSs are mostly restricted to personal computer systems; most other DBMSs are multiuser. For example, an airline reservations system is used by hundreds of travel agents and reservation clerks concurrently. Systems in banks, insurance agencies, stock exchanges, supermarkets, and the like are also operated on by many users who submit transactions concurrently to the system.

Multiple users can access databases—and use computer systems—simultaneously because of the concept of **multiprogramming**, which allows the computer to execute multiple programs—or **processes**—at the same time. If only a single central processing unit (CPU) exists, it can actually execute at most one process at a time. However, **multiprogramming operating systems** execute some commands from one process, then suspend that process and execute some commands from the next process, and so on. A process is resumed at the point where it was suspended whenever it gets its turn to use the CPU again. Hence, concurrent execution of processes is actually **interleaved**, as illustrated in Figure 11.1, which shows two processes A and B executing concurrently in an interleaved fashion. Interleaving keeps the CPU busy when a process requires an input or output (I/O) operation, such as reading a block from disk. The CPU is switched to execute another process rather than remaining idle during I/O time. Interleaving also prevents a long process from delaying other processes.

FIGURE 11.1 Interleaved processing versus parallel processing of concurrent transactions.

If the computer system has multiple hardware processors (CPUs), **parallel processing** of multiple processes is possible, as illustrated by processes C and D in Figure 11.1. Most of the theory concerning concurrency control in databases is developed in terms of interleaved concurrency, so for the remainder of this chapter we assume this model. In a multiuser DBMS, the stored data items are the primary resources that may be accessed concurrently by interactive users or application programs, which are constantly retrieving information from and modifying the database.

11.1.2 Transactions, Read and Write Operations, and DBMS Buffers

A transaction is an executing program that forms a logical unit of database processing. A transaction includes one or more database access operations—these can include insertion, deletion, modification, or retrieval operations. The database operations that form a transaction can either be embedded within an application program or they can be specified interactively via a high-level query language such as SQL. One way of specifying the transaction boundaries is by specifying explicit **begin transaction** and **end transaction** statements in an application program; in this case, all database access operations between the two are considered as forming one transaction. A single application program may contain more than one transaction if it contains several transaction boundaries. If the database operations in a transaction do not update the database but only retrieve data, the transaction is called a **read-only transaction**.

The model of a database that is used to explain transaction processing concepts is much simplified. A **database** is basically represented as a collection of **named data items**. The size of a data item is called its **granularity**, and it can be a field of some record in the database, or it may be a larger unit such as a record or even a whole disk block, but the concepts we discuss are independent of the data item granularity. Using this simplified database model, the basic database access operations that a transaction can include are as follows:

- **read_item (X):** Reads a database item named X into a program variable. To simplify our notation, we assume that the *program variable is also named* X.

- **write_item (X):** Writes the value of program variable X into the database item named X.

As we discussed in Chapter 9, the basic unit of data transfer from disk to main memory is one block. Executing a read_item (X) command includes the following steps:

1. Find the address of the disk block that contains item X.
2. Copy that disk block into a buffer in main memory (if that disk block is not already in some main memory buffer).
3. Copy item X from the buffer to the program variable named X.

Executing a write_item (X) command includes the following steps:

1. Find the address of the disk block that contains item X.
2. Copy that disk block into a buffer in main memory (if that disk block is not already in some main memory buffer).
3. Copy item X from the program variable named X into its correct location in the buffer.
4. Store the updated block from the buffer back to disk (either immediately or at some later point in time).

Step 4 is the one that actually updates the database on disk. In some cases the buffer is not immediately stored to disk, in case additional changes are to be made to the buffer. Usually, the decision about when to store back a modified disk block that is in a main memory buffer is handled by the recovery manager of the DBMS in cooperation with the underlying operating system. The DBMS will generally maintain a number of buffers in main memory that hold database disk blocks containing the database items being processed. When these buffers are all occupied, and additional database blocks must be copied into memory, some buffer replacement policy is used to choose which of the current buffers is to be replaced. If the chosen buffer has been modified, it must be written back to disk before it is reused.[1]

A transaction includes read_item and write_item operations to access and update the database. Figure 11.2 shows examples of two very simple transactions. The **read-set** of a transaction is the set of all items that the transaction reads, and the **write-set** is the set of all items that the transaction writes. For example, the read-set of T_1 in Figure 11.2 is $\{X, Y\}$ and its write-set is also $\{X, Y\}$.

Concurrency control and recovery mechanisms are mainly concerned with the database access commands in a transaction. Transactions submitted by the various users may execute concurrently and may access and update the same database items. If this concurrent execution is uncontrolled, it may lead to problems, such as an inconsistent database. In the next section we informally introduce some of the problems that may occur.

11.1.3 Why Concurrency Control is Needed

Several problems can occur when concurrent transactions execute in an uncontrolled manner. We illustrate some of these problems by referring to a much simplified airline reservations database in which a record is stored for each airline flight. Each record includes the number of reserved seats on that flight as a *named data item*, among other information. Figure 11.2a shows a transaction T_1 that *transfers N reservations* from one flight whose number of reserved seats is stored in the database item named X to another flight whose number of reserved seats is stored in the database item named Y. Figure 11.2b shows a simpler transaction T_2 that just *reserves M seats* on the first flight (X) referenced in transaction T_1.[2] To simplify our example, we do not show additional portions of the transactions, such as checking whether a flight has enough seats available before reserving additional seats.

(a) T_1

```
read_item (X);
X:=X-N;
write_item (X);
read_item (Y);
Y:=Y+N;
write_item (Y);
```

(b) T_2

```
read_item (X);
X:=X+M;
write_item (X);
```

FIGURE 11.2 Two sample transactions. (a) Transaction T_1. (b) Transaction T_2.

When a database access program is written, it has the flight numbers, their dates, and the number of seats to be booked as parameters; hence, the same program can be used to execute many transactions, each with different flights and numbers of seats to be booked. For concurrency control purposes, a transaction is

---

1. We will not discuss buffer replacement policies here as these are typically discussed in operating systems textbooks.

2. A similar, more commonly used example assumes a bank database, with one transaction doing a transfer of funds from account X to account Y and the other transaction doing a deposit to account X.

a *particular execution* of a program on a specific date, flight, and number of seats. In Figure 11.2a and b, the transactions T_1 and T_2 are *specific executions* of the programs that refer to the specific flights whose numbers of seats are stored in data items X and Y in the database. We now discuss the types of problems we may encounter with these two transactions if they run concurrently.

The Lost Update Problem. This problem occurs when two transactions that access the same database items have their operations interleaved in a way that makes the value of some database items incorrect. Suppose that transactions T_1 and T_2 are submitted at approximately the same time, and suppose that their operations are interleaved as shown in Figure 11.3a; then the final value of item X is incorrect, because T_2 reads the value of X before T_1 changes it in the database, and hence the updated value resulting from T_1 is lost. For example, if $X = 80$ at the start (originally there were 80 reservations on the flight), $N = 5$ (T_1 transfers 5 seat reservations from the flight corresponding to X to the flight corresponding to Y), and $M = 4$ (T_2 reserves 4 seats on X), the final result should be $X = 79$; but in the interleaving of operations shown in Figure 11.3a, it is $X = 84$ because the update in T_1 that removed the five seats from X was lost.

(a)

(b)

FIGURE 11.3 Some problems that occur when concurrent execution is uncontrolled. (a) The lost update problem. (b) The temporary update problem.

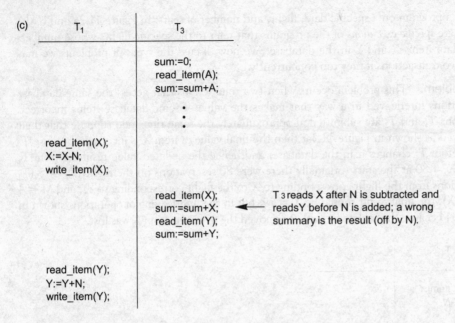

(c)

	T_1	T_3

		sum:=0;
		read_item(A);
		sum:=sum+A;
		⋮

	read_item(X);
	X:=X-N;
	write_item(X);	

		read_item(X);
		sum:=sum+X;
		read_item(Y);
		sum:=sum+Y;

	read_item(Y);
	Y:=Y+N;
	write_item(Y);	

T_3 reads X after N is subtracted and readsY before N is added; a wrong summary is the result (off by N).

FIGURE 11.3(CONTINUED) Some problems that occur when concurrent execution is uncontrolled. (c) The incorrect summary problem.

The Temporary Update (or Dirty Read) Problem. This problem occurs when one transaction updates a database item and then the transaction fails for some reason (see Section 11.1.4). The updated item is accessed by another transaction before it is changed back to its original value. Figure 11.3b shows an example where T_1 updates item X and then fails before completion, so the system must change X back to its original value. Before it can do so, however, transaction T_2 reads the "temporary" value of X, which will not be recorded permanently in the database because of the failure of T_1. The value of item X that is read by T_2 is called *dirty data*, because it has been created by a transaction that has not completed and committed yet; hence, this problem is also known as the *dirty read problem*.

The Incorrect Summary Problem. If one transaction is calculating an aggregate summary function on a number of records while other transactions are updating some of these records, the aggregate function may calculate some values before they are updated and others after they are updated. For example, suppose that a transaction T_3 is calculating the total number of reservations on all the flights; meanwhile, transaction T_1 is executing. If the interleaving of operations shown in Figure 11.3c occurs, the result of T_3 will be off by an amount N because T_3 reads the value of X *after* N seats have been subtracted from it but reads the value of Y *before* those N seats have been added to it.

Another problem that may occur is called **unrepeatable read**, where a transaction T reads an item twice and the item is changed by another transaction T' between the two reads. Hence, T receives *different values* for its two reads of the same item. This may occur, for example, if during an airline reservation transaction, a customer is inquiring about seat availability on several flights. When the customer decides on a particular flight, the transaction then reads the number of seats on that flight a second time before completing the reservation.

11.1.4   Why Recovery Is Needed

Whenever a transaction is submitted to a DBMS for execution, the system is responsible for making sure that either (1) all the operations in the transaction are completed successfully and their effect is recorded permanently in the database, or (2) the transaction has no effect whatsoever on the database or on any other transactions. The DBMS must not permit some operations of a transaction T to be applied to the database while other operations of T are not. This may happen if a transaction **fails** after executing some of its operations but before executing all of them.

Types of Failures.   Failures are generally classified as transaction, system, and media failures. There are several possible reasons for a transaction to fail in the middle of execution:

1. *A computer failure (system crash)*: A hardware, software, or network error occurs in the computer system during transaction execution. Hardware crashes are usually media failures—for example, main memory failure.

2. *A transaction or system error*: Some operation in the transaction may cause it to fail, such as integer overflow or division by zero. Transaction failure may also occur because of erroneous parameter values or because of a logical programming error.[3] In addition, the user may interrupt the transaction during its execution.

3. *Local errors or exception conditions detected by the transaction*: During transaction execution, certain conditions may occur that necessitate cancellation of the transaction. For example, data for the transaction may not be found. Notice that an exception condition,[4] such as insufficient account balance in a banking database, may cause a transaction, such as a fund withdrawal, to be canceled. This exception should be programmed in the transaction itself, and hence would not be considered a failure.

4. *Concurrency control enforcement*: The concurrency control method (see Section 11.4) may decide to abort the transaction, to be restarted later, because it violates serializability (see Section 11.3.2) or because several transactions are in a state of deadlock.

5. *Disk failure*: Some disk blocks may lose their data because of a read or write malfunction or because of a disk read/write head crash. This may happen during a read or a write operation of the transaction.

6. *Physical problems and catastrophes*: This refers to an endless list of problems that includes power or air-conditioning failure, fire, theft, sabotage, overwriting disks or tapes by mistake, and mounting of a wrong tape by the operator.

Failures of types 1, 2, 3, and 4 are more common than those of types 5 or 6. Whenever a failure of type 1 through 4 occurs, the system must keep sufficient information to recover from the failure. Disk failure or other catastrophic failures of type 5 or 6 do not happen frequently; if they do occur, recovery is a major task. We discuss recovery from failure in Sections 11.5 and 11.6.

The concept of transaction is fundamental to many techniques for concurrency control and recovery from failures.

11.2   Transaction and System Concepts

In this section we discuss additional concepts relevant to transaction processing. Section 11.2.1 describes the various states a transaction can be in, and discusses additional relevant operations needed in transaction

---

3. In general, a transaction should be thoroughly tested to ensure that it has no bugs (logical programming errors).

4. Exception conditions, if programmed correctly, do not constitute transaction failures.

processing. Section 11.2.2 discusses the system log, which keeps information needed for recovery. Section 11.2.3 describes the concept of commit points of transactions, and why they are important in transaction processing. Section 11.2.4 describes the desirable properties of a transaction.

11.2.1 Transaction States and Additional Operations

A transaction is an atomic unit of work that is either completed in its entirety or not done at all. For recovery purposes, the system needs to keep track of when the transaction starts, terminates, and commits or aborts (see Section 11.2.3). Hence, the recovery manager keeps track of the following operations:

- BEGIN_TRANSACTION: This marks the beginning of transaction execution.

- READ OR WRITE: These specify read or write operations on the database items that are executed as part of a transaction.

- END_TRANSACTION: This specifies that READ and WRITE transaction operations have ended and marks the end of transaction execution. However, at this point it may be necessary to check whether the changes introduced by the transaction can be permanently applied to the database (committed) or whether the transaction has to be aborted because it violates serializability (see Section 11.3.2) or for some other reason.

- COMMIT_TRANSACTION: This signals a *successful end* of the transaction so that any changes (updates) executed by the transaction can be safely **committed** to the database and will not be undone.

- ROLLBACK (OR ABORT): This signals that the transaction has *ended unsuccessfully*, so that any changes or effects that the transaction may have applied to the database must be undone.

Figure 11.4 shows a state transition diagram that describes how a transaction moves through its execution states. A transaction goes into an **active state** immediately after it starts execution, where it can issue READ and WRITE operations. When the transaction ends, it moves to the **partially committed state**. At this point, some recovery protocols need to ensure that a system failure will not result in an inability to record the changes of the transaction permanently (usually by recording changes in the system log, discussed in the next section).[5] Once this check is successful, the transaction is said to have reached its commit point and enters

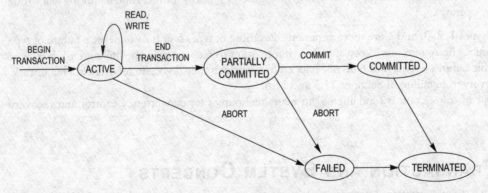

FIGURE 11.4 State transition diagram illustrating the states for transaction execution.

---

5. Optimistic concurrency control (see Section 11.4.4) also requires that certain checks be made at this point to ensure that the transaction did not interfere with other executing transactions.

the committed state. Commit points are discussed in more detail in Section 11.2.3. Once a transaction is committed, it has concluded its execution successfully and all its changes must be recorded permanently in the database.

However, a transaction can go to the **failed state** if one of the checks fails or if the transaction is aborted during its active state. The transaction may then have to be rolled back to undo the effect of its WRITE operations on the database. The **terminated state** corresponds to the transaction leaving the system. The transaction information that is maintained in system tables while the transaction has been running is removed when the transaction terminates. Failed or aborted transactions may be *restarted* later—either automatically or after being resubmitted by the user—as brand new transactions.

11.2.2 The System Log

To be able to recover from failures that affect transactions, the system maintains a log[6] to keep track of all transaction operations that affect the values of database items. This information may be needed to permit recovery from failures. The log is kept on disk, so it is not affected by any type of failure except for disk or catastrophic failure. In addition, the log is periodically backed up to archival storage (tape) to guard against such catastrophic failures. We now list the types of entries—called **log records**—that are written to the log and the action each performs. In these entries, T refers to a unique **transaction-id** that is generated automatically by the system and is used to identify each transaction:

1. [start_transaction,T]: Indicates that transaction T has started execution.

2. [write_item,T,X,*old_value*,*new_value*]: Indicates that transaction T has changed the value of database item X from *old_value* to *new_value*.

3. [read_item, T,X]: Indicates that transaction T has read the value of database item X.

4. [commit,T]: Indicates that transaction T has completed successfully, and affirms that its effect can be committed (recorded permanently) to the database.

5. [abort,T]: Indicates that transaction T has been aborted.

Protocols for recovery that avoid cascading rollbacks (see Section 11.3.1.2)—which include nearly all practical protocols—do not require that READ operations be written to the system log. However, if the log is also used for other purposes—such as auditing (keeping track of all database operations)—then such entries can be included. In addition, some recovery protocols require simpler WRITE entries that do not include new_value (see Section 11.3.1.2).

Notice that we assume here that all permanent changes to the database occur within transactions, so the notion of recovery from a transaction failure amounts to either undoing or redoing transaction operations individually from the log. If the system crashes, we can recover to a consistent database state by examining the log and using one of the techniques described in section 11.6. Because the log contains a record of every WRITE operation that changes the value of some database item, it is possible to **undo** the effect of these WRITE operations of a transaction T by tracing backward through the log and resetting all items changed by a WRITE operation of T to their old_values. **Redoing** the operations of a transaction may also be needed if all its updates are recorded in the log but a failure occurs before we can be sure that all these new_values have been written permanently in the actual database on disk.[7] Redoing the operations of transaction T is applied by tracing forward through the log and setting all items changed by a WRITE operation of T to their new_values.

---

6. The log has sometimes been called the DBMS journal.

7. Undo and redo are discussed more fully in Sections 11.5 and 11.6.

11.2.3 Commit Point of a Transaction

A transaction T reaches its **commit point** when all its operations that access the database have been executed successfully *and* the effect of all the transaction operations on the database have been recorded in the log. Beyond the commit point, the transaction is said to be **committed**, and its effect is assumed to be *permanently recorded* in the database. The transaction then writes a commit record [commit,T] into the log. If a system failure occurs, we search back in the log for all transactions T that have written a [start_transaction,T] record into the log but have not written their [commit,T] record yet; these transactions may have to be rolled back to undo their effect on the database during the recovery process. Transactions that have written their commit record in the log must also have recorded all their WRITE operations in the log, so their effect on the database can be *redone* from the log records.

Notice that the log file must be kept on disk. As discussed in Chapter 9, updating a disk file involves copying the appropriate block of the file from disk to a buffer in main memory, updating the buffer in main memory, and copying the buffer to disk. It is common to keep one or more blocks of the log file in main memory buffers until they are filled with log entries and then to write them back to disk only once, rather than writing to disk every time a log entry is added. This saves the overhead of multiple disk writes of the same log file block. At the time of a system crash, only the log entries that have been *written back to disk* are considered in the recovery process because the contents of main memory may be lost. Hence, *before* a transaction reaches its commit point, any portion of the log that has not been written to the disk yet must now be written to the disk. This process is called **force-writing** the log file before committing a transaction.

11.2.4 Desirable Properties of Transactions

Transactions should possess several properties. These are often called the ACID **properties**, and they should be enforced by the concurrency control and recovery methods of the DBMS. The following are the ACID properties:

1. **Atomicity:** A transaction is an atomic unit of processing; it is either performed in its entirety or not performed at all.

2. **Consistency preservation:** A transaction is consistency preserving if its complete execution take(s) the database from one consistent state to another.

3. **Isolation:** A transaction should appear as though it is being executed in isolation from other transactions. That is, the execution of a transaction should not be interfered with by any other transactions executing concurrently.

4. **Durability or permanency:** The changes applied to the database by a committed transaction must persist in the database. These changes must not be lost because of any failure.

The atomicity property requires that we execute a transaction to completion. It is the responsibility of the transaction recovery subsystem of a DBMS to ensure atomicity. If a transaction fails to complete for some reason, such as a system crash in the midst of transaction execution, the recovery technique must undo any effects of the transaction on the database.

The preservation of consistency is generally considered to be the responsibility of the programmers who write the database programs or of the DBMS module that enforces integrity constraints. Recall that a **database state** is a collection of all the stored data items (values) in the database at a given point in time. A **consistent state** of the database satisfies the constraints specified in the schema as well as any other constraints that should hold on the database. A database program should be written in a way that guarantees that, if the database is in a consistent state before executing the transaction, it will be in a consistent state after the *complete* execution of the transaction, assuming that *no interference with other transactions* occurs.

Isolation is enforced by the concurrency control subsystem of the DBMS.[8] If every transaction does not make its updates visible to other transactions until it is committed, one form of isolation is enforced that solves the temporary update problem and eliminates cascading rollbacks (see Section 11.6). There have been attempts to define the *level of isolation* of a transaction. A transaction is said to have level 0 (zero) isolation if it does not overwrite the dirty reads of higher-level transactions. Level 1 (one) isolation has no lost updates; and level 2 isolation has no lost updates and no dirty reads. Finally, level 3 isolation (also called *true isolation*) has, in addition to degree 2 properties, repeatable reads.

Finally, the durability property is the responsibility of the recovery subsystem of the DBMS. We will discuss how recovery protocols enforce durability and atomicity in Section 11.6.

11.3   CHARACTERIZING SCHEDULES

11.3.1   Characterizing Schedules Based on Recoverability

When transactions are executing concurrently in an interleaved fashion, then the order of execution of operations from the various transactions is known as a **schedule** (or **history**). In this section, we first define the concept of schedule, and then we characterize the types of schedules that facilitate recovery when failures occur. In Section 11.3.2, we characterize schedules in terms of the interference of participating transactions, leading to the concepts of serializability and serializable schedules.

11.3.1.1   Schedules (histories) of transactions
A **schedule** (or **history**) S of n transactions $T_1, T_2, \ldots, T_n$ is an ordering of the operations of the transactions subject to the constraint that, for each transaction T_i that participates in S, the operations of T_i in S must appear in the same order in which they occur in T_i. Note, however, that operations from other transactions T_j can be interleaved with the operations of T_i in S. For now, consider the order of operations in S to be a *total ordering*, although it is possible theoretically to deal with schedules whose operations form *partial orders* (as we discuss later).

For the purpose of recovery and concurrency control, we are mainly interested in the read_item and write_item operations of the transactions, as well as the commit and abort operations. A shorthand notation for describing a schedule uses the symbols r, w, c, and a for the operations read_item, write_item, commit, and abort, respectively, and appends as subscript the transaction id (transaction number) to each operation in the schedule. In this notation, the database item X that is read or written follows the r and w operations in parentheses. For example, the schedule of Figure 11.3(a), which we shall call S_a, can be written as follows in this notation:

S_a: $r_1(X)$; $r_2(X)$; $w_1(X)$; $r_1(Y)$; $w_2(X)$; $w_1(Y)$;

Similarly, the schedule for Figure 11.3(b), which we call S_b, can be written as follows, if we assume that transaction T_1 aborted after its read_item(Y) operation:

S_b: $r_1(X)$; $w_1(X)$; $r_2(X)$; $w_2(X)$; $r_1(Y)$; a_1;

---

8. We will discuss concurrency control protocols in Section 11.4.

Two operations in a schedule are said to **conflict** if they satisfy all three of the following conditions: (1) they belong to different transactions; (2) they access the same item X; and (3) at least one of the operations is a write_item(X). For example, in schedule S_a, the operations $r_1(X)$ and $w_2(X)$ conflict, as do the operations $r_2(X)$ and $w_1(X)$, and the operations $w_1(X)$ and $w_2(X)$. However, the operations $r_1(X)$ and $r_2(X)$ do not conflict, since they are both read operations; the operations $w_2(X)$ and $w_1(Y)$ do not conflict, because they operate on distinct data items X and Y; and the operations $r_1(X)$ and $w_1(X)$ do not conflict, because they belong to the same transaction.

A schedule S of n transactions $T_1, T_2, \ldots, T_n$, is said to be a **complete schedule** if the following conditions hold:

1. The operations in S are exactly those operations in $T_1, T_2, \ldots, T_n$, including a commit or abort operation as the last operation for each transaction in the schedule.

2. For any pair of operations from the same transaction T_i, their order of appearance in S is the same as their order of appearance in T_i.

3. For any two conflicting operations, one of the two must occur before the other in the schedule.[9]

The preceding condition (3) allows for two *nonconflicting operations* to occur in the schedule without defining which occurs first, thus leading to the definition of a schedule as a **partial order** of the operations in the n transactions.[10] However, a total order must be specified in the schedule for any pair of conflicting operations (condition 3) and for any pair of operations from the same transaction (condition 2). Condition 1 simply states that all operations in the transactions must appear in the complete schedule. Since every transaction has either committed or aborted, a complete schedule will not contain any active transactions at the end of the schedule.

In general, it is difficult to encounter complete schedules in a transaction processing system, because new transactions are continually being submitted to the system. Hence, it is useful to define the concept of the **committed projection** C(S) of a schedule S, which includes only the operations in S that belong to committed transactions—that is, transactions T_i whose commit operation c_i is in S.

11.3.1.2 Characterizing schedules based on recoverability

For some schedules it is easy to recover from transaction failures, whereas for other schedules the recovery process can be quite involved. Hence, it is important to characterize the types of schedules for which recovery is possible, as well as those for which recovery is relatively simple. These characterizations do not actually provide the recovery algorithm but instead only attempt to theoretically characterize the different types of schedules.

First, we would like to ensure that, once a transaction T is committed, it should *never* be necessary to roll back T. The schedules that theoretically meet this criterion are called *recoverable schedules* and those that do not are called **nonrecoverable**, and hence should not be permitted. A schedule S is recoverable if no transaction T in S commits until all transactions T' that have written an item that T reads have committed. A transaction T reads from transaction T' in a schedule S if some item X is first written by T' and later read by T. In addition, T' should not have been aborted before T reads item X, and there should be no transactions that write X after T' writes it and before T reads it (unless those transactions, if any, have aborted before T reads X).

---

9. Theoretically, it is not necessary to determine an order between pairs of nonconflicting operations.

10. In practice, most schedules have a total order of operations. If parallel processing is employed, it is theoretically possible to have schedules with partially-ordered nonconflicting operations.

Recoverable schedules require a complex recovery process as we shall see, but if sufficient information is kept (in the log), a recovery algorithm can be devised. The (partial) schedules S_a and S_b from the preceding section are both recoverable, since they satisfy the above definition. Consider the schedule S_a' given below, which is the same as schedule S_a except that two commit operations have been added to S_a:

S_a': $r_1(X)$; $r_2(X)$; $w_1(X)$; $r_1(Y)$; $w_2(X)$; c_2; $w_1(Y)$; c_1;

S_a' is recoverable, even though it suffers from the lost update problem. However, consider the two (partial) schedules S_c and S_d that follow:

S_c: $r_1(X)$; $w_1(X)$; $r_2(X)$; $r_1(Y)$; $w_2(X)$; c_2; a_1;
S_d: $r_1(X)$; $w_1(X)$; $r_2(X)$; $r_1(Y)$; $w_2(X)$; $w_1(Y)$; c_1; c_2;
S_e: $r_1(X)$; $w_1(X)$; $r_2(X)$; $r_1(Y)$; $w_2(X)$; $w_1(Y)$; a_1; a_2;

S_c is not recoverable, because T_2 reads item X from T_1, and then T_2 commits before T_1 commits. If T_1 aborts after the c_2 operation in S_c, then the value of X that T_2 read is no longer valid and T_2 must be aborted *after* it had been committed, leading to a schedule that is not recoverable. For the schedule to be recoverable, the c_2 operation in S_c must be postponed until after T_1 commits, as shown in S_d; if T_1 aborts instead of committing, then T_2 should also abort as shown in S_e, because the value of X it read is no longer valid.

In a recoverable schedule, no committed transaction ever needs to be rolled back. However, it is possible for a phenomenon known as **cascading rollback** (or **cascading abort**) to occur, where an *uncommitted* transaction has to be rolled back because it read an item from a transaction that failed. This is illustrated in schedule S_e, where transaction T_2 has to be rolled back because it read item X from T_1, and T_1 then aborted.

Because cascading rollback can be quite time-consuming—since numerous transactions can be rolled back (see Section 11.6)—it is important to characterize the schedules where this phenomenon is guaranteed not to occur. A schedule is said to be **cascadeless**, or **to avoid cascading rollback**, if every transaction in the schedule reads only items that were written by committed transactions. In this case, all items read will not be discarded, so no cascading rollback will occur. To satisfy this criterion, the $r_2(X)$ command in schedules S_d and S_e must be postponed until after T_1 has committed (or aborted), thus delaying T_2 but ensuring no cascading rollback if T_1 aborts.

Finally, there is a third, more restrictive type of schedule, called a **strict schedule**, in which transactions can *neither read nor write* an item X until the last transaction that wrote X has committed (or aborted). Strict schedules simplify the recovery process. In a strict schedule, the process of undoing a write_item(X) operation of an aborted transaction is simply to restore the **before image** (*old_value* or BFIM) of data item X. This simple procedure always works correctly for strict schedules, but it may not work for recoverable or cascadeless schedules. For example, consider schedule S_f:

S_f: $w_1(X, 5)$; $w_2(X, 8)$; a_1;

Suppose that the value of X was originally 9, which is the before image stored in the system log along with the $w_1(X, 5)$ operation. If T_1 aborts, as in S_f, the recovery procedure that restores the before image of an aborted write operation will restore the value of X to 9, even though it has already been changed to 8 by transaction T_2, thus leading to potentially incorrect results. Although schedule S_f is cascadeless, it is not a strict schedule, since it permits T_2 to write item X even though the transaction T_1 that last wrote X had not yet committed (or aborted). A strict schedule does not have this problem.

We have now characterized schedules according to the following terms: (1) recoverability, (2) avoidance of cascading rollback, and (3) strictness. We have thus seen that those properties of schedules are successively more stringent conditions. Thus condition (2) implies condition (1), and condition (3) implies both (2) and (1). Thus, all strict schedules are cascadeless, and all cascadeless schedules are recoverable.

11.3.2 Characterizing Schedules Based on Serializability

In the previous section, we characterized schedules based on their recoverability properties. We now characterize the types of schedules that are considered correct when concurrent transactions are executing. Suppose that two users—two airline reservation clerks—submit to the DBMS transactions T_1 and T_2 of Figure 11.2 at approximately the same time. If no interleaving of operations is permitted, there are only two possible outcomes:

1. Execute all the operations of transaction T_1 (in sequence) followed by all the operations of transaction T_2 (in sequence).

2. Execute all the operations of transaction T_2 (in sequence) followed by all the operations of transaction T_1 (in sequence).

FIGURE 11.5 Examples of serial and nonserial schedules involving transactions T_1 and T_2. (a) Serial schedule A: T_1 followed by T_2. (b) Serial schedule B: T_2 followed by T_1. (c) Two nonserial schedules C and D with interleaving of operations.

These alternatives are shown in Figure 11.5a and b, respectively. If interleaving of operations is allowed, there will be many possible orders in which the system can execute the individual operations of the transactions. Two possible schedules are shown in Figure 11.5c. The concept of serializability of schedules is used to identify which schedules are correct when transaction executions have interleaving of their operations in the schedules. This section defines serializability and discusses how it may be used in practice.

11.3.2.1 Serial, nonserial, and conflict-serializable schedules

Schedules A and B in Figure 11.5a and b are called *serial* because the operations of each transaction are executed consecutively, without any interleaved operations from the other transaction. In a serial schedule, entire transactions are performed in serial order: T_1 and then T_2 in Figure 11.5a, and T_2 and then T_1 in Figure 11.5b. Schedules C and D in Figure 11.5c are called *nonserial* because each sequence interleaves operations from the two transactions.

Formally, a schedule S is **serial** if, for every transaction T participating in the schedule, all the operations of T are executed consecutively in the schedule; otherwise, the schedule is called **nonserial**. Hence, in a serial schedule, only one transaction at a time is active—the commit (or abort) of the active transaction initiates execution of the next transaction. No interleaving occurs in a serial schedule. One reasonable assumption we can make, if we consider the transactions to be *independent*, is that every serial schedule is considered correct. We can assume this because every transaction is assumed to be correct if executed on its own (according to the consistency preservation property of Section 11.2.4). Hence, it does not matter which transaction is executed first. As long as every transaction is executed from beginning to end without any interference from the operations of other transactions, we get a correct end result on the database. The problem with serial schedules is that they limit concurrency or interleaving of operations. In a serial schedule, if a transaction waits for an I/O operation to complete, we cannot switch the CPU processor to another transaction, thus wasting valuable CPU processing time. In addition, if some transaction T is quite long, the other transactions must wait for T to complete all its operations before commencing. Hence, serial schedules are generally considered unacceptable in practice.

To illustrate our discussion, consider the schedules in Figure 11.5, and assume that the initial values of database items are $X = 90$ and $Y = 90$ and that $N = 3$ and $M = 2$. After executing transactions T_1 and T_2, we would expect the database values to be $X = 89$ and $Y = 93$, according to the meaning of the transactions. Sure enough, executing either of the serial schedules A or B gives the correct results. Now consider the nonserial schedules C and D. Schedule C (which is the same as Figure 11.3a) gives the results $X = 92$ and $Y = 93$, in which the X value is erroneous, whereas schedule D gives the correct results.

Schedule C gives an erroneous result because of the lost update problem discussed in Section 11.1.3; transaction T_2 reads the value of X *before* it is changed by transaction T_1, so only the effect of T_2 on X is reflected in the database. The effect of T_1 on X is *lost*, overwritten by T_2, leading to the incorrect result for item X. However, some nonserial schedules give the correct expected result, such as schedule D. We would like to determine which of the nonserial schedules *always* give a correct result and which may give erroneous results. The concept used to characterize schedules in this manner is that of serializability of a schedule.

A schedule S of n transactions is **serializable** if it is *equivalent to some serial schedule* of the same n transactions. We will define the concept of equivalence of schedules shortly. Notice that there are $n!$ possible serial schedules of n transactions and many more possible nonserial schedules. We can form two disjoint groups of the nonserial schedules: those that are equivalent to one (or more) of the serial schedules, and hence are serializable; and those that are not equivalent to *any* serial schedule and hence are not serializable.

Saying that a nonserial schedule S is serializable is equivalent to saying that it is correct, because it is equivalent to a serial schedule, which is considered correct. The remaining question is: When are two schedules considered "equivalent"? There are several ways to define equivalence of schedules. The simplest, but least satisfactory, definition of schedule equivalence involves comparing the effects of the schedules on the database. Two schedules are called **result equivalent** if they produce the same final state of the database. However, two different schedules may accidentally produce the same final state. For example, in Figure 11.6, schedules S_1 and S_2 will produce the same final database state if they execute on a database with an initial value of $X = 100$; but for other initial values of X, the schedules are *not* result equivalent. In addition, these two schedules execute different transactions, so they definitely should not be considered equivalent. Hence, result equivalence alone cannot be used to define equivalence of schedules. The safest and most general approach to defining schedule equivalence is not to make any assumption about the types of operations included in the transactions. For two schedules to be equivalent, the operations applied to each data item affected by the schedules should be applied to that item in both schedules in the *same order*. Two definitions of equivalence of schedules are generally used: *conflict equivalence and view equivalence*. We discuss conflict equivalence next, which is the more commonly used definition.

Two schedules are said to be **conflict equivalent** if the order of any two *conflicting operations* is the same in both schedules. Recall from Section 11.3.1.1 that two operations in a schedule are said to *conflict* if they belong to different transactions, access the same database item, and at least one of the two operations is a write_item operation. If two conflicting operations are applied in *different orders* in two schedules, the effect can be different on the database or on other transactions in the schedule, and hence the schedules are not conflict equivalent. For example, if a read and write operation occur in the order $r_1(X)$, $w_2(X)$ in schedule S_1, and in the reverse order $w_2(X)$, $r_1(X)$ in schedule S_2, the value read by $r_1(X)$ can be different in the two schedules. Similarly, if two write operations occur in the order $w_1(X)$, $w_2(X)$ in S_1, and in the reverse order $w_2(X)$, $w_1(X)$ in S_2, the next $r(X)$ operation in the two schedules will read potentially different values; or if these are the last operations writing item X in the schedules, the final value of item X in the database will be different.

Using the notion of conflict equivalence, we define a schedule S to be **conflict serializable**[11] if it is (conflict) equivalent to some serial schedule S'. In such a case, we can reorder the *nonconflicting* operations in S until we form the equivalent serial schedule S'. According to this definition, schedule D of Figure 11.5c is equivalent to the serial schedule A of Figure 11.5a. In both schedules, the read_item(X) of T_2 reads the value of X written by T_1, while the other read_item operations read the database values from the initial database state. In addition, T_1 is the last transaction to write Y, and T_2 is the last transaction to write X in both schedules. Because A is a serial schedule and schedule D is equivalent to A, D is a *serializable schedule*. Notice that the operations $r_1(Y)$ and $w_1(Y)$ of schedule D do not conflict with the operations $r_2(X)$ and $w_2(X)$, since they access different data items. Hence, we can move $r_1(Y)$, $w_1(Y)$ before $r_2(X)$, $w_2(X)$, leading to the equivalent serial schedule T_1, T_2.

S_1	S_2
read_item(X);	read_item(X);
X:=X+10;	X:=X*1.1;
write_item(X);	write_item(X);

FIGURE 11.6 Two schedules that are result equivalent for the initial value of $X = 100$ but are not result equivalent in general.

Schedule C of Figure 11.5c is not equivalent to either of the two possible serial schedules A and B, and hence is *not serializable*. Trying to reorder the operations of schedule C to find an equivalent serial schedule fails, because $r_2(X)$ and $w_1(X)$ conflict, which means that we cannot move $r_2(X)$ down to get the equivalent

---

11. We will use *serializable* to mean conflict serializable. Another definition of serializable used in practice (see Section 11.7) is to have repeatable reads, no dirty reads, and no phantom records (see Section 11.4.7.1 for a discussion on phantoms).

serial schedule T_1, T_2. Similarly, because $w_1(X)$ and $w_2(X)$ conflict, we cannot move $w_1(X)$ down to get the equivalent serial schedule T_2, T_1.

Another, more complex definition of equivalence—called *view equivalence*, which leads to the concept of *view serializability*—is discussed in Section 11.3.2.4.

11.3.2.2 Testing for conflict serializability of a schedule
There is a simple algorithm for determining the conflict serializability of a schedule. Most concurrency control methods do *not* actually test for serializability. Rather protocols, or rules, are developed that guarantee that a schedule will be serializable. We discuss the algorithm for testing conflict serializability of schedules here to gain a better understanding of these concurrency control protocols, which are discussed in Section 11.4.

Algorithm 11.1 can be used to test a schedule for conflict serializability. The algorithm looks at only the read_item and write_item operations in a schedule to construct a **precedence graph** (or **serialization graph**), which is a **directed graph** $G = (N, E)$ that consists of a set of nodes $N = \{T_1, T_2, \ldots, T_n\}$ and a set of directed edges $E = \{e_1, e_2, \ldots, e_m\}$. There is one node in the graph for each transaction T_i in the schedule. Each edge e_i in the graph is of the form $(T_j \rightarrow T_k)$, $1 \leq j \leq n$, $1 \leq k \leq n$, where T_j is the **starting node** of e_i and T_k is the **ending node** of e_i. Such an edge is created if one of the operations in T_j appears in the schedule *before some conflicting operation* in T_k.

Algorithm 11.1: Testing conflict serializability of a schedule S.

1. For each transaction T_i participating in schedule S, create a node labeled T_i in the precedence graph.
2. For each case in S where T_j executes a read_item(X) after T_i executes a write_item(X), create an edge $(T_i \rightarrow T_j)$ in the precedence graph.
3. For each case in S where T_j executes a write_item(X) after T_i executes a read_item(X), create an edge $(T_i \rightarrow T_j)$ in the precedence graph.
4. For each case in S where T_j executes a write_item(X) after T_i executes a write_item(X), create an edge $(T_i \rightarrow T_j)$ in the precedence graph.
5. The schedule S is serializable if and only if the precedence graph has no cycles.

The precedence graph is constructed as described in Algorithm 11.1. If there is a cycle in the precedence graph, schedule S is not (conflict) serializable; if there is no cycle, S is serializable. A **cycle** in a directed graph is a **sequence of edges** $C = ((T_j \rightarrow T_k), (T_k \rightarrow T_p), \ldots, (T_i \rightarrow T_j))$ with the property that the starting node of each edge—except the first edge—is the same as the ending node of the previous edge, and the starting node of the first edge is the same as the ending node of the last edge (the sequence starts and ends at the same node).

In the precedence graph, an edge from T_i to T_j means that transaction T_i must come before transaction T_j in any serial schedule that is equivalent to S, because two conflicting operations appear in the schedule in that order. If there is no cycle in the precedence graph, we can create an **equivalent serial schedule** S' that is equivalent to S, by ordering the transactions that participate in S as follows: Whenever an edge exists in the precedence graph from T_i to T_j, T_i must appear before T_j in the equivalent serial schedule S'.[12] Notice that the edges $(T_i \rightarrow T_j)$ in a precedence graph can optionally be labeled by the name(s) of the data item(s) that led to creating the edge. Figure 11.7 shows such labels on the edges.

In general, several serial schedules can be equivalent to S if the precedence graph for S has no cycle. However, if the precedence graph has a cycle, it is easy to show that we cannot create any equivalent serial schedule, so S is not serializable. The precedence graphs created for schedules A to D, respectively, of Figure

---

12. This process of ordering the nodes of an acyclic graph is known as topological sorting.

FIGURE 11.7 Constructing the precedence graphs for schedules A to D from Figure 11.5 to test for conflict serializability. (a) Precedence graph for serial schedule A. (b) Precedence graph for serial schedule B. (c) Precedence graph for schedule C (not serializable). (d) Precedence graph for schedule D (serializable, equivalent to schedule A).

11.5 appear in Figure 11.7a to d. The graph for schedule C has a cycle, so it is not serializable. The graph for schedule D has no cycle, so it is serializable, and the equivalent serial schedule is T_1 followed by T_2. The graphs for schedules A and B have no cycles, as expected, because the schedules are serial and hence serializable.

Another example, in which three transactions participate, is shown in Figure 11.8. Figure 11.8a shows the read_item and write_item operations in each transaction. Two schedules E and F for these transactions are shown in Figure 11.8b and c, respectively, and the precedence graphs for schedules E and F are shown in parts d and e. Schedule E is not serializable, because the corresponding precedence graph has cycles. Schedule F is serializable, and the serial schedule equivalent to F is shown in Figure 11.8e. Although only one equivalent serial schedule exists for F, in general there may be *more than one equivalent serial schedule* for a serializable schedule. Figure 11.8f shows a precedence graph representing a schedule that has two equivalent serial schedules.

11.3.2.3 Uses of serializability

As we discussed earlier, saying that a schedule S is (conflict) serializable—that is, S is (conflict) equivalent to a serial schedule—is tantamount to saying that S is correct. Being *serializable* is distinct from being *serial*, however. A serial schedule represents inefficient processing because no interleaving of operations from different transactions is permitted. This can lead to low CPU utilization while a transaction waits for disk I/O, or for another transaction to terminate, thus slowing down processing considerably. A serializable schedule gives the benefits of concurrent execution without giving up any correctness. In practice, it is quite difficult to test for the serializability of a schedule. The interleaving of operations from concurrent transactions—which are usually executed as processes by the operating system—is typically determined by the operating system scheduler, which allocates resources to all processes. Factors such as system load, time of transaction submission, and priorities of processes contribute to the ordering of operations in a schedule. Hence, it is difficult to determine how the operations of a schedule will be interleaved beforehand to ensure serializability.

If transactions are executed at will and then the resulting schedule is tested for serializability, we must cancel the effect of the schedule if it turns out not to be serializable. This is a serious problem that makes this approach impractical. Hence, the approach taken in most practical systems is to determine methods

(a)

(b)

Schedule E

(c)

Schedule F

FIGURE 11.8 Another example of serializability testing. (a) The READ and WRITE operations of three transactions T_1, T_2, and T_3. (b) Schedule E. (c) Schedule F.

FIGURE 11.8(CONTINUED) Another example of serializability testing. Another example of serializability testing. (d) Precedence graph for schedule E. (e) Precedence graph for schedule F. (f) Precedence graph with two equivalent serial schedules.

that ensure serializability, without having to test the schedules themselves. The approach taken in most commercial DBMSs is to design **protocols** (sets of rules) that—if followed by *every* individual transaction or if enforced by a DBMS concurrency control subsystem—will ensure serializability of *all schedules in which the transactions participate.*

Another problem appears here: When transactions are submitted continuously to the system, it is difficult to determine when a schedule begins and when it ends. Serializability theory can be adapted to deal with this problem by considering only the committed projection of a schedule S. Recall from Section 11.3.1 that the *committed projection* C(S) of a schedule S includes only the operations in S that belong to committed transactions. We can theoretically define a schedule S to be serializable if its committed projection C(S) is equivalent to some serial schedule, since only committed transactions are guaranteed by the DBMS.

In Section 11.4, we discuss a number of different concurrency control protocols that guarantee serializability. The most common technique, called *two-phase locking*, is based on locking data items to prevent concurrent transactions from interfering with one another, and enforcing an additional condition that guarantees serializability. This is used in the majority of commercial DBMSs. Other protocols have been proposed;[13] these include *timestamp ordering*, where each transaction is assigned a unique timestamp and the protocol ensures that any conflicting operations are executed in the order of the transaction timestamps; *multiversion protocols*, which are based on maintaining multiple versions of data items; and *optimistic* (also called *certification* or *validation*) *protocols*, which check for possible serializability violations after the transactions terminate but before they are permitted to commit.

11.3.2.4 View equivalence and view serializability

In Section 11.5.1, we defined the concepts of conflict equivalence of schedules and conflict serializability. Another less restrictive definition of equivalence of schedules is called *view equivalence*. This leads to another definition of serializability called *view serializability*. Two schedules S and S' are said to be view equivalent if the following three conditions hold:

1. The same set of transactions participates in S and S', and S and S' include the same operations of those transactions.

2. For any operation $r_i(X)$ of T_i in S, if the value of X read by the operation has been written by an operation $w_j(X)$ of T_j (or if it is the original value of X before the schedule started), the same condition must hold for the value of X read by operation $r_i(X)$ of T_i in S'.

3. If the operation $w_k(Y)$ of T_k is the last operation to write item Y in S, then $w_k(Y)$ of T_k must also be the last operation to write item Y in S'.

The idea behind view equivalence is that, as long as each read operation of a transaction reads the result of the same write operation in both schedules, the write operations of each transaction must produce the same results. The read operations are hence said to *see the same view* in both schedules. Condition 3 ensures that the final write operation on each data item is the same in both schedules, so the database state should be the same at the end of both schedules. A schedule S is said to be **view serializable** if it is view equivalent to a serial schedule.

The definitions of conflict serializability and view serializability are similar if a condition known as the **constrained write assumption** holds on all transactions in the schedule. This condition states that any write operation $w_i(X)$ in T_i is preceded by a $r_i(X)$ in T_i and that the value written by $w_i(X)$ in T_i depends only on the value of X read by $r_i(X)$. This assumes that computation of the new value of X is a function $f(X)$ based on the old value of X read from the database. However, the definition of view serializability is less restrictive than that of conflict serializability under the **unconstrained write assumption**, where the value written by an operation $w_i(X)$ in T_i can be independent of its old value from the database. This is called a **blind write**, and it is illustrated by the following schedule S_g of three transactions T_1: $r_1(X)$; $w_1(X)$; T_2: $w_2(X)$; and T_3: $w_3(X)$:

S_g: $r_1(X)$; $w_2(X)$; $w_1(X)$; $w_3(X)$; c_1; c_2; c_3;

In S_g the operations $w_2(X)$ and $w_3(X)$ are blind writes, since T_2 and T_3 do not read the value of X. The schedule S_g is view serializable, since it is view equivalent to the serial schedule T_1, T_2, T_3. However, S_g

---

13. These other protocols have not been used much in practice so far; most systems use some variation of the two-phase locking protocol.

is not conflict serializable, since it is not conflict equivalent to any serial schedule. It has been shown that any conflict-serializable schedule is also view serializable but not vice versa, as illustrated by the preceding example. There is an algorithm to test whether a schedule S is view serializable or not. However, the problem of testing for view serializability has been shown to be NP-hard, meaning that finding an efficient polynomial time algorithm for this problem is highly unlikely.

11.3.2.5 Other types of equivalence of schedules

Serializability of schedules is sometimes considered to be too restrictive as a condition for ensuring the correctness of concurrent executions. Some applications can produce schedules that are correct by satisfying conditions less stringent than either conflict serializability or view serializability. An example is the type of transactions known as **debit-credit transactions**—for example, those that apply deposits and withdrawals to a data item whose value is the current balance of a bank account. The semantics of debit-credit operations is that they update the value of a data item X by either subtracting from or adding to the value of the data item. Because addition and subtraction operations are commutative—that is, they can be applied in any order—it is possible to produce correct schedules that are not serializable. For example, consider the following two transactions, each of which may be used to transfer an amount of money between two bank accounts:

T_1: $r_1(X)$; $X := X - 10$; $w_1(X)$; $r_1(Y)$; $Y := Y + 10$; $w_1(Y)$;
T_2: $r_2(Y)$; $Y := Y - 20$; $w_2(Y)$; $r_2(X)$; $X := X + 20$; $w_2(X)$;

Consider the following nonserializable schedule S_h for the two transactions:

S_h: $r_1(X)$; $w_1(X)$; $r_2(Y)$; $w_2(Y)$; $r_1(Y)$; $w_1(Y)$; $r_2(X)$; $w_2(X)$;

With the additional knowledge, or **semantics**, that the operations between each $r_i(I)$ and $w_i(I)$ are commutative, we know that the order of executing the sequences consisting of (read, update, write) is not important as long as each (read, update, write) sequence by a particular transaction T_i on a particular item I is not interrupted by conflicting operations. Hence, the schedule S_h is considered to be correct even though it is not serializable. Researchers have been working on extending concurrency control theory to deal with cases where serializability is considered to be too restrictive as a condition for correctness of schedules.

11.4 CONCURRENCY CONTROL TECHNIQUES

In this section, we discuss a number of concurrency control techniques that are used to ensure the noninterference or isolation property of concurrently executing transactions. Most of these techniques ensure serializability of schedules (see Section 11.3.2), using **protocols** (that is, sets of rules) that guarantee serializability. One important set of protocols employs the technique of **locking** data items to prevent multiple transactions from accessing the items concurrently; a number of locking protocols are described in Section 11.4.1. Locking protocols are used in most commercial DBMSs. Another set of concurrency control protocols use **timestamps.** A timestamp is a unique identifier for each transaction, generated by the system. Concurrency control protocols that use timestamp ordering to ensure serializability are described in Section 11.4.2. In Section 11.4.3, we discuss **multiversion** concurrency control protocols that use multiple versions of a data item. In Section 11.4.4, we present a protocol based on the concept of **validation** or **certification** of a transaction after it executes its operations; these are sometimes called **optimistic protocols.**

Another factor that affects concurrency control is the **granularity** of the data items—that is, what portion of the database a data item represents. An item can be as small as a single attribute (field) value or as large as a disk block, or even a whole file or the entire database. We discuss granularity of items in Section 11.4.5. In Section 11.4.6, we discuss concurrency control issues that arise when indexes are used to process transactions. Finally, in Section 11.4.7 we discuss some additional concurrency control issues.

11.4.1   Two-phase Locking Techniques for Concurrency Control

Some of the main techniques used to control concurrent execution of transactions are based on the concept of locking data items. A **lock** is a variable associated with a data item that describes the status of the item with respect to possible operations that can be applied to it. Generally, there is one lock for each data item in the database. Locks are used as a means of synchronizing the access by concurrent transactions to the database items. In Section 11.4.1.1 we discuss the nature and types of locks. Then, in Section 11.4.1.2, we present protocols that use locking to guarantee serializability of transaction schedules. Finally, in Section 11.4.1.3 we discuss two problems associated with the use of locks— namely, deadlock and starvation—and show how these problems are handled.

11.4.1.1   Types of locks and system lock tables
Several types of locks are used in concurrency control. To introduce locking concepts gradually, we first discuss binary locks, which are simple but restrictive and so are not used in practice. We then discuss shared/exclusive locks, which provide more general locking capabilities and are used in practical database locking schemes. In Section 11.4.3.2, we describe a certify lock and show how it can be used to improve performance of locking protocols.

Binary Locks.   A **binary lock** can have two **states** or **values:** locked and unlocked (or 1 and 0, for simplicity). A distinct lock is associated with each database item X. If the value of the lock on X is 1, item X *cannot be accessed* by a database operation that requests the item. If the value of the lock on X is 0, the item can be accessed when requested. We refer to the current value (or state) of the lock associated with item X as **LOCK(X).** Two operations, lock_item and unlock_item, are used with binary locking. A transaction requests access to an item X by first issuing a **lock_item (X)** operation. If LOCK (X) = 1, the transaction is forced to wait. If LOCK (X) = 0, it is set to 1 (the transaction **locks** the item) and the transaction is allowed to access item X. When the transaction is through using the item, it issues an **unlock_item (X)** operation, which sets LOCK (X) to 0 (**unlocks** the item) so that X may be accessed by other transactions. Hence, a binary lock enforces **mutual exclusion** on the data item. A description of the lock_item (X) and unlock_item (X) operations is shown in Figure 11.9.

Notice that the lock_item and unlock_item operations must be implemented as indivisible units (known as **critical sections** in operating systems); that is, no interleaving should be allowed once a lock or unlock operation is started until the operation terminates or the transaction waits. In Figure 11.9, the wait command within the lock_item (X) operation is usually implemented by putting the transaction on a waiting queue for item X until X is unlocked and the transaction can be granted access to it. Other transactions that also want to access X are placed on the same queue. Hence, the wait command is considered to be outside the lock_item operation.

```
lock_item(X):
     B: If LOCK(X)=0 (*item is unlocked*)
        then LOCK(X)←1(*lock the item*)
        else begin
            wait (until lock(X)=o and
                the lock manager wakes up the transaction);
            go to B
        end;
```

```
unlock_item(X):
     LOCK(X)←0; (*unlock the item*)
     if any transactions are waiting
        then wakeup one of the waiting transactions;
```

Figure 11.9 Lock and unlock operations for binary locks.

Notice that it is quite simple to implement a binary lock; all that is needed is a binary-valued variable, LOCK, associated with each data item X in the database. In its simplest form, each lock can be a record with three fields: < data item name, LOCK, locking transaction > plus a queue for transactions that are waiting to access the item. The system needs to maintain only these records for the items that are currently locked in a **lock table,** which could be organized as a hash file. Items not in the lock table are considered to be unlocked. The DBMS has a **lock manager subsystem** to keep track of and control access to locks.

If the simple binary locking scheme described here is used, every transaction must obey the following rules:

1. A transaction T must issue the operation lock_item(X) before any read_item(X) or write_item(X) operations are performed in T.

2. A transaction T must issue the operation unlock_item(X) after all read_item(X) and write_item(X) operations are completed in T.

3. A transaction T will not issue a lock_item(X) operation if it already holds the lock on item X.[14]

4. A transaction T will not issue an unlock_item(X) operation unless it already holds the lock on item X.

These rules can be enforced by the lock manager module of the DBMS. Between the lock_item(X) and unlock_item(X) operations in transaction T, T is said to **hold the lock** on item X. At most one transaction can hold the lock on a particular item. Thus no two transactions can access the same item concurrently.

Shared/Exclusive (or Read/Write) Locks. The preceding binary locking scheme is too restrictive for database items, because at most one transaction can hold a lock on a given item. We should allow several transactions to access the same item X if they all access X for *reading purposes only.* However, if a transaction is to write an item X, it must have exclusive access to X. For this purpose, a different type of lock called a **multiplemode lock** is used. In this scheme—called **shared/exclusive** or **read/write locks**—there are three locking operations: read_lock(X), write_lock(X), and unlock(X). A lock associated with an item X, LOCK(X), now has three possible states: "read-locked," "writelocked," or "unlocked." A **read-locked item** is also called **share-locked,** because other transactions are allowed to read the item, whereas a **write-locked item** is called **exclusive-locked,** because a single transaction exclusively holds the lock on the item.

---

14. This rule may be removed if we modify the lock_item(X) operation in Figure 11.9 so that if the item is currently locked *by the requesting transaction,* the lock is granted.

One method for implementing the preceding three operations on a read/write lock is to keep track of the number of transactions that hold a shared (read) lock on an item in the lock table. Each record in the lock table will have four fields: <data item name, LOCK, no_of_reads, locking_transaction(s)>. Again, to save space, the system need maintain lock records only for locked items in the lock table. The value (state) of LOCK is either read-locked or write-locked, suitably coded (if we assume no records are kept in the lock table for unlocked items). If LOCK(X)=write-locked, the value of locking_transaction(s) is a single transaction that holds the exclusive (write) lock on X. If LOCK(X)=readlocked, the value of locking transaction(s) is a list of one or more transactions that hold the shared (read) lock on X. The three operations read_lock(X), write_lock(X), and unlock(X) are described in Figure 11.10.[15] As before, each of the three operations should be considered indivisible; no interleaving should be allowed once one of the operations is started until either the operation terminates by granting the lock or the transaction is placed on a waiting queue for the item.

When we use the shared/exclusive locking scheme, the system must enforce the following rules:

1. A transaction T must issue the operation read_lock(X) or write_lock(X) before any read_item(X) operation is performed in T.

2. A transaction T must issue the operation write_lock(X) before any write_item(X) operation is performed in T.

3. A transaction T must issue the operation unlock(X) after all read_item(X) and write_item(X) operations are completed in T.[16]

4. A transaction T will not issue a read_lock(X) operation if it already holds a read (shared) lock or a write (exclusive) lock on item X. This rule may be relaxed, as we discuss shortly.

5. A transaction T will not issue a write_lock(X) operation if it already holds a read (shared) lock or write (exclusive) lock on item X. This rule may be relaxed, as we discuss shortly.

6. A transaction T will not issue an unlock(X) operation unless it already holds a read (shared) lock or a write (exclusive) lock on item X.

Conversion of Locks. Sometimes it is desirable to relax conditions 4 and 5 in the preceding list in order to allow **lock conversion;** that is, a transaction that already holds a lock on item X is allowed under certain conditions to **convert** the lock from one locked state to another. For example, it is possible for a transaction T to issue a read_lock(X) and then later on to **upgrade** the lock by issuing a write_lock(X) operation. If T is the only transaction holding a read lock on X at the time it issues the write_lock(X) operation, the lock can be upgraded; otherwise, the transaction must wait. It is also possible for a transaction T to issue a write_lock(X) and then later on to **downgrade** the lock by issuing a read_lock(X) operation. When upgrading and downgrading of locks is used, the lock table must include transaction identifiers in the record structure for each lock (in the locking_transaction(s) field) to store the information on which transactions hold locks on the item. The descriptions of the read_lock(X) and write_lock(X) operations in Figure 11.10 must be changed appropriately. We leave this as an exercise for the reader.

Using binary locks or read/write locks in transactions, as described earlier, does *not guarantee serializability* of schedules on its own. Figure 11.11 shows an example where the preceding locking rules are followed but a nonserializable schedule may result. This is because in Figure 11.11a the items Y in T_1 and X in T_2 were *unlocked too early*. This allows a schedule such as the one shown in Figure 11.11c to occur, which is not a serializable schedule and hence gives incorrect results. To guarantee serializability, we must follow *an additional*

---

15. These algorithms do not allow *upgrading* or *downgrading* of locks, as described later in this section. The reader can extend the algorithms to allow these additional operations.

16. This rule may be relaxed to allow a transaction to unlock an item, then lock it again later.

read_lock (X);

B: if LOCK (X) = "unlocked"
   then begin LOCK (X) ←"read-locked"
         no_of_reads (X) ←1
   end
   else if LOCK (X) = "read-locked"
         then no_of_reads (X) ←   no_of_reads (X) + 1
         else begin wait (until locked (X) = "unlocked" and
                  the lock manager wakes up the transaction);
               go to **B**
            end;

write_lock (X);

B: if LOCK (X) = "unlocked"
   then LOCK (X) ←1 "write-locked"
   else begin
      wait (untill LOCK (X) = "unlocked" and
      the lock manager wakes up the transaction);
      go to **B**
      end;

Unlock (X);

if LOCK (X) = "write-locked"
   then begin LOCK (X) ←1 "unlocked"
      wakeup one of the waiting transactions, if any
      end
   else if LOCK (X) = "read-locked"
      then begin
            no_of_reads (X) ←no_of_reads (X) – 1
            if no_of_reads (X) = 0
               then begin LOCK(X) = "unlocked";
                  wakeup one of the waiting transactions, if any
                  end;
               end

FIGURE 11.10 Locking and unlocking operations for two-mode (read-write or shared-exclusive) locks.

protocol concerning the positioning of locking and unlocking operations in every transaction. The best known protocol, two-phase locking, is described in the next section.

11.4.1.2 Guaranteeing serializability by two-phase locking
A transaction is said to follow the **two-phase locking protocol** if *all* locking operations (read_lock, write_lock) precede the *first* unlock operation in the transaction. Such a transaction can be divided into two phases: an **expanding or growing (first) phase,** during which new locks on items can be acquired but none can be released; and a **shrinking (second) phase,** during which existing locks can be released but no new locks can be acquired. If lock conversion is allowed, then upgrading of locks (from read-locked to write-locked) must be done during the expanding phase, and downgrading of locks (from write-locked to read-locked) must be done in the shrinking phase. Hence, a read_lock(X) operation that downgrades an already held write lock on X can appear only in the shrinking phase.

Transactions T_1 and T_2 of Figure 11.11a do not follow the two-phase locking protocol. This is because the write_lock(X) operation follows the unlock(Y) operation in T_1, and similarly the write_lock(Y) operation follows the unlock(X) operation in T_2. If we enforce two-phase locking, the transactions can be rewritten as T_1' and T_2', as shown in Figure 11.12. Now, the schedule shown in Figure 11.11(c) is not permitted for T_1' and T_2' (with their modified order of locking and unlocking operations) under the rules of locking described in Section 11.4.1.1. This is because T_1' will issue its write_lock(X) *before* it unlocks item Y; consequently, when T_2' issues its read_lock(X), it is forced to wait until T_1' releases the lock by issuing an unlock(X) in the schedule.

(a)

T_1	T_2
read_lock(Y);	read_lock(X);
read_item(Y);	read_item(X);
unlock(Y);	unlock(X);
write_lock(X);	write_lock(Y);
read_item(X);	read_item(Y);
X:=X+Y;	Y:=Y+Y;
write_item(X);	write_item(Y);
unlock(X);	unlock(Y);

(b)

Initial values: X=20, Y=30
Result of by schedule T_1 followed serial T
X=50, Y=80
Result of by schedule T_2 followed serial T
X=70, Y=50

(c)

	T_1	T_2
	read_lock(Y);	
	read_item(Y);	
	unlock(Y);	
		read_lock(X);
		read_item(X);
		unlock(X);
		write_lock(X);
		read_item(Y);
		Y:=X+Y;
		write_item(X);
		unlock(Y);
	write_lock(X);	
	read_item(Y);	
	X:=X+Y;	
	write_item(X);	
	unlock(X);	

Time

Result of schedule S:
X=50, Y=50
(nonserializable)

FIGURE 11.11 Transactions that do not obey two-phase locking. (a) Two transactions T_1 and T_2. (b) Results of possible serial schedules of T_1 and T_2. (c) A nonserializable schedule S that uses locks.

T'_1	T'_2
read_lock(Y);	read_lock(X);
read_item(Y);	read_item(X);
write_lock(X);	write_lock(Y);
unlock(Y);	unlock(X);
read_item	read_item(Y);
X:=X+Y;	Y:=X+Y;
write_item(X);	write_item(Y);
unlock(X);	unlock(Y);

FIGURE 11.12 Transactions T_1' and T_2', which are the same as T_1 and T_2 of Figure 11.11 but which follow the two-phase locking protocol. Note that they can produce a deadlock.

It can be proved that, if *every* transaction in a schedule follows the two-phase locking protocol, the schedule is *guaranteed to be serializable*, obviating the need to test for serializability of schedules any more. The locking mechanism, by enforcing two-phase locking rules, also enforces serializability.

Two-phase locking may limit the amount of concurrency that can occur in a schedule. This is because a transaction T may not be able to release an item X after it is through using it if T must lock an additional item Y later on; or conversely, T must lock the additional item Y before it needs it so that it can release X. Hence, X must remain locked by T until all items that the transaction needs to read or write have been locked; only then can X be released by T. Meanwhile, another transaction seeking to access X may be forced to wait, even though T is done with X; conversely, if Y is locked earlier than it is needed, another transaction seeking to access Y is forced to wait even though T is not using Y yet. This is the price for guaranteeing serializability of all schedules without having to check the schedules themselves.

Basic, Conservative, Strict, and Rigorous Two-Phase Locking. There are a number of variations of two-phase locking (2PL). The technique just described is known as **basic 2PL.** A variation known as **conservative 2PL** (or **static 2PL**) requires a transaction to lock all the items it accesses *before the transaction begins execution*, by **predeclaring** its *readset* and *write-set*. Recall from Section 11.1.2 that the **read-set** of a transaction is the set of all items that the transaction reads, and the **write-set** is the set of all items that it writes. If any of the predeclared items needed cannot be locked, the transaction does not lock any item; instead, it waits until all the items are available for locking. Conservative 2PL is a deadlock-free protocol, as we shall see in Section 11.4.1.3 when we discuss the deadlock problem. However, it is difficult to use in practice because of the need to predeclare the read-set and write-set, which is not possible in most situations.

In practice, the most popular variation of 2PL is **strict 2PL,** which guarantees strict schedules (see Section 11.3.2). In this variation, a transaction T does not release any of its exclusive (write) locks until after it commits or aborts. Hence, no other transaction can read or write an item that is written by T unless T has committed, leading to a strict schedule for recoverability. Strict 2PL is not deadlock-free. A more restrictive variation of strict 2PL is **rigorous 2PL,** which also guarantees strict schedules. In this variation, a transaction T does not release any of its locks (exclusive or shared) until after it commits or aborts, and so it is easier to implement than strict 2PL. Notice the difference between conservative and rigorous 2PL; the former must lock all its items *before it starts* so once the transaction starts it is in its shrinking phase, whereas the latter does not unlock any of its items until *after it terminates* (by committing or aborting) so the transaction is in its expanding phase until it ends.

In many cases, the **concurrency control subsystem** itself is responsible for generating the read_lock and write_lock requests. For example, suppose the system is to enforce the strict 2PL protocol. Then, whenever transaction T issues a read_item(X), the system calls the read_lock(X) operation on behalf of T. If the state of LOCK(X) is write_locked by some other transaction T', the system places T on the waiting queue for item X; otherwise, it grants the read_lock(X) request and permits the read_item(X) operation of T to execute. On the other hand, if transaction T issues a write_item(X), the system calls the write_lock(X) operation on behalf of T. If the state of LOCK(X) is write_locked or read_locked by some other transaction T', the system places T on the waiting queue for item X; if the state of LOCK(X) is read_locked *and* T itself is the only transaction holding the read lock on X, the system upgrades the lock to write_locked and permits the write_item(X) operation by T; finally, if the state of LOCK(X) is unlocked, the system grants the write_lock(X) request and permits the write_item(X) operation to execute. After each action, the system must update its lock table appropriately.

Although the two-phase locking protocol guarantees serializability (that is, every schedule that is permitted is serializable), it does not permit *all possible* serializable schedules (that is, some serializable schedules will be prohibited by the protocol). In addition, the use of locks can cause two additional problems: deadlock and starvation. We discuss these problems and their solutions in the next section.

11.4.1.3 Dealing with deadlock and starvation

Deadlock occurs when *each* transaction T in a set of *two or more transactions* is waiting for some item that is locked by some other transaction T′ in the set. Hence, each transaction in the set is on a waiting queue, waiting for one of the other transactions in the set to release the lock on an item. A simple example is shown in Figure 11.13a, where the two transactions T_1' and T_2' are deadlocked in a partial schedule; T_1' is on the waiting queue for X, which is locked by T_2', while T_2' is on the waiting queue for Y, which is locked by T_1'. Meanwhile, neither T_1' nor T_2 nor any other transaction can access items X and Y.

FIGURE 11.13 Illustrating the deadlock problem. (a) A partial schedule of T_1' and T_2' that is in a state of deadlock. (b) A wait for graph for the partial schedule in (a).

Deadlock Prevention Protocols. One way to prevent deadlock is to use a **deadlock prevention protocol**.[17] One deadlock prevention protocol, which is used in conservative two-phase locking, requires that every transaction *lock all the items it needs in advance* (which is generally not a practical assumption)—if any of the items cannot be obtained, none of the items are locked. Rather, the transaction waits and then tries again to lock all the items it needs. This solution obviously further limits concurrency. A second protocol, which also limits concurrency, involves *ordering all the items* in the database and making sure that a transaction that needs several items will lock them according to that order. This requires that the programmer (or the system) be aware of the chosen order of the items, which is also not practical in the database context.

A number of other deadlock prevention schemes have been proposed that make a decision about what to do with a transaction involved in a possible deadlock situation: Should it be blocked and made to wait or should it be aborted, or should the transaction preempt and abort another transaction? These techniques use the concept of **transaction timestamp** TS(T), which is a unique identifier assigned to each transaction. The timestamps are typically based on the order in which transactions are started; hence, if transaction T_1 starts before transaction T_2, then $TS(T_1) < TS(T_2)$. Notice that the *older* transaction has the *smaller* timestamp value. Two schemes that prevent deadlock are called wait-die and wound-wait. Suppose that transaction T_i tries to lock an item X but is not able to because X is locked by some other transaction T_j with a conflicting lock. The rules followed by these schemes are as follows:

- **Wait-die:** If $TS(T_i) < TS(T_j)$, then (T_i older than T_j) T_i is allowed to wait; otherwise (T_i younger than T_j) abort T_i (T_i *dies*) and restart it later *with the same timestamp*.

- **Wound-wait:** If $TS(T_i) < TS(T_j)$, then (T_i older than T_j) abort T_j (T_i *wounds* T_j) and restart it later *with the same timestamp*; otherwise (T_i younger than T_j) T_i is allowed to wait.

---

17. These protocols are not generally used in practice, either because of unrealistic assumptions or because of their possible overhead. Deadlock detection and timeouts (see below) are more practical.

In wait-die, an older transaction is allowed to wait on a younger transaction, whereas a younger transaction requesting an item held by an older transaction is aborted and restarted. The wound-wait approach does the opposite: A younger transaction is allowed to wait on an older one, whereas an older transaction requesting an item held by a younger transaction *preempts* the younger transaction by aborting it. Both schemes end up aborting the *younger* of the two transactions that *may be involved* in a deadlock. It can be shown that these two techniques are deadlock-free, since in wait-die, transactions only wait on younger transactions so no cycle is created. Similarly, in wound-wait, transactions only wait on older transactions so no cycle is created. However, both techniques may cause some transactions to be aborted and restarted needlessly, even though those transactions may *never actually cause a deadlock*.

Another group of protocols that prevent deadlock do not require timestamps. These include the no waiting (NW) and cautious waiting (CW) algorithms. In the **no waiting algorithm,** if a transaction is unable to obtain a lock, it is immediately aborted and then restarted after a certain time delay without checking whether a deadlock will actually occur or not. Because this scheme can cause transactions to abort and restart needlessly, the **cautious waiting** algorithm was proposed to try to reduce the number of needless aborts/restarts. Suppose that transaction T_i tries to lock an item X but is not able to do so because X is locked by some other transaction T_j with a conflicting lock. The cautious waiting rules are as follows:

- **Cautious waiting:** If T_j is not blocked (not waiting for some other locked item), then T_i is blocked and allowed to wait; otherwise abort T_i.

It can be shown that cautious waiting is deadlock-free, by considering the time $b(T)$ at which each blocked transaction T was blocked. If the two transactions T_i and T_j above both become blocked, and T_i is waiting on T_j, then $b(T_i) < b(Tj)$, since T_i can only wait on T_j at a time when T_j is not blocked. Hence, the blocking times form a total ordering on all blocked transactions, so no cycle that causes deadlock can occur.

Deadlock Detection and Timeouts. A second—more practical—approach to dealing with deadlock is **deadlock detection,** where the system checks if a state of deadlock actually exists. This solution is attractive if we know there will be little interference among the transactions—that is, if different transactions will rarely access the same items at the same time. This can happen if the transactions are short and each transaction locks only a few items, or if the transaction load is light. On the other hand, if transactions are long and each transaction uses many items, or if the transaction load is quite heavy, it may be advantageous to use a deadlock prevention scheme.

A simple way to detect a state of deadlock is for the system to construct and maintain a **wait-for graph.** One node is created in the wait-for graph for each transaction that is currently executing. Whenever a transaction T_i is waiting to lock an item X that is currently locked by a transaction T_j, a directed edge $(T_i \rightarrow T_j)$ is created in the wait-for graph. When T_j releases the lock(s) on the items that T_i was waiting for, the directed edge is dropped from the wait-for graph. We have a state of deadlock if and only if the wait-for graph has a cycle. One problem with this approach is the matter of determining *when* the system should check for a deadlock. Criteria such as the number of currently executing transactions or the period of time several transactions have been waiting to lock items may be used. Figure 11.13b shows the wait-for graph for the (partial) schedule shown in Figure 11.13a. If the system is in a state of deadlock, some of the transactions causing the deadlock must be aborted. Choosing which transactions to abort is known as **victim selection.** The algorithm for victim selection should generally avoid selecting transactions that have been running for a long time and that have performed many updates, and it should try instead to select transactions that have not made many changes.

Another simple scheme to deal with deadlock is the use of **timeouts.** This method is practical because of its low overhead and simplicity. In this method, if a transaction waits for a period longer than a system-defined timeout period, the system assumes that the transaction may be deadlocked and aborts it—regardless of whether a deadlock actually exists or not.

Starvation. Another problem that may occur when we use locking is **starvation,** which occurs when a transaction cannot proceed for an indefinite period of time while other transactions in the system continue normally. This may occur if the waiting scheme for locked items is unfair, giving priority to some transactions over others. One solution for starvation is to have a fair waiting scheme, such as using a **first-come-first-served** queue; transactions are enabled to lock an item in the order in which they originally requested the lock. Another scheme allows some transactions to have priority over others but increases the priority of a transaction the longer it waits, until it eventually gets the highest priority and proceeds. Starvation can also occur because of victim selection if the algorithm selects the same transaction as victim repeatedly, thus causing it to abort and never finish execution. The algorithm can use higher priorities for transactions that have been aborted multiple times to avoid this problem. The wait-die and wound-wait schemes discussed previously avoid starvation.

11.4.2 Concurrency Control Based on Timestamp Ordering

The use of locks, combined with the 2PL protocol, guarantees serializability of schedules. The serializable schedules produced by 2PL have their equivalent serial schedules based on the order in which executing transactions lock the items they acquire. If a transaction needs an item that is already locked, it may be forced to wait until the item is released. A different approach that guarantees serializability involves using transaction timestamps to order transaction execution for an equivalent serial schedule. In Section 11.4.2.1 we discuss timestamps and in Section 11.4.2.2 we discuss how serializability is enforced by ordering transactions based on their timestamps.

11.4.2.1 Timestamps
Recall that a **timestamp** is a unique identifier created by the DBMS to identify a transaction. Typically, timestamp values are assigned in the order in which the transactions are submitted to the system, so a timestamp can be thought of as the *transaction start time*. We will refer to the timestamp of transaction T as **TS(T)**. Concurrency control techniques based on timestamp ordering do not use locks; hence, *deadlocks cannot occur.*

Timestamps can be generated in several ways. One possibility is to use a counter that is incremented each time its value is assigned to a transaction. The transaction timestamps are numbered 1, 2, 3, . . . in this scheme. A computer counter has a finite maximum value, so the system must periodically reset the counter to zero when no transactions are executing for some short period of time. Another way to implement timestamps is to use the current date/time value of the system clock and ensure that no two timestamp values are generated during the same tick of the clock.

11.4.2.2 The timestamp ordering algorithm
The idea for this scheme is to order the transactions based on their timestamps. A schedule in which the transactions participate is then serializable, and the equivalent serial schedule has the transactions in order of their timestamp values. This is called **timestamp ordering (TO).** Notice how this differs from 2PL, where a schedule is serializable by being equivalent to *some* serial schedule allowed by the locking protocols. In timestamp ordering, however, the schedule is equivalent to the *particular serial order* corresponding to the order of the transaction timestamps. The algorithm must ensure that, for each item accessed by *conflicting operations* in the schedule, the order in which the item is accessed does not violate the serializability order. To do this, the algorithm associates with each database item X two timestamp (TS) values:

1. **Read_TS(X):** The **read timestamp** of item X; this is the largest timestamp among all the timestamps of transactions that have successfully read item X—that is, read_TS(X) = TS(T), where T is the *youngest* transaction that has read X successfully.

2. **Write_TS(X):** The **write timestamp** of item X; this is the largest of all the timestamps of transactions that have successfully written item X—that is, write_TS(X) = TS(T), where T is the *youngest* transaction that has written X successfully.

Basic Timestamp Ordering. Whenever some transaction T tries to issue a read_item(X) or a write_item(X) operation, the **basic TO** algorithm compares the timestamp of T with read_TS(X) and write_TS(X) to ensure that the timestamp order of transaction execution is not violated. If this order is violated, then transaction T is aborted and resubmitted to the system as a new transaction with a *new timestamp*. If T is aborted and rolled back, any transaction T_1 that may have used a value written by T must also be rolled back. Similarly, any transaction T_2 that may have used a value written by T_1 must also be rolled back, and so on. This effect is known as **cascading rollback** and is one of the problems associated with basic TO, since the schedules produced are not guaranteed to be recoverable. An *additional protocol* must be enforced to ensure that the schedules are recoverable, cascadeless, or strict. We first describe the basic TO algorithm here. The concurrency control algorithm must check whether conflicting operations violate the timestamp ordering in the following two cases:

1. Transaction T issues a write_item(X) operation:
   a. If read_TS(X) >TS(T) or if write_TS(X) > TS(T), then abort and roll back T and reject the operation. This should be done because some younger transaction with a timestamp greater than TS(T)—and hence *after* T in the timestamp ordering—has already read or written the value of item X before T had a chance to write X, thus violating the timestamp ordering.
   b. If the condition in part (a) does not occur, then execute the write_item(X) operation of T and set write_TS(X) to TS(T).

2. Transaction T issues a read_item(X) operation:
   a. If write_TS(X) > TS(T), then abort and roll back T and reject the operation. This should be done because some younger transaction with timestamp greater than TS(T)—and hence *after* T in the timestamp ordering—has already written the value of item X before T had a chance to read X.
   b. If write_TS(X) $\leq$ TS(T), then execute the read_item(X) operation of T and set read_TS(X) to the *larger* of TS(T) and the current read_TS(X).

Hence, whenever the basic TO algorithm detects two *conflicting operations* that occur in the incorrect order, it rejects the later of the two operations by aborting the transaction that issued it. The schedules produced by basic TO are hence guaranteed to be conflict serializable, like the 2PL protocol. However, some schedules are possible under each protocol that are not allowed under the other. Hence, neither protocol allows *all possible* serializable schedules. As mentioned earlier, deadlock does not occur with timestamp ordering. However, cyclic restart (and hence starvation) may occur if a transaction is continually aborted and restarted.

Strict Timestamp Ordering. A variation of basic TO called **strict TO** ensures that the schedules are both **strict** (for easy recoverability) and (conflict) serializable. In this variation, a transaction T that issues a read_item(X) or write_item(X) such that TS(T) >write_TS(X) has its read or write operation *delayed* until the transaction T' that *wrote* the value of X (hence TS(T') = write_TS(X)) has committed or aborted. To implement this algorithm, it is necessary to simulate the locking of an item X that has been written by transaction T' until T' is either committed or aborted. This algorithm does not cause deadlock, since T waits for T' only if TS(T) > TS(T').

Thomas's Write Rule.   A modification of the basic TO algorithm, known as **Thomas's write rule,** does not enforce conflict serializability; but it rejects fewer write operations, by modifying the checks for the write_item(X) operation as follows:

1. If read_TS(X) > TS(T), then abort and roll back T and reject the operation.

2. If write_TS(X) > TS(T), then do not execute the write operation but continue processing. This is because some transaction with timestamp greater than TS(T)—and hence after T in the timestamp ordering—has already written the value of X. Hence, we must ignore the write_item(X) operation of T because it is already outdated and obsolete. Notice that any conflict arising from this situation would be detected by case (1).

3. If neither the condition in part (1) nor the condition in part (2) occurs, then execute the write_item(X) operation of T and set write_TS(X) to TS(T).

11.4.3   Multiversion Concurrency Control Techniques

Other protocols for concurrency control keep the old values of a data item when the item is updated. These are known as **multiversion concurrency control,** because several versions (values) of an item are maintained. When a transaction requires access to an item, an *appropriate* version is chosen to maintain the serializability of the currently executing schedule, if possible. The idea is that some read operations that would be rejected in other techniques can still be accepted by reading an *older version* of the item to maintain serializability. When a transaction writes an item, it writes a *new version* and the old version of the item is retained. Some multiversion concurrency control algorithms use the concept of view serializability rather than conflict serializability.

An obvious drawback of multiversion techniques is that more storage is needed to maintain multiple versions of the database items. However, older versions may have to be maintained anyway—for example, for recovery purposes. In addition, some database applications require older versions to be kept to maintain a history of the evolution of data item values. The extreme case is a *temporal database*, which keeps track of all changes and the times at which they occurred. In such cases, there is no additional storage penalty for multiversion techniques, since older versions are already maintained.

Several multiversion concurrency control schemes have been proposed. We discuss two schemes here, one based on timestamp ordering and the other based on 2PL.

11.4.3.1   Multiversion technique based on timestamp ordering   In this method, several versions X_1, X_2, ..., X_k of each data item X are maintained. For *each version*, the value of version X_i and the following two timestamps are kept:

1. **read_TS(X_i):** The **read timestamp** of X_i is the largest of all the timestamps of transactions that have successfully read version X_i.

2. **write_TS(X_i):** The **write timestamp** of X_i is the timestamp of the transaction that wrote the value of version X_i.

Whenever a transaction T is allowed to execute a write_item(X) operation, a new version X_{k+1} of item X is created, with both the write_TS(X_{k+1}) and the read_TS(X_{k+1}) set to TS(T). Correspondingly, when a transaction T is allowed to read the value of version X_i, the value of read_TS(X_i) is set to the larger of the current read_TS(X_i) and TS(T).

To ensure serializability, the following two rules are used:

1. If transaction T issues a write_item(X) operation, and version i of X has the highest write_TS(X$_i$) of all versions of X that is also *less than or equal to* TS(T), and read_TS(X$_i$) > TS(T), then abort and roll back transaction T; otherwise, create a new version X$_j$ of X with read_TS(X$_j$) = write_TS(X$_j$) = TS(T).

2. If transaction T issues a read_item(X) operation, find the version i of X that has the highest write_TS(X$_i$) of all versions of X that is also *less than or equal to* TS(T); then return the value of X$_i$ to transaction T, and set the value of read_ TS(X$_i$) to the larger of TS(T) and the current read_TS(X$_i$).

As we can see in case 2, a read_item(X) is always successful, since it finds the appropriate version X$_i$ to read based on the write_TS of the various existing versions of X. In case 1, however, transaction T may be aborted and rolled back. This happens if T is attempting to write a version of X that should have been read by another transaction T' whose timestamp is read_TS(X$_i$); however, T' has already read version X$_i$, which was written by the transaction with timestamp equal to write_TS(X$_i$). If this conflict occurs, T is rolled back; otherwise, a new version of X, written by transaction T, is created. Notice that, if T is rolled back, cascading rollback may occur. Hence, to ensure recoverability, a transaction T should not be allowed to commit until after all the transactions that have written some version that T has read have committed.

11.4.3.2 Multiversion two-phase locking using certify locks

In this multiple-mode locking scheme, there are *three locking modes* for an item: read, write, and certify, instead of just the two modes (read, write) discussed previously. Hence, the state of LOCK(X) for an item X can be one of read-locked, write-locked, certifylocked, or unlocked. In the standard locking scheme with only read and write locks (see Section 11.4.1.1), a write lock is an exclusive lock. We can describe the relationship between read and write locks in the standard scheme by means of the **lock compatibility table** shown in Figure 11.14a. An entry of *yes* means that, if a transaction T holds the type of lock specified in the column header on item X and if transaction T' requests the type of lock specified in the row header on the same item X, then T' can *obtain the lock* because the locking modes are compatible. On the other hand, an entry of *no* in the table indicates that the locks are not compatible, so T' must wait until T releases the lock.

In the standard locking scheme, once a transaction obtains a write lock on an item, no other transactions can access that item. The idea behind multiversion 2PL is to allow other transactions T' to read an item X while a single transaction T holds a write lock on X. This is accomplished by allowing *two versions* for each item X; one version must always have been written by some committed transaction. The second version X' is created when a transaction T acquires a write lock on the item. Other transactions can continue to read the *committed version* of X while T holds the write lock. Transaction T can write the value of X' as needed, without affecting the value of the committed version X. However, once T is ready to commit, it must obtain a **certify lock** on all items that it currently holds write locks on before it can commit. The certify lock is not compatible with read locks, so the transaction may have to delay its commit until all its write-locked items are released by any reading transactions in order to obtain the certify locks. Once the certify locks—which are exclusive locks—are acquired, the committed version X of the data item is set to the value of version X', version X' is discarded, and the certify locks are then released. The lock compatibility table for this scheme is shown in Figure 11.14b.

In this multiversion 2PL scheme, reads can proceed concurrently with a single write operation—an arrangement not permitted under the standard 2PL schemes. The cost is that a transaction may have to delay its commit until it obtains exclusive certify locks on *all the items* it has updated. It can be shown that this scheme avoids cascading aborts, since transactions are only allowed to read the version X that was written by a committed transaction. However, deadlocks may occur if upgrading of a read lock to a write lock is allowed, and these must be handled by variations of the techniques discussed in Section 11.4.1.3.

(a)

	Read	Write
Read	yes	no
Write	no	no

(b)

	Read	Write	Certify
Read	yes	yes	no
Write	yes	no	no
Certify	no	no	no

FIGURE 11.14 Lock compatibility tables. (a) A compatibility table for read/write locking scheme. (b) A compatibility table for read/write/certify locking scheme.

11.4.4 Validation (Optimistic) Concurrency Control Techniques

In all the concurrency control techniques we have discussed so far, a certain degree of checking is done *before* a database operation can be executed. For example, in locking, a check is done to determine whether the item being accessed is locked. In timestamp ordering, the transaction timestamp is checked against the read and write timestamps of the item. Such checking represents overhead during transaction execution, with the effect of slowing down the transactions.

In **optimistic concurrency control techniques,** also known as **validation** or **certification techniques,** *no checking* is done while the transaction is executing. Several proposed concurrency control methods use the validation technique. We will describe only one scheme here. In this scheme, updates in the transaction are *not* applied directly to the database items until the transaction reaches its end. During transaction execution, all updates are applied to *local copies* of the data items that are kept for the transaction.[18] At the end of transaction execution, a **validation phase** checks whether any of the transaction's updates violate serializability. Certain information needed by the validation phase must be kept by the system. If serializability is not violated, the transaction is committed and the database is updated from the local copies; otherwise, the transaction is aborted and then restarted later.

There are three phases for this concurrency control protocol:

1. **Read phase:** A transaction can read values of committed data items from the database. However, updates are applied only to local copies (versions) of the data items kept in the transaction workspace.

2. **Validation phase:** Checking is performed to ensure that serializability will not be violated if the transaction updates are applied to the database.

---

18. Note that this can be considered as keeping multiple versions of items!

3. Write phase: If the validation phase is successful, the transaction updates are applied to the database; otherwise, the updates are discarded and the transaction is restarted.

The idea behind optimistic concurrency control is to do all the checks at once; hence, transaction execution proceeds with a minimum of overhead until the validation phase is reached. If there is little interference among transactions, most will be validated successfully. However, if there is much interference, many transactions that execute to completion will have their results discarded and must be restarted later. Under these circumstances, optimistic techniques do not work well. The techniques are called "optimistic" because they assume that little interference will occur and hence that there is no need to do checking during transaction execution.

The optimistic protocol we describe uses transaction timestamps and also requires that the write_sets and read_sets of the transactions be kept by the system. In addition, *start* and *end* times for some of the three phases need to be kept for each transaction. Recall that the **write_set** of a transaction is the set of items it writes, and the **read_set** is the set of items it reads. In the validation phase for transaction T_i, the protocol checks that T_i does not interfere with any committed transactions or with any other transactions currently in their validation phase. The validation phase for T_i checks that, for *each* such transaction T_j that is either committed or is in its validation phase, *one* of the following conditions holds:

1. Transaction T_j completes its write phase before T_i starts its read phase.

2. Ti starts its write phase after T_j completes its write phase, and the read_set of T_i has no items in common with the write_set of T_j.

3. Both the read_set and write_set of T_i have no items in common with the write_ set of T_j, and T_j completes its read phase before T_i completes its read phase.

When validating transaction T_i, the first condition is checked first for each transaction T_j, since (1) is the simplest condition to check. Only if condition (1) is false is condition (2) checked, and only if (2) is false is condition (3)—the most complex to evaluate—checked. If any one of these three conditions holds, there is no interference and T_i is validated successfully. If none of these three conditions holds, the validation of transaction T_i fails and it is aborted and restarted later because interference *may* have occurred.

11.4.5 Granularity of Data Items and Multiple Granularity Locking

All concurrency control techniques assumed that the database was formed of a number of named data items. A database item could be chosen to be one of the following:

- A database record.
- A field value of a database record.
- A disk block.
- A whole file.
- The whole database.

The granularity can affect the performance of concurrency control and recovery. In Section 11.4.5.1, we discuss some of the tradeoffs with regard to choosing the granularity level used for locking, and, in Section 11.4.5.2, we discuss a multiple granularity locking scheme, where the granularity level (size of the data item) may be changed dynamically.

11.4.5.1 Granularity level considerations for locking

The size of data items is often called the **data item granularity**. *Fine granularity* refers to small item sizes, whereas *coarse granularity* refers to large item sizes. Several tradeoffs must be considered in choosing the data item size. We shall discuss data item size in the context of locking, although similar arguments can be made for other concurrency control techniques.

First, notice that the larger the data item size is, the lower the degree of concurrency permitted. For example, if the data item size is a disk block, a transaction T that needs to lock a record B must lock the whole disk block X that contains B because a lock is associated with the whole data item (block). Now, if another transaction S wants to lock a different record C that happens to reside in the same block X in a conflicting lock mode, it is forced to wait. If the data item size was a single record, transaction S would be able to proceed, because it would be locking a different data item (record).

On the other hand, the smaller the data item size is, the more the number of items in the database. Because every item is associated with a lock, the system will have a larger number of active locks to be handled by the lock manager. More lock and unlock operations will be performed, causing a higher overhead. In addition, more storage space will be required for the lock table. For timestamps, storage is required for the read_TS and write_TS for each data item, and there will be similar overhead for handling a large number of items.

Given the above tradeoffs, an obvious question can be asked: What is the best item size? The answer is that *it depends on the types of transactions involved.* If a typical transaction accesses a small number of records, it is advantageous to have the data item granularity be one record. On the other hand, if a transaction typically accesses many records in the same file, it may be better to have block or file granularity so that the transaction will consider all those records as one (or a few) data items.

11.4.5.2 Multiple granularity level locking

Since the best granularity size depends on the given transaction, it seems appropriate that a database system support multiple levels of granularity, where the granularity level can be different for various mixes of transactions. Figure 11.15 shows a simple granularity hierarchy with a database containing two files, each file containing several pages, and each page containing several records. This can be used to illustrate a **multiple granularity level** 2PL protocol, where a lock can be requested at any level. However, additional types of locks will be needed to efficiently support such a protocol.

FIGURE 11.15 A granularity hierarchy for illustrating multiple granularity level locking.

Consider the following scenario, with only shared and exclusive lock types, that refers to the example in Figure 11.15. Suppose transaction T_1 wants to update *all the records* in file f_1, and T_1 requests and is granted an exclusive lock for f_1. Then all of f_1's pages (p_{11} through p_{1n})—and the records contained on those pages—are locked in exclusive mode. This is beneficial for T_1 because setting a single file-level lock is more efficient than setting n page-level locks or having to lock each individual record. Now suppose another transaction T_2 only wants to read record r_{1nj} from page p_{1n} of file f_1; then T_2 would request a shared record-level lock on r_{1nj}. However, the database system (that is, the transaction manager or more specifically the lock manager) must verify the compatibility of the requested lock with already held locks. One way to verify this is to traverse the tree from the leaf r_{1nj} to p_{1n} to f_1 to db. If at any time a conflicting lock is held on any of those items, then the lock request for r_{1nj} is denied and T_2 is blocked and must wait. This traversal would be fairly efficient.

However, what if transaction T_2's request came *before* transaction T_1's request? In this case, the shared record lock is granted to T_2 for r_{1nj}, but when T_1's file-level lock is requested, it is quite difficult for the lock manger to check all nodes (pages and records) that are descendants of node f_1 for a lock conflict. This would be very inefficient and would defeat the purpose of having multiple granularity level locks.

To make multiple granularity level locking practical, additional types of locks, called **intention locks,** are needed. The idea behind intention locks is for a transaction to indicate, along the path from the root to the desired node, what type of lock (shared or exclusive) it will require from one of the node's descendants. There are three types of intention locks:

1. **Intention-shared (IS)** indicates that a shared lock(s) will be requested on some descendant node(s).

2. **Intention-exclusive (IX)** indicates that an exclusive lock(s) will be requested on some descendant node(s).

3. **Shared-intention-exclusive (SIX)** indicates that the current node is locked in shared mode but an exclusive lock(s) will be requested on some descendant node(s).

The compatibility table of the three intention locks, and the shared and exclusive locks, is shown in Figure 11.16. Besides the introduction of the three types of intention locks, an appropriate locking protocol must be used. The **multiple granularity locking (MGL)** protocol consists of the following rules:

1. The lock compatibility (based on Figure 11.16) must be adhered to.

2. The root of the tree must be locked first, in any mode.

3. A node N can be locked by a transaction T in S or IS mode only if the parent node N is already locked by transaction T in either IS or IX mode.

4. A node N can be locked by a transaction T in X, IX, or SIX mode only if the parent of node N is already locked by transaction T in either IX or SIX mode.

5. A transaction T can lock a node only if it has not unlocked any node (to enforce the 2PL protocol).

6. A transaction T can unlock a node, N, only if none of the children of node N are currently locked by T.

Rule 1 simply states that conflicting locks cannot be granted. Rules 2, 3, and 4 state the conditions when a transaction may lock a given node in any of the lock modes. Rules 5 and 6 of the MGL protocol enforce 2PL rules to produce serializable schedules. To illustrate the MGL protocol with the database hierarchy in Figure 11.15, consider the following three transactions:

1. T_1 wants to update record r_{111} and record r_{211}.

2. T_2 wants to update all records on page p_{12}.

3. T_3 wants to read record r_{11j} and the entire f_2 file.

Figure 11.17 shows a possible serializable schedule for these three transactions. Only the lock operations are shown. The notation <lock_type>(<item>) is used to display the locking operations in the schedule.

	IS	IX	S	SIX	X
IS	yes	yes	yes	yes	no
IX	yes	yes	no	no	no
S	yes	no	yes	no	no
SIX	yes	no	no	no	no
X	no	no	no	no	no

FIGURE 11.16 Lock compatibility matrix for multiple granularity locking.

T_1	T_2	T_3
IX(db)		
IX(f_1)		
	IX(db)	
		IS(db)
		IS(f_1)
		IS(p_{11})
IX(p_{11})		
X(r_{111})		
	IX(f_1)	
	X(p_{12})	
		S(r_{11j})
IX(f_2)		
IX(p_{21})		
X(r_{211})		
unlock(r_{211})		
unlock(p_{21})		
unlock(f_2)		
		S(f_2)
	unlock(p_{12})	
	unlock(f_1)	
	unlock(db)	
unlock(r_{111})		
unlock(p_{11})		
unlock(f_1)		
unlock(db)		
		unlock(r_{11j})
		unlock(p_{11})
		unlock(f_1)
		unlock(f_2)
		unlock(db)

FIGURE 11.17 Lock operations to illustrate a serializable schedule.

The multiple granularity level protocol is especially suited when processing a mix of transactions that include: (1) short transactions that access only a few items (records or fields), and (2) long transactions that access entire files. In this environment, less transaction blocking and less locking overhead is incurred by such a protocol when compared to a single level granularity locking approach.

11.4.6 Using Locks for Concurrency Control in Indexes

Two-phase locking can also be applied to indexes (see Chapter 9), where the nodes of an index correspond to disk pages. However, holding locks on index pages until the shrinking phase of 2PL could cause an undue amount of transaction blocking. This is because searching an index always *starts at the root*, so if a transaction wants to insert a record (write operation), the root would be locked in exclusive mode, so all other conflicting lock requests for the index must wait until the transaction enters its shrinking phase. This blocks all other transactions from accessing the index, so in practice other approaches to locking an index must be used.

The tree structure of the index can be taken advantage of when developing a concurrency control scheme. For example, when an index search (read operation) is being executed, a path in the tree is traversed from the root to a leaf. Once a lower-level node in the path has been accessed, the higher-level nodes in that path will not be used again. So once a read lock on a child node is obtained, the lock on the parent can be released. Second, when an insertion is being applied to a leaf node (that is, when a key and a pointer are inserted), then a specific leaf node must be locked in exclusive mode. However, if that node is not full, the insertion will not cause changes to higher-level index nodes, which implies that they need not be locked exclusively.

A conservative approach for insertions would be to lock the root node in exclusive mode and then to access the appropriate child node of the root. If the child node is not full, then the lock on the root node can be released. This approach can be applied all the way down the tree to the leaf, which is typically three or four levels from the root. Although exclusive locks are held, they are soon released. An alternative, more optimistic approach would be to request and hold shared locks on the nodes leading to the leaf node, with an exclusive lock on the leaf. If the insertion causes the leaf to split, insertion will propagate to a higher level node(s). Then, the locks on the higher level node(s) can be upgraded to exclusive mode.

Another approach to index locking is to use a variant of the B$^+$-tree, called the **B-link tree.** In a B-link tree, sibling nodes on the same level are linked together at every level. This allows shared locks to be used when requesting a page and requires that the lock be released before accessing the child node. For an insert operation, the shared lock on a node would be upgraded to exclusive mode. If a split occurs, the parent node must be relocked in exclusive mode. One complication is for search operations executed concurrently with the update. Suppose that a concurrent update operation follows the same path as the search, and inserts a new entry into the leaf node. In addition, suppose that the insert causes that leaf node to split. When the insert is done, the search process resumes, following the pointer to the desired leaf, only to find that the key it is looking for is not present because the split has moved that key into a new leaf node, which would be the *right sibling* of the original leaf node. However, the search process can still succeed if it follows the pointer (link) in the original leaf node to its right sibling, where the desired key has been moved.

Handling the deletion case, where two or more nodes from the index tree merge, is also part of the B-link tree concurrency protocol. In this case, locks on the nodes to be merged are held as well as a lock on the parent of the two nodes to be merged.

11.4.7 Other Concurrency Control Issues

In this section, we discuss some other issues relevant to concurrency control. In Section 11.4.7.1, we discuss problems associated with insertion and deletion of records and the so-called *phantom problem*, which may occur when records are inserted. This problem was described as a potential problem requiring a concurrency control measure in Section 11.7. Then, in Section 11.4.7.2, we discuss problems that may occur when a transaction outputs some data to a monitor before it commits, and then the transaction is later aborted.

11.4.7.1 Insertion, deletion, and phantom records

When a new data item is **inserted** in the database, it obviously cannot be accessed until after the item is created and the insert operation is completed. In a locking environment, a lock for the item can be created and set to exclusive (write) mode; the lock can be released at the same time as other write locks would be released, based on the concurrency control protocol being used. For a timestamp-based protocol, the read and write timestamps of the new item are set to the timestamp of the creating transaction.

Next, consider **deletion operation** that is applied on an existing data item. For locking protocols, again an exclusive (write) lock must be obtained before the transaction can delete the item. For timestamp ordering, the protocol must ensure that no later transaction has read or written the item before allowing the item to be deleted.

A situation known as the **phantom problem** can occur when a new record that is being inserted by some transaction T satisfies a condition that a set of records accessed by another transaction T' must satisfy. For example, suppose that transaction T is inserting a new EMPLOYEE record whose DNO = 5, while transaction T' is accessing all EMPLOYEE records whose DNO = 5 (say, to add up all their SALARY values to calculate the personnel budget for department 5). If the equivalent serial order is T followed by T', then T' must read the new EMPLOYEE record and include its SALARY in the sum calculation. For the equivalent serial order T' followed by T, the new salary should not be included. Notice that although the transactions logically conflict, in the latter case there is really no record (data item) in common between the two transactions, since T' may have locked all the records with DNO = 5 *before* T inserted the new record. This is because the record that causes the conflict is a **phantom record** that has suddenly appeared in the database on being inserted. If other operations in the two transactions conflict, the conflict due to the phantom record may not be recognized by the concurrency control protocol.

One solution to the phantom record problem is to use **index locking,** as discussed in Section 11.4.6. Recall from Chapter 9 that an index includes entries that have an attribute value, plus a set of pointers to all records in the file with that value. For example, an index on DNO of EMPLOYEE would include an entry for each distinct DNO value, plus a set of pointers to all EMPLOYEE records with that value. If the index entry is locked *before* the record itself can be accessed, then the conflict on the phantom record can be detected. This is because transaction T' would request a read lock on the *index entry* for DNO = 5, and T would request a write lock on the same entry *before* they could place the locks on the actual records. Since the index locks conflict, the phantom conflict would be detected.

A more general technique, called **predicate locking,** would lock access to all records that satisfy an *arbitrary predicate* (condition) in a similar manner; however predicate locks have proved to be difficult to implement efficiently.

11.4.7.2 Interactive transactions

Another problem occurs when interactive transactions read input and write output to an interactive device, such as a monitor screen, before they are committed. The problem is that a user can input a value of a data item to a transaction T that is based on some value written to the screen by transaction T', which may not have committed. This dependency between T and T' cannot be modeled by the system concurrency control method, since it is only based on the user interacting with the two transactions.

An approach to dealing with this problem is to postpone output of transactions to the screen until they have committed.

11.4.7.3 Latches Locks held for a short duration are typically called **latches.** Latches do not follow the usual concurrency control protocol such as two-phase locking. For example, a latch can be used to guarantee the physical integrity of a page when that page is being written from the buffer to disk. A latch would be acquired for the page, the page written to disk, and then the latch is released.

11.5 DATABASE RECOVERY CONCEPTS

In this section we discuss some of the techniques that can be used for database recovery from failures. We have already discussed the different causes of failure, such as system crashes and transaction errors, in Section 11.1.4. We have also covered many of the concepts that are used by recovery processes, such as the system log and commit points, in Section 11.2.

We start Section 11.5.1 with an outline of a typical recovery procedures and a categorization of recovery algorithms, and then discuss several recovery concepts, including write-ahead logging, in-place versus shadow updates, and the process of rolling back (undoing) the effect of an incomplete or failed transaction. In Section 11.6, we present recovery techniques based on *deferred update,* also known as the NO-UNDO/REDO technique. In Section 11.6.2, we discuss recovery techniques based on immediate update; these include the UNDO/REDO and UNDO/NO-REDO algorithms. We discuss the technique known as shadowing or shadow paging, which can be categorized as a NO-UNDO/NO-REDO algorithm in Section 11.6.3. An example of a practical DBMS recovery scheme, called ARIES, is presented in Section 11.6.4. Recovery in multidatabases is briefly discussed in Section 11.6.5. Finally, techniques for recovery from catastrophic failure are discussed in Section 11.6.6.

Our emphasis is on conceptually describing several different approaches to recovery. For descriptions of recovery features in specific systems, the reader should consult the bibliographic notes and the user manuals for those systems. Recovery techniques are often intertwined with the concurrency control mechanisms. Certain recovery techniques are best used with specific concurrency control methods. We will attempt to discuss recovery concepts independently of concurrency control mechanisms, but we will discuss the circumstances under which a particular recovery mechanism is best used with a certain concurrency control protocol.

11.5.1 Recovery Outline and Categorization of Recovery Algorithms

Recovery from transaction failures usually means that the database is *restored* to the most recent consistent state just before the time of failure. To do this, the system must keep information about the changes that were applied to data items by the various transactions. This information is typically kept in the **system log,** as we discussed in Section 11.2.2. A typical strategy for recovery may be summarized informally as follows:

1. If there is extensive damage to a wide portion of the database due to catastrophic failure, such as a disk crash, the recovery method restores a past copy of the database that was *backed up* to archival storage (typically tape) and reconstructs a more current state by reapplying or *redoing* the operations of committed transactions from the *backed up* log, up to the time of failure.

2. When the database is not physically damaged but has become inconsistent due to noncatastrophic failures of types 1 through 4 of Section 11.1.4, the strategy is to reverse any changes that caused the inconsistency by *undoing* some operations. It may also be necessary to *redo* some operations in order to restore a consistent state of the database, as we shall see. In this case we do not need a complete archival copy of the database. Rather, the entries kept in the online system log are consulted during recovery.

Conceptually, we can distinguish two main techniques for recovery from noncatastrophic transaction failures: (1) deferred update and (2) immediate update. The **deferred update** techniques do not physically update the database on disk until *after* a transaction reaches its commit point; then the updates are recorded in the database. Before reaching commit, all transaction updates are recorded in the local transaction workspace (or buffers). During commit, the updates are first recorded persistently in the log and then written to the database. If a transaction fails before reaching its commit point, it will not have changed the database in any way, so UNDO is not needed. It may be necessary to REDO the effect of the operations of a committed transaction from the log, because their effect may not yet have been recorded in the database. Hence, deferred update is also known as the **NO-UNDO/REDO algorithm.** We discuss this technique in Section 11.6.1.

In the **immediate update** techniques, the database may be updated by some operations of a transaction *before* the transaction reaches its commit point. However, these operations are typically recorded in the log *on disk* by force writing *before* they are applied to the database, making recovery still possible. If a transaction fails after recording some changes in the database but before reaching its commit point, the effect of its operations on the database must be undone; that is, the transaction must be rolled back. In the general case of immediate update, both *undo* and *redo* may be required during recovery. This technique, known as the **UNDO/REDO algorithm,** requires both operations, and is used most often in practice. A variation of the algorithm where all updates are recorded in the database before a transaction commits requires *undo* only, so it is known as the **UNDO/NO-REDO algorithm.** We discuss these techniques in Section 11.6.2.

11.5.2 Caching (Buffering) of Disk Blocks

The recovery process is often closely intertwined with operating system functions—in particular, the buffering and caching of disk pages in main memory. Typically, one or more disk pages that include the data items to be updated are **cached** into main memory buffers and then updated in memory before being written back to disk. The caching of disk pages is traditionally an operating system function, but because of its importance to the efficiency of recovery procedures, it is handled by the DBMS by calling low-level operating systems routines.

In general, it is convenient to consider recovery in terms of the database disk pages (blocks). Typically a collection of in-memory buffers, called the **DBMS cache,** is kept under the control of the DBMS for the purpose of holding these buffers. A **directory** for the cache is used to keep track of which database items are in the buffers.[19] This can be a table of <disk page address, buffer location> entries. When the DBMS requests action on some item, it first checks the cache directory to determine whether the disk page containing the item is in the cache. If it is not, then the item must be located on disk, and the appropriate disk pages are copied into the cache. It may be necessary to **replace** (or **flush**) some of the cache buffers to make space available for the new item. Some page-replacement strategy from operating systems, such as least recently used (LRU) or first-in-first-out (FIFO), can be used to select the buffers for replacement.

Associated with each buffer in the cache is a **dirty bit,** which can be included in the directory entry, to indicate whether or not the buffer has been modified. When a page is first read from the database disk into a cache buffer, the cache directory is updated with the new disk page address, and the dirty bit is set to 0 (zero).

---

19. This is somewhat similar to the concept of *page tables* used by the operating system.

As soon as the buffer is modified, the dirty bit for the corresponding directory entry is set to 1 (one). When the buffer contents are replaced (flushed) from the cache, the contents must first be written back to the corresponding disk page *only if its dirty bit is 1*. Another bit, called the **pin-unpin** bit, is also needed—a page in the cache is **pinned** (bit value 1 (one)) if it cannot be written back to disk as yet.

Two main strategies can be employed when flushing a modified buffer back to disk. The first strategy, known as **in-place updating,** writes the buffer back to the *same original disk location*, thus overwriting the old value of any changed data items on disk.[20] Hence, a single copy of each database disk block is maintained. The second strategy, known as **shadowing,** writes an updated buffer at a different disk location, so multiple versions of data items can be maintained. In general, the old value of the data item before updating is called the **before image (BFIM),** and the new value after updating is called the **after image (AFIM).** In shadowing, both the BFIM and the AFIM can be kept on disk; hence, it is not strictly necessary to maintain a log for recovering. We briefly discuss recovery based on shadowing in Section 11.6.3.

11.5.3 Write-Ahead Logging, Steal/No-Steal, and Force/No-Force

When in-place updating is used, it is necessary to use a log for recovery (see Section 11.2.2). In this case, the recovery mechanism must ensure that the BFIM of the data item is recorded in the appropriate log entry and that the log entry is flushed to disk before the BFIM is overwritten with the AFIM in the database on disk. This process is generally known as **write-ahead logging.** Before we can describe a protocol for write-ahead logging, we need to distinguish between two types of log entry information included for a write command: (1) the information needed for UNDO and (2) that needed for REDO. A **REDO-type log entry** includes the **new value** (AFIM) of the item written by the operation since this is needed to *redo* the effect of the operation from the log (by setting the item value in the database to its AFIM). The **UNDO-type log entries** include the **old value** (BFIM) of the item since this is needed to *undo* the effect of the operation from the log (by setting the item value in the database back to its BFIM). In an UNDO/REDO algorithm, both types of log entries are combined. In addition, when cascading rollback is possible, read_item entries in the log are considered to be UNDO-type entries (see Section 11.2.5).

As mentioned, the DBMS cache holds the cached database disk blocks, which include not only *data blocks* but also *index blocks* and *log blocks* from the disk. When a log record is written, it is stored in the current log block in the DBMS cache. The log is simply a sequential (append-only) disk file and the DBMS cache may contain several log blocks (for example, the last *n* log blocks) that will be written to disk. When an update to a data block—stored in the DBMS cache—is made, an associated log record is written to the last log block in the DBMS cache. With the write-ahead logging approach, the log blocks that contain the associated log records for a particular data block update must first be written to disk before the data block itself can be written back to disk.

Standard DBMS recovery terminology includes the terms **steal/no-steal** and **force/no force,** which specify when a page from the database can be written to disk from the cache:

1. If a cache page updated by a transaction *cannot* be written to disk before the transaction commits, this is called a **no-steal approach.** The pin-unpin bit indicates if a page cannot be written back to disk. Otherwise, if the protocol allows writing an updated buffer *before* the transaction commits, it is called **steal.** Steal is used when the DBMS cache (buffer) manager needs a buffer frame for another transaction and the buffer manager replaces an existing page that has been updated but whose transaction has not committed.

---

20. In-place updating is used in most systems in practice.

2. If all pages updated by a transaction are immediately written to disk when the transaction commits, this is called a **force approach.** Otherwise, it is called **no-force.**

The deferred update recovery scheme in Section 11.6.1 follows a *no-steal* approach. However, typical database systems employ a *steal/no-force* strategy. The advantage of steal is that it avoids the need for a very large buffer space to store all updated pages in memory. The advantage of no-force is that an updated page of a committed transaction may still be in the buffer when another transaction needs to update it, thus eliminating the I/O cost to read that page again from disk. This may provide a substantial saving in the number of I/O operations when a specific page is updated heavily by multiple transactions.

To permit recovery when in-place updating is used, the appropriate entries required for recovery must be permanently recorded in the logon disk before changes are applied to the database. For example, consider the following **write-ahead logging (WAL)** protocol for a recovery algorithm that requires both UNDO and REDO:

1. The before image of an item cannot be overwritten by its after image in the database on disk until all UNDO-type log records for the updating transaction—up to this point in time—have been force-written to disk.

2. The commit operation of a transaction cannot be completed until all the REDO-type and UNDO-type log records for that transaction have been force-written to disk.

To facilitate the recovery process, the DBMS recovery subsystem may need to maintain a number of lists related to the transactions being processed in the system. These include a list for **active transactions** that have started but not committed as yet, and it may also include lists of all **committed** and **aborted transactions** since the last checkpoint (see next section). Maintaining these lists makes the recovery process more efficient.

11.5.4   Checkpoints in the System Log and Fuzzy Checkpointing

Another type of entry in the log is called a **checkpoint.**[21] A [checkpoint] record is written into the log periodically at that point when the system writes out to the database on disk all DBMS buffers that have been modified. As a consequence of this, all transactions that have their [commit,T] entries in the log before a [checkpoint] entry do not need to have their WRITE operations *redone* in case of a system crash, since all their updates will be recorded in the database on disk during checkpointing.

The recovery manager of a DBMS must decide at what intervals to take a checkpoint. The interval may be measured in time—say, every m minutes—or in the number t of committed transactions since the last checkpoint, where the values of m or t are system parameters. Taking a checkpoint consists of the following actions:

1. Suspend execution of transactions temporarily.

2. Force-write all main memory buffers that have been modified to disk.

3. Write a [checkpoint] record to the log, and force-write the log to disk.

4. Resume executing transactions.

---

21. The term *checkpoint* has been used to describe more restrictive situations in some systems, such as DB2. It has also been used in the literature to describe entirely different concepts.

As a consequence of step 2, a checkpoint record in the log may also include additional information, such as a list of active transaction ids, and the locations (addresses) of the first and most recent (last) records in the log for each active transaction. This can facilitate undoing transaction operations in the event that a transaction must be rolled back.

The time needed to force-write all modified memory buffers may delay transaction processing because of step 1. To reduce this delay, it is common to use a technique called **fuzzy checkpointing** in practice. In this technique, the system can resume transaction processing after the [checkpoint] record is written to the log without having to wait for step 2 to finish. However, until step 2 is completed, the previous [checkpoint] record should remain valid. To accomplish this, the system maintains a pointer to the valid checkpoint, which continues to point to the previous [checkpoint] record in the log. Once step 2 is concluded, that pointer is changed to point to the new checkpoint in the log.

11.5.5 Transaction Rollback

If a transaction fails for whatever reason after updating the database, it may be necessary to **roll back** the transaction. If any data item values have been changed by the transaction and written to the database, they must be restored to their previous values (BFIMs). The undo-type log entries are used to restore the old values of data items that must be rolled back.

If a transaction T is rolled back, any transaction S that has, in the interim, read the value of some data item X written by T must also be rolled back. Similarly, once S is rolled back, any transaction R that has read the value of some data item Y written by S must also be rolled back; and so on. This phenomenon is called **cascading rollback,** and can occur when the recovery protocol ensures *recoverable* schedules but does not ensure *strict* or *cascadeless* schedules (see Section 11.3.1.2). Cascading rollback, understandably, can be quite complex and time-consuming. That is why almost all recovery mechanisms are designed such that cascading rollback *is never required.*

Figure 11.18 shows an example where cascading rollback is required. The read and write operations of three individual transactions are shown in Figure 11.18a. Figure 11.18b shows the system log at the point of a system crash for a particular execution schedule of these transactions. The values of data items A, B, C, and D, which are used by the transactions, are shown to the right of the system log entries. We assume that the original item values, shown in the first line, are A = 30, B = 15, C = 40, and D = 20. At the point of system failure, transaction T_3 has not reached its conclusion and must be rolled back. The WRITE operations of T_3, marked by a single * in Figure 11.18b, are the T_3 operations that are undone during transaction rollback. Figure 11.18c graphically shows the operations of the different transactions along the time axis.

We must now check for cascading rollback. From Figure 11.18c we see that transaction T_2 reads the value of item B that was written by transaction T_3; this can also be determined by examining the log. Because T_3 is rolled back, T_2 must now be rolled back, too. The WRITE operations of T_2, marked by ** in the log, are the ones that are undone. Note that only write_item operations need to be undone during transaction rollback; read_item operations are recorded in the log only to determine whether cascading rollback of additional transactions is necessary.

In practice, cascading rollback of transactions is *never* required because practical recovery methods guarantee cascadeless or strict schedules. Hence, there is also no need to record any read_item operations in the log, because these are needed only for determining cascading rollback.

(a)

T_1	T_2	T_3
read_item(A)	read_item(B)	read_item(C)
read_item(D)	write_item(B)	write_item(B)
write_item(D)	read_item(D)	read_item(A)
	write_item(D)	write_item(A)

(b)

		A	B	C	D
		30	15	40	20
	[start_transaction, T_3]				
	[read_item, T_3, C]				
*	[write_item, T_2, B, 15, 12]		12		
	[start_transaction, T_2]				
	[read_item, T_2, B]				
**	[write_item, T_2, B, 12, 18]		18		
	[start_transaction, T_1]				
	[read_item, T_1, A]				
	[read_item, T_1, D]				
	[write_item, T_1, D, 20, 25]				25
	[read_item, T_2, D]				
**	[write_item, T_2, D, 25, 26]				26
	[read_item, T_3, A]				

←system crash

* T_3 is rolled back because it did not reach its commit point.

** T_2 is rolled back because it reads the value of item B written by T_3

(c)

FIGURE 11.18 Illustrating cascading rollback (a process that never occurs in strict or cascadeless schedules). (a) The read and write operations of three transactions. (b) System log at point of crash. (c) Operations before the crash.

11.6 RECOVERY TECHNIQUES

11.6.1 Recovery Techniques Based on Deferred Update

The idea behind deferred update techniques is to defer or postpone any actual updates to the database until the transaction completes its execution successfully and reaches its commit point.[22] During transaction execution, the updates are recorded only in the log and in the cache buffers. After the transaction reaches its commit point and the log is force-written to disk, the updates are recorded in the database. If a transaction fails before reaching its commit point, there is no need to undo any operations, because the transaction has not affected the database on disk in any way. Although this may simplify recovery, it cannot be used in practice unless transactions are short and each transaction changes few items. For other types of transactions, there is the potential for running out of buffer space because transaction changes must be held in the cache buffers until the commit point.

We can state a typical deferred update protocol as follows:

1. A transaction cannot change the database on disk until it reaches its commit point.

2. A transaction does not reach its commit point until all its update operations are recorded in the log *and* the log is force-written to disk.

Notice that step 2 of this protocol is a restatement of the write-ahead logging (WAL) protocol. Because the database is never updated on disk until after the transaction commits, there is never a need to UNDO any operations. Hence, this is known as the **NO-UNDO/REDO recovery algorithm.** REDO is needed in case the system fails after a transaction commits but before all its changes are recorded in the database on disk. In this case, the transaction operations are redone from the log entries.

Usually, the method of recovery from failure is closely related to the concurrency control method in multiuser systems. First we discuss recovery in single-user systems, where no concurrency control is needed, so that we can understand the recovery process independently of any concurrency control method. We then discuss how concurrency control may affect the recovery process.

11.6.1.1 Recovery using deferred update in a single-user environment

In such an environment, the recovery algorithm can be rather simple. The algorithm RDU_S (Recovery using Deferred Update in a Single-user environment) uses a REDO procedure, given subsequently, for redoing certain write_item operations; it works as follows:

PROCEDURE RDU_S: Use two lists of transactions: the committed transactions since the last checkpoint, and the active transactions (at most one transaction will fall in this category, because the system is single-user). Apply the REDO operation to all the WRITE_ITEM operations of the committed transactions from the log in the order in which they were written to the log. Restart the active transactions.

The REDO procedure is defined as follows:

REDO(WRITE_OP): Redoing a write_item operation WRITE_OP consists of examining its log entry [write_item,T,X,new_value] and setting the value of item X in the database to new_value, which is the after image (AFIM).

The REDO operation is required to be **idempotent**—that is, executing it over and over is equivalent to executing it just once. In fact, the whole recovery process should be idempotent. This is so because, if the

---

22. Hence deferred update can generally be characterized as a *no-steal approach*.

system were to fail during the recovery process, the next recovery attempt might REDO certain write_item operations that had already been redone during the first recovery process. The result of recovery from a system crash *during recovery* should be the same as the result of recovering *when there is no crash during recovery!*

Notice that the only transaction in the active list will have had no effect on the database because of the deferred update protocol, and it is ignored completely by the recovery process because none of its operations were reflected in the database on disk. However, this transaction must now be restarted, either automatically by the recovery process or manually by the user.

Figure 11.19 shows an example of recovery in a single-user environment, where the first failure occurs during execution of transaction T_2, as shown in Figure 11.19b. The recovery process will redo the [write_item,T1,D,20] entry in the log by resetting the value of item D to 20 (its new value). The [write,T2, ...] entries in the log are ignored by the recovery process because T_2 is not committed. If a second failure occurs during recovery from the first failure, the same recovery process is repeated from start to finish, with identical results.

(a)

T_1	T_2
read_item(A)	read_item(B)
read_item(D)	write_item(B)
write_item(D)	read_item(D)
	write_item(D)

(b)
[start_transaction, T_1]
[write_item, T_1, D, 20]
[commit, T_1]
[start_transaction, T_2]
[write_item, T_2, B, 10]
[write_item, T_2, D, 25] ← system c

FIGURE 11.19 An example of recovery using deferred update in a single-user environment. (a) The READ and WRITE operations of two transactions. (b) The system log at the point of crash.

11.6.1.2 Deferred update with concurrent execution in a multiuser environment

For multiuser systems with concurrency control, the recovery process may be more complex, depending on the protocols used for concurrency control. In many cases, the concurrency control and recovery processes are interrelated. In general, the greater the degree of concurrency we wish to achieve, the more time consuming the task of recovery becomes.

Consider a system in which concurrency control uses strict two-phase locking, so the locks on items remain in effect *until the transaction reaches its commit point*. After that, the locks can be released. This ensures strict and serializable schedules. Assuming that [checkpoint] entries are included in the log, a possible recovery algorithm for this case, which we call RDU_M (Recovery using Deferred Update in a Multiuser environment), is given next. This procedure uses the REDO procedure defined earlier.

PROCEDURE RDU_M (WITH CHECKPOINTS): Use two lists of transactions maintained by the system: the committed transactions T since the last checkpoint (**commitlist**), and the active transactions T' (**active list**). REDO all the WRITE operations of the committed transactions from the log, *in the order in which they were written into the log*. The transactions that are active and did not commit are effectively canceled and must be resubmitted.

Figure 11.20 shows a possible schedule of executing transactions. When the checkpoint was taken at time t_1, transaction T_1 had committed, whereas transactions T_3 and T_4 had not. Before the system crash at time t_2, T_3 and T_2 were committed but not T_4 and T_5. According to the RDU_M method, there is no need to redo the write_item operations of transaction T_1—or any transactions committed before the last checkpoint time t_1. Write_ item operations of T_2 and T_3 must be redone, however, because both transactions reached their commit points after the last checkpoint. Recall that the log is force-written before committing a transaction. Transactions T_4 and T_5 are ignored: They are effectively canceled or rolled back because none of their write_ item operations were recorded in the database under the deferred update protocol. We will refer to Figure 11.20 later to illustrate other recovery protocols.

FIGURE 11.20 An example of recovery in a multiuser environment.

We can make the NO-UNDO/REDO recovery algorithm *more efficient* by noting that, if a data item X has been updated—as indicated in the log entries—more than once by committed transactions since the last checkpoint, it is only necessary to REDO *the last update of* X from the log during recovery. The other updates would be overwritten by this last REDO in any case. In this case, we start from *the end of the log;* then, whenever an item is redone, it is added to a list of redone items. Before REDO is applied to an item, the list is checked; if the item appears on the list, it is not redone again, since its last value has already been recovered.

If a transaction is aborted for any reason (say, by the deadlock detection method), it is simply resubmitted, since it has not changed the database on disk. A drawback of the method described here is that it limits the concurrent execution of transactions because *all items remain locked until the transaction reaches its commit point.* In addition, it may require excessive buffer space to hold all updated items until the transactions commit. The method's main benefit is that transaction operations *never need to be undone,* for two reasons:

1. A transaction does not record any changes in the database on disk until after it reaches its commit point—that is, until it completes its execution successfully. Hence, a transaction is never rolled back because of failure during transaction execution.

2. A transaction will never read the value of an item that is written by an uncommitted transaction, because items remain locked until a transaction reaches its commit point. Hence, no cascading rollback will occur.

Figure 11.21 shows an example of recovery for a multiuser system that utilizes the recovery and concurrency control method just described.

11.6.1.3 Transaction actions that do not affect the database

In general, a transaction will have actions that do *not* affect the database, such as generating and printing messages or reports from information retrieved from the database. If a transaction fails before completion, we may not want the user to get these reports, since the transaction has failed to complete. If such erroneous reports are produced, part of the recovery process would have to inform the user that these reports are wrong, since the user may take an action based on these reports that affects the database. Hence, such reports should be generated only *after the transaction reaches its commit point.* A common method of dealing with such actions is to issue the commands that generate the reports but keep them as batch jobs, which are executed only after the transaction reaches its commit point. If the transaction fails, the batch jobs are canceled.

11.6.2 Recovery Techniques Based on Immediate Update

In these techniques, when a transaction issues an update command, the database can be updated "immediately," without any need to wait for the transaction to reach its commit point. In these techniques, however, an update operation must still be recorded in the log (on disk) *before* it is applied to the database—using the write-ahead logging protocol—so that we can recover in case of failure.

Provisions must be made for *undoing* the effect of update operations that have been applied to the database by a *failed transaction.* This is accomplished by rolling back the transaction and undoing the effect of the transaction's write_item operations. Theoretically, we can distinguish two main categories of immediate update algorithms. If the recovery technique ensures that all updates of a transaction are recorded in the database on disk *before the transaction commits,* there is never a need to REDO any operations of committed transactions. This is called the **UNDO/NO-REDO recovery algorithm.** On the other hand, if the transaction is allowed to commit before all its changes are written to the database, we have the most general case, known as the

(a)

T_1	T_2	T_3	T_4
read_item(A)	read_item(B)	read_item(A)	read_item(B)
read_item(D)	write_item(B)	write_item(A)	write_item(B)
write_item(D)	read_item(D)	read_item(C)	read_item(A)
	write_item(D)	write_item(C)	write_item(A)

(b)

[start_transaction, T_1]
[write_item, T_1, D, 20]
[commit, T_1]
[checkpoint]
[start_transaction, T_4]
[write_item, T_4, B, 15]
[write_item, T_4, A, 20]
[commit, T_2]
[start_transaction, T_2]
[start_transaction, T_3]
[write_item, T_2, A, 12]
[write_item, T_3, A, 30]
[write_item, T_2, d, 25] ←system crash

T_2 and T_3 are ignored because they did not reach their commit point.
T_4 is redone because its commit point is after the last system checkpoint.

FIGURE 11.21 An example of recovery using deferred update with concurrent transactions. (a) The READ and WRITE operations of four transactions. (b) System log at the point of crash.

UNDO/REDO recovery algorithm. This is also the most complex technique. Next, we discuss two examples of **UNDO/REDO** algorithms and leave it as an exercise for the reader to develop the **UNDO/NO-REDO** variation. In Section 11.5, we describe a more practical approach known as the ARIES recovery technique.

11.6.2.1 UNDO/REDO recovery based on immediate update in a single-user environment   In a single-user system, if a failure occurs, the executing (active) transaction at the time of failure may have recorded some changes in the database. The effect of all such operations must be undone. The recovery algorithm RIU_S (Recovery using Immediate Update in a Single-user environment) uses the REDO procedure defined earlier, as well as the UNDO procedure defined below.

PROCEDURE RIU_S

1. Use two lists of transactions maintained by the system: the committed transactions since the last checkpoint and the active transactions (at most one transaction will fall in this category, because the system is single-user).
2. Undo all the write_item operations of the *active* transaction from the log, using the UNDO procedure described below.
3. Redo the write_item operations of the *committed* transactions from the log, in the order in which they were written in the log, using the REDO procedure described earlier.

The UNDO procedure is defined as follows:

UNDO(WRITE_OP): Undoing a write_item operation write_op consists of examining its log entry [write_item,T,X,old_value,new_value] and setting the value of item X in the database to old_value which is the before image (BFIM). Undoing a number of write_item operations from one or more transactions from the log must proceed in the *reverse order* from the order in which the operations were written in the log.

11.6.2.2 UNDO/REDO recovery based on immediate update with concurrent execution   When concurrent execution is permitted, the recovery process again depends on the protocols used for concurrency control. The procedure RIU_M (Recovery using Immediate Updates for a Multiuser environment) outlines a recovery algorithm for concurrent transactions with immediate update. Assume that the log includes checkpoints and that the concurrency control protocol produces *strict schedules*—as, for example, the strict two-phase locking protocol does. Recall that a strict schedule does not allow a transaction to read or write an item unless the transaction that last wrote the item has committed (or aborted and rolled back). However, deadlocks can occur in strict two-phase locking, thus requiring abort and UNDO of transactions. For a strict schedule, UNDO of an operation requires changing the item back to its old value (BFIM).

PROCEDURE RIU_M

1. Use two lists of transactions maintained by the system: the committed transactions since the last checkpoint and the active transactions.
2. Undo all the write_item operations of the *active* (uncommitted) transactions, using the UNDO procedure. The operations should be undone in the reverse of the order in which they were written into the log.
3. Redo all the write_item operations of the *committed* transactions from the log, in the order in which they were written into the log.

As we discussed in Section 11.6.1.2, step 3 is more efficiently done by starting from the *end of the log* and redoing only *the last update of each item* X. Whenever an item is redone, it is added to a list of redone items and is not redone again. A similar procedure can be devised to improve the efficiency of step 2.

11.6.3   Shadow Paging

This recovery scheme does not require the use of a log in a single-user environment. In a multiuser environment, a log may be needed for the concurrency control method. Shadow paging considers the database to be made up of a number of fixed-size disk pages (or disk blocks)—say, *n*—for recovery purposes. A **directory** with *n* entries[23] is constructed, where the ith entry points to the ith database page on disk. The directory is kept in main memory if it is not too large, and all references—reads or writes—to database pages on disk go through it. When a transaction begins executing, the **current directory**—whose entries point to the most recent or current database pages on disk—is copied into a **shadow directory.** The shadow directory is then saved on disk while the current directory is used by the transaction.

During transaction execution, the shadow directory is *never* modified. When a write_item operation is performed, a new copy of the modified database page is created, but the old copy of that page is *not overwritten*. Instead, the new page is written elsewhere—on some previously unused disk block. The current directory entry is modified to point to the new disk block, whereas the shadow directory is not modified and continues to point to the old unmodified disk block. Figure 11.22 illustrates the concepts of shadow and current directories. For pages updated by the transaction, two versions are kept. The old version is referenced by the shadow directory, and the new version by the current directory.

To recover from a failure during transaction execution, it is sufficient to free the modified database pages and to discard the current directory. The state of the database before transaction execution is available through the shadow directory, and that state is recovered by reinstating the shadow directory. The database thus is returned to its state prior to the transaction that was executing when the crash occurred, and any modified pages are discarded. Committing a transaction corresponds to discarding the previous shadow directory. Since recovery involves neither undoing nor redoing data items, this technique can be categorized as a NO-UNDO/NO-REDO technique for recovery.

In a multiuser environment with concurrent transactions, logs and checkpoints must be incorporated into the shadow paging technique. One disadvantage of shadow paging is that the updated database pages change location on disk. This makes it difficult to keep related database pages close together on disk without complex storage management strategies. Furthermore, if the directory is large, the overhead of writing shadow directories to disk as transactions commit is significant. A further complication is how to handle **garbage collection** when a transaction commits. The old pages referenced by the shadow directory that have been updated must be released and added to a list of free pages for future use. These pages are no longer needed after the transaction commits. Another issue is that the operation to migrate between current and shadow directories must be implemented as an atomic operation.

11.6.4   The ARIES Recovery Algorithm

We now describe the ARIES algorithm as an example of a recovery algorithm used in database systems. ARIES uses a steal/no-force approach for writing, and it is based on three concepts: (1) write-ahead logging, (2)

---

23. The directory is similar to the **page table** maintained by the operating system for each process.

repeating history during redo, and (3) logging changes during undo. We already discussed write-ahead logging in Section 11.5.3. The second concept, **repeating history,** means that ARIES will retrace all actions of the database system prior to the crash to reconstruct the database state *when the crash occurred.*

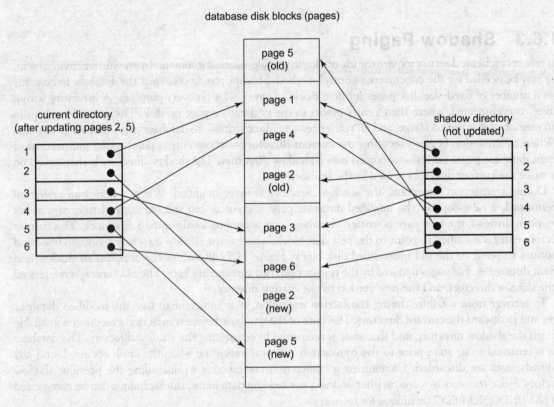

FIGURE 11.22 An example of shadow paging.

Transactions that were uncommitted at the time of the crash (active transactions) are undone. The third concept, **logging during undo,** will prevent ARIES from repeating the completed undo operations if a failure occurs during recovery, which causes a restart of the recovery process.

The ARIES recovery procedure consists of three main steps: (1) analysis, (2) REDO and (3) UNDO. The **analysis step** identifies the dirty (updated) pages in the buffer,[24] and the set of transactions active at the time of the crash. The appropriate point in the log where the REDO operation should start is also determined. The **REDO phase** actually reapplies updates from the log to the database. Generally, the REDO operation is applied to only committed transactions. However, in ARIES, this is not the case. Certain information in the ARIES log will provide the start point for REDO, from which REDO operations are applied until the end of the log is reached. In addition, information stored by ARIES and in the data pages will allow ARIES to determine whether the operation to be redone has actually been applied to the database and hence need not be reapplied. Thus *only the necessary* REDO *operations* are applied during recovery. Finally, during the **UNDO phase,** the log is scanned backwards and the operations of transactions that were active at the time of the

---

24. The actual buffers may be lost during a crash, since they are in main memory. Additional tables stored in the log during checkpointing (Dirty Page Table, Transaction Table) allow ARIES to identify this information (see next page).

crash are undone in reverse order. The information needed for ARIES to accomplish its recovery procedure includes the log, the Transaction Table, and the Dirty Page Table. In addition, checkpointing is used. These two tables are maintained by the transaction manager and written to the log during checkpointing.

In ARIES, every log record has an associated **log sequence number** (LSN) that is monotonically increasing and indicates the address of the log record on disk. Each LSN corresponds to a *specific change* (action) of some transaction. In addition, each data page will store the LSN of the *latest log record corresponding to a change for that page*. A log record is written for any of the following actions: updating a page (write), committing a transaction (commit), aborting a transaction (abort), undoing an update (undo), and ending a transaction (end). The need for including the first three actions in the log has been discussed, but the last two need some explanation. When an update is undone, a *compensation log record* is written in the log. When a transaction ends, whether by committing or aborting, an *end log record* is written.

Common fields in all log records include: (1) the previous LSN for that transaction, (2) the transaction ID, and (3) the type of log record. The previous LSN is important because it links the log records (in reverse order) for each transaction. For an update (write) action, additional fields in the log record include: (4) the page ID for the page that includes the item, (5) the length of the updated item, (6) its offset from the beginning of the page, (7) the before image of the item, and (8) its after image.

Besides the log, two tables are needed for efficient recovery: the **Transaction Table** and the **Dirty Page Table,** which are maintained by the transaction manager. When a crash occurs, these tables are rebuilt in the analysis phase of recovery. The Transaction Table contains an entry for *each active transaction*, with information such as the transaction ID, transaction status, and the LSN of the most recent log record for the transaction. The Dirty Page Table contains an entry for each dirty page in the buffer, which includes the page ID and the LSN corresponding to the earliest update to that page.

Checkpointing in ARIES consists of the following: (1) writing a begin_checkpoint record to the log, (2) writing an end_checkpoint record to the log, and (3) writing *the LSN of* the begin_checkpoint record to a special file. This special file is accessed during recovery to locate the last checkpoint information. With the end_checkpoint record, the contents of both the Transaction Table and Dirty Page Table are appended to the end of the log. To reduce the cost, **fuzzy checkpointing** is used so that the DBMS can continue to execute transactions during checkpointing (see Section 11.5.4). In addition, the contents of the DBMS cache do not have to be flushed to disk during checkpoint, since the Transaction Table and Dirty Page Table—which are appended to the log on disk—contain the information needed for recovery. Notice that if a crash occurs during checkpointing, the special file will refer to the previous checkpoint, which is used for recovery.

After a crash, the ARIES recovery manager takes over. Information from the last checkpoint is first accessed through the special file. The **analysis phase** starts at the begin_checkpoint record and proceeds to the end of the log. When the end_checkpoint record is encountered, the Transaction Table and Dirty Page Table are accessed (recall that these tables were written in the log during checkpointing). During analysis, the log records being analyzed may cause modifications to these two tables. For instance, if an end log record was encountered for a transaction T in the Transaction Table, then the entry for T is deleted from that table. If some other type of log record is encountered for a transaction T', then an entry for T' is inserted into the Transaction Table, if not already present, and the last LSN field is modified. If the log record corresponds to a change for page P, then an entry would be made for page P (if not present in the table) and the associated LSN field would be modified. When the analysis phase is complete, the necessary information for REDO and UNDO has been compiled in the tables.

The **REDO phase** follows next. To reduce the amount of unnecessary work, ARIES starts redoing at a point in the log where it knows (for sure) that previous changes to dirty pages *have already been applied to the database on disk*. It can determine this by finding the smallest LSN, M, of all the dirty pages in the Dirty Page Table, which indicates the log position where ARIES needs to start the REDO phase. Any changes corresponding to a LSN < M, for redoable transactions, must have already been propagated to disk or already been overwritten in the buffer; otherwise, those dirty pages with that LSN would be in the buffer (and the Dirty Page Table). So, REDO starts at the log record with LSN = M and scans forward to the end of the log. For each change recorded in the log, the REDO algorithm would verify whether or not the change has to be reapplied. For example, if a change recorded in the log pertains to page P that is not in the Dirty Page Table, then this change is already on disk and need not be reapplied. Or, if a change recorded in the log (with LSN = N, say) pertains to page P and the Dirty Page Table contains an entry for P with LSN greater than N, then the change is already present. If neither of these two conditions hold, page P is read from disk and the LSN stored on that page, $LSN(P)$, is compared with N. If $N < LSN(P)$, then the change has been applied and the page need not be rewritten to disk.

Once the REDO phase is finished, the database is in the exact state that it was in when the crash occurred. The set of active transactions—called the **undo_set**—has been identified in the Transaction Table during the analysis phase. Now, the **UNDO phase** proceeds by scanning backward from the end of the log and undoing the appropriate actions. A compensating log record is written for each action that is undone. The UNDO reads backward in the log until every action of the set of transactions in the undo_set has been undone. When this is completed, the recovery process is finished and normal processing can begin again.

Consider the recovery example shown in Figure 11.23. There are three transactions: T_1, T_2, and T_3. T_1 updates page C, T_2 updates pages B and C, and T_3 updates page A. Figure 11.23 (a) shows the partial contents of the log and (b) shows the contents of the Transaction Table and Dirty Page Table. Now, suppose that a crash occurs at this point.

(a)

LSN	LAST_LSN	TRAN_ID	TYPE	PAGE_ID	OTHER INFORMATION
1	0	T_1	update	C	...
2	0	T_2	update	B	...
3	1	T_1	commit		...
4			begin checkpoint		
5			end checkpiont		
6	0	T_3	update	A	...
7	2	T_2	update	C	...
8	7	T_2	commit		...

(b)

TRANSACTION TABLE			DIRTY PAGE TABLE	
TRANSACTION ID	LAST LSN	STATUS	PAGE ID	LSN
T_1	3	commit	C	1
T_2	2	in progress	B	2

(c)

TRANSACTION TABLE			DIRTY PAGE TABLE	
TRANSACTION ID	LAST LSN	STATUS	PAGE ID	LSN
T_1	3	commit	C	1
T_2	8	commit	B	2
T_3	6	in progress	A	6

FIGURE 11.23 An example of recovery in ARIES. (a) The log at point of crash. (b) The Transaction and Dirty Page Tables at time of checkpoint. (c) The Transaction and Dirty Page Tables after the analysis phase.

Since a checkpoint has occurred, the address of the associated begin_checkpoint record is retrieved, which is location 4. The analysis phase starts from location 4 until it reaches the end. The end_checkpoint record would contain the Transaction Table and Dirty Page table in Figure 11.23b, and the analysis phase will further reconstruct these tables. When the analysis phase encounters log record 6, a new entry for transaction T_3 is made in the Transaction Table and a new entry for page A is made in the Dirty Page table. After log record 8 is analyzed, the status of transaction T_2 is changed to committed in the Transaction Table. Figure 11.23c shows the two tables after the analysis phase.

For the REDO phase, the smallest LSN in the Dirty Page table is 1. Hence the REDO will start at log record 1 and proceed with the REDO of updates. The LSNs {1, 2, 6, 7} corresponding to the updates for pages C, B, A, and C, respectively, are not less than the LSNs of those pages (as shown in the Dirty Page table). So those data pages will be read again and the updates reapplied from the log (assuming the actual LSNs stored on those data pages are less then the corresponding log entry). At this point, the REDO phase is finished and the UNDO phase starts. From the Transaction Table (Figure 11.23c), UNDO is applied only to the active transaction T_3. The UNDO phase starts at log entry 6 (the last update for T_3) and proceeds backward in the log. The backward chain of updates for transaction T_3 (only log record 6 in this example) is followed and undone.

11.6.5   Recovery in Multidatabase Systems

So far, we have implicitly assumed that a transaction accesses a single database. In some cases a single transaction, called a **multidatabase transaction,** may require access to multiple databases. These databases may even be stored on different types of DBMSs; for example, some DBMSs may be relational, whereas others are object-oriented, hierarchical, or network DBMSs. In such a case, each DBMS involved in the multidatabase transaction may have its own recovery technique and transaction manager separate from those of the other DBMSs. This situation is somewhat similar to the case of a distributed database management system, where parts of the database reside at different sites that are connected by a communication network.

To maintain the atomicity of a multidatabase transaction, it is necessary to have a two-level recovery mechanism. A **global recovery manager,** or **coordinator,** is needed to maintain information needed for recovery, in addition to the local recovery managers and the information they maintain (log, tables). The coordinator usually follows a protocol called the **two-phase commit protocol,** whose two phases can be stated as follows:

- **Phase 1:** When all participating databases signal the coordinator that the part of the multidatabase transaction involving each has concluded, the coordinator sends a message "prepare for commit" to each participant to get ready for committing the transaction. Each participating database receiving that message will force-write all log records and needed information for local recovery to disk and then send a "ready to commit" or "OK" signal to the coordinator. If the force-writing to disk fails or the local transaction cannot commit for some reason, the participating database sends a "cannot commit" or "not OK" signal to the coordinator. If the coordinator does not receive a reply from a database within a certain time out interval, it assumes a "not OK" response.

- **Phase 2:** If *all* participating databases reply "OK," and the coordinator's vote is also "OK," the transaction is successful, and the coordinator sends a "commit" signal for the transaction to the participating databases. Because all the local effects of the transaction and information needed for local recovery have been recorded in the logs of the participating databases, recovery from failure is now possible. Each participating database completes transaction commit by writing a [commit] entry for the transaction in the log and permanently updating the database if needed. On the other hand, if one or more of the participating databases or the coordinator have a "not OK" response, the transaction has failed, and the coordinator sends a message to "roll back" or UNDO the local effect of the transaction to each participating database. This is done by undoing the transaction operations, using the log.

The net effect of the two-phase commit protocol is that either all participating databases commit the effect of the transaction or none of them do. In case any of the participants—or the coordinator—fails, it is always possible to recover to a state where either the transaction is committed or it is rolled back. A failure during or before Phase 1 usually requires the transaction to be rolled back, whereas a failure during Phase 2 means that a successful transaction can recover and commit.

11.6.6 Database Backup and Recovery from Catastrophic Failures

So far, all the techniques we have discussed apply to noncatastrophic failures. A key assumption has been that the system log is maintained on the disk and is not lost as a result of the failure. Similarly, the shadow directory must be stored on disk to allow recovery when shadow paging is used. The recovery techniques we have discussed use the entries in the system log or the shadow directory to recover from failure by bringing the database back to a consistent state.

The recovery manager of a DBMS must also be equipped to handle more catastrophic failures such as disk crashes. The main technique used to handle such crashes is that of **database backup.** The whole database and the log are periodically copied onto a cheap storage medium such as magnetic tapes. In case of a catastrophic system failure, the latest backup copy can be reloaded from the tape to the disk, and the system can be restarted.

To avoid losing all the effects of transactions that have been executed since the last backup, it is customary to back up the system log at more frequent intervals than full database backup by periodically copying it to magnetic tape. The system log is usually substantially smaller than the database itself and hence can be backed up more frequently. Thus users do not lose all transactions they have performed since the last database backup. All committed transactions recorded in the portion of the system log that has been backed up to tape can have their effect on the database redone. A new log is started after each database backup. Hence, to recover from disk failure, the database is first recreated on disk from its latest backup copy on tape. Following that, the effects of all the committed transactions whose operations have been recorded in the backed-up copies of the system log are reconstructed.

11.7 TRANSACTION SUPPORT IN SQL

The definition of an SQL-transaction is similar to our already defined concept of a transaction. That is, it is a logical unit of work and is guaranteed to be atomic. A single SQL statement is always considered to be atomic—either it completes execution without error or it fails and leaves the database unchanged.

With SQL, there is no explicit Begin_Transaction statement. Transaction initiation is done implicitly when particular SQL statements are encountered. However, every transaction must have an explicit end statement, which is either a COMMIT or a ROLLBACK. Every transaction has certain characteristics attributed to it. These characteristics are specified by a SET TRANSACTION statement in SQL. The characteristics are the *access mode,* the *diagnostic area size,* and the *isolation level.*

The **access mode** can be specified as READ ONLY or READ WRITE. The default is READ WRITE, unless the isolation level of READ UNCOMMITTED is specified, in which case READ ONLY is assumed. A mode of READ WRITE allows update, insert, delete and create commands to be executed. A mode of READ ONLY, as the name implies, is simply for data retrieval.

The **diagnostic area size** option, DIAGNOSTIC SIZE n, specifies an integer value n, indicating the number of conditions that can be held simultaneously in the diagnostic area. These conditions supply feedback information (errors or exceptions) to the user or program on the most recently executed SQL statement.

The **isolation level** option is specified using the statement ISOLATION LEVEL <isolation>, where the value for <isolation> can be READ UNCOMMITTED, READ COMMITTED, REPEATABLE READ, or SERIALIZABLE.[25] The default isolation level is SERIALIZABLE, although some systems use as READ COMMITTED their default. The use of the term SERIALIZABLE here is based on not allowing violations that cause dirty read, unrepeatable read, and phantoms,[26] and it is thus not identical to the way serializability was defined earlier in Section 11.3.2. If a transaction executes at a lower isolation level than SERIALIZABLE, then one or more of the following three violations may occur:

1. **Dirty read:** A transaction T_1 may read the update of a transaction T_2, which has not yet committed. If T_2 fails and is aborted, then T_1 would have read a value that does not exist and is incorrect.

2. **Nonrepeatable read:** A transaction T_1 may read a given value from a table. If another transaction T_2 later updates that value and T_1 reads that value again, T_1 will see a different value.

3. **Phantoms:** A transaction T_1 may read a set of rows from a table, perhaps based on some condition specified in the SQL WHERE-clause. Now suppose that a transaction T_2 inserts a new row that also satisfies the WHERE-clause condition used in T_1, into the table used by T_1. If T_1 is repeated, then T_1 will see a phantom, a row that previously did not exist.

Table 11.1 summarizes the possible violations for the different isolation levels. An entry of "yes" indicates that a violation is possible and an entry of "no" indicates that it is not possible.

TABLE 11.1 POSSIBLE VIOLATIONS BASED ON ISOLATION LEVELS AS DEFINED IN SQL

	Type of Violation		
Isolation level	Dirty read	Nonrepeatable read	Phantom
READ UNCOMMITTED	yes	yes	yes
READ COMMITTED	no	yes	yes
REPEATABLE READ	no	no	yes
SERIALIZABLE	no	no	no

A sample SQL transaction might look like the following:

```
EXEC   SQL WHENEVER SQLERROR GOTO UNDO;
EXEC   SQL SET TRANSACTION
       READ WRITE
       DIAGNOSTIC SIZE 5
       ISOLATION LEVEL SERIALIZABLE;
EXEC   SQL INSERT INTO EMPLOYEE (FNAME, LNAME, ENO, DNO, SALARY)
       VALUES ('ROBERT', 'SMITH', '991004321', 2, 35000);
EXEC   SQL UPDATE EMPLOYEE
       SET SALARY = SALARY * 1.1 WHERE DNO = 2;
EXEC   SQL COMMIT;
GOTO   THE_END;
UNDO:  EXEC SQL ROLLBACK;
THE_END: ...;
```

---

25. These are similar to the *isolation levels* discussed briefly at the end of Section 11.2.4.

26. The dirty read and unrepeatable read problems were discussed in Section 11.1.3. Phantoms are discussed in Section 11.4.7.1.

The above transaction consists of first inserting a new row in the EMPLOYEE table and then updating the salary of all employees who work in department 2. If an error occurs on any of the SQL statements, the entire transaction is rolled back. This implies that any updated salary (by this transaction) would be restored to its previous value and that the newly inserted row would be removed.

As we have seen, SQL provides a number of transaction-oriented features. The DBA or database programmers can take advantage of these options to try improving transaction performance by relaxing serializability if that is acceptable for their applications.

11.8 SUMMARY

In this chapter, we discussed DBMS concepts for transaction processing. We introduced the concept of a database transaction and the operations relevant to transaction processing.

We then introduced the typical states that a transaction passes through during execution, and discussed several concepts that are used in recovery and concurrency control methods. We presented an overview of the desirable properties of transactions—which are often referred to as the ACID properties.

We then defined a schedule as an execution sequence of the operations of several transactions with possible interleaving. We characterized schedules in terms of their recoverability. We then defined equivalence of schedules and saw that a serializable schedule is equivalent to some serial schedule.

We then discussed DBMS techniques for concurrency control. We started by discussing lock-based protocol, *which are by far the most commonly used in practice.* We described the two-phase locking protocol and a number of its variations. We then presented other concurrency control protocols that are not used often in practice but are important for the theoretical alternatives they show for solving problem. These include the timestamp ordering protocols and two multiversion protocols. We then turned our attention to the important practical issue of data item granularity.

We then discussed the techniques for recovery from transaction failures. The main goal of recovery is to ensure the atomicity property of a transaction. We discussed two different approaches to recovery: deferred update and immediate update. We discussed the shadow paging technique for recovery, which keeps track of old database pages by using a shadow directory.

Finally, we gave a brief overview of how transaction concepts are used in practice within SQL.

Review Questions

11.1. What is meant by the concurrent execution of database transactions in a multiuser system? Discuss why concurrency control is needed, and give informal examples.

11.2. Discuss the different types of failures. What is meant by catastrophic failure?

11.3. Discuss the actions taken by the read_item and write_item operations on a database.

11.4. Draw a state diagram, and discuss the typical states that a transaction goes through during execution.

11.5. What is the system log used for? What are the typical kinds of records in a system log? What are transaction commit points, and why are they important?

11.6. Discuss the atomicity, durability, isolation, and consistency preservation properties of a database transaction.

11.7. What is a schedule (history)? Define the concepts of recoverable, cascadeless, and strict schedules, and compare them in terms of their recoverability.

11.8. Discuss the different measures of transaction equivalence. What is the difference between conflict equivalence and view equivalence?

11.9. What is a serial schedule? What is a serializable schedule? Why is a serial schedule considered correct? Why is a serializable schedule considered correct?

11.10. What is the difference between the constrained write and the unconstrained write assumptions? Which is more realistic?

11.11. Discuss how serializability is used to enforce concurrency control in a database system. Why is serializability sometimes considered too restrictive as a measure of correctness for schedules?

11.12. Describe the four levels of isolation in SQL.

11.13. Define the violations caused by each of the following: dirty read, nonrepeatable read, and phantoms.

11.14. What is the two-phase locking protocol? How does it guarantee serializability?

11.15. What are some variations of the two-phase locking protocol? Why is strict or rigorous two-phase locking often preferred?

11.16. Discuss the problems of deadlock and starvation, and the different approaches to dealing with these problems.

11.17. Compare binary locks to exclusive/shared locks. Why is the latter type of locks preferable?

11.18. Describe the wait-die and wound-wait protocols for deadlock prevention.

11.19. Describe the cautious waiting, no waiting, and timeout protocols for deadlock prevention.

11.20. What is a timestamp? How does the system generate timestamps?

11.21. Discuss the timestamp ordering protocol for concurrency control. How does strict timestamp ordering differ from basic timestamp ordering?

11.22. Discuss two multiversion techniques for concurrency control.

11.23. What is a certify lock? What are the advantages and disadvantages of using certify locks?

11.24. How do optimistic concurrency control techniques differ from other concurrency control techniques? Why are they also called validation or certification techniques? Discuss the typical phases of an optimistic concurrency control method.

11.25. How does the granularity of data items affect the performance of concurrency control? What factors affect selection of granularity size for data items?

11.26. What type of locks are needed for insert and delete operations?

11.27. What is multiple granularity locking? Under what circumstances is it used?

11.28. What are intention locks?

11.29. When are latches used?

11.30. What is a phantom record? Discuss the problem that a phantom record can cause for concurrency control.

11.31. How does index locking resolve the phantom problem?

11.32. What is a predicate lock?

11.33. Discuss the different types of transaction failures. What is meant by catastrophic failure?

11.34. Discuss the actions taken by the read_item and write_item operations on a database.

11.35. What is the system log used for? What are the typical kinds of entries in a system log? What are checkpoints, and why are they important? What are transaction commit points, and why are they important?

11.36. How are buffering and caching techniques used by the recovery subsystem?

11.37. What are the before image (BFIM) and after image (AFIM) of a data item? What is the difference between in-place updating and shadowing, with respect to their handling of BFIM and AFIM?

11.38. What are UNDO-type and REDO-type log entries?

11.39. Describe the write-ahead logging protocol.

11.40. Identify three typical lists of transactions that are maintained by the recovery subsystem.

11.41. What is meant by transaction rollback? What is meant by cascading rollback? Why do practical recovery methods use protocols that do not permit cascading rollback? Which recovery techniques do not require any rollback?

11.42. Discuss the UNDO and REDO operations and the recovery techniques that use each.

11.43. Discuss the deferred update technique of recovery. What are the advantages and disadvantages of this technique? Why is it called the NO-UNDO/REDO method?

11.44. How can recovery handle transaction operations that do not affect the database, such as the printing of reports by a transaction?

11.45. Discuss the immediate update recovery technique in both single-user and multiuser environments. What are the advantages and disadvantages of immediate update?

11.46. What is the difference between the UNDO/REDO and the UNDO/NO-REDO algorithms for recovery with immediate update? Develop the outline for an UNDO/NO-REDO algorithm.

11.47. Describe the shadow paging recovery technique. Under what circumstances does it not require a log?

11.48. Describe the three phases of the ARIES recovery method.

11.49. What are log sequence numbers (LSNs) in ARIES? How are they used? What information does the Dirty Page Table and Transaction Table contain? Describe how fuzzy checkpointing is used in ARIES.

11.50. What do the terms steal/no-steal and force/no-force mean with regard to buffer management for transaction processing.

11.51. Describe the two-phase commit protocol for multidatabase transactions.

11.52. Discuss how recovery from catastrophic failures is handled.

11.53. Change transaction T_2 in Figure 11.2b to read

read_item(X);
$X := X+M$;
if $X > 90$ then exit
else write_item(X);

Discuss the final result of the different schedules in Figure 11.3(a) and (b), where $M = 2$ and $N = 2$, with respect to the following questions. Does adding the above condition change the final outcome? Does the outcome obey the implied consistency rule (that the capacity of X is 90)?

11.54. Repeat Exercise 11.53, adding a check in T_1 so that Y does not exceed 90.

11.55. Add the operation commit at the end of each of the transactions T_1 and T_2 from Figure 11.2; then list all possible schedules for the modified transactions. Determine which of the schedules are recoverable, which are cascadeless, and which are strict.

11.56. List all possible schedules for transactions T_1 and T_2 from Figure 11.2, and determine which are conflict serializable (correct) and which are not.

11.57. How many *serial* schedules exist for the three transactions in Figure 11.8(a)? What are they? What is the total number of possible schedules?

11.58. Write a program to create all possible schedules for the three transactions in Figure 11.8(a), and to determine which of those schedules are conflict serializable and which are not. For each conflict serializable schedule, your program should print the schedule and list all equivalent serial schedules.

11.59. Why is an explicit transaction end statement needed in SQL but not an explicit begin statement?

11.60. Describe situations where each of the different isolation levels would be useful for transaction processing.

11.61. Prove that the basic two-phase locking protocol guarantees conflict serializability of schedules. (*Hint:* Show that, if a serializability graph for a schedule has a cycle, then at least one of the transactions participating in the schedule does not obey the two-phase locking protocol.)

11.62. Modify the data structures for multiple-mode locks and the algorithms for read_lock(X), write_lock(X), and unlock(X) so that upgrading and downgrading of locks are possible. (*Hint:* The lock needs to check the transaction id(s) that hold the lock, if any.)

11.63. Prove that strict two-phase locking guarantees strict schedules.

11.64. Prove that the wait-die and wound-wait protocols avoid deadlock and starvation.

11.65. Prove that cautious waiting avoids deadlock.

11.66. Apply the timestamp ordering algorithm to the schedules of Figure 11.8(b) and (c), and determine whether the algorithm will allow the execution of the schedules.

11.67. Repeat Exercise 11.66, but use the multiversion timestamp ordering method.

11.68. Why is two-phase locking not used as a concurrency control method for indexes such as B+-trees?

11.69. The compatibility matrix of Figure 11.16 shows that IS and IX locks are compatible. Explain why this is valid.

11.70. The MGL protocol states that a transaction T can unlock a node N, only if none of the children of node N are still locked by transaction T. Show that without this condition, the MGL protocol would be incorrect.

11.71. Which of the following schedules is (conflict) serializable? For each serializable schedule, determine the equivalent serial schedules.

a. $r_1(X); r_3(X); w_1(X); r_2(X); w_3(X);$

b. $r_1(X); r3(X); w_3(X); w_1(X); r_2(X);$

c. $r_3(X); r_2(X); w_3(X); r_1(X); w_1(X);$

d. $r_3(X); r_2(X); r_1(X); w_3(X); w_1(X);$

11.72. Consider the three transactions T_1, T_2, and T_3, and the schedules S_1 and S_2 given below. Draw the serializability (precedence) graphs for S_1 and S_2, and state whether each schedule is serializable or not. If a schedule is serializable, write down the equivalent serial schedule(s).

T_1: r_1 (X); r_1 (Z); w_1 (X);

T_2: r_2 (Z); r_2 (Y); w_2 (Z); w_2 (Y);

T_3: r_3 (X); r_3 (Y); w_3 (Y);

S_1: r_1 (X); r_2 (Z); r_1 (Z); r_3 (X); r_3 (Y); w_1 (X); w_3 (Y); r_2 (Y); w_2 (Z); w_2 (Y);

S_2: r_1 (X); r_2 (Z); r_3 (X); r_1 (Z); r_2 (Y); r_3 (Y); w_1 (X); w_2 (Z); w_3 (Y); w_2 (Y);

11.73. Consider schedules S_3, S_4, and S_5 below. Determine whether each schedule is strict, cascadeless, recoverable, or nonrecoverable. (Determine the strictest recoverability condition that each schedule satisfies.)

S_3: r_1 (X); r_2 (Z); r_1 (Z); r_3 (X); r_3 (Y); w_1 (X); c_1; w_3 (Y); c_3; r_2 (Y); w_2 (Z); w_2 (Y); c_2;

S_4: r_1 (X); r_2 (Z); r_1 (Z); r_3 (X); r_3 (Y); w_1 (X); w_3 (Y); r_2 (Y); w_2 (Z); w_2 (Y); c_1; c_2; c_3;

S_5: r_1 (X); r_2 (Z); r_3 (X); r_1 (Z); r_2 (Y); r_3 (Y); w_1 (X); c_1; w_2 (Z); w_3 (Y); w_2 (Y); c_3; c_2;

11.74. Suppose that the system crashes before the [read_item,T3,A] entry is written to the log in Figure 11.18b. Will that make any difference in the recovery process?

11.75. Suppose that the system crashes before the [write_item,T2,D,25,26] entry is written to the log in Figure 11.18b. Will that make any difference in the recovery process?

11.76. Figure 11.24 shows the log corresponding to a particular schedule at the point of a system crash for four transactions T_1, T_2, T_3, and T_4. Suppose that we use the *immediate update protocol* with checkpointing. Describe the recovery process from the system crash. Specify which transactions are rolled back, which operations in the log are redone and which (if any) are undone, and whether any cascading rollback takes place.

11.77. Suppose that we use the deferred update protocol for the example in Figure 11.24. Show how the log would be different in the case of deferred update by removing the unnecessary log entries; then describe the recovery process, using your modified log. Assume that only REDO operations are applied, and specify which operations in the log are redone and which are ignored.

11.78. How does checkpointing in ARIES differ from checkpointing.

11.79. How are log sequence numbers used by ARIES to reduce the amount of REDO work needed for recovery? Illustrate with an example using the information shown in Figure. You can make your own assumptions as to when a page is written to disk.

[start_transaction, T_1]
[read_item, T_1,A]
[read_item, T_1,D]
[write_item, T_1,D, 20, 25]
[commit, T_1]
[checkpoint]
[start_transaction, T_2]
[read_item, T_2,B]
[write_item, T_2,B,12,18]
[start_transaction, T_4]
[read_item, T_4,D]
[write_item, T_4,D, 25,15]
[start_transaction, T_3]

[write_item, T_3, C, 30,40]

[read_item, T_4, A]

[write_item, T_4, A, 30, 20]

[commit, T_4]

[read_item, T_2, D]

[write_item, T_2, D, 15, 25] ← system crash

FIGURE 11.24 An example schedule and its corresponding log.

11.80. What implications would a no-steal/force buffer management policy have on checkpointing and recovery?

Choose the correct answer for each of the following multiple-choice questions:

11.81. Incremental logging with deferred updates implies that the recovery system must necessarily

a. store the old value of the updated item in the log.

b. store the new value of the updated item in the log.

c. store both the old and new value of the updated item in the log.

d. store only the Begin Transaction and Commit Transaction records in the log.

11.82. The write ahead logging (WAL) protocol simply means that

a. the writing of a data item should be done ahead of any logging operation.

b. the log record for an operation should be written before the actual data is written.

c. all log records should be written before a new transaction begins execution.

d. the log never needs to be written to disk.

11.83. In case of transaction failure under a deferred update incremental logging scheme, which of the following will be needed:

a. an undo operation.

b. a redo operation.

c. an undo and redo operation.

d. none of the above.

11.84. For incremental logging with immediate updates, a log record for a transaction would contain:

a. a transaction name, data item name, old value of item, new value of item.

b. a transaction name, data item name, old value of item.

c. a transaction name, data item name, new value of item.

d. a transaction name and a data item name.

11.85. For correct behavior during recovery, undo and redo operations must be

a. commutative.

b. associative.

c. idempotent.

d. distributive.

11.86. When a failure occurs, the log is consulted and each operation is either undone or redone. This is a problem because

    a. searching the entire log is time consuming.

    b. many redo's are unnecessary.

    c. both (a) and (b).

    d. none of the above.

11.87. When using a log based recovery scheme, it might improve performance as well as providing a recovery mechanism by

    a. writing the log records to disk when each transaction commits.

    b. writing the appropriate log records to disk during the transaction's execution.

    c. waiting to write the log records until multiple transactions commit and writing them as a batch.

    d. never writing the log records to disk.

11.88. There is a possibility of a cascading rollback when

    a. a transaction writes items that have been written only by a committed transaction.

    b. a transaction writes an item that is previously written by an uncommitted transaction.

    c. a transaction reads an item that is previously written by an uncommitted transaction.

    d. both (b) and (c).

11.89. To cope with media (disk) failures, it is necessary

    a. for the DBMS to only execute transactions in a single user environment.

    b. to keep a redundant copy of the database.

    c. to never abort a transaction.

    d. all of the above.

11.90. If the shadowing approach is used for flushing a data item back to disk, then

    a. the item is written to disk only after the transaction commits.

    b. the item is written to a different location on disk.

    c. the item is written to disk before the transaction commits.

    d. the item is written to the same disk location from which it was read.

11.91. B^+ Trees are preferred to binary trees in database because

    a. disk capacities are greater than memory capacities

    b. disk access is much slower than memory access

    c. Disk data transfer rates are much less than memory data transfer rates

    d. Disks are more reliable than memory

11.92. Which of the following is correct?

    a. *B-trees* are for storing data on disk and B^+ trees are for main memory

    b. Range queries are faster on B^+ trees

    c. B^+ trees are primary indexes and B^+ trees are secondary indexes

    d. The height of B^+ tree is independent of the number of records

11.93. _____ have one key pointer pair for each block of the data file.

 a. sparse indexes   b. dense indexes

 c. secondary indexes   d. inverted indexes

11.94. If blocks hold either three records or 10 key-pointer pairs. As a function of n, the number records, how many blocks are needed to hold a data file in the case of dense index?

 a. 13n/30 blocks   b. n/3   c. n/10   d. n^2/30

11.95. If blocks hold either three records or 10 key-pointer pairs. As a function of n, the number records, how many blocks are needed to hold a data file in the case of sparse index?

 a. 13n/30   b. n/3   c. 11n/30   d. n^2/30

11.96. Consider a file of 1,000,000 records and are hashed into a table with 1000 buckets. Assume that 100 records will fit in a block. Also assume that all blocks are kept as full as possible but no two buckets share a block. What are the maximum and minimum number of blocks that needs to store this hash table?

11.97. How many I/Os are needed to access a page in B$^+$ tree of height h?

 a. h   b. h+1   c. h-1   d. 1

11.98. Which of the following is false?

 a. A secondary index is an index that is a primary index

 b. A secondary index can contain duplicates

 c. At most one sparse index can exist on a data file

 d. More than one sparse index can exist on a data file

11.99. Which of the following is false?

 a. A clustered index is one in which the ordering of data entries is the same as the ordering of data records

 b. At most one clustered index can exist on a data file

 c. Several un clustered indexes can exist on a data file

 d. At most one un clustered index can exist on a data file

11.100. If an index contains data records as 'data entries', then which of the following statements are correct?

 I.   the index is clustered

 II. the index is un clustered

 III. the index is dense

 IV. the index is sparse

 a. (I and Ill) are correct

 b. (1, IV) are correct

 c. II and Ill) are correct

 d. (II, IV) are correct

Selected Bibliography

The concept of transaction is discussed in Gray (1981). Bernstein, Hadzilacos, and Goodman (1987) focus on concurrency control and recovery techniques in both centralized and distributed database systems; it is an excellent reference. Papadimitriou (1986) offers a more theoretical perspective. A large reference book of more than a thousand pages by Gray and Reuter (1993) offers a more practical perspective of transaction processing concepts and techniques. Elmagarmid (1992) and Bhargava (1989) offer collections of research papers on transaction processing. Transaction support in SQL is described in Date and Darwen (1993). The concepts of serializability are introduced in Gray et al. (1975). View serializability is defined in Yannakakis (1984). Recoverability of schedules is discussed in Hadzilacos (1983, 1988).

The two-phase locking protocol, and the concept of predicate locks was first proposed by Eswaran et al. (1976). Bernstein et al. (1987), Gray and Reuter (1993), and Papadimitriou (1986) focus on concurrency control and recovery. Kumar (1996) focuses on performance of concurrency control methods. Locking is discussed in Gray et al. (1975), Lien and Weinberger (1978), Kedem and Silbershatz (1980), and Korth (1983). Deadlocks and wait-for graphs were formalized by Holt (1972), and the wait-wound and wound-die schemes are presented in Rosenkrantz et al. (1978). Cautious waiting is discussed in Hsu et al. (1992). Helal et al. (1993) compares various locking approaches. Timestamp-based concurrency control techniques are discussed in Bernstein and Goodman (1980) and Reed (1983). Optimistic concurrency control is discussed in Kung and Robinson (1981) and Bassiouni (1988). Papadimitriou and Kanellakis (1979) and Bernstein and Goodman (1983) discuss multiversion techniques. Multiversion timestamp ordering was proposed in Reed (1978, 1983), and multiversion two-phase locking is discussed in Lai and Wilkinson (1984). A method for multiple locking granularities was proposed in Gray et al. (1975), and the effects of locking granularities are analyzed in Ries and Stonebraker (1977). Bhargava and Reidl (1988) presents an approach for dynamically choosing among various concurrency control and recovery methods. Concurrency control methods for indexes are presented in Lehman and Yao (1981) and in Shasha and Goodman (1988). A performance study of various B+ tree concurrency control algorithms is presented in Srinivasan and Carey (1991).

Other recent work on concurrency control includes semantic-based concurrency control (Badrinath and Ramamritham, 1992), transaction models for long running activities (Dayal et al., 1991), and multilevel transaction management (Hasse and Weikum, 1991).

The books by Bernstein et al. (1987) and Papadimitriou (1986) are devoted to the theory and principles of concurrency control and recovery. The book by Gray and Reuter (1993) is an encyclopedic work on concurrency control, recovery, and other transaction processing issues.

Verhofstad (1978) presents a tutorial and survey of recovery techniques in database systems. Categorizing algorithms based on their UNDO/REDO characteristics is discussed in Haerder and Reuter (1983) and in Bernstein et al. (1983). Gray (1978) discusses recovery, along with other system aspects of implementing operating systems for databases. The shadow paging technique is discussed in Lorie (1977), Verhofstad (1978), and Reuter (1980). Gray et al. (1981) discuss the recovery mechanism in SYSTEM R. Lockeman and Knutsen (1968), Davies (1972), and Bjork (1973) are early papers that discuss recovery. Chandy et al. (1975) discuss transaction rollback. Lilien and Bhargava (1985) discuss the concept of integrity block and its use to improve the efficiency of recovery.

Recovery using write-ahead logging is analyzed in Jhingran and Khedkar (1992) and is used in the ARIES system (Mohan et al. 1992a). More recent work on recovery includes compensating transactions (Korth et al. 1990) and main memory database recovery (Kumar 1991). The ARIES recovery algorithms (Mohan et al. 1992) have been quite successful in practice. Franklin et al. (1992) discusses recovery in the EXODUS system. Two recent books by Kumar and Hsu (1998) and Kumar and Son (1998) discuss recovery in detail and contain descriptions of recovery methods used in a number of existing relational database products.

6
FURTHER TOPICS

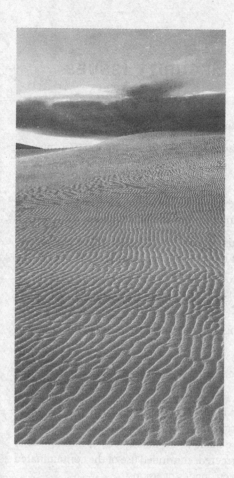

12

Database Security
and Authorization

This chapter discusses the techniques used for protecting the database against persons who are not authorized to access either certain parts of a database or the whole database. Section 12.1 provides an introduction to security issues and the threats to databases and an overview of the countermeasures that are covered in the rest of this chapter. Section 12.2 discusses the mechanisms used to grant and revoke privileges in relational database systems and in SQL, mechanisms that are often referred to as **discretionary access control**. Section 12.3 offers an overview of the mechanisms for enforcing multiple levels of security—a more recent concern in database system security that is known as **mandatory access control**. It also introduces the more recently developed strategy of **role-based access control**. Section 12.4 briefly discusses the security problem in statistical databases. Section 12.5 introduces flow control and mentions problems associated with covert channels. Section 12.6 is a brief summary of encryption and public key infrastructure schemes. Section 12.7 summarizes the chapter.

12.1 INTRODUCTION TO DATABASE SECURITY ISSUES

12.1.1 Types of Security

Database security is a very broad area that addresses many issues, including the following:

- Legal and ethical issues regarding the right to access certain information. Some information may be deemed to be private and cannot be accessed legally by unauthorized persons. In the United States, there are numerous laws governing privacy of information.

- Policy issues at the governmental, institutional, or corporate level as to what kinds of information should not be made publicly available—for example, credit ratings and personal medical records.

- System-related issues such as the *system levels* at which various security functions should be enforced—for example, whether a security function should be handled at the physical hardware level, the operating system level, or the DBMS level.

- The need in some organizations to identify multiple *security levels* and to categorize the data and users based on these classifications—for example, top secret, secret, confidential, and unclassified. The security policy of the organization with respect to permitting access to various classifications of data must be enforced.

Threats to Databases. Threats to databases result in the loss or degradation of some or all of the following security goals: integrity, availability, and confidentiality.

- *Loss of integrity*: Database integrity refers to the requirement that information be protected from improper modification. Modification of data includes creation, insertion, modification, changing the status of data, and deletion. Integrity is lost if unauthorized changes are made to the data by either intentional or accidental acts. If the loss of system or data integrity is not corrected, continued use of the contaminated system or corrupted data could result in inaccuracy, fraud, or erroneous decisions.

- *Loss of availability*: Database availability refers to making objects available to a human user or a program to which they have a legitimate right.

- *Loss of confidentiality*: Database confidentiality refers to the protection of data from unauthorized disclosure. The impact of unauthorized disclosure of confidential information can range from violation of the Data Privacy Act to the jeopardization of national security. Unauthorized, unanticipated, or unintentional disclosure could result in loss of public confidence, embarrassment, or legal action against the organization.

To protect databases against these types of threats four kinds of countermeasures can be implemented: access control, inference control, flow control, and encryption. We discuss each of these in this chapter.

In a multiuser database system, the DBMS must provide techniques to enable certain users or user groups to access selected portions of a database without gaining access to the rest of the database. This is particularly important when a large integrated database is to be used by many different users within the same organization. For example, sensitive information such as employee salaries or performance reviews should be kept confidential from most of the database system's users. A DBMS typically includes a **database security and authorization subsystem** that is responsible for ensuring the security of portions of a database against unauthorized access. It is now customary to refer to two types of database security mechanisms:

- *Discretionary security mechanisms*: These are used to grant privileges to users, including the capability to access specific data files, records, or fields in a specified mode (such as read, insert, delete, or update).

- *Mandatory security mechanisms*: These are used to enforce multilevel security by classifying the data and users into various security classes (or levels) and then implementing the appropriate security policy of the organization. For example, a typical security policy is to permit users at a certain classification level to see only the data items classified at the user's own (or lower) classification level. An extension of this is *role-based security*, which enforces policies and privileges based on the concept of roles.

We discuss discretionary security in Section 12.2 and mandatory and role-based security in Section 12.3.

A second security problem common to all computer systems is that of preventing unauthorized persons from accessing the system itself, either to obtain information or to make malicious changes in a portion of the database. The security mechanism of a DBMS must include provisions for restricting access to the database system as a whole. This function is called **access control** and is handled by creating user accounts and passwords to control the login process by the DBMS. We discuss access control techniques in Section 12.1.3.

A third security problem associated with databases is that of controlling the access to a **statistical database**, which is used to provide statistical information or summaries of values based on various criteria. For example, a database for population statistics may provide statistics based on age groups, income levels, size of household, education levels, and other criteria. Statistical database users such as government statisticians or market research firms are allowed to access the database to retrieve statistical information about a population but not to access the detailed confidential information on specific individuals. Security for statistical databases must ensure that information on individuals cannot be accessed. It is sometimes possible to deduce or infer certain facts concerning individuals from queries that involve only summary statistics on groups; consequently, this must not be permitted either. This problem, called **statistical database security**, is discussed briefly in Section 12.4. The corresponding countermeasures are called **inference control** measures.

Another security issue is that of **flow control**, which prevents information from flowing in such a way that it reaches unauthorized users. It is discussed in Section 12.5. Channels that are pathways for information to flow implicitly in ways that violate the security policy of an organization are called **covert channels**. We briefly discuss some issues related to covert channels in Section 12.5.1.

A final security issue is **data encryption**, which is used to protect sensitive data (such as credit card numbers) that is being transmitted via some type of communications network. Encryption can be used to provide additional protection for sensitive portions of a database as well. The data is **encoded** using some coding algorithm. An unauthorized user who accesses encoded data will have difficulty deciphering it, but authorized users are given decoding or decrypting algorithms (or keys) to decipher the data. Encrypting techniques that are very difficult to decode without a key have been developed for military applications. Section 12.6 briefly discusses encryption techniques, including popular techniques such as public key encryption, which is heavily used to support Web-based transactions against databases, and digital signatures, which are used in personal communications.

A complete discussion of security in computer systems and databases is outside the scope of this textbook. We give only a brief overview of database security techniques here. The interested reader can refer to several of the references discussed in the selected bibliography at the end of this chapter for a more comprehensive discussion.

12.1.2 Database Security and the DBA

As we discussed in Chapter 1, the database administrator (DBA) is the central authority for managing a database system. The DBA's responsibilities include granting privileges to users who need to use the system and classifying users and data in accordance with the policy of the organization. The DBA has a **DBA account** in the DBMS, sometimes called a **system** or **superuser account**, which provides powerful capabilities that are not made available to regular database accounts and users.[1] DBA-privileged commands include commands for

---

1. This account is similar to the *root* or *superuser* accounts that are given to computer system administrators, allowing access to restricted operating system commands.

granting and revoking privileges to individual accounts, users, or user groups and for performing the following types of actions:

1. *Account creation*: This action creates a new account and password for a user or a group of users to enable access to the DBMS.

2. *Privilege granting*: This action permits the DBA to grant certain privileges to certain accounts.

3. *Privilege revocation*: This action permits the DBA to revoke (cancel) certain privileges that were previously given to certain accounts.

4. *Security level assignment*: This action consists of assigning user accounts to the appropriate security classification level.

The DBA is responsible for the overall security of the database system. Action 1 in the preceding list is used to control access to the DBMS as a whole, whereas actions 2 and 3 are used to control *discretionary* database authorization, and action 4 is used to control *mandatory* authorization.

12.1.3 Access Protection, User Accounts, and Database Audits

Whenever a person or a group of persons needs to access a database system, the individual or group must first apply for a user account. The DBA will then create a new **account number** and **password** for the user if there is a legitimate need to access the database. The user must **log in** to the DBMS by entering the account number and password whenever database access is needed. The DBMS checks that the account number and password are valid; if they are, the user is permitted to use the DBMS and to access the database. Application programs can also be considered as users and can be required to supply passwords.

It is straightforward to keep track of database users and their accounts and passwords by creating an encrypted table or file with the two fields AccountNumber and Password. This table can easily be maintained by the DBMS. Whenever a new account is created, a new record is inserted into the table. When an account is canceled, the corresponding record must be deleted from the table.

The database system must also keep track of all operations on the database that are applied by a certain user throughout each **login session**, which consists of the sequence of database interactions that a user performs from the time of logging in to the time of logging off. When a user logs in, the DBMS can record the user's account number and associate it with the terminal from which the user logged in. All operations applied from that terminal are attributed to the user's account until the user logs off. It is particularly important to keep track of update operations that are applied to the database so that, if the database is tampered with, the DBA can find out which user did the tampering.

To keep a record of all updates applied to the database and of the particular user who applied each update, we can modify the *system log*. Recall from Chapter 11 that the **system log** includes an entry for each operation applied to the database that may be required for recovery from a transaction failure or system crash. We can expand the log entries so that they also include the account number of the user and the online terminal ID that applied each operation recorded in the log. If any tampering with the database is suspected, a **database audit** is performed, which consists of reviewing the log to examine all accesses and operations applied to the database during a certain time period. When an illegal or unauthorized operation is found, the DBA can determine the account number used to perform this operation. Database audits are particularly important for sensitive databases that are updated by many transactions and users, such as a banking database that is updated by many bank tellers. A database log that is used mainly for security purposes is sometimes called an **audit trail**.

12.2 DISCRETIONARY ACCESS CONTROL BASED ON GRANTING AND REVOKING PRIVILEGES

The typical method of enforcing **discretionary access control** in a database system is based on the granting and revoking of **privileges**. Let us consider privileges in the context of a relational DBMS. In particular, we will discuss a system of privileges somewhat similar to the one originally developed for the SQL language (see Chapter 7). Many current relational DBMSs use some variation of this technique. The main idea is to include statements in the query language that allow the DBA and selected users to grant and revoke privileges.

12.2.1 Types of Discretionary Privileges

In SQL2, the concept of an **authorization identifier** is used to refer, roughly speaking, to a user account (or group of user accounts). For simplicity, we will use the words *user* or *account* interchangeably in place of *authorization identifier*. The DBMS must provide selective access to each relation in the database based on specific accounts. Operations may also be controlled; thus, having an account does not necessarily entitle the account holder to all the functionality provided by the DBMS. Informally, there are two levels for assigning privileges to use the database system:

- *The account level*: At this level, the DBA specifies the particular privileges that each account holds independently of the relations in the database.

- *The relation (or table) level*: At this level, the DBA can control the privilege to access each individual relation or view in the database.

The privileges at the **account level** apply to the capabilities provided to the account itself and can include the CREATE SCHEMA or CREATE TABLE privilege, to create a schema or base relation; the CREATE VIEW privilege; the ALTER privilege, to apply schema changes such as adding or removing attributes from relations; the DROP privilege, to delete relations or views; the MODIFY privilege, to insert, delete, or update tuples; and the SELECT privilege, to retrieve information from the database by using a SELECT query. Notice that these account privileges apply to the account in general. If a certain account does not have the CREATE TABLE privilege, no relations can be created from that account. Account-level privileges are not defined as part of SQL2; they are left to the DBMS implementers to define. In earlier versions of SQL, a CREATETAB privilege existed to give an account the privilege to create tables (relations).

The second level of privileges applies to the **relation level**, whether they are base relations or virtual (view) relations. These privileges *are* defined for SQL2. In the following discussion, the term *relation* may refer either to a base relation or to a view, unless we explicitly specify one or the other. Privileges at the relation level specify for each user the individual relations on which each type of command can be applied. Some privileges also refer to individual columns (attributes) of relations. SQL2 commands provide privileges at the *relation and attribute level only*. Although this is quite general, it makes it difficult to create accounts with limited privileges. The granting and revoking of privileges generally follow an authorization model for discretionary privileges known as the **access matrix model**, where the rows of a matrix M represent *subjects* (users, accounts, programs) and the columns represent *objects* (relations, records, columns, views, operations). Each position M(i, j) in the matrix represents the types of privileges (read, write, update) that subject i holds on object j.

To control the granting and revoking of relation privileges, each relation R in a database is assigned an **owner account**, which is typically the account that was used when the relation was created in the first place. The owner of a relation is given *all* privileges on that relation. In SQL2, the DBA can assign an owner to a whole schema by creating the schema and associating the appropriate authorization identifier with that schema, using the CREATE SCHEMA command (see Section 7.1.1). The owner account holder can pass privileges on any of the owned relations to other users by **granting** privileges to their accounts. In SQL the following types of privileges can be granted on each individual relation R:

- SELECT (retrieval or read) privilege on R: Gives the account retrieval privilege. In SQL this gives the account the privilege to use the SELECT statement to retrieve tuples from R.

- MODIFY privileges on R: This gives the account the capability to modify tuples of R. In SQL this privilege is further divided into UPDATE, DELETE, and INSERT privileges to apply the corresponding SQL command to R. In addition, both the INSERT and UPDATE privileges can specify that only certain attributes of R can be updated by the account.

- REFERENCES privilege on R: This gives the account the capability to reference relation R when specifying integrity constraints. This privilege can also be restricted to specific attributes of R.

Notice that to create a view, the account must have SELECT privilege on *all relations* involved in the view definition.

12.2.2 Specifying Privileges Using Views

The mechanism of **views** is an important discretionary authorization mechanism in its own right. For example, if the owner A of a relation R wants another account B to be able to retrieve only some fields of R, then A can create a view V of R that includes only those attributes and then grant SELECT on V to B. The same applies to limiting B to retrieving only certain tuples of R; a view V' can be created by defining the view by means of a query that selects only those tuples from R that A wants to allow B to access. We shall illustrate this discussion with the example given in Section 12.2.5.

12.2.3 Revoking Privileges

In some cases it is desirable to grant a privilege to a user temporarily. For example, the owner of a relation may want to grant the SELECT privilege to a user for a specific task and then revoke that privilege once the task is completed. Hence, a mechanism for **revoking** privileges is needed. In SQL a REVOKE command is included for the purpose of canceling privileges. We will see how the REVOKE command is used in the example in Section 12.2.5.

12.2.4 Propagation of Privileges Using the GRANT OPTION

Whenever the owner A of a relation R grants a privilege on R to another account B, the privilege can be given to B *with* or *without* the **GRANT OPTION**. If the GRANT OPTION is given, this means that B can also grant that privilege on R to other accounts. Suppose that B is given the GRANT OPTION by A and that B then grants the privilege on R to a third account C, also with GRANT OPTION. In this way, privileges on R can **propagate** to other accounts without the knowledge of the owner of R. If the owner account A now revokes the privilege granted to B, all the privileges that B propagated based on that privilege should automatically be revoked by the system.

It is possible for a user to receive a certain privilege from two or more sources. For example, A4 may receive a certain UPDATE R privilege from *both* A2 and A3. In such a case, if A2 revokes this privilege from A4, A4 will still continue to have the privilege by virtue of having been granted it from A3. If A3 later revokes the privilege from A4, A4 totally loses the privilege. Hence, a DBMS that allows propagation of privileges must keep track of how all the privileges were granted so that revoking of privileges can be done correctly and completely.

12.2.5   An Example

Suppose that the DBA creates four accounts—A1, A2, A3, and A4—and wants only A1 to be able to create base relations; then the DBA must issue the following GRANT command in SQL:

GRANT CREATETAB **TO** A1;

The CREATETAB (create table) privilege gives account A1 the capability to create new database tables (base relations) and is hence an *account privilege*. This privilege was part of earlier versions of SQL but is now left to each individual system implementation to define.

In SQL2, the same effect can be accomplished by having the DBA issue a CREATE SCHEMA command, as follows:

CREATE SCHEMA EXAMPLE **AUTHORIZATION** A1;

Now user account A1 can create tables under the schema called EXAMPLE. To continue our example, suppose that A1 creates the two base relations EMPLOYEE and DEPARTMENT shown in Figure 12.1; A1 is then the **owner** of these two relations and hence has *all the relation privileges* on each of them.

EMPLOYEE

NAME	ENO	DOB	ADDRESS	SEX	SALARY	DNO

DEPARTMENT

DNUMBER	DNAME	MGRENO

FIGURE 12.1 Schemas for the two relations EMPLOYEE and DEPARTMENT.

Next, suppose that account A1 wants to grant to account A2 the privilege to insert and delete tuples in both of these relations. However, A1 does not want A2 to be able to propagate these privileges to additional accounts. A1 can issue the following command:

GRANT INSERT, DELETE **ON** EMPLOYEE, DEPARTMENT **TO** A2;

Notice that the owner account A1 of a relation automatically has the GRANT OPTION, allowing it to grant privileges on the relation to other accounts. However, account A2 cannot grant INSERT and DELETE privileges on the EMPLOYEE and DEPARTMENT tables, because A2 was not given the GRANT OPTION in the preceding command.

Next, suppose that A1 wants to allow account A3 to retrieve information from either of the two tables and also to be able to propagate the SELECT privilege to other accounts. A1 can issue the following command:

GRANT SELECT **ON** EMPLOYEE, DEPARTMENT **TO** A3 **WITH GRANT OPTION**;

The clause WITH GRANT OPTION means that A3 can now propagate the privilege to other accounts by using GRANT. For example, A3 can grant the SELECT privilege on the EMPLOYEE relation to A4 by issuing the following command:

GRANT SELECT **ON** EMPLOYEE **TO** A4;

Notice that A4 cannot propagate the SELECT privilege to other accounts because the GRANT OPTION was not given to A4.

Now suppose that A1 decides to revoke the SELECT privilege on the EMPLOYEE relation from A3; A1 then can issue this command:

REVOKE SELECT **ON** EMPLOYEE **FROM** A3;

The DBMS must now automatically revoke the SELECT privilege on EMPLOYEE from A4, too, because A3 granted that privilege to A4 and A3 does not have the privilege any more.

Next, suppose that A1 wants to give back to A3 a limited capability to SELECT from the EMPLOYEE relation and wants to allow A3 to be able to propagate the privilege. The limitation is to retrieve only the NAME, BDATE, and ADDRESS attributes and only for the tuples with DNO = 5. A1 then can create the following view:

CREATE VIEW A3EMPLOYEE **AS**

SELECT NAME, DOB, ADDRESS

FROM EMPLOYEE

WHERE DNO = 5;

After the view is created, A1 can grant SELECT on the view A3EMPLOYEE to A3 as follows:

GRANT SELEC **ON** A3EMPLOYEE **TO** A3 **WITH GRANT OPTION**;

Finally, suppose that A1 wants to allow A4 to update only the SALARY attribute of EMPLOYEE; A1 can then issue the following command:

GRANT UPDATE **ON** EMPLOYEE (SALARY) TO A4;

The UPDATE or INSERT privilege can specify particular attributes that may be updated or inserted in a relation. Other privileges (SELECT, DELETE) are not attribute specific, because this specificity can easily be controlled by creating the appropriate views that include only the desired attributes and granting the corresponding privileges on the views. However, because updating views is not always possible (see Chapter 7), the UPDATE and INSERT privileges are given the option to specify particular attributes of a base relation that may be updated.

12.2.6 Specifying Limits on Propagation of Privileges

Techniques to limit the propagation of privileges have been developed, although they have not yet been implemented in most DBMSs and are not a part of SQL. Limiting **horizontal propagation** to an integer number i means that an account B given the GRANT OPTION can grant the privilege to at most i other accounts. **Vertical propagation** is more complicated; it limits the depth of the granting of privileges. Granting a privilege with a vertical propagation of zero is equivalent to granting the privilege with *no* GRANT OPTION.

If account A grants a privilege to account B with the vertical propagation set to an integer number $j > 0$, this means that the account B has the GRANT OPTION on that privilege, but B can grant the privilege to other accounts only with a vertical propagation *less than j*. In effect, vertical propagation limits the sequence of GRANT OPTIONs that can be given from one account to the next based on a single original grant of the privilege.

We now briefly illustrate horizontal and vertical propagation limits—which are *not available* currently in SQL or other relational systems—with an example. Suppose that A1 grants SELECT to A2 on the EMPLOYEE relation with horizontal propagation equal to 1 and vertical propagation equal to 2. A2 can then grant SELECT to at most one account because the horizontal propagation limitation is set to 1. In addition, A2 cannot grant the privilege to another account except with vertical propagation set to 0 (no GRANT OPTION) or 1; this is because A2 must reduce the vertical propagation by at least 1 when passing the privilege to others. As this example shows, horizontal and vertical propagation techniques are designed to limit the propagation of privileges.

12.3   MANDATORY ACCESS CONTROL AND ROLE-BASED ACCESS CONTROL FOR MULTILEVEL SECURITY[2]

The discretionary access control technique of granting and revoking privileges on relations has traditionally been the main security mechanism for relational database systems. This is an all-or-nothing method: A user either has or does not have a certain privilege. In many applications, an *additional security policy* is needed that classifies data and users based on security classes. This approach, known as **mandatory access control**, would typically be *combined* with the discretionary access control mechanisms described in Section 12.2. It is important to note that most commercial DBMSs currently provide mechanisms only for discretionary access control. However, the need for multilevel security exists in government, military, and intelligence applications, as well as in many industrial and corporate applications.

Typical **security classes** are top secret (TS), secret (S), confidential (C), and unclassified (U), where TS is the highest level and U the lowest. Other more complex security classification schemes exist, in which the security classes are organized in a lattice. For simplicity, we will use the system with four security classification levels, where $TS \geq S \geq C \geq U$, to illustrate our discussion. The commonly used model for multilevel security, known as the Bell-LaPadula model, classifies each **subject** (user, account, program) and **object** (relation, tuple, column, view, operation) into one of the security classifications TS, S, C, or U. We will refer to the **clearance** (classification) of a subject S as **class(S)** and to the classification of an object O as **class(O)**. Two restrictions are enforced on data access based on the subject/object classifications:

1. A subject S is not allowed read access to an object O unless class(S) ≥ class(O). This is known as the **simple security property**.

2. A subject S is not allowed to write an object O unless class(S) ≤ class(O). This is known as the **star property** (or *-property).

The first restriction is intuitive and enforces the obvious rule that no subject can read an object whose security classification is higher than the subject's security clearance. The second restriction is less intuitive. It prohibits a subject from writing an object at a lower security classification than the subject's security clearance. Violation of this rule would allow information to flow from higher to lower classifications, which violates a basic tenet of multilevel security. For example, a user (subject) with TS clearance may make a copy of an

---

2. The contribution of Fariborz Farahmand to this and subsequent sections is appreciated.

object with classification TS and then write it back as a new object with classification U, thus making it visible throughout the system.

To incorporate multilevel security notions into the relational database model, it is common to consider attribute values and tuples as data objects. Hence, each attribute A is associated with a **classification attribute** C in the schema, and each attribute value in a tuple is associated with a corresponding security classification. In addition, in some models, a **tuple classification** attribute TC is added to the relation attributes to provide a classification for each tuple as a whole. Hence, a **multilevel relation** schema R with n attributes would be represented as

$$R(A_1, C_1, A_2, C_2, \ldots, A_n, C_n, TC)$$

where each C_i represents the *classification attribute* associated with attribute A_i.

The value of the TC attribute in each tuple t—which is the *highest* of all attribute classification values within t—provides a general classification for the tuple itself, whereas each C_i provides a finer security classification for each attribute value within the tuple. The **apparent key** of a multilevel relation is the set of attributes that would have formed the primary key in a regular (single-level) relation. A multilevel relation will appear to contain different data to subjects (users) with different clearance levels. In some cases, it is possible to store a single tuple in the relation at a higher classification level and produce the corresponding tuples at a lower-level classification through a process known as **filtering**. In other cases, it is necessary to store two or more tuples at different classification levels with the same value for the *apparent key*. This leads to the concept of **polyinstantiation**,[3] where several tuples can have the same apparent key value but have different attribute values for users at different classification levels.

We illustrate these concepts with the simple example of a multilevel relation shown in Figure 12.2a, where we display the classification attribute values next to each attribute's value. Assume that the **Name** attribute is the apparent key, and consider the query **SELECT*** FROM employee. A user with security clearance S would see the same relation shown in Figure 12.2a, since all tuple classifications are less than or equal to S. However, a user with security clearance C would not be allowed to see values for Salary of Gaurav and JobPerformance of Mahesh, since they have higher classification. The tuples would be *filtered* to appear as shown in Figure 12.2b, with Salary and JobPerformance *appearing* as *null*. For a user with security clearance U, the filtering allows only the Name attribute of Mahesh to appear, with all the other attributes appearing as null (Figure 12.2c). Thus, filtering introduces null values for attribute values whose security classification is higher than the user's security clearance.

In general, the **entity integrity** rule for multilevel relations states that all attributes that are members of the apparent key must not be null and must have the *same* security classification within each individual tuple. In addition, all other attribute values in the tuple must have a security classification greater than or equal to that of the apparent key. This constraint ensures that a user can see the key if the user is permitted to see any part of the tuple at all. Other integrity rules, called **null integrity** and **interinstance integrity**, informally ensure that if a tuple value at some security level can be filtered (derived) from a higher-classified tuple, then it is sufficient to store the higher-classified tuple in the multilevel relation.

To illustrate polyinstantiation further, suppose that a user with security clearance C tries to update the value of JobPerformance of Mahesh in Figure 12.2 to 'Excellent'; this corresponds to the following SQL update being issued:

```
UPDATE   EMPLOYEE
SET      JobPerformance = 'Excellent'
WHERE    Name = 'Mahesh';
```

---

3. This is similar to the notion of having multiple versions in the database that represent the same real-world object.

(a) EMPLOYEE

Name		Salary		JobPerformance		TC
Mahesh	U	40000	C	Fair	S	S
Gaurav	C	80000	S	Good	C	S

(b) EMPLOYEE

Name		Salary		JobPerformance		TC
Mahesh	U	40000	C	null	C	C
Gaurav	C	null	C	Good	C	C

(c) EMPLOYEE

Name		Salary		JobPerformance		TC
Mahesh	U	null	U	null	U	U

(d) EMPLOYEE

Name		Salary		JobPerformance		TC
Mahesh	U	40000	C	Fair	S	S
Mahesh	U	40000	C	Excellent	C	C
Gaurav	C	80000	S	Good	C	S

FIGURE 12.2 A multilevel relation to illustrate multilevel security. (a) The original EMPLOYEE tuples. (b) Appearance of EMPLOYEE after filtering for classification C users. (c) Appearance of EMPLOYEE after filtering for classification U users. (d) Polyinstantiation of the Mahesh tuple.

Since the view provided to users with security clearance C (see Figure 12.2b) permits such an update, the system should not reject it; otherwise, the user could infer that some nonnull value exists for the JobPerformance attribute of Mahesh rather than the null value that appears. This is an example of inferring information through what is known as a **covert channel**, which should not be permitted in highly secure systems (see Section 12.5.1). However, the user should not be allowed to overwrite the existing value of JobPerformance at the higher classification level. The solution is to create a **polyinstantiation** for the Mahesh tuple at the lower classification level C, as shown in Figure 12.2d. This is necessary since the new tuple cannot be filtered from the existing tuple at classification S.

The basic update operations of the relational model (insert, delete, update) must be modified to handle this and similar situations, but this aspect of the problem is outside the scope of our presentation: We refer the interested reader to the end-of-chapter bibliography for further details.

12.3.1 Comparing Discretionary Access Control and Mandatory Access Control

Discretionary Access Control (DAC) policies are characterized by a high degree of flexibility, which makes them suitable for a large variety of application domains. The main drawback of DAC models is their vulnerability to malicious attacks, such as Trojan horses embedded in application programs. The reason is that discretionary authorization models do not impose any control on how information is propagated and used once it has been accessed by users authorized to do so. By contrast, mandatory policies ensure a high degree of protection—in a way, they prevent any illegal flow of information. They are therefore suitable for military types of applications, which require a high degree of protection. However, mandatory policies have the drawback of being too rigid in that they require a strict classification of subjects and objects into security levels, and therefore they are applicable to very few environments. In many practical situations, discretionary policies are preferred because they offer a better trade-off between security and applicability.

12.3.2   Role-Based Access Control

Role-based access control (RBAC) emerged rapidly in the 1990s as a proven technology for managing and enforcing security in large-scale enterprisewide systems. Its basic notion is that permissions are associated with roles, and users are assigned to appropriate roles. Roles can be created using the CREATE ROLE and DESTROY ROLE commands. The GRANT and REVOKE commands discussed under DAC can then be used to assign and revoke privileges from roles.

RBAC appears to be a viable alternative to traditional discretionary and mandatory access controls; it ensures that only authorized users are given access to certain data or resources. Users create sessions during which they may activate a subset of roles to which they belong. Each session can be assigned to many roles, but it maps to only one user or a single subject. Many DBMSs have allowed the concept of roles, where privileges can be assigned to roles.

Role hierarchy in RBAC is a natural way of organizing roles to reflect the organization's lines of authority and responsibility. By convention, junior roles at the bottom are connected to progressively senior roles as one moves up the hierarchy. The hierarchic diagrams are partial orders, so they are reflexive, transitive, and antisymmetric.

Another important consideration in RBAC systems is the possible temporal constraints that may exist on roles, such as the time and duration of role activations, and timed triggering of a role by an activation of another role. Using an RBAC model is a highly desirable goal for addressing the key security requirements of Web-based applications. Roles can be assigned to workflow tasks so that a user with any of the roles related to a task may be authorized to execute it and may play a certain role for a certain duration only.

RBAC models have several desirable features, such as flexibility, policy neutrality, better support for security management and administration, and other aspects that make them attractive candidates for developing secure Web-based applications. In contrast, DAC and mandatory access control (MAC) models lack capabilities needed to support the security requirements of emerging enterprises and Web-based applications. In addition, RBAC models can represent traditional DAC and MAC policies as well as user-defined or organization-specific policies. Thus, RBAC becomes a superset model that can in turn mimic the behavior of DAC and MAC systems. Furthermore, an RBAC model provides a natural mechanism for addressing the security issues related to the execution of tasks and workflows. Easier deployment over the Internet has been another reason for the success of RBAC models.

12.3.3   Access Control Policies for E-Commerce and the Web

Electronic commerce (**E-commerce**) environments are characterized by any transactions that are done electronically. They require elaborate access control policies that go beyond traditional DBMSs. In conventional database environments, access control is usually performed using a set of authorizations stated by security officers or users according to some security policies. Such a simple paradigm is not well suited for a dynamic environment like e-commerce. Furthermore, in an e-commerce environment the resources to be protected are not only traditional data but also knowledge and experience. Such peculiarities call for more flexibility in specifying access control policies. The access control mechanism must be flexible enough to support a wide spectrum of heterogeneous protection objects.

A second related requirement is the support for content-based access control. Content-based access control allows one to express access control policies that take the protection object content into account. In order to support content-based access control, access control policies must allow inclusion of conditions based on the object content.

A third requirement is related to the heterogeneity of subjects, which requires access control policies based on user characteristics and qualifications rather than on very specific and individual characteristics (e.g., user IDs). A possible solution, to better take into account user profiles in the formulation of access control policies, is to support the notion of credentials. A **credential** is a set of properties concerning a user that are relevant for security purposes (for example, age, position within an organization). For instance, by using credentials, one can simply formulate policies such as "Only permanent staff with 5 or more years of service can access documents related to the internals of the system."

It is believed that the XML language can play a key role in access control for e-commerce applications.[4] The reason is that XML is becoming the common representation language for document interchange over the Web, and is also becoming the language for e-commerce. Thus, on the one hand there is the need to make XML representations secure, by providing access control mechanisms specifically tailored to the protection of XML documents. On the other hand, access control information (that is, access control policies and user credentials) can be expressed using XML itself. The Directory Service Markup Language provides a foundation for this: a standard for communicating with the directory services that will be responsible for providing and authenticating user credentials. The uniform presentation of both protection objects and access control policies can be applied to policies and credentials themselves. For instance, some credential properties (such as the user name) may be accessible to everyone, whereas other properties may be visible only to a restricted class of users. Additionally, the use of an XML-based language for specifying credentials and access control policies facilitates secure credential submission and export of access control policies.

12.4 INTRODUCTION TO STATISTICAL DATABASE SECURITY

Statistical databases are used mainly to produce statistics on various populations. The database may contain confidential data on individuals, which should be protected from user access. However, users are permitted to retrieve statistical information on the populations, such as averages, sums, counts, maximums, minimums, and standard deviations. The techniques that have been developed to protect the privacy of individual information are outside the scope of this book. We will only illustrate the problem with a very simple example, which refers to the relation shown in Figure 12.3. This is a PERSON relation with the attributes NAME, ENO, INCOME, ADDRESS, CITY, STATE, ZIP, SEX, and LAST_DEGREE.

A **population** is a set of tuples of a relation (table) that satisfy some selection condition. Hence each selection condition on the PERSON relation will specify a particular population of PERSON tuples. For example, the condition SEX = 'M' specifies the male population; the condition ((SEX = 'M') AND (LAST_DEGREE = 'M.S.' OR LAST_DEGREE = 'PH.D.')) specifies the female population that has an M.S. or PH.D. degree as their highest degree; and the condition CITY = 'Hyderabad' specifies the population that lives in Hyderabad.

---

4. See Thuraisingham et al. (2001).

PERSON

NAME	ENO	INCOME	ADDRESS	CITY	STATE	ZIP	SEX	LAST_DEGREE

FIGURE 12.3 The PERSON relation schema for illustrating statistical database security.

Statistical queries involve applying statistical functions to a population of tuples. For example, we may want to retrieve the number of individuals in a population or the average income in the population. However, statistical users are not allowed to retrieve individual data, such as the income of a specific person. **Statistical database security** techniques must prohibit the retrieval of individual data. This can be achieved by prohibiting queries that retrieve attribute values and by allowing only queries that involve statistical aggregate functions such as COUNT, SUM, MIN, MAX, AVERAGE, and STANDARD DEVIATION. Such queries are sometimes called **statistical queries.**

It is the responsibility of a database management system to ensure the confidentiality of information about individuals, while still providing useful statistical summaries of data about those individuals to users. Provision of **privacy protection** of users in a statistical database is paramount; its violation is illustrated in the following example.

In some cases it is possible to **infer** the values of individual tuples from a sequence of statistical queries. This is particularly true when the conditions result in a population consisting of a small number of tuples. As an illustration, consider the following two statistical queries:

Q1: **SELECT COUNT** (*) **FROM** PERSON
WHERE <CONDITION>;

Q2: **SELECT AVG** (INCOME) **FROM** PERSON
WHERE <CONDITION>;

Now suppose that we are interested in finding the SALARY of 'Mahesh Kumar', and we know that he has a PH.D. degree and that he lives in the city of Hyderabad, AP. We issue the statistical query Q1 with the following condition:

(LAST_DEGREE='PH.D.' AND SEX='M' AND CITY='HYDERABAD' AND
STATE='AP')

If we get a result of 1 for this query, we can issue Q2 with the same condition and find the income of Mahesh Kumar. Even if the result of Q1 on the preceding condition is not 1 but is a small number—say, 2 or 3—we can issue statistical queries using the functions MAX, MIN, and AVERAGE to identify the possible range of values for the INCOME of MAHESH KUMAR.

The possibility of inferring individual information from statistical queries is reduced if no statistical queries are permitted whenever the number of tuples in the population specified by the selection condition falls below some threshold. Another technique for prohibiting retrieval of individual information is to prohibit sequences of queries that refer repeatedly to the same population of tuples. It is also possible to introduce slight inaccuracies or "noise" into the results of statistical queries deliberately, to make it difficult to deduce individual information from the results. Another technique is partitioning of the database. Partitioning implies that records are stored in groups of some minimum size; queries can refer to any complete group or set of groups, but never to subsets of records within a group. The interested reader is referred to the bibliography for a discussion of these techniques.

12.5 INTRODUCTION TO FLOW CONTROL

Flow control regulates the distribution or flow of information among accessible objects. A flow between object X and object Y occurs when a program reads values from X and writes values into Y. **Flow controls** check that information contained in some objects does not flow explicitly or implicitly into less protected objects. Thus, a user cannot get indirectly in Y what he or she cannot get directly from X. Active flow control began in the early 1970s. Most flow controls employ some concept of security class; the transfer of information from a sender to a receiver is allowed only if the receiver's security class is at least as privileged as the sender's. Examples of a flow control include preventing a service program from leaking a customer's confidential data, and blocking the transmission of secret military data to an unknown classified user.

A **flow policy** specifies the channels along which information is allowed to move. The simplest flow policy specifies just two classes of information: confidential (C) and nonconfidential (N), and allows all flows except those from class C to class N. This policy can solve the confinement problem that arises when a service program handles data such as customer information, some of which may be confidential. For example, an income-tax computing service might be allowed to retain the customer's address and the bill for services rendered, but not the customer's income or deductions.

Access control mechanisms are responsible for checking users' authorizations for resource access: Only granted operations are executed. Flow controls can be enforced by an extended access control mechanism, which involves assigning a security class (usually called the *clearance*) to each running program. The program is allowed to read a particular memory segment only if its security class is as high as that of the segment. It is allowed to write in a segment only if its class is as low as that of the segment. This automatically ensures that no information transmitted by the person can move from a higher to a lower class. For example, a military program with a secret clearance can read only from objects that are unclassified and confidential and it can only write into objects that are secret or top secret.

Two types of flow can be distinguished: *explicit flows*, occurring as a consequence of assignment instructions, such as $Y := f(X_1, X_n)$; and *implicit flows* generated by conditional instructions, such as if $f(X_{m+1}, \ldots, X_n)$ then $y := f(X_1, X_m)$.

Flow control mechanisms must verify that only authorized flows, both explicit and implicit, are executed. A set of rules must be satisfied to ensure secure information flows. Rules can be expressed using flow relations among classes and assigned to information, stating the authorized flows within a system. (An information flow from A to B occurs when information associated with A affects the value of information associated with B. The flow results from operations that cause information transfer from one object to another.) These relations can define, for a class, the set of classes where information (classified in that class) can flow, or can state the specific relations to be verified between two classes to allow information flow from one to the other. In general, flow control mechanisms implement the controls by assigning a label to each object and by specifying the security class of the object. Labels are then used to verify the flow relations defined in the model.

12.5.1 Covert Channels

A covert channel allows a transfer of information that violates the security or the policy. Specifically, a **covert channel** allows information to pass from a higher classification level to a lower classification level through improper means. Covert channels can be classified into two broad categories: storage and timing channels. The distinguishing feature between the two is that in a **timing channel** the information is conveyed by the timing of events or processes, whereas **storage channels** do not require any temporal synchronization, in that information is conveyed by accessing system information or what is otherwise inaccessible to the user.

In a simple example of a covert channel, consider a distributed database system in which two nodes have user security levels of secret (S) and unclassified (U). In order for a transaction to commit, both nodes must agree to commit. They mutually can only do operations that are consistent with the *-property, which states that in any transaction, the S site cannot write or pass information to the U site. However, if these two sites collude to set up a covert channel between them, a transaction involving secret data may be committed unconditionally by the U site, but the S site may do so in some predefined agreed-upon way so that certain information may be passed on from the S site to the U site, violating the *-property. This may be achieved where the transaction runs repeatedly, but the actions taken by the S site implicitly convey information to the U site. Measures such as locking that we discussed in Chapter 11 prevent concurrent writing of the information by users with different security levels into the same objects, preventing the storage-type covert channels. Operating systems and distributed databases provide control over the multiprogramming of operations that allow a sharing of resources without the possibility of encroachment of one program or process into another's memory or other resources in the system, thus preventing timing-oriented covert channels. In general, covert channels are not a major problem in well-implemented robust database implementations. However, certain schemes may be contrived by clever users that implicitly transfer information.

Some security experts believe that one way to avoid covert channels is for programmers to not actually gain access to sensitive data that a program is supposed to process after the program has been put into operation. For example, a programmer for a bank has no need to access the names or balances in depositors' accounts. Programmers for brokerage firms do not need to know what buy and sell orders exist for clients. During program testing, access to a form of real data or some sample test data may be justifiable, but not after the program has been accepted for regular use.

12.6 ENCRYPTION AND PUBLIC KEY INFRASTRUCTURES

The previous methods of access and flow control, despite being strong countermeasures, may not be able to protect databases from some threats. Suppose we communicate data, but our data falls into the hands of some nonlegitimate user. In this situation, by using encryption we can disguise the message so that even if the transmission is diverted, the message will not be revealed. Encryption is a means of maintaining secure data in an insecure environment. Encryption consists of applying an **encryption algorithm** to data using some prespecified **encryption key**. The resulting data has to be **decrypted** using a **decryption key** to recover the original data.

12.6.1 The Data and Advanced Encryption Standards

The Data Encryption Standard (DES) is a system developed by the U.S. government for use by the general public. It has been widely accepted as a cryptographic standard both in the United States and abroad. DES can provide end-to-end encryption on the channel between the sender A and receiver B. The DES algorithm is a careful and complex combination of two of the fundamental building blocks of encryption: substitution and permutation (transposition). The algorithm derives its strength from repeated application of these two techniques for a total of 16 cycles. Plaintext (the original form of the message) is encrypted as blocks of 64 bits. Although the key is 64 bits long, in effect the key can be any 56-bit number. After questioning the adequacy of DES, the National Institute of Standards (NIST) introduced the Advanced Encryption Standards (AES). This algorithm has a block size of 128 bits, compared with DES's 56-block size, and can use keys of 128, 192, or 256 bits, compared with DES's 56-bit key. AES introduces more possible keys, compared with DES, and thus takes a much longer time to crack.

12.6.2   Public Key Encryption

In 1976 Diffie and Hellman proposed a new kind of cryptosystem, which they called **public key encryption**. Public key algorithms are based on mathematical functions rather than operations on bit patterns. They also involve the use of two separate keys, in contrast to conventional encryption, which uses only one key. The use of two keys can have profound consequences in the areas of confidentiality, key distribution, and authentication. The two keys used for public key encryption are referred to as the **public key** and the **private key**. Invariably, the private key is kept secret, but it is referred to as a private key rather than a *secret key* (the key used in conventional encryption) to avoid confusion with conventional encryption.

A public key encryption scheme, or infrastructure, has six ingredients:

1. *Plaintext*: This is the data or readable message that is fed into the algorithm as input.
2. *Encryption algorithm*: The encryption algorithm performs various transformations on the plaintext.
3. and 4. *Public and private keys*: These are a pair of keys that have been selected so that if one is used for encryption, the other is used for decryption. The exact transformations performed by the encryption algorithm depend on the public or private key that is provided as input.
5. *Ciphertext*: This is the scrambled message produced as output. It depends on the plaintext and the key. For a given message, two different keys will produce two different ciphertexts.
6. *Decryption algorithm*: This algorithm accepts the ciphertext and the matching key and produces the original plaintext.

As the name suggests, the public key of the pair is made public for others to use, whereas the private key is known only to its owner. A general-purpose public key cryptographic algorithm relies on one key for encryption and a different but related one for decryption. The essential steps are as follows:

1. Each user generates a pair of keys to be used for the encryption and decryption of messages.
2. Each user places one of the two keys in a public register or other accessible file. This is the public key. The companion key is kept private.
3. If a sender wishes to send a private message to a receiver, the sender encrypts the message using the receiver's public key.
4. When the receiver receives the message, he or she decrypts it using the receiver's private key. No other recipient can decrypt the message because only the receiver knows his or her private key.

The RSA Public Key Encryption Algorithm.   One of the first public key schemes was introduced in 1978 by Ron Rivest, Adi Shamir, and Len Adleman at MIT and is named after them as the RSA scheme. The RSA scheme has since then reigned supreme as the most widely accepted and implemented approach to public key encryption. The RSA encryption algorithm incorporates results from number theory, combined with the difficulty of determining the prime factors of a target. The RSA algorithm also operates with modular arithmetic—mod n.

Two keys, d and e, are used for decryption and encryption. An important property is that they can be interchanged. n is chosen as a large integer that is a product of two large distinct prime numbers, a and b. The encryption key e is a randomly chosen number between 1 and n that is relatively prime to $(a-1) \times (b-1)$. The plaintext block P is encrypted as P^e mod n. Because the exponentiation is performed mod n, factoring P^e to uncover the encrypted plaintext is difficult. However, the decrypting key d is carefully chosen so that $(P^e)^d$ mod $n = P$. The decryption key d can be computed from the condition that $d \times e = 1 \ mod \ ((a-1) \times (b-1))$. Thus, the legitimate receiver who knows d simply computes $(P^e)^d \ mod \ n = P$ and recovers P without having to factor P^e.

12.6.3 Digital Signatures

A digital signature is an example of using encryption techniques to provide authentication services in electronic commerce applications. Like a handwritten signature, a **digital signature** is a means of associating a mark unique to an individual with a body of text. The mark should be unforgettable, meaning that others should be able to check that the signature does come from the originator.

A digital signature consists of a string of symbols. If a person's digital signature were always the same for each message, then one could easily counterfeit it by simply copying the string of symbols. Thus, signatures must be different for each use. This can be achieved by making each digital signature a function of the message that it is signing, together with a time stamp. To be unique to each signer and counterfeitproof, each digital signature must also depend on some secret number that is unique to the signer. Thus, in general, a counterfeitproof digital signature must depend on the message and a unique secret number of the signer. The verifier of the signature, however, should not need to know any secret number. Public key techniques are the best means of creating digital signatures with these properties.

12.7 SUMMARY

This chapter discussed several techniques for enforcing security in database systems. It presented the different threats to databases in terms of loss of integrity, availability, and confidentiality. The four types of countermeasures to deal with these problems are access control, inference control, flow control, and encryption. We discussed all of these measures in this chapter.

Security enforcement deals with controlling access to the database system as a whole and controlling authorization to access specific portions of a database. The former is usually done by assigning accounts with passwords to users. The latter can be accomplished by using a system of granting and revoking privileges to individual accounts for accessing specific parts of the database. This approach is generally referred to as discretionary access control. We presented some SQL commands for granting and revoking privileges, and we illustrated their use with examples. Then we gave an overview of mandatory access control mechanisms that enforce multilevel security. These require the classifications of users and data values into security classes and enforce the rules that prohibit flow of information from higher to lower security levels. Some of the key concepts underlying the multilevel relational model, including filtering and polyinstantiation, were presented. Role-based access control was introduced, which assigns privileges based on roles that users play. We briefly discussed the problem of controlling access to statistical databases to protect the privacy of individual information while concurrently providing statistical access to populations of records. The issues related to flow control and the problems associated with covert channels were discussed next. Finally, we covered the area of encryption of data, including the public key infrastructure and digital signatures.

Review Questions

12.1. Discuss what is meant by each of the following terms: *database authorization, access control, data encryption, privileged (system) account, database audit, audit trail.*

   a. Discuss the types of privileges at the account level and those at the relation level.

12.2. Which account is designated as the owner of a relation? What privileges does the owner of a relation have?

12.3. How is the view mechanism used as an authorization mechanism?

12.4. What is meant by granting a privilege?

12.5. What is meant by revoking a privilege?

12.6. Discuss the system of propagation of privileges and the restraints imposed by horizontal and vertical propagation limits.

12.7. List the types of privileges available in SQL.

12.8. What is the difference between *discretionary* and *mandatory* access control?

12.9. What are the typical security classifications? Discuss the simple security property and the *-property, and explain the justification behind these rules for enforcing multilevel security.

12.10. Describe the multilevel relational data model. Define the following terms: *apparent key, polyinstantiation, filtering.*

12.11. What are the relative merits of using DAC or MAC?

12.12. What is role-based access control? In what ways is it superior to DAC and MAC?

12.13. What is a statistical database? Discuss the problem of statistical database security.

12.14. How is privacy related to statistical database security? What meaures can be taken to ensure some degree of privacy in statistical databases?

12.15. What is flow control as a security measure? What types of flow control exist?

12.16. What are covert channels? Give an example of a covert channel.

12.17. What is the goal of encryption? What process is involved in encrypting data and then recovering it at the other end?

12.18. Give an example of an encryption algorithm and explain how it works.

12.19. Repeat the previous question for the popular RSA algorithm.

12.20. What is the public key infrastructure scheme? How does it provide security?

12.21. What are digital signatures? How do they work?

Exercises

12.22. Consider the relational database schema of Figure 4.5. Suppose that all the relations were created by (and hence are owned by) user X, who wants to grant the following privileges to user accounts A, B, C, D, and E:

   a. Account A can retrieve or modify any relation except dependent and can grant any of these privileges to other users.

   b. Account B can retrieve all the attributes of employee and department except for salary, mgreno, and mgrstartdate.

   c. Account C can retrieve or modify WORKS_ON but can only retrieve the FNAME, INITIAL, LNAME, and ENO attributes of EMPLOYEE and the PNAME and PNUMBER attributes of PROJECT.

   d. Account D can retrieve any attribute of EMPLOYEE or dependent and can modify DEPENDENT.

   e. Account E can retrieve any attribute of EMPLOYEE but only for EMPLOYEE tuples that have DNO=3.

   f. Write SQL statements to grant these privileges. Use views where appropriate.

12.23. Suppose that privilege (a) of Exercise 12.1 is to be given with GRANT OPTION but only so that account A can grant it to at most five accounts, and each of these accounts can propagate the privilege to other accounts but *without* the GRANT OPTION privilege. What would the horizontal and vertical propagation limits be in this case?

12.24. Consider the relation shown in Figure 12.2d. How would it appear to a user with classification U? Suppose a classification U user tries to update the salary of 'Kumar' to Rs. 50,000; what would be the result of this action?

Selected Bibliography

Authorization based on granting and revoking privileges was proposed for the SYSTEM R experimental DBMS and is presented in Griffiths and Wade (1976). Several books discuss security in databases and computer systems in general, including the books by Leiss (1982a) and Fernandez et al. (1981). Denning and Denning (1979) is a tutorial paper on data security.

Many papers discuss different techniques for the design and protection of statistical databases. These include McLeish (1989), Chin and Ozsoyoglu (1981), Leiss (1982), Wong (1984), and Denning (1980). Ghosh (1984) discusses the use of statistical databases for quality control. There are also many papers discussing cryptography and data encryption, including Diffie and Hellman (1979), Rivest et al. (1978), Akl (1983), Pfleeger (1997), Omura et al. (1990), and Stalling (2000).

Multilevel security is discussed in Jajodia and Sandhu (1991), Denning et al. (1987), Smith and Winslett (1992), Stachour and Thuraisingham (1990), Lunt et al. (1990), and Bertino et al. (2001). Overviews of research issues in database security are given by Lunt and Fernandez (1990), Jajodia and Sandhu (1991), Bertino et al. (1998), Castano et al. (1995), and Thuraisingham et al. (2001). The effects of multilevel security on concurrency control are discussed in Atluri et al. (1997). Security in next-generation, semantic, and object-oriented databases is discussed in Rabbiti et al. (1991), Jajodia and Kogan (1990), and Smith (1990). Oh (1999) presents a model for both discretionary and mandatory security. Security models for Web-based applications and role-based access control are discussed in Joshi et al. (2001). Security issues for managers in the context of e-commerce applications and the need for risk assessment models for selection of appropriate security countermeasures are discussed in Farahmand et al. (2002).

13

Enhanced Data Models for Advanced Applications

As the use of database systems has grown, users have demanded additional functionality from these software packages, with the purpose of making it easier to implement more advanced and complex user applications. Object-oriented databases and object-relational systems do provide features that allow users to extend their systems by specifying additional abstract data types for each application. However, it is quite useful to identify certain common features for some of these advanced applications and to create models that can represent these common features. In addition, specialized storage structures and indexing methods can be implemented to improve the performance of these common features. These features can then be implemented as abstract data type or class libraries and separately purchased with the basic DBMS software package. The term **datablade** has been used in Informix and **cartridge** in Oracle to refer to such optional submodules that can be included in a DBMS package. Users can utilize these features directly if they are suitable for their applications, without having to reinvent, reimplement, and reprogram such common features.

This chapter introduces database concepts for some of the common features that are needed by advanced applications and that are starting to have widespread use. The features we will cover are *active rules* that are used in active database applications, *temporal concepts* that are used in temporal database applications, and briefly some of the issues involving *multimedia databases*. We will also discuss *deductive databases*. It is important to note that each of these topics is very broad, and we can give only a brief introduction to each area. In fact, each of these areas can serve as the sole topic for a complete book.

Before discussing these topics, we first describe concepts for object databases, object database standards, languages and design and object relational and extended relational systems briefly in Sections 13.1, 13.2 and 13.3 respectively.

In Section 13.4, we will introduce the topic of active databases, which provide additional functionality for specifying **active rules.** These rules can be automatically triggered by events that occur, such as a database update or a certain time being reached, and can initiate certain actions that have been specified in the rule declaration if certain conditions are met. Many commercial packages already have some of the functionality provided by active databases in the form of **triggers.** Triggers are now part of the SQL-99 standard.

In Section 13.5, we will introduce the concepts of **temporal databases,** which permit the database system to store a history of changes, and allow users to query both current and past states of the database. Some temporal database models also allow users to store future expected information, such as planned schedules. It is important to note that many database applications are already temporal, but are often implemented without having much temporal support from the DBMS package—that is, the temporal concepts were implemented in the application programs that access the database.

Section 13.6 will give a brief overview of spatial and multimedia databases. **Spatial databases** provide concepts for databases that keep track of objects in a multidimensional space. For example, cartographic databases that store maps include two-dimensional spatial positions of their objects, which include countries, states, rivers, cities, roads, seas, and so on. Other databases, such as meteorological databases for weather information, are three-dimensional, since temperatures and other meteorological information are related to three-dimensional spatial points. **Multimedia databases** provide features that allow users to store and query different types of multimedia information, which includes **images** (such as pictures or drawings), **video clips** (such as movies, news reels, or home videos), **audio clips** (such as songs, phone messages, or speeches), and **documents** (such as books or articles).

In Section 13.7, we discuss briefly about deductive databases, an area that is at the intersection of databases, logic, and artificial intelligence or knowledge bases. A **deductive database system** is a database system that includes capabilities to define **(deductive) rules,** which can deduce or infer additional information from the facts that are stored in a database. Because part of the theoretical foundation for some deductive database systems is mathematical logic, such rules are often referred to as **logic databases.** Other types of systems, referred to as **expert database systems** or **knowledge-based systems,** also incorporate reasoning and inferencing capabilities; such systems use techniques that were developed in the field of artificial intelligence, including semantic networks, frames, production systems, or rules for capturing domain-specific knowledge.

Readers may choose to peruse the particular topics they are interested in, as the sections in this chapter are practically independent of one another.

13.1 CONCEPTS FOR OBJECT DATABASES

In this section and the next, we discuss object-oriented data models and database systems.[1] Traditional data models and systems, such as relational, network, and hierarchical, have been quite successful in developing the database technology required for many traditional business database applications. However, they have certain shortcomings when more complex database applications must be designed and implemented—for example, databases for engineering design and manufacturing (CAD/CAM and CIM[2]), scientific experiments, telecommunications, geographic information systems, and multimedia.[3] These newer applications have

---

1. These databases are often referred to as **Object Databases** and the systems are referred to as **Object Database Management Systems (ODBMS).** However, because this chapter discusses many general object-oriented concepts, we will use the term *object-oriented* instead of just *object*.

2. Computer-Aided Design/Computer-Aided Manufacturing and Computer-Integrated Manufacturing.

3. Multimedia databases must store various types of multimedia objects, such as video, audio, images, graphics, and documents (see section 13.6).

requirements and characteristics that differ from those of traditional business applications, such as more complex structures for objects, longer-duration transactions, new data types for storing images or large textual items, and the need to define nonstandard application-specific operations. Object-oriented databases were proposed to meet the needs of these more complex applications. The object-oriented approach offers the flexibility to handle some of these requirements without being limited by the data types and query languages available in traditional database systems. A key feature of object-oriented databases is the power they give the designer to specify both the *structure* of complex objects and the *operations* that can be applied to these objects.

Another reason for the creation of object-oriented databases is the increasing use of object-oriented programming languages in developing software applications. Databases are now becoming fundamental components in many software systems, and traditional databases were difficult to use with object-oriented software applications that are developed in an object-oriented programming language such as C++, SMALLTALK, or JAVA. Object-oriented databases are designed so they can be directly—or *seamlessly*— integrated with software that is developed using object-oriented programming languages.

The need for additional data modeling features has also been recognized by relational DBMS vendors, and newer versions of relational systems are incorporating many of the features that were proposed for object-oriented databases. This has led to systems that are characterized as *object-relational* or *extended relational* DBMSs (see section 13.3). The latest version of the SQL standard for relational DBMSs includes some of these features.

The experimental prototypes included the ORION system developed at MCC,[4] OPENOODB at Texas Instruments, the IRIS system at Hewlett-Packard laboratories, the ODE system at AT&T Bell Labs,[5] and the ENCORE/ObServer project at Brown University. Commercially available systems included GEMSTONE/ OPAL of GemStone Systems, ONTOS of Ontos, Objectivity of Objectivity Inc., Versant of Versant Object Technology, ObjectStore of Object Design, ARDENT of ARDENT Software,[6] and POET of POET Software. These represent only a partial list of the experimental prototypes and commercial object-oriented database systems that were created.

As commercial object-oriented DBMSs became available, the need for a standard model and language was recognized. Because the formal procedure for approval of standards normally takes a number of years, a consortium of object-oriented DBMS vendors and users, called ODMG,[7] proposed a standard that is known as the ODMG-93 standard, which has since been revised. We will describe some features of the ODMG standard in section 13.2.

Object-oriented databases have adopted many of the concepts that were developed originally for object-oriented programming languages.[8] In Section 13.1.1, we examine the origins of the object-oriented approach and discuss how it applies to database systems. Then, in Sections 13.1.2 through 13.1.6, we describe the key concepts utilized in many object-oriented database systems. Section 13.1.2 discusses *object identity*, *object structure*, and *type constructors*. Section 13.1.3 presents the concepts of *encapsulation of operations* and definition of *methods* as part of class declarations, and also discusses the mechanisms for storing objects in a database by making them persistent. Section 13.1.4 describes *type and class hierarchies* and *inheritance* in object-oriented databases, and Section 13.1.5 provides an overview of the issues that arise when *complex objects* need to be represented and stored. Section 13.1.6 discusses additional concepts, including *polymorphism, operator overloading, dynamic binding, multiple and selective inheritance*, and *versioning* and *configuration* of objects. Section 13.1.7 provides summary of this section.

---

4. Microelectronics and Computer Technology Corporation, Austin, Texas.

5. Now called Lucent Technologies.

6. Formerly O2 of O2 Technology.

7. Object Database Management Group.

8. Similar concepts were also developed in the fields of semantic data modeling and knowledge representation.

13.1.1 Overview of Object-Oriented Concepts

This section gives a quick overview of the history and main concepts of object-oriented databases, or OODBs for short. The OODB concepts are then explained in more detail in Sections 13.1.2 through 13.1.6. The term *object-oriented*—abbreviated by OO or O-O—has its origins in OO programming languages, or OOPLs. Today OO concepts are applied in the areas of databases, software engineering, knowledge bases, artificial intelligence, and computer systems in general. OOPLs have their roots in the SIMULA language, which was pro-posed in the late 1960s. In SIMULA, the concept of a *class* groups together the internal data structure of an object in a class declaration. Subsequently, researchers proposed the concept of *abstract data type*, which hides the internal data structures and specifies all possible external operations that can be applied to an object, leading to the concept of *encapsulation*. The programming language SMALLTALK, developed at Xerox PARC[9] in the 1970s, was one of the first languages to explicitly incorporate additional OO concepts, such as message passing and inheritance. It is known as a *pure* OO programming language, meaning that it was explicitly designed to be object-oriented. This contrasts with *hybrid* OO programming languages, which incorporate OO concepts into an already existing language. An example of the latter is C++, which incorporates OO concepts into the popular C programming language.

An **object** typically has two components: state (value) and behavior (operations). Hence, it is somewhat similar to a *program variable* in a programming language, except that it will typically have a *complex data structure* as well as *specific operations* defined by the programmer.[10] Objects in an OOPL exist only during program execution and are hence called *transient objects*. An OO database can extend the existence of objects so that they are stored permanently, and hence the objects persist beyond program termination and can be retrieved later and shared by other programs. In other words, OO databases store *persistent objects* permanently on secondary storage, and allow the sharing of these objects among multiple programs and applications. This requires the incorporation of other well-known features of database management systems, such as indexing mechanisms, concurrency control, and recovery. An OO database system interfaces with one or more OO programming languages to provide persistent and shared object capabilities.

One goal of OO databases is to maintain a direct correspondence between real-world and database objects so that objects do not lose their integrity and identity and can easily be identified and operated upon. Hence, OO databases provide a unique system-generated *object identifier* (OID) for each object. We can compare this with the relational model where each relation must have a primary key attribute whose value identifies each tuple uniquely. In the relational model, if the value of the primary key is changed, the tuple will have a new identity, even though it may still represent the same real-world object. Alternatively, a real-world object may have different names for key attributes in different relations, making it difficult to ascertain that the keys represent the same object (for example, the object identifier may be represented as EMP_ID in one relation and as ENO in another).

Another feature of OO databases is that objects may have an *object structure* of *arbitrary complexity* in order to contain all of the necessary information that describes the object. In contrast, in traditional database systems, information about a complex object is often *scattered* over many relations or records, leading to loss of direct correspondence between a real-world object and its database representation.

The internal structure of an object in OOPLs includes the specification of **instance variables**, which hold the values that define the internal state of the object. Hence, an instance variable is similar to the concept of an *attribute* in the relational model, except that instance variables may be encapsulated within the object and thus are not necessarily visible to external users. Instance variables may also be of arbitrarily complex data types. Object-oriented systems allow definition of the operations or functions (behavior) that can be

---

9. Palo Alto Research Center, Palo Alto, California.

10. Objects have many other characteristics, as we discuss in the rest of this section.

applied to objects of a particular type. In fact, some OO models insist that all operations a user can apply to an object must be predefined. This forces a *complete encapsulation* of objects. This rigid approach has been relaxed in most OO data models for several reasons. First, the database user often needs to know the attribute names so they can specify selection conditions on the attributes to retrieve specific objects. Second, complete encapsulation implies that any simple retrieval requires a predefined operation, thus making ad hoc queries difficult to specify on the fly.

To encourage encapsulation, an operation is defined in two parts. The first part, called the *signature* or *interface* of the operation, specifies the operation name and arguments (or parameters). The second part, called the *method* or *body*, specifies the *implementation* of the operation. Operations can be invoked by passing a *message* to an object, which includes the operation name and the parameters. The object then executes the method for that operation. This encapsulation permits modification of the internal structure of an object, as well as the implementation of its operations, without the need to disturb the external programs that invoke these operations. Hence, encapsulation provides a form of data and operation independence.

Another key concept in OO systems is that of type and class hierarchies and *inheritance*. This permits specification of new types or classes that inherit much of their structure and/or operations from previously defined types or classes. Hence, specification of object types can proceed systematically. This makes it easier to develop the data types of a system incrementally, and to *reuse* existing type definitions when creating new types of objects.

One problem in early OO database systems involved representing *relationships* among objects. The insistence on complete encapsulation in early OO data models led to the argument that relationships should not be explicitly represented, but should instead be described by defining appropriate methods that locate related objects. However, this approach does not work very well for complex databases with many relationships, because it is useful to identify these relationships and make them visible to users. The ODMG standard has recognized this need and it explicitly represents binary relationships via a pair of *inverse references*—that is, by placing the OIDs of related objects within the objects themselves, and maintaining referential integrity, as we shall describe in section 13.2.

Some OO systems provide capabilities for dealing with *multiple versions* of the same object—a feature that is essential in design and engineering applications. For example, an old version of an object that represents a tested and verified design should be retained until the new version is tested and verified. A new version of a complex object may include only a few new versions of its component objects, whereas other components remain unchanged. In addition to permitting versioning, OO databases should also allow for *schema evolution*, which occurs when type declarations are changed or when new types or relationships are created. These two features are not specific to OODBs and should ideally be included in all types of DBMSs.[11]

Another OO concept is *operator overloading*, which refers to an operation's ability to be applied to different types of objects; in such a situation, an *operation name* may refer to several distinct *implementations*, depending on the type of objects it is applied to. This feature is also called *operator polymorphism*. For example, an operation to calculate the area of a geometric object may differ in its method (implementation), depending on whether the object is of type triangle, circle, or rectangle. This may require the use of *late binding* of the operation name to the appropriate method at run-time, when the type of object to which the operation is applied becomes known.

This section provided an overview of the main concepts of OO databases. In Sections 13.1.2 through 13.1.6, we discuss these concepts in more detail.

---

11. Several schema evolution operations, such as ALTER TABLE, are already defined in the relational SQL standard (see section 7.3).

13.1.2 Object Identity, Object Structure, and Type Constructors

In this section we first discuss the concept of object identity, and then we present the typical structuring operations for defining the structure of the state of an object. These structuring operations are often called **type constructors**. They define basic data-structuring operations that can be combined to form complex object structures.

13.1.2.1 Object identity An OO database system provides a **unique identity** to each independent object stored in the database. This unique identity is typically implemented via a unique, system-generated **object identifier**, or **OID**. The value of an OID is not visible to the external user, but it is used internally by the system to identify each object uniquely and to create and manage inter-object references. The OID can be assigned to program variables of the appropriate type when needed.

The main property required of an OID is that it be **immutable**; that is, the OID value of a particular object should not change. This preserves the identity of the real-world object being represented. Hence, an OO database system must have some mechanism for generating OIDs and preserving the immutability property. It is also desirable that each OID be used only once; that is, even if an object is removed from the database, its OID should not be assigned to another object. These two properties imply that the OID should not depend on any attribute values of the object, since the value of an attribute may be changed or corrected. It is also generally considered inappropriate to base the OID on the physical address of the object in storage, since the physical address can change after a physical reorganization of the database. However, some systems do use the physical address as OID to increase the efficiency of object retrieval. If the physical address of the object changes, an *indirect pointer* can be placed at the former address, which gives the new physical location of the object. It is more common to use long integers as OIDs and then to use some form of hash table to map the OID value to the current physical address of the object in storage.

Some early OO data models required that everything—from a simple value to a complex object—be represented as an object; hence, every basic value, such as an integer, string, or Boolean value, has an OID. This allows two basic values to have different OIDs, which can be useful in some cases. For example, the integer value 50 can be used sometimes to mean a weight in kilograms and at other times to mean the age of a person. Then, two basic objects with distinct OIDs could be created, but both objects would represent the integer value 50. Although useful as a theoretical model, this is not very practical, since it may lead to the generation of too many OIDs. Hence, most OO database systems allow for the representation of both objects and **values**. Every object must have an immutable OID, whereas a value has no OID and just stands for itself. Hence, a value is typically stored within an object and *cannot be referenced* from other objects. In some systems, complex structured values can also be created without having a corresponding OID if needed.

13.1.2.2 Object structure In OO databases, the state (current value) of a complex object may be constructed from other objects (or other values) by using certain **type constructors**. One formal way of representing such objects is to view each object as a triple (i, c, v), where i is a unique *object identifier* (the OID), c is a *type constructor*[12] (that is, an indication of how the object state is constructed), and v is the object state (or *current value*). The data model will typically include several type constructors. The three most basic constructors are **atom**, **tuple**, and **set**. Other commonly used constructors include **list**, **bag**, and **array**. The atom constructor is used to represent all basic atomic values, such as integers, real numbers, character strings, Booleans, and any other basic data types that the system supports directly.

---

12. This is different from the constructor operation that is used in C++ and other OOPLs to create new objects.

The object state v of an object (i, c, v) is interpreted based on the constructor c. If c = atom, the state (value) v is an atomic value from the domain of basic values supported by the system. If c = set, the state v is a set *of object identifiers* $\{i_1, i_2, \ldots, i_n\}$, which are the OIDs for a set of objects that are typically of the same type. If c = tuple, the state v is a tuple of the form $<a_1{:}i_1, a_2{:}i_2, \ldots, a_n{:}i_n>$, where each a_j is an attribute name[13] and each i_j is an OID. If c = list, the value v is an *ordered list* $[i_1, i_2, \ldots, i_n]$ of OIDs of objects of the same type. A list is similar to a set except that the OIDs in a list are *ordered*, and hence we can refer to the first, second, or j^{th} object in a list. For c = array, the state of the object is a single-dimensional array of object identifiers. The main difference between array and list is that a list can have an arbitrary number of elements whereas an array typically has a maximum size. The difference between *set* and *bag*[14] is that all elements in a set must be distinct whereas a bag can have duplicate elements.

This model of objects allows arbitrary nesting of the set, list, tuple, and other constructors. The state of an object that is not of type atom will refer to other objects by their object identifiers. Hence, the only case where an actual value appears is in *the state of an object of type atom.*[15]

The type constructors **set**, **list**, **array**, and **bag** are called **collection types** (or **bulk types**), to distinguish them from basic types and tuple types. The main characteristic of a collection type is that the state of the object will be a *collection of objects* that may be unordered (such as a set or a bag) or ordered (such as a list or an array). The **tuple** type constructor is often called a **structured type**, since it corresponds to the **struct** construct in the C and C++ programming languages.

EXAMPLE 1: A Complex Object

We now represent some objects from the relational database shown in Figure 4.6, using the preceding model, where an object is defined by a triple (OID, type constructor, state) and the available type constuctors are atom, set, and tuple. We use $i_1, i_2, i_3, \ldots$ to stand for unique system-generated object identifiers. Consider the following objects:

$o_1 = (i_1, \text{atom}, \text{'Hyderabad'})$
$o_2 = (i_2, \text{atom}, \text{'Bangalore'})$
$o_3 = (i_3, \text{atom}, \text{'New Delhi'})$
$o_4 = (i_4, \text{atom}, 5)$
$o_5 = (i_5, \text{atom}, \text{'Research'})$
$o_6 = (i_6, \text{atom}, \text{'22-05-1988'})$
$o_7 = (i_7, \text{set}, \{i_1, i_2, i_3\})$
$o_8 = (i_8, \text{tuple}, <\text{DNAME}{:}i_5, \text{DNUMBER}{:}i_4, \text{MGR}{:}i_9, \text{LOCATIONS}{:}i_7, \text{EMPLOYEES}{:}i_{10}, \text{PROJECTS}{:}i_{11}>)$
$o_9 = (i_9, \text{tuple}, <\text{MANAGER}{:}i_{12}, \text{MANAGER\_START\_DATE}{:}i_6>)$
$o_{10} = (i_{10}, \text{set}, \{i_{12}, i_{13}, i_{14}\})$
$o_{11} = (i_{11}, \text{set} \{i_{15}, i_{16}, i_{17}\})$
$o_{12} = (i_{12}, \text{tuple}, <\text{FNAME}{:}i_{18}, \text{INITIAL}{:}i_{19}, \text{LNAME}{:}i_{20}, \text{ENO}{:}i_{21}, \ldots, \text{SALARY}{:}i_{26}, \text{SUPERVISOR}{:}i_{27}, \text{DEPT}{:}i_8>)$
$\ldots$

The first six objects (o_1–o_6) listed here represent atomic values. There will be many similar objects, one for each distinct constant atomic value in the database.[16] Object o_7 is a set-valued object that represents the

---

13. Also called an *instance variable name* in OO terminology.

14. Also called a *multiset.*

15. As we noted earlier, it is not practical to generate a unique system identifier for every value, so real systems allow for both OIDs and *structured value*, which can be structured by using the same type constructors as objects, except that a value *does not have* an OID.

16. These atomic objects are the ones that may cause a problem, due to the use of too many object identifiers, if this model is implemented directly.

set of locations for department 5; the set $\{i_1, i_2, i_3\}$ refers to the atomic objects with values {'Hyderabad', 'Bangalore', 'New Delhi'}. Object o_8 is a tuple-valued object that represents department 5 itself, and has the attributes DNAME, DNUMBER, MGR, LOCATIONS, and so on. The first two attributes DNAME and DNUMBER have atomic objects o_5 and o_4 as their values. The MGR attribute has a tuple object o_9 as its value, which in turn has two attributes. The value of the MANAGER attribute is the object whose OID is i_{12}, which represents the employee 'Mahesh B. Kumar' who manages the department, whereas the value of MANAGER_START_DATE is another atomic object whose value is a date. The value of the EMPLOYEES attribute of o_8 is a set object with OID $= i_{10}$, whose value is the set of object identifiers for the employees who work for the DEPARTMENT (objects i_{12}, plus i_{13} and i_{14}, which are not shown). Similarly, the value of the PROJECTS attribute of o_8 is a set object with OID $= i_{11}$, whose value is the set of object identifiers for the projects that are controlled by department number 5 (objects i_{15}, i_{16}, and i_{17}, which are not shown). The object whose OID $= i_{12}$ represents the employee 'Mahesh B. Kumar' with all its atomic attributes (FNAME, INITIAL, LNAME, ENO, . . ., SALARY, that are referencing the atomic objects i_{18}, i_{19}, i_{20}, i_{21}, . . ., i_{26}, respectively (not shown)) plus SUPERVISOR which references the employee object with OID $= i_{27}$ (this represents 'Gaurav E. Kishan' who supervises 'Mahesh B. Kumar' but is not shown) and DEPT which references the department object with OID $= i_8$ (this represents department number 5 where 'Mahesh B. Kumar' works).

In this model, an object can be represented as a graph structure that can be constructed by recursively applying the type constructors. The graph representing an object o_i can be constructed by first creating a node for the object o_i itself. The node for o_i is labeled with the OID and the object constructor c. We also create a node in the graph for each basic atomic value. If an object o_i has an atomic value, we draw a directed arc from the node representing o_i to the node representing its basic value. If the object value is constructed, we draw directed arcs from the object node to a node that represents the constructed value. Figure 13.1 shows the graph for the example DEPARTMENT object o_8 given earlier.

The preceding model permits two types of definitions in a comparison of the *states of two objects* for equality. Two objects are said to have **identical states** (deep equality) if the graphs representing their states are identical in every respect, including the OIDs at every level. Another, weaker definition of equality is when two objects have **equal states** (shallow equality). In this case, the graph structures must be the same, and all the corresponding atomic values in the graphs should also be the same. However, some corresponding internal nodes in the two graphs may have objects with *different OIDs*.

EXAMPLE 2: Identical Versus Equal Objects

A example can illustrate the difference between the two definitions for comparing object states for equality. Consider the following objects o_1, o_2, o_3, o_4, o_5, and o_6:

$o_1 = (i_1, \text{tuple}, <a_1{:}i_4, a_2{:}i_6>)$
$o_2 = (i_2, \text{tuple}, <a_1{:}i_5, a_2{:}i_6>)$
$o_3 = (i_3, \text{tuple}, <a_1{:}i_4, a_2{:}i_6>)$
$o_4 = (i_4, \text{atom}, 10)$
$o_5 = (i_5, \text{atom}, 10)$
$o_6 = (i_6, \text{atom}, 20)$

The objects o_1 and o_2 have *equal* states, since their states at the atomic level are the same but the values are reached through distinct objects o_4 and o_5. However, the states of objects o_1 and o_3 are *identical*, even though the objects themselves are not because they have distinct OIDs. Similarly, although the states of o_4 and o_5 are identical, the actual objects o_4 and o_5 are equal but not identical, because they have distinct OIDs.

13.1.2.3   Type constructors

An **object definition language (ODL)**[17] that incorporates the preceding type constructors can be used to define the object types for a particular database application. In Section 13.2, we shall describe the standard ODL of ODMG, but we first introduce the concepts gradually in this

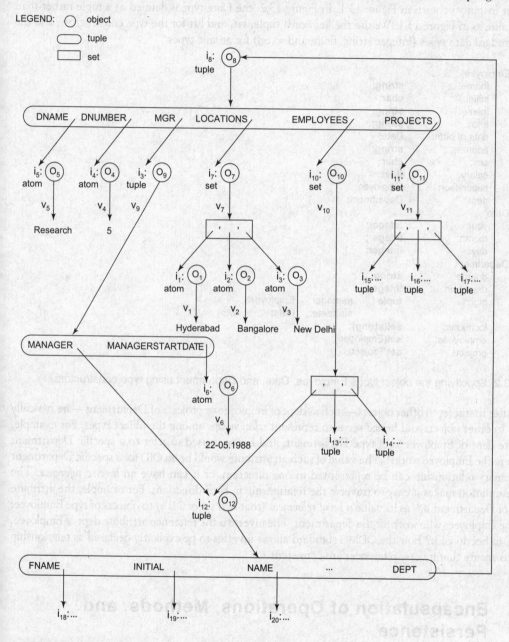

FIGURE 13.1 Representation of a DEPARTMENT complex object as a graph.

---

17. This would correspond to the DDL (Data Definition Language) of the database system (see Chapter 2).

section using a simpler notation. The type constructors can be used to define the *data structures* for an OO *database schema*. In Section 13.1.3 we will see how to incorporate the definition of operations (or methods) into the OO schema. Figure 13.2 shows how we may declare Employee and Department types corresponding to the object instances shown in Figure 13.1. In Figure 13.2, the Date type is defined as a tuple rather than an atomic value as in Figure 13.1. We use the keywords tuple, set, and list for the type constructors, and the available standard data types (integer, string, float, and so on) for atomic types.

```
define type Employee:
    tuple (      fname:          string;
                 initial:        char;
                 lname:          string;
                 eno:            string;
                 date of birth:  Date;
                 address:        string;
                 sex:            char;
                 salary:         float;
                 supervisor:     Employee;
                 dept:           Department;        );
define type Date
    tuple (      year:           integer;
                 month:          integer;
                 day:            integer;    );
define type Department
    tuple (      dname:          string;
                 dnumber:        integer;
                 mgr:            tuple (   manager:    Employee;
                                          startdate:  Date;         );
                 locations:      set(string);
                 employees:      set(Employee);
                 projects        set(Project);   );
```

FIGURE 13.2 Specifying the object types Employee, Date, and Department using type constructors.

Attributes that refer to other objects—such as dept of Employee or projects of Department—are basically **references** to other objects and hence serve to represent *relationships* among the object types. For example, the attribute dept of Employee is of type Department, and hence is used to refer to a specific Department object (where the Employee works). The value of such an attribute would be an OID for a specific Department object. A binary relationship can be represented in one direction, or it can have an *inverse reference*. The latter representation makes it easy to traverse the relationship in both directions. For example, the attribute employees of Department has as its value a *set of references* (that is, a set of OIDs) to objects of type Employee; these are the employees who work for the department. The inverse is the reference attribute dept of Employee. We will see in Section 13.2 how the ODMG standard allows inverses to be explicitly declared as relationship attributes to ensure that inverse references are consistent.

13.1.3 Encapsulation of Operations, Methods, and Persistence

The concept of *encapsulation* is one of the main characteristics of OO languages and systems. It is also related to the concepts of *abstract data types* and *information hiding* in programming languages. In traditional database models and systems, this concept was not applied, since it is customary to make the structure of database objects visible to users and external programs. In these traditional models, a number of standard database operations are applicable to objects of all types. For example, in the relational model, the operations for selecting, inserting, deleting, and modifying tuples are generic and may be applied to *any relation* in the database. The relation and its attributes are visible to users and to external programs that access the relation by using these operations.

13.1.3.1 Specifying object behavior via class operations The concepts of information hiding and encapsulation can be applied to database objects. The main idea is to define the **behavior** of a type of object based on the **operations** that can be externally applied to objects of that type. The internal structure of the object is hidden, and the object is accessible only through a number of predefined operations. Some operations may be used to create (insert) or destroy (delete) objects; other operations may update the object state; and others may be used to retrieve parts of the object state or to apply some calculations. Still other operations may perform a combination of retrieval, calculation, and update. In general, the **implementation** of an operation can be specified in a *general-purpose programming language* that provides flexibility and power in defining the operations.

The external users of the object are only made aware of the **interface** of the object type, which defines the name and arguments (parameters) of each operation. The implementation is hidden from the external users; it includes the definition of the internal data structures of the object and the implementation of the operations that access these structures. In OO terminology, the interface part of each operation is called the **signature,** and the operation implementation is called a **method.** Typically, a method is invoked by sending a **message** to the object to execute the corresponding method. Notice that, as part of executing a method, a subsequent message to another object may be sent, and this mechanism may be used to return values from the objects to the external environment or to other objects.

For database applications, the requirement that all objects be completely encapsulated is too stringent. One way of relaxing this requirement is to divide the structure of an object into **visible** and **hidden** attributes (instance variables). Visible attributes may be directly accessed for reading by external operators, or by a high-level query language. The hidden attributes of an object are completely encapsulated and can be accessed only through predefined operations. Most OODBMSs employ high-level query languages for accessing visible attributes. In Section 13.2, we will describe the OQL query language that is proposed as a standard query language for OODBs.

In most cases, operations that *update* the state of an object are encapsulated. This is a way of defining the update semantics of the objects, given that in many OO data models, few integrity constraints are predefined in the schema. Each type of object has its integrity constraints *programmed into the methods* that create, delete, and update the objects by explicitly writing code to check for constraint violations and to handle exceptions. In such cases, all update operations are implemented by encapsulated operations. More recently, the ODL for the ODMG standard allows the specification of some common constraints such as keys and inverse relationships (referential integrity) so that the system can automatically enforce these constraints (see Section 13.2).

The term **class** is often used to refer to an object type definition, along with the definitions of the operations for that type.[18] Figure 13.3 shows how the type definitions of Figure 13.2 may be extended with operations to define classes. A number of operations are declared for each class, and the signature (interface) of each operation is included in the class definition. A method (implementation) for each operation must be defined elsewhere, using a programming language. Typical operations include the **object constructor** operation, which is used to create a new object, and the **destructor** operation, which is used to destroy an

---

18. This definition of *class* is similar to how it is used in the popular C++ programming language. The ODMG standard uses the word *interface* in addition to *class* (see Section 13.2). In the EER model, the term *class* was used to refer to an object type, along with the set of all objects of that type (see Chapter 3).

object. A number of **object modifier** operations can also be declared to modify the states (values) of various attributes of an object. Additional operations can **retrieve** information about the object.

```
define class Employee:
    type tuple(   fname:              string;
                  initial:            char;
                  lname:              string;
                  eno:                string;
                  data of birth:      Date;
                  address:            string;
                  sex:                char;
                  salary:             float;
                  supervisor:         Employee;
                  dept:               Department;           );
    operations age:                   integer;
                  create_emp:         Employee;
                  destroy_emp:        boolean;
end Employee;

define class Department
    type tuple(   dname:              string;
                  dnumber:            integer;
                  mgr:                tuple (   manager: Employee;
                                               startdate: Date;          );
                  locations:          set(string);
                  employees:          set(Employee);
                  projects:           set(Project);     );
    operations no_of_emps:            integer;
                  create_dept:        Department;
                  destroy_dept:       boolean;
                  assign_emp(e: Employee): boolean;
            (* adds an employee to the department *)
                  remove_emp(e: Employee): boolean;
            (* removes an employee from the department *)
end Department;
```

FIGURE 13.3 Adding operations to the definitions of Employee and Department.

An operation is typically applied to an object by using the **dot notation.** For example, if d is a reference to a department object, we can invoke an operation such as no_of_emps by writing d.no_of_emps. Similarly, by writing d.destroy_dept, the object referenced by d is destroyed (deleted). The only exception is the constructor operation, which returns a reference to a new Department object. Hence, it is customary to have a default name for the constructor operation that is the name of the class itself, although this was not used in Figure 13.3.[19] The dot notation is also used to refer to attributes of an object—for example, by writing d.dnumber or d.mgr.startdate.

13.1.3.2 Specifying object persistence via naming and reachability
An OODBMS is often closely coupled with an OOPL. The OOPL is used to specify the method implementations as well as other application code. An object is typically created by some executing application program, by invoking the

---

19. Default names for the constructor and destructor operations exist in the C++ programming language. For example, for class Employee, the *default constructor name* is Employee and the *default destructor name* is ~Employee. It is also common to use the *new* operation to create new objects.

object constructor operation. Not all objects are meant to be stored permanently in the database. **Transient objects** exist in the executing program and disappear once the program terminates. **Persistent objects** are stored in the database and persist after program termination. The typical mechanisms for making an object persistent are *naming* and *reachability*.

The **naming mechanism** involves giving an object a unique persistent name through which it can be retrieved by this and other programs. This persistent object name can be given via a specific statement or operation in the program, as illustrated in Figure 13.4. All such names given to objects must be unique within a particular database. Hence, the named persistent objects are used as **entry points** to the database through which users and applications can start their database access. Obviously, it is not practical to give names to all objects in a large database that includes thousands of objects, so most objects are made persistent by using the second mechanism, called **reachability.** The reachability mechanism works by making the object reachable from some persistent object. An object B is said to be **reachable** from an object A if a sequence of references in the object graph lead from object A to object B. For example, all the objects in Figure 13.1 are reachable from object o_8; hence, if o_8 is made persistent, all the other objects in Figure 13.1 also become persistent.

If we first create a named persistent object N, whose state is a *set* or *list* of objects of some class C, we can make objects of C persistent by *adding them* to the set or list, and thus making them reachable from N. Hence, N defines a **persistent collection** of objects of class C. For example, we can define a class DepartmentSet (see Figure 13.4) whose objects are of type **set**(Department).[20] Suppose that an object of type DepartmentSet is created, and suppose that it is named AllDepartments and thus made persistent, as illustrated in Figure 13.4. Any Department object that is added to the set of AllDepartments by using the add_dept operation becomes

```
define class DepartmentSet:
    type        set(Department);
    operations  add_dept(d: Department): boolean;
             (* adds a department to the DepartmentSet object *)
                remove_dept(d: Department): boolean;
             (* removes a department from the DepartmentSet object *)
                create_dept_set:      DepartmentSet;
                destroy_dept_set:     boolean;
end DepartmentSet;

...

persistent name AllDepartments: DepartmentSet;
(* AllDepartments is a persistent named object of type DepartmentSet *)

...

d:= create_dept;
(* create a new Department object in the variable d *)

...

b:= AllDepartments.add_dept(d);
(* make d persistent by adding it to the persistent set AllDepartments *)

...
```

FIGURE 13.4 Creating persistent objects by naming and reachability.

---

20. As we shall see in Section 13.2, the ODMG ODL syntax uses **set**<Department> instead of **set**(Department).

persistent by virtue of its being reachable from AllDepartments. The AllDepartments object is often called the **extent** of the class Department, as it will hold all persistent objects of type Department. As we shall see in Section 13.2, the ODMG ODL standard gives the schema designer the option of naming an extent as part of class definition.

Notice the difference between traditional database models and OO databases in this respect. In traditional database models, such as the relational model or the EER model, *all* objects are assumed to be persistent. Hence, when an entity type or class such as EMPLOYEE is defined in the EER model, it represents both the *type declaration* for EMPLOYEE and a *persistent set* of *all* EMPLOYEE objects. In the OO approach, a class declaration of EMPLOYEE specifies only the type and operations for a class of objects. The user must separately define a persistent object of type set(EMPLOYEE) or list(EMPLOYEE) whose value is the *collection of references* to all persistent EMPLOYEE objects, if this is desired, as illustrated in Figure 13.4.[21] This allows transient and persistent objects to follow the same type and class declarations of the ODL and the OOPL. In general, it is possible to define several persistent collections for the same class definition, if desired.

13.1.4 Type and Class Hierarchies and Inheritance

Another main characteristic of OO database systems is that they allow type hierarchies and inheritance. Type hierarchies in databases usually imply a constraint on the extents corresponding to the types in the hierarchy. We first discuss type hierarchies (in Section 13.1.4.1), and then the constraints on the extents (in Section 13.1.4.2). We use a different OO model in this section—a model in which attributes and operations are treated uniformly—since both attributes and operations can be inherited. In Section 13.2, we will discuss the inheritance model of the ODMG standard, which differs from the model discussed here.

13.1.4.1 Type hierarchies and inheritance

In most database applications, there are numerous objects of the same type or class. Hence, OO databases must provide a capability for classifying objects based on their type, as do other database systems. But in OO databases, a further requirement is that the system permit the definition of new types based on other predefined types, leading to a **type** (or **class**) **hierarchy.**

Typically, a type is defined by assigning it a type name and then defining a number of attributes (instance variables) and operations (methods) for the type.[22] In some cases, the attributes and operations are together called *functions*, since attributes resemble functions with zero arguments. A function name can be used to refer to the value of an attribute or to refer to the resulting value of an operation (method). In this section, we use the term **function** to refer to both attributes *and* operations of an object type, since they are treated similarly in a basic introduction to inheritance.[23]

A type in its simplest form can be defined by giving it a **type name** and then listing the names of its visible (*public*) **functions.** When specifying a type in this section, we use the following format, which does not specify arguments of functions, to simplify the discussion:

TYPE_NAME: function, function, . . ., function

For example, a type that describes characteristics of a PERSON may be defined as follows:

PERSON: Name, Address, Date of Birth, Age, ENO

---

21. Some systems, such as POET, automatically create the extent for a class.

22. In this section, we will use the terms *type* and *class* as meaning the same thing—namely, the attributes *and* operations of some type of object.

23. We will see in Section 13.2 that types with functions are similar to the interfaces used in ODMG ODL.

In the PERSON type, the Name, Address, ENO, and Date of Birth functions can be implemented as stored attributes, whereas the Age function can be implemented as a method that calculates the Age from the value of the Date of Birth attribute and the current date.

The concept of **subtype** is useful when the designer or user must create a new type that is similar but not identical to an already defined type. The subtype then inherits all the functions of the predefined type, which we shall call the **supertype.** For example, suppose that we want to define two new types EMPLOYEE and STUDENT as follows:

EMPLOYEE: Name, Address, Date of Birth, Age, ENO, Salary, HireDate, Seniority
STUDENT: Name, Address, Date of Birth, Age, ENO, Major, GPA

Since both STUDENT and EMPLOYEE include all the functions defined for PERSON plus some additional functions of their own, we can declare them to be **subtypes** of PERSON. Each will inherit the previously defined functions of PERSON—namely, Name, Address, Date of Birth, Age, and ENO. For STUDENT, it is only necessary to define the new (local) functions Major and GPA, which are not inherited. Presumably, Major can be defined as a stored attribute, whereas GPA may be implemented as a method that calculates the student's grade point average by accessing the Grade values that are internally stored (hidden) within each STUDENT object as *private attributes*. For EMPLOYEE, the Salary and HireDate functions may be stored attributes, whereas Seniority may be a method that calculates Seniority from the value of HireDate.

The idea of defining a type involves defining all of its functions and implementing them either as attributes or as methods. When a subtype is defined, it can then inherit all of these functions and their implementations. Only functions that are specific or **local** to the subtype, and hence are not specified in the supertype, need to be defined and implemented. Therefore, we can declare EMPLOYEE and STUDENT as follows:

EMPLOYEE **subtype**-of PERSON: Salary, HireDate, Seniority
STUDENT **subtype**-of PERSON: Major, GPA

In general, a subtype includes *all* of the functions that are defined for its supertype plus some additional functions that are specific only to the subtype. Hence, it is possible to generate a **type hierarchy** to show the supertype/subtype relationships among all the types declared in the system.

As another example, consider a type that describes objects in plane geometry, which may be defined as follows:

GEOMETRY_OBJECT: Shape, Area, ReferencePoint

For the GEOMETRY_OBJECT type, Shape is implemented as an attribute (its domain can be an enumerated type with values 'triangle', 'rectangle', 'circle', and so on), and Area is a method that is applied to calculate the area. ReferencePoint specifies the coordinates of a point that determines the object location. Now suppose that we want to define a number of subtypes for the GEOMETRY_OBJECT type, as follows:

RECTANGLE **subtype**-of GEOMETRY_OBJECT: Width, Height
TRIANGLE **subtype**-of GEOMETRY_OBJECT: Side1, Side2, Angle
CIRCLE **subtype**-of GEOMETRY_OBJECT: Radius

Notice that the Area operation may be implemented by a different method for each subtype, since the procedure for area calculation is different for rectangles, triangles, and circles. Similarly, the attribute ReferencePoint may have a different meaning for each subtype; it might be the center point for RECTANGLE and CIRCLE objects, and the vertex point between the two given sides for a TRIANGLE object. Some OO database systems allow the **renaming** of inherited functions in different subtypes to reflect the meaning more closely.

An alternative way of declaring these three subtypes is to specify the value of the Shape attribute as a condition that must be satisfied for objects of each subtype:

RECTANGLE **subtype-of** GEOMETRY_OBJECT (Shape='rectangle'): Width, Height
TRIANGLE **subtype-of** GEOMETRY_OBJECT (Shape='triangle'): Side1, Side2, Angle
CIRCLE **subtype-of** GEOMETRY_OBJECT (Shape='circle'): Radius

Here, only GEOMETRY_OBJECT objects whose Shape='rectangle' are of the subtype RECTANGLE, and similarly for the other two subtypes. In this case, all functions of the GEOMETRY_OBJECT supertype are inherited by each of the three subtypes, but the value of the Shape attribute is restricted to a specific value for each.

Notice that type definitions describe objects but *do not* generate objects on their own. They are just declarations of certain types; and as part of that declaration, the implementation of the functions of each type is specified. In a database application, there are many objects of each type. When an object is created, it typically belongs to one or more of these types that have been declared. For example, a circle object is of type CIRCLE and GEOMETRY_OBJECT (by inheritance). Each object also becomes a member of one or more persistent collections of objects (or extents), which are used to group together collections of objects that are meaningful to the database application.

13.1.4.2 Constraints on extents corresponding to a type hierarchy[24]

In most OO databases, the collection of objects in an extent has the same type or class. However, this is not a necessary condition. For example, SMALLTALK, a so-called *typeless* OO language, allows a collection of objects to contain objects of different types. This can also be the case when other non-object-oriented typeless languages, such as LISP, are extended with OO concepts. However, since the majority of OO databases support types, we will assume that **extents** are collections of objects of the same type for the remainder of this section.

It is common in database applications that each type or subtype will have an extent associated with it, which holds the collection of all persistent objects of that type or subtype. In this case, the constraint is that every object in an extent that corresponds to a subtype must also be a member of the *extent* that corresponds to its supertype. Some OO database systems have a predefined system type (called the ROOT class or the OBJECT class) whose extent contains all the objects in the system.[25] Classification then proceeds by assigning objects into additional subtypes that are meaningful to the application, creating a **type hierarchy** or **class hierarchy** for the system. All extents for system- and user-defined classes are subsets of the extent corresponding to the class OBJECT, directly or indirectly. In the ODMG model (see Section 13.2), the user may or may not specify an extent for each class (type), depending on the application.

In most OO systems, a distinction is made between persistent and transient objects and collections. A **persistent collection** holds a collection of objects that is stored permanently in the database and hence can be accessed and shared by multiple programs. A **transient collection** exists temporarily during the execution of a program but is not kept when the program terminates. For example, a transient collection may be created in a program to hold the result of a query that selects some objects from a persistent collection and copies those objects into the transient collection. The transient collection holds the same type of objects as the persistent collection. The program can then manipulate the objects in the transient collection, and once the program terminates, the transient collection ceases to exist. In general, numerous collections—transient or persistent—may contain objects of the same type.

---

24. In the second edition of this book, we used the title *Class Hierarchies* to describe these extent constraints. Because the word *class* has too many different meanings, *extent* is used in this edition. This is also more consistent with ODMG terminology (see Section 13.2).

25. This is called OBJECT in the ODMG model (see Section 13.2)

Notice that the type constructors discussed in Section 13.1.2 permit the state of one object to be a collection of objects. Hence, collection objects whose types are based on the *set constructor* can define a number of collections—one corresponding to each object. The set-valued objects themselves are members of another collection. This allows for multilevel classification schemes, where an object in one collection has as its state a collection of objects of a different class.

As we shall see in Section 13.2, the ODMG model distinguishes between type inheritance—called interface inheritance and denoted by the ":" symbol—and the extent inheritance constraint—denoted by the keyword EXTEND.

13.1.5 Complex Objects

A principal motivation that led to the development of OO systems was the desire to represent complex objects. There are two main types of complex objects: structured and unstructured. A structured complex object is made up of components and is defined by applying the available type constructors recursively at various levels. An unstructured complex object typically is a data type that requires a large amount of storage, such as a data type that represents an image or a large textual object.

13.1.5.1 Unstructured complex objects and type extensibility An **unstructured complex object** facility provided by a DBMS permits the storage and retrieval of large objects that are needed by the database application. Typical examples of such objects are *bitmap images* and *long text strings* (such as documents); they are also known as **binary large objects,** or **BLOBs** for short. Character strings are also known as **character large objects,** or **CLOBs** for short. These objects are unstructured in the sense that the DBMS does not know what their structure is—only the application that uses them can interpret their meaning. For example, the application may have functions to display an image or to search for certain keywords in a long text string. The objects are considered complex because they require a large area of storage and are not part of the standard data types provided by traditional DBMSs. Because the object size is quite large, a DBMS may retrieve a portion of the object and provide it to the application program before the whole object is retrieved. The DBMS may also use buffering and caching techniques to prefetch portions of the object before the application program needs to access them.

The DBMS software does not have the capability to directly process selection conditions and other operations based on values of these objects, unless the application provides the code to do the comparison operations needed for the selection. In an OODBMS, this can be accomplished by defining a new abstract data type for the uninterpreted objects and by providing the methods for selecting, comparing, and displaying such objects. For example, consider objects that are two-dimensional bitmap images. Suppose that the application needs to select from a collection of such objects only those that include a certain pattern. In this case, the user must provide the pattern recognition program as a method on objects of the bitmap type. The OODBMS then retrieves an object from the database and runs the method for pattern recognition on it to determine whether the object includes the required pattern

Because an OODBMS allows users to create new types, and because a type includes both structure and operations, we can view an OODBMS as having an **extensible type system.** We can create libraries of new types by defining their structure and operations, including complex types. Applications can then use or modify these types, in the latter case by creating subtypes of the types provided in the libraries. However, the DBMS internals must provide the underlying storage and retrieval capabilities for objects that require large amounts of storage so that the operations may be applied efficiently. Many OODBMSs provide for the storage and retrieval of large unstructured objects such as character strings or bit strings, which can be passed "as is" to the application program for interpretation. Recently, relational and extended relational DBMSs have also been able to provide such capabilities. Special indexing techniques are also being developed.

13.1.5.2 Structured complex objects A **structured complex object** differs from an unstructured complex object in that the object's structure is defined by repeated application of the type constructors provided by the OODBMS. Hence, the object structure is defined and known to the OODBMS. As an example, consider the DEPARTMENT object shown in Figure 13.1. At the first level, the object has a tuple structure with six attributes: DNAME, DNUMBER, MGR, LOCATIONS, EMPLOYEES, and PROJECTS. However, only two of these attributes—namely, DNAME and DNUMBER—have basic values; the other four have complex structure and hence build the second level of the complex object structure. One of these four (MGR) has a tuple structure, and the other three (LOCATIONS, EMPLOYEES, PROJECTS) have set structures. At the third level, for a MGR tuple value, we have one basic attribute (MANAGERSTARTDATE) and one attribute (MANAGER) that refers to an employee object, which has a tuple structure. For a LOCATIONS set, we have a set of basic values, but for both the EMPLOYEES and the PROJECTS sets, we have sets of tuple-structured objects.

Two types of reference semantics exist between a complex object and its components at each level. The first type, which we can call **ownership semantics,** applies when the sub-objects of a complex object are encapsulated within the complex object and are hence considered part of the complex object. The second type, which we can call **reference semantics,** applies when the components of the complex object are themselves independent objects but may be referenced from the complex object. For example, we may consider the DNAME, DNUMBER, MGR, and LOCATIONS attributes to be owned by a DEPARTMENT, whereas EMPLOYEES and PROJECTS are references because they reference independent objects. The first type is also referred to as the *is-part-of* or *is-component-of* relationship; and the second type is called the *is-associated-with* relationship, since it describes an equal association between two independent objects. The is-part-of relationship (ownership semantics) for constructing complex objects has the property that the component objects are encapsulated within the complex object and are considered part of the internal object state. They need not have object identifiers and can only be accessed by methods of that object. They are deleted if the object itself is deleted. On the other hand, referenced components are considered as independent objects that can have their own identity and methods. When a complex object needs to access its referenced components, it must do so by invoking the appropriate methods of the components, since they are not encapsulated within the complex object. Hence, reference semantics represents *relationships* among independent objects. In addition, a referenced component object may be referenced by more than one complex object and hence is not automatically deleted when the complex object is deleted.

An OODBMS should provide storage options for **clustering** the component objects of a complex object together on secondary storage in order to increase the efficiency of operations that access the complex object. In many cases, the object structure is stored on disk pages in an uninterpreted fashion. When a disk page that includes an object is retrieved into memory, the OODBMS can build up the structured complex object from the information on the disk pages, which may refer to additional disk pages that must be retrieved. This is known as **complex object assembly.**

13.1.6 Other Objected-oriented Concepts

In this section we give an overview of some additional OO concepts, including polymorphism (operator overloading), multiple inheritance, selective inheritance, versioning, and configurations.

13.1.6.1 Polymorphism (Operator overloading)

Another characteristic of OO systems is that they provide for **polymorphism** of operations, which is also known as **operator overloading.** This concept allows the same *operator name* or *symbol* to be bound to two or more different *implementations* of the operator, depending on the type of objects to which the operator is applied. A simple example from programming languages can illustrate this concept. In some languages, the operator symbol "+" can mean different things when applied to operands (objects) of different types. If the operands of "+" are of type *integer,* the operation invoked is integer addition. If the operands of "+" are of type *floating point,* the operation invoked is floating point addition. If the operands of "+" are of type *set,* the operation invoked is set union. The compiler can determine which operation to execute based on the types of operands supplied.

In OO databases, a similar situation may occur. We can use the GEOMETRY_OBJECT example discussed in Section 13.1.4 to illustrate polymorphism[26] in OO databases. Suppose that we declare GEOMETRY_OBJECT and its subtypes as follows:

GEOMETRY_OBJECT: Shape, Area, ReferencePoint
RECTANGLE **subtype-of** GEOMETRY_OBJECT (Shape='rectangle'): Width, Height
TRIANLE **subtype-of** GEOMETRY_OBJECT (Shape='triangle'): Side1, Side2, Angle
CIRCLE **subtype-of** GEOMETRY_OBJECT (Shape='circle'): Radius

Here, the function Area is declared for all objects of type GEOMETRY_OBJECT. However, the implementation of the method for Area may differ for each subtype of GEOMETRY_OBJECT. One possibility is to have a general implementation for calculating the area of a generalized GEOMETRY_OBJECT (for example, by writing a general algorithm to calculate the area of a polygon) and then to rewrite more efficient algorithms to calculate the areas of specific types of geometric objects, such as a circle, a rectangle, a triangle, and so on. In this case, the Area function is *overloaded* by different implementations.

The OODBMS must now select the appropriate method for the Area function based on the type of geometric object to which it is applied. In strongly typed systems, this can be done at compile time, since the object types must be known. This is termed **early** (or **static**) **binding.** However, in systems with weak typing or no typing (such as SMALLTALK and LISP), the type of the object to which a function is applied may not be known until runtime. In this case, the function must check the type of object at runtime and then invoke the appropriate method. This is often referred to as **late** (or **dynamic**) **binding.**

13.1.6.2 Multiple inheritance and selective inheritance

Multiple inheritance in a type hierarchy occurs when a certain subtype T is a subtype of two (or more) types and hence inherits the functions (attributes and methods) of both supertypes. For example, we may create a subtype ENGINEERING_MANAGER that is a subtype of both MANAGER and ENGINEER. This leads to the creation of a **type lattice** rather than a type hierarchy. One problem that can occur with multiple inheritance is that the supertypes from which the subtype inherits may have distinct functions of the same name, creating an ambiguity. For example, both MANAGER and ENGINEER may have a function called Salary. If the Salary function is implemented by different methods in the MANAGER and ENGINEER supertypes, an ambiguity exists as to which of the two is inherited by the subtype ENGINEERING_MANAGER. It is possible, however, that both ENGINEER and MANAGER inherit Salary from the same supertype (such as EMPLOYEE) higher up in the lattice. The general rule is that if a function is inherited from some *common supertype,* then it is inherited only once. In such a case, there is no ambiguity; the problem only arises if the functions are distinct in the two supertypes.

---

26. In programming languages, there are several kinds of polymorphism. The interested reader is referred to the bibliographic notes for works that include a more thorough discussion.

There are several techniques for dealing with ambiguity in multiple inheritance. One solution is to have the system check for ambiguity when the subtype is created, and to let the user explicitly choose which function is to be inherited at this time. Another solution is to use some system default. A third solution is to disallow multiple inheritance altogether if name ambiguity occurs, instead forcing the user to change the name of one of the functions in one of the supertypes. Indeed, some OO systems do not permit multiple inheritance at all.

Selective inheritance occurs when a subtype inherits only some of the functions of a supertype. Other functions are not inherited. In this case, an EXCEPT clause may be used to list the functions in a supertype that are *not* to be inherited by the subtype. The mechanism of selective inheritance is not typically provided in OO database systems, but it is used more frequently in artificial intelligence applications.[27]

13.1.6.3 Versions and configurations

Many database applications that use OO systems require the existence of several **versions** of the same object.[28] For example, consider a database application for a software engineering environment that stores various software artifacts, such as *design modules, source code modules,* and *configuration information* to describe which modules should be linked together to form a complex program, and *test cases* for testing the system. Commonly, *maintenance activities* are applied to a software system as its requirements evolve. Maintenance usually involves changing some of the design and implementation modules. If the system is already operational, and if one or more of the modules must be changed, the designer should create a **new version** of each of these modules to implement the changes. Similarly, new versions of the test cases may have to be generated to test the new versions of the modules. However, the existing versions should not be discarded until the new versions have been thoroughly tested and approved; only then should the new versions replace the older ones.

Notice that there may be more than two versions of an object. For example, consider two programmers working to update the same software module concurrently. In this case, two versions, in addition to the original module, are needed. The programmers can update their own versions of the same software module concurrently. This is often referred to as **concurrent engineering.** However, it eventually becomes necessary to merge these two versions together so that the new (hybrid) version can include the changes made by both programmers. During merging, it is also necessary to make sure that their changes are compatible. This necessitates creating yet another version of the object: one that is the result of merging the two independently updated versions.

As can be seen from the preceding discussion, an OODBMS should be able to store and manage multiple versions of the same conceptual object. Several systems do provide this capability, by allowing the application to maintain multiple versions of an object and to refer explicitly to particular versions as needed. However, the problem of merging and reconciling changes made to two different versions is typically left to the application developers, who know the semantics of the application. Some DBMSs have certain facilities that can compare the two versions with the original object and determine whether any changes made are incompatible, in order to assist with the merging process. Other systems maintain a **version graph** that shows the relationships among versions. Whenever a version v_1 originates by copying another version v, a directed arc can be drawn from v to v_1. Similarly, if two versions v_2 and v_3 are merged to create a new version v_4, directed arcs are drawn from v_2 and v_3 to v_4. The version graph can help users understand the relationships among the various versions and can be used internally by the system to manage the creation and deletion of versions.

---

27. In the ODMG model, type inheritance refers to inheritance of operations only, not attributes (see Section 13.2).

28. Versioning is not a problem that is unique to OODBs and it can be applied to relational or other types of DBMSs.

When versioning is applied to complex objects, further issues arise that must be resolved. A complex object, such as a software system, may consist of many modules. When versioning is allowed, each of these modules may have a number of different versions and a version graph. A **configuration** of the complex object is a collection consisting of one version of each module arranged in such a way that the module versions in the configuration are compatible and together form a valid version of the complex object. A new version or configuration of the complex object does not have to include new versions for every module. Hence, certain module versions that have not been changed may belong to more than one configuration of the complex object. Notice that a configuration is a collection of versions of *different* objects that together make up a complex object, whereas the version graph describes versions of the *same* object. A configuration should follow the type structure of a complex object; multiple configurations of the same complex object are analogous to multiple versions of a component object.

13.1.7   Section Summary

In this section we discussed the concepts of the object-oriented approach to database systems, which was proposed to meet the needs of complex database applications and to add database functionality to object-oriented programming languages such as C++. We first discussed the main concepts used in OO databases, which include the following:

- *Object identity:* Objects have unique identities that are independent of their attribute values.

- *Type constructors:* Complex object structures can be constructed by recursively applying a set of basic constructors, such as tuple, set, list, and bag.

- *Encapsulation of operations:* Both the object structure and the operations that can be applied to objects are included in the object class definitions.

- *Programming language compatibility:* Both persistent and transient objects are handled seamlessly. Objects are made persistent by being attached to a persistent collection or by explicit naming.

- *Type hierarchies and inheritance:* Object types can be specified by using a type hierarchy, which allows the inheritance of both attributes and methods of previously defined types. Multiple inheritance is allowed in some models.

- *Extents:* All persistent objects of a particular type can be stored in an extent. Extents corresponding to a type hierarchy have set/subset constraints enforced on them.

- *Support for complex objects:* Both structured and unstructured complex objects can be stored and manipulated.

- *Polymorphism and operator overloading:* Operations and method names can be overloaded to apply to different object types with different implementations.

- *Versioning:* Some OO systems provide support for maintaining several versions of the same object.

In the next section, we show how some of these concepts are realized in the ODMG standard.

13.2   OBJECT DATABASE STANDARDS, LANGUAGES, AND DESIGN

As we discussed at the beginning of Chapter 7, having a standard for a particular type of database system is very important, because it provides support for portability of database applications. **Portability** is generally defined as the capability to execute a particular application program on different systems with minimal modifications to the program itself. In the object database field,[29] portability would allow a program written to access one Object Database Management System (ODBMS) package to access another ODBMS package as long as both packages support the standard faithfully. This is important to database users because they are generally wary of investing in a new technology if the different vendors do not adhere to a standard. To illustrate why portability is important, suppose that a particular user invests thousands of dollars in creating an application that runs on a particular vendor's product and is then dissatisfied with that product for some reason—say the performance does not meet their requirements. If the application was written using the standard language constructs, it is possible for the user to convert the application to a different vendor's product—which adheres to the same language standards but may have better performance for that user's application—without having to do major modifications that require time and a major monetary investment.

A second potential advantage of having and adhering to standards is that it helps in achieving **interoperability,** which generally refers to the ability of an application to access multiple distinct systems. In database terms, this means that the same application program may access some data stored under one ODBMS package, and other data stored under another package. There are different levels of interoperability. For example, the DBMSs could be two distinct DBMS packages of the same type—for example, two object database systems—or they could be two DBMS packages of different types—say one relational DBMS and one object DBMS. A third advantage of standards is that it allows customers to *compare commercial products* more easily by determining which parts of the standard are supported by each product.

As we discussed in the introduction to Chapter 7, one of the reasons for the success of commercial relational DBMSs is the SQL standard. The lack of a standard for ODBMSs for several years may have caused some potential users to shy away from converting to this new technology. Subsequently, a consortium of ODBMS vendors, called ODMG (Object Data Management Group), proposed a standard that is known as the ODMG-93 or ODMG 1.0 standard. This was revised into ODMG 2.0, which we will describe in this section. The standard is made up of several parts: the **object model**, the **object definition language (ODL)**, the **object query language (OQL)**, and the **bindings** to object-oriented programming languages. Language bindings have been specified for several object-oriented programming languages including C++, SMALLTALK, and JAVA. Some vendors only offer specific language bindings, without offering the full capabilities of ODL and OQL. We will describe the ODMG object model in Section 13.2.1, ODL in Section 13.2.2, OQL in Section 13.2.3, and the C++ language binding in Section 13.2.4. Examples of how to use ODL, OQL, and the C++ language binding will use the UNIVERSITY database example introduced in Chapter 3. In our description, we will follow the ODMG 2.0 object model as described in Cattell et al. (1997).[30] It is important to note that many of the ideas embodied in the ODMG object model are based on two decades of research into conceptual modeling and object-oriented databases by many researchers.

Following the description of the ODMG model, we will describe a technique for object database conceptual design in Section 13.2.5. We will discuss how object-oriented databases differ from relational databases and show how to map a conceptual database design in the EER model to the ODL statements of the ODMG model.

The reader may skip Sections 13.2.3 through 13.2.7 if a less detailed introduction to the topic is desired.

---

29. In this section, we will use *object* database instead of *object-oriented* database (as in the previous section), since this is now more commonly accepted terminology.

30. The earlier version of the object model was published in 1993.

13.2.1   Overview of the Object Model of ODMG

The ODMG **object model** is the data model upon which the object definition language (ODL) and object query language (OQL) are based. In fact, this object model provides the data types, type constructors, and other concepts that can be utilized in the ODL to specify object database schemas. Hence, it is meant to provide a standard data model for object-oriented databases, just as SQL describes a standard data model for relational databases. It also provides a standard terminology in a field where the same terms were sometimes used to describe different concepts. We will try to adhere to the ODMG terminology in this section. Many of the concepts in the ODMG model have already been discussed in Section 13.1, and we assume the reader has already gone through Sections 13.1.1. Through 13.1.5. We will point out whenever the ODMG terminology differs from that used in Section 13.1.

13.2.1.1   Objects and literals

Objects and literals are the basic building blocks of the object model. The main difference between the two is that an object has both an object identifier and a **state** (or current value), whereas a literal has only a value but *no object identifier*.[31] In either case, the value can have a complex structure. The object state can change over time by modifying the object value. A literal is basically a constant value, possibly having a complex structure, that does not change.

An **object** is described by four characteristics: (1) **identifier**, (2) **name**, (3) **lifetime**, and (4) **structure**. The **object identifier** is a unique system-wide identifier (or OBJECT_ID).[32] Every object must have an object identifier. In addition to the OBJECT_ID, some objects may optionally be given a unique **name** within a particular database—this name can be used to refer to the object in a program, and the system should be able to locate the object given that name.[33] Obviously, not all individual objects will have unique names. Typically, a few objects, mainly those that hold collections of objects of a particular object type—such as extents—will have a name. These names are used as **entry points** to the database; that is, by locating these objects by their unique name, the user can then locate other objects that are referenced from these objects. Other important objects in the application may also have unique names. All such names within a particular database must be unique. The **lifetime** of an object specifies whether it is a *persistent object* (that is, a database object) or *transient object* (that is, an object in an executing program that disappears after the program terminates). Finally, the **structure** of an object specifies how the object is constructed by using the type constructors. The structure specifies whether an object is *atomic* or a *collection object*.[34] The term atomic object is different than the way we defined the *atom constructor* in Section 13.1.2.2, and it is quite different from an atomic literal (see below). In the ODMG model, an atomic object is any object that is not a collection, so this also covers *structured objects* created using the *struct* constructor.[35] We will discuss collection objects in Section 13.2.1.2 and atomic objects in Section 13.2.1.3. First, we define the concept of a literal.

In the object model, a **literal** is a value that *does not have* an object identifier. However, the value may have a simple or complex structure. There are three types of literals: (1) atomic, (2) collection, and (3) structured. **Atomic literals**[36] correspond to the values of basic data types and are predefined. The basic data types of the

---

31. We will use the terms value and state interchangeably here.

32. Corresponds to the OID of Section 13.1.

33. This corresponds to the naming mechanism described in Section 13.1.3.

34. In the ODMG model, *atomic objects* do not correspond to objects whose values are basic data types. All basic values (integers, reals, etc.) are considered to be *literals*.

35. The *struct* construct corresponds to the *tuple* constructor of Section 13.1.

36. The use of the word atomic in *atomic literal* **does** correspond to the way we used *atom constructor* in Section 13.1.2.2.

object model include long, short, and unsigned integer numbers (these are specified by the keywords Long, Short, Unsigned Long, Unsigned Short in ODL), regular and double precision floating point numbers (Float, Double), boolean values (Boolean), single characters (Char), character strings (String), and enumeration types (Enum), among others. **Structured literals** correspond roughly to values that are constructed using the tuple constructor described in Section 13.1.2.2. They include Date, Interval, Time, and Timestamp as built in structures (see Figure 13.5B), as well as any additional user-defined type structures as needed by each application.[37] User-defined structures are created using the **Struct** keyword in ODL, as in the C and C++ programming languages. **Collection literals** specify a value that is a collection of objects or values but the collection itself does not have an OBJECT_ID. The collections in the object model are SET<T>, BAG<T>, LIST<T>, and ARRAY<T>, where T is the type of objects or values in the collection.[38] Another collection type is Dictionary <K,V>, which is a collection of associations <K,V> where each K is a key (a unique search value) associated with a value V; this can be used to create an index on a collection of values.

Figure 13.5 gives a simplified view of the basic components of the object model. The notation of ODMG uses the keyword *interface* where we had used the keywords type and class in Section 13.1. In fact, interface is a more appropriate term, since it describes the interface of types of objects—namely, their visible attributes, relationships, and operations.[39] These interfaces are typically noninstantiable (that is, no objects are created for an interface) but they serve to define operations that can be *inherited* by the user-defined objects for a particular application. The keyword *class* in the object model is reserved for user-specified class declarations that form a database schema and are used for creating application objects. Figure 13.5 is a simplified version of the object model. For the full specifications, see Cattell et al. (1997). We will describe the constructs shown in Figure 13.5 as we describe the object model.

```
interface Object{
    ...
    boolean        same_as(in Object other_Object);
    Object         copy()
    void           delete(0;
};
```

FIGURE 13.5A Overview of the interface definitions for part of the ODMG object model. The basic Object interface, inherited by all objects.

```
interface Date : Object {
    enum           Weekday
    {Sunday, Monday, Tuesday, Wednesday, Thursday, Friday, Saturday};
    enum           Month
    {January, February, March, April, May, June, July, August, September, October, November, December};
    unsigned short year();
    unsigned short month();
    unsigned short day();
    ...
    boolean        is_equal(in Date other_Date);
    boolean        is_greater(in Date other_Date);
    ...
};
```

FIGURE 13.5B Overview of the interface definitions for part of the ODMG object model. Some standard interfaces for structured literals.

---

37. The structures for Date, Interval, Time, and Timestamp can be used to create either literal values or objects with identifiers.

38. These are similar to the corresponding type constructors described in Section 13.1.2.2.

39. Interface is also the keyword used in the CORBA standard (see Section 13.2.5) and the JAVA programming language.

```
interface Time : Object {
    ...
    unsigned short     hour();
    unsigned short     minute();
    unsigned short     second();
    unsigned short     millisecond();

    ...
    boolean            is_equal(in Time other_Time);
    boolean            is_greater(in Time other_Time);

    ...
    Time               add_interval(in Interval some_Interval);
    Time               subtract_interval(in Interval some_Interval);
    Interval           subtract_time(in Time other_Time);
};

interface Timestamp : Object {
    ...
    unsigned short     year();
    unsigned short     month();
    unsigned short     day();
    unsigned short     hour();
    unsigned short     minute();
    unsigned short     second();
    unsigned short     millisecond();

    ...
    Timestamp          plus(in Interval some_Interval);
    Timestamp          minus(in Interval some_Interval);
    boolean            is_equal(in Timestamp other_Timestamp);
    boolean            is_greater(in Timestamp other_Timestamp);
    ...
};

interface Interval : Object {
    unsigned short     day();
    unsigned short     hour();
    unsigned short     minute();
    unsigned short     second();
    unsigned short     millisecond();

    ...
    Interval           plus(in Interval some_Interval);
    Interval           minus(in Interval some_Interval);
    Interval           product(in long some_value);
    Interval           quotient(in long some_value);
    boolean            is_equal(in Interval other_Interval);
    boolean            is_greater(in Interval other_Interval);
    ...
};
```

FIGURE 13.5B(CONTINUED) Overview of the interface definitions for part of the ODMG object. Some standard interfaces for structured literals.

```
interface Collection : Object {
    ...
    exception      ElementNotFound{any element; };
    unsigned long  cardinality();
    boolean        is_empty();
    ...
    boolean        contains_element(in any element);
    void           insert_element(in any element);
    void           remove_element(in any element)
                       raises(ElementNotFound);
    Iterator       create_iterator(in boolean stable);
    ...
};

interface Iterator {
    exception      NoMoreElements();
    ...
    boolean        is_stable();
    boolean        at_end();
    void           reset();
    any            get_element() raises(NoMoreElements);
    void           next_position() raises(NoMoreElements);
    ...
};

interface Set : Collection {
    Set            create_union(in Set other_set);
    ...
    boolean        is_subset_of(in Set other_set);
    ...
};

interface Bag : Collection {
    unsigned long  occurrences_of(in any element);
    Bag            create_union(in Bag other_bag);
    ...
};

interface List : Collection {
    exception      Invalid_Index{unsigned_long index; };
    any            remove_element_at(in unsigned long position)
                       raises(InvalidIndex);
    any            retrieve_element_at(in unsigned long position)
                       raises(InvalidIndex);
    void           replace_element_at(in any element, in unsigned long position)
                       raises(InvalidIndex);
    void           insert_element_after(in any element, in unsigned long position)
                       raises(InvalidIndex);
    ...
    void           insert_element_first(in any element);
    ...
    any            remove_first_element() raises(InvalidIndex);
    ...
    any            retrieve_first_element() raises(InvalidIndex);
    ...
    List           concat(in List other_list);
    void           append(in List other_list);
};
```

FIGURE 13.5C Overview of the interface definitions for part of the ODMG object model. Interface definitions for collection objects.

```
interface Array : Collection {
    exception        Invalid_Index{unsigned_long index; };
    any              remove_element_at(in unsigned long index)
                            raises(InvalidIndex);
    any              retrieve_element_at(in unsigned long index)
                            raises(InvalidIndex);
    void             replace_element_at(in unsigned long index, in any element)
                            raises(InvalidIndex);
    void             resize(in unsigned long new_size);
};

struct Association {any key; any value; };

interface Dictionary : Collection {
    exception        KeyNotFound{any key; };
    void             bind(in any key, in any value);
    void             unbind(in any key) raises(KeyNotFound);
    any              lookup(in any key) raises(KeyNotFound);
    boolean          contains_key(in any key);
};
```

FIGURE 13.5C(CONTINUED) Overview of the interface definitions for part of the ODMG object model. Interface definitions for collection objects.

In the object model, all objects inherit the basic interface of Object, shown in Figure 13.5A. Hence, the basic operations that are inherited by all objects (from the Object interface) are copy (creates a new copy of the object), delete (deletes the object), and same_as (compares the object's identity to another object).[40] In general, operations are applied to objects using the **dot notation**. For example, given an object o, to compare it with another object p, we write

   o.same_as(p)

The result returned by this expression is Boolean and would be true if the identity of p is the same as that of o, and false otherwise. Similarly, to create a copy p of object o, we write

   p = o.copy()

An alternative to the dot notation is the **arrow notation**: o->same_as(p) or o->copy().

Type inheritance, which is used to define type/subtype relationships, is specified in the object model using the colon (:) notation, as in the C++ programming language. Hence, in Figure 13.5, we can see that all interfaces, such as Collection, Date, and Time, inherit the basic Object interface. In the object model, there are two main types of objects: (1) collection objects, described in Section 13.2.1.2, and (2) atomic (and structured) objects, described in Section 13.2.1.3.

13.2.1.2 Built-in interfaces for collection objects Any collection object inherits the basic Collection interface shown in Figure 13.5C, which shows the operations for all collection objects. Given a collection object O, the o.cardinality() operation returns the number of elements in the collection. The operation o.is_empty() returns true if the collection o is empty, and false otherwise. The operations o.insert_element(e) and o.remove_element(e) insert or remove an element e from the collection o. Finally, the operation o.contains_element(e) returns true if the collection o includes element e, and returns false otherwise. The op-

---

40. Additional operations are defined on objects for *locking* purposes, which are not shown in Figure 13.5. We discuss locking concepts for databases in Section 13.1.

eration i = o.create_iterator() creates an **iterator object** i for the collection object o, which can iterate over each element in the collection. The interface for iterator objects is also shown in Figure 13.5C. The i.reset() operation sets the iterator at the first element in a collection (for an unordered collection, this would be some arbitrary element), and i.next_position() sets the iterator to the next element. The i.get_element() retrieves the **current element**, which is the element at which the iterator is currently positioned.

The ODMG object model uses **exceptions** for reporting errors or particular conditions. For example, the ElementNotFound exception in the Collection interface would be raised by the o.remove_element(e) operation if e is not an element in the collection o. The NoMoreElements exception in the iterator interface would be raised by the i.next_ position() operation if the iterator is currently positioned at the last element in the collection, and hence no more elements exist for the iterator to point to.

Collection objects are further specialized into Set, List, Bag, Array, and Dictionary, which inherit the operations of the Collection interface. A Set<t> object type can be used to create objects such that the value of object o is a *set whose elements are of type* t. The Set interface includes the additional operation p = o.create_ union(s) (see Figure 13.5C), which returns a new object p of type Set<t> that is the union of the two sets o and s. Other operations similar to create_union (not shown in Figure 13.5C) are create_intersection(s) and create_difference(s). Operations for set comparison include the o.is_subset_of(s) operation, which returns true if the set object o is a subset of some other set object s, and returns false otherwise. Similar operations (not shown in Figure 13.5C) are is_proper_subset_of(s), is_superset_of(s), and is_proper_superset_of(s). The Bag<t> object type allows duplicate elements in the collection and also inherits the Collection interface. It has three operations—create_union(b), create_intersection(b), and create_difference(b)—that all return a new object of type Bag<t>. For example, p = o.create_union(b) returns a Bag object p that is the union of o and b (keeping duplicates). The o.occurrences_of(e) operation returns the number of duplicate occurrences of element e in bag o.

A List<t> object type inherits the Collection operations and can be used to create collections where the order of the elements is important. The value of each such object o is an *ordered list whose elements are of type* t. Hence, we can refer to the first, last, and i^{th} element in the list. Also, when we add an element to the list, we must specify the position in the list where the element is inserted. Some of the List operations are shown in Figure 13.5C. If o is an object of type List<t>, the operation o.insert_element_first(e) (see Figure 13.5C) inserts the element e before the first element in the list o, so that e becomes the first element in the list. A similar operation (not shown) is o.insert_element_last(e). The operation o.insert_element_after(e,i) in Figure 13.5C inserts the element e after the ith element in the list o and will raise the exception InvalidIndex if no i^{th} element exists in o. A similar operation (not shown) is o.insert_element_before(e,i). To remove elements from the list, the operations are e = o.remove_first_element(), e = o.remove_last_element(), and e = o.remove_element_ at(i); these operations remove the indicated element from the list *and* return the element as the operation's result. Other operations retrieve an element without removing it from the list. These are e = o.retrieve_first_ element(), e = o.retrieve_last_element(), and e = o.retrieve_element_at(i). Finally, two operations to manipulate lists are defined. These are p = o.concat(1), which creates a new list p that is the concatenation of lists o and 1 (the elements in list o followed by those in list 1), and o.append(1), which appends the elements of list 1 to the end of list o (without creating a new list object).

The Array<t> object type also inherits the Collection operations. It is similar to a list except that an array has a fixed number of elements. The specific operations for an Array object o are o.replace_element_at(i,e), which replaces the array element at position i with element e; e = o.remove_element_at(i), which retrieves the ith element and replaces it with a null value; and e = o.retrieve_element_at(i), which simply retrieves the ith element of the array. Any of these operations can raise the exception InvalidIndex if i is greater than the array's size. The operation o.resize(n) changes the number of array elements to n.

The last type of collection objects are of type Dictionary<k, v>. This allows the creation of a collection of association pairs <k, v>, where all k (key) values are unique. This allows for associative retrieval of a particular pair given its key value (similar to an index). If o is a collection object of type Dictionary<k,v>, then o.bind(k,v) binds value v to the key k as an association <k,v> in the collection, whereas o.unbind(k) removes the association with key k from o, and v = o.lookup(k) returns the value v associated with key k in o. The latter two operations can raise the exception KeyNotFound. Finally, o.contains_key(k) returns true if key k exists in o, and returns false otherwise.

Figure 13.6 is a diagram that illustrates the inheritance hierarchy of the built-in constructs of the object model. Operations are inherited from the supertype to the subtype. The collection object interfaces described above are *not directly instantiable*; that is, one cannot directly create objects based on these interfaces. Rather, the interfaces can be used to specify user-defined collection objects—of type Set, Bag, List, Array, or Dictionary—for a particular database application. When a user designs a database schema, they will declare their own object interfaces and classes that are relevant to the database application. If an interface or class is one of the collection objects, say a Set, then it will inherit the operations of the Set interface. For example, in a UNIVERSITY database application, the user can specify a class for Set<Student>, whose objects would be sets of Student objects. The programmer can then use the operations for Set<t> to manipulate an object of type Set<Student>. Creating application classes is typically done by utilizing the object definition language ODL (see Section 13.2.2).

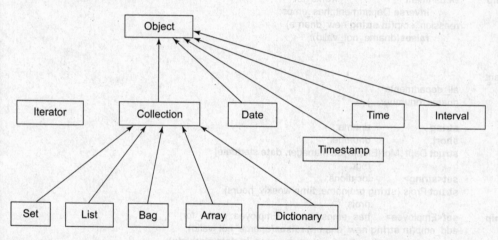

FIGURE 13.6 Inheritance hierarchy for the built-in interfaces of the object model.

It is important to note that all objects in a particular collection *must be of the same type*. Hence, although the keyword any appears in the specifications of collection interfaces in Figure 13.5C, this does not mean that objects of any type can be intermixed within the same collection. Rather, it means that any type can be used when specifying the type of elements for a particular collection (including other collection types!).

13.2.1.3 Atomic (user-defined) objects The previous section described the built-in collection types of the object model. We now discuss how object types for *atomic objects* can be constructed. These are specified using the keyword **class** in ODL. In the object model, any user-defined object that is not a collection object is called an **atomic object**.[41] For example, in a UNIVERSITY database application, the user can specify an object type (class) for Student objects. Most such objects will be **structured objects**; for example, a Student object will have a complex structure, with many attributes, relationships, and operations, but it is still considered atomic because it is not a collection. Such a user-defined atomic object type is defined as a class by specifying its **properties** and **operations**. The properties define the state of the object and are further distinguished into **attributes** and **relationships**. In this subsection, we elaborate on the three types of components—attributes, relationships, and operations—that a user-defined object type for atomic (structured) objects can include. We illustrate our discussion with the two classes Employee and Department shown in Figure 13.7.

```
class Employee
(    extent    all_employees
     key        )
{
     attribute    string            name;
     attribute    string            eno;
     attribute    date              date of birth;
     attribute    enum Gender{M, F}  sex;
     attribute    short             age;
     relationship  Department         works_for
                       inverse Department::has_emps;
     void         reassign_emp(in string new_dname)
                       raises(dname_not_valid);
};

class Department
(    extent    all_departments
     key        dname, dnumber   )
{
     attribute    string            dname;
     attribute    short             dnumber;
     attribute    struct Dept_Mgr{Employee manager, date startdate}
                       mgr;
     attribute    set<string>       locations;
     attribute    struct Projs {string projname, time weekly_hours}
                       projs;
     relationship  set<Employee>     has_emps inverse Employee::works_for;
     void         add_emp(in string new_ename) raises(ename_not_valid);
     void         change_manager(in string new_mgr_name; in date startdate);
};
```

FIGURE 13.7 The attributes, relationships, and operations in a class definition.

An **attribute** is a property that describes some aspect of an object. Attributes have values, which are typically literals having a simple or complex structure, that are stored within the object. However, attribute values can also be Object_Ids of other objects. Attribute values can even be specified via methods that are used to calculate the attribute value. In Figure 13.7,[42] the attributes for Employee are name, eno, date of birth,

---

41. As mentioned earlier, this definition of *atomic object* in the ODMG object model is different from the definition of atom constructor given in Section 13.1, which is the definition used in much of the object-oriented database literature.

42. We are using the Object Definition Language (ODL) notation in Figure 13.7, which will be discussed in more detail in Section 13.2.2.

sex, and age, and those for Department are dname, dnumber, mgr, locations, and projs. The mgr and projs attributes of Department have complex structure and are defined via **struct**, which corresponds to the *tuple constructor* of Section 13.1. Hence, the value of mgr in each Department object will have two components: manager, whose value is an Object_Id that references the Employee object that manages the Department, and startdate, whose value is a date. The locations attribute of Department is defined via the set constructor, since each Department object can have a set of locations.

A **relationship** is a property that specifies that two objects in the database are related together. In the object model of ODMG, only binary relationships (see Chapter 3) are explicitly represented, and each binary relationship is represented by a *pair of inverse references* specified via the keyword relationship. In Figure 13.7, one relationship exists that relates each Employee to the Department in which he or she works—the works_for relationship of Employee. In the inverse direction, each Department is related to the set of Employees that work in the Department—the has_emps relationship of Department. The keyword inverse specifies that these two properties specify a single conceptual relationship in inverse directions.[43] By specifying inverses, the database system can maintain the referential integrity of the relationship automatically. That is, if the value of works_for for a particular Employee e refers to Department d, then the value of has_emps for Department d must include a reference to e in its set of Employee references. If the database designer desires to have a relationship to be represented in *only one direction*, then it has to be modeled as an attribute (or operation). An example is the manager component of the mgr attribute in Department.

In addition to attributes and relationships, the designer can include **operations** in object type (class) specifications. Each object type can have a number of **operation signatures**, which specify the operation name, its argument types, and its returned value, if applicable. Operation names are unique within each object type, but they can be overloaded by having the same operation name appear in distinct object types. The operation signature can also specify the names of **exceptions** that can occur during operation execution. The implementation of the operation will include the code to raise these exceptions. In Figure 13.7, the Employee class has one operation, reassign_emp, and the Department class has two operations, add_emp and change_manager.

13.2.1.4 Interfaces, classes, and inheritance   In the ODMG object model, two concepts exist for specifying object types: interfaces and classes. In addition, two types of inheritance relationships exist. In this section, we discuss the differences and similarities among these concepts. Following the ODMG terminology, we use the word **behavior** to refer to operations, and **state** to refer to properties (attributes and relationships).

An **interface** is a specification of the abstract behavior of an object type, which specifies the operation signatures. Although an interface may have state properties (attributes and relationships) as part of its specifications, these cannot be inherited from the interface, as we shall see. An interface also is **noninstantiable**—that is, one cannot create objects that correspond to an interface definition.[44]

A **class** is a specification of both the abstract behavior and abstract state of an object type, and is **instantiable**—that is, one can create individual object instances corresponding to a class definition. Because interfaces are noninstantiable, they are mainly used to specify abstract operations that can be inherited by classes or by other interfaces. This is called **behavior inheritance** and is specified by the "**:**" symbol.[45] Hence, in the ODMG object model, behavior inheritance requires the supertype to be an interface, whereas the subtype could be either a class or another interface.

---

43. Chapter 3 discussed how a relationship can be represented by two attributes in inverse directions.

44. This is somewhat similar to the concept of abstract class in the C++ programming language.

45. The ODMG report also calls interface inheritance as type/subtype, is-a, and generalization/specialization relationships, although, in the literature, these terms have been used to describe inheritance of both state and operations (see Chapter 3 and Section 13.1).

Another inheritance relationship, called **EXTENDS** and specified by the **extends** keyword, is used to inherit both state and behavior strictly among classes. In an EXTENDS inheritance, both the supertype and the subtype must be classes. Multiple inheritance via EXTENDS is not permitted. However, multiple inheritance is allowed for behavior inheritance via ":". Hence, an interface may inherit behavior from several other interfaces. A class may also inherit behavior from several interfaces via ":", in addition to inheriting behavior and state from *at most one* other class via EXTENDS. We will give examples in Section 13.2.2 of how these two inheritance relationships—":" and EXTENDS—may be used.

13.2.1.5 Extents, keys, and factory objects

In the ODMG object model, the database designer can declare an **extent** for any object type that is defined via a **class** declaration. The extent is given a name, and it will contain all persistent objects of that class. Hence, the extent behaves as a *set object* that holds all persistent objects of the class. In Figure 13.7, the Employee and Department classes have extents called all_employees and all_departments, respectively. This is similar to creating two objects—one of type Set<Employee> and the second of type Set<Department>—and making them persistent by naming them all_employees and all_departments. Extents are also used to automatically enforce the set/subset relationship between the extents of a supertype and its subtype. If two classes A and B have extents all_A and all_B, and class B is a subtype of class A (that is, class B EXTENDS class A), then the collection of objects in all_B must be a subset of those in all_A at any point in time. This constraint is automatically enforced by the database system.

A class with an extent can have one or more keys. A **key** consists of one or more properties (attributes or relationships) whose values are constrained to be unique for each object in the extent. For example, in Figure 13.7, the Employee class has the eno attribute as key (each Employee object in the extent must have a unique eno value), and the Department class has two distinct keys: dname and dnumber (each Department must have a unique dname and a unique dnumber). For a composite key[46] that is made of several properties, the properties that form the key are contained in parentheses. For example, if a class Vehicle with an extent all_vehicles has a key made up of a combination of two attributes state and license_number, they would be placed in parentheses as (state, license_number) in the key declaration.

Next, we present the concept of **factory object**—an object that can be used to generate or create individual objects via its operations. Some of the interfaces of factory objects that are part of the ODMG object model are shown in Figure 13.8. The interface ObjectFactory has a single operation, new(), which returns a new object with an Object_Id. By inheriting this interface, users can create their own factory interfaces for each user-defined (atomic) object type, and the programmer can implement the operation *new* differently for each type of object. Figure 13.8 also shows a DateFactory interface, which has additional operations for creating a new calendar_date, and for creating an object whose value is the current_date, among other operations (not shown in Figure 13.8). As we can see, a factory object basically provides the **constructor operations** for new objects.

Finally, we discuss the concept of a **database**. Because a ODBMS can create many different databases, each with its own schema, the ODMG object model has interfaces for DatabaseFactory and Database objects, as shown in Figure 13.8. Each database has its own *database name*, and the **bind** operation can be used to assign individual unique names to persistent objects in a particular database. The **lookup** operation returns an object from the database that has the specified object_name, and the **unbind** operation removes the name of a persistent named object from the database.

---

46. A composite key is called a *compound key* in the ODMG report.

```
interface ObjectFactory {
    Object            new();
};

interface DateFactory : ObjectFactory {
    exception        InvalidDate{};
    ...
    Date             calendar_date(  in unsigned short year,
                                     in unsigned short month,
                                     in unsigned short day)
                     raises(InvalidDate);
    ...
    Date             current();
};

interface DatabaseFactory {
    Database         new();
};

interface Database {
    void             open(in string database_name);
    void             close();
    void             bind(in any some_object, in string object_name);
    Object           unbind(in string name);
    Object           lookup(in string object_name)
                            raises(ElementNotFound);
    ...
};
```

FIGURE 13.8 Interfaces to illustrate factory objects and database objects.

13.2.2   The Object Definition Language ODL

After our overview of the ODMG object model in the previous section, we now show how these concepts can be utilized to create an object database schema using the object definition language ODL.[47] The ODL is designed to support the semantic constructs of the ODMG object model and is independent of any particular programming language. Its main use is to create object specifications—that is, classes and interfaces. Hence, ODL is not a full programming language. A user can specify a database schema in ODL independently of any programming language, then use the specific language bindings to specify how ODL constructs can be mapped to constructs in specific programming languages, such as C++, SMALLTALK, and JAVA. We will give an overview of the C++ binding in Section 13.2.4.

Figure 13.9b shows a possible object schema for part of the UNIVERSITY database, which was presented in Chapter 3. We will describe the concepts of ODL using this example, and the one in Figure 13.11. The graphical notation for Figure 13.9b is shown in Figure 13.9a and can be considered as a variation of EER diagrams (see Chapter 3) with the added concept of interface inheritance but without several EER concepts, such as categories (union types) and attributes of relationships.

Figure 13.10 shows one possible set of ODL class definitions for the UNIVERSITY database. In general, there may be several possible mappings from an object schema diagram (or EER schema diagram) into ODL classes. We will discuss these options further in Section 13.2.5.

---

47. The ODL syntax and data types are meant to be compatible with the Interface Definition Language (IDL) of CORBA (Common Object Request Broker Architecture), with extensions for relationships and other database concepts.

Figure 13.10 shows the straightforward way of mapping part of the UNIVERSITY database from Chapter 3. Entity types are mapped into ODL classes, and inheritance is done using EXTENDS. However, there is no direct way to map categories (union types) or to do multiple inheritance. In Figure 13.10, the classes Person, Faculty, Student, and GradStudent have the extents persons, faculty, students, and grad_students, respectively. Both Faculty and Student EXTENDS Person, and GradStudent EXTENDS Student. Hence, the collection of students (and the collection of faculty) will be constrained to be a subset of the collection of persons at any point in time. Similarly, the collection of grad_students will be a subset of students. At the same time, individual Student and Faculty objects will inherit the properties (attributes and relationships) and operations of Person, and individual GradStudent objects will inherit those of Student.

The classes Department, Course, Section, and CurrSection in Figure 13.10 are straightforward mappings of the corresponding entity types in Figure 13.9b. However, the class Grade requires some explanation. The Grade class corresponds to the M:N relationship between Student and Section in Figure 13.9b. The reason it was made into a separate class (rather than as a pair of inverse relationships) is because it includes the relationship attribute grade.[48] Hence, the M:N relationship is mapped to the class Grade, and a pair of 1:N relationships, one between Student and Grade and the other between Section and Grade.[49] These two relationships are represented by the following relationship properties: completed_sections of Student; section and student of Grade; and students of Section (see Figure 13.10). Finally, the class Degree is used to represent the composite, multivalued attribute degrees of GradStudent (see Figure 3.26).

Because the previous example did not include any interfaces, only classes, we now utilize a different example to illustrate interfaces and interface (behavior) inheritance. Figure 13.11 is part of a database schema for storing geometric objects. An interface GeometryObject is specified, with operations to calculate the perimeter and area of a geometric object, plus operations to translate (move) and rotate an object. Several classes (Rectangle, Triangle, Circle, ...) inherit the GeometryObject interface. Since GeometryObject is an interface, it is *noninstantiable*—that is, no objects can be created based on this interface directly. However, objects of type Rectangle, Triangle, Circle, ... can be created, and these objects inherit all the operations of the GeometryObject interface. Note that with interface inheritance, only operations are inherited, not properties (attributes, relationships). Hence, if a property is needed in the inheriting class, it must be repeated in the class definition, as with the reference_point attribute in Figure 13.11. Notice that the inherited operations can have different implementations in each class. For example, the implementations of the area and perimeter operations may be different for Rectangle, Triangle, and Circle.

Multiple inheritance of interfaces by a class is allowed, as is multiple inheritance of interfaces by another interface. However, with the EXTENDS (class) inheritance, multiple inheritance is *not permitted*. Hence, a class can inherit via EXTENDS from at most one class (in addition to inheriting from zero or more interfaces).

13.2.3 The Object Query Language OQL

The object query language (OQL) is the query language proposed for the ODMG object model. It is designed to work closely with the programming languages for which an ODMG binding is defined, such as C++, SMALLTALK, and JAVA. Hence, an OQL query embedded into one of these programming languages can return

---

48. We will discuss alternative mappings for attributes of relationships in Section 13.2.5.

49. This is similar to how an M:N relationship is mapped in the relational model (see Chapter 6) and in the legacy network model (see Appendix C).

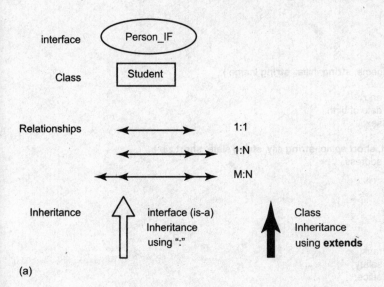

interface   Person_IF

Class   Student

Relationships   1:1

1:N

M:N

Inheritance   interface (is-a)   Class
Inheritance   Inheritance
using ":"   using **extends**

(a)

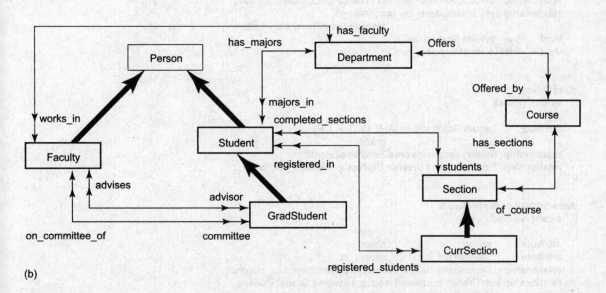

(b)

FIGURE 13.9 An example of a database schema. (a) Graphical notation for representing ODL schemas. (b) A graphical object database schema for part of the UNIVERSITY database.

```
class Person
(   extent   persons
    key       eno  )
{
    attribute         struct Pname {string fname, string initial, string lname }
                                name;
    attribute         string                eno;
    attribute         date                  date of birth;
    attribute         enum Gender{M, F}     sex;
    attribute         struct Address
                         {short no, string street, short aptno, string city, string state, short zip }
                                address;
    short   age();
};

class Faculty extends Person
(   extent   faculty   )
{
    attribute         string                rank;
    attribute         float                 salary;
    attribute         string                office;
    attribute         string                phone;
    relationship      Department            works_in inverse Department::has_faculty;
    relationship set<GradStudent> advises inverse GradStudent::advisor;
    relationship set<GradStudent> on_committee_of
                                inverse GradStudent::committee;
    void    give_raise(in float raise);
    void    promote(in string new_rank);
};

class Grade
(   extent   grades   )
{
    attribute         enum Grade Values{A, B, C, D, F, I, P}
                                grade;
    relationship  Section section inverse Section::students;
    relationship  Student student inverse Student::completed_sections;
};

class Student extends Person
(   extent   students   )
{
    attribute         string                class;
    attribute         Department            minors_in;
    relationship      Department majors_in inverse Department::has_majors;
    relationship set<Grade> completed_sections inverse Grade::student;
    relationship set<CurrSection> registered_in
                                inverse CurrSection::registered_students;
    void    change_major(in string dname) raises(dname_not_valid);
    float   gpa();
    void    register(in short secno) raises(section_not_valid);
    void    assign_grade(in short secno; in GradeValue grade)
                                raises(section_not_valid, grade_not_valid);
```

FIGURE 13.10 Possible ODL schema for the UNIVERSITY database of Figure 13.9(b). (Continued)

```
class Degree
{
    attribute       string              college;
    attribute       string              degree;
    attribute       string              year;
};

class GradStudent extends Student
(   extent  grad_students   )
{
    attribute       set<Degree>         degrees;
    relationship   Faculty advisor inverse Faculty::advises;
    relationship set<Faculty> committee inverse Faculty::on_committee_of;
    void            assign_advisor(in string lname; in string fname)
                                raises(faculty_not_valid);
    void            assign_committee_member(in string lname; in string fname)
                                raises(faculty_not_valid);
};

class Department
(   extent  departments key dname   )
{
    attribute       string              dname;
    attribute       string              dphone;
    attribute       string              doffice;
    attribute       string              college;
    attribute       Faculty             chair;
    relationship set<Faculty> has_faculty inverse Faculty::works_in;
    relationship set<Student> has_majors inverse Student::majors_in;
    relationship set<Course> offers inverse Course::offered_by;
};

class Course
(   extent  course key cno   )
{
    attribute       string              cname;
    attribute       string              cno;
    attribute       string              description;
    relationship set<Section> has_sections inverse Section::of_course;
    relationship Department offered_by inverse Department::offers;
};

class Section
(   extent  section   )
{
    attribute       short               secno;
    attribute       string              year;
    attribute       enum Quarter{Fall, Winter, Spring, Summer} qtr;
    relationship set<Grade> students inverse Grade::section;
    relationship Course of_course inverse Course::has_sections;
};

class CurrSection extends Section
(   extent  current_sections   )
{
    relationship set<Student> registered_students inverse Student::registered_in
    void            register_student(in string ssn)
                        raises(student_not_valid, section_full);
};
```

FIGURE 13.10 Possible ODL schema for the UNIVERSITY database of Figure 13.9(b).

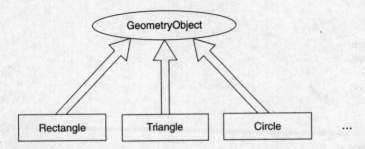

FIGURE 13.11A An illustration of interface inheritance via ":". Graphical schema representation.

```
interface GeometryObject
{
    attribute        enum Shape{Rectangle,Triangle,Circle,...} shape;
    attribute        struct Point {short x, short y}      reference_point;
    float    perimeter();
    float    area();
    void     translate(in short x_translation; in short y_translation);
    void     rotate(in float angle_of_rotation);
};

class Rectangle : GeometryObject
(  extent rectangles      )
{
    attribute        struct Point {short x, short y}      reference_point;
    attribute        short             length;
    attribute        short             height;
    attribute        float             orientation_angle;
};

class Triangle : GeometryObject
(  extent triangles   )
{
    attribute        struct Point {short x, short y}      reference_point;
    attribute        short             side_1;
    attribute        short             side_2;
    attribute        float             side1_side2_angle;
    attribute        float             side1_orientation_angle;
};

class Circle : GeometryObject
(  extent circles    )
{
    attribute        struct Point {short x, short y}      reference_point;
    attribute        short             radius;
};
```

FIGURE 13.11B An illustration of interface inheritance via ":". Corresponding interface and class definitions in ODL.

objects that match the type system of that language. In addition, the implementations of class operations in an ODMG schema can have their code written in these programming languages. The OQL syntax for queries is similar to the syntax of the relational standard query language SQL, with additional features for ODMG concepts, such as object identity, complex objects, operations, inheritance, polymorphism, and relationships.

We will first discuss the syntax of simple OQL queries and the concept of using named objects or extents as database entry points in Section 13.2.3.1. Then in Section 13.2.3.2, we discuss the structure of query results and the use of path expressions to traverse relationships among objects. Other OQL features for handling object identity, inheritance, polymorphism, and other object oriented concepts are discussed in Section 13.2.3.3. The examples to illustrate OQL queries are based on the UNIVERSITY database schema given in Figure 13.10.

13.2.3.1 Simple OQL queries, database entry points, and iterator variables   The basic OQL syntax is a **select** . . . **from** . . . **where** . . . structure, as for SQL. For example, the query to retrieve the names of all departments in the college of 'Engineering' can be written as follows:

```
Q0:   SELECT   d.dname
      FROM     d in departments
      WHERE    d.college = 'Engineering';
```

In general, an **entry point** to the database is needed for each query, which can be any *named persistent object*. For many queries, the entry point is the name of the **extent** of a class. Recall that the extent name is considered to be the name of a persistent object whose type is a collection (in most cases, a set) of objects from the class. Looking at the extent names in Figure 13.10, the named object departments is of type set<Department>; persons is of type set<Person>; faculty is of type set<Faculty>; and so on.

The use of an extent name—departments in Q0—as an entry point refers to a persistent collection of objects. Whenever a collection is referenced in an OQL query, we should define an **iterator variable**[50]—d in Q0—that ranges over each object in the collection. In many cases, as in Q0, the query will select certain objects from the collection, based on the conditions specified in the where-clause. In Q0, only persistent objects d in the collection of departments that satisfy the condition d.college = 'Engineering' are selected for the query result. For each selected object d, the value of d.dname is retrieved in the query result. Hence, the *type of the result* for Q0 is bag<string>, because the type of each dname value is string (even though the actual result is a set because dname is a key attribute). In general, the result of a query would be of type *bag* for select . . . from . . . and of type set for select distinct . . . from . . . , as in SQL (adding the keyword distinct eliminates duplicates).

Using the example in Q0, there are three syntactic options for specifying iterator variables:

d **in** departments
departments d
departments **as** d

We will use the first construct in our examples.[51]

The named objects used as database entry points for OQL queries are not limited to the names of extents. Any named persistent object, whether it refers to an atomic (single) object or to a collection object can be used as a database entry point.

---

50. This is similar to the tuple variables that range over tuples in SQL queries.
51. Note that the latter two options are similar to the syntax for specifying tuple variables in SQL queries.

13.2.3.2 Query results and path expressions
The result of a query can in general be of any type that can be expressed in the ODMG object model. A query does not have to follow the select . . . from . . . where . . . structure; in the simplest case, any persistent name on its own is a query, whose result is a reference to that persistent object. For example, the query

Q1: departments;

returns a reference to the collection of all persistent department objects, whose type is set<Department>. Similarly, suppose we had given (via the database bind operation, see Figure 13.8) a persistent name csdepartment to a single department object (the computer science department); then, the query:

Q1a: csdepartment;

returns a reference to that individual object of type Department. Once an entry point is specified, the concept of a **path expression** can be used to specify a *path* to related attributes and objects. A path expression typically starts at a *persistent object name*, or at the iterator variable that ranges over individual objects in a collection. *This name will be followed by zero or more relationship names or attribute names connected using the dot notation.* For example, referring to the UNIVERSITY database of Figure 13.10, the following are examples of path expressions, which are also valid queries in OQL:

Q2:   csdepartment.chair;
Q2a: csdepartment.chair.rank;
Q2b: csdepartment.has_faculty;

The first expression Q2 returns an object of type Faculty, because that is the type of the attribute chair of the Department class. This will be a reference to the Faculty object that is related to the department object whose persistent name is csdepartment via the attribute chair; that is, a reference to the Faculty object who is chairperson of the computer science department. The second expression Q2a is similar, except that it returns the rank of this Faculty object (the computer science chair) rather than the object reference; hence, the type returned by Q2a is string, which is the data type for the rank attribute of the Faculty class.

Path expressions Q2 and Q2a return single values, because the attributes chair (of Department) and rank (of Faculty) are both single-valued and they are applied to a single object. The third expression Q2b is different; it returns an object of type set<Faculty> even when applied to a single object, because that is the type of the relationship has_faculty of the Department class. The collection returned will include references to all Faculty objects that are related to the department object whose persistent name is csdepartment via the relationship has_faculty; that is, references to all Faculty objects who are working in the computer science department. Now, to return the ranks of computer science faculty, we cannot write

Q3': csdepartment.has_faculty.rank;

This is because it is not clear whether the object returned would be of type set<string> or bag<string> (the latter being more likely, since multiple faculty may share the same rank). Because of this type of ambiguity problem, OQL does not allow expressions such as Q3'. Rather, one must use an iterator variable over these collections, as in Q3a or Q3b below:

Q3a: select   f.rank
       from   f **in** csdepartment.has_faculty;
Q3b: **select**   **distinct** f.rank
       from   f **in** csdepartment.has_faculty;

Here, Q3a returns bag<string> (duplicate rank values appear in the result), whereas Q3b returns set<string> (duplicates are eliminated via the distinct keyword). Both Q3a and Q3b illustrate how an iterator variable can be defined in the from-clause to range over a restricted collection specified in the query. The variable f in Q3a and Q3b ranges over the elements of the collection csdepartment.has_faculty, which is of type set<Faculty>, and includes only those faculty that are members of the computer science department.

In general, an OQL query can return a result with a complex structure specified in the query itself by utilizing the struct keyword. Consider the following two examples:

```
Q4:    csdepartment.chair.advises;
Q4a:   select struct  (name:struct(last_name: s.name.lname,
                                    first_name: s.name.fname),
                        degrees:(select struct (deg: d.degree,
                                                yr: d.year,
                                                college: d.college)
                                 from d in s.degrees)
               from s in csdepartment.chair.advises;
```

Here, Q4 is straightforward, returning an object of type set<GradStudent> as its result; this is the collection of graduate students that are advised by the chair of the computer science department. Now, suppose that a query is needed to retrieve the last and first names of these graduate students, plus the list of previous degrees of each. This can be written as in Q4a, where the variable s ranges over the collection of graduate students advised by the chairperson, and the variable d ranges over the degrees of each such student s. The type of the result of Q4a is a collection of (firstlevel) structs where each struct has two components: name and degrees.[52] The name component is a further struct made up of last_name and first_name, each being a single string. The degrees component is defined by an embedded query and is itself a collection of further (second level) structs, each with three string components: deg, yr, and college.

Note that OQL is *orthogonal* with respect to specifying path expressions. That is, attributes, relationships, and operation names (methods) can be used interchangeably within the path expressions, as long as the type system of OQL is not compromised. For example, one can write the following queries to retrieve the grade point average of all senior students majoring in computer science, with the result ordered by gpa, and within that by last and first name:

```
Q5a:   select struct (last_name: s.name.lname, first_name:
                       s.name.fname, gpa: s.gpa)
               from s in csdepartment.has_majors
               where s.class = 'senior'
               order by gpa desc, last_name asc, first_name asc;
Q5b:   select struct (last_name: s.name.lname, first_name:
                       s.name.fname, gpa: s.gpa)
               from s in students
               where s.majors_in.dname = 'Computer Science' and
                     s.class = 'senior'
               order by gpa desc, last_name asc, first_name asc;
```

Q5a used the named entry point csdepartment to directly locate the reference to the computer science department and then locate the students via the relationship has_majors, whereas Q5b searches the students extent to locate all students majoring in that department. Notice how attribute names, relationship names, and operation (method) names are all used interchangeably (in an orthogonal manner) in the path expressions: gpa is an operation; majors_in and has_majors are relationships; and class, name, dname, lname, and fname are attributes. The implementation of the gpa operation computes the grade point average and returns its value as a float type for each selected student.

The order by clause is similar to the corresponding SQL construct, and specifies in which order the query result is to be displayed. Hence, the collection returned by a query with an order by clause is of type *list*.

---

52. As mentioned earlier, struct corresponds to the tuple constructor discussed in Section 13.1.

13.2.3.3 Other features of OQL

Specifying Views as Named Queries.   The view mechanism in OQL uses the concept of a **named query.** The *define* keyword is used to specify an identifier of the named query, which must be a unique name among all named objects, class names, method names, or function names in the schema. If the identifier has the same name as an existing named query, then the new definition replaces the previous definition. Once defined, a query definition is persistent until it is redefined or deleted. A view can also have parameters (arguments) in its definition.

For example, the following view V1 defines a named query has_minors to retrieve the set of objects for students minoring in a given department:

```
V1:  define has_minors(deptname) as
     select s
     from s in students
     where s.minors_in.dname = deptname;
```

Because the ODL schema in Figure 13.10 only provided a unidirectional minors_in attribute for a Student, we can use the above view to represent its inverse without having to explicitly define a relationship. This type of view can be used to represent inverse relationships that are not expected to be used frequently. The user can now utilize the above view to write queries such as

```
has_minors('Computer Science');
```

which would return a bag of students minoring in the Computer Science department. Note that in Figure 13.10, we did define has_majors as an explicit relationship, presumably because it is expected to be used more often.

Extracting Single Elements from Singleton Collections.   An OQL query will, in general, return a collection as its result, such as a bag, set (if distinct is specified), or list (if the order by clause is used). If the user requires that a query only return a single element, there is an *element* operator in OQL that is guaranteed to return a single element e from a singleton collection c that contains only one element. If c contains more than one element or if c is empty, then the element operator *raises an exception*. For example, Q6 returns the single object reference to the computer science department:

```
Q6:  element (select d
             from d in departments
             where d.dname = 'Computer Science');
```

Since a department name is unique across all departments, the result should be one department. The type of the result is d:Department.

Collection Operators (Aggregate Functions, Quantifiers).   Because many query expressions specify collections as their result, a number of operators have been defined that are applied to such collections. These include aggregate operators as well as membership and quantification (universal and existential) over a collection.

The aggregate operators (min, max, count, sum, and avg) operate over a collection.[53] The operator count returns an integer type. The remaining aggregate operators (min, max, sum, avg) return the same type as the type of the operand collection. Two examples follow. The query Q7 returns the number of students minoring in 'Computer Science,' while Q8 returns the average gpa of all seniors majoring in computer science.

---

53. These correspond to aggregate functions in SQL.

Q7: **count** (s **in** has_minors('Computer Science'));
Q8: **avg** (**select** s.gpa
         from s **in** students
         where s.majors_in.dname = 'Computer Science' **and**
               s.class = 'senior');

Notice that aggregate operations can be applied to any collection of the appropriate type and can be used in any part of a query. For example, the query to retrieve all department names that have more that 100 majors can be written as in Q9:

Q9: **select**   d.dname
       from   d **in** departments
       where   count (d.has_majors) > 100;

The *membership* and *quantification* expressions return a boolean type—that is, true or false. Let v be a variable, c a collection expression, b an expression of type boolean (that is, a boolean condition), and e an element of the type of elements in collection c. Then:

(**e in** c) returns true if element e is a member of collection c.
(**for all** v **in** c: b) returns true if *all* the elements of collection c satisfy b.
(**exists** v **in** c: b) returns true if there is at least one element in c satisfying b.

To illustrate the membership condition, suppose we want to retrieve the names of all students who completed the course called 'Database Systems I'. This can be written as in Q10, where the nested query returns the collection of course names that each student s has completed, and the membership condition returns true if 'Database Systems I' is in the collection for a particular student s:

Q10: **select** s.name.lname, s.name.fname
        from s **in** students
        where 'Database Systems I' in
             (**select** c.cname
             from c **in** s.completed_sections.section.of_course);

Q10 also illustrates a simpler way to specify the select clause of queries that return a collection of structs; the type returned by Q10 is bag<struct(string, string)>.

One can also write queries that return true/false results. As an example, let us assume that there is a named object called Jeremy of type Student. Then, query Q11 answers the following question: "Is Jeremy a computer science minor?" Similarly, Q12 answers the question "Are all computer science graduate students advised by computer science faculty?". Both Q11 and Q12 return true or false, which are interpreted as yes or no answers to the above questions:

Q11:   Jeremy **in** has_minors('Computer Science');
Q12:   **for all** g **in**
             (**select** s
             from s **in** grad_students
             where s.majors_in.dname = 'Computer Science')
        : g.advisor **in** csdepartment.has_faculty;

Note that query Q12 also illustrates how attribute, relationship, and operation inheritance applies to queries. Although s is an iterator that ranges over the extent grad_students, we can write s.majors_in because the majors_in relationship is inherited by GradStudent from Student via EXTENDS (see Figure 13.10). Finally, to illustrate the exists quantifier, query Q13 answers the following question: "Does any graduate computer science major have a 4.0 gpa?" Here, again, the operation gpa is inherited by GradStudent from Student via EXTENDS.

Q13: **exists** g **in**
      (**select** s
      from s **in** grad_students
      where s.majors_in.dname = 'Computer Science')
   : g.gpa = 4;

Ordered (Indexed) Collection Expressions.

As we discussed in Section 13.1.2.2, collections that are lists and arrays have additional operations, such as retrieving the ith, first and last elements. In addition, operations exist for extracting a subcollection and concatenating two lists. Hence, query expressions that involve lists or arrays can invoke these operations. We will illustrate a few of these operations using example queries. Q14 retrieves the last name of the faculty member who earns the highest salary:

Q14: **first (select**   **struct**(faculty: f.name.lname, salary:
                      f.salary)
      from   f **in** faculty
      order by   f.salary **desc**);

Q14 illustrates the use of the first operator on a list collection that contains the salaries of faculty members sorted in descending order on salary. Thus the first element in this sorted list contains the faculty member with the highest salary. This query assumes that only one faculty member earns the maximum salary. The next query, Q15, retrieves the top three computer science majors based on gpa.

Q15: (**select struct**(last_name: s.name.lname, first_name:
                   s.name.fname, gpa: s.gpa)
    from s **in** csdepartment.has_majors
    order by gpa **desc**) [0:2];

The select-from-order-by query returns a list of computer science students ordered by gpa in descending order. The first element of an ordered collection has an index position of 0, so the expression [0:2] returns a list containing the first, second and third elements of the select-from-order-by result.

The Grouping Operator.

The group by clause in OQL, although similar to the corresponding clause in SQL, provides explicit reference to the collection of objects within each *group* or *partition*. First we give an example, then describe the general form of these queries.

Q16 retrieves the number of majors in each department. In this query, the students are grouped into the same partition (group) if they have the same major; that is, the same value for s.majors_in.dname:

Q16: **select**   **struct**(deptname, number_of_majors:
                   count (partition))
    from   s **in** students
    group by deptname: s.majors_in.dname;

The result of the grouping specification is of type set<struct(deptname: string, partition: bag<struct(s: Student)>)>, which contains a struct for each group (PARTITION) that has two components: the grouping attribute value (deptname) and the bag of the student objects in the group (partition). The select clause returns the grouping attribute (name of the department), and a count of the number of elements in each partition (that is, the number of students in each department), where **partition** is the keyword used to refer to each partition. The result type of the select clause is set<struct(deptname: string, number_of_majors: integer)>. In general, the syntax for the group by clause is

    group by f_1: e_1, f_2: e_2, ... , f_k: e_k

where f_1: e_1, f_2: e_2, ... , fk: e_k is a list of partitioning (grouping) attributes and each partitioning attribute specification fi:ei defines an attribute (field) name fi and an expression ei.

The result of applying the grouping (specified in the group by clause) is a set of structures:

set<struct(f_1: t_1, f_2: t_2, . . ., f_k: t_k, partition: bag<B>)>

where ti is the type returned by the expression ei, partition is a distinguished field name (a keyword), and B is a structure whose fields are the iterator variables (s in Q16) declared in the from clause having the appropriate type.

Just as in SQL, a *having* clause can be used to filter the partitioned sets (that is, select only some of the groups based on group conditions). In Q17, the previous query is modified to illustrate the having clause (and also shows the simplified syntax for the select clause). Q17 retrieves for each department having more than 100 majors, the average gpa of its majors. The having clause in Q17 selects only those partitions (groups) that have more than 100 elements (that is, departments with more than 100 students).

Q17: **select**   deptname, avg_gpa: **avg** (**select** p.s.gpa **from** p
                                         in partition)
     from   s **in** students
     group by deptname: s.majors_in.dname
     having   **count** (**partition**) > 100;

Note that the select clause of Q17 returns the average gpa of the students in the partition. The expression

select p.s.gpa **from** p **in partition**

returns a bag of student gpas for that partition. The from clause declares an iterator variable p over the partition collection, which is of type bag<struct(s: Student)>. Then the path expression p.s.gpa is used to access the gpa of each student in the partition.

13.2.4   Overview Of The C++ Language Binding

The C++ language binding specifies how ODL constructs are mapped to C++ constructs. This is done via a C++ class library that provides classes and operations that implement the ODL constructs. An Object Manipulation Language (OML) is needed to specify how database objects are retrieved and manipulated within a C++ program, and this is based on the C++ programming language syntax and semantics. In addition to the ODL/OML bindings, a set of constructs called *physical pragmas* are defined to allow the programmer some control over physical storage issues, such as clustering of objects, utilizing indices, and memory management.

The class library added to C++ for the ODMG standard uses the prefix d_ for class declarations that deal with database concepts.[54] The goal is that the programmer should think that only one language is being used, not two separate languages. For the programmer to refer to database objects in a program, a class d_Ref<T> is defined for each database class T in the schema. Hence, program variables of type d_Ref<T> can refer to both persistent and transient objects of class T.

In order to utilize the various built-in types in the ODMG Object Model such as collection types, various template classes are specified in the library. For example, an abstract class d_Object<T> specifies the operations to be inherited by all objects. Similarly, an abstract class d_Collection<T> specifies the operations of collections. These classes are not instantiable, but only specify the operations that can be inherited by all objects and by collection objects, respectively. A template class is specified for each type of collection; these include d_Set<T>, d_List<T>, d_Bag<T>, d_Varray<T>, and d_Dictionary<T>, and correspond to the collection types in the Object Model (see Section 13.2.1.1). Hence, the programmer can create classes of types such

---

54. Presumably, d_ stands for *database* classes.

as d_Set<d_Ref<Student>> whose instances would be sets of references to Student objects, or d_ Set<String> whose instances would be sets of Strings. In addition, a class d_Iterator corresponds to the Iterator class of the Object Model.

The C++ ODL allows a user to specify the classes of a database schema using the constructs of C++ as well as the constructs provided by the object database library. For specifying the data types of attributes,[55] basic types such as d_Short (short integer), d_UShort (unsigned short integer), d_Long (long integer), and d_Float (floating point number) are provided. In addition to the basic data types, several structured literal types are provided to correspond to the structured literal types of the ODMG Object Model. These include d_String, d_Interval, d_Date, d_Time, and d_Timestamp (see Figure 13.5B).

To specify relationships, the keyword Rel_ is used within the prefix of type names; for example, by writing

    d_Rel_Ref<Department, _has_majors> majors_in;

in the Student class, and

    d_Rel_Set<Student, _majors_in> has_majors;

in the Department class, we are declaring that majors_in and has_majors are relationship properties that are inverses of one another and hence represent a 1:N binary relationship between Department and Student.

For the OML, the binding overloads the operation *new* so that it can be used to create either persistent or transient objects. To create persistent objects, one must provide the database name and the persistent name of the object. For example, by writing

    d_Ref<Student> s = new(DB1, 'Mahesh_Kumar') Student;

the programmer creates a named persistent object of type Student in database DB1 with persistent name Mahesh_Kumar. Another operation, delete_object() can be used to delete objects. Object modification is done by the operations (methods) defined in each class by the programmer.

The C++ binding also allows the creation of extents by using the library class d_Extent. For example, by writing

    d_Extent<Person> AllPersons(DB1);

the programmer would create a named collection object AllPersons—whose type would be d_Set<Person>—in the database DB1 that would hold persistent objects of type Person. However, key constraints are not supported in the C++ binding, and any key checks must be programmed in the class methods.[56] Also, the C++ binding does not support persistence via reachability; the object must be statically declared to be persistent at the time it is created.

13.2.5 Object Database Conceptual Design

Section 13.2.5.1 discusses how Object Database (ODB) design differs from Relational Database (RDB) design. Section 13.2.5.2 outlines a mapping algorithm that can be used to create an ODB schema, made of ODMG ODL class definitions, from a conceptual EER schema.

---

55. That is, *member variables* in object-oriented programming terminology.
56. We have only provided a brief overview of the C++ binding. For full details, see Cattell et al. (1997).

13.2.5.1 Differences between conceptual design of ODB and RDB One of the main differences between ODB and RDB design is how relationships are handled. In ODB, relationships are typically handled by having relationship properties or reference attributes that include OID(s) of the related objects. These can be considered as OID references to the related objects. Both single references and collections of references are allowed. References for a binary relationship can be declared in a single direction, or in both directions, depending on the types of access expected. If declared in both directions, they may be specified as inverses of one another, thus enforcing the ODB equivalent of the relational referential integrity constraint.

In RDB, relationships among tuples (records) are specified by attributes with matching values. These can be considered as *value references* and are specified via *foreign keys*, which are values of primary key attributes repeated in tuples of the referencing relation. These are limited to being single-valued in each record because multivalued attributes are not permitted in the basic relational model. Thus, M:N relationships must be represented not directly but as a separate relation (table), as discussed in Section 6.1.

Mapping binary relationships that contain attributes is not straightforward in ODBs, since the designer must choose in which direction the attributes should be included. If the attributes are included in both directions, then redundancy in storage will exist and may lead to inconsistent data. Hence, it is sometimes preferable to use the relational approach of creating a separate table by creating a separate class to represent the relationship. This approach can also be used for n-ary relationships, with degree n > 2.

Another major area of difference between ODB and RDB design is how inheritance is handled. In ODB, these structures are built into the model, so the mapping is achieved by using the inheritance constructs, such as *derived* (:) and EXTENDS. In relational design, as we discussed in Section 6.2, there are several options to choose from since no built-in construct exists for inheritance in the basic relational model. It is important to note, though, that object-relational and extended-relational systems are adding features to directly model these constructs as well as to include operation specifications in abstract data types (see Section 13.3).

The third major difference is that in ODB design, it is necessary to specify the operations early on in the design since they are part of the class specifications. Although it is important to specify operations during the design phase for all types of databases, it may be delayed in RDB design as it is not strictly required until the implementation phase.

13.2.5.2 Mapping an EER schema to an ODB schema It is relatively straightforward to design the type declarations of object classes for an ODBMS from an EER schema that contains *neither* categories *nor* n-ary relationships with n > 2. However, the operations of classes are not specified in the EER diagram and must be added to the class declarations after the structural mapping is completed. The outline of the mapping from EER to ODL is as follows:

Step 1:   Create an ODL *class* for each EER entity type or subclass. The type of the ODL class should include all the attributes of the EER class.[57] *Multivalued attributes* are declared by using the set, bag, or list constructors.[58] If the values of the multivalued attribute for an object should be ordered, the list constructor is chosen; if duplicates are allowed, the bag constructor should be chosen; otherwise, the set constructor is chosen. Composite attributes are mapped into a tuple constructor (by using a struct declaration in ODL).

---

57. This implicitly uses a tuple constructor at the top level of the type declaration, but in general, the tuple constructor is not explicitly shown in the ODL class declarations.

58. Further analysis of the application domain is needed to decide on which constructor to use because this information is not available from the EER schema.

Declare an extent for each class, and specify any key attributes as keys of the extent. (This is possible only if an extent facility and key constraint declarations are available in the ODBMS.)

Step 2: Add relationship properties or reference attributes for each *binary* relationship into the ODL classes that participate in the relationship. These may be created in one or both directions. If a binary relationship is represented by references in both directions, declare the references to be relationship properties that are inverses of one another, if such a facility exists.[59] If a binary relationship is represented by a reference in only *one* direction, declare the reference to be an attribute in the referencing class whose type is the referenced class name.

Depending on the cardinality ratio of the binary relationship, the relationship properties or reference attributes may be single-valued or collection types. They will be single-valued for binary relationships in the 1:1 or N:1 directions; they are collection types (set-valued or list-valued[60]) for relationships in the 1:N or M:N direction. An alternative way for mapping binary M:N relationships is discussed in Step 7 below.

If relationship attributes exist, a tuple constructor (struct) can be used to create a structure of the form <reference, relationship attributes>, which may be included instead of the reference attribute. However, this does not allow the use of the inverse constraint. In addition, if this choice is represented in *both directions*, the attribute values will be represented twice, creating redundancy.

Step 3: Include appropriate operations for each class. These are not available from the EER schema and must be added to the database design by referring to the original requirements. A constructor method should include program code that checks any constraints that must hold when a new object is created. A destructor method should check any constraints that may be violated when an object is deleted. Other methods should include any further constraint checks that are relevant.

Step 4: An ODL class that corresponds to a subclass in the EER schema inherits (via EXTENDS) the type and methods of its superclass in the ODL schema. Its *specific* (noninherited) attributes, relationship references, and operations are specified, as discussed in Steps 1, 2, and 3.

Step 5: Weak entity types can be mapped in the same way as regular entity types. An alternative mapping is possible for weak entity types that do not participate in any relationships except their identifying relationship; these can be mapped as though they were *composite multivalued attributes* of the owner entity type, by using the set<struct<...>> or list<struct<...>> constructors. The attributes of the weak entity are included in the struct<...> construct, which corresponds to a tuple constructor. Attributes are mapped as discussed in Steps 1 and 2.

Step 6: Categories (union types) in an EER schema are difficult to map to ODL. It is possible to create a mapping similar to the EER-to-relational mapping (see Section 6.2) by declaring a class to represent the category and defining 1:1 relationships between the category and each of its superclasses. Another option is to use a union type, if it is available.

Step 7: An *n*-ary relationship with degree $n > 2$ can be mapped into a separate class, with appropriate references to each participating class. These references are based on mapping a 1:N relationship from each class that represents a participating entity type to the class that represents the n-ary relationship. An M:N binary relationship, especially if it contains relationship attributes, may also use this mapping option, if desired.

---

59. The ODL standard provides for the explicit definition of inverse relationships. Some ODBMS products may not provide this support; in such a case, the programmers must maintain every relationship explicitly by coding the methods that update the objects appropriately.

60. The decision whether to use set or list is not available from the EER schema and must be determined from the requirements.

The mapping has been applied to a subset of the UNIVERSITY database schema of Figure 4.10 in the context of the ODMG object database standard.

13.2.6 Section Summary

In this section we discussed the proposed standard for object-oriented databases. We started by describing the various constructs of the ODMG object model. The various built-in types, such as Object, Collection, Iterator, Set, List, and so on were described by their interfaces, which specify the built-in operations of each type. These built-in types are the foundation upon which the object definition language (ODL) and object query language (OQL) are based. We also described the difference between objects, which have an ObjectId, and literals, which are values with no OID. Users can declare classes for their application that inherit operations from the appropriate built-in interfaces. Two types of properties can be specified in a user-defined class—attributes and relationships—in addition to the operations that can be applied to objects of the class. The ODL allows users to specify both interfaces and classes, and permits two different types of inheritance—interface inheritance via ":" and class inheritance via EXTENDS. A class can have an extent and keys.

A description of ODL then followed, and an example database schema for the UNIVERSITY database was used to illustrate the ODL constructs. We then presented an overview of the object query language (OQL). The OQL follows the concept of orthogonality in constructing queries, meaning that an operation can be applied to the result of another operation as long as the type of the result is of the correct input type for the operation. The OQL syntax follows many of the constructs of SQL but includes additional concepts such as path expressions, inheritance, methods, relationships, and collections. Examples of how to use OQL over the UNIVERSITY database were given.

We then gave an overview of the C++ language binding, which extends C++ class declarations with the ODL type constructors but permits seamless integration of C++ with the ODBMS.

Following the description of the ODMG model, we described a general technique for designing object-oriented database schemas. We discussed how object-oriented databases differ from relational databases in three main areas: references to represent relationships, inclusion of operations, and inheritance. We showed how to map a conceptual database design in the EER model to the constructs of object databases.

13.3 OBJECT-RELATIONAL AND EXTENDED-RELATIONAL SYSTEMS

In the preceding chapters we have primarily discussed three data models—the Entity-Relationship (ER) model and its enhanced version, the EER model, in Chapter 3; the relational data model and its languages and systems in Chapters 4 through 8; and the object-oriented data model and object database languages and standards in Sections 13.1 and 13.2. We discussed how all these data models have been thoroughly developed in terms of the following features:

- Modeling constructs for developing schemas for database applications.

- Constraints facilities for expressing certain types of relationships and constraints on the data as determined by application semantics.

- Operations and language facilities to manipulate the database.

Out of these three models, the ER model and its variations, has been primarily employed in CASE tools that are used for database and software design, whereas the other two models have been used as the basis for commercial DBMSs. This section discusses the emerging class of commercial DBMSs that are called *object-relational* or *enhanced relational systems*, and some of the conceptual foundations for these systems. These systems—which are often called object-relational DBMSs (ORDBMSs)—emerged as a way of enhancing the capabilities of relational DBMSs (RDBMSs) with some of the features that appeared in object DBMSs (ODBMSs).

We start in Section 13.3.1 by giving an overview of the SQL standard, which provides extended and object capabilities to the SQL standard for RDBMS. In Section 13.3.2 we give a historical perspective of database technology evolution and current trends to understand why these systems emerged. Section 13.3.3 gives an overview of the Informix database server as an example of a commercial extended ORDBMS. Section 13.3.4 discusses the object-relational and extended features of Oracle. Section 13.3.5 discusses some issues related to the implementation of extended relational systems and Section 13.3.6 presents an overview of the nested relational model, which provides some of the theoretical foundations behind extending the relational model with complex objects. Section 13.3.7 provides summary of this section.

13.3.1 Overview of SQL and its Object-relational Features

We introduced SQL as the standard language for RDBMSs in Chapter 7. As we discussed, SQL was first specified in the 1970s and underwent enhancements in 1989 and 1992. The language continued its evolution toward a new standard called SQL3, which adds object-oriented and other features. A subset of the SQL3 standard, now known as SQL:99, was approved. This section highlights some of the features of SQL3 and SQL:99 with a particular emphasis on the object-relational concepts.

13.3.1.1 The SQL standard and its components
We will briefly point out what each part of the SQL standard deals with, then describe some SQL features that are relevant to the object extensions to SQL. The SQL standard now includes the following parts:[61]

- SQL/Framework, SQL/Foundation, SQL/Bindings, SQL/Object.
- New parts addressing temporal, transaction aspects of SQL.
- SQL/CLI (Call Level Interface).
- SQL/PSM (Persistent Stored Modules).

SQL/Foundation deals with new data types, new predicates, relational operations, cursors, rules and triggers, user-defined types, transaction capabilities, and stored routines. SQL/CLI (Call Level Interface) (see Chapter 7) provides rules that allow execution of application code without providing source code and avoids the need for preprocessing. It contains about 50 routines for tasks such as connection to the SQL server, allocating and deallocating resources, obtaining diagnostic and implementation information, and controlling termination of transactions. SQL/PSM (Persistent Stored Modules) specifies facilities for partitioning an application between a client and a server. The goal is to enhance performance by minimizing network traffic. SQL/Bindings includes Embedded SQL and Direct Invocation. Embedded SQL has been

---

61. The discussion about the standard is largely based on Melton and Mattos (1996).

enhanced to include additional exception declarations. SQL/Temporal deals with historical data, time series data, and other temporal extensions, and it is being proposed by the TSQL2 committee.[62] SQL/Transaction specification formalizes the XA interface for use by SQL implementors.

13.3.1.2 Object-relational support in SQL-99

The SQL/Object specification extends SQL-92 to include object-oriented capabilities. We will discuss some of these features by referring to the corresponding object-oriented concepts that we discussed in Section 13.1. The following are some of the features that have been included in SQL-99:

- Some **type constructors** have been added to specify complex objects. These include the *row type*, which corresponds to the tuple (or struct) constructor of Section 13.1. An *array type* for specifying collections is also provided. Other collection type constructors, such as set, list, and bag constructors, are not yet part of the SQL-99 specifications, although some systems include them and they are expected to be in future versions of the standard.

- A mechanism for specifying **object identity** through the use of *reference type* is included.

- **Encapsulation of operations** is provided through the mechanism of user-defined types that may include operations as part of their declaration.

- **Inheritance** mechanisms are provided.

We now discuss each of these concepts in more detail.

Type Constructors. The type constructors *row* and *array* are used to specify complex types. These are also known as **user-defined types**, or **UDTs**, since the user defines them for a particular application. A **row type** may be specified using the following syntax:

CREATE TYPE row_type_name **AS [ROW]** (<component declarations>);

The keyword ROW is optional. An example for specifying a row type for addresses and employees may be done as follows:

```
CREATE TYPE Addr_type AS (
    street VARCHAR (45),
    city VARCHAR (25),
    zip CHAR (5)
    );
CREATE TYPE Emp_type AS (
    name VARCHAR (35),
    addr Addr_type,
    age INTEGER
    );
```

Notice that we can use a previously defined type as a type for an attribute, as illustrated by the addr attribute above. An **array type** may be specified for an attribute whose value will be a collection. For example, suppose that a company has up to ten locations. Then a row type for company may be defined as follows:

```
CREATE TYPE Comp_type AS (
    compname VARCHAR (20),
    location VARCHAR (20) ARRAY [10]
    );
```

---

62. The full proposal appears in Snodgrass and Jensen (1996). We discuss temporal modeling and introduce TSQL2 in Section 13.5.

Fixed-length array types have their elements referenced using the common notation of square brackets. For example, location[1] refers to the first location value in a location attribute. For row types, the common dot notation is used to refer to components. For example, addr.city refers to the city component of an addr attribute. Currently, array elements cannot be arrays themselves, thus limiting the complexity of the object structures that can be created.

Object Identifiers Using References. A user defined type can be used either as type for an attribute, as illustrated by the addr attribute of Emp_type, or it can be used to specify the row types of tables. For example, we can create two tables based on the row type declarations given earlier as follows:

```
CREATE TABLE Employee OF Emp_type REF IS emp_id SYSTEM GENERATED;
CREATE TABLE Company OF Comp_type (
REF IS comp_id SYSTEM GENERATED,
PRIMARY KEY (compname));
```

The above examples also illustrate how the user can specify that system-generated object identifiers for the individual rows in a table should be created. By using the syntax:

```
REF IS <oid_attribute> <value_generation_method> ;
```

the user declares that the attribute named <oid_attribute> will be used to identify individual tuples in the table. The options for <value_generation_method> are SYSTEM GENERATED or DERIVED. In the former case, the system will automatically generate a unique identifier for each tuple. In the latter case, the traditional method of using the user-provided primary key value to identify tuples is applied.

A component attribute of one tuple may be a **reference** (specified using the keyword REF) to a tuple of another (or possibly the same) table. For example, we can define the following additional row type and corresponding table to relate an employee to a company:

```
CREATE TYPE Employment_type AS (
    employee REF (Emp_type) SCOPE (Employee),
    company REF (Comp_type) SCOPE (Company)
);
CREATE TABLE Employment OF Employment_type;
```

The keyword SCOPE specifies the name of the table whose tuples can be referenced by the reference attribute. Notice that this is similar to a foreign key, except that the system generated value is used rather than the primary key value.

SQL uses a **dot notation** to build **path expressions** that refer to the component attributes of tuples and row types. However, for an attribute whose type is REF, the dereferencing symbol -> is used. For example, the query below retrieves employees working in the company named 'ABCXYZ' by querying the Employment table:

```
SELECT e.employee->name
FROM Employment AS e
WHERE e.company->compname = 'ABCXYZ';
```

In SQL, -> is used for **dereferencing** and has the same meaning assigned to it in the C programming language. Thus if r is a reference to a tuple and a is a component attribute in that tuple, $r -> a$ is the value of attribute a in that tuple.

Object identifiers can also be explicitly declared in the type definition rather than in the table declaration. For example, the definition of Emp_type may be changed as follows:

```
CREATE TYPE Emp_type AS (
    name CHAR (35),
    addr Addr_type,
```

```
    age INTEGER,
    emp_id REF (Emp_type)
);
```

In the above example, the emp_id values may be specified to be system generated by using the command:

CREATE TABLE Employee **OF** Emp_type
VALUES FOR emp_id **ARE SYSTEM GENERATED;**

If several relations of the same row type exist, SQL provides the SCOPE keyword by which a reference attribute may be made to point to a specific table of that type by using:

SCOPE FOR <attribute> **IS** <relation>

Encapsulation of Operations in SQL.

In SQL a construct similar to class definition is provided whereby the user can create a named user-defined type with its own behavioral specification by specifying methods (or operations) in addition to the attributes. The general form of an UDT specification with methods is:

CREATE TYPE <type-name> (
    list of component attributes with individual types
    declaration of EQUAL and LESS THAN functions
    declaration of other functions (methods)
);

For example, suppose we would like to extract the apartment number (if given) from a string that forms the street attribute component of the Addr_type row type declared previously. We can specify a method for Addr_type as follows:

CREATE TYPE Addr_type **AS** (
    street VARCHAR (45),
    city VARCHAR (25),
    zip CHAR (5)
)
METHOD apt_no() **RETURNS** CHAR (8);

The code for implementing the method still has to be written. We can refer to the method implementation by specifying the file that contains the code for the method as follows:

METHOD
CREATE FUNCTION apt_no() **RETURNS** CHAR (8) **FOR** Addr_type **AS**
EXTERNAL NAME '/x/y/aptno.class' **LANGUAGE** 'java';

In this example, the implementation is in the JAVA language, and the code is stored in the specified file path name.

SQL provides certain built-in functions for user defined types. For a UDT called Type_T, the **constructor function** Type_T() returns a new object of that type. In the new UDT object, every attribute is initialized to its default value. An **observer function** A is implicitly created for each attribute A to read its value. Hence, A(X) or X.A returns the value of attribute A of Type_T if X is of type Type_T. A **mutator function** for updating an attribute sets the value of the attribute to a new value. SQL allows these functions to be blocked from public use; an EXECUTE privilege is needed to have access to these functions.

In general, a UDT can have a number of user-defined functions associated with it. The syntax is

METHOD <name> (<argument_list>) **RETURNS** <type>;

Two types of functions can be defined: internal SQL and external. Internal functions are written in the extended PSM language of SQL (see Chapter 7). External functions are written in a host language, with only their signature (interface) appearing in the UDT definition. An external function definition can be declared as follows:

DECLARE EXTERNAL <function_name> <signature>
LANGUAGE <language_name>;

Many ORBDMSs have taken the approach of defining a package of Abstract Data Types (ADTs) and associated functions for specific application domains. These could be purchased separately from the basic system. For example, the Data Blades in Informix Universal Server, the Data Cartridges in Oracle, and the Extenders in DB2 can be considered as such packages or libraries of ADTs for specific application domains.

UDTs can be used as the types for attributes in SQL and the parameter types in a function or procedure, and as a source type in a distinct type. **Type Equivalence** is defined in SQL at two levels. Two types are **name equivalent** if and only if they have the same name. Two types are **structurally equivalent** if and only if they have the same number of components and the components are pairwise type equivalent.

Attributes and functions in UDTs are divided into three categories:

- PUBLIC (visible at the UDT interface).
- PRIVATE (not visible at the UDT interface).
- PROTECTED (visible only to subtypes).

It is also possible to define virtual attributes as part of UDTs, which are computed and updated using functions.

Inheritance and Overloading of Functions in SQL. Recall that we already discussed many of the principles of inheritance in Section 13.1. SQL has rules for dealing with inheritance (specified via the UNDER keyword). Associated with inheritance are the rules for overloading of function implementations, and for resolution of function names. These rules can be summarized as follows:

- All attributes are inherited.
- The order of supertypes in the UNDER clause determines the inheritance hierarchy.
- An instance of a subtype can be used in every context in which a supertype instance is used.
- A subtype can redefine any function that is defined in its supertype, with the restriction that the signature be the same.
- When a function is called, the best match is selected based on the types of all arguments.
- For dynamic linking, the runtime types of parameters is considered.

Consider the following example to illustrate type inheritance. Suppose that we want to create a subtype Manager_type that inherits all the attributes (and methods) of Emp_type but has an additional attribute dept_managed. Then we can write:

CREATE TYPE Manager_type **UNDER** Emp_type **AS** (
    dept_managed CHAR (20)
);

This inherits all the attributes and methods of the supertype Emp_type, and has an additional specific attribute dept_managed. We could also specify additional specific methods for the subtype.

Another facility in SQL is the supertable/subtable facility, which is similar to the class or extends inheritance discussed in Section 13.1. Here, a subtable inherits every column from its supertable; every row of a subtable corresponds to one and only one row in the supertable; every row in the supertable corresponds to at most one row in a subtable. INSERT, DELETE, and UPDATE operations are appropriately propagated. For example, consider the real_estate_info table defined as follows:

```
CREATE TABLE real_estate_info (
    property real_estate,
    owner CHAR(25),
    price MONEY,
);
```

The following subtables can be defined:

```
CREATE TABLE american_real_estate UNDER real_estate_info;
CREATE TABLE georgia_real_estate UNDER american_real_estate;
CREATE TABLE atlanta_real_estate UNDER georgia_real_estate;
```

In this example, every tuple in the subtable american_real_estate must exist in its supertable real_estate_info; every tuple in the subtable georgia_real_estate must exist in its supertable american_real _estate, and so on. However, tuples can exist in a supertable without being in the subtable.

Unstructured Complex Objects in SQL. SQL has new data types for binary large objects (LOBs), and large object locators. Two variations exist for binary large objects (BLOBs) and character large objects (CLOBs). SQL proposes LOB manipulation within the DBMS without having to use external files. Certain operators do not apply to LOB-valued attributes—for example, arithmetic comparisons, group by, and order by. On the other hand, retrieval of partial value, LIKE comparison, concatenation, substring, position, and length are operations that can be applied to LOBs. We will see how large objects are used in Oracle 8.

We have given an overview of the proposed object-oriented facilities in SQL. At this time, both the SQL/Foundations and SQL/Object specification have been standardized. It is evident that the facilities that make SQL object-oriented closely follow what has been implemented in commercial ORDBMSs. SQL/MM (multimedia) is being proposed as a separate standard for multimedia database management with multiple parts: framework, full text, spatial, general purpose facilities, and still image. We will discuss the use of the two-dimensional data types and the image and text Datablades in Informix Universal Server.

13.3.1.3 Some new operations and features in SQL

A major new operation is **linear recursion** for specifying recursive queries. To illustrate this, suppose we have a table called PART_TABLE(Part1, Part2), which contains a tuple <p1, p2> whenever part p1 contains part p2 as a component. A query to produce the **bill of materials** for some part p1 (that is, all component parts needed to produce p1) is written as a recursive query as follows:

```
WITH RECURSIVE
BILL_MATERIAL (Part1, Part2) AS
    (SELECT Part1, Part2
    FROM PART_TABLE
    WHERE Part1 = 'p1'
        UNION ALL
    SELECT PART_TABLE(Part1), PART_TABLE(Part2)
    FROM BILL_MATERIAL, PART_TABLE
    WHERE PART_TABLE.Part1 = BILL_MATERIAL(Part2))

SELECT * FROM BILL_MATERIAL
ORDER BY Part1, Part2;
```

The final result is contained in BILL_MATERIAL(Part1, Part2). The UNION ALL operation is evaluated by taking a union of all tuples generated by the inner block until no new tuples can be generated. Because SQL2 lacks recursion, it was left to the programmer to accomplish it by appropriate iteration.

For security in SQL3, the concept of **role** is introduced, which is similar to a "job description" and is subject to authorization of privileges. The actual persons (user accounts) that are assigned to a role may change, but the role authorization itself does not have to be changed. SQL3 also includes syntax for the specification and use of **triggers** (see Section 13.4) as active rules. Triggering events include the INSERT, DELETE, and UPDATE operations on a table. The trigger can be specified to be considered BEFORE or AFTER the triggering event. The concept of **trigger granularity** is included in SQL3, which allows the specification of both row-level triggers (the trigger is considered for each affected row) or statement-level trigger (the trigger is considered only once for each triggering event).[63] For distributed (client-server) databases (see Chapter 14), the concept of a **client module** is included in SQL3. A client module may contain externally invoked procedures, cursors, and temporary tables, which can be specified using SQL3 syntax.

SQL3 also is being extended with programming language facilities. Routines written in SQL/CLI with full matching of data types and an integrated environment are referred to as SQL **routines.** To make the language computationally complete, the following programming control structures are included in the SQL3 syntax: CALL/RETURN, BEGIN/END, FOR/END_FOR, IF/THEN/ELSE/END_IF, CASE/END_CASE, LOOP/END_LOOP, WHILE/END_WHILE, REPEAT/UNTIL/END_REPEAT, and LEAVE. Variables are declared using DECLARE, and assignments are specified using SET. **External routines** refer to programs written in a host language (ADA, C, COBOL, PASCAL, etc.), possibly containing embedded SQL and having possible type mismatches. The advantage of external routines is that there are existing libraries of such routines that are broadly used, which can cut down a lot of implementation effort for applications. On the other hand, SQL routines are more "pure," but they have not been in wide use. SQL routines can be used for server routines (schema-level routines or modules) or as client modules, and they may be procedures or functions that return values. SQL/ CLI is described in Chapter 7.

13.3.2 Evolution and Current Trends of Database Technology

In the commercial world today, there are several families of DBMS products available. Two important ones are RDBMS and ODBMS, which subscribe to the relational and the object data models respectively. Two other major types of DBMS products—hierarchical and network—are now being referred to as **legacy DBMSs;** these are based on the hierarchical and the network data models, both of which were introduced in the mid-1960s. The hierarchical family primarily has one dominant product—IMS of IBM, whereas the network family includes a large number of DBMSs, such as IDS II (Honeywell), IDMS (Computer Associates), IMAGE (Hewlett Packard), VAX-DBMS (Digital), and TOTAL/SUPRA (Cincom), to name a few. The hierarchical and network data models are summarized in Appendixes E and F.[64]

As database technology evolves, the legacy DBMSs will be gradually replaced by newer offerings. In the interim, we must face the major problem of **interoperability**—the interoperation of a number of databases belonging to all of the disparate families of DBMSs—as well as to legacy file management systems. A whole series of new systems and tools to deal with this problem are emerging as well. More recently, XML has emerged as a new standard for data exchange on the Web (see Chapter 15).

The main forces behind the development of extended ORDBMSs stem from the inability of the legacy DBMSs and the basic relational data model as well as the earlier RDBMSs to meet the challenges of new applications. These are primarily in areas that involve a variety of types of data—for example, text in computer-

---

63. These concepts are discussed in more detail in Section 13.4.
64. Those chapters devoted to the Network Data Model and the Hierarchical Data Model are available at the Web site for this book.

aided desktop publishing; images in satellite imaging or weather forecasting; complex nonconventional data in engineering designs, in the biological genome information, and in architectural drawings; time series data in history of stock market transactions or sales histories; and spatial and geographic data in maps, air/water pollution data, and traffic data. Hence there is a clear need to design databases that can develop, manipulate, and maintain the complex objects arising from such applications. Furthermore, it is becoming necessary to handle digitized information that represents audio and video data streams (partitioned into individual frames) requiring the storage of BLOBs (binary large objects) in DBMSs.

The popularity of the relational model is helped by a very robust infrastructure in terms of the commercial DBMSs that have been designed to support it. However, the basic relational model and earlier versions of its SQL language proved inadequate to meet the above challenges. Legacy data models like the network data model have a facility to model relationships explicitly, but they suffer from a heavy use of pointers in the implementation and have no concepts like object identity, inheritance, encapsulation, or the support for multiple data types and complex objects. The hierarchical model fits well with some naturally occurring hierarchies in nature and in organizations, but it is too limited and rigid in terms of built-in hierarchical paths in the data. Hence, a trend was started to combine the best features of the object data model and languages into the relational data model so that it can be extended to deal with the challenging applications of today.

In the remainder of this section we highlight the features of two representative DBMSs that exemplify the ORDBMS approach: Informix Universal Server and Oracle 8. We conclude by briefly discussing the nested relational model, which has its origin in a series of research proposals and prototype implementations; this provides a theoretical framework of embedding hierarchically structured complex objects within the relational framework.

13.3.3   The Informix Universal Server[65]

The Informix Universal Server is an ORDBMS that combines relational and object database technologies from two previously existing products: Informix and Illustra. The latter system originated from the POSTGRES DBMS, which was a research project at the University of California at Berkeley that was commercialized as the Montage DBMS and went through the name Miro before being named Illustra. Illustra was then acquired by Informix, integrated into its RDBMS, and introduced as the Informix Universal Server—an ORDBMS.

To see why ORDBMSs emerged, we start by focusing on one way of classifying DBMS applications according to two dimensions or axes: (1) complexity of data—the X dimension—and (2) complexity of querying—the Y-dimension. We can arrange these axes into a simple 0-1 space having four quadrants:

Quadrant 1 ($X = 0$, $Y = 0$): Simple data, simple querying
Quadrant 2 ($X = 0$, $Y = 1$): Simple data, complex querying
Quadrant 3 ($X = 1$, $Y = 0$): Complex data, simple querying
Quadrant 4 ($X = 1$, $Y = 1$): Complex data, complex querying

Traditional RDBMSs belong to Quadrant 2. Although they support complex ad hoc queries and updates (as well as transaction processing), they can deal only with simple data that can be modeled as a set of rows in a table. Many object databases (ODBMSs) fall in Quadrant 3, since they concentrate on managing complex data but have somewhat limited querying capabilities based on navigation.[66] In order to move into the fourth

---

65. The discussion in this section is primarily based on the book *Object-Relational DBMSs* by Michael Stonebraker and Dorothy Moore (1996), and on the input provided by Magdi Morsi of Informix, Inc. Our discussion may refer to earlier versions of Informix that may not be the most recent.

66. Quadrant 1 includes any software packages that deal with data handling without sophisticated data retrieval and manipulation features. These include spreadsheets like EXCEL, word processors like Microsoft Word, or any file management software.

quadrant to support both complex data and querying, RDBMSs have been incorporating more complex data objects while ODBMSs have been incorporating more complex querying (for example, the OQL high-level query language, discussed in Section 13.2). The Informix Universal Server belongs to Quadrant 4 because it has extended its basic relational model by incorporating a variety of features that make it object-relational.

Other current ORDBMSs that evolved from RDBMSs include Oracle from Oracle Corporation, Universal DB (UDB) from IBM, Odapter by Hewlett Packard (HP) (which extends Oracle's DBMS), and Open ODB from HP (which extends HP's own Allbase/SQL product). The more successful products seem to be those that maintain the option of working as an RDBMS while introducing the additional functionality. Our intent here is not to provide a comparative analysis of these products but only to give an overview of two representative systems.

How Informix Universal Server Extends the Relational Data Model. The extensions to the relational data model provided by Illustra and incorporated into Informix Universal Server fall into the following categories:

- Support for additional or extensible data types.
- Support for user-defined routines (procedures or functions).
- Implicit notion of inheritance.
- Support for indexing extensions.
- Data Blades Application Programming Interface (API).[67]

We give an overview of each of these features in the following sections. We have already introduced in a general way the concepts of data types, type constructors, complex objects, and inheritance in the context of object-oriented models (see Section 13.1).

13.3.3.1 Extensible data types The architecture of Informix Universal Server comprises the basic DBMS plus a number of **Data Blade modules.** The idea is to treat the DBMS as a razor into which a particular blade is inserted for the support of a specific data type. A number of data types have been provided, including two-dimensional geometric objects (such as points, lines, circles, and ellipses), images, time series, text, and Web pages. When Informix announced the Universal Server, 29 Data Blades were already available.[68] It is also possible for an application to create its own types, thus making the data type notion fully extendible. In addition to the built-in types, Informix Universal Server provides the user with the following four constructs to declare additional types:

1. Opaque type.
2. Distinct type.
3. Row type.
4. Collection type.

When creating a type based on one of the first three options, the user has to provide functions and routines for manipulation and conversion, including built-in, aggregate, and operator functions as well as any additional user-defined functions and routines. The details of these four types are presented in the following sections.

---

67. Data Blades provides extensions to the basic system, as we shall discuss later in Section 13.3.3.6.

68. For more information on the Data Blades for Informix Universal Server, consult the Web site http://www.informix.com/informix/.

Opaque Type. The opaque type has its internal representation hidden, so it is used for encapsulating a type. The user has to provide casting functions to convert an opaque object between its hidden representation in the server (database) and its visible representation as seen by the client (calling program). The user functions *send/receive* are needed to convert to/from the server internal representation from/to the client representation. Similarly, *import/export* functions are used to convert to/from an external representation for bulk copy from/to the internal representation. Several other functions may be defined for processing the opaque types, including *assign()*, *destroy()*, and *compare()*.

The specification of an opaque type includes its name, internal length if fixed, maximum internal length if it is variable length, alignment (which is the byte boundary), as well as whether or not it is hashable (for creating a hash access structure). If we write

```
CREATE OPAQUE TYPE fixed_opaque_udt (INTERNALLENGTH = 8,
    ALIGNMENT = 4, CANNOTHASH);
CREATE OPAQUE TYPE var_opaque_udt (INTERNALLENGTH = variable,
    MAXLEN=1024, ALIGNMENT = 8);
```

then the first statement creates a fixed-length user-defined opaque type, named fixed_opaque_udt, and the second statement creates a variable length one, named var_opaque_udt. Both are described in an implementation with internal parameters that are not visible to the client.

Distinct Type. The distinct data type is used to extend an existing type through inheritance. The newly defined type inherits the functions/routines of its base type, if they are not overridden. For example, the statement

```
CREATE DISTINCT TYPE hiring_date AS DATE;
```

creates a new user-defined type, hiring_date, which can be used like any other built-in type.

Row Type. The row type, which represents a composite attribute, is analogous to a *struct* type in the C programming language.[69] It is a composite type that contains one or more fields. Row type is also used to support inheritance by using the keyword UNDER, but the type system supports single inheritance only. By creating tables whose tuples are of a particular row type, it is possible to treat a relation as part of an object-oriented schema and establish inheritance relationships among the relations. In the following row type declarations, employee_t and student_t inherit (or are *declared under*) person_t:

```
CREATE ROW TYPE person_t(name VARCHAR(60), social_security
    NUMERIC(9), birth_date DATE);
CREATE ROW TYPE employee_t(salary NUMERIC(10,2), hired_on
    hiring_date) UNDER person_t;
CREATE ROW TYPE student_t(gpa NUMERIC(4,2), address
    VARCHAR(200)) UNDER person_t;
```

Collection Type. Informix Universal Server collections include lists, sets, and multisets (bags) of built-in types as well as user-defined types.[70] A collection can be the type of either a field in a row type or a column in a table. The elements of a **set** collection cannot contain duplicate values, and have no specific order. The **list** may contain duplicate elements, and order is significant. Finally, the **multiset** may include duplicates and has no specific order. Consider the following example:

---

69. This is similar to the *tuple constructor* discussed in Section 13.1.
70. These are similar to the *collection types* discussed in Sections 13.1 and 13.2.

```
CREATE TABLE employee (name VARCHAR(50) NOT NULL, commission
    MULTISET (MONEY));
```

Here, the employee table contains the commission column, which is of type multiset.

13.3.3.2 Support for user-defined routines

Informix Universal Server supports user-defined functions and routines to manipulate the user defined types. The implementation of these functions can be in either Stored Procedure Language (SPL), or in the C or JAVA programming languages. User-defined functions enable the user to define operator functions such as *plus()*, *minus()*, *times()*, *divide()*, *positive()*, and *negate()*, built-in functions such as *cos()* and *sin()*, aggregate functions such as *sum()* and *avg()*, and user-defined routines. This enables Informix Universal Server to handle user-defined types as a built-in type whenever the required functions are defined. The following example specifies an equal function to compare two objects of the fixed_opaque_udt type declared earlier:

```
CREATE FUNCTION equal (arg1 fixed_opaque_udt, arg2
    fixed_opaque_udt) RETURNING BOOLEAN;
EXTERNAL NAME "/usr/lib/informix/libopaque.so
    (fixed_opaque_udt_equal)" LANGUAGE C;
END FUNCTION;
```

Informix Universal Server also supports **cast**—a function that converts objects from a source type to a target type. There are two types of user-defined casts: (1) implicit and (2) explicit. Implicit casts are invoked automatically, whereas explicit casts are invoked only when the cast operator is specified explicitly by using "::" or CAST AS. If the source and target types have the same internal structure (such as when using the *distinct types* specification), no user-defined functions are needed.

Consider the following example to illustrate explicit casting, where the employee table has a col1 column of type var_opaque_udt and a col2 column of type fixed_opaque_udt.

```
SELECT col1 FROM employee WHERE fixed_opaque_udt::col1 = col2;
```

In order to compare col1 with col2, the cast operator is applied to col1 to convert it from var_opaque_udt to fixed_opaque_udt.

13.3.3.3 Support for inheritance

Inheritance is addressed at two levels in Informix Universal Server: (1) data (attribute) inheritance and (2) function (operation) inheritance.

Data Inheritance. To create subtypes under existing row types, we use the UNDER keyword as discussed earlier. Consider the following example:

```
CREATE ROW TYPE employee_type (
    ename VARCHAR(25),
    eno CHAR(9),
    salary INT) ;
CREATE ROW TYPE engineer_type (
    degree VARCHAR(10),
    license VARCHAR(20))
    UNDER employee_type;
CREATE ROW TYPE engr_mgr_type (
    manager_start_date VARCHAR(10),
    dept_managed VARCHAR(20))
    UNDER engineer_type;
```

The above statements create an employee_type and a subtype called engineer_type, which represents employees who are engineers and hence inherits all attributes of employees and has additional properties of degree and license. Another type called engr_mgr_type is a subtype under engineer_type, and hence inherits from engineer_type and implicitly from employee_type as well. Informix Universal Server does not support multiple inheritance. We can now create tables called employee, engineer, and engr_mgr based on these row types.

Note that storage options for storing type hierarchies in tables vary. Informix Universal Server provides the option to store instances in different combinations—for example, one instance (record) at each level or one instance that consolidates all levels— these correspond to the mapping options in Section 6.2. The inherited attributes are either represented repeatedly in the tables at lower levels or are represented with a reference to the object of the supertype. The processing of SQL commands is appropriately modified based on the type hierarchy. For example, the query

```
SELECT *
FROM employee
WHERE salary > 100000;
```

returns the employee information from all tables where each selected employee is represented. Thus the scope of the employee table extends to all tuples under employee. As a default, queries on the supertable return columns from the supertable as well as those from the subtables that inherit from that supertable. In contrast, the query

```
SELECT *
FROM ONLY (employee)
WHERE salary > 100000;
```

returns instances from only the employee table because of the keyword ONLY.

It is possible to query a supertable using a *correlation variable* so that the result contains not only supertable_type columns of the subtables but also subtype-specific columns of the subtables. Such a query returns rows of different sizes; the result is called a **jagged row result**. Retrieving all information about an employee from all levels in a "jagged form" is accomplished by

```
SELECT e
FROM employee e ;
```

For each employee, depending on whether he or she is an engineer or some other subtype(s), it will return additional sets of attributes from the appropriate subtype tables.

Views defined over supertables cannot be updated because placement of inserted rows is ambiguous.

Function Inheritance.
In the same way that data is inherited among tables along a type hierarchy, functions can also be inherited in an ORDBMS. For example, a function overpaid may be defined on employee_type to select those employees making a higher salary than Bill Brown as follows:

```
CREATE FUNCTION overpaid (employee_type)
RETURNS BOOLEAN AS
RETURN $1.salary > (SELECT salary
                    FROM employee
                    WHERE ename = 'Bill Brown');
```

The tables under the employee table automatically inherit this function. However, the same function may be redefined for the engr_mgr_type as those employees making a higher salary than Jack Jones as follows:

```
CREATE FUNCTION overpaid (engr_mgr_type)
RETURNS BOOLEAN AS
```

```
RETURN $1.salary > (SELECT salary
                    FROM employee
                    WHERE ename = 'Jack Jones');
```

For example, consider the query

```
SELECT e.ename
FROM ONLY (employee) e
WHERE overpaid (e);
```

which is evaluated with the first definition of overpaid. The query

```
SELECT g.ename
FROM engineer g
WHERE overpaid (g);
```

also uses the first definition of overpaid (because it was not redefined for engineer), whereas

```
SELECT gm.ename
FROM engr_mgr gm
WHERE overpaid (gm);
```

uses the second definition of overpaid, which overrides the first. This is called **operation** (or **function**) **overloading**, as was discussed in Section 13.1.6 under polymorphism. Note that overpaid—and other functions—can also be treated as virtual attributes; hence overpaid may be referenced as employee.overpaid or engr_mgr.overpaid in a query.

13.3.3.4 Support for indexing extensions
Informix Universal Server supports indexing on user-defined routines on either a single table or a table hierarchy. For example,

```
CREATE INDEX empl_city ON employee (city (address));
```

creates an index on the table employee using the value of the city function.

In order to support user-defined indexes, Informix Universal Server supports operator classes, which are used to support user-defined data types in the generic B-tree as well as other secondary access methods such as R-trees.

13.3.3.5 Support for external data source
Informix Universal Server supports external data sources (such as data stored in a file system) that are mapped to a table in the database called the **virtual table interface**. This interface enables the user to define operations that can be used as *proxies* for the other operations, which are needed to access and manipulate the row or rows associated with the underlying data source. These operations include open, close, fetch, insert, and delete. Informix Universal Server also supports a set of functions that enables calling SQL statements within a user-defined routine without the overhead of going through a client interface.

13.3.3.6 Support for data blades application programming interface
The Data Blades Application Programming Interface (API) of Informix Universal Server provides new data types and functions for specific types of applications. We will review the extensible data types for two-dimensional operations (required in GIS or CAD applications),[71] the data types related to image storage and management, the

---

71. Recall that GIS stands for Geographic Information Systems and CAD for Computer Aided Design.

time series data type, and a few features of the text data type. The strength of ORDBMSs to deal with the new unconventional applications is largely attributed to these special data types and the tailored functionality that they provide.

Two-Dimensional (Spatial) Data Types.   For a two-dimensional application, the relevant data types would include the following:

- A **point** defined by (X, Y) coordinates.
- A **line** defined by its two end points.
- A **polygon** defined by an ordered list of n points that form its vertices.
- A **path** defined by a sequence (ordered list) of points.
- A **circle** defined by its center point and radius.

Given the above as data types, a function such as *distance* may be defined between two points, a point and a line, a line and a circle, and so on, by implementing the appropriate mathematical expressions for distance in a programming language. Similarly, a Boolean cross function—which returns true or false depending on whether two geometric objects cross (or intersect)—can be defined between a line and a polygon, a path and a polygon, a line and a circle, and so on. Other relevant Boolean functions for GIS applications would be *overlap* (polygon, polygon), *contains* (polygon, polygon), *contains* (point, polygon), and so on. Note that the concept of overloading (operation polymorphism) applies when the same function name is used with different argument types.

Image Data Types.   Images are stored in a variety of standard formats—such as TIFF, GIF, JPEG, photoCD, GROUP 4, and FAX—so one may define a data type for each of these formats and use appropriate library functions to input images from other media or to render images for display. Alternately, IMAGE can be regarded as a single data type with a large number of options for storage of data. The latter option would allow a column in a table to be of type IMAGE and yet accept images in a variety of different formats. The following are some possible functions (operations) on images:

```
rotate (image, angle) returns image.
crop (image, polygon) returns image.
enhance (image) returns image.
```

The *crop* function extracts the portion of an image that intersects with a polygon. The *enhance* function improves the quality of an image by performing contrast enhancement. Multiple images may be supplied as parameters to the following functions:

```
common (image1, image2) returns image.
union (image1, image2) returns image.
similarity (image1, image2) returns number.
```

The *similarity* function typically takes into account the distance between two vectors with components <color, shape, texture, edge> that describe the content of the two images. The VIR Data Blade in Informix Universal Server can be used to accomplish a search on images by content based on the above similarity measure.

Time Series Data Type.   Informix Universal Server supports a time series data type that makes the handling of time series data much more simplified than storing it in multiple tables. For example, consider storing the closing stock price on the New York Stock Exchange for more than 3,000 stocks for each workday when the market is open. Such a table can be defined as follows:

```
CREATE TABLE stockprices (
company-name VARCHAR(30),
symbol VARCHAR(5),
prices TIME_SERIES OF FLOAT);
```

Regarding the stock price data for all 3,000 companies over an entire period of, say, several years, only one relation is adequate thanks to the time series data type for the prices attribute. Without this data type, each company would need one table. For example, a table for the coca_cola company (symbol KO) may be declared as follows:

```
CREATE TABLE coca_cola (
recording_date DATE,
price FLOAT);
```

In this table, there would be approximately 260 tuples per year—one for each business day. The time series data type takes into account the calendar, starting time, recording interval (for example, daily, weekly, monthly), and so on. Functions such as extracting a subset of the time series (for example, closing prices during January 1999), summarizing at a coarser granularity (for example, average weekly closing price from the daily closing prices), and constructing moving averages are appropriate. A query on the stockprices table that gives the moving average for 30 days starting at June 1, 1999 for the coca_cola stock can use the MOVING-AVG function as follows:

```
SELECT MOVING-AVG(prices, 30, '01-06-1999')
FROM stockprices
WHERE symbol = "KO";
```

The same query in SQL on the table coca_cola would be much more complicated to write and would access numerous tuples, whereas the above query on the stockprices table deals with a single row in the table corresponding to this company. It is claimed that using the time series data type provides an order of magnitude performance gain in processing such queries.

Text Data Type. The text DataBlade supports storage, search, and retrieval for text objects. It defines a single data type called **doc**, whose instances are stored as large objects that belong to the built-in data type large-text. We will briefly discuss a few important features of this data type.

The underlying storage for large-text is the same as that for the large-object data type. References to a single large object are recorded in the 'refcount' system table, which stores information such as number of rows referring to the large object, its OID, its storage manager, its last modification time, and its archive storage manager. Automatic conversion between large-text and text data types enables any functions with text arguments to be applied to large-text objects. Thus concatenation of large-text objects as strings as well as extraction of substrings from a large-text object are possible.

The Text DataBlade parameters include format for which the default is ASCII, with other possibilities such as postscript, dvipostscript, nroff, troff, and text. A Text Conversion DataBlade, which is separate from the Text DataBlade, is needed to convert documents among the various formats. An External File parameter instructs the internal representation of doc to store a pointer to an external file rather than copying it to a large object.

For manipulation of doc objects, functions such as the following are used:

```
Import_doc (doc, text) returns doc.
Export_doc (doc, text) returns text.
Assign (doc) returns doc.
Destroy (doc) returns void.
```

The Assign and Destroy functions already exist for the built-in large-object and large-text data types, but they must be redefined by the user for objects of type doc. The following statement creates a table called legaldocuments, where each row has a title of the document in one column and the document itself as the other column:

```
CREATE TABLE legaldocuments(
title TEXT,
document DOC);
```

To insert a new row into this table of a document called 'lease.contract,' the following statement can be used:

```
INSERT INTO legaldocuments (title, document)
VALUES ('lease.contract', 'format {troff}:/user/local/
            documents/lease');
```

The second value in the values clause is the path name specifying the file location of this document; the format specification signifies that it is a troff document. To search the text, an index must be created, as in the following statement:

```
CREATE INDEX legalindex
ON legaldocuments
USING dtree(document text_ops);
```

In the above, text_ops is an op-class (operator class) applicable to an access structure called a dtree index, which is a special index structure for documents. When a document of the doc data type is inserted into a table, the text is parsed into individual words. The Text DataBlade is case insensitive; hence, Housenumber, HouseNumber, or housenumber are all considered the same word. Words are *stemmed* according to the WORDNET thesaurus. For example, houses or housing would be stemmed to house, quickly to quick, and talked to talk. A **stopword** file is kept, which contains insignificant words such as articles or prepositions that are ignored in the searches. Examples of stopwords include is, not, a, the, but, for, and, if, and so on.

Informix Universal Server provides two sets of routines—the **contains routines** and **text-string functions**—to enable applications to determine which documents contain a certain word or words and which documents are similar. When these functions are used in a search condition, the data is returned in descending order of how well the condition matches the documents, with the best match showing first. There is Weight-Contains(index to use, tuple-id of the document, input string) function and a similar WeightContainsWords function that returns a precision number between 0 and 1 indicating the closeness of the match between the input string or input words and the specific document for that tuple-id. To illustrate the use of these functions, consider the following query: Find the titles of legal documents that contain the top ten terms in the document titled 'lease contract', which can be specified as follows:

```
SELECT d.title
FROM legaldocuments d, legaldocuments l
WHERE contains (d.document, AndTerms (TopNTerms(l.document,10)))
AND l.title = 'lease.contract' AND d.title <> 'lease.contract';
```

This query illustrates how SQL can be enhanced with these data type specific functions to yield a very powerful capability of handing text-related functions. In this query, variable d refers to the entire legal corpus whereas l refers to the specific document whose title is 'lease.contract'. TopNTerms extracts the top ten terms from the 'lease.contract' document (l); AndTerms combines these terms into a list; and contains compares the terms in that list with the stemwords in every other document (d) in the table legaldocuments.

Summary of Data Blades. As we can see, Data Blades enhance an RDBMS by providing various constructors for abstract data types (ADTs) that allow a user to operate on the data as if it were stored in an

ODBMS using the ADTs as classes. This makes the relational system *behave* as an ODBMS, and drastically cuts down the programming effort needed when compared with achieving the same functionality with just SQL embedded in a programming language.

13.3.4 Object-relational Features of Oracle 8

In this section we will review a number of features related to the version of the Oracle DBMS product called Release 8.X, which has been enhanced to incorporate object relational features. Additional features may have been incorporated into subsequent versions of Oracle. A number of additional data types with related manipulation facilities called **cartridges** have been added.[72] For example, the spatial cartridge allows mapbased and geographic information to be handled. Management of multimedia data has been facilitated with new data types. Here we highlight the differences between the release 8.X of Oracle (as available at the time of this writing) from the preceding version in terms of the new object-oriented features and data types as well as some storage options. Portions of the language SQL-99, which we discussed in Section 13.2.1, will be applicable to Oracle. We do not discuss these features here.

13.3.4.1 Some examples of object-relational features of oracle
As an ORDBMS, Oracle 8 continues to provide the capabilities of an RDBMS and additionally supports object-oriented concepts. This provides higher levels of abstraction so that application developers can manipulate application objects as opposed to constructing the objects from relational data. The complex information about an object can be hidden, but the properties (attributes, relationships) and methods (operations) of the object can be identified in the data model. Moreover, object type declarations can be reused via inheritance, thereby reducing application development time and effort. To facilitate object modeling, Oracle introduced the following features (as well as some of the SQL-99 features in Section 13.3.1).

Representing Multivalued Attributes Using VARRAY. Some attributes of an object/entity could be multivalued. In the relational model, the multivalued attributes would have to be handled by forming a new table (see Section 7.1 and Section 8.3.2 on first normal form). If ten attributes of a large table were multivalued, we would have eleven tables generated from a single table after normalization. To get the data back, the developer would have to do ten joins across these tables. This does not happen in an object model since all the attributes of an object—including multivalued ones—are encapsulated within the object. Oracle 8 achieves this by using a varying length array (VARRAY) data type, which has the following properties:

1. COUNT: Current number of elements.

2. LIMIT: Maximum number of elements the VARRAY can contain. This is user defined.

Consider the example of a customer VARRAY entity with attributes name and phone_numbers, where phone_numbers is multivalued. First, we need to define an object type representing a phone_number as follows:

    CREATE TYPE phone_num_type **AS OBJECT** (phone_number CHAR(10));

Then we define a VARRAY whose elements would be objects of type phone_num_type:

    CREATE TYPE phone_list_type as VARRAY (5) **OF** phone_num_type;

---

72. Cartridges in Oracle are somewhat similar to Data Blades in Informix.

Now we can create the customer_type data type as an object with attributes customer_name and phone_numbers:

CREATE TYPE customer_type **AS**
OBJECT (customer_name VARCHAR(20),
            phone_numbers phone_list_type);

It is now possible to create the customer table as

CREATE TABLE customer **OF** customer_type;

To retrieve a list of all customers and their phone numbers, we can issue a simple query without any joins:

SELECT customer_name, phone_numbers
FROM customers;

Using Nested Tables to Represent Complex Objects.

In object modeling, some attributes of an object could be objects themselves. Oracle 8 accomplishes this by having **nested tables** (see Section 13.1.6). Here, columns (equivalent to object attributes) can be declared as tables. In the above example let us assume that we have a description attached to every phone number (for example, home, office, cellular). This could be modeled using a nested table by first redefining phone_num_type as follows:

CREATE TYPE phone_num_type **AS**
OBJECT (phone_number CHAR(10), description CHAR(30));

We next redefine phone_list_type as a table of phone_number_type as follows:

CREATE TYPE phone_list_type **AS TABLE OF** phone_number_type;

We can then create the type customer_type and the customer table as before. The only difference is that phone_list_type is now a nested table instead of a VARRAY. Both structures have similar functions with a few differences. Nested tables do *not* have an upper bound on the number of items whereas VARRAYs do have a limit. Individual items can be retrieved from the nested tables, but this is not possible with VARRAYs. Additional indexes can also be built on nested tables for faster data access.

Object Views.

Object views can be used to build virtual objects from relational data, thereby enabling programmers to evolve existing schemas to support objects. This allows relational and object applications to coexist on the same database. In our example, let us say that we had modeled our customer database using a relational model, but management decided to do all future applications in the object model. Moving over to the object view of the same existing relational data would thus facilitate the transition.

13.3.4.2 Managing large objects and other storage features

Oracle can now store extremely large objects like video, audio, and text documents. New data types have been introduced for this purpose. These include the following:

- BLOB (binary large object).
- CLOB (character large object).
- BFILE (binary file stored outside the database).
- NCLOB (fixed-width multibyte CLOB).

All of the above except for BFILE, which is stored outside the database, are stored inside the database along with other data. Only the directory name for a BFILE is stored in the database.

Index Only Tables. Standard Oracle 7.X involves keeping indexes as a B+-tree that contains pointers to data blocks (see Chapter 9). This gives good performance in most situations. However, both the index and the data block must be accessed to read the data. Moreover, key values are stored twice—in the table and in the index—increasing the storage costs. Oracle 8 supports both the standard indexing scheme and also **index only tables,** where the data records and index are kept together in a B-tree structure (see Chapter 9). This allows faster data retrieval and requires less storage space for small- to medium-sized files where the record size is not too large.

Partitioned Tables and Indexes. Large tables and indexes can be broken down into smaller partitions. The table now becomes a logical structure and the partitions become the actual physical structures that hold the data. This gives the following advantages:

- Continued data availability in the event of partial failures of some partitions.
- Scalable performance allowing substantial growth in data volumes.
- Overall performance improvement in query and transaction processing.

13.3.5 Implementation and Related Issues for Extended Type Systems

There are various implementation issues regarding the support of an extended type system with associated functions (operations). We briefly summarize them here.[73]

- The ORDBMS must dynamically link a user-defined function in its address space only when it is required. As we saw in the case of the two ORDBMSs, numerous functions are required to operate on two- or three-dimensional spatial data, images, text, and so on. With a static linking of all function libraries, the DBMS address space may increase by an order of magnitude. Dynamic linking is available in the two ORDBMSs that we studied.

- Client-server issues deal with the placement and activation of functions. If the server needs to perform a function, it is best to do so in the DBMS address space rather than remotely, due to the large amount of overhead. If the function demands computation that is too intensive or if the server is attending to a very large number of clients, the server may ship the function to a separate client machine. For security reasons, it is better to run functions at the client using the user ID of the client. In the future functions are likely to be written in interpreted languages like JAVA.

- It should be possible to run queries inside functions. A function must operate the same way whether it is used from an application using the application program interface (API), or whether it is invoked by the DBMS as a part of executing SQL with the function embedded in an SQL statement. Systems should support a nesting of these "callbacks."

- Because of the variety in the data types in an ORDBMS and associated operators, efficient storage and access of the data is important. For spatial data or multidimensional data, new storage structures such as R-trees, quad trees, or Grid files may be used. The ORDBMS must allow new types to be defined with new access structures. Dealing with large text strings or binary files also opens up a number of storage and search options. It should be possible to explore such new options by defining new data types within the ORDBMS.

---

73. This discussion is derived largely from Stonebraher and Mooro (1996).

Other Issues Concerning Object-Relational Systems. In the above discussion of Informix Universal Server and Oracle 8, we have concentrated on how an ORDBMS extends the relational model. We discussed the features and facilities it provides to operate on relational data stored as tables as if it were an object database. There are other obvious problems to consider in the context of an ORDBMS:

- *Object-relational database design*: We described a procedure for designing object schemas in Section 13.2.5. Object-relational design is more complicated because we have to consider not only the underlying design considerations of application semantics and dependencies in the relational data model (which we discussed in Chapter 8) but also the object-oriented nature of the extended features that we have just discussed.

- *Query processing and optimization*: By extending SQL with functions and rules, this problem is further compounded beyond the query optimization overview that we discuss for the relational model in Chapter 10.

- *Interaction of rules with transactions*: Rule processing as implied in SQL covers more than just the update-update rules (see Section 13.4.1), which are implemented in RDBMSs as triggers. Moreover, RDBMSs currently implement only immediate execution of triggers. A deferred execution of triggers involves additional processing.

13.3.6 The Nested Relational Model

To complete this discussion, we summarize in this section an approach that proposes the use of nested tables, also known as nonnormal form relations. No commercial DBMS has chosen to implement this concept in its original form. The **nested relational model** removes the restriction of first normal form (1NF, see Chapter 8) from the basic relational model, and thus is also known as the **Non-1NF** or **Non-First Normal Form (NFNF)** or **NF²** relational model. In the basic relational model—also called the **flat relational model**—attributes are required to be single-valued and to have atomic domains. The nested relational model allows composite and multivalued attributes, thus leading to complex tuples with a hierarchical structure. This is useful for representing objects that are naturally hierarchically structured. In Figure 13.12, part (a) shows a nested relation schema DEPT based on part of the COMPANY database, and part (b) gives an example of a Non-1NF tuple in DEPT.

To define the DEPT schema as a nested structure, we can write the following:

```
dept = (dno, dname, manager, employees, projects, locations)
employees = (ename, dependents)
projects = (pname, ploc)
locations = (dloc)
dependents = (dname, age)
```

First, all attributes of the DEPT relation are defined. Next, any nested attributes of DEPT—namely, EMPLOYEES, PROJECTS, and LOCATIONS—are themselves defined. Next, any second-level nested attributes, such as DEPENDENTS of EMPLOYEES, are defined, and so on. All attribute names must be distinct in the nested relation definition. Notice that a nested attribute is typically a **multivalued composite attribute,** thus leading to a "nested relation" *within each tuple.* For example, the value of the PROJECTS attribute within each DEPT tuple is a relation with two attributes (PNAME, PLOC). In the DEPT tuple of Figure 13.12b, the PROJECTS attribute contains three tuples·as its value. Other nested attributes may be **multivalued simple attributes,** such as LOCATIONS of DEPT. It is also possible to have a nested attribute that is **single-valued and composite,** although most nested relational models treat such an attribute as though it were multivalued.

When a nested relational database schema is defined, it consists of a number of external relation schemas; these define the top level of the individual nested relations. In addition, nested attributes are called **internal relation schemas,** since they define relational structures that are nested inside another relation. In our example, DEPT is the only external relation. All the others—EMPLOYEES, PROJECTS, LOCATIONS, and DEPENDENTS—are internal relations. Finally, **simple attributes** appear at the leaf level and are not nested. We can represent each relation schema by means of a tree structure, as shown in Figure 13.12c, where the root is an external relation schema, the leaves are simple attributes, and the internal nodes are internal relation schemas. Notice the similarity between this representation and a hierarchical schema (see Appendix E) and XML (see Chapter 15).

(a)

DNO	DNAME	MANAGER	EMPLOYEES			PROJECTS		LOCATIONS
			ENAME	DEPENDENTS		PNAME	PLOC	DLOC
				DNAME	AGE			

(b)

4	Administration	Ganesh	Narayan	Thomas	8	New benefits	chennai	chennai
				Priya	6	Computerization	chennai	Greenway
			Ganesh	Jack	18	Phone System	Greenway	
				Robert	15			
				Mary	10			
			Jabbar					

(c)

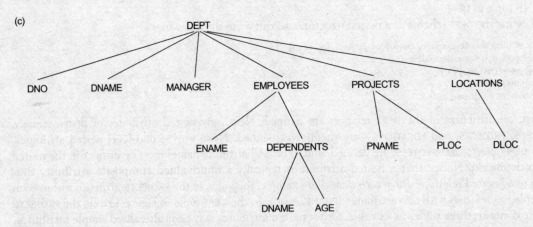

FIGURE 13.12 Illustrating a nested relation. (a) DEPT schema. (b) Example of a Non-1NF tuple of DEPT. (c) Tree representation of DEPT schema.

It is important to be aware that the three first-level nested relations in DEPT represent *independent information*. Hence, EMPLOYEES represents the employees *working for* the department, PROJECTS represents the projects *controlled by* the department, and LOCATIONS represents the various department locations. The relationship between EMPLOYEES and PROJECTS is not represented in the schema; this is an M:N relationship, which is difficult to represent in a hierarchical structure.

Extensions to the relational algebra and to the relational calculus, as well as to SQL, have been proposed for nested relations. The interested reader is referred to the selected bibliography at the end of this chapter for details. Here, we illustrate two operations, **NEST** and **UNNEST,** that can be used to augment standard relational algebra operations for converting between nested and flat relations. Consider the flat EMP_PROJ relation of Figure 8.3, and suppose that we project it over the attributes ENO, PNUMBER, HOURS, ENAME as follows:

$$EMP\_PROJ\_FLAT \leftarrow \pi_{ENO, ENAME, PNUMBER, HOURS} (EMP\_PROJ)$$

To create a nested version of this relation, where one tuple exists for each employee and the (PNUMBER, HOURS) are nested, we use the NEST operation as follows:

$$EMP\_PROJ\_NESTED \leftarrow NEST_{PROJS = (PNUMBER, HOURS)}(EMP\_PROJ\_FLAT)$$

The effect of this operation is to create an internal nested relation PROJS = (PNUMBER, HOURS) within the external relation EMP_PROJ_NESTED. Hence, NEST groups together the tuples *with the same value* for the attributes that are *not specified* in the NEST operation; these are the ENO and ENAME attributes in our example. For each such group, which represents one employee in our example, a single nested tuple is created with an internal nested relation PROJS = (PNUMBER, HOURS). Hence, the EMP_PROJ_NESTED relation looks like the EMP_PROJ relation shown in Figure 8.9a and b.

Notice the similarity between nesting and grouping for aggregate functions. In the former, each group of tuples becomes a single nested tuple; in the latter, each group becomes a single summary tuple after an aggregate function is applied to the group.

The UNNEST operation is the inverse of NEST. We can reconvert EMP_PROJ_NESTED to EMP_PROJ_FLAT as follows:

$$EMP\_PROJ\_FLAT \leftarrow UNNEST_{PROJS = (PNUMBER, HOURS)}(EMP\_PROJ\_NESTED)$$

Here, the PROJS nested attribute is flattened into its components PNUMBER, HOURS.

13.3.7   Section Summary

In this section, we first gave an overview of the object-oriented features in SQL-99, which are applicable to object-relational systems. Then we discussed the history and current trends in database management systems that led to the development of object-relational DBMSs (ORDBMSs). We then focused on some of the features of Informix Universal Server and of Oracle 8 in order to illustrate how commercial RDBMSs are being extended with object features. Other commercial RDBMSs are providing similar extensions. We saw that these systems also provide Data Blades (Informix) or Cartridges (Oracle) that provide specific type extensions for newer application domains, such as spatial, time series, or text/document databases. Because of the extendibility of ORDBMSs, these packages can be included as abstract data type (ADT) libraries whenever the users need to implement the types of applications they support. Users can also implement their own extensions as needed by using the ADT facilities of these systems. We briefly discussed some implementation issues for ADTs. Finally, we gave an overview of the nested relational model, which extends the flat relational model with hierarchically structured complex objects.

13.4 ACTIVE DATABASE CONCEPTS AND TRIGGERS

Rules that specify actions that are automatically triggered by certain events have been considered as important enhancements to a database system for quite some time. In fact, the concept of **triggers**—a technique for specifying certain types of active rules—has existed in early versions of the SQL specification for relational databases and triggers are now part of the SQL-99 standard. Commercial relational DBMSs—such as Oracle, DB2, and SYBASE—have had various versions of triggers available. However, much research into what a general model for active databases should look like has been done since the early models of triggers were proposed. In Section 13.4.1, we will present the general concepts that have been proposed for specifying rules for active databases. We will use the syntax of the Oracle commercial relational DBMS to illustrate these concepts with specific examples, since Oracle triggers are close to the way rules are specified in the SQL standard. Section 13.4.2 will discuss some general design and implementation issues for active databases. We then give examples of how active databases are implemented in the STARBURST experimental DBMS in Section 13.4.3, since STARBURST provides for many of the concepts of generalized active databases within its framework. Section 13.4.4 discusses possible applications of active databases. Finally, Section 13.4.5 describes how triggers are declared in the SQL-99 standard.

13.4.1 Generalized Model for Active Databases and Oracle Triggers

The model that has been used for specifying active database rules is referred to as the **Event-Condition-Action,** or **ECA** model. A rule in the ECA model has three components:

1. The **event** (or events) that triggers the rule: These events are usually database update operations that are explicitly applied to the database. However, in the general model, they could also be temporal events[74] or other kinds of external events.

2. The **condition** that determines whether the rule action should be executed: Once the triggering event has occurred, an *optional* condition may be evaluated. If *no condition* is specified, the action will be executed once the event occurs. If a condition is specified, it is first evaluated, and only *if it evaluates to true* will the rule action be executed.

3. The **action** to be taken: The action is usually a sequence of SQL statements, but it could also be a database transaction or an external program that will be automatically executed.

Let us consider some examples to illustrate these concepts. The examples are based on a much simplified variation of the COMPANY database application from Figure 4.7, which is shown in Figure 13.13, with each employee having a name (NAME), employee's number (ENO) salary (SALARY), department to which they are currently assigned (DNO, a foreign key to DEPARTMENT), and a direct supervisor (SUPERVISOR_ENO, a (recursive) foreign key to EMPLOYEE). For this example, we assume that null is allowed for DNO, indicating that an employee may be temporarily unassigned to any department. Each department has a name (DNAME), number (DNO), the total salary of all employees assigned to the department (TOTAL_SAL), and a manager (MANAGER_ENO, a foreign key to EMPLOYEE).

---

74. An example would be a temporal event specified as a periodic time, such as: Trigger this rule every day at 5:30 A.M.

Notice that the TOTAL_SAL attribute is really a derived attribute, whose value should be the sum of the salaries of all employees who are assigned to the particular department. Maintaining the correct value of such a derived attribute can be done via an active rule. We first have to determine the **events** that *may cause* a change in the value of TOTAL_SAL, which are as follows:

1. Inserting (one or more) new employee tuples.
2. Changing the salary of (one or more) existing employees.
3. Changing the assignment of existing employees from one department to another.
4. Deleting (one or more) employee tuples.

EMPLOYEE

NAME	ENO	SALARY	DNO	SUPERVISOR_ENO

DEPARTMENT

DNAME	DNO	TOTAL_SAL	MANAGER_ENO

FIGURE 13.13 A simplified COMPANY database used for active rule examples.

In the case of event 1, we only need to recompute TOTAL_SAL if the new employee is immediately assigned to a department—that is, if the value of the DNO attribute for the new employee tuple is not null (assuming null is allowed for DNO). Hence, this would be the **condition** to be checked. A similar condition could be checked for event 2 (and 4) to determine whether the employee whose salary is changed (or who is being deleted) is currently assigned to a department. For event 3, we will always execute an action to maintain the value of TOTAL_SAL correctly, so no condition is needed (the action is always executed).

The **action** for events 1, 2, and 4 is to automatically update the value of TOTAL_SAL for the employee's department to reflect the newly inserted, updated, or deleted employee's salary. In the case of event 3, a twofold action is needed; one to update the TOTAL_SAL of the employee's old department and the other to update the TOTAL_SAL of the employee's new department.

The four active rules (or triggers) R1, R2, R3, and R4—corresponding to the above situation—can be specified in the notation of the Oracle DBMS as shown in Figure 13.14a. Let us consider rule R1 to illustrate the syntax of creating triggers in Oracle. The CREATE TRIGGER statement specifies a trigger (or active rule) name—TOTALSAL1 for R1. The AFTER-clause specifies that the rule will be triggered *after* the events that trigger the rule occur. The triggering events—an insert of a new employee in this example—are specified following the AFTER keyword.[75] The ON-clause specifies the relation on which the rule is specified—EMPLOYEE for R1. The *optional* keywords FOR EACH ROW specify that the rule will be triggered *once for each row* that is affected by the triggering event.[76] The *optional* WHEN-clause is used to specify any conditions that need to be checked after the rule is triggered but before the action is executed. Finally, the action(s) to be taken are specified as a PL/SQL block, which typically contains one or more SQL statements or calls to execute external procedures.

---

75. As we shall see later, it is also possible to specify BEFORE instead of AFTER, which indicates that the rule is triggered *before the triggering event is executed.*

76. Again, we shall see later that an alternative is to trigger the rule *only once* even if multiple rows (tuples) are affected by the triggering event.

(a)   **R1:**   **CREATE TRIGGER** TOTALSAL1
              AFTER INSERT ON EMPLOYEE
              FOR EACH ROW
              WHEN (NEW.DNO **IS NOT NULL**)
                    UPDATE DEPARTMENT
                    SET TOTAL_SAL= TOTAL_SAL + **NEW**.SALARY
                    WHERE DNO=**NEW**.DNO;

     R2:   **CREATE TRIGGER** TOTALSAL2
              AFTER UPDATE OF SALARY **ON** EMPLOYEE
              FOR EACH ROW
              WHEN (NEW.DNO IS NOT NULL)
                    UPDATE DEPARTMENT
                    SET TOTAL_SAL=TOTAL_SAL + **NEW**.SALARY - **OLD**.SALARY
                    WHERE DNO=**NEW**.DNO;

     R3:   **CREATE TRIGGER** TOTALSAL3
              AFTER UPDATE OF DNO **ON** EMPLOYEE
              FOR EACH ROW
                    BEGIN
                    UPDATE DEPARTMENT
                    SET TOTAL_SAL= TOTAL_SAL + NEW.SALARY
                    WHERE DNO=**NEW**.DNO;
                    UPDATE DEPARTMENT
                    SET TOTAL_SAL= TOTAL_SAL- **OLD**.SALARY
                    WHERE DNO=**OLD**.DNO;
                    END;

     R4:   **CREATE TRIGGER** TOTALSAL4
              AFTER DELETE ON EMPLOYEE
              FOR EACH ROW
              WHEN (OLD.DNO **IS NOT NULL**)
                    UPDATE DEPARTMENT
                    SET TOTAL_SAL= TOTAL_SAL - **OLD**. SALARY
                    WHERE DNO=**OLD**.DNO;

(b)   **R5:**   **CREATE TRIGGER** INFORM_SUPERVISOR1
              BEFORE INSERT OR UPDATE OF SALARY, SUPERVISOR_ENO **ON** EMPLOYEE
              FOR EACH ROW
               WHEN
              (**NEW**. SALARY > (**SELECT** SALARY **FROM** EMPLOYEE
              WHERE ENO=**NEW**.SUPERVISOR_ENO))
              INFORM_SUPERVISOR(**NEW**. SUPERVISOR_ENO, **NEW**.ENO);

FIGURE 13.14 Specifying active rules as triggers in Oracle notation. (a) Triggers for automatically maintaining the consistency of TOTAL_SAL of DEPARTMENT. (b) Trigger for comparing an employee's salary with that of his or her supervisor.

The four triggers (active rules) R1, R2, R3, and R4 illustrate a number of features of active rules. First, the basic **events** that can be specified for triggering the rules are the standard SQL update commands: **INSERT,** DELETE, and UPDATE. These are specified by the keywords **INSERT, DELETE,** and **UPDATE** in Oracle notation. In the case of **UPDATE** one may specify the attributes to be updated—for example, by writing **UPDATE OF** SALARY, DNO. Second, the rule designer needs to have a way to refer to the tuples that have been inserted, deleted, or modified by the triggering event. The keywords **NEW** and **OLD** are used in Oracle notation; NEW is used to refer to a newly inserted or newly updated tuple, whereas OLD is used to refer to a deleted tuple or to a tuple before it was updated.

Thus rule R1 is triggered after an INSERT operation is applied to the EMPLOYEE relation. In R1, the condition (**NEW.**DNO **IS NOT NULL**) is checked, and if it evaluates to true, meaning that the newly inserted employee tuple is related to a department, then the action is executed. The action updates the DEPARTMENT tuple(s) related to the newly inserted employee by adding their salary (**NEW.**SALARY) to the TOTAL_SAL attribute of their related department.

Rule R2 is similar to R1, but it is triggered by an UPDATE operation that updates the SALARY of an employee rather than by an INSERT. Rule R3 is triggered by an update to the DNO attribute of EMPLOYEE, which signifies changing an employee's assignment from one department to another. There is no condition to check in R3, so the action is executed whenever the triggering event occurs. The action updates both the old department and new department of the reassigned employees by adding their salary to TOTAL_SAL of their *new* department and subtracting their salary from TOTAL_SAL of their *old* department. Note that this should work even if the value of DNO was null, because in this case no department will be selected for the rule action.[77]

It is important to note the effect of the optional FOR EACH ROW clause, which signifies that the rule is triggered separately *for each tuple.* This is known as a **row-level trigger.** If this clause was left out, the trigger would be known as a **statement-level trigger** and would be triggered once for each triggering statement. To see the difference, consider the following update operation, which gives a 10 percent raise to all employees assigned to department 5. This operation would be an event that triggers rule R2:

```
UPDATE      EMPLOYEE
SET         SALARY = 1.1 * SALARY
WHERE       DNO = 5;
```

Because the above statement could update multiple records, a rule using row-level semantics, such as R2 in Figure 13.14, would be triggered *once for each row,* whereas a rule using statement-level semantics is triggered *only once.* The Oracle system allows the user to choose which of the above two options is to be used for each rule. Including the optional FOR EACH ROW clause creates a row-level trigger, and leaving it out creates a statement-level trigger. Note that the keywords NEW and OLD can only be used with row-level triggers.

As a second example, suppose we want to check whenever an employee's salary is greater than the salary of his or her direct supervisor. Several events can trigger this rule: inserting a new employee, changing an employee's salary, or changing an employee's supervisor. Suppose that the action to take would be to call an external procedure INFORM_SUPERVISOR,[78] which will notify the supervisor. The rule could then be written as in R5 (see Figure 13.14b).

Figure 13.15 shows the syntax for specifying some of the main options available in Oracle triggers. We will describe the syntax for triggers in the SQL-99 standard in Section 13.4.5.

---

77. R1, R2, and R4 can also be written without a condition. However, they may be more efficient to execute with the condition since the action is not invoked unless it is required.

78. Assuming that an appropriate external procedure has been declared. This is a feature that is now available in SQL.

13.4.2 Design and Implementation Issues for Active Databases

The previous section gave an overview of some of the main concepts for specifying active rules. In this section, we discuss some additional issues concerning how rules are designed and implemented. The first issue concerns activation, deactivation, and grouping of rules. In addition to creating rules, an active database system should allow users to *activate, deactivate,* and *drop* rules by referring to their rule names. A **deactivated rule** will not be triggered by the triggering event. This feature allows users to selectively deactivate rules for certain periods of time when they are not needed. The **activate command** will make the rule active again. The **drop command** deletes the rule from the system. Another option is to group rules into named **rule sets,** so the whole set of rules could be activated, deactivated, or dropped. It is also useful to have a command that can trigger a rule or rule set via an explicit **PROCESS RULES** command issued by the user.

```
<trigger> ::= CREATE TRIGGER <trigger name>
              (AFTER | BEFORE) <triggering events> ON <table name>
              [FOR EACH ROW]
              [WHEN <condition>]
<trigger actions>;
<triggering events> ::= <trigger events> {OR <trigger event>}
<trigger event> ::= INSERT | DELETE | UPDATE [OF <column name>{, <column name>}
<trigger action> ::= <PL/SQL block>
```

FIGURE 13.15 A syntax summary for specifying triggers in the Oracle system (main options only).

The second issue concerns whether the triggered action should be executed *before, after,* or *concurrently with* the triggering event. A related issue is whether the action being executed should be considered as a *separate transaction* or whether it should be part of the same transaction that triggered the rule. We will first try to categorize the various options. It is important to note that not all options may be available for a particular active database system. In fact, most commercial systems are *limited to one or two of the options* that we will now discuss.

Let us assume that the triggering event occurs as part of a transaction execution. We should first consider the various options for how the triggering event is related to the evaluation of the rule's condition. The rule *condition evaluation* is also known as **rule consideration,** since the action is to be executed only after considering whether the condition evaluates to true or false. There are three main possibilities for rule consideration:

1. *Immediate consideration:* The condition is evaluated as part of the same transaction as the triggering event, and is evaluated *immediately.* This case can be further categorized into three options:

   - Evaluate the condition *before* executing the triggering event.

   - Evaluate the condition *after* executing the triggering event.

   - Evaluate the condition *instead of* executing the triggering event.

2. *Deferred consideration:* The condition is evaluated at the end of the transaction that included the triggering event. In this case, there could be many triggered rules waiting to have their conditions evaluated.

3. *Detached consideration:* The condition is evaluated as a separate transaction, spawned from the triggering transaction.

The next set of options concerns the relationship between evaluating the rule condition and *executing* the rule action. Here, again, three options are possible: **immediate, deferred,** and **detached** execution. However, most active systems use the first option. That is, as soon as the condition is evaluated, if it returns true, the action is *immediately* executed.

The Oracle system (see Section 13.4.1) uses the *immediate consideration* model, but it allows the user to specify for each rule whether the *before* or *after* option is to be used with immediate condition evaluation. It also uses the *immediate execution* model. The STARBURST system (see Section 13.4.3) uses the *deferred consideration* option, meaning that all rules triggered by a transaction wait until the triggering transaction reaches its end and issues its COMMIT WORK command before the rule conditions are evaluated.[79]

Another issue concerning active database rules is the distinction between *row-level rules* versus *statement-level rules*. Because SQL update statements (which act as triggering events) can specify a set of tuples, one has to distinguish between whether the rule should be considered once for the *whole statement* or whether it should be considered separately *for each row* (that is, tuple) affected by the statement. The SQL-99 standard (see Section 13.4.5) and the Oracle system (see Section 13.4.1) allow the user to choose which of the above two options is to be used for each rule, whereas STARBURST uses statement-level semantics only. We will give examples of how statement-level triggers can be specified in Section 13.4.3.

One of the difficulties that may have limited the widespread use of active rules, in spite of their potential to simplify database and software development, is that there are no easy-to-use techniques for designing, writing, and verifying rules. For example, it is quite difficult to verify that a set of rules is **consistent,** meaning that two or more rules in the set do not contradict one another. It is also difficult to guarantee **termination** of a set of rules under all circumstances. To briefly illustrate the termination problem, consider the rules in Figure 13.16. Here, rule R1 is triggered by an INSERT event on TABLE1 and its action includes an update event on ATTRIBUTE1 of TABLE2. However, rule R2's triggering event is an UPDATE event on ATTRIBUTE1 of TABLE2, and its action includes an INSERT event on TABLE1. It is easy to see in this example that these two rules can trigger one another indefinitely, leading to nontermination. However, if dozens of rules are written, it is very difficult to determine whether termination is guaranteed or not.

If active rules are to reach their potential, it is necessary to develop tools for the design, debugging, and monitoring of active rules that can help users in designing and debugging their rules.

13.4.3   Examples of Statement-Level Active Rules in STARBURST

We now give some examples to illustrate how rules can be specified in the STARBURST experimental DBMS. This will allow us to demonstrate how statement-level rules can be written, since these are the only types of rules allowed in STARBURST.

The three active rules R1S, R2S, and R3S in Figure 13.17 correspond to the first three rules in Figure 13.14, but use STARBURST notation and statement-level semantics. We can explain the rule structure using rule R1S. The CREATE RULE statement specifies a rule name—TOTALSAL1 for R1S. The ON-clause specifies the relation on which the rule is specified—EMPLOYEE for R1S. The WHEN-clause is used to specify the **events** that trigger the rule.[80] The *optional* IF-clause is used to specify any **conditions** that need to be checked. Finally, the THEN-clause is used to specify the **action** (or actions) to be taken, which are typically one or more SQL statements.

---

79. STARBURST also allows the user to explicitly start rule consideration via a PROCESS RULES command.

80. Note that the WHEN keyword specifies *events* in STARBURST but is used to specify the rule *condition* in SQL and Oracle triggers.

RI: **CREATE TRIGGER** T1
        AFTER INSERT ON TABLE1
        FOR EACH ROW
            UPDATE TABLE2
            SET ATTRIBUTE1=...;

R2:   **CREATE TRIGGER** T2
        AFTER UPDATE OF ATTRIBUTE1 **ON** TABLE2
        FOR EACH ROW
            INSERT INTO TABLE1 **VALUES** (...);

FIGURE 13.16 An example to illustrate the termination problem for active rules.

RIS: **CREATE RULE** TOTALSAL1 **ON** EMPLOYEE
        WHEN INSERTED
        IF   **EXISTS(SELECT * FROM INSERTED WHERE** DNO **IS NOT NULL)**
        THEN   **UPDATE**   DEPARTMENT **AS D**
                  SET   D.TOTAL_SAL=D.TOTAL_SAL +
                        (SELECT SUM(T.SALARY) **FROM INSERTED AS** I
                  WHERE   D.DNO = I.DNO)
                  WHERE   D.DNO **IN (SELECT** DNO **FROM INSERTED)**;

R2S: **CREATE RULE** TOTALSAL2 **ON** EMPLOYEE
        WHEN UPDATED (SALARY)
        IF   **EXISTS(SELECT * FROM NEW-UPDATED WHERE** DNO **IS NOT NULL)**
                OR **EXISTS(SELECT * FROM OLD-UPDATED WHERE** DNO **IS NOT NULL)**
        THEN   **UPDATE** DEPARTMENT **AS D**
                  SET   D.TOTAL_SAL=D.TOTAL_SAL +
                        (SELECT SUM(N.SALARY) **FROM NEW-UPDATED AS** N **WHERE**
                              D.DNO =N.DNO) –
                        (SELECT SUM(O.SALARY) **FROM OLD-UPDATED AS** 0 **WHERE**
                              D.DNO=O.DNO)
                  WHERE   D.DNO **IN (SELECT** DNO **FROM NEW-UPDATED) OR**
                              D.DNO **IN (SELECT** DNO **FROM OLD-UPDATED)**;

R3S: **CREATE RULE** TOTALSAL3 **ON** EMPLOYEE
        WHEN UPDATED(DNO)
        THEN   **UPDATE** DEPARTMENT **AS D**
                  SET   D.TOTAL_SAL=D.TOTAL_SAL +
                        (SELECT SUM(N.SALARY) **FROM NEW-UPDATED AS** N **WHERE**
                              D.DNO=N.DNO)
                  WHERE   D.DNO **IN (SELECT** DNO **FROM NEW-UPDATED)**;
                  UPDATE   DEPARTMENT **AS D**
                  SET   D.TOTAL_SAL=D.TOTAL_SAL-.
                        (SELECT SUM(O.SALARY) **FROM OLD-UPDATED AS** 0 **WHERE**
                            D.DNO=O.DNO)
                  WHERE   D.DNO **IN (SELECT** DNO **FROM OLD-UPDATED)**;

FIGURE 13.17 Active rules using statement-level semantics in STARBURST notation.

In STARBURST, the basic events that can be specified for triggering the rules are the standard SQL update commands: INSERT, DELETE, and UPDATE. These are specified by the keywords **INSERTED, DELETED,** and **UPDATED** in STARBURST notation. Second, the rule designer needs to have a way to refer to the tuples that have been modified. The keywords **INSERTED, DELETED, NEW-UPDATED,** and **OLD-UPDATED** are used in STARBURST notation to refer to four **transition tables** (relations) that include the newly inserted tuples, the deleted tuples, the updated tuples *before* they were updated, and the updated tuples *after* they were updated, respectively. Obviously, depending on the triggering events, only some of these transition tables may be available. The rule writer can refer to these tables when writing the condition and action parts of the rule. Transition tables contain tuples of the same type as those in the relation specified in the ON-clause of the rule—for R1S, R2S, and R3S, this is the EMPLOYEE relation.

In statement-level semantics, the rule designer can only refer to the transition tables as a whole and the rule is triggered only once, so the rules must be written differently than for row-level semantics. Because multiple employee tuples may be inserted in a single insert statement, we have to check if *at least one* of the newly inserted employee tuples is related to a department. In R1S, the condition

EXISTS(SELECT * FROM INSERTED WHERE DNO **IS NOT NULL)**

is checked, and if it evaluates to true, then the action is executed. The action updates in a single statement the DEPARTMENT tuple(s) related to the newly inserted employee(s) by adding their salaries to the TOTAL_SAL attribute of each related department. Because more than one newly inserted employee may belong to the same department, we use the SUM aggregate function to ensure that all their salaries are added.

Rule R2S is similar to R1S, but is triggered by an UPDATE operation that updates the salary of one or more employees rather than by an INSERT. Rule R3S is triggered by an update to the DNO attribute of EMPLOYEE, which signifies changing one or more employees' assignment from one department to another. There is no condition in R3S, so the action is executed whenever the triggering event occurs.[81] The action updates both the old department(s) and new department(s) of the reassigned employees by adding their salary to TOTAL_SAL of each *new* department and subtracting their salary from TOTAL_SAL of each *old* department.

In our example, it is more complex to write the statement-level rules than the row-level rules, as can be illustrated by comparing Figures 13.14 and 13.17. However, this is not a general rule, and other types of active rules may be easier to specify using statement-level notation than when using row-level notation.

The execution model for active rules in STARBURST uses **deferred consideration.** That is, all the rules that are triggered within a transaction are placed in a set—called the **conflict set**—which is not considered for evaluation of conditions and execution until the transaction ends (by issuing its COMMIT WORK command). STARBURST also allows the user to explicitly start rule consideration in the middle of a transaction via an explicit PROCESS RULES command. Because multiple rules must be evaluated, it is necessary to specify an order among the rules. The syntax for rule declaration in STARBURST allows the specification of *ordering* among the rules to instruct the system about the order in which a set of rules should be considered.[82] In addition, the transition tables—INSERTED, DELETED, NEW-UPDATED, and OLD-UPDATED—contain the *net effect* of all the operations within the transaction that affected each table, since multiple operations may have been applied to each table during the transaction.

---

81. As in the Oracle examples, rules R1S and R2S can be written without a condition. However, they may be more efficient to execute with the condition since the action is not invoked unless it is required.

82. If no order is specified between a pair of rules, the system default order is based on placing the rule declared first ahead of the other rule.

13.4.4 Potential Applications for Active Databases

We now briefly discuss some of the potential applications of active rules. Obviously, one important application is to allow **notification** of certain conditions that occur. For example, an active database may be used to monitor, say, the temperature of an industrial furnace. The application can periodically insert in the database the temperature reading records directly from temperature sensors, and active rules can be written that are triggered whenever a temperature record is inserted, with a condition that checks if the temperature exceeds the danger level, and the action to raise an alarm.

Active rules can also be used to **enforce integrity constraints** by specifying the types of events that may cause the constraints to be violated and then evaluating appropriate conditions that check whether the constraints are actually violated by the event or not. Hence, complex application constraints, often known as **business rules** may be enforced that way. For example, in the UNIVERSITY database application, one rule may monitor the grade point average of students whenever a new grade is entered, and it may alert the advisor if the GPA of a student falls below a certain threshold; another rule may check that course prerequisites are satisfied before allowing a student to enroll in a course; and so on.

Other applications include the automatic **maintenance of derived data,** such as the examples of rules R1 through R4 that maintain the derived attribute TOTAL_SAL whenever individual employee tuples are changed. A similar application is to use active rules to maintain the consistency of **materialized views** (see Chapter 7) whenever the base relations are modified. This application is also relevant to the new data warehousing technologies (see Chapter 17). A related application is to maintain **replicated tables** consistent by specifying rules that modify the replicas whenever the master table is modified.

13.4.5 Triggers in SQL-99

Triggers in the SQL-99 standard are quite similar to the examples we discussed in Section 13.4.1, with some minor syntactic differences. The basic **events** that can be specified for triggering the rules are the standard SQL update commands: INSERT, DELETE, and UPDATE. In the case of UPDATE one may specify the attributes to be updated. Both row-level and statement-level triggers are allowed, indicated in the trigger by the clauses FOR EACH ROW and FOR EACH STATEMENT, respectively. One syntactic difference is that the trigger may specify particular tuple variable names for the old and new tuples instead of using the keywords NEW and OLD as in Figure 13.13. Trigger T1 in Figure 13.18 shows how the row-level trigger R2 from Figure 13.13(a) may be specified in SQL-99. Inside the REFERENCING clause, we named tuple variables (aliases) O and N to refer to the OLD tuple (before modification) and NEW tuple (after modification), respectively. Trigger T2 in Figure 13.18 shows how the statement-level trigger R2S from Figure 13.17 may be specified in SQL-99. For a statement-level trigger, the REFERENCING clause is used to refer to the table of all new tuples (newly inserted or newly updated) as N, whereas the table of all old tuples (deleted tuples or tuples before they were updated) is referred to as O.

13.5 TEMPORAL DATABASE CONCEPTS

Temporal databases, in the broadest sense, encompass all database applications that require some aspect of time when organizing their information. Hence, they provide a good example to illustrate the need for developing a set of unifying concepts for application developers to use. Temporal database applications have been developed since the early days of database usage. However, in creating these applications, it was mainly left to the application designers and developers to discover, design, program, and implement the temporal concepts they need. There are many examples of applications where some aspect of time is needed to maintain the information in a database. These include *healthcare,* where patient histories need to be maintained; *insurance,* where claims and accident histories are required as well as information on the times when insurance policies are in effect; *reservation systems* in general (hotel, airline, car rental, train, etc.), where information on the dates and times when reservations are in effect are required; *scientific databases,* where data collected from experiments includes the time when each data is measured; an so on. Even the two examples used in this book may be easily expanded into temporal applications. In the COMPANY database, we may wish to keep SALARY, JOB, and PROJECT histories on each employee. In the UNIVERSITY database, time is already included in the SEMESTER and YEAR of each SECTION of a COURSE; the grade history of a STUDENT; and the information on research grants. In fact, it is realistic to conclude that the majority of database applications have some temporal information. Users often attempted to simplify or ignore temporal aspects because of the complexity that they add to their applications.

In this section, we will introduce some of the concepts that have been developed to deal with the complexity of temporal database applications. Section 13.5.1 gives an overview of how time is represented in databases, the different types of temporal information, and some of the different dimensions of time that may be needed. Section 13.5.2 discusses how time can be incorporated into relational databases. Section 13.5.3 gives some additional options for representing time that are possible in database models that allow complex-structured objects, such as object databases. Section 13.5.4 introduces operations for querying temporal databases, and gives a brief overview of the TSQL2 language, which extends SQL with temporal concepts. Section 13.5.5 focuses on time series data, which is a type of temporal data that is very important in practice.

```
T1:     CREATE TRIGGER TOTALSAL1
        AFTER. UPDATE OF SALARY ON EMPLOYEE
        REFERENCING OLD ROW AS 0, NEW ROW AS N
        FOR EACH ROW
        WHEN (N.DNO IS NOT NULL)
                UPDATE DEPARTMENT
                SET TOTAL_SAL = TOTAL_SAL + N.SALARY - O.SALARY
                WHERE DNO = N.DNO;
T2:     CREATE TRIGGER TOTALSAL2
        AFTER UPDATE OF SALARY ON EMPLOYEE
        REFERENCING OLD TABLE AS 0, NEW TABLE AS N
        FOR EACH STATEMENT.
        WHEN EXISTS(SELECT * FROM N WHERE N.DNO IS NOT NULL) OR
                EXISTS(SELECT * FROM 0 WHERE O.DNO IS NOT NULL)
                UPDATE DEPARTMENT AS D
                SET D.TOTAL_SAL = D.TOTAL_SAL
                + (SELECT SUM(N.SALARY) FROM N WHERE D.DNO=N.DNO)
                - (SELECT SUM(O.SALARY) FROM 0 WHERE D.DNO=O.DNO)
                WHERE DNO IN ((SELECT DNO FROM N) UNION (SELECT DNO FROM 0»;
```

FIGURE 13.18 Trigger T1 illustrating the syntax for defining triggers in SQL-99.

13.5.1 Time Representation, Calendars, and Time Dimensions

For temporal databases, time is considered to be an *ordered sequence* of **points** in some **granularity** that is determined by the application. For example, suppose that some temporal application never requires time units that are less than one second. Then, each time point represents one second in time using this granularity. In reality, each second is a (short) *time duration*, not a point, since it may be further divided into milliseconds, microseconds, and so on. Temporal database researchers have used the term **chronon** instead of point to describe this minimal granularity for a particular application. The main consequence of choosing a minimum granularity—say, one second—is that events occurring within the same second will be considered to be *simultaneous events*, even though in reality they may not be.

Because there is no known beginning or ending of time, one needs a reference point from which to measure specific time points. Various calendars are used by various cultures (such as Gregorian (Western), Chinese, Islamic, Hindu, Jewish, Coptic, etc.) with different reference points. A **calendar** organizes time into different time units for convenience. Most calendars group 60 seconds into a minute, 60 minutes into an hour, 24 hours into a day (based on the physical time of earth's rotation around its axis), and 7 days into a week. Further grouping of days into months and months into years either follow solar or lunar natural phenomena, and are generally irregular. In the Gregorian calendar, which is used in most Western countries, days are grouped into months that are either 28, 29, 30, or 31 days, and 12 months are grouped into a year. Complex formulas are used to map the different time units to one another.

In SQL2, the temporal data types (see Chapter 7) include DATE (specifying Day, Month, and Year as DD-MM-YYYY), TIME (specifying Hour, Minute, and Second as HH:MM:SS), TIMESTAMP (specifying a Date/Time combination, with options for including sub-second divisions if they are needed), INTERVAL (a relative time duration, such as 10 days or 250 minutes), and PERIOD (an *anchored* time duration with a fixed starting point, such as the 10-day period from January 1, 1999, to January 10, 1999, inclusive).[83]

Event Information Versus Duration (or State) Information. A temporal database will store information concerning when certain events occur, or when certain facts are considered to be true. There are several different types of temporal information. **Point events** or **facts** are typically associated in the database with a **single time point** in some granularity. For example, a bank deposit event may be associated with the timestamp when the deposit was made, or the total monthly sales of a product (fact) may be associated with a particular month (say, February 1999). Note that even though such events or facts may have different granularities, each is still associated with a *single time value* in the database. This type of information is often represented as **time series data** as we shall discuss in Section 13.4.5. **Duration events** or **facts,** on the other hand, are associated with a specific **time period** in the database.[84] For example, an employee may have worked in a company from August 15, 1993, till November 20, 1998.

A **time period** is represented by its **start** and **end time points** [START-TIME, END-TIME]. For example, the above period is represented as [15-08-1993, 20-11-1998]. Such a time period is often interpreted to mean the *set of all time points* from start-time to end-time, inclusive, in the specified granularity. Hence, assuming day granularity, the period [15-08-1993, 20-11-1998] represents the set of all days from August 15, 1993, until November 20, 1998, inclusive.[85]

---

83. Unfortunately, the terminology has not been used consistently. For example, the term *interval* is often used to denote an anchored duration. For consistency, we shall use the SQL terminology.

84. This is the same as an anchored duration. It has also been frequently called a **time interval**, but to avoid confusion we will use **period** to be consistent with SQL terminology.

85. The representation [15-08-1993, 20-11-1998] is called a *closed interval* representation. One can also use an *open interval*, denoted [15-08-1993, 21-11-1998), where the set of points *does not include* the end point. Although the latter representation is sometimes more convenient, we shall use closed intervals throughout to avoid confusion.

Valid Time and Transaction Time Dimensions. Given a particular event or fact that is associated with a particular time point or time period in the database, the association may be interpreted to mean different things. The most natural interpretation is that the associated time is the time that the event occurred, or the period during which the fact was considered to be true *in the real world*. If this interpretation is used, the associated time is often referred to as the **valid time**. A temporal database using this interpretation is called a **valid time database.**

However, a different interpretation can be used, where the associated time refers to the time when the information was actually stored in the database; that is, it is the value of the system time clock when the information is valid *in the system*.[86] In this case, the associated time is called the **transaction time**. A temporal database using this interpretation is called a **transaction time database.**

Other interpretations can also be intended, but these two are considered to be the most common ones, and they are referred to as **time dimensions.** In some applications, only one of the dimensions is needed and in other cases both time dimensions are required, in which case the temporal database is called a **bitemporal database.** If other interpretations are intended for time, the user can define the semantics and program the applications appropriately, and it is called a **user-defined time.**

The next section shows with examples how these concepts can be incorporated into relational databases, and Section 13.4.3 shows an approach to incorporate temporal concepts into object databases.

13.5.2 Incorporating Time in Relational Databases Using Tuple Versioning

Valid Time Relations. Let us now see how the different types of temporal databases may be represented in the relational model. First, suppose that we would like to include the history of changes as they occur in the real world. Consider again the database in Figure 13.13, and let us assume that, for this application, the granularity is day. Then, we could convert the two relations EMPLOYEE and DEPARTMENT into **valid time relations** by adding the attributes VST (Valid Start Time) and VET (Valid End Time), whose data type is DATE in order to provide day granularity. This is shown in Figure 13.19a, where the relations have been renamed EMP_VT and DEPT_VT, respectively.

Consider how the EMP_VT relation differs from the nontemporal EMPLOYEE relation (Figure 13.13).[87] In EMP_VT, each tuple V represents a **version** of an employee's information that is valid (in the real world) only during the time period [V.VST, V.VET], whereas in EMPLOYEE each tuple represents only the current state or current version of each employee. In EMP_VT, the current version of each employee typically has a special value, *now*, as its valid end time. This special value, *now*, is a **temporal variable** that implicitly represents the current time as time progresses. The nontemporal EMPLOYEE relation would only include those tuples from the EMP_VT relation whose VET is *now*.

Figure 13.20 shows a few tuple versions in the valid-time relations EMP_VT and DEPT_VT. There are two versions of Kumar, three versions of Chandra, one version of Agarwal, and one version of Narayan. We can now see how a valid time relation should behave when information is changed. Whenever one or more attributes of an employee are **updated,** rather than actually overwriting the old values, as would happen in a nontemporal relation, the system should create a new version and **close** the current version by changing its VET to the end time. Hence, when the user issued the command to update the salary of Kumar effective on June 1, 2003, to Rs. 30000, the second version of Kumar was created (see Figure 13.20). At the time of this update, the first version of Kumar was the current version, with *now* as its VET, but after the update *now* was

---

86. The explanation is more involved, as we shall see in Section 13.4.3.

87. A nontemporal relation is also called a **snapshot relation** as it shows only the *current snapshot* or *current state* of the database.

changed to May 31, 2003 (one less than June 1, 2003, in day granularity), to indicate that the version has become a **closed** or **history version** and that the new (second) version of Kumar is now the current one.

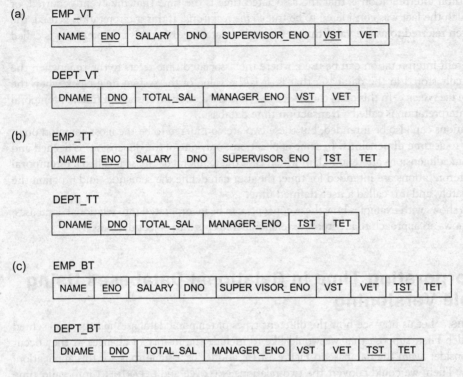

(a) **EMP_VT**

NAME	ENO	SALARY	DNO	SUPERVISOR_ENO	VST	VET

DEPT_VT

DNAME	DNO	TOTAL_SAL	MANAGER_ENO	VST	VET

(b) **EMP_TT**

NAME	ENO	SALARY	DNO	SUPERVISOR_ENO	TST	TET

DEPT_TT

DNAME	DNO	TOTAL_SAL	MANAGER_ENO	TST	TET

(c) **EMP_BT**

NAME	ENO	SALARY	DNO	SUPER VISOR_ENO	VST	VET	TST	TET

DEPT_BT

DNAME	DNO	TOTAL_SAL	MANAGER_ENO	VST	VET	TST	TET

FIGURE 13.19 Different types of temporal relational databases. (a) Valid time database schema. (b) Transaction time database schema. (c) Bitemporal database schema.

EMP_VT

NAME	ENO	SALARY	DNO	SUPER VISOR_ENO	VST	VET
Kumar	123456789	25000	5	333445555	15-06-2002	31-05-2003
Kumar	123456789	30000	5	333445555	01-06-2003	now
Chandra	333445555	25000	4	999887777	20-08-1999	31-01-2001
Chandra	333445555	30000	5	999887777	01-02-2001	31-03-2002
Chandra	333445555	40000	5	888665555	01-04-2002	now
Agarwal	222447777	28000	4	999887777	01-05-2001	10-08-2002
Narayan	666884444	38000	5	333445555	01-08-2003	now

. . .

DEPT_VT

DNAME	DNO	MANAGER_ENO	VST	VET
Research	5	888665555	20-09-2001	31-03-2002
Research	5	333445555	01-04-2002	now

. . .

FIGURE 13.20 Some tuple versions in the valid time relations EMP_VT and DEPT_VT.

It is important to note that in a valid time relation, the user must generally provide the valid time of an update. For example, the salary update of Kumar may have been entered in the database on May 15, 2003, at 8:52:12 A.M., say, even though the salary change in the real world is effective on June 1, 2003. This is called a **proactive update,** since it is applied to the database *before* it becomes effective in the real world. If the update was applied to the database *after* it became effective in the real world, it is called a **retroactive update.** An update that is applied at the same time when it becomes effective is called a **simultaneous update.**

The action that corresponds to **deleting** an employee in a nontemporal database would typically be applied to a valid time database by *closing the current version* of the employee being deleted. For example, if Kumar leaves the company effective January 19, 2004, then this would be applied by changing VET of the current version of Kumar from *now* to 19-01-2004. In Figure 13.8, there is no current version for Agarwal, because he presumably left the company on 10-08-2002 and was *logically deleted.* However, because the database is temporal, the old information on Agarwal is still there.

The operation to **insert** a new employee would correspond to *creating the first tuple version* for that employee, and making it the current version, with the VST being the effective (real world) time when the employee starts work. In Figure 13.20, the tuple on Narayan illustrates this, since the first version has not been updated yet.

Notice that in a valid time relation, the *nontemporal key,* such as ENO in EMPLOYEE, is no longer unique in each tuple (version). The new relation key for EMP_VT is a combination of the nontemporal key and the valid start time attribute VST,[88] so we use (ENO, VST) as primary key. This is because, at any point in time, there should be *at most one valid version* of each entity. Hence, the constraint that any two tuple versions representing the same entity should have *nonintersecting valid time periods* should hold on valid time relations. Notice that if the nontemporal primary key value may change over time, it is important to have a unique **surrogate key attribute,** whose value never changes for each real world entity, in order to relate together all versions of the same real world entity.

Valid time relations basically keep track of the history of changes as they become effective in the *real world.* Hence, if all real-world changes are applied, the database keeps a history of the *real-world states* that are represented. However, because updates, insertions, and deletions may be applied retroactively or proactively, there is no record of the actual *database state* at any point in time. If the actual database states are more important to an application, then one should use *transaction time relations.*

Transaction Time Relations.   In a transaction time database, whenever a change is applied to the database, the actual **timestamp** of the transaction that applied the change (insert, delete, or update) is recorded. Such a database is most useful when changes are applied *simultaneously* in the majority of cases—for example, real-time stock trading or banking transactions. If we convert the nontemporal database of Figure 13.13 into a transaction time database, then the two relations EMPLOYEE and DEPARTMENT are converted into **transaction time relations** by adding the attributes TST (Transaction Start Time) and TET (Transaction End Time), whose data type is typically TIMESTAMP. This is shown in Figure 13.19b, where the relations have been renamed EMP_TT and DEPT_TT, respectively.

In EMP_TT, each tuple V represents a *version* of an employee's information that was created at actual time V.TST and was (logically) removed at actual time V.TET (because the information was no longer correct). In EMP_TT, the *current version* of each employee typically has a special value, *uc* (**Until Changed**), as its transaction end time, which indicates that the tuple represents correct information *until it is changed* by some other transaction.[89] A transaction time database has also been called a **rollback database,**[90] because a user

---

88. A combination of the nontemporal key and the valid end time attribute VET could also be used.

89. The *uc* variable in transaction time relations corresponds to the *now* variable in valid time relations. The semantics are slightly different though.

90. The term rollback here does not have the same meaning as *transaction rollback* (see Chapter 11) during recovery, where the transaction updates are *physically undone.* Rather, here the updates can be *logically undone,* allowing the user to examine the database as it appeared at a previous time point.

can logically roll back to the actual database state at any past point in time T by retrieving all tuple versions V whose transaction time period [V.TST, V.TET] includes time point T.

Bitemporal Relations. Some applications require both valid time and transaction time, leading to **bitemporal relations.** In our example, Figure 13.19c shows how the EMPLOYEE and DEPARTMENT non-temporal relations in Figure 13.13 would appear as bitemporal relations EMP_BT and DEPT_BT, respectively. Figure 13.21 shows a few tuples in these relations. In these tables, tuples whose transaction end time TET is *uc* are the ones representing currently valid information, whereas tuples whose TET is an absolute timestamp are tuples that were valid until (just before) that timestamp. Hence, the tuples with *uc* in Figure 13.21 correspond to the valid time tuples in Figure 13.19. The transaction start time attribute TST in each tuple is the timestamp of the transaction that created that tuple.

EMP_BT

NAME	ENO	SALARY	DNO	SUPERVISOR_ENO	VST	VET	TST	TET
Kumar	123456789	25000	5	333445555	15-06-2002	now	08-06-2002, 13:05:58	04-06-2003, 08:56:12
Kumar	123456789	25000	5	333445555	15-06-2002	31-05-1998	04-06-2003, 08:56:12	uc
Kumar	123456789	30000	5	333445555	01-06-2003	now	04-06-2003, 08:56:12	uc
Chandra	333445555	25000	4	999887777	20-08-1999	now	20-08-1999, 11:18:23	07-01-2001, 14:33:02
Chandra	333445555	25000	4	999887777	20-08-1999	31-01-1996	07-01-2001, 14:33:02	uc
Chandra	333445555	30000	5	999887777	01-02-2001	now	28-03-2002, 14:33:02	28-03-2002, 09:23:57
Chandra	333445555	30000	5	999887777	01-02-2001	31-03-1997	27-04-2001, 09:23:57	uc
Chandra	333445555	40000	5	888665555	01-04-2002	now	28-03-2002, 09:23:57	uc
Agarwal	222447777	28000	4	999887777	01-05-2001	now	28-03-2002, 16:22:05	12-08-2002, 10:11:07
Agarwal	222447777	28000	4	999887777	01-05-2001	10-08-1997	27-04-2001, 10:11:07	uc
Narayan	666884444	38000	5	333445555	01-08-2003	now	28-07-2003, 09:25:37	uc

EMP_BT

DNAME	DNO	MANAGER_ENO	VST	VET	TST	TET
Research	5	888665555	20-09-2001	now	15-09-2001, 14:52:12	28-03-2001, 09:23:57
Research	5	888665555	20-09-2001	31-03-1997	28-03-2002, 09:23:57	uc
Research	5	333445555	01-04-2002	now	28-03-2002, 09:23:57	uc

FIGURE 13.21 Some tuple versions in the bitemporal relations EMP_BT and DEPT_BT.

Now consider how an **update operation** would be implemented on a bitemporal relation. In this model of bitemporal databases,[91] *no attributes are physically changed* in any tuple except for the transaction end time attribute TET with a value of *uc*.[92] To illustrate how tuples are created, consider the EMP_BT relation. The *current version* V of an employee has *uc* in its TET attribute and *now* in its VET attribute. If some attribute—say, SALARY—is updated, then the transaction T that performs the update should have two parameters: the new value of SALARY and the valid time VT when the new salary becomes effective (in the real world). Assume that VT$^-$ is the time point before VT in the given valid time granularity and that transaction T has a timestamp TS(T). Then, the following physical changes would be applied to the EMP_BT table:

1. Make a copy V2 of the current version V; set V2.VET to VT$^-$, V2.TST to TS(T), V2.TET to *uc*, and insert V2 in EMP_BT; V2 is a copy of the previous current version V *after it is closed* at valid time VT$^-$.

---

91. There have been many proposed temporal database models. We are describing specific models here as examples to illustrate the concepts.

92. Some bitemporal models allow the VET attribute to be changed also, but the interpretations of the tuples are different in those models.

2. Make a copy V3 of the current version V; set V3.VST to VT, V3.VET to *now*, V3.SALARY to the new salary value, V3.TST to TS(T), V3.TET to *uc*, and insert V3 in EMP_BT; V3 represents the new current version.

3. Set V.TET to TS(T) since the current version is no longer representing correct information.

As an illustration, consider the first three tuples V1, V2, and V3 in EMP_BT in Figure 13.21. Before the update of Kumar's salary from 25000 to 30000, only V1 was in EMP_BT and it was the current version and its TET was *uc*. Then, a transaction T whose timestamp TS(T) is 04-06-2003,08:56:12 updates the salary to 30000 with the effective valid time of 01-06-2003. The tuple V2 is created, which is a copy of V1 except that its VET is set to 31-05-2003, one day less than the new valid time and its TST is the timestamp of the updating transaction. The tuple V3 is also created, which has the new salary, its VST is set to 01-06-2003, and its TST is also the timestamp of the updating transaction. Finally, the TET of V1 is set to the timestamp of the updating transaction, 04-06-2003,08:56:12. Note that this is a *retroactive update*, since the updating transaction ran on June 4, 2003, but the salary change is effective on June 1, 2003.

Similarly, when Chandra's salary and department are updated (at the same time) to 30000 and 5, the updating transaction's timestamp is 07-01-2001,14:33:02 and the effective valid time for the update is 01-02-2001. Hence, this is a *proactive update* because the transaction ran on January 7, 2001, but the effective date was February 1, 2001. In this case, tuple V4 is logically replaced by V5 and V6.

Next, let us illustrate how a **delete operation** would be implemented on a bitemporal relation by considering the tuples V9 and V10 in the EMP_BT relation of Figure 13.21. Here, employee Agarwal left the company effective August 10, 2002, and the logical delete is carried out by a transaction T with TS(T) = 12-08-2002,10:11:07. Before this, V9 was the current version of Agarwal, and its TET was *uc*. The logical delete is implemented by setting V9.TET to 12-08-2002,10:11:07 to invalidate it, and creating the *final version* V10 for Agarwal, with its VET = 10-08-2002 (see Figure 13.21). Finally, an **insert operation** is implemented by creating the *first version* as illustrated by V11 in the EMP_BT table.

Implementation Considerations.   There are various options for storing the tuples in a temporal relation. One is to store all the tuples in the same table, as in Figures 13.21 and 13.20. Another option is to create two tables: one for the currently valid information and the other for the rest of the tuples. For example, in the bitemporal EMP_BT relation, tuples with *uc* for their TET and *now* for their VET would be in one relation, the *current table*, since they are the ones currently valid (that is, represent the current snapshot), and all other tuples would be in another relation. This allows the database administrator to have different access paths, such as indexes for each relation, and keeps the size of the current table reasonable. Another possibility is to create a third table for corrected tuples whose TET is not *uc*.

Another option that is available is to *vertically partition* the attributes of the temporal relation into separate relations. The reason for this is that, if a relation has many attributes, a whole new tuple version is created whenever any one of the attributes is updated. If the attributes are updated asynchronously, each new version may differ in only one of the attributes, thus needlessly repeating the other attribute values. If a separate relation is created to contain only the attributes that *always change synchronously*, with the primary key replicated in each relation, the database is said to be in **temporal normal form.** However, to combine the information, a variation of join known as **temporal intersection join** would be needed, which is generally expensive to implement.

It is important to note that bitemporal databases allow a complete record of changes. Even a record of corrections is possible. For example, it is possible that two tuple versions of the same employee may have the same valid time but different attribute values as long as their transaction times are disjoint. In this case, the tuple with the later transaction time is a **correction** of the other tuple version. Even incorrectly entered valid times may be corrected this way. The incorrect state of the database will still be available as a previous database state for querying purposes. A database that keeps such a complete record of changes and corrections has been called an **append only database.**

13.5.3 Incorporating Time in Object-oriented Databases Using Attribute Versioning

The previous section discussed the **tuple versioning approach** to implementing temporal databases. In this approach, whenever one attribute value is changed, a whole new tuple version is created, even though all the other attribute values will be identical to the previous tuple version. An alternative approach can be used in database systems that support **complex structured objects,** such as object databases or object-relational systems. This approach is called **attribute versioning.**[93]

```
class Temporal_Salary
{
    attribute    Date          valid_start_time;
    attribute    Date          valid_end_time;
    attribute    float         salary;
};

class Temporal_Dept
{
    attribute    Date          valid_start_time;
    attribute    Date          valid_end_time;
    attribute    Department_VT dept;
};

class Temporal_Supervisor
{
    attribute    Date          valid_start_time;
    attribute    Date          valid_end_time;
    attribute    Employee_VT   supervisor;
};

class Temporal_Lifespan
{
    attribute    Date          valid_ start_time;
    attribute    Date          valid_end_time;
};

class Employee_VT
(    extent    employees)
{
    attribute    list<Temporal_Lifespan>      lifespan;
    attribute    string                       name;
    attribute    string                       eno;
    attribute    list<Temporal_Salary>        sal_history;
    attribute    list<Temporal_Dept>          dept_history;
    attribute    list<Temporal_Supervisor>    supervisor_history;
};
```

FIGURE 13.22 Possible ODL schema for a temporal valid time Employee_VT object class using attribute versioning.

---

93. Attribute versioning can also be used in the nested relational model.

In attribute versioning, a single complex object is used to store all the temporal changes of the object. Each attribute that changes over time is called a **time-varying attribute,** and it has its values versioned over time by adding temporal periods to the attribute. The temporal periods may represent valid time, transaction time, or bitemporal, depending on the application requirements. Attributes that do not change are called **non-time-varying** and are not associated with the temporal periods. To illustrate this, consider the example in Figure 13.22, which is an attribute versioned valid time representation of EMPLOYEE using the ODL notation for object databases. Here, we assumed that name and employee number are non-time-varying attributes (they do not change over time), whereas salary, department, and supervisor are time-varying attributes (they may change over time). Each time-varying attribute is represented as a list of tuples <VALID_START_TIME, VALID_END_TIME, VALUE>, ordered by valid start time.

Whenever an attribute is changed in this model, the current attribute version is *closed* and a **new attribute version** for this attribute only is appended to the list. This allows attributes to change asynchronously. The current value for each attribute has *now* for its VALID_END_TIME. When using attribute versioning, it is useful to include a **lifespan temporal attribute** associated with the whole object whose value is one or more valid time periods that indicate the valid time of existence for the whole object. Logical deletion of the object is implemented by closing the lifespan. The constraint that any time period of an attribute within an object should be a subset of the object's lifespan should be enforced.

For bitemporal databases, each attribute version would have a tuple with five components:

<valid_start_time, valid_end_time, trans_start_time, trans_end_time, value>

The object lifespan would also include both valid and transaction time dimensions. The full capabilities of bitemporal databases can hence be available with attribute versioning. Mechanisms similar to those discussed earlier for updating tuple versions can be applied to updating attribute versions.

13.5.4   Temporal Querying Constructs and the TSQL2 Language

So far, we have discussed how data models may be extended with temporal constructs. We now give a brief overview of how query operations need to be extended for temporal querying. Then we briefly discuss the TSQL2 language, which extends SQL for querying valid time, transaction time, and bitemporal relational databases.

In nontemporal relational databases, the typical selection conditions involve attribute conditions, and tuples that satisfy these conditions are selected from the set of *current tuples.* Following that, the attributes of interest to the query are specified by a *projection operation* (see Chapter 4). For example, in the query to retrieve the names of all employees working in department 5 whose salary is greater than 30000, the selection condition would be:

((SALARY > 30000) AND (DNO = 5))

The projected attribute would be NAME. In a temporal database, the conditions may involve time in addition to attributes. A **pure time condition** involves only time—for example, to select all employee tuple versions that were valid on a certain *time point* T or that were valid *during a certain time period* [T1, T2]. In this case, the specified time period is compared with the valid time period of each tuple version [T.VST, T.VET], and only those tuples that satisfy the condition are selected. In these operations, a period is considered to be equivalent to the set of time points from T1 to T2 inclusive, so the standard set comparison operations can be used. Additional operations, such as whether one time period ends *before* another starts are also needed.[94] Some of the more common operations used in queries are as follows:

[t.VST, t.VET] **INCLUDES** [t1, t2]	Equivalent to t1 $\geq$ t.VST AND t2 $\leq$ t.VET
[t.VST, t.VET] **INCLUDED_IN** [t1, t2]	Equivalent to t1 $\leq$ t.VST AND t2 $\geq$ t.VET
[t.VST, t.VET] **OVERLAPS** [t1, t2]	Equivalent to (t1 $\leq$ t.VET AND t2 $\geq$ t.VST)[95]
[t.VST, t.VET] **BEFORE** [t1, t2]	Equivalent to t1 $\geq$ t.VET
[t.VST, t.VET] **AFTER** [t1, t2]	Equivalent to t2 $\leq$ t.VST
[t.VST, t.VET] **MEETS_BEFORE** [t1, t2]	Equivalent to t1 = t.VET + 1[96]
[t.VST, t.VET] **MEETS_AFTER** [t1, t2]	Equivalent to t2 + 1 = t.VST

In addition, operations are needed to manipulate time periods, such as computing the union or intersection of two time periods. The results of these operations may not themselves be periods, but rather **temporal elements**—a collection of one or more *disjoint* time periods such that no two time periods in a temporal element are directly adjacent. That is, for any two time periods [τ1, τ2] and [τ3, τ4] in a temporal element, the following three conditions must hold:

- [τ1, τ2] **intersection** [τ3, τ4] is empty.

- τ3 is not the time point following τ2 in the given granularity.

- τ1 is not the time point following τ4 in the given granularity.

The latter conditions are necessary to ensure unique representations of temporal elements. If two time periods [τ1, τ2] and [τ3, τ4] are adjacent, they are combined into a single time period [τ1, τ4]. This is called **coalescing** of time periods. Coalescing also combines intersecting time periods.

To illustrate how pure time conditions can be used, suppose a user wants to select all employee versions that were valid at any point during 2002. The appropriate selection condition applied to the relation in Figure 13.20 would be

[T.VST, T.VET] **OVERLAPS** [01-01-2002, 31-12-2002]

Typically, most temporal selections are applied to the valid time dimension. For a bitemporal database, one usually applies the conditions to the currently correct tuples with *uc* as their transaction end times. However, if the query needs to be applied to a previous database state, an AS_OF τ clause is appended to the query, which means that the query is applied to the valid time tuples that were correct in the database at time τ.

In addition to pure time conditions, other selections involve **attribute and time conditions.** For example, suppose we wish to retrieve all EMP_VT tuple versions τ for employees who worked in department 5 at any time during 2002. In this case, the condition is

([T.VST, T.VET] **OVERLAPS** [01-01-2002, 31-12-2002]) AND (T.DNO = 5)

Finally, we give a brief overview of the TSQL2 query language, which extends SQL with constructs for temporal databases. The main idea behind TSQL2 is to allow users to specify whether a relation is nontemporal

---

94. A complete set of operations, known as **Allen's algebra,** has been defined for comparing time periods.

95. This operation returns true if the *intersection* of the two periods is not empty; it has also been called INTERSECTS_WITH.

96. Here, 1 (one) refers to one time point in the specified granularity. The MEETS operations basically specify if one period starts immediately after the other period ends.

(that is, a standard SQL relation) or temporal. The CREATE TABLE statement is extended with an *optional* AS-clause to allow users to declare different temporal options. The following options are available:

- AS VALID STATE <GRANULARITY> (valid time relation with valid time period)

- AS VALID EVENT <GRANULARITY> (valid time relation with valid time point)

- AS TRANSACTION (transaction time relation with transaction time period)

- AS VALID STATE <GRANULARITY> AND TRANSACTION (bitemporal relation, valid time period)

- AS VALID EVENT <GRANULARITY> AND TRANSACTION (bitemporal relation, valid time point)

The keywords STATE and EVENT are used to specify whether a time *period* or time *point* is associated with the valid time dimension. In TSQL2, rather than have the user actually see how the temporal tables are implemented (as we discussed in the previous sections), the TSQL2 language adds query language constructs to specify various types of temporal selections, temporal projections, temporal aggregations, transformation among granularities, and many other concepts. The book by Snodgrass et al. (1995) describes the language.

13.5.5   Time Series Data

Time series data is used very often in financial, sales, and economics applications. They involve data values that are recorded according to a specific predefined sequence of time points. They are hence a special type of **valid event data,** where the event time points are predetermined according to a fixed calendar. Consider the example of closing daily stock prices of a particular Stock Exchange company. The granularity here is day, but the days that the stock market is open are known (nonholiday weekdays). Hence, it has been common to specify a computational procedure that calculates the particular **calendar** associated with a time series. Typical queries on time series involve **temporal aggregation** over higher granularity intervals—for example, finding the average or maximum *weekly* closing stock price or the maximum and minimum *monthly* closing stock price from the *daily* information.

As another example, consider the daily sales amount at each store of a chain of stores owned by a particular company. Again, typical temporal aggregates would be retrieving the weekly, monthly, or yearly sales from the daily sales information (using the sum aggregate function), or comparing same store monthly sales with previous monthly sales, and so on.

Because of the specialized nature of time series data, and the lack of support in older DBMSs, it has been common to use specialized **time series management systems** rather than general purpose DBMSs for managing such information. In such systems, it has been common to store time series values in sequential order in a file, and apply specialized time series procedures to analyze the information. The problem with this approach is that the full power of high-level querying in languages such as SQL will not be available in such systems.

More recently, some commercial DBMS packages are offering time series extensions, such as the time series datablade of Informix Universal Server. In addition, the TSQL2 language provides some support for time series in the form of event tables.

13.6   MULTIMEDIA DATABASES

Because the two topics discussed in this section are very broad, we can give only a very brief introduction to these fields. Section 13.6.1 introduces spatial databases, and Section 13.6.2 briefly discusses multimedia databases.

13.6.1 Introduction to Spatial Database Concepts

Spatial databases provide concepts for databases that keep track of objects in a multidimensional space. For example, cartographic databases that store maps include two-dimensional spatial descriptions of their objects—from countries and states to rivers, cities, roads, seas, and so on. These applications are also known as Geographical Information Systems (GIS), and are used in areas such as environmental, emergency, and battle management. Other databases, such as meteorological databases for weather information, are three-dimensional, since temperatures and other meteorological information are related to three-dimensional spatial points. In general, a spatial database stores objects that have spatial characteristics that describe them. The spatial relationships among the objects are important, and they are often needed when querying the database. Although a spatial database can in general refer to an n-dimensional space for any n, we will limit our discussion to two dimensions as an illustration.

The main extensions that are needed for spatial databases are models that can interpret spatial characteristics. In addition, special indexing and storage structures are often needed to improve performance. Let us first discuss some of the model extensions for two-dimensional spatial databases. The basic extensions needed are to include two-dimensional geometric concepts, such as points, lines and line segments, circles, polygons, and arcs, in order to specify the spatial characteristics of objects. In addition, spatial operations are needed to operate on the objects' spatial characteristics—for example, to compute the distance between two objects—as well as spatial Boolean conditions—for example, to check whether two objects spatially overlap. To illustrate, consider a database that is used for emergency management applications. A description of the spatial positions of many types of objects would be needed. Some of these objects generally have static spatial characteristics, such as streets and highways, water pumps (for fire control), police stations, fire stations, and hospitals. Other objects have dynamic spatial characteristics that change over time, such as police vehicles, ambulances, or fire trucks.

The following categories illustrate three typical types of spatial queries:

- *Range query:* Finds the objects of a particular type that are within a given spatial area or within a particular distance from a given location. (For example, finds all hospitals within the Hyderabad city area, or finds all ambulances within five miles of an accident location.)

- *Nearest neighbor query:* Finds an object of a particular type that is closest to a given location. (For example, finds the police car that is closest to a particular location.)

- *Spatial joins or overlays:* Typically joins the objects of two types based on some spatial condition, such as the objects intersecting or overlapping spatially or being within a certain distance of one another. (For example, finds all cities that fall on a major highway or finds all homes that are within two miles of a lake.)

For these and other types of spatial queries to be answered efficiently, special techniques for spatial indexing are needed. One of the best known techniques is the use of **R-trees** and their variations. R-trees group together objects that are in close spatial physical proximity on the same leaf nodes of a tree-structured index. Since a leaf node can point to only a certain number of objects, algorithms for dividing the space into rectangular subspaces that include the objects are needed. Typical criteria for dividing the space include minimizing the rectangle areas, since this would lead to a quicker narrowing of the search space. Problems such as having objects with overlapping spatial areas are handled in different ways by the many different variations of R-trees. The internal nodes of R-trees are associated with rectangles whose area covers all the rectangles in its subtree. Hence, R-trees can easily answer queries, such as find all objects in a given area by limiting the tree search to those subtrees whose rectangles intersect with the area given in the query.

Other spatial storage structures include quadtrees and their variations. **Quadtrees** generally divide each space or subspace into equally sized areas, and proceed with the subdivisions of each subspace to identify the positions of various objects. Recently, many newer spatial access structures have been proposed, and this area is still an active research area.

13.6.2 Introduction to Multimedia Database Concepts

Multimedia databases provide features that allow users to store and query different types of multimedia information, which includes *images* (such as photos or drawings), *video clips* (such as movies, newsreels, or home videos), *audio clips* (such as songs, phone messages, or speeches), and *documents* (such as books or articles). The main types of database queries that are needed involve locating multimedia sources that contain certain objects of interest. For example, one may want to locate all video clips in a video database that include a certain person in them, say Bill Clinton. One may also want to retrieve video clips based on certain activities included in them, such as a video clips where a goal is scored in a soccer game by a certain player or team.

The above types of queries are referred to as **content-based retrieval**, because the multimedia source is being retrieved based on its containing certain objects or activities. Hence, a multimedia database must use some model to organize and index the multimedia sources based on their contents. *Identifying the contents* of multimedia sources is a difficult and time-consuming task. There are two main approaches. The first is based on **automatic analysis** of the multimedia sources to identify certain mathematical characteristics of their contents. This approach uses different techniques depending on the type of multimedia source (image, text, video, or audio). The second approach depends on **manual identification** of the objects and activities of interest in each multimedia source and on using this information to index the sources. This approach can be applied to all the different multimedia sources, but it requires a manual preprocessing phase where a person has to scan each multimedia source to identify and catalog the objects and activities it contains so that they can be used to index these sources.

In the remainder of this section, we will very briefly discuss some of the characteristics of each type of multimedia source—images, video, audio, and text sources, in that order.

An **image** is typically stored either in raw form as a set of pixel or cell values, or in compressed form to save space. The image *shape descriptor* describes the geometric shape of the raw image, which is typically a rectangle of **cells** of a certain width and height. Hence, each image can be represented by an m by n grid of cells. Each cell contains a pixel value that describes the cell content. In black/white images, pixels can be one bit. In gray scale or color images, a pixel is multiple bits. Because images may require large amounts of space, they are often stored in compressed form. Compression standards, such as GIF or JPEG, use various mathematical transformations to reduce the number of cells stored but still maintain the main image characteristics. The mathematical transforms that can be used include Discrete Fourier Transform (DFT), Discrete Cosine Transform (DCT), and wavelet transforms.

To identify objects of interest in an image, the image is typically divided into homogeneous segments using a *homogeneity predicate*. For example, in a color image, cells that are adjacent to one another and whose pixel values are close are grouped into a segment. The homogeneity predicate defines the conditions for how to automatically group those cells. Segmentation and compression can hence identify the main characteristics of an image. A typical image database query would be to find images in the database that are similar to a given image. The given image could be an isolated segment that contains, say, a pattern of interest, and the query is to locate other images that contain that same pattern. There are two main techniques for this type of search. The first approach uses a **distance function** to compare the given image with the stored images and their segments. If the distance value returned is small, the probability of a match is high. Indexes can be created to group together stored images that are close in the distance metric so as to limit the search space. The second approach, called the **transformation approach**, measures image similarity by having a small number of transformations that can transform one image's cells to match the other image. Transformations include rotations, translations, and scaling. Although the latter approach is more general, it is also more time consuming and difficult.

A **video source** is typically represented as a sequence of frames, where each frame is a still image. However, rather than identifying the objects and activities in every individual frame, the video is divided into **video segments,** where each segment is made up of a sequence of contiguous frames that includes the same objects/activities. Each segment is identified by its starting and ending frames. The objects and activities identified in each video segment can be used to index the segments. An indexing technique called *frame segment trees* has been proposed for video indexing. The index includes both objects, such as persons, houses, cars, and activities, such as a person *delivering* a speech or two people *talking*. Videos are also often compressed using standards such as MPEG.

A **text/document source** is basically the full text of some article, book, or magazine. These sources are typically indexed by identifying the keywords that appear in the text and their relative frequencies. However, filler words are eliminated from that process. Because there could be too many keywords when attempting to index a collection of documents, techniques have been developed to reduce the number of keywords to those that are most relevant to the collection. A technique called *singular value decompositions* (SVD), which is based on matrix transformations, can be used for this purpose. An indexing technique called *telescoping vector trees,* or TV-trees, can then be used to group similar documents together.

Audio sources include stored recorded messages, such as speeches, class presentations, or even surveillance recording of phone messages or conversations by law enforcement. Here, discrete transforms can be used to identify the main characteristics of a certain person's voice in order to have similarity based indexing and retrieval. Audio characteristic features include loudness, intensity, pitch, and clarity.

13.7 INTRODUCTION TO DEDUCTIVE DATABASES

13.7.1 Overview of Deductive Databases

In a deductive database system, we typically specify rules through a **declarative language**—a language in which we specify what to achieve rather than how to achieve it. An **inference engine** (or **deduction mechanism**) within the system can deduce new facts from the database by interpreting these rules. The model used for deductive databases is closely related to the relational data model, and particularly to the domain relational calculus formalism (see Section 5.6). It is also related to the field of **logic programming** and the **Prolog** language. The deductive database work based on logic has used Prolog as a starting point. A variation of Prolog called **Datalog** is used to define rules declaratively in conjunction with an existing set of relations, which are themselves treated as literals in the language. Although the language structure of Datalog resembles that of Prolog, its operational semantics—that is, how a Datalog program is to be executed—is still different.

A deductive database uses two main types of specifications: facts and rules. **Facts** are specified in a manner similar to the way relations are specified, except that it is not necessary to include the attribute names. Recall that a tuple in a relation describes some real-world fact whose meaning is partly determined by the attribute names. In a deductive database, the meaning of an attribute value in a tuple is determined solely by its *position* within the tuple. **Rules** are somewhat similar to relational views. They specify virtual relations that are not actually stored but that can be formed from the facts by applying inference mechanisms based on the rule specifications. The main difference between rules and views is that rules may involve recursion and hence may yield virtual relations that cannot be defined in terms of basic relational views.

The evaluation of Prolog programs is based on a technique called *backward chaining,* which involves a top-down evaluation of goals. In the deductive databases that use Datalog, attention has been devoted to handling large volumes of data stored in a relational database. Hence, evaluation techniques have been devised that resemble those for a bottom-up evaluation. Prolog suffers from the limitation that the order of specification of facts and rules is significant in evaluation; moreover, the order of literals (defined later in Section 13.7.3) within a rule is significant. The execution techniques for Datalog programs attempt to circumvent these problems.

13.7.2 Prolog/Datalog Notation

The notation used in Prolog/Datalog is based on providing predicates with unique names. A **predicate** has an implicit meaning, which is suggested by the predicate name, and a fixed number of **arguments.** If the arguments are all constant values, the predicate simply states that a certain fact is true. If, on the other hand, the predicate has variables as arguments, it is either considered as a query or as part of a rule or constraint. Throughout this chapter, we adopt the Prolog convention that all **constant values** in a predicate are either *numeric* or character strings; they are represented as identifiers (or names) starting with *lowercase letters* only, whereas **variable names** always start with an *uppercase letter.*

Consider the example shown in Figure 13.23, which is based on the relational database of Figure 4.6, but in a much simplified form. There are three predicate names: *supervise, superior,* and *subordinate.* The supervise predicate is defined via a set of facts, each of which has two arguments: a supervisor name, followed by the name of a *direct* supervisee (subordinate) of that supervisor. These facts correspond to the actual data that is stored in the database, and they can be considered as constituting a set of tuples in a relation SUPERVISE with two attributes whose schema is

SUPERVISE(Supervisor,Supervisee)

Thus, supervise(X,Y) states the fact that "X supervises Y." Notice the omission of the attribute names in the Prolog notation. Attribute names are only represented by virtue of the position of each argument in a predicate: the first argument represents the supervisor, and the second argument represents a direct subordinate.

(a)

Facts
supervise(karthik, mahesh).
supervise(karthik, ramesh).
supervise(karthik, kiran).
supervise(priya, swetha).
supervise(priya, jitendra).
supervise(gaurav, karthik).
supervise(gaurav, priya).
...

Rules
supervise(X, Y) :-supervise(X, Y).
supervise(X, Y) :- supervise(X, Z), superior(Z,Y).
subordinate(X,Y) :- superior(Y,X).

Queries
superior(Gaurav,Y)?
superior(Gaurav, Kiran)?

(b)

Gaurav
Karthik   Priya
Mahesh Ramesh   Kiran   Swetha   Jitendra

FIGURE 13.23 (a) Prolog notation. (b) The supervisory tree.

The other two predicate names are defined by rules. The main contribution of deductive databases is the ability to specify recursive rules, and to provide a framework for inferring new information based on the specified rules. A rule is of the form **head :- body,** where :- is read as "if and only if." A rule usually has a **single predicate** to the left of the :- symbol—called the **head** or **left-hand side** (LHS) or **conclusion** of the rule—and **one or more predicates** to the right of the :- symbol—called the **body** or **right-hand side** (RHS) or **premise(s)** of the rule. A predicate with constants as arguments is said to be **ground;** we also refer to it as an **instantiated predicate.** The arguments of the predicates that appear in a rule typically include a number of variable symbols, although predicates can also contain constants as arguments. A rule specifies that, if a particular assignment or **binding** of constant values to the variables in the body (RHS predicates) makes *all* the RHS predicates **true,** it also makes the head (LHS predicate) true by using the same assignment of constant values to variables. Hence, a rule provides us with a way of generating new facts that are instantiations of the head of the rule. These new facts are based on facts that already exist, corresponding to the instantiations (or bindings) of predicates in the body of the rule. Notice that by listing multiple predicates in the body of a rule we implicitly apply the **logical and** operator to these predicates. Hence, the commas between the RHS predicates may be read as meaning "and."

Consider the definition of the predicate superior in Figure 13.23, whose first argument is an employee name and whose second argument is an employee who is either a *direct* or an *indirect* subordinate of the first employee. By *indirect subordinate,* we mean the subordinate of some subordinate down to any number of levels. Thus superior(X,Y) stands for the fact that "X is a superior of Y" through direct or indirect supervision. We can write two rules that together specify the meaning of the new predicate. The first rule under Rules in the figure states that, for every value of X and Y, if supervise(X,Y)—the rule body—is true, then superior(X,Y)—the rule head—is also true, since Y would be a direct subordinate of X (at one level down). This rule can be used to generate all direct superior/subordinate relationships from the facts that define the supervise predicate. The second recursive rule states that, if supervise(X, Z) *and* superior(Z, Y) are *both* true, then superior(X,Y) is also true. This is an example of a **recursive rule,** where one of the rule body predicates in the RHS is the same as the rule head predicate in the LHS. In general, the rule body defines a number of premises such that, if they are all true, we can deduce that the conclusion in the rule head is also true. Notice that, if we have two (or more) rules with the same head (LHS predicate), it is equivalent to saying that the predicate is true (that is, that it can be instantiated) if *either one* of the bodies is true; hence, it is equivalent to a **logical or** operation. For example, if we have two rules X :- Y and X :- Z, they are equivalent to a rule X :- Y **or** Z. The latter form is not used in deductive systems, however, because it is not in the standard form of rule, called a Horn clause, as we discuss in Section 13.5.4.

A Prolog system contains a number of **built-in** predicates that the system can interpret directly. These typically include the equality comparison operator =(X,Y), which returns true if X and Y are identical and can also be written as X=Y by using the standard infix notation.[97] Other comparison operators for numbers, such as $<, <=, >$, and $>=$, can be treated as binary predicates. Arithmetic functions such as $+, \_, *$, and $/$ can be used as arguments in predicates in Prolog. In contrast, Datalog (in its basic form) does *not* allow functions such as arithmetic operations as arguments; indeed, this is one of the main differences between Prolog and Datalog. However, later extensions to Datalog have been proposed to include functions.

A **query** typically involves a predicate symbol with some variable arguments, and its meaning (or "answer") is to deduce all the different constant combinations that, when **bound** (assigned) to the variables, can make the predicate true. For example, the first query in Figure 13.23 requests the names of all subordinates of

---

97. A Prolog system typically has a number of different equality predicates that have different interpretations.

"gaurav" at any level. A different type of query, which has only constant symbols as arguments, returns either a true or a false result, depending on whether the arguments provided can be deduced from the facts and rules. For example, the second query in Figure 13.23 returns true, since superior(gaurav, kiran) can be deduced.

13.7.3 Datalog Notation

In Datalog, as in other logic-based languages, a program is built from basic objects called **atomic formulas.** It is customary to define the syntax of logic-based languages by describing the syntax of atomic formulas and identifying how they can be combined to form a program. In Datalog, atomic formulas are **literals** of the form $p(a_1, a_2, ..., a_n)$, where p is the predicate name and n is the number of arguments for predicate p. Different predicate symbols can have different numbers of arguments, and the number of arguments n of predicate p is sometimes called the **arity** or **degree** of p. The arguments can be either constant values or variable names. As mentioned earlier, we use the convention that constant values either are numeric or start with a *lowercase* character, whereas variable names always start with an *uppercase* character.

A number of **built-in predicates** are included in Datalog, which can also be used to construct atomic formulas. The built-in predicates are of two main types: the binary comparison predicates <(less), <=(less_ or_equal), >(greater), and >= (greater_or_equal) over ordered domains; and the comparison predicates = (equal) and /= (not_equal) over ordered or unordered domains. These can be used as binary predicates with the same functional syntax as other predicates—for example by writing less(X, 3)—or they can be specified by using the customary infix notation X<3. Notice that, because the domains of these predicates are potentially infinite, they should be used with care in rule definitions. For example, the predicate greater(X, 3), if used alone, generates an infinite set of values for X that satisfy the predicate (all integer numbers greater than 3).

A **literal** is either an atomic formula as defined earlier—called a **positive literal**—or an atomic formula preceded by **not.** The latter is a negated atomic formula, called a **negative literal.** Datalog programs can be considered to be a *subset* of the **predicate calculus** formulas, which are somewhat similar to the formulas of the domain relational calculus (see Section 5.7). In Datalog, however, these formulas are first converted into what is known as **clausal form** before they are expressed in Datalog; and only formulas given in a restricted clausal form, called Horn clauses,[98] can be used in Datalog.

13.7.4 Clausal Form and Horn Clauses

Recall from Section 5.6 that a formula in the relational calculus is a condition that includes predicates called *atoms* (based on relation names). In addition, a formula can have quantifiers—namely, the *universal quantifier* (for all) and the *existential quantifier* (there exists). In clausal form, a formula must be transformed into another formula with the following characteristics:

- All variables in the formula are universally quantified. Hence, it is not necessary to include the universal quantifiers (for all) explicitly; the quantifiers are removed, and all variables in the formula are *implicitly* quantified by the universal quantifier.

- In clausal form, the formula is made up of a number of clauses, where each **clause** is composed of a number of *literals* connected by OR logical connectives only. Hence, each clause is a *disjunction* of literals.

- The *clauses themselves* are connected by AND logical connectives only, to form a formula. Hence, the *clausal form of a formula* is a *conjunction* of clauses.

---

98. Named after the mathematician Alfred Horn.

It can be shown that *any formula can be converted into clausal form.* For our purposes, we are mainly interested in the form of the individual clauses, each of which is a disjunction of literals. Recall that literals can be positive literals or negative literals. Consider a clause of the form:

$$not(P_1) \text{ OR } not(P_2) \text{ OR } \ldots \text{ OR } not(P_n) \text{ OR } Q_1 \text{ OR } Q_2 \text{ OR } \ldots \text{ OR } Q_m \tag{1}$$

This clause has n negative literals and m positive literals. Such a clause can be transformed into the following equivalent logical formula:

$$P_1 \text{ AND } P_2 \text{ AND } \ldots \text{ AND } P_n => Q_1 \text{ OR } Q_2 \text{ OR } \ldots \text{ OR } Q_m \tag{2}$$

where $=>$ is the **implies** symbol. The formulas (1) and (2) are equivalent, meaning that their truth values are always the same. This is the case because, if all the P_i literals (i = 1, 2, ..., n) are true, the formula (2) is true only if at least one of the Q_i's is true, which is the meaning of the $=>$ (implies) symbol. For formula (1), if all the P_i literals (i = 1, 2, ..., n) are true, their negations are all false; so in this case formula (1) is true only if at least one of the Q_i's is true. In Datalog, rules are expressed as a restricted form of clauses called **Horn clauses,** in which a clause can contain *at most one* positive literal. Hence, a Horn clause is either of the form

$$not(P_1) \text{ OR } not(P_2) \text{ OR } \ldots \text{ OR } not(P_n) \text{ OR } Q \tag{3}$$

or of the form

$$not(P_1) \text{ OR } not(P_2) \text{ OR } \ldots \text{ OR } not(P_n) \tag{4}$$

The Horn clause in (3) can be transformed into the clause

$$P_1 \text{ AND } P_2 \text{ AND } \ldots \text{ AND } P_n => Q \tag{5}$$

which is written in Datalog as the following rule

$$Q :- P_1, P_2, \ldots, P_n. \tag{6}$$

The Horn clause in (4) can be transformed into

$$P_1 \text{ AND } P_2 \text{ AND } \ldots \text{ AND } P_n => \tag{7}$$

which is written in Datalog as follows:

$$P_1, P_2, \ldots, P_n. \tag{8}$$

A Datalog rule, as in (6), is hence a Horn clause, and its meaning, based on formula (5), is that if the predicates P_1 and P_2 and ... and P_n are all true for a particular binding to their variable arguments, then Q is also true and can hence be inferred. The Datalog expression (8) can be considered as an integrity constraint, where all the predicates must be true to satisfy the query.

In general, a query in Datalog consists of two components:

• A Datalog program, which is a finite set of rules.

• A literal $P(X_1, X_2, \ldots, X_n)$, where each Xi is a variable or a constant.

A Prolog or Datalog system has an internal **inference engine** that can be used to process and compute the results of such queries. Prolog inference engines typically return one result to the query (that is, one set of values for the variables in the query) at a time and must be prompted to return additional results. On the contrary, Datalog returns results set-at-a-time.

13.7.5 Interpretations of Rules

There are two main alternatives for interpreting the theoretical meaning of rules: *prooftheoretic* and *model-theoretic*. In practical systems, the inference mechanism within a system defines the exact interpretation, which may not coincide with either of the two theoretical interpretations. The inference mechanism is a computational procedure and hence provides a computational interpretation of the meaning of rules. In this section, we first discuss the two theoretical interpretations. Inference mechanisms are then discussed briefly as a way of defining the meaning of rules.

In the **proof-theoretic** interpretation of rules, we consider the facts and rules to be true statements, or **axioms. Ground axioms** contain no variables. The facts are ground axioms that are given to be true. Rules are called **deductive axioms,** since they can be used to deduce new facts. The deductive axioms can be used to construct proofs that derive new facts from existing facts. For example, Figure 13.24 shows how to prove the fact superior(gaurav, jitendra) from the rules and facts given in Figure 13.23. The proof-theoretic interpretation gives us a procedural or computational approach for computing an answer to the Datalog query. The process of proving whether a certain fact (theorem) holds is known as *theorem proving*.

1. superior(X,Y) :- supervise(X,Y).	(rule 1)
2. superior(X,Y) :- supervise(X,Z), superior(Z,Y).	(rule 2)
3. supervise(priya, jitendra).	(ground axiom, given)
4. supervise(gaurav, priya).	(ground axiom, given)
5. superior(priya, jitendra).	(apply rule 1 on 3)
6. superior(gaurav, jitendra).	(apply rule 2 on 4 and 5)

FIGURE 13.24 Proving a new fact.

The second type of interpretation is called the **model-theoretic** interpretation. Here, given a finite or an infinite domain of constant values,[99] we assign to a predicate every possible combination of values as arguments. We must then determine whether the predicate is true or false. In general, it is sufficient to specify the combinations of arguments that make the predicate true, and to state that all other combinations make the predicate false. If this is done for every predicate, it is called an **interpretation** of the set of predicates. For example, consider the interpretation shown in Figure 13.25 for the predicates supervise and superior. This interpretation assigns a truth value (true or false) to every possible combination of argument values (from a finite domain) for the two predicates.

An interpretation is called a **model** for a *specific set of rules* if those rules are *always true* under that interpretation; that is, for any values assigned to the variables in the rules, the head of the rules is true when we substitute the truth values assigned to the predicates in the body of the rule by that interpretation. Hence, whenever a particular substitution (binding) to the variables in the rules is applied, if all the predicates in the body of a rule are true under the interpretation, the predicate in the head of the rule must also be true. The interpretation shown in Figure 13.25 is a model for the two rules shown, since it can never cause the rules to be violated. Notice that a rule is violated if a particular binding of constants to the variables makes all the predicates in the rule body true but makes the predicate in the rule head false. For example, if supervise(a,b) and superior(b,c) are both true under some interpretation, but superior(a,c) is not true, the interpretation cannot be a model for the recursive rule:

superior(X,Y) :- supervise(X,Z), superior(Z,Y)

---

99. The most commonly chosen domain is finite and is called the *Herbrand Universe*.

In the model-theoretic approach, the meaning of the rules is established by providing a model for these rules. A model is called a **minimal model** for a set of rules if we cannot change any fact from true to false and still get a model for these rules. For example, consider the interpretation in Figure 13.25, and assume that the supervise predicate is defined by a set of known facts, whereas the superior predicate is defined as an interpretation (model) for the rules. Suppose that we add the predicate superior(gaurav, bob) to the true predicates. This remains a model for the rules shown, but it is not a minimal model, since changing the truth value of superior(gaurav, bob) from true to false still provides us with a model for the rules. The model shown in Figure 13.25 is the minimal model for the set of facts that are defined by the supervise predicate.

Rules

superior(X,Y) :- supervise(X,Y).
superior(X,Y) :- supervise(X,Z), superior(Z,Y).

Interpretation

Known Facts:

supervise(karthik, mahesh) is **true**.
supervise(karthik,ramesh) is **true**.
supervise(karthik, kiran) is **true**.
supervise(priya, swetha) is **true**.
supervise(priya, jitendra) is **true**.
supervise(gaurav, karthik) is **true**.
supervise(gaurav, priya) is **true**.
supervise(X,Y) is **false** for all other possible (X,Y) combinations.

Derived Facts:

supervise(karthik, mahesh) is **true**.
supervise(karthik,ramesh) is **true**.
supervise(karthik, kiran) is **true**.
supervise(priya, swetha) is **true**.
supervise(priya, jitendra) is **true**.
supervise(gaurav, karthik) is **true**.
supervise(gaurav, priya) is **true**.
supervise(gaurav, mahesh) is **true**.
supervise(gaurav, ramesh) is **true**.
supervise(gaurav, kiran) is **true**.
supervise(gaurav, swetha) is **true**.
supervise(gaurav, jitendra) is **true**.
superior(X,Y) is false for all other possible (X,Y) combinations.

FIGURE 13.25 An interpretation that is a minimal model.

In general, the minimal model that corresponds to a given set of facts in the model-theoretic interpretation should be the same as the facts generated by the proof-theoretic interpretation for the same original set of ground and deductive axioms. However, this is generally true only for rules with a simple structure. Once we allow negation in the specification of rules, the correspondence between interpretations *does not* hold. In fact, with negation, numerous minimal models are possible for a given set of facts.

A third approach to interpreting the meaning of rules involves defining an inference mechanism that is used by the system to deduce facts from the rules. This inference mechanism would define a **computational interpretation** to the meaning of the rules. The Prolog logic programming language uses its inference mechanism to define the meaning of the rules and facts in a Prolog program. Not all Prolog programs correspond to the prooftheoretic or model-theoretic interpretations; it depends on the type of rules in the program. However, for many simple Prolog programs, the Prolog inference mechanism infers the facts that correspond either to the proof-theoretic interpretation or to a minimal model under the model-theoretic interpretation.

13.7.6 Datalog Programs and their Safety

There are two main methods of defining the truth values of predicates in actual Datalog programs. **Fact-defined predicates** (or **relations**) are defined by listing all the combinations of values (the tuples) that make the predicate true. These correspond to base relations whose contents are stored in a database system. Figure 13.26 shows the fact-defined predicates employee, male, female, department, supervise, project, and workson, which correspond to part of the relational database shown in Figure 4.6. **Rule-defined predicates** (or **views**) are defined by being the head (LHS) of one or more Datalog rules; they correspond to *virtual relations* whose contents can be inferred by the inference engine. Figure 13.27 shows a number of rule-defined predicates.

employee(mahesh).
employee(karthik).
employee(swetha).
employee(priya).
employee(ramesh).
employee(kiran).
employee(jitendra).
employee(gaurav).

male(mahesh).
male(karthik).
male(ramesh).
male(jitendra).
male(gaurav).

female(swetha).
female(priya).
female(kiran).

salary(mahesh,30000).
salary(karthik,40000).
salary(swetha,25000).
salary(priya,43000).
salary(ramesh,38000).
salary(kiran,25000).
salary(jitendra,25000).
salary(gaurav,55000).

project(productx).
project(producty).
project(productz).
project(computerization).
project(reorganization).
project(newbenefits).

department(mahesh,research).
department(karthik,research).
department(swetha,administration).
department(priya,administration).
department(ramesh,research).
department(kiran,research).
department(jitendra,administration).
department(gaurav,headquarters).

workson(mahesh,productx,32).
workson(mahesh,producty,8).
workson(ramesh,productz,40).
workson(kiran,productx,20).
workson(kiran,producty,20).
workson(karthik,producty,10).
workson(karthik,productz,10).
workson(karthik,computer ization,10).
workson(karthik,reorganization,10).
workson(swetha,newbenefits,30).
workson(swetha,computerization,10).
workson(jitendra,computerization,35).
workson(jitendra,newbenefits,5).
workson(priya,newbenefits,20).
workson(priya,reorganization,15).
workson(gaurav,reorganization,10).

supervise(karthik,mahesh).
supervise(karthik,ramesh).
supervise(karthik,kiran).
supervise(priya,swetha).
supervise(priya,jitendra).
supervise(gaurav, karthik).
supervise(gaurav,priya).

FIGURE 13.26 Fact predicates for part of the database from Figure 4.6.

A program or a rule is said to be **safe** if it generates a *finite* set of facts. The general theoretical problem of determining whether a set of rules is safe is undecidable. However, one can determine the safety of restricted forms of rules. For example, the rules shown in Figure 13.28 are safe. One situation where we get unsafe rules that can generate an infinite number of facts arises when one of the variables in the rule can range over an infinite domain of values, and that variable is not limited to ranging over a finite relation. For example, consider the rule

> big_salary(Y) :- Y>60000

Here, we can get an infinite result if Y ranges over all possible integers. But suppose that we change the rule as follows:

> big_salary(Y) :- employee(X), salary(X,Y), Y>60000

In the second rule, the result is not infinite, since the values that Y can be bound to are now restricted to values that are the salary of some employee in the database—presumably, a finite set of values. We can also rewrite the rule as follows:

> big_salary(Y) :- Y>60000, employee(X), salary(X,Y)

In this case, the rule is still theoretically safe. However, in Prolog or any other system that uses a top-down, depth-first inference mechanism, the rule creates an infinite loop, since we first search for a value for Y and then check whether it is a salary of an employee. The result is generation of an infinite number of Y values, even though these, after a certain point, cannot lead to a set of true RHS predicates. One definition of Datalog considers both rules to be safe, since it does not depend on a particular inference mechanism. Nonetheless, it is generally advisable to write such a rule in the safest form, with the predicates that restrict possible bindings of variables placed first. As another example of an unsafe rule, consider the following rule:

> has_something(X,Y) :- employee(X)

Here, an infinite number of Y values can again be generated, since the variable Y appears only in the head of the rule and hence is not limited to a finite set of values. To define safe rules more formally, we use the concept of a limited variable. A variable X is **limited** in a rule if (1) it appears in a regular (not built-in) predicate in the body of the rule; (2) it appears in a predicate of the form X=c or c=X or (c1<=X and X<=c2) in the rule body, where c, c1, and c2 are constant values; or (3) it appears in a predicate of the form X=Y or Y=X in the rule body, where Y is a limited variable. A rule is said to be **safe** if all its variables are limited.

13.7.7 Use of Relational Operations

It is straightforward to specify many operations of the relational algebra in the form of Datalog rules that define the result of applying these operations on the database relations (fact predicates). This means that relational queries and views can easily be specified in Datalog. The additional power that Datalog provides is in the specification of recursive queries, and views based on recursive queries. In this section, we show how some of the standard relational operations can be specified as Datalog rules. Our examples will use the base relations (fact-defined predicates) rel_one, rel_two, and rel_three, whose schemas are shown in Figure 13.28. In Datalog, we do not need to specify the attribute names as in Figure 13.28; rather, the arity (degree) of each predicate is the important aspect. In a practical system, the domain (data type) of each attribute is also important for operations such as UNION, INTERSECTION, and JOIN, and we assume that the attribute types are compatible for the various operations, as discussed in Chapter 4.

Figure 13.28 illustrates a number of basic relational operations. Notice that, if the Datalog model is based on the relational model and hence assumes that predicates (fact relations and query results) specify sets of tuples, duplicate tuples in the same predicate are automatically eliminated. This may or may not be true, depending on the Datalog inference engine. However, it is definitely *not* the case in Prolog, so any of the rules in Figure 13.28 that involve duplicate elimination are not correct for Prolog. For example, if we want to specify Prolog rules for the UNION operation with duplicate elimination, we must rewrite them as follows:

```
union_one_two(X,Y,Z) :- rel_one(X,Y,Z).
union_one_two(X,Y,Z) :- rel_two(X,Y,Z), not(rel_one(X,Y,Z)).
```

```
superior(X,Y) :- supervise(X,Y).
superior(X,Y) :- supervise(X,Z), superior(Z,Y).

subordinate(X,Y) :- superior(Y,X).

supervisor(X) :- employee(X), supervise(X,Y).

over_40K_emp(X) :- employee(X), salary(X,Y), Y>=40000.
under_40K_supervisor(X) :- supervisor(X), not(over_40_K_emp(X)).
main_productx_emp(X) :- employee(X), workson(X,productx,Y), Y>=20.
president(X) :- employee(X), not(supervise(Y,X)).
```

FIGURE 13.27 Rule-defined predicates.

However, the rules shown in Figure 13.28 should work for Datalog, if duplicates are automatically eliminated. Similarly, the rules for the PROJECT operation shown in Figure 13.28 should work for Datalog in this case, but they are not correct for Prolog, since duplicates would appear in the latter case.

```
rel_one(A,B,C).
rel_two(D,E,F).
rel_three(G,H,I,J).

select_one_A_eq_c(X,Y,Z) :- rel_one(c,Y,Z).
select_one_B_less_5(X,Y,Z) :- rel_one(X,Y,Z), Y<5.
select_one_A_eq_c_and_B_less_5(X,Y,Z) :- rel_one(c,Y,Z), Y<5.

select_one_A_eq_c_or_B_less_5(X,Y,Z) :- rel_one(c,Y,Z).
select_one_A_eq_c_or_B_less_5(X,Y,Z) :- rel_one(X,Y,Z), Y<5.

project_three_on_G_H(W,X) :- rel_three(W,X,Y,Z).

union_one_two(X,Y,Z) :- rel_one(X,Y,Z).
union_one_two(X,Y,Z) :- rel_two(X,Y,Z).

intersect_one_two(X,Y,Z) :- rel_one(X,Y,Z), rel_two(X,Y,Z).

difference_two_one(X,Y,Z) :- rel_two(X,Y,Z), not(rel_one(X,Y,Z)).

cart_prod_one_three(T,U,V,W,X,Y,Z) :-
                    rel_one(T,U,V), rel_three(W,X,Y,Z).

natural_join_one_three_C_eq_G(U,V,W,X,Y,Z) :-
                    rel_one(U,V,W), rel_three(W,X,Y,Z).
```

FIGURE 13.28 Predicates for illustrating relational operations.

13.7.8 Evaluation of Nonrecursive Datalog Queries

In order to use Datalog as a deductive database system, it is appropriate to define an inference mechanism based on relational database query processing concepts. The inherent strategy involves a bottom-up evaluation, starting with base relations; the order of operations is kept flexible and subject to query optimization. In this section, we discuss an inference mechanism based on relational operations that can be applied to **nonrecursive** Datalog queries. We use the fact and rule base shown in Figures 13.26 and 13.27 to illustrate our discussion.

If a query involves only fact-defined predicates, the inference becomes one of searching among the facts for the query result. For example, a query such as

department(X,research)?

is a selection of all employee names X who work for the research department. In relational algebra, it is the query:

$$\pi_{Rs.\,1} \left(\sigma_{Rs.\,2\,=\,\text{``Research''}} \left(\text{department} \right) \right)$$

which can be answered by searching through the fact-defined predicate department(X,Y). The query involves relational SELECT and PROJECT operations on a base relation, and it can be handled by the database query processing and optimization techniques discussed in Chapter 10.

When a query involves rule-defined predicates, the inference mechanism must compute the result based on the rule definitions. If a query is nonrecursive and involves a predicate p that appears as the head of a rule p :- p_1, p_2, ..., p_n, the strategy is first to compute the relations corresponding to p_1, p_2, ..., p_n and then to compute the relation corresponding to p. It is useful to keep track of the dependency among the predicates of a deductive database in a **predicate dependency graph.** Figure 13.29 shows the graph for the fact and rule predicates shown in Figures 13.26 and 13.27. The dependency graph contains a **node** for each predicate. Whenever a predicate A is specified in the body (RHS) of a rule, and the head (LHS) of that rule is the predicate B, we say that B **depends on** A, and we draw a directed edge from A to B. This indicates that, in order to compute the facts for the predicate B (the rule head), we must first compute the facts for all the predicates A in the rule body. If the dependency graph has no cycles, we call the rule set **nonrecursive.** If there is at least one cycle, the rule set is called **recursive.** In Figure 13.29, there is one recursively defined predicate—namely, superior—which has a recursive edge pointing back to itself. In addition, because the predicate subordinate depends on superior, it also requires recursion in computing its result.

A query that includes only nonrecursive predicates is called a **nonrecursive query.** In this section, we discuss only inference mechanisms for nonrecursive queries. In Figure 13.29, any query that does not involve the predicates subordinate or superior is nonrecursive. In the predicate dependency graph, the nodes corresponding to fact-defined predicates do not have any incoming edges, since all fact-defined predicates have their facts stored in a database relation. The contents of a fact-defined predicate can be computed by directly retrieving the tuples in the corresponding database relation.

The main function of an inference mechanism is to compute the facts that correspond to query predicates. This can be accomplished by generating a **relational expression** involving relational operators as SELECT, PROJECT, JOIN, UNION, and SET DIFFERENCE (with appropriate provision for dealing with safety issues) that, when executed, provides the query result. The query can then be executed by utilizing the internal query processing and optimization operations of a relational database management system. Whenever the inference mechanism needs to compute the fact set corresponding to a nonrecursive rule-defined predicate p, it first locates all the rules that have p as their head. The idea is to compute the fact set for each such rule and then to apply the UNION operation to the results, since UNION corresponds to a logical OR operation. The dependency graph indicates all predicates q on which each p depends, and since we assume that the predicate is nonrecursive, we can always determine a partial order among such predicates q. Before computing the fact set for p, we first compute the fact sets for all predicates q on which p̄ depends, based on their partial order.

For example, if a query involves the predicate under_40K_supervisor, we must first compute both supervisor and over_40K_emp. Since the latter two depend only on the fact-defined predicates employee, salary, and supervise, they can be computed directly from the stored database relations.

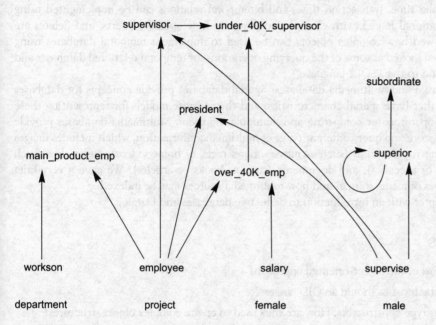

FIGURE 13.29 Predicate dependency graph for Figures 13.26 and 13.27.

This concludes our introduction to deductive databases. Additional material may be found at the book Web site, where the complete Chapter 14 from the third edition is available. This includes a discussion on algorithms for recursive query processing.

13.8 SUMMARY

In this chapter, we introduced database concepts for some of the common features that are needed by advanced applications: object databases, active databases, temporal databases, and spatial and multimedia databases. It is important to note that each of these topics is very broad and warrants a complete textbook.

We first introduced the topic of active databases, which provide additional functionality for specifying active rules. We introduced the event-condition-action or ECA model for active databases. The rules can be automatically triggered by events that occur—such as a database update—and they can initiate certain actions that have been specified in the rule declaration if certain conditions are true. Many commercial packages already have some of the functionality provided by active databases in the form of triggers. We discussed the different options for specifying rules, such as row-level versus statement-level, before versus after, and immediate versus deferred. We gave examples of row-level triggers in the Oracle commercial system, and statement-level rules in the STARBURST experimental system. The syntax for triggers in the SQL-99 standard was also discussed. We briefly discussed some design issues and some possible applications for active databases.

We then introduced some of the concepts of temporal databases, which permit the database system to store a history of changes and allow users to query both current and past states of the database. We discussed how time is represented and distinguished between the valid time and transaction time dimensions. We then discussed how valid time, transaction time, and bitemporal relations can be implemented using tuple versioning in the relational model, with examples to illustrate how updates, inserts, and deletes are implemented. We also showed how complex objects can be used to implement temporal databases using attribute versioning. We then looked at some of the querying operations for temporal relational databases and gave a very brief introduction to the TSQL2 language.

We then turned to spatial and multimedia databases. Spatial databases provide concepts for databases that keep track of objects that have spatial characteristics, and they require models for representing these spatial characteristics and operators for comparing and manipulating them. Multimedia databases provide features that allow users to store and query different types of multimedia information, which includes images (such as pictures or drawings), video clips (such as movies, news reels, or home videos), audio clips (such as songs, phone messages, or speeches), and documents (such as books or articles). We gave a very brief overview of the various types of media sources and how multimedia sources may be indexed.

We concluded the chapter with an introduction to deductive databases and Datalog.

Review Questions

13.1. What are the origins of the object-oriented approach?

13.2. What primary characteristics should an OID possess?

13.3. Discuss the various type constructors. How are they used to create complex object structures?

13.4. Discuss the concept of encapsulation, and tell how it is used to create abstract data types.

13.5. Explain what the following terms mean in object-oriented database terminology: *method, signature, message, collection, extent*.

13.6. What is the relationship between a type and its subtype in a type hierarchy? What is the constraint that is enforced on extents corresponding to types in the type hierarchy?

13.7. What is the difference between persistent and transient objects? How is persistence handled in typical OO database systems?

13.8. How do regular inheritance, multiple inheritance, and selective inheritance differ?

13.9. Discuss the concept of polymorphism/operator overloading.

13.10. What is the difference between structured and unstructured complex objects?

13.11. What is the difference between ownership semantics and reference semantics in structured complex objects?

13.12. What is versioning? Why is it important? What is the difference between versions and configurations?

13.13. What are the differences and similarities between objects and literals in the ODMG Object Model?

13.14. List the basic operations of the following built-in interfaces of the ODMG Object Model: Object, Collection, Iterator, Set, List, Bag, Array, and Dictionary.

13.15. Describe the built-in structured literals of the ODMG Object Model and the operations of each.

13.16. What are the differences and similarities of attribute and relationship properties of a user-defined (atomic) class?

13.17.   What are the differences and similarities of EXTENDS and interface ":" inheritance?

13.18.   Discuss how persistence is specified in the ODMG Object Model in the C++ binding.

13.19.   Why are the concepts of extents and keys important in database applications?

13.20.   Describe the following OQL concepts: *database entry points, path expressions, iterator variables, named queries (views), aggregate functions, grouping, and quantifiers.*

13.21.   What is meant by the type orthogonality of OQL?

13.22.   Discuss the general principles behind the C++ binding of the ODMG standard.

13.23.   What are the main differences between designing a relational database and an object database?

13.24.   Describe the steps of the algorithm for object database design by EER-to-OO mapping.

13.25.   What are the differences between row-level and statement-level active rules?

13.26.   What are the differences among immediate, deferred, and detached *consideration* of active rule conditions?

13.27.   What are the differences among immediate, deferred, and detached *execution* of active rule actions?

13.28.   Briefly discuss the consistency and termination problems when designing a set of active rules.

13.29.   Discuss some applications of active databases.

13.30.   Discuss how time is represented in temporal databases and compare the different time dimensions.

13.31.   What are the differences between valid time, transaction time, and bitemporal relations?

13.32.   Describe how the insert, delete, and update commands should be implemented on a valid time relation.

13.33.   Describe how the insert, delete, and update commands should be implemented on a bitemporal relation.

13.34.   Describe how the insert, delete, and update commands should be implemented on a transaction time relation.

13.35.   What are the main differences between tuple versioning and attribute versioning?

13.36.   How do spatial databases differ from regular databases?

13.37.   What are the different types of multimedia sources?

13.38.   How are multimedia sources indexed for content-based retrieval?

Exercises

13.39.   Convert the example of GEOMETRY_OBJECTs given in Section 13.1.4.1 from the functional notation to the notation given in Figure 13.3 that distinguishes between attributes and operations. Use the keyword INHERIT to show that one class inherits from another class.

13.40.   Compare inheritance in the EER model (see Chapter 3) to inheritance in the OO model described in Section 13.1.4.

13.41.   Consider the UNIVERSITY EER schema of Figure 3.26. Think of what operations are needed for the entity types/classes in the schema. Do not consider constructor and destructor operations.

13.42.   Consider the COMPANY ER schema of Figure 3.2. Think of what operations are needed for the entity types/classes in the schema. Do not consider constructor and destructor operations.

13.43. Design an OO schema for a database application that you are interested in. First construct an EER schema for the application; then create the corresponding classes in ODL. Specify a number of methods for each class, and then specify queries in OQL for your database application.

13.44. Consider the AIRPORT database described in Exercise 3.43. Specify a number of operations/methods that you think should be applicable to that application. Specify the ODL classes and methods for the database.

13.45. Map the COMPANY ER schema of Figure 3.2 into ODL classes. Include appropriate methods for each class.

13.46. Specify in OQL the queries in the exercises to Chapter 7 that apply to the COMPANY database.

13.47. Consider the COMPANY database described in Figure 4.6. Using the syntax of Oracle triggers, write active rules to do the following:

a. Whenever an employee's project assignments are changed, check if the total hours per week spent on the employee's projects are less than 30 or greater than 40; if so, notify the employee's direct supervisor.

b. Whenever an EMPLOYEE is deleted, delete the PROJECT tuples and DEPENDENT tuples related to that employee, and if the employee is managing a department or supervising any employees, set the MGRENO for that department to null and set the SUPERENO for those employees to null.

13.48. Repeat 13.47 but use the syntax of STARBURST active rules.

13.49. Consider the relational schema shown in Figure 13.30. Write active rules for keeping the SUM_COMMISSIONS attribute of SALES_PERSON equal to the sum of the COMMISSION attribute in SALES for each sales person. Your rules should also check if the SUM_COMMISSIONS exceeds 100000; if it does, call a procedure NOTIFY_MANAGER(S_ID). Write both statement-level rules in STARBURST notation and row-level rules in Oracle.

SALES

S_ID	V_ID	COMMISSION

SALES_PERSON

SALESPERSON_ID	NAME	TITLE	PHONE	SUM_COMMISSION

FIGURE 13.30 Database schema for sales and salesperson commissions in Exercise 13.49.

13.50. Consider the UNIVERSITY EER schema of Figure 3.26. Write some rules (in English) that could be implemented via active rules to enforce some common integrity constraints that you think are relevant to this application.

13.51. Discuss which of the updates that created each of the tuples shown in Figure 13.21 were applied retroactively and which were applied proactively.

13.52. Show how the following updates, if applied in sequence, would change the contents of the bitemporal EMP_BT relation in Figure 13.21. For each update, state whether it is a retroactive or proactive update.

    a. On 10-03-2004,17:30:00, the salary of NARAYAN is updated to 40000, effective on 01-03-2004.

    b. On 30-07-2003,08:31:00, the salary of KUMAR was corrected to show that it should have been entered as 31000 (instead of 30000 as shown), effective on 01-06-2003.

    c. On 18-03-2004,08:31:00, the database was changed to indicate that NARAYAN was leaving the company (i.e., logically deleted) effective 31-03-2004.

    d. On 20-04-2004,14:07:33, the database was changed to indicate the hiring of a new employee called JOHNSON, with the tuple <'JOHNSON', '334455667', 1, NULL> effective on 20-04-2004.

    e. On 28-04-2004,12:54:02, the database was changed to indicate that CHANDRA was leaving the company (i.e., logically deleted) effective 2004-06-01.

    f. On 05-05-2004,13:07:33, the database was changed to indicate the rehiring of AGARWAL, with the same department and supervisor but with salary 35000 effective on 01-05-2004.

13.53. Show how the updates given in Exercise 13.52, if applied in sequence, would change the contents of the valid time EMP_VT relation in Figure 13.20.

13.54. Add the following facts to the example database in Figure 13.15

supervise (Jitendra,bob), supervise (Karthik,gwen).

First modify the supervisory tree in Figure 13.13b to reflect this change. Then modify the diagram in Figure 13.16 showing the top-down evaluation of the query superior(gaurav,Y).

13.55. Consider the following set of facts for the relation parent(X,Y), where Y is the parent of X:

parent(a,aa), parent(a,ab), parent(aa,aaa), parent(aa,aab),

parent(aaa,aaaa), parent(aaa,aaab).

Consider the rules

r1: ancestor(X,Y) :- parent(X,Y)

r2: ancestor(X,Y) :- parent(X,Z), ancestor(Z,Y)

which define ancestor Y of X as above.

    a. Show how to solve the Datalog query

       ancestor(aa,X)?

    using the naive strategy. Show your work at each step.

    b. Show the same query by computing only the changes in the ancestor relation and using that in rule 2 each time.

    [This question is derived from Bancilhon and Ramakrishnan (1986).]

13.56. Consider a deductive database with the following rules:

ancestor(X,Y) :- father(X,Y)

ancestor(X,Y) :- father(X,Z), ancestor(Z,Y)

Notice that "father(X,Y)" means that Y is the father of X; "ancestor(X,Y)" means that Y is the ancestor of X. Consider the fact base

father(Harry,Issac), father(Issac,John), father(John,Kurt).

    a. Construct a model theoretic interpretation of the above rules using the given facts.

    b. Consider that a database contains the above relations father(X,Y), another relation brother(X,Y), and a third relation birth(X,B), where B is the birthdate of person X. State a rule that computes the first cousins of the following variety: their fathers must be brothers.

c. Show a complete Datalog program with fact-based and rule-based literals that computes the following relation: list of pairs of cousins, where the first person is born after 1960 and the second after 1970. You may use "greater than" as a built-in predicate. (*Note:* Sample facts for brother, birth, and person must also be shown.)

13.57. Consider the following rules:

reachable(X,Y) :- flight(X,Y)

reachable(X,Y) :- flight(X,Z), reachable(Z,Y)

where reachable(X,Y) means that city Y can be reached from city X, and flight(X,Y) means that there is a flight to city Y from city X.

a. Construct fact predicates that describe the following:

   i. Los Angeles, New York, Chicago, Atlanta, Frankfurt, Paris, Singapore, Sydney are cities.

   ii. The following flights exist: LA to NY, NY to Atlanta, Atlanta to Frankfurt, Frankfurt to Atlanta, Frankfurt to Singapore, and Singapore to Sydney. (*Note:* No flight in reverse direction can be automatically assumed.)

b. Is the given data cyclic? If so, in what sense?

c. Construct a model theoretic interpretation (that is, an interpretation similar to the one shown in Figure 14.3) of the above facts and rules.

d. Consider the query

reachable(Atlanta,Sydney)?

How will this query be executed using naive and seminaive evaluation? List the series of steps it will go through.

e. Consider the following rule-defined predicates:

round-trip-reachable(X,Y) :- reachable(X,Y), reachable(Y,X) duration(X,Y,Z)

Draw a predicate dependency graph for the above predicates. (*Note:* duration(X,Y,Z) means that you can take a flight from X to Y in Z hours.)

f. Consider the following query: What cities are reachable in 12 hours from Atlanta? Show how to express it in Datalog. Assume built-in predicates like greater-than(X,Y). Can this be converted into a relational algebra statement in a straightforward way? Why or why not?

g. Consider the predicate population(X,Y) where Y is the population of city X. Consider the following query: List all possible bindings of the predicate pair (X,Y), where Y is a city that can be reached in two flights from city X, which has over 1 million people. Show this query in Datalog. Draw a corresponding uery tree in relational algebraic terms.

Selected Bibliography

Object-oriented database concepts are an amalgam of concepts from OO programming languages and from database systems and conceptual data models. A number of textbooks describe OO programming languages—for example, Stroustrup (1986) and Pohl (1991) for C++, and Goldberg (1989) for SMALLTALK. Recent books by Cattell (1994) and Lausen and Vossen (1997) describe OO database concepts.

There is a vast bibliography on OO databases, so we can only provide a representative sample here. The October 1991 issue of CACM and the December 1990 issue of *IEEE Computer* describe object-oriented database concepts and systems. Dittrich (1986) and Zaniolo et al. (1986) survey the basic concepts of object-oriented data models. An early paper on object-oriented databases is Baroody and DeWitt (1981). Su et al. (1988) presents an object-oriented data model that is being used in CAD/CAM applications. Mitschang (1989) extends the relational algebra to cover complex objects. Query languages and graphical user interfaces for OO are described in Gyssens et al. (1990), Kim (1989), Alashqur et al. (1989), Bertino et al. (1992), Agrawal et al. (1990), and Cruz (1992).

Polymorphism in databases and object-oriented programming languages is discussed in Osborn (1989), Atkinson and Buneman (1987), and Danforth and Tomlinson (1988). Object identity is discussed in Abiteboul and Kanellakis (1989). OO programming languages for databases are discussed in Kent (1991). Object constraints are discussed in Delcambre et al. (1991) and Elmasri et al. (1993). Authorization and security in OO databases are examined in Rabitti et al. (1991) and Bertino (1992).

Cattell et al. (1997) describes the ODMG 2.0 standard and Cattell et al. (1993) describes the earlier versions of the standard. Several books describe the CORBA architecture—for example, Baker (1996).

The O2 system is described in Deux et al. (1991) and Bancilhon et al. (1992) includes a list of references to other publications describing various aspects of O2. The O2 model was formalized in Velez et al. (1989). The ObjectStore system is described in Lamb et al. (1991). Fishman et al. (1987) and Wilkinson et al. (1990) discuss IRIS, an bjectoriented DBMS developed at Hewlett-Packard laboratories. Maier et al. (1986) and Butterworth et al. (1991) describe the design of GEMSTONE. An OO system supporting open architecture developed at Texas Instruments is described in Thompson et al. (1993). The ODE system developed at ATT Bell Labs is described in Agrawal and Gehani (1989). The ORION system developed at MCC is described in Kim et al. (1990). Morsi et al. (1992) describes an OO testbed.

Stonebraker and Moore (1996) provides a comprehensive reference for object-relational DBMSs. The discussion about concepts related to Illustra in that book are mostly applicable to the current Informix Universal Server. Kim (1995) discusses many issues related to modern database systems that include object orientation. For the most current information on Informix and Oracle, consult their Web sites: www.informix.com and www.oracle.com, respectively.

The SQL3 standard is described in various publications of the ISO WG3 (Working Group 3) reports; for example, see Kulkarni et al. (1995) and Melton et al. (1991). An excellent tutorial on SQL3 was given at the Very Large Data Bases Conference by Melton and Mattos (1996). Ullman and Widom (1997) have a good discussion of SQL3 with examples.

For issues related to rules and triggers, Widom and Ceri (1995) have a collection of chapters on active databases. Some comparative studies—for example, Ketabchi et al. (1990)—compare relational DBMSs with object DBMSs; their conclusion shows the superiority of the object-oriented approach for nonconventional applications. The nested relational model is discussed in Schek and Scholl (1985), Jaeshke and Schek (1982), Chen and Kambayashi (1991), and Makinouchi (1977), among others. Algebras and query languages for nested relations are presented in Paredaens and VanGucht (1992), Pistor and Andersen (1986), Roth et al. (1988), and Ozsoyoglu et al. (1987), among others. Implementation of prototype nested relational systems is described in Dadam et al. (1986), Deshpande and VanGucht (1988), and Schek and Scholl (1989).

The book by Zaniolo et al. (1997) consists of several parts, each describing an advanced atabase concept such as active, temporal, and spatial/text/multimedia databases. Widom nd Ceri (1996) and Ceri and Fraternali (1997) focus on active database concepts and ystems. Snodgrass et al. (1995) describe the TSQL2 language and data model. Hoshafian nd Baker (1996), Faloutsos (1996), and Subrahmanian (1998) describe multimedia atabase concepts. Tansel et al. (1992) is a collection of chapters on temporal databases.

STARBURST rules are described in Widom and Finkelstein (1990). Early work on ctive databases includes the HiPAC project, discussed in Chakravarthy et al. (1989) and Chakravarthy (1990). A glossary for temporal databases is given in Jensen et al. (1994). Snodgrass (1987) focuses on TQuel, an early temporal query language.

608 | Fundamentals of Database Systems

Temporal normalization is defined in Navathe and Ahmed (1989). Paton (1999) and Paton and Diaz (1999) survey active databases. Chakravarthy et al. (1994) describe SENTINEL, and object-based active systems. Lee et al. (1998) discuss time series management.

The early developments of the logic and database approach are surveyed by Gallaire et al. (1984). Reiter (1984) provides a reconstruction of relational database theory, while Levesque (1984) provides a discussion of incomplete knowledge in light of logic. Gallaire and Minker (1978) provide an early book on this topic. A detailed treatment of logic and databases appears in Ullman (1989, vol. 2), and there is a related chapter in Volume 1 (1988). Ceri, Gottlob, and Tanca (1990) present a comprehensive yet concise treatment of logic and databases. Das (1992) is a comprehensive book on deductive databases and logic programming. The early history of Datalog is covered in Maier and Warren (1988). Clocksin and Mellish (1994) is an excellent reference on Prolog language.

Aho and Ullman (1979) provide an early algorithm for dealing with recursive queries, using the least fixed-point operator. Bancilhon and Ramakrishnan (1986) give an excellent and detailed description of the approaches to recursive query processing, with detailed examples of the naive and seminaive approaches. Excellent survey articles on deductive databases and recursive query processing include Warren (1992) and Ramakrishnan and Ullman (1993). A complete description of the seminaive approach based on relational algebra is given in Bancilhon (1985). Other approaches to recursive query processing include the recursive query/subquery strategy of Vieille (1986), which is a top-down interpreted strategy, and the Henschen-Naqvi (1984) top-down compiled iterative strategy. Balbin and Rao (1987) discuss an extension of the seminaive differential approach for multiple predicates.

The original paper on magic sets is by Bancilhon et al. (1986). Beeri and Ramakrishnan (1987) extend it. Mumick et al. (1990) show the applicability of magic sets to nonrecursive nested SQL queries. Other approaches to optimizing rules without rewriting them appear in Vieille (1986, 1987). Kifer and Lozinskii (1986) propose a different technique. Bry (1990) discusses how the top-down and bottom-up approaches can be reconciled. Whang and Navathe (1992) describe an extended disjunctive normal form technique to deal with recursion in relational algebra expressions for providing an expert system interface over a relational DBMS.

Chang (1981) describes an early system for combining deductive rules with relational databases. The LDL system prototype is described in Chimenti et al. (1990). Krishnamurthy and Naqvi (1989) introduce the "choice" notion in LDL. Zaniolo (1988) discusses the language issues for the LDL system. A language overview of CORAL is provided in Ramakrishnan et al. (1992), and the implementation is described in Ramakrishnan et al. (1993). An extension to support object-oriented features, called CORAL++, is described in Srivastava et al. (1993). Ullman (1985) provides the basis for the NAIL! system, which is described in Morris et al. (1987). Phipps et al. (1991) describe the GLUE-NAIL! deductive database system.

Zaniolo (1990) reviews the theoretical background and the practical importance of deductive databases. Nicolas (1997) gives an excellent history of the developments leading up to DOODs. Falcone et al. (1997) survey the DOOD landscape. References on the VALIDITY system include Friesen et al. (1995), Vieille (1997), and Dietrich et al. (1999).

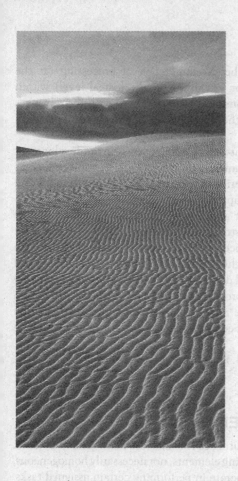

14

Distributed Databases and Client–Server Architectures

In this chapter we turn our attention to distributed databases (DDBs), distributed database management systems (DDBMSs), and how the client-server architecture is used as a platform for database application development. The DDB technology emerged as a merger of two technologies: (1) database technology, and (2) network and data communication technology. The latter has made tremendous strides in terms of wired and wireless technologies—from satellite and cellular communications and Metropolitan Area Networks (MANs) to the standardization of protocols like Ethernet, TCP/IP, and the Asynchronous Transfer Mode (ATM) as well as the explosion of the Internet. While early databases moved toward centralization and resulted in monolithic gigantic databases in the seventies and early eighties, the trend reversed toward more decentralization and autonomy of processing in the late eighties. With advances in distributed processing and distributed computing that occurred in the operating systems arena, the database research community did considerable work to address the issues of data distribution, distributed query and transaction processing, distributed database metadata management, and other topics, and developed many research prototypes. However, a full-scale comprehensive DDBMS that implements the functionality and techniques proposed in DDB research never emerged as a commercially viable product. Most major vendors redirected their efforts from developing a "pure" DDBMS product into developing systems based on client-server, or toward developing technologies for accessing distributed heterogeneous data sources.

Organizations, however, have been very interested in the *decentralization* of processing (at the system level) while achieving an *integration* of the information resources (at the logical level) within their geographically distributed systems of databases, applications, and users. Coupled with the advances in communications, there is now a general endorsement of the client-server approach to application development, which assumes many of the DDB issues.

In this chapter we discuss both distributed databases and client-server architectures,[1] in the development of database technology that is closely tied to advances in communications and network technology. Details of the latter are outside our scope; the reader is referred to a series of texts on data communications and networking (see the Selected Bibliography at the end of this chapter).

Section 14.1 introduces distributed database management and related concepts. Detailed issues of distributed database design, involving fragmenting of data and distributing it over multiple sites with possible replication, are discussed in Section 14.2. Section 14.3 introduces different types of distributed database systems, including federated and multidatabase systems and highlights the problems of heterogeneity and the needs of autonomy in federated database systems, which will dominate for years to come. Sections 14.4 and 14.5 introduce distributed database query and transaction processing techniques, respectively. Section 14.6 discusses how the client-server architectural concepts are related to distributed databases. Section 14.7 elaborates on future issues in client-server architectures. Section 14.8 discusses distributed database features of the Oracle RDBMS.

For a short introduction to the topic, only sections 14.1, 14.3, and 14.6 may be covered.

14.1 DISTRIBUTED DATABASE CONCEPTS

Distributed databases bring the advantages of distributed computing to the database management domain. A **distributed computing system** consists of a number of processing elements, not necessarily homogeneous, that are interconnected by a computer network, and that cooperate in performing certain assigned tasks. As a general goal, distributed computing systems partition a big, unmanageable problem into smaller pieces and solve it efficiently in a coordinated manner. The economic viability of this approach stems from two reasons: (1) more computer power is harnessed to solve a complex task, and (2) each autonomous processing element can be managed independently and develop its own applications.

We can define a **distributed database (DDB)** as a collection of multiple logically interrelated databases distributed over a computer network, and a **distributed database management system (DDBMS)** as a software system that manages a distributed database while making the distribution transparent to the user.[2] A collection of files stored at different nodes of a network and the maintaining of interrelationships among them via hyperlinks has become a common organization on the Internet, with files of Web pages. The common functions of database management, including uniform query processing and transaction processing, *do not* apply to this scenario yet. The technology is, however, moving in a direction such that distributed World Wide Web (WWW) databases will become a reality in the near future. We shall discuss issues of accessing databases on the Web in Chapter 15. None of those qualifies as DDB by the definition given earlier.

---

1. The reader should review the introduction to client-server architecture in Section 2.5.

2. This definition and some of the discussion in this section are based on Ozsu and Valduriez (1999).

14.1.1 Parallel Versus Distributed Technology

Turning our attention to parallel system architectures, there are two main types of multiprocessor system architectures that are commonplace:

- *Shared memory (tightly coupled) architecture:* Multiple processors share secondary (disk) storage and also share primary memory.

- *Shared disk (loosely coupled) architecture:* Multiple processors share secondary (disk) storage but each has their own primary memory.

These architectures enable processors to communicate without the overhead of exchanging messages over a network.[3] Database management systems developed using the above types of architectures are termed **parallel database management systems** rather than DDBMS, since they utilize parallel processor technology. Another type of multiprocessor architecture is called **shared nothing architecture.** In this architecture, every processor has its own primary and secondary (disk) memory, no common memory exists, and the processors communicate over a high-speed interconnection network (bus or switch). Although the shared nothing architecture resembles a distributed database computing environment, major differences exist in the mode of operation. In shared nothing multiprocessor systems, there is symmetry and homogeneity of nodes; this is not true of the distributed database environment where heterogeneity of hardware and operating system at each node is very common. Shared nothing architecture is also considered as an environment for parallel databases. Figure 14.1 contrasts these different architectures.

14.1.2 Advantages of Distributed Databases

Distributed database management has been proposed for various reasons ranging from organizational decentralization and economical processing to greater autonomy. We highlight some of these advantages here.

1. *Management of distributed data with different levels of transparency:* Ideally, a DBMS should be **distribution transparent** in the sense of hiding the details of where each file (table, relation) is physically stored within the system. Consider the company database in Figure 4.5 that we have been discussing throughout the book. The EMPLOYEE, PROJECT, and WORKS_ON tables may be fragmented horizontally (that is, into sets of rows, as we shall discuss in Section 14.2) and stored with possible replication as shown in Figure 14.2. The following types of transparencies are possible:

- *Distribution or network transparency:* This refers to freedom for the user from the operational details of the network. It may be divided into location transparency and naming transparency. **Location transparency** refers to the fact that the command used to perform a task is independent of the location of data and the location of the system where the command was issued. **Naming transparency** implies that once a name is specified, the named objects can be accessed unambiguously without additional specification.

- *Replication transparency:* As we show in Figure 14.2, copies of data may be stored at multiple sites for better availability, performance, and reliability. Replication transparency makes the user unaware of the existence of copies.

- *Fragmentation transparency:* Two types of fragmentation are possible. **Horizontal fragmentation** distributes a relation into sets of tuples (rows). **Vertical fragmentation** distributes a relation into subrelations where each subrelation is defined by a subset of the columns of the original relation. A global query by the user must be transformed into several fragment queries. Fragmentation transparency makes the user unaware of the existence of fragments.

---

3. If both primary and secondary memories are shared, the architecture is also known as **shared everything architecture.**

FIGURE 14.1 Some different database system architectures. (a) Shared nothing architecture. (b) A networked architecture with a centralized database at one of the sites. (c) A truly distributed database architecture.

EMPLOYEES-Mumbai
and New Delhi
PROJECTS-Mumbai
WORKS_ON-Mumbai
Employees

EMPLOYES-All
PROJECTS-All
WORKS_ON-All

EMPLOYES-Calcutta
PROJECTS-All
WORKS_ON-Calcutta
Employees

EMPLOYEES-New Delhi
PROJECTS-New Delhi and
Mumbai
WORKS_ON-New Delhi
Employees

EMPLOYEES-Chennai
PROJECTS-Chennai
WORKS_ON-Chennai
Employees

FIGURE 14.2 Data distribution and replication among distributed databases.

2. *Increased reliability and availability:* These are two of the most common potential advantages cited for distributed databases. **Reliability** is broadly defined as the probability that a system is running (not down) at a certain time point, whereas **availability** is the probability that the system is continuously available during a time interval. When the data and DBMS software are distributed over several sites, one site may fail while other sites continue to operate. Only the data and software that exist at the failed site cannot be accessed. This improves both reliability and availability. Further improvement is achieved by judiciously *replicating* data and software at more than one site. In a centralized system, failure at a single site makes the whole system unavailable to all users. In a distributed database, some of the data may be unreachable, but users may still be able to access other parts of the database.

3. *Improved performance:* A distributed DBMS fragments the database by keeping the data closer to where it is needed most. **Data localization** reduces the contention for CPU and I/O services and simultaneously reduces access delays involved in wide area networks. When a large database is distributed over multiple sites, smaller databases exist at each site. As a result, local queries and transactions accessing data at a single site have better performance because of the smaller local databases. In addition, each site has a smaller number of transactions executing than if all transactions are submitted to a single centralized database. Moreover, interquery and intraquery parallelism can be achieved by executing multiple queries at different sites, or by breaking up a query into a number of subqueries that execute in parallel. This contributes to improved performance.

4. *Easier expansion:* In a distributed environment, expansion of the system in terms of adding more data, increasing database sizes, or adding more processors is much easier.

The transparencies we discussed in (1) above lead to a compromise between ease of use and the overhead cost of providing transparency. Total transparency provides the global user with a view of the entire DDBS as if it is a single centralized system. Transparency is provided as a complement to **autonomy,** which gives the users tighter control over their own local databases. Transparency features may be implemented as a part of the user language, which may translate the required services into appropriate operations. In addition, transparency impacts the features that must be provided by the operating system and the DBMS.

14.1.3   Additional Functions of Distributed Databases

Distribution leads to increased complexity in the system design and implementation. To achieve the potential advantages listed previously, the DDBMS software must be able to provide the following functions in addition to those of a centralized DBMS:

- *Keeping track of data:* The ability to keep track of the data distribution, fragmentation, and replication by expanding the DDBMS catalog.

- *Distributed query processing:* The ability to access remote sites and transmit queries and data among the various sites via a communication network.

- *Distributed transaction management:* The ability to devise execution strategies for queries and transactions that access data from more than one site and to synchronize the access to distributed data and maintain integrity of the overall database.

- *Replicated data management:* The ability to decide which copy of a replicated data item to access and to maintain the consistency of copies of a replicated data item.

- *Distributed database recovery:* The ability to recover from individual site crashes and from new types of failures such as the failure of a communication links.

- *Security:* Distributed transactions must be executed with the proper management of the security of the data and the authorization/access privileges of users.

- *Distributed directory (catalog) management:* A directory contains information (metadata) about data in the database. The directory may be global for the entire DDB, or local for each site. The placement and distribution of the directory are design and policy issues.

These functions themselves increase the complexity of a DDBMS over a centralized DBMS. Before we can realize the full potential advantages of distribution, we must find satisfactory solutions to these design issues and problems. Including all this additional functionality is hard to accomplish, and finding optimal solutions is a step beyond that.

At the physical **hardware** level, the following main factors distinguish a DDBMS from a centralized system:

- There are multiple computers, called **sites** or **nodes**.

- These sites must be connected by some type of **communication network** to transmit data and commands among sites, as shown in Figure 14.1c.

The sites may all be located in physical proximity—say, within the same building or group of adjacent buildings—and connected via a **local area network,** or they may be geographically distributed over large distances and connected via a **long-haul** or **wide area network.** Local area networks typically use cables, whereas long-haul networks use telephone lines or satellites. It is also possible to use a combination of the two types of networks.

Networks may have different **topologies** that define the direct communication paths among sites. The type and topology of the network used may have a significant effect on performance and hence on the strategies for distributed query processing and distributed database design. For high-level architectural issues, however, it does not matter which type of network is used; it only matters that each site is able to communicate, directly or indirectly, with every other site. For the remainder of this chapter, we assume that some type of communication network exists among sites, regardless of the particular topology. We will not address any network specific issues, although it is important to understand that for an efficient operation of a DDBS, network design and performance issues are very critical.

14.2   DATA FRAGMENTATION, REPLICATION, AND ALLOCATION TECHNIQUES FOR DISTRIBUTED DATABASE DESIGN

In this section we discuss techniques that are used to break up the database into logical units, called **fragments,** which may be assigned for storage at the various sites. We also discuss the use of **data replication,** which permits certain data to be stored in more than one site, and the process of **allocating** fragments—or replicas of fragments—for storage at the various sites. These techniques are used during the process of **distributed database design.** The information concerning data fragmentation, allocation, and replication is stored in a **global directory** that is accessed by the DDBS applications as needed.

14.2.1   Data Fragmentation

In a DDB, decisions must be made regarding which site should be used to store which portions of the database. For now, we will assume that there is *no replication;* that is, each relation—or portion of a relation—is to be stored at only one site. We discuss replication and its effects later in this section. We also use the terminology of relational databases—similar concepts apply to other data models. We assume that we are starting with a relational database schema and must decide on how to distribute the relations over the various sites. To illustrate our discussion, we use the relational database schema in Figure 4.5.

Before we decide on how to distribute the data, we must determine the *logical units* of the database that are to be distributed. The simplest logical units are the relations themselves; that is, each *whole* relation is to be stored at a particular site. In our example, we must decide on a site to store each of the relations EMPLOYEE, DEPARTMENT, PROJECT, WORKS_ON, and DEPENDENT of Figure 4.5. In many cases, however, a relation can be divided into smaller logical units for distribution. For example, consider the company database shown in Figure 4.6, and assume there are three computer sites—one for each department in the company.[4] We may want to store the database information relating to each department at the computer site for that department. A technique called *horizontal fragmentation* can be used to partition each relation by department.

Horizontal Fragmentation.   A **horizontal fragment** of a relation is a subset of the tuples in that relation. The tuples that belong to the horizontal fragment are specified by a condition on one or more attributes of the relation. Often, only a single attribute is involved. For example, we may define three horizontal fragments on the EMPLOYEE relation of Figure 4.6 with the following conditions: (DNO = 5), (DNO = 4), and (DNO = 1)—each fragment contains the EMPLOYEE tuples working for a particular department. Similarly, we may define three horizontal fragments for the PROJECT relation, with the conditions (DNUM = 5), (DNUM = 4), and (DNUM = 1)— each fragment contains the PROJECT tuples controlled by a particular department. **Horizontal fragmentation** divides a relation "horizontally" by grouping rows to create subsets of tuples, where each subset has a certain logical meaning. These fragments can then be assigned to different sites in the distributed system. **Derived horizontal fragmentation** applies the partitioning of a primary relation (DEPARTMENT in our example) to other secondary relations (EMPLOYEE and PROJECT in our example), which are related to the primary via a foreign key. This way, related data between the primary and the secondary relations gets fragmented in the same way.

Vertical Fragmentation.   Each site may not need all the attributes of a relation, which would indicate the need for a different type of fragmentation. **Vertical fragmentation** divides a relation "vertically" by columns. A **vertical fragment** of a relation keeps only certain attributes of the relation. For example, we may want to

---

4. Of course, in an actual situation, there will be many more tuples in the relations than those shown in Figure 4.6.

fragment the EMPLOYEE relation into two vertical fragments. The first fragment includes personal information—NAME, DOB, ADDRESS, and SEX—and the second includes work-related information—ENO, SALARY, SUPERENO, DNO. This vertical fragmentation is not quite proper because, if the two fragments are stored separately, we cannot put the original employee tuples back together, since there is *no common attribute* between the two fragments. It is necessary to include the primary key or some candidate key attribute in *every* vertical fragment so that the full relation can be reconstructed from the fragments. Hence, we must add the ENO attribute to the personal information fragment.

Notice that each horizontal fragment on a relation R can be specified by a $\sigma_{Ci}(R)$ operation in the relational algebra. A set of horizontal fragments whose conditions C1, C2, . . . , Cn include all the tuples in R—that is, every tuple in R satisfies (C1 OR C2 OR . . . OR Cn)—is called a **complete horizontal fragmentation** of R. In many cases a complete horizontal fragmentation is also **disjoint;** that is, no tuple in R satisfies (Ci AND Cj) for any i ≠ j. Our two earlier examples of horizontal fragmentation for the EMPLOYEE and PROJECT relations were both complete and disjoint. To reconstruct the relation R from a *complete* horizontal fragmentation, we need to apply the UNION operation to the fragments.

A vertical fragment on a relation R can be specified by a $\pi_{Li}(R)$ operation in the relational algebra. A set of vertical fragments whose projection lists L1, L2, . . . , Ln include all the attributes in R but share only the primary key attribute of R is called a **complete vertical fragmentation** of R. In this case the projection lists satisfy the following two conditions:

- L1 ∪ L2 ∪ . . . ∪ Ln = ATTRS(R).

- Li ∩ Lj = PK(R) for any i ≠ j, where ATTRS(R) is the set of attributes of R and PK(R) is the primary key of R.

To reconstruct the relation R from a *complete* vertical fragmentation, we apply the OUTER UNION operation to the vertical fragments (assuming no horizontal fragmentation is used). Notice that we could also apply a FULL OUTER JOIN operation and get the same result for a complete vertical fragmentation, even when some horizontal fragmentation may also have been applied. The two vertical fragments of the EMPLOYEE relation with projection lists L1 = {ENO, NAME, DOB, ADDRESS, SEX} and L2 = {ENO, SALARY, SUPERENO, DNO} constitute a complete vertical fragmentation of EMPLOYEE.

Two horizontal fragments that are neither complete nor disjoint are those defined on the EMPLOYEE relation of Figure 4.5 by the conditions (SALARY > 50000) and (DNO = 4); they may not include all EMPLOYEE tuples, and they may include common tuples. Two vertical fragments that are not complete are those defined by the attribute lists L1 = {NAME, ADDRESS} and L2 = {ENO, NAME, SALARY}; these lists violate both conditions of a complete vertical fragmentation.

Mixed (Hybrid) Fragmentation. We can intermix the two types of fragmentation, yielding a **mixed fragmentation.** For example, we may combine the horizontal and vertical fragmentations of the EMPLOYEE relation given earlier into a mixed fragmentation that includes six fragments. In this case the original relation can be reconstructed by applying UNION *and* OUTER UNION (or OUTER JOIN) operations in the appropriate order. In general, a **fragment** of a relation R can be specified by a SELECT-PROJECT combination of operations $\pi_L(\sigma_C(R))$. If C = TRUE (that is, all tuples are selected) and L ≠ ATTRS(R), we get a vertical fragment, and if C ≠ TRUE and L = ATTRS(R), we get a horizontal fragment. Finally, if C ≠ TRUE and L ≠ ATTRS(R), we get a mixed fragment. Notice that a relation can itself be considered a fragment with C = TRUE and L = ATTRS(R). In the following discussion, the term *fragment* is used to refer to a relation or to any of the preceding types of fragments.

A **fragmentation schema** of a database is a definition of a set of fragments that includes *all* attributes and tuples in the database and satisfies the condition that the whole database can be reconstructed from the fragments by applying some sequence of OUTER UNION (or OUTER JOIN) and UNION operations. It is also sometimes useful—although not necessary—to have all the fragments be disjoint except for the repetition of primary keys among vertical (or mixed) fragments. In the latter case, all replication and distribution of fragments is clearly specified at a subsequent stage, separately from fragmentation.

An **allocation schema** describes the allocation of fragments to sites of the DDBS; hence, it is a mapping that specifies for each fragment the site(s) at which it is stored. If a fragment is stored at more than one site, it is said to be **replicated.** We discuss data replication and allocation next.

14.2.2 Data Replication and Allocation

Replication is useful in improving the availability of data. The most extreme case is replication of the *whole database* at every site in the distributed system, thus creating a **fully replicated distributed database.** This can improve availability remarkably because the system can continue to operate as long as at least one site is up. It also improves performance of retrieval for global queries, because the result of such a query can be obtained locally from any one site; hence, a retrieval query can be processed at the local site where it is submitted, if that site includes a server module. The disadvantage of full replication is that it can slow down update operations drastically, since a single logical update must be performed on every copy of the database to keep the copies consistent. This is especially true if many copies of the database exist. Full replication makes the concurrency control and recovery techniques more expensive than they would be if there were no replication, as we shall see in Section 14.5.

The other extreme from full replication involves having **no replication**—that is, each fragment is stored at exactly one site. In this case all fragments *must be* disjoint, except for the repetition of primary keys among vertical (or mixed) fragments. This is also called **nonredundant allocation.**

Between these two extremes, we have a wide spectrum of **partial replication** of the data—that is, some fragments of the database may be replicated whereas others may not. The number of copies of each fragment can range from one up to the total number of sites in the distributed system. A special case of partial replication is occurring heavily in applications where mobile workers—such as sales forces, financial planners, and claims adjustors—carry partially replicated databases with them on laptops and personal digital assistants and synchronize them periodically with the server database.[5] A description of the replication of fragments is sometimes called a **replication schema.**

Each fragment—or each copy of a fragment—must be assigned to a particular site in the distributed system. This process is called **data distribution** (or **data allocation**). The choice of sites and the degree of replication depend on the performance and availability goals of the system and on the types and frequencies of transactions submitted at each site. For example, if high availability is required and transactions can be submitted at any site and if most transactions are retrieval only, a fully replicated database is a good choice. However, if certain transactions that access particular parts of the database are mostly submitted at a particular site, the corresponding set of fragments can be allocated at that site only. Data that is accessed at multiple sites can be replicated at those sites. If many updates are performed, it may be useful to limit replication. Finding an optimal or even a good solution to distributed data allocation is a complex optimization problem.

14.2.3 Example of Fragmentation, Allocation, and Replication

We now consider an example of fragmenting and distributing the company database of Figures 4.5 and 4.6. Suppose that the company has three computer sites—one for each current department. Sites 2 and 3 are for departments 5 and 4, respectively. At each of these sites, we expect frequent access to the EMPLOYEE and PROJECT information for the employees *who work in that department* and the projects *controlled by that department*. Further, we assume that these sites mainly access the NAME, ENO, SALARY, and SUPERENO attributes

---

5. For a scalable approach to synchronize partially replicated databases, see Mahajan et al. (1998).

of EMPLOYEE. Site 1 is used by company headquarters and accesses all employee and project information regularly, in addition to keeping track of DEPENDENT information for insurance purposes.

According to these requirements, the whole database of Figure 4.6 can be stored at site 1. To determine the fragments to be replicated at sites 2 and 3, we can first horizontally fragment DEPARTMENT by its key DNUMBER. We then apply derived fragmentation to the relations EMPLOYEE, PROJECT, and DEPT_LOCATIONS relations based on their foreign keys for department number—called DNO, DNUM, and DNUMBER, respectively,

(a)

EMPD5	FNAME	INITIAL	LNAME	ENO	SALARY	SUPERENO	DNO
	Mahesh	B	Kumar	123456789	30000	333445555	5
	Karthik	T	Chandra	333445555	40000	888665555	5
	Ramesh	K	Narayan	666884444	38000	333445555	5
	Kiran	A	Goyal	453453453	25000	333445555	5

DEP5	DNAME	DNUMBER	MGRENO	MGRSTARTDATE
	Research	5	333445555	22-05-1988

DEP5_LOCS	DNUMBER	LOCATION
	5	Bangalore
	5	New Delhi
	5	Hyderabad

WORKS_ON5	EENO	PNO	HOURS
	123456789	1	32.5
	123456789	2	7.5
	666884444	3	40.0
	453453453	1	20.0
	453453453	2	20.0
	333445555	2	10.0
	333445555	3	10.0
	333445555	10	10.0
	333445555	20	10.0

PROJS5	PNAME	PNUMBER	PLOCATION	DNUM
	Product X	1	Bangalore	5
	Product Y	2	New Delhi	5
	Product Z	3	Hyderabad	5

Data at Site 2

(b)

EMPD4	FNAME	INITIAL	LNAME	ENO	SALARY	SUPERENO	DNO
	Swetha	J	Narayan	999887777	25000	987654321	4
	Priya	S	Ganesh	987654321	43000	888665555	4
	Jitendra	V	Nath	987987987	25000	987654321	4

DEP4	DNAME	DNUMBER	MGRENO	MGRSTARTDATE
	Administration	4	987654321	01-01-1995

DEP4_LOCS	DNUMBER	LOCATION
	4	Chennai

WORKS_ON4	EENO	PNO	HOURS
	333445555	10	10.0
	999887777	30	30.0
	999887777	10	10.0
	987987987	10	35.0
	987987987	30	5.0
	987654321	30	20.0
	987654321	20	15.0

PROJS4	PNAME	PNUMBER	PLOCATION	DNUM
	Computerization	10	Chennai	4
	Newbenefits	30	Chennai	4

Data at Site 3

FIGURE 14.3 Allocation of fragments to sites. (a) Relation fragments at site 2 corresponding to department 5. (b) Relation fragments at site 3 corresponding to department 4.

in Figure 4.5. We can then vertically fragment the resulting EMPLOYEE fragments to include only the attributes {NAME, ENO, SALARY, SUPERENO, DNO}. Figure 14.3 shows the mixed fragments EMPD5 and EMPD4, which include the EMPLOYEE tuples satisfying the conditions DNO = 5 and DNO = 4, respectively. The horizontal fragments of PROJECT, DEPARTMENT, and DEPT_LOCATIONS are similarly fragmented by department number. All these fragments—stored at sites 2 and 3—are replicated because they are also stored at the headquarters site 1.

We must now fragment the WORKS_ON relation and decide which fragments of WORKS_ON to store at sites 2 and 3. We are confronted with the problem that no attribute of WORKS_ON directly indicates the department to which each tuple belongs. In fact, each tuple in WORKS_ON relates an employee **e** to a project **p**. We could fragment WORKS_ON based on the department **d** in which **e** works *or* based on the department **d'** that controls **p**. Fragmentation becomes easy if we have a constraint stating that **d** = **d'** for all WORKS_ON tuples—that is, if employees can work only on projects controlled by the department they work for. However, there is no such constraint in our database of Figure 4.6. For example, the WORKS_ON tuple <333445555, 10, 10.0> relates an employee who works for department 5 with a project controlled by department 4. In this case we could fragment WORKS_ON based on the department in which the employee works (which is expressed by the condition C) and then fragment further based on the department that controls the projects that employee is working on, as shown in Figure 14.4.

In Figure 14.4, the union of fragments G1, G2, and G3 gives all WORKS_ON tuples for employees who work for department 5. Similarly, the union of fragments G4, G5, and G6 gives all WORKS_ON tuples for employees who work for department 4. On the other hand, the union of fragments G1, G4, and G7 gives all WORKS_ON tuples for projects controlled by department 5. The condition for each of the fragments G1 through G9 is shown in Figure 14.4. The relations that represent M:N relationships, such as WORKS_ON, often have several possible logical fragmentations. In our distribution of Figure 14.3, we choose to include all fragments that can be joined to either an EMPLOYEE tuple or a PROJECT tuple at sites 2 and 3. Hence, we place the union of fragments G1, G2, G3, G4, and G7 at site 2 and the union of fragments G4, G5, G6, G2, and G8 at site 3. Notice that fragments G2 and G4 are replicated at both sites. This allocation strategy permits the join between the local EMPLOYEE or PROJECT fragments at site 2 or site 3 and the local WORKS_ON fragment to be performed completely locally. This clearly demonstrates how complex the problem of database fragmentation and allocation is for large databases. The Selected Bibliography at the end of this chapter discusses some of the work done in this area.

14.3   TYPES OF DISTRIBUTED DATABASE SYSTEMS

The term distributed database management system can describe various systems that differ from one another in many respects. The main thing that all such systems have in common is the fact that data and software are distributed over multiple sites connected by some form of communication network. In this section we discuss a number of types of DDBMSs and the criteria and factors that make some of these systems different.

The first factor we consider is the **degree of homogeneity** of the DDBMS software. If all servers (or individual local DBMSs) use identical software and all users (clients) use identical software, the DDBMS is called **homogeneous;** otherwise, it is called **heterogeneous.** Another factor related to the degree of homogeneity is the **degree of local autonomy.** If there is no provision for the local site to function as a stand-alone DBMS, then the system has **no local autonomy.** On the other hand, if *direct access* by local transactions to a server is permitted, the system has some degree of local autonomy.

At one extreme of the autonomy spectrum, we have a DDBMS that "looks like" a centralized DBMS to the user. A single conceptual schema exists, and all access to the system is obtained through a site that is part of the DDBMS—which means that no local autonomy exists. At the other extreme we encounter a type of DDBMS called a *federated DDBMS* (or a *multidatabase system*). In such a system, each server is an independent and autonomous centralized DBMS that has its own local users, local transactions, and DBA and hence has a

(a)

G1	EENO	PNO	HOURS
	123456789	1	32.5
	123456789	2	7.5
	666884444	3	40.0
	453453453	1	20.0
	453453453	2	20.0
	333445555	2	10.0
	333445555	3	10.0

C1=C AND (PNO IN (SELECT PNUMBER
FROM PROJECT
WHERE DNUM=5))

G2	EENO	PNO	HOURS
	333445555	10	10.0

C2=C AND (PNO IN (SELECT PNUMBER
FROM PROJECT
WHERE DNUM=4))

G3	EENO	PNO	HOURS
	333445555	20	10.0

C3=C AND (PNO IN (SELECT PNUMBER
FROM PROJECT
WHERE DNUM=1))

Employees in Department 5

(b)

G4	EENO	PNO	HOURS

C4=C AND (PNO IN (SELECT PNUMBER
FROM PROJECT
WHERE DNUM=5))

G5	EENO	PNO	HOURS
	999887777	30	30.0
	999887777	10	10.0
	987987987	10	35.0
	987987987	30	5.0
	987654321	30	20.0

C5=C AND (PNO IN (SELECT PNUMBER
FROM PROJECT
WHERE DNUM=4))

G6	EENO	PNO	HOURS
	987654321	20	15.0

C6=C AND (PNO IN (SELECT PNUMBER
FROM PROJECT
WHERE DNUM=1))

Employees in Department 4

(c)

G7	EENO	PNO	HOURS

C7=C AND (PNO IN (SELECT PNUMBER
FROM PROJECT
WHERE DNUM=5))

G8	EENO	PNO	HOURS

C8=C AND (PNO IN (SELECT PNUMBER
FROM PROJECT
WHERE DNUM=4))

G9	EENO	PNO	HOURS
	888665555	20	null

C9=C AND (PNO IN (SELECT PNUMBER
FROM PROJECT
WHERE DNUM=1))

Employees in Department 1

FIGURE 14.4 Complete and disjoint fragments of the WORKS_ON relation. (a) Fragments of WORKS_ON for employees working in department 5 (C=[EENO IN (SELECT ENO FROM EMPLOYEE WHERE DNO=5)]). (b) Fragments of WORKS_ ON for employees working in department 4 (C=[EENO IN (SELECT ENO FROM EMPLOYEE WHERE DNO=4)]). (c) Fragments of WORKS_ON for employees working in department 1 (C=[EENO IN (SELECT ENO FROM EMPLOYEE WHERE DNO=1)]).

very high degree of *local autonomy*. The term **federated database system (FDBS)** is used when there is some global view or schema of the federation of databases that is shared by the applications. On the other hand, a **multidatabase system** does not have a global schema and interactively constructs one as needed by the application. Both systems are hybrids between distributed and centralized systems and the distinction we made between them is not strictly followed. We will refer to them as FDBSs in a generic sense.

In a heterogeneous FDBS, one server may be a relational DBMS, another a network DBMS, and a third an object or hierarchical DBMS; in such a case it is necessary to have a canonical system language and to include language translators to translate subqueries from the canonical language to the language of each server. We briefly discuss the issues affecting the design of FDBSs below.

Federated Database Management Systems Issues.   The type of heterogeneity present in FDBSs may arise from several sources. We discuss these sources first and then point out how the different types of autonomies contribute to a semantic heterogeneity that must be resolved in a heterogeneous FDBS.

- *Differences in data models:* Databases in an organization come from a variety of data models including the so-called legacy models (network and hierarchical, see Appendixes E and F), the relational data model, the object data model, and even files. The modeling capabilities of the models vary. Hence, to deal with them uniformly via a single global schema or to process them in a single language is challenging. Even if two databases are both from the RDBMS environment, the same information may be represented as an attribute name, as a relation name, or as a value in different databases. This calls for an intelligent query-processing mechanism that can relate information based on metadata.

- *Differences in constraints:* Constraint facilities for specification and implementation vary from system to system. There are comparable features that must be reconciled in the construction of a global schema. For example, the relationships from ER models are represented as referential integrity constraints in the relational model. Triggers may have to be used to implement certain constraints in the relational model. The global schema must also deal with potential conflicts among constraints.

- *Differences in query languages:* Even with the same data model, the languages and their versions vary. For example, SQL has multiple versions like SQL-89, SQL-92, and SQL-99, and each system has its own set of data types, comparison operators, string manipulation features, and so on.

Semantic Heterogeneity.   Semantic heterogeneity occurs when there are differences in the meaning, interpretation, and intended use of the same or related data. Semantic heterogeneity among component database systems (DBSs) creates the biggest hurdle in designing global schemas of heterogeneous databases. The **design autonomy** of component DBSs refers to their freedom of choosing the following design parameters, which in turn affect the eventual complexity of the FDBS:

- *The universe of discourse from which the data is drawn:* For example, two customer accounts, databases in the federation may be from United States and Japan with entirely different sets of attributes about customer accounts required by the accounting practices. Currency rate fluctuations would also present a problem. Hence, relations in these two databases which have identical names—CUSTOMER or ACCOUNT— may have some common and some entirely distinct information.

- *Representation and naming:* The representation and naming of data elements and the structure of the data model may be prespecified for each local database.

- *The understanding, meaning, and subjective interpretation of data.* This is a chief contributor to semantic heterogeneity.

- *Transaction and policy constraints:* These deal with serializability criteria, compensating transactions, and other transaction policies.

- *Derivation of summaries:* Aggregation, summarization, and other data-processing features and operations supported by the system.

   Communication autonomy of a component DBS refers to its ability to decide whether to communicate with another component DBS. **Execution autonomy** refers to the ability of a component DBS to execute local operations without interference from external operations by other component DBSs and its ability to decide the order in which to execute them. The **association autonomy** of a component DBS implies that it has the ability to decide whether and how much to share its functionality (operations it supports) and resources (data it manages) with other component DBSs. The major challenge of designing FDBSs is to let component DBSs interoperate while still providing the above types of autonomies to them.

A typical five-level schema architecture to support global applications in the FDBS environment is shown in Figure 14.5. In this architecture, the **local schema** is the conceptual schema (full database definition) of a component database, and the **component schema** is derived by translating the local schema into a canonical data model or common data model (CDM) for the FDBS. Schema translation from the local schema to the component schema is accompanied by generation of mappings to transform commands on a component schema into commands on the corresponding local schema. The **export schema** represents the subset of a component schema that is available to the FDBS. The **federated schema** is the global schema or view, which is the result of integrating all the shareable export schemas. The **external schemas** define the schema for a user group or an application, as in the three-level schema architecture.[6]

All the problems related to query processing, transaction processing, and directory and metadata management and recovery apply to FDBSs with additional considerations. It is not within our scope to discuss them in detail here.

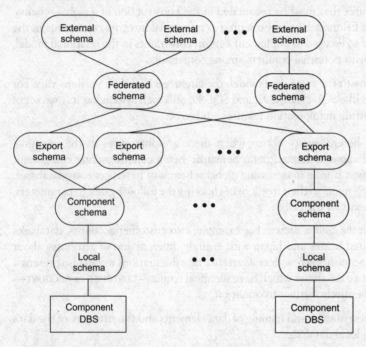

FIGURE 14.5 The five-level schema architecture in a federated database system (FDBS). Source: Adapted from Sheth and Larson, Federated Database Systems for Managing Distributed Heterogeneous Autonomous Databases. ACM Computing Surveys (Vol. 22: No. 3, September 1990).

14.4 QUERY PROCESSING IN DISTRIBUTED DATABASES

We now give an overview of how a DDBMS processes and optimizes a query. We first discuss the communication costs of processing a distributed query; we then discuss a special operation, called a *semijoin*, that is used in optimizing some types of queries in a DDBMS.

---

6. For a detailed discussion of the autonomies and the five-level architecture of FDBMSs, see Sheth and Larson (1990).

14.4.1   Data Transfer Costs of Distributed Query Processing

We discussed the issues involved in processing and optimizing a query in a centralized DBMS in Chapter 10. In a distributed system, several additional factors further complicate query processing. The first is the cost of transferring data over the network. This data includes intermediate files that are transferred to other sites for further processing, as well as the final result files that may have to be transferred to the site where the query result is needed. Although these costs may not be very high if the sites are connected via a high-performance local area network, they become quite significant in other types of networks. Hence, DDBMS query optimization algorithms consider the goal of reducing the *amount of data transfer* as an optimization criterion in choosing a distributed query execution strategy.

We illustrate this with two simple example queries. Suppose that the EMPLOYEE and DEPARTMENT relations of Figure 4.5 are distributed as shown in Figure 14.6. We will assume in this example that neither relation is fragmented. According to Figure 14.6, the size of the EMPLOYEE relation is 100 * 10,000 = 10^6 bytes, and the size of the DEPARTMENT relation is 35 * 100 = 3500 bytes. Consider the query Q: "For each employee, retrieve the employee name and the name of the department for which the employee works." This can be stated as follows in the relational algebra:

Q: $\pi_{\text{FNAME, LNAME, DNAME}}$ (EMPLOYEE $\bowtie_{\text{DNO=DNUMBER}}$ DEPARTMENT)

The result of this query will include 10,000 records, assuming that every employee is related to a department. Suppose that each record in the query result is *40 bytes long*. The query is submitted at a distinct site 3, which is called the **result site** because the query result is needed there. Neither the EMPLOYEE nor the DEPARTMENT relations reside at site 3. There are three simple strategies for executing this distributed query:

1. Transfer both the EMPLOYEE and the DEPARTMENT relations to the result site, and perform the join at site 3. In this case a total of 1,000,000 + 3500 = 1,003,500 bytes must be transferred.

SITE 1:

EMPLOYEE

FNAME	MINIT	INITIAL	<u>ENO</u>	DOB	ADDRESS	SEX	SALARY	SUPERENO	DNO

10,000 records
each record is 100 bytes long
ENO field is 9 bytes long   FNAME field is 15 bytes long
DNO field is 4 bytes long   LNAME field is 15 bytes long

SITE 2:

DEPARTMENT

DNAME	<u>DNUMBER</u>	MGRENO	MGRSTARTDATE

100 records
each record is 35 bytes long
DNUMBER field is 4 bytes long   DNAME field is 10 bytes long
MGRENO field is 9 bytes long

FIGURE 14.6 Example to illustrate volume of data transferred.

2. Transfer the EMPLOYEE relation to site 2, execute the join at site 2, and send the result to site 3. The size of the query result is 40 * 10,000 = 400,000 bytes, so 400,000 + 1,000,000 = 1,400,000 bytes must be transferred.

3. Transfer the DEPARTMENT relation to site 1, execute the join at site 1, and send the result to site 3. In this case 400,000 + 3500 = 403,500 bytes must be transferred.

If minimizing the amount of data transfer is our optimization criterion, we should choose strategy 3. Now consider another query Q_: "For each department, retrieve the department name and the name of the department manager." This can be stated as follows in the relational algebra:

$$Q': \pi_{FNAME, LNAME, DNAME} (DEPARTMENT \bowtie_{MGRENO=ENO} EMPLOYEE)$$

Again, suppose that the query is submitted at site 3. The same three strategies for executing query Q apply to Q', except that the result of Q' includes only 100 records, assuming that each department has a manager:

1. Transfer both the EMPLOYEE and the DEPARTMENT relations to the result site, and perform the join at site 3. In this case a total of 1,000,000 + 3500 = 1,003,500 bytes must be transferred.

2. Transfer the EMPLOYEE relation to site 2, execute the join at site 2, and send the result to site 3. The size of the query result is 40 * 100 = 4000 bytes, so 4000 + 1,000,000 = 1,004,000 bytes must be transferred.

3. Transfer the DEPARTMENT relation to site 1, execute the join at site 1, and send the result to site 3. In this case 4000 + 3500 = 7500 bytes must be transferred.

Again, we would choose strategy 3—in this case by an overwhelming margin over strategies 1 and 2. The preceding three strategies are the most obvious ones for the case where the result site (site 3) is different from all the sites that contain files involved in the query (sites 1 and 2). However, suppose that the result site is site 2; then we have two simple strategies:

1. Transfer the EMPLOYEE relation to site 2, execute the query, and present the result to the user at site 2. Here, the same number of bytes—1,000,000—must be transferred for both Q and Q'.

2. Transfer the DEPARTMENT relation to site 1, execute the query at site 1, and send the result back to site 2. In this case 400,000 + 3500 = 403,500 bytes must be transferred for Q and 4000 + 3500 = 7500 bytes for Q'.

A more complex strategy, which sometimes works better than these simple strategies, uses an operation called **semijoin**. We introduce this operation and discuss distributed execution using semijoins next.

14.4.2 Distributed Query Processing Using Semijoin

The idea behind distributed query processing using the *semijoin operation* is to reduce the number of tuples in a relation before transferring it to another site. Intuitively, the idea is to send the *joining column* of one relation R to the site where the other relation S is located; this column is then joined with S. Following that, the join attributes, along with the attributes required in the result, are projected out and shipped back to the original site and joined with R. Hence, only the joining column of R is transferred in one direction, and a subset of S with no extraneous tuples or attributes is transferred in the other direction. If only a small fraction of the tuples in S participate in the join, this can be quite an efficient solution to minimizing data transfer.

To illustrate this, consider the following strategy for executing Q or Q':

1. Project the join attributes of DEPARTMENT at site 2, and transfer them to site 1. For Q, we transfer $F = \pi_{DNUMBER}(DEPARTMENT)$, whose size is 4 * 100 = 400 bytes, whereas, for Q', we transfer $F' = \pi_{MGRENO}$ (DEPARTMENT), whose size is 9 * 100 = 900 bytes.

2. Join the transferred file with the EMPLOYEE relation at site 1, and transfer the required attributes from the resulting file to site 2. For Q, we transfer $R = \pi_{DNO, FNAME, LNAME} (F \ltimes_{DNUMBER=DNOEMPLOYEE})$, whose size is 34 * 10,000 = 340,000 bytes, whereas, for Q_, we transfer $R' = \pi_{MGRENO, FNAME, LNAME} (F \ltimes_{MGRENO=ENO} EMPLOYEE)$, whose size is 39 * 100 = 3900 bytes.

3. Execute the query by joining the transferred file R or R′ with DEPARTMENT, and present the result to the user at site 2.

Using this strategy, we transfer 340,400 bytes for Q and 4800 bytes for Q′. We limited the EMPLOYEE attributes and tuples transmitted to site 2 in step 2 to only those that will *actually be joined* with a DEPARTMENT tuple in step 3. For query Q, this turned out to include all EMPLOYEE tuples, so little improvement was achieved. However, for Q′ only 100 out of the 10,000 EMPLOYEE tuples were needed.

The semijoin operation was devised to formalize this strategy. A **semijoin operation** $R \ltimes_{A=B} S$, where A and B are domain-compatible attributes of R and S, respectively, produces the same result as the relational algebra expression $\pi_R(R\bowtie_{A=B}S)$. In a distributed environment where R and S reside at different sites, the semijoin is typically implemented by first transferring $F = \pi_B(S)$ to the site where R resides and then joining F with R, thus leading to the strategy discussed here.

Notice that the semijoin operation is not commutative; that is,

$$R \ltimes S \neq S \ltimes R$$

14.4.3   Query and Update Decomposition

In a DDBMS with *no distribution transparency*, the user phrases a query directly in terms of specific fragments. For example, consider another query Q: "Retrieve the names and hours per week for each employee who works on some project controlled by department 5," which is specified on the distributed database where the relations at sites 2 and 3 are shown in Figure 14.3, and those at site 1 are shown in Figure 4.6, as in our earlier example. A user who submits such a query must specify whether it references the PROJS5 and WORKS_ON5 relations at site 2 (Figure 14.3) or the PROJECT and WORKS_ON relations at site 1 (Figure 4.6). The user must also maintain consistency of replicated data items when updating a DDBMS with *no replication transparency.*

On the other hand, a DDBMS that supports *full distribution, fragmentation,* and *replication transparency* allows the user to specify a query or update request on the schema of Figure 4.5 just as though the DBMS were centralized. For updates, the DBMS is responsible for maintaining *consistency among replicated items* by using one of the distributed concurrency control algorithms to be discussed in Section 14.5. For queries, a **query decomposition** module must break up or **decompose** a query into **subqueries** that can be executed at the individual sites. In addition, a strategy for combining the results of the subqueries to form the query result must be generated. Whenever the DDBMS determines that an item referenced in the query is replicated, it must choose or **materialize** a particular replica during query execution.

To determine which replicas include the data items referenced in a query, the DDBMS refers to the fragmentation, replication, and distribution information stored in the DDBMS catalog. For vertical fragmentation, the attribute list for each fragment is kept in the catalog. For horizontal fragmentation, a condition, sometimes called a **guard,** is kept for each fragment. This is basically a selection condition that specifies which tuples exist in the fragment; it is called a guard because *only tuples that satisfy this condition* are permitted to be stored in the fragment. For mixed fragments, both the attribute list and the guard condition are kept in the catalog.

In our earlier example, the guard conditions for fragments at site 1 (Figure 4.6) are TRUE (all tuples), and the attribute lists are * (all attributes). For the fragments shown in Figure 14.3, we have the guard conditions and attribute lists shown in Figure 14.7. When the DDBMS decomposes an update request, it can determine which fragments must be updated by examining their guard conditions. For example, a user request to insert a new EMPLOYEE tuple <"Amarnath', 'B', 'Reddy', '345671239', '22-APR-64', '3306' Park Street, Calcutta, WB', M, 33000, '987654321', 4> would be decomposed by the DDBMS into two insert requests: the first inserts the preceding tuple in the EMPLOYEE fragment at site 1, and the second inserts the projected tuple <'Amarnath', 'B', 'Reddy', '345671239', 33000, '987654321', 4> in the EMPD4 fragment at site 3.

(a) EMPD5
  attribute list: FNAME,INITIAL,LNAME,ENO,SALARY,SUPERENO, DNO
  guard condition: DNO=5
 DEP5
  attribute list: ∗ (all attributes DNAME,DNUMBER,MGRENO,MGRSTARTDATE)
  guard condition: DNUMBER=5
 DEP5_LOCS
  attribute list: ∗ (all attributes DNUMBER,LOCATION)
  guard condition: DNUMBER=5
 PROJS5
  attribute list: ∗ (all attributes PNAME,PNUMBER,PLOCATION,DNUM)
  guard condition: DNUM=5
 WORKS_ON5
  attribute list: ∗ (all attributes EENO,PNO,HOURS)
  guard condition: EENO IN (π_{ENO} (EMPD5)) OR PNO IN ($\pi_{PNUMBER}$ (PROJS5))

  EMPD4
(b) attribute list: FNAME,MINIT,LNAME,ENO,SALARY,SUPERENO, DNO
  guard condition: DNO=4
 DEP4
  attribute list: ∗ (all attributes DNAME,DNUMBER,MGRENO,MGRSTARTDATE)
  guard condition: DNUMBER=4
 DEP4_LOCS
  attribute list: ∗ (all attributes DNUMBER,LOCATION)
  guard condition: DNUMBER=4
 PROJS4
  attribute list: ∗ (all attributes PNAME,PNUMBER,PLOCATION,DNUM)
  guard condition: DNUM=4
 WORKS_ON4
  attribute list: ∗ (all attributes EENO,PNO,HOURS)
  guard condition: EENO IN (π_{ENO} (EMPD4))
  OR PNO IN ($\pi_{PNUMBER}$ (PROJS4))

FIGURE 14.7 Guard conditions and attributes lists for fragments. (a) Site 2 fragments. (b) Site 3 fragments.

For query decomposition, the DDBMS can determine which fragments may contain the required tuples by comparing the query condition with the guard conditions. For example, consider the query Q: "Retrieve the names and hours per week for each employee who works on some project controlled by department 5"; this can be specified in SQL on the schema of Figure 4.5 as follows:

Q: SELECT FNAME,   LNAME,   HOURS
  FROM   EMPLOYEE, PROJECT, WORKS_ON
  WHERE DNUM=5 **AND** PNUMBER=PNO **AND** EENO=ENO;

Suppose that the query is submitted at site 2, which is where the query result will be needed. The DDBMS can determine from the guard condition on PROJS5 and WORKS_ON5 that all tuples satisfying the conditions (DNUM = 5 AND PNUMBER = PNO) reside at site 2. Hence, it may decompose the query into the following relational algebra subqueries:

T1 ← p_{EENO} (PROJS5 ⋈$_{PNUMBER=PNO}$WORKS_ON5)
T2 ← $p_{EENO, FNAME, LNAME}$ (T1 ⋈$_{EENO=ENO}$EMPLOYEE)
RESULT ← $p_{FNAME, LNAME, HOURS}$(T2 ∗ WORKS_ON5)

This decomposition can be used to execute the query by using a semijoin strategy. The DDBMS knows from the guard conditions that PROJS5 contains exactly those tuples satisfying (DNUM = 5) and that WORKS_ON5 contains all tuples to be joined with PROJS5; hence, subquery T1 can be executed at site 2, and the projected column EENO can be sent to site 1. Subquery T2 can then be executed at site 1, and the result can be sent back to site 2, where the final query result is calculated and displayed to the user. An alternative strategy would be to send the query Q itself to site 1, which includes all the database tuples, where it would be executed locally and from which the result would be sent back to site 2. The query optimizer would estimate the costs of both strategies and would choose the one with the lower cost estimate.

14.5   OVERVIEW OF CONCURRENCY CONTROL AND RECOVERY IN DISTRIBUTED DATABASES

For concurrency control and recovery purposes, numerous problems arise in a distributed DBMS environment that are not encountered in a centralized DBMS environment. These include the following:

- *Dealing with* **multiple copies** *of the data items:* The concurrency control method is responsible for maintaining consistency among these copies. The recovery method is responsible for making a copy consistent with other copies if the site on which the copy is stored fails and recovers later.

- *Failure of individual sites:* The DDBMS should continue to operate with its running sites, if possible, when one or more individual sites fail. When a site recovers, its local database must be brought up to date with the rest of the sites before it rejoins the system.

- *Failure of communication links:* The system must be able to deal with failure of one or more of the communication links that connect the sites. An extreme case of this problem is that **network partitioning** may occur. This breaks up the sites into two or more partitions, where the sites within each partition can communicate only with one another and not with sites in other partitions.

- *Distributed commit:* Problems can arise with committing a transaction that is accessing databases stored on multiple sites if some sites fail during the commit process. The **two-phase commit protocol** (see Chapter 11) is often used to deal with this problem.

- *Distributed deadlock:* Deadlock may occur among several sites, so techniques for dealing with deadlocks must be extended to take this into account. Distributed concurrency control and recovery techniques must deal with these and other problems. In the following subsections, we review some of the techniques that have been suggested to deal with recovery and concurrency control in DDBMSs.

14.5.1   Distributed Concurrency Control Based on a Distinguished Copy of a Data Item

To deal with replicated data items in a distributed database, a number of concurrency control methods have been proposed that extend the concurrency control techniques for centralized databases. We discuss these techniques in the context of extending centralized *locking*. Similar extensions apply to other concurrency control techniques. The idea is to designate *a particular copy* of each data item as a **distinguished copy**. The locks for this data item are associated *with the distinguished copy,* and all locking and unlocking requests are sent to the site that contains that copy.

A number of different methods are based on this idea, but they differ in their method of choosing the distinguished copies. In the **primary site technique,** all distinguished copies are kept at the same site. A modification of this approach is the primary site with a **backup site.** Another approach is the **primary copy** method, where the distinguished copies of the various data items can be stored in different sites. A site that includes a distinguished copy of a data item basically acts as the **coordinator site** for concurrency control on that item. We discuss these techniques next.

Primary Site Technique.   In this method a single **primary site** is designated to be the **coordinator site** *for all database items.* Hence, all locks are kept at that site, and all requests for locking or unlocking are sent there. This method is thus an extension of the centralized locking approach. For example, if all transactions follow the two-phase locking protocol, serializability is guaranteed. The advantage of this approach is that it is a simple extension of the centralized approach and hence is not overly complex. However, it has certain inherent disadvantages. One is that all locking requests are sent to a single site, possibly overloading that site and causing a system bottleneck. A second disadvantage is that failure of the primary site paralyzes the system, since all locking information is kept at that site. This can limit system reliability and availability.

Although all locks are accessed at the primary site, the items themselves can be accessed at any site at which they reside. For example, once a transaction obtains a READ_LOCK on a data item from the primary site, it can access any copy of that data item. However, once a transaction obtains a WRITE_LOCK and updates a data item, the DDBMS is responsible for updating *all copies* of the data item before releasing the lock.

Primary Site with Backup Site.   This approach addresses the second disadvantage of the primary site method by designating a second site to be a **backup site.** All locking information is maintained at both the primary and the backup sites. In case of primary site failure, the backup site takes over as primary site, and a new backup site is chosen. This simplifies the process of recovery from failure of the primary site, since the backup site takes over and processing can resume after a new backup site is chosen and the lock status information is copied to that site. It slows down the process of acquiring locks, however, because all lock requests and granting of locks must be recorded at *both the primary and the backup sites* before a response is sent to the requesting transaction. The problem of the primary and backup sites becoming overloaded with requests and slowing down the system remains undiminished.

Primary Copy Technique.   This method attempts to distribute the load of lock coordination among various sites by having the distinguished copies of different data items *stored at different sites.* Failure of one site affects any transactions that are accessing locks on items whose primary copies reside at that site, but other transactions are not affected. This method can also use backup sites to enhance reliability and availability.

Choosing a New Coordinator Site in Case of Failure.   Whenever a coordinator site fails in any of the preceding techniques, the sites that are still running must choose a new coordinator. In the case of the primary site approach with *no* backup site, all executing transactions must be aborted and restarted in a tedious recovery process. Part of the recovery process involves choosing a new primary site and creating a lock manager process and a record of all lock information at that site. For methods that use backup sites, transaction processing is suspended while the backup site is designated as the new primary site and a new backup site is chosen and is sent copies of all the locking information from the new primary site.

If a backup site X is about to become the new primary site, X can choose the new backup site from among the system's running sites. However, if no backup site existed, or if both the primary and the backup sites are down, a process called **election** can be used to choose the new coordinator site. In this process, any site Y that attempts to communicate with the coordinator site repeatedly and fails to do so can assume that the coordinator is down and can start the election process by sending a message to all running sites proposing that Y become the new coordinator. As soon as Y receives a majority of yes votes, Y can declare that it is the new coordinator. The election algorithm itself is quite complex, but this is the main idea behind the election method. The algorithm also resolves any attempt by two or more sites to become coordinator at the same time. The references in the Selected Bibliography at the end of this chapter discuss the process in detail.

14.5.2 Distributed Concurrency Control Based on Voting

The concurrency control methods for replicated items discussed earlier all use the idea of a distinguished copy that maintains the locks for that item. In the **voting method,** there is no distinguished copy; rather, a lock request is sent to all sites that includes a copy of the data item. Each copy maintains its own lock and can grant or deny the request for it. If a transaction that requests a lock is granted that lock by *a majority* of the copies, it holds the lock and informs *all copies* that it has been granted the lock. If a transaction does not receive a majority of votes granting it a lock within a certain *time-out period,* it cancels its request and informs all sites of the cancellation.

The voting method is considered a truly distributed concurrency control method, since the responsibility for a decision resides with all the sites involved. Simulation studies have shown that voting has higher message traffic among sites than do the distinguished copy methods. If the algorithm takes into account possible site failures during the voting process, it becomes extremely complex.

14.5.3 Distributed Recovery

The recovery process in distributed databases is quite involved. We give only a very brief idea of some of the issues here. In some cases it is quite difficult even to determine whether a site is down without exchanging numerous messages with other sites. For example, suppose that site X sends a message to site Y and expects a response from Y but does not receive it. There are several possible explanations:

- The message was not delivered to Y because of communication failure.

- Site Y is down and could not respond.

- Site Y is running and sent a response, but the response was not delivered.

Without additional information or the sending of additional messages, it is difficult to determine what actually happened.

Another problem with distributed recovery is distributed commit. When a transaction is updating data at several sites, it cannot commit until it is sure that the effect of the transaction on *every* site cannot be lost. This means that every site must first have recorded the local effects of the transactions permanently in the local site log on disk. The two-phase commit protocol, discussed in Section 11.6, is often used to ensure the correctness of distributed commit.

14.6 AN OVERVIEW OF 3-TIER CLIENT-SERVER ARCHITECTURE

As we pointed out in the chapter introduction, full-scale DDBMSs have not been developed to support all the types of functionalities that we discussed so far. Instead, distributed database applications are being developed in the context of the client-server architectures. We already introduced the two-tier client-server architecture in Section 2.5. It is now more common to use a three-tier architecture, particular in Web applications. This architecture is illustrated in Figure 14.8.

FIGURE 14.8 The three-tier client-server architecture.

In the three-tier client-server architecture, the following three layers exist:

1. Presentation layer (client): This provides the user interface and interacts with the user. The programs at this layer present Web interfaces or forms to the client in order to interface with the application. Web browsers are often utilized, and the languages used include HTML, JAVA, JavaScript, PERL, Visual Basic, and so on. This layer handles user input, output, and navigation by accepting user commands and displaying the needed information, usually in the form of static or dynamic Web pages. The latter are employed when the interaction involves database access. When a Web interface is used, this layer typically communicates with the application layer via the HTTP protocol.

2. Application layer (business logic): This layer programs the application logic. For example, queries can be formulated based on user input from the client, or query results can be formatted and sent to the client for presentation. Additional application functionality can be handled at this layer, such as security checks, identity verification, and other functions. The application layer can interact with one or more databases or data sources as needed by connecting to the database using ODBC, JDBC, SQL/CLI or other database access techniques.

3. Database server: This layer handles query and update requests from the application layer, processes the requests, and send the results. Usually SQL is used to access the database if it is relational or object-relational and stored database procedures may also be invoked. Query results (and queries) may be formatted into XML (see Chapter 15) when transmitted between the application server and the database server.

Exactly how to divide the DBMS functionality between client, application server, and database server may vary. The common approach is to include the functionality of a centralized DBMS at the database server level. A number of relational DBMS products have taken this approach, where an SQL server is provided. The application server must then formulate the appropriate SQL queries and connect to the database server when needed. The client provides the processing for user interface interactions. Since SQL is a relational standard, various SQL servers, possibly provided by different vendors, can accept SQL commands through standards such as ODBC, JDBC, SQL/CLI (see Chapter 7).

In this architecture, the application server may also refer to a data dictionary that includes information on the distribution of data among the various SQL servers, as well as modules for decomposing a global query into a number of local queries that can be executed at the various sites. Interaction between application server and database server might proceed as follows during the processing of an SQL query:

1. The application server formulates a user query based on input from the client layer and decomposes it into a number of independent site queries. Each site query is sent to the appropriate database server site.

2. Each database server processes the local query and sends the results to the application server site. Increasingly, XML is being touted as the standard for data exchange (see Chapter 15) so the database server may format the query result into XML before sending it to the application server.

3. The application server combines the results of the subqueries to produce the result of the originally required query, formats it into HTML or some other form accepted by the client, and sends it to the client site for display.

The application server is responsible for generating a distributed execution plan for a multisite query or transaction and for supervising distributed execution by sending commands to servers. These commands include local queries and transactions to be executed, as well as commands to transmit data to other clients or servers. Another function controlled by the application server (or coordinator) is that of ensuring consistency of replicated copies of a data item by employing distributed (or global) concurrency control techniques. The application server must also ensure the atomicity of global transactions by performing global recovery when certain sites fail. We discussed distributed recovery and concurrency control in Section 14.5.

If the DDBMS has the capabilty to *hide* the details of data distribution from the application server, then it enables the application server to execute global queries and transactions as though the database were centralized, without having to specify the sites at which the data referenced in the query or transaction resides. This property is called **distribution transparency.** Some DDBMSs do not provide distribution transparency, instead requiring that applications be aware of the details of data distribution.

14.7   DISTRIBUTED DATABASES IN ORACLE

In the client-server architecture, the Oracle database system is divided into two parts: (1) a front-end as the client portion, and (2) a back-end as the server portion. The client portion is the front-end database application that interacts with the user. The client has no data access responsibility and merely handles the requesting, processing, and presentation of data managed by the server. The server portion runs Oracle and handles the functions related to concurrent shared access. It accepts SQL and PL/SQL statements originating from client applications, processes them, and sends the results back to the client. Oracle client-server applications provide location transparency by making location of data transparent to users; several features like views, synonyms, and procedures contribute to this. Global naming is achieved by using <TABLENAME.@,DATABASENA ME> to refer to tables uniquely. Oracle uses a two-phase commit protocol to deal with concurrent distributed transactions. The COMMIT statement triggers the two-phase commit mechanism. The RECO (recoverer) background process automatically resolves the outcome of those distributed transactions in which the commit was interrupted. The RECO of each local Oracle Server automatically commits or rolls back any "in-doubt" distributed transactions consistently on all involved nodes. For long-term failures, Oracle allows each local DBA to manually commit or roll back any in-doubt transactions and free up resources. Global consistency can be maintained by restoring the database at each site to a predetermined fixed point in the past.

Oracle's distributed database architecture is shown in Figure 14.9. A node in a distributed database system can act as a client, as a server, or both, depending on the situation. The figure shows two sites where databases called HQ (headquarters) and Sales are kept. For example, in the application shown running at the headquarters, for an SQL statement issued against local data (for example, DELETE FROM DEPT ...), the HQ computer acts as a server, whereas for a statement against remote data (for example, INSERT INTO EMP@SALES), the HQ computer acts as a client.

All Oracle databases in a distributed database system (DDBS) use Oracle's networking software Net8 for interdatabase communication. Net8 allows databases to communicate across networks to support remote and distributed transactions. It packages SQL statements into one of the many communication protocols to facilitate client to server communication and then packages the results back similarly to the client. Each database has a unique global name provided by a hierarchical arrangement of network domain names that is prefixed to the database name to make it unique.

Oracle supports database links that define a one-way communication path from one Oracle database to another. For example,

CREATE DATABASE LINK   sales.us.americas;

establishes a connection to the sales database in Figure 14.9 under the network domain us that comes under domain India.

Data in an Oracle DDBS can be replicated using snapshots or replicated master tables. Replication is provided at the following levels:

- *Basic replication:* Replicas of tables are managed for read-only access. For updates, data must be accessed at a single primary site.

- *Advanced (symmetric) replication:* This extends beyond basic replication by allowing applications to update table replicas throughout a replicated DDBS. Data can be read and updated at any site. This requires additional software called Oracle's advanced replication option. A **snapshot** generates a copy of a part of the table by means of a query called the *snapshot defining query.* A simple snapshot definition looks like this:

CREATE SNAPSHOT sales.orders AS
SELECT   * FROM sales.orders@hq.us.americas;

Oracle groups snapshots into refresh groups. By specifying a refresh interval, the snapshot is automatically refreshed periodically at that interval by up to ten **Snapshot Refresh Processes (SNPs).** If the defining query of a snapshot contains a distinct or aggregate function, a GROUP BY or CONNECT BY clause, or join or set operations, the snapshot is termed a **complex snapshot** and requires additional processing. Oracle (up to version 7.3) also supports ROWID snapshots that are based on physical row identifiers of rows in the master table.

Heterogeneous Databases in Oracle.

In a heterogeneous DDBS, at least one database is a non-Oracle system. **Oracle Open Gateways** provides access to a non-Oracle database from an Oracle server, which uses a database link to access data or to execute remote procedures in the non-Oracle system. The Open Gateways feature includes the following:

- *Distributed transactions:* Under the two-phase commit mechanism, transactions may span Oracle and non-Oracle systems.

- *Transparent SQL access:* SQL statements issued by an application are transparently transformed into SQL statements understood by the non-Oracle system.

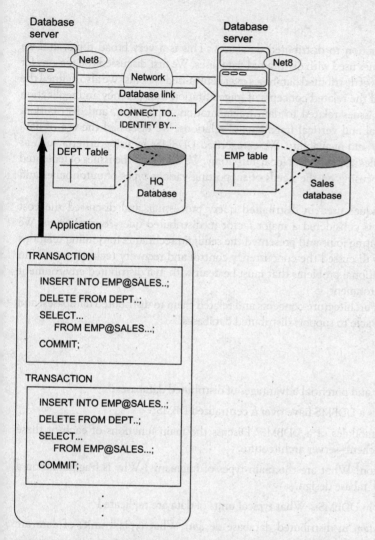

FIGURE 25.9 Oracle distributed database systems. Source: From Oracle (1997a). Copyright © Oracle Corporation 1997. All rights reserved.

- *Pass-through* SQL *and stored procedures:* An application can directly access a non-Oracle system using that system's version of SQL. Stored procedures in a non-Oracle SQL-based system are treated as if they were PL/SQL remote procedures.

- *Global query optimization:* Cardinality information, indexes, etc., at the non-Oracle system are accounted for by the Oracle Server query optimizer to perform global query optimization.

- *Procedural access:* Procedural systems like messaging or queuing systems are accessed by the Oracle server using PL/SQL remote procedure calls.

In addition to the above, data dictionary references are translated to make the non-Oracle data dictionary appear as a part of the Oracle Server's dictionary. Character set translations are done between national language character sets to connect multilingual databases.

14.8 SUMMARY

In this chapter we provided an introduction to distributed databases. This is a very broad topic, and we discussed only some of the basic techniques used with distributed databases. We first discussed the reasons for distribution and the potential advantages of distributed databases over centralized systems. We also defined the concept of distribution transparency and the related concepts of fragmentation transparency and replication transparency. We discussed the design issues related to data fragmentation, replication, and distribution, and we distinguished between horizontal and vertical fragments of relations. We discussed the use of data replication to improve system reliability and availability. We categorized DDBMSs by using criteria such as degree of homogeneity of software modules and degree of local autonomy. We discussed the issues of federated database management in some detail focusing on the needs of supporting various types of autonomies and dealing with semantic heterogeneity.

We illustrated some of the techniques used in distributed query processing, and discussed the cost of communication among sites, which is considered a major factor in distributed query optimization. We compared different techniques for executing joins and presented the semijoin technique for joining relations that reside on different sites. We briefly discussed the concurrency control and recovery techniques used in DDBMSs. We reviewed some of the additional problems that must be dealt with in a distributed environment that do not appear in a centralized environment.

We then discussed the client-server architecture concepts and related them to distributed databases, and we described some of the facilities in Oracle to support distributed databases.

Review Questions

14.1. What are the main reasons for and potential advantages of distributed databases?

14.2. What additional functions does a DDBMS have over a centralized DBMS?

14.3. What are the main software modules of a DDBMS? Discuss the main functions of each of these modules in the context of the client–server architecture.

14.4. What is a fragment of a relation? What are the main types of fragments? Why is fragmentation a useful concept in distributed database design?

14.5. Why is data replication useful in DDBMSs? What typical units of data are replicated?

14.6. What is meant by *data allocation* in distributed database design? What typical units of data are distributed over sites?

14.7. How is a horizontal partitioning of a relation specified? How can a relation be put back together from a complete horizontal partitioning?

14.8. How is a vertical partitioning of a relation specified? How can a relation be put back together from a complete vertical partitioning?

14.9. Discuss what is meant by the following terms: *degree of homogeneity of a* DDBMS, *degree of local autonomy of a* DDBMS, *federated DBMS, distribution transparency, fragmentation transparency, replication transparency, multidatabase system.*

14.10. Discuss the naming problem in distributed databases.

14.11. Discuss the different techniques for executing an equijoin of two files located at different sites. What main factors affect the cost of data transfer?

14.12. Discuss the semijoin method for executing an equijoin of two files located at different sites. Under what conditions is an equijoin strategy efficient?

14.13. Discuss the factors that affect query decomposition. How are guard conditions and attribute lists of fragments used during the query decomposition process?

14.14. How is the decomposition of an update request different from the decomposition of a query? How are guard conditions and attribute lists of fragments used during the decomposition of an update request?

14.15. Discuss the factors that do not appear in centralized systems that affect concurrency control and recovery in distributed systems.

14.16. Compare the primary site method with the primary copy method for distributed concurrency control. How does the use of backup sites affect each?

14.17. When are voting and elections used in distributed databases?

14.18. What are the software components in a client-server DDBMS? Compare the two-tier and three-tier client-server architectures.

Exercises

14.19. Consider the data distribution of the COMPANY database, where the fragments at sites 2 and 3 are as shown in Figure 14.3 and the fragments at site 1 are as shown in Figure 4.6. For each of the following queries, show at least two strategies of decomposing and executing the query. Under what conditions would each of your strategies work well?

   a. For each employee in department 5, retrieve the employee name and the names of the employee's dependents.

   b. Print the names of all employees who work in department 5 but who work on some project *not* controlled by department 5.

14.20. Consider the following relations:

BOOKS (Book#, Primary_author, Topic, Total_stock, $price)
BOOKSTORE (Store#, City, State, Zip, Inventory_value)
STOCK (Store#, Book#, Qty)

TOTAL_STOCK is the total number of books in stock, and INVENTORY_VALUE is the total inventory value for the store.

   a. Give an example of two simple predicates that would be meaningful for the BOOKSTORE relation for horizontal partitioning.

   b. How would a derived horizontal partitioning of STOCK be defined based on the partitioning of BOOKSTORE?

   c. Show predicates by which BOOKS may be horizontally partitioned by topic.

   d. Show how the STOCK may be further partitioned from the partitions in (b) by adding the predicates in (c).

14.21. Consider a distributed database for a bookstore chain called National Books with 3 sites called EAST, MIDDLE, and WEST. The relation schemas are given in question 14.20. Consider that BOOKS are fragmented by $PRICE amounts into:

B1: BOOK1: up to $20.

B2: BOOK2: from $20.01 to $50.

B3: BOOK3: from $50.01 to $100.

B4: BOOK4: $100.01 and above.

Similarly, BOOKSTORES are divided by Zipcodes into:

S_1: EAST: Zipcodes up to 35000.

S_2: MIDDLE: Zipcodes 35001 to 70000.

S_3: WEST: Zipcodes 70001 to 99999.

Assume that STOCK is a derived fragment based on BOOKSTORE only.

a. Consider the query:

```
SELECT Book#, Total_stock
FROM Books
WHERE $price > 15 and $price < 55;
```

Assume that fragments of BOOKSTORE are non-replicated and assigned based on region. Assume further that BOOKS are allocated as:

EAST: B_1, B_4

MIDDLE: B_1, B_2

WEST: B_1, B_2, B_3, B_4

Assuming the query was submitted in EAST, what remote subqueries does it generate? (write in SQL).

b. If the bookprice of BOOK#= 1234 is updated from $45 to $55 at site MIDDLE, what updates does that generate? Write in English and then in SQL.

c. Given an example query issued at WEST that will generate a subquery for MIDDLE.

d. Write a query involving selection and projection on the above relations and show two possible query trees that denote different ways of execution.

14.22. Consider that you have been asked to propose a database architecture in a large organization, General Motors, as an example, to consolidate all data including legacy databases (from Hierarchical and Network models, which are explained in Appendices C and D; no specific knowledge of these models is needed) as well as relational databases, which are geographically distributed so that global applications can be supported. Assume that alternative one is to keep all databases as they are, while alternative two is to first convert them to relational and then support the applications over a distributed integrated database.

a. Draw two schematic diagrams for the above alternatives showing the linkages among appropriate schemas. For alternative one, choose the approach of providing export schemas for each database and constructing unified schemas for each application.

b. List the steps one has to go through under each alternative from the present situation until global applications are viable.

c. Compare these from the issues of: (i) design time considerations, and (ii) runtime considerations.

Selected Bibliography

The textbooks by Ceri and Pelagatti (1984a) and Ozsu and Valduriez (1999) are devoted to distributed databases. Halsaal (1996), Tannenbaum (1996), and Stallings (1997) are textbooks on data communications and computer networks. Comer (1997) discusses networks and internets. Dewire (1993) is a textbook on client-server computing. Ozsu et al. (1994) has a collection of papers on distributed object management.

Distributed database design has been addressed in terms of horizontal and vertical fragmentation, allocation, and replication. Ceri et al. (1982) defined the concept of minterm horizontal fragments. Ceri et al. (1983) developed an integer programming based optimization model for horizontal fragmentation and allocation. Navathe et al. (1984) developed algorithms for vertical fragmentation based on attribute affinity and showed a variety of contexts for vertical fragment allocation. Wilson and Navathe (1986) present an analytical model for optimal allocation of fragments. Elmasri et al. (1987) discuss fragmentation for the ECR model; Karlapalem et al. (1994) discuss issues for distributed design of object databases. Navathe et al. (1996) discuss mixed fragmentation by combining horizontal and vertical fragmentation; Karlapalem et al. (1996) present a model for redesign of distributed databases.

Distributed query processing, optimization, and decomposition are discussed in Hevner and Yao (1979), Kerschberg et al. (1982), Apers et al. (1983), Ceri and Pelagatti (1984), and Bodorick et al. (1992). Bernstein and Goodman (1981) discuss the theory behind semijoin processing. Wong (1983) discusses the use of relationships in relation fragmentation. Concurrency control and recovery schemes are discussed in Bernstein and Goodman (1981a). Kumar and Hsu (1998) have some articles related to recovery in distributed databases. Elections in distributed systems are discussed in Garcia-Molina (1982). Lamport (1978) discusses problems with generating unique timestamps in a distributed system.

A concurrency control technique for replicated data that is based on voting is presented by Thomas (1979). Gifford (1979) proposes the use of weighted voting, and Paris (1986) describes a method called voting with witnesses. Jajodia and Mutchler (1990) discuss dynamic voting. A technique called *available copy* is proposed by Bernstein and Goodman (1984), and one that uses the idea of a group is presented in ElAbbadi and Toueg (1988). Other recent work that discusses replicated data includes Gladney (1989), Agrawal and ElAbbadi (1990), ElAbbadi and Toueg (1990), Kumar and Segev (1993), Mukkamala (1989), and Wolfson and Milo (1991). Bassiouni (1988) discusses optimistic protocols for DDB concurrency control. Garcia-Molina (1983) and Kumar and Stonebraker (1987) discuss techniques that use the semantics of the transactions. Distributed concurrency control techniques based on locking and distinguished copies are presented by Menasce et al. (1980) and Minoura and Wiederhold (1982). Obermark (1982) presents algorithms for distributed deadlock detection.

A survey of recovery techniques in distributed systems is given by Kohler (1981). Reed (1983) discusses atomic actions on distributed data. A book edited by Bhargava (1987) presents various approaches and techniques for concurrency and reliability in distributed systems.

Federated database systems were first defined in McLeod and Heimbigner (1985). Techniques for schema integration in federated databases are presented by Elmasri et al. (1986), Batini et al. (1986), Hayne and Ram (1990), and Motro (1987). Elmagarmid and Helal (1988) and Gamal-Eldin et al. (1988) discuss the update problem in heterogeneous DDBSs. Heterogeneous distributed database issues are discussed in Hsiao and Kamel (1989). Sheth and Larson (1990) present an exhaustive survey of federated database management.

Recently, multidatabase systems and interoperability have become important topics. Techniques for dealing with semantic incompatibilities among multiple databases are examined in DeMichiel (1989), Siegel and Madnick (1991), Krishnamurthy et al. (1991), and Wang and Madnick (1989). Castano et al. (1998) present an excellent survey of techniques for analysis of schemas. Pitoura et al. (1995) discuss object orientation in multidatabase systems.

Transaction processing in multidatabases is discussed in Mehrotra et al. (1992), Georgakopoulos et al. (1991), Elmagarmid et al. (1990), and Brietbart et al. (1990), among others. Elmagarmid et al. (1992) discuss transaction processing for advanced applications, including engineering applications discussed in Heiler et al. (1992).

The workflow systems, which are becoming popular to manage information in complex organizations, use multilevel and nested transactions in conjunction with distributed databases. Weikum (1991) discusses multilevel transaction management. Alonso et al. (1997) discuss limitations of current workflow systems.

A number of experimental distributed DBMSs have been implemented. These include distributed INGRES (Epstein et al., 1978), DDTS (Devor and Weeldreyer, 1980), SDD-1 (Rothnie et al., 1980), System R* (Lindsay et al., 1984), SIRIUS-DELTA (Ferrier and Stangret, 1982), and MULTIBASE (Smith et al., 1981). The OMNIBASE system (Rusinkiewicz et al., 1988) and the Federated Information Base developed using the Candide data model (Navathe et al., 1994) are examples of federated DDBMS. Pitoura et al. (1995) present a comparative survey of the federated database system prototypes. Most commercial DBMS vendors have products using the client-server approach and offer distributed versions of their systems. Some system issues concerning client-server DBMS architectures are discussed in Carey et al. (1991), DeWitt et al. (1990), and Wang and Rowe (1991). Khoshafian et al. (1992) discuss design issues for relational DBMSs in the client-server environment. Client-server management issues are discussed in many books, such as Zantinge and Adriaans (1996).

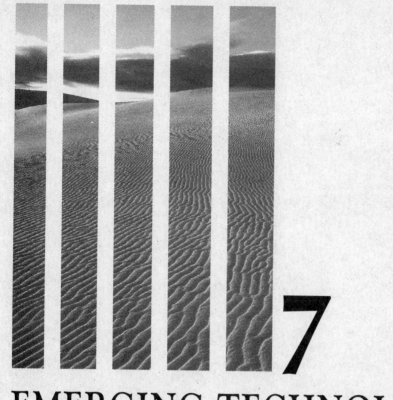

7
EMERGING TECHNOLOGIES

15

XML and Internet Databases

We now turn our attention to how databases are used and accessed from the Internet. Many electronic commerce (e-commerce) and other Internet applications provide Web interfaces to access information stored in one or more databases. These databases are often referred to as **data sources.** It is common to use two-tier and three-tier clientserver architectures for Internet applications (see Section 2.5). In some cases, other variations of the clientserver model are used. E-commerce and other Internet database applications are designed to interact with the user through Web interfaces that display Web pages. The common method of specifying the contents and formatting of Web pages is through the use of **hyperlink documents.** There are various languages for writing these documents, the most common being HTML (Hypertext Markup Language). Although HTML is widely used for formatting and structuring Web *documents*, it is not suitable for specifying *structured data* that is extracted from databases. Recently, a new language—namely, XML (Extended Markup Language)—has emerged as the standard for structuring and exchanging data over the Web. XML can be used to provide information about the structure and meaning of the data in the Web pages rather than just specifying how the Web pages are formatted for display on the screen. The formatting aspects are specified separately—for example, by using a formatting language such as XSL (Extended Stylesheet Language).

This chapter describes the basics of accessing and exchanging information over the Internet. We start in Section 15.1 by discussing how traditional Web pages differ from structured databases, and discuss the differences between structured, semistructured, and unstructured data. Then in Section 15.2 we turn our attention to the XML standard and its tree-structured (hierarchical) data model. Section 15.3 discusses XML documents and the languages for specifying the structure of these documents, namely, XML DTD (Document Type Definition) and XML schema. Section 15.4 presents the various approaches for storing XML documents, whether in their native (text) format, in a compressed form, or in relational and other types of databases. Section 15.5 gives an overview of the languages proposed for querying XML data. Section 15.6 summarizes the chapter.

15.1 STRUCTURED, SEMISTRUCTURED, AND UNSTRUCTURED DATA

The information stored in databases is known as **structured data** because it is represented in a strict format. For example, each record in a relational database table—such as the EMPLOYEE table in Figure 4.6—follows the same format as the other records in that table. For structured data, it is common to carefully design the database using techniques such as those described in Chapters 3, 6 and 8 in order to create the database schema. The DBMS then checks to ensure that all data follows the structures and constraints specified in the schema.

However, not all data is collected and inserted into carefully designed structured databases. In some applications, data is collected in an ad-hoc manner before it is known how it will be stored and managed. This data may have a certain structure, but not all the information collected will have identical structure. Some attributes may be shared among the various entities, but other attributes may exist only in a few entities. Moreover, additional attributes can be introduced in some of the newer data items at any time, and there is no predefined schema. This type of data is known as **semistructured data.** A number of data models have been introduced for representing semistructured data, often based on using tree or graph data structures rather than the flat relational model structures.

A key difference between structured and semistructured data concerns how the schema constructs (such as the names of attributes, relationships, and entity types) are handled. In semistructured data, the schema information is *mixed in* with the data values, since each data object can have different attributes that are not known in advance. Hence, this type of data is sometimes referred to as **self-describing data.** Consider the following example. We want to collect a list of bibliographic references related to a certain research project. Some of these may be books or technical reports, others may be research articles in journals or conference proceedings, and still others may refer to complete journal issues or conference proceedings. Clearly, each of these may have different attributes and different types of information. Even for the same type of reference— say, conference articles—we may have different information. For example, one article citation may be quite complete, with full information about author names, title, proceedings, page numbers, and so on, whereas another citation may not have all the information available. New types of bibliographic sources may appear in the future—for example, references to Web pages or to conference tutorials—and these may have new attributes that describe them.

Semistructured data may be displayed as a directed graph, as shown in Figure 15.1. The information shown in Figure 15.1 corresponds to some of the structured data shown in Figure 4.6. As we can see, this model somewhat resembles the object model in its ability to represent complex objects and nested structures. In Figure 15.1, the **labels** or **tags** on the directed edges represent the schema names: the *names of attributes, object types (or entity types or classes),* and *relationships* . The internal nodes represent individual objects or composite attributes. The leaf nodes represent actual data values of simple (atomic) attributes.

There are two main differences between the semistructured model and the object model.

1. The schema information—names of attributes, relationships, and classes (object types) in the semistructured model is intermixed with the objects and their data values in the same data structure.

2. In the semistructured model, there is no requirement for a predefined schema to which the data objects must conform.

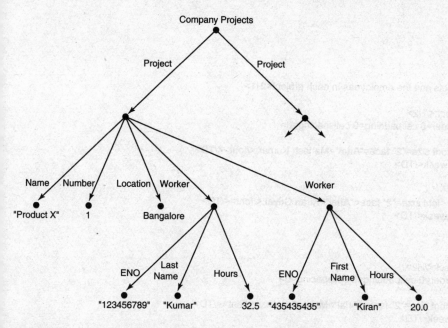

FIGURE 15.1 Representing semistructured data as a graph.

In addition to structured and semistructured data, a third category exists, known as **unstructured data** because there is very limited indication of the type of data. A typical example is a text document that contains information embedded within it. Web pages in HTML that contain some data are considered to be unstructured data. Consider part of an HTML file, shown in Figure 15.2. Text that appears between angled brackets, <...>, is an **HTML tag**. A tag with a backslash, </...>, indicates an **end tag**, which represents the ending of the effect of a matching **start tag**. The tags **mark up** the document[1] in order to instruct an HTML processor how to display the text between a start tag and a matching end tag. Hence, the tags specify document formatting rather than the meaning of the various data elements in the document. HTML tags specify information, such as font size and style (boldface, italics, and so on), color, heading levels in documents, and so on. Some tags provide text structuring in documents, such as specifying a numbered or unnumbered list or a table. Even these structuring tags specify that the embedded textual data is to be displayed in a certain manner, rather than indicating the type of data represented in the table.

HTML uses a large number of predefined tags, which are used to specify a variety of commands for formatting Web documents for display. The start and end tags specify the range of text to be formatted by each command. A few examples of the tags shown in Figure 15.2 follow:

- The <html> ... </html> tags specify the boundaries of the document.

- The **document header** information—within the <head> ... </head> tags—specifies various commands that will be used elsewhere in the document. For example, it may specify various **script functions** in a language such as JAVA Script or PERL, or certain **formatting styles** (fonts, paragraph styles, header styles, and so on) that can be used in the document. It can also specify a title to indicate what the HTML file is for, and other similar information that will not be displayed as part of the document.

---

1. That is why it is known as Hypertext *Markup* Language.

```
<html>
<head>
...
</head>
<body>
<H1>List of company projects and the employees in each project<\H1>

  <H2>The ProductX project:</H2>
  <table width="100%" border=0 cellpadding=0 cellspacing=0>
   <TR>
     <TD width="50%"><font size="2" face="Arial">Mahesh Kumar:</font></TD>
     <TD>32.5 hours per week</TD>
     </TR>
   <TR>
     <TD width="50%%"><font size="2" face="Arial">Kiran Goyal:</font></TD>
     <TD>20.0 hours per week</TD>
     </TR>
  </table>

  <H2>The ProductY project:</H2>
  <table width="100%" border=0 cellpadding=0 cellspacing=0>
   <TR>
     <TD width="50%"><font size="2" face="Arial">Mahesh Kumar:</font></TD>
     <TD>7.5 hours per week</TD>
     </TR>
   <TR>
     <TD width="50%%"><font size="2" face="Arial">Kiran Goyal:</font></TD>
     <TD>20.0 hours per week</TD>
     </TR>
   <TR>
     <TD width="50%%"><font size="2" face="Arial">Karthik Chandra:</font></TD>
     <TD>10.0 hours per week</TD>
     </TR>
  </table>

...
</body>
</html>
```

FIGURE 15.2 Part of an HTML document representing unstructured data.

- The **body** of the document—specified within the <body> ... </body> tags—includes the document text and the markup tags that specify how the text is to be formatted and displayed. It can also include references to other objects, such as images, videos, voice messages, and other documents.

- The <H1> ... </H1> tags specify that the text is to be displayed as a level 1 heading. There are many heading levels (<H2>, <H3>, and so on), each displaying text in a less prominent heading format.

- The <table> ... </table> tags specify that the following text is to be displayed as a table. Each row in the table is enclosed within <TR> ... </TR> tags, and the actual text data in a row is displayed within <TD> ... </TD> tags.[2]

---

2. <TR> stands for table row, and <TD> for table data.

- Some tags may have **attributes,** which appear within the start tag and describe additional properties of the tag.[3] In Figure 15.2, the <table> start tag has four attributes describing various characteristics of the table. The following <TD> and <font> start tags have one and two attributes, respectively.

HTML has a very large number of predefined tags, and whole books are devoted to describing how to use these tags. If designed properly, HTML documents can be formatted so that humans are able to easily understand the document contents, and are able to navigate through the resulting Web documents. However, the source HTML text documents are very difficult to interpret automatically by *computer programs* because they do not include schema information about the type of data in the documents. As e-commerce and other Internet applications become increasingly automated, it is becoming crucial to be able to exchange Web documents among various computer sites and to interpret their contents automatically. This need was one of the reasons that led to the development of XML, which we discuss in the next section.

15.2   XML HIERARCHICAL (TREE) DATA MODEL

We now introduce the data model used in XML. The basic object is XML in the **XML document.** Two main structuring concepts are used to construct an XML document: **elements** and **attributes.** It is important to note right away that the term *attribute* in XML is not used in the same manner as is customary in database terminology, but rather as it is used in document description languages such as HTML and SGML.[4] Attributes in XML provide additional information that describes elements, as we shall see. There are additional concepts in XML, such as entities, identifiers, and references, but we first concentrate on describing elements and attributes to show the essence of the XML model.

Figure 15.3 shows an example of an XML element called <projects>. As in HTML, elements are identified in a document by their **start tag** and **end tag.** The tag names are enclosed between angled brackets <...>, and end tags are further identified by a backslash, </...>.[5] **Complex elements** are constructed from other elements hierarchically, whereas **simple elements** contain data values. A major difference between XML and HTML is that XML tag names are defined to describe the meaning of the data elements in the document, rather than to describe how the text is to be displayed. This makes it possible to process the data elements in the XML document automatically by computer programs.

It is straightforward to see the correspondence between the XML textual representation shown in Figure 15.3 and the tree structure shown in Figure 15.1. In the tree representation, internal nodes represent complex elements, whereas leaf nodes represent simple elements. That is why the XML model is called a **tree model** or a **hierarchical model.** In Figure 15.3, the simple elements are the ones with the tag names <Name>, <Number>, <Location>, <DeptNo>, <ENO>, <LastName>, <FirstName>, and <hours>. The complex elements are the ones with the tag names <projects>, <project>, and <Worker>. In general, there is no limit on the levels of nesting of elements.

In general, it is possible to characterize three main types of XML documents:

- *Data-centric XML documents:* These documents have many small data items that follow a specific structure and hence may be extracted from a structured database. They are formatted as XML documents in order to exchange them or display them over the Web.

---

3. This is how the term *attribute* is used in document markup languages, which differs from how it is used in database models.

4. SGML (Standard Generalized Markup Language) is a more general language for describing documents and provides capabilities for specifying new tags. However, it is more complex than HTML and XML.

5. The left and right angled bracket characters (< and >) are reserved characters, as are the ampersand (&), apostrophe ('), and single quotation marks ('). To include them within the text of a document, they must be encoded as <, >, &, ', and ", respectively.

- *Document-centric XML documents:* These are documents with large amounts of text, such as news articles or books. There are few or no structured data elements in these documents.

- *Hybrid XML documents:* These documents may have parts that contain structured data and other parts that are predominantly textual or unstructured.

It is important to note that data-centric XML documents can be considered either as semistructured data or as structured data. If an XML document conforms to a predefined XML schema or DTD (see Section 15.3), then the document can be considered as *structured data*. On the other hand, XML allows documents that do not conform to any schema; and these would be considered as *semistructured data*. The latter are also known as *schemaless XML documents*. When the value of the STANDALONE attribute in an XML document is "YES", as in the first line of Figure 15.3, the document is standalone and schemaless.

```
<?xml version="1.0" standalone="yes"?>
<projects>

    <project>
      <Name>ProductX</Name>
      <Number>1</Number>
      <Location>Bangalore</Location>
      <DeptNo>5</DeptNo>
      <Worker>
        <ENO>123456789</ENO>
        <LastName>Kumar</LastName>
        <hours>32.5</hours>
      </Worker>
      <Worker>
        <ENO>453453453</ENO>
        <FirstName>Kiran</FirstName>
        <hours>20.0</hours>
      </Worker>
    </project>
    </project>
      <Name>ProductY</Name>
      <Number>2</Number>
      <Location>New Delhi</Location>
      <DeptNo >5</DeptNo >
      <Worker>
        <ENO>123456789</ENO>
        <hours>7.5</hours>
      </Worker>
      <Worker>
        <ENO>453453453</ENO>
        <hours>20.0</hours>
      </Worker>
      <Worker>
        <ENO>333445555</ENO>
        <hours>10.0</hours>
      </Worker>
    </project>

    ...

</projects>
```

FIGURE 15.3 A complex XML element called <projects>.

XML attributes are generally used in a manner similar to how they are used in HTML (see Figure 15.2), namely, to describe properties and characteristics of the elements (tags) within which they appear. It is also possible to use XML attributes to hold the values of simple data elements; however this is definitely not recommended. We discuss XML attributes further in Section 15.3 when we discuss XML schema and DTD.

15.3   XML DOCUMENTS, DTD, AND XML SCHEMA

15.3.1   Well-Formed and Valid XML Documents and XML DTD

In Figure 15.3, we saw what a simple XML document may look like. An XML document is **well formed** if it follows a few conditions. In particular, it must start with an **XML declaration** to indicate the version of XML being used as well as any other relevant attributes, as shown in the first line of Figure 15.3. It must also follow the syntactic guidelines of the tree model. This means that there should be a *single root element*, and every element must include a matching pair of start and end tags within the start and end tags *of the parent element*. This ensures that the nested elements specify a well-formed tree structure.

A well-formed XML document is syntactically correct. This allows it to be processed by generic processors that traverse the document and create an internal tree representation. A standard set of API (application programming interface) functions called DOM (Document Object Model) allows programs to manipulate the resulting tree representation corresponding to a well-formed XML document. However, the whole document must be parsed beforehand when using DOM. Another API called SAX allows processing of XML documents on the fly by notifying the processing program whenever a start or end tag is encountered. This makes it easier to process large documents and allows for processing of so-called **streaming XML documents,** where the processing program can process the tags as they are encountered.

A well-formed XML document can have any tag names for the elements within the document. There is no predefined set of elements (tag names) that a program processing the document knows to expect. This gives the document creator the freedom to specify new elements, but limits the possibilities for automatically interpreting the elements within the document.

A stronger criterion is for an XML document to be **valid.** In this case, the document must be well formed, and in addition the element names used in the start and end tag pairs must follow the structure specified in a separate XML **DTD (Document Type Definition)** file or XML schema file. We first discuss XML DTD here, then give an overview of XML schema in Section 15.3.2. Figure 15.4 shows a simple XML DTD file, which specifies the elements (tag names) and their nested structures. Any valid documents conforming to this DTD should follow the specified structure. A special syntax exists for specifying DTD files, as illustrated in Figure 15.4. First, a name is given to the **root tag** of the document, which is called projects in the first line of Figure 15.4. Then the elements and their nested structure are specified.

When specifying elements, the following notation is used:

- A * following the element name means that the element can be repeated zero or more times in the document. This kind of element is known as an *optional multivalued (repeating) element.*

- A + following the element name means that the element can be repeated one or more times in the document. This kind of element is a *required multivalued (repeating) element.*

- A? following the element name means that the element can be repeated zero or one times. This kind is an *optional single-valued (nonrepeating) element.*

- An element appearing without any of the preceding three symbols must appear exactly once in the document. This kind is a *required single-valued (nonrepeating) element.*

```
<!DOCTYPE projects [
  <!ELEMENT projects (project+)>
  <!ELEMENT project (Name, Number, Location, DeptNo?, Workers)>
  <!ELEMENT Name (#PCDATA)>
  <!ELEMENT Number (#PCDATA)>
  <!ELEMENT Location (#PCDATA)>
  <!ELEMENT DeptNo (#PCDATA)>
  <!ELEMENT Workers (Worker*)>
  <!ELEMENT Worker (ENO, LastName?, FirstName?, hours)>
  <!ELEMENT ENO (#PCDATA)>
  <!ELEMENT LastName (#PCDATA)>
  <!ELEMENT FirstName (#PCDATA)>
  <!ELEMENT hours (#PCDATA)>
] >
```

FIGURE 15.4 An XML DTD file called projects.

- The **type** of the element is specified via parentheses following the element. If the parentheses include names of other elements, these latter elements are the *children* of the element in the tree structure. If the parentheses include the keyword #PCDATA or one of the other data types available in XML DTD, the element is a leaf node. PCDATA stands for *parsed character data*, which is roughly similar to a string data type.

- Parentheses can be nested when specifying elements.

- A bar symbol ($e_1 \mid e_2$) specifies that either e_1 or e_2 can appear in the document.

We can see that the tree structure in Figure 15.1 and the XML document in Figure 15.3 conform to the XML DTD in Figure 15.4. To require that an XML document be checked for conformance to a DTD, we must specify this in the declaration of the document. For example, we could change the first line in Figure 15.3 to the following:

```
<?xml version="1.0" standalone="no"?>
<!DOCTYPE projects SYSTEM "proj.dtd">
```

When the value of the standalone attribute in an XML document is "no", the document needs to be checked against a separate DTD document. The DTD file shown in Figure 15.4 should be stored in the same file system as the XML document, and should be given the file name "proj.dtd". Alernatively, we could include the DTD document text at the beginning of the XML document itself to allow the checking.

Although XML DTD is quite adequate for specifying tree structures with required, optional, and repeating elements, it has several limitations. First, the data types in DTD are not very general. Second, DTD has its own special syntax and thus requires specialized processors. It would be advantageous to specify XML schema documents using the syntax rules of XML itself so that the same processors used for XML documents could process XML schema descriptions. Third, all DTD elements are always forced to follow the specified ordering of the document, so unordered elements are not permitted. These drawbacks led to the development of XML schema, a more general language for specifying the structure and elements of XML documents.

15.3.2 XML Schema

The XML schema language is a standard for specifying the structure of XML documents. It uses the same syntax rules as regular XML documents, so that the same processors can be used on both. To distinguish the two types of documents, we will use the term XML *instance document* or XML *document* for a regular XML document, and XML *schema document* for a document that specifies an XML schema. Figure 15.5 shows an XML schema document corresponding to the COMPANY database shown in Figures 3.2 and 4.5. Although it is unlikely that we would want to display the whole database as a single document, there have been proposals to store data in native XML format as an alternative to storing the data in relational databases. The schema in Figure 15.5 would serve the purpose of specifying the structure of the COMPANY database if it were stored in a native XML system. We discuss this topic further in Section 15.4.

As with XML DTD, XML schema is based on the tree data model, with elements and attributes as the main structuring concepts. However, it borrows additional concepts from database and object models, such as keys, references, and identifiers. We here describe the features of XML schema in a step-by-step manner, referring to the example XML schema document of Figure 15.5 for illustration. We introduce and describe some of the schema concepts in the order in which they are used in Figure 15.5.

1. *Schema descriptions and XML namespaces:* It is necessary to identify the specific set of XML schema language elements (tags) being used by specifying a file stored at a Web site location. The second line in Figure 15.5 specifies the file used in this example, which is "http://www.w3.org/2001/XMLSchema". This is the most commonly used standard for XML schema commands. Each such definition is called an **XML namespace,** because it defines the set of commands (names) that can be used. The file name is assigned to the variable xsd (XML schema description) using the attribute xmlns (XML namespace), and this variable is used as a prefix to all XML schema commands (tag names). For example, in Figure 15.5, when we write xsd:element or xsd:sequence, we are referring to the definitions of the element and sequence tags as defined in the file "http://www.w3.org/ 2001/XMLSchema".

2. *Annotations, documentation, and language used:* The next couple of lines in Figure 15.5 illustrate the XML schema elements (tags) xsd:annotation and xsd:documentation, which are used for providing comments and other descriptions in the XML document. The attribute xml:lang of the xsd:documentation element specifies the language being used, where "en" stands for the English language.

```
<?xml version="1.0" encoding="UTF-8" ?>
<xsd:schema xmlns:xsd="http://www.w3.org/2001/XMLSchema">
   <xsd:annotation>
        <xsd:documentation xml:lang="en">Company Schema (Element Approach) –
            Prepared by Babak Hojabri</xsd:documentation>
   </xsd:annotation>
<xsd:element name="company">
    <xsd:complexType>
        <xsd:sequence>
          <xsd:element name="department" type="Department" minOccurs="0"
                maxOccurs="unbounded" />
          <xsd:element name="employee" type="Employee" minOccurs="0"
                maxOccurs="unbounded">
            <xsd:unique name="dependentNameUnique">
                <xsd:selector xpath="employeeDependent" />
                <xsd:field xpath="dependentName" />
            </xsd:unique>
          </xsd:element>
          <xsd:element name="project" type="Project" minOccurs="0"
                maxOccurs="unbounded" />
        </xsd:sequence>
    </xsd:complexType>
</xsd:element>
```

FIGURE 15.5 An XML schema file called company.

```xml
    <xsd:unique name="departmentNameUnique">
        <xsd:selector xpath="department" />
        <xsd:field xpath="departmentName" />
    </xsd:unique>
    <xsd:unique name="projectNameUnique">
        <xsd:selector xpath="project" />
        <xsd:field xpath="projectName" />
    </xsd:unique>
    <xsd:key name="projectNumberKey">
        <xsd:selector xpath="project" />
        <xsd:field xpath="projectNumber" />
    </xsd:key>
    <xsd:key name="departmentNumberKey">
        <xsd:selector xpath="department" />
        <xsd:field xpath="departmentNumber" />
    </xsd:key>
    <xsd:key name="employeeENOKey">
        <xsd:selector xpath="employee" />
        <xsd:field xpath="employeeENO" />
    </xsd:key>
    <xsd:keyref name="departmentManagerENOKeyRef " refer="employeeENOKey">
        <xsd:selector xpath="department" />
        <xsd:field xpath="departmentManagerENO" />
    </xsd:keyref>
    <xsd:keyref name="employeeDepartmentNumberKeyRef"
        refer="departmentNumberKey">
        <xsd:selector xpath="employee" />
        <xsd:field xpath="employeeDepartmentNumber" />
    </xsd:keyref>
    <xsd:keyref name="employeeSupervisorENOKeyRef" refer="employeeENOKey">
        <xsd:selector xpath="employee" />
        <xsd:field xpath="employeeSupervisorENO" />
    </xsd:keyref>
    <xsd:keyref name="projectDepartmentNumberKeyRef"
        refer="departmentNumberKey">
        <xsd:selector xpath="project" />
        <xsd:field xpath="projectDepartmentNumber" />
    </xsd:keyref>
    <xsd:keyref name="projectWorkerENOKeyRef" refer="employeeENOKey">
        <xsd:selector xpath="project/projectWorker" />
        <xsd:field xpath="ENO" />
    </xsd:keyref>
    <xsd:keyref name="employeeWorksOnProjectNumberKeyRef"
        refer="projectNumberKey">
        <xsd:selector xpath="employee/employeeWorksOn" />
        xsd:field xpath="projectNumber" />
    </xsd:keyref>
</xsd:element>
```

FIGURE 15.5(CONTINUED) An XML schema file called company.

```
<xsd:complexType name="Department">
    <xsd:sequence>
        <xsd:element name="departmentName" type="xsd:string" />
        <xsd:element name="departmentNumber" type="xsd:string" />
        <xsd:element name="departmentManagerENO" type="xsd:string" />
        <xsd:element name="departmentManagerStartDate" type="xsd:date" />
        <xsd:element name="departmentLocation" type="xsd:string"
            minOccurs="0" maxOccurs="unbounded" />
    </xsd:sequence>
</xsd:complexType>
<xsd:complexType name="Employee">
    <xsd:sequence>
        <xsd:element name="employeeName" type="Name" />
        <xsd:element name="employeeENO" type="xsd:string" />
        <xsd:element name="employeeSex" type="xsd:string" />
        <xsd:element name="employeeSalary" type="xsd:unsignedInt" />
        <xsd:element name="employeeDOB" type="xsd:date" />
        <xsd:element name="employeeDepartmentNumber" type="xsd:string" />
        <xsd:element name="employeeSupervisorENO" type="xsd:string" />
        <xsd:element name="employeeAddress" type="Address" />
        <xsd:element name="employeeWorksOn" type="WorksOn" minOccurs="1"
            maxOccurs="unbounded" />
        <xsd:element name="employeeDependent" type="Dependent" minOccurs="0"
            maxOccurs="unbounded" />
    </xsd:sequence>
</xsd:complexType>
<xsd:complexType name="Project">
    <xsd:sequence>
        <xsd:element name="projectName" type="xsd:string" />
        <xsd:element name="projectNumber" type="xsd:string" />
        <xsd:element name="projectLocation" type="xsd:string" />
        <xsd:element name="projectDepartmentNumber" type="xsd:string" />
        <xsd:element name="projectWorker" type="Worker" minOccurs="1"
            maxOccurs="unbounded" />
    </xsd:sequence>
</xsd:complexType>
<xsd:complexType name="Dependent">
    <xsd:sequence>
        <xsd:element name="dependentName" type="xsd:string" />
        <xsd:element name="dependentSex" type="xsd:string" />
        <xsd:element name="dependentDOB" type="xsd:date" />
        <xsd:element name="dependentRelationship" type="xsd:string" />
    </xsd:sequence>
</xsd:complexType>
<xsd:complexType name="Address">
    <xsd:sequence>
        <xsd:element name="number" type="xsd:string" />
        <xsd:element name="street" type="xsd:string" />
        <xsd:element name="city" type="xsd:string" />
        <xsd:element name="state" type="xsd:string" />
    </xsd:sequence>
```

FIGURE 15.5(CONTINUED) An XML schema file called company.

```
        </xsd:complexType>
        <xsd:complexType name="Name">
            <xsd:sequence>
                <xsd:element name="firstName" type="xsd:string" />
                <xsd:element name="initial" type="xsd:string" />
                <xsd:element name="lastName" type="xsd:string" />
            </xsd:sequence>
        </xsd:complexType>
        <xsd:complexType name="Worker">
            <xsd:sequence>
                <xsd:element name="ENO" type="xsd:string" />
                <xsd:element name="hours" type="xsd:float" />
            </xsd:sequence>
        </xsd:complexType>
        <xsd:complexType name="WorksOn">
            <xsd:sequence>
                <xsd:element name="projectNumber" type="xsd:string" />
                <xsd:element name="hours" type="xsd:float" />
            </xsd:sequence>
        </xsd:complexType>
    </xsd:schema>
```

FIGURE 15.5(CONTINUED) An XML schema file called company.

3. *Elements and types:* Next, we specify the *root element* of our XML schema. In XML schema, the name attribute of the xsd:element tag specifies the element name, which is called company for the root element in our example (see Figure 15.5). The structure of the company root element can then be specified, which in our example is xsd:complexType. This is further specified to be a sequence of departments, employees, and projects using the xsd:sequence structure of XML schema. It is important to note here that this is not the only way to specify an XML schema for the COMPANY database. We will discuss other options in Section 15.4.

4. *First-level elements in the COMPANY database:* Next, we specify the three first-level elements under the company root element in Figure 15.5. These elements are named employee, department, and project, and each is specified in an xsd:element tag. Notice that if a tag has only attributes and no further subelements or data within it, it can be ended with the backslash symbol (/>) directly instead of having a separate matching end tag. These are called **empty elements;** examples are the xsd:element elements named department and project in Figure 15.5.

5. *Specifying element type and minimum and maximum occurrences:* In XML schema, the attributes type, minOccurs, and maxOccurs in the xsd:element tag specify the type and multiplicity of each element in any document that conforms to the schema specifications. If we specify a type attribute in an xsd:element, the structure of the element must be described separately, typically using the xsd:complexType element of XML schema. This is illustrated by the employee, department, and project elements in Figure15.5. On the other hand, if no type attribute is specified, the element structure can be defined directly following the tag, as illustrated by the company root element in Figure 15.5. The minOccurs and maxOccurs tags are used for specifying lower and upper bounds on the number of occurrences of an element in any document that conforms to the schema specifi-cations. If they are not specified, the default is exactly one occurrence. These serve a similar role to the *, +, and ? symbols of XML DTD, and to the (min, max) constraints of the ER model (see Section 3.7.4).

6. *Specifying keys:* In XML schema, it is possible to specify constraints that correspond to unique and primary key constraints in a relational database (see Section 4.2.2), as well as foreign keys (or referential integrity)

constraints (see Section 4.2.4). The xsd:unique tag specifies elements that correspond to unique attributes in a relational database that are not primary keys. We can give each such uniqueness constraint a name, and we must specify xsd:selector and xsd:field tags for it to identify the element type that contains the unique element and the element name within it that is unique via the xpath attribute. This is illustrated by the departmentNameUnique and projectNameUnique elements in Figure 15.5. For specifying **primary keys,** the tag xsd:key is used instead of xsd:unique, as illustrated by the projectNumberKey, departmentNumberKey, and employeeENOKey elements in Figure 15.5. For specifying **foreign keys,** the tag xsd:keyref is used, as illustrated by the six xsd:keyref elements in Figure 15.5. When specifying a foreign key, the attribute refer of the xsd:keyref tag specifies the referenced primary key, whereas the tags xsd:selector and xsd:field specify the referencing element type and foreign key (see Figure 15.5).

7. *Specifying the structures of complex elements via complex types:* The next part of our example specifies the structures of the complex elements Department, Employee, Project, and Dependent, using the tag xsd:complexType (see Figure 15.5). We specify each of these as a sequence of subelements corresponding to the database attributes of each entity type (see Figures 3.2 and 4.7) by using the xsd:sequence and xsd:element tags of XML schema. Each element is given a name and type via the attributes name and type of xsd:element. We can also specify minOccurs and maxOccurs attributes if we need to change the default of exactly one occurrence. For (optional) database attributes where null is allowed, we need to specify minOccurs = 0, whereas for multivalued database attributes we need to specify maxOccurs = "unbounded" on the corresponding element. Notice that if we were not going to specify any key constraints, we could have embedded the subelements within the parent element definitions directly without having to specify complex types. However, when unique, primary key, and foreign key constraints need to be specified, we must define complex types to specify the element structures.

8. *Composite (compound) attributes:* Composite attributes from Figure 3.2 are also specified as complex types in Figure 15.5, as illustrated by the Address, Name, Worker, and WorksOn complex types. These could have been directly embedded within their parent elements.

This example illustrates some of the main features of XML schema. There are other features, but they are beyond the scope of our presentation. In the next section, we discuss the different approaches to creating XML documents from relational databases and storing XML documents.

15.4   XML DOCUMENTS AND DATABASES

We now discuss how various types of XML documents can be stored and retrieved. Section 15.4.1 gives an overview of the various approaches for storing XML documents. Section 15.4.2 discusses one of these approaches, in which data-centric XML documents are extracted from existing databases, in more detail. In particular, we show how tree structured documents can be created from graph-structured databases. Section 15.4.3 discusses the problem of cycles and how it can be dealt with.

15.4.1   Approaches to Storing XML Documents

Several approaches to organizing the contents of XML documents to facilitate their subsequent querying and retrieval have been proposed. The following are the most common approaches:

1. *Using a DBMS to store the documents as text:* A relational or object DBMS can be used to store whole XML documents as text fields within the DBMS records or objects. This approach can be used if the DBMS has

a special module for document processing, and would work for storing schemaless and document-centric DBMS documents. The keyword indexing functions of the document processing module can be used to index and speed up search and retrieval of the documents.

2. *Using a DBMS to store the document contents as data elements:* This approach would work for storing a collection of documents that follow a specific XML DTD or XML schema. Because all the documents have the same structure, one can design a relational (or object) database to store the leaf-level data elements within the XML documents. This approach would require mapping algorithms to design a database schema that is compatible with the XML document structure as specified in the XML schema or DTD and to recreate the XML documents from the stored data. These algorithms can be implemented either as an internal DBMS module or as separate middleware that is not part of the DBMS.

3. *Designing a specialized system for storing native XML data:* A new type of database system based on the hierarchical (tree) model could be designed and implemented. The system would include specialized indexing and querying techniques, and would work for all types of XML documents. It could also include data compression techniques to reduce the size of the documents for storage.

4. *Creating or publishing customized XML documents from preexisting relational databases:* Because there are enormous amounts of data already stored in relational databases, parts of this data may need to be formatted as documents for exchanging or displaying over the Web. This approach would use a separate middleware software layer to handle the conversions needed between the XML documents and the relational database.

All four of these approaches have received considerable attention over the past few years. We focus on approach 4 in the next subsection, because it gives a good conceptual understanding of the differences between the XML tree data model and the traditional database models based on flat files (relational model) and graph representations (ER model).

15.4.2 Extracting XML Documents from Relational Databases

This section discusses the representational issues that arise when converting data from a database system into XML documents. As we have discussed, XML uses a hierarchical (tree) model to represent documents. The database systems with the most widespread use follow the flat relational data model. When we add referential integrity constraints, a relational schema can be considered to be a graph structure (for example, see Figure 4.7). Similarly, the ER model represents data using graphlike structures (for example, see Figure 3.2). We saw in Chapter 6 that there are straightforward mappings between the ER and relational models, so we can conceptually represent a relational database schema using the corresponding ER schema. Although we will use the ER model in our discussion and examples to clarify the conceptual differences between tree and graph models, the same issues apply to converting relational data to XML.

We will use the simplified UNIVERSITY ER schema shown in Figure 15.6 to illustrate our discussion. Suppose that an application needs to extract XML documents for student, course, and grade information from the UNIVERSITY database. The data needed for these documents is contained in the database attributes of the entity types COURSE, SECTION, and STUDENT from Figure 15.6, and the relationships S-S and C-S between them. In general, most documents extracted from a database will only use a subset of the attributes, entity types, and relationships in the database. In this example, the subset of the database that is needed is shown in Figure 15.7.

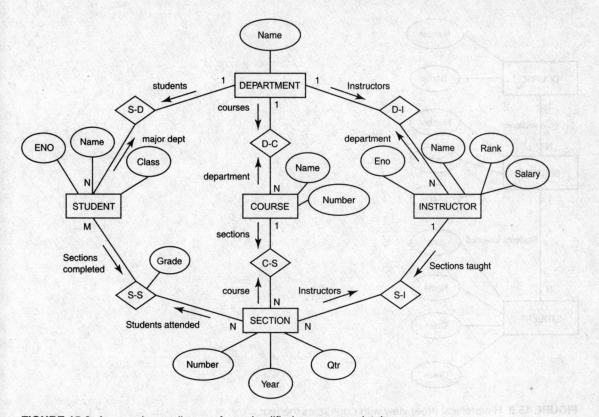

FIGURE 15.6 An ER schema diagram for a simplified UNIVERSITY database.

FIGURE 15.7 Subset of the UNIVERSITY database schema needed for XML document extraction.

At least three possible document hierarchies can be extracted from the database subset in Figure 15.7. First, we can choose COURSE as the root, as illustrated in Figure 15.8. Here, each course entity has the set of its sections as subelements, and each section has its students as subelements. We can see one consequence of modeling the information in a hierarchical tree structure. If a student has taken multiple sections, that student's information will appear multiple times in the document—once under each section. A possible simplified XML schema for this view is shown in Figure 15.9. The Grade database attribute in the S-S relationship is migrated to the STUDENT element. This is because STUDENT becomes a child of SECTION in this hierarchy, so each STUDENT element under a specific SECTION element can have a specific grade in that section. In this document hierarchy, a student taking more than one section will have several replicas, one under each section, and each replica will have the specific grade given in that particular section.

FIGURE 15.8 Hierarchical (tree) view with COURSE as the root.

```
<xsd:element name="root">
<xsd:sequence>
    <xsd:element name="course" minOccurs="0" maxOccurs="unbounded">
        <xsd:sequence>
        <xsd:element name="cname" type="xsd:string" />
        <xsd:element name="cnumber" type="xsd:unsignedInt" />
        <xsd:element name="section" minOccurs="0" maxOccurs="unbounded">
<xsd:sequence>
        <xsd:element name="secnumber" type="xsd:unsignedInt" />
        <xsd:element name="year" type="xsd:string" />
        <xsd:element name="quarter" type="xsd:string" />
        <xsd:element name="student" minOccurs="0" maxOccurs="unbounded">
<xsd:sequence>
        <xsd:element name="sno" type="xsd:string" />
        <xsd:element name="sname" type="xsd:string" />
        <xsd:element name="class" type="xsd:string" />
        <xsd:element name="grade" type="xsd:string" />
</xsd:sequence>
    </xsd:element>
        </xsd:sequence>
        </xsd:element>
    </xsd:sequence>
</xsd:element>
</xsd:sequence>
</xsd:element>
```

FIGURE 15.9 XML schema document with COURSE as the root.

In the second hierarchical document view, we can choose STUDENT as root (Figure 15.10). In this hierarchical view, each student has a set of sections as its child elements, and each section is related to one course as its child, because the relationship between SECTION and COURSE is N:1. We can hence merge the COURSE and SECTION elements in this view, as shown in Figure 15.10. In addition, the GRADE database attribute can be migrated to the SECTION element. In this hierarchy, the combined COURSE/SECTION information is replicated under each student who completed the section. A possible simplified XML schema for this view is shown in Figure 15.11.

FIGURE 15.10 Hierarchical (tree) view with STUDENT as the root.

The third possible way is to choose SECTION as the root, as shown in Figure 15.12. Similar to the second hierarchical view, the COURSE information can be merged into the SECTION element. The GRADE database attribute can be migrated to the STUDENT element. As we can see, even in this simple example, there can be numerous hierarchical document views, each corresponding to a different root and a different XML document structure.

```
<xsd:element name="root">
<xsd:sequence>
<xsd:element name="student" minOccurs="0" maxOccurs="unbounded">
    <xsd:sequence>
        <xsd:element name="sno" type="xsd:string" />
        <xsd:element name="sname" type="xsd:string" />
        <xsd:element name="class" type="xsd:string" />
        <xsd:element name="section" minOccurs="0" maxOccurs="unbounded">
            <xsd:sequence>
                <xsd:element name="secnumber" type="xsd:unsignedInt" />
                <xsd:element name="year" type="xsd:string" />
                <xsd:element name="quarter" type="xsd:string" />
                <xsd:element name="cnumber" type="xsd:unsignedInt" />
                <xsd:element name="cname" type="xsd:string" />
                <xsd:element name="grade" type="xsd:string" />
            </xsd:sequence>
        </xsd:element>
    </xsd:sequence>
</xsd:element>
</xsd:sequence>
</xsd:element>
```

FIGURE 15.11 XML schema document with STUDENT as the root.

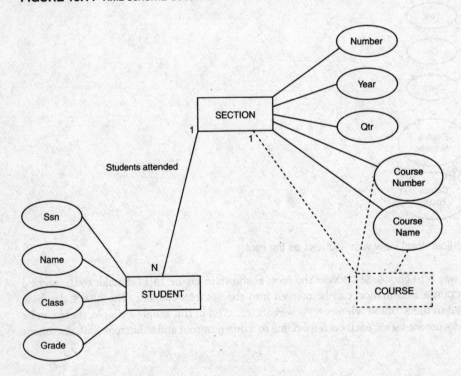

FIGURE 15.12 Hierarchical (tree) view with SECTION as the root.

15.4.3   Breaking Cycles to Convert Graphs into Trees

In the previous examples, the subset of the database of interest had no cycles. It is possible to have a more complex subset with one or more cycles, indicating multiple relationships among the entities. In this case, it is more complex to decide how to create the document hierarchies. Additional duplication of entities may be needed to represent the multiple relationships. We shall illustrate this with an example using the ER schema in Figure 15.6.

Suppose that we need the information in all the entity types and relationships of Figure 15.6 for a particular XML document, with STUDENT as the root element. Figure 15.13 illustrates how a possible hierarchical tree structure can be created for this document. First, we get a lattice with STUDENT as the root, as shown in part (1) of Figure 15.13. This is not a tree structure because of the cycles. One way to break the cycles is to replicate the entity types involved in the cycles. First, we replicate INSTRUCTOR as shown in part (2) of Figure 15.13, calling the replica to the right INSTRUCTOR1. The INSTRUCTOR replica on the left represents the relationship between instructors and the sections they teach, whereas the INSTRUCTOR1 replica on the right represents the relationship between instructors and the department each works in. After this, we still have the cycle involving COURSE, so we can replicate COURSE in a similar manner, leading to the hierarchy shown in part (3) of Figure 15.13. The COURSE1 replica to the left represents the relationship between courses and their sections, whereas the COURSE replica to the right represents the relationship between courses and the department that offers each course.

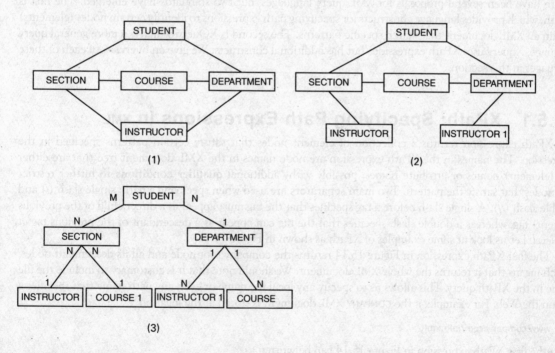

FIGURE 15.13 Converting a graph with cycles into a hierarchical (tree) structure.

In part (3) of Figure 15.13, we have converted the initial graph to a hierarchy. We can do further merging if desired (as in our previous example) before creating the final hierarchy and the corresponding XML schema structure.

15.4.4 Other Steps for Extracting XML Documents from Databases

In addition to creating the appropriate XML hierarchy and corresponding XML schema document, several other steps are needed to extract a particular XML document from a database:

1. It is necessary to create the correct query in SQL to extract the desired information for the XML document.

2. Once the query is executed, its result must be structured from the flat relational form to the XML tree structure.

3. The query can be customized to select either a single object or multiple objects into the document. For example, in the view of Figure 15.11, the query can select a single student entity and create a document corresponding to that single student, or it may select several—or even all of—the students and create a document with multiple students.

15.5 XML QUERYING

There have been several proposals for XML query languages, but two standards have emerged. The first is XPath, which provides language constructs for specifying path expressions to identify certain nodes (elements) within an XML document that match specific patterns. The second is XQuery, which is a more general query language. Xquery uses XPath expressions but has additional constructs. We give an overview of each of these languages in this section.

15.5.1 XPath: Specifying Path Expressions in XML

An XPath expression returns a collection of element nodes that satisfy certain patterns specified in the expression. The names in the XPath expression are node names in the XML document tree that are either tag (element) names or attribute names, possibly with additional **qualifier conditions** to further restrict the nodes that satisfy the pattern. Two main **separators** are used when specifying a path: single slash (/) and double slash (//). A single slash before a tag specifies that the tag must appear as a direct child of the previous (parent) tag, whereas a double slash specifies that the tag can appear as a descendant of the previous tag *at any level*. Let us look at some examples of XPath as shown in Figure 15.14.

The first XPath expression in Figure 15.14 returns the company root node and all its descendant nodes, which means that it returns the whole XML document. We should note that it is customary to include the file name in the XPath query. This allows us to specify any local file name or even any path name that specifies a file on the Web. For example, if the COMPANY XML document is stored at the location

    www.company.com/info.xml

then the first XPath expression in Figure 15.14 can be written as

    doc(www.company.com/info.xml)/company

This prefix would also be included in the other examples.

The second example in Figure 15.14 returns all department nodes (elements) and their descendant subtrees. Note that the nodes (elements) in an XML document are ordered, so the XPath result that returns multiple nodes will do so in the same order in which the nodes are ordered in the document tree.

The third XPath expression in Figure 15.14 illustrates the use of //, which is convenient to use if we do not know the full path name we are searching for, but do know the name of some tags of interest within the XML document. This is particularly useful for schemaless XML documents or for documents with many nested levels of nodes.[6] The expression returns all employeeName nodes that are direct children of an employee node, such that the employee node has another child element employeeSalary whose value is greater than 70000. This illustrates the use of qualifier conditions, which restrict the nodes selected by the XPath expression to those that satisfy the condition. XPath has a number of comparison operations for use in qualifier conditions, including standard arithmetic, string, and set comparison operations.

1. /company
2. /company/department
3. //employee [employeeSalary gt 70000]/employeeName
4. /company/employee [employeeSalary gt 70000]/employeeName
5. /company/project/projectWorker [hours ge 20.0]

FIGURE 15.14 Some examples of XPath expressions on XML documents that follow the XML schema file COMPANY in Figure 15.5.

The fourth XPath expression should return the same result as the previous one, except that we specified the full path name in this example. The fifth expression in Figure 15.14 returns all projectWorker nodes and their descendant nodes that are children under a path /company/project and have a child node hours with a value greater than 20.0 hours.

15.5.2   XQuery: Specifying Queries in XML

XPath allows us to write expressions that select nodes from a tree-structured XML document. XQuery permits the specification of more general queries on one or more XML documents. The typical form of a query in XQuery is known as a **FLWR expression,** which stands for the four main clauses of XQuery and has the following form:

```
FOR <variable bindings to individual nodes (elements)>
LET <variable bindings to collections of nodes (elements)>
WHERE <qualifier conditions>
RETURN <query result specification>
```

Figure 15.15 includes some examples of queries in XQuery that can be specified on XML instance documents that follow the XML schema document in Figure 15.5. The first query retrieves the first and last names of employees who earn more than $70,000. The variable $x is bound to each employeeName element that is a child of an employee element, but only for employee elements that satisfy the qualifier that their employeeSalary value is greater than $70,000. The result retrieves the firstName and lastName child elements of the selected employeeName elements. The second query is an alternative way of retrieving the same elements retrieved by the first query.

---

6. We are using the terms *node, tag,* and *element* interchangeably here.

1. FOR $x IN
    doc(www.company.com/info.xml)
    //employee [employeeSalary gt 70000]/employeeName
    RETURN <res> $x/firstName, $x/lastName </res>
2. FOR $x IN
    doc(www.company.com/info.xml)/company/employee
    WHERE $x/employeeSalary gt 70000
    RETURN <res> $x/employeeName/firstName,
                 $x/employeeName/lastName </res>
3. FOR $x IN
    doc(www.company.com/info.xml)/company
                /project[projectNumber = 5]/projectWorker,
        $y IN
    doc(www.company.com/info.xml)/company/employee
    WHERE $x/hours gt 20.0 AND $y.ssn = $x.ssn
    RETURN <res> $y/employeeName/firstName,
                 $y/employeeName/lastName, $x/hours </res>

FIGURE 15.15 Some examples of XQuery queries on XML documents that follow the XML schema file COMPANY in Figure 15.5.

The third query illustrates how a join operation can be performed by having more than one variable. Here, the $x variable is bound to each projectWorker element that is a child of project number 5, whereas the $y variable is bound to each employee element. The join condition matches ENO values in order to retrieve the employee names.

This concludes our brief introduction to XQuery. The interested reader is referred to the Web site www.w3.org, which contains documents describing the latest standards related to XML.

15.6 SUMMARY

This chapter gave an overview of the standard for representing and exchanging data over the Internet. We started by discussing the differences between structured, semistructured, and unstructured data, then discussed why there was a need for a specification language such as XML. We described the XML standard and its tree-structured (hierarchical) data model, and discussed XML documents and the languages for specifying the structure of these documents, namely, XML DTD (Document Type Definition) and XML schema. We then gave an overview of the various approaches for storing XML documents, whether in their native (text) format, in a compressed form, or in relational and other types of databases, and discussed the mapping issues that arise when there is need to convert data stored in traditional databases into XML documents. Finally, we gave an overview of the XPath and XQuery languages proposed for querying XML data.

Review Questions

15.1. What are the differences between structured, semistructured, and unstructured data?

15.2. Under which of the above categories do XML documents fall? What about self-describing data?

15.3. What are the differences between the use of tags in XML versus HTML?

15.4. What is the difference between data-centric and document-centric XML documents?

15.5. What is the difference between attributes and elements in XML? List some of the important attributes used in specifying elements in XML schema.

15.6. What is the difference between XML schema and XML DTD?

Exercises

15.7. Create an XML instance document to correspond to the data stored in the relational database shown in Figure 4.6 such that the XML document conforms to the XML schema document in Figure 15.5.

15.8. Create XML schema documents to correspond to the hierarchies shown in Figures 15.12 and 15.13 part (3).

15.9. Consider the LIBRARY relational database schema of Figure 4.20. Create an XML schema document that corresponds to this database schema.

15.10. Specify the following views as queries in XQuery on the COMPANY XML schema shown in Figure 15.5.

 a. A view that has the department name, manager name, and manager salary for every department.

 b. A view that has the employee name, supervisor name, and employee salary for each employee who works in the Research department.

 c. A view that has the project name, controlling department name, number of employees, and total hours worked per week on the project for each project.

 d. A view that has the project name, controlling department name, number of employees, and total hours worked per week on the project for each project with more than one employee working on it.

Selected Bibliography

There are so many articles and books on various aspects of XML that it would be impossible to make even a modest list. We will mention one book: Chaudhri, Rashid, and Zicari, eds (2003). This book discusses various aspects of XML and contains a list of some recent references to XML research and practice.

16

Data Mining Concepts

Over the last three decades, many organizations have generated a large amount of machine-readable data in the form of files and databases. To process this data, we have the database technology available that supports query languages like SQL. The problem with SQL is that it is a structured language that assumes the user is aware of the database schema. SQL supports operations of relational algebra that allow a user to select rows and columns of data from tables or join related information from tables based on common fields. In the next chapter, we shall see that *data warehousing technology* affords several types of functionality: that of consolidation, aggregation, and summarization of data. Data warehouses let us view the same information along multiple dimensions. In this chapter, we will focus our attention on another very popular area of interest known as data mining. As the term connotes, **data mining** refers to the mining or discovery of new information in terms of patterns or rules from vast amounts of data. To be practically useful, data mining must be carried out efficiently on large files and databases.

We will briefly review the state of the art of this rather extensive field of data mining, which uses techniques from such areas as machine learning, statistics, neural networks, and genetic algorithms. We will highlight the nature of the information that is discovered, the types of problems faced when trying to mine databases, and the types of applications of data mining. We also survey the state of the art of a large number of commercial tools available (see Section 16.2.5) and describe a number of research advances that are needed to make this area viable.

16.1 OVERVIEW OF DATA MINING TECHNOLOGY

In reports such as the very popular Gartner Report,[1] data mining has been hailed as one of the top technologies for the near future. In this section we relate data mining to the broader area called knowledge discovery and contrast the two by means of an illustrative example.

Data Mining versus Data Warehousing. The goal of a data warehouse (see Chapter 17) is to support decision making with data. Data mining can be used in conjunction with a data warehouse to help with certain types of decisions. Data mining can be applied to operational databases with individual transactions. To make data mining more efficient, the data warehouse should have an aggregated or summarized collection of data. Data mining helps in extracting meaningful new patterns that cannot be found necessarily by merely querying or processing data or metadata in the data warehouse. Data mining applications should therefore be strongly considered early, during the design of a data warehouse. Also, data mining tools should be designed to facilitate their use in conjunction with data warehouses. In fact, for very large databases running into terabytes of data, successful use of data mining applications will depend first on the construction of a data warehouse.

Data Mining as a Part of the Knowledge Discovery Process. **Knowledge Discovery in Databases,** frequently abbreviated as **KDD,** typically encompasses more than data mining. The knowledge discovery process comprises six phases: [2] data selection, data cleansing, enrichment, data transformation or encoding, data mining, and the reporting and display of the discovered information.

As an example, consider a transaction database maintained by a specialty consumer goods retailer. Suppose the client data includes a customer name, zip code, phone number, date of purchase, item code, price, quantity, and total amount. A variety of new knowledge can be discovered by KDD processing on this client database. During *data selection*, data about specific items or categories of items, or from stores in a specific region or area of the country, may be selected. The *data cleansing* process then may correct invalid zip codes or eliminate records with incorrect phone prefixes. *Enrichment* typically enhances the data with additional sources of information. For example, given the client names and phone numbers, the store may purchase other data about age, income, and credit rating and append them to each record. *Data transformation* and encoding may be done to reduce the amount of data. For instance, item codes may be grouped in terms of product categories into audio, video, supplies, electronic gadgets, camera, accessories, and so on. Zip codes may be aggregated into geographic regions, incomes may be divided into ranges, and so on. In Figure 17.1, we will show a step called *cleaning* as a precursor to the data warehouse creation. If data mining is based on an existing warehouse for this retail store chain, we would expect that the cleaning has already been applied. It is only after such preprocessing that *data mining* techniques are used to mine different rules and patterns.

The result of mining may be to discover the following type of "new" information:

a. Association rules—for example, whenever a customer buys video equipment, he or she also buys another electronic gadget.

b. Sequential patterns—for example, suppose a customer buys a camera, and within three months he or she buys photographic supplies, then within six months he is likely to buy an accessory item. This defines a sequential pattern of transactions. A customer who buys more than twice in the lean periods may be likely to buy at least once during the Christmas period.

---

1. The Gartner Report is one example of the many technology survey publications that corporate managers rely on to make their technology selection decisions.

2. This discussion is largely based on Adriaans and Zantinge (1996).

    c. Classification trees—for example, customers may be classified by frequency of visits, by types of financing used, by amount of purchase, or by affinity for types of items, and some revealing statistics may be generated for such classes.

We can see that many possibilities exist for discovering new knowledge about buying patterns, relating factors such as age, income group, place of residence, to what and how much the customers purchase. This information can then be utilized to plan additional store locations based on demographics, to run store promotions, to combine items in advertisements, or to plan seasonal marketing strategies. As this retail store example shows, data mining must be preceded by significant data preparation before it can yield useful information that can directly influence business decisions.

The results of data mining may be reported in a variety of formats, such as listings, graphic outputs, summary tables, or visualizations.

Goals of Data Mining and Knowledge Discovery.   Data mining is typically carried out with some end goals or applications. Broadly speaking, these goals fall into the following classes: prediction, identification, classification, and optimization.

- **Prediction**—Data mining can show how certain attributes within the data will behave in the future. Examples of predictive data mining include the analysis of buying transactions to predict what consumers will buy under certain discounts, how much sales volume a store would generate in a given period, and whether deleting a product line would yield more profits. In such applications, business logic is used coupled with data mining. In a scientific context, certain seismic wave patterns may predict an earthquake with high probability.

- **Identification**—Data patterns can be used to identify the existence of an item, an event, or an activity. For example, intruders trying to break a system may be identified by the programs executed, files accessed, and CPU time per session. In biological applications, existence of a gene may be identified by certain sequences of nucleotide symbols in the DNA sequence. The area known as *authentication* is a form of identification. It ascertains whether a user is indeed a specific user or one from an authorized class, and involves a comparison of parameters or images or signals against a database.

- **Classification**—Data mining can partition the data so that different classes or categories can be identified based on combinations of parameters. For example, customers in a supermarket can be categorized into discount-seeking shoppers, shoppers in a rush, loyal regular shoppers, shoppers attached to name brands, and infrequent shoppers. This classification may be used in different analyses of customer buying transactions as a post-mining activity. Sometimes classification based on common domain knowledge is used as an input to decompose the mining problem and make it simpler. For instance, health foods, party foods, or school lunch foods are distinct categories in the supermarket business. It makes sense to analyze relationships within and across categories as separate problems. Such categorization may be used to encode the data appropriately before subjecting it to further data mining.

- **Optimization**—One eventual goal of data mining may be to optimize the use of limited resources such as time, space, money, or materials and to maximize output variables such as sales or profits under a given set of constraints. As such, this goal of data mining resembles the objective function used in operations research problems that deals with optimization under constraints.

The term data mining is popularly being used in a very broad sense. In some situations it includes statistical analysis and constrained optimization as well as machine learning. There is no sharp line separating data mining from these disciplines. It is beyond our scope, therefore, to discuss in detail the entire range of applications that make up this vast body of work. For a detailed understanding of the area, readers are referred to specialized books devoted to data mining.

Types of Knowledge Discovered During Data Mining. The term "knowledge" is very broadly interpreted as involving some degree of intelligence. There is a progression from raw data to information to knowledge as we go through additional processing. Knowledge is often classified as inductive versus deductive. **Deductive knowledge** deduces new information based on applying *pre-specified* logical rules of deduction on the given data. Data mining addresses **inductive knowledge**, which discovers new rules and patterns from the supplied data. Knowledge can be represented in many forms: In an unstructured sense, it can be represented by rules or propositional logic. In a structured form, it may be represented in decision trees, semantic networks, neural networks, or hierarchies of classes or frames. It is common to describe the knowledge discovered during data mining in five ways, as follows.

- **Association rules**—These rules correlate the presence of a set of items with another range of values for another set of variables. Examples: (1) When a female retail shopper buys a handbag, she is likely to buy shoes. (2) An X-ray image containing characteristics a and b is likely to also exhibit characteristic c.

- **Classification hierarchies**—The goal is to work from an existing set of events or transactions to create a hierarchy of classes. Examples: (1) A population may be divided into five ranges of credit worthiness based on a history of previous credit transactions. (2) A model may be developed for the factors that determine the desirability of location of a store on a 1–10 scale. (3) Mutual funds may be classified based on performance data using characteristics such as growth, income, and stability.

- **Sequential patterns**—A sequence of actions or events is sought. Example: If a patient underwent cardiac bypass surgery for blocked arteries and an aneurysm and later developed high blood urea within a year of surgery, he or she is likely to suffer from kidney failure within the next 18 months. Detection of sequential patterns is equivalent to detecting associations among events with certain temporal relationships.

- **Patterns within time series**—Similarities can be detected within positions of a **time series** of data, which is a sequence of data taken at regular intervals such as daily sales or daily closing stock prices. Examples: (1) Stocks of a utility company, ABC Power, and a financial company, XYZ Securities, showed the same pattern during 2002 in terms of closing stock price. (2) Two products show the same selling pattern in summer but a different one in winter. (3) A pattern in solar magnetic wind may be used to predict changes in earth atmospheric conditions.

- **Clustering**—A given population of events or items can be partitioned (segmented) into sets of "similar" elements. Examples: (1) An entire population of treatment data on a disease may be divided into groups based on the similarity of side effects produced. (2) The adult population in the United States may be categorized into five groups from "most likely to buy" to "least likely to buy" a new product. (3) The web accesses made by a collection of users against a set of documents (say, in a digital library) may be analyzed in terms of the keywords of documents to reveal clusters or categories of users.

For most applications, the desired knowledge is a combination of the above types. We expand on each of the above knowledge types in the following sections.

16.2 ASSOCIATION RULES

16.2.1 Market-Basket Model, Support, and Confidence

One of the major technologies in data mining involves the discovery of association rules. The database is regarded as a collection of transactions, each involving a set of items. A common example is that of **market-basket data**. Here the market basket corresponds to the sets of items a consumer buys in a supermarket during one visit. Consider four such transactions in a random sample shown in Figure 16.1.

An **association rule** is of the form $X \Rightarrow Y$, where $X = \{x_1, x_2, \ldots, x_n\}$, and $Y = \{y_1, y_2, \ldots, y_m\}$ are sets of items, with x_i and y_j being distinct items for all i and all j. This association states that if a customer buys X, he or she is also likely to buy Y. In general, any association rule has the form LHS (left-hand side) $\Rightarrow$ RHS (right-hand side), where LHS and RHS are sets of items. The set LHS $\cup$ RHS is called an **itemset**, the set of items purchased by customers. For an association rule to be of interest to a data miner, the rule should satisfy some interest measure. Two common interest measures are support and confidence.

Transaction-id	Time	Items-Bought
101	6:35	milk, bread, cookies, juice
792	7:38	milk, juice
1130	8:05	milk, eggs
1735	8:40	bread, cookies, coffee

FIGURE 16.1 Example transactions in market-basket model.

The **support** for a rule LHS $\Rightarrow$ RHS is with respect to the itemset; it refers to how frequently a specific itemset occurs in the database. That is, the support is the percentage of transactions that contain all of the items in the itemset, LHS $\cup$ RHS. If the support is low, it implies that there is no overwhelming evidence that items in LHS $\cup$ RHS occur together, because the itemset occurs in only a small fraction of transactions. Another term for support is *prevalence* of the rule.

The **confidence** is with regard to the implication shown in the rule. The confidence of the rule LHS $\Rightarrow$ RHS is computed as the support(LHS $\cup$ RHS)/support(LHS). We can think of it as the probability that the items in RHS will be purchased given that the items in LHS are purchased by a customer. Another term for confidence is *strength* of the rule.

As an example of support and confidence, consider the following two rules: Milk $\Rightarrow$ Juice and Bread $\Rightarrow$ Juice. Looking at our four sample transactions in Figure 16.1, we see that the support of {Milk, Juice} is 50% and the support of {Bread, Juice} is only 25%. The confidence of Milk $\Rightarrow$ Juice is 66.7% (meaning that, of three transactions in which milk occurs, two contain juice) and the confidence of Bread $\Rightarrow$ Juice is 50% (meaning that one of two transactions containing bread also contains juice). Table 16.1 shows the support and confidence for various association rules.

TABLE 16.1 SUPPORT AND CONFIDENCE FOR SOME ASSOCIATION RULES

LHS $\Rightarrow$ RHS	s	c
bread $\Rightarrow$ cookies	(2/4) 50%	2/2 (100%)
milk $\Rightarrow$ juice	(2/4) 50%	2/3 (66%)
cookies $\Rightarrow$ coffee	(1/4) 25%	1/2 (50%)
milk $\Rightarrow$ eggs	1/4 (25%)	11/3 (33%)

As we can see, support and confidence do not necessarily go hand in hand. The goal of mining association rules, then, is to generate all possible rules that exceed some minimum user-specified support and confidence thresholds. The problem is thus decomposed into two subproblems:

a. Generate all itemsets that have a support that exceeds the threshold. These sets of items are called **large** (or **frequent**) **itemsets.** Note that large here means large support.

b. For each large itemset, all the rules that have a minimum confidence are generated as follows: For a large itemset X and $Y \subset X$, let $Z = X - Y$; then if support(X)/support(Z) > minimum confidence, the rule Z $\Rightarrow$ Y (that is, $X - Y \Rightarrow Y$) is a valid rule.

Generating rules by using all large itemsets and their supports is relatively straightforward. However, discovering all large itemsets together with the value for their support is a major problem if the cardinality of the set of items is very high. A typical supermarket has thousands of items. The number of distinct itemsets is 2^m, where m is the number of items, and counting support for all possible itemsets becomes very computation-intensive. To reduce the combinatorial search space, algorithms for finding association rules utilize the following properties:

- A subset of a large itemset must also be large (that is, each subset of a large itemset exceeds the minimum required support).

- Conversely, a superset of a small itemset is also small (implying that it does not have enough support).

The first property is referred to as **downward closure**. The second property, called the **antimonotonicity** property, helps in reducing the search space of possible solutions. That is, once an itemset is found to be small (not a large itemset), then any extension to that itemset, formed by adding one or more items to the set, will also yield a small itemset.

16.2.2 Apriori Algorithm

The first algorithm to use the downward closure and antimontonicity properties was the **Apriori algorithm,** shown as Algorithm 16.1.

Algorithm 16.1: Apriori algorithm for finding frequent (large) itemsets

Input: database of m transactions, D, and a minimum support, *mins*, represented as a fraction of m

Output: frequent itemsets, $L_1, L_2, ..., L_k$

Begin

compute support(i_j) = count$(i_j)/m$ for each individual item, $i_1, i_2, . . . , i_n$ by scanning the database once and counting the number of transactions that item i_j appears in (that is, count(i_j));

the candidate frequent 1-itemset, C_1, will be the set of items $i_1, i_2, . . . , i_n$.

the subset of items containing i_j from C_1 where support(i_j) >= mins becomes the frequent 1-itemset, L_1;

k = 1;

termination = false;

repeat

    $L_{k+1} = $;

    create the candidate frequent (k+1)-itemset, C_{k+1}, by combining members of L_k that have k-1 items in common; (this forms candidate frequent (k+1)-itemsets by selectively extending frequent k-itemsets by one item)

    in addition, only consider as elements of C_{k+1} those k+1 items such that every subset of size k appears in L_k;

    scan the database once and compute the support for each member of C_{k+1}; if the support for a member of C_{k+1} >= mins then add that member to L_{k+1};

    if L_{k+1} is empty then termination = true

      else k = k + 1;

until termination;

End;

We illustrate Algorithm 16.1 using the transaction data in Figure 16.1 using a minimum support of 0.5. The candidate 1-itemsets are {milk, bread, juice, cookies, eggs, coffee} and their respective supports are 0.75, 0.5, 0.5, 0.5, 0.25 and 0.25. The first four items qualify for L_1 since each support is greater than or equal to 0.5. In the first iteration of the repeat-loop, we extend the frequent 1-itemsets to create the candidate frequent 2-itemsets, C_2. C_2 contains {milk , bread}, {milk, juice}, {bread, juice}, {milk, cookies}, {bread, cookies} and {juice, cookies}. Notice, for example that {milk, eggs} does not appear in C_2 since {eggs} is small (by the antimonotonicity property) and does not appear in L_1. The supports for the six sets contained in C_2 are 0.25, 0.5, 0.25, 0.25, 0.5 and 0.25 and are computed by scanning the set of transactions. Only the second 2-itemset {milk, juice} and the fifth 2-itemset {bread, cookies} have support greater than or equal to 0.5. These two 2-itemsets form the frequent 2-itemsets, L_2.

In the next iteration of the repeat-loop, we construct candidate frequent 3-itemsets by adding additional items to sets in L_2. However, for no extension of itemsets in L_2 will all 2-item subsets be contained in L_2. For example, consider {milk, juice, bread}; the 2-itemset {milk, bread} is not in L_2, hence {milk, juice, bread} cannot be a frequent 3-itemset by the downward closure property. At this point the algorithm terminates with L_1 equal to {{milk}, {bread}, {juice}, {cookies}} and L_2 equal to {{milk, juice}, {bread, cookies}}.

Several other algorithms have been proposed to mine association rules. They vary mainly in terms of how the candidate itemsets are generated, and how the supports for the candidate itemsets are counted. Some algorithms use such data structures as bitmaps and hashtrees to keep information about itemsets. Several algorithms have been proposed that use multiple scans of the database because the potential number of itemsets, 2^m can be too large to set up counters during a single scan. We will examine three improved algorithms (compared to the Apriori algorithm) for association rule mining: a sampling algorithm, the frequent-pattern tree algorithm, and the partition algorithm.

16.2.3 Sampling Algorithm

The main idea for the **Sampling algorithm** is to select a small sample, one that fits in main memory, of the database of transactions and to determine the frequent itemsets from that sample. If those frequent itemsets form a superset of the frequent itemsets for the entire database, then we can determine the real frequent itemsets by scanning the remainder of the database in order to compute the exact support values for the superset itemsets. A superset of the frequent itemsets can usually be found from the sample by using, for example, the Apriori algorithm, with a lowered minimum support.

In some rare cases, some frequent itemsets may be missed and a second scan of the database is needed. To decide whether any frequent itemsets have been missed, the concept of the negative border is used. The negative border with respect to a frequent itemset, S, and set of items, I, is the minimal itemsets contained in PowerSet(I) and not in S. The basic idea is that the negative border of a set of frequent itemsets contains the closest itemsets that could also be frequent. Consider the case where a set X is not contained in the frequent itemsets. If all subsets of X are contained in the set of frequent itemsets, then X would be in the negative border.

We illustrate this with the following example. Consider the set of items I = {A, B, C, D, E} and let the combined frequent itemsets of size 1 to 3 be S = {{A}, {B}, {C}, {D}, {AB}, {AC}, {BC}, {AD}, {CD}, {ABC}}. The negative border is {{E}, {BD}, {ACD}}. The set {E} is the only 1-itemset not contained in S, {BD} is the only 2-itemset not in S but whose 1-itemset subsets are, and {ACD} is the only 3-itemset whose 2-itemset subsets are all in S. The negative border is important since it is necessary to determine the support for those itemsets in the negative border to ensure that no large itemsets are missed from analyzing the sample data.

Support for the negative border is determined when the remainder of the database is scanned. If we find that an itemset, X, in the negative border belongs in the set of all frequent itemsets, then there is a potential for a superset of X to also be frequent. If this happens, then a second pass over the database is needed to make sure that all frequent itemsets are found.

16.2.4 Frequent-Pattern Tree Algorithm

The **Frequent-pattern tree algorithm** is motivated by the fact that Apriori based algorithms may generate and test a very large number of candidate itemsets. For example, with 1000 frequent 1-itemsets, the Apriori algorithm would have to generate $\binom{1000}{2}$ or 499,500 candidate 2-itemsets. The FP-growth algorithm is one approach that eliminates the generation of a large number of candidate itemsets.

The algorithm first produces a compressed version of the database in terms of an FP-tree (frequent pattern tree). The FP-tree stores relevant itemset information and allows or the efficient discovery of frequent itemsets. The actual mining process adopts a divide and conquer strategy where the mining process is decomposed into a set of smaller tasks that each operate on a conditional FP-tree, a subset (projection) of the original tree. To start with, we examine how the FP-tree is constructed. The database is first scanned and the frequent 1-itemsets along with their support are computed. With this algorithm, the support is the *count* of transactions containing the item rather than the fraction of transactions containing the item. The frequent 1-itemsets are then sorted in nonincreasing order of their support. Next, the root of the FP-tree is created with a "null" label. The database is scanned a second time and for each transaction T in the database, the frequent 1-itemsets in T are placed in order as was done with the frequent 1-itemsets. We can designate this sorted list for T as consisting of a first item, the head, and the remaining items, the tail. The itemset information (head, tail) is inserted into the FP-tree recursively, starting at the root node, as follows:

1. if the current node, N, of the FP-tree has a child with an item name = head, then increment the count associated with node N by 1 else create a new node, N, with a count of 1, link N to it's parent and link N with the item header table (used for efficient tree traversal).

2. if tail is nonempty, then repeat step (1) using as the sorted list only the tail, i.e., the old head is removed and the new head is the first item from the tail and the remaining items become the new tail.

The item header table, created during the process of building the FP-tree, contains three fields per entry for each frequent item, which are item identifier, support count, and node link. The item identifier and support count are self-explanatory. The node link is a pointer to an occurrence of that item in the FP-tree. Since multiple occurrences of a single item may appear in the FP-tree, these items are linked together as a list where the start of the list is pointed to by the node link in the item header table. We illustrate the building of the FP-tree using the transaction data in Figure 16.1. Let us use a minimum support of 2. One pass over the four transactions yields the following frequent 1-itemsets with associated support: {{(milk,3)}, {(bread,2)}, {(cookies,2)}, {(juice,2)}}. The database is scanned a second time and each transaction will be processed again.

For the first transaction, we create the sorted list, T = {milk, bread, cookies, juice}. The items in T are the frequent 1-itemsets from the first transaction. The items are ordered based on the nonincreasing ordering of the count of the 1-itemsets found in pass 1, (i.e., milk first, bread second, etc.). We create a null root node for the FP-tree and insert "milk" as a child of the root, "bread" as a child of "milk", "cookies" as a child of "bread" and "juice" as a child of "cookies". We adjust the entries for the frequent items in the item header table.

For the second transaction, we have the sorted list {milk, juice}. Starting at the root, we see that a child node with label "milk" exists, so we move to that node and update its count (to account for the second transaction that contains milk). We see that there is no child of the current node with label "juice," so we create a new node with label "juice." The item header table is adjusted.

The third transaction only has 1-frequent item, {milk}. Again, starting at the root, we see that the node with label "milk" exists, so we move to that node, increment its count, and adjust the item header table. The final transaction contains frequent items, {bread, cookies}. At the root node, we see that there does not exist a child with label "bread." Thus, we create a new child of the root, initialize its counter, and then insert "cookies" as a child of this node and initialize its count. After the item header table is updated, we end up with the FP-tree and item header table as shown in Figure 16.2. If we examine this FP-tree, we see that it indeed represents the original transactions in a compressed format (that is, only showing the items from each transaction that are large 1-itemsets).

Algorithm 16.2: FP-growth Algorithm for finding frequent itemsets

Input: Fp-tree and a minimum support, mins
Output: frequent patterns (itemsets)
procedure FP-growth (tree, alpha);
Begin
if tree contains a single path P then
for each combination, beta, of the nodes in the path
    generate pattern (beta ∪ alpha)
    with support = minimum support of nodes in beta
else
for each item, i, in the header of the tree do
  begin
    generate pattern beta = (i ∪ alpha) with support = i.support;
    construct beta's conditional pattern base;
    construct beta's conditional FP-tree, beta_tree;
    if beta_tree is not empty then
      FP-growth(beta_tree, beta);
  end;
  End;

FIGURE 16.2 FP-tree and item header table.

Algorithm 16.2 is used for mining the FP-tree for frequent patterns. With the FP-tree, it is possible to find all frequent patterns that contain a given frequent item by starting from the item header table for that item and traversing the node links in the FP-tree. The algorithm starts with a frequent 1-itemset (suffix pattern), constructs its conditional pattern base and then its conditional FP-tree. The conditional pattern base is made up of a set of prefix paths, i.e., where the frequent item is a suffix. For example, if we consider the item juice, we see from Figure 16.2. that there are two paths in the FP-tree that end with juice: (milk, bread, cookies, juice) and (milk, juice). The two associated prefix paths are (milk, bread, cookies) and (milk). The conditional FP-tree is constructed from the patterns in the conditional pattern base. The mining is recursively performed on this FP-tree. The frequent patterns are formed by concatenating the suffix pattern with the frequent patterns produced from a conditional FP-tree.

We illustrate the algorithm using the data in Figure 16.1 and the tree in Figure 16.2. The procedure FP-growth is called with the two parameters: the original FP-tree and null for the variable alpha. Since the original FP-tree has more than a single path, we execute the else part of the first if statement. We start with the frequent item, juice. We will examine the frequent items in order of lowest support (that is, from the last entry in the table to the first). The variable beta is set to juice with support equal to 2.

Following the node link in the item header table, we construct the conditional pattern base consisting of two paths (with juice as suffix). These are (milk, bread, cookies: 1) and (milk: 1). The conditional FP-tree consists of only a single node, milk:2. This is due to a support of only 1 for node bread and cookies, which is below the minimal support of 2. The algorithm is called recursively with an FP-tree of only a single node (i.e., milk:2) and a beta value of juice. Since this FP-tree only has one path, all combinations of beta and nodes in the path are generated, (that is, {milk, juice}) with support of 2.

Next, the frequent item, cookies, is used. The variable beta is set to cookies with support = 2. Following the node link in the item header table, we construct the conditional pattern base consisting of two paths. These are (milk, bread: 1) and (bread: 1). The conditional FP-tree is only a single node, bread:2. The algorithm is called recursively with an FP-tree of only a single node (that is, bread:2) and a beta value of cookies. Since this FP-tree only has one path, all combinations of beta and nodes in the path are generated, that is, {bread, cookies} with support of 2. The frequent item, bread, is considered next. The variable beta is set to bread with support = 2. Following the node link in the item header table, we construct the conditional pattern base consisting of one path, which is (milk: 1). The conditional FP-tree is empty since the count is less than the minimum support. Since the conditional FP-tree is empty, no frequent patterns will be generated.

The last frequent item to consider is milk. This is the top item in the item header table and as such has an empty conditional pattern base and empty conditional FP-tree. As a result, no frequent patterns are added. The result of executing the algorithm is the following frequent patterns (or itemsets) with their support: { {milk:3}, {bread:2}, {cookies:2}, {juice:2}, {milk,juice:2}, {bread,cookies:2} }.

16.2.5 Partition Algorithm

Another algorithm, called the **Partition algorithm**,[3] is summarized below. If we are given a database with a small number of potential large itemsets, say, a few thousand, then the support for all of them can be tested in one scan by using a partitioning technique. Partitioning divides the database into nonoverlapping subsets; these are individually considered as separate databases and all large itemsets for that partition, called *local frequent itemsets*, are generated in one pass. The Apriori algorithm can then be used efficiently on each partition if it fits entirely in main memory. Partitions are chosen in such a way that each partition can be accommodated in main memory. As such, a partition is read only once in each pass. The only caveat with

---

3. See Savasere et al. (1995) for details of the algorithm, the data structures used to implement it, and its performance comparisons.

the partition method is that the minimum support used for each partition has a slightly different meaning from the original value. The minimum support is based on the size of the partition rather than the size of the database for determining local frequent (large) itemsets. The actual support threshold value is the same as given earlier, but the support is computed only for a partition.

At the end of pass one, we take the union of all frequent itemsets from each partition. These form the global candidate frequent itemsets for the entire database. When these lists are merged, they may contain some false positives. That is, some of the itemsets that are frequent (large) in one partition may not qualify in several other partitions and hence may not exceed the minimum support when the original database is considered. Note that there are no false negatives; no large itemsets will be missed. The global candidate large itemsets identified in pass one are verified in pass two; that is, their actual support is measured for the *entire* database. At the end of phase two, all global large itemsets are identified. The Partition algorithm lends itself naturally to a parallel or distributed implementation for better efficiency. Further improvements to this algorithm have been suggested.[4]

16.2.6 Other Types of Association Rules

Association Rules among Hierarchies. There are certain types of associations that are particularly interesting for a special reason. These associations occur among hierarchies of items. Typically, it is possible to divide items among disjoint hierarchies based on the nature of the domain. For example, foods in a supermarket, items in a department store, or articles in a sports shop can be categorized into classes and subclasses that give rise to hierarchies. Consider Figure 16.3, which shows the taxonomy of items in a supermarket. The figure shows two hierarchies—beverages and desserts, respectively. The entire groups may not produce associations of the form beverages ⇒ desserts, or desserts ⇒ beverages. However, associations of the type Healthy-brand frozen yoghurt ⇒ bottled water, or Richcream-brand ice cream ⇒ wine cooler may produce enough confidence and support to be valid association rules of interest.

FIGURE 16.3 Taxonomy of items in a supermarket.

---

4. See Cheung et al. (1996) and Lin and Dunham (1998).

Therefore, if the application area has a natural classification of the itemsets into hierarchies, discovering associations *within* the hierarchies is of no particular interest. The ones of specific interest are associations *across* hierarchies. They may occur among item groupings at different levels.

Multidimensional Associations.   Discovering association rules involves searching for patterns in a file. At the beginning of the data mining section, we have an example of a file of customer transactions with three dimensions, Transaction-Id, Time and Items-Bought. However, our data mining tasks and algorithms introduced up to this point only involve one dimension: the items-bought. The following rule is an example, where we include the label of the single dimension: Items-Bought(milk) ⇒ Items-Bought(juice). It may be of interest to find association rules that involve multiple dimensions, e.g., Time(6:30...8:00) ⇒ Items-Bought(milk). Rules like these are called multidimensional association rules. The dimensions represent attributes of records of a file or, in terms of relations, columns of rows of a relation, and can be categorical or quantitative. Categorical attributes have a finite set of values that display no ordering relationship. Quantitative attributes are numeric and whose values display an ordering relationship, e.g., $<$. Items-Bought is an example of a categorical attribute and Transaction-Id and Time are quantitative.

One approach to handling a quantitative attribute is to partition its values into nonoverlapping intervals that are assigned labels. This can be done in a static manner based on domain specific knowledge. For example, a concept hierarchy may group values for salary into three distinct classes: low income (0 < salary < 29,999), middle income (30,000 < salary < 74,999) and high income (salary > 75,000). From here, the typical Apriori type algorithm or one of its variants can be used for the rule mining since the quantitative attributes now look like categorical attributes. Another approach to partitioning is to group attribute values together based on data distribution, for example, equi-depth partitioning, and to assign integer values to each partition. The partitioning at this stage may be relatively fine, that is, a larger number of intervals. Then during the mining process, these partitions may combine with other adjacent partitions if their support is less than some predefined maximum value. An Apriori-type algorithm can be used here as well for the data mining.

Negative Associations.   The problem of discovering a negative association is harder than that of discovering a positive association. A negative association is of the following type: "60% of customers who buy potato chips do not buy bottled water." (Here, the 60% refers to the confidence for the negative association rule.) In a database with 10,000 items, there are 2^{10000} possible combinations of items, a majority of which do not appear even once in the database. If the absence of a certain item combination is taken to mean a negative association, then we potentially have millions and millions of negative association rules with RHSs that are of no interest at all. The problem, then, is to find only *interesting* negative rules. In general, we are interested in cases in which two specific sets of items appear very rarely in the same transaction. This poses two problems.

1. For a total item inventory of 10,000 items, the probability of any two being bought together is (1/10,000) * (1/10,000) = 10^{-8}. If we find the actual support for these two occurring together to be zero, that does not represent a significant departure from expectation and hence is not an interesting (negative) association.

2. The other problem is more serious. We are looking for item combinations with very low support, and there are millions and millions with low or even zero support. For example, a data set of 10 million transactions has most of the 2.5 billion pairwise combinations of 10,000 items missing. This would generate billions of useless rules.

Therefore, to make negative association rules interesting, we must use prior knowledge about the itemsets. One approach is to use hierarchies. Suppose we use the hierarchies of soft drinks and chips shown in Figure 16.4.

A strong positive association has been shown between soft drinks and chips. If we find a large support for the fact that when customers buy Days chips they predominantly buy Topsy and *not* Joke and *not* Wakeup, that would be interesting. This is so because we would normally expect that if there is a strong association between Days and Topsy, there should also be such a strong association between Days and Joke or Days and Wakeup.[5]

In the frozen yoghurt and bottled water groupings in Figure 16.3, suppose the Reduce versus Healthy-brand division is 80–20 and the Plain and Clear brands division is 60–40 among respective categories. This would give a joint probability of Reduce frozen yoghurt being purchased with Plain bottled water as 48% among the transactions containing a frozen yoghurt and a bottled water. If this support, however, is found to be only 20%, that would indicate a significant negative association among Reduce yoghurt and Plain bottled water; again, that would be interesting.

FIGURE 16.4 Simple hierarchy of soft drinks and chips.

The problem of finding negative association is important in the above situations given the domain knowledge in the form of item generalization hierarchies (that is, the beverage given and desserts hierarchies shown in Figure 16.3), the existing positive associations (such as between the frozen yoghurt and bottled water groups), and the distribution of items (such as the name brands within related groups). Work has been reported by the database group at Georgia Tech in this context (see bibliographic notes). The scope of discovery of negative associations is limited in terms of knowing the item hierarchies and distributions. Exponential growth of negative associations remains a challenge.

16.2.7 Additional Considerations for Association Rules

Mining association rules in real-life databases is complicated by the following factors.

- The cardinality of itemsets in most situations is extremely large, and the volume of transactions is very high as well. Some operational databases in retailing and communication industries collect tens of millions of transactions per day.

- Transactions show variability in such factors as geographic location and seasons, making sampling difficult.

- Item classifications exist along multiple dimensions. Hence, driving the discovery process with domain knowledge, particularly for negative rules, is extremely difficult.

- Quality of data is variable; significant problems exist with missing, erroneous, con-flicting, as well as redundant data in many industries.

---

5. For simplicity we are assuming a uniform distribution of transactions among members of a hierarchy.

16.3   CLASSIFICATION

Classification is the process of learning a model that describes different classes of data. The classes are predetermined. For example, in a banking application, customers who apply for a credit card may be classified as a "poor risk," a "fair risk," or a "good risk." Hence this type of activity is also called **supervised learning.** Once the model is built, then it can be used to classify new data. The first step, of learning the model, is accomplished by using a training set of data that has already been classified. Each record in the training data contains an attribute, called the class label, that indicates which class the record belongs to. The model that is produced is usually in the form of a decision tree or a set of rules. Some of the important issues with regard to the model and the algorithm that produces the model include the model's ability to predict the correct class of new data, the computational cost associated with the algorithm, and the scalability of the algorithm.

We will examine the approach where our model is in the form of a decision tree. A decision tree is simply a graphical representation of the description of each class or in other words, a representation of the classification rules. An example decision tree is pictured in Figure 16.5. We see from Figure 16.5 that if a customer is "married" and their salary $>= 50K$, then they are a good risk for a credit card from the bank. This is one of the rules that describe the class "good risk." Other rules for this class and the two other classes are formed by traversing the decision tree from the root to each leaf node. Algorithm 16.3 shows the procedure for constructing a decision tree from a training data set. Initially, all training samples are at the root of the tree. The samples are partitioned recursively based on selected attributes. The attribute used at a node to partition the samples is the one with the best splitting criterion, for example, the one that maximizes the information gain measure.

Algorithm 16.3: Algorithm for decision tree induction

Input: set of training data Records: $R_1, R_2, \ldots, R_m$ and set of Attributes: $A_1, A_2, \ldots, A_n$
Output: decision tree

procedure Build_tree (Records, Attributes);
Begin
create a node N;

if all Records belong to the same class, C then
Return N as a leaf node with class label C;

if Attributes is empty then
Return N as a leaf node with class label C, such that the majority of Records belong to it;

select attribute A_i *(with the highest information gain)* from Attributes;

label node N with A_i;
for each known value, V_j, of A_i do
    begin
        add a branch from node N for the condition $A_i = V_j$;
        S_j = subset of Records where $A_i = V_j$;
        if S_j is empty then
        add a leaf, L, with class label C, such that the majority of
           Records belong to it and Return L
        else add the node returned by Build_tree $(S_j, \text{Attributes} - A_i)$;
    end;
End;

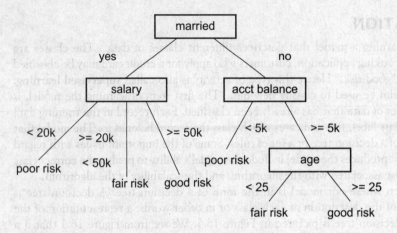

FIGURE 16.5 Example decision tree for credit card applications.

Before we illustrate Algorithm 16.3, we will explain in more detail the **information gain** measure. The use of **entropy** as the information gain measure is motivated by the goal of minimizing the information needed to classify the sample data in the resulting partitions and thus minimizing the expected number of conditional tests needed to classify a new record. The expected information needed to classify training data of s samples, where the Class attribute has n values $(v_1,...,v_n)$ and s_i is the number of samples belonging to Class label v_i, is given by

$$I(S_1, S_2,...,S_n) = -\sum_{i=1}^{n} p_i \log_2 p_i$$

where p_i is the probability that a random sample belongs to class with label v_i. An estimate for p_i is s_i/s. Consider an attribute A with values $\{v_1,...,v_m\}$ used as the test attribute for splitting in the decision tree. Attribute A partitions the samples into the subsets S_1, ..., S_m where samples in each S_i have a value of v_i for attribute A. Each S_i may contain samples that belong to any of the classes. The number of samples in S_i that belong to class j can be denoted as s_{ji}. The entropy associated with using attribute A as the test attribute is defined as

$$E(A) = \sum_{j=1}^{n} \frac{S_{j1} + ... + S_{jn}}{S} \bullet I(S_{j1}, S_{j2},...,S_{jn})$$

$I(s_{j1},...,s_{jn})$ can be defined using the formulation for $I(s_1,...s_n)$ with p_i being replaced by p_{ji} where $p_{ji} = s_{ji}/s$. Now the information gain by partitioning on attribute A, Gain(A), is defined as $I(s_1,...,s_n)$ - E(A). We can use the sample training data from Figure 16.6 to illustrate Algorithm.

The attribute RID represents the record identifier used for identifying an individual record and is an internal attribute. We use it to identify a particular record in our example. First, we compute the expected information needed to classify the training data of 6 records as $I(s_1,s_2)$ where the first class label value corresponds to "yes" and the second to "no". So,

$$I(3,3) = -0.5\log_2 0.5 - 0.5\log_2 0.5 = 1.$$

Now, we compute the entropy for each of the 4 attributes as shown below. For Married = yes, we have $s_{11} = 2$, $s_{21} = 1$ and $I(s_{11},s_{12}) = 0.92$. For Married = no, we have $s_{12} = 1$, $s_{22} = 2$ and $I(s_{12}, s_{22}) = 0.92$. So, the expected information needed to classify a sample using attribute married as the partitioning attribute is

$$E(Married) \bullet = 3/6\ I(s_{11},s_{21}) + 3/6\ I(s_{12},s_{22}) = 0.92.$$

RID	Married	Salary	Acct Balance	Age	Loanworthy
1	no	>=50k	<5k	>=25	yes
2	yes	>=50k	>=5k	>=25	yes
3	yes	20k...50k	<5k	<25	no
4	no	<20k	>=5k	<25	no
5	no	<20k	<5k	>=25	no
6	yes	20k...50k	>=5k	>=25	yes

FIGURE 16.6 Sample training data for classification algorithm.

The gain in information, Gain(Married), would be $1 - 0.92 = 0.08$. If we follow similar steps for computing the gain with respect to the other three attributes we end up with

$$E(Salary) = 0.33 \quad \text{and} \quad Gain(Salary) = 0.67$$
$$E(Acct\ Balance) = 0.82 \quad \text{and} \quad Gain(Acct\ Balance) = 0.18$$
$$E(Age) = 0.81 \quad \text{and} \quad Gain(Age) = 0.19$$

Since the greatest gain occurs for attribute Salary, it is chosen as the partitioning attribute. The root of the tree is created with label Salary and has three branches, one for each value of Salary. For two of the three values, i.e., <20k and >=50k, all the samples that are partitioned accordingly (records with RIDs 4 and 5 for <20k and records with RIDs 1 and 2 for >=50k) fall within the same class "loanworthy no" and "loanworthy yes," respectively for those two values. So we create a leaf node for each. The only branch that needs to be expanded is for the value 20k...50k with two samples, records with RIDs 3 and 6 in the training data. Continuing the process using these two records, we find that Gain(Married) is 0, Gain(Acct Balance) is 1 and Gain(Age) is 1.

We can choose either Age or Acct Balance since they both have the largest gain. Let us choose Age as the partitioning attribute. We add a node with label Age that has two branches, less than 25, and greater or equal to 25. Each branch partitions the remaining sample data such that one sample record belongs to each branch and hence one class. Two leaf nodes are created and we are finished. The final decision tree is pictured in Figure 16.7.

16.4   CLUSTERING

The previous data mining task of classification deals with partitioning data based on using a pre-classified training sample. However, it is often useful to partition data without having a training sample; this is also known as **unsupervised learning**. For example, in business, it may be important to determine groups of customers who have similar buying patterns, or in medicine, it may be important to determine groups of patients who show similar reactions to prescribed drugs. The goal of clustering is to place records into groups, such that records in a group are similar to each other and dissimilar to records in other groups. The groups are usually *disjoint*.

An important facet of clustering is the similarity function that is used. When the data is numeric, a similarity function based on distance is typically used. For example, the Euclidean distance can be used to measure similarity. Consider two n-dimensional data points (records) r_j and r_k. We can consider the value for the ith dimension as r_{ji} and r_{ki} for the two records. The Euclidean distance between points r_j and r_k in n-dimensional space is calculated as:

$$\text{Distance}\left(r_j, r_k\right) = \sqrt{\left|r_{j1} - r_{k1}\right|^2 + \left|r_{j2} - r_{k2}\right|^2 + \cdots + \left|r_{jn} - r_{kn}\right|^2}t$$

The smaller the distance between two points, the greater is the similarity as we think of them. A classic clustering algorithm is the k-Means algorithm, Algorithm 16.4.

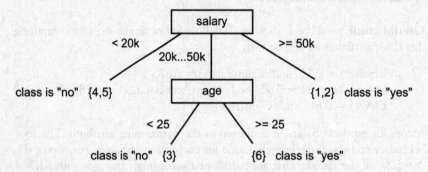

FIGURE 16.7 Decision tree based on sample training data where the leaf nodes are represented by a set of RIDs of the partitioned records.

Algorithm 16.4: K-means clustering algorithm

Input: a database D, of m records, $r_1, \ldots, r_m$ and a desired number of clusters k
Output: set of k clusters that minimizes the squared error criterion

Begin
randomly choose k records as the centroids for the k clusters;

repeat

assign each record, r_i, to a cluster such that the distance between r_i
    and the cluster centroid (mean) is the smallest among the k clusters;

recalculate the centroid (mean) for each cluster based on the records assigned to the cluster;

until no change;

End;

The algorithm begins by randomly choosing k records to represent the centroids (means), $m_1, \ldots, m_k$, of the clusters, $C_1, \ldots, C_k$. All the records are placed in a given cluster based on the distance between the record and the cluster mean. If the distance between m_i and record r_j is the smallest among all cluster means, then record r_j is placed in cluster C_i. Once all records have been initially placed in a cluster, the mean for each cluster is recomputed. Then the process repeats, by examining each record again and placing it in the cluster whose mean is closest. Several iterations may be needed, but the algorithm will converge, although it may terminate at a local optimum. The terminating condition is usually the squared-error criterion. For clusters $C_1, \ldots, C_k$ with means $m_1, \ldots, m_k$, the error is defined as:

$$\text{Error} = \sum_{i=1}^{k} \sum_{\forall r_j \in C_i} \text{Distance}(r_j, m_i)^2$$

We will examine how Algorithm 16.4 works with the (2-dimensional) records in Figure 16.8. Assume that the number of desired clusters k is 2. Let the algorithm choose records with RID 3 for cluster C_1 and RID 6 for cluster C_2 as the initial cluster centroids. The remaining records will be assigned to one of those clusters during the first iteration of the repeat loop. The record with RID 1 has a distance from C_1 of 22.4 and a distance from C_2 of 32.0, so it joins cluster C_1. The record with RID 2 has a distance from C_1 of 10.0 and a distance from C_2 of 5.0, so it joins cluster C_2. The record with RID 4 has a distance from C_1 of 25.5 and a distance from C_2 of 36.6, so it joins cluster C_1. The record with RID 5 has a distance from C_1 of 20.6 and a distance from C_2 of 29.2, so it joins cluster C_1. Now, the new means (centroids) for the two clusters are computed. The mean for a cluster, C_i, with n records of m dimensions is the vector:

$$\bar{C}_i = \left(\frac{1}{n} \sum_{\forall r_j \in C_i} r_{ji}, \ldots, \frac{1}{n} \sum_{\forall r_j \in C_i} r_{jm} \right)$$

The new mean for C_1 is (33.75, 8.75) and the new mean for C_2 is (52.5, 25). A second iteration proceeds and the six records are placed into the two clusters as follows: records with RIDs 1, 4, 5 are placed in C_1 and records with RIDs 2, 3, 6 are placed in C_2. The mean for C_1 and C_2 is recomputed as (28.3, 6.7) and (51.7, 21.7), respectively. In the next iteration, all records stay in their previous clusters and the algorithm terminates.

RID	Age	Years of Service
1	30	5
2	50	25
3	50	15
4	25	5
5	30	10
6	55	25

FIGURE 16.8 Sample 2-dimensional records for clustering example (the RID column is not considered).

Traditionally, clustering algorithms assume that the entire data set fits in main memory. More recently, researchers have been developing algorithms that are efficient and are scalable for very large databases. One such algorithm is called BIRCH. BIRCH is a hybrid approach that uses both a hierarchical clustering approach, which builds a tree representation of the data, as well as additional clustering methods, which are applied to the leaf nodes of the tree. Two input parameters are used by the BIRCH algorithm. One specifies the amount of available main memory and the other is an initial threshold for the radius of any cluster. Main memory is used to store descriptive cluster information such as the center (mean) of a cluster and the radius of the cluster (clusters are assumed to be spherical in shape). The radius threshold affects the number of clusters that are produced. For example, if the radius threshold value is large, then few clusters of many records will be formed. The algorithm tries to maintain the number of clusters such that their radius is below the radius threshold. If available memory is insufficient, then the radius threshold is increased.

The BIRCH algorithm reads the data records sequentially and inserts them into an in-memory tree structure, which tries to preserve the clustering structure of the data. The records are inserted into the appropriate leaf nodes (potential clusters) based on the distance between the record and the cluster center. The leaf node where the insertion happens may have to split, depending upon the updated center and radius of the cluster and the radius threshold parameter. In addition, when splitting, extra cluster information is stored and if memory becomes insufficient, then the radius threshold will be increased. Increasing the radius threshold may actually produce a side effect of reducing the number of clusters since some nodes may be merged.

Overall, BIRCH is an efficient clustering method with a linear computational complexity in terms of the number of records to be clustered.

16.5 APPROACHES TO OTHER DATA MINING PROBLEMS

16.5.1 Discovery of Sequential Patterns

The discovery of sequential patterns is based on the concept of a sequence of itemsets. We assume that transactions such as the supermarket-basket transactions we discussed previously are ordered by time of purchase. That ordering yields a sequence of itemsets. For example, {milk, bread, juice}, {bread, eggs}, {cookies, milk, coffee} may be such a **sequence of itemsets** based on three visits of the same customer to the store. The **support** for a sequence S of itemsets is the percentage of the given set U of sequences of which S is a subsequence. In this example, {milk, bread, juice} {bread, eggs} and {bread, eggs} {cookies, milk, coffee} are considered **subsequences.** The problem of identifying sequential patterns, then, is to find all subsequences from the given sets of sequences that have a user-defined minimum support. The sequence S_1, $S_2, S_3, \ldots$ is a **predictor** of the fact that a customer who buys itemset S_1 is likely to buy itemset S_2 and then S_3, and so on. This prediction is based on the frequency (support) of this sequence in the past. Various algorithms have been investigated for sequence detection.

16.5.2 Discovery of Patterns in Time Series

Time series are sequences of events; each event may be a given fixed type of a transaction. For example, the closing price of a stock or a fund is an event that occurs every weekday for each stock and fund. The sequence of these values per stock or fund constitutes a time series. For a time series, one may look for a variety of patterns by analyzing sequences and subsequences as we did above. For example, we might find the period during which the stock rose or held steady for n days, or we might find the longest period over which the stock had a fluctuation of no more than 1% over previous closing price, or we might find the quarter during which the stock had the most percentage gain or percentage loss. Time series may be compared by establishing measures of similarity to identify companies whose stocks behave in a similar fashion. Analysis and mining of time series is an extended functionality of temporal data management (see Chapter 13).

16.5.3 Regression

Regression is a special application of the classification rule. If a classification rule is regarded as a function over the variables that maps these variables into a target class variable, the rule is called a **regression rule.** A general application of regression occurs when, instead of mapping a tuple of data from a relation to a specific class, the value of a variable is predicted based on that tuple. For example, consider a relation

LAB_TESTS (patient ID, test 1, test 2, . . . , test n)

which contains values that are results from a series of n tests for one patient. The target variable that we wish to predict is P, the probability of survival of the patient. Then the rule for regression takes the form:

(test 1 in range$_1$) and (test 2 in range$_2$) and . . . (test n in range$_n$) $\Rightarrow P = x$, or $x < P \le y$

The choice depends on whether we can predict a unique value of P or a range of values for P. If we regard P as a function:

$P = f$ (test 1, test 2, . . . , test n)

the function is called a **regression function** to predict P. In general, if the function appears as

$Y = f(x_1, x_2, . . . , X_n)$,

and f is linear in the domain variables x_i, the process of deriving f from a given set of tuples for $< x_1, x_2, . . . , x_n, y >$ is called **linear regression.** Linear regression is a commonly used statistical technique for fitting a set of observations or points in n dimensions with the target variable y.

Regression analysis is a very common tool for analysis of data in many research domains. The discovery of the function to predict the target variable is equivalent to a data mining operation.

16.5.4   Neural Networks

Neural network is a technique derived from artificial intelligence research that uses generalized regression and provides an iterative method to carry it out. Neural networks use the curve-fitting approach to infer a function from a set of samples. This technique provides a "learning approach"; it is driven by a test sample that is used for the initial inference and learning. With this kind of learning method, responses to new inputs may be able to be interpolated from the known samples. This interpolation however, depends on the world model (internal representation of the problem domain) developed by the learning method.

Neural networks can be broadly classified into two categories: supervised and unsupervised networks. Adaptive methods that attempt to reduce the output error are **supervised learning** methods, whereas those that develop internal representations without sample outputs are called **unsupervised learning** methods.

Neural networks self-adapt; that is, they learn from information on a specific problem. They perform well on classification tasks and are therefore useful in data mining. Yet, they are not without problems. Although they learn, they do not provide a good representation of *what* they have learned. Their outputs are highly quantitative and not easy to understand. As another limitation, the internal representations developed by neural networks are not unique. Also, in general, neural networks have trouble modeling time series data. Despite these shortcomings, they are popular and frequently used by several commercial vendors.

16.5.5   Genetic Algorithms

Genetic algorithms (GAs) are a class of randomized search procedures capable of adaptive and robust search over a wide range of search space topologies. Modeled after the adaptive emergence of biological species from evolutionary mechanisms, and introduced by Holland,[6] GAs have been successfully applied in such diverse fields such as image analysis, scheduling, and engineering design.

---

6. Holland's seminal work (1975) entitled "Adaptation in Natural and Artificial Systems" introduced the idea of genetic algorithms.

Genetic algorithms extend the idea from human genetics of the four-letter alphabet (based on the A, C, T, G nucleotides) of the human DNA code. The construction of a genetic algorithm involves devising an alphabet that encodes the solutions to the decision problem in terms of strings of that alphabet. Strings are equivalent to individuals. A fitness function defines which solutions can survive and which cannot. The ways in which solutions can be combined are patterned after the cross-over operation of cutting and combining strings from a father and a mother. An initial population of well-varied population is provided, and a game of evolution is played in which mutations occur among strings. They combine to produce a new generation of individuals; the fittest individuals survive and mutate until a family of successful solutions develops.

The solutions produced by genetic algorithms (GAs) are distinguished from most other search techniques by the following characteristics:

- A GA search uses a set of solutions during each generation rather than a single solution.

- The search in the string-space represents a much larger parallel search in the space of encoded solutions.

- The memory of the search done is represented solely by the set of solutions available for a generation.

- A genetic algorithm is a randomized algorithm since search mechanisms use probabilistic operators.

- While progressing from one generation to the next, a GA finds near-optimal balance between knowledge acquisition and exploitation by manipulating encoded solutions.

Genetic algorithms are used for problem solving and clustering problems. Their ability to solve problems in parallel provides a powerful tool for data mining. The drawbacks of GAs include the large overproduction of individual solutions, the random character of the searching process, and the high demand on computer processing. In general, substantial computing power is required to achieve anything of significance with genetic algorithms.

16.6 APPLICATIONS OF DATA MINING

Data mining technologies can be applied to a large variety of decision-making contexts in business. In particular, areas of significant payoffs are expected to include the following:

- Marketing—Applications include analysis of consumer behavior based on buying patterns; determination of marketing strategies including advertising, store location, and targeted mailing; segmentation of customers, stores, or products; and design of catalogs, store layouts, and advertising campaigns.

- Finance—Applications include analysis of creditworthiness of clients, segmentation of account receivables, performance analysis of finance investments like stocks, bonds, and mutual funds; evaluation of financing options; and fraud detection.

- Manufacturing—Applications involve optimization of resources like machines, manpower, and materials; optimal design of manufacturing processes, shop-floor layouts, and product design, such as for automobiles based on customer requirements.

- Health Care—Applications include discovering patterns in radiological images, analysis of microarray (gene-chip) experimental data to relate to diseases, analyzing side effects of drugs, and effectiveness of certain treatments; optimization of processes within a hospital, relating patient wellness data with doctor qualifications.

16.7   COMMERCIAL DATA MINING TOOLS

At the present time, commercial data mining tools use several common techniques to extract knowledge. These include association rules, clustering, neural networks, sequencing, and statistical analysis. We have discussed these earlier. Also used are decision trees, which are a representation of the rules used in classification or clustering, and statistical analyses, which may include regression and many other techniques. Other commercial products use advanced techniques such as genetic algorithms, case-based reasoning, Bayesian networks, nonlinear regression, combinatorial optimization, pattern matching, and fuzzy logic. In this chapter we have already discussed some of these.

Most data mining tools use the ODBC (Open Database Connectivity) interface. ODBC is an industry standard that works with databases; it enables access to data in most of the popular database programs such as Access, dBASE, Informix, Oracle, and SQL Server. Some of these software packages provide interfaces to specific database programs; the most common are Oracle, Access, and SQL Server. Most of the tools work in the Microsoft Windows environment and a few work in the UNIX operating system. The trend is for all products to operate under the Microsoft Windows environment. One tool, Data Surveyor, mentions ODMG compliance.

In general, these programs perform sequential processing in a single machine. Many of these products work in the client-server mode. Some products incorporate parallel processing in parallel computer architectures and work as a part of online analytical processing (OLAP) tools.

User Interface.   Most of the tools run in a graphical user interface (GUI) environment. Some products include sophisticated visualization techniques to view data and rules (e.g., MineSet of SGI), and are even able to manipulate data this way interactively. Text interfaces are rare and are more common in tools available for UNIX, such as IBM's Intelligent Miner.

Application Programming Interface.   Usually, the application programming interface (API) is an optional tool. Most products do not permit using their internal functions. However, some of them allow the application programmer to reuse their code. The most common interfaces are C libraries and Dynamic Link Libraries (DLLs). Some tools include proprietary database command languages.

In Table 16.2 we list 11 representative data mining tools. To date there are almost a hundred commercial data mining products available worldwide. Non-U.S. products include Data Surveyor from the Netherlands and Polyanalyst from Russia.

Future Directions.   Data mining tools are continually evolving, building on ideas from the latest scientific research. Many of these tools incorporate the latest algorithms taken from artificial intelligence (AI), statistics, and optimization.

At present, fast processing is done using modern database techniques—such as distributed processing—in client-server architectures, in parallel databases, and in data warehousing. For the future, the trend is toward developing Internet capabilities more fully. In addition, hybrid approaches will become commonplace, and processing will be done using all resources available. Processing will take advantage of both parallel and distributed computing environments. This shift is especially important because modern databases contain very large amounts of information. Not only are multimedia databases growing, but image storage and retrieval are both slow operations. Also, the cost of secondary storage is decreasing, so massive information storage will be feasible, even for small companies. Thus, data mining programs will have to deal with larger sets of data of more companies.

TABLE 16.2 SOME REPRESENTATIVE DATA MINING TOOLS

COMPANY	PRODUCT	TECHNIQUE	PLATFORM	INTERFACE*
Acknosoft	Kate	Decision trees, Case-based reasoning	Win NT UNIX	Microsoft Access
Angoss	Knowledge Seeker	Decision trees, Statistics	Win NT	ODBC
Business Objects	Business Miner	Neural nets, Machine learning	Win NT	ODBC
CrossZ	QueryObject	Statistical Analysis Optimization algorithm	Win NT MVS UNIX	ODBC
Data Distilleries	Data Surveyor	Comprehensive, Can mix DM	UNIX	ODBC ODMG-compliant
DBMiner Technology Inc.	DBMiner	OLAP analysis, Associations, Classification, Clustering algorithms	Win NT	Microsoft 7.0 OLAP MGr
IBM	Intelligent Miner	Classification, Association rules, Predictive models	UNIX (AIX)	IBM DB2
Megaputer Intelligence	Polyanalyst	Symbolic knowledge acquisition, Evolutionary programming	Win NT OS/2	ODBC Oracle DB2
NCR	Management Discovery Tool (MDT)	Association rules	Win NT	ODBC
SAS	Enterprise Miner	Decision trees, Association rules, Neural nets, Regression, Clustering	UNIX (Solaris) Win NT Macintosh	ODBC Oracle AS/400
Silicon Graphics	MineSet	Decision trees, Association rules	UNIX (Irix)	Oracle Sybase Informix

*ODBC: Open Data Base Connectivity;
ODMG: Object Data Management Group

In the near future it seems that Microsoft Windows NT and UNIX will be the standard platforms, with NT being dominant. Most of data mining software will use the ODBC standard to extract data from business databases; proprietary input formats can be expected to disappear. There is a definite need to include nonstandard data, including images and other multimedia data, as source data for data mining. However, the algorithmic developments for nonstandard data mining have not reached a maturity level sufficient for commercialization.

16.8   SUMMARY

In this chapter we surveyed the important discipline of data mining, which uses database technology to discover additional knowledge or patterns in the data. We gave an illustrative example of knowledge discovery in databases, which has a wider scope than data mining. For data mining, among the various techniques, we focused on the details of association rule mining classificaion and clustering. We presented algorithms in each of these areas and illustrated how those algorithms work with the aid of examples.

A variety of other techniques, including the AI-based neural networks and genetic algorithms, were also briefly discussed. Active research is ongoing in data mining and we have outlined some of the expected research directions. In the future database technology products market, a great deal of data mining activity is expected. We summarized 11 out of nearly a hundred data mining tools available today; future research is expected to extend the number and functionality significantly.

Review Questions

16.1. What are the different phases of the knowledge discovery from databases? Describe a complete application scenario in which new knowledge may be mined from an existing database of transactions.

16.2. What are the goals or tasks that data mining attempts to facilitate?

16.3. What are the five types of knowledge produced from data mining?

16.4. What are association rules as a type of knowledge? Give a definition of support and confidence and use them to define an association rule.

16.5. What is the downward closure property? How does it aid in developing an efficient algorithm for finding association rules, i.e., with regard to finding large itemsets?

16.6. What was the motivating factor for the development of the FP-tree algorithm for association rule mining?

16.7. Describe an association rule among hierarchies with an example.

16.8. What is a negative association rule in the context of the hierarchy of Figure 16.3?

16.9. What are the difficulties of mining association rules from large databases?

16.10. What are classification rules and how are decision trees related to them?

16.11. What is entropy and how is it used in building decision trees?

16.12. How does clustering differ from classification?

16.13. Describe neural networks and genetic algorithms as techniques for data mining. What are the main difficulties in using these techniques?

Exercises

16.14. Apply the Apriori algorithm to the following data set.

Trans ID	Items Purchased
101	milk, bread, eggs
102	milk, juice
103	juice, butter
104	milk, bread, eggs
105	coffee, eggs
106	coffee
107	coffee, juice
108	milk, bread, cookies, eggs
109	cookies, butter
110	milk, bread

The set of items is {milk, bread, cookies, eggs, butter, coffee, juice}. Use 0.2 for the minimum support value.

16.15. Show two rules that have a confidence of 0.7 or greater for an itemset containing three items from Exercise 16.14.

16.16. For the Partition algorithm, prove that any frequent itemset in the database must appear as a local frequent itemset in at least one partition.

16.17. Show the P-tree that would be made for the data from Exercise 16.14.

16.18. Apply the FP-growth algorithm to the FP-tree from Exercise 16.17 and show the frequent itemsets.

16.19. Apply the classification algorithm to the following set of data records. The lass attribute is Repeat Customer.

RID	Age	City	Gender	Education	Repeat Customer
101	20..30	NY	F	college	YES
102	20..30	SF	M	graduate	YES
103	31..40	NY	F	college	YES
104	51..60	NY	F	college	NO
105	31..40	LA	M	high school	NO
106	41..50	NY	F	college	YES
107	41..50	NY	F	graduate	YES
108	20..30	LA	M	college	YES
109	20..30	NY	F	high school	NO
110	20..30	NY	F	college	YES

16.20. Consider the following set of two-dimensional records:

RID	Dimension1	Dimension2
1	8	4
2	5	4
3	2	4
4	2	6
5	2	8
6	8	6

Also consider two different clustering schemes: (1) where Cluster$_1$ contains records {1,2,3} and Cluster$_2$ contains records {4,5,6} and (2) where Cluster$_1$ contains records {1,6} and Cluster$_2$ contains records {2,3,4,5}. Which scheme is better and why?

16.21. Use the K-means algorithm to cluster the data from Exercise 16.20. We can use a value of 3 for K and can assume that the records with RIDs 1, 3 and 5 are used for the initial cluster centroids (means).

16.22. The K-means algorithm uses a similarity metric of distance between a record and a cluster centroid. If the attributes of the records are not quantitative but categorical in nature, such as Income Level with values {low, medium, high} or Married with values {Yes, No} or State of Residence with values {Alabama, Alaska, . . . , Wyoming} then the distance metric is not meaningful. Define a more suitable similarity metric that can be used for clustering data records that contain categorical data.

Selected Bibliography

Literature on data mining comes from several fields, including statistics, mathematical optimization, machine learning, and artificial intelligence. Data mining has only recently become a topic in the database literature. We, therefore, mention only a few database-related works. Chen et al. (1996) give a good summary of the database perspective on data mining. The book by Han and Kamber (2001) is an excellent text, describing in detail the different algorithms and techniques used in the data mining area. Work at IBM Almaden research has produced a large number of early concepts and algorithms as well as results from some performance studies. Agrawal et al. (1993) report the first major study on association rules. Their Apriori algorithm for market basket data in Agrawal and Srikant (1994) is improved by using partitioning in Savasere et al. (1995); Toivonen (1996) proposes sampling as a way to reduce the processing effort. Cheung et al. (1996) extends the partitioning to distributed environments; Lin and Dunham (1998) propose techniques to overcome problems with data skew. Agrawal et al. (1993b) discuss the performance perspective on association rules. Mannila et al. (1994), Park et al. (1995), and Amir et al. (1997) present additional efficient algorithms related to association rules. Han et al. (2000) present the FP tree algorithm discussed in this chapter. Srikant (1995) proposes mining generalized rules. Savasere et al. (1998) present the first approach to mining negative associations. Agrawal et al. (1996) describe the Quest system at IBM. Sarawagi et al. (1998) describe an implementation where association rules are integrated with a relational database management system. Piatesky-Shapiro and Frawley (1992) have contributed papers from a wide range of topics related to knowledge discovery. Zhang et al. (1996) present the BIRCH algorithm for clustering large databases. Information about decision tree learning and the classification algorithm presented in this chapter can be found in Mitchell (1997).

Adriaans and Zantinge (1996) and Weiss and Indurkhya (1998) are two recent books devoted to the different aspects of data mining and its use in prediction. The idea of genetic algorithms was proposed by Holland (1975); a good survey of genetic algorithms appears in Srinivas and Patnaik (1974). Neural networks have a vast literature; a comprehensive introduction is available in Lippman (1987).

17

Overview of Data Warehousing and OLAP

The increasing processing power and sophistication of analytical tools and techniques have resulted in the development of what are known as data warehouses. These data warehouses provide storage, functionality, and responsiveness to queries beyond the capabilities of transaction-oriented databases. Accompanying this ever-increasing power has come a great demand to improve the data access performance of databases. As we have seen throughout the book, traditional databases balance the requirement of data access with the need to ensure integrity of data. In modern organizations, users of data are often completely removed from the data sources. Many people only need read-access to data, but still need a very rapid access to a larger volume of data than can conveniently be downloaded to the desktop. Often such data comes from multiple databases. Because many of the analyses performed are recurrent and predictable, software vendors and systems support staff have begun to design systems to support these functions. At present there is a great need to provide decision makers from middle management upward with information at the correct level of detail to support decision making. *Data warehousing, online analytical processing* (OLAP), and *data mining* provide this functionality. We already gave an introduction to data mining techniques in Chapter 16. In this chapter we give a broad overview of data warehousing and OLAP technologies.

17.1 INTRODUCTION, DEFINITIONS, AND TERMINOLOGY

In Chapter 1 we defined database as a collection of related data and a database system as a database and database software together. A data warehouse is also a collection of information as well as a supporting system. However, a clear distinction exists. Traditional databases are transactional (relational, object-oriented, network, or hierarchical). Data warehouses have the distinguishing characteristic that they are mainly intended for decision-support applications. They are optimized for data retrieval, not routine transaction processing.

Because data warehouses have been developed in numerous organizations to meet particular needs, there is no single, canonical definition of the term data warehouse. Professional magazine articles and books in the popular press have elaborated on the meaning in a variety of ways. Vendors have capitalized on the popularity of the term to help market a variety of related products, and consultants have provided a large variety of services, all under the data warehousing banner. However, data warehouses are quite distinct from traditional databases in their structure, functioning, performance, and purpose.

W. H. Inmon[1] characterized a **data warehouse** as "a subject-oriented, integrated, nonvolatile, time-variant collection of data in support of management's decisions." Data warehouses provide access to data for complex analysis, knowledge discovery, and decision making. They support high-performance demands on an organization's data and information. Several types of applications—OLAP, DSS, and data mining applications— are supported. We define each of these next.

OLAP (online analytical processing) is a term used to describe the analysis of complex data from the data warehouse. In the hands of skilled knowledge workers, OLAP tools use distributed computing capabilities for analyses that require more storage and processing power than can be economically and efficiently located on an individual desktop.

DSS (decision-support systems) also known as **EIS** (executive information systems) (not to be confused with enterprise integration systems) support an organization's leading decision makers with higher level data for complex and important decisions. Data mining (which we discussed in detail in Chapter 16) is used for knowledge discovery, the process of searching data for unanticipated new knowledge.

Traditional databases support **online transaction processing (OLTP)**, which includes insertions, updates, and deletions, while also supporting information query requirements. Traditional relational databases are optimized to process queries that may touch a small part of the database and transactions that deal with insertions or updates of a few tuples per relation to process. Thus, they cannot be optimized for OLAP, DSS, or data mining. By contrast, data warehouses are designed precisely to support efficient extraction, processing, and presentation for analytic and decision-making purposes. In comparison to traditional databases, data warehouses generally contain very large amounts of data from multiple sources that may include databases from different data models and sometimes files acquired from independent systems and platforms.

17.2   CHARACTERISTICS OF DATA WAREHOUSES

To discuss data warehouses and distinguish them from transactional databases calls for an appropriate data model. The multidimensional data model (explained in more detail in Section 17.3) is a good fit for OLAP and decision-support technologies. In contrast to multidatabases, which provide access to disjoint and usually heterogeneous databases, a data warehouse is frequently a store of integrated data from multiple sources, processed for storage in a multidimensional model. Unlike most transactional databases, data warehouses typically support time-series and trend analysis, both of which require more historical data than is generally maintained in transactional databases.

Compared with transactional databases, data warehouses are nonvolatile. That means that information in the data warehouse changes far less often and may be regarded as non-real–time with periodic updating. In transactional systems, transactions are the unit and are the agent of change to the database; by contrast, data

---

1. Inmon (1992) has been credited with initially using the term data warehouse.

warehouse information is much more coarse grained and is refreshed according to a careful choice of refresh policy, usually incremental. Warehouse updates are handled by the warehouse's acquisition component that provides all required preprocessing.

We can also describe data warehousing more generally as "a collection of decision support technologies, aimed at enabling the knowledge worker (executive, manager, analyst) to make better and faster decisions."[2] Figure 17.1 gives an overview of the conceptual structure of a data warehouse. It shows the entire data warehousing process. This process includes possible cleaning and reformatting of data before its warehousing. At the back end of the process, OLAP, data mining, and DSS may generate new relevant information such as rules; this information is shown in the figure going back into the warehouse. The figure also shows that data sources may include files.

FIGURE 17.1 Example transactions in market-basket model.

Data warehouses have the following distinctive characteristics: [3]

- multidimensional conceptual view
- generic dimensionality
- unlimited dimensions and aggregation levels
- unrestricted cross-dimensional operations
- dynamic sparse matrix handling
- client-server architecture
- multi-user support
- accessibility
- transparency
- intuitive data manipulation
- consistent reporting performance
- flexible reporting

---

2. Chaudhuri and Dayal (1997) provide an excellent tutorial on the topic, with this as a starting definition.

3. Codd (1993) coined the term OLAP and mentioned these characteristics. We have reordered Codd's original list.

Because they encompass large volumes of data, data warehouses are generally an order of magnitude (sometimes two orders of magnitude) larger than the source databases. The sheer volume of data (likely to be in terabytes) is an issue that has been dealt with through enterprise-wide data warehouses, virtual data warehouses, and data marts:

- **Enterprise-wide data warehouses** are huge projects requiring massive investment of time and resources.

- **Virtual data warehouses** provide views of operational databases that are materialized for efficient access.

- **Data marts** generally are targeted to a subset of the organization, such as a department, and are more tightly focused.

17.3   DATA MODELING FOR DATA WAREHOUSES

Multidimensional models take advantage of inherent relationships in data to populate data in multidimensional matrices called data cubes. (These may be called hypercubes if they have more than three dimensions.) For data that lends itself to dimensional formatting, query performance in multidimensional matrices can be much better than in the relational data model. Three examples of dimensions in a corporate data warehouse would be the corporation's fiscal periods, products, and regions.

A standard spreadsheet is a two-dimensional matrix. One example would be a spreadsheet of regional sales by product for a particular time period. Products could be shown as rows, with sales revenues for each region comprising the columns. (Figure 17.2 shows this two-dimensional organization.) Adding a time dimension, such as an organization's fiscal quarters, would produce a three-dimensional matrix, which could be represented using a data cube.

In Figure 17.3 there is a three-dimensional data cube that organizes product sales data by fiscal quarters and sales regions. Each cell could contain data for a specific product, specific fiscal quarter, and specific region. By including additional dimensions, a data hypercube could be produced, although more than three dimensions cannot be easily visualized at all or presented graphically. The data can be queried directly in any combination of dimensions, bypassing complex database queries. Tools exist for viewing data according to the user's choice of dimensions.

FIGURE 17.2 Two-dimensional matrix model.

FIGURE 17.3 A three-dimensional data cube model.

Changing from one dimensional hierarchy (orientation) to another is easily accomplished in a data cube by a technique called **pivoting** (also called rotation). In this technique the data cube can be thought of as rotating to show a different orientation of the axes. For example, you might pivot the data cube to show

FIGURE 17.4 Pivoted version of the data cube from Figure 17.3.

regional sales revenues as rows, the fiscal quarter revenue totals as columns, and the company's products in the third dimension (Figure 17.4). Hence, this technique is equivalent to having a regional sales table for each product separately, where each table shows quarterly sales for that product region by region.

FIGURE 17.5 The roll-up operation.

FIGURE 17.6 The drill-down operation.

Multidimensional models lend themselves readily to hierarchical views in what is known as roll-up display and drill-down display. **Roll-up display** moves up the hierarchy, grouping into larger units along a dimension (e.g., summing weekly data by quarter, or by year). Figure 17.5 shows a roll-up display that moves from individual products to a coarser grain of product categories. Shown in Figure 17.6, a **drill-down display** provides the opposite capability, furnishing a finer-grained view, perhaps disaggregating country sales by region and then regional sales by subregion and also breaking up products by styles.

The multidimensional storage model involves two types of tables: dimension tables and fact tables. A **dimension table** consists of tuples of attributes of the dimension. A **fact table** can be thought of as having tuples, one per a recorded fact. This fact contains some measured or observed variable(s) and identifies it (them) with pointers to dimension tables. The fact table contains the data, and the dimensions identify each tuple in that data. Figure 17.7 contains an example of a fact table that can be viewed from the perspective of multiple dimension tables.

Two common multidimensional schemas are the star schema and the snowflake schema. The **star schema** consists of a fact table with a single table for each dimension (Figure 17.7). The **snowflake schema** is a variation on the star schema in which the dimensional tables from a star schema are organized into a hierarchy by normalizing them (Figure 17.8). Some installations are normalizing data warehouses up to the third normal form so that they can access the data warehouse to the finest level of detail. A **fact constellation** is a set of fact tables that share some dimension tables. Figure 17.9 shows a fact constellation with two fact tables, business results and business forecast. These share the dimension table called product. Fact constellations limit the possible queries for the warehouse.

Data warehouse storage also utilizes indexing techniques to support high performance access (see Chapter 5 for a discussion of indexing). A technique called **bitmap indexing** constructs a bit vector for each value in a domain (column) being indexed. It works very well for domains of low cardinality. There is a 1 bit placed in the jth position in the vector if the jth row contains the value being indexed. For example, imagine an inventory of 100,000 cars with a bitmap index on car size. If there are four car sizes—economy, compact, midsize, and fullsize—there will be four bit vectors, each containing 100,000 bits (12.5 K) for a total index size of 50K. Bitmap indexing can provide considerable input/output and storage space advantages in low-cardinality domains. With bit vectors a bitmap index can provide dramatic improvements in comparison, aggregation, and join performance.

In a star schema, dimensional data can be indexed to tuples in the fact table by **join indexing.** Join indexes are traditional indexes to maintain relationships between primary key and foreign key values. They relate the values of a dimension of a star schema to rows in the fact table. For example, consider a sales fact table that has city and fiscal quarter as dimensions. If there is a join index on city, for each city the join index maintains the tuple IDs of tuples containing that city. Join indexes may involve multiple dimensions.

Data warehouse storage can facilitate access to summary data by taking further advantage of the nonvolatility of data warehouses and a degree of predictability of the analyses that will be performed using them. Two approaches have been used: (1) smaller tables including summary data such as quarterly sales or revenue by product line, and (2) encoding of level (e.g., weekly, quarterly, annual) into existing tables. By comparison, the overhead of creating and maintaining such aggregations would likely be excessive in a volatile, transaction-oriented database.

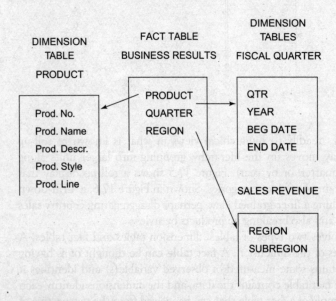

FIGURE 17.7 A star schema with fact and dimensional tables.

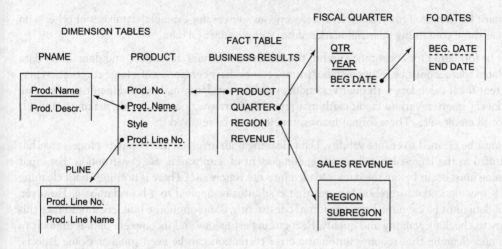

FIGURE 17.8 A snowflake schema.

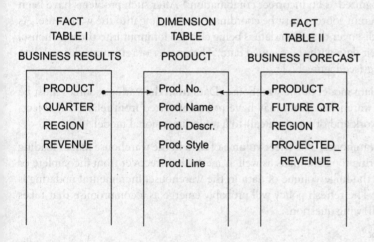

FIGURE 17.9 A fact constellation.

17.4   BUILDING A DATA WAREHOUSE

In constructing a data warehouse, builders should take a broad view of the anticipated use of the warehouse. There is no way to anticipate all possible queries or analyses during the design phase. However, the design should specifically support **ad-hoc querying,** that is, accessing data with any meaningful combination of values for the attributes in the dimension or fact tables. For example, a marketing-intensive consumer-products company would require different ways of organizing the data warehouse than would a nonprofit charity focused on fund raising. An appropriate schema should be chosen that reflects anticipated usage.

Acquisition of data for the warehouse involves the following steps:

- The data must be extracted from multiple, heterogeneous sources, for example, databases or other data feeds such as those containing financial market data or environmental data.

- Data must be formatted for consistency within the warehouse. Names, meanings, and domains of data from unrelated sources must be reconciled. For instance, subsidiary companies of a large corporation may have different fiscal calendars with quarters ending on different dates, making it difficult to aggregate financial data by quarter. Various credit cards may report their transactions differently, making it difficult to compute all credit sales. These format inconsistencies must be resolved.

- The data must be cleaned to ensure validity. Data cleaning is an involved and complex process that has been identified as the largest labor-demanding component of data warehouse construction. For input data, cleaning must occur before the data is loaded into the warehouse. There is nothing about cleaning data that is specific to data warehousing and that could not be applied to a host database. However, since input data must be examined and formatted consistently, data warehouse builders should take this opportunity to check for validity and quality. Recognizing erroneous and incomplete data is difficult to automate, and cleaning that requires automatic error correction can be even tougher. Some aspects, such as domain checking, are easily coded into data cleaning routines, but automatic recognition of other data problems can be more challenging. (For example, one might require that City = 'San Francisco' together with State = 'CT' be recognized as an incorrect combination.) After such problems have been taken care of, similar data from different sources must be coordinated for loading into the warehouse. As data managers in the organization discover that their data is being cleaned for input into the warehouse, they will likely want to upgrade their data with the cleaned data. The process of returning cleaned data to the source is called **backflushing** (see Figure 17.1).

- The data must be fitted into the data model of the warehouse. Data from the various sources must be installed in the data model of the warehouse. Data may have to be converted from relational, object-oriented, or legacy databases (network and/or hierarchical) to a multidimensional model.

- The data must be loaded into the warehouse. The sheer volume of data in the warehouse makes loading the data a significant task. Monitoring tools for loads as well as methods to recover from incomplete or incorrect loads are required. With the huge volume of data in the warehouse, incremental updating is usually the only feasible approach. The refresh policy will probably emerge as a compromise that takes into account the answers to the following questions:

  - How up-to-date must the data be?

  - Can the warehouse go off-line, and for how long?

  - What are the data interdependencies?

  - What is the storage availability?

  - What are the distribution requirements (such as for replication and partitioning)?

  - What is the loading time (including cleaning, formatting, copying, transmitting, and overhead such as index rebuilding)?

As we have said, databases must strike a balance between efficiency in transaction processing and supporting query requirements (ad hoc user requests), but a data warehouse is typically optimized for access from a decision maker's needs. Data storage in a data warehouse reflects this specialization and involves the following processes:

- Storing the data according to the data model of the warehouse

- Creating and maintaining required data structures
- Creating and maintaining appropriate access paths
- Providing for time-variant data as new data are added
- Supporting the updating of warehouse data
- Refreshing the data
- Purging data

Although adequate time can be devoted initially to constructing the warehouse, the sheer volume of data in the warehouse generally makes it impossible to simply reload the warehouse in its entirety later on. Alternatives include selective (partial) refreshing of data and separate warehouse versions (requiring double storage capacity for the warehouse!). When the warehouse uses an incremental data refreshing mechanism, data may need to be periodically purged; for example, a warehouse that maintains data on the previous twelve business quarters may periodically purge its data each year.

Data warehouses must also be designed with full consideration of the environment in which they will reside. Important design considerations include the following:

- Usage projections
- The fit of the data model
- Characteristics of available sources
- Design of the metadata component
- Modular component design
- Design for manageability and change
- Considerations of distributed and parallel architecture

We discuss each of these in turn. Warehouse design is initially driven by usage projections; that is, by expectations about who will use the warehouse and in what way. Choice of a data model to support this usage is a key initial decision. Usage projections and the characteristics of the warehouse's data sources are both taken into account. Modular design is a practical necessity to allow the warehouse to evolve with the organization and its information environment. In addition, a well-built data warehouse must be designed for maintainability, enabling the warehouse managers to effectively plan for and manage change while providing optimal support to users.

You may recall the term metadata from Chapter 2; metadata was defined as the description of a database including its schema definition. The **metadata repository** is a key data warehouse component. The metadata repository includes both technical and business metadata. The first, technical metadata, covers details of acquisition processing, storage structures, data descriptions, warehouse operations and maintenance, and access support functionality. The second, business metadata, includes the relevant business rules and organizational details supporting the warehouse.

The architecture of the organization's distributed computing environment is a major determining characteristic for the design of the warehouse.

There are two basic distributed architectures: the distributed warehouse and the federated warehouse. For a **distributed warehouse,** all the issues of distributed databases are relevant, for example, replication, partitioning, communications, and consistency concerns. A distributed architecture can provide benefits particularly important to warehouse performance, such as improved load balancing, scalability of performance, and higher availability. A single replicated metadata repository would reside at each distribution site. The idea of the **federated warehouse** is like that of the federated database: a decentralized confederation of autonomous data warehouses, each with its own metadata repository. Given the magnitude of the challenge inherent to data warehouses, it is likely that such federations will consist of smaller scale components, such as data marts. Large organizations may choose to federate data marts rather than build huge data warehouses.

17.5 TYPICAL FUNCTIONALITY OF A DATA WAREHOUSE

Data warehouses exist to facilitate complex, data-intensive, and frequent ad hoc queries. Accordingly, data warehouses must provide far greater and more efficient query support than is demanded of transactional databases. The data warehouse access component supports enhanced spreadsheet functionality, efficient query processing, structured queries, ad hoc queries, data mining, and materialized views. In particular, enhanced spreadsheet functionality includes support for state-of-the-art spreadsheet applications (e.g., MS Excel) as well as for OLAP applications programs. These offer preprogrammed functionalities such as the following:

- Roll-up: Data is summarized with increasing generalization (e.g., weekly to quarterly to annually).

- Drill-down: Increasing levels of detail are revealed (the complement of roll-up).

- Pivot: Cross tabulation (also referred as rotation) is performed.

- Slice and dice: Performing projection operations on the dimensions.

- Sorting: Data is sorted by ordinal value.

- Selection: Data is available by value or range.

- Derived (computed) attributes: Attributes are computed by operations on stored and derived values.

Because data warehouses are free from the restrictions of the transactional environment, there is an increased efficiency in query processing. Among the tools and techniques used are query transformation, index intersection and union, special **ROLAP** (relational OLAP) and **MOLAP** (multidimensional OLAP) functions, SQL extensions, advanced join methods, and intelligent scanning (as in piggy-backing multiple queries).

Improved performance has also been attained with parallel processing. Parallel server architectures include symmetric multiprocessor (SMP), cluster, and massively parallel processing (MPP), and combinations of these.

Knowledge workers and decision makers use tools ranging from parametric queries to ad hoc queries to data mining. Thus, the access component of the data warehouse must provide support for structured queries (both parametric and ad hoc). These together make up a managed query environment. Data mining itself uses techniques from statistical analysis and artificial intelligence. Statistical analysis can be performed by advanced spreadsheets, by sophisticated statistical analysis software, or by custom-written programs. Techniques such as lagging, moving averages, and regression analysis are also commonly employed. Artificial intelligence techniques, which may include genetic algorithms and neural networks, are used for classification and are employed to discover knowledge from the data warehouse that may be unexpected or difficult to specify in queries. (We treat data mining in detail in Chapter 16.)

17.6 DATA WAREHOUSE VERSUS VIEWS

Some people have considered data warehouses to be an extension of database views. Earlier we mentioned materialized views as one way of meeting requirements for improved access to data (see Chapter 7 for a discussion of views). Materialized views have been explored for their performance enhancement. Views, however, provide only a subset of the functions and capabilities of data warehouses. Views and data warehouses are alike in that they both have read-only extracts from databases and subject-orientation. However, data warehouses are different from views in the following ways:

- Data warehouses exist as persistent storage instead of being materialized on demand.

- Data warehouses are not usually relational, but rather multidimensional. Views of a relational database are relational.

- Data warehouses can be indexed to optimize performance. Views cannot be indexed independent of the underlying databases.

- Data warehouses characteristically provide specific support of functionality; views cannot.

- Data warehouses provide large amounts of integrated and often temporal data, generally more than is contained in one database, whereas views are an extract of a database.

17.7   PROBLEMS AND OPEN ISSUES IN DATA WAREHOUSES

17.7.1   Difficulties of Implementing Data Warehouses

Some significant operational issues arise with data warehousing: construction, administration, and quality control. Project management—the design, construction, and implementation of the warehouse—is an important and challenging consideration that should not be underestimated. The building of an enterprise-wide warehouse in a large organization is a major undertaking, potentially taking years from conceptualization to implementation. Because of the difficulty and amount of lead time required for such an undertaking, the widespread development and deployment of data marts may provide an attractive alternative, especially to those organizations with urgent needs for OLAP, DSS, and/or data mining support.

The administration of a data warehouse is an intensive enterprise, proportional to the size and complexity of the warehouse. An organization that attempts to administer a data warehouse must realistically understand the complex nature of its administration. Although designed for read-access, a data warehouse is no more a static structure than any of its information sources. Source databases can be expected to evolve. The warehouse's schema and acquisition component must be expected to be updated to handle these evolutions.

A significant issue in data warehousing is the quality control of data. Both quality and consistency of data are major concerns. Although the data passes through a cleaning function during acquisition, quality and consistency remain significant issues for the database administrator. Melding data from heterogeneous and disparate sources is a major challenge given differences in naming, domain definitions, identification numbers, and the like. Every time a source database changes, the data warehouse administrator must consider the possible interactions with other elements of the warehouse.

Usage projections should be estimated conservatively prior to construction of the data warehouse and should be revised continually to reflect current requirements. As utilization patterns become clear and change over time, storage and access paths can be tuned to remain optimized for support of the organization's use of its warehouse. This activity should continue throughout the life of the warehouse in order to remain ahead of demand. The warehouse should also be designed to accommodate addition and attrition of data sources without major redesign. Sources and source data will evolve, and the warehouse must accommodate such change. Fitting the available source data into the data model of the warehouse will be a continual challenge, a task that is as much art as science. Because there is continual rapid change in technologies, both the requirements and capabilities of the warehouse will change considerably over time. Additionally, data warehousing technology itself will continue to evolve for some time so that component structures and functionalities will continually be upgraded. This certain change is excellent motivation for having fully modular design of components.

Administration of a data warehouse will require far broader skills than are needed for traditional database administration. A team of highly skilled technical experts with overlapping areas of expertise will likely be needed, rather than a single individual. Like database administration, data warehouse administration is only partly technical; a large part of the responsibility requires working effectively with all the members of the organization with an interest in the data warehouse. However difficult that can be at times for database administrators, it is that much more challenging for data warehouse administrators, as the scope of their responsibilities is considerably broader.

Design of the management function and selection of the management team for a database warehouse are crucial. Managing the data warehouse in a large organization will surely be a major task. Many commercial tools are already available to support management functions. Effective data warehouse management will certainly be a team function, requiring a wide set of technical skills, careful coordination, and effective leadership. Just as we must prepare for the evolution of the warehouse, we must also recognize that the skills of the management team will, of necessity, evolve with it.

17.7.2 Open Issues in Data Warehousing

There has been much marketing hyperbole surrounding the term "data warehouse"; the exaggerated expectations will probably subside, but the concept of integrated data collections to support sophisticated analysis and decision support will undoubtedly endure.

Data warehousing as an active research area is likely to see increased research activity in the near future as warehouses and data marts proliferate. Old problems will receive new emphasis; for example, data cleaning, indexing, partitioning, and views could receive renewed attention.

Academic research into data warehousing technologies will likely focus on automating aspects of the warehouse that currently require significant manual intervention, such as the data acquisition, data quality management, selection and construction of appropriate access paths and structures, self-maintainability, functionality, and performance optimization. Application of active database functionality (see Section 12.1) into the warehouse is likely also to receive considerable attention. Incorporation of domain and business rules appropriately into the warehouse creation and maintenance process may make it more intelligent, relevant, and self- governing.

Commercial software for data warehousing is already available from a number of vendors, focusing principally on management of the data warehouse and OLAP/DSS applications. Other aspects of data warehousing, such as design and data acquisition (especially cleaning), are being addressed primarily by teams of in-house IT managers and consultants.

17.8 SUMMARY

In this chapter we surveyed the field known as data warehousing. Data warehousing can be seen as a process that requires a variety of activities to precede it. In contrast, data mining (see Chapter 16) may be thought of as an activity that draws knowledge from an existing data warehouse. We introduced key concepts related to data warehousing and we discussed the special functionality associated with a multidimensional view of data. We also discussed the ways in which data warehouses supply decision makers with information at the correct level of detail, based on an appropriate organization and perspective.

Review Questions

17.1.   What is a data warehouse? How does it differ from a database?

17.2.   Define the terms: OLAP (Online Analytical Processing), ROLAP (Relational OLAP), and MOLAP (Multidimensional OLAP), DSS (Decision support Systems).

17.3.   Describe the characteristics of a data warehouse. Divide them into functionality of a warehouse and advantages users derive from it.

17.4.   What is the multidimensional data model? How is it used in data warehousing?

17.5.   Define these terms: Star Schema, Snowflake Schema, Fact Constellation, Data Marts.

17.6.   What types of indexes are built for a warehouse? Illustrate the uses for each with an example.

17.7.   Describe the steps of building a warehouse.

17.8.   What considerations play a major role in the design of a warehouse?

17.9.   Describe the functions a user can perform on a data warehouse and illustrate the results of these functions on a sample multidimensional data warehouse.

17.10.   How is the concept of a relational view related to data warehouse and data marts? In what way are they different?

17.11.   List the difficulties in implementing a data warehouse.

17.12.   List the open issues and research problems in data warehousing.

Selected Bibliography

Data warehousing has become a very popular topic and has appeared in many publications in the last few years. Inmon (1992) is credited for giving this term wide acceptance. Codd (1993) popularized the term online analytical processing (OLAP) and defined a set of characteristics for data warehouses to support OLAP. Mattison (1996) is one of the several books on data warehousing that gives a comprehensive analysis of techniques available in data warehouses and the strategies companies should use in deploying them. Bischoff and Alexander (1997) is a compilation of advice from experts. Chaudhuri and Dayal (1997) give an excellent tutorial on the topic, while Widom (1995) points to a number of outstanding research problems.

18

Emerging Database Technologies and Applications

Throughout this book we have discussed a variety of issues related to the modeling, design, and functions of databases as well as to the internal structure and performance issues related to database management systems. In Chapter 15 we covered the internet databases that provide universal access to data and discussed the use of XML that will facilitate development of applications involving many disimilar databases and different DBMS platforms. In the previous two chapters we considered variations of database management technology, such as data mining and data warehouses, that provide very large databases and tools for decision support. We now turn our attention in this chapter to two categories of continuously evolving developments in the database field: (1) emerging database technologies, and (2) the major application domains. We do not claim to do so exhaustively and only address some prominent technological and application advances. The first deals with creating new functionality in DBMSs so that a variety of new applications can be supported, including mobile databases to allow users widespread and flexible access to data while being mobile, and multimedia databases providing support for storage and processing of multimedia information. Sections 18.1 and 18.2 will briefly introduce and discuss the issues and approaches to solving the specific problems that arise in the mobile and multimedia database technologies.

We next consider two application domains that have historically relied upon manual processing of file systems, or tailored system solutions. Section 18.3 discusses geographic information systems, which deal with geographic data alone or spatial data combined with non-spatial data, such as census counts. Section 18.4 discusses biological databases and their applications, particularly containing genetic data on different organisms, including the human genome data. A common characteristic of all these applications is the domain-specific nature of data in each specific application domain. Furthermore, they are all characterized by their "static" nature—a situation where the end user can only retrieve from the database; updating with new information is limited to database domain experts who supervise and analyze the new data being entered.

18.1 MOBILE DATABASES[1]

Recent advances in portable and wireless technology have led to **mobile computing**, a new dimension in data communication and processing. Portable computing devices coupled with wireless communications allow clients to access data from virtually anywhere and at any time. This feature is especially useful to geographically dispersed organizations. Typical examples might include electronic valets, news reporting, brokerage services, and automated salesforces. However, there are a number of hardware and software problems that must be resolved before the capabilities of mobile computing can be fully utilized.

Some of the software problems—which may involve data management, transaction management, and database recovery—have their origins in distributed database systems. In mobile computing, however, these problems are more difficult, mainly because of the limited and intermittent connectivity afforded by wireless communications, the limited life of the power supply (battery) of mobile units, and the changing topology of the network. In addition, mobile computing introduces new architectural possibilities and challenges.

18.1.1 Mobile Computing Architecture

The general architecture of a mobile platform is illustrated in Figure 18.1. It is a distributed architecture where a number of computers, generally referred to as **Fixed Hosts** and **Base Stations,** are interconnected through a high-speed wired network. Fixed hosts are general purpose computers that are not typically equipped to manage mobile units but can be configured to do so. Base stations function as gateways to the fixed network for the **Mobile Units.** They are equipped with wireless interfaces and offer network access services of which mobile units are clients.

Wireless Communications. The wireless medium on which mobile units and base stations communicate have bandwidths significantly lower than those of a wired network. The current generation of wireless technology has data rates that range from the tens to hundreds of kilobits per second (2G cellular telephony) to tens of megabits per second (wireless Ethernet, popularly known as WiFi). Modern (wired) Ethernet, by comparison, provides data rates on the order of hundreds of megabits per second.

Besides data rates, other characteristics also distinguish wireless connectivity options. Some of these characteristics include range, interference, locality of access, and support for packet switching. Some wireless access options allow seamless roaming throughout a geographical region (e.g., cellular networks), whereas WiFi networks are localized around a base station. Some wireless networks, such as WiFi and Bluetooth, use unlicensed areas of the frequency spectrum, which may cause interference with other appliances, such as cordless telephones. Finally, modern wireless networks can transfer data in units called packets, that are commonly used in wired networks in order to conserve bandwidth. Wireless applications must consider these characteristics when choosing a communication option. For example, physical objects block infrared frequencies. While inconvenient for some applications, such blockage allows for secure wireless communications within a closed room.

---

1. The contribution of Waigen Yee and Wanxia Xie to this section is appreciated.

FIGURE 18.1 A general architecture of a mobile platform (Adapted from Dunham and Helal (1995)).

Client/Network Relationships. Mobile units can move freely in a **geographic mobility domain,** an area that is circumscribed by wireless network coverage. To manage the mobility of units, the entire geographic mobility domain is divided into one or more smaller domains, called **cells,** each of which is supported by at least one base station. The mobile discipline requires that the movement of mobile units be unrestricted throughout the cells of a geographic mobility domain, while maintaining information **access contiguity**—i.e., movement, especially intercell movement, does not negatively affect the data retrieval process.

The communication architecture just described is designed to give the mobile unit the impression that it is attached to a fixed network, emulating a traditional client-server architecture. Wireless communications, however, make other architectures possible. One alternative is a mobile ad-hoc network (MANET), illustrated in Figure 18.2.[2] In a MANET, co-located mobile units do not need to communicate via a fixed network, but instead, form their own using cost-effective technologies such as Bluetooth. In a MANET, mobile units are responsible for routing their own data, effectively acting as base stations as well as clients. Moreover, they must be robust enough to handle changes in the network topology, such as the arrival or departure of other mobile units.

MANET applications can be considered as peer-to-peer, meaning that a mobile unit is simultaneously a client and a server. Transaction processing and data consistency control become more difficult since there is no central control in this architecture. Resource discovery and data routing by mobile units make computing in a MANET even more complicated. Sample MANET applications are multi-user games, shared whiteboards,

---

2. This architecture is based on the IETF proposal in IETF(1999) with comments by Carson and Macker (1999)

distributed calendars, and battle information sharing. The expectation is that these networks and related applications will become dominant in a few years. Currently MANETs are an active research area in both academia and industry. This research is still in its infancy, so the following discussion will focus on the basic mobile computing architecture described previously.

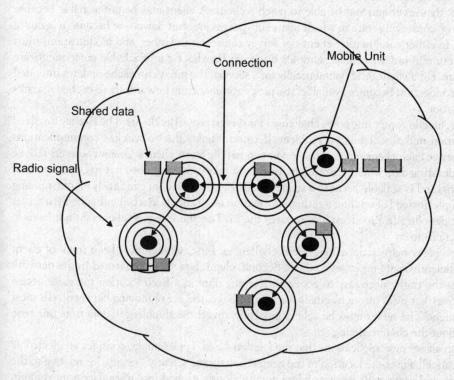

FIGURE 18.2 The architecture of a mobile ad-hoc network.

18.1.2   Characteristics of Mobile Environments

As we discussed in the previous section, the characteristics of mobile computing include high communication latency, intermittent wireless connectivity, limited battery life, and, of course, changing client location. Latency is caused by the processes unique to the wireless medium, such as coding data for wireless transfer, and tracking and filtering wireless signals at the receiver. Battery life is directly related to battery size, and indirectly related to the mobile device's capabilities. Intermittent connectivity can be intentional or unintentional. Unintentional disconnections happen in areas wireless signals cannot reach, e.g., elevator shafts or subway tunnels. Intentional disconnections occur by user intent, e.g., during an airplane takeoff, or when the mobile device is powered down. Finally, clients are expected to move, which alters the network topology and may cause their data requirements to change. All of these characteristics impact data management, and robust mobile applications must consider them in their design.[3]

---

3. This architecture is based on the IETF proposal in IETF(1999) with comments by Carson and Macker (1999).

To compensate for high latencies and unreliable connectivity, clients cache replicas of important, frequently accessed data, and work offline, if necessary. Besides increasing data availability and response time, caching can also reduce client power consumption by eliminating the need to make energy-consuming wireless data transmissions for each data access.

On the other hand, the server may not be able to reach a client. A client may be unreachable because it is **dozing**—in an energy-conserving state in which many subsystems are shut down—or because it is out of range of a base station. In either case, neither client nor server can reach the other, and modifications must be made to the architecture in order to compensate for this case. **Proxies** for unreachable components are added to the architecture. For a client (and symmetrically for a server), the proxy can cache updates intended for the server. When a connection becomes available, the proxy automatically forwards these cached updates to their ultimate destination.

As suggested above, mobile computing poses challenges for servers as well as clients. The latency involved in wireless communication makes scalability a problem. Because latency due to wireless communications increases the time to service each client request, the server can handle fewer clients. One way servers relieve this problem is by **broadcasting** data whenever possible. Broadcast takes advantage of a natural characteristic of radio communications, and is scalable because a single broadcast of a data item can satisfy all outstanding requests for it. For example, instead of sending weather information to all clients in a cell individually, a server can simply broadcast it periodically. Broadcast also reduces the load on the server, as clients do not have to maintain active connections to it.

Client mobility also poses many data management challenges. First, servers must keep track of client locations in order to efficiently route messages to them. Second, client data should be stored in the network location that minimizes the traffic necessary to access it. Keeping data in a fixed location increases access latency if the client moves "far away" from it. Finally, as stated above, the act of moving between cells must be transparent to the client. The server must be able to gracefully divert the shipment of data from one base station to another, without the client noticing.

Client mobility also allows new applications that are *location-based*. For example, consider an electronic valet application that can tell a user the location of the nearest restaurant. Clearly, "nearest" is relative to the client's current position, and movement can invalidate any previously cached responses. Upon movement, the client must efficiently invalidate parts of its cache and request updated data from the database.

18.1.3 Data Management Issues

From a data management standpoint, mobile computing may be considered a variation of distributed computing. Mobile databases can be distributed under two possible scenarios:

1. The entire database is distributed mainly among the wired components, possibly with full or partial replication. A base station or fixed host manages its own database with a DBMS-like functionality, with additional functionality for locating mobile units and additional query and transaction management features to meet the requirements of mobile environments.

2. The database is distributed among wired and wireless components. Data management responsibility is shared among base stations or fixed hosts and mobile units.

Hence, the distributed data management issues we discussed in Chapter 13 can also be applied to mobile databases with the following additional considerations and variations:

- *Data distribution and replication:* Data is unevenly distributed among the base stations and mobile units. The consistency constraints compound the problem of cache management. Caches attempt to provide the most frequently accessed and updated data to mobile units that process their own transactions and may be disconnected over long periods.

- *Transaction models:* Issues of fault tolerance and correctness of transactions are aggravated in the mobile environment. A mobile transaction is executed sequentially through several base stations and possibly on multiple data sets depending upon the movement of the mobile unit. Central coordination of transaction execution is lacking, particularly in scenario (2) above. Moreover, a mobile transaction is expected to be long-lived because of disconnection in mobile units. Hence, traditional ACID properties of transactions (see Chapter 11) may need to be modified and new transaction models must be defined.

- *Query processing:* Awareness of where data is located is important and affects the cost/benefit analysis of query processing. Query optimization is more complicated because of mobility and rapid resource changes of mobile units. The query response needs to be returned to mobile units that may be in transit or may cross cell boundaries yet must receive complete and correct query results.

- *Recovery and fault tolerance:* The mobile database environment must deal with site, media, transaction, and communication failures. Site failure of a mobile unit is frequent due to limited battery power. A voluntary shutdown of a mobile unit should *not* be treated as a failure. Transaction failures are routine during handoff when a mobile unit crosses cells. The transaction manager should be able to deal with such frequent failures.

- *Mobile database design:* The global name resolution problem for handling queries is compounded because of mobility and frequent shutdown. Mobile database design must consider many issues of metadata management—for example, the constant updating of location information.

- *Location-based service:* As clients move, location-dependent cache information may become stale. Eviction techniques are important in this case. Furthermore, frequently updating location dependent queries, then applying these (spatial) queries in order to refresh the cache poses a problem.

- *Division of labor:* Certain characteristics of the mobile environment force a change in the division of labor in query processing. In some cases, the client must function independent of the server. However, what are the consequences of allowing full independent access to replicated data? The relationship between client responsibilities and their consequences has yet to be developed.

- *Security:* Mobile data is less secure than that which is left at the fixed location. Proper techniques for managing and authorizing access to critical data become more important in this environment. Data is also more volatile, and techniques must be able to compensate for its loss.

18.1.4 Application: Intermittently Synchronized Databases

One mobile computing scenario is becoming increasingly commonplace as people conduct their work away from their offices and homes and perform a wide range of activities and functions: all kinds of sales, particularly in pharmaceuticals, consumer goods, and industrial parts; law enforcement; insurance and financial consulting and planning; real estate or property management activities; courier and transportation services, and so on. In these applications, a server or a group of servers manages the central database and the clients carry laptops or palmtops with a resident DBMS software to do "local" transaction activity for most of the time. The clients connect via a network or a dial-up connection (or possibly even through the Internet) with the server, typically for a short session—say, 30 to 60 minutes. They send their updates to the server, and the server must in turn enter them in its central database, which must maintain up-to-date data and prepare appropriate copies for all clients on the system. Thus, whenever clients connect—through a process known in the industry as *synchronization* of a client with a server—they receive a batch of updates to be installed on their local database. The primary characteristic of this scenario is that the clients are mostly disconnected; the server is not necessarily able to reach them. This environment has problems similar to those in distributed and client/server databases, and some from mobile databases, but presents several additional research problems for investigation. We refer to this environment as **Intermittently Synchronized Database Environment** (ISDBE), and the corresponding databases as Intermittently Synchronized Databases (ISDBs).

Together, the following characteristics of ISDB's make them *distinct* from the mobile databases we have discussed thus far:

1. A client connects to the server when it wants to exchange updates. This communication may be *unicast*—one-on-one communication between the server and the client—or *multicast*—one sender or server may periodically communicate to a set of receivers or update a group of clients.

2. A server cannot connect to a client at will.

3. Issues of wireless versus wired client connections and power conservation are generally immaterial.

4. A client is free to manage its own data and transactions while it is disconnected. It can also perform its own recovery to some extent.

5. A client has multiple ways of connecting to a server and, in case of many servers, may choose a particular server to connect to based on proximity, communication nodes available, resources available, etc.

Because of such differences, there is a need to address a number of problems related to ISDBs that are different from those typically involving mobile database systems. These include server database design for server databases, consistency and synchronization management among client and server databases, transaction and update processing, efficient use of the server bandwidth, and achieving scalability in the ISDB environments.

18.1.5 Selected Bibliography for Mobile Databases

There has been a sudden surge of interest in mobile computing, and research on mobile databases has had a significant growth for the last five to six years. The June 1995 issue of *Byte* magazine discusses many aspects of mobile computing. Among books written on this topic, Dhawan (1997) is an excellent source on mobile computing. Wireless networks and their future are discussed in Holtzman and Goodman (1993). Imielinski and Badrinath (1994) provide a good survey of mobile database issues and also discuss in Imielinski and Badrinath (1992) data and metadata allocation in a mobile architecture. Dunham and Helal (1995) discuss problems of query processing, data distribution, and transaction management for mobile databases. Foreman and Zahorjan (1994) describe the capabilities and the problems of mobile computing and make a convincing argument in its favor as a viable solution for many information system applications of the future. Pitoura and Samaras (1998) describe all aspects of mobile database problems and solutions. Chrysanthis (1993) describes a transaction model that is designed to operate in an environment with mobile clients. In particular, this model allows a client to share the transaction processing load with proxies in order to facilitate mobility. Bertino et al. (1998) discuss approaches to fault tolerance and recovery in mobile databases. Acharya et al. (1995) consider broadcast schedules that minimize average query latency, and explore the impact of such schedules on optimal client caching strategies. Milojicic et al. (2002) present a tutorial on peer-to-peer computing. Corson and Macker (1999) is a response to IETF(1999) report that discusses the mobile ad-hoc networking protocol performance issues. Broadcasting (or pushing) data as a means of scalably disseminating information to clients is covered in Yee et al. (2002). Chintalapati et al. (1997) provide an adaptive location management algorithm. Jensen et al. (2001) discuss data management issues as they pertain to location-based services. Wolfson (2001) describes a novel way of efficiently modeling object mobility by describing position using trajectories instead of points. For an initial discussion of the ISDB scalability issues and an approach by aggregation of data and grouping of clients, see Mahajan et al. (1998). Specific aggregation algorithms for grouping data at the server in ISDB applications are described in Yee et al. (2001). Gray et al. (1993) discuss ISDB update conflicts and resolution techniques under various ISDB architectures. Breibart et al. (1999) go into further detail about deferred synchronization algorithms for replicated data.

18.2   MULTIMEDIA DATABASES

In the years ahead multimedia information systems are expected to dominate our daily lives. Our houses will be wired for bandwidth to handle interactive multimedia applications. Our high-definition TV/computer workstations will have access to a large number of databases, including digital libraries, image and video databases that will distribute vast amounts of multisource multimedia content.

18.2.1   The Nature of Multimedia Data and Applications

In Section 13.3 we discussed the advanced modeling issues related to multimedia data. DBMSs have been constantly adding to the types of data they support. Today the following types of multimedia data are available in current systems:

- *Text:* May be formatted or unformatted. For ease of parsing structured documents, standards like SGML and variations such as HTML are being used.

- *Graphics:* Examples include drawings and illustrations that are encoded using some descriptive standards (e.g., CGM, PICT, postscript).

- *Images:* Includes drawings, photographs, and so forth, encoded in standard formats such as bitmap, JPEG, and MPEG. Compression is built into JPEG and MPEG. These images are not subdivided into components. Hence querying them by content (e.g., find all images containing circles) is nontrivial.

- *Animations:* Temporal sequences of image or graphic data.

- *Video:* A set of temporally sequenced photographic data for presentation at specified rates—for example, 30 frames per second.

- *Structured audio:* A sequence of audio components comprising note, tone, duration, and so forth.

- *Audio:* Sample data generated from aural recordings in a string of bits in digitized form. Analog recordings are typically converted into digital form before storage.

- *Composite or mixed multimedia data:* A combination of multimedia data types such as audio and video which may be physically mixed to yield a new storage format or logically mixed while retaining original types and formats. Composite data also contains additional control information describing how the information should be rendered.

Nature of Multimedia Applications.   Multimedia data may be stored, delivered, and utilized in many different ways. Applications may be categorized based on their data management characteristics as follows:

- *Repository applications:* A large amount of multimedia data as well as metadata is stored for retrieval purposes. A central repository containing multimedia data may be maintained by a DBMS and may be organized into a hierarchy of storage levels—local disks, tertiary disks and tapes, optical disks, and so on. Examples include repositories of satellite images, engineering drawings and designs, space photographs, and radiology scanned pictures.

- *Presentation applications:* A large number of applications involve delivery of multimedia data subject to temporal constraints. Audio and video data are delivered this way; in these applications optimal viewing or listening conditions require the DBMS to deliver data at certain rates offering "quality of service" above a certain threshold. Data is consumed as it is delivered, unlike in repository applications, where it may be processed later (e.g., multimedia electronic mail). Simple multimedia viewing of video data, for example, requires a system to simulate VCR-like functionality. Complex and interactive multimedia presentations involve orchestration directions to control the retrieval order of components in a series or in parallel. Interactive environments must support capabilities such as real-time editing analysis or annotating of video and audio data.

- *Collaborative work using multimedia information:* This is a new category of applications in which engineers may execute a complex design task by merging drawings, fitting subjects to design constraints, and generating new documentation, change notifications, and so forth. Intelligent healthcare networks as well as telemedicine will involve doctors collaborating among themselves, analyzing multimedia patient data and information in real time as it is generated.

All of these application areas present major challenges for the design of multimedia database systems.

18.2.2 Data Management Issues

Multimedia applications dealing with thousands of images, documents, audio and video segments, and free text data depend critically on appropriate modeling of the structure and content of data and then designing appropriate database schemas for storing and retrieving multimedia information. Multimedia information systems are very complex and embrace a large set of issues, including the following:

- *Modeling:* This area has the potential for applying database versus information retrieval techniques to the problem. There are problems of dealing with complex objects made up of a wide range of types of data: numeric, text, graphic (computer- generated image), animated graphic image, audio stream, and video sequence. Documents constitute a specialized area and deserve special consideration.

- *Design:* The conceptual, logical, and physical design of multimedia databases has not been addressed fully, and it remains an area of active research. The design process can be based on the general methodology but the performance and tuning issues at each level are far more complex.

- *Storage:* Storage of multimedia data on standard disklike devices presents problems of representation, compression, mapping to device hierarchies, archiving, and buffering during the input/output operation. Adhering to standards such as JPEG or MPEG is one way most vendors of multimedia products are likely to deal with this issue. In DBMSs, a "BLOB" (Binary Large Object) facility allows untyped bitmaps to be stored and retrieved. Standardized software will be required to deal with synchronization and compression/decompression, and will be coupled with indexing problems, which are still in the research domain.

- *Queries and retrieval:* The "database" way of retrieving information is based on query languages and internal index structures. The "information retrieval" way relies strictly on keywords or predefined index terms. For images, video data, and audio data, this opens up many issues, among them efficient query formulation, query execution, and optimization. The standard optimization techniques need to be modified to work with multimedia data types.

- *Performance:* For multimedia applications involving only documents and text, performance constraints are subjectively determined by the user. For applications involving video playback or audio-video synchronization, physical limitations dominate. For instance, video must be delivered at a steady rate of 60 frames per second. Techniques for query optimization may compute expected response time before evaluating the query. The use of parallel processing of data may alleviate some problems, but such efforts are currently subject to further experimentation.

Such issues have given rise to a variety of open research problems. We look at a few representative problems now.

18.2.3   Open Research Problems

Information Retrieval Perspective in Querying Mutimedia Databases.   Modeling data content has not been an issue in database models and systems because the data has a rigid structure and the meaning of a data instance can be inferred from the schema. In contrast, information retrieval (IR) is mainly concerned with modeling the content of text documents (through the use of keywords, phrasal indexes, semantic networks, word frequencies, soundex encoding, and so on) for which structure is generally neglected. By modeling content, the system can determine whether a document is relevant to a query by examining the content-descriptors of the document. Consider, for instance, an insurance company's accident claim report as a multimedia object: it includes images of the accident, structured insurance forms, audio recordings of the parties involved in the accident, the text report of the insurance company's representative, and other information. Which data model should be used to represent multimedia information such as this? How should queries be formulated against this data? Efficient execution thus becomes a complex issue, and the semantic heterogeneity and representational complexity of multimedia information gives rise to many new problems.

Requirements of Multimedia/Hypermedia Data Modeling and Retrieval.   To capture the full expressive power of multimedia data modeling, the system should have a general construct that lets the user specify links between any two arbitrary nodes. **Hypermedia links,** or hyperlinks, have a number of different characteristics:

- Links can be specified with or without associated information, and they may have large descriptions associated with them.

- Links can start from a specific point within a node or from the whole node.

- Links can be directional or nondirectional when they can be traversed in either direction.

The link capability of the data model should take into account all of these variations. When content-based retrieval of multimedia data is needed, the query mechanism should have access to the links and the link-associated information. The system should provide facilities for defining views over all links—private and public. Valuable contextual information can be obtained from the structural information. Automatically generated hypermedia links do not reveal anything new about the two nodes, and in contrast to manually generated hypermedia links, would have different significance. Facilities for creating and utilizing such links, as well as developing and using navigational query languages to utilize the links, are important features of any system permitting effective use of multimedia information. This area is important to interlinked databases on the WWW.

The World Wide Web presents an opportunity to access a vast amount of information via an array of unstructured and structured databases that are interlinked. The phenomenal success and growth of the web has made the problem of finding, accessing, and maintaining this information extremely challenging. For the last few years several projects are attempting to define frameworks and languages that will allow us to define the semantic content of the web that will be machine processable. The effort is collectively known by the term **semantic web.** The RDF (resource description framework), XHTML (Extensible Hypertext Markup

Language), DAML (DARPA Agent Markup Language), and OIL (Ontology Inference Layer) are among some of its major components.[4] Further details are outside the scope of our discussion.

Indexing of Images.   There are two approaches to indexing images: (1) identifying objects automatically through image-processing techniques, and (2) assigning index terms and phrases through manual indexing. An important problem in using image-processing techniques to index pictures relates to scalability. The current state of the art allows the indexing of only simple patterns in images. Complexity increases with the number of recognizable features. Another important problem relates to the complexity of the query. Rules and inference mechanisms can be used to derive higher-level facts from simple features of images. Similarly, abstraction can be used to capture concepts that are not simply possible to define in terms of a set of <attribute, value> pairs. This allows high-level queries like "find hotel buildings that have open foyers and allow maximum sunshine in the front desk area" in an architectural application.

The information-retrieval approach to image indexing is based on one of three indexing schemes:

1. *Classificatory systems:* Classifies images hierarchically into predetermined categories. In this approach, the indexer and the user should have a good knowledge of the available categories. Finer details of a complex image and relationships among objects in an image cannot be captured.

2. *Keyword-based systems:* Uses an indexing vocabulary similar to that used in the indexing of textual documents. Simple facts represented in the image (like "icecapped region") and facts derived as a result of high-level interpretation by humans (like permanent ice, recent snowfall, and polar ice) can be captured.

3. *Entity-attribute-relationship systems:* All objects in the picture and the relationships between objects and the attributes of the objects are identified.

In the case of text documents, an indexer can choose the keywords from the pool of words available in the document to be indexed. This is not possible in the case of visual and video data.

Problems in Text Retrieval.   Text retrieval has always been the key feature in business applications and library systems, and although much work has gone into some of the following problems, there remains an ongoing need for improvement, especially regarding the following issues:

- *Phrase indexing:* Substantial improvements can be realized if phrase descriptors (as opposed to single-word index terms) are assigned to documents and used in queries, provided that these descriptors are good indicators of document content and information need.

- *Use of thesaurus:* One reason for the poor recall of current systems is that the vocabulary of the user differs from the vocabulary used to index the documents. One solution is to use a thesaurus to expand the user's query with related terms. The problem then becomes one of finding a thesaurus for the domain of interest. Another resource in this context is **ontologies**. An ontology necessarily entails or embodies some sort of world view with respect to a given domain. The world view is often conceived as a set of concepts (e.g. entities, attributes, process), their definitions and their interrelationships which describe a target world. An ontology can be constructed in two ways, domain dependent and generic. The purpose of generic ontologies is to make a general framework for all (or most) categories encountered by human existence. A variety of domain ontologies such as gene ontology (see Section 18.4) or ontology for electronic components have been constructed.[5]

---

4. See Fensel (2000) for an overview of these terms.

5. A good discussion of ontologies is given in Uschold and Gruninger (1996).

- *Resolving ambiguity:* One of the reasons for low precision (the ratio of the number of relevant items retrieved to the total number of retrieved items) in text information retrieval systems is that words have multiple meanings. One way to resolve ambiguity is to use an online dictionary or ontology; another is to compare the contexts in which the two words occur.

In the first three decades of DBMS development—roughly from 1965 to 1995—the primary focus had been on the management of mostly numeric business and industrial data. In the next few decades, nonnumeric textual information will probably dominate database content. The text retrieval problem is becoming very relevant in the context of HTML and XML documents. The web currently contains several billion of these pages. Search engines find relevant documents given lists of words which is a case of free form natural language query. Obtaining the corrrect result that meets the requirements of both precision (% of retrieved documents that are relevant) and recall (% of total relevant documents that are retrieved), which are standard metrics in information retrieval, remains a challenge. As a consequence, a variety of functionalities involving comparison, conceptualization, understanding, indexing, and summarization of documents will be added to DBMSs. Multimedia information systems promise to bring about a joining of disciplines that have historically been separate areas: information retrieval and database management.

18.2.4   Multimedia Database Applications

Large-scale applications of multimedia databases can be expected to encompass a large number of disciplines and enhance existing capabilities. Some important applications will be involved:

- *Documents and records management:* A large number of industries and businesses keep very detailed records and a variety of documents. The data may include engineering design and manufacturing data, medical records of patients, publishing material, and insurance claim records.

- *Knowledge dissemination:* The multimedia mode, a very effective means of knowledge dissemination, will encompass a phenomenal growth in electronic books, catalogs, manuals, encyclopedias and repositories of information on many topics.

- *Education and training:* Teaching materials for different audiences—from kindergarten students to equipment operators to professionals—can be designed from multimedia sources. Digital libraries are expected to have a major influence on the way future students and researchers as well as other users will access vast repositories of educational material.

- *Marketing, advertising, retailing, entertainment, and travel:* There are virtually no limits to using multimedia information in these applications—from effective sales presentations to virtual tours of cities and art galleries. The film industry has already shown the power of special effects in creating animations and synthetically designed animals, aliens, and special effects. The use of predesigned stored objects in multimedia databases will expand the range of these applications.

- *Real-time control and monitoring:* Coupled with active database technology (see Chapter 13), multimedia presentation of information can be a very effective means for monitoring and controlling complex tasks such as manufacturing operations, nuclear power plants, patients in intensive care units, and transportation systems.

Commercial Systems for Multimedia Information Management.   There are no DBMSs designed for the sole purpose of multimedia data management, and therefore there are none that have the range of functionality required to fully support all of the multimedia information management applications that we discussed above. However, several DBMSs today support multimedia data types; these include Informix

Dynamic Server, DB2 Universal database (UDB) of IBM, Oracle 9 and 10, CA- JASMINE, Sybase, ODB II. All of these DBMSs have support for objects, which is essential for modeling a variety of complex multimedia objects. One major problem with these systems is that the "blades, cartridges, and extenders" for handling multimedia data are designed in a very ad hoc manner. The functionality is provided without much apparent attention to scalability and performance. There are products available that operate either stand-alone or in conjunction with other vendors' systems to allow retrieval of image data by content. They include Virage, Excalibur, and IBM's QBIC. Operations on multimedia need to be standardized. The MPEG-7 and other standards are addressing some of these issues.

18.2.5 Selected Bibliography on Multimedia Databases

Multimedia database management is becoming a very heavily researched area with several industrial projects on the way. Grosky (1994, 1997) provides two excellent tutorials on the topic. Pazandak and Srivastava (1995) provide an evaluation of database systems related to the requirements of multimedia databases. Grosky et al. (1997) contains contributed articles including a survey on content-based indexing and retrieval by Jagadish (1997). Faloutsos et al. (1994) also discuss a system for image querying by content. Li et al. (1998) introduce image modeling in which an image is viewed as a hierarchical structured complex object with both semantics and visual properties. Nwosu et al. (1996) and Subramanian and Jajodia (1997) have written books on the topic. Lassila (1998) discusses the need for metadata for accessing mutimedia information on the web; the semantic web effort is summarized in Fensel (2000). Khan (2000) did a dissertation on ontology-based information retrieval. Uschold and Gruninger (1996) is a good resource on ontologies Corcho et al. (2003) compare ontology languages and discuss methodologies to build ontologies. Multimedia content analysis, indexing, and filtering are discussed in Dimitrova (1999). A survey of content-based multimedia retrieval is provided by Yoshitaka and Ichikawa (1999). The following WWW references may be consulted for additional information:

CA- JASMINE (Multimedia ODBMS): http://www.cai.com/products/jasmine.htm

Excalibur technologies: http://www.excalib.com

Virage, Inc (Content based image retrieval): http://www.virage.com

IBM's QBIC (Query by Image Content) product: http://qbic.almaden.ibm.com

18.3 GEOGRAPHIC INFORMATION SYSTEMS

Geographic information systems (GIS) are used to collect, model, store, and analyze information describing physical properties of the geographical world. The scope of GIS broadly encompasses two types of data: (1) spatial data, originating from maps, digital images, administrative and political boundaries, roads, transportation networks; physical data such as rivers, soil characteristics, climatic regions, land elevations, and (2) nonspatial data, such as socio-economic data (like census counts), economic data, and sales or marketing information. GIS is a rapidly developing domain that offers highly innovative approaches to meet some challenging technical demands.

18.3.1 GIS Applications

It is possible to divide GISs into three categories: (1) cartographic applications, (2) digital terrain modeling applications, and (3) geographic objects applications. Figure 18.3 summarizes these categories.

In cartographic and terrain modeling applications, variations in spatial attributes are captured—for example, soil characteristics, crop density, and air quality. In geographic objects applications, objects of interest are identified from a physical domain—for example, power plants, electoral districts, property parcels, product distribution districts, and city landmarks. These objects are related with pertinent application data—which may be, for this specific example, power consumption, voting patterns, property sales volumes, product sales volume, and traffic density.

The first two categories of GIS applications require a field-based representation, whereas the third category requires an object-based one. The cartographic approach involves special functions that can include the overlapping of layers of maps to combine attribute data that will allow, for example, the measuring of distances in three-dimensional space and the reclassification of data on the map. Digital terrain modeling requires a digital representation of parts of earth's surface using land elevations at sample points that are connected to yield a surface model such as a three-dimensional net (connected lines in 3D) showing the surface terrain. It requires functions of interpolation between observed points as well as visualization. In object-based geographic applications, additional spatial functions are needed to deal with data related to roads, physical pipelines, communication cables, power lines, and such. For example, for a given region, comparable maps can be used for comparison at various points of time to show changes in certain data such as locations of roads, cables, buildings, and streams.

FIGURE 18.3 A possible classification of GIS applications (Adapted from Adam and Gangopadhyay (1997))

18.3.2   Data Management Requirements of GIS

The functional requirements of the GIS applications above translate into the following database requirements.

Data Modeling and Representation. GIS data can be broadly represented in two formats: (1) vector and (2) raster. Vector data represents geometric objects such as points, lines, and polygons. Thus a lake may be represented as a polygon, a river by a series of line segments. Raster data is characterized as an array of points, where each point represents the value of an attribute for a real-world location. Informally, raster images are n-dimensional arrays where each entry is a unit of the image and represents an attribute. Two-dimensional units are called *pixels*, while three-dimensional units are called *voxels*. Three-dimensional elevation data is stored in a raster-based **digital elevation model** (DEM) format. Another raster format called **triangular irregular network (**TIN) is a topological vector-based approach that models surfaces by connecting sample points as vertices of triangles and has a point density that may vary with the roughness of the terrain. Rectangular grids (or elevation matrices) are two-dimensional array structures. In **digital terrain modeling** (DTM), the model also may be used by substituting the elevation with some attribute of interest such as population density or air temperature. GIS data often includes a temporal structure in addition to a spatial structure. For example, traffic flow or average vehicular speeds in traffic may be measured every 60 seconds at a set of points in a roadway network.

Data Analysis. GIS data undergoes various types of analysis. For example, in applications such as soil erosion studies, environmental impact studies, or hydrological runoff simulations, DTM data may undergo various types of **geomorphometric analysis**—measurements such as slope values, *gradients* (the rate of change in altitude), *aspect* (the compass direction of the gradient), *profile convexity* (the rate of change of gradient), *plan convexity* (the convexity of contours and other parameters). When GIS data is used for decision support applications, it may undergo aggregation and expansion operations using data warehousing, as we discussed in Section 17.3. In addition, geometric operations (to compute distances, areas, volumes), topological operations (to compute overlaps, intersections, shortest paths), and temporal operations (to compute internal-based or event-based queries) are involved. Analysis involves a number of temporal and spatial operations, which were discussed in Chapter 13.

Data Integration. GISs must integrate both vector and raster data from a variety of sources. Sometimes edges and regions are inferred from a raster image to form a vector model, or conversely, raster images such as aerial photographs are used to update vector models. Several coordinate systems such as Universal Transverse Mercator (UTM), latitude/longitude, and local cadastral systems are used to identify locations. Data originating from different coordinate systems requires appropriate transformations. Major public sources of geographic data, including the TIGER files maintained by U.S. Department of Commerce, are used for road maps by many Web-based map drawing tools (e.g., http:// maps.yahoo.com). Often there are high-accuracy, attribute-poor maps that have to be merged with low-accuracy, attribute-rich maps. This is done with a process called "rubber-banding" where the user defines a set of control points in both maps and the transformation of the low accuracy map is accomplished by lining up the control points. A major integration issue is to create and maintain attribute information (such as air quality or traffic flow), which can be related to and integrated with appropriate geographical information over time as both evolve.

Data Capture. The first step in developing a spatial database for cartographic modeling is to capture the two-dimensional or three-dimensional geographical information in digital form—a process that is sometimes impeded by source map characteristics such as resolution, type of projection, map scales, cartographic licensing, diversity of measurement techniques, and coordinate system differences. Spatial data can also be captured from remote sensors in satellites such as Landsat, NORA, and Advanced Very High Resolution Radiometer (AVHRR) as well as SPOT HRV (High Resolution Visible Range Instrument), which is free of interpretive bias and very accurate. For digital terrain modeling, data capture methods range from manual to fully automated. Ground surveys are the traditional approach and the most accurate, but they are very time consuming. Other techniques include photogrammetric sampling and digitizing cartographic documents.

18.3.3   Specific GIS Data Operations

GIS applications are conducted through the use of special operators such as the following:

1. *Interpolation:* This process derives elevation data for points at which no samples have been taken. It includes computation at single points, computation for a rectangular grid or along a contour, and so forth. Most interpolation methods are based on triangulation that uses the TIN method for interpolating elevations inside the triangle based on those of its vertices.

2. *Interpretation:* Digital terrain modeling involves the interpretation of operations on terrain data such as editing, smoothing, reducing details, and enhancing. Additional operations involve patching or zipping the borders of triangles (in TIN data), and merging, which implies combining overlapping models and resolving conflicts among attribute data. Conversions among grid models, contour models, and TIN data are involved in the interpretation of the terrain.

3. *Proximity analysis:* Several classes of proximity analysis include computations of "zones of interest" around objects, such as the determination of a buffer around a car on a highway. Shortest path algorithms using 2D or 3D information is an important class of proximity analysis.

4. *Raster image processing:* This process can be divided into two categories: (1) map algebra, which is used to integrate geographic features on different map layers to produce new maps algebraically; and (2) digital image analysis, which deals with analysis of a digital image for features such as edge detection and object detection. Detecting roads in a satellite image of a city is an example of the latter.

5. *Analysis of networks:* Networks occur in GIS in many contexts that must be analyzed and may be subjected to segmentations, overlays, and so on. Network overlay refers to a type of spatial join where a given network—for example, a highway network—is joined with a point database—for example, incident locations—to yield, in this case, a profile of high-incident roadways.

Other Database Functionality.   The functionality of a GIS database is also subject to other considerations.

- *Extensibility:* GISs are required to be extensible to accommodate a variety of constantly evolving applications and corresponding data types. If a standard DBMS is used, it must allow a core set of data types with a provision for defining additional types and methods for those types.

- *Data quality control:* As in many other applications, quality of source data is of paramount importance for providing accurate results to queries. This problem is particularly significant in the GIS context because of the variety of data, sources, and measurement techniques involved and the absolute accuracy expected by applications users.

6. *Visualization:* A crucial function in GIS is related to visualization—the graphical display of terrain information and the appropriate representation of application attributes to go with it. Major visualization techniques include (1) *contouring* through the use of *isolines,* spatial units of lines or arcs of equal attribute values; (2) *hillshading,* an illumination method used for qualitative relief depiction using varied light intensities for individual facets of the terrain model; and (3) *perspective displays,* three-dimensional images of terrain model facets using perspective projection methods from computer graphics. These techniques impose cartographic data and other three-dimensional objects on terrain data providing animated scene renderings such as those in flight simulations and animated movies.

Such requirements clearly illustrate that standard RDBMSs or ODBMSs do not meet the special needs of GIS. It is therefore necessary to design systems that support the vector and raster representations and the spatial functionality as well as the required DBMS features. A popular GIS software called ARC-INFO, which is *not* a DBMS but integrates RDBMS functionality in the INFO part of the system, is briefly discussed in the subsection that follows. More systems are likely to be designed in the future to work with relational or object databases that will contain some of the spatial and most of the nonspatial information.

18.3.4 An Example of a GIS Software: ARC-INFO

ARC/INFO—a popular GIS software launched in 1981 by Environmental System Research Institute (ESRI)—uses the arc node model to store spatial data. A geographic layer—called *coverage* in ARC/INFO—consists of three primitives: (1) nodes (points), (2) arcs (similar to lines), and (3) polygons. The arc is the most important of the three and stores a large amount of topological information. An arc has a start node and an end node (and it therefore has direction too). In addition, the polygons to the left and the right of the arc are also stored along with each arc. As there is no restriction on the shape of the arc, shape points that have no topological information are also stored along with each arc. The database managed by the INFO RDBMS thus consists of three required tables: (1) node attribute table (NAT), (2) arc attribute table (AAT), and (3) polygon attribute table (PAT). Additional information can be stored in separate tables and joined with any of these three tables.

The NAT contains an internal ID for the node, a user-specified ID, the coordinates of the node, and any other information associated with that node (e.g., names of the intersecting roads at the node). The AAT contains an internal ID for the arc, a user-specified ID, the internal ID of the start and end nodes, the internal ID of the polygons to the left and the right, a series of coordinates of shape points (if any), the length of the arc, and any other data associated with the arc (e.g., the name of the road the arc represents). The PAT contains an internal ID for the polygon, a user-specified ID, the area of the polygon, the perimeter of the polygon, and any other associated data (e.g., name of the county the polygon represents).

Typical spatial queries are related to adjacency, containment, and connectivity. The arc node model has enough information to satisfy all three types of queries, but the RDBMS is not ideally suited for this type of querying. A simple example will highlight the number of times a relational database has to be queried to extract adjacency information. Assume that we are trying to determine whether two polygons, A and B, are adjacent to each other. We would have to exhaustively look at the entire AAT to determine whether there is an edge that has A on one side and B on the other. The search cannot be limited to the edges of either polygon as we do not explicitly store all the arcs that make a polygon in the PAT. Storing all the arcs in the PAT would be redundant because all the information is already there in the AAT.

ESRI has released Arc/Storm (Arc Store Manager) which allows multiple users to use the same GIS, handles distributed databases, and integrates with other commercial RDBMSs like ORACLE, INFORMIX, and SYBASE. While it offers many performance and functional advantages over ARC/INFO, it is essentially an RDBMS embedded within a GIS.

18.3.5 Problems and Future Issues in GIS

GIS is an expanding application area of databases, reflecting an explosion in the number of end users using digitized maps, terrain data, space images, weather data, and traffic information support data. As a consequence, an increasing number of problems related to GIS applications has been generated and will need to be solved:

1. *New architectures:* GIS applications will need a new client-server architecture that will benefit from existing advances in RDBMS and ODBMS technology. One possible solution is to separate spatial from nonspatial data and to manage the latter entirely by a DBMS. Such a process calls for appropriate modeling and integration as both types of data evolve. Commercial vendors find that it is more viable to keep a small number of independent databases with an automatic posting of updates across them. Appropriate tools for data transfer, change management, and workflow management will be required.

2. *Versioning and object life-cycle approach:* Because of constantly evolving geographical features, GISs must maintain elaborate cartographic and terrain data—a management problem that might be eased by incremental updating coupled with update authorization schemes for different levels of users. Under

the object life-cycle approach, which covers the activities of creating, destroying, and modifying objects as well as promoting versions into permanent objects, a complete set of methods may be predefined to control these activities for GIS objects.

3. *Data standards:* Because of the diversity of representation schemes and models, formalization of data transfer standards is crucial for the success of GIS. The international standardization body (ISO TC211) and the European standards body (CEN TC278) are now in the process of debating relevant issues— among them conversion between vector and raster data for fast query performance.

4. *Matching applications and data structures:* Looking again at Figure 16.5, we see that a classification of GIS applications is based on the nature and organization of data. In the future, systems covering a wide range of functions—from market analysis and utilities to car navigation—will need boundary-oriented data and functionality. On the other hand, applications in environmental science, hydrology, and agriculture will require more area-oriented and terrain model data. It is not clear that all this functionality can be supported by a single general-purpose GIS. The specialized needs of GISs will require that general purpose DBMSs must be enhanced with additional data types and functionality before full-fledged GIS applications can be supported.

5. *Lack of semantics in data structures:* This is evident especially in maps. Information such as highway and road crossings may be difficult to determine based on the stored data. One-way streets are also hard to represent in the present GISs. Transportation CAD systems have incorporated such semantics into GIS.

18.3.6   Selected Bibliography for GIS

There are a number of books written on GIS. Adam and Gangopadhyay (1997) and Laurini and Thompson (1992) focus on GIS database and information management problems. Kemp (1993) gives an overview of GIS issues and data sources. Huxhold (1991) gives an introduction to Urban GIS. Maguire et al. (1991) have a very good collection of GIS-related papers. Antenucci (1998) presents a discussion of the GIS technologies. Shekhar and Chawla (2002) discusses issues and approaches to spatial data management which is at the core of all GIS. Demers (2002) is another recent book on the fundamentals of GIS. Bossomaier and Green (2002) is a primer on GIS operations, languages, metadata paradigms and standards. Peng and Tsou (2003) discusses Internet GIS which includes a suite of emerging new technologies aimed at making GIS more mobile, powerful, and flexible, as well as better able to share and communicate geographic information. The TIGER files for road data in the United States are managed by the U.S. Department of Commerce (1993). Laser-Scan's Web site (http://www.lsl.co.uk/papers) is a good source of information.

Environmental System Research Institute (ESRI) has an excellent library of GIS books for all levels at http://www.esri.com. The GIS terminology is defined at http:// www.esri.com/library/glossary/glossary.html. The university of Edinburgh maintains a GIS WWW resource list at http://www.geo.ed.ac.uk/home/giswww.html

18.4   GENOME DATA MANAGEMENT

18.4.1   Biological Sciences and Genetics

The biological sciences encompass an enormous variety of information. Environmental science gives us a view of how species live and interact in a world filled with natural phenomena. Biology and ecology study particular species. Anatomy focuses on the overall structure of an organism, documenting the physical aspects of individual bodies. Traditional medicine and physiology break the organism into systems and tissues and strive to collect information on the workings of these systems and the organism as a whole. Histology and cell biology delve into the tissue and cellular levels and provide knowledge about the inner structure and function of the cell. This wealth of information that has been generated, classified, and stored for centuries has only recently become a major application of database technology.

Genetics has emerged as an ideal field for the application of information technology. In a broad sense, it can be thought of as the construction of models based on information about genes—which can be defined as basic units of heredity—and populations and the seeking out of relationships in that information. The study of genetics can be divided into three branches: (1) Mendelian genetics, (2) molecular genetics, and (3) population genetics. Mendelian genetics is the study of the transmission of traits between generations. Molecular genetics is the study of the chemical structure and function of genes at the molecular level. Population genetics is the study of how genetic information varies across populations of organisms.

Molecular genetics provides a more detailed look at genetic information by allowing researchers to examine the composition, structure, and function of genes. The origins of molecular genetics can be traced to two important discoveries. The first occurred in 1869 when Friedrich Miescher discovered nuclein and its primary component, deoxyribonucleic acid (DNA). In subsequent research DNA and a related compound, ribonucleic acid (RNA), were found to be composed of nucleotides (a sugar, a phosphate, and a base, which combined to form nucleic acid) linked into long polymers via the sugar and phosphate. The second discovery was the demonstration in 1944 by Oswald Avery that DNA was indeed the molecular substance carrying genetic information. Genes were thus shown to be composed of chains of nucleic acids arranged linearly on chromosomes and to serve three primary functions: (1) replicating genetic information between generations, (2) providing blueprints for the creation of polypeptides, and (3) accumulating changes—thereby allowing evolution to occur. Waston and Crick found the double-helix structure of the DNA in 1953, which gave molecular genetics research a new direction.[6] Discovery of the DNA and its structure is hailed as probably the most important biological work of the last 100 years, and the field it opened may be the scientific frontier for the next 100. In 1962, Watson, Crick, and Wilkins won the Nobel Prize for physiology/medicine for this breakthrough.[7]

18.4.2 Characteristics of Biological Data

Biological data exhibits many special characteristics that make management of biological information a particularly challenging problem. We will thus begin by summarizing the characteristics related to biological information, and focusing on a multidisciplinary field called **bioinformatics** that has emerged, with graduate degree programs now in place in several universities. Bioinformatics addresses information management of genetic information with special emphasis on DNA sequence analysis. It needs to be broadened into a wider scope to harness all types of biological information—its modeling, storage, retrieval, and management. Moreover, applications of bioinformatics span design of targets for drugs, study of mutations and related diseases, anthropological investigations on migration patterns of tribes, and therapeutic treatments.

Characteristic 1: *Biological data is highly complex when compared with most other domains or applications.* Definitions of such data must thus be able to represent a complex substructure of data as well as relationships and to ensure that no information is lost during biological data modeling. The structure of biological data often provides an additional context for interpretation of the information. Biological information systems must be able to represent any level of complexity in any data schema, relationship, or schema substructure—

---

6. See Nature, 171:737 1953.

7. http://www.pbs.org/wgbh/aso/databank/entries/do53dn.html

not just hierarchical, binary, or table data. As an example, MITOMAP is a database documenting the human mitochondrial genome.[8] This single genome is a small, circular piece of DNA encompassing information about 16,569 nucleotide bases; 52 gene loci encoding messenger RNA, ribosomal RNA, and transfer RNA; 1000 known population variants; over 60 known disease associations; and a limited set of knowledge on the complex molecular interactions of the biochemical energy producing pathway of oxidative phosphorylation. As might be expected, its management has encountered a large number of problems; we have been unable to use the traditional RDBMS or ODBMS approches to capture all aspects of the data.

Characteristic 2: *The amount and range of variability in data is high.* Hence, biological systems must be flexible in handling data types and values. With such a wide range of possible data values, placing constraints on data types must be limited since this may exclude unexpected values—e.g., outlier values—that are particularly common in the biological domain. Exclusion of such values results in a loss of information. In addition, frequent exceptions to biological data structures may require a choice of data types to be available for a given piece of data.

Characteristic 3: *Schemas in biological databases change at a rapid pace.* Hence, for improved information flow between generations or releases of databases, schema evolution and data object migration must be supported. The ability to extend the schema, a frequent occurrence in the biological setting, is unsupported in most relational and object database systems. Presently systems such as GenBank rerelease the entire database with new schemas once or twice a year rather than incrementally changing the system as changes become necessary. Such an evolutionary database would provide a timely and orderly mechanism for following changes to individual data entities in biological databases over time. This sort of tracking is important for biological researchers to be able to access and reproduce previous results.

Characteristic 4: *Representations of the same data by different biologists will likely be different (even when using the same system).* Hence, mechanisms for "aligning" different biological schemas or different versions of schemas should be supported. Given the complexity of biological data, there are a multitude of ways of modeling any given entity, with the results often reflecting the particular focus of the scientist. While two individuals may produce different data models if asked to interpret the same entity, these models will likely have numerous points in common. In such situations, it would be useful to biological investigators to be able to run queries across these common points. By linking data elements in a network of schemas, this could be accomplished.

Characteristic 5: *Most users of biological data do not require write access to the database; read-only access is adequate.* Write access is limited to privileged users called *curators*. For example, the database created as part of the MITOMAP project has on average more than 15,000 users per month on the Internet. There are fewer than twenty noncurator generated submissions to MITOMAP every month. In other words, the number of users requiring write access is small. Users generate a wide variety of read-access patterns into the database, but these patterns are not the same as those seen in traditional relational databases. User requested ad hoc searches demand indexing of often unexpected combinations of data instance classes.

Characteristic 6: *Most biologists are not likely to have any knowledge of the internal structure of the database or about schema design.* Biological database interfaces should display information to users in a manner that is applicable to the problem they are trying to address and that reflects the underlying data structure. Biological users usually know which data they require, but they have no technical knowledge of the data structure or how a DBMS represents the data. They rely on technical users to provide them with views into the database. Relational schemas fail to provide cues or any intuitive information to the user regarding the meaning of their schema. Web interfaces in particular often provide preset search interfaces, which may limit access into the database. However, if these interfaces are generated directly from database structures, they are likely to produce a wider possible range of access, although they may not guarantee usability.

---

8. Details of MITOMAP and its information complexity can be seen in Kogelnik et al. (1997, 1998) and at http://www. mitomap.org.

Characteristic 7: *The context of data gives added meaning for its use in biological applications.* Hence, context must be maintained and conveyed to the user when appropriate. In addition, it should be possible to integrate as many contexts as possible to maximize the interpretation of a biological data value. Isolated values are of less use in biological systems. For example, the sequence of a DNA strand is not particularly useful without additional information describing its organization, function, and such. A single nucleotide on a DNA strand, for example, seen in context with nondisease-causing DNA strands, could be seen as a causative element for sickle cell anemia.

Characteristic 8: *Defining and representing complex queries is extremely important to the biologist.* Hence, biological systems must support complex queries. Without any knowledge of the data structure (see Characteristic 6), average users cannot construct a complex query across data sets on their own. Thus, in order to be truly useful, systems must provide some tools for building these queries. As mentioned previously, many systems provide predefined query templates.

Characteristic 9: *Users of biological information often require access to "old" values of the data—particularly when verifying previously reported results.* Hence, changes to the values of data in the database must be supported through a system of archives. Access to both the most recent version of a data value and its previous version are important in the biological domain. Investigators consistently want to query the most up-to-date data, but they must also be able to reconstruct previous work and reevaluate prior and current information. Consequently, values that are about to be updated in a biological database cannot simply be thrown away.

All of these characteristics clearly point to the fact that today's DBMSs do not fully cater to the requirements of complex biological data. A new direction in database management systems is necessary.[9]

18.4.3 The Human Genome Project and Existing Biological Databases

The term *genome* is defined as the total genetic information that can be obtained about an entity. The **human genome**, for example, generally refers to the complete set of genes required to create a human being— estimated to be more than 30,000 genes spread over 23 pairs of chromosomes, with an estimated 3 to 4 billion nucleotides. The goal of the Human Genome Project (HGP) has been to obtain the complete sequence—the ordering of the bases—of those nucleotides. A rough draft of entire human genome sequence was announced in June 2000 and the 13-year effort will end in year 2003 with the completion of the human genetic sequence. In isolation, the human DNA sequence is not particularly useful. The sequence can however be combined with other data and used as a powerful tool to help address questions in genetics, biochemistry, medicine, anthropology, and agriculture. In the existing genome databases, the focus has been on "curating" (or collecting with some initial scrutiny and quality check) and classifying information about genome sequence data. In addition to the human genome, numerous organisms such as *E.coli*, *Drosophila*, and *C.elegans* have been investigated. We will briefly discuss some of the existing database systems that are supporting or have grown out of the Human Genome Project.

GenBank. The preeminent DNA sequence database in the world today is GenBank, maintained by the National Center for Biotechnology Information (NCBI) of the National Library of Medicine (NLM). It was established in 1978 as a central repository for DNA sequence data. Since then it has expanded somewhat in scope to include expressed sequence tag data, protein sequence data, three-dimensional protein structure, taxonomy, and links to the biomedical literature (MEDLINE). As of release 135.0 in April 2003, GenBank contains over 31 billion nucleotide bases of more than 24 million sequences from over 100,000 species

---

9. See Kogelnik et al. (1997, 1998) for further details.

with roughly 1400 new organisms being added each month. The database size in flat file format is over 100 GB uncompressed and has been doubling every 15 months. Through international collaboration with the European Molecular Biology Laboratory(EMBL) in the U.K. and the DNA Data Bank of Japan (DDBJ), data are exchanged among the three sites on a daily basis. The mirroring of sequence data at the three sites affords fast access to this data to scientists in varous geographical parts of the world.

While it is a complex, comprehensive database, the scope of its coverage is focused on human sequences and links to the literature. Other limited data sources (e.g. three-dimensional structure and OMIM, discussed below), have been added recently by reformatting the existing OMIM and PDB databases and redesigning the structure of the GenBank system to accommodate these new data sets.

The system is maintained as a combination of flat files, relational databases, and files containing **Abstract Syntax Notation One** (ASN.1)—a syntax for defining data structures developed for the telecommunications industry. Each GenBank entry is assigned a unique identifier by the NCBI. Updates are assigned a new identifier, with the identifier of the original entity remaining unchanged for archival purposes. Older references to an entity thus do not inadvertently indicate a new and possibly inappropriate value. The most current concepts also receive a second set of unique identifiers (UIDs), which mark the most up-to-date form of a concept while allowing older versions to be accessed via their original identifier.

The average user of the database is not able to access the structure of the data directly for querying or other functions, although complete snapshots of the database are available for export in a number of formats, including ASN.1. The query mechanism provided is via the Entrez application (or its World Wide Web version), which allows keyword, sequence, and GenBank UID searching through a static interface.

The Genome Database (GDB). Created in 1989, the Genome Database (GDB) is a catalog of human gene mapping data, a process that associates a piece of information with a particular location on the human genome. The degree of precision of this location on the map depends upon the source of the data, but it is usually not at the level of individual nucleotide bases. GDB data includes data describing primarily map information (distance and confidence limits), and Polymerase Chain Reaction (PCR) probe data (experimental conditions, PCR primers, and reagents used). More recently efforts have been made to add data on mutations linked to genetic loci, cell lines used in experiments, DNA probe libraries, and some limited polymorphism and population data.

The GDB system is built around SYBASE, a commercial relational DBMS, and its data are modeled using standard Entity-Relationship techniques (see Chapter 3). The implementors of GDB have noted difficulties in using this model to capture more than simple map and probe data. In order to improve data integrity and to simplify the programming for application writers, GDB distributes a Database Access Toolkit. However, most users use a Web interface to search the ten interlinked data managers. Each manager keeps track of the links (relationships) for one of the ten tables within the GDB system. As with GenBank, users are given only a very high-level view of the data at the time of searching and thus cannot easily make use of any knowledge gleaned from the structure of the GDB tables. Search methods are most useful when users are simply looking for an index into map or probe data. Exploratory ad hoc searching of the database is not encouraged by present interfaces. Integration of the database structures of GDB and OMIM (see below) was never fully established.

Online Mendelian Inheritance in Man.   Online Mendelian Inheritance in Man (OMIM) is an electronic compendium of information on the genetic basis of human disease. Begun in hard-copy form by Victor McCusick in 1966 with 1500 entries, it was converted to a full-text electronic form between 1987 and 1989 by the GDB. In 1991 its administration was transferred from Johns Hopkins University to the NCBI, and the entire database was converted to NCBI's GenBank format. Today it contains more than 14,000 entries.

OMIM covers material on five disease areas based loosely on organs and systems. Any morphological, biochemical, behavioral, or other properties under study are referred to as **phenotype** of an individual (or a cell). Mendel realized that genes can exist in numerous different forms known as **alleles.** A **genotype** refers to the actual allelic composition of an individual.

The structure of the phenotype and genotype entries contains textual data loosely structured as general descriptions, nomenclature, modes of inheritance, variations, gene structure, mapping, and numerous lesser categories. The full-text entries were converted to an ASN.1 structured format when OMIM was transferred to the NCBI. This greatly improved the ability to link OMIM data to other databases and it also provided a rigorous structure for the data. However, the basic form of the database remained difficult to modify.

EcoCyc. The Encyclopedia of *Escherichia coli* Genes and Metabolism (EcoCyc) is a recent experiment in combining information about the genome and the metabolism of *E. coli* K-12. The database was created in 1996 as a collaboration between Stanford Research Institute and the Marine Biological Laboratory. It catalogs and describes the known genes of *E.coli*, the enzymes encoded by those genes, and the biochemical reactions catalyzed by each enzyme and their organization into metabolic pathways. In so doing, EcoCyc spans the sequence and function domains of genomic information. It contains 1283 compounds with 965 structures as well as lists of bonds and atoms, molecular weights, and empirical formulas. It contains 3038 biochemical reactions described using 269 data classes.

An object-oriented data model was first used to implement the system, with data stored on Ocelot, a frame knowledge representation system. EcoCyc data was arranged in a hierarchy of object classes based on the observations that (1) the properties of a reaction are independent of an enzyme that catalyzes it, and (2) an enzyme has a number of properties that are "logically distinct" from its reactions.

EcoCyc provides two methods of querying: (1) direct (via predefined queries) and (2) indirect (via hypertext navigation). Direct queries are performed using menus and dialogs that can initiate a large but finite set of queries. No navigation of the actual data structures is supported. In addition, no mechanism for evolving the schema is documented.

Table 18.1 summarizes the features of the major genome-related databases, as well as HGMDB and ACEDB databases. Some additional protein databases exist; they contain information about protein structures. Prominent protein databases include SWISSPROT at the University of Geneva, Protein Data Bank (PDB) at Brookhaven National Laboratory, and Protein Identification Resource (PIR) at National Biomedical Research Foundation.

Over the past ten years, there has been an increasing interest in the applications of databases in biology and medicine. GenBank, GDB, and OMIM have been created as central repositories of certain types of biological data but, while extremely useful, they do not yet cover the complete spectrum of the Human Genome Project data. However, efforts are under way around the world to design new tools and techniques that will alleviate the data management problem for the biological scientists and medical researchers.

Gene Ontology. We already explained the concept of ontologies in Section 18.2.3 in the context of modeling of multimedia information. Gene Ontology (GO) Consortium was formed in 1998 as a collaboration among three model organism databases: FlyBase, Mouse Genome Informatics (MGI) and Saccharomyces or yeast Genome Database (SGD). Its goal is to produce a structured, precisely defined, common, controlled vocabulary for describing the roles of genes and gene products in any organism. With the completion of genome sequencing of many species, it has been observed that a large fraction of genes among organisms display similarity in biological roles and biologists have acknowledge that there is likely to be a single limited universe of genes and proteins that are conserved in most or all living cells. On the other hand, genome data is increasing exponentially and there is no uniform way to interpret and conceptualize the shared biological elements. Gene Ontology makes possible the annotation of gene products using a common vocabulary based on their shared biological attributes and interoperability between genomic databases.

The GO Consortium has developed three ontologies: Molecular function, biological process, and cellular component, to describe attributes of genes, gene products or gene product groups. Molecular function is defined as the biochemical activity of a gene product. Biological process refers to a biological objective to which the gene or gene product contributes. Cellular component refers to the place in the cell where a gene product is active. Each ontology comprises a set of well-defined vocabularies of terms and relationships. The terms are organized in the form of directed acyclic graphs (DAGs), in which a term node may have multiple parents and multiple children. A child term can be an *instance of (is a)* or a *part of* its parent. In the latest release of the GO database, there are over 13,000 terms and more than 18,000 relationships between terms. The annotation of gene products is operated independently by each of the collaborating databases. A subset of the annotations is included in GO database, which contains over 1,386,000 gene products and 5,244,000 associations between gene products and GO terms.

TABLE 18.1 SUMMARY OF THE MAJOR GENOME-RELATED DATABASES

DATABASE NAME	MAJOR CONTENT	INITIAL TECHNOLOGY	CURRENT TECHNOLOGY	DB PROBLEM AREAS	PRIMARY DATA TYPES
Genbank	DNA/RNA sequence, protein	Text files	Flat-file/ASN.1	Schema browsing, schema evolution, linking to other dbs	Text, numeric, some complex types
OMIM	Disease phenotypes and genotypes, etc.	Index cards/text files	Flat-ile/ASN.1	Unstructured, free text entries linking to other dbs	Text
GDB	Genetic map linkage data	Flat file	Relational	Schema expansion/ evolution, complex objects, linking to other dbs	Text, numeric
ACEDB	Genetic map linkage data, sequence data (non-human)	OO	OO	Schema expansion/ evolution, linking to other dbs	Text, numeric
HGMDB	Sequence and sequence variants	Flat file— application specific	Flat-file— application specific	Schema expansion/ evolution, linking to other dbs	Text
EcoCyc	Biochemical reactions and pathways	OO	OO	Locked into class hierarchy, schema evolution	Complex types, text, numeric

The Gene Ontology was implemented using MySQL, an open source relational DBMS and a monthly database release is available in SQL and XML formats. A set of tools and libraries, written in C, Java, Perl and XML etc, is available for database access and development of applications. Web-based and stand-alone GO browsers are available from the GO consortium.

18.4.4   Selected Bibliography for Genome Databases

Bioinformatics has become a popular area of research in recent years and many workshops and conferences are being organized around this topic. Robbins (1993) gives a good overview while Frenkel (1991) surveys the human genome project with its special role in bioinformatics at large. Cutticchia et al. (1993), Benson et al. (2002), and Pearson et al. (1994) are references on GDB, GenBank, and OMIM. In an international collaboration among GeneBank (USA), DNA Data Bank of Japan (DDBJ) (http: // www.ddbj.nig.ac.jp/E-mail/ homology.html), and Euporean Molecular Biology Laborarory (EBML) (Stoesser G, 2003), data are exchanged amongst the collaborating databases on a daily basis to achieve optimal synchronization Wheeler et al. (2000) discuss the various tools that currently allow users access and analysis of the data available in the databases.

Wallace (1995) has been a pioneer in the mitochondrial genome research, which deals with a specific part of the human genome; the sequence and organizational details of this area appear in Anderson et al. (1981) Recent work in Kogelnik et al. (1997, 1998) and Kogelnik (1998) addresses the development of a generic solution to the data management problem in biological sciences by developing a prototype solution. Apweiler et al. (2003) review the core Bioinformatics resources maintained at the European Bioinformatics Institute (EBI) (such as Swiss-prot + TrEMBL) and summarize important issues of database management of such resources. They discuss three main types of databases: Sequence Databases such as DDBJ/EMBL/GENEBANK Nucleotide Sequence Database; Secondary Databases such as PROSITE, PRINTS and Pfam; and Integrated Databases such as InterPro, that integrates data from six major protein signature databases (Pfam, PRINTS, ProDom, PROSITE, SMART, and TIGRFAMs).

The European Bioinformatics Institute Macromolecular Structure Database (EMSD), which is a relational database (http://www.ebi.ac.uk/msd) (Boutselakis et al., 2003) is designed to be a single access point for protein and nucleic acid structures and related information. The database is derived from Protein Data Bank (PDB) entries. The search database contains an extensive set of derived properties, goodness-of-fit indicators, and links to other EBI databases including InterPro, GO, and SWISS-PROT, together with links to SCOP, CATH, PFAM and PROSITE. Karp (1996) discusses the problems of interlinking the variety of databases mentioned in this section. He defines two types of links: those that integrate the data and those that relate the data between databases. These were used to design the Ecocyc database.

Some of the important web links include the following: The Human Genome sequence information can be found at: http://www.ncbi.nlm.nih.gov/genome/seq/.

The MITOMAP database developed in Kogelnik (1998) can be accessed at http://www.mitomap.org/. The biggest protein database SWISS-PROT can be accessed from http://expasy.hcuge.ch/sprot/. The ACEDB database information is available at http://probe.nalusda.gov:8080/acedocs/.

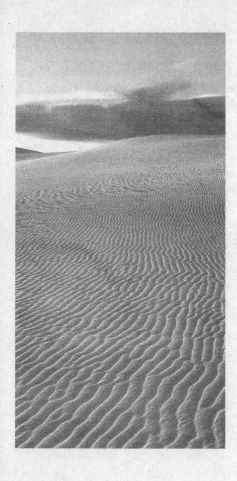

A

Alternative Diagrammatic Notations for ER Models

Figure A.1 shows a number of different diagrammatic notations for representing ER and EER model concepts. Unfortunately, there is no standard notation: different database design practitioners prefer different notations. Similarly, various **CASE** (computer-aided software engineering) tools and **OOA** (object-oriented analysis) methodologies use various notations. Some notations are associated with models that have additional concepts and constraints beyond those of the ER and EER models described in Chapter 3, while other models have fewer concepts and constraints. The notation we used in Chapter 3 is quite close to the original notation for ER diagrams, which is still widely used. We discuss some alternate notations here.

Figure A.1 (a) shows different notations for displaying entity types/classes, attributes, and relationships. In Chapter 3, we used the symbols marked (i) in Figure A.1 (a)—namely, rectangle, oval, and diamond. Notice that symbol (ii) for entity types/ classes, symbol (ii) for attributes, and symbol (ii) for relationships are similar, but they are used by different methodologies to represent three different concepts. The straight line symbol (iii) for representing relationships is used by several tools and methodologies.

Figure A. 1(b) shows some notations for attaching attributes to entity types. We used notation (i). Notation (ii) uses the third notation (iii) for attributes from Figure A.1 (a). The last two notations in Figure A.1 (b)—(iii) and (iv)—are popular in OOA methodologies and in some CASE tools. In particular, the last notation displays both the attributes and the methods of a class, separated by a horizontal line.

Figure A.1(c) shows various notations for representing the cardinality ratio of binary relationships. We used notation (i) in Chapter 3. Notation (ii)—known as the *chicken feet* notation—is quite popular. Notation (iv) uses the arrow as a functional reference (from the N to the 1 side) and resembles our notation for foreign keys in the relational model (see Figure 6.7); notation (v)—used in *Bachman diagrams*— uses the arrow in *the reverse direction* (from the 1 to the N side). For a 1:1 relationship, (ii) uses a straight line without any chicken feet; (iii) makes both halves of the diamond white; and (iv) places arrowheads on both sides. For an M:N relationship, (ii) uses chicken feet at both ends of the line; (iii) makes both halves of the diamond black; and (iv) does not display any arrowheads.

FIGURE A.1 Alternative notations. (a) Symbols for entity type/class, attribute, and relationship. (b) Displaying attributes. (c) Displaying cardinality ratios. (d) Various (min, max) notations. (e) Notations for displaying specialization/generalization.

Figure A.l (d) shows several variations for displaying (min, max) constraints, which are used to display both cardinality ratio and total/partial participation. Notation (ii) is the alternative notation we used in Figure 3.15 and discussed in Section 3.7.4. Recall that our notation specifies the constraint that each entity must participate in at least min and at most max relationship instances. Hence, for a 1:1 relationship, both max values are 1; and for M:N, both max values are n. A min value greater than 0 (zero) specifies total participation (existence dependency). In methodologies that use the straight line for displaying relationships, it is common to *reverse the positioning* of the (min, max) constraints, as shown in (iii). Another popular technique—which follows the same positioning as (iii)—is to display the *min* as o ("oh" or circle, which stands for zero) or as | (vertical dash, which stands for 1), and to display the max as | (vertical dash, which stands for 1) or as chicken feet (which stands for n), as shown in (iv).

Figure A.l (e) shows some notations for displaying specialization/generalization. We used notation (i) in Chapter 3, where a d in the circle specifies that the subclasses (S1, S2, and S3) are disjoint and an o specifies overlapping subclasses. Notation (ii) uses G (for generalization) to specify disjoint, and Gs to specify overlapping; some notations use the solid arrow, while others use the empty arrow (shown at the side). Notation (iii) uses a triangle pointing toward the superclass, and notation (v) uses a triangle pointing toward the subclasses; it is also possible to use both notations in the same methodology, with (iii) indicating generalization and (v) indicating specialization. Notation (iv) places the boxes representing subclasses within the box representing the superclass. Of the notations based on (vi), some use a single-lined arrow, and others use a double-lined arrow (shown at the side).

The notations shown in Figure A.1 show only some of the diagrammatic symbols that have been used or suggested for displaying database conceptual schemes. Other notations, as well as various combinations of the preceding, have also been used. It would be useful to establish a standard that everyone would adhere to, in order to prevent misunderstandings and reduce confusion.

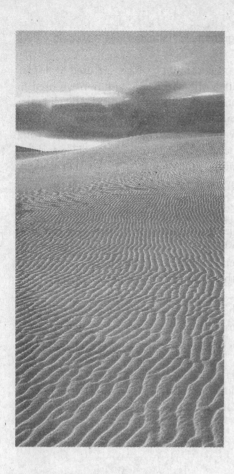

C

Parameters of Disks

The most important disk parameter is the time required to locate an arbitrary disk block, given its block address, and then to transfer the block between the disk and a main memory buffer. This is the **random access time** for accessing a disk block. There are three time components to consider:

1. **Seek time (s):** This is the time needed to mechanically position the read/write head on the correct track for movable-head disks. (For fixed-head disks, it is the time needed to electronically switch to the appropriate read/write head.) For movable head disks this time varies, depending on the distance between the current track under the read/write head and the track specified in the block address. Usually, the disk manufacturer provides an average seek time in milliseconds. The typical range of average seek time is 10 to 60 msec. This is the main "culprit" for the delay involved in transferring blocks between disk and memory.

2. **Rotational delay (rd):** Once the read/write head is at the correct track, the user must wait for the beginning of the required block to rotate into position under the read/write head. On the average, this takes about the time for half a revolution of the disk, but it actually ranges from immediate access (if the start of the required block is in position under the read/write head right after the seek) to a full disk revolution (if the start of the required block just passed the read/write head after the seek). If the speed of disk rotation is p revolutions per minute (rpm), then the average rotational delay rd is given by

   $$rd = (1/2)*(1/p) \text{ min} = (60*1000)/(2*p) \text{ msec}$$

   A typical value for p is 10,000 rpm, which gives a rotational delay of rd = 3 msec. For fixed-head disks, where the seek time is negligible, this component causes the greatest delay in transferring a disk block.

3. **Block transfer time (btt):** Once the read/write head is at the beginning of the required block, some time is needed to transfer the data in the block. This block transfer time depends on the block size, the track size, and the rotational speed. If the **transfer rate** for the disk is tr bytes/msec and the block size is B bytes, then

> btt = B/tr msec

If we have a track size of 50 Kbytes and p is 3600 rpm, the transfer rate in bytes/ msec is

> tr = (50*1000)/(60*1000/3600) = 3000 bytes/msec

In this case, btt = B/3000 msec, where B is the block size in bytes.

The average time needed to find and transfer a block, given its block address, is estimated by

> (s + rd + btt) msec

This holds for either reading or writing a block. The principal method of reducing this time is to transfer several blocks that are stored on one or more tracks of the same cylinder; then the seek time is required only for the first block. To transfer consecutively k *noncontiguous* blocks that are on the *same cylinder*, we need approximately

> s + (k * (rd + btt)) msec

In this case, we need two or more buffers in main storage, because we are continuously reading or writing the k blocks. The transfer time per block is reduced even further when *consecutive blocks* on the same track or cylinder are transferred. This eliminates the rotational delay for all but the first block, so the estimate for transferring k consecutive blocks is

> s + rd + (k * btt) msec

A more accurate estimate for transferring consecutive blocks takes into account the interblock gap (see Chapter 9), which includes the information that enables the read/ write head to determine which block it is about to read. Usually, the disk manufacturer provides a **bulk transfer rate** (btr) that takes the gap size into account when reading consecutively stored blocks. If the gap size is G bytes, then

> btr = (B/(B + G)) * tr bytes/msec

The bulk transfer rate is the rate of transferring *useful bytes* in the data blocks. The disk read/write head must go over all bytes on a track as the disk rotates, including the bytes in the interblock gaps, which store control information but not real data. When the bulk transfer rate is used, the time needed to transfer the useful data in one block out of several consecutive blocks is B/btr. Hence, the estimated time to read k blocks consecutively stored on the same cylinder becomes

> s + rd + (k * (B/btr)) msec

Another parameter of disks is the **rewrite time.** This is useful in cases when we read a block from the disk into a main memory buffer, update the buffer, and then write the buffer back to the same disk block on which it was stored. In many cases, the time required to update the buffer in main memory is less than the time required for one disk revolution. If we know that the buffer is ready for rewriting, the system can keep the disk heads on the same track, and during the next disk revolution the updated buffer is rewritten back to the disk block. Hence, the rewrite time T_{rw}, is usually estimated to be the time needed for one disk revolution:

> $T_{rw} = $ 2 * rd msec

To summarize, here is a list of the parameters we have discussed and the symbols we use for them:

seek time: s msec
rotational delay: rd msec
block transfer time: btt msec
rewrite time: T_{rw} msec
transfer rate: tr bytes/msec
bulk transfer rate: btr bytes/msec
block size: B bytes
interblock gap size: G bytes

Overview of the QBE Languages

The Query-By-Example (QBE) language is important because it is one of the first graphical query languages with minimum syntax developed for database systems. It was developed at IBM Research and is available as an IBM commercial product as part of the QMF (Query Management Facility) interface option to DB2. The language was also implemented in the PARADOX DBMS, and is related to a point-and-click type interface in the ACCESS DBMS. It differs from SQL in that the user does not have to specify a structured query explicitly; rather, the query is formulated by filling in **templates** of relations that are displayed on a monitor screen. Figure D.1 shows how these templates may look for the database of Figure 4.6. The user does not have to remember the names of attributes or relations, because they are displayed as part of these templates. In addition, the user does not have to follow any rigid syntax rules for query specification; rather, constants and variables are entered in the columns of the templates to construct an **example** related to the retrieval or update request. QBE is related to the domain relational calculus, as we shall see, and its original specification has been shown to be relationally complete.

D.1 BASIC RETRIEVALS IN QBE

In QBE, retrieval queries are specified by filling in one or more rows in the templates of the tables. For a single relation query, we enter either constants or **example elements** (a QBE term) in the columns of the template of that relation. An example element stands for a domain variable and is specified as an example value preceded by the underscore character (_). Additionally, a P. prefix (called the P dot operator) is entered in certain columns to indicate that we would like to print (or display) values in those columns for our result. The constants specify values that must be exactly matched in those columns.

EMPLOYEE	FNAME	INITIAL	LNAME	ENO	DOB	ADDRESS	SEX	SALARY	SUPERENO	DNO

DEPARTMENT	DNAME	DNUMBER	MGRENO	MGRSTARTDATE

DEPT_LOCATION	DNUMBER	DLOCATION

WORKS_ON	EENO	PNO	HOURS

PROJECT	PNAME	PNUMBER	PLOCATION	DNUM

DEPENDENT	EENO	DEPENDENT_NAME	SEX	BDATE	RELATIONSHIP

FIGURE D.1 The relational schema of Figure 4.6 as it may be displayed by QBE.

For example, consider the query QO: "Retrieve the date of birth and address of Mahesh B. Kumar." We show in Figures D.2(a) through D.2(d) how this query can be specified in a progressively more terse form in QBE. In Figure D.2(a) an example of an employee is presented as the type of row that we are interested in. By

(a)

EMPLOYEE	FNAME	INITIAL	LNAME	ENO	DOB	ADDRESS	SEX	SALARY	SUPERENO	DNO
	Mahesh	B	Kumar	_123456789	P._9/1/65	P._731, Ameerpet, Hyderabad, AP	_M	_30000	_123456789	_3

(b)

EMPLOYEE	FNAME	INITIAL	LNAME	ENO	DOB	ADDRESS	SEX	SALARY	SUPERENO	DNO
	Mahesh	B	Kumar		P._9/1/65	P._731, Ameerpet, Hyderabad, AP				

(c)

EMPLOYEE	FNAME	INITIAL	LNAME	ENO	DOB	ADDRESS	SEX	SALARY	SUPERENO	DNO
	Mahesh	B	Kumar		P._X	P._Y				

(d)

EMPLOYEE	FNAME	INITIAL	LNAME	ENO	DOB	ADDRESS	SEX	SALARY	SUPERENO	DNO
	Mahesh	B	Kumar		P.	P.				

FIGURE D.2 Four ways of specifying the query Q0 in QBE.

leaving Mahesh B. Kumar as constants in the FNAME, INITIAL, and LNAME columns, we are specifying an exact match in those columns. All the rest of the columns are preceded by an underscore indicating that they are domain variables (example elements). The P. prefix is placed in the DOB and ADDRESS columns to indicate that we would like to output value(s) in those columns.

Q0 can be abbreviated as shown in Figure D.2(b). There is no need to specify example values for columns in which we are not interested. Moreover, because example values are completely arbitrary, we can just specify variable names for them, as shown in Figure D.2(c). Finally, we can also leave out the example values entirely, as shown in Figure D.2(d) and just specify a P. under the columns to be retrieved.

To see how retrieval queries in QBE are similar to the domain relational calculus, compare Figure D.2(d) with Q0 (simplified) in domain calculus, which is as follows:

Q0: { uv | EMPLOYEE (qrstuvwxyz) **and** q='Mahesh' **and** r='B' **and** s='Kumar'}

We can think of each column in a QBE template as an *implicit domain variable*; hence, FNAME corresponds to the domain variable q, INITIAL corresponds to r, . . ., and DNO corresponds to z. In the QBE query, the columns with P. correspond to variables specified to the left of the bar in domain calculus, whereas the columns with constant values correspond to tuple variables with equality selection conditions on them. The condition EMPLOYEE (qrstuvwxyz) and the existential quantifiers are implicit in the QBE query because the template corresponding to the EMPLOYEE relation is used.

In QBE, the user interface first allows the user to choose the tables (relations) needed to formulate a query by displaying a list of all relation names. The templates for the chosen relations are then displayed. The user moves to the appropriate columns in the templates and specifies the query. Special function keys were provided to move among templates and perform certain functions.

We now give examples to illustrate basic facilities of QBE. Comparison operators other than = (such as > or ≥) may be entered in a column before typing a constant value. For example, the query Q0A: "List the employee's numbers of employees who work more than 20 hours per week on project number 1," can be specified as shown in Figure D.3(a). For more complex conditions, the user can ask for a **condition box,** which is created by pressing a particular function key. The user can then type the complex condition.[1] For example, the query Q0B—"List the empoloyee's numbers of employees who work more than 20 hours per week on either project 1 or project 2"—can be specified as shown in Figure D.3(b).

Some complex conditions can be specified without a condition box. The rule is that all conditions specified on the same row of a relation template are connected by the **and** logical connective (*all* must be satisfied by a selected tuple), whereas conditions specified on distinct rows are connected by **or** (*at least one* must be satisfied). Hence, Q0B can also be specified, as shown in Figure D.3(c), by entering two distinct rows in the template.

Now consider query Q0C: "List the employee's numbers of employees who work on *both* project 1 and project 2"; this cannot be specified as in Figure D.4(a), which lists those who work on *either* project 1 or project 2. The example variable _ES will bind itself to EENO values in < −, 1, − > tuples *as well as* to those in < −, 2, − > tuples. Figure D.4(b) shows how to specify Q0C correctly, where the condition (_EX = _EY) in the box makes the _EX and _EY variables bind only to identical EENO values.

In general, once a query is specified, the resulting values are displayed in the template under the appropriate columns. If the result contains more rows than can be displayed on the screen, most QBE implementations have function keys to allow scrolling up and down the rows. Similarly, if a template or several templates are too wide to appear on the screen, it is possible to scroll sideways to examine all the templates.

---

1. Negation with the ¬ symbol is *not* allowed in a condition box.

(a)

WORKS_ON	EENO	PNO	HOURS
	P.		>20

(b)

WORKS_ON	EENO	PNO	HOURS
	P.	_PX	_HX

CONDITIONS

_HX>20 AND (_PX = 1 OR _PX = 2)

(c)

WORKS_ON	EENO	PNO	HOURS
	P.		>20

FIGURE D.3 Specifying complex conditions in QBE. (a) The same query Q0A. (b) The query Q0B with a condition box. (c) The query Q0B without a condition box.

(a)

WORKS_ON	EENO	PNO	HOURS
	P._ES	1	
	P._ES	2	

(b)

WORKS_ON	EENO	PNO	HOURS
	P._EX	1	
	P._EY	2	

CONDITIONS

_EX=_EY

FIGURE D.4 Specifying EMPLOYEES who work on both projects. (a) Incorrect specification of an AND condition. (b) Correct specification.

A join operation is specified in QBE by using the *same variable* [2] in the columns to be joined. For example, the query Q1: "List the name and address of all employees who work for the 'Research' department," can be specified as shown in Figure D.5(a). Any number of joins can be specified in a single query. We can also specify a **result table** to display the result of the join query, as shown in Figure D.5(a); this is needed if the result includes attributes from two or more relations. If no result table is specified, the system provides the query result in the columns of the various relations, which may make it difficult to interpret. Figure D.5(a) also illustrates the feature of QBE for specifying that all attributes of a relation should be retrieved, by placing the P. operator under the relation name in the relation template.

To join a table with itself, we specify different variables to represent the different references to the table. For example, query Q8—"For each employee retrieve the employee's first and last name as well as the first and last name of his or her immediate supervisor"— can be specified as shown in Figure D.5(b), where the variables starting with E refer to an employee and those starting with S refer to a supervisor.

---

2. A variable is called an **example element** in QBE manuals.

(a)

EMPLOYEE	FNAME	INITIAL	LNAME	ENO	DOB	ADDRESS	SEX	SALARY	SUPERENO	DNO
	_FN		_LN			_ADDR				_DX

DEPARTMENT	DNAME	DNUMBER	MGRENO	MGRSTARTDATE
	Research	_DX		

RESULT			
P.	_FN	_LN	_ADDR

(b)

EMPLOYEE	FNAME	INITIAL	LNAME	ENO	DOB	ADDRESS	SEX	SALARY	SUPERENO	DNO
	_E1 _S1		_E2 _S2	_XENO					_XENO	

RESULT				
P.	_E1	_E2	_S1	_S2

FIGURE D.5 Illustrating JOIN and result relations in QBE. (a) The query Q1. (b) The query Q8.

D.2 GROUPING, AGGREGATION, AND DATABASE MODIFICATION IN QBE

Next, consider the types of queries that require grouping or aggregate functions. A grouping operator G. can be specified in a column to indicate that tuples should be grouped by the value of that column. Common functions can be specified, such as AVG., SUM., CNT. (count), MAX., and MIN. In QBE the functions AVG., SUM., and CNT. are applied to distinct values within a group in the default case. If we want these functions to apply to all values, we must use the prefix ALL.[3] This convention is *different* in SQL, where the default is to apply a function to all values.

Figure D.6(a) shows query Q23, which counts the number of *distinct* salary values in the EMPLOYEE relation. Query Q23A (Figure D.6(b)) counts all salary values, which is the same as counting the number of employees. Figure D.6(c) shows Q24, which retrieves each department number and the number of employees and average salary within each department; hence, the DNO column is used for grouping as indicated by the G. function. Several of the operators G., P., and ALL can be specified in a single column. Figure D.6(d) shows query Q26, which displays each project name and the number of employees working on it for projects on which more than two employees work.

QBE has a negation symbol, ¬, which is used in a manner similar to the NOT EXISTS function in SQL. Figure D.7 shows query Q6, which lists the names of employees who have no dependents. The negation symbol ¬ says that we will select values of the _SX variable from the EMPLOYEE relation only if they do not occur in the DEPENDENT relation. The same effect can be produced by placing a ¬ _SX in the EENO column.

---

3. ALL in QBE is unrelated to the universal quantifier.

(a)

EMPLOYEE	FNAME	INITIAL	LNAME	ENO	DOB	ADDRESS	SEX	SALARY	SUPERENO	DNO
								P.CNT		

(b)

EMPLOYEE	FNAME	INITIAL	LNAME	ENO	DOB	ADDRESS	SEX	SALARY	SUPERENO	DNO
								P.CNT.ALL		

(c)

EMPLOYEE	FNAME	INITIAL	LNAME	ENO	DOB	ADDRESS	SEX	SALARY	SUPERENO	DNO
				P.CNT.ALL				P.AVG.ALL		P.G.

(d)

PROJECT	PNAME	PNUMBER	PLOCATION	DNUM
	P	_PX		

WORKS_ON	EENO	PNO	HOURS
	P.CNT_EX	G._PX	

CONDITIONS

CNT._EX>2

FIGURE D.6 Functions and grouping in QBE. (a) The query Q23. (b) The query Q23A. (c) The query Q24. (d) The query Q26.

EMPLOYEE	FNAME	INITIAL	LNAME	eno	DOB	ADDRESS	SEX	SALARY	SUPERENO	DNO
	P.		_P.	_SX						

DEPENDENT	EENO	DEPENDENT_NAME	SEX	DOB	RELATIONSHIP
	_SX				

FIGURE D.7 Illustrating negation by the query Q6.

Although the QBE language as originally proposed was shown to support the equivalent of the EXISTS and NOT EXISTS functions of SQL, the QBE implementation in QMF (under the DB2 system) does *not* provide this support. Hence, the QMF version of QBE, which we discuss here, is *not relationally complete*. Queries such as Q3—"Find employees who work on *all* projects controlled by department 5"—*cannot* be specified.

There are three QBE operators for modifying the database: I. for insert, D. for delete, and U. for update. The insert and delete operators are specified in the template column under the relation name, whereas the update operator is specified under the columns to be updated. Figure D.8(a) shows how to insert a new EMPLOYEE tuple. For deletion, we first enter the D. operator and then specify the tuples to be deleted by a condition (Figure D.8 (b)). To update a tuple, we specify the U. operator under the attribute name, followed by the new value of the attribute. We should also select the tuple or tuples to be updated in the usual way. Figure D.8(c) shows an update request to increase the salary of 'Mahesh Kumar' by 10 percent and also to reassign him to department number 4.

QBE also has data definition capabilities. The tables of a database can be specified interactively, and a table definition can also be updated by adding, renaming, or removing a column. We can also specify various characteristics for each column, such as whether it is a key of the relation, what its data type is, and whether an index should be created on that field. QBE also has facilities for view definition, authorization, storing query definitions for later use, and so on.

(a)

EMPLOYEE	FNAME	INITIAL	LNAME	ENO	DOB	ADDRESS	SEX	SALARY	SUPERENO	DNO
I.	Gaurav	K	Gupta	653298653	30-DEC-52	98, Infantry Rd, Bangalore, KA	M	37000	987654321	4

(b)

EMPLOYEE	FNAME	INITIAL	LNAME	ENO	DOB	ADDRESS	SEX	SALARY	SUPERENO	DNO
D.				653298653						

(c)

EMPLOYEE	FNAME	INITIAL	LNAME	ENO	DOB	ADDRESS	SEX	SALARY	SUPERENO	DNO
	Mahesh		Kumar					U.S_1.1		U.4

FIGURE D.8 Modifying the database in QBE. (a) Insertion. (b) Deletion. (c) Update in QBE.

QBE does not use the "linear" style of SQL; rather, it is a "two-dimensional" language, because users specify a query moving around the full area of the screen. Tests on users have shown that QBE is easier to learn than SQL, especially for nonspecialists. In this sense, QBE was the first user-friendly "visual" relational database language.

More recently, numerous other user-friendly interfaces have been developed for commercial database systems. The use of menus, graphics, and forms is now becoming quite common. Visual query languages, which are still not so common, are likely to be offered with commercial relational databases in the future.

Selected Bibliography

Abbreviations Used in the Bibliography

ACM: Association for Computing Machinery

AFIPS: American Federation of Information Processing Societies

CACM: Communications of the ACM (journal)

CIKM: Proceedings of the International Conference on Information and Knowledge Management

EDS: Proceedings of the International Conference on Expert Database Systems

ER Conference: Proceedings of the International Conference on Entity-Relationship Approach (now called International Conference on Conceptual Modeling)

ICDE: Proceedings of the IEEE International Conference on Data Engineering

IEEE: Institute of Electrical and Electronics Engineers

IEEE Computer: Computer magazine (journal) of the IEEE CS

IEEE CS: IEEE Computer Society

IFIP: International Federation for Information Processing

JACM: Journal of the ACM

KDD: Knowledge Discovery in Databases

LNCS: Lecture Notes in Computer Science

NCC: Proceedings of the National Computer Conference (published by AFIPS)

OOPSLA: Proceedings of the ACM Conference on Object-Oriented Programming Systems, Languages, and Applications

PODS: Proceedings of the ACM Symposium on Principles of Database Systems
SIGMOD: Proceedings of the ACM SIGMOD International Conference on Management of Data
TKDE: IEEE Transactions on Knowledge and Data Engineering (journal)
TOCS: ACM Transactions on Computer Systems (journal)
TODS: ACM Transactions on Database Systems (journal)
TOIS: ACM Transactions on Information Systems (journal)
TOOIS: ACM Transactions on Office Information Systems (journal)
TSE: IEEE Transactions on Software Engineering (journal)
VLDB: Proceedings of the International Conference on Very Large Data Bases (issues after 1981 available from Morgan Kaufmann, Menlo Park, California)

Format for Bibliographic Citations

Book titles are in boldface—for example, **Database Computers**. Conference proceedings names are in italics—for example, ACM *Pacific Conference*. Journal names are in boldface—for example, **TODS** or **Information Systems**. For journal citations, we give the volume number and issue number (within the volume, if any) and date of issue. For example "**TODS**, 3:4, December 1978" refers to the December 1978 issue of ACM *Transactions on Database Systems*, which is Volume 3, Number 4. Articles that appear in books or conference proceedings that are themselves cited in the bibliography are referenced as "in" these references—for example, "in VLDB [1978]" or "in Rustin [1974]." Page numbers (abbreviated "pp.") are provided with pp. at the end of the citation whenever available. For citations with more than four authors, we will give the first author only followed by et al. In the selected bibliography at the end of each chapter, we use et al. if there are more than two authors.

BIBLIOGRAPHIC REFERENCES

Abbott, R., and Garcia-Molina, H. [1989] "Scheduling Real-Time Transactions with Disk Resident Data," in VLDB [1989].

Abiteboul, S., and Kanellakis, P. [1989] "Object Identity as a Query Language Primitive," in SIGMOD [1989].

Abiteboul, S. Hull, R., and Vianu, V. [1995] **Foundations of Databases,** Addison-Wesley, 1995.

Abrial, J. [1974] "Data Semantics," in Klimbie and Koffeman [1974].

Adam, N., and Gongopadhyay, A. [1993] "Integrating Functional and Data Modeling in a Computer Integrated Manufacturing System," in ICDE [1993].

Adriaans, P., and Zantinge, D. [1996] **Data Mining,** Addison-Wesley, 1996.

Afsarmanesh, H., McLeod, D., Knapp, D., and Parker, A. [1985] "An Extensible Object-Oriented Approach to Databases for VLSI /CAD," in VLDB [1985].

Agrawal, D., and ElAbbadi, A. [1990] "Storage Efficient Replicated Databases," **TKDE,** 2:3, September 1990.

Agrawal, R., Gehani, N., and Srinivasan, J. [1990] "OdeView: The Graphical Interface to Ode," in SIGMOD [1990].

Agrawal, R., Imielinski, T., and Swami A. [1993] "Mining Association Rules Between Sets of Items in Databases," in SIGMOD [1993].

Agrawal, R., Imielinski, T., and Swami, A. [1993b] "Database Mining: A Performance Perspective," **IEEE TKDE** 5:6, December 1993.

Agrawal, R., Mehta, M., and Shafer, J., and Srikant, R. [1996] "The Quest Data Mining System," in KDD [1996].

Agrawal, R., and Srikant, R. [1994] "Fast Algorithms for Mining Association Rules in Large Databases," in VLDB [1994].

Ahad, R., and Basu, A. [1991] "ESQL: A Query Language for the Relational Model Supporting Image Domains," in ICDE [1991].

Aho, A., Beeri, C., and Ullman, J. [1979] "The Theory of Joins in Relational Databases," **TODS,** 4:3, September 1979.

Aho, A., Sagiv, Y., and Ullman, J. [1979a] "Efficient Optimization of a Class of Relational Expressions," **TODS,** 4:4, December 1979.

Aho, A. and Ullman, J. [1979] "Universality of Data Retrieval Languages," *Proceedings of the POPL Conference,* San Antonio TX, ACM, 1979.

Akl, S. [1983] "Digital Signatures: A Tutorial Survey," **IEEE Computer,** 16:2, February 1983.

Alashqur, A., Su, S., and Lam, H. [1989] "OQL: A Query Language for Manipulating Object-Oriented Databases," in VLDB [1989].

Albano, A., Cardelli, L., and Orsini, R. [1985] "GALILEO: A Strongly Typed Interactive Conceptual Language," **TODS,** 10:2, June 1985.

Allen, F., Loomis, M., and Mannino, M. [1982] "The Integrated Dictionary/Directory System," **ACM Computing Surveys,** 14:2, June 1982.

Alonso, G., Agrawal, D., El Abbadi, A., and Mohan, C. [1997] "Functionalities and Limitations of Current Workflow Management Systems," **IEEE Expert,** 1997.

Amir, A., Feldman, R., and Kashi, R. [1997] "A New and Versatile Method for Association Generation," Information Systems, 22:6, September 1997.

Anderson, S., Bankier, A., Barrell, B., deBruijn, M., Coulson, A., Drouin, J., Eperon, I., Nierlich, D., Rose, B., Sanger, F., Schreier, P., Smith, A., Staden, R., Young, I. [1981] "Sequence and Organization of the Human Mitochondrial Genome." **Nature,** 290:457–465, 1981.

Andrews, T., and Harris, C. [1987] "Combining Language and Database Advances in an Object-Oriented Development Environment," OOPSLA, 1987.

ANSI [1975] American National Standards Institute Study Group on Data Base Management Systems: Interim Report, FDT, 7:2, ACM, 1975.

ANSI [1986] American National Standards Institute: The Database Language SQL, Document ANSI X3.135, 1986.

ANSI [1986a] American National Standards Institute: The Database Language NDL, Document ANSI X3.133, 1986.

ANSI [1989] American National Standards Institute: Information Resource Dictionary Systems, Document ANSI X3.138, 1989.

Anwar, T., Beck, H., and Navathe, S. [1992] "Knowledge Mining by Imprecise Querying: A Classification Based Approach," in ICDE [1992].

Apers, P., Hevner, A., and Yao, S. [1983] "Optimization Algorithms for Distributed Queries," **TSE,** 9:1, January 1983.

Armstrong, W. [1974] "Dependency Structures of Data Base Relationships," *Proceedings of the IFIP Congress,* 1974.

Astrahan, M., et al. [1976] "System R: A Relational Approach to Data Base Management," **TODS,** 1:2, June 1976.

Atkinson, M., and Buneman, P. [1987] "Types and Persistence in Database Programming Languages" in **ACM Computing Surveys,** 19:2, June 1987.

Atluri, V., Jajodia, S., Keefe, T.F., McCollum, C., and Mukkamala, R. [1997] "Multilevel Secure Transaction Processing: Status and Prospects," in **Database Security: Status and Prospects,** Chapman and Hall, 1997, pp. 79–98.

Atzeni, P., and De Antonellis, V. [1993] **Relational Database Theory,** Benjamin/Cummings, 1993.

Atzeni, P., Mecca, G., and Merialdo, P. [1997] "To Weave the Web," in VLDB [1997].

Bachman, C. [1969] "Data Structure Diagrams," **Data Base** (Bulletin of ACM SIGFIDET), 1:2, March 1969.

Bachman, C. [1973] "The Programmer as a Navigator," **CACM,** 16:1, November 1973.

Bachman, C. [1974] "The Data Structure Set Model," in Rustin [1974].

Bachman, C., and Williams, S. [1964] "A General Purpose Programming System for Random Access Memories," *Proceedings of the Fall Joint Computer Conference,* AFIPS, 26, 1964.

Badal, D., and Popek, G. [1979] "Cost and Performance Analysis of Semantic Integrity Validation Methods," in SIGMOD [1979].

Badrinath, B. and Ramamritham, K. [1992] "Semantics-Based Concurrency Control: Beyond Commutativity," **TODS,** 17:1, March 1992.

Baeza-Yates, R., and Larson, P. A. [1989] "Performance of B1-trees with Partial Expansions," **TKDE,** 1:2, June 1989.

Baeza-Yates, R., and Ribero-Neto, B. [1999] Modern Information Retrieval, Addison- Wesley, 1999.

Balbin, I., and Ramamohanrao, K. [1987] "A Generalization of the Different Approach to Recursive Query Evaluation," **Journal of Logic Programming,** 15:4, 1987.

Bancilhon, F., and Buneman, P., eds. [1990] **Advances in Database Programming Languages,** ACM Press, 1990.

Bancilhon, F., Maier, D., Sagiv, Y., and Ullman, J. [1986] "Magic sets and other strange ways to implement logic programs," PODS [1986].

Bancilhon, F., and Ramakrishnan, R. [1986] "An Amateur's Introduction to Recursive Query Processing Strategies, " in SIGMOD [1986].

Banerjee, J., et al. [1987] "Data Model Issues for Object-Oriented Applications," **TOOIS,** 5:1, January 1987.

Banerjee, J., Kim, W., Kim, H., and Korth, H. [1987a] "Semantics and Implementation of Schema Evolution in Object-Oriented Databases," in SIGMOD [1987].

Baroody, A., and DeWitt, D. [1981] "An Object-Oriented Approach to Database System Implementation," **TODS,** 6:4, December 1981.

Barsalou, T., Siambela, N., Keller, A., and Wiederhold, G. [1991] "Updating Relational Databases Through Object-Based Views," in SIGMOD [1991].

Bassiouni, M. [1988] "Single-Site and Distributed Optimistic Protocols for Concurrency Control," **TSE,** 14:8, August 1988.

Batini, C., Ceri, S., and Navathe, S. [1992] **Database Design: An Entity-Relationship Approach,** Benjamin/ Cummings, 1992.

Batini, C., Lenzerini, M., and Navathe, S. [1987] "A Comparative Analysis of Methodologies for Database Schema Integration," **ACM Computing Surveys,** 18:4, December 1987.

Batory, D., and Buchmann, A. [1984] "Molecular Objects, Abstract Data Types, and Data Models: A Framework," in VLDB [1984].

Batory, D., et al. [1988] "GENESIS: An Extensible Database Management System," **TSE,** 14:11, November 1988.

Bayer, R., Graham, M., and Seegmuller, G., eds. [1978] **Operating Systems: An Advanced Course,** Springer-Verlag, 1978.

Bayer, R., and McCreight, E. [1972] "Organization and Maintenance of Large Ordered Indexes," **Acta Informatica,** 1:3, February 1972.

Beck, H., Anwar, T., and Navathe, S. [1993] "A Conceptual Clustering Algorithm for Database Schema Design," **TKDE,** to appear.

Beck, H., Gala, S., and Navathe, S. [1989] "Classification as a Query Processing Technique in the CANDIDE Semantic Data Model," in ICDE [1989].

Beeri, C., Fagin, R., and Howard, J. [1977] "A Complete Axiomatization for Functional and Multivalued Dependencies," in SIGMOD [1977].

Beeri, C., and Ramakrishnan, R. [1987] "On the Power of Magic" in PODS [1987].

Benson, D., Boguski, M., Lipman, D., and Ostell, J., "GenBank," **Nucleic Acids Research,** 24:1, 1996.

Ben-Zvi, J. [1982] "The Time Relational Model," Ph.D. dissertation, University of California, Los Angeles, 1982.

Berg, B. and Roth, J. [1989] **Software for Optical Disk,** Meckler, 1989.

Berners-Lee, T., Caillian, R., Grooff, J., Pollermann, B. [1992] "World-Wide Web: The Information Universe," **Electronic Networking: Research, Applications and Policy,** 1:2, 1992.

Berners-Lee, T., Caillian, R., Lautonen, A., Nielsen, H., and Secret, A. [1994] "The World Wide Web," CACM, 13:2, August 1994.

Bernstein, P. [1976] "Synthesizing Third Normal Form Relations from Functional Dependencies," **TODS,** 1:4, December 1976.

Bernstein, P., Blaustein, B., and Clarke, E. [1980] "Fast Maintenance of Semantic Integrity Assertions Using Redundant Aggregate Data," in VLDB [1980].

Bernstein, P., and Goodman, N. [1980] "Timestamp-Based Algorithms for Concurrency Control in Distributed Database Systems," in VLDB [1980].

Bernstein, P., and Goodman, N. [1981] "The Power of Natural Semijoins," **SIAM Journal of Computing,** 10:4, December 1981.

Bernstein, P., and Goodman, N. [1981a] "Concurrency Control in Distributed Database Systems," **ACM Computing Surveys,** 13:2, June 1981.

Bernstein, P., and Goodman, N. [1984] "An Algorithm for Concurrency Control and Recovery in Replicated Distributed Databases," **TODS,** 9:4, December 1984.

Bernstein, P., Hadzilacos, V., and Goodman, N. [1988] **Concurrency Control and Recovery in Database Systems,** Addison-Wesley, 1988.

Bertino, E. [1992] "Data Hiding and Security in Object-Oriented Databases," in ICDE [1992].

Bertino, E., Catania, B., and Ferrari, E. [2001] "A Nested Transaction Model for Multilevel Secure Database Management Systems," **ACM Transactions on Information and System Security,** 4:4, November 2001, pp. 321–370.

Bertino, E., and Ferrari, E. [1998] "Data Security," *Twenty-Second Annual International Conference on Computer Software and Applications,* August 1998, pp. 228–237.

Bertino, E., and Kim, W. [1989] "Indexing Techniques for Queries on Nested Objects," **TKDE,** 1:2, June 1989.

Bertino, E., Negri, M., Pelagatti, G., and Sbattella, L. [1992] "Object-Oriented Query Languages: The Notion and the Issues," **TKDE,** 4:3, June 1992.

Bertino, E., Pagani, E., and Rossi, G. [1992] "Fault Tolerance and Recovery in Mobile Computing Systems, in Kumar and Han [1992].

Bertino, F., Rabbitti and Gibbs, S. [1988] "Query Processing in a Multimedia Environment," **TOIS,** 6, 1988.

Bhargava, B., ed. [1987] **Concurrency and Reliability in Distributed Systems,** Van Nostrand-Reinhold, 1987.

Bhargava, B., and Helal, A. [1993] "Efficient Reliability Mechanisms in Distributed Database Systems," CIKM, November 1993.

Bhargava, B., and Reidl, J. [1988] "A Model for Adaptable Systems for Transaction Processing," in ICDE [1988].

Biliris, A. [1992] "The Performance of Three Database Storage Structures for Managing Large Objects," in SIGMOD [1992].

Biller, H. [1979] "On the Equivalence of Data Base Schemas—A Semantic Approach to Data Translation," **Information Systems,** 4:1, 1979.

Bischoff, J., and T. Alexander, eds., **Data Warehouse: Practical Advice from the Experts,** Prentice-Hall, 1997.

Biskup, J., Dayal, U., and Bernstein, P. [1979] "Synthesizing Independent Database Schemas," in SIGMOD [1979].

Bjork, A. [1973] "Recovery Scenario for a DB/DC System," *Proceedings of the* ACM *National Conference,* 1973.

Bjorner, D., and Lovengren, H. [1982] "Formalization of Database Systems and a Formal Definition of IMS," in VLDB [1982].

Blaha, M., Premerlani, W. [1998] **Object-Oriented Modeling and Design for Database Applications,** Prentice-Hall, 1998.

Blakeley, J., Coburn, N., and Larson, P. [1989] "Updated Derived Relations: Detecting Irrelevant and Autonomously Computable Updates," **TODS,** 14:3, September 1989.

Blakeley, J., and Martin, N. [1990] "Join Index, Materialized View, and Hybrid-Hash Join: A Performance Analysis," in ICDE [1990].

Blasgen, M., and Eswaran, K. [1976] "On the Evaluation of Queries in a Relational Database System," **IBM Systems Journal,** 16:1, January 1976.

Blasgen, M., et al. [1981] "System R: An Architectural Overview," **IBM Systems Journal,** 20:1, January 1981.

Bleier, R., and Vorhaus, A. [1968] "File Organization in the SDC TDMS," *Proceedings of the IFIP Congress.*

Bocca, J. [1986] "EDUCE—A Marriage of Convenience: Prolog and a Relational DBMS," *Proceedings of the Third International Conference on Logic Programming,* Springer-Verlag, 1986.

Bocca, J. [1986a] "On the Evaluation Strategy of EDUCE," in SIGMOD [1986].

Bodorick, P., Riordon, J., and Pyra, J. [1992] "Deciding on Correct Distributed Query Processing," **TKDE,** 4:3, June 1992.

Booch, G., Rumbaugh, J., and Jacobson, I., **Unified Modeling Language User Guide,** Addison-Wesley, 1999.

Borgida, A., Brachman, R., McGuinness, D., and Resnick, L. [1989] "CLASSIC: A Structural Data Model for Objects," in SIGMOD [1989].

Borkin, S. [1978] "Data Model Equivalence," in VLDB [1978].

Bouzeghoub, M., and Metais, E. [1991] "Semantic Modelling of Object-Oriented Databases," in VLDB [1991].

Boyce, R., Chamberlin, D., King, W., and Hammer, M. [1975] "Specifying Queries as Relational Expressions," **CACM,** 18:11, November 1975.

Bracchi, G., Paolini, P., and Pelagatti, G. [1976] "Binary Logical Associations in Data Modelling," in Nijssen [1976].

Brachman, R., and Levesque, H. [1984] "What Makes a Knowledge Base Knowledgeable? A View of Databases from the Knowledge Level," in EDS [1984].

Bratbergsengen, K. [1984] "Hashing Methods and Relational Algebra Operators," in VLDB [1984].

Bray, O. [1988] **Computer Integrated Manufacturing—The Data Management Strategy,** Digital Press, 1988.

Breitbart, Y., Silberschatz, A., and Thompson, G. [1990] "Reliable Transaction Management in a Multidatabase System," in SIGMOD [1990].

Brodie, M., and Mylopoulos, J., eds. [1985] **On Knowledge Base Management Systems,** Springer-Verlag, 1985.

Brodie, M., Mylopoulos, J., and Schmidt, J., eds. [1984] **On Conceptual Modeling,** Springer-Verlag, 1984.

Brosey, M., and Shneiderman, B. [1978] "Two Experimental Comparisons of Relational and Hierarchical Database Models," **International Journal of Man-Machine Studies,** 1978.

Bry, F. [1990] "Query Evaluation in Recursive Databases: Bottom-up and Top-down Reconciled," TKDE, 2, 1990.

Bukhres, O. [1992] "Performance Comparison of Distributed Deadlock Detection Algorithms," in ICDE [1992].

Buneman, P., and Frankel, R. [1979] "FQL: A Functional Query Language," in SIGMOD [1979].

Burkhard, W. [1976] "Hashing and Trie Algorithms for Partial Match Retrieval," **TODS,** 1:2, June 1976, pp. 175–87.

Burkhard, W. [1979] "Partial-match Hash Coding: Benefits of Redunancy," **TODS,** 4:2, June 1979, pp. 228–39.

Bush, V. [1945] "As We May Think," *Atlantic Monthly,* 176:1, January 1945. Reprinted in Kochen, M., ed., **The Growth of Knowledge,** Wiley, 1967.

Byte [1995] Special Issue on Mobile Computing, June 1995.

CACM [1995] Special issue of the **Communications of the ACM,** on Digital Libraries, 38:5, May 1995.

CACM [1998] Special issue of the **Communications of the ACM** on Digital Libraries: Global Scope and Unlimited Access, 41:4, April 1998.

Cammarata, S., Ramachandra, P., and Shane, D. [1989] "Extending a Relational Database with Deferred Referential Integrity Checking and Intelligent Joins," in SIGMOD [1989].

Campbell, D., Embley, D., and Czejdo, B. [1985] "A Relationally Complete Query Language for the Entity-Relationship Model," in ER Conference [1985].

Cardenas, A. [1985] **Data Base Management Systems,** 2nd ed., Allyn and Bacon, 1985.

Carey, M., et al. [1986] "The Architecture of the EXODUS Extensible DBMS," in Dittrich and Dayal [1986].

Carey, M., DeWitt, D., Richardson, J. and Shekita, E. [1986a] "Object and File Management in the EXODUS Extensible Database System," in VLDB [1986].

Carey, M., DeWitt, D., and Vandenberg, S. [1988] "A Data Model and Query Language for Exodus," in SIGMOD [1988].

Carey, M., Franklin, M., Livny, M., and Shekita, E. [1991] "Data Caching Tradeoffs in Client-Server DBMS Architectures," in SIGMOD [1991].

Carlis, J. [1986] "HAS, a Relational Algebra Operator or Divide Is Not Enough to Conquer," in ICDE [1986].

Carlis, J., and March, S. [1984] "A Descriptive Model of Physical Database Design Problems and Solutions," in ICDE [1984].

Carroll, J. M., [1995] **Scenario Based Design: Envisioning Work and Technology in System Development,** Wiley, 1995.

Casanova, M., Fagin, R., and Papadimitriou, C. [1981] "Inclusion Dependencies and Their Interaction with Functional Dependencies," in PODS [1981].

Casanova, M., Furtado, A., and Tuchermann, L. [1991] "A Software Tool for Modular Database Design," **TODS,** 16:2, June 1991.

Casanova, M., Tuchermann, L., Furtado, A., and Braga, A. [1989] "Optimization of Relational Schemas Containing Inclusion Dependencies," in VLDB [1989].

Casanova, M., and Vidal, V. [1982] "Toward a Sound View Integration Method," in PODS [1982].

Cattell, R., and Skeen, J. [1992] "Object Operations Benchmark," **TODS,** 17:1, March 1992.

Castano, S., DeAntonellio, V., Fugini, M.G., and Pernici, B. [1998] "Conceptual Schema Analysis: Techniques and Applications," TODS, 23:3, September 1998, pp. 286–332.

Castano, S., Fugini, M., Martella G., and Samarati, P. [1995] **Database Security,** ACM Press and Addison-Wesley, 1995.

Catarci, T., Costabile, M. F., Santucci, G., and Tarantino, L., eds. [1998] *Proceedings of the Fourth International Workshop on Advanced Visual Interfaces,* ACM Press, 1998.

Catarci, T., Costabile, M. F., Levialdi, S., and Batini, C. [1997] "Visual Query Systems for Databases: A Survey," **Journal of Visual Languages and Computing,** 8:2, June 1997, pp. 215–60.

Ceri, S., and Fraternali, P. [1997] **Designing Database Applications with Objects and Rules: The IDEA Methodology,** Addison-Wesley, 1997.

Ceri, S., Gottlob, G., Tanca, L. [1990], **Logic Programming and Databases,** Springer- Verlag, 1990.

Ceri, S., Navathe, S., and Wiederhold, G. [1983] "Distribution Design of Logical Database Schemas," **TSE,** 9:4, July 1983.

Ceri, S., Negri, M., and Pelagatti, G. [1982] "Horizontal Data Partitioning in Database Design," in SIGMOD [1982].

Ceri, S., and Owicki, S. [1983] "On the Use of Optimistic Methods for Concurrency Control in Distributed Databases," *Proceedings of the Sixth Berkeley Workshop on Distributed Data Management and Computer Networks,* February 1983.

Ceri, S., and Pelagatti, G. [1984] "Correctness of Query Execution Strategies in Distributed Databases," **TODS,** 8:4, December 1984.

Ceri, S., and Pelagatti, G. [1984a] **Distributed Databases: Principles and Systems,** McGraw-Hill, 1984.

Ceri, S., and Tanca, L. [1987] "Optimization of Systems of Algebraic Equations for Evaluating Datalog Queries," in VLDB [1987].

Cesarini, F., and Soda, G. [1991] "A Dynamic Hash Method with Signature," **TODS,** 16:2, June 1991.

Chakravarthy, S. [1990] "Active Database Management Systems: Requirements, State-of-the-Art, and an Evaluation," in ER Conference [1990].

Chakravarthy, S. [1991] "Divide and Conquer: A Basis for Augmenting a Conventional Query Optimizer with Multiple Query Processing Capabilities," in ICDE [1991].

Chakravarthy, S., Anwar, E., Maugis, L., and Mishra, D. [1994] Design of Sentinel: An Object-oriented DBMS with Event-based Rules, **Information and Software Technology,** 36:9, 1994.

Chakravarthy, S., et al. [1989] "HiPAC: A Research Project in Active, Time Constrained Database Management," Final Technical Report, XAIT-89-02, Xerox Advanced Information Technology, August 1989.

Chakravarthy, S., Karlapalem, K., Navathe, S., and Tanaka, A. [1993] "Database Supported Co-operative Problem Solving," in **International Journal of Intelligent Cooperative Information Systems,** 2:3, September 1993.

Chakravarthy, U., Grant, J., and Minker, J. [1990] "Logic-Based Approach to Semantic Query Optimization," **TODS,** 15:2, June 1990.

Chalmers, M., and Chitson, P. [1992] "Bead: Explorations in Information Visualization," *Proceedings of the ACM SIGIR International Conference,* June 1992.

Chamberlin, D., and Boyce, R. [1974] "SEQUEL: A Structured English Query Language," in SIGMOD [1984].

Chamberlin, D., et al. [1976] "SEQUEL 2: A Unified Approach to Data Definition, Manipulation, and Control," **IBM Journal of Research and Development,** 20:6, November 1976.

Chamberlin, D., et al. [1981] "A History and Evaluation of System R," **CACM,** 24:10, October 1981.

Chan, C., Ooi, B., and Lu, H. [1992] "Extensible Buffer Management of Indexes," in VLDB [1992].

Chandy, K., Browne, J., Dissley, C., and Uhrig, W. [1975] "Analytical Models for Rollback and Recovery Strategies in Database Systems," **TSE,** 1:1, March 1975.

Chang, C. [1981] "On the Evaluation of Queries Containing Derived Relations in a Relational Database" in Gallaire et al. [1981].

Chang, C., and Walker, A. [1984] "PROSQL: A Prolog Programming Interface with SQL/DS," in EDS [1984].

Chang, E., and Katz, R. [1989] "Exploiting Inheritance and Structure Semantics for Effective Clustering and Buffering in Object-Oriented Databases," in SIGMOD [1989].

Chang, N., and Fu, K. [1981] "Picture Query Languages for Pictorial Databases," IEEE **Computer,** 14:11, November 1981.

Chang, P., and Myre, W. [1988] "OS/2 EE Database Manager: Overview and Technical Highlights," **IBM Systems Journal,** 27:2, 1988.

Chang, S., Lin, B., and Walser, R. [1979] "Generalized Zooming Techniques for Pictorial Database Systems," NCC, AFIPS, 48, 1979.

Chen, M., and Yu, P. [1991] "Determining Beneficial Semijoins for a Join Sequence in Distributed Query Processing," in ICDE [1991].

Chatzoglu, P. D., and McCaulay, L. A. [1997] "Requirements Capture and Analysis: A Survey of Current Practice," **Requirements Engineering,** 1997, pp. 75–88.

Chaudhuri, S., and Dayal, U. [1997] "An Overview of Data Warehousing and OLAP Technology," **SIGMOD Record,** Vol. 26, No. 1, March 1997.

Chen, M., Han, J., Yu, P.S., [1996] " Data Mining: An Overview from a Database Perspective," IEEE TKDE, 8:6, December 1996.

Chen, P. [1976] "The Entity Relationship Mode—Toward a Unified View of Data," **TODS,** 1:1, March 1976.

Chen, P., Lee E., Gibson G., Katz, R., and Patterson, D. [1994] RAID High Performance, Reliable Secondary Storage, **ACM Computing Surveys,** 26:2, 1994.

Chen, P., and Patterson, D. [1990]. "Maximizing performance in a striped disk array," in *Proceedings of Symposium on Computer Architecture, IEEE,* New York, 1990.

Cheng, J. [1991] "Effective Clustering of Complex Objects in Object-Oriented Databases," in SIGMOD [1991].

Cheung, D., Han, J., Ng, V., Fu, A.W., and Fu, A.Y., "A Fast and Distributed Algorithm for Mining Association Rules," in *Proceedings of International Conference on Parallel and Distributed Information Systems,* PDIS [1996].

Childs, D. [1968] "Feasibility of a Set Theoretical Data Structure—A General Structure Based on a Reconstituted Definition of Relation," *Proceedings of the IFIP Congress,* 1968.

Chimenti, D., et al. [1987] "An Overview of the LDL System," MCC Technical Report #ACA-ST-370-87, Austin, TX, November 1987.

Chimenti, D., et al. [1990] "The LDL System Prototype," **TKDE,** 2:1, March 1990.

Chin, F. [1978] "Security in Statistical Databases for Queries with Small Counts," **TODS,** 3:1, March 1978.

Chin, F., and Ozsoyoglu, G. [1981] "Statistical Database Design," **TODS,** 6:1, March 1981.

Chintalapati, R. Kumar, V. and Datta, A. [1997] "An Adaptive Location Management Algorithm for Mobile Computing," *Proceedings of 22nd Annual Conference on Local Computer Networks (LCN '97),* Minneapolis, 1997.

Chou, H., and Kim, W. [1986] "A Unifying Framework for Version Control in a CAD Environment," in VLDB [1986].

Christodoulakis, S., et al. [1984] "Development of a Multimedia Information System for an Office Environment," in VLDB [1984].

Christodoulakis, S., and Faloutsos, C. [1986] "Design and Performance Considerations for an Optical Disk-Based Multimedia Object Server," **IEEE Computer,** 19:12, December 1986.

Chu, W., and Hurley, P. [1982] "Optimal Query Processing for Distributed Database Systems," IEEE **Transactions on Computers,** 31:9, September 1982.

Ciborra, C., Migliarese, P., and Romano, P. [1984] "A Methodological Inquiry of Organizational Noise in Socio Technical Systems," **Human Relations,** 37:8, 1984.

Claybrook, B. [1983] **File Management Techniques,** Wiley, 1983.

Claybrook, B. [1992] **OLTP: OnLine Transaction Processing Systems,** Wiley, 1992.

Clifford, J., and Tansel, A. [1985] "On an Algebra for Historical Relational Databases: Two Views," in SIGMOD [1985].

Clocksin, W. F., and Mellish, C. S. [1984] **Programming in Prolog,** 2nd ed., Springer Verlag, 1984.

CODASYL [1978] Data Description Language Journal of Development, Canadian Government Publishing Centre, 1978.

Codd, E. [1970] "A Relational Model for Large Shared Data Banks," **CACM,** 13:6, June 1970.

Codd, E. [1971] "A Data Base Sublanguage Founded on the Relational Calculus," *Proceedings of the ACM SIGFIDET Workshop on Data Description, Access, and Control,* November 1971.

Codd, E. [1972] "Relational Completeness of Data Base Sublanguages," in Rustin [1972].

Codd, E. [1972a] "Further Normalization of the Data Base Relational Model," in Rustin [1972].

Codd, E. [1974] "Recent Investigations in Relational Database Systems," *Proceedings of the IFIP Congress,* 1974.

Codd, E. [1978] "How About Recently? (English Dialog with Relational Data Bases Using Rendezvous Version 1)," in Shneiderman [1978].

Codd, E. [1979] "Extending the Database Relational Model to Capture More Meaning," **TODS,** 4:4, December 1979.

Codd, E. [1982] "Relational Database: A Practical Foundation for Productivity," **CACM,** 25:2, December 1982.

Codd, E. [1985] "Is Your DBMS Really Relational?" and "Does Your DBMS Run By the Rules?," **COMPUTER WORLD,** October 14 and October 21, 1985.

Codd, E. [1986] "An Evaluation Scheme for Database Management Systems That Are Claimed to Be Relational," in ICDE [1986].

Codd, E. [1990] **Relational Model for Data Management-Version 2,** Addison-Wesley, 1990.

Codd, E. F., Codd, S. B., and Salley, C. T. [1993] "Providing OLAP (On-Line Analytical Processing) to User Analyst: An IT Mandate," a white paper at http://www.arborsoft. com/OLAP.html, 1993.

Comer, D. [1979] "The Ubiquitous B-tree," **ACM Computing Surveys,** 11:2, June 1979. Comer, D. [1997] **Computer Networks and Internets,** Prentice-Hall, 1997.

Cornelio, A. and Navathe, S. [1993] "Applying Active Database Models for Simulation," in *Proceedings of 1993 Winter Simulation Conference,* IEEE, Los Angeles, December 1993.

Cosmadakis, S., Kanellakis, P. C., and Vardi, M. [1990] "Polynomial-time Implication Problems for Unary Inclusion Dependencies," JACM, 37:1, 1990, pp. 15–46.

Cruz, I. [1992] "Doodle: A Visual Language for Object-Oriented Databases," in SIGMOD [1992].

Curtice, R. [1981] "Data Dictionaries: An Assessment of Current Practice and Problems," in VLDB [1981].

Cuticchia, A., Fasman, K., Kingsbury, D., Robbins, R., and Pearson, P. [1993] "The GDB Human Genome Database Anno 1993." **Nucleic Acids Research,** 21:13, 1993.

Czejdo, B., Elmasri, R., Rusinkiewicz, M., and Embley, D. [1987] "An Algebraic Language for Graphical Query Formulation Using an Extended Entity-Relationship Model," *Proceedings of the ACM Computer Science Conference,* 1987.

Dahl, R., and Bubenko, J. [1982] "IDBD: An Interactive Design Tool for CODASYL DBTG Type Databases," in VLDB [1982].

Dahl, V. [1984] "Logic Programming for Constructive Database Systems," in EDS [1984].

Das, S. [1992] **Deductive Databases and Logic Programming,** Addison-Wesley, 1992.

Date, C. [1983] **An Introduction to Database Systems,** Vol. 2, Addison-Wesley, 1983.

Date, C. [1983a] "The Outer Join," *Proceedings of the Second International Conference on Databases (ICOD-2),* 1983.

Date, C. [1984] "A Critique of the SQL Database Language," **ACM SIGMOD Record,** 14:3, November 1984.

Date, C. [1995] **An Introduction Database Systems,** 6th ed., Addison-Wesley, 1995.

Date, C. J., and Darwen, H. [1993] **A Guide to the SQL Standard,** 3rd ed., Addison-Wesley.

Date, C., and White, C. [1989] **A Guide to DB2,** 3rd ed., Addison-Wesley, 1989.

Date, C., and White, C. [1988a] **A Guide to SQL/DS,** Addison-Wesley, 1988.

Davies, C. [1973] "Recovery Semantics for a DB/DC System," *Proceedings of the ACM National Conference,* 1973.

Dayal, U., and Bernstein, P. [1978] "On the Updatability of Relational Views," in VLDB [1978].

Dayal, U., Hsu, M., and Ladin, R. [1991] "A Transaction Model for Long-Running Activities," in VLDB [1991].

Dayal, U., et al. [1987] "PROBE Final Report," Technical Report CCA-87-02, Computer Corporation of America, December 1987.

DBTG [1971] Report of the CODASYL Data Base Task Group, ACM, April 1971.

Delcambre, L., Lim, B., and Urban, S. [1991] "Object-Centered Constraints," in ICDE [1991].

DeMarco, T. [1979] **Structured Analysis and System Specification,** Prentice-Hall, 1979.

DeMichiel, L. [1989] "Performing Operations Over Mismatched Domains," in ICDE [1989].

Denning, D. [1980] "Secure Statistical Databases with Random Sample Queries," **TODS,** 5:3, September 1980.

Denning, D., and Denning, P. [1979] "Data Security," **ACM Computing Surveys,** 11:3, September 1979, pp. 227–249.

Devor, C., and Weeldreyer, J. [1980] "DDTS: A Testbed for Distributed Database Research," *Proceedings of the ACM Pacific Conference,* 1980.

Dewire, D. [1993] **Client Server Computing,** McGraw-Hill, 1993.

DeWitt, D., et al. [1984] "Implementation Techniques for Main Memory Databases," in SIGMOD [1984].

DeWitt, D., et al. [1990] "The Gamma Database Machine Project," **TKDE,** 2:1, March 1990.

DeWitt, D., Futtersack, P., Maier, D., and Velez, F. [1990] "A Study of Three Alternative Workstation Server Architectures for Object-Oriented Database Systems," in VLDB [1990].

Dhawan, C. [1997] **Mobile Computing,** McGraw-Hill, 1997.

Dietrich, S., Friesen, O., W. Calliss [1998] On Deductive and Object Oriented Databases: The VALIDITY Experience," Technical Report, Arizona State University, 1999.

Diffie, W., and Hellman, M. [1979] "Privacy and Authentication," **Proceedings of the IEEE,** 67:3, March 1979.

Dipert, B., and Levy M. [1993] **Designing with Flash Memory,** Annabooks 1993.

Dittrich, K. [1986] "Object-Oriented Database Systems: The Notion and the Issues," in Dittrich and Dayal [1986].

Dittrich, K., and Dayal, U., eds. [1986] *Proceedings of the International Workshop on Object-Oriented Database Systems,* IEEE CS, Pacific Grove, CA, September 1986.

Dittrich, K., Kotz, A., and Mulle, J. [1986] "An Event/Trigger Mechanism to Enforce Complex Consistency Constraints in Design Databases," in SIGMOD Record, 15:3, 1986.

Dodd, G. [1969] "APL—A Language for Associative Data Handling in PL/I," *Proceedings of the Fall Joint Computer Conference,* AFIPS, 29, 1969.

Dodd, G. [1969] "Elements of Data Management Systems," ACM **Computing Surveys,** 1:2, June 1969.

Dogac, A., Ozsu, M. T., Bilins, A., Sellis, T., eds. [1994] **Advances in Object-oriented Databases Systems,** Springer-Verlag, 1994.

Dogac, A., [1998] Special Section on Electronic Commerce, **ACM Sigmod Record** 27:4, December 1998.

Dos Santos, C., Neuhold, E., and Furtado, A. [1979] "A Data Type Approach to the Entity-Relationship Model," in ER Conference [1979].

Du, D., and Tong, S. [1991] "Multilevel Extendible Hashing: A File Structure for Very Large Databases," **TKDE,** 3:3, September 1991.

Du, H., and Ghanta, S. [1987] "A Framework for Efficient IC/VLSI CAD Databases," in ICDE [1987].

Dumas, P., et al. [1982] "MOBILE-Burotique: Prospects for the Future," in Naffah [1982].

Dumpala, S., and Arora, S. [1983] "Schema Translation Using the Entity-Relationship Approach," in ER Conference [1983].

Dunham, M., and Helal, A. [1995] "Mobile Computing and Databases: Anything New?" **SIGMOD Record,** 24:4, December 1995.

Dwyer, S., et al. [1982] "A Diagnostic Digital Imaging System," *Proceedings of the IEEE CS Conference on Pattern Recognition and Image Processing,* June 1982.

Eastman, C. [1987] "Database Facilities for Engineering Design," **Proceedings of the IEEE,** 69:10, October 1981.

EDS [1984] **Expert Database Systems,** Kerschberg, L., ed. (*Proceedings of the First International Workshop on Expert Database Systems,* Kiawah Island, SC, October 1984), Benjamin/Cummings, 1986.

EDS [1986] **Expert Database Systems,** Kerschberg, L., ed. (*Proceedings of the First International Conference on Expert Database Systems,* Charleston, SC, April 1986), Benjamin/Cummings, 1987.

EDS [1988] **Expert Database Systems,** Kerschberg, L., ed. (*Proceedings of the Second International Conference on Expert Database Systems,* Tysons Corner, VA, April 1988), Benjamin/Cummings (forthcoming).

Eick, C. [1991] "A Methodology for the Design and Transformation of Conceptual Schemas," in VLDB [1991].

ElAbbadi, A., and Toueg, S. [1988] "The Group Paradigm for Concurrency Control," in SIGMOD [1988].

ElAbbadi, A., and Toueg, S. [1989] "Maintaining Availability in Partitioned Replicated Databases," **TODS,** 14:2, June 1989.

Ellis, C., and Nutt, G. [1980] "Office Information Systems and Computer Science," **ACM Computing Surveys,** 12:1, March 1980.

Elmagarmid A. K., ed. [1992] **Database Transaction Models for Advanced Applications,** Morgan Kaufmann, 1992.

Elmagarmid, A., Leu, Y., Litwin, W., and Rusinkiewicz, M. [1990] "A Multidatabase Transaction Model for Interbase," in VLDB [1990].

Elmasri, R., James, S., and Kouramajian, V. [1993] "Automatic Class and Method Generation for Object-Oriented Databases," *Proceedings of the Third International Conference on Deductive and Object-Oriented Databases (DOOD-93),* Phoenix, AZ, December 1993.

Elmasri, R., Kouramajian, V., and Fernando, S. [1993] "Temporal Database Modeling: An Object-Oriented Approach," *CIKM,* November 1993.

Elmasri, R., and Larson, J. [1985] "A Graphical Query Facility for ER Databases," in ER Conference [1985].

Elmasri, R., Larson, J., and Navathe, S. [1986] "Schema Integration Algorithms for Federated Databases and Logical Database Design," Honeywell CSDD, Technical Report CSC-86-9: 8212, January 1986.

Elmasri, R., Srinivas, P., and Thomas, G. [1987] "Fragmentation and Query Decomposition in the ECR Model," in ICDE [1987].

Elmasri, R., Weeldreyer, J., and Hevner, A. [1985] "The Category Concept: An Extension to the Entity-Relationship Model," **International Journal on Data and Knowledge Engineering,** 1:1, May 1985.

Elmasri, R., and Wiederhold, G. [1979] "Data Model Integration Using the Structural Model," in SIGMOD [1979].

Elmasri, R., and Wiederhold, G. [1980] "Structural Properties of Relationships and Their Representation," *NCC, AFIPS*, 49, 1980.

Elmasri, R., and Wiederhold, G. [1981] "GORDAS: A Formal, High-Level Query Language for the Entity-Relationship Model," in ER Conference [1981].

Elmasri, R., and Wuu, G. [1990] "A Temporal Model and Query Language for ER Databases," in ICDE [1990], in VLDB [1990].

Elmasri, R., and Wuu, G. [1990a] "The Time Index: An Access Structure for Temporal Data," in VLDB [1990].

Engelbart, D., and English, W. [1968] "A Research Center for Augmenting Human Intellect," *Proceedings of the Fall Joint Computer Conference*, AFIPS, December 1968.

Epstein, R., Stonebraker, M., and Wong, E. [1978] "Distributed Query Processing in a Relational Database System," in SIGMOD [1978].

ER Conference [1979] **Entity-Relationship Approach to Systems Analysis and Design,** Chen, P., ed. (*Proceedings of the First International Conference on Entity-Relationship Approach*, Los Angeles, December 1979), North-Holland, 1980.

ER Conference [1981] **Entity-Relationship Approach to Information Modeling and Analysis,** Chen, P., eds. (*Proceedings of the Second International Conference on Entity-Relationship Approach*, Washington, October 1981), Elsevier Science, 1981.

ER Conference [1983] **Entity-Relationship Approach to Software Engineering,** Davis, C., Jajodia, S., Ng, P., and Yeh, R., eds. (*Proceedings of the Third International Conference on Entity-Relationship Approach*, Anaheim, CA, October 1983), North-Holland, 1983.

ER Conference [1985] *Proceedings of the Fourth International Conference on Entity-Relationship Approach*, Liu, J., ed., Chicago, October 1985, IEEE CS.

ER Conference [1986] *Proceedings of the Fifth International Conference on Entity Relationship Approach*, Spaccapietra, S., ed., Dijon, France, November 1986, Express-Tirages.

ER Conference [1987] *Proceedings of the Sixth International Conference on Entity-Relationship Approach*, March, S., ed., New York, November 1987.

ER Conference [1988] *Proceedings of the Seventh International Conference on Entity-Relationship Approach*, Batini, C., ed., Rome, November 1988.

ER Conference [1989] *Proceedings of the Eighth International Conference on Entity Relationship Approach*, Lochovsky, F., ed., Toronto, October 1989.

ER Conference [1990] *Proceedings of the Ninth International Conference on Entity-Relationship Approach*, Kangassalo, H., ed., Lausanne, Switzerland, September 1990.

ER Conference [1991] *Proceedings of the Tenth International Conference on Entity-Relationship Approach*, Teorey, T., ed., San Mateo, CA, October 1991.

ER Conference [1992] *Proceedings of the Eleventh International Conference on Entity Relationship Approach*, Pernul, G., and Tjoa, A., eds., Karlsruhe, Germany, October 1992.

ER Conference [1993] *Proceedings of the Twelfth International Conference on Entity-Relationship Approach*, Elmasri, R., and Kouramajian, V., eds., Arlington, TX, December 1993.

ER Conference [1994] *Proceedings of the Thirteenth International Conference on Entity-Relationship Approach*, Loucopoulos, P., and Theodoulidis, B., eds., Manchester, England, December 1994.

ER Conference [1995] *Proceedings of the Fourteenth International Conference on ER-OO Modeling*, Papazouglou, M., and Tari, Z., eds., Brisbane, Australia, December 1995.

ER Conference [1996] *Proceedings of the Fifteenth International Conference on Conceptual Modeling*, Thalheim, B., ed., Cottbus, Germany, October 1996.

ER Conference [1997] *Proceedings of the Sixteenth International Conference on Conceptual Modeling*, Embley, D., ed., Los Angeles, October 1997.

ER Conference [1998] *Proceedings of the Seventeenth International Conference on Conceptual Modeling,* Ling, T.-K., ed., Singapore, November 1998.

Eswaran, K., and Chamberlin, D. [1975] "Functional Specifications of a Subsystem for Database Integrity," in VLDB [1975].

Eswaran, K., Gray, J., Lorie, R., and Traiger, I. [1976] "The Notions of Consistency and Predicate Locks in a Data Base System," **CACM,** 19:11, November 1976.

Everett, G., Dissly, C., and Hardgrave, W. [1971] *RFMS User Manual,* TRM-16, Computing Center, University of Texas at Austin, 1981.

Fagin, R. [1977] "Multivalued Dependencies and a New Normal Form for Relational Databases," **TODS,** 2:3, September 1977.

Fagin, R. [1979] "Normal Forms and Relational Database Operators," in SIGMOD [1979].

Fagin, R. [1981] "A Normal Form for Relational Databases That Is Based on Domains and Keys," TODS, 6:3, September 1981.

Fagin, R., Nievergelt, J., Pippenger, N., and Strong, H. [1979] "Extendible Hashing—A Fast Access Method for Dynamic Files," **TODS,** 4:3, September 1979.

Falcone, S., and Paton, N. [1997]. "Deductive Object-Oriented Database Systems: A Survey," *Proceedings of the 3rd International Workshop Rules in Database Systems (RIDS'97),* Skovde, Sweden, June 1997.

Faloutsos, C. [1996] **Searching Multimedia Databases by Content,** Kluwer, 1996.

Faloutsos, G., and Jagadish, H. [1992] "On B-Tree Indices for Skewed Distributions," in VLDB [1992].

Faloutsos, C., Barber, R., Flickner, M., Hafner, J., Niblack, W., Perkovic, D., and Equitz, W. [1994] Efficient and effective querying by image content," in **Journal of Intelligent Information Systems,** 3:4, 1994.

Farag, W., and Teorey, T. [1993] "FunBase: A Function-based Information Management System," *CIKM,* November 1993.

Farahmand, F., Navathe, S. B., and Enslow, P. H. [2002] "Electronic Commerce and Security—Management Perspective," *INFORMS 7th Annual Conference on Informations Systems and Technology, CIST 2002,* November 2002 (http://www.sba.uconn.edu/OPIM/CIST/).

Fernandez, E., Summers, R., and Wood, C. [1981] **Database Security and Integrity,** Addison-Wesley, 1981.

Ferrier, A., and Stangret, C. [1982] "Heterogeneity in the Distributed Database Management System SIRIUS-DELTA," in VLDB [1982].

Fishman, D., et al. [1986] "IRIS: An Object-Oriented DBMS," **TOOIS,** 4:2, April 1986.

Folk, M. J., Zoellick, B., and Riccardi, G. [1998] **File Structures: An Object Oriented Approach with C++,** 3rd ed., Addison-Wesley, 1998.

Ford, D., Blakeley, J., and Bannon, T. [1993] "Open OODB: A Modular Object-Oriented DBMS," in SIGMOD [1993].

Ford, D., and Christodoulakis, S. [1991] "Optimizing Random Retrievals from CLV Format Optical Disks," in VLDB [1991].

Foreman, G., and Zahorjan, J. [1994] "The Challenges of Mobile Computing" **IEEE Computer,** April 1994.

Fowler, M., and Scott, K. [1997] **UML distilled,** Addison-Wesley, 1997.

Franaszek, P., Robinson, J., and Thomasian, A. [1992] "Concurrency Control for High Contention Environments," **TODS,** 17:2, June 1992.

Franklin, F., et al. [1992] "Crash Recovery in Client-Server EXODUS," in SIGMOD [1992].

Fraternali, P. [1999] Tools and Approaches for Data Intensive Web Applications: A Survey, ACM *Computing Surveys,* 31:3, September 1999.

Frenkel, K. [1991] "The Human Genome Project and Informatics," **CACM,** November 1991.

Friesen, O., Gauthier-Villars, G., Lefelorre, A., and Vieille, L., "Applications of Deductive Object-Oriented Databases Using DEL," in Ramakrishnan (1995).

Furtado, A. [1978] "Formal Aspects of the Relational Model," **Information Systems,** 3:2, 1978.

Gadia, S. [1988] "A Homogeneous Relational Model and Query Language for Temporal Databases," **TODS,** 13:4, December 1988.

Gait, J. [1988] "The Optical File Cabinet: A Random-Access File System for Write-Once Optical Disks," **IEEE Computer,** 21:6, June 1988.

Gallaire, H., and Minker, J., eds. [1978] **Logic and Databases,** Plenum Press, 1978.

Gallaire, H., Minker, J., and Nicolas, J. [1984] "Logic and Databases: A Deductive Approach," **ACM Computing Surveys,** 16:2, June 1984.

Gallaire, H., Minker, J., and Nicolas, J., eds. [1981], **Advances in Database Theory,** vol. 1, Plenum Press, 1981.

Gamal-Eldin, M., Thomas, G., and Elmasri, R. [1988] "Integrating Relational Databases with Support for Updates," *Proceedings of the International Symposium on Databases in Parallel and Distributed Systems,* IEEE CS, December 1988.

Gane, C., and Sarson, T. [1977] **Structured Systems Analysis: Tools and Techniques,** Improved Systems Technologies, 1977.

Gangopadhyay, A., and Adam, N. [1997]. **Database Issues in Geographic Information Systems,** Kluwer Academic Publishers, 1997.

Garcia-Molina, H. [1982] "Elections in Distributed Computing Systems," **IEEE Transactions on Computers,** 31:1, January 1982.

Garcia-Molina, H. [1983] "Using Semantic Knowledge for Transaction Processing in a Distributed Database," **TODS,** 8:2, June 1983.

Gehani, N., Jagdish, H., and Shmueli, O. [1992] "Composite Event Specification in Active Databases: Model and Implementation," in VLDB [1992].

Georgakopoulos, D., Rusinkiewicz, M., and Sheth, A. [1991] "On Serializability of Multidatabase Transactions Through Forced Local Conflicts," in ICDE [1991].

Gerritsen, R. [1975] "A Preliminary System for the Design of DBTG Data Structures," **CACM,** 18:10, October 1975.

Ghosh, S. [1984] "An Application of Statistical Databases in Manufacturing Testing," in ICDE [1984].

Ghosh, S. [1986] "Statistical Data Reduction for Manufacturing Testing," in ICDE [1986].

Gifford, D. [1979] "Weighted Voting for Replicated Data," *Proceedings of the Seventh ACM Symposium on Operating Systems Principles,* 1979.

Gladney, H. [1989] "Data Replicas in Distributed Information Services," **TODS,** 14:1, March 1989.

Gogolla, M., and Hohenstein, U. [1991] "Towards a Semantic View of an Extended Entity-Relationship Model," **TODS,** 16:3, September 1991.

Goldberg, A., and Robson, D. [1983] **Smalltalk-80: The Language and Its Implementation,** Addison-Wesley, 1983.

Goldfine, A., and Konig, P. [1988] A *Technical Overview of the Information Resource Dictionary System (IRDS),* 2nd ed., NBS IR 88-3700, National Bureau of Standards.

Gotlieb, L. [1975] "Computing Joins of Relations," in SIGMOD [1975].

Graefe, G. [1993] "Query Evaluation Techniques for Large Databases," ACM Computing Surveys, 25:2, June 1993.

Graefe, G., and DeWitt, D. [1987] "The EXODUS Optimizer Generator," in SIGMOD [1987].

Gravano, L., and Garcia-Molina, H. [1997] "Merging Ranks from Heterogeneous Sources," in VLDB [1997].

Gray, J. [1978] "Notes on Data Base Operating Systems," in Bayer, Graham, and Seegmuller [1978].

Gray, J. [1981] "The Transaction Concept: Virtues and Limitations," in VLDB [1981].

Gray, J., Lorie, R., and Putzulo, G. [1975] "Granularity of Locks and Degrees of Consistency in a Shared Data Base," in Nijssen [1975].

Gray, J., McJones, P., and Blasgen, M. [1981] "The Recovery Manager of the System R Database Manager," **ACM Computing Surveys,** 13:2, June 1981.

Gray, J., and Reuter, A. [1993] **Transaction Processing: Concepts and Techniques,** Morgan Kaufmann, 1993.

Griffiths, P., and Wade, B. [1976] "An Authorization Mechanism for a Relational Database System," **TODS,** 1:3, September 1976.

Grochowski, E., and Hoyt, R. F. [1996] "Future Trends in Hard Disk Drives," **IEEE Transactions on Magnetics,** 32:3, May 1996.

Grosky, W. [1994] "Multimedia Information Systems," in **IEEE Multimedia,** 1:1, Spring 1994.

Grosky, W. [1997] "Managing Multimedia Information in Database Systems," in **CACM,** 40:12, December 1997.

Grosky, W., Jain, R., and Mehrotra, R., eds. [1997], **The Handbook of Multimedia Information Management,** Prentice-Hall PTR, 1997.

Guttman, A. [1984] "R-Trees: A Dynamic Index Structure for Spatial Searching," in SIGMOD [1984].

Gwayer, M. [1996] **Oracle Designer/2000 Web Server Generator Technical Overview** (version 1.3.2), Technical Report, Oracle Corporation, September 1996.

Halsaal, F. [1996] **Data Communications, Computer Networks and Open Systems,** 4th ed., Addison-Wesley, 1996.

Haas, P., Naughton, J., Seshadri, S. and Stokes, L. [1995] Sampling-based Estimation of the Number of Distinct Values of an Attribute," in VLDB [1995].

Haas, P., and Swami, A.[1995] "Sampling-based Selectivity Estimation for Joins Using Augmented Frequent Value Statistics," in ICDE [1995].

Hachem, N. and Berra, P. [1992] "New Order Preserving Access Methods for Very Large Files Derived from Linear Hashing," **TKDE,** 4:1, February 1992.

Hadzilacos, V. [1983] "An Operational Model for Database System Reliability," in *Proceedings of SIGACT-SIGMOD Conference,* March 1983.

Hadzilacos, V. [1986] "A Theory of Reliability in Database Systems," 1986.

Haerder, T., and Rothermel, K. [1987] "Concepts for Transaction Recovery in Nested Transactions," in SIGMOD [1987].

Haerder, T., and Reuter, A. [1983] "Principles of Transaction Oriented Database Recovery—A Taxonomy," **ACM Computing Surveys,** 15:4, September 1983, pp. 287–318.

Hall, P. [1976] "Optimization of a Single Relational Expression in a Relational Data Base System," **IBM Journal of Research and Development,** 20:3, May 1976.

Hamilton, G., Catteli, R., and Fisher, M. [1997] **JDBC Database Access with Java–A Tutorial and Annotated Reference,** Addison Wesley, 1997.

Hammer, M., and McLeod, D. [1975] "Semantic Integrity in a Relational Data Base System," in VLDB [1975].

Hammer, M., and McLeod, D. [1981] "Database Description with SDM: A Semantic Data Model," **TODS,** 6:3, September 1981.

Hammer, M., and Sarin, S. [1978] "Efficient Monitoring of Database Assertions," in SIGMOD [1978].

J. Han and M. Kamber, *Data Mining: Concepts and Techniques*, Morgan Kaufmann, San Francisco, 2001.

J. Han, J. Pei and Y. Yin, "Mining Frequent Patterns without Candidate Generation," Proc. ACM SIGMOD Conference, 2000.

Hanson, E. [1992] "Rule Condition Testing and Action Execution in Ariel," in SIGMOD [1992].

Hardgrave, W. [1984] "BOLT: A Retrieval Language for Tree-Structured Database Systems," in TOU [1984].

Hardgrave, W. [1980] "Ambiguity in Processing Boolean Queries on TDMS Tree Structures: A Study of Four Different Philosophies," **TSE,** 6:4, July 1980.

Harrington, J. [1987] **Relational Database Management for Microcomputer: Design and Implementation,** Holt, Rinehart, and Winston, 1987.

Harris, L. [1978] "The ROBOT System: Natural Language Processing Applied to Data Base Query," *Proceedings of the ACM National Conference,* December 1978.

Haskin, R., and Lorie, R. [1982] "On Extending the Functions of a Relational Database System," in SIGMOD [1982].

Hasse, C., and Weikum, G. [1991] "A Performance Evaluation of Multi-Level Transaction Management," in VLDB [1991].

Hayes-Roth, F., Waterman, D., and Lenat, D., eds. [1983] **Building Expert Systems,** Addison-Wesley, 1983.

Hayne, S., and Ram, S. [1990] "Multi-User View Integration System: An Expert System for View Integration," in ICDE [1990].

Heiler, S., and Zdonick, S. [1990] "Object Views: Extending the Vision," in ICDE [1990].

Heiler, S., Hardhvalal, S., Zdonik, S., Blaustein, B., and Rosenthal, A. [1992] "A Flexible Framework for Transaction Management in Engineering Environment," in Elmagarmid [1992].

Helal, A., Hu, T., Elmasri, R., and Mukherjee, S. [1993] "Adaptive Transaction Scheduling," *CIKM,* November 1993.

Held, G., and Stonebraker, M. [1978] "B-Trees Reexamined," **CACM,** 21:2, February 1978.

Henschen, L., and Naqvi S. [1984], "On Compiling Queries in Recursive First-Order Databases," **JACM,** 31:1, January 1984.

Hernandez, H., and Chan., E. [1991] "Constraint-Time-Maintainable BCNF Database Schemes," **TODS,** 16:4, December 1991.

Herot, C. [1980] "Spatial Management of Data," **TODS,** 5:4, December 1980.

Hevner, A., and Yao, S. [1979] "Query Processing in Distributed Database Systems," **TSE,** 5:3, May 1979.

Hoffer, J. [1982] "An Empirical Investigation with Individual Differences in Database Models," *Proceedings of the Third International Information Systems Conference,* December 1982.

Holland, J. [1975] **Adaptation in Natural and Artificial Systems,** University of Michigan Press, 1975.

Holsapple, C., and Whinston, A., eds. [1987] **Decisions Support Systems Theory and Application,** Springer-Verlag, 1987.

Holtzman J. M., and Goodman D. J., eds. [1993] **Wireless Communications: Future Directions,** Kluwer, 1993.

Hsiao, D., and Kamel, M. [1989] "Heterogeneous Databases: Proliferation, Issues, and Solutions," **TKDE,** 1:1, March 1989.

Hsu, A., and Imielinsky, T. [1985] "Integrity Checking for Multiple Updates," in SIGMOD [1985].

Hull, R., and King, R. [1987] "Semantic Database Modeling: Survey, Applications, and Research Issues," **ACM Computing Surveys,** 19:3, September 1987.

IBM [1978] QBE Terminal Users Guide, Form Number SH20-2078-0.

IBM [1992] Systems Application Architecture Common Programming Interface Database Level 2 Reference, Document Number SC26-4798-01.

ICDE [1984] *Proceedings of the IEEE CS International Conference on Data Engineering,* Shuey, R., ed., Los Angeles, CA, April 1984.

ICDE [1986] *Proceedings of the IEEE CS International Conference on Data Engineering,* Wiederhold, G., ed., Los Angeles, February 1986.

ICDE [1987] *Proceedings of the IEEE CS International Conference on Data Engineering,* Wah, B., ed., Los Angeles, February 1987.

ICDE [1988] *Proceedings of the IEEE CS International Conference on Data Engineering,* Carlis, J., ed., Los Angeles, February 1988.

ICDE [1989] *Proceedings of the IEEE CS International Conference on Data Engineering,* Shuey, R., ed., Los Angeles, February 1989.

ICDE [1990] *Proceedings of the IEEE CS International Conference on Data Engineering,* Liu, M., ed., Los Angeles, February 1990.

ICDE [1991] *Proceedings of the IEEE CS International Conference on Data Engineering,* Cercone, N., and Tsuchiya, M., eds., Kobe, Japan, April 1991.

ICDE [1992] *Proceedings of the IEEE CS International Conference on Data Engineering,* Golshani, F., ed., Phoenix, AZ, February 1992.

ICDE [1993] *Proceedings of the IEEE CS International Conference on Data Engineering,* Elmagarmid, A., and Neuhold, E., eds., Vienna, Austria, April 1993.

ICDE [1994] *Proceedings of the IEEE CS International Conference on Data Engineering.*

ICDE [1995] *Proceedings of the IEEE CS International Conference on Data Engineering,* Yu, P. S., and Chen, A. L. A., eds., Taipei, Taiwan, 1995.

ICDE [1996] *Proceedings of the IEEE CS International Conference on Data Engineering,* Su, S. Y. W., ed., New Orleans, 1996.

ICDE [1997] *Proceedings of the IEEE CS International Conference on Data Engineering,* Gray, A., and Larson, P. A., eds., Birmingham, England, 1997.

ICDE [1998] *Proceedings of the IEEE CS International Conference on Data Engineering,* Orlando, FL, 1998.

ICDE [1999] *Proceedings of the IEEE CS International Conference on Data Engineering,* Sydney, Australia, 1999.

ICDE [1983] International Graphics Exchange Specification Version 2, National Bureau of Standards, U.S. Department of Commerce, January 1983.

Imielinski, T., and Badrinath, B. [1994] "Mobile Wireless Computing: Challenges in Data Management," **CACM,** 37:10, October 1994.

Imielinski, T., and Lipski, W. [1981] "On Representing Incomplete Information in a Relational Database," in VLDB [1981].

Informix [1998] "Web Integration Option for Informix Dynamic Server," available at http://www.infomix. com.

Inmon, W. H. [1992] **Building the Data Warehouse,** Wiley, 1992.

Ioannidis, Y., and Kang, Y. [1990] "Randomized Algorithms for Optimizing Large Join Queries," in SIGMOD [1990].

Ioannidis, Y., and Kang, Y. [1991] "Left-Deep vs. Bushy Trees: An Analysis of Strategy Spaces and Its Implications for Query Optimization," in SIGMOD [1991].

Ioannidis, Y., and Wong, E. [1988] "Transforming Non-Linear Recursion to Linear Recursion," in EDS [1988].

Iossophidis, J. [1979] "A Translator to Convert the DDL of ERM to the DDL of System 2000," in ER Conference [1979].

Irani, K., Purkayastha, S., and Teorey, T. [1979] "A Designer for DBMS-Processable Logical Database Structures," in VLDB [1979].

Jacobson, I., Christerson, M., Jonsson, P., Overgaard, G. [1992] **Object Oriented Software Engineering: A Use Case Driven Approach,** Addison-Wesley, 1992.

Jagadish, H. [1989] "Incorporating Hierarchy in a Relational Model of Data," in SIGMOD [1989].

Jagadish, H. [1997] "Content-based Indexing and Retrieval," in Grosky et al. [1997].

Jajodia, S., and Kogan, B. [1990] "Integrating an Object-oriented Data Model with Multilevel Security," *IEEE Symposium on Security and Privacy,* May 1990, pp. 76–85.

Jajodia, S., and Mutchler, D. [1990] "Dynamic Voting Algorithms for Maintaining the Consistency of a Replicated Database," **TODS,** 15:2, June, 1990.

Jajodia, S., Ng, P., and Springsteel, F. [1983] "The Problem of Equivalence for Entity- Relationship Diagrams," **TSE,** 9:5, September, 1983.

Jajodia, S., and Sandhu, R. [1991] "Toward a Multilevel Secure Relational Data Model," in SIGMOD [1991].

Jardine, D., ed. [1977] **The ANSI/SPARC DBMS Model,** North-Holland, 1977.

Jarke, M., and Koch, J. [1984] "Query Optimization in Database Systems," **ACM Computing Surveys,** 16:2, June 1984.

Jensen, C., and Snodgrass, R. [1992] "Temporal Specialization," in ICDE [1992].

Jensen, C., et al. [1994] "A Glossary of Temporal Database Concepts," **ACM SIGMOD Record,** 23:1, March 1994.

Johnson, T., and Shasha, D. [1993] "The Performance of Current B-Tree Algorithms," **TODS,** 18:1, March 1993.

Joshi, J. B. D., Aref, W. G., Ghafoor, A., and Spafford, E. H. [2001] "Security Models for Web-Based Applications," **Communications of the ACM,** February 2001, pp. 38–44.

Kaefer, W., and Schoening, H. [1992] "Realizing a Temporal Complex-Object Data Model," in SIGMOD [1992].

Kamel, I., and Faloutsos, C. [1993] "On Packing R-trees," *CIKM,* November 1993.

Kamel, N., and King, R. [1985] "A Model of Data Distribution Based on Texture Analysis," in SIGMOD [1985].

Kapp, D., and Leben, J. [1978] **IMS Programming Techniques,** Van Nostrand-Reinhold, 1978.

Kappel, G., and Schrefl, M. [1991] "Object/Behavior Diagrams," in ICDE [1991].

Karlapalem, K., Navathe, S. B., and Ammar, M. [1996] "Optimal Redesign Policies to Support Dynamic Processing of Applications on a Distributed Relational Database System," **Information Systems,** 21:4, 1996, pp. 353–67.

Katz, R. [1985] **Information Management for Engineering Design: Surveys in Computer Science,** Springer-Verlag, 1985.

Katz, R., and Wong, E. [1982] "Decompiling CODASYL DML into Relational Queries," **TODS,** 7:1, March 1982.

KDD [1996] *Proceedings of the Second International Conference on Knowledge Discovery in Databases and Data Mining,* Portland, Oregon, August 1996.

Kedem, Z., and Silberschatz, A. [1980] "Non-Two Phase Locking Protocols with Shared and Exclusive Locks," in VLDB [1980].

Keller, A. [1982] "Updates to Relational Database Through Views Involving Joins," in Scheuermann [1982].

Kemp, K. [1993]. "Spatial Databases: Sources and Issues," in **Environmental Modeling with GIS,** Oxford University Press, New York, 1993.

Kemper, A., Lockemann, P., and Wallrath, M. [1987] "An Object-Oriented Database System for Engineering Applications," in SIGMOD [1987].

Kemper, A., Moerkotte, G., and Steinbrunn, M. [1992] "Optimizing Boolean Expressions in Object Bases," in VLDB [1992].

Kemper, A., and Wallrath, M. [1987] "An Analysis of Geometric Modeling in Database Systems," **ACM Computing Surveys,** 19:1, March 1987.

Kent, W. [1978] **Data and Reality,** North-Holland, 1978.

Kent, W. [1979] "Limitations of Record-Based Information Models," **TODS,** 4:1, March 1979.

Kent, W. [1991] "Object-Oriented Database Programming Languages," in VLDB [1991].

Kerschberg, L., Ting, P., and Yao, S. [1982] "Query Optimization in Star Computer Networks," **TODS,** 7:4, December 1982.

Ketabchi, M. A., Mathur, S., Risch, T., and Chen, J. [1990] "Comparative Analysis of RDBMS and OODBMS: A Case Study," *IEEE International Conference on Manufacturing,* 1990.

Khoshafian, S. and Baker A., [1996] **Multimedia and Imaging Databases,** Morgan Kaufmann, 1996.

Khoshafian, S., Chan, A., Wong, A., and Wong, H. K. T. [1992] **Developing Client Server Applications,** Morgan Kaufmann, 1992.

Kifer, M., and Lozinskii, E. [1986] "A Framework for an Efficient Implementation of Deductive Databases," *Proceedings of the Sixth Advanced Database Symposium,* Tokyo, August 1986.

Kim, P. [1996] "A Taxonomy on the Architecture of Database Gateways for the Web," Working Paper TR-96-U-10, Chungnam National University, Taejon, Korea (available from http://grigg.chungnam.ac.kr/projects/UniWeb).

Kim, W. [1982] "On Optimizing an SQL-like Nested Query," **TODS,** 3:3, September 1982.

Kim, W. [1989] "A Model of Queries for Object-Oriented Databases," in VLDB [1989].

Kim, W. [1990] "Object-Oriented Databases: Definition and Research Directions," **TKDE,** 2:3, September 1990.

Kim W. [1995] **Modern Database Systems: The Object Model, Interoperability, and Beyond,** ACM Press, Addison-Wesley, 1995.

Kim, W., Reiner, D., and Batory, D., eds. [1985] **Query Processing in Database Systems,** Springer-Verlag, 1985.

Kim, W. et al. [1987] "Features of the ORION Object-Oriented Database System," Microelectronics and Computer Technology Corporation, Technical Report ACA-ST-308-87, September 1987.

Kimball, R. [1996] **The Data Warehouse Toolkit,** Wiley, Inc. 1996.

King, J. [1981] "QUIST: A System for Semantic Query Optimization in Relational Databases," in VLDB [1981].

Kitsuregawa, M., Nakayama, M., and Takagi, M. [1989] "The Effect of Bucket Size Tuning in the Dynamic Hybrid GRACE Hash Join Method," in VLDB [1989].

Klimbie, J., and Koffeman, K., eds. [1974] **Data Base Management,** North-Holland, 1974.

Klug, A. [1982] "Equivalence of Relational Algebra and Relational Calculus Query Languages Having Aggregate Functions," **JACM,** 29:3, July 1982.

Knuth, D. [1973] **The Art of Computer Programming, Vol. 3: Sorting and Searching,** Addison-Wesley, 1973.

Kogelnik, A. [1998] "Biological Information Management with Application to Human Genome Data," Ph.D. dissertation, Georgia Institute of Technology and Emory University, 1998.

Kogelnik, A., Lott, M., Brown, M., Navathe, S., Wallace, D. [1998] "MITOMAP: A human mitochondrial genome database—1998 update." **Nucleic Acids Research,** 26:1, January 1998.

Kogelnik, A., Navathe, S., Wallace, D. [1997] "GENOME: A system for managing Human Genome Project Data." *Proceedings of Genome Informatics '97, Eighth Workshop on Genome Informatics,* Tokyo, Japan, Sponsor: Human Genome Center, University of Tokyo, December 1997.

Kohler, W. [1981] "A Survey of Techniques for Synchronization and Recovery in Decentralized Computer Systems," **ACM Computing Surveys,** 13:2, June 1981.

Konsynski, B., Bracker, L., and Bracker, W. [1982] "A Model for Specification of Office Communications," **IEEE Transactions on Communications,** 30:1, January 1982.

Korfhage, R. [1991] "To See, or Not to See: Is that the Query?" in *Proceedings of the ACM SIGIR International Conference,* June 1991.

Korth, H. [1983] "Locking Primitives in a Database System," **JACM,** 30:1, January 1983.

Korth, H., Levy, E., and Silberschatz, A. [1990] "A Formal Approach to Recovery by Compensating Transactions," in VLDB [1990].

Kotz, A., Dittrich, K., Mulle, J. [1988] "Supporting Semantic Rules by a Generalized Event/Trigger Mechanism," in VLDB [1988].

Krishnamurthy, R., Litwin, W., and Kent, W. [1991] "Language Features for Interoperability of Databases with Semantic Discrepancies," in SIGMOD [1991].

Krishnamurthy, R., and Naqvi, S., [1988] "Database Updates in Logic Programming, Rev. 1," MCC Technical Report #ACA-ST-010-88, Rev. 1, September 1988.

Krishnamurthy, R., and Naqvi, S. [1989] "Non-Deterministic Choice in Datalog," *Proceeedings of the 3rd International Conference on Data and Knowledge Bases,* Jerusalem, June 1989.

Krovetz, R., and Croft B. [1992] "Lexical Ambiguity and Information Retrieval" in **TOIS,** 10, April 1992.

Kumar, A. [1991] "Performance Measurement of Some Main Memory Recovery Algorithms," in ICDE [1991].

Kumar, A., and Segev, A. [1993] "Cost and Availability Tradeoffs in Replicated Concurrency Control," **TODS,** 18:1, March 1993.

Kumar, A., and Stonebraker, M. [1987] "Semantics Based Transaction Management Techniques for Replicated Data," in SIGMOD [1987].

Kumar, V., and Han, M., eds. [1992] **Recovery Mechanisms in Database Systems,** Prentice-Hall, 1992.

Kumar, V., and Hsu, M. [1998] **Recovery Mechanisms in Database Systems,** Prentice-Hall (PTR), 1998.

Kumar, V., and Song, H. S. [1998] Database Recovery, Kluwer Academic, 1998.

Kung, H., and Robinson, J. [1981] "Optimistic Concurrency Control," **TODS,** 6:2, June 1981.

Lacroix, M., and Pirotte, A. [1977] "Domain-Oriented Relational Languages," in VLDB [1977].

Lacroix, M., and Pirotte, A. [1977a] "ILL: An English Structured Query Language for Relational Data Bases," in Nijssen [1977].

Lamport, L. [1978] "Time, Clocks, and the Ordering of Events in a Distributed System," **CACM,** 21:7, July 1978.

Langerak, R. [1990] "View Updates in Relational Databases with an Independent Scheme," **TODS,** 15:1, March 1990.

Lanka, S., and Mays, E. [1991] "Fully Persistent B1-Trees," in SIGMOD [1991].

Larson, J. [1983] "Bridging the Gap Between Network and Relational Database Management Systems," **IEEE Computer,** 16:9, September 1983.

Larson, J., Navathe, S., and Elmasri, R. [1989] "Attribute Equivalence and its Use in Schema Integration," **TSE,** 15:2, April 1989.

Larson, P. [1978] "Dynamic Hashing," **BIT,** 18, 1978.

Larson, P. [1981] "Analysis of Index-Sequential Files with Overflow Chaining," **TODS,** 6:4, December 1981.

Laurini, R., and Thompson, D. [1992] **Fundamentals of Spatial Information Systems,** Academic Press, 1992.

Lehman, P., and Yao, S. [1981] "Efficient Locking for Concurrent Operations on B-Trees," **TODS,** 6:4, December 1981.

Lee, J., Elmasri, R., and Won, J. [1998] " An Integrated Temporal Data Model Incorporating Time Series Concepts," Data and Knowledge Engineering, 24, 1998, pp. 257–276.

Lehman, T., and Lindsay, B. [1989] "The Starburst Long Field Manager," in VLDB [1989].

Leiss, E. [1982] "Randomizing: A Practical Method for Protecting Statistical Databases Against Compromise," in VLDB [1982].

Leiss, E. [1982a] **Principles of Data Security,** Plenum Press, 1982.

Lenzerini, M., and Santucci, C. [1983] "Cardinality Constraints in the Entity Relationship Model," in ER Conference [1983].

Leung, C., Hibler, B., and Mwara, N. [1992] "Picture Retrieval by Content Description," in **Journal of Information Science,** 1992, pp. 111–19.

Levesque, H. [1984] " The Logic of Incomplete Knowledge Bases," in Brodie et al., ch. 7 [1984].

Li, W., Seluk Candan, K., Hirata, K., and Hara, Y. [1998] Hierarchical Image Modeling for Object-based Media Retrieval in DKE, 27:2, September 1998, pp. 139–76.

Lien, E., and Weinberger, P. [1978] "Consistency, Concurrency, and Crash Recovery," in SIGMOD [1978].

Lieuwen, L., and DeWitt, D. [1992] "A Transformation-Based Approach to Optimizing Loops in Database Programming Languages," in SIGMOD [1992].

Lilien, L., and Bhargava, B. [1985] "Database Integrity Block Construct: Concepts and Design Issues," **TSE,** 11:9, September 1985.

Lin, J., and Dunham, M. H. [1998] "Mining Association Rules," in ICDE [1998].

Lindsay, B., et al. [1984] "Computation and Communication in R*: A Distributed Database Manager," **TOCS,** 2:1, January 1984.

Lippman R. [1987] "An Introduction to Computing with Neural Nets," **IEEE ASSP Magazine,** April 1987.

Lipski, W. [1979] "On Semantic Issues Connected with Incomplete Information," TODS, 4:3, September 1979.

Lipton, R., Naughton, J., and Schneider, D. [1990] "Practical Selectivity Estimation through Adaptive Sampling," in SIGMOD [1990].

Liskov, B., and Zilles, S. [1975] "Specification Techniques for Data Abstractions," **TSE,** 1:1, March 1975.

Litwin, W. [1980] "Linear Hashing: A New Tool for File and Table Addressing," in VLDB [1980].

Liu, K., and Sunderraman, R. [1988] "On Representing Indefinite and Maybe Information in Relational Databases," in ICDE [1988].

Liu, L., and Meersman, R. [1992] "Activity Model: A Declarative Approach for Capturing Communication Behavior in Object-Oriented Databases," in VLDB [1992].

Livadas, P. [1989] **File Structures: Theory and Practice,** Prentice-Hall, 1989.

Lockemann, P., and Knutsen, W. [1968] "Recovery of Disk Contents After System Failure," **CACM,** 11:8, August 1968.

Lorie, R. [1977] "Physical Integrity in a Large Segmented Database," **TODS,** 2:1, March 1977.

Lorie, R., and Plouffe, W. [1983] "Complex Objects and Their Use in Design Transactions," in SIGMOD [1983].

Lozinskii, E. [1986] "A Problem-Oriented Inferential Database System," **TODS,** 11:3, September 1986.

Lu, H., Mikkilineni, K., and Richardson, J. [1987] "Design and Evaluation of Algorithms to Compute the Transitive Closure of a Database Relation," in ICDE [1987].

Lubars, M., Potts, C., and Richter, C. [1993] " A Review of the State of Practice in Requirements Modeling," *IEEE International Symposium on Requirements Engineering,* San Diego, CA, 1993.

Lucyk, B. [1993] **Advanced Topics in DB2,** Addison-Wesley, 1993.

Maguire, D., Goodchild, M. and Rhind D., eds. [1997] **Geographical Information Systems: Principles and Applications.** vols. 1 and 2, Longman Scientific and Technical, New York.

Mahajan, S., Donahoo. M. J., Navathe, S. B., Ammar, M., Malik, S. [1998] "Grouping Techniques for Update Propagation in Intermittently Connected Databases," in ICDE [1998].

Maier, D. [1983] **The Theory of Relational Databases,** Computer Science Press, 1983.

Maier, D., Stein, J., Otis, A., and Purdy, A. [1986] "Development of an Object-Oriented DBMS," *OOPSLA,* 1986.

Malley, C. and Zdonick, S. [1986] "A Knowledge-Based Approach to Query Optimization," in EDS [1986].

Maier, D., and Warren, D. S. [1988] **Computing with Logic,** Benjamin Cummings, 1988.

Mannila, H., Toivonen, H., and Verkamo A. [1994] "Efficient Algorithms for Discovering Association Rules," in *KDD-94, AAAI Workshop on Knowledge Discovery in Databases,* Seattle, 1994.

Manola. F. [1998] "Towards a Richer Web Object Model," in **SIGMOD Record,** 27:1, March 1998.

March, S., and Severance, D. [1977] "The Determination of Efficient Record Segmentations and Blocking Factors for Shared Files," **TODS,** 2:3, September 1977.

Mark, L., Roussopoulos, N., Newsome, T., and Laohapipattana, P. [1992] "Incrementally Maintained Network to Relational Mappings," **Software Practice & Experience,** 22:12, December 1992.

Markowitz, V., and Raz, Y. [1983] "ERROL: An Entity-Relationship, Role Oriented, Query Language," in ER Conference [1983].

Martin, J., Chapman, K., and Leben, J. [1989] **DB2-Concepts, Design, and Programming,** Prentice-Hall, 1989.

Martin, J., and Odell, J. [1992] **Object Oriented Analysis and Design,** Prentice Hall, 1992.

Maryanski, F. [1980] "Backend Database Machines," **ACM Computing Surveys,** 12:1, March 1980.

Masunaga, Y. [1987] "Multimedia Databases: A Formal Framework," *Proceedings of the IEEE Office Automation Symposium,* April 1987.

Mattison, R., **Data Warehousing: Strategies, Technologies, and Techniques,** McGraw-Hill, 1996.

McFadden, F. and Hoffer, J. [1988] **Database Management,** 2nd ed., Benjamin/Cummings, 1988.

McFadden, F. R., and Hoffer, J. A. [1994] **Modern Database Management,** 4th ed., Benjamin Cummings, 1994.

McGee, W. [1977] "The Information Management System IMS/VS, Part I: General Structure and Operation," **IBM Systems Journal,** 16:2, June 1977.

McLeish, M. [1989] "Further Results on the Security of Partitioned Dynamic Statistical Databases," **TODS,** 14:1, March 1989.

McLeod, D., and Heimbigner, D. [1985] "A Federated Architecture for Information Systems," **TOOIS,** 3:3, July 1985.

Mehrotra, S., et al. [1992] "The Concurrency Control Problem in Multidatabases: Characteristics and Solutions," in SIGMOD [1992].

Melton, J., Bauer, J., and Kulkarni, K. [1991] "Object ADTs (with improvements for value ADTs)," *ISO WG3 Report X3H2-91-083,* April 1991.

Melton, J., and Mattos, N. [1996] *An Overview of SQL3—The Emerging New Generation of the SQL Standard,* Tutorial No. T5, VLDB, Bombay, September 1996.

Melton, J., and Simon, A. R. [1993] **Understanding the New SQL: A Complete Guide,** Morgan Kaufmann.

Menasce, D., Popek, G., and Muntz, R. [1980] "A Locking Protocol for Resource Coordination in Distributed Databases," **TODS,** 5:2, June 1980.

Mendelzon, A., and Maier, D. [1979] "Generalized Mutual Dependencies and the Decomposition of Database Relations," in VLDB [1979].

Mendelzon, A., Mihaila, G., Milo, T. [1997] "Querying the World Wide Web," **Journal of Digital Libraries,** 1:1, April 1997.

Metais, E., Kedad, Z., Comyn-Wattiau, C., Bouzeghoub, M., "Using Linguistic Knowledge in View Integration: Toward a Third Generation of Tools," in DKE 23:1, June 1977.

Mikkilineni, K., and Su, S. [1988] "An Evaluation of Relational Join Algorithms in a Pipelined Query Processing Environment," **TSE,** 14:6, June 1988.

Miller, N. [1987] **File Structures Using PASCAL,** Benjamin Cummings, 1987.

Minoura, T., and Wiederhold, G. [1981] "Resilient Extended True-Copy Token Scheme for a Distributed Database," **TSE,** 8:3, May 1981.

Missikoff, M., and Wiederhold, G. [1984] "Toward a Unified Approach for Expert and Database Systems," in EDS [1984].

T. Mitchell, *Machine Learning,* McGraw Hill, New York, 1997.

Mitschang, B. [1989] "Extending the Relational Algebra to Capture Complex Objects," in VLDB [1989].

Mohan, C. [1993] "IBM's Relational Database Products: Features and Technologies," in SIGMOD [1993].

Mohan, C., Haderle, D., Lindsay, B., Pirahesh, H. and Schwarz, P. [1992] "ARIES: A Transaction Recovery Method Supporting Fine-Granularity Locking and Partial Rollbacks using Write-Ahead Logging," **TODS,** 17:1, March 1992.

Mohan, C., and Levine, F. [1992] "ARIEL/IM: An Efficient and High-Concurrency Index Management Method Using Write-Ahead Logging," in SIGMOD [1992].

Mohan, C., and Narang, I. [1992] "Algorithms for Creating Indexes for Very Large Tables without Quiescing Updates," in SIGMOD [1992].

Mohan, C. et al. [1992] "ARIEL: A Transaction Recovery Method Supporting Fine-Granularity Locking and Partial Rollbacks Using Write-Ahead Logging," **TODS,** 17:1, March 1992.

Morris, K., Ullman, J., and VanGelden, A. [1986] "Design Overview of the NAIL! System," *Proceedings of the Third International Conference on Logic Programming,* Springer-Verlag, 1986.

Morris, K., et al. [1987] "YAWN! (Yet Another Window on NAIL!), in ICDE [1987].

Morris, R. [1968] "Scatter Storage Techniques," **CACM,** 11:1, January 1968.

Morsi, M., Navathe, S., and Kim, H. [1992] "An Extensible Object-Oriented Database Testbed," in ICDE [1992].

Moss, J. [1982] "Nested Transactions and Reliable Distributed Computing," *Proceedings of the Symposium on Reliability in Distributed Software and Database Systems,* IEEE CS, July 1982.

Motro, A. [1987] "Superviews: Virtual Integration of Multiple Databases," **TSE,** 13:7, July 1987.

Mukkamala, R. [1989] "Measuring the Effect of Data Distribution and Replication Models on Performance Evaluation of Distributed Systems," in ICDE [1989].

Mumick, I., Finkelstein, S., Pirahesh, H., and Ramakrishnan, R. [1990] "Magic Is Relevant," in SIGMOD [1990].

Mumick, I., Pirahesh, H., and Ramakrishnan, R. [1990] "The Magic of Duplicates and Aggregates," in VLDB [1990].

Muralikrishna, M. [1992] "Improved Unnesting Algorithms for Join and Aggregate SQL Queries," in VLDB [1992].

Muralikrishna, M., and DeWitt, D. [1988] "Equi-depth Histograms for Estimating Selectivity Factors for Multi-dimensional Queries," in SIGMOD [1988].

Mylopolous, J., Bernstein, P., and Wong, H. [1980] "A Language Facility for Designing Database-Intensive Applications," **TODS,** 5:2, June 1980.

Naish, L., and Thom, J. [1983] "The MU-PROLOG Deductive Database," Technical Report 83/10, Department of Computer Science, University of Melbourne, 1983.

Navathe, S. [1980] "An Intuitive View to Normalize Network-Structured Data," in VLDB [1980].

Navathe, S., and Ahmed, R. [1989] "A Temporal Relational Model and Query Language," **Information Sciences,** 47:2, March 1989, pp. 147–75.

Navathe, S., Ceri, S., Wiederhold, G., and Dou, J. [1984] "Vertical Partitioning Algorithms for Database Design," **TODS,** 9:4, December 1984.

Navathe, S., Elmasri, R., and Larson, J. [1986] "Integrating User Views in Database Design," **IEEE Computer,** 19:1, January 1986.

Navathe, S., and Gadgil, S. [1982] "A Methodology for View Integration in Logical Database Design," in VLDB [1982].

Navathe, S. B. Karlapalem, K., and Ra, M.Y. [1996] "A Mixed Fragmentation Methodology for the Initial Distributed Database Design," **Journal of Computers and Software Engineering,** 3:4, 1996.

Navathe, S., and Kerschberg, L. [1986] "Role of Data Dictionaries in Database Design," **Information and Management,** 10:1, January 1986.

Navathe, S., and Pillalamarri, M. [1988] "Toward Making the ER Approach Object-Oriented," in ER Conference [1988].

Navathe, S., Sashidhar, T., and Elmasri, R. [1984a] "Relationship Merging in Schema Integration," in VLDB [1984].

Navathe, S., and Savasere, A. [1996] "A Practical Schema Integration Facility using an Object Oriented Approach," in **Multidatabase Systems** (A. Elmagarmid and O. Bukhres, eds.), Prentice-Hall, 1996.

Navathe, S. B., Savasere, A., Anwar, T. M., Beck, H., and Gala, S. [1994] "Object Modeling Using Classification in CANDIDE and Its Application," in Dogac et al. [1994].

Navathe, S., and Schkolnick, M. [1978] "View Representation in Logical Database Design," in SIGMOD [1978].

Negri, M., Pelagatti, S., and Sbatella, L. [1991] "Formal Semantics of SQL Queries," **TODS,** 16:3, September 1991.

Ng, P. [1981] "Further Analysis of the Entity-Relationship Approach to Database Design," **TSE,** 7:1, January 1981.

Nicolas, J. [1978] "Mutual Dependencies and Some Results on Undecomposable Relations," in VLDB [1978].

Nicolas, J. [1997] "Deductive Object-oriented Databases, Technology, Products, and Applications: Where Are We?" *Proceedings of the Symposium on Digital Media Information Base (DMIB'97),* Nara, Japan, November 1997.

Nicolas, J., Phipps, G., Derr, M., and Ross, K. [1991] "Glue-NAIL!: A Deductive Database System," in SIGMOD [1991].

Nievergelt, J. [1974] "Binary Search Trees and File Organization," **ACM Computing Surveys,** 6:3, September 1974.

Nievergelt, J., Hinterberger, H., and Seveik, K. [1984]. "The Grid File: An Adaptable Symmetric Multikey File Structure," TODS, 9:1, March 1984, pp. 38–71.

Nijssen, G., ed. [1976] **Modelling in Data Base Management Systems,** North-Holland, 1976.

Nijssen, G., ed. [1977] **Architecture and Models in Data Base Management Systems,** North-Holland, 1977.

Nwosu, K., Berra, P., Thuraisingham, B., eds. [1996], **Design and Implementation of Multimedia Database Management Systems,** Kluwer Academic, 1996.

Obermarck, R. [1982] "Distributed Deadlock Detection Algorithms," **TODS,** 7:2, June 1982.

Oh, Y-C., [1999] "Secure Database Modeling and Design," Ph.D. dissertation, College of Computing, Georgia Institute of Technology, March 1999.

Ohsuga, S. [1982] "Knowledge Based Systems as a New Interactive Computer System of the Next Generation," in **Computer Science and Technologies,** North-Holland, 1982.

Olle, T. [1978] **The CODASYL Approach to Data Base Management,** Wiley, 1978.

Olle, T., Sol, H., and Verrijn-Stuart, A., eds. [1982] **Information System Design Methodology,** North-Holland, 1982.

Omiecinski, E., and Scheuermann, P. [1990] "A Parallel Algorithm for Record Clustering," **TODS,** 15:4, December 1990.

Omura, J. K. [1990] *Novel Applications of Cryptography in Digital Communications,* **IEEE Communications** 28:5, May 1990, pp. 21–29.

O'Neill, P. [1994] **Database: Principles, Programming, Performance,** Morgan Kaufmann, 1994.

Oracle [1992a] **RDBMS Database Administrator's Guide,** ORACLE, 1992.

Oracle [1992 b] **Performance Tuning Guide,** Version 7.0, ORACLE, 1992.

Oracle [1997a] **Oracle 8 Server Concepts,** vols. 1 and 2, Release 8-0, Oracle Corporation, 1997.

Oracle [1997b] **Oracle 8 Server Distributed Database Systems,** Release 8.0, 1997.

Oracle [1997c] **PL/SQL User's Guide and Reference,** Release 8.0, 1997.

Oracle [1997d] **Oracle 8 Server SQL Reference,** Release 8.0, 1997.

Oracle [1997e] **Oracle 8 Parallel Server, Concepts and Administration,** Release 8.0, 1997.

Oracle [1997f] **Oracle 8 Server Spatial Cartridge, User's Guide and Reference,** Release 8.0.3, 1997.

Osborn, S. [1977] **Normal Forms for Relational Databases,** Ph.D. dissertation, University of Waterloo, 1977.

Osborn, S. [1979] "Towards a Universal Relation Interface," in VLDB [1979].

Osborn, S. [1989] "The Role of Polymorphism in Schema Evolution in an Object-Oriented Database," **TKDE,** 1:3, September 1989.

Ozsoyoglu, G., Ozsoyoglu, Z., and Matos, V. [1985] "Extending Relational Algebra and Relational Calculus with Set Valued Attributes and Aggregate Functions," **TODS,** 12:4, December 1987.

Ozsoyoglu, Z., and Yuan, L. [1987] "A New Normal Form for Nested Relations," **TODS,** 12:1, March 1987.

Ozsu, M. T., and Valduriez, P. [1999] **Principles of Distributed Database Systems,** 2nd ed., Prentice-Hall, 1999.

Papadimitriou, C. [1979] "The Serializability of Concurrent Database Updates," **JACM,** 26:4, October 1979.

Papadimitriou, C. [1986] **The Theory of Database Concurrency Control,** Computer Science Press, 1986.

Papadimitriou, C., and Kanellakis, P. [1979] "On Concurrency Control by Multiple Versions," **TODS,** 9:1, March 1974.

Papazoglou, M., and Valder, W. [1989] **Relational Database Management: A Systems Programming Approach,** Prentice-Hall, 1989.

Paredaens, J., and Van Gucht, D. [1992] "Converting Nested Algebra Expressions into Flat Algebra Expressions," **TODS,** 17:1, March 1992.

Parent, C., and Spaccapietra, S. [1985] "An Algebra for a General Entity-Relationship Model," **TSE,** 11:7, July 1985.

Paris, J. [1986] "Voting with Witnesses: A Consistency Scheme for Replicated Files," in ICDE [1986].

Park, J., Chen, M., and Yu, P. [1995] "An Effective Hash Based Algorithm for Mining Association Rules," in SIGMOD [1995].

Paton, A. W., ed. [1999] **Active Rules in Database Systems,** Springer Verlag, 1999.

Paton, N. W., and Diaz, O. [1999] Survey of Active Database Systems, **ACM Computing Surveys,** to appear.

Patterson, D., Gibson, G., and Katz, R. [1988]. "A Case for Redundant Arrays of Inexpensive Disks (RAID)," in SIGMOD [1988].

Paul, H., et al. [1987] "Architecture and Implementation of the Darmstadt Database Kernel System," in SIGMOD [1987].

Pazandak, P., and Srivastava, J., "Evaluating Object DBMSs for Multimedia," **IEEE Multimedia,** 4:3, pp. 34–49.

PDES [1991] "A High-Lead Architecture for Implementing a PDES/STEP Data Sharing Environment." Publication Number PT 1017.03.00, PDES Inc., May 1991.

Pearson, P., Francomano, C., Foster, P., Bocchini, C., Li, P., and McKusick, V. [1994] *"The Status of Online Mendelian inheritance in Man (OMIM) Medio 1994"* **Nucleic Acids Research** 22:17, 1994.

Peckham, J., and Maryanski, F. [1988] "Semantic Data Models," **ACM Computing Surveys,** 20:3, September 1988, pp. 153–89.

Pfleeger, C. P. [1997] **Security in Computing,** Prentice Hall, 1997.

Phipps, G., Derr, M., Ross, K. [1991] "Glue-NAIL!: A Deductive Database System," in SIGMOD [1991].

Piatesky-Shapiro, G., and Frauley, W., eds. [1991] **Knowledge Discovery in Databases,** AAAI Press/MIT Press, 1991.

Pitoura, E., Bukhres, O., and Elmagarmid, A. [1995] "Object Orientation in Multidatabase Systems," **ACM Computing Surveys,** 27:2, June 1995.

Pitoura, E., and Samaras, G. [1998] **Data Management for Mobile Computing,** Kluwer, 1998.

Poosala, V., Ioannidis, Y., Haas, P., and Shekita, E. [1996] "Improved Histograms for Selectivity Estimation of Range Predicates," in SIGMOD [1996].

Potter, B., Sinclair, J., Till, D. [1991] **An Introduction to Formal Specification and Z,** Prentice-Hall, 1991.

Rabitti, F., Bertino, E., Kim, W., and Woelk, D. [1991] "A Model of Authorization for Next-Generation Database Systems," **TODS,** 16:1, March 1991.

Ramakrishnan, R., ed. [1995] **Applications of Logic Databases,** Kluwer Academic, 1995.

Ramakrishnan, R. [1997] **Database Management Systems,** McGraw-Hill, 1997.

Ramakrishnan, R., Srivastava, D. and Sudarshan, S. [1992] "{CORAL}: {C}ontrol, {R}elations and {L}ogic," in VLDB [1992].

Ramakrishnan, R., Srivastava, D., Sudarshan, S. and Sheshadri, P. [1993] "Implementation of the {CORAL} deductive database system," in SIGMOD [1993].

Ramakrishnan, R., and Ullman, J. [1995] "Survey of Research in Deductive Database Systems," **Journal Of Logic Programming,** 23:2, 1995, pp. 125–49.

Ramamoorthy, C., and Wah, B. [1979] "The Placement of Relations on a Distributed Relational Database," *Proceedings of the First International Conference on Distributed Computing Systems,* IEEE CS, 1979.

Ramesh, V., and Ram, S. [1997] "Integrity Constraint Integration in Heterogeneous Databases an Enhanced Methodology for Schema Integration," **Information Systems,** 22:8, December 1997, pp. 423–46.

Reed, D. [1983] "Implementing Atomic Actions on Decentralized Data," **TOCS,** 1:1, February 1983.

Reisner, P. [1977] "Use of Psychological Experimentation as an Aid to Development of a Query Language," **TSE,** 3:3, May 1977.

Reisner, P. [1981] "Human Factors Studies of Database Query Languages: A Survey and Assessment," **ACM Computing Surveys,** 13:1, March 1981.

Reiter, R. [1984] "Towards a Logical Reconstruction of Relational Database Theory," in Brodie et al., ch. 8. [1984].

Ries, D., and Stonebraker, M. [1977] "Effects of Locking Granularity in a Database Management System," **TODS,** 2:3, September 1977.

Rissanen, J. [1977] "Independent Components of Relations," **TODS,** 2:4, December 1977.

Robbins, R. [1993] "Genome Informatics: Requirements and Challenges," *Proceedings of the Second International Conference on Bioinformatics, Supercomputing and Complex Genome Analysis,* World Scientific Publishing, 1993.

Roth, M., and Korth, H. [1987] "The Design of Non-1NF Relational Databases into Nested Normal Form," in SIGMOD [1987].

Rothnie, J., et al. [1980] "Introduction to a System for Distributed Databases (SDD-1)," **TODS,** 5:1, March 1980.

Roussopoulos, N. [1991] "An Incremental Access Method for View-Cache: Concept, Algorithms, and Cost Analysis," **TODS,** 16:3, September 1991.

Rozen, S., and Shasha, D. [1991] "A Framework for Automating Physical Database Design," in VLDB [1991].

Rudensteiner, E. [1992] "Multiview: A Methodology for Supporting Multiple Views in Object-Oriented Databases," in VLDB [1992].

Ruemmler, C., and Wilkes, J. [1994] "An Introduction to Disk Drive Modeling," IEEE Computer, 27:3, March 1994, pp. 17–27.

Rumbaugh, J., Blaha, M., Premerlani, W., Eddy, F., and Lorensen, W. [1991] **Object Oriented Modelng and Design,** Prentice-Hall, 1991.

Rusinkiewicz, M., et al. [1988] "OMNIBASE—A Loosely Coupled: Design and Implementation of a Multidatabase System," **IEEE Distributed Processing Newsletter,** 10:2, November 1988.

Rustin, R., ed. [1972] **Data Base Systems,** Prentice-Hall, 1972.

Rustin, R., ed. [1974] *Proceedings of the BJNAV2.*

Sacca, D., and Zaniolo, C. [1987] "Implementation of Recursive Queries for a Data Language Based on Pure Horn Clauses," *Proceedings of the Fourth International Conference on Logic Programming,* MIT Press, 1986.

Sadri, F., and Ullman, J. [1982] "Template Dependencies: A Large Class of Dependencies in Relational Databases and Its Complete Axiomatization," **JACM,** 29:2, April 1982.

Sagiv, Y., and Yannakakis, M. [1981] "Equivalence among Relational Expressions with the Union and Difference Operators," **JACM,** 27:4, November 1981.

Sakai, H. [1980] "Entity-Relationship Approach to Conceptual Schema Design," in SIGMOD [1980].

Salzberg, B. [1988] **File Structures: An Analytic Approach,** Prentice-Hall, 1988.

Salzberg, B., et al. [1990] "FastSort: A Distributed Single-Input Single-Output External Sort," in SIGMOD [1990].

Salton, G., and Buckley, C. [1991] "Global Text Matching for Information Retrieval" in **Science,** 253, August 1991.

Samet, H. [1990] **The Design and Analysis of Spatial Data Structures,** Addison Wesley, 1990.

Samet, H. [1990a] **Applications of Spatial Data Structures: Computer Graphics, Image Processing and GIS,** Addison-Wesley, 1990.

Sammut, C., and Sammut, R. [1983] "The Implementation of UNSW-PROLOG," **The Australian Computer Journal,** May 1983.

Sarasua, W., and O'Neill, W. [1999]. GIS in Transportation, in Taylor and Francis [1999].

Sarawagi, S., Thomas, S., Agrawal, R. [1998] "Integrating Association Rules Mining with Relational Database systems: Alternatives and Implications," in SIGMOD [1998].

Savasere, A., Omiecinski, E., and Navathe, S. [1995] "An Efficient Algorithm for Mining Association Rules," in VLDB [1995].

Savasere, A., Omiecinski, E., and Navathe, S. [1998] "Mining for Strong Negative Association in a Large Database of Customer Transactions," in ICDE [1998].

Schatz, B. [1995] "Information Analysis in the Net: The Interspace of the Twenty-First Century," *Keynote Plenary Lecture at American Society for Information Science (ASIS) Annual Meeting,* Chicago, October 11, 1995.

Schatz, B. [1997] "Information Retrieval in Digital Libraries: Bringing Search to the Net," **Science,** vol. 275, 17 January 1997.

Schek, H. J., and Scholl. M. H. [1986] "The Relational Model with Relation-valued Attributes," **Information Systems,** 11:2, 1986.

Scheuermann, P., Schiffner, G., and Weber, H. [1979] "Abstraction Capabilities and Invariant Properties Modeling within the Entity-Relationship Approach," in ER Conference [1979].

Schlimmer, J., Mitchell, T., McDermott, J. [1991] "Justification Based Refinement of Expert Knowledge" in Piatesky-Shapiro and Frawley [1991].

Schmidt, J., and Swenson, J. [1975] "On the Semantics of the Relational Model," in SIGMOD [1975].

Sciore, E. [1982] "A Complete Axiomatization for Full Join Dependencies," **JACM,** 29:2, April 1982.

Selinger, P., et al. [1979] "Access Path Selection in a Relational Database Management System," in SIGMOD [1979].

Senko, M. [1975] "Specification of Stored Data Structures and Desired Output in DIAM II with FORAL," in VLDB [1975].

Senko, M. [1980] "A Query Maintenance Language for the Data Independent Accessing Model II," **Information Systems,** 5:4, 1980.

Shapiro, L. [1986] "Join Processing in Database Systems with Large Main Memories," TODS, 11:3, 1986.

Shasha, D. [1992] **Database Tuning: A Principled Approach,** Prentice-Hall, 1992.

Shasha, D., and Goodman, N.[1988] "Concurrent Search Structure Algorithms," **TODS,** 13:1, March 1988.

Shekita, E., and Carey, M. [1989] "Performance Enhancement Through Replication in an Object-Oriented DBMS," in SIGMOD [1989].

Shenoy, S., and Ozsoyoglu, Z. [1989] "Design and Implementation of a Semantic Query Optimizer," **TKDE,** 1:3, September 1989.

Sheth, A., Gala, S., Navathe, S. [1993]" On Automatic Reasoning for Schema Integration," in **International Journal of Intelligent Co-operative Information Systems,** 2:1, March 1993.

Sheth, A. P., and Larson, J. A. [1990] "Federated Database Systems for Managing Distributed, Heterogeneous, and Autonomous Databases," **ACM Computing Surveys,** 22:3, September 1990, pp. 183–236.

Sheth, A., Larson, J., Cornelio, A., and Navathe, S. [1988] "A Tool for Integrating Conceptual Schemas and User Views," in ICDE [1988].

Shipman, D. [1981] "The Functional Data Model and the Data Language DAPLEX," **TODS,** 6:1, March 1981.

Shlaer, S., Mellor, S. [1988] **Object-Oriented System Analysis: Modeling the World in Data,** Yourdon Press, 1988.

Shneiderman, B., ed. [1978] **Databases: Improving Usability and Responsiveness,** Academic Press, 1978.

Sibley, E., and Kerschberg, L. [1977] "Data Architecture and Data Model Considerations," *NCC, AFIPS,* 46, 1977.

Siegel, M., and Madnick, S. [1991] "A Metadata Approach to Resolving Semantic Conflicts," in VLDB [1991].

Siegel, M., Sciore, E., and Salveter, S. [1992] "A Method for Automatic Rule Derivation to Support Semantic Query Optimization," **TODS,** 17:4, December 1992.

SIGMOD [1974] *Proceedings of the ACM SIGMOD-SIGFIDET Conference on Data Description, Access, and Control,* Rustin, R., ed., May 1974.

SIGMOD [1975] *Proceedings of the 1975 ACM SIGMOD International Conference on Management of Data,* King, F., ed., San Jose, CA, May 1975.

SIGMOD [1976] *Proceedings of the 1976 ACM SIGMOD International Conference on Management of Data,* Rothnie, J., ed., Washington, June 1976.

SIGMOD [1977] *Proceedings of the 1977 ACM SIGMOD International Conference on Management of Data,* Smith, D., ed., Toronto, August 1977.

SIGMOD [1978] *Proceedings of the 1978 ACM SIGMOD International Conference on Management of Data,* Lowenthal, E. and Dale, N., eds., Austin, TX, May/June 1978.

SIGMOD [1979] *Proceedings of the 1979 ACM SIGMOD International Conference on Management of Data,* Bernstein, P., ed., Boston, MA, May/June 1979.

SIGMOD [1980] *Proceedings of the 1980 ACM SIGMOD International Conference on Management of Data,* Chen, P. and Sprowls, R., eds., Santa Monica, CA, May 1980.

SIGMOD [1981] *Proceedings of the 1981 ACM SIGMOD International Conference on Management of Data,* Lien, Y., ed., Ann Arbor, MI, April/May 1981.

SIGMOD [1982] *Proceedings of the 1982 ACM SIGMOD International Conference on Management of Data,* Schkolnick, M., ed., Orlando, FL, June 1982.

SIGMOD [1983] *Proceedings of the 1983 ACM SIGMOD International Conference on Management of Data,* DeWitt, D. and Gardarin, G., eds., San Jose, CA, May 1983.

SIGMOD [1984] *Proceedings of the 1984 ACM SIGMOD Internaitonal Conference on Management of Data,* Yormark, E., ed., Boston, MA, June 1984.

SIGMOD [1985] *Proceedings of the 1985 ACM SIGMOD International Conference on Management of Data,* Navathe, S., ed., Austin, TX, May 1985.

SIGMOD [1986] *Proceedings of the 1986 ACM SIGMOD Internaitonal Conference on Management of Data,* Zaniolo, C., ed., Washington, May 1986.

SIGMOD [1987] *Proceedings of the 1987 ACM SIGMOD International Conference on Management of Data*, Dayal, U. and Traiger, I., eds., San Francisco, CA, May 1987.

SIGMOD [1988] *Proceedings of the 1988 ACM SIGMOD International Conference on Management of Data*, Boral, H., and Larson, P., eds., Chicago, June 1988.

SIGMOD [1989] *Proceedings of the 1989 ACM SIGMOD International Conference on Management of Data*, Clifford, J., Lindsay, B., and Maier, D., eds., Portland, OR, June 1989.

SIGMOD [1990] *Proceedings of the 1990 ACM SIGMOD International Conference on Management of Data*, Garcia-Molina, H., and Jagadish, H., eds., Atlantic City, NJ, June 1990.

SIGMOD [1991] *Proceedings of the 1991 ACM SIGMOD International Conference on Management of Data*, Clifford, J. and King, R., eds., Denver, CO, June 1991.

SIGMOD [1992] *Proceedings of the 1992 ACM SIGMOD International Conference on Management of Data*, Stonebraker, M., ed., San Diego, CA, June 1992.

SIGMOD [1993] *Proceedings of the 1993 ACM SIGMOD International "Conference on Management of Data*, Buneman, P. and Jajodia, S., eds., Washington, June 1993.

SIGMOD [1994] *Proceedings of 1994 ACM SIGMOD International Conference on Management of Data*, Snodgrass, R. T., and Winslett, M., eds., Minneapolis, MN, June 1994.

SIGMOD [1995] *Proceedings of 1995 ACM SIGMOD International Conference on Management of Data*, Carey, M., and Schneider, D. A., eds., Minneapolis, MN, June 1995.

SIGMOD [1996] *Proceedings of 1996 ACM SIGMOD International Conference on Management of Data*, Jagadish, H. V., and Mumick, I. P., eds., Montreal, June 1996.

SIGMOD [1997] *Proceedings of 1997 ACM SIGMOD International Conference on Management of Data*, Peckham, J., ed., Tucson, AZ, May 1997.

SIGMOD [1998] *Proceedings of 1998 ACM SIGMOD International Conference on Management of Data*, Haas, L., and Tiwary, A., eds., Seattle, WA. June 1998.

SIGMOD [1999] *Proceedings of 1999 ACM SIGMOD International Conference on Management of Data*, Faloutsos, C., ed., Philadelphia, PA, May 1999.Silberschatz, A., Stonebraker, M., and Ullman, J. [1990] "Database Systems: Achievements and Opportunities," in **ACM SIGMOD Record,** 19:4, December 1990.

Silberschatz, A., Korth, H., and Sudarshan, S. [2001] Database System Concepts, 4th ed., McGraw-Hill, 2001.

Smith, G. [1990] "The Semantic Data Model for Security: Representing the Security Semantics of an Application," in ICDE [1990].

Smith, J., and Chang, P. [1975] "Optimizing the Performance of a Relational Algebra Interface," **CACM,** 18:10, October 1975.

Smith, J., and Smith, D. [1977] "Database Abstractions: Aggregation and Generalization," **TODS,** 2:2, June 1977.

Smith, J., et al. [1981] "MULTIBASE: Integrating Distributed Heterogeneous Database Systems," NCC, AFIPS, 50, 1981.

Smith, K., and Winslett, M. [1992] "Entity Modeling in the MLS Relational Model," in VLDB [1992].

Smith, P., and Barnes, G. [1987] **Files and Databases: An Introduction,** Addison-Wesley, 1987.

Snodgrass, R. [1987] "The Temporal Query Language TQuel," **TODS,** 12:2, June 1987.

Snodgrass, R., ed. [1995] **The TSQL2 Temporal Query Language,** Kluwer, 1995.

Snodgrass, R., and Ahn, I. [1985] "A Taxonomy of Time in Databases," in SIGMOD [1985].

Soutou, G. [1998] "Analysis of Constraints for N-ary Relationships," in ER 98.

Spaccapietra, S., and Jain, R., eds. [1995] *Proceedings of the Visual Database Workshop*, Lausanne, Switzerland, October 1995.

Spooner D., Michael, A., and Donald, B. [1986] "Modeling CAD Data with Data Abstraction and Object Oriented Technique," in ICDE [1986].

Srikant, R., and Agrawal, R. [1995] "Mining Generalized Association Rules," in VLDB [1995].

Srinivas, M., and Patnaik, L. [1994] "Genetic Algorithms: A Survey," **IEEE Computer,** June 1994.

Srinivasan, V., and Carey, M. [1991] "Performance of B-Tree Concurrency Control Algorithms," in SIGMOD [1991].

Srivastava, D., Ramakrishnan, R., Sudarshan, S., and Sheshadri, P. [1993] "Coral++: Adding Object-orientation to a Logic Database Language," in VLDB [1993].

Stachour, P., and Thuraisingham, B. [1990] "The Design and Implementation of INGRES," **TKDE,** 2:2, June 1990.

Stallings, W. [1997] Data and Computer Communications, 5th ed., Prentice-Hall, 1997.

Stallings, W. [2000] **Network Security Essentials: Applications and Standards,** Prentice Hall, 2000.

Stonebraker, M. [1975] "Implementation of Integrity Constraints and Views by Query Modification," in SIGMOD [1975].

Stonebraker, M. [1993] "The Miro DBMS" in SIGMOD [1993].

Stonebraker, M., ed. [1994] **Readings in Database Systems,** 2nd ed., Morgan Kaufmann, 1994.

Stonebraker, M., Hanson, E., and Hong, C. [1987] "The Design of the POSTGRES Rules System," in ICDE [1987].

Stonebraker, M., and Rowe, L. [1986] "The Design of POSTGRES," in SIGMOD [1986].

Stonebraker, M., Wong, E., Kreps, P., and Held, G. [1976] "The Design and Implementation of INGRES," **TODS,** 1:3, September 1976.

Su, S. [1985] "A Semantic Association Model for Corporate and Scientific-Statistical Databases," **Information Science,** 29, 1985.

Su, S. [1988] **Database Computers,** McGraw-Hill, 1988.

Su, S., Krishnamurthy, V., and Lam, H. [1988] "An Object-Oriented Semantic Association Model (OSAM*)," in **AI in Industrial Engineering and Manufacturing: Theoretical Issues and Applications,** American Institute of Industrial Engineers, 1988.

Subrahmanian, V. [1998] **Principles of Multimedia Databases Systems,** Morgan Kaufmann, 1998.

Subramanian V. S., and Jajodia, S., eds. [1996] **Multimedia Database Systems: Issues and Research Directions,** Springer Verlag. 1996.

Sunderraman, R. [1999] **ORACLE Programming: A Primer,** Addison Wesley Longman, 1999.

Swami, A., and Gupta, A. [1989] "Optimization of Large Join Queries: Combining Heuristics and Combinatorial Techniques," in SIGMOD [1989].

Tanenbaum, A. [1996] **Computer Networks,** Prentice Hall PTR, 1996.

Tansel, A., et al., eds. [1993] **Temporal Databases: Theory, Design, and Implementation,** Benjamin Cummings, 1993.

Teorey, T. [1994] **Database Modeling and Design: The Fundamental Principles,** 2nd ed., Morgan Kaufmann, 1994.

Teorey, T., Yang, D., and Fry, J. [1986] "A Logical Design Methodology for Relational Databases Using the Extended Entity-Relationship Model," **ACM Computing Surveys,** 18:2, June 1986.

Thomas, J., and Gould, J. [1975] "A Psychological Study of Query by Example," NCC AFIPS, 44, 1975.

Thomas, R. [1979] "A Majority Consensus Approach to Concurrency Control for Multiple Copy Data Bases," **TODS,** 4:2, June 1979.

Thomasian, A. [1991] "Performance Limits of Two-Phase Locking," in ICDE [1991].

Thuraisingham, B., et al. [2001] "Directions for Web and E-Commerce Applications Security," Tenth IEEE International Workshops on Enabling Technologies: Infrastructure for Collaborative Enterprises, 2001, pp. 200–204.

Todd, S. [1976] "The Peterlee Relational Test Vehicle—A System Overview," **IBM Systems Journal,** 15:4, December 1976.

Toivonen, H., "Sampling Large Databases for Association Rules," in VLDB [1996].

Tou, J., ed. [1984] **Information Systems COINS-IV,** Plenum Press, 1984.

Tsangaris, M., and Naughton, J. [1992] "On the Performance of Object Clustering Techniques," in SIGMOD [1992].

Tsichritzis, D. [1982] "Forms Management," **CACM,** 25:7, July 1982.

Tsichritzis, D., and Klug, A., eds. [1978] **The ANSI/X3/SPARC DBMS Framework,** AFIPS Press, 1978.

Tsichritzis, D., and Lochovsky, F. [1976] "Hierarchical Data-base Management: A Survey," **ACM Computing Surveys,** 8:1, March 1976.

Tsichritzis, D., and Lochovsky, F. [1982] **Data Models,** Prentice-Hall, 1982.

Tsotras, V., and Gopinath, B. [1992] "Optimal Versioning of Object Classes," in ICDE [1992].

Tsou, D. M., and Fischer, P. C. [1982] "Decomposition of a Relation Scheme into Boyce Codd Normal Form," *SIGACT News,* 14:3, 1982, pp. 23–29.

Ullman, J. [1982] **Principles of Database Systems,** 2nd ed., Computer Science Press, 1982.

Ullman, J. [1985] "Implementation of Logical Query Languages for Databases," **TODS,** 10:3, September 1985.

Ullman, J. [1988] **Principles of Database and Knowledge-Base Systems,** vol. 1, Computer Science Press, 1988.

Ullman, J. [1989] **Principles of Database and Knowledge-Base Systems,** vol. 2, Computer Science Press, 1989.

Ullman, J. D. and Widom, J. [1997] **A First Course in Database Systems,** Prentice-Hall, 1997.

U.S. Congress [1988] "Office of Technology Report, Appendix D: Databases, Repositories, and Informatics," in **Mapping Our Genes: Genome Projects: How Big, How Fast?** John Hopkins University Press, 1988.

U.S. Department of Commerce [1993]. **TIGER/Line Files,** Bureau of Census, Washington, 1993.

Valduriez, P., and Gardarin, G. [1989] **Analysis and Comparison of Relational Database Systems,** Addison-Wesley, 1989.

Vassiliou, Y. [1980] "Functional Dependencies and Incomplete Information," in VLDB [1980].

Verheijen, G., and VanBekkum, J. [1982] "NIAM: An Information Analysis Method," in Olle et al. [1982].

Verhofstadt, J. [1978] "Recovery Techniques for Database Systems," **ACM Computing Surveys,** 10:2, June 1978.

Vielle, L. [1986] "Recursive Axioms in Deductive Databases: The Query-Subquery Approach," in EDS [1986].

Vielle, L. [1987] "Database Complete Proof Production Based on SLD-resolution," in *Proceedings of the Fourth International Conference on Logic Programming,* 1987.

Vielle, L. [1988] "From QSQ Towards QoSaQ: Global Optimization of Recursive Queries," in EDS [1988].

Vieille, L. [1998] "VALIDITY: Knowledge Independence for Electronic Mediation," invited paper, in *Practical Applications of Prolog/Practical Applications of Constraint Technology (PAP/PACT '98),* London, March 1998, available from lvieille@computer.org.

Vin, H., Zellweger, P., Swinehart, D., and Venkat Rangan, P. [1991] "Multimedia Conferencing in the Etherphone Environment," **IEEE Computer,** Special Issue on Multimedia Information Systems, 24:10, October 1991.

VLDB [1975] *Proceedings of the First International Conference on Very Large Data Bases,* Kerr, D., ed., Framingham, MA, September 1975.

VLDB [1976] **Systems for Large Databases,** Lockemann, P. and Neuhold, E., eds., in *Proceedings of the Second International Conference on Very Large Data Bases,* Brussels, Belgium, July 1976, North-Holland, 1976.

VLDB [1977] *Proceedings of the Third International Conference on Very Large Data Bases,* Merten, A., ed., Tokyo, Japan, October 1977.

VLDB [1978] *Proceedings of the Fourth International Conference on Very Large Data Bases*, Bubenko, J., and Yao, S., eds., West Berlin, Germany, September 1978.

VLDB [1979] *Proceedings of the Fifth International Conference on Very Large Data Bases*, Furtado, A., and Morgan, H., eds., Rio de Janeiro, Brazil, October 1979.

VLDB [1980] *Proceedings of the Sixth International Conference on Very Large Data Bases*, Lochovsky, F., and Taylor, R., eds., Montreal, Canada, October 1980.

VLDB [1981] *Proceedings of the Seventh International Conference on Very Large Data Bases*, Zaniolo, C., and Delobel, C., eds., Cannes, France, September 1981.

VLDB [1982] *Proceedings of the Eighth International Conference on Very Large Data Bases*, McLeod, D., and Villasenor, Y., eds., Mexico City, September 1982.

VLDB [1983] *Proceedings of the Ninth International Conference on Very Large Data Bases*, Schkolnick, M., and Thanos, C., eds., Florence, Italy, October/November 1983.

VLDB [1984] *Proceedings of the Tenth International Conference on Very Large Data Bases*, Dayal, U., Schlageter, G., and Seng, L., eds., Singapore, August 1984.

VLDB [1985] *Proceedings of the Eleventh International Conference on Very Large Data Bases*, Pirotte, A., and Vassiliou, Y., eds., Stockholm, Sweden, August 1985.

VLDB [1986] *Proceedings of the Twelfth International Conference on Very Large Data Bases*, Chu, W., Gardarin, G., and Ohsuga, S., eds., Kyoto, Japan, August 1986.

VLDB [1987] *Proceedings of the Thirteenth International Conference on Very Large Data Bases*, Stocker, P., Kent, W., and Hammersley, P., eds., Brighton, England, September 1987.

VLDB [1988] *Proceedings of the Fourteenth International Conference on Very Large Data Bases*, Bancilhon, F., and DeWitt, D., eds., Los Angeles, August/September 1988.

VLDB [1989] *Proceedings of the Fifteenth International Conference on Very Large Data Bases*, Apers, P., and Wiederhold, G., eds., Amsterdam, August 1989.

VLDB [1990] *Proceedings of the Sixteenth International Conference on Very Large Data Bases*, McLeod, D., Sacks-Davis, R., and Schek, H., eds., Brisbane, Australia, August 1990.

VLDB [1991] *Proceedings of the Seventeenth International Conference on Very Large Data Bases*, Lohman, G., Sernadas, A., and Camps, R., eds., Barcelona, Catalonia, Spain, September 1991.

VLDB [1992] *Proceedings of the Eighteenth International Conference on Very Large Data Bases*, Yuan, L., ed., Vancouver, Canada, August 1992.

VLDB [1993] *Proceedings of the Nineteenth International Conference on Very Large Data Bases*, Agrawal, R., Baker, S., and Bell, D.A., eds., Dublin, Ireland, August 1993.

VLDB [1994] *Proceedings of the 20th International Conference on Very Large Data Bases*, Bocca, J., Jarke, M., and Zaniolo, C., eds., Santiago, Chile, September 1994.

VLDB [1995] *Proceedings of the 21st International Conference on Very Large Data Bases*, Dayal, U., Gray, P.M.D., and Nishio, S., eds., Zurich, Switzerland, September 1995.

VLDB [1996] *Proceedings of the 22nd International Conference on Very Large Data Bases*, Vijayaraman, T. M., Buchman, A. P., Mohan, C., and Sarda, N. L., eds., Bombay, India, September 1996.

VLDB [1997] *Proceedings of the 23rd International Conference on Very Large Data Bases*, Jarke, M., Carey, M. J., Dittrich, K. R., Lochovsky, F. H., and Loucopoulos, P.(editors), Zurich, Switzerland, September 1997.

VLDB [1998] *Proceedings of the 24th International Conference on Very Large Data Bases*, Gupta, A., Shmueli, O., and Widom, J., eds., New York, September 1998.

VLDB [1999] *Proceedings of the 25th International Conference on Very Large Data Bases*, Zdonik, S. B., Valduriez, P., and Orlowska, M., eds., Edinburgh, Scotland, September 1999.

Vorhaus, A., and Mills, R. [1967] "The Time-Shared Data Management System: A New Approach to Data Management," System Development Corporation, Report SP-2634, 1967.

Wallace, D. [1995] "1994 William Allan Award Address: Mitochondrial DNA Variation in Human Evolution, Degenerative Disease, and Aging." **American Journal of Human Genetics,** 57:201–223, 1995.

Walton, C., Dale, A., and Jenevein, R. [1991] "A Taxonomy and Performance Model of Data Skew Effects in Parallel Joins," in VLDB [1991].

Wang, K. [1990] "Polynomial Time Designs Toward Both BCNF and Efficient Data Manipulation," in SIGMOD [1990].

Wang, Y., and Madnick, S. [1989] "The Inter-Database Instance Identity Problem in Integrating Autonomous Systems," in ICDE [1989].

Wang, Y. and Rowe, L. [1991] "Cache Consistency and Concurrency Control in a Client/ Server DBMS Architecture," in SIGMOD [1991].

Warren, D. [1992] "Memoing for Logic Programs," CACM, 35:3, ACM, March 1992.

Weddell, G. [1992] "Reasoning About Functional Dependencies Generalized for Semantic Data Models," TODS, 17:1, March 1992.

Weikum, G. [1991] "Principles and Realization Strategies of Multilevel Transaction Management," TODS, 16:1, March 1991.

Weiss, S. and Indurkhya, N. [1998] **Predictive Data Mining: A Practical Guide,** Morgan Kaufmann, 1998.

Whang, K. [1985] "Query Optimization in Office By Example," IBM Research Report RC 11571, December 1985.

Whang, K., Malhotra, A., Sockut, G., and Burns, L. [1990] "Supporting Universal Quantification in a Two-Dimensional Database Query Language," in ICDE [1990].

Whang, K., and Navathe, S. [1987] "An Extended Disjunctive Normal Form Approach for Processing Recursive Logic Queries in Loosely Coupled Environments," in VLDB [1987].

Whang, K., and Navathe, S. [1992] "Integrating Expert Systems with Database Management Systems—an Extended Disjunctive Normal Form Approach," **Information Sciences,** 64, March 1992.

Whang, K., Wiederhold, G., and Sagalowicz, D. [1982] "Physical Design of Network Model Databases Using the Property of Separability," in VLDB [1982].

Widom, J., "Research Problems in Data Warehousing," CIKM, November 1995.

Widom, J., and Finkelstein, S. [1990] "Set Oriented Production Rules in Relational Database Systems" in SIGMOD [1990].

Wiederhold, G. [1983] **Database Design,** 2nd ed., McGraw-Hill, 1983.

Wiederhold, G. [1984] "Knowledge and Database Management," **IEEE Software,** January 1984.

Wiederhold, G. [1995] "Digital Libraries, Value, and Productivity," **CACM,** April 1995.

Wiederhold, G., Beetem, A., and Short, G. [1982] "A Database Approach to Communication in VLSI Design," **IEEE Transactions on Computer-Aided Design of Integrated Circuits and Systems,** 1:2, April 1982.

Wiederhold, G., and Elmasri, R. [1979] "The Structural Model for Database Design," in ER Conference [1979].

Willshire, M. [1991] "How Spacey Can They Get? Space Overhead for Storage and Indexing with Object-Oriented Databases," in ICDE [1991].

Wilson, B., and Navathe, S. [1986] "An Analytical Framework for Limited Redesign of Distributed Databases," *Proceedings of the Sixth Advanced Database Symposium,* Tokyo, August 1986.

Wiorkowski, G., and Kull, D. [1992] **DB2-Design and Development Guide,** 3rd ed., Addison-Wesley, 1992.

Wirth, N. [197] **Algorithms + Data Structures = Programs,** Prentice-Hall, 1972.

Wood, J., and Silver, D. [1989] **J Joint Application Design: How to Design Quality Systems in 40% Less Time,** Wiley, 1989.

Wong, E. [1983] "Dynamic Rematerialization-Processing Distributed Queries Using Redundant Data," TSE, 9:3, May 1983.

Wong, E., and Youssefi, K. [1976] "Decomposition—A Strategy for Query Processing," TODS, 1:3, September 1976.

Wong, H. [1984] "Micro and Macro Statistical/Scientific Database Management," in ICDE [1984].

Wu, X., and Ichikawa, T. [1992] "KDA: A Knowledge-based Database Assistant with a Query Guiding Facility," **TKDE** 4:5, October 1992.

Yannakakis, Y. [1984] "Serializability by Locking," **JACM,** 31:2, 1984.

Yao, S. [1979] "Optimization of Query Evaluation Algorithms," **TODS,** 4:2, June 1979.

Yao, S., ed. [1985] **Principles of Database Design,** vol. 1: **Logical Organizations,** Prentice-Hall, 1985.

Youssefi, K., and Wong, E. [1979] "Query Processing in a Relational Database Management System," in VLDB [1979].

Zadeh, L. [1983] "The Role of Fuzzy Logic in the Management of Uncertainty in Expert Systems," **Fuzzy Sets and Systems,** 11, North-Holland, 1983.

Zaniolo, C. [1976] "Analysis and Design of Relational Schemata for Database Systems," Ph.D. dissertation, University of California, Los Angeles, 1976.

Zaniolo, C. [1988] "Design and Implementation of a Logic Based Language for Data Intensive Applications," MCC Technical Report #ACA-ST-199-88, June 1988.

Zaniolo, C., et al. [1986] "Object-Oriented Database Systems and Knowledge Systems," in EDS [1984].

Zaniolo, C., et al. [1997] **Advanced Database Systems,** Morgan Kaufmann, 1997. Zave, P. [1997] "Classification of Research Efforts in Requirements Engineering," **ACM Computing Surveys,** 29:4, December 1997.

T. Zhang, R. Ramakrishnan and M. Livny, "Birch: An Efficient Data Clustering Method for Very Large Databases," Proc. ACM SIGMOD Conference, 1996.

Zicari, R. [1991] "A Framework for Schema Updates in an Object-Oriented Database System," in ICDE [1991].

Zloof, M. [1975] "Query by Example," *NCC, AFIPS,* 44, 1975.

Zloof, M. [1982] "Office By Example: A Business Language That Unifies Data, Word Processing, and Electronic Mail," **IBM Systems Journal,** 21:3, 1982.

Zobel, J., Moffat, A., and Sacks-Davis, R. [1992] "An Efficient Indexing Technique for Full-Text Database Systems," in VLDB [1992].

Zook, W., et al. [1977] **INGRES Reference Manual,** Department of EECS, University of California at Berkeley, 1977.

Zvieli, A. [1986] "A Fuzzy Relational Calculus," in EDS [1986].

Index